PROFESSIONALS PRESS

CHARACTER ANIMATION
In Depth

DOUG KELLY

The Coriolis Group, Inc.
An International Thomson Publishing Company
14455 N. Hayden Road, Suite 220
Scottsdale, Arizona 85260

602/483-0192
FAX 602/483-0193
http://www.coriolis.com

Library of Congress Cataloging-In-Publication Data
Kelly, Doug
    Character animation in depth / by Doug Kelly.
       p. cm
    Includes index
    ISBN 1-56604-771-4
    1. Computer animation 2. Computer graphics
I. Title
TR897.7.K448 1998   97-41587
006.6'96--DC21   CIP
Printed in the United States of America
10 9 8 7 6 5 4 3 2 1

Publisher

Keith Weiskamp

Acquisitions

Stephanie Wall

Project Editor

Michelle Stroup

Marketing Specialist

Dylan Zoller

Production Coordinator

Wendy Littley

Cover Design

Anthony Stock

Layout Design

April Nielsen

CD-ROM Development

Robert Clarfield

Albany, NY • Belmont, CA • Bonn • Boston • Cincinnati • Detroit • Johannesburg
London • Madrid • Melbourne • Mexico City • New York • Paris • Singapore
Tokyo • Toronto • Washington

Jared Bendis
A friend in need is a friend, indeed.

Patty Koenig
A pearl beyond price.

CHARACTER
ANIMATION
IN DEPTH

CHARACTER
ANIMATION
IN DEPTH

ACKNOWLEDGMENTS

This book, more than most, would not have been possible without the contributions of a great many people. Special thanks to those who contributed directly to this book's contents: Steph Greenberg, Sandra Frame, Ken Cope, Mike Comet, Kim Oravecz, Bill Fleming, Adam Pletcher, Robert Terrell, Dylan Crooke, and Mark Riddell. Thanks also to Chris Grams, who believed in this book before anyone else, and worked above and beyond the call to keep it alive. Special recognition should also go to Michelle Stroup, Robert Clarfield, Tony Stock and Wendy Littley at Coriolis, who had this orphan dropped in their laps and made it feel welcome.

My sincere thanks go out to all those animators who made themselves and their hard-won expertise available to me, both in correspondence and interviews, and to the many publishers and vendors who made their products available for review. They are listed in no particular order, and if I have omitted anyone, the fault is entirely mine and in no way reflects on the value of their contribution.

Chris Bailey, Sylvain Taillon, Steve Sappington, Steve Roberts, Stephen Price, Shai Hinitz, Rick May, Peter Ryce, Paul Salvini, Patrick Kelly, Brian Kelly, Miguel Grinberg, Michael Kass, Mark Thomas, Mark Mayerson, Kevin Clark, Jeremy Cantor, Harold Harris, Frank Falcone, Colin Withers, Donna Teggart, Chris Wallace, Brick Eksten, Alex Walsh, Mary Alice, Armando Afre, Dan Kraus, Diana Cruz, Dolores Santos, Doug Griffin, Erica Schisler, Jeff Bunker, Jeff Yates, Kellie-Bea Rainey, Mairi Welman, Tammy Neske, Marshall Hash, Mike Caputo, Terry Cotant, Erin Mohan, Vincent Liggio, Cecilia Chien, David Addelman, Sue Addelman, Karen Raz, Barry Robbins, Melissa Bell, Leona Lopez, Brad Peebler, Dennis Derrick, Rachel Levine, Jeffrey Lew, Gene Sexton, Cheyenne Bloomfield, Colin Doncaster, Brent Malnack, Brian Gillespie, Craig A. Carson, Dan Laguardia, Danny Shapiro, David Hague, Doug Cooper, Eden Rain, Genevieve Laberge, Chris Landreth, Jane Perratt, Keith Lango, Jeremy Birn, Ken F. Morton, Lisa Brimo, Michelle Fink, Paul Franklin, Peter Loveday, Peter Plantec, Rob Skiena, Wave Johnson, Roger Helman, Ron L. Dutcher, Shaun Elstob, Hal Hickel, Steve Levin, Toshio Ishibashi, Zero Z. Batzell Dean, Shane Olson, Pari Natarajan, Roman Ormandy, Owen O. Owen, Frank Capezzuto, Steve Bloom, Jonathan Roberts, Kathleen Gavin, Steven S. Wilson, Pete Docter, Robert A. Heinlein, Jim Studt, James Doohan, Phil South, Domenic DiGiorgio, Stephen Evans, Bill Allen, and the members of the CG-CHAR mailing list.

CHARACTER ANIMATION IN DEPTH

CHARACTER
ANIMATION
IN DEPTH

Animation tools that were once available exclusively as the expensive product of highly competitive research and development teams are now a hobbyist's hot key or icon click away. Most animation packages no longer require the skills of a programmer to be exploited to their fullest capacity. Computer animators push the envelope of science and technology and create magic. Our skill is best measured by how compellingly we suspend disbelief.

How do you learn to suspend disbelief compellingly with a computer? Since the computer does not animate any more than does pencil or clay, of what discipline should you be a student in order to best prepare for the challenge?

With some accommodation to the technology, a stop motion animator can work much the same way as always. A cel animator, in a different way, can find much in the computer that is familiar and powerful. Yet, neither will fully realize the potential of their new environment so long as they remain frustrated by how it differs from their old; struggling to retain their old habits and practices rather than embracing new ones.

The computer animator's environment is as spatially dimensional and texturally rich as you choose to make it, like stop motion, with any point in the temporal dimension multiply revisitable for revision, more like cel animation. With laws of physics that need to be contended with for good or ill in stop motion, or synthesized by the cel animator to the limits of one's skill and intention, a middle ground is possible in CG. The parameters of the laws of physics are arbitrarily applicable, to the extent of the animator's skill at manipulating dynamics conditionally, or by a communicator's skill at conveying the abstract notion of physics entertainingly.

To take advantage of all this freedom and responsibility, an artist coming from either tradition would do well to learn from the opposite school. A stop motion animator, used to working straight ahead, who now has the capacity to revise some regrettable artifacts of that mode rather than starting all over from frame one, soon learns when not to set a key for every single frame.

The cel animator, used to thinking in terms of color separations, silhouettes, outrageous exaggeration and implication (and fresh assistant animators), is now working in an arena of explicit detail and complexity, more like that focused by a stop motion camera's lens. The cues that promote verisimilitude highlight with jarring clarity any minor discrepancy from the level of complexity established.

Both disciplines have to deal with the paradox that the more you want to control, the more you have to keep track of. We could all profit from a deeper understanding of how to generalize the responses of a character model to our control. How do we get it to do what we *meant* it to do? Sometimes, we want it to take its mutable nature and environment into consideration automatically, and just as often, we don't, frequently both in the same scene or frame. The fanciful freedom of an animator's whim has to be somehow built into the creature's capacity to resolve multiple and conflicting cues. We need to find a happy medium on a scale of explicit control vs. creature complexity. That scale spans the range from explicitly controlling each vertex, one tedious pixel at a time on every frame, nearly all the way to creating and winding up an artificially intelligent automaton.

Computer animation isn't merely a new work environment for the unaltered procedures of one older medium or another. It is an infant, discovering itself and its surroundings one bit at a time; a monster baby taking its faltering first steps wearing concrete diapers.

Ken Cope

CHARACTER ANIMATION IN DEPTH

Silent animations are boring. Even a little generic background music will liven them up, and synchronized sound effects will do wonders.

PART II MODELING

Chapter 5
Character Design   113

This chapter tells you about the process of designing characters, including the people involved, rules of thumb, mistakes to avoid, and useful tools. To assist you in designing realistic and cartoon characters, this chapter also explains the underlying muscle and bone structure of the human face and figure, plus dimples, wrinkles, flab, and fat.

Chapter 6
Modeling Tools   147

The influence of your modeling tools doesn't stop at your character's outward appearance. Modeling tools can limit or expand your options for animation, too. This chapter guides you through choices of surface type, work strategies, and critical tools you'll need to model characters effectively.

Chapter 7
Advanced Modeling Tools

Modeling characters for animation requires that you go beyond the standard tools. You need to know how to digitize a maquette or life cast, work with laser-scan data, and make a heavy mesh more efficient to set up and animate.

PART III TEXTURING

Chapter 8
Material Basics

This chapter is like a quick tour through the makeup department of a motion picture studio. Just as actors need makeup before going in front of the cameras, your models need appropriate surface materials.

Chapter 9
Character Cartography:
Making And Applying Maps 257

2D maps are important to character animation in direct proportion to the realism of the characters. Learn to make and use cartoon and realistic maps, and your characters will be more effective storytellers.

Chapter 10
Advanced Material Tools 297

If you are creating characters to appear in high-resolution media, if you have tight deadlines, or if you are a perfectionist, you'll want to use these tools.

PART IV SETUP

Chapter 11
Essential Setups 325

Setups are the flesh and bone of animated characters. You need to understand how animation works before you can set up a character, and you need to understand how a character is set up before you can animate it.

Chapter 12
Advanced Setups With Constraints 397

A humanoid character is too complex to efficiently animate by manually keyframing every control. This chapter shows how to link controls to one another using constraints. A constraint setup enables the animator to use a small fraction of the total controls to pose the character faster, more intuitively, and with more consistent results.

Chapter 13
Power-Tool Setups   533

Power tools and procedural setups, like any animation tools, are worse than useless if they get in the animator's way. As a setup person, you need to know when a power tool can save the animator work, and when it's a counter-productive geek toy.

PART V ANIMATING

Chapter 14
Essential Character Animation   583

To create the illusion of life, you need to animate characters with the basic principles of timing: anticipation, snap, ease, cushion, squash, stretch, follow through, overlapping action, secondary action, and holds. To animate efficiently, you need to understand spline and keyframe controls. To communicate effectively, you need to compose your shots. Finally, you need to animate your characters with uniquely characteristic actions to keep your audience entertained and interested.

Chapter 15
Advanced Animation Using Constraints   657

The best setup in the world is useless unless you can make your characters act
through posing and timing. This chapter shows you how to pose your characters for
best effect, mimic weight and balance, create walks, runs, and other motion cycles,
and use the animation hierarchy effectively. You'll also learn to analyze and
caricature motion, including the classic cartoon repertoire of takes, sneaks,
staggers, and zips.

Chapter 16
Power-Tool Animation 723

Power tools and procedural setups, like any animation tools, are only as good as the animator applying them. You need to know when a power tool will save you work without reducing the quality of the final animation, and when the power tool will drag down the quality of your work. Power tools are seductive, and you need to have a well-developed suspicion of inflated claims or inappropriate applications.

PART VI   POST-ANIMATION PRODUCTION

Chapter 17
Lighting And Rendering 763

All your test renderings are no more than dress rehearsals. Your final lighting and rendering are opening night: here are the results you will place before your audience.

Chapter 18
Compositing Effects 787

Compositing is a means to add your CGI creations to live-action footage, or to combine effects you couldn't render in one pass. Add compositing to your personal toolkit, and you'll more than double utility and effectiveness of all your other tools.

Chapter 19
Title Design And Finishing Touches 817

Good title design and readable credits add to the professional appearance of your animations. Take the time to do them right, especially for your demo reel or an independent short.

Chapter 20
Final Output

Even the best character animation is worthless if an audience can't see it. How you record, distribute, and play back your animations will depend on your resources and your target audience.

PART VII   TAKING CARE OF BUSINESS

Chapter 21
Starting Out

When you're trying to break into the business, you need to know what employers are looking for and where to find animation industry information.

Chapter 22
Being An Employee 863

Once you've landed a job in animation, you'll have to work to keep it. You'll also need to look after yourself, if you want to avoid being underpaid, exploited, obsolete, or disabled.

Chapter 23
Running Your Own Shop 871

If you really love doing the best work you can, making your own creative decisions, setting your own rules, and working on your own schedule, you may want to work for yourself.

PART VIII   APPENDIXES

Appendix A
Glossary 889

Animation is a special form of that most human of arts, storytelling. It is perhaps the furthest extrapolation of the hand gestures used by the fireside storyteller to draw pictures in the minds of the audience. Just as the storyteller uses a physical language to emphasize and embellish their tale, animation can use a variety of techniques to accomplish the same goals.

An animator creates the illusion of motion with a series of images. Whether those images are created by the pen of a cartoonist, the knife of a sculptor, the posing of a living body, or the pixel manipulation of the computer artist, the principles of animation are the same. Every branch of animation can learn from every other. Computer generated imagery, or CGI, is the youngest shoot on the family tree, and therefore has the greatest amount to learn from the older forms.

The last 30 years have seen great advances in CGI, from abstract light patterns on vector graphic displays to the photorealism of *The Lost World* and *Dragonheart* and character development of *Toy Story*. Older forms of animation were restrained by the limits of the physical materials they relied on, whether paper, cel, clay, or even the film itself. Now it is possible for CGI to overcome the limits of that materiality, to literally animate anything we can imagine, to make our dreams and fantasies live on the screen.

CGI animation development has thrived in the area of motion picture special effects, animating spacecraft and astronomic phenomena, energy weapons and the explosions they produce. These effects have pushed CGI to very high levels of cinematic realism, but they cannot tell an engaging story by themselves. People aren't interested in watching special effects unless they advance the story line. Effects are window dressing, not premise.

If CGI animation is to tell an engaging story, it must be a story about anthropomorphic characters: digital models of humans, creatures, artifacts, or even inanimate objects caricatured into the semblance of life. This is the highest and most difficult form of CGI: Character Animation.

Character animation has always been the apex of any form of animation. Even in the most abstract of line drawings or the most minimalist of stop-motion cinematography, the creative workload of character animation is overwhelming. Each image must first be composed with the obsessively detailed care of any other animation. On top of this, the animator must give the characters that breath of life, the posing, timing, and expressiveness that will convince the audience that the characters are moving of their own volition.

Character animation is a combination of talents so rare that *Fortune*, *The Wall Street Journal*, and *The New York Times* have published profiles of top animators. Salaries for lead animators have more than doubled in the last few years. Even considering the cyclical nature of the business, the prospects for CGI character animators have never been better. The viewing public has responded well to the use of CGI character animation, so advertising agencies, video game developers, and motion picture studios are pushing the demand for character animators. How long this market will last is anyone's guess, but the current reality is that demand for competent character animators is far outstripping the supply.

Training for CGI character animation has been almost exclusively on-the-job or by way of traditional animation approaches. Until very recently, the hardware and software necessary for CGI character animation have been prohibitively expensive, animation schools have been slow to offer courses including CGI, and there have been few books or videos on the topic.

CGI Software And Character Animation

Recent software development has made character animation tools affordable for even the beginning animator. The hardware necessary can be purchased for a fraction of the price of a good used car, and several software packages are priced for the hobbyist or student. Most of the programs reviewed here will continue to support you in growing an animation business all the way up to television and feature films.

Many of these programs have already been used to produce character animation for film, television or games. The commercial success of these programs has helped build the demand for character animators who can use them. Some studios use a variety of software, while other use only one or two packages. You can refer to the Artist and Studio Directory in the appendixes for information about which studios use what software. If you have your heart set on working for a particular studio, you'd do well to learn the software they're already using.

Who Needs This Book?

This book is intended to bridge the gap between the CGI artist and the traditional animator. It is designed to introduce you to the vocabulary and techniques used by both approaches. If you are already an animator, you will learn the CGI software tools designed to support character animation. If you are a CGI artist, you will learn the essential techniques of character animation as they apply to CGI tools.

If you are a beginner in both fields, I suggest that you complete the exercises in your software's manuals before you start to work through this book. At the least, they will contain the technical information you'll need regarding system requirements, software installation and troubleshooting. Many vendors also include tutorials that introduce you to the basic functions of the software. Vendors put a lot of time and effort into these user and reference manuals; if you never read them, you're not getting your money's worth. Once you have worked through the materials that came with your software, you will be much better prepared for the projects in this book.

If a vendor has included a particularly helpful tutorial with their manuals, I'll refer to it at the appropriate point. There's no sense in my repeating what's been written elsewhere, I'd rather provide you with original projects that go beyond the vendor's manuals.

If you're trying to use this book as a "manual" for pirated software, don't. Don't email me for advice about "cracks" or "warez," either; I'll just refer you to: **http://www.spa.org/piracy/ q&a.htm**.

Throughout this book, each concept is reinforced with projects designed to build your expertise without overwhelming you. Completing all the projects will enable you to produce complete character animation, from storyboard to video or film. This book also shows you how to assemble a demo reel and look for employment as an animator or technical director.

What's Inside?

This introduction is your guide to using this book to your best advantage. The path you follow through the projects will depend on what you already know, and what you want to learn. Whether you are a beginner, an expert CGI artist, or a traditional animator, you should read this chapter first.

The bulk of this book is organized in pretty much the same order as an animation production. If you are new to animation, you would do well to read through this book in order from first to last. If you are more experienced, you may choose to skim over areas with which you are already familiar, and move on to the more challenging new areas. If you are a traditional animator making the transition to CGI, I recommend that you also read through this book in order, noting where the CGI process is similar to traditional processes and where it differs.

The first chapter provides an overview of the production team, something especially useful to freelancers and beginners who have not yet been part of a larger studio. Chapters 2, 3, and 4 provide step-by-step development of the story, script, storyboard, soundtrack and timing sheets that are necessary before you can begin to animate the characters. Chapters 5, 6, and 7 cover character design and modeling, proceeding from general guidelines to specific procedures with advanced software and hardware tools like 3D scanners and digitizers. Chapters 8, 9, and 10 cover materials and maps, the tools you'll use to control the surface appearance of your characters.

Chapters 11, 12, and 13 introduce the principles of character setup, the critical process of articulating the character so the animator can pose it as intuitively and easily as possible. Chapters 14, 15, and 16 present the principles of character animation, keyed to the corresponding setups in the preceding three chapters. Each project closes with tips on practicing, sometimes recommending that you repeat the project (with interesting changes) and sometimes referring you to other activities that will help hone your skills.

The next part, Chapters 17, 18, 19, and 20, wraps up with projects that teach you how to light your scenes, do titles and credits, compositing and move matching, and transfer your animations to the final output format.

Along the way, and especially in Chapters 21, 22, and 23, you'll find advice from professional animators about the business of animation. You'll learn what to expect from studio, freelance, or independent work, getting your career started, when not to take a job or project, and other maps through the minefield.

As you might expect, at the back of this book you'll find a glossary, index, and a number of useful appendices.

Platform Wars

I've used just about every desktop computing hardware and operating system developed since the mid-80s, and I have no religious convictions about any of them. The only criteria I use for choosing a platform are current functionality, compatibility with colleagues, longevity, upgrade path, and vendor support.

- Current functionality means the platform has to work right now, and do what you need to get your work done. Neither promises nor fond memories can cut it in the working world.

- Compatibility with colleagues means you can share files, either across the cubicle or across the world (usually via the Internet). If you can't play well with others, you won't be invited to play as often.

- Longevity means your system will still be productively viable for the three years it takes to depreciate into a boat anchor.

- Upgrade path means you can put a third of the system's purchase price into it each year in the form of new parts, and thereby keep it from becoming a boat anchor for another year.

- Vendor support means the system runs software that is commercially available without paying consultants or programmers to tweak it. Personally, I also like being able to run general business software. This enables me to focus my investment in a single machine, rather than creating CGI on one and doing bookkeeping and taxes on another.

That said, I've got a few words of advice about choosing hardware and software for character animation. The general trend in the industry is towards the Microsoft Windows NT platform. For good or ill, that's where the lion's share of the market is headed, and that's where you will continue to find the broadest selection of software, hardware and vendor support. This trend does not mean you have to immediately abandon whatever investment you have made in another platform, it just means you should seriously reevaluate your hardware purchases any time you upgrade in the future. Vendor support becomes even more important, and you should make sure you buy or lease your system from a dealer who understands your needs. For example, if you need an SGI machine, MicroMadness (**www.madness.net**) in New York has character animators on staff who understand what you need, and can provide well-informed advice about software and hardware options. Vince Liggio, the owner, has been active and supportive in the character animation community, and understands the issues involved.

There is still a large installed base of SGI and Mac machines in studios around the world, and as long as a colleague, client, employer or software publisher is still using a system that's compatible with yours, you're doing all right. Who knows, by the time all the forthcoming NT ports are shipping, there may actually be a new operating system that will give Microsoft a run for its money.

Character Animation Software

The following thumbnail software reviews are my opinions, based on my efforts to duplicate the character animation projects in this book with each software package. Your mileage may vary. If you have a markedly different opinion (and can back it up objectively), I'd like to hear it!

3D Studio MAX

Kinetix (**www.ktx.com**) currently holds the largest installed base for software capable of character animation. The combination of the base 3D Studio MAX program and Character Studio plug-ins makes a powerful toolset that is popular in game development and is making inroads in television and film production.

The major disadvantage to MAX is that plug-ins are necessary for serious character animation. This is partially balanced by the large number of third-party developers who publish plug-ins for

MAX. The base program has a fairly steep learning curve, but lots of help is available in the excellent MAX manuals, third-party books and videotapes, and a cornucopia of online resources.

MAX (plus the necessary plug-ins) has a steep price for hobbyists, but is reasonable for shops or working professionals. Mastering MAX is a good step toward steady employment, and owning a copy can be the foundation of your own business. If you are looking for Hollywood-level employment, however, you will need to show competence with Softimage, Alias, or Houdini.

Alias

As of this writing, Alias|Wavefront, an SGI subsidiary, (**www.aw.sgi.com**) just released Maya, the next generation of the Alias family of software. This release will probably make most of this book's references to Alias obsolete, as they refer mostly to PowerAnimator version 8. You can check my Web site (**http://home.earthlink.net/~dakelly/index.htm**) for online updates, reviews and projects for Maya as they become available.

Alias has been highly regarded for modeling, and the most common software combination I've found in Hollywood-level shops is Alias for modeling and Softimage for animation. The new Maya may change that, but probably not overnight, especially considering the per-seat license cost. At present, Maya is only available on the SGI platform, although SGI is supposed to be manufacturing NT boxes in the near future. At the moment, an Alias/Maya seat is beyond the financial reach of most individuals, a steep investment for small shops, and still a significant cost of doing business for the large studios that rely on Alias|Wavefront products.

On the positive side, the Alias development team is talented and well-funded, and work produced with Alias software has won nearly every major award from the Oscar on down. Chris Landreth, creator of *The End* and other award-winning character animations, is on staff at Alias, and with other staff animators has made a significant impact on the direction of software development. The basic Alias package includes a well-written, exhaustive 35-pound set of manuals, and online resources and classes fill in the few remaining gaps. There is very little character animation you can't do with Alias. Whether it's suitable for your purposes is only a matter of finance and workflow preferences.

Animation:Master

You'll be able to judge Hash, Inc.'s Animation:Master (**www.hash.com**) for yourself, since there's a demo version of Animation:Master '98 on this book's companion CD-ROM. The most significant difference from other software is that A:M is entirely spline-based, it uses no polygons. This is a major advantage for characters that you want to squash, stretch and bend without the angular artifacts of polygonal models.

There are several movie clips on the CD-ROM of films produced with A:M, including *Fluffy, Balls & Blocks,* and *Nightwalk.* For pure character animation, A:M can challenge Softimage in most respects. The primary complaint of A:M users has been its instability, but the staff at Hash has been working on that. A:M is available on both Intel and PowerMac platforms, which makes it one of the few serious character animation packages still available to Mac users.

The current entry-level price for A:M is $199, but educational discounts can reduce that to $139. Animation:Master is definitely the most bang for your buck for character animation. If you are just getting started in character animation, this is the software I recommend.

Electric Image Animation System

Electric Image (**www.electricimg.com**) just released EIAS version 2.8, unfortunately too close to this book's print deadline for me to do it justice in a review. Judging from the development version I saw last August, they have made major improvements to the tools most needed by character animators, especially keyframe editing and joint setup. As with Maya, check my Web site for online updates, reviews and projects as they become available.

Extreme 3D 2

I can't recommend that you use Macromedia's Extreme 3D for character animation. Technically, the software is capable of rendering an animated character. Practically, the tools you need to model, set up and animate a character are either missing entirely or are simply too difficult to use. Character animation with Extreme 3D is harder than traditional puppet or cel animation, and that's defeating the whole purpose of CGI animation.

If you're stuck with Macromedia products and you have to animate a character, there are a couple of things you can do to make your job less difficult. One of the most frustrating things about learning to use Extreme 3D is trying to figure out what the publisher decided to call a particular feature or function. I recommend that you read the manual with a highlighter or pen in hand and mark odd terms with synonyms and *See Also* references in the index. Also, Macromedia products do not play well with others. You will need to use only native Macromedia file formats, if you want to avoid nasty incompatibility problems. Last, using Extreme 3D makes it more important than ever to plan your work so you have a chance of getting it right the first time. Extreme 3D (and several other Macromedia products) are not at all tolerant of errors, and rather than a simple Undo, you will often have to start over when you make a mistake.

Even if you got it free as part of a Macromedia bundle, Extreme 3D is no bargain for character animation.

Houdini

Side Effects Software (**www.sidefx.com**) publishes what is arguably the most powerful, top-of-the-heap character animation software available. It is entirely procedural, which means everything is controlled by variables and expressions and is therefore continuously editable. This has the great advantage of enabling you to change each detail, right up to the final rendering, without having to rebuild any other work. This is an invaluable benefit if you have micromanaging clients or impossible deadlines. The disadvantage is that all this power demands that you know what you're doing in order to control it all.

Houdini is a program for the true power user. I do not recommend it as the first character animation software you buy, even if you can afford it. If you already have a working shop, your clients demand top-notch results, and you're comfortable with the theories behind CGI, then you should definitely consider Houdini. The open architecture of this software means that you can duplicate any feature of any other package with a little ingenuity on your part.

If you're comfortable with off-the-shelf CGI software and want to stretch your mind in a more technical direction, Houdini is a wonderful learning tool. It's not impossible, or even difficult, for a new user to learn. It simply requires you to commit time to actually reading and understanding the manuals. The staff at Side Effects Software has done a laudable job in compiling the *Reference* and *Tutorial* manuals for Houdini. The text is phrased as simply as the subject matter permits, and jargon is defined clearly when it first appears. This documentation is like an outline for a Master's degree in computer graphics.

At present, Houdini is available only for the SGI platform, although an NT version is in development.

If your work (or your dedication to your hobby) justifies it, the premium price for Houdini is well worth it. This software is a literally unlimited tool for character animation or any other form of CGI.

Imagine

Impulse has been in the desktop graphics software business for a number of years. It's unfortunate that it's management hasn't learned more from experience. The version of Imagine that I was provided to review for this book did not correspond at all to the documentation that came with it, and my subsequent inquiries to Impulse went unanswered. I have seen at least one example of character animation reportedly created with Imagine. However, since I could not duplicate even basic hierarchical setups with this software, I have to recommend that you avoid it. I wish I could say something more positive, as my first CGI animation experience was with Imagine's predecessor, Turbo Silver, on the Amiga platform, and it's sad to see a favorite tool fall by the wayside. I'm sorry to see that Impulse hasn't kept up with the rest of the industry.

Infini-D

MetaCreations' (**www.metacreations.com**) Infini-D is an adequate program for learning the basics of modeling, lighting, rendering, and simple hierarchical animation. However, it's short on deformation animation tools, and therefore limits you to marionette-style characters with visible seams. The manuals are good, and the price is reasonable for hobbyists or students. This is an acceptable entry-level program for learning basic CGI and character animation on the PowerMac, but it's not really suitable for a production environment.

LightWave 3D

NewTek's LightWave 3D (**www.newtek.com**) program for the Intel, Alpha, and PowerMac platforms is a staple of the game, TV, and film production environment. It's entirely suitable for character animation as is, but if you're new to the software you may find some of its approaches less than intuitive. Plug-ins are available that make character animation easier, but you can do just fine with the base package. In quality of rendering, LW can stand up to nearly any program, but in ease of use and availability of character animation functions it's a little behind MAX, A:M, and Softimage. Since it's also priced well below MAX and Softimage, it has more character animation bang for the buck than anything except Animation:Master.

For a more detailed set of tutorials on character animation with LightWave 3D, I refer you to my first book, *LightWave 3D 5 Character Animation F/X*, to my regular column "The Character Shop," in LightWavin' magazine, and to my Web site.

Poser

This program, also from MetaCreations, was one of the biggest (and most pleasant) surprises in this book. I originally had it pegged as a low-end form of 3D clip art, but it turns out to be one of the most easy-to-use and versatile education tools for character animation that I've ever seen. The pre-built characters included with the program enable beginners to start animating a full humanoid without hassling with a setup first. The keyframe animation controls are rather rudimentary, but they get the job done. The lighting and rendering are simple and straightforward, and the end results can be exported to other software. This is a serious character animation learning tool and, at about $150 list, a bargain. If you received it as part of a software bundle, you're missing out if you haven't tried it.

The only disadvantage to Poser is that it achieves its ease of use through cutting off options, so once you've reached the limits of the software or models, there's no place to go. No plug-ins, no open architecture. However, by that time you'll be ready for a higher level of character animation software.

Ray Dream Studio 5

You might think of this program as Poser's big brother. RD5, also published by MetaCreations, is a full-featured CGI package with all the tools you'd expect of a polygonal modeler, keyframe animator, and versatile renderer. The manual, complete and colorful in the original Fractal Design style, is a very user-friendly introduction to CGI in general and, along the way, to the basic concepts of character animation. While not as versatile or powerful as MAX or Softimage, it's certainly adequate for the hobbyist, small business or student, and at about $300 list is very reasonably priced.

Softimage 3D

Softimage (**www.softimage.com**) was a favorite of the character animation community long before Microsoft purchased it. This software is definitely in the CGI big leagues. It requires serious hardware (SGI or NT) to run it, and forget multitasking. Softimage takes over your system, fixes your screen resolution, and pretty much demands acceleration from officially approved video cards like Dynamic Pictures' Oxygen series. If you don't have a serious accelerator card, you can go nuts waiting for screen refresh on complex character setups.

Despite these drawbacks, Softimage is the character animation program of choice among working pros in top studios. For an example of what's possible, take a look at the clips from Steph Greenberg's short film, *The Physics of Cartoons, Part 1*, in the PHYSICS directory of the CD-ROM. You can do things in Softimage that are difficult or impossible in most other character animation programs, and that production edge is what sells a lot of Softimage licenses. The support, documentation and online resources are also superlative, and once you've mastered the program you'll discover that Softimage animators are almost always in demand.

According to several professional character animators who have worked with both programs, Animation:Master and Softimage are currently the best choices for character animation using complex constraint setups as described in Chapter 12. Considering the price difference, you might want to try A:M before you invest in Softimage. A major new release of Softimage, code named Sumatra, is currently in the works, but don't hold your breath. As with Alias' Maya, major releases of software at this level of development are few and far between.

Strata Studio Pro

Strata's StudioPro (**www.strata.com**), now available for both Mac and NT, is acceptable as a general CGI animation program but falls a little short on character setup and animation tools. Judging from the level of documentation, support, and usability of features, this program seems overpriced and underpowered. At $1,495 list, you can get a lot more power and functionality with LightWave, or chuck the polygons and try Animation:Master for a fraction of the price.

trueSpace3

As with Animation:Master, you can try out Caligari's (**www.caligari.com**) trueSpace3 with the demo version on the CD-ROM. TS requires plug-ins for morphing, but other than that it's a pretty complete character animation package. One especially nice touch is the import and export compatibility with multiple object file formats like Wavefront OBJ, Kinetix 3DS and LightWave LWO. TrueSpace3 is available for Windows 95 and runs comfortably on NT as well. At $695 list, this program falls somewhere between LightWave and Ray Dream 5, and that's about where it falls functionally, too.

About The CD-ROM

The CD-ROM enclosed with this book contains all the electronic files you will need to complete the projects. You will also find examples of completed work from the projects for you to compare to your own efforts. In addition to scripts, storyboards, sounds, exposure sheets, models, backgrounds, images, and scenes, there are finished animations, artwork, software, and other samples from a number of vendors and artists.

About Online Updates

Software changes rapidly, so I'm offering free updates to projects and files from this book as software development continues. When software developers announce a new feature or program, I'll do my best to update the relevant sections of this book online. I'll also provide links to various CGI resources on the Internet, including discussion groups, newsgroups, databases, and more, at **http://home.earthlink.net/~dakelly/index.htm**.

Hardware And Software Requirements

To complete the projects, you'll need whatever hardware is necessary to run your software on the platform of your choice. Many of the projects use software written for the Intel platform, and equivalent tools for Alpha, PowerPC, or SGI hardware and operating systems may not be available. In each case, sample output from the project is provided on the CD-ROM so you can complete any dependent projects.

So What Are You Waiting For?

By now, I'm certain you're eager to get started. When you've completed all the projects, or just have a few nice examples you want to show off, I'd like to hear from you. You can reach me via email at **dakelly@earthlink.net**, or c/o Coriolis Group.

Best of luck, and welcome to the wonderful world of character animation!

Doug Kelly

CHARACTER ANIMATION

IN DEPTH

PART I

PRE-PRODUCTION

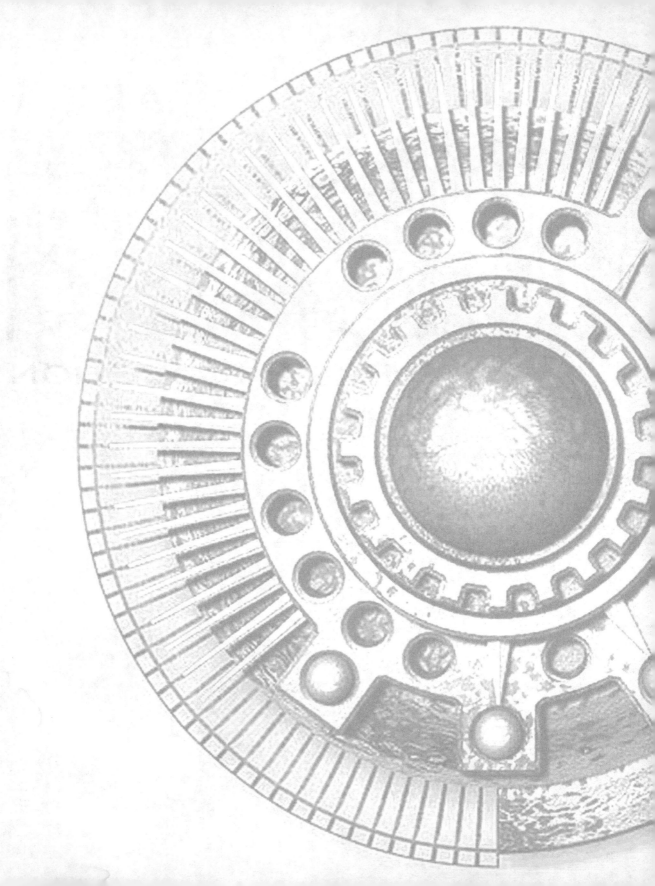

Hats Can You Wear?

If you have never worked as an animator before, this chapter is a good place to find out what the job is like, either in an animation production house or as a freelance artist.

One of the most liberating aspects about the revolution in desktop animation software is that you really can do it all yourself. There are software tools that can assist you in doing screenwriting, storyboard and layout art, modeling, texturing, audio digitizing, track reading, animation, rendering, record keeping, financial and scheduling project management, music composition and recording, audio and video mixing and editing, title design, and film or video recording.

The question is, do you want to handle it all?

If you really have a driving, unique artistic vision that you feel only you can realize, then more power to you (just don't try to be your own agent and attorney, as well!). If you prefer to concentrate on one specialty and do it well, then more power to you also. Whatever your approach, this book shows you how to put all the necessary pieces together to create character animation.

Along the way, you'll learn a little more about the other professions and trades associated with animated film production. I hope this information will help you become a more effective animator or technical director (TD), whether you pursue an independent career or join one of the growing number of animation production houses.

Meet The Team

Most production studios have an organizational structure with similar job titles, although the actual responsibilities of the people vary from studio to studio. Generally, the larger the organization, or the bigger the project, the more people will specialize. For smaller shops and shorter projects, each person may handle several different jobs. Whatever the size or scope of the production, there are a few basic job descriptions you can depend on, including director, writer, storyboard artist, art director, supervising animator, animator, technical director, track reader, sheet timer, layout artist, production assistants, gofers, and peons.

Director

The director is the person responsible for the overall product—for keeping the "big picture" clearly in sight. In smaller shops or on shorter projects, the director will hand you the storyboards and exposure sheets, and go over the intent of the shot to make sure you understand the characterization they are looking for. The director will also pass final judgment on your animation.

In effect, the director is a minor deity, answerable only to the executive producer or the client. Some directors will remind you of their status at every opportunity. Others will remind you of their rank only if you do something inadvisable, like continuing to disagree with them after they've made a decision. Voice your opinion once, diplomatically, then go along with whatever the director decides. Making the final decision is what the director gets paid for.

Directors can also be your best mentors. They generally have the most on-the-job experience of anyone on a production team, and can be a treasure trove of knowledge and advice. Listen to their critiques carefully, consider their advice, and do your best to learn from their experience.

Writer

The writer develops the script. Unless there are rewrites, the writer has the least influence on the difficulty of your work as an animator. In many cases, once the script has been translated to storyboards, all further development is done visually and the script is obsolete. The writer may still participate in story sessions, but any revisions from that point are collaborative efforts.

Storyboard Artist

The storyboard artist translates the written script to a series of sketches (see Chapter 3) and revises, adds, or deletes sketches during story sessions. Because storyboard artists work in 2D, they can "cheat" or draw character actions that are difficult to animate. If you see a story sketch that is going to be a problem, point it out (diplomatically, of course) at the first opportunity. It's a lot easier to get a story sketch revised than the finished model and exposure sheets!

Art Director

The art director (and the entire art department, in larger organizations) is responsible for developing the overall look—the visual style—of the product. Like the storyboard artist, the art director can create 2D drawings that are nearly impossible to replicate in 3D. Character design is especially difficult to adapt; you will need to work closely with the TD in negotiating with the art director to make sure the proposed characters can be built and animated.

Supervising Animator

If the project is a large one, you may be working under a supervising animator. Job titles and authorities vary, but typical examples are directing animator, lead animator, or animation supervisor. Usually, these are senior animators who act as deputies for the director. You will probably receive your shot materials from the supervising animator rather than the director. If you are new to the profession, the supervising animator may become your mentor, helping you out on problem shots and giving you the benefit of his or her experience. Take advantage of the opportunity to learn from them!

Animator

When you strip away the technology, finance, and politics of making an animated film, the animator's job is the heart of it. Whether working solo or as part of a production team, the animator's task is to breathe the illusion of life into a model by creating a sequence of poses that communicate character. You can program a computer to make a model lip sync any line of dialogue, but if the accompanying action is not convincing, the characterization fails. The rest of the production team relies on you to get the animation right.

The materials the animator uses to create a CGI animation can include storyboards, exposure sheets, model sheets, film footage to be matched, objects and scenes. Who provides these on the job can vary from studio to studio. For this book's exercises, the necessary materials are included in the appendices and this book's CD-ROM. The results your director expects you to produce are finished animation files, ready to be lighted and rendered.

Technical Director

The technical director (TD) can make or break your animation work. In most shops, the TD builds, textures, and lights the models you will be animating, and may develop custom software tools as well. In larger shops, lighting, textures and character setup may be separate job descriptions. In smaller shops, you may be doing all these tasks yourself.

The TD will usually provide you, the animator, with the model sheets and other notes on the construction of the characters. This information can make your work much easier, so cultivate your TD and treat him or her well. TDs tend to have more computer skills and a more analytical and engineering approach than animators, which has led to industry stereotypes about cultural conflicts between the two "tribes."

When you take a problem to a TD, be diplomatic (as with all team members), and make an attempt to understand the TD's side of the problem. One of the goals of this book is to teach you the professional vocabulary of the TD, since people are generally more receptive to suggestions if you speak their language. As an animator, you do not need to know absolutely everything about CGI software or the particular computer hardware you use, just as you don't need to know how to make a pencil in order to use it effectively. However, more knowledge can be a good thing; just as in other arts, the artist who does not understand how their tools function and are made is at a disadvantage.

Track Reader

Track reading has traditionally been performed by specialists, with the director or supervising animator transcribing the completed analysis to exposure sheets, which are then passed on to the animator. In some studios, the track reader may fill in the exposure sheets directly. Software developers have recently produced several different tools to automate most of the track analysis process (see Chapter 4), so this specialty may not survive much longer.

Sheet Timer

You will usually find sheet timers working in television production, where they take over some of the traditional timing work of directors. After the storyboards are done, the sheet timer marks the musical beats, foley (sound effect) hits, and actions on the exposure sheets. The sheet timer determines the overall timing of the animation; they sometimes have more influence on the final appearance of the action than either the director or the animator.

Layout Artist

Layout artist is a job title that you will only find in larger organizations. In smaller ones, the job is generally split between the director, TD, and animator. The layout artist translates each 2D story sketch to one or more composed 3D shots, setting the scene with camera, characters, sets, and basic lighting. This is the CGI equivalent of cinematic or theatrical *blocking*.

Layout can be a difficult job, especially if the storyboard artist "cheated" shots in ways that can't be modeled in 3D. Once the layouts are done, it's possible to substitute rendered frames for the story sketches in the story reel (see Chapter 4). In some studios, layout can also refer to character layout or setup—working with the TD and animator to assemble the model, skeleton and controls for each character (see Part IV).

Production Assistants, Gofers, And Peons

Somebody has to pick up and deliver stuff, keep track of schedules and checklists, and make sure nothing falls through the cracks. Animation production is even more detail-sensitive than live-action cinematography. Don't underestimate the importance of, or try to complete a major project without, these invaluable assistants. And treat them well, someday you might be working for them!

Working With A Team

Production workflows seem to be one of the most closely-guarded secrets in the animation business. As I was researching this book, I found questions about production practices to be the one sure way to get a source to clam up. Whenever you have a job interview, be sure to ask questions about workflow and creative opportunities—it shows you are interested in doing the work, and the answers will tell you a lot about the organization.

Every shop is different, and even the same shop can vary from project to project. An advertising project may come from a micromanaging client or agency with very specific ideas about everything, or they may ask the production team to come up with the whole concept. A feature or short may start out very nebulous, with the creative team soliciting story ideas from everyone down to the janitor, or the director may have one of those crystalline, burning visions that dictates every detail. As an animator or TD, you need to stay flexible and adapt your working style to your employer or client.

For example, many studios will leave the fine details of character design until later in the process. Animators often do early tests with rough or low-resolution models of the characters, which are gradually refined as the action shows where changes are needed. This gives the studio a margin of error, so if a character is not working out it can be revised or discarded at no great loss. In this type of workflow, you need to provide feedback to the TDs responsible for the character modeling, pointing out problems and suggesting solutions, so the final model is one you can animate well and easily. Conversely, some studios (Mainframe Entertainment, for one) lock the character designs early, so they can do layout, blocking and storyboard sessions completely in the computer. Studios can get away with this in producing a series because the cast and sets don't change very much. Once you've ironed out the characters for the first episode, you can take advantage of stock character setups to speed up the story and layout processes. As an animator, you'll have to make your critiques and suggestions before the director locks the models, so you're not stuck with a character that's difficult to animate. Make sure you know how your studio works, and think ahead!

Depending on shop policy (and your seniority), your supervisor may simply hand you exposure and model sheets and tell you to animate them. This kind of creative restriction is intolerable to some animators, but others don't seem to mind. In more flexible shops, you may be allowed or encouraged to contribute ideas in story meetings, storyboard sessions and other creative collaborations. These are good opportunities to practice your diplomacy and teamwork skills.

You should also keep in mind the ground rules for these meetings, which can vary a great deal between shops, teams, and even directors. One common approach is to separate the creative, brainstorming part of a meeting from the analytical, critical part. If a meeting is being run with this approach, the fastest way to make yourself *persona non grata* is to break the rules, either criticizing during the brainstorming session or throwing in new ideas after the analysis has begun. In any case, don't hare off on topics that aren't on the agenda, don't chime in if you don't have anything constructive to contribute, and never play devil's advocate just for the sake of starting an argument. Try not to think out loud, either; give yourself a moment to phrase an observation or suggestion as concisely as possible, and think about the effect your suggestions may have on the other people in the meeting. If you are not sure of what you have to say, and especially if your remarks may offend someone in another department, consider making discreet suggestions through channels (i.e., your supervisor) after the meeting. You're better off having your supervisor take credit for one of your ideas (yes, that happens) than offending a coworker through ignorance. Diplomacy and tact are essential to all production

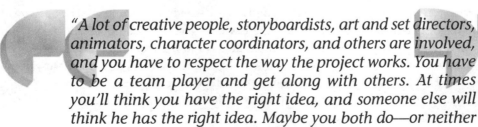

"A lot of creative people, storyboardists, art and set directors, animators, character coordinators, and others are involved, and you have to respect the way the project works. You have to be a team player and get along with others. At times you'll think you have the right idea, and someone else will think he has the right idea. Maybe you both do—or neither of you is close."

Steve Bloom, screenwriter

team members. You want to build a reputation as a person of few words and good ideas, so when you do speak up your team members will listen.

Pay attention to the person running the meeting, too. Some people run very good meetings where most participants leave with a positive attitude, good ideas are created, and a lot of work gets done. Try to emulate these people; someday you're going to be the one leading the meeting.

Plan Your Work, Work Your Plan

Character animation, like many other complex endeavors, benefits from thorough planning. For any complicated project involving different talents or groups of people, a successful plan evolves and grows. It never springs full-grown from the mind of even the most Zeus-like director. The plan starts with a basic idea, that idea is fleshed out and detailed, and those details are in turn filled out to the next level of detail. At each level, changes and revisions can be made with a minimum of disturbance to the rest of the plan. If a level were skipped over or not developed completely, revisions to later levels would echo catastrophically back through every part of the project.

In animation, the initial idea is usually a story to be told, and the final level of detail is the individual frame. Getting from one to the other is a series of logical steps—story, script, storyboard, bar sheets, exposure sheets, animation.

Different members of the production team may contribute revisions at each step in the process, depending on the studio and project. Each step produces its own characteristic set of documents, a record of the work completed that also forms the skeleton for the next level to flesh out. Take each of these steps one at a time, with a little thought and practice, and you will be able to master them all.

Organization: Getting There And Staying There

If you are producing your own demo reel or leading a small production team, you are responsible for creating and maintaining the project plan. This may be as simple as keeping track of your own notes, or as complex as managing all the working documents and files for your entire team. The larger the project, and the more people involved, the more critical this task becomes.

Small projects can get along with storyboards and a basic schedule showing which shots are at each stage in the production process. That's the low end. The high end goes all the way up through conventional production boards to integrated computer systems like Disney's CAPS, designed to manage projects that employ hundreds of people for years at a time. Most of the time, you'll find yourself somewhere between these extremes. In any case, you can save yourself lots of headaches and redundant effort if you use whatever organizational tools are available. Here are a few general guidelines:

- Keep all the project's working documents stored safely and in an order that enables you to find things quickly.

- Store older versions and backups safely out of the way, at least until the project is finished. You never know what you might need again.

- Don't be cute or cryptic with labels or file names. If several people are creating files, use consistent rules for naming them. You need to be able to tell what a file contains just by reading its name.

- Back up files regularly, and label the storage media when you record it. Few things are more tedious or annoying than having to play "feed the toaster" with a stack of unmarked disks, just to find one file.

- If more than one person is to use a character, setup, or other complex file, document that file. The time you save may be your own.

- If you're using a revised version of a file, keep careful track of which version is the most current, back up older versions and remove them from your computer to avoid confusion.

- When in doubt, print it out. Keeping hard copies of critical files is cheap insurance against system failures, and you can always recycle the paper after the project is over.

- If your project has any kind of deadline, put a calendar on your wall that shows the current date, the deadline date and all the days in between. Mark your milestones, delivery and receipt dates, deadlines, and payment dates. Marking important dates like anniversaries, birthdays and holidays can save you some grief, too, especially if you're a workaholic.

- Put one person in charge of maintaining the project plan and materials. Choose the most trustworthy, reliable, and detail-oriented person on the production team. If that isn't you, then keep your fingers out of it and let them do their job!

Goals

The point of all this effort is usually an animated film. Sometimes there are other goals, too; a better job, a distribution deal, a film contract, political statement, fame, fortune, or just getting credit for a class. Whatever your goal is, make it clear from the start, and keep an eye on it. No project ever goes perfectly, and when you have to choose what to sacrifice, you'll appreciate a clear picture of what's necessary to your goal and what can be discarded. When you're embroiled in all the details of producing an animation, it's very easy to lose sight of your original goal. Once you're no longer focused on the goal, your project can veer off into directions you won't want it to take. At the least, the story and execution may lose focus and not be as powerful as you intended; at worst, the project may come apart completely.

Keep an eye on your goal!

Moving On

I hope this chapter has given you a better idea of what your day-to-day work will be like, and that it hasn't scared you away from being an animator. Like most art forms, the thrill of seeing your animations played for an appreciative audience is worth the sacrifices. In the next chapter, you'll learn how to create the story and script that will be the foundation for your animation.

STORY **AND SCRIPT**

This chapter shows you how to build a strong foundation for your character animation. It's possible to create an excellent bit of character animation without a story or script, but the odds are against it.

You can bypass the steps of creating a story or script if you're doing motion tests or exercises, because those aren't necessarily telling a story. For anything more complex, do yourself a favor, and work through the story and script process first.

Even the most prominent names in the field of character animation follow this process. Pixar had already moved into production on parts of *Toy Story* when they found the story had major problems. They put most of the production team on hiatus while the story team hammered out the problem, then resumed production. If they had bulled through production with the original, flawed story, the film would most likely have bombed at the theaters.

First things first!

The Importance Of A Story

A good story, even if it is very small, is crucial to a successful animation. Thirty-second TV commercials, video game cut scenes, even five-second television station identifications all have stories to tell. If you want clients, employers, or any other audience to pay attention to your animation, make sure you are telling an interesting story. This is especially important for your demo reel. A series of brief, unrelated clips is simply not going to hold the reviewer's attention as well as a good, coherent story built around an engaging character.

Every good story must have a premise, which must suggest character, conflict, and a conclusion. The premise should be simple, as in "haste makes waste," "love conquers all," or, the premise selected for the example script, "easy come, easy go." A complex premise generally leads to a muddled and confusing story, and should therefore be avoided.

The premise is also crucial to pitching the story, if you need to convince investors, producers, talent, or distributors. The premise is your one-line pitch—the hook to interest your audience and get them to listen to the rest of your presentation.

Some film schools put their students through a tough but educational process of making their first film. The student has to choose an event in her own life that was embarrassing, traumatic, or otherwise emotionally very strong, then write it up as a

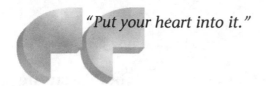

"Put your heart into it."

Harold Harris, TOPIX

script, and produce it as a film. This is an extension of the old writer's dictum, "Write what you know." Harold Harris, creative director at TOPIX, advises beginning animators to "Put your heart into it." If you want to make an outstanding film or demo reel, you've got to put something of yourself into it.

This approach has its merits. You will certainly have a personal interest in the production, and you should be able to identify the various emotional states the character goes through. The difficulty lies in extracting the premise of the story. Without that, it's just a disconnected anecdote, a slice of life quickly forgotten by all but the participants.

The essential element of a story for character animation is, appropriately enough, character. Other dramatic forms may emphasize different elements of the storytelling traditions, but this book—and your work—are about character animation.

Character

Character is defined by action. When we first see a character, we have no idea what he will do next. An undefined character can perform any action or speak any line of dialogue, without having the least effect on your audience. It is your job as an animator to make that character tell us about himself, to define who he is, so that the actions you animate and the lines your character lip-syncs have an effect on the audience and so advance your story. This can be a daunting task. For some television commercials, you may have as little as 2 seconds, a mere 60 frames, to define a character. In longer formats, you may have the luxury of developing your character in terms of physiology, sociology, and psychology. For example, Quasimodo in Disney's remake of *The Hunchback of Notre Dame* is the unique product of all three factors. Had Quasimodo been of a more average appearance (physiology), associated freely with people outside the church (sociology), or raised under different principles than those imposed by Frollo (psychology), his character would be different and so would the story. In the shorter formats, you usually must resort to caricature and stereotype to establish your character as quickly as possible.

Conflict builds character. Sounds like what they tell you as they cart you off the field, doesn't it? Nevertheless, it's true. Conflict is the friction between the character and his environment (including other characters) that forces the character to change and grow. This change and growth must be in a direction consistent with what we have already seen of the character. A miser shouldn't suddenly empty his wallet into the nearest charity box unless we first tell the whole series of conflicts leading up to his redemption, as in Dickens' *A Christmas Carol*. Ebenezer Scrooge must incrementally perceive the error of his ways, showing a plausible progression from hard-hearted miser to contrite benefactor, in order for the audience to accept Scrooge's epiphany on Christmas morning.

Conflict also serves to draw the characters more clearly. Even if the change through conflict is very small, with each conflict, your audience will see the character a little more clearly.

So, how do you devise a conflict? No need, the characters create their own plots. If the character is initially a miser, then obviously the strongest conflict would be if the miser's property were threatened. Depict your character strongly, and conflicts will present themselves.

Transition

Another concept I'd like to introduce here is the transition. While the term means something different in screenwriting and editing, in the dramatic sense the word refers to the dominant emotional state of a character. A transition occurs when a character expressing one emotion progresses through a conflict and changes to expressing a different emotion. Leaving out the transition, or shortening it so the audience does not see it clearly, makes a jump in the character's development that can ruin the story. This is especially important for character animation, because emotions must be displayed more obviously than in live action and require a good deal of planning from the animator. For example, there are several strong, visual emotional transitions for the title character in *How the Grinch Stole Christmas*:

- Frustration to evil glee when he gets his "wonderful, awful idea"
- Guilty surprise to smooth craftiness when Cindy Lou Who surprises him and he recovers by telling her lies
- Anger to enlightenment when he discovers the true meaning of Christmas

These transitions are worth studying. How many other pivotal transitions can you remember from your favorite films, both live-action and animated?

The end of the story should follow naturally from the growth of the original character through conflict. Don't try to get fancy, outfoxing your audience with surprise endings and bizarre last-act plot twists. Your audience won't thank you for it. Just finish the story with the last transition, in a manner that completes the premise, and leave it at that.

PROJECT 2.1 Develop A Story Line

Select a simple premise, and develop a brief story line from it. If you like, choose an incident from your own life that has strong potential for good character animation. Conflicts and transitions should be physically obvious, not internalized philosophical debates. If the story would work as a voiced-over exposition, throw it out. This is character animation, not a radio play.

Is your premise 10 words or less? Is the premise one you, personally, can believe in? (Remember, you're going to be spending a lot of quality time with the little monster.)

Can your character fulfill the premise? Is your conflict one that will expose the character more fully, or force the character to grow? Does the story provide for interesting transitions that will hold your audience's attention? Does the end of the story follow naturally from the character's growth or exposition, and does it fulfill the premise?

If all your answers are Yes, why aren't you a screenwriter? Just kidding! Let's take your story to the next level.

Drafting The Script

So, now you have an interesting story to tell. The sheer expense of character animation, whether measured in money or work-hours, demands that the story be told as succinctly and effectively as possible.

If you want to tell your story effectively, you need to have a plan, a blueprint that lays out all the parts in their proper places. The script is your blueprint. A properly formatted script tells each member of the production team what has to happen in order to tell the story. From this information, each specialist can plan the work she will contribute to the project.

If you can't write up your story as a script, you don't have a clear idea of what you are trying to say. The act of putting words on paper has a great clarifying effect on even the most obscure daydreams. It is also a useful test of the writer's creative vision: if the vision can't survive being translated into a script, it certainly isn't robust enough to survive the rigors of animation production.

Reshooting to correct problems that should have been caught in the script is a good way to blow your budget, your schedule, and your career as a director. A well-formatted script can go a long way toward preventing that kind of disaster. Each conflict and transition is written there in black and white, and if more than one member of the production team can't "see" a particular shot, that's an excellent indication that a rewrite is needed. Paper's cheap, but time and film aren't.

The script is intended as a working tool, not a literary form. Get used to writing in the standard format expected by Hollywood and Madison Avenue. Even as an independent or hobbyist, you may find it useful to consult a working professional or two about some production matter. If you show them an unkempt collection of odd formatting that you call a script, they are not as likely to take you seriously. Writing in the standard format costs you nothing in creativity, helps you stay organized, and makes your eventual transition to professional work that much easier.

The correct format for a shooting script is an easy thing to master. Get a copy of Blacker's *The Elements of Screenwriting*. This slender but dense volume covers the simple mechanics of punctuation and formatting in less than 10 pages.

One modification I would make to Blacker's advice, specifically for animation scripts: go ahead and direct the camera. Especially if you are playing Omnipotent Person Wearing All Hats, you probably have some idea of the camera angles and lenses you want for each shot. If not, trust me, you'll get those ideas while you're typing the script. Put them in; it's easier to line them out later than to pencil them in.

The sample script reprinted at the end of this chapter was formatted with the Script Maker template for Microsoft Word. This shareware template was distributed by Impact Pictures, but they seem to have vanished. There are a lot of similar products out there, both shareware and commercial. For links to demos and shareware, try:

http://elaine.teleport.com/~cdeemer/Software.html

For commercial screenwriting and production software, check out The Writer's Computer Store at:

http://writerscomputer.com/store/production_storyboard_software.htm

Take a look at the sample script. Note that each character, sound effect, and animated prop or live set is typed in all caps. This is an extension of the standard script format. The characters are capped so the animators for each character can see their shots, the sounds are capped so the sound crew can plan their work, and the sets and props are capped so the TD and animator can plan for the additional modeling and animation. If you are given a more traditional script to animate from, you may want to amplify it along these lines.

You should be aware that different studios may use slightly different terminology for *shot* and *scene*. Generally, and almost always in live-action cinematography, a scene is a collection of shots all in the same set or location, and a shot is the footage between one camera cut and the next. In animation, a scene sometimes refers only to what can be filmed without a change in background. This makes sense, if you consider that traditional animation requires the background to be redrawn whenever the camera moves. For the purposes of this book, I will use the live-action definition of shot and scene.

In the sample script, each shot is described by camera lens, angle, and the subjects contained in the shot. This is over-directing for live action, but it really helps for animation. If you're not familiar with camera directions, jump ahead to Chapter 14's section on camera animation, then come back here.

Each emotional transition is clearly written out. You wouldn't want to be this heavy-handed with directing live actors, but for animation, it's a necessity. After months of looking at dozens of shots, often out of order, you will have no idea what emotion was supposed to be portrayed unless it's written down somewhere. You might as well start with the script. Also, if there is to be any dialog, the written transition instructions will help the voice talent replace the normal interaction between the actors. In many animation productions, the voice talent record their own parts of the dialog in separate sessions, and don't interact with each other during recording. This can be a challenge, and the transition notes can help.

"Some people say your script should be sparse and flow. We detail a lot."
Steve Bloom and Jonathan Roberts, screenwriters

The level of detail in your script can vary according to your production team. For larger teams that are accustomed to a collaborative story process, the script should be less detailed. Other team members from the director all the way down to assistant animators may expect to contribute their own ideas to flesh out the script, and if you write in too much detail, they may resent it.

If you are writing a script for a video game cut scene, you should preface each shot with a brief summary of the preceding and following actions. This summary might include what the player has accomplished, which characters are present and any pertinent changes in their appearance, and the situation that will face the player after the cut scene concludes. This information makes it easier to write a cut scene script that will enhance the game play. For example, if the following action is a surprise attack by a horde of monsters, you wouldn't want the player's companions to decide that it's safe to take a nap. On the other hand, if the next action is solving an intricate puzzle, the game characters shouldn't end the scene by prepping weapons and hyperventilating.

No scene is complete until it advances character development, story, and premise at the same time. If you develop the character alone, perhaps in a vignette, the story will lag, and your audience will lose interest. If you develop the story without showing the character's growth, the character becomes two-dimensional and you lose the audience's empathy. If you ignore the premise in developing either story or character, your film loses focus and wanders away from your goal.

PROJECT 2.2 Draft A Script

Expand the brief story line from Project 2.1 into a properly formatted animation shooting script. When you are writing your shot descriptions, remember the principles of composition and character motion. If you need to review these principles, refer to the character animation section in Chapter 14.

If you don't want to script your own story, select and videotape a 30- or 60-second television commercial, then translate it to a script. The purpose of this exercise is to make you familiar with screenwriting conventions. Whether you write your own or work exclusively with other writers' scripts, you need to be able to read these blueprints accurately.

Have your script read by at least three other people. Be polite when they suggest plot changes, "improvements," or make other comments; people seem incapable of resisting the urge to muck up somebody else's writing. All you need to do is get answers to these three questions:

- Could you visualize each shot?
- Did the characters act consistently?
- Did you have an emotional reaction to any part of the story?

If you get a lot of "No" answers, you probably need to rewrite. If that seems too much for you, set your script aside and try to rewrite it later. You can complete the exercises by using the example script provided, you don't have to create everything from scratch. This book is about animation, after all, not screenwriting.

Sample Script

The script shown in Figures 2.1 through 2.6 is included to assist you in completing the exercises in the rest of this book, in case you don't want to write your own script. The premise of the story is also the title, "Easy Come, Easy Go."

This script is copyright © 1996 Douglas A. Kelly. Your permission to use the script is subject to the following conditions:

- Permission is granted to purchasers of this book to use this script for educational purposes only.

- Purchasers of this book are specifically granted permission to use this script for completing the exercises in this book in the production of a not-for-resale animated motion picture.

- If you use this script "as is" or in any revised or derivative form, you are required to display the phrase "Written by Doug Kelly" in the credits.

- If the finished work will be used for any commercial purpose or public display, including any advertisement or solicitation regarding animation services or employment, copyright law requires that you get my permission in advance.

- If you use this script to create a demo reel, you can secure my permission by sending me a letter of request and a copy of the demo reel.

Whether you use it or not, I hope you enjoy the story.

Moving On

You should now have a practical working knowledge of stories and scripts for animation. The next step in the animation process is the storyboard. Chapter 3 will show you the essentials of storyboarding for animation, including a complete sample storyboard for "Easy Come, Easy Go" and advice from professional storyboard artist Sandra Frame.

"EASY COME, EASY GO"

Written by

Doug Kelly

Doug Kelly
1531 Warren Road
Lakewood, OH 44107

Copyright © 1996 Douglas A. Kelly

REVISED DRAFT
May 25, 1996

dakelly@earthlink.com

Figure 2.1 Title page of script.

1

"EASY COME, EASY GO"

FADE IN:

EXT CLOSE SHOT PUDDLE DESERTED CITY STREET LATE AFTERNOON

Heavy rain is falling on a city sidewalk. Puddle reflects
blinking neon in ripples. NEON BUZZES. Rainfall tapers
off, stops.

Truck back, pan up to MEDIUM TRACKING SHOT of FRED.
Storefronts are brick with large plate glass windows. FRED
looks down on his luck. Almost emaciated, holes and tears
in clothing, dirty, unshaven, overlong hair peeking out
under a stoved-in hat, flapping shoe sole, glasses askew.
FRED walks along sidewalk, head down, dragging feet.

THREE-QUARTER MEDIUM SHOT FRED as he glances in darkened
shop window, then pauses. He sees his REFLECTION, stops and
faces window.

CLOSE SHOT REFLECTION over FRED's shoulder. Reflection
morphs to well-fed, well-dressed, happy-looking version of
FRED.

MEDIUM SHOT REVERSE ANGLE THROUGH WINDOW FRED as he perks
up, smiling, tips hat to reflection.

CLOSE SHOT REFLECTION over FRED's shoulder, as reflection
morphs back to Fred's current image.

MEDIUM SHOT REVERSE ANGLE THROUGH WINDOW FRED as he sighs,
slouches again. Fred turns and begins to walk out of frame.

MEDIUM TRACKING SHOT FRED as he shuffles along sidewalk.
Trash blows past. BILL blows into frame, plasters itself
across FRED's glasses. FRED staggers.

CLOSE SHOT FRED as he peels bill off glasses, tries to clear
glasses.

THREE-QUARTER CLOSE SHOT FRED as he looks at bill. FRED
blinks, momentarily baffled.

Figure 2.2   First page of script.

2

CLOSE SHOT over FRED's shoulder ZOOM to EXTREME CLOSE SHOT on BILL in FRED's hands. We can read bill as $1000.

THREE-QUARTER MEDIUM SHOT FRED as he looks at bill. Wild take, as he stretches bill flat between both hands.

THREE-QUARTER CLOSE SHOT FRED recovers, looks up and into the middle distance, as if at a wonderful vision.

CLOSE SHOT FRED'S FACE. FRED's eyes reflect images of dollar signs, then a rich dinner, then bubbling champagne, then the well-dressed image from the storefront.

THREE-QUARTER MEDIUM SHOT FRED clutching bill as he looks around, reading storefront signs. FRED sees shop he wants, anticipates and zips out of frame.

REAR MEDIUM SHOT FRED as he brakes to a screeching halt and performs a 90-degree zip into Restaurant doorway. DOOR SWINGING. ARGUMENT, ON RISING NOTE. Door opens forcefully as FRED reappears, arcing out of doorway in midair and landing on his rump in the middle of the sidewalk, still clutching bill. FRED protests. BOUNCER'S HAND appears from doorway, pointing to sign in window.

CLOSE SHOT SIGN with pointing hand. Sign reads, "PROPER ATTIRE REQUIRED" in elegant script.

MEDIUM SHOT FRED as BOUNCER'S HAND withdraws, SLAMMING DOOR. FRED gets to feet, dusts himself off, looking disgruntled, then transitions to determination. FRED looks around at storefront signs again. He sees the shop he wants across the street. FRED marches determinedly out of frame, stepping off the curb.

MEDIUM SHOT TAILOR SHOP as FRED marches up to door and enters.

HELD SHOT ON TAILOR SHOP. We hear MEASURING TAPE, SCISSORS, SEWING MACHINE, CASH REGISTER.

Figure 2.3 Second page of script.

3

                                        MATCH DISSOLVE TO:

MEDIUM SHOT BARBER SHOP with spinning barber pole. By the
light, it is visibly later in the evening, nearly sunset. We
hear SCISSORS, HAIR TONIC, LATHER BRUSH, RAZOR STROP,
SHAVING, CASH REGISTER. Door opens. FRED exits with a
jaunty strut, clean-shaven and with slicked-down, neatly-
parted hair. (Possibly insert humorous cameo from weiner-
dog) FRED turns to find restaurant again, and jauntily walks
out of frame, back across street.

MEDIUM SHOT RESTAURANT as FRED jauntily walks up and enters.

INT MEDIUM SHOT TABLE RESTAURANT EVENING

WAITRESS'S HANDS hold chair as FRED sits down. WAITRESS'S
HANDS present MENU. FRED peruses menu, making a great show
of it. FRED smiles broadly, holds menu open toward WAITRESS
(OS) and points to several items, nodding rapidly.
WAITRESS'S HANDS retrieve menu. WAITRESS'S HANDS serve
heaping plates of food, pour champagne.

MONTAGE

fred making pig of self, waistline expanding

drinking more

becoming boisterous

gesturing and calling to other tables (OS)

dishes stacking

champagne magnums accumulating

increasingly tight close shots on Fred, mouth opening wider
in eating and talking, actions more broad and out of control

loosening collar, clothing becoming disarrayed

CASH REGISTER RINGING repeatedly

MEDIUM SHOT TABLE FRED as WAITRESS' HANDS gesture Fred to
settle down. FRED transitions from gluttonous to irate,
then fascinated with WAITRESS(OS), then leering. FRED makes
grab for WAITRESS(OS). WAITRESS' HANDS withdraw, fending
off FRED, who nearly falls out of chair. FRED, grumbling,
resumes guzzling champagne. BOUNCER'S HAND reaches into
frame, tap FRED on shoulder. FRED looks up, bleary and
obviously in his cups. His reaction time is severely
impaired.

Figure 2.4 Third page of script.

4

EXT MEDIUM SHOT RESTAURANT DESERTED CITY STREET NIGHT

CRASHING and THUDS. DOOR OPENS forcefully as FRED reappears, arcing out of doorway in midair. Camera tracks FRED, does zip pan as he COLLIDES headfirst with LAMPPOST. DOOR SLAMS forcefully. FRED defies gravity for a moment, then falls, SPLAT, facefirst onto sidewalk.

CLOSE SHOT MOVING HOLD FRED, left flat on face across sidewalk. Hat is now crumpled, clothing partially soiled from contact with sidewalk and lamppost.(Possibly insert another humorous cameo from weiner-dog) FRED slowly sits up, holds head and weaves a bit. FRED climbs shakily to his feet. He GAGS, but can't hold it in and the camera pans to follow his rush for the alley entrance next to RESTAURANT. FRED drops to knees with head and upper torso out of sight in alley, and GAGS repeatedly.

MEDIUM SHOT ALLEY FRED as he drags himself across the alley on hands and knees to a patch of wall between garbage cans and props himself there.

CLOSE SHOT FRED TRASH CANS His color is slightly better, although still pale. His clothing is now thoroughly soiled and torn. His eyelids flicker a few times, then fall shut as FRED begins to snore.

                              DISSOLVE TO:

MEDIUM SHOT ALLEY FRED as morning light filters into the alley, showing all the damage. FRED's snoring changes, he wakes, blinks repeatedly, winces at the light, shakes his head and immediately clutches it in pain. He is badly hung over.

FULL SHOT ALLEY RESTAURANT SHOP as FRED staggers onto sidewalk in front of store.

CLOSE SHOT FRED as he transitions from bewilderment to total recall, and then to crushing remorse. His shoulders sag.

THREE-QUARTER MEDIUM SHOT FRED as FRED glances in darkened shop window. He sees his reflection again, and turns to face window.

CLOSE SHOT MOVING HOLD REFLECTION over FRED's shoulder. Reflection morphs to well-fed, well-dressed version of FRED. REFLECTION's expression is stern and disapproving, an

Figure 2.5 Fourth page of script.

5

unflinching glare.

THREE-QUARTER MEDIUM SHOT FRED as REFLECTION morphs back to
real reflection.   FRED SIGHS, slouches further.

MEDIUM TRACKING SHOT FRED as he turns, SIGHS again, and
shuffles down the sidewalk, very much as we first saw him,
holes and tears in clothing, dirty, unshaven, hat stoved in
and glasses askew. TRACKING slows to let FRED pass gradually
out of frame.

                                                    FADE OUT

Figure 2.6   Fifth and last page of script.

STORYBOARDING

Storyboards bridge the gap between script and animation, providing the next level of detail in visualization. If the script is a film's blueprint, the storyboard is a set of detailed engineering drawings. Storyboard artists are crucial to production teams, and storyboarding skills are assets even for solo animators.

A *storyboard* is a collection of individual story sketches, each illustrating a particular shot from the script as it would appear to the camera. The storyboard itself can be a large piece of board or section of wall with the sketches pinned to it, a portfolio with a few sketches on each page, or even a loose-leaf binder intended to show only one story sketch at a time. If the storyboard is only for yourself, you can draw each sketch on a 4×6 file card and write your ideas and descriptions on the back. You can easily shuffle them into the right order and hold them in place with a rubber band; a low tech, cheap and portable solution. You can even photocopy and enlarge your sketches onto larger sheets later, if you need to give your sketches to a storyboard artist.

Storyboards were developed in the Disney studio in the late 1920s as a way of visualizing the shot flow of the entire story at once. By the mid-1930s, most Hollywood studios were using them as a means of preplanning and managing film production. As you will see, the storyboard is one of the most valuable tools used by an animation director.

The Storyboard As A Tool

A well-done storyboard bridges the gap between the script and the actual animation, providing the next level of detail in visualization. If the script is a film's blueprint, the storyboard is a set of detailed engineering drawings. As with the script, if you have trouble creating the storyboard, you may want to revise or clarify your ideas.

Storyboards are also necessary for dealing with most employers and partners. If you are working in feature films, television, or advertising, the producers and other team members will need to see the storyboards. In advertising, even the client will see the storyboards; ad agencies are notorious for over-approving everything. For an animated ad, expect to produce detailed, finished artwork for storyboards, and be prepared to have it all second-guessed and revised repeatedly. Although it's true that CGI animation can often be laid out and rendered faster than an artist can produce the finished storyboards, speed is not the issue. Client approval and agency c.y.a. are the issues.

If a particular employer requires more storyboarding than you want to do, plan to hire a storyboard artist to do the extra work, and increase your fee accordingly. If there will be several cycles of storyboarding and approval before you can get down to animating, make sure your contract spells out your compensation for the delays and extra work. Pay particular attention to the clause that states that you will get paid for out-of-pocket expenses and work completed, even if the client changes their mind or cancels the project.

If you are working on an independent project like a demo reel, you have a lot more leeway in the production values of your storyboards. Stick figures and rough sketches are adequate if you are doing a solo project but putting in more information will make your work easier later on. After months of posing and tweaking, it's sometimes difficult to remember exactly what you had in mind for a particular shot. A detailed story sketch is one of the best memory joggers you can have.

You can also abbreviate storyboards by using a single sketch for several shots (or a *traveling shot*) of the same backgrounds and characters. Place numbered frame outlines in the sketch, especially if the shots use complex cuts or travel. For example, Shot 17 in the sample storyboards (presented at the end of this chapter) uses a frame outline to show a zoom in, rather than having another complete sketch for the zoomed view.

I still recommend using complete storyboards, both to help clarify your vision of the story and as evidence that the work is actually yours. Some animation houses will ask you to prove that you created the work on your demo reel. You should save the script drafts, story sketches, and other production notes and take them to your interviews.

Now that you understand the importance of storyboards, let's move on to practical methods for creating your own.

Script To Storyboard

Exactly how do you expand a script into a storyboard? There are almost as many approaches as there are professional storyboard artists. You can choose the size, medium, and style to suit yourself, and several books listed in the Bibliography can give you ideas. If you have access to a good art supply store, you can buy storyboard panels already printed with television cutoff. These panels are designed for TV commercials, but the proper aspect ratio is there.

My personal approach is, I think, simple and effective. Once I have the finished script in a Word document, I save a copy of the script and make the following page layout changes to the duplicate:

1. Change the page orientation to landscape.
2. Change the page number in the header to read *SHOT #*.
3. Immediately after the shot number, insert a carriage return and create an 8×6 frame that is centered in the header, flush against the top margin, and spaced 0.2 inches from following text.

4. Change the cover page to read *DRAFT STORYBOARD* rather than FIRST (or whatever) DRAFT.

To see an example of this formatting, open the EASYSHO2.DOC file in the Chapter 3 directory on this book's CD-ROM.

This starts off every page (except the cover) with a blank 8×6 frame, which is the standard aspect ratio for film work. If you are going to be working in another aspect ratio, change the dimensions of the frame to match. Working with landscape format 8-1/2×11 inch paper also enables you to put the storyboard in a standard three-ring binder. A number of directors prefer working this way because they can flip through the pages rapidly to get an idea of the timing for shot flow.

This format is much larger than most studios work with. I like the extra space, but many storyboard artist are more comfortable with 4×6, or even smaller, sketches. There are alternative storyboard layouts that can fit three or more sketches on a single page. Choose the format you like best, but be prepared to work in other formats if a studio or client requests it.

The shots will be numbered automatically. If you need to insert a new shot later, it will probably be easier to hand-letter on a blank page than to fool around with reformatting the entire document. This was the procedure used for the montage (Shot 49) of Fred's excesses in the restaurant. The composite shot was numbered from the original script breakout. The individual shots used to compose the montage (which was edited together in post-production) were designed later, their descriptions handwritten on blank sheets, and the finished sketches numbered 49A, 49B, and so on. In a more professional production, this whole scene would have been worked out in story sketches first. Independent production lets you cheat in lots of little ways like this.

To create blank story sketch pages in Word, follow these steps:

1. Add a section break and a page break after the last FADE OUT.
2. Turn off the Same As Previous toggle.
3. Change the new section's header to replace the page number with a few underscores.
4. Add the label *SHOT DESCRIPTION*: under the frame.
5. Print a single copy of this last page and photocopy it or print off a lot of copies so that you can keep the blank pages handy in your binder for making changes.

If you don't want to fool around with making your own story sketch blanks, you can print copies of the SKETCH.PDF file located in the Chapter 3 directory on this book's CD-ROM.

The next step is to go through the script line by line and insert a page break after each shot. I carry this a little further for character animation storyboards by breaking after each action or moving hold.

Let's look at an example from an earlier draft of the "Easy Come, Easy Go" script. Originally, the shot in which Fred leaves the barber shop was much longer and involved a visible barber character. Although it was an opportunity to animate some interesting actions, the sequence was cut because it didn't advance the story's premise. This shot broke down into five sketches, even though, cinematically, it's a single shot. From a character animator's viewpoint, the actions to be animated are very different and can be handled as a series of separate shots connected by overlapping action:

1. The door opens and Fred exits the barbershop with a particular gait. The main action ends when Fred halts, just before beginning the turn. All the overlapping actions that are part of Fred continue into the next main action.

2. Fred turns and bows to the barber. This should be a single action, flowing and graceful (if a trifle overacted). The action ends when Fred straightens into a moving hold, which overlaps the next action.

3. The barber's hands wave. The action ends when the door closes. The overlapping action is Fred's reaction, which begins just before the door is completely closed.

4. Fred turns again and scans the storefronts. This turn is slightly different from the second action in both timing and emphasis, because he now has another purpose in mind. The action ends when he identifies his goal and sets himself to begin walking. Again, the overlapping actions are all associated with Fred.

5. The last action is Fred walking out of the frame. There is no overlapping action, because the set is empty of characters.

As you can see, this breakout increases the number of story sketches. I prefer this approach because it helps bridge the transition from storyboard to bar sheet or exposure sheet, giving you more breaking points than a simpler shot breakout. This makes it a little easier to time each action, and you can pencil your timing estimates right on the story sketch margin. This is a big help when you first meet with the music director or composer.

If I'm doing the entire production myself, I prefer working in pencil (and so do most board artists I've asked). I'm not a graphic artist by any stretch of the definition, so most of my storyboards are simple perspective layouts of the sets populated by somewhat-proportional stick figures. For the example production presented in this chapter, I planned to work with a production team and therefore arranged for a professional artist to do the storyboards.

At some point during the script revision process, you will need to do the preliminary character design, as detailed in Chapter 5. The storyboard artist will need a copy of the character model sheets plus whatever concept sketches are available for sets and props. Figure 3.1 shows a design sketch for the Fred character.

If the project is a continuation of a series using existing sets, it's helpful to provide the artist with some appropriate rendered backgrounds from previous projects. There's no need to expend creative effort on a stock interior that has appeared in 12 episodes already—at least, not if you want to stay on good terms with your storyboard artist.

You should also have sketched *plans* and *elevations* (overhead and side views) of the original set elements called for in the script. If you mention a storefront, make sure the storyboard artist

Figure 3.1   Preliminary character designs for Fred.

has some idea of what kind of storefront you mean. A trendy big-city designer boutique will have a very different look than a small-town barber shop.

At this point, you may find it useful to make some schematic sketches of the objects and their eventual positioning in your CGI software. A simple plan sketched on scaled grid paper, as shown in Figure 3.2, will greatly reduce the time you spend setting up the master scene.

It's important that you discuss with the artist any moods, specific camera angles, or other limitations you want to keep in mind. For example, because everything described in the sample script was to be constructed from scratch, I wanted to limit extraneous backgrounds. One way to do this is to limit camera angles. If the camera is always looking below the horizon line and buildings are in the near foreground, you'll never have to create a sky. Similarly, if the camera is on a slight down angle in a medium shot of a building, nothing above the first floor needs to be modeled. A matter of a few degrees in panning the camera can mean the difference between modeling an entire street scene and being able to get away with a few false-front shops and a dozen feet of road and sidewalk.

It may help if you think of the camera view as a pyramid, with the point at the focal plane (just behind the lens) of the camera, and the base way out at infinity. The frame of the shot is a slice through the pyramid. Anything within the volume of that pyramid is something you are going to have to model, buy, or fake. It's in your interest to keep that pyramid as empty as possible while still telling an engaging story.

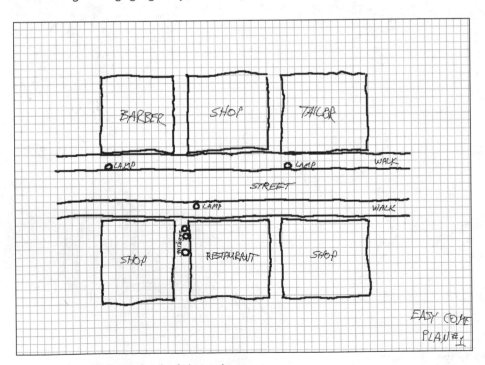

Figure 3.2 A simple preliminary sketch of object placement.

You can't always get away with dodges like these, but for a character animation demo reel, you should concentrate on the animation and avoid having to re-create the whole world.

In the next section, I'll turn you over to storyboard artist Sandra Frame for an inside look at this part of the animation business.

Advice From The Trenches: Storyboard Artist Sandra Frame

Hello. My name is Sandra, and I'm a storyboard artist. (Response: "Hello Sandra!") In this section, I'll try to explain the theory of storyboards. It's a lot easier to explain how a board works when one has an example, and even though I am going to be doing that as well, a brief review of ground rules is necessary.

Knowing how to do boards is becoming more and more important in the traditional animation industry, since most actual layout and animation is done by studios overseas. At least that's true for the TV animation industry. Even though TV doesn't have the prestige that features do, it creates the bulk of the jobs for the industry. A lot of people who are now getting into the traditional animation industry aren't going to be able to cut their teeth doing character layout or animation, unless they work for a commercial house. I personally think it'd be better for the artists and the industry if domestic layouts were brought back to the U.S., but it's not up to me. I feel that way because it's easier to understand how to do the job just before it gets to someone if they're at the next level down. It's easier to absorb what's needed to know when one has time and opportunity to absorb it, instead of being expected to know how a studio-system show is put together from the get-go. Granted, there are a few who can hit the ground running and can do brilliant boards even though it's their first job in the industry, but that's the minority.

You may be wondering why a traditional animation board artist is contributing to this book as opposed to someone who does boards for computer animation. Well, I have done a board for a computer animation, "The Physics of Cartoons." I also did the character design, despite the fact that I've never done 3D animation before in my life. The reason I was able to do this was that I don't see a great difference between doing a presentation with pencil, computer, clay, or live-action. The general rules apply no matter what. Some of the terms may be different, but the reasons for doing a film to begin with are usually the same; something having to do with entertainment or something.

If you're thinking of doing your boards on computer, I'd advise against it, just for the simple reason that it always manages to take forever to do boards in the computer.

People get caught up in getting the angle *just* right, or the proportions on the characters looking *really* cool, or worrying about the backgrounds, or any other such potentially secondary worries. Your board is a blueprint, but it doesn't need to be a perfectly rendered blueprint (unless you're using it for presentation purposes), it needs to be a jumping-off place to bring your film to life.

> *Author's Note:* At least one studio, Mainframe Entertainment (Reboot, Beast Wars), uses the computer for storyboards, layout, and blocking straight from the script. This is a special case, as they have established sets, characters, and a large library of existing poses and actions from which to choose. If you're doing a series, you might consider doing the same; for a first project, you are better off following Sandra's advice.

You don't need to be a brilliant artist with a pencil; if these boards are going to be seen by a minimum amount of people, you just need to be able to draw the character with the correct general proportions, and in correct ratio to the backgrounds. Once you look at the example board that I drew for this book (see the end of this chapter), you'll see that my line quality isn't too fantastic, my perspective is kind of off, and I don't draw the backgrounds for every single panel. However, you will notice that it's very clear as to what is supposed to be going on, and that's what counts.

First off, however, I'm going to tell you guys what I know about boards. Which isn't a lot, but what the heck, I still manage to get paid to do boards for a living. I've been doing boards for television animation for a few years now, at several different studios, including Warner Bros., Film Roman, and Classy Scup. I haven't done boards for feature films, but the basics are the same. I'm going to compare how boards are done in both TV and feature, to let you decide what tools and ideas you can use when you do your own boards.

Creating TV Storyboards

Here's the step-by-step on what I do for my day job boards. This varies a little bit from studio to studio; some places try to baby-sit the board artist every step of the way, others just throw the script at the board artist and expect a finished board in two weeks. However, like I've said before, the basics are the same, and that's what really counts; the picky stuff is easily grasped.

The board artist gets the script of the show they're going to be boarding on. Hopefully they'll talk to the director and/or producer to find out if there are any specifics for any sequences that the artist needs to board in a particular way. Usually the artist is given approximately two weeks to board out the assignment. What I try to do before I use the actual board paper is get scratch paper and do some thumbnail sketches of what I think the sequence should look like, and then work out the rough staging. Then I draw away on the official board paper (Figure 3.3), putting in dialogue and scene descriptions as needed. Hopefully a dialogue track is provided at this point, as there tend to be less in the way of revisions if the artist knows what the characters sound like, and can do the appropriate acting for the board.

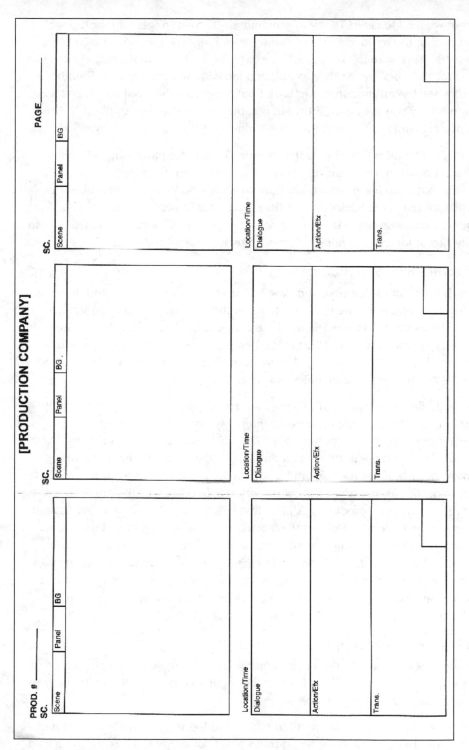

Figure 3.3 Sample board paper.

The scripts that we tend to get in TV are approximately 30 to 40 pages for a half-hour show. Unfortunately, the trend seems to be toward even longer scripts, which creates more work for the artist. This wouldn't be a problem except for the fact that the artist doesn't get more time for the work, unless they complain a lot. Also, what usually ends up happening is that when the animation comes back from overseas, whole sequences end up being cut. So not only was the board artist put out, but also the background artists, the overseas animators, and most importantly, the budget.

After two weeks, the board is turned in to the director. The director makes any notes and changes either on post-it notes on the original board, or directly onto a copy of the board. Then it gets sent to the producers, who make their notes as well. When the producers are done, the artist gets the board back and does the requested changes as fast as possible. Usually no more than two weeks are given for revisions. Then the board gets turned back in and hopefully except for any last minute changes, the board artist is done for that episode.

Creating Feature Film Storyboards

Feature is much more labor-intensive and time-intensive. The board artists and directors work closer together, and there are more meetings on the story in general. The script doesn't need to be as strictly adhered to, until the dialogue tracks are laid down. The artists are given a greater amount of time to do their job, as well. It takes longer to make sure that the sequences will all work together, so the viewer isn't unnecessarily jarred by differences in style and presentation, unless it's called for.

The artists usually do some thumbnails before they actually start boarding. When they do start boarding, they tend to use index cards, probably around 4×6 size. This way, if there's a panel that doesn't work, it's easy to get rid of, without having to rearrange the rest of the cards. The cards are numbered on the back to keep track of them. When a board is being critiqued, it's pinned up onto a bulletin board or wall or whatever, so that you can start to get the feeling of the flow of the whole thing. Usually, the artist *pitches* the board to the director and producers. A pitch involves the artist verbally going though the board panel by panel and acting out the action, including saying any dialogue, and even doing facial expressions, jumping, running, or any other action called for in the board. The artist then gets instant feedback from the director and producer, and changes are worked out from there. There's a greater chance of whole sequences being redone in feature than TV, but that's what doing a feature is all about; doing something over and over until it's the best it can be.

Career Path: How I Got From There To Here

I know that you probably bought this book so that you can be a really cool director or producer, because that's what everyone wants to be—well, except me. I like doing boards, but then some might consider me insane.

Anyway, this is how I got to be in the position that I'm in today (i.e., employed): a lot of hard work. No duh, I know. But, considering that when I got out of CalArts, I had no idea what I wanted to do, it's amazing I got anywhere. Luckily, I got a job doing character layout on a television show called *The Critic*. Maybe you remember it. It was actually kind of funny, especially the second season. When doing character layout for *The Critic*, the artist would sit down with the director and go through the section to be done with the storyboard. That's where I began to learn where cuts go, how many ways one can do an establishing shot, how far one can go with a truck-in or truck-out (defined in the next section), and how to keep camera direction consistent so that the viewer doesn't get confused as to the action that's taking place or where the character is supposed to be.

After two seasons of working on *The Critic* and a few months of doing layout on *The Samisens*, I was pretty good at character layout. Then I lost my job. Oops. More like, "What do you mean, *The Critic* wasn't picked up for a third season? Don't they know I need the money!" That wasn't good, especially since the job of character layout was being phased out by every other studio at the time. Double oops. Luckily for me, however, I was about to get a break.

One of my coworkers went from *The Critic* to another show, called *The Klutter*, at the same studio. *The Klutter* was created by "Savage" Steve Holland, the same guy who created *Eek! The Cat*. Anyway, this new show wasn't going to have character layouts, just boards to be sent to the overseas studios. There happened to be a couple of young punks such as myself who were in need of a change of pace and (bonus for the studio), were cheap as dirt, so we were hired to try out doing storyboards. Every job I've gotten, except for my very first one, I got not because of my portfolio, but because I knew someone who would recommend me. Friends are a beautiful thing!

When I was hired to work on *The Klutter*, I was told that I'd be doing storyboard *clean-up*, which consists of taking a board that has gone through its first round of revisions and putting in any changes, backgrounds, etc. that need to be done before it gets passed on to the next phase of production. Sounded cool to me, so I didn't even ask for a raise from my previous salary, because this isn't considered as good as being a full-fledged board artist. Well, it ended up that I had a trial by fire waiting for me!

Because the director (the guy who helped me get this job to begin with) and the producer were both busy doing other things, such as meetings, vacations and the like, I was just given the script and told to start doing thumbnails. Okay, no problem. I thumbnailed the entire section I was assigned to. The director and producer then critiqued it, and butchered the entire section, with me sitting right there! I could see my career going down in flames at this point, and it was very hard to control the urge to go on a shooting spree through the whole studio.

Now, you have to understand at this point, that even though it was indeed my first attempt at putting together a board, and it certainly could use improvement, it wasn't entirely my fault this first board was torn apart so much. The producer and director didn't hold it against me that there were so many changes. Why didn't they? Because they were busy having different ideas on how the show would look to begin with. If they had talked to each other about style before I was given my assignment, I would've done a different board, one which would've been more of what it was supposed to look like. In other words, I was given the wrong direction to go in. Things like this aren't rare, unfortunately for us. At any rate, the producer came by later and apologized.

From that point on, I try to make it a point to understand where the directors and producers I work with are coming from; it makes my life a heck of a lot easier. Which isn't to say my boards haven't been reamed from time to time, but I roll with the punches a lot easier, and I learn a heck of a lot from it. Apparently it works, for I've been able to stay almost constantly employed for quite a while now.

Do's And Don'ts—Some Board Advice

When you do your board, you'll hopefully know some basic terms and definitions in relation to filmmaking, which will help you figure out exactly how to put the pictures of the film in your head onto the blank paper in front of you.

I noticed that when I started storyboarding, my instincts for deciding what kind of shot to use in a particular section were already developing. Working as a character layout artist with other storyboards from other shows helped to prepare me. In addition, I realized I learned quite a bit from just watching movies and television shows. Once you start doing a little research on filmmaking, you'll most likely realize that you already have a feeling of what will work.

Here are some basic terms that you should know:

- *Establishing shot*—This shows where the action of the film is to be taking place for each change of venue. It can be incorporated into a pan where the character walks into a scene, or it can be a very wide shot, or even a not so wide shot.

- *Cut*—A cut shows where a change of camera stationing takes place, whether it's from one view of the character to a different view of the same character, or if it's a change of viewpoint, or a change in locale, and so forth.

- *Cross-Dissolve*—This is used in situations between scenes where you want to show that time has passed from one scene to the next.

- *Wipe*—A wipe is another method of showing that time has passed from one scene to the next. A wipe can go from one side of the screen to the other, or it can go around like a hand on a clockface, or it can even move diagonally, if you're feeling really fancy.

- *Fade-in and Fade-out*—Usually this is used at the beginning and end of a film. It indicates that the picture is fading in from black screen (usually) or fading out to black.

- *Scene/Shot*—Apparently, the definition of scene is different between live action and animation. In live action, a scene is a segment that takes place in the same locale. In animation, a scene is a piece of uninterrupted action between cuts, cross-dissolves, wipes, and so on. A shot for live-action is the same as a scene for animation. Confusing? Yep. For the purpose of this book, we're going the live-action way for these two definitions.

- *Pan*—Pans are shots that cover more than one field of the screen. Pans are used for a variety of reasons: to establish a shot, to follow the action of something going through the shot, such as a character running through or an object flying through. A pan can go from side to side, or up and down, or even diagonally.

- *Zip pan*—A variation of a pan, a zip pan can be used as a transition between scenes or shots, but I usually use it as a sped up pan. When there's supposed to be a great deal of distance between the starting point and ending point of the pan, the middle is usually the zip part. Everything between the start and end point of a zip pan usually looks something like drybrush speed lines.

- *Truck-in/Truck-out*—These are used to help focus the viewer's eye on an aspect of a shot. For instance, in the sample board, the character Fred finds some money. There's a shot that shows a close-up of the bill in Fred's hands, then the camera trucks in even closer on the bill. An example of a truck-out may be something like starting close on a sign on a building that hasn't been established before, then having the camera pull back to reveal the building. In live action, a truck out is sometimes called a *reveal*.

- *Close, Medium, and Wide shot*—The easiest way to explain these is in reference to how you would place a character in a shot. A close shot would be the face of a character, maybe the whole head. A medium shot would be a character from the waist up. A wide shot could be anything with the entire character visible in the shot.

- *OS*—This is an abbreviation of *off screen*. This can be used to indicate when an object or character is leaving the shot. You'd draw an arrow indicating direction and write OS by the arrow. It's also useful for indicating a noise or dialogue that happens to be off-screen for a particular shot.

- *POV*—This is an abbreviation for *point of view*. This is a shot that is from the view of the character. These can be really fun if your character is either exceptionally short or tall, or if the character is in an unusual situation, such as hanging upside down.

- *Up-shot/Down-shot*—An up-shot is a shot where the camera is tilted up. A down-shot has the camera tilted down. These can be used for fun effects; an up-shot can be used to make the viewer feel intimidated, as looking up is like the view of a helpless child. The opposite is true of a down shot, it makes the shot/angle feel very powerful.

Now that you have an idea of some of the industry's terms, I'll tell you the only hard-and-fast rule that I've learned. It's called the *180 Rule*.

The 180 Rule

Visualize it like this: Look at the setting of your scene from straight above. Visualize the setting like a circle. A circle has 360 degrees—if you split a circle straight down the middle, you have 180 degrees. Now, in relation to your scene, imagine keeping all camera moves and angles to one side or another of that imaginary line that bisects your space. This helps to keep the characters and scene grounded, and ensures that the viewer doesn't lose sight of where everyone and everything is supposed to be in the scene. Now, when you use the same setting for different scenes, you can set up your imaginary 180 line differently each time. The rule applies to a single scene not to the entire film. You just want to keep everything consistent for the viewer.

With the shot description terms and the 180 Rule in mind, you're ready to draw your boards.

Drawing Your Boards

You may not be thrilled with the idea of having to draw out your board if you feel you can't draw to save your life. Don't let a little thing like lack of talent or experience stop you from going full blast on your board! If you read this book thoroughly, you'll learn stuff like line of action and silhouette that you can use for your characters. Those can be used in your boards as well, it'll help you be inspired when you get around to animating your characters. You don't need pretty drawings, you can use stick figures with the approximate proportions of your characters, and if you have a french or flexi-curve tool (both can be found at your local art store), you can use those to get the line of action your characters need to enhance their actions. The boards should be able to put across your story idea no matter what, even with stick figures.

Also remember that even though the storyboard is the blueprint for your film, small changes can be made to your film even after you're done with the board and are animating.

Sometimes there are unforeseen problems or just a change of opinion on your part that make you want to change something. Just suppress the urge to change the board to a great degree when you're animating, or you'll never get the darned thing done. When working on the "Physics of Cartoons," we had a problem. The animators wanted to make changes to the film, which would've been no problem under normal circumstances. However, we had to record the entire soundtrack before any animation was done, which locked everyone into the timing that was set up for the animatic. Usually, if there is dialogue, the animator should get the recording of it before he starts animating; all other sounds such as music and effects are done after the animation is done, for convenience sake. For additional help, I suggest that you read *Film Directing: Shot By Shot,* by Steven Katz. Even though it's geared toward live action, you'll get an idea of what further terms are, and of the film making process in general. It can also give you ideas on what kind of look you can get out of certain shots for an intended impact.

Doug has already given his opinion on what tools he likes to use to do boards, so I will give mine. For my own boards, I prefer using 4"×6" index cards and a dark Prismacolor pencil. It's easier to pin up the cards to get an idea of how it's going to look than to have the panels in a notebook. Of course, everyone has their own way of working; there's no absolute correct way of doing it, so explore what feels most comfortable to you

Storyboard Critique

The story sketches presented in this section follow a revised version of the script presented in Chapter 2, so you will find small differences where shots were cut, added, or changed.

This enables you to see how the story changed during script revisions. Gaps or additional letters in the shot numbering show where shots were deleted or added in the storyboard sessions; shots 3, 36, 37, 49, 63, and 72 were cut, and shots 18A, 19A, 28A and B, 34A, 49A through M, and 71A were inserted.

Standard screenwriting abbreviations are used in the script and storyboard. For complete details on style and abbreviation usage, consult Irwin Blacker's *Elements of Screenwriting*, listed in this book's bibliography. In the storyboard captions presented here, the abbreviations EXT, INT, OTS, and OS mean, respectively, Exterior, Interior, Over The Shoulder and Offscreen.

Following is my shot-by-shot critique of the first-draft storyboards for "Easy Come, Easy Go," with my comments appearing in italics after each original shot caption. I don't say these things to put anyone down, they're common mistakes that anyone can make. If you'd like to follow along with the original sketches, they are stored as a series of TIF files in the Chapter 3 directory on this book's CD-ROM. Notice how (and if) I take my own advice when you see the revised board I did at the end of this chapter. Does the board work? If so, how? Start analyzing the storyboard now—it'll help you later.

Be sure to put in a panel at the very beginning to show the fade-in.

Shot 1: FADE IN: EXT CLOSE SHOT PUDDLE DESERTED CITY STREET NIGHT. Heavy rain is falling on a city sidewalk. Puddle reflects blinking neon in ripples. NEON BUZZES. Rainfall tapers off, stops.
No problem.

Shot 2: Truck back, pan up to MEDIUM TRACKING SHOT of FRED. Storefronts are brick with large plate glass windows. FRED looks down on his luck. Almost emaciated, holes and tears in clothing, dirty, unshaven, overlong hair peeking out under a stoved-in hat, flapping shoe sole, glasses askew.
If this is a truck-out, it should be seen where the starting field is and have arrows indicating where the camera pulls out to full frame.

Shot 4: THREE-QUARTER MEDIUM SHOT FRED as he glances in darkened shop window, then pauses. He sees his REFLECTION, stops, and faces window.
Multiple images like this aren't generally done unless the character's action is supposed to be very rapid or if the character is moving fully from one side of the shot to the other.

Shot 5: CLOSE SHOT REFLECTION over FRED's shoulder. Reflection morphs to well-fed, well-dressed, happy-looking version of FRED.
There's no reason to cut closer at this point. The previous shot's setup would do just fine.

Shot 6: THREE-QUARTER MEDIUM SHOT THROUGH WINDOW FRED as he perks up, smiling, tips hat.
I'd put this shot on more of an angle. I'd have the camera still in the store, but more on Fred's left side. It keeps Fred facing to the left of the screen constant.

Shot 7: CLOSE SHOT REFLECTION over FRED's shoulder, as reflection morphs back to Fred's current image.
Use the same setup as Shot 4. There's no need to be this close.

Shot 8: THREE-QUARTER MEDIUM SHOT THROUGH WINDOW FRED as face falls, he sighs, slouches again.
Use the same setup that I suggested for Shot 6.

Shot 9: FRED turns and walks out of frame.
Same suggestion as for Shot 8.

Shot 10: MEDIUM TRACKING SHOT FRED as he shuffles along sidewalk. Trash blows past.
Really emphasize Fred's posture. He looks to be strongly striding along, but he's supposed to be miserable! Have him slouched and sad-looking.

Shot 11: BILL blows into frame, plasters itself across FRED's glasses. FRED staggers.
It appears that the camera has moved in closer. It should stay in the wide shot.

Shot 12: CLOSE SHOT FRED as he peels bill off glasses, tries to clear glasses.
Again, stay in the wide shot of Shot 10.

Shot 13: THREE-QUARTER CLOSE SHOT FRED as he looks at bill. FRED blinks, momentarily baffled.
Same suggestion as Shot 12.

Shot 14: CLOSE SHOT OTS STAGGER ZOOM to EXTREME CLOSE SHOT on BILL in FRED's hands. We can read bill as $1,000.
No problem.

Shot 15: THREE-QUARTER MEDIUM SHOT FRED as he looks at bill. Wild take, as he stretches bill flat between both hands.
Fred looks mighty cramped in this shot. Go back to the wide shot or use a medium shot.

Shot 16: FRED recovers, looks up and into the middle distance, as if at a wonderful vision.
The cut is fine, but I'd lose the dream bubble. Let the expression on his face do the talking.

Shot 17: CLOSE SHOT FRED'S FACE. FRED's eyes reflect images of dollar signs, then a rich dinner, then bubbling champagne, then the well-dressed image from the storefront.
There are several things that are supposed to be reflected in Fred's eyes, yet they're not represented in a panel for each item like they should be.

Shot 18: THREE-QUARTER MEDIUM SHOT FRED clutching bill as he looks around, reading storefront signs.
This doesn't look like the medium shot that the description says it should be. I'd go back to the wide shot and have Fred look around then, with only one head per panel.

Shot 18A: FRED sees shop he wants, anticipates, and zips out of frame.
Three panels are described, yet only one has been drawn. You have to draw out what you describe!

Shot 19: REAR MEDIUM SHOT FRED as he brakes to a screeching halt and performs a 90-degree zip into restaurant doorway.
Again, break the action down into more panels. Have one panel where he skids to a halt, then the next panel should show where he runs into the restaurant.

Shot 19A: DOOR SWINGING. ARGUMENT, ON RISING NOTE.
Just have the door shut instead of swinging. It's not a saloon but a supposedly fancy restaurant.

Shot 20: Door opens forcefully as FRED reappears, arcing out of doorway in midair and landing on his rump in the middle of the sidewalk, still clutching bill.
Fred looks a little bit too big to me. If he stood up as drawn in this panel, he'd have to stoop over to go through the door.

Shot 21: FRED protests.
Make Fred's gestures clear. It would work better if you see him shake his fist (something you can do on one panel with multiple images of his fist), then have another panel showing how upset he is.

Shot 22: BOUNCER'S HAND appears from doorway, pointing to sign in window.
Is Fred warding off a blow? Make this gesture clear.

Shot 23: CLOSE SHOT SIGN with pointing hand. Sign reads, "PROPER ATTIRE REQUIRED" in elegant script.
Make this shot appear more of a POV from where Fred is sitting. It would appear as more of an up-shot and make it more foreboding and effective.

Shot 24: MEDIUM SHOT FRED as BOUNCER'S HAND withdraws, SLAMMING DOOR.
This cut breaks the 180 degree rule. Fred was facing the right of the screen after he was thrown out of the restaurant, and there's no compelling reason to change that now. You could cut back to the setup previous to Shot 23.

Shot 25: FRED gets to feet, dusts himself off, looking disgruntled, then transitions to determination.
Same suggestion as Shot 24.

Shot 26: FRED looks around at storefront signs again. He sees the shop he wants, across the street.
Same suggestion as Shot 24 for composition. Also, don't do the multiple images like this. Split it up into two panels.

Shot 27: FRED marches determinedly out of frame, stepping off curb.
Instead of this composition, use the previous suggestion for composition and just have Fred walk off screen.

Shot 28: MEDIUM SHOT TAILOR SHOP as FRED marches up to door and enters.
Except for Fred's gesture at the window, this is fine. The gesture is unnecessary, in my opinion, because he should be stridently marching to the tailor's shop, it should be obvious as to his intent.

Shot 28A: HELD SHOT TAILOR SHOP. We hear MEASURING TAPE, SCISSORS, SEWING MACHINE, CASH REGISTER.
No problem.

Shot 28B: MATCH DISSOLVE TO MEDIUM SHOT BARBER SHOP, visibly later by lighting, now near dusk. SOUNDS continuous, bridge from TAILOR sounds to BARBER sounds.
Put in a panel indicating the cross-dissolve. Don't let the barber sounds start yet. It needs to be established that Fred has gone to the barber's. I'd put in a pan move to the barber shop (conveniently next door to the tailor).

Shot 34A: HELD SHOT BARBER SHOP with spinning barber pole. We hear SCISSORS, HAIR TONIC, LATHER BRUSH, RAZOR STROP, SHAVING, CASH REGISTER.
Flop the image of the barber shop to match with the angle of the tailor shop next door.

Shot 35: BARBER SHOP door opens. FRED exits with a jaunty strut, clean-shaven, and with slicked-down, neatly-parted hair.
Same suggestion as Shot 34A of flopping the image.

Shot 38: FRED turns and scans storefronts, finds restaurant again.
Instead of having Fred stop and scan the storefronts again, he should be so confident at this point that he'd just strut on over to the restaurant.

Shot 39: FRED jauntily walks out of frame, back across street.
This is what Shot 38 should look like, except for the flopping of the barber shop, of course.

Shot 40: MEDIUM SHOT RESTAURANT as FRED jauntily walks up and enters.
It would be more fun if there was a low shot of the restaurant (something like having the camera across the street from the restaurant about foot-level), and then having Fred walk past camera, off in the distance towards the restaurant.

Shot 41: INT MEDIUM SHOT TABLE RESTAURANT EVENING as WAITRESS'S HANDS hold chair as FRED crosses in front of table, makes slight bow to WAITRESS, sits down as WAITRESS places chair.
Instead of torturing the animator by doing this scene, just wipe to Fred sitting at his table in the restaurant.

Shot 42: CLOSE SHOT TABLE FRED, as WAITRESS'S HANDS present MENU.
No problem.

Shot 43: CLOSE SHOT MENU FRED as he peruses menu, making a great show of it.
Have Fred's reading of the menu be a little more natural looking. Most people don't turn to the side and flop open their menu to read it. You can keep the silhouette of the character clear even when a prop is partly covering the character like this.

Shot 44: CLOSE SHOT TABLE FRED as he smiles broadly, holds menu open toward WAITRESS (OS, RIGHT), and points to several items, nodding rapidly.
Because Fred is pointing to multiple items on the menu, you should have multiple panels showing him pointing to each different item.

Shot 45: WAITRESS'S HANDS retrieve menu.
No problem.

Shot 48: MEDIUM SHOT FRED TABLE as WAITRESS'S HANDS serve heaping plates of food, pour champagne.
Again, the action described needs to be seen in the board panels. Have the waitress put the food down in front of Fred. Then, have the waitress pour the champagne. There should be two or three panels for the action described here.

Shots 49A through 49M: MONTAGE: FRED making pig of self, waistline expanding, drinking more, becoming boisterous, gesturing and calling to other tables (OS), dishes stacking, champagne magnums accumulating, increasingly tight close shots on FRED, mouth opening wider in eating and talking, actions more broad and out of control, loosening collar, clothing becoming disarrayed, CASH REGISTER RINGING repeatedly. Evening light dims to night during montage.
The whole montage sequence needs to be boarded out to some degree; even if you don't strictly adhere to the order you establish at this stage, you'll have something to work off of when you're animating. If you showed the board panel to someone who doesn't know your story idea, they probably wouldn't get the full impact of your intent for the scene. When in doubt, board it out!

Shot 50: MEDIUM SHOT TABLE FRED as WAITRESS'S HANDS (OS, RIGHT) gesture FRED to settle down.
Make Fred more belligerent-looking here.

Shot 51: FRED transitions from gluttonous to irate, then fascinated with WAITRESS (OS), then leering.
Again, break down the action described, and lose the multiple positions of Fred here.

Shot 52: FRED makes grab for WAITRESS (OS). WAITRESS'S HANDS withdraw, fending off FRED, who nearly falls out of chair.
Yet again, break down the actions into more panels. Also, add a panel where Fred catches himself before he falls over, as described in this panel.

Shot 53: FRED, grumbling, resumes guzzling champagne.
Again, lose the multiple images of Fred, unless he's doing some speed drinking.

Shot 54: BOUNCER'S HAND reaches into frame from OS RIGHT, taps FRED on shoulder.
Have Fred facing directly away from the bouncer—it makes for a better silhouette.

Shot 55: FRED looks up, bleary-eyed and obviously intoxicated . His reaction time is severely impaired.
This shot can be accomplished in the previous panel.

Shot 56: EXT MEDIUM SHOT RESTAURANT DESERTED CITY STREET NIGHT as we hear CRASHING and THUDS.
This is a fun angle but, considering what happens in Shot 57, it serves no purpose.

Shot 57: DOOR OPENS forcefully as FRED reappears, arcing out of doorway in midair.
Do this in more of a low angle, and have the lamppost closer to camera, so that Fred comes sailing more toward camera.

Shot 58: Camera tracks FRED, does zip pan as he COLLIDES headfirst with LAMPPOST.
Don't put the lamppost too close to camera, or it will end up looking more cramped than it needs to be.

Shot 59: DOOR SLAMS forcefully.
Don't cut here like this. Keep this sequence in one shot.

Shot 60: FRED defies gravity for a moment, then rear end sags accordion-style down to sidewalk, followed by body, head, and hat.
Pull the camera back just a little bit more, so it doesn't feel so claustrophobic.

Shot 61: FRED is left flat across sidewalk. Hat is now crumpled, clothing partially soiled from contact with sidewalk and LAMPPOST. MOVING HOLD.
Same suggestion as Shot 60.

Shot 62: FRED slowly sits up, holds head, and weaves a bit.
Keep this and Shot 64 in the same composition as Shot 60. Also, cut the multiple images out.

Shot 64: FRED climbs shakily to his feet.
Except for the earlier composition note, this is fine.

Shot 65: FRED GAGS, but can't hold it in, and the camera pans to follow his rush for the alley entrance next to RESTAURANT.
Even though this is a cool angle, I'd not use this. For this part of the story, I'd cut close on Fred's face to show him looking nauseous. Then, I'd cut wide and have Fred turn and run away from camera to the alleyway in the background, where he'd retch.

Shot 66: FRED drops to knees with head and upper torso out of sight in alley, and GAGS repeatedly.
A good angle for this shot, I'd just have Fred stagger into the alley after already retching in the previous shot.

Shot 67: MEDIUM SHOT ALLEY FRED as he drags himself across the alley on hands and knees to a patch of wall between garbage cans and props himself there.
For consistency's sake, have Fred face to the right side of the screen instead of the left.

Shot 68: CLOSE SHOT FRED TRASH CANS. FRED's color is slightly better, although still pale. His clothing is now thoroughly soiled and torn. His eyelids flicker a few times, then fall shut as FRED begins to snore.
Instead of cutting close, stay wide, and just have Fred pass out.

Shot 69: MATCH DISSOLVE to MEDIUM SHOT ALLEY FRED as morning light filters into the alley, showing all the damage.
Add a panel indicating the cross-dissolve to daylight. Stay wide as in the suggestion for the previous shot, then cut close on Fred's face.

Shot 70: FRED wakes, blinks repeatedly, winces at the light, shakes his head and immediately clutches it in pain. He is badly hung over.
Break this action down into separate panels. The part where Fred shakes his head is appropriate for the multiple image idea.

Shot 71A: THREE-QUARTER MEDIUM SHOT FRED ALLEY ENTRANCE as he staggers onto sidewalk in front of store.
Use the same angle as Shot 66—it hooks up better and is more visually interesting than what's shown.

Shot 73: CLOSE SHOT FRED as he transitions from incomprehension to total recall, and then to crushing remorse. His shoulders sag.
Instead of cutting close like this at this point, have Fred stagger out of the alley and look into the store window before cutting closer for any facial reactions.

Shot 74: THREE-QUARTER MEDIUM SHOT FRED as FRED glances in darkened shop window. He sees his reflection again, and turns to face window.
Except for the multiple heads, this is fine.

Shot 75: CLOSE SHOT REFLECTION over FRED's shoulder.
No need to cut closer like this, you could stay in the composition of Shot 74.

Shot 76: REFLECTION morphs to well-fed, well-dressed version of FRED. REFLECTION's expression is stern and disapproving, an unflinching glare. MOVING HOLD.
Same composition note as Shot 75, but looks fine otherwise.

Shot 77: THREE-QUARTER MEDIUM SHOT FRED as REFLECTION morphs back to real reflection. FRED SIGHS, slouches further.
Have the action work with the description given. The action should probably be broken down into more than one panel anyway.

Shot 78: MEDIUM SHOT STOREFRONT FRED as he turns, SIGHS again.
Cut back to the composition that I suggest for Shot 73, and have the actions of Fred's turning and walking away broken down into separate panels.

Shot 79: FRED shuffles down the sidewalk and out of frame, very much as we first saw him, holes and tears in clothing, dirty, unshaven, hat stoved in and glasses askew. FADE OUT.
Have Fred forlornly walk off-screen at this point, and add a panel indicating the fade-out for the end.

That wraps up my comments on the first-draft storyboard. At the end of this chapter is the revised board I've done based on the sample script in this book. This isn't the only way this board could have been staged; if it had been handed to a different board artist, it would have been boarded differently. However, notice how the example is staged, and see if you can follow this board with minimal reading of the description. If you'd like to learn more about storyboarding, or get a different perspective to analyze the sample boards, here are a few resources you can try.

Storyboard Artist Resources: Films And Books

There isn't a lot out there that pertains solely to storyboards. I've already mentioned Steven Katz's book *Shot By Shot,* and how handy its small but effective storyboard section is. Additionally, there is a section in Katz's book that lists book titles that would help you. Some of these that are in my own little library include *The Illusion Of Life* (of course), the Preston Blair books, Tony White's *Animation Workbook, Animation: From Script To Screen* by Shamus Culhane, and *Chuck Amuck* and *Chuck Reducks,* by Chuck Jones.

I also have various books about Warner Bros. cartoons (such as *Bugs Bunny: 50 Years And Only One Grey Hare*), out-of-print how-to animation books, and books that aren't directly animation-related, but show different styles that can be incorporated into animation. For instance, I'm slowly collecting Shel Silverstein's books. His drawings are nice and simple, and show a line of action, even though they don't move. Any collection of *New Yorker* cartoons is a must for me, as well as Charles Addams' work. Comic strip collections worth noting include *Bloom County, Outland,* and *Calvin and Hobbes,* as they all show nice movement even when they're not moving. I also collect books on costume and fashion from different historical eras (for reference and inspiration).

Since I have a laser disc player at home, I have a large supply of cartoons to watch frame-by-frame or go through at half-speed or whatever I need to do. These include all of the box sets for the *Golden Age of Looney Tunes,* the Tex Avery box set, several Disney films including *The Lion King, Dumbo, Aladdin,* and *Pinocchio.*

For beginners, I especially recommend that you look at the Disney films to get the Disney "formula"—it's the same in just about every film, so it doesn't matter which one you watch. They definitely break down the film into three parts: the set-up, (introducing the characters and situation), the action (where the main part of the story takes place, where the villain puts the main obstacle in the hero's way), and the end, where everything is wrapped up very nicely, the villain vanquished, and everybody's happy. Also, if you look at the "new wave" of Disney features (from *The Little Mermaid* on), you'll notice that they even have songs in the same places with the same themes. They have the introductory song, then they have the hero's "I want" song, which usually consists of the hero wanting to get out of the current locale. Next, they'll have the main dance number song, which includes the cuddly side characters. Then, they'll have the villain's song, which usually has the villain explain his evil ways, and usually some sort of ballady love song, which personally makes me want to puke. I'm not the biggest Disney fan, but they obviously have great success with this formula.

One time I was taken through the Dreamworks feature studio. Nice place, and incredible artwork! They had something which I'd not seen before, and I don't know if other places such as Disney use them, but here it is. They had a wall graph for each main character of the film, and the graph showed what emotional high the character would be at in every phase of the film. It was rather intriguing, and great for those who need to go look at the graph and get some inspiration for any scene they're doing.

There is one last piece of animation that warrants mentioning, and it's one of the best examples of storytelling I've seen: *My Neighbor Totoro*. The reason I say this is because when I first saw this film, it was in its original Japanese, without dubbing or subtitles. I was able to follow the story with minimal problems, despite the fact that I had no idea what the characters were saying. When a film can tell its story despite language barriers, it's worth noting. If you can get a copy of this film, I strongly suggest that you do so.

I'm also getting a collection of live-action films together. In school, we were shown quite a few clips from Alfred Hitchcock's films, for he was a genius in story and staging. His classic films are a must to see for this. Another notable live-action film is Orson Welles' *Touch Of Evil*. This movie contains one of the best film openings I've ever seen. The opening shows the character and activities of a small Mexican border town, and it does this without a single cut for about six minutes. It's amazing.

Citizen Kane is of course every film class's darling. I fell asleep the two times I saw it, but there is one sequence that I later saw in my storyboarding class that shows the disintegration of Kane's marriage to his first wife. The sequence has no dialogue, which is why it's so great to watch, to see the emotions, or lack of them become evident. It takes place at the dinner table. It starts with the characters seated side-by-side. Then the scene cross-dissolves to the characters sitting farther apart. Then they're sitting even farther apart. Finally, they're sitting at opposite ends of the long table, not even acknowledging each other.

Other live-action films I've got include a few by Humphrey Bogart such as *Treasure of the Sierra Madre* and *African Queen*. Of course I have *Pulp Fiction* and *Reservoir Dogs*. *Pulp Fiction* is a brilliant display of how to take apart a story according to its chronological order, rearrange it, and still have it be a complete film. The opening sequence of *Reservoir Dogs* really sets up who each of the characters are, and considering how hard it is to show a group clearly when they're sitting around a table, this sequence is just brilliant (and funny as heck). I've also got a couple of Sergio Leoni films, my favorite being *Once Upon A Time In The West*. The film takes its time in showing and developing its characters and plot, and does it so that the viewer couldn't possibly be bored. I am a sucker for character-driven films, and this is one of the best. A recent film that I enjoyed as a "character film" is called *Amateur*. Another example of slow, steady character development with an interesting story.

Other films I was shown in my storyboarding class included two of Steven Spielberg's greatest: *Jaws* and *E.T.*. The specific sequences shown to us included one in *Jaws* where Roy Scheider is on shark-watch, and he thinks he sees the shark's fin in the water. You get some good POV shots as well as good reaction shots of his face when he thinks he sees the shark, and drives the beachgoers into a panic when he yells at them to evacuate. From *E.T.*, we were shown the sequence where Drew Barrymore's character first sees E.T. Her expressions are delightful, and the viewer feels the same wonder she does. Spielberg, in general, is great at drawing the viewer in to feel exactly what he wants them to feel at any point in his films.

One of my now-favorite films is *GoodFellas*. Gangster films in general reek of character. They're great, and just about everybody loves them. *Goodfellas* is yet another example of distinct characters that are appealing, even though they do very unappealing things. The first two *Godfather* films also accomplish this, and, to top it off, the cinematography is excellent.

You probably noticed that I started talking a lot about character in this section. It's because when you have characters that have appealing personalities, their personalities and reactions help drive the film and keep the viewers interested.

Now that you have read theory and seen examples of storyboarding, it's time for you to practice doing your own boards.

Sandra Frame is a storyboard artist who has worked on shows such as "Pinky and the Brain," "Animaniacs," and "Duckman." She also created the characters and storyboards for the independent production "The Physics of Cartoons, Part 1." Sandra lives in Los Angeles with her husband and two cats. If you want to make fun of her writing, email her at SFrame13@aol.com.

Make A Storyboard

This exercise is intended to get you thinking visually, converting the shot descriptions in the script into images that are closer to what you want in the final film.

Break out your script from Project 2.2 into a properly formatted storyboard. Stick figures are acceptable, but try to keep them in proportion. If the characters are interacting with part of the set (looking out a window, opening a door), draw that part of the set.

If you don't want to storyboard your own script, either use the sample script provided in Chapter 2 or select at least four pages from a motion picture or television script. Break it out as if you will be animating it, even if the script is for a live-action show. If your shot descriptions are longer than two or three short sentences, they are probably too long. Break them down even further.

If you use the sample script, make your version of Fred markedly different. How would you compose the shots if Fred were tall and thin? Short and fat? Make all the action work from the opposite side of the street. Do *not* simply copy the storyboard from this chapter!

Use a blank sheet of paper to cover the shot description under each sketch. At random, pick a sketch, and see if you can tell what the action is and what the character is expressing. Repeat this test for several of the shots.

Flip through the storyboard in order, looking only at the sketches. Are you starting to get a sense of the rhythm, the timing for the shot flow? Are there gaps or jumps in the shot flow? If you jump from one camera location to another without a strong common visual reference, you may lose your audience. If you have to make a big jump, make sure you have an object or character that appears in both shots, so the audience can immediately orient themselves to the new point of view. For example, the cut from Shot 22 to Shot 23 in the first-draft storyboard does not lose the audience, because the "Proper Attire" sign is in the middle of both shots. The cut is a kind of super-fast zoom in. By contrast, the cut between Shot 23 and Shot 24 can lose the audience, because there is no common reference point. To correct this, you could widen or shift the frame in Shot 24 to include the "Proper Attire" sign again.

If you can, show your storyboard to someone you know who can think visually. Ask them to tell you the story represented by the boards, in their own words.

If the responses to all three of these critiques are close to what you intended, your storyboard is working. If not, remember that storyboarding, like writing or animating, is a skill that improves with practice. Keep at it! And, as with all the other techniques discussed in this book, be *ruthless* with your editing.

Putting The Storyboard To Work

So you've got a storyboard. Now what? Put it to work, of course, saving you time and effort!

The number one value of a storyboard is that it saves effort for the production team. For example, if there are no shots in the storyboard where the camera is closer than a hundred feet to a particular object, you don't have to build any details into that object that aren't visible at a hundred feet. If every camera angle cuts off at first-floor height, there's no use in modeling and texturing the upper floors and roofs.

This is really where "limitations" are considered and put to use. The first round of storyboards should be fairly free of constraints. It's always easier to scale back than to build up.

Take another look at the revised sample storyboard printed at the end of this chapter. This time, look at the sketches from the point of view of the technical director. Fred is the only character who needs to have a head, feet, or a body—the bouncer and waitress are represented by disembodied hands and arms that appear from off-screen. This is an enormous savings in modeling and animation. There is a slight cost in terms of expressive range, as you can only communicate so much with hand gestures (we have to assume most of the audience doesn't read American Sign Language).

The sets are almost all false-front shops, with simple (and reusable) sections of sidewalk, street, and alley connecting them. The single interior is also deliberately vague and simple, kept shadowy by lighting so minor details need not be modeled.

Take a look at your own storyboards. Look at each sketch. Is there any object in this sketch that doesn't appear somewhere else? Is there a different way to compose the shot so that object doesn't have to be modeled? Will cropping it out have a negative effect on telling the story? Could a simpler or stock object be substituted? There's no reason to custom-build a 1931 Duesenberg if it's only in one shot for a few seconds and the character could just as easily be stepping out of a stock-model taxi.

Storyboards force you to make these important decisions early on, and are therefore an absolute requirement for any sizable animation. Budgets can be broken and deadlines blown by a few overly complex shots. If these shots are necessary to tell the story effectively, the finance people might accept the overrun; if the shots are superfluous, you are likely to hear phrases like "Heaven's Gate" or "Waterworld" as they tell you to clean out your desk.

Sample Storyboard

The following storyboard is included to assist you in completing the exercises in the rest of the book, in case you don't want to draw your own storyboards. These story sketches originally followed a revised version of the script presented in Chapter 2, roughly the third draft. More additions, changes, and deletions came from storyboard revisions—this storyboard is the second full revision. You will find many differences from the script, which enable you to see how the story changed through the development process.

This storyboard is copyright © 1996-1997 Douglas A. Kelly. Your permission to use the storyboard is subject to the following conditions:

- Permission is granted to purchasers of this book to use this storyboard for educational purposes only.

- Purchasers of this book are specifically granted permission to use this storyboard for completing the projects in this book in the production of a not-for-resale animated motion picture.

- If you use this storyboard "as is" or in any revised or derivative form, you are required to display the phrases "Written by Doug Kelly" and "Storyboards: Sandra Frame and Brian Kelly" in the credits.

- If the finished work will be used for any commercial purpose or public display, including any advertisement or solicitation regarding animation services or employment, copyright law requires that you get my permission in advance.

- If you use this storyboard to create a demo reel, you can secure my permission by sending me a letter of request and a copy of the demo reel. You can contact me through The Coriolis Group, or email me at **dakelly@earthlink.net**.

Fade in...

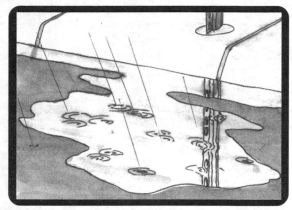

Shot 1: Same as Shot 1 in old board.

Shot 2: Truck out wide. See Fred shuffle into scene.

Shot 3: Cut to the storefront window.

Shot 4: Fred walks into scene.

Shot 5: Fred notices his reflection in the window.

Shot 6: Fred turns to face his reflection.

Shot 7: The reflection morphs into a nicely dressed, snappy looking Fred.

Shot 10: The reflection morphs back to reality.

Shot 11: Fred looks dismayed.

Shot 13A: Fred starts shuffling forward again.

Shot 14: Cut wide, see the wind blowing leaves and garbage by Fred.

Shot 8: Cut to the interior of the store window, see Fred puff his chest out, completely involved in his little fantasy.

Shot 9: Cut back to over-the-shoulder shot of Fred and his fantasy reflection.

Shot 12: Fred sighs, and slumps down.

Shot 13: Fred turns away.

Shot 15: A money bill flies into scene and slaps Fred right across his eyes.

Shot 16: Fred grabs the money, and readjusts his glasses.

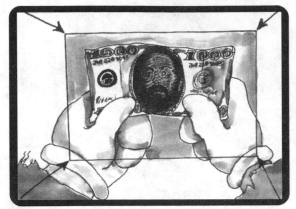

Shot 17: Cut to Fred's POV of the money in his hand. Truck in to see it's a big denomination. (Same as Shot 14 from the old board.)

Shot 18: Cut back to a medium shot of Fred, as he does a take.

Shot 21: Dollar signs are reflected in Fred's pupils.

Shot 22: The dollar signs morph into a hot dinner, and Fred starts to smile.

Shot 25: Cut wide as Fred snaps out of his reverie, and looks around.

Shot 19: Fred recovers, still unable to believe his eyes.

Shot 20: Close on Fred as he looks up, his eyes huge.

Shot 23: The hot dinner morphs into a glass of champagne, and Fred's smile grows.

Shot 24: The glass morphs into the snappy well-dressed visage of Fred himself, as his smile grows even more.

Shot 26: Fred's POV as the camera pans across the street until it stops at a restaurant.

Shot 27: Cut back to Fred, who appears ecstatic.

Shot 28: Fred antics back.

Shot 31: Fred skids to a stop at the front door.

Shot 32: Fred runs inside.

Shots 35 and 36: Fred protests his treatment by shaking his fist and waving his arms.

Shot 29: Fred runs OS.

Shot 30: Cut to downshot of the restaurant as Fred runs into scene.

Shot 33: The door slams. An argument is heard coming from inside.

Shot 34: The door opens, and Fred is tossed out on his bum.

Shot 37: A huge bouncer's arm shoots out of the doorway, pointing to a sign in the window.

Shot 38: Cut close to a slight up-shot on the sign.

Shot 39: Cut to an over-the-shoulder shot of Fred, as the restaurant door is slammed shut.

Shot 40: Cut wide as Fred picks himself up off the ground.

Shot 43: Fred reacts when he sees what he's looking for.

Shot 44: Fred steps off the curb.

Shot 47: The door shuts, and the sounds of a sewing machine and scissors heard.

Cross-dissolve.

Shots 41 and 42: Fred brushes himself off and looks around.

Shot 42

Shot 45: Cut to a tailor shop.

Shot 46: Fred walks into scene and goes into the shop.

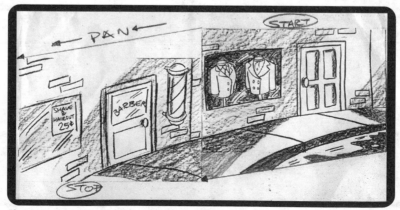

Shot 48: Same shot of the tailor shop, but at night. Pan over to the barber shop next door, where the sounds of a razor and scissors are heard.

Shot 49: Fred walks out, looking as snappy as his fantasy reflection.

Shot 50: Cut to a low shot of the restaurant, as Fred walks into scene and away from camera, towards the restaurant.

Shot 51: Fred reads the menu, with the waitress waiting with pad in hand.

Shots 52, 53, and 54: Fred points to different items on the menu as the waitress scribbles them down on her pad.

Shot 55: Fred hands the menu back to the waitress. (Same as Shot 45 from old board.)

Shot 56: The waitress pours a glass of champagne as Fred waits.

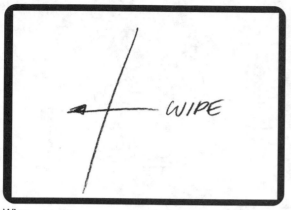

Wipe.

Shot 50A: Medium shot of Fred seated in the restaurant. A waitress hands him a menu. (Same as Shot 42 from old board.)

Shot 53

Shot 54

Shot 57: Fred grabs the champagne.

Shot 58: As Fred drinks, the waitress puts a big plate of food down in front of him.

Shot 59: Fred puts the glass down and grabs his fork.

Shot 60: Fred's glass is refilled as he starts to eat.

Shot 63: Cut to a medium shot of Fred as he picks up the chicken leg to take a bite.

Shot 64: Cut closer as Fred takes a sip of champagne.

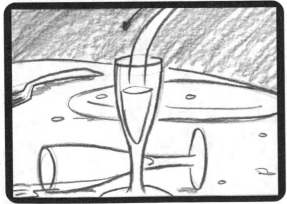

Shot 67: Cut close on the table as champagne is being poured.

Shot 68: Cut close to Fred's hand swinging into scene with a full glass.

Shot 61: More plates of food are set down onto the table.

Shot 62: [Beginning of montage sequence] Cut close on the table as a plate of chicken and mashed potatoes is set down.

Shot 65: Cut to extreme close-up on Fred's mouth as he eats green beans.

Shot 66: Cut to a close shot of another bottle of champagne being opened.

Shot 69: Cut to the tabletop as a huge pizza is set down.

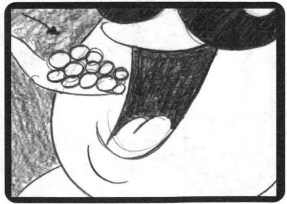

Shot 70: Cut to extreme close-up on Fred's mouth as he eats some peas.

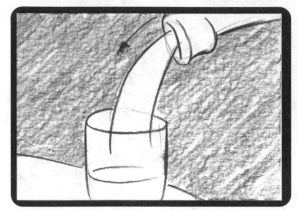

Shot 71: Cut to extreme close-up as more champagne is poured into a glass.

Shot 72: Cut back to medium shot of Fred still sitting at the table, empty dishes around him, as he's very drunk, and still drinking.

Shot 75

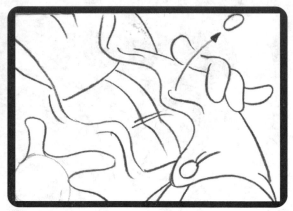

Shot 76

Shot 79: Cut to medium shot of the table. Empty dishes are stacked high, and Fred is still drinking. The waitress motions with her hands to tell him to quiet down.

Shot 80: Fred turns to look at her.

Shot 73: Cut to close shot of Fred with his mouth full of food.

Shots 74, 75, 76, and 77: Cut to a close shot on his belly. The buttons on his blazer pop off one by one due to his increased girth.

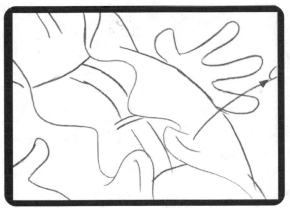

Shot 77

Shot 78: Cut to medium shot of Fred, obviously drunk, yelling. [End of montage]

Shot 81: Fred sets his glass down and argues with the waitress.

Shot 82: Fred's face softens.

Shot 83: Fred starts to waggle his eyebrows at the waitress in a lascivious manner.

Shot 84: Fred kisses the waitress's hand.

Shot 87: Fred catches himself on the edge of the table.

Shot 88: Fred sits up, grumbling, and grabs his glass of champagne again.

Shot 91: Fred turns to face the bouncer, as the bouncer's hand withdraws.

Shot 92: Cut to a wide, low shot of the restaurant.

Shot 85: The waitress snatches her hand away.

Shot 86: Fred is caught off-balance.

Shot 89: Fred turns and starts drinking again.

Shot 90: The bouncer's huge arm reaches into scene and taps Fred on the shoulder.

Shot 93: The door flies open, and the bouncer sends Fred flying out the door.

Shot 94: Fred hits the lamppost in the foreground.

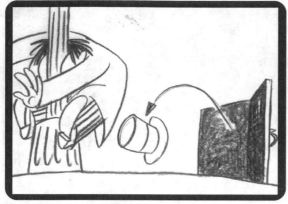

Shot 95: Fred's top hat comes flying out, too.

Shot 96: The door slams shut.

Shot 99: Fred hits the ground, squashing his hat.

Shot 100: Fred's arms and legs flop to the ground.

Shot 103: Fred leans against the lamppost, feeling sick.

Shot 104: Cut close to Fred's face, who looks miserable.

Shot 97: Cut to a side shot of Fred still stuck to the lamppost.

Shot 98: Fred starts to fall, stiff as a board.

Shot 101: Fred sits up, hand to his head

Shot 102: Fred starts to get up, holding the lamppost for support.

Shot 105: Fred feels very nauseous.

Shot 106: Cut low and wide, as Fred still momentarily holds onto the lamppost.

Shot 107: Fred quickly turns away and starts to run.

Shot 108: Fred runs to the alleyway.

Shot 111: Fred starts to slide to the ground.

Shot 112: Fred slumps on the ground and passes out.

Shot 114: Cut close on Fred as he wakes up, wincing.

Shot 115: Fred puts his hand to his head.

Shot 109: Fred retches.

Shot 110: Cut closer on the alleyway as Fred stumbles in.

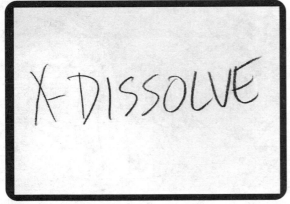

Cross-dissolve.

Shot 113: It's bright morning in the alleyway.

Shot 116: Fred shakes his head.

Shot 117: Fred grabs his head in pain.

Shot 118: Cut wide on the street as Fred totters out of the alley, still woozy.

Shot 119: Fred passes a storefront window.

Shot 122: Fred's reflection morphs into the fantasy well-dressed version of Fred, who is looking very stern and disapproving.

Shot 123: The reflection morphs back to Fred's shabby appearance. He looks sad and crestfallen.

Shot 126: Fred turns away, and starts slowly walking away.

Shot 127: Fred continues walking OS.

Shot 120: Fred turns to look at his reflection.

Shot 121: Cut to a medium over-the-shoulder shot of Fred looking at his shabby appearance.

Shot 124: Fred sighs and slumps down.

Shot 125: Cut back to the wide shot. Fred is still standing in front of the window.

Fade Out.

Moving On

If you've read and completed the exercise for this chapter, you should have a good idea of the importance and utility of a storyboard for your character animation. The examples shown here should help you avoid making the same mistakes in your own production.

The next level of detail is the timing of each shot, writing up the actions, music and sound effects on bar sheets and exposure sheets. Chapter 4 will guide you through this step in the production process.

EXPOSURE SHEETS

Silent animations are boring. Even a little generic background music will liven them up, and synchronized sound effects will do wonders.

If you are producing a demo reel, you can increase your chances of an interview if you pay a little attention to your soundtrack. The reviewer is more likely to watch your reel, and less likely to cut it off short, if the audio track adds to the flow and continuity of your animations. Just as the script and storyboard document the story development of your film, the bar sheets and exposure sheets document the development of music, sound, and dialog.

Making Sound Decisions

You have a variety of options for adding sound to your animation: do without, borrow, buy, or make it yourself. You can always opt for a silent piece, a bad idea in general but sometimes necessary if your resources are limited.

General background music and sound effects are the next step up. At minimum, try to dub a song that has similar mood and length to your animation. If your animation has been laid out to a steady beat, you may even be able to find prerecorded music that will match your animation's accents.

If you intend to send your demo reel only to potential employers, you may be able to get away with using commercial recordings; this is a gray area of the fair use doctrine regarding copyright. You definitely cannot use a copyrighted work to make money or in a public performance, and any use on a demo reel must be strictly for "educational or research purposes." That is, a student piece, even if you are self-taught. If you are already in the graphics business, and the reel is distributed to advertise your services, you can't use the fair use defense. Also, if there is any chance that your reel will be shown in public, you need to comply with all the copyright restrictions or prepare to be sued. To play it safe, if you can afford it, you should buy an appropriate piece from a music or sound effects library.

Custom music and sound effects, synchronized to the action, are the most expensive but highest quality sounds for animation. If you don't have the budget to hire professionals, find a friendly musician or composer who is willing to work with you, or even try to do the music yourself. The same is true of sound effects and vocal tracks; locate people willing to help, or do it yourself if you can. *Foley* work (recording sound effects) can still be done effectively by non-professionals. You don't need a license to play the coconut halves, and most theater arts schools will have books on low-end sound effect recording techniques.

Animation and sound are a chicken-and-egg problem. Which should be done first? The answer is an unsatisfying "That depends."

The most common tool in coordinating sound and animation is the *bar sheet*.

Using Bar Sheets

A bar sheet (shown in Figure 4.1) is similar to the blank sheets a composer would use, except the three middle staff lines are missing. The measures are marked, and the number of beats to each measure is penciled in.

The director uses the bar sheets to plan the flow of the whole animation, condensing a hundred or more story sketches down to a few pages of cryptically penciled notations. This is where the mood and tempo of the finished film are determined. Prior to this, there has been a great deal of flexibility in how shots are paced and connected and what the mood of each segment can be. Once the director establishes the rhythm and timing of every shot via the bar sheet, the flow of the film is much more definite.

The bar sheets are especially useful because the director, composer, and other members of the production team can easily see if a particular action, sound, or musical passage will fit properly in the time allotted. This helps in negotiating the inevitable tradeoffs and compromises necessary to make the sound and animation work together. All these changes are also recorded on the bar sheets. Other people may contribute during the bar sheets' revision, but the final responsibility is the director's.

The bar sheets track most of the information needed to coordinate the entire animation production team. The director, animator, and most of the rest of the crew will live and breathe by

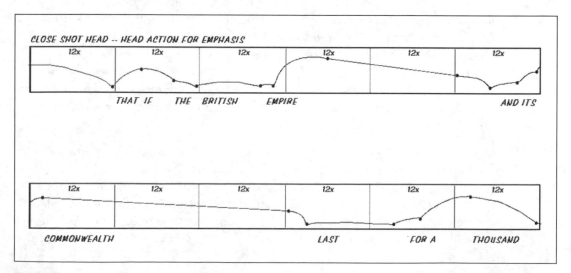

Figure 4.1 Part of a bar sheet.

these sheets before the project is completed. Keeping track of the sheets is an important job, whether you are being paid to do it as an assistant director or are doing it all yourself on a private project.

Modern cartoon production has diverged from this "classic" mode of animation timing. If the relation of the musical score to the animation is not critical, or if the animation is a short one, it's possible to dispense with the bar sheets and go directly to the exposure sheets (more about exposure sheets later). This is standard practice for television cartoon production, where most of the responsibility for the animation's timing resides with the sheet timer. The timer's influence on the finished animation is similar to that of the film editor in live action: the director may be the front man, but the timer or editor can make or break the finished product. Later in this chapter you'll learn to use exposure sheets, but for now let's stick to the classic methods and work with bar sheets first.

There are four basic approaches to coordinating sound and animation, plus combinations of two or more of the basics. All of them depend on accurate bar sheets:

- Music first. Compose and record the music first, using a strictly regular beat. The director lays out the musical beat in the bar sheets, so the animators can match the action to it without hearing the score. This approach can force animation into the realm of choreography. It can be challenging for the animator to squeeze a long action into a fast passage, or stretch to fill up a slow one. This approach is best used only when there is a strong reason to adhere to a prerecorded piece of music.

- Music first, but this time with a variable tempo. The music track is analyzed as if it were dialog, and the beats noted on the bar sheets.

- The director and composer negotiate between the director's timing of planned actions and the composer's scoring of individual phrases or passages.

- Scoring to the action. The action is laid out in the bar sheets with each accent marked in a dummy score. Then the composer writes a free tempo score to match the actions' emphasis with the music's beat.

Timing For Bar Sheets

For any approach that includes voice or sound effects, you are going to need timing information to help build your bar sheets. If you have recorded dialog, you should have several takes of each line from the script. Extracting timing information from these takes is called *sentence measurement*. In addition to extracting the amount of time each line of dialog takes, you also need to note the interval between the line being measured and both the preceding line and the following line.

One way to do sentence measurement is to digitize each usable take from the recording session, then open up the digitized files in a sound editor. It's fairly simple, then, to note the time of each sentence. Exactly how the information is organized depends on your working style, but I prefer typing it all into a spreadsheet with session, take, time, intervals, clip file name, and comments organized in separate columns. This is probably overkill on small projects, but it can save you a lot of hassle on big ones by enabling you to sort and search for just the right clip. It's a good idea to do the same for any sound effects you plan to use. If you will be matching action to the sounds, it's essential.

If you are following the last method listed above, or are animating a sequence with no sound effects, musical, or vocal timing guidelines, you will have to wing it. That is, you'll have to estimate each action's timing to the best of your ability. In the past, veteran animators became masters at this, partly through necessity. Management pressures at some studios dictated the precise length of animated shorts, and directors quickly learned to time an animation exactly to the frame. Similar pressures still exist today in advertising and television, but there is a lot more slack in independent and feature-length productions. You can develop your ability to time actions accurately by working through the exercises in Part V of this book.

In learning to time action, use any technique that helps. I recommend acting the actions out, and using a stopwatch to time them. Repeat each action until you are satisfied with your performance, then take three more timings and average them to get your working time.

You should modify the timing of your characters' actions based on the style of the animation and the character whose role you are acting out. Typically, caricatures or cartoons move much more rapidly than real-world creatures, with a great deal of snap and exaggerated acceleration and deceleration. On the other hand, if you are animating Gulliver among the Brobdignagians, the hapless adventurer should move at a normal pace while his giant captors move as ponderously as elephants.

Other useful tools for acting out timing include a videotape recorder and camera with a SMPTE timecode display, a laser disc player and a collection of discs with appropriate action sequences, or a metronome (for you traditionalists). There are special stopwatches that are marked in frames; if you will be doing this a lot, consider acquiring one.

Professional animators time their work at 24 frames per second (fps), the *frame rate* of standard 35mm motion picture film. NTSC video runs at 29.97 (usually rounded to 30) fps, PAL video at 25 fps, and game or multimedia animations at anywhere from 6 to 30 fps. Even if you plan to work entirely in video or multimedia formats, you should learn and practice timing at 24 fps. All television and film animation is done on film at 24 fps. The repertoire of most experienced animators and timers for a given move (for example, snap the arm up in 4 frames, then cushion for 8 frames) is learned for 24 fps, and it is difficult and counterproductive to relearn or translate this hard-won experience into 30 fps timing. Also, many people who intend to eventually transfer animation to film, or who are using video until the film is ready to be transferred, animate at 24 fps.

24 fps footage can be converted to 30 fps using a process called *3:2 pulldown*, which is discussed in more technical detail in Chapter 18. This conversion allows the footage to retain the appearance that it was originally shot on film. In the opinion of most TV viewers, 3:2 pulldown conversion looks superior to video originally shot at 30 fps, although no one seems to know why. The effect of 3:2 pulldown on animation timing is considered negligible, and can't really

be detected by viewing animation in real time. In summary, there are several good reasons to animate at 24 fps, and no good reason not to.

Timing The Sketches

PROJECT 4.1

This exercise gives you some practice at rough timing story sketches. You will use the complete rough timing to assemble the story reel, the next step in revising and "tightening up" the timing of your film.

1. Beg, borrow, or otherwise acquire access to a stopwatch or a VTR with timecode display.
2. Act out each shot in the sample storyboards. Repeat each action at least three times. Record the time for each action.
3. Average the performances to give a working time for each action.
4. Convert the working time to frames at 24 frames per second.
5. Note the working time in the margin of the page next to each story sketch.

Repeat this exercise with your own storyboards, if you have any. Practice your sketch timing at every opportunity. This hones your sense of timing for actions and contributes to your abilities as an animator. As mentioned earlier, sheet timers in television production sometimes have more influence on the final animation than the director.

So, how do you know if your timings are any good? One way to check them is to make a *story reel*.

The Story Reel

A story reel is a motion picture assembled using the story sketches. This is sometimes called a *Leica reel*, after the camera commonly used to produce it. Each sketch is held on screen for the exact length of time the action depicted is supposed to take. No illusion of motion is created, but the overall timing and shot flow of the animation becomes obvious.

Fortunately, modern technology has made the task of assembling a story reel almost trivial. The first requirement is to convert the story sketches to electronic image files. You can do this with a scanner, a video camera and digitizer, or my favorite low-tech approach: a fax machine!

If you are strapped for cash and don't have access to a scanner, a cheap used fax machine can be just what the doctor ordered. There are a lot of old fax machines out there designed to print on the slick, expensive thermal paper that everybody hates. These machines are usually retired as quickly as possible, and you may even be able to pick one up for free.

"Ideally, you want to complete the storyboards, then have it all on a story reel before you even start production."

Kathleen Gavin, co-producer,
Nightmare Before Christmas

The other side of this technique is the fact that most machines capable of running CGI software include a fax modem as standard equipment.

The trick that makes this possible is that you can hook a fax machine directly into your fax modem without tying up your phone line. Just drop your sketches in the hopper, tell your fax software to pick up, and press the fax machine's send button. Presto, you've got scanned sketches in your computer!

The disadvantages to this technique are that the resolution on fax machines is around 200 dpi, and you still have to translate or export the page images from your fax software to an image format that your CGI software can work with.

PROJECT 4.2 Check Your Rough Timing With A Silent Story Reel

This exercise puts your rough timing into a form that you (and others) can readily critique and revise. The story reel is an important development tool throughout the rest of your film's production, and knowing how to build and edit your reel is a valuable skill. You will find digitized story sketches in TIFF format in the Chapter 3 directory on this book's CD-ROM. Use them for this exercise.

1. Make a duplicate of all the story sketch files in their own directory on your hard drive. You'll need about 13MB of free space.

2. Using the timing notations from Project 4.1, calculate the beginning frame number for each story sketch.

   For example, if the first and second sketches are each to be held for 60 frames, and the third is held for 120 frames, the fourth would start at 60+60+120, or frame 240. The easiest way to keep track of this is by using a printing calculator that prints the running total as you add in each sketch's timing.

3. Rename each duplicate story sketch to match the appropriate beginning frame number, for example: SHOT0090.TIF.

   You should end up with a numbered sequence of images. The preceding three steps are common to this process for most software, the remaining steps will differ. Steps 4 through 9 are explicit for LightWave, followed by summary instructions for other programs.

4. In LightWave 3D Layout, open a new scene, and click the Images button. In the Images panel, click on Load Sequence. Select the first image in the sequence you just created, and click on Continue.

5. Click on the Scene button to call up the Scene panel. Set the number of frames equal to (or slightly greater than) the total of the story sketch times. Click on Continue.

6. Click on the Effects button to call up the Effects panel. In the Compositing layer of the Effects panel, set the Background Image to the image sequence you loaded in Step 4. Click on Continue.

7. Click on the Record button to open the Record panel. Choose a directory, file name, and format for the animation you are about to render, and click on Continue.

8. Click on the Camera button. In the Camera panel, set rendering to Wireframe, antialiasing off, and whatever resolution your machine can play back at 24 frames per second. Click on Continue. (You don't need antialiasing or anything other than Wireframe, because the only purpose of this scene is to duplicate the background images into an animation.)

9. Render the animation.

Make sure you've got plenty of disk space available. Even though the sketches mostly have very small *deltas* (changes in pixel values between successive frames), AVI, and FLC compression algorithms are not very efficient with this sort of file.

This approach is adequate only for a really quick timing check, as it has no provision for music or other sound tracks. However, it's handy, quick, and doesn't require any software besides LightWave 3D. Almost all CGI software capable of character animation shares this ability to load a sequence of background images.

In 3D Studio MAX, the quickest method is to use the Video Post utility to load the story sketches and render them as an AVI file. Chapter 36 of the User Manual provides an adequate tutorial on using this utility. Unfortunately, neither background map rendering nor Video Post in MAX pays any attention to the image sequence numbers; if frames 20 through 29 are missing, they will render the animation so frame 30 follows immediately after frame 19. This behavior is dictated by the IFL file that Video Post creates when you tell it what directory and root file name you want to use. Video Post looks for sequential files in the directory and makes the IFL list of only the file names it finds. The workaround for this problem, therefore, is to load the image sequence as usual, then use a text editor, such as Notepad, to edit the IFL file to pad it out, repeating the images to cover the gaps in the sequence. The first part of the raw sequence might look like this:

```
shot0001.bmp
shot0005.bmp
shot0006.bmp
shot0007.bmp
shot0010.bmp
```

The same part of the revised IFL file would look like this:

```
shot0001.bmp
shot0001.bmp
shot0001.bmp
shot0001.bmp
shot0005.bmp
shot0006.bmp
shot0007.bmp
```

```
shot0007.bmp
shot0007.bmp
shot0010.bmp
```

This makes Video Post or background mapping re-render each image in the sequence until the next one is available, covering the gaps in the sketch sequence. This is a little extra cut-and-paste work, but it goes quickly and takes about as much effort as the Premiere-based editing described in Project 4.4.

Incidentally, you can use this technique to pad out image sequences for lip sync and other animation tasks where you have images for keyframes but not for in-betweens.

Page 107 of trueSpace3's manual describes how to set up an image sequence as a background.

In SoftImage, you can load a sequence of background images into a scene using Rotoscope View mode (Reference Guide, pp. 37-40). For quickest results, render the scene in Rotoscope Wire mode (Rendering, pp. 21-23), and use the Sync Frame option to synchronize the story sketch numbers (SHOT0001, SHOT0072, and so forth) to the output image sequence. View the output image sequence with the Flipbook tool or standalone (Animating, p. 26).

In Alias, you can load the story sketches as a Pix File Backdrop sequence (Rendering, p. 99) and render a QuickTime, MPEG-1, or other animation file. Alternatively, you can use ComposerLite's MultiFlip function (Complimentary Applications, pp. 295-296) to play back the sequence from a temporary disk file.

Strata Studio Pro loads background images primarily for environment reflection maps. It does not allow accurate, consistent image proportions and placement, so it's not really usable for rendering a story reel.

Extreme 3D can only render a single background image throughout an animation, so it can't create a story reel using this technique. It also insists on locking the loaded image to the upper-left corner of the screen, at a forced 1:1 pixel ratio. If you want to render anything other than the exact size of the background image, you'll get borders or cutoffs at the right and bottom edges. This is a serious oversight by Macromedia, and they should correct it at the first opportunity.

Infini-D includes an easy step-by-step procedure for loading PICT sequences or QuickTime movies as backgrounds on pages 27 and 28 of Chapter 3 in the tutorial manual.

Electric Image's Projector application has a function, Append Animations, that enables you to compile an animation from a collection of images. This feature is described on pages 11-31 through 11-33 of the Projector manual. You simply open the first story sketch image file to be appended, specify the number of frames the sketch will occupy in the End field of the Editing dialog, and repeat for the remaining sketches. This is an easy and painless way to precisely control each sketch's duration.

If I haven't mentioned your software, check your user or reference manual for the exact procedures.

Writing Up Your Bar Sheets

The purpose of this exercise is to create bar sheets from your demo reel storyboards.

1. First, get some blank bar sheets, or draw up your own. Set the space between bar lines equal to 12 frames.

This gives you one-half second per measure at standard film speed of 24 frames per second. This is arbitrary, but I like it since it gets an adequate amount of animation onto a single sheet while leaving room for a moderate amount of scribbled notes.

2. Mark the important accents, especially the beats the composer needs to match. Footsteps, strong actions, starts or peaks of sounds, and dialog accents should all be noted.

    Refer to Figure 4.1 for an example of a filled-in bar sheet.

3. From each accent, arrange the boundaries of the sound effects and dialog, using the sentence measurements you performed earlier.

This should immediately show any glaring inconsistencies, like a seven-second speech that is supposed to match an action timed for five seconds, or an originally brief interval between sentences that now stretches interminably.

4. Interpolate minor actions and accents in between the major ones.

    As you will do later with the actual animation, work from the most important element down to the least significant. The important actions have to be timed to certain frames or musical *hits*; the less important actions can slide around the bar sheets more without adversely affecting the story.

Depending on the approach you are taking to coordinate sound and music, you may want your composer or other musical talent to have a hand in developing the bar sheets.

When the bar sheets are complete, you are ready to put together your next production tool, the story reel.

Checking Your Plan: The Story Reel

For a better idea of how your film is progressing and to assist in making various production decisions, you will want to make a more complete story reel. This requires an almost complete set of sound tracks, including voices, music, and sound effects. You will also need the completed bar sheets and digitized story sketches.

Assemble A Story Reel

This exercise is written for Adobe Premiere 4.2. Other compositing and editing software may be usable if it has similar functions. You'll be assembling the sound clips, story sketches, and music to match the timing you've written up in your bar sheets. If you are using a different editing software, read through these instructions, then consult your software's user or reference manuals to learn how to duplicate this process.

1. Start Adobe Premiere. Choose the Presentation-160x120 Preset for the new project. Set the timebase to 24 fps.

The Project, Info, Preview, Construction, and Transitions windows will appear. You can immediately close the Transitions window, as you won't be using any transitions for this exercise and there's no sense in cluttering your workspace.

2. Choose the File|Import|File option, or press Ctrl+I. The Import dialog appears.

3. Drag-select all the story sketch TIFF files from the Chapter 3 directory on this book's CD-ROM. Click on Open to import the images.

   The story sketch files appear in the Project window as *thumbnails*, or smaller versions of images that are more suitable for on-screen viewing.

4. Repeat Step 3 for the sound effects, voice tracks, and music tracks, as appropriate.

The sound files also appear in the Project window, but as audio waveform thumbnails. Soundtrack WAV files created to accompany the sample storyboard are included in the Chapter 4 directory on this book's CD-ROM. These include sound effects, voice tracks, and original music, and are © 1996-1997 Patrick Q. Kelly. If you use any part of these files in a production for profit or public display, you must contact him at PQKelly@aol.com, or 509 Division St., Madison, WI 53704 for permission. If you use these files in a nonprofit demo reel, your end credits must include the MUSICOPY.BMP, MUSIC.BMP, and FOLEY.BMP images (or equivalent wording) from the Chapter 19 directory on the CD-ROM. You must also send the copyright holder a courtesy copy of the demo reel.

So far, so good. Now you need to set the duration of each story sketch. Premiere has a default setting of one second for still images, which is probably too short for any of the shots from the sample storyboards.

5. Double-click on the first story sketch in the Project window. The Clip window opens. Click on the Duration button at the lower left. The Duration dialog appears.

6. Enter a duration for the first sketch. This should be equal to the number of frames penciled in the sketch margin from Project 4.1.

7. Click on OK. Close the Clip window. Double-click on the next sketch in the Project window.

8. Repeat the process until you have set the duration for each sketch. Save the project with an appropriate name.

9. Drag the first story sketch from the Project window to the top row of the Construction window. Drag the sketch to the left until it is flush with the first frame of the time ruler.

10. Drag the next story sketch from the Project window to the top row of the Construction window. Drag the sketch to the left until it is flush with the right edge of the preceding frame.

The duration you set for each sketch automatically sets the timing for the whole story reel.

11. Repeat until all the sketches are loaded in the Construction window. Save the project again.

At this point, you have the same results as when you rendered a sequence of background images in Project 4.2. The next step adds synchronized sound, which some character animation software can't handle—yet.

12. Drag the first sound clip from the Project window to the top track of the Audio part of the Construction window. Drag it left or right until it matches the timing laid out in the bar sheets.

13. Repeat Step 12 for the rest of the sound clips. If the timing marked in the bar sheets indicates two or more sounds will overlap, position one of the overlapping sound clips in a lower track.

Premiere can handle up to 99 audio tracks at once, so you shouldn't have any problems with overloading.

14. When everything is set up according to the bar sheets, save the project again. Choose Make|Make Movie. The Make Movie dialog appears. Choose the directory and file name for the movie, then click on the Output Options button.

15. Set the options to create a movie that can play back at full 24 fps on your system. Click on OK, then repeat with the Compression options. Click on OK again.

This may limit you to a 160x120 preview, or you may be using a monster machine that can handle full-screen 24 fps playback with stereo sound and lossless compression. Use whatever works—this is just for a working preview!

16. Click on OK in the Make Movie dialog to begin compiling the story reel. When it's complete, open and play it.

Are all the sounds synchronized correctly? Does the story reel "read" well? Does it give you a better idea of the effect of timing on how the story reads? Is there anything you want to change?

Adjusting The Timing Of Individual Sketches

You can adjust the timing of sounds by dragging them left and right in the audio tracks. Adjusting the timing of the individual sketches is a little trickier:

1. In Adobe Premiere, double-click on the thumbnail you want to re-time in the Construction window. The Clip window appears.

2. Enter a revised duration for the sketch, and click on OK.

3. Select and drag the thumbnails to either side of the re-timed clip, if necessary, until they are all flush again.

Re-timing the story sketches is a lot easier than re-animating finished sequences, isn't it? That's why story reels are an integral part of the workflow for most animators. It's standard procedure, because it pays off.

When you start producing finished renderings, you can selectively substitute them for the corresponding story sketches and recompile the movie. This way, the movie fills out as you make progress, and at any time you can view the whole thing. It's a wonderful feeling to watch your creative efforts grow this way.

Make Your Own Story Reel

Repeat Project 4.4, but use your own story sketches, bar sheets, and sound files.

Synchronizing Sound

You can add synchronized sound effects to an animation by noting where a sound should start and pasting the appropriate sound file into a sound track at that frame.

Synchronizing A Sound Effect To An Animation Using Adobe Premiere

This exercise synchs a simple "boing" sound (BOING.WAV) to an animation of a vibrating desk lamp, BOING.AVI. Both files can be found in the Chapter 4 directory on this book's CD-ROM. Again, most AV editing software can handle a simple edit like this. Consult your software's manual for specific procedures.

1. Start Adobe Premiere. Choose the Preset and Timebase for the new project.

2. Choose File|Import|File, or press Ctrl+I. The Import dialog appears.

3. Select the BOING.AVI file. Click on OK.

   The AVI file appears in the Project window as a thumbnail.

4. Choose File|Import|File again. Select the BOING.WAV sound clip. Click on OK.

   The sound file appears in the Project window. Note the spike at the beginning of the waveform.

5. Drag BOING.AVI from the Project window to the top row of the Construction window. Drag the thumbnail to the left until it is flush with the first frame of the time ruler.

6. Drag the BOING.WAV sound clip from the Project window to the top track of the Audio part of the Construction window.

7. Watch the Preview window as you drag the pointer to find the exact frame where the desk lamp is first hit. This is where the sound of the impact should also occur.

8. Slide the WAV file along the Audio track until the boing spike lines up with the frame where the desk lamp is hit.

9. Compile the animation. When it's complete, play it back.

Sometimes it's a good idea to add a two- or three-frame delay from a visual cue to the matching sound. For some reason, this "reads" better with most audiences. This is known as *slipping* the track.

You can also synchronize a longer sound effect within an animation. Simply note where a significant point (preferably a peak in the waveform) in the sound should appear in the animation, and slide the sound file in Premiere's audio track until the chosen point lines up with the correct frame number. For example, a long slide-whistle sound ending in a splat, and immediately followed by clanking and crashing, could quickly be synchronized by the initial spike in the waveform at the beginning of the splat.

If it's necessary to precisely position a sound, use the time unit selector at the bottom of the Construction window to zoom in on the frames in question. This will make it much easier to match the sound to a particular frame.

In addition to Premiere, there are several character animation software packages that you can use to import sound files.

Importing Sound To Your Animation Software

Some software packages are designed to make it easier for you to synchronize your animation to music, dialog, or sound effects.

For 3D Studio MAX, pages 29-22 and 29-23 of the User Guide explain how to load an audio file into the Track View. This is a very nice implementation of audio support; I wish more 3D software was this easy to sync in!

You can load a mono or stereo sound file into the Audio Track of Infini-D's Sequencer window, using the File|Import|Audio menu option. This enables you to sync to a visible point in the waveform(s), and to play back the sound file. There is no detailed documentation of this feature, but it's pretty simple. The only real glitch I found was an apparent problem in loading sound files other than QuickTime. If you try to load an AIFF or WAV file first, the waveform will display as a lot of blocks of black. If you first load a QuickTime sound, the waveform displays properly for all succeeding sound files. Unfortunately, Infini-D can't play back a sound file during a preview of the animation, so you can't use the Sequencer as a scrub bar to examine the matching of sound to action. This sound-loading feature is better than no sound at all, but it's only halfway to being the sound tool a character animator really needs.

Electric Image uses the File|Add|Sound menu option to add visible waveforms and playable audio to a project. This is very similar to Infini-D's audio feature, including the inability to play the audio in sync with a preview. Again, this is useful, but only half the tool we really need.

SoftImage currently has a very limited ability to import audio files to assist in synching. The Effects|Splound command in the Motion module creates a linear curve that describes the amplitude or "high spots" of the audio file. This is barely adequate for matching animation to major audibles like door slams or loud footsteps. For lip sync or musical cues, this isn't as useful as it should be. Keep your fingers crossed, SoftImage says they have greatly improved audio support in the next major release. Meanwhile, if you're running SoftImage on NT, you may want to experiment with Magpie (see Chapter 15) for lip sync.

Alias has two ways of using audio files to sync an animation. The most basic is the Sound Options in Playback, which enable you to hear an audio file as a preview plays. This isn't as useful as a full waveform display in the scene window would be; it reduces synching to a series of cut-and-try exercises, but it's better than no support at all. The other way is with the SoundSync application, which is essentially a lip sync power tool, and is therefore covered in Chapter 15.

At this time, Strata Studio Pro, Extreme 3D, Imagine, trueSpace3, MH3D, and LightWave have no ability to load sound files into scenes to assist with synchronizing animation. If you really need to see the waveform, Project 4.7 shows a trick you can use to fake it.

Faking Sound Import

1. Take screenshots of the audio file you want to import. Crop the screenshots to just the waveform, plus any reference marks or divisions. Make a note of the total length of the waveform, in frames at your chosen frame rate.

2. Assemble the screenshots into a continuous horizontal image, and save it in an image format that your 3D software can display as a map in its camera view.

3. Make a note of the dimensions of the waveform map. Create a simple plane object with the same proportions.

   Alternatively, if your 3D software can import a bitmap and turn it into an object, you can simply convert the waveform to a transparent or faceless object.

4. Load the new object into the scene you want to sync to the sound. Apply the waveform map to the object, and make the map visible in your preview mode, so you can see it while setting keyframes.

   It's usually best to parent the waveform to the camera, so the waveform is always visible in the same place in the camera view window. I like to put the waveform along the bottom edge of the camera view, just high enough to read clearly while leaving most of the scene visible. If you are using TV-safe guides, you can generally fit the waveform object into the lower cutoff area.

   You may find it helpful to add a very small primitive cone to the scene, positioned as a pointer at the top edge of the waveform, centered in the camera view.

5. Set a keyframe for the waveform's position so the left edge of the waveform is centered in the camera view (or aligned with the pointer object) in frame 1.

6. Set a keyframe for the waveform's position so the right edge of the waveform is centered in the camera view (or aligned with the pointer object) in the last frame.

This should move the waveform through the scene in sync with the current frame. Alternatively, if your 3D software can import a bitmap and turn it into an object, you can simply convert the waveform to a faceless wireframe object. This usually gives a faster screen redraw than a map.

Once you've mastered synchronizing your animations to simple sounds, you are ready to tackle the more complex tasks of lip sync.

Exposure Sheets For Lip Sync

Lip sync is essentially the same as synchronizing the bouncing ball to the music's beat. But instead of just a ball's position and maybe a little squash-and-stretch, you have to match the appropriate mouth and face shape to the phoneme being pronounced.

This is a lot more complicated, with many more opportunities for error. If you want to make as few mistakes as possible, you should plan your lip sync work using an *exposure sheet*. This is a table that is laid out with a line for each frame and a column for each kind of information needed to plan and track the production of the animation.

The exposure sheet, or *x-sheet*, tracks the frame-by-frame information needed by the animator. For the animator, and to a lesser degree the technical director, the exposure sheets are crucial. These sheets are an order of magnitude more detailed than the bar sheets, and are therefore not as useful to most other members of the production team. There's just too much information! Most of the team will be working in units of a complete shot, or of tens of seconds at least. An exposure sheet gets pretty crowded if it contains as much as three seconds' worth of information.

Different production houses use different forms for exposure sheets. I have made up a document that I like to use for character animation with CGI software, and included it in the Chapter 4 directory on this book's CD-ROM in Microsoft Word (XSHEET24.DOC, XSHEET30.DOC) and Adobe Acrobat (X_SHEET.PDF) formats. Several filled-in examples are printed at the end of this chapter.

To fill in your own exposure sheets, you can print multiple copies from the Word or Acrobat files and pencil in all your notes and changes. This is helpful when you need to make revisions later on, because you can easily erase the pencil marks while leaving the printed form intact.

The sheets should be labeled with enough information to keep them in order and to know who is responsible for any changes to their contents. At a minimum, the project name, the animator's name, and the scene number should be written in. Since most scenes will run longer than three seconds, the sheet number is also a requirement. It is advisable to write in the sheet numbers as "1 of 4," "2 of 4," et cetera, so you know how many sheets should be attached.

The sample exposure sheet is long enough to hold 90 frames, or three seconds of NTSC video, on each page. The first column of the sheet contains a waveform of the audio track. A little later, we'll go through the steps needed to capture these waveform images.

The second column is titled *PH* for phoneme. Here, the breakdown editor will write in the phonetic spelling of the sound being pronounced and mark duration and transitions, as well. This process is called *track analysis*, and it takes a good deal of practice.

The next column, *DIALOG*, is for the dialog and sound effects from the script. These words are written with their usual spellings and begin on the frame when the word or sound begins.

The fourth column is labeled *ACTION*. This is where the director or their assistant writes in a description of the action that must take place during the indicated frames. A door slamming, for instance, requires the complete closure of the door to be written at the frame where the sound of the slam begins.

The column labeled *SMPTE* is for the convenience of those who are synchronizing their work to film or video footage. Some foley (sound effects) artists or composers will also work with *SMPTE timecodes*, which usually appear as hours, minutes, seconds, and frames in the format HH:MM:SS:FF.

The next column, *FRAME*, is intended for the frame count of this specific scene or shot. Note that the numbering begins with frame one, and only the last digit is preprinted in the form. You can pencil in your own leading digits; typically, only the tens line is actually filled in.

As with all CGI animation, it is safest if you establish all your baseline keyframes in frame zero, but do not render it. This prevents a number of problems. The exposure sheet begins with frame 1, so the beginning of the audio track can simply be matched to the first frame of the rendered animation for perfect sync.

The *BACKGROUND* column provides a place for you to note any image sequences or stills that are to be used as backdrops. This is especially useful for compositing with other animations, digitized video sequences, or "matched" stills.

The last column, *CAMERA*, is a place to put your notes about special camera, post-processing plug-in, or compositing effects. In traditional animation, this information was used by the camera operator. You should list here any changes in lens size or other parameters for camera zooms, tracking, and pans.

Exposure sheets differ from studio to studio, and you may want to make your own.

Making Your Own Exposure Sheets

The next exercise shows you how to make exposure sheets like those included on the CD-ROM, and how to customize x-sheets for your particular needs and preferences.

Before you get started, take a look at the sample exposure sheets at the end of this chapter. Then ask yourself the following questions:

- How much of that information will you want to have in your own sheets?
- What information do you need to track that doesn't appear here?
- How many frames do you need to fit on a single sheet?
- How small can you read and write?
- What size paper can your printer handle?

These are all questions you should have definite answers to before you start building your own exposure sheet.

Make A Custom Exposure Sheet In Microsoft Word 6

These instructions are specific to Microsoft Word 6, but the principles can be adapted to any word processor or spreadsheet manager that allows you to embed linked graphics.

1. Open a New document.

2. Choose File|Page Setup. The Page Setup dialog appears, as shown in Figure 4.2.

   You will want to use as much of each page as possible, and you don't need much margin since your notes are supposed to fit in the exposure sheet itself.

3. Set all the margins to zero, and click on OK. A warning dialog gives you the option to use the Fix function. This automatically sets the page margins to the maximum printing area for your printer. Click on the Fix button.

   Because there are many kinds of printers, there is no one set of dimensions guaranteed to work with all systems. This procedure finds the best dimensions for your particular system.

4. The margins will have changed to the minimum. Depending on your printer, the left margin may be less than 1/2 inch. Change the left margin to at least 0.5 if you want to hole-punch your exposure sheets for a loose-leaf binder. When you are done, click on the OK button.

   I tend to design all my working papers with a loose-leaf binder punch in mind. For most purposes, it's one of the better ways of keeping projects organized. The exception is original artwork, which no one in their right mind would punch holes through. I keep those items in binder-punched document envelopes.

5. Choose Edit|Select All. You want the next few steps to affect the entire document.

6. Choose Format|Columns. The Columns dialog appears, as shown in Figure 4.3.

7. Choose 2 columns and turn off Equal Column Width. Set the first column to 1-inch wide with zero spacing. The second column defaults to the remainder of the print area. Make a note of the second column's width. Click on OK.

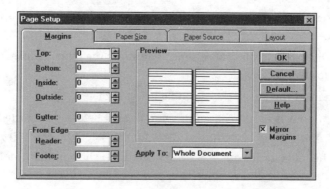

Figure 4.2 Page Setup dialog with all margins set to zero.

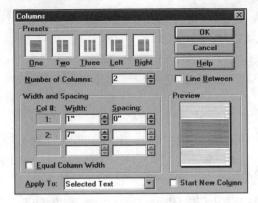

Figure 4.3 Columns dialog with all settings made.

The first column will be used for the waveform image file. The second column will hold the table that organizes the rest of the exposure sheet's information.

8. Insert three carriage returns. After the second carriage return, choose Insert|Frame.

   You'll be positioning a frame to hold the waveform image. It's not absolutely critical, but it makes the printed sheet look a little neater.

9. The cursor changes to the Frame crosshair. This tells you the program is ready for you to draw the frame. Click and hold in the upper-left corner of the first column, and drag down and to the right, approximately the width of the first column. Release, and the new frame will be drawn (see Figure 4.4).

10. Choose Format|Frame. The Frame dialog appears.

11. In the Frame dialog, set Horizontal to Left, Margin, and Distance From Text=0. Set Vertical to 0", Paragraph, and Distance From Text =0, and turn on Move With Text. Set Size Width to Exactly and 0.95", and set Size Height to Exactly and 9.0" (see Figure 4.5). Click on OK.

   Some of these settings will be changed later, but set them to these values for now. The goal is to have the frame aligned with the table as closely as possible, as if the waveform were actually printed as part of the table.

12. Position the cursor below the Frame. Choose Insert|Break, then choose Column Break. Click on OK.

   This leaves the frame in the first column, and starts the next column, where you'll be putting the table.

13. At the last paragraph mark, choose Table|Insert Table.

   Did you figure out how many columns you'd need before you started these instructions? If not, stop and get a definite answer now or you'll be wasting your time.

14. Set the number of columns and rows you want, then click on the AutoFormat button. The AutoFormat Table dialog appears.

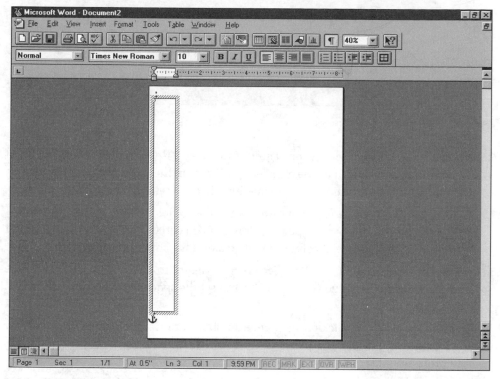

Figure 4.4 Frame added.

I like to get an even three seconds of animation on a single x-sheet, so 72 rows for film or 90 for 30 fps video is a good setting.

15. From the Formats list, select Grid1. Click on OK.

This will draw a simple grid of fine lines around each cell of the table. This is easy to read and doesn't take up much space. You can choose something fancier if you like, but remember that form should follow function.

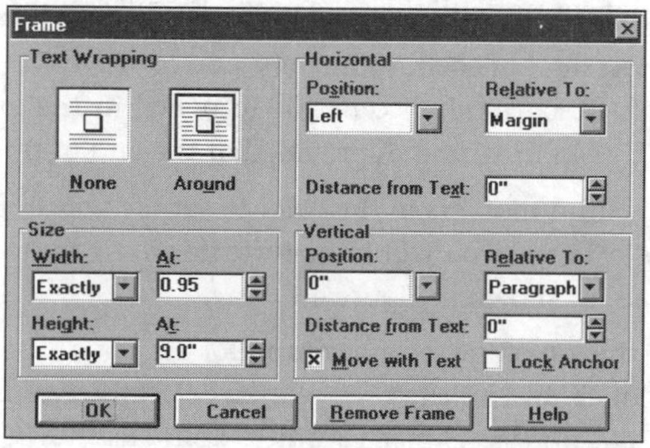

Figure 4.5 Frame format settings.

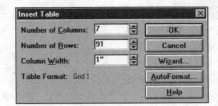

Figure 4.6 Table settings. Where's the salad fork?

16. Remember the width of the second column (from Step 7)? Calculate the total width of the second column divided by the number of columns in the table. Set the table column width to this figure. You should have something like the settings shown in Figure 4.6.

17. Click on OK. Now just a few more tweaks for the table. Choose Table|Select Table. Change the table font to Arial 7 point, or larger if you can fit it in. 7 point is the largest that would fit in a 91-row, 7-column table on standard paper for my system.

18. Choose Table|Cell Height & Width. Set the Row Height to Exactly 7 point, and leave Column Width to the value you set earlier, but set the space between columns to 0.1. Click on OK.

19. Select the top row, and click on the Center toolbar button. This centers the labels for the columns. Again, this is a personal preference; I think it's more legible and looks more professional.

20. Select the top cell of the first column. Type the column label. Repeat for the other columns. I prefer making the column labels all caps; at 7 point size, you need all the help you can get!

21. Select the column for the frame numbers, then click on the Align Right toolbar button. This keeps the last digits of the frame numbers aligned. Select the top cell, containing the column label, and reset it to Center.

22. In the second row of the FRAMES column (assuming you have one), type the number *1*. Type *2* in the third row, and so on up to *0* in the eleventh row. Select the 10 cells you just filled in, and copy them. Select the next 10 empty cells, and paste the copied values into them. Repeat until all the cells in the Frame column are filled in.

    This preprints the last digit of each frame for you. You have only to pencil in the tens and hundreds digits. It is usually acceptable to pencil in the extra digits just at the frames ending in 0, as in the samples provided at the end of this chapter.

23. Drag each of the column markers in the ruler to set the width of the columns. Leave extra space for the columns you will have to write words in; leave less space if only numbers are needed, as shown in Figure 4.7.

24. Move the cursor to the top of the second column of the page, above the table. Type the sheet information labels and underscored blanks. Select the entire line, and change the font to a readable style and size. I prefer Arial 10 point, as shown in the examples. Add a carriage return after the blanks, to separate them from the table (see Figure 4.8).

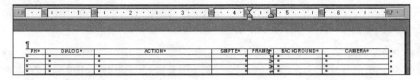

Figure 4.7   Setting the table column margin.

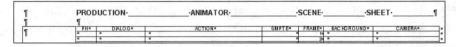

Figure 4.8   Sheet information blanks.

The types of information you use to track your projects will depend on the kind of work you do. If you are an independent or student, you may need little more than your name, the project, and the scene and shot. On the other hand, if you are one of several animators working on a long and complex animation project, you may need details like lead animator, technical director, and revision numbers.

Here are some examples of information that can be useful in heading an exposure sheet:

- Producer
- Director
- Lead animator
- Animator
- Technical director
- Art director
- Layout artist
- Camera operator/rendering supervisor
- Assistants (various)
- Project
- Client
- Agency
- Account or billing number
- Scene
- Shot
- Sheet number
- Date (start, due, and finish)
- Approvals/checkoffs/initials.
  And that's the short list!

25. Select the paragraphs above the frame in the first column. Change the font and size to match the changes you just made in the second column.

26. Add another carriage return above the frame. Select the paragraph immediately above the frame, and change the font and size to match the first row of the table. This should bring the top of the frame level with the top of the second row of the table.

27. Type the label *WAVEFORM* in the paragraph above the frame.

    This makes the frame look like an extension of the table, because it is now aligned with the other columns and headed in the same style. Now, you're ready to add the waveform image.

28. Click on the inside of the frame to set the cursor. Choose Insert|Picture. The Insert Picture dialog appears.

    It's a good idea to keep the waveform images in a temp file directory or similar location. Generally, the waveform images will be used only once, and there's no need to clutter your system with obsolete images. Since they are so similar, keeping them around can be a definite hazard to your track analysis.

29. Select the waveform image file to paste into the frame. Turn on the Link To File option. Turn off the Save Picture In Document option (see Figure 4.9). Click on OK.

30. Scroll to the bottom of the page. Select the frame. Drag the bottom of the frame until it is exactly level with the bottom of the table.

31. Choose Format|Frame, and then turn on Lock Anchor (see Figure 4.10).

    This should keep the frame the same size, even if the waveform image changes size. This means you should not have to resize the frame or image each time you reload this document.

32. Choose Edit|Links. The Links dialog appears. Turn on the Locked option, as shown in Figure 4.11.

    This tells Word to reload the image file every time something happens to either document. This is how the procedures in the next exercise can produce a stack of exposure

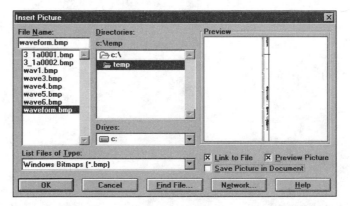

Figure 4.9 Options for inserting the waveform picture.

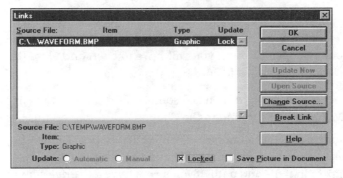

Figure 4.10 Locking the frame anchor.

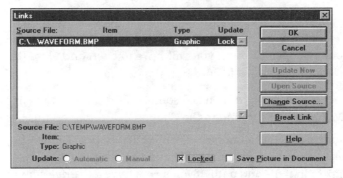

Figure 4.11 Locking the picture link.

sheets—complete with preprinted waveforms—so quickly. It's an example of an appropriate use of computers: automating repetitive work to free up human creative resources.

33. Save the document.

That's it. You are now the proud owner of a brand-new exposure sheet. Go find a track to analyze!

 Track Analysis

This exercise will show you the basics of track analysis, the craft of breaking out sounds for the animator's exposure sheets.

To begin filling in the exposure sheet, we'll need a clean image of the waveform. It's easy to do this in either the Windows or MacOS environment. Just open the sound file in an editing program that displays the waveform, take a screenshot, and cut-and-paste the image of the waveform into an exposure sheet.

Most sound editors can display a waveform. It will be to your advantage if the editor you use can display a timecode or frame count alongside the waveform. My preference is for a shareware package called GoldWave. It has a lot of useful tools for sound editing, the waveform ruler is clear and legible, and the screen colors can be customized for the best printing contrast. The only downside is that the ruler is marked in decimal units of time rather than frames.

The GoldWave home page (www.cs.mun.ca/~chris3/goldwave) contains the latest information and updates for GoldWave. GoldWave and its documentation are © 1993-1995 by Chris S. Craig, all rights reserved. GoldWave is a trademark of Chris S. Craig. Questions, comments, and suggestions are welcome. You can send them via email to chris3@cs.mun.ca and regular mail to:

Chris Craig
P.O. Box 51
St. John's, NF
Canada A1C 5H5

This exercise requires that you keep Word, Photoshop (or other graphics software), and your sound editor open at the same time. This requires a significant amount of memory. If you can't keep all the programs open at once, you will have to open and close them in turn for each three-second waveform image—a tedious business, at best.

For this exercise, we'll be using a digitized sample from a speech by Sir Winston Churchill, THISHOUR.WAV, which you can find in the Chapter 4 directory on this book's CD-ROM.

1. Copy the sample waveform image file WAVEFORM.BMP from the Chapter 4 directory on this book's CD-ROM to your C:\TEMP directory. The exposure sheet document has a built-in link to that file and path. If you do not have a C: drive, you may have to edit the exposure sheet to change the link path.

2. Open THISHOUR.WAV in the sound editor.

3. Adjust the waveform display for full screen width resolution of a three-second selection, as in Figure 4.12.

4. Start Photoshop. (If you use different graphics software, make sure it can paste from the system clipboard.)

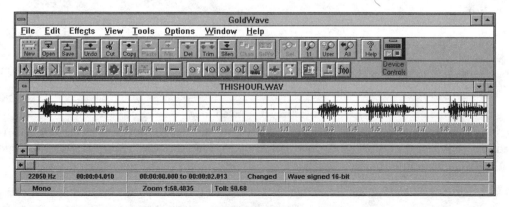

Figure 4.12   GoldWave sound editor showing THISHOUR.WAV.

5. Open X_SHEET.DOC in Microsoft Word. Note whether the document found the WAVEFORM.BMP image file in the C:\TEMP directory. If not, you will have to change the link to the exposure sheet document before proceeding with the rest of the exercise. To do this, select Edit|Links to call up the Links dialog. Click on the Change Source button, and choose the directory and file name you want to link to. Press Enter, or click on OK to return to the exposure sheet. The image you specified appears in the waveform column. You may have to resize it. If you have further difficulties, review Project 4.8.

6. If everything seems to be in order, press Alt+Esc to switch back to the sound editor.

7. Click on the Print Screen button to take a screenshot of the sound editor display.

8. Press Alt+Esc again to switch back to Photoshop.

9. Press Ctrl+N to open a new document. Accept the default values Photoshop suggests (they match the image currently held in the system clipboard).

10. Press Ctrl+V to paste the clipboard contents into the new blank document. Deselect the pasted area.

11. Zoom in, if necessary, to see details. Drag-select the three-second waveform section you want to paste into the exposure sheet. Make sure you precisely outline the start and stop points. Include the frame numbers if they are displayed. They will be useful later on.

Steps 11 through 14 can be saved as a macro. This saves a great deal of time when you have minutes of audio track digitized and waiting for analysis. It cuts the cut-copy-paste-print cycle down to less than a minute per sheet, once you really get rolling.

If you'd like to try it, I've included my own Photoshop macro on this book's CD-ROM, file WAVEFORM.REC.

12. Choose Edit|Crop. This gets rid of everything outside your selection area and resizes the document.

13. Choose Image|Rotate|90 Degrees Clockwise. This changes the waveform image from horizontal to vertical, which is much easier to use in exposure sheets.

14. Choose Mode|Grayscale. This gets rid of stray pixels of odd colors, which can sometimes cause problems with a black-and-white laser printer.

15. Choose File|Save As, and type in the file name and path C:\TEMP\WAVEFORM.BMP. The system asks if you want to replace the older file with the new one of the same name. Click on Yes.

16. Press Alt+Esc again to switch back to Word. The X_SHEET document has a locked link to the original WAVEFORM.BMP image, so it will automatically update to the one you just saved.

    I set up this exposure sheet for exactly three seconds of animation. Make sure each of your drag-selects clips out precisely three seconds worth of audio waveform, or the sound and the frames won't match up. Note that it will sometimes be necessary to append a small amount of silence to the end of each audio sample to bring it up to the next three-second mark. It's easier to deal with exact measures than to readjust the size of the pasted-in waveform for each sheet.

17. Click on the Print icon button to print the exposure sheet. Number it immediately— you'll be printing several, and you don't want to get them mixed up.

18. Return to the sound editor, and adjust the waveform display for full screen width resolution of the next three-second selection.

19. Repeat Steps 6 through 17 until you have all the sound files laid out in a series of exposure sheets. You might want to make photocopies of these sheets, just in case you ruin one.

You now have the raw materials for the track analysis. The only other tools you may need are more patience, quiet surroundings, sharp pencils, and a good dictionary.

Track analysis is not really difficult, just painstaking. There are a relatively small number of *phonemes*, or unique sounds, that are used by all spoken human languages. If you are only working in one language, your task is even simpler.

You can find a pronunciation guide in the front of any good dictionary. This guide will list all the phonemes for the dictionary's language, and explain the letters and diacritical marks used in phonetic spelling. I highly recommend keeping a good dictionary like this handy while analyzing vocal tracks; it can save you a lot of time while you are developing your track-reading skills. Until you can rely on those skills, I recommend that you cheat.

20. Make up a copy of the script for the vocal track, double- or even triple-spaced so you can write legibly under or over each word.

21. Look up each word in the dictionary. Copy the phonetic spelling of each word under the normal spelling in the script. Now you know exactly what phonetic symbols you need to write in the PH column of the exposure sheet; all that's left is figuring out exactly where to put them!

What you will be doing next is looking—and listening—for characteristic shapes in the waveform that correspond to phonemes. Human speech is made up mostly of clicks, buzzes, and hisses. For example, a sharp spike—a click—can represent a plosive sound such as P or B. The word *baby* would therefore have two spikes, and you would mark the frames next to those spikes with the letter B. Buzzing phonemes like M or N show up as relatively even zigzags with very similar individual waveforms, sustained over a number of frames. Hissing Ss or Cs look a lot like static, just a little louder.

Rather than go into a rambling theoretical discussion of all the different phonemes and how they are produced, I'm going to encourage you to experiment and develop your own rules. This all goes back to the principles discussed in Part V of this book. You can take someone else's word for it, or you can observe and draw your own conclusions. Observing speech is a wonderful way to lose your preconceptions about how people communicate.

22. Using the sound editor and the sample WAV file, highlight and play back one word at a time. When you have located the actual beginning of a word (which can be difficult when they are slurred together), write the complete word, spelled normally, on the exposure sheet frame where the word starts. Do *not* simply copy from the filled-in exposure sheets at the end of this chapter. You can check your work with it later, but don't look at it now.

23. Find the plosives and clicks. Look for peaks or other sharp changes within the word. Select and play them back until you can identify their start at a particular frame. Mark the frame.

24. Find the buzzes and hisses. These will appear as relatively even areas, drawn out over several frames. Mark the beginning with the appropriate phonetic symbol, and draw a short line through the succeeding frames to the end of the phoneme.

25. Find and write in the phonetic symbols for the remaining sounds, which will probably be mostly vowels. They tend to fill in everywhere but the clicks, buzzes, and hisses. They are also the most visible mouth shapes to animate, as they are held longer and generally require more facial distortion.

Congratulations! You've completed your first track analysis.

Compare your exposure sheet for THISHOUR.WAV to the exposure sheet at the end of this chapter. Did you differ by more than a frame or two for the beginning of any word? Did you use any different phonetic symbols?

Don't worry about minor differences, this is largely a matter of opinion. People use a variety of dialects and personal speech idiosyncrasies that make insistence on absolute answers in track analysis a moot point. However, if your reading of the track was significantly different, you might want to recheck your work.

Analyzing Your Own Voice

Repeat the previous exercise, but analyze a sample of your own voice giving a brief dramatic reading. Compare your pronunciation to the phonetic guidelines in the dictionary. What phonetic symbols might you change in the exposure sheet to represent your own speech patterns?

Power Tools For Lip Sync

Depending on your software, you may have tools available to you that automate part of the lip-sync process. These tools are explained in Chapter 15, because lip sync is only a part of what you can do with them. If you'd like to use these tools for your initial lip sync, jump ahead to Chapter 15, then come back here to finish your track analysis.

Using Your Exposure Sheets

Now that you've got the basics of track analysis, you're ready to make up the exposure sheets for your demo reel.

1. If your story depends on synchronized speech, sound effects, or existing music, digitize the sound track, and analyze it.

2. Write it all up on the exposure sheets, or use your software's sound sync tools as detailed in Chapter 15.

How close did you get? Was the lip sync convincing? Try slipping the audio track two or three frames in dubbing it to see if the lip sync looks better delayed than with a precise match. Many studios slip the track as a general policy.

If you had trouble, go back over the track analysis exercises, and see if you can spot what's going wrong. If it's just a matter of a few frames here and there seeming "off," don't worry about it. Your track analysis will improve with practice, as with so many other aspects of animation.

Moving On

If you've worked through the exercises in this chapter and all your exposure sheets are filled in, congratulations! Your preproduction work is finished. If production issues force a change in story or soundtrack, you may have to revise some of this work; otherwise, you should now have a complete script, storyboard, bar sheets, story reel, and exposure sheets. Part II of this book takes you through the next step, building your characters and sets.

Sample Exposure Sheets

The filled-in exposure sheets document a quote from the "Finest Hour" speech by Sir Winston Churchill. A three-second clip from the speech is digitized in the file THISHOUR.WAV, which you can find in the Chapter 4 directory on this book's CD-ROM. A longer version is in FINESTHR.WAV. Both are used in lip-sync exercises in this book.

The shorter quote is: "This...was their finest hour."

The full quote is: "So bear ourselves that if the British Empire, and its Commonwealth, last for a thousand years, men will still say, 'This...was their finest hour.'"

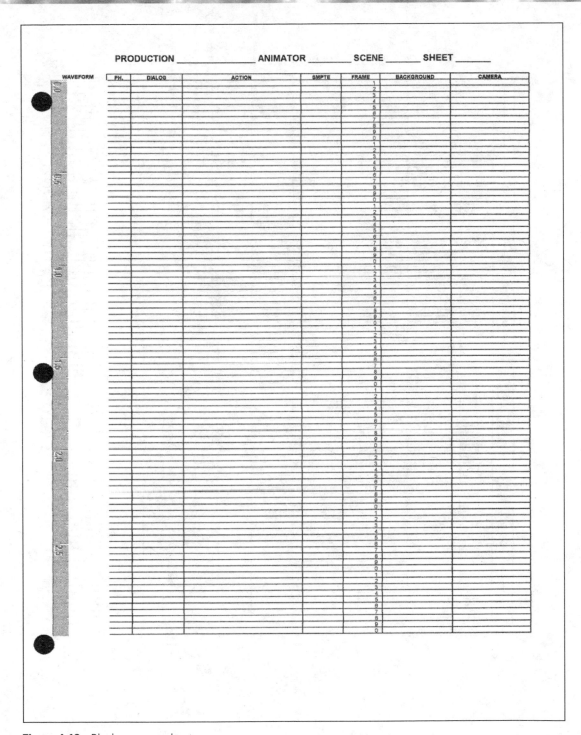

Figure 4.13   Blank exposure sheet.

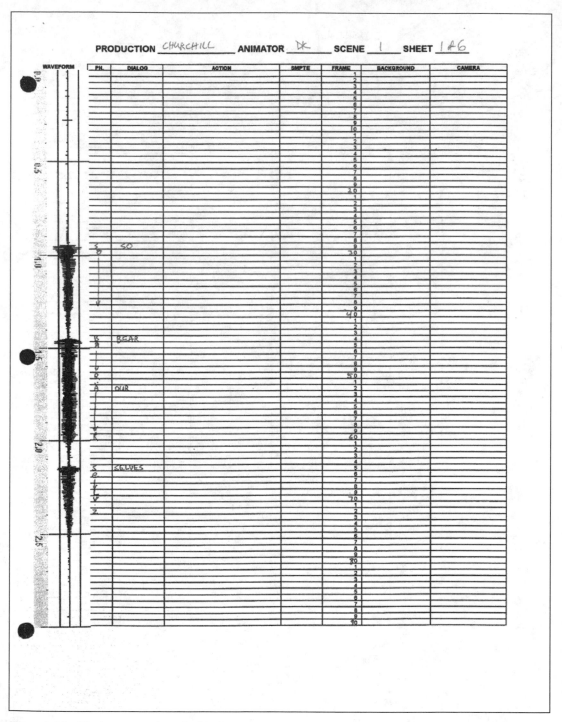

Figure 4.14 Filled exposure sheet 1 of 6.

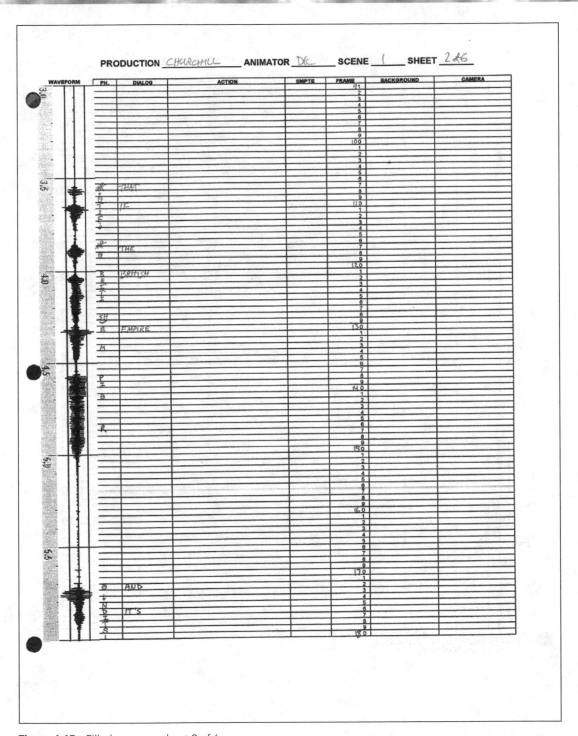

Figure 4.15 Filled exposure sheet 2 of 6.

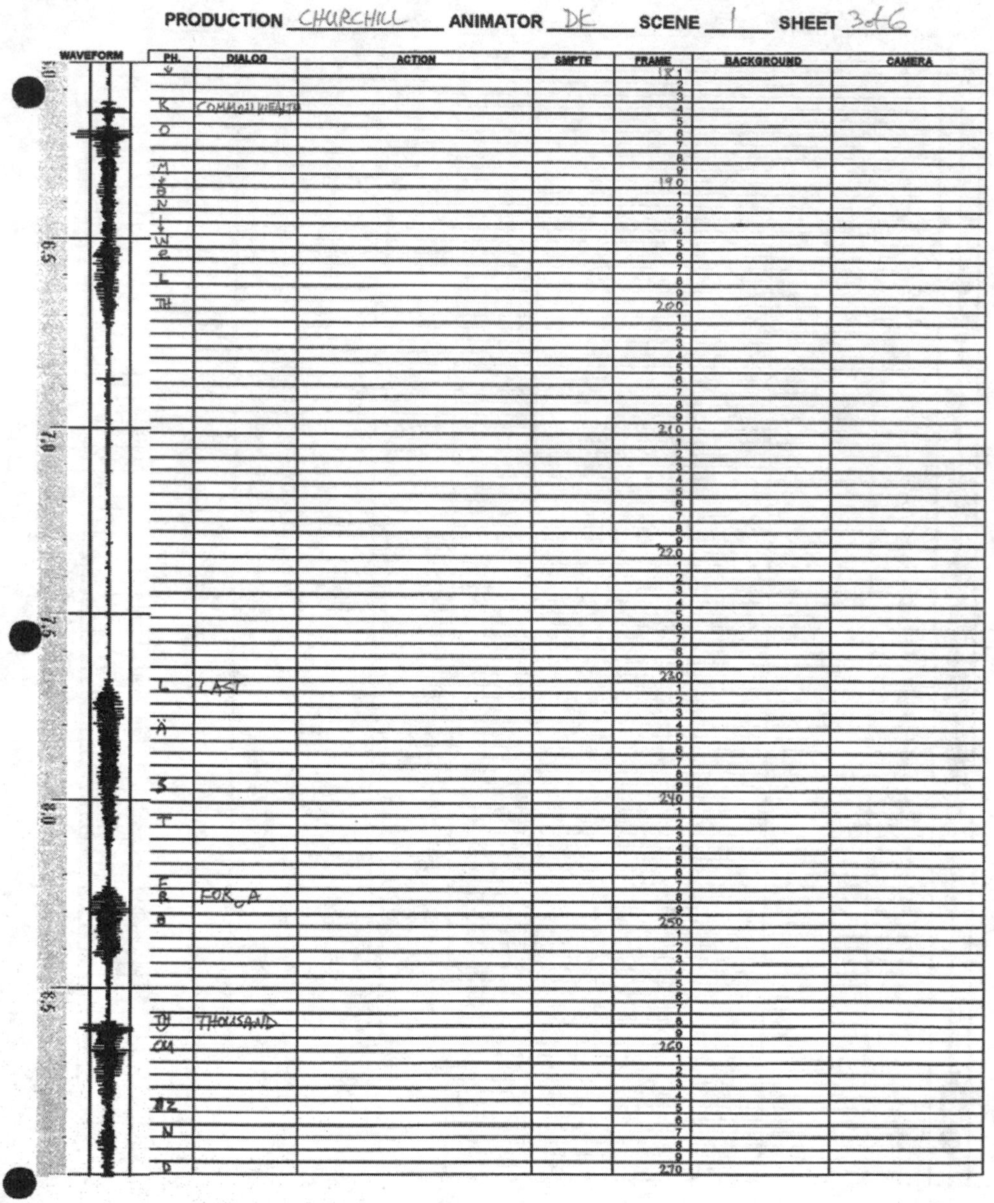

Figure 4.16 Filled exposure sheet 3 of 6.

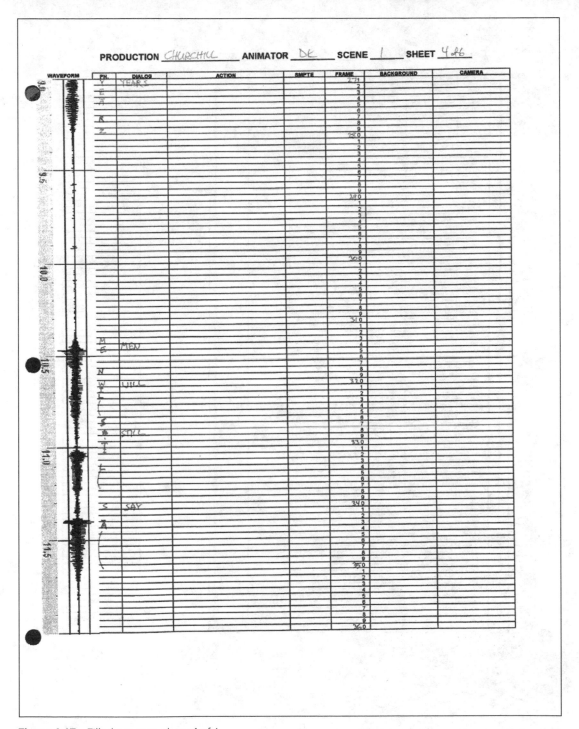

Figure 4.17 Filled exposure sheet 4 of 6.

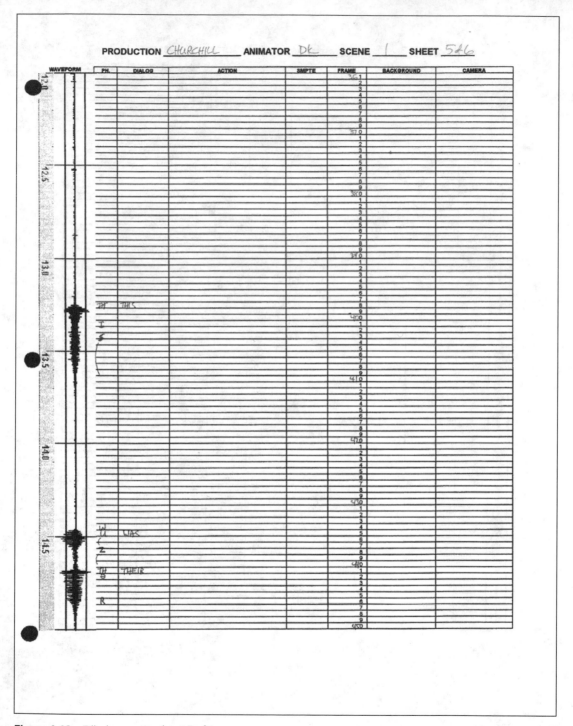

Figure 4.18 Filled exposure sheet 5 of 6.

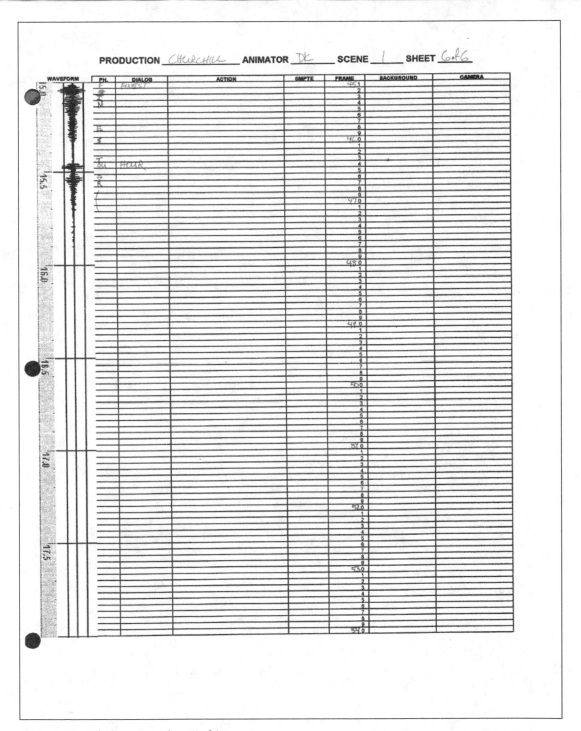

Figure 4.19 Filled exposure sheet 6 of 6.

PART II

MODELING

CHARACTER DESIGN

This chapter tells you about the process of designing characters, including the people involved, rules of thumb, mistakes to avoid, and useful tools. To assist you in designing realistic and cartoon characters, this chapter also explains the underlying muscle and bone structure of the human face and figure, plus dimples, wrinkles, flab, and fat.

As you learned in Chapter 1, character animation is almost always a group effort. Good character design, as part of that larger effort, is also a cooperative process that you need to understand.

The Typical Character Design Process

In most studios, you will work with a variety of people to design the characters the animators will use. You will have to cope with suggestions and directions from just about everybody, from the director, technical director, layout artist, animator, and, sometimes it seems, the janitor. Everybody will have a different idea of how the character should look and work.

> **TEAMWORK**
>
> **As a team member, your performance in design meetings is just as important as your performance with software.**

As a team member, your performance in design meetings is just as important as your performance with software. You can exercise and develop your sense of tact by carefully questioning parts of the proposed script, storyboard, or layout that have a disproportionate effect on your workload.

For example, suppose the storyboard calls for a character to reach into a trouser pocket, extract a key, open the door with it, and the camera then cuts to the next shot, where the character drops the key on the entryway table. Nowhere else does the character pull anything out of that pocket, nor do the key or lock have any further effect on the story. It's a throw-away, and should be discarded if possible.

You might propose that the character stage the action of reaching into a pocket, then cut on that action to an interior shot of the door, with the sound of the key going into the lock and turning. The rest of the shot is just as before. This approach would save all the expense of modeling and animating the trouser pocket and the complex arm-and-hand movement of fishing for the key.

Always try to have a better idea to suggest before you criticize or complain about something, and if you must complain, state your reasons for doing so in as productive and team-spirited a way as possible. You're much more likely to get your way if you point out where a change will save money, effort, or time for others as well as yourself. Keeping a positive tone doesn't cost you a thing, and keeping a production team's morale up through a long project is a lot more important than saving a couple of hours' work on a one-shot model.

Balance is critical to the character design process. The penultimate goal of the entire production team is to put the character animation in front of an audience. Creatively, most members of the team want to contribute their best work, see their own contributions prominently in the final product, and will naturally tend to favor their own ideas. Practically, there are a number of constraints, limits and harsh realities in the production process that will weed out many of these ideas. Part of your job is to help negotiate the delicate balance between creative vision and real-world production. To do this, you need a clear picture of all the checks and balances affecting character design.

Character Design Guidelines

Whenever you discuss character design, you should keep a few critical factors about character construction in mind. These factors will determine the levels of detail, flexibility, and versatility you must build into the character's model, setup, motion, and map libraries. They may not make a lot of difference to the rest of the production team, but they can make or break the character construction.

Medium

Is this character going to be shown forty feet tall on motion picture screens, or two hundred pixels tall on a video game screen? Whether the character will be used in film, TV, multimedia, or video games, the medium dictates the level of detail and the constraints on your tools and other resources. Generally, film work is the most demanding, but it also enables you to use whatever tricks and tools get the job done. Television is much lower resolution, so you can cut corners on fine details, but the realities of TV production mean you will have fewer tools and less time to do the work. Multimedia covers a range of resolution, frame rates, and color depths, from near-TV to lower than video games, and your resources can vary just as widely. In several ways, video games can be the most demanding form of character animation: you have to contend with low face count models, few mapping options, restricted timing options (no anticipation or follow-through), and low production budgets.

Distance

How far will this character be from the camera? How much screen space will it actually occupy, in the closest shot? If the character is just an extra, seen only in the distance and occupying only a few dozen pixels of screen resolution, you can cut all kinds of corners, save lots of time and effort, and the finished product will look just as good. If the character will appear in several extreme close shots, you must plan for more detailed modeling, higher resolution maps, and more subtle animation controls in the face.

Speed

If the character is to move very fast, you can rely on motion blur to obscure any minor flaws or crudeness in the character design for the faster sequences, and focus your resources on more detailed modeling for the slower intervals. A character who always runs at top speed, for example, will require little more for those sequences than a detailed anticipation pose, a follow through pose for stopping, and a run pose that will look good in motion blur (perhaps with multiple legs in different positions).

Range Of Movement

Ideally, every character you build should have at least the range of movement of the equivalent real creature or person. Practically, building such characters would break every deadline and budget you ever come up against. You must find every possible compromise you can make in the construction of the character, without affecting the quality of the finished image. If the storyboards never show the character raising its arms above shoulder level, you may not have to build that range of motion into the character.

At the same time, you shouldn't design restrictive motion in from the start. It takes experience to know how to build the model in anticipation of how it will move, and it frequently happens that the model can't be said to be fully completed until it has been animated and sent back with a more complete understanding of what it really needs to do. The storyboard is the place to start, but only the animator knows what he needs it to do, after the pre-production phase. Build that into your schedule and don't be surprised. Revisions happen!

Range of movement includes emotional or dramatic range, especially if you need to build separate models for the character's facial expressions. If the character is written as surly and nasty, you will probably not have to build its face to express benevolence or compassion. On the other hand, if the character is extraordinarily flexible or mutable (a classic cartoon wiseguy, for example), you can plan on creating several times the usual number of models, setups, and maps. A villain can be far more sinister when there is a full range of emotion in his face, particularly useful for contrast. A frown is all the more malevolent when it started as a smile. The villain is the hammiest, juiciest role in the picture! It's often the parts that are just off a bit that make a villain creepy—a smile that goes just too far, like the Coachman in *Pinocchio*. This is where weighted shapes come in so handy. A raised smile from a neutral closed mouth turns into a lowered frown when the target is used in the negative direction. Push that mouth widening target too far, and it gets scary with no additional modeling required!

Style

Is the character to have a very abstract style, or does the director favor photorealism? Can you get by with a simple surface color, or will you have to plan more complex models and layers of maps to get a realistic skin appearance? Can the surfaces remain relatively rigid and look artificial, or must you build them to be fully animated and appear organic?

The style of the character (and the rest of the production) must be compatible with the story you are trying to tell. A bright, primary-colored cartoon is unsuitable for a *film noir* hardboiled detective, just as a dark, Gothic design is inappropriate for a cheerful comedy. Appropriate character style makes storytelling easier by preparing the audience. A character wearing a tin star and a sixgun is obviously the sheriff. Poor design means the animation has to work harder— a man in a nondescript suit doesn't lead the audience to expect anything, and only becomes a character through subsequent actions.

Appeal

Every character you design should have visual appeal. This doesn't mean cutesy, nice, or conventionally attractive; appeal means the character's appearance grabs and holds your audience's attention. Villains, monsters, comics and even major props and sets must have visual appeal. You want every shot in your film to be able to stand on its own as a piece of art, with the interaction of characters and sets providing the detail and composition that will hold your audience's eyes.

You can give your characters appeal by keeping them strong and simple. Design them for strong poses, with clear lines of action. Keep the details of face and figure as simple as possible, so you can animate expressions and actions directly and clearly. Don't clutter your characters with a lot of extraneous detail that muddies their outlines and diverts attention from their expressions. If your character can't communicate, it's worthless.

Line Of Action

In a strong key pose, you should be able to draw an arc or broad s-curve from the visual base of the character, up through its center and out to the goal of the action. This is the *line of action*. If this line is broken, bent too sharply or veers off in different directions, it is more difficult for your audience to read the pose.

Each part of a character should enhance your ability to pose it with a strong line of action. If part of the character is jutting out at an angle, that part breaks up the visual flow of the pose. In the early 2D drawing stages of character design, the line of action can be drawn first, and the character sketch built around the line.

As soon as you have a general concept of the character's proportions, you should make a series of pose sketches, building the figure along characteristic strong lines of action. You can choose these poses from the script, selecting shots that define the character's development or exposition. Once you have a design that will fit the character's most typical or defining actions, you have a better idea of the necessary mesh and joint layout that you will have to build in 3D.

Silhouette

It's important to test your designs in silhouette. If a posed character does not read well as an outline, your audience will have to rely on much more subtle clues to understand what the character is trying to do or say. That takes more time, makes your audience work harder, and is generally poor animation practice. On the other hand, a character that reads well in silhouette will only get better and stronger as you add color, depth, and surface details within the silhouette.

You can test a character design sketch in silhouette by laying tracing paper over it and tracing only the outline of the figure. Cover the original sketch, and look only at the traced outline. If you can still "read" the pose, the sketch works. If not, go back to the drawing board; how can you make the outline cleaner, less cluttered, and with a strong line of action?

You still need to check your character's silhouette in the 3D modeling phase of character design. Fortunately, most 3D software enables you to mimic silhouette tracing automatically, by rendering an alpha channel image (see Figure 5.1).

Character Design Tools

If you want to design characters professionally, you need to be familiar with the design tools commonly used in studios. Even if you are doing this for fun, learning to use these tools is good practice, and will help you focus more efficiently on the critical factors in designing your characters.

The most commonly used character design tools are sketches, maquettes, and photographs. Just as you develop a story from premise to script to storyboard, you can develop an original character design from sketch to maquette to 3D computer model. If your character has to match an existing real-world actor, photographs become a crucial part of the design process.

Looks A Little Sketchy To Me

The first tool for discussing character design is the sketch. Even if you are a lightning-fast modeler, anyone deserving the word *artist* in their job title will be able to sketch a figure faster than you can model it. Get used to pencils and paper, if you aren't already. And don't be shy about not being able to draw, if you come from the "propeller-head" side of computer graphics. I rarely attempt anything more character-oriented than a stick figure, myself, and there are plenty of working CGI professionals who could say the same.

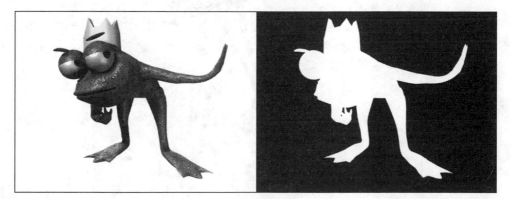

Figure 5.1 A posed character with a clear silhouette.

The obvious advantages of pencil sketching are that it's cheap; you don't need electricity or a computer; everybody in a meeting can have one; it's easy to make revisions; you can start with a fairly light, hesitant line and firm it up or change it as the discussion progresses; and the product is easy to reproduce, fax, or digitize.

The disadvantage to pencil sketching is that it's not a 3D medium, so something that looks good on paper can turn out to be completely worthless in the computer. Caveat emptor.

While you have your design factors firmly in mind, the other members of the design team have their own ideas and concerns. The character usually evolves with a lot of pushing and grinding: everybody pushes their own agenda and grinds their own axe. If things go well, the character develops toward a design that will help tell the story, be economical to model, and be reasonably easy to animate. Sometimes the end design is rather far from the first concept, and sometimes it's pretty close to the original.

Figure 5.2 Early character sketch for "Easy Come, Easy Go."

Figure 5.2 is one of the earliest character sketches for Fred, the lead character in the example script. This was drawn by the film's technical director, Mike Comet, based on some verbal descriptions and a really simple stick-figure of my own, which I won't inflict on you. Even a simple figure like this can communicate the actions that define a character.

Figure 5.3 is another step in Fred's evolution, as drawn by storyboard artist Brian Kelly. Again, the drawing captures an action that defines the character. At this point, the drawings also refine the surface appearances and ranges of motion that the TD will be called on to create.

Figure 5.4 is a collage of various stages in the modeling process. Mike roughed out the head first (inset left), and I ran some animation tests on it and came back with some suggestions. In between that, we discussed body proportions and clothing (center), and Mike ran range-of-motion experiments on Fred's knee, hip, shoulder, and elbow joints. Finally, Mike put together all the changes and modeled the head's details (inset right): glasses, hat, hair, and mustache.

Figure 5.3 Section of storyboard sketch for "Easy Come, Easy Go."

Figure 5.4 Collage of early character objects.

This is not too far from the finished version of Fred, and is certainly good enough for more detailed animation and layout tests. If we had tried to jump straight from the script or storyboards to modeling and animating Fred, I don't think we would have ever gotten this far.

> **CAST IN STONE**
>
> **Once you start putting models into the computer, there is a very strong temptation to leave them alone.**

Once you start putting models into the computer, there is a very strong temptation to leave them alone. The pencil sketch design process is cheap enough that it enables you to go back and revise or throw out materials without cutting out that "pound of flesh nearest one's heart."

Maquettes

A maquette is a three-dimensional physical model, usually constructed of clay, plaster or other easily-worked material. The process of creating a maquette allows the design team to visualize, modify and detail the character in ways that 2D sketches can't support.

Maquettes have been used for many years in animation studios, and they show no sign of disappearing. In fact, maquettes have become even more important to CGI work, because 3D digitizers and scanners now provide a means of bringing the maquette directly into the computer. Maquette sculptors are a traditional and respected part of the design team at many studios, and those that don't have on-staff sculptors often hire freelancers.

You can build maquettes from a variety of materials, using standard sculpture techniques. Some of the more popular brand-name materials are Sculpey, Fimo, and Cernit synthetic-firing clays, and Van Aiken and Plastilina oil-based clays. Water-based clays are generally unsuitable for maquettes, as they don't fire well and tend to dry out and crack. You can work all of these materials with common sculpting tools of wood, metal or hard plastic.

Oil-based modeling clays like Van Aiken and Plastilina are suitable for initial model studies that will need lots of revision. These clays stay malleable for a long time, and can be reworked repeatedly before they start to lose the proper feel. However, the only way to harden one of these maquettes is to cast a mold of the clay, then make a positive casting in a more rigid and durable material. This is more bother, but does allow you to make a short production run of identical maquettes so everybody can have a copy.

Sculpey is a family of synthetic clays that can be molded like ordinary clay, then fired at relatively low temperatures to harden them. Fired Sculpey maquettes are very lightweight and durable, and can take paints and other finishes. This material is better for one-off models, as it is faster, less expensive and avoids the restrictions of mold-making.

The original Sculpey is plain white and has a slightly crumbly texture. Sculpey III is not as pliable as the original, so it retains the modeled shape better and doesn't stick to your fingers as much. Super Sculpey is also less sticky and easier to work with. Sculpey III comes in a variety of colors, as does Fimo. Fimo is similar to Sculpey, but can be better for fine details because it is harder and less pliable. It is also more difficult to work because it crumbles more easily. Fimo and Cernit have a more waxy appearance than Sculpey, and they tend to scorch or burn more in firing.

You can buy these materials in most art, ceramic, or craft stores. If you can't find a local supplier, you can call Polyform Products (the makers of Sculpey) at 847-427-0020 for more information or the address of the nearest distributor.

To fire Super Sculpey, put it in a temperature-controlled oven at 250 to 275 degrees Fahrenheit for 15 to 20 minutes. If you will be firing a lot of maquettes, think about buying an inexpensive toaster oven that you can use exclusively for firing clay. If you overheat Sculpey, it can give off toxic fumes and leave a nasty residue, both on the inside of the oven and on any dishes you used to hold the maquette. Don't use a microwave—the maquette will explode!

Firing time and temperature will depend on the thickness of the Sculpey. Thicker layers take longer and should be fired at lower temperatures to avoid cracking due to uneven heating. On the other hand, if you leave thin spots in the Sculpey, they can scorch and burn.

If parts of your maquette will be very thick, you should consider layering the Sculpey over an armature. The armature can be wads of aluminum foil, bent coat hanger wire, or anything else that won't melt or distort during firing. A good armature helps hold the maquette together, lowers total weight, and saves clay that would otherwise be wasted on interior volumes.

If any part of your maquette is hollow, you need to leave passages for air to escape during firing. Trapped air will expand when heated, blowing your maquette apart. This is also a good reason to thoroughly knead the clay before modeling the maquette and make sure you press out all the air bubbles. Make sure the Sculpey isn't overage, either. Check the dates on the side of the box. If you get a bad or overage batch by mistake, contact your distributor or Polyform Products for a replacement.

Once you've fired the Sculpey, you need to cool it down carefully. If you cool it too rapidly, your maquette will crack. You can prevent this by leaving the maquette in the oven with the heat turned off and the door open, so the maquette cools at the same rate as the oven. You can also remove the maquette from the oven and immediately wrap it in one or more thick towels, which will insulate it and allow it to cool more slowly and evenly.

Once the maquette has cooled completely, inspect it for scorches, burns, and cracks. Super Sculpey can be repaired by cutting off the bad part, smoothing on a new layer and re-firing. Small burns can be sanded off with a nail file or emery board.

The fired maquettes sometimes don't hold up well over time, cracking in spots and crumbling around the edges. You can make your maquette last longer by coating it with sanding sealer or clear nail polish, which will reduce dusting and crumbling problems.

Once you have your finished maquette, there are several ways you can use it as a reference for creating a computer model. The simplest (and least accurate) is to simply refer to it while you model freehand in the computer. If you want to be slightly more accurate, you can photograph the maquette from different angles, digitize the photos, then load the digitized images as backdrops in your modeling software. Finally, you can be accurate down to machine-shop tolerances by using a digitizer or laser scanner to convert the maquette directly to a 3D mesh. The next two chapters go into more detail about each of these techniques.

Photo Reference

If you are working from a live subject or finished maquette, photographs can be a great help during the construction of the character model, setups, and maps. The same digitizing techniques described in Chapter 9 can be used to get these photos into your computer. Getting useful 3D data from these 2D photographs requires a slightly different setup.

One of the goals of reference photography is to enable you to locate any vertex or node on the model by referring to two or more photographs. Loading the photos in your 3D modeling software and placing vertices or nodes to create the model is a process discussed in detail in Chapter 6. The goal of this section is to show you how to get adequate photos for the 3D process.

You can make your work much simpler by marking your subject with a series of reference points or a grid. If you are working from a maquette, you can mark it with a fine felt-tip pen in a contrasting color. For a live subject, you will need some kind of non-toxic marker that leaves a fine line. An eyeliner pen works well. If you don't have one handy, ask at the nearest makeup counter.

Place reference marks where the curves of the subject change rapidly. You don't need to mark large flat areas—it's the sharp curves and edges where you'll need help in modeling. You'll get better at this with practice. You may want to mark up and photograph several practice subjects before you try a critical maquette or live subject. Halloween masks make inexpensive practice subjects.

Don't make more marks than you need. If the reference marks overlap and it's difficult to tell them apart, you'll have a harder time matching the vertices or nodes to the correct marks.

Take two sets of photos, one with and one without reference marks. Try to make the photos as similar in camera setup as possible.

The farther the separation in camera viewpoints, the easier it is to accurately place vertices. If two photos are shot from only 5 degrees apart, it will be difficult to see a change in the reference marks. If the separation is 45 degrees, the change will be more obvious, and your margin for error will be more generous, too.

The more photos you use, the more checks you can make to confirm the placement of each vertex. Unfortunately, every extra photo also adds the possibility of error, so you can easily find yourself noodling back and forth between two mutually exclusive errors for the same vertex. In general, you should use the minimum number of photos you need to cover the subject. For human faces, I recommend four shots as the minimum: 0 degree face-on, 90 degree profile (either side), left 45 degrees, and right 45 degrees.

These four basic shots should be taken with the camera level at the middle of the subject's height, with as long a lens as possible. Keeping the camera level allows you to ignore the lateral axes, so, in modeling, you will only have to rotate the model on the vertical axis to match the angle of the background photo. Using a long lens minimizes the distortion due to perspective. The farther away the camera is from the subject, the flatter and more accurate the photo will be.

If you need to get finicky about details or undercuts, such as the back of the subject's ears or the underside of the nose, chin, or eyebrow ridge, take close-up photos. Try to keep the camera as close to level as you can. Ideally, you want to secure the subject and the camera, then take all the shots without disturbing either. Practically, you will have to move at least one or use a multicamera setup to take all the photos simultaneously.

It's important that you match the horizontal and vertical registration of the entire series of photos before you begin modeling. The easiest way to do this is to load the photos into separate layers in image-processing software, like Photoshop, and then move the images around until the reference marks match. A good place to start is the top of the head for both profile and face-on, and the tip of the nose and back of the head for profiles.

You should be especially careful to match the photos vertically, so the tip of the nose, top of the head, and underside of the chin are each at exactly the same height in each photo. If at all possible, you should also match the centerline of the subject's images horizontally. That is, the center of the view should pass through the vertical axis of rotation of the subject. This is hard to do with a live subject, because you can't accurately measure to the center of the head. If possible, you can try using spirit gum or other cosmetic adhesive to attach an upside-down golf tee to the crown of your subject's head, as a marker for the vertical axis of rotation. If this isn't possible, you'll simply have to make your best estimate and practice to get better at it.

Aside from the photos used to build the 3D model, you will need reference photos for texture, color, and specularity. You can use the same procedures outlined in Chapter 9. I recommend using a camcorder with its own spotlight to capture specularity patterns; you can get all the data you need by making a few passes around your subject at different up- and down-angles to record the highlights from the entire face or figure.

Once you have your photographs, I recommend that you have them processed onto a PhotoCD. Other methods of digitizing or scanning generally have lower resolution, and you want these images to be as sharp as possible. The limit of your modeling accuracy is directly proportional to the quality of the reference images.

Designing The Figure

If you are building characters from scratch, you'll need to study proportion and dimension from life and from caricature. "Winging it" is an excellent recipe for rebuilding models repeatedly. You should at least have a rough pencil sketch before you start modeling.

The best resources on proportion from life are not the artist's books but the industrial designer's and engineer's. When you're planning joints and range of motion, there is no substitute for hard numbers. Henry Dreyfuss' work on ergonomics is still worth consulting, and his *Measure of Man* is usually available from your local public or university library. References on anthropometry can also help you decide on just how long to model that arm or how high to place the ankle bone.

On the artistic side, several of the books in the Bibliography may be of use. Peck's *Human Anatomy for the Artist* for the realists, and, for you game developers, Lee and Buscema's *How to Draw Comics*. If you are leaning toward a cartoon style, the three Brian Lemay handbooks give excellent advice on construction and animation of the figure. Blair's *Cartoon Animation* and the various compilations from the Warner and Disney studios have lots of examples.

And don't forget original inspiration! If all you are going to model is a 3D version of the same old caricatures, you might as well stay with ink and paint. 3D animation is a new medium. Why not push the boundaries and develop a completely original character design that belongs only to 3D CGI?

The following sections outline some of the basic design considerations for parts of the character.

Pelvis

The pelvis (see Figure 5.5) is the largest single bone in the human body and the nearest to the *center of gravity*, or CG. Because the CG is the first layer of the *animation hierarchy* (see Part IV in this book), the place where all actions begin, you should consider the pelvis as the starting point for your character design.

The pelvis provides attachments for the base of the spine and for the upper ball-and-socket joint of the legs. The pelvis itself normally rotates on all three axes. You can test this yourself. Stand, take a long step forward, and keep both feet planted at full extension—your pelvis will swivel on the vertical axis of your spine. Stand straight again, and bend forward or back at the hips—your pelvis will pitch, bisecting the angle between your thighs and torso. Stand straight again, then bend one knee slightly, taking your full weight on the other leg—your pelvis will tilt down toward the bent leg.

The pelvis doesn't rotate very much on any of the three axes, but a small rotation at the pelvis makes a big difference in the position of a hand, foot, or head. Because the movements are so small and the effects are so large, you should spend extra time studying and animating the movement of the pelvis.

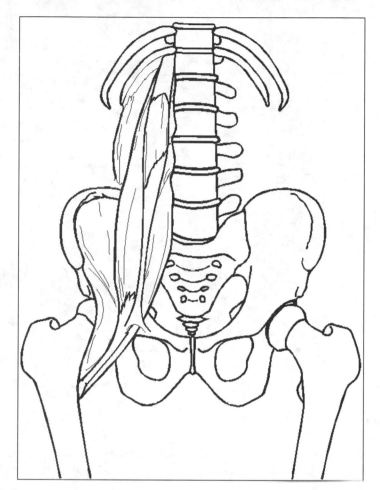

Figure 5.5   Pelvis in the human skeleton.

When modeling the pelvis, you should keep gender differences in mind. Although the human race includes wide variations in body type, men generally have a pelvis that is narrower than their rib cage, while in women the opposite is true.

Spine

The spine, or spinal column (see Figure 5.6), connects the pelvis to the head through the rib cage. The spine usually provides at least half the character's line of action. In actual anatomy, the spine is a series of many small bones called *vertebrae*, which can rotate only slightly in relation to their neighboring bones. This arrangement provides support yet allows a great deal of flexibility. The accumulation of small angles can add up to 180 degrees in a very flexible character.

In most character designs, the spine is not simulated with an anatomically correct number of vertebral joints. For simple characters, joints at the pelvis, waist, rib cage, and neck can provide

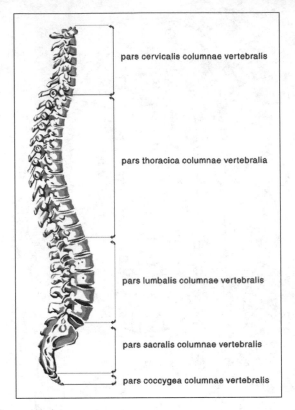

pars cervicalis columnae vertebralis

pars thoracica columnae vertebralia

pars lumbalis columnae vertebralis

pars sacralis columnae vertebralis

pars coccygea columnae vertebralis

Figure 5.6 Spine in the human skeleton.

most of the flexibility necessary to the character's range of movement. If you are creating a more flexible character, such as a snake or dragon, you will have to build more detail into the spine.

Rib Cage

The rib cage, or upper torso (see Figure 5.7), is attached to the spine between the pelvis and the head. In animation, it's an odd combination of rigid and flexible. It must be expandable enough for your character to breathe deeply, yet rigid enough to maintain the character's profile as the rib cage moves with the spine's curvature.

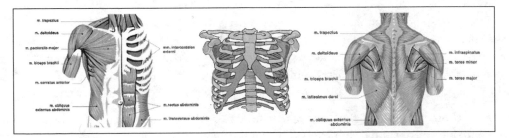

Figure 5.7 Rib cage in the human skeleton.

How you model and set up the rib cage depends entirely on your character's intended range. If it needs to breathe deeply, you will have to provide controls to expand and contract the upper torso without displacing other joints. If the character is to swell up in an attempt to bully or impress another character, you need to be able to animate that, too. If none of this is necessary, you may be able to leave the upper torso rigid, with the minimum rotational joints at the spine (or waist and neck, depending on how you construct the hierarchy).

Legs

The legs (see Figure 5.8) are relatively easy to design for most characters. The knee joint is a simple hinge that can rotate from straight (or a little past, in hyperextension) to 150 degrees or so, limited more by the mass of the calf muscle than by the joint structure. The hip joint connects the leg to the pelvis and is a true ball-and-socket, enabling free rotation in any combination of the three axes.

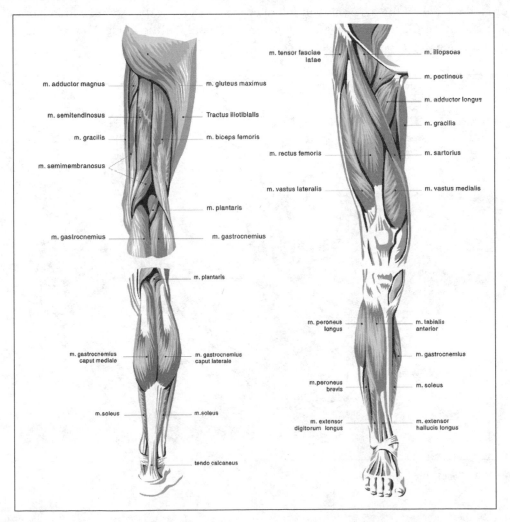

Figure 5.8   Legs in the human skeleton.

The two major challenges to modeling and setting up the legs are the appearance of the knee-cap, or *patella*, and the deformation of the mesh around the hip, buttock, and thigh. These difficulties are directly proportional to the realism of the character. For caricatures and primitives, the hip joint is the first place you should cheat.

Feet

Feet in real-world humans (see Figure 5.9) are nearly as complex and flexible as the hands. The toes are articulated just like fingers, and the arch can flex and stretch to change the entire shape of the foot. The ankle can rotate in two axes, and with the torsion of the lower leg, it can appear to rotate in the third axis as well. Modeling and setup for a realistic foot is complex enough that you shouldn't attempt it unless it's essential for the character's performance.

If you are designing a caricature or primitive, the first details you want to lose are the toes. Abridge the end of the foot to a shoe or similar uniform lump, with a joint to flex the mesh around the ball of the foot. This will still allow heel-and-toe walks. For an extreme primitive, you can make the foot a single rigid lump, rotating only at the ankle; however, this makes heel-and-toe walks look excessively robotic.

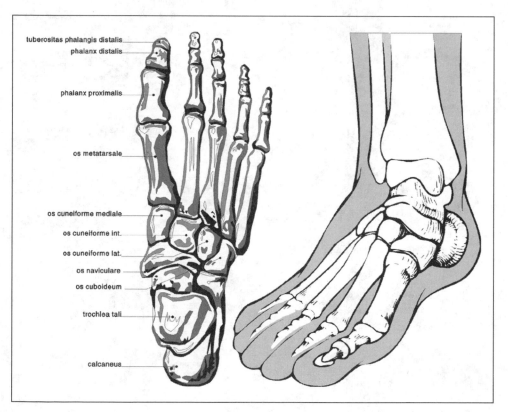

tuberositas phalangis distalis
phalanx distalis
phalanx proximalis
os metatarsale
os cuneiforme mediale
os cuneiforme int.
os cuneiforme lat.
os naviculare
os cuboideum
trochlea tali
calcaneus

Figure 5.9   Feet in the human skeleton.

Arms

Arms are similar to the legs (see Figure 5.10). The elbow, like the knee joint, is a simple hinge that can rotate from straight (or a little past, in hyperextension) to 160 degrees or so, limited more by the mass of the biceps muscle than by the joint structure. The shoulder joint is not a true ball-and-socket, it is actually a hinge-and-pivot. The upper arm is not actually connected to the rib cage or collarbone, it's connected to the shoulder blade which has its own range of movement across the back of the rib cage. The shoulder is a complex setup for characters approaching realism and merits special treatment in Part IV of this book.

You can cheat on the arms for a caricature or primitive by using the old cartoon method of *rubber hose* construction. In this style, the limb has no fixed joint—it simply bends in an arc to connect the torso to the hand or foot.

Hands

Hands (see Figure 5.11) are tough to model and set up, but they are almost always critical to the character's expressive range. People do talk with their hands, and even a primitive character can benefit from a mitt with an opposable thumb.

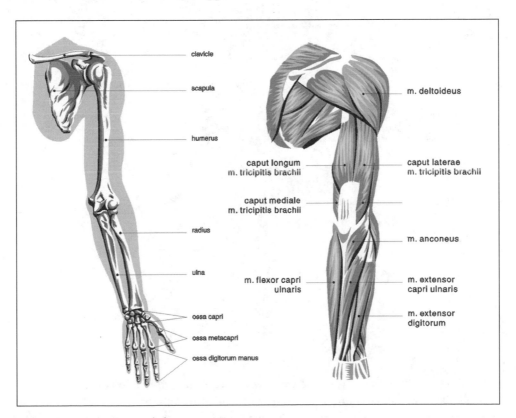

Figure 5.10 Arms in the human skeleton.

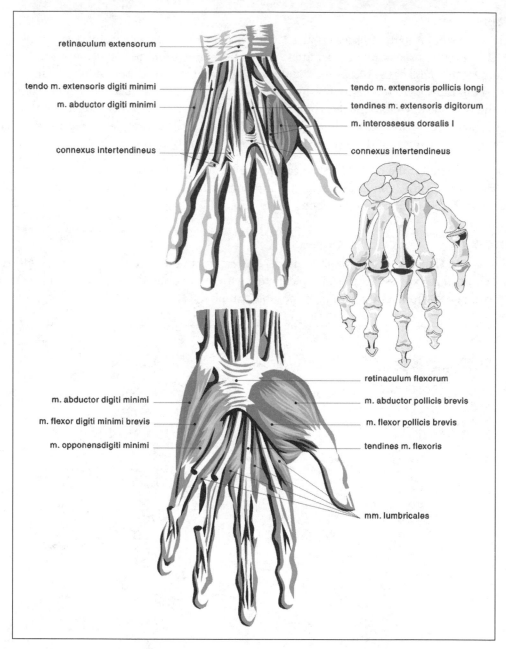

Figure 5.11   Hands in the human skeleton.

The hands connect to the arms at the wrist, which can pitch almost 90 degrees up and down and head about 45 degrees right-to-left, but banks only through the torsion of the forearm. The wrinkles and folds of the wrist are bothersome enough that a cartoon character's rolled-cuff glove is a welcome cheat to hide the wrist joint entirely.

The hands and feet are the tail-end layer of the animation hierarchy, posed last because they don't drive any other part of the hierarchy. They are also the most likely candidates for IK and constraints, as they are the parts that interact with surfaces and objects.

Realistic hands are a genuine technical challenge, especially for close-ups. Knuckle protrusion, tendons, skin folds and wrinkles, and the pad of muscle at the base of the thumb are all tricky things to emulate. A common cheat is to use carefully modeled morph targets for the major poses.

Caricature and primitive hands are easier and more fun. Later on, we'll look at simple ways to build the traditional three-fingered cartoon glove shown in Figure 5.12.

Creature Appendages: Tails, Claws, Extra Limbs

If you're designing a creature with more appendages than a normal human, you'll need to look at the animal kingdom for reference. Tails and snakes are relatively straightforward, simply extensions of the spine (see Figure 5.13).

Claws, exoskeletal plates, and other rigid body parts are easier than the equivalent human appendages, because you only have to set up rotation controls at the obvious joints—no deformation controls are necessary.

Invertebrates like slugs, worms, octopi, and sharks are more of a challenge since you don't have definite joints or bones to provide a structure. It's *all* deformation controls! You have to design the mesh to accept *depth-charge* controls to drive the meat, as detailed in Part V of this book. This technique is handy for articulating a realistic tongue, too.

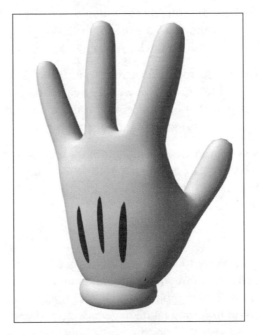

Figure 5.12 Traditional three-fingered cartoon glove.

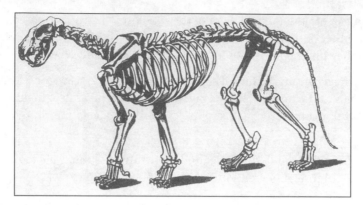

Figure 5.13 Claws and tail in the African lion skeleton.

Designing Character Faces

You can model the simplest version of an animatable character face after a traditional puppet or ventriloquist's dummy. The eyes should rotate; the upper eyelids are useful for blinks, winks, and a variety of emotional expressions; and you can animate a simple hinged jaw for lip sync. That's a total of five objects in a parented hierarchy. This approach is so simple that I'm not even going to illustrate it with an exercise. If you want to build a Pinnochio, you can refer to the later sections of this chapter on proportion and expression and plan one for yourself.

The problem with a very simple puppet head is that you can't easily animate the full range of human emotion. For real people, more subtle emotion is communicated by the softer tissues of the face than by the simple angle of the eyes or jaw. If you want to mimic emotional expression, you must try to re-create the subtlety of motion of a real human face. If you want your character to lip-sync as convincingly as possible, you must be able to deform the lips to match the *sibilants* and *fricatives* of the dialog track.

It's possible to assemble a more complex face from separate objects—some traditional puppets have many moving parts in their faces. You would have to accept the seams between objects, however, which rules out parented objects for any animation that hopes to create a higher realism or a smoother style than traditional marionettes.

The two remaining design approaches to facial animation are mesh deformation controls and morph targets (see Chapters 11, 12 and 13 for details). Proper modeling, setup, and animation of either approach can give you results from the caricatured to the photorealistic, depending only on the time and effort you put into it.

First Principles

Observing nature is the best way to begin. It's very easy to go wrong if you try to work from memory or from your own ideas about how a creature should function. Go to the source! When you are first considering a modeling project, even if it is pure caricature or fantasy, study everything you can lay hands on that may relate to your project. If you will be modeling animals, study their physiology, and visit the zoo to observe how they move. If you will be modeling people, do the same—although just about any street corner will do as well as a zoo, for people-watching.

There are a handful of resources I have found invaluable for modeling and animating faces. On my desk, I keep a mirror and a model human skull, one to study the live play of muscles and skin, and the other to study the underlying structures. Both items are cheap, available nearly everywhere, and last a long time. I also keep several books handy when designing character's heads, the most useful being Faigin's *The Artist's Complete Guide to Facial Expression* (see the Bibliography for details). The language is clear, technical only when necessary, and the illustrations seem designed especially for 3D construction. A paperback edition of Gray's *Anatomy* gets regular use, too. For caricature and more traditional cartoon design, the materials mentioned in the following section on proportion give plenty of ideas.

All these resources boil down to a relatively small number of guidelines you should keep in mind when designing a character's head and face.

Proportion

The first guide is proportion—the size and relationship of the head's parts can make or break your character. Audiences expect a certain amount of stereotype in animated films. Characters are expected to act as they look. If the eyes are a bit too close together, the nose hooked, and the forehead too low, the audience will expect a different type of behavior than that of a normally proportioned character. If you choose a realistic style, you must be especially careful to model accurate human proportions.

The baseline for the head is the *orbit*, or socket, of the eye. A line drawn horizontally through the eyes should divide the head in half. One of the most common mistakes is to put the eyes too far up the forehead, making the character look small-brained. Once the eyes are located, use the rule of thirds to divide the face: the top of the forehead (the hairline) to the eyebrow ridge is the upper third, the eyebrow ridge to the base of the nose is the middle third, and the base of the nose to the bottom of the chin is the lower third. If you get these proportions right, modeling the rest of the head goes more easily.

Bone Structure

The second guideline is to start with the bone structure. Even if you are designing a very flexible fantasy character, you need to understand and borrow from normal human bone structure to create a character your audience can understand. For example, in a normal human, the distances between the eye sockets, base of the nose, and upper teeth are all firmly fixed by bone (see Figure 5.14). If a realistic character's eyes, upper teeth and nose float around, the effect is very disturbing. Even if a cartoony character will squash and stretch to extremes, you should establish the same fixed relationships between facial parts before you create any distortions.

Make a baseline, then play with it any way you like, and the audience will be able to follow along. Jump straight into distorted and variable proportions without that baseline, and your audience will be so busy trying to figure out the character's face they will completely miss the story.

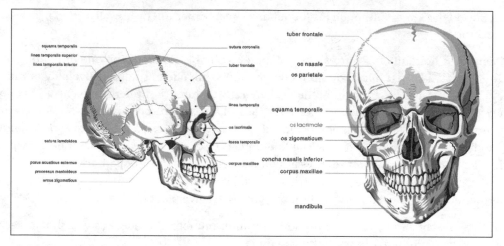

Figure 5.14 Human skull.

Muscles

The third guideline is to follow the muscles. Muscles (and their associated fat and skin attachments) provide most of the surface distortion we use to create facial expressions, so you need to understand the musculature in order to simulate it with your models (see Figure 5.15).

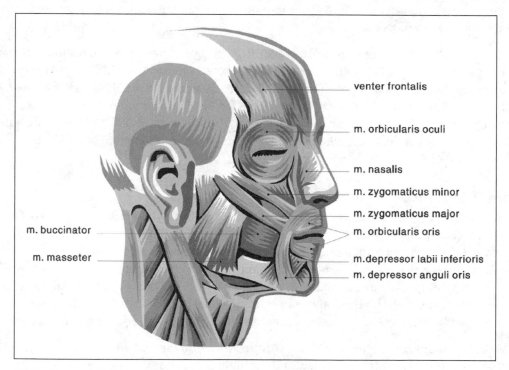

Figure 5.15 Human facial musculature.

Even if you are building a dragon or other fantastic creature, you must model it with believable muscle action or the character will look like a rubber toy. This is why life drawing and anatomy are so important for artists. If you have a very focused CGI background, this may be an area where you can learn from coworkers with more traditional art training.

Feature By Feature

This section examines the proportion, bone, musculature, and range of motion of each part of the face, including tips on designing them for animation and opportunities for caricature and exaggeration.

Eyebrows

Eyebrows are controlled by two sets of muscles, the *frontalis* and the *corrugator*. The frontalis runs in two vertical broad bands from the hairline straight down to the brow ridge. The main effect of this muscle is to lift the eyebrows toward the hairline, producing wrinkles in the fore-head. Each half of the frontalis can be controlled independently, raising one eyebrow at a time and wrinkling only the half of the forehead above the raised eyebrow. The corrugator is a collection of three smaller bands of muscle connecting the bridge of the nose, the lower center of the forehead, and the center of each eyebrow. These muscles pull the eyebrows together and down over the bridge of the nose, forming deep folds.

Realistic eyebrows do not have a very large range of motion. On the average, they can move up or down only about half an inch, and the outer ends of the eyebrows hardly move at all. As the eyebrows lower, they tend to compress inwards slightly. Caricature eyebrows, however, can be exaggerated to such an extent that you can actually separate them from the face and animate them as individual objects.

The eyebrows can be very important for a character's nonverbal communication, as any fan of Groucho Marx or Leonard Nimoy can attest. Eyebrows contribute to many expressions, usually in combination with the eyes and eyelids.

Nose

The realistic human nose is nearly rigid. The *septum*, at the base of the nose just above the upper lip, does not move, nor does the entire bridge. The tip can deflect slightly when the nostrils flare or compress or the upper lip moves radically. The root (between the brows) can be wrinkled deeply by the corrugator muscles of the eyebrows. Some people can flare open or partially close their nostrils by flexing the *nasalis* muscle that runs from each wing of the nose across the crest. Since the perimeter of the nose is mostly attached to underlying bone, the nose doesn't affect surrounding tissues very much. On the contrary, the nose is usually moved inci-dentally by strong motions of the cheeks or upper lip.

The nose has little to do with most realistic character animation. Humans are not generally attuned to flared nostrils as a sign of anger or alertness or constricted nostrils as a reaction to unpleasant smells. The phrase "wrinkling one's nose" is a bit misleading. The wrinkles are formed at the nose's root by the eyebrow's corrugators, and the nose's midsection is compressed by the *angular head* of the *quadratus labii superiorus* muscle that runs along the *nasolabial furrows* that divide the nose from the cheeks. In other words, the wrinkles are all formed by muscles around the nose not part of it.

Caricature animation can easily employ the nose to humorous effect. Exaggerate the nose to a fleshy mass, make it bob and wobble in overlapping action, and every facial motion becomes laughable.

Eyes: Realistic

Realistic eyeballs are paradoxically the easiest and among the most difficult parts to animate. On one hand, they are nearly perfect spheres, easy to model, position, and rotate. On the other hand, they are such a crucial part of nonverbal communication that your audience will be examining your character's eyes more closely than any other part of the scene. That means you can often cheat other parts of the scene, as long as you model and animate the eyes well.

If you're going for realism, you can't get away with modeling the eyeball as a simple sphere. You need to model the corneal bulge, and, if the eye is going to be seen in extreme close shots, you will probably want to model the iris complete with a variable pupil opening and set the *index of refraction* for the cornea and the vitreous humor (the liquid filling the eyeball, visible through the pupil) to something near the real values. For ordinary concentric pupils, you have two basic choices: a set of image maps with a variety of pupil sizes or a pupil opening that can be animated with mesh controls. If you want to get completely obsessive about realism, consult an ophthalmologist. Then, there are all the interesting possibilities for creature eyeballs, from a relatively prosaic cat's-eye slit pupil to weird glowing effects and hypnotically flowing iris maps.

Eyelids: Realistic

Eyelids convey a significant fraction of the eyes' expressiveness. Rotation and pupil dilation are the limits of the eyeball's repertoire, so the eyelids and brows have to do the rest of the work. As with any action involving the eyes, the tiniest changes can make a big difference in the meaning of an expression.

The eyelids are controlled by two muscles, the *levator palpebrae,* which raises the upper lid, and the *orbicularis oculi,* which encircles the eye and squeezes the lids together in squinting. The normal position of the upper lid is between the upper edge of the pupil and the upper edge of the iris. Usually, the upper lid just covers the edge of the iris. If the upper lid covers any part of the pupil, the eyes look sleepy, depressed, intoxicated, or slow. If the upper lid raises far enough to expose the *sclera*, or white of the eye, the eyes look surprised or alert.

The lower lid has much less influence on expression. Normally, the lower lid simply follows the edge of the iris, within the lid's range of motion. If the eyeball rotates upward, the lower lid cannot follow very far and often leaves part of the sclera exposed. Unlike the upper lid, exposing the sclera above the lower lid has no particular emotional message. Even when squinting, the lower lid rarely covers more than the lower part of the iris and, sometimes, the lowest edge of the pupil. Neither eyelid ever slants beyond its natural angle. This is an effect used sometimes in caricature, but in reality, the illusion of a slant upwards in distress or downwards in anger is created by an extreme position of the eyebrows that deepens the shadows in the eye socket.

Modeling and setting up the eyelids can be easy or hard, depending on the style of modeling you choose for the character. Exact realism is difficult because of the wrinkling and folding of the lids. Mimicking this precisely would require a plethora of controls and take forever to animate. If you need realistic eyelids, I recommend modeling a series of morph target objects and making good use of bump maps.

A much easier approach is to treat the eyelids as simple hemispheres and allow them to interpenetrate the face. The seam along the penetration will show, but appropriate texture maps can partially disguise it. This makes animation a breeze, and the right setup can automate most of the eyelids' actions.

Eyes: Cartoon

Cartoon eyes behave just like real eyes, only more so. The limits of various expressions are the same, but you have to model the eyeball, lids, and brows so the animator can distort them to exaggerate and emphasize the central traits of the expression. For example, a very angry scowl for a realistic character would require drawn-down eyebrows, lowered upper eyelids, and the eyes' tracking null positioned on the object of the anger. A caricature of the same expression may require the brows to be pushed farther down the nose, deeper wrinkles across the bridge, swelling and thrusting forward of the brows to make them appear larger and more threatening, and bulging of the eyeballs and lids toward the object of the anger. Obviously, cartoon eyes will require more than a simple rotating-sphere setup.

The need for flexibility means the shape of a cartoon eye depends on the character and the expression. Most cartoon eyeballs are drawn as distorted ovoids, like soft-boiled eggs with the point up, but different characters may require flattened, elongated, or even triangular eyeballs. Because the shape will probably not be suitable for rotating, you don't need to model the eyeball separately from the face. You don't even need to animate the sclera, except for gross distortions, like bulging and stretch-and-squash. You can create the illusion of a moving eyeball by simply animating the iris and pupil across the unmoving surface of the sclera. Therefore, you can model a cartoon eyeball as just another bulge in the face, but you need to define it as a separate surface. If there is any way you can use a regular ellipsoid (a stretched-out sphere) for a sclera, it can really make setup and animation easier.

Eyelids: Cartoon

One of the problems with cartoon-style eyes and eyelids is the difficulty of keeping an animated pupil underneath a relatively thin modeled eyelid. Mapping the iris to the sclera is a handy way to solve this problem. If at all possible, design your cartoon characters with very thin eyelids that can be faked with color and bump maps applied directly to the sclera surface.

If your character needs thicker eyelids, you may have to model a series of morph targets. This gives you the flexibility to match irregular sclera shapes but complicates setup and animation. Either a spherical eyeball or a mapped eyelid will save you effort. An irregular eyeball with thick, modeled eyelids is a tough combination.

Jaw

Most of the expression in a person's face is due to muscles and other soft tissues. Very little unique expression is contributed by the position of the jaw, but it acts as a modifier for many emotions and is important for lip sync. A human jaw is basically a hinge on the local X axis, with a small amount of play allowing X-axis and Z-axis movement. The jaw does not pivot on either Y or Z axes, unless it has been broken or dislocated. The pivot of the jaw is located just under the rear end of the zygomatic arch, the ridge of bone that runs from the cheekbone back toward the ear. If you draw a horizontal line from underneath the eye socket to the opening of the ear, the pivot will be on that line and just forward of the ear.

The jaw carries the lower mouth, lower teeth, and the tongue along when it moves or rotates, and stretches the cheeks between their upper attachments and the jawline. You can get a better feel for this if you run a finger inside your mouth, along the outside surface of your lower gums, pushing outward on the cheek to note where the flesh is fixed to the jaw and where it stretches to meet the rest of the face. You may be surprised at just how much of your face isn't really attached to anything. From just below the orbits to the jawline, it's all hanging loose. This is one of the times a model skull comes in handy, to correlate what your fingers are telling you with what the bone structure looks like.

The upper palate and teeth are locked to the rest of the skull. You should never try to animate them, unless you're trying to upset your audience with a really unnatural character. The upper front teeth are handy as reference points for facial maps, as they are visible in wireframe, do not move, and are near the center of the face.

When you model the lower face, remember that the lower jaw, teeth, lower edge of cheeks, and the base of the tongue are all attached and should share the same parent in the hierarchy, with the lateral axis of rotation at the hinge of the jaw.

The tongue itself is extremely fluid and versatile, a mass of muscle with no limiting bone structure. It may be best to limit its use to phonemes that prominently display the tongue, or use morph targets to enable you to make detailed models of different tongue poses.

Mouth

The mouth is one of the most complex areas of a character's face, and it contributes almost as much expression as the eyes. In nature, the mouth is a ring of muscle, the *orbicularis oris*, which forms the lips. There are at least five other major groups of muscles that pull, push, or otherwise affect some part of the mouth. The mouth can be complex enough to justify its own animation hierarchy, depending on how realistic you want your character's face to be.

The mouth is bounded by the rigid septum of the nose above and the equally rigid attachments to the chin and jawline below. Between these extremes, the musculature of the mouth is almost completely free. This shows us where to begin to model and set up the mouth. Parent the upper mouth to the root of the head and the lower mouth to the jaw. This takes care of the grosser movements required for lip sync and extreme emotions. Leaving the larger motions to a parent control also leaves you more flexibility in setting child controls to animate the subsidiary surfaces.

The next level of the animation hierarchy is the lips. Generally, you can get away with leaving the upper surface of the upper lip and the lower surface of the lower lip to fend for themselves. Overlapping influence between the lips' controls and those for the jawline and upper face will stretch the intervening surface enough for most expressions. The lips proper need a fair number of controls, but this setup is important enough to justify the extra effort.

Keep in mind that the corners of the mouth will have to move somewhere between the lower jaw's position and the rest of the face, but not exactly halfway. The lower lip usually stretches more with the jaw opening, and the upper lip stays relatively close to the upper face. The lips also should be able to pucker outwards or suck in, especially for pronouncing Ps, Vs, and Fs.

Cheeks

The cheeks are an interesting challenge after the complexities of the mouth. They can be deceptively simple. The main purpose of the cheeks is to bridge the distance between jaw and eye socket. For a low-resolution character, cheeks can even be single polygons or patches stretched between the jawline, nose, mouth, and lower eyelids. Cheeks bulge up and out near the top when the corners of the lips are pulled up or the eyes squint. They stretch when the jaw is opened and bulge from air pressure just before *plosive* phonemes or when the character is making a face.

The dual role of the cheeks requires a special solution. The stretching to connect the jaw is pretty easily handled, simply by being careful with positioning of vertices or nodes in the cheek surfaces. Air pressure bulging, on the other hand, is a bit of a challenge. I recommend tackling it with an additional set of controls designed specifically to puff out the cheeks.

The cheek controls should influence the lips, the upper lip to the base of the nose, the lower lip to the chin, the cheeks up to the lower eyelids and down to the jawline, and up to the edges of the nose on both sides. This is the outline of attachment for the loose skin of the cheeks. The cheek controls should not influence the nose, eyeballs, jawline, chin, eyelids, eyebrows, or any part of the top of the head above the eyes or back of the head behind the temples. These are either firmly attached to underlying bone or beyond the cheeks' range of influence. The preceding sections laid out guidelines for character design based on the character's desired appearance and its relation to the workings of real-world creatures. The next section takes a look at guidelines for designing a character for efficient production.

Nuts And Bolts

When you choose a style for your character, you need to consider what the story requires. If you are creating a digital stuntman to take the fall for a recognizable actor, you've got a lot of work to do just to make the character look acceptable, let alone animate well.

If your story can work with a more abstract or primitive character, you can focus your energy and resources on timing, posing, and actually telling the story. Somewhere between photorealism and stick figures, you'll find the style that suits your story.

Character designs fall into three general levels of complexity and difficulty: primitive, caricature, and realistic.

Primitives

Primitive characters are hierarchies of separate objects, like a skeleton or puppet hinged at the joints. Any software that supports hierarchies can be used to animate a primitive character.

The challenge for a primitive hierarchical character is that you have to use joint rotation to fake squash-and-stretch. This demands an excellent sense of timing, as exemplified in Pixar's "Luxo, Jr." Similarly, the character's limited emotional range, even with a fully articulated marionette face, means your character will have to act more with posture and gesture than with facial expression. This has the benefit of forcing you to improve your timing and posing skills, which makes primitives excellent practice characters.

Primitive hierarchies are relatively easy to model and are fast and simple to animate, as well. The individual objects don't have to be designed to deform. The animator simply moves and rotates the objects "as is."

Unfortunately, the joints between objects are difficult to conceal, and they destroy the illusion of life unless the character is supposed to have visible seams. Parented hierarchies are best suited for puppets, robots, machines, and creatures with external skeletons like insects, arachnids, and silly English kinniggits.

A new style of character construction, unique to CGI character animation, is the invisible joint. This approach simply omits the mating parts of the joint, so there is a visible gap between parent and child object. This approach has been used in a number of CGI character animations, including Steph Greenberg's "The Physics of Cartoons, Part I" (shown in Figure 5.16) and Doug Aberle's "Fluffy" (which you can find in the Hash directory on this book's CD-ROM).

The tools for building an object for a primitive hierarchy are so basic that I won't go into a step-by-step tutorial describing them. Essentially, you can create the sliding surface of any rotating joint by using a lathe tool, or create a round primitive and modify it as necessary.

There are three basic joint types for character animation: hinge, universal joint, and the ball-and-socket joint.

Figure 5.16 Slim and Tubbs from "The Physics of Cartoons, Part I," showing invisible joints.

The simplest is the hinge, a joint with a single degree of freedom. That is, it can only rotate around one axis. The human knee and elbow are examples of hinge joints, for while they can move slightly in other axes, this is a strain on the joint.

You can model a hinge with a simple cylinder. The socket (the hollow part of the joint) must be cut away enough to allow the pin (the cylindrical center) to rotate through the intended range of motion. For example, a hinged knee requires that the thigh and shin objects be cut away at the back, so the calf of the lower leg does not overlap the back of the thigh when the knee is bent. Look at the objects in the Puppet character shown in Figure 5.17 for other examples of hinge joint cutaways.

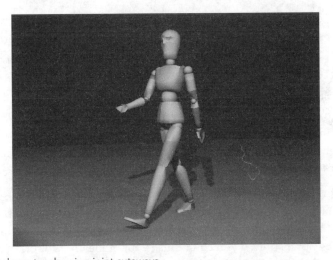

Figure 5.17 Puppet character showing joint cutaways.

The next joint type is the universal joint, or U-joint, which has two degrees of freedom. The wrist and shoulder are universal joints. The wrist can rotate the hand up and down and side to side, but twisting is a job for the forearm. The shoulder can rotate the arm to the side, on the dorsal axis, and forward and back on the lateral axis.

You can model a universal joint with two interdependent hinge joints, but I recommend skipping straight to a spherical socket. It's much simpler. If you really want to do a universal joint, take a look at a marine gimbal or a car's driveshaft U-joint.

Despite the apparent flexibility of the shoulder's combination of motions, it is not a true ball-and-socket joint like the hip. The hip has three degrees of freedom—it can rotate both forward and to the side, and also twist around the long axis of the upper leg.

Modeling the ball-and-socket joint is nearly self-explanatory. Create a spherical cap for one object, usually the child. Use the spherical part of the object as a Boolean tool to carve a matching cavity in the parent object. That's it—you have a ball-and-socket joint.

Incidentally, any joint with more degrees of freedom can substitute for lower-order joints. You can animate a ball-and-socket as any of the three types, a universal joint can move as itself and as a hinge, but the hinge construction can only move as a hinge. I prefer to build ball-and-socket joints for everything, just in case the character will be called on to perform an action the joints weren't designed for.

To help align the objects during setup, I like to mark the center of a joint's rotation with a 3D crosshair. I build one of these into a parent object wherever a child object will be attached. You can build a crosshair by adding six vertices or nodes in three perpendicular pairs, one pair each on the X, Y, and Z axes. Space the points just far enough apart that you will be able to see them, but try to keep them inside the parent object. This forms a 3D crosshair, like a toy jack, which is much easier to work with during setup than a single reference point.

If you're really eager for some practice at constructing primitive object hierarchies, try building a bug. Insect, lobster, arachnid, whatever—just make sure it's got an external skeleton.

PROJECT 5.1 Is There An Entomologist In The House? (Optional Project)

Check out a book on comparative entomology from your local library. I like Fox and Fox, *Introduction to Comparative Entomology*, for its line drawings, but a volume with more photographs would probably be more helpful. For range of motion and other constraints, you should refer to the resources on animal studies in the Bibliography.

Failing that, get down to your nearest seafood restaurant, and buy a lobster or crab dinner. Insist that they bring out the whole thing. Hang out by the tank for a while, and watch how they move, too. Take your study model apart carefully when you eat, and bring the shell home in a doggy bag for closer study. If you can't finish your model in a couple of days, you'll need to make sure the shell is completely clean.

Welcome To Toon Town: Design For Caricature

The next level of complexity is the caricature. This is usually a more complete character, with full articulation in the hands and face and often built from a single seamless mesh or patch. This requires your 3D software to support mesh deformation tools like bones, spline patches, or free-form deformations. If your software can't handle this, you are pretty much stuck with primitive characters.

Cartoons or caricatures are a very popular style of character animation. Shading and rendering options enable you to create caricatures for a variety of environments, from the photorealism of *The Mask* to cel shading that mimics traditional 2D drawn animation. Some animators have succeeded in emulating the visual style of classic cartoon animators like Tex Avery, Friz Freleng, and Chuck Jones, while others are intent on breaking new ground in ways unique to the computer medium.

The dramatic strengths of the caricature style lie in stereotype, archetypes and exaggeration. If your character is a villain, he'll have to look like a villain. Don't try to fool with your audience by making a perfectly nice-looking character turn out to be the bad guy. If your story premise is understated or subtle, you may want to consider another style. A notable example is the character of Gaston in *Beauty and the Beast*. Andreas Deja, the animator, originally wanted a darker, bigger chinned heavy with a mustache and dark circles under his eyes. Producer Jeffrey Katzenberg wanted to emphasize the 'beauty is only skin deep' moral, by showing how ugly Gaston was with his behavior rather than with his appearance, the perfect complement to the Beast. And yet, many people act surprised when reminded that Gaston was not the hero! "But he was so good looking!" Commercial audiences, especially in the U.S., generally aren't expecting subtlety or irony in an animation, and your more refined dramatic efforts may be lost on them.

Exaggeration means you'll have to design and build the character to exceed the limits of a merely human character. A caricature must be able to pop eyes in surprise, recoil like rubber in a *wild take*, and generally move as if the laws of physics are as mutable as their anatomy. The key to designing a caricature for exaggeration is finding what defines the character and its actions, then pushing that definition to the breaking point. For example, a primitive or realistic character might reach for a doorknob by straightening out his arm and stepping forward until his hand reaches the knob. The caricatured character would fling out his arm, hyperextending the elbow, and stretching his arm until his hand meets the doorknob, at which point the elasticity of his stretched arm snaps him forward, perhaps off his feet. The essence of this action was the extension of the arm with the goal of the doorknob—the exaggeration was in putting all of the character's energy and form into attaining that goal.

Caricatures never do things halfway; it's several hundred percent effort, every time. Even a caricature's casual saunter is an exaggeration of the essential actions of the real-life motion.

Facial design is especially important for the caricature style. You'll almost never see a stone-faced or neutral caricature face; even at rest, the character must be saying, loudly, exactly who they are and what they are intending. Fortunately, the caricature style can borrow heavily from the existing body of work on 2D cartoon animation. The references in the Bibliography contain many excellent examples of 2D caricature design, and the majority can be adapted (more or less) to the 3D environment. I especially recommend Brian Lemay's *Designing Cartoon Characters for Animation* and any of Preston Blair's books.

Better Than Life?

Realism is the most technically demanding character style, at least for modeling and setup. It is also the style least suited to traditional animation methods and most suited to *mocap*, or motion capture. Before you decide on realism as your character's style, you should be absolutely sure that your story requires this high level of modeling and rendering detail. If so, are there also compelling reasons why you shouldn't simply make it a live-action film rather than animate it?

Modeling and setup for a realistic human is possibly the most complex job in character animation. Your software must support nearly every modeling, texturing, setup, animation, and rendering tool available. It's almost impossible to do a realistic human in just one software package. It's more common for studios to use a variety of software and hardware tools, each in its strongest area, to assemble a realistic character.

The design process is mostly a matter of choosing a subject, then research and data capture. If you are simulating a particular person, you will have to capture complete geometry, map, and range-of-motion (if not actual mocap) data. Even if you are building a unique character rather than a digital stuntman, you will find it more efficient to capture as much geometry, map, and movement data from similar real-life subjects as possible. Trying to model and texture a realistic human from scratch is work for a master, and a gifted one at that.

Finicky attention to detail is the prime requirement for realistic character creation. Subtleties, like specularity maps, skin folds, and the translucency of fingernails, can make or break an illusion. The same is true for animating the finished character. You must create absolutely perfect timing, or the illusion of life is destroyed.

If your realistic character is not human, you will have to do the equivalent research on animals. If the character is fantastic, you'll need to find the most similar bits and pieces in real-life creatures and adapt them with as much wit and talent as you can muster. Concocting a Draco from an artist's sketch is the sort of work you'll find at the very top of the field.

If you're just starting out in character animation or you're making the transition to the computer from traditional animation, don't jump straight into realism or even caricature. Go back to the primitives, get your setup and animation skills up to speed, then start adding complexity to your characters. If you're brand-new to computer animation, the most forgiving and least demanding place to start modeling is in building your own sets.

Set Design

Most sets don't have to move or interact very much. In fact, many of them can just as easily be painted backdrops. You won't have to build in many controls, and the ones you do can usually be automated.

Set design also gives you the opportunity to match your story's environment to its characters. If you use the same tools and techniques to create the sets as you will use later to build the characters, you will get the same visual style throughout your production.

You can make scene layout a lot easier if you combine all the immovable objects in a scene into a single object. Furniture, walls, and architectural details rarely need to be animated. You can also delete unnecessary polygons or nodes once you know they won't be seen in a shot, thereby conserving memory and saving redraw and rendering time. You can also add simple looping actions to a set as child objects. You can set fan rotation, clock hands, even dripping water to simple repeating cycles.

If you think ahead about set construction, you can build reusable objects that you can customize with a minimum of effort. Suppose you assigned mesh controls to lock down all the vertices defining a window opening. You could drag the controls to move the window and have a new room layout. With a judicious placement of controls and definition of surfaces, you can make a chameleon room that you can transform into the basis of almost any interior set.

When you're ready to furnish a set, don't neglect 3D clip art. If the animation's style is very quirky and unique, you'll probably have to model everything from scratch. But if the sets are at all "normal," you can probably find some clip art that will save you modeling time. CD-ROM collections are available, including inexpensive compilations from Internet FTP sites. Those sites are also good hunting grounds, if you have the time to browse.

Building A Simplified Set

1. Assemble a generic office set as a single object in Modeler, with floor, ceiling, walls, door, window, desk, chairs, credenza, shelves, and lamp, using prebuilt objects. Cull objects from the Internet, your software's CD-ROMs, and any other sources you find useful.

2. Define surfaces so you can select the individual parts, as necessary.

3. Build child objects for clock hands, a ceiling fan, or other objects that will make cyclical motions. Set up a looping action.

Moving On

You should now be able to make well-informed decisions about how you want your characters to look and move. The next chapter will show you some of the most useful modeling tools appropriate to building animatable characters.

MODELING TOOLS

The influence of your modeling tools doesn't stop at your character's outward appearance. Modeling tools can limit or expand your options for animation, too. This chapter guides you through choices of surface type, work strategies, and critical tools you'll need to model characters effectively.

Before you work through this chapter and the following one, you should be comfortably familiar with the modeling tools in your 3D software of choice. Modeling is so basic to animation that most software manuals have adequate tutorials. If your manuals seem a little short on modeling tutorials, you might consider some of the more general 3D resources. A book on special effects, flying logos, and zooming spacecraft is a perfectly good resource for learning basic modeling skills. If I attempted to duplicate all that general information in this book, there wouldn't be enough room for the specifics of character modeling. Once you have mastered the construction of rigid objects, moving up to deformable meshes and complex hierarchies will be much easier. This chapter provides the information you need to successfully choose modeling software based on your project's requirements.

Evaluating Modeling Tools

Nearly every 3D software package now includes some form of modeling toolkit. The choice for you is to determine which tools suit the way you work and enable you to create the characters and other models you need. Very few character animators model, set up, and animate all within a single software suite. Most studios rely on a collection of tools, applying whatever gets the job done to the task at hand. Whether you are just starting out or you've been involved in 3D animation from its beginnings, you can use a few guidelines to select and judge your modeling tools:

- Look for software that minimizes the number of steps you have to follow to perform a single task. Each step, or *therblig*, costs you time. If you have to go through three or four therbligs to re-scale an object, that will be a less efficient use of your time than software that only requires one therblig to perform the same task. It may not seem like much of a difference, but repeated hundreds, even thousands, of times during an animation production will drive you crazy.

- Never buy or use a modeler without multiple levels of Undo. There's no excuse for not having this feature—it's an industry standard. It's both a safety net and an encouragement to your creativity. Use as many levels of Undo as your system's memory can support.

- Slow feedback is sometimes worse than no feedback at all. If the redraw rates on your machine are fine in animation but lousy in modeling, find a new modeler. The best ones enable you to work in modes ranging from bounding box to realtime shaded, depending on your current needs.

- Being able to label and recall collections of vertices or control nodes is very handy, especially if the selection sets can overlap irrespective of material or surface settings.

- User-definable magnetism and other soft deformation tools are highly valuable for modeling characters, especially when you are hand-modeling morph targets.

- Controls for *tessellating* (subdividing or breaking down), triangulating, merging, and welding points are useful for optimizing models, especially if you need to export them for use in other software.

- If you are working from photos, drawings, or maquettes, accurate registration of the 3D windows with background template images is a must-have.

- Remember that modeling and setup are closely related iterative processes. Make sure your tools are compatible, that you can import and export your models in both directions from whatever tools you are using. Any one-way ports will make it much more difficult to revise your models.

The tools and procedures you choose or develop will depend on the type of character animation you do and the resources you have available to do it. A work strategy that succeeds for a sizable commercial shop like Foundation Imaging is not necessarily a good one for a one-person shop doing local TV ads. And vice versa—a work strategy that you have been using successfully as a solo animator may fail when you try to apply it to a larger production team. Fit the tools to the job.

I have a short list of criteria you can use to develop a work strategy that is best for your particular situation:

- Reduce redundant work
- Support incremental detailing
- Provide rapid feedback
- Create documents for decision-makers
- Stay flexible

Before you make changes to the way you work, check the new procedures against these criteria. If your proposed changes don't measure up, you should fix the problem before you go any further.

Reducing redundant work means you shouldn't have to repeat any work that isn't creative. Bringing a revised low-resolution model up to hi-res is the kind of work you should automate, if possible. Doing it once is a learning experience, doing it twice is annoying, and doing it a couple times a week can be a sentence in Purgatory. Work smart. Find ways to create macros, batch files, programs, or other tools that can do most of the repetitive work for you. This is the type of work that computers excel at—repetitive, complex tasks with no artistic judgment required. If you don't use the computer for these tasks, you're not using CG character animation's primary advantage over traditional methods. You might as well be using pencils or clay.

Supporting incremental detailing means your work strategy should enable you to rough out the entire model before making revisions and changes. For example, the first rough should be a sketch. A sketch is very easy to change, because it's only lines on paper. Odds are good that you, your production team, or the client are going to make some major changes to the character design. It's almost unheard of for a first draft design to be identical to the final character in a film. Because you can be certain of changes, you should make as many of them as you can at the lowest, cheapest level of detail. You should be able to revise the character sketches to the decision-makers' satisfaction before you start to work on the next level of detail. If your work strategy requires you to complete a detailed character model before the sketches are approved, you will almost certainly be wasting a lot of that effort. The same is true of the rest of the character design process: maquette, rough model, setup and animation tests, fine model, materials, and lighting. Every step in the process depends on the preceding steps. A mistake in design that goes uncorrected until final animation can waste many, many hours and sink your budget.

Providing rapid feedback means being able to make go/no-go decisions as soon as a task is completed. This is one of the problems with traditional cel or clay animation that computer-generated animation can eliminate almost entirely. Traditional pencil tests, which have to be filmed, processed, edited, and projected, give feedback with a 24-hour turnaround. You can render full-color images of a model in a matter of minutes. If you design your character setups properly, you can rapidly test new character objects in existing animations. These tests can tell you if the object is going to work properly or if it will have to be remodeled to eliminate creases, intersections, or other unwanted artifacts.

Creating documents for decision-makers has two purposes for your work strategy: to make your work more efficient and to limit your risks. The first purpose is reason enough for you to habitually document your work. When you have a concrete document to refer to, whether sketch, maquette, model sheet, or rendering, you can concentrate better and waste less misdirected effort than if you were winging it from memory alone. When you get bogged down in the details of character animation, it's almost impossible to keep everything straight in your head.

When you're building a character for a client, the second purpose becomes more important. Nothing can guarantee that you won't have to make major changes once you're in the later stages of production. Clients and studio execs are rarely noted for either their far-sightedness or deep understanding of the production process. You can expect decision-makers to waffle and change their minds right up to the last minute and sometimes beyond. Commercial animations have, on occasion, been completed and paid for by clients, then trashed, never to see the light of day. The important criteria for your work strategy is to have firm, contractually binding approvals at each level of detail, based on the documents you produce. When the client signs off on the maquette, you need to be confident that you can go ahead with building and setting up the model. A good contract will spell out how you are paid for each deliverable, including the sketches, maquettes, rough model, setup, and animation tests. If the client wants to make changes after they've already approved the work, they should pay you to do the work over. If it's not in your contract, you'll end up either eating the costs or having an irate client. When the client makes an expensive decision, you don't want to be the one paying the bill.

Staying flexible means just that. If your work strategy is too rigid, it's likely to snap on you someday. You shouldn't get too attached to any part of the project plan. You have to be prepared to deal with the setbacks and roadblocks that happen to every project. You should get in the habit of trying out alternatives, experimenting with different approaches to typical character design and modeling problems. When your usual approach doesn't work, you'll have a spare, and you'll sometimes find an application for a procedure you never expected to use.

Work strategy is just the beginning of selecting your modeling tools. You should also evaluate tools based on the type of surface you want to use, splines, polygons or some combination of the two.

Polygons Vs. Splines

There are two major approaches to 3D modeling, with some techniques that draw from both approaches. The older and more common approach is polygonal modeling, in which every surface is described as a group of vertices located by 3D coordinates and connected by straight lines. The newer and less common approach is spline modeling, in which surfaces are described as a group of control points or nodes located by 3D coordinates and connected by 3D curves. The most important difference between polygonal and spline modeling is that polygons can only approximate curves, and they require many vertices and edges to do so, while splines can define 3D compound curves with only a few nodes, as shown in Figure 6.1.

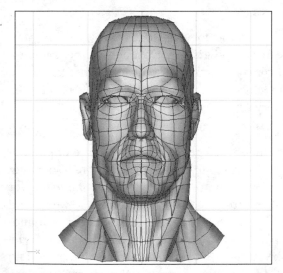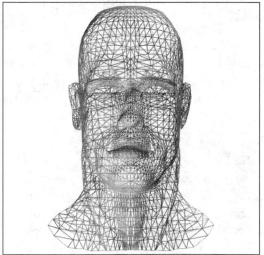

Figure 6.1 Polygonal head model compared to spline model.

This difference is important for character animation, since most styles require characters built from compound curves. The trade-off is that splines are more difficult to manage, requiring more advanced software than polygonal modelers. Polygons are simple to manage. You manipulate the surfaces by changing the location of the vertices, and the edges automatically follow along. Spline modelers require that you manage the 3D coordinates of each node plus the tension, bias, and continuity variables that define each spline curve passing through that node. Deeper technical details of splines versus polygons are beyond the scope of this book, but you can find more information in the Bibliography. All you need to understand as a character animator is how your 3D software handles polygons, splines, and their related techniques.

Polygons are simple to work with. You add and delete vertices, connect them with edges to form faces, and push them around in 3D coordinate space to build a character model. If you need to change the model, you can select the appropriate vertices, change their position, add or delete them, and save the new model. Most polygonal modeling software provides a selection of tools to make these processes easier, especially for modifying large numbers of vertices in a single operation.

Polygonal modeling requires you to be able to visualize and manage your model in terms of vertices, edges, and faces to build up complex organic curves from collections of flat faces. This is generally not difficult for people with technical illustration, drafting, or engineering educations, where orthographic projection is a basic technique. It can be more difficult for people from art or design backgrounds, where the tools have traditionally been better suited to managing 3D curves as single entities rather than by segments.

Splines are more powerful and versatile in modeling curved surfaces, but you need a better understanding of how they work in order to use them effectively. For example, it's possible to create a model using splines exactly as you'd use vertices and edges, keeping every spline perfectly straight and editing the model by moving nodes around just like vertices. This would be a grossly wasteful approach, ignoring all the flexibility and power available through manipulating the splines as curves. Used properly, you could use a small fraction of the nodes, with curved splines, to more accurately describe a complex model.

The real strength of spline models lies in their ability to describe complex shapes with minimal data. Some 3D software also enables you to animate splines, so you never have to deal with polygons at all. This is an enormously labor-saving process, although it does require more advanced software and a different approach to modeling and animation.

Some 3D software enables you to model with both approaches. You can use spline tools to create most of a model, then tessellate the curves into a regular sequence of polygons, and complete the model using polygonal tools. Some software allows you to do almost all modeling in splines, then tessellates the model for rendering. Each of these hybrid approaches has its advantages and disadvantages. If you understand the options your software makes available to you, you'll be able to choose the approach that is most effective for your current project.

Maquettes And Drawings And Scans, Oh My!

There is no arguing against the use of clay and pencil and paper in the design process. The utility of traditional media compared to the computer environment says more about our negative expectations for the computer than it does about the computer's potential as a design tool. The more effective you are at using 3D tools in CG, the more comfortable it will be to extend and refine the design process in the computer.

Most people are not as effective as they might be when they use clay to visualize three dimensions. There isn't a nondestructive undo button. While maquettes are incredibly effective for obtaining client signoff, they are not going to solve most of the critical problems you'll face in the creation of a CG model for animation.

It's one thing to acquire a cloud of points from an object in the real world and quite another to organize them into an intelligible, manageable group of surfaces. Scanning devices aren't terribly selective in the number of vertices nor are they helpful with their initial connectivity.

When modeling a character, it's up to you to determine where to put the detail. There should be detail sufficient both to reveal the shape and to allow for proper deformation when it moves. There are a number of issues to consider before you even get that far. First, what are you building the model for? A limited-detail, real-time 3D game? A low-resolution pre-rendered image? A high-resolution film? Will your model need to function in more than one of those environments? Can you or do you need to plan for resolution independence? How much geometric detail can be provided by textures and shaders, volume, bump, or displacement maps? How much do you like to punish your machine? How long are you willing to wait for a screen refresh? You have only *how* much time available? What have you already got in a morgue file that you can kit-bash? Will anybody ever see that part you were just obsessing about? What does the model need to be able to do that can be built in from the start, rather than later, when it would be a pain in the butt to change?

Of course, you'll want to begin with a clear plan, one that accommodates both form and function, before approaching the computer. As with anything you undertake, your strategies will improve with experience. Once you have learned to feel comfortable in this evolving medium, you'll thrive in that zone between drawing and sculpture that exists nowhere else.

The first step to using modeling software effectively is to make yourself comfortable in the 3D environment.

Getting Around In Flatland

You need to internalize your software's navigation techniques, reducing them to the point of trained reflexes, so you don't have to interrupt the creative process to remember things like which way is up. Here are a few useful tips for learning to maneuver in three-space:

- *Is Y up or out, and why?* Pick an up axis. Character animators prefer Y up, a stage with a proscenium arch with Z facing forward. Flight simulator builders and industrial designers prefer Z up because a pilot is looking at the ground as an XY map. Alias defaults to Z up. In Softimage, Y is up.

- *Internalize your coordinate system.* Front, right, and top views allow for point maneuvering by dragging in the windows. Memorize the planes in which you drag points in each window. In a Y-up system, the front view is the XY plane, right view is YZ, and top view is XZ. Some programs allow you to customize your own coordinate and view layouts, while other set it for you. Experiment with the available alternatives until you find a system that works intuitively for you, then stick with it.

- *Keep your work in perspective.* If you drag in the perspective window, you're going to be moving the point in a plane not necessarily congruent with one of those planes. If you keep four windows open, you're going to be leaning hard on the CPU. If you keep only the perspective window active, you can use hotkeys to maneuver your camera and manipulate surfaces intuitively. You can keep track of your movements as long as you set your initial modeling conditions properly.

- *Tag it locally, orbit while you translate it globally.* Tag vertices with the T hotkey, singly or multiply, making sure you're in Tag mode in the modeling module. You can highlight translation mode either with the mouse or by hitting the V key (just as the X key will pop you into the Scale mode). Make sure you've selected Global (sometimes Local is appropriate also) for your move mode, and you can work all day like this. Start with a primitive shape, like a sphere. Move points by tagging them (T), then moving them in X (left mouse button), Y (middle), or Z (right mouse) while orbiting your object using the O hotkey to see what you're doing.

Whatever modeling tools you choose, you should be familiar with the basic underlying principles common to most of the currently available modeling software.

Surface Type Pros And Cons

Modeling is essentially about defining surfaces, so it's useful to categorize modeling tools by the way they define and manipulate surfaces. Common surface types for character animation include polygons, splines, Non-Uniform Rational B-Splines (NURBS), and Hash patches. The following section provides a quick overview and evaluation of these surfaces as they apply to character animation.

Connect The Dots, La, La, La, La

Even animators would like modeling if it weren't for the problem of connecting the dots. As if dot placement alone weren't a big enough problem, where should the resultant surface be in relation to the points, through them or near them? How will the surface deform when vertices are moved? How can adjacent surfaces be adjoined? How will it light? Why does everything have to be an infinitely subdivisible grid? Shouldn't I be able to place detail where I need it without all that adjacent baggage? What is the balance between too little detail and too much? How many animation packages can use that type of surface? What's the proper balance between detail sufficient to define the surface yet simple enough to control it as an animator? Why don't *you* model and set it up and call me when it's ready for an animator? Modeling can be tedious, often frustrating work. If you understand common problems and the solutions provided by each surface type, your modeling will go much more smoothly.

Before discussing the merits of each surface in various stages of modeling, I want to mention a few key points about Hash splines.

A Word About Hash Splines

I love Hash splines. If you don't know whether you can visualize in three dimensions, yet if you can draw and/or sculpt moderately, you may find that Hash splines give results closest to the traditional tools with which you are familiar. Hash patches, a variation of Coon's splines, are not an available surface type outside of Animation:Master, but you may find it useful to know how they differ from the types of surfaces available in other packages.

Alias offers NURBS and polygons, which Softimage also offers. Softimage also offers additional types of patch surfaces, including Bezier, b-splines, linear splines, and cardinal splines (see Figure 6.2). Softimage patches can also be combinations, such as cardinal patches on the U axis, and b-splines on the V axis.

While Hash splines are similar to cardinal patches, they also differ from cardinal patches in significant ways. Cardinal patches are always regular grids, containing a minimum number of control points. In Hash splines, a surface can consist of as few as three points in a closed line. The simplest cardinal patch contains 16 control vertices, arrayed like a tic-tac-toe grid to define the square in the center. Using Hash splines to make a similar surface would require four lines, each containing four points, with each two in the center connected to define the center square,

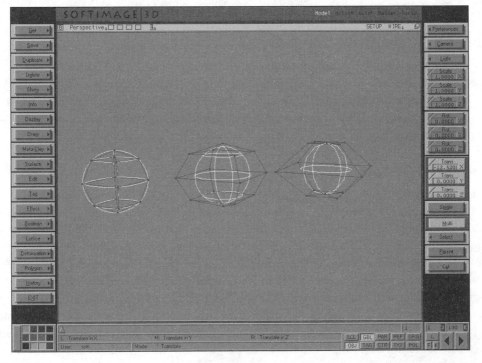

Figure 6.2 Splines.

using 12 control vertices. What Hash splines, cardinal patches, and polygons have in common is that the surface contains vertices that are always congruent with the surface—vertices that are always part of the surface. NURBS or B-Splines use control vertices that modify but are not directly part of the surface they define. This can be annoying when trying to locate the vertices that will make the surface go where you want it to be, and you can't just move that U and V intersection to where you need it.

Figure 6.3 shows an example of the same mesh as a cardinal surface, NURBS surface, and polygonal surface. You can see a textured and rendered polygonal version in the Color Studio.

For the simple reason that you can add or subtract detail where you want it, polygons and Hash splines are the simplest way to work. Of course, surfaces made with the same number of control vertices in Hash will be smooth and rounded, and the polygonal models will be quite faceted. But polygonal surfaces can be rounded up with a button push in Softimage (as in Figure 6.4), and, if you do so procedurally (using plug-ins you get from your software vendor), your low-detail polygonal model can drive the high-detailed model used for final render.

The other patch surfaces can be UV mapped, unlike polys and Hash splines. Having pointed out the differences, I'll get back to discussing the merits of each in various stages of modeling.

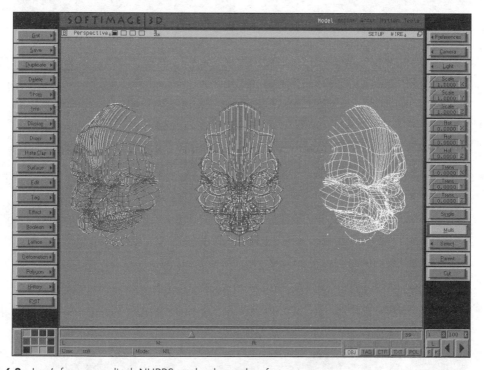

Figure 6.3 Imp's face as cardinal, NURBS, and polygonal surfaces.

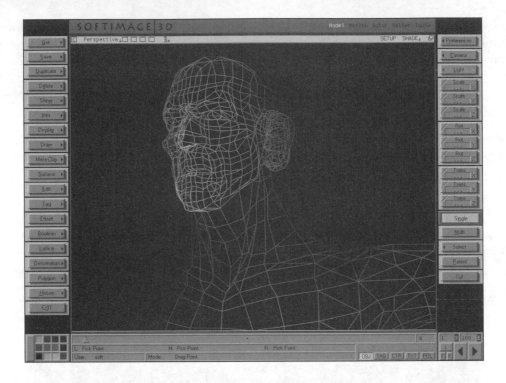

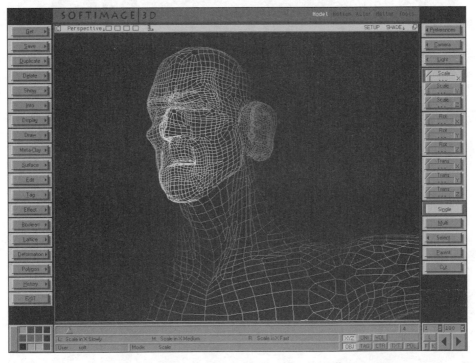

Figure 6.4 A polygonal surface subdivided using the Softimage rounding effect.

Why Polygons At All?

Anybody who has played a realtime 3D game is very familiar with the look of polygonal surfaces. As geometry engines become more powerful, they'll be capable of slinging even more polygons, until even games lose that trademark polygonal look. Polygons aren't yet history. Even if polygons can't be detected in your final product, they have much utility in the production pipeline.

An appropriately sized polygonal cube is a stand-in for a more highly detailed prop or character until you drop in the finished model. Using only a few simple commands and some talent, you can turn that cube into a finished model.

I'm now in the habit of modeling in low-polygonal detail to block out basic shapes and proportions, rounding up to higher detail and using the resultant smoothed shape as a virtual maquette template for a cardinal patch/NURBS surface.

With a low-detailed polygonal surface, I can focus entirely on shape and proportion, and easily refine it without worrying about Us and Vs, putting detail only where I want it. Proportions are easier to change than clay, at low enough detail.

That way, I can focus on one problem at a time. Shape with polygons, and then focus on the surface properties of the patch surface while magnet snapping its points to the polygonal model. I can focus on how it should bend and where the Us and Vs of the patch surface should line up, without worrying about trying to define a shape at the same time.

Polygonal Modeling

I've seen too many modelers that offered the utility of inputting the first point in a triangle, the next, the last, and then you track down the "close face" icon. Next, you select the "new face" icon and do it again. Then, you weld the two triangles together, and you have a complex surface. I hope you entered the points in the expected clockwise or counterclockwise manner. I could never remember which was which. Oh well, you get what you pay for.

For polys, you don't need a whole lot more than that, but a little bit goes a long way. For instance, let's look at what happens when you subdivide a quad into triangles. In Softimage, pull up a cube primitive, and select Polygon|Edge. Left-click on two of the vertices of the top face, adding an edge diagonally across the top. Now, tag one of the vertices, and move it up, by translating the tagged vertex along the Y axis. Depending on whether you raised a vertex to which the diagonal is connected or one of the others, you have one of two very different shapes. See Figures 6.5 and 6.6.

Suppose the shape isn't the one you wanted. Go back to Object mode from Tag, middle-click on the polygon box (reselecting the last choice inside that box, in this case Edge), and right-click on the diagonal edge you added, deleting it. Left-click on the two vertices that define the other possible way to cut that quad into two triangles.

Perhaps you've scanned a mesh for a human face (see Chapter 7, for details), and you now have a quad mesh. Duplicate it, scale it to -1 in the X axis, freeze the scale transform, and

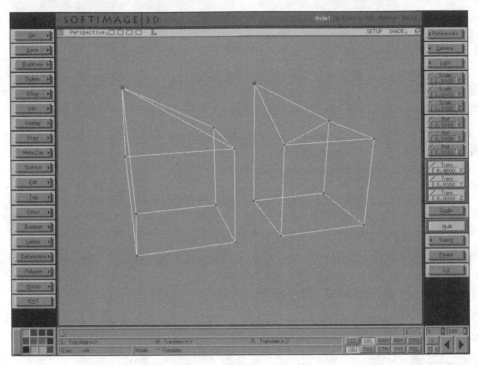

Figure 6.5 Wireframe view of quads divided into triangles.

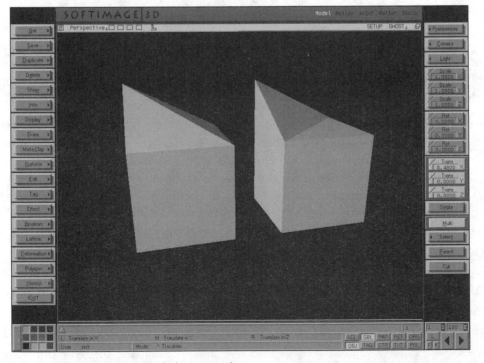

Figure 6.6 Shaded view of quads divided into triangles.

invert the surface. Weld the two halves into one mesh, resulting in edges only on the boundaries, with no seam in the middle. You can triangulate the resulting mesh, but one side will look better than the other. That's because triangles will cut the quads along natural folds, such as the naso-labial, on one side and not on the other side. For that reason, if your final work is triangles, make sure the triangles define the shape you want first, then scale the duplicate on the X axis.

Taking Advantage Of Polygons

When you need to define a surface with the least amount of detail, polygons are the way to go if you don't care about harsh edges in your silhouette. You can always hit the Rounding button in Softimage, the one Viewpoint charges you substantially for when they use it. Even if you're never, ever going to make game art and all your finished models are going to be made of NURBS, there is still much utility in polygonal modeling that can't be readily dismissed.

Generally, patch surfaces are great for generating smooth, rounded surfaces with far less detail than it would take to model the same surface in polygons. Patch surfaces are regular grids. If you need to add resolution in an area of high detail, you have more detail to manage than you want in simpler areas that don't require the detail. Polygons allow for flexibility of resolution in the planning stages, letting you design with the least amount of detail to manage.

Low-detail patch grids don't map readily onto complex surfaces, like the folds and openings of a human face (see Figure 6.7). If you design with polygons to begin with, you can increase or

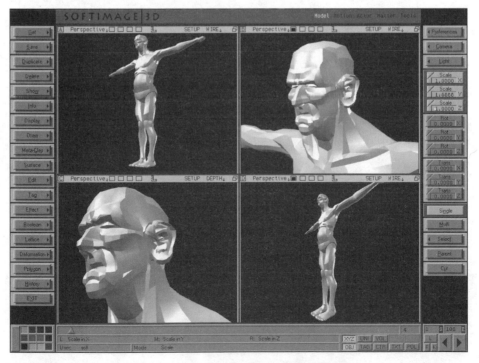

Figure 6.7   A sculptural approach is easier with polygons than with NURBS.

decrease detail as you go and then later apply a patch surface. Sometimes you have to deliver NURBS, but if your software can handle it, polygons can be the best choice, particularly for something as highly detailed as a face.

Surface Subdivision

On its way to picking up an Oscar, Pixar's *Geri's Game* generated some buzz about how it was made (as if it were the tools that gave it its edge). You can read about Geri's suit elsewhere in this book. You could drive yourself crazy trying to model Geri's face in NURBS, let alone manage that amount of detail for animation. Pixar's trick was to subdivide a comparatively simple polygonal surface at render, using proprietary code that let them predict the shape and mapping attributes of the surface without having to do iterative subdivision beforehand. Just hitting the round button a few times until you have a surface black with vertices that's a nightmare to light and weight doesn't cut it. Many plug-ins exist that let you work with a low-detail polygonal mesh that drives a multiply subdivided surface for use at lighting and render time, freeing you from dealing with higher levels of detail until critical. Whether you want triangles or quads, one vendor claims to allow for UV mapping on surfaces that did not start out as regular grids. Don't let anybody tell you that polygons are dead. A polygon is merely the simplest type of patch.

While commercially available tools won't be identical to those generated at Pixar, your tool palette can be every bit as full as theirs. You may have to jump through a few more hoops in

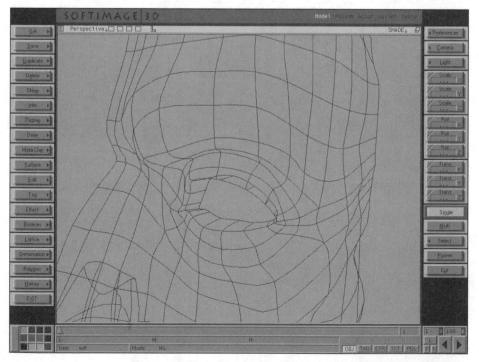

Figure 6.8 In three places, five edges radiate from one vertex (multiple separate but adjacent cardinal patch surfaces).

some apps than others to accomplish with polygons what you can do so easily with Hashsplines. You can approximate the utility of Hashsplines with subdivided polygonal surfaces more readily than you can with any kind of patch surface, except perhaps with David Forsey's hierarchical b-splines. H-splines require a great deal more planning, and are not as forgiving as either subdivided polygons or Hashsplines. If you are used to NURBS, hierarchical b-splines may be the best thing to happen to you in a long time.

The trick that is the most difficult to achieve in anything other than polygons or Hashsplines is the problem of adding a row of detail in one area without increasing it elsewhere (see Figure 6.8). In the film *Contact,* a dimensional math puzzle momentarily stumps our heroes: Sure you can connect the corners of four grids at a single-vertex intersection, but what happens with the intersection of three grids, or five? In most real-world cases, you get a big ugly surface discontinuity. In other words, it'll light funny, with highlights not matching (see Figure 6.9). The artifact occurs when you can only obtain tangency across two but not three, or four but not five, of the surfaces. You can design around this problem in just about any area other than a human face, or a human hand. Active blends connecting multiple trimmed surfaces create other kinds of problems in a face. A single mesh affords far greater control, with fewer problems to solve.

Faces are elastic surfaces that don't fold neatly along the U and the V isoparms. A hexagonal mesh, the type that one can see overlayed on any triangular mesh, is perhaps more analogous to the way skin stretches and folds. A tube, radial from the mouth, gives a close approximation

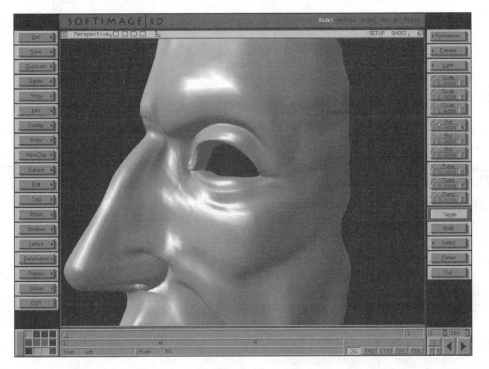

Figure 6.9 Lighting discontinuity.

to what we want, with lines matching up around the mouth. What we really want is something that matches more of the muscular structure of the face, with lines radial from the mouth, the nose, and each eye. This is why I always suggest starting out in Hash, where you can focus on the shape that you want, and how little detail to use to achieve your goals, until you feel at all comfortable in 3D. Every other approach is process heavy, plug-in reliant, or requires the beginner to muster a lot of lateral thinking where basic concepts are difficult enough to grasp.

Patching It Up: Cardinals And NURBS

A cardinal patch has the advantage (over NURBS or b-splines) of containing control vertices that the spline surface passes *through* rather than *near*. The disadvantage is that splines overshoot when two points are too close to each other while the third point of the spline is at too wide an angle from the others. Unlike NURBS surfaces, adding a row of vertices in the U or V direction puts control points at the linear midpoint between its neighbors. This puts a nasty divot in your smooth surface that you'll need to modify.

If you add a row in the U or V direction on a NURBS surface, the shape of the surface will remain unmodified while providing a new row of control vertices (CVs) for you to tweak. Because the CVs of a NURBS surface lie near but never congruent with a surface, they can be difficult to manage when trying to build or modify a shape. It would be better to have a NURBS surface that is modifiable by both its CVs and at the intersections of its Us and Vs directly on the surface. There is a way of working that lets you take advantage of cardinal surface *and* NURBS surface properties when you need them. Conversion from one type of surface to another is a one-way street, so it would appear, at first glance, that you can't conveniently go back and forth when it would be so desirable to do so. I'll explain how to do it, and why.

Usually, you'll want to use NURBS for your final skinned objects, particularly for character animation. The CVs lie above but never directly on the actual surface, yet you can see rows of Us and Vs on the surface itself that look very much like the previously discussed cardinal surface. You can look at these *isoparms*, but you can't touch them directly. You can change a cardinal surface into a NURBS surface or polygonal mesh using Convert in the Effects box.

> ### THERE CAN BE ONLY ONE
>
> **Be sure to lower all subdivisions to 1 in the Get Info dialogue before converting a cardinal surface into a NURBS surface or polygonal mesh. If you use subdivisions higher than 1, you'll redundantly multiply the density of the mesh.**

If you start with a cardinal patch and convert it to NURBS, the points you edited as a cardinal surface are still where the Us and Vs intersect. Now, the CVs have jumped above that surface. Sadly, you can only convert a NURBS surface into polygonal quads. You can't change it back into a cardinal surface. That's OK, because if we convert it to a polygonal surface (don't forget to change subdivisions down to 1), we can use the result, with a little bit of editing to update our previously converted cardinal surface.

Start with a cardinal surface, and move its points around until you want to convert it to a NURBS surface. Duplicate the cardinal version, then (remembering to lower the subdivisions of the copy to 1) convert it to a NURBS surface. Add Us or Vs, and modify away. If your original cardinal surface was undesirably irregular, you can see where to smooth it more readily as a NURBS surface. The CVs of the NURBS surface show any irregularities with far more exaggeration, making it much easier to correct (you shouldn't need it to be *that* smooth, anyway). Of course, the CVs that control the part of the surface on which you're concentrating could be anywhere in that forest of vertices, especially in folded areas around the mouth, nose, and eyes. If you plan to make weighted shape targets for facial animation, it will be easier to do so if you keep the original target that you edit a cardinal patch. Now, you're ready to convert the NURBS surface back to cardinal.

For safety, duplicate the NURBS surface first. Lower its subdivisions to one, and convert it to polygons. You now have a mesh of polygonal quads that can be used as a template to edit the earlier cardinal surface that you kept. With only the cardinal and polygonal surfaces visible in your full-screen perspective window, single select the cardinal surface. In the window's ruler menu, toggle magnet points to on, unselected objects only. Now, using Edit|Move, you can snap points on the cardinal surface to their new locations quickly and easily. Where you need a new row, simply Edit|Add one, and snap those new vertices to where they belong. You might be able to script this, by swapping out the X, Y, and Z triplet values in a new cardinal grid that starts with the right number of Us and Vs. A problem remains, due to the nature of cardinal patches, that would need to be taken into account, or this might already have been a simple button option.

You may have noticed this feature, unique to cardinal patches. Extending the grid is one row of vertices bordering the surface, on each of its four outer edges, connected at the corners. These control the tangency of the splines through the edge vertices. I've started calling them *phantom points*, because they aren't part of the surface. You need to pay attention to them in the aforementioned conversion cycle. If you have changed the position of the edge very much, that polygonal mesh won't help you to reposition these phantom vertices. You can touch it up pretty easily.

You should be aware that a cardinal patch sphere is actually an open cylinder. The poles appear to be smooth and unbroken, because all the points on the surface edge are congruent at the pole, but that isn't all. Each phantom point in an even-numbered cardinal sphere starts out congruent with the vertex adjacent to the pole, on the side opposite the direction from which it came. Moving one of the phantom points that define the tangency of each longitude line, from the pole through its next latitude, immediately changes the shape near the pole on the opposite side. Choosing an uneven number of rows when creating a cardinal sphere places the phantom vertices near, but not on, those surface points. This also happens if you add a row to an extant sphere. In this case, it makes sense to add rows in pairs.

Phantom points can be used to make two adjacent cardinal grids light smoothly across their borders, as if they are one surface. Unlike two imperfectly aligned NURBS surfaces, a cardinal can be offset from another, with a few rows extending past its neighbor. As long as the phantom vertices maintain congruency with the vertex opposite its border and its opposite number does the same, no seams will be visible. They will light as if they are one surface. This can be handy if you're comfortable using cardinals for your finished object and you want to avoid using active blends. You can obtain a high degree of control with this, in a manner not too unlike Hash splines, and still use UV texture maps. It can be really tough to keep track of all those phantom points when it's time to weight the vertices during animation setup.

Start with a primitive, usually a low-detail sphere made with a cardinal patch. Change it into a cylinder, by deleting the poles and the next latitude row, and you'll have a small number of points that you can tag and translate until it assumes the shape you want. You'll need to use curve controls with U and V edge visibility toggled on so that you can put the start/end edge where you want it, generally at the point of symmetry on the XY axis. A cardinal patch has the advantage (over NURBS or b-splines) of containing points that the spline surface passes through rather than near. It has the disadvantage of surfaces overshooting when points get too close. If your control points are getting to the point where they're that close, you should consider changing the surface type to NURBS. A cardinal patch can be changed to a NURBS or polygonal surface. A NURBS surface cannot be changed back to a cardinal surface, but it can be changed to a polygonal surface, first quads, then to triangles.

Creating Symmetry

There are several ways in Softimage to model one side of an object and see what it looks like in symmetry while modeling, without having to match tagged points. You can duplicate one side of the face using an instance and scale it -1 in the X axis. That will update while you work on the original, though adding or subtracting vertices, edges, or polygons should be done before you instance one side of the face. This is useful primarily for translating tagged vertices so that you can see the proportions properly. Of course, when it's time to finish the face properly, you'll have to remove the symmetry by working on the other side of the final mesh.

Strategies For Face Modeling

You'll achieve better results with a single mesh for the face. Facial expressions affect much of the face at the same time. If you're raising the corners of the mouth, you're also raising the cheeks, nostrils, eyelids, and associated wrinkles.

Multiple surfaces with blends connecting them, such as a separate nose, mouth, eyes, and mask, can be done but at the cost of isolating parts of the face that don't really behave by themselves.

Most cyber-scanned faces start with a regular grid, and you can achieve success with that same approach. You may achieve better success with a radial half sphere, radial from the opening of the mouth. The advantage is that natural folds can be defined with lines that already are where you need them.

Case Study: Modeling A Realistic Human Head In 3DS MAX

By Adam Pletcher

For our upcoming PC game, FreeSpace, we needed a quick-and-easy way to make high-detail CG heads for the many cinematics that will appear throughout the game. These heads not only have to look good, but they have to deform properly for the facial animation and lip sync. Following is a basic explanation of how I modeled my own head in MAX.

I started by taking two reference photographs of myself, using an ordinary 35mm camera (see Figure 6.10). I then took the film to a local photo lab and had it developed onto a Kodak Photo-CD. These two photos served as the only real-world reference for the head.

I needed to work with the reference photos close-up, so I created two perpendicular boxes in MAX and applied them as textures in the realtime viewport. This has an advantage over using Background Images, because it enables you to zoom in/out of the details.

INCREASING VIEWPORT RESOLUTION

By adding GFXTexSize=1024 under the [Performance] section of your 3DSMAX.INI file, you can greatly increase the viewport resolution used for realtime textures like this one. This adds a small speed penalty to your viewport, but it can also accept smaller powers of 2.

Using Edit Spline 2 (part of Surface Tools by Peter Watje, available from Digimation) and the standard MAX spline tools, I created a grid of splines in the front viewport. From a side viewport, I then pulled the vertices back into the scene, attempting to match the contours on the side reference photo. One thing I wanted to avoid here was to put too much detail into the splines. I only made lines for the major contours of the face and for details around the eyelids and lips. The final spline head can be seen in Figure 6.11.

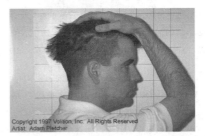

Figure 6.10 Front and side reference photos of Adam Pletcher.

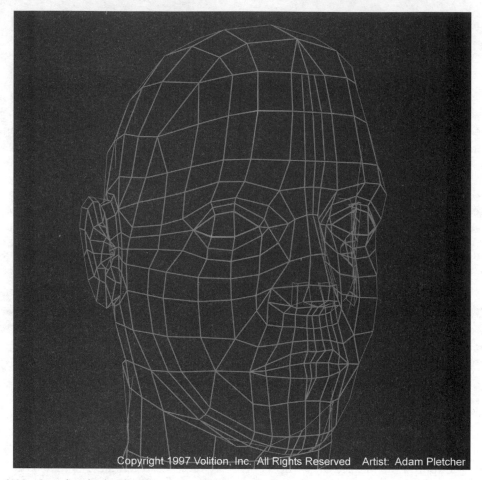

Figure 6.11 Completed spline head.

Next, I applied the Surface modifier (found in Surface Tools, mentioned earlier). It pays to keep a close eye on the Step setting. You want to use the lowest setting you can get away with, dependent on the amount of detail you'd like in the final polygon mesh. The resulting polygon-based head can be seen in Figure 6.12. At this point, I went back and made many small tweaks to the splines until it looked as accurate as possible.

When the mesh was finalized, I applied a cylindrical UVW Map modifier to the whole head. I fit the cylinder gizmo as close as possible to the head, keeping the seam in the back. I then applied an Unwrap to the head, using the freeware plug-in by Peter Watje (see Chapter 9 for details). This created a bitmap with gridlines, as shown in Figure 6.13, onto which I could place texture details.

Using Photoshop 4, I then used the original reference photos to place texture details over the gridlines shown in the Unwrap bitmap. I used the Rubber Stamp tool heavily and was careful to avoid using blurring tools, such as Smudge. I wanted to keep the realistic grain

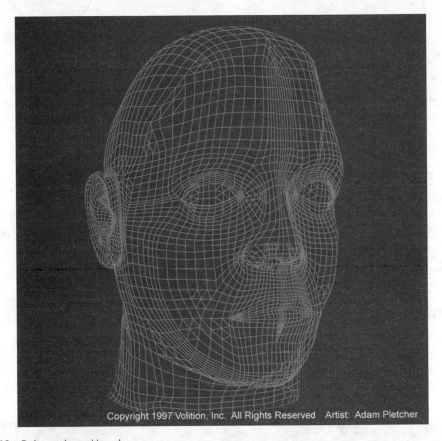

Figure 6.12 Polygon-based head.

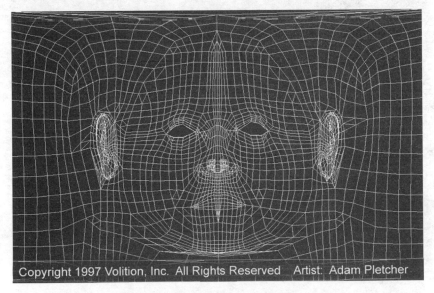

Figure 6.13 Unwrapped bitmap template for texture map placement.

of the skin intact. The resulting texture was then used as the Diffuse Map for the head material, as shown in Figure 6.14. From this texture, I generated bitmaps to use as Bump and Shininess maps in the same head material.

I made several minor changes to the textures until they lined up exactly the way I wanted. The result can be seen in Figure 6.15. The whole modeling and texturing process only took about 24 hours of work. Once we had a base head to work from, we were able to reshape it into other heads in even less time. From there, the heads went to our character animators for use in the FreeSpace cut scenes.

*Adam Pletcher has worked for Volition, Inc./Parallax Software for four years as a Lead Artist. He did a great deal of 2D and 3D artwork for their first two games, Descent and Descent 2, published by Interplay Productions. He's largely self-taught, having graduated from Purdue University in 1993 with a BS in Computer Technology. Adam can be reached at **adam@volition-inc.com**.*

Roughing Out A Reference Figure

If you start with a cube, you can turn it into any shape you need. Pull up a primitive polygonal cube. You'll use only a handful of polygonal tools, so familiarize yourself with them now. Use the vertex tool to add a vertex to any point on an edge depending on where you left-click. Middle-clicking adds a vertex at the midpoint of the edge. Right-clicking deletes the edge, which

Figure 6.14 Diffuse texture map.

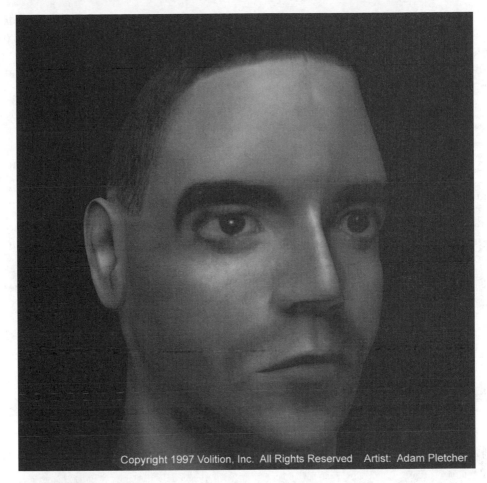

Figure 6.15 Final head.

can have varying results depending on how many edges are attached to it. Using the edge tool allows you to connect two vertices that share a face with a left-click on each vertex. If you have quite a few vertices you'd like to string edges across, you can middle-click until the last vertex.

Select a face, and, in Polygon mode (as opposed to Obj or Tag mode), duplicate it, and translate it. You have lofted that polygon's shape from the body it occupied, with edges connecting each new vertex of the new polygon to the original body.

Take your cube, and add vertices to the midpoint of each of the vertical edges. Connect them with four new edges, so that your cube now has an equator. Scale it up in Y and down in Z so that it is roughly torso shaped. Freeze the scaling operation in effect, and then use the rounding operation, also in the Effect menu, using the default value of 0.5. You should now have a rounded lozenge affair, divided roughly in thirds.

Now, select Tag, so that any scaling or translation will apply only to tagged vertices rather than the whole object, and make sure you've selected Global rather than Drag. Tag vertices (using the T hotkey), and scale the lower third so that it's more like a pelvic shape, and move other points to where they need to be for a chest area. Loft polys for the arms, legs, and head, and you're set.

PROJECT 6.1 Turning A Cube Into A Superhero

In this project, start with a cube, and slowly res it up as you go. Add detail where you need it. Grab polygons, and duplicate them to add arms, legs, and a neck. Cut polys as you need them to define the shape as you go. Refer to Figures 6.16 through 6.25 as a guide, as you work your way through the process.

Be sure to take advantage of rounding tagged vertices when appropriate, rather than rounding the entire object, so you can get additional detail where you want it without overcomplicating the object.

Pay attention to what happens when you bevel selected areas to maintain harder edges that you don't want to lose when you round up your object.

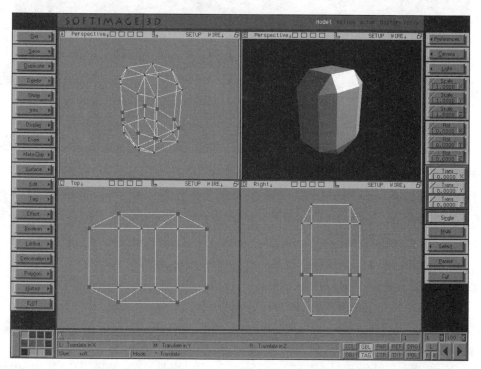

Figure 6.16 Round a polygonal cube, add vertices at the midpoints of the eight edges, connect, tag, and translate them down.

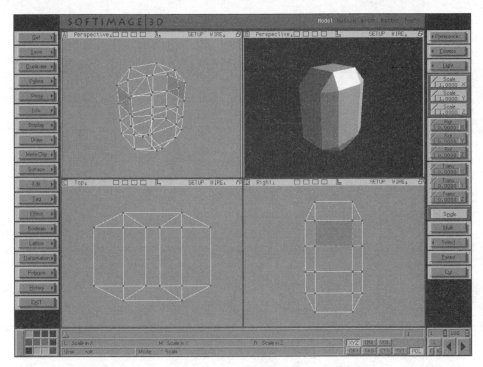

Figure 6.17   Add one more edge row, select polygon mode, and find the faces you'll extrude for arms and legs.

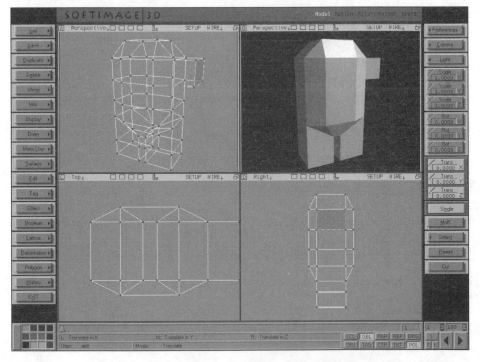

Figure 6.18   Extrude a selected face in polygon mode by duplicating and translating it.

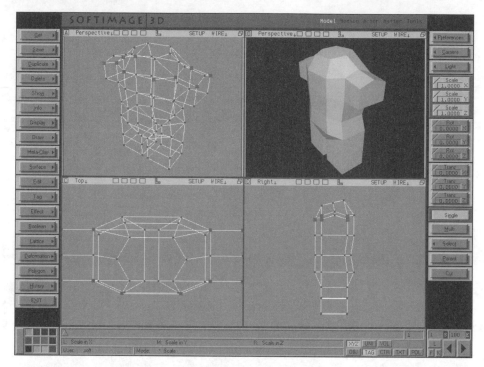

Figure 6.19 Add edges tag vertices and globally translate them.

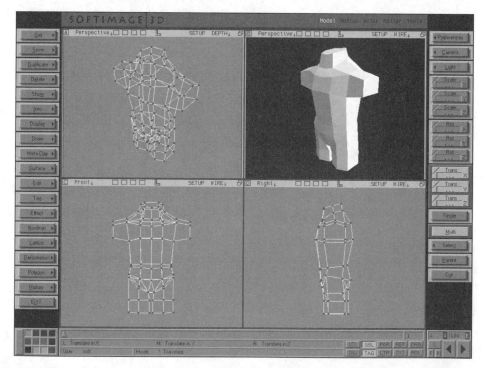

Figure 6.20 A bit blocky, though it's ready for texturing if you're making a 3D game.

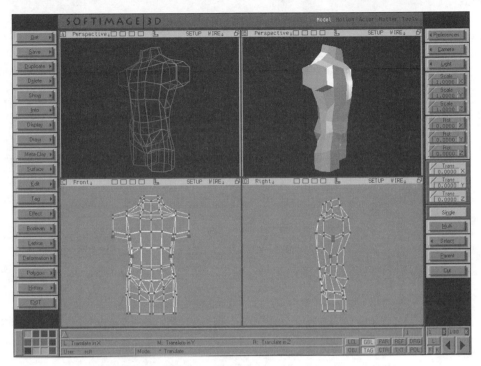

Figure 6.21   It's easier to rough out proportions with just a little more detail.

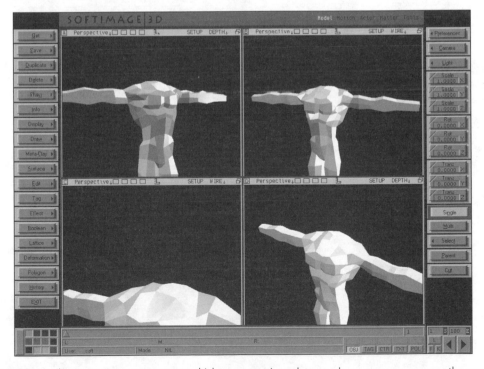

Figure 6.22   At this stage, it starts to matter which way you triangulate quads, as you can see near the armpit.

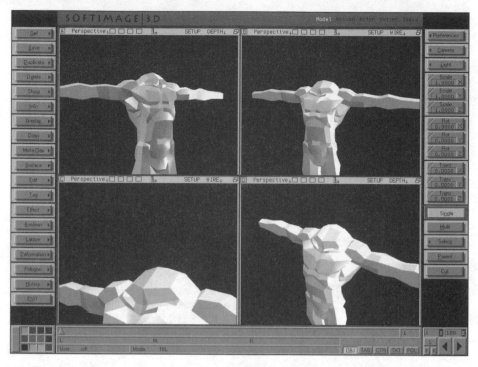

Figure 6.23 Stylize and exaggerate the abstract idea of superheroic musculature.

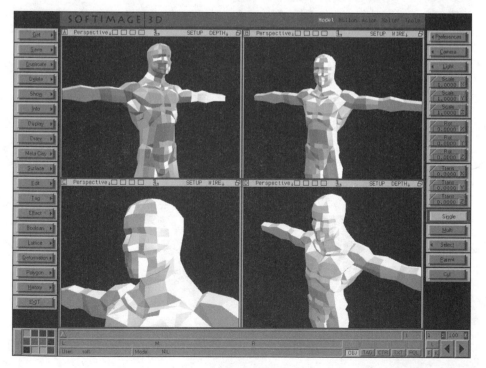

Figure 6.24 Move vertices around on a polygonal sphere for a head, merge it, and weld it.

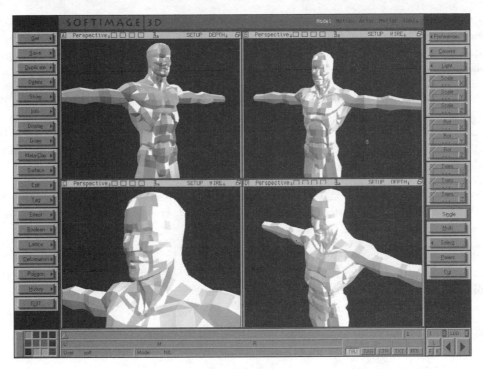

Figure 6.25 Slap on a mask and a catchy Icon on his leotards, after you've modeled the hands.

Case Study: Modeling The Iguana Using LightWave's MetaNURBS

By Kim Oravecz

I started by creating a rectangular shaped box (using the box primitive in LightWave) with seven segments on Z, three segments on Y, and five segments on X. I used

Figure 6.26 Kim Oravecz's You "Wanna Iguana?"

LightWave's MetaNURBS to create the entire body, tail, arms, legs, fingers, and head as one seamless object. The spikes on his back were added later, after I froze the object by Boolean-adding the spikes one at a time. Well, sometimes two or three at a time, to speed things up.

The legs and arms were created by using the bevel tool to pull out polygons from the side of the body portion of the object. You could also use LightWave's smooth shift tool, as well. The fingers and toes were created the same way, by beveling out polygons off of the hands and feet. And the claws were beveled out of the ends of the fingers and toes and then shaped into a point.

Once all of this was complete, I froze the MetaNURBS object to make it a polygonal object. I no longer had to keep all the polygons four sided. This is when I created the spike object and Boolean-added them down his back.

After I completed the spikes and did some other tweaking here and there, I realized that, if I animate him, I may want his mouth to open and close. But I had Boolean-added the spikes, and the object was no longer made up of just four-sided polygons. So, how was I going to create the inside of his mouth?

Well, I remembered a little article that I had read in *3D Artist* on how someone had created the inside of a dolphin's mouth using Boolean operations. So, I set out to do the same thing.

To create the Boolean object, I decided to paint a grayscale image to be used as a displacement map on top of a subdivided cube object to create the shape of the inside of the mouth. Refer to Figure 6.27 to see how I painted it.

I created a cube in Modeler and subdivided the heck out of the top polygon of the cube. I brought that object into Layout and applied my mouth map as a displacement map on

Figure 6.27 Displacement mouth map.

top of the cube (with the texture axis on Y). This displaced the polygons on the top of the cube to form the inside of the bottom jaw of the iguana. I went into the objects panel and did a Save Transformed.

I loaded that object into a background layer in Modeler and lined it up with the bottom portion of the iguana's head, so I could do the Boolean intersect operation to give me the bottom jaw (refer to Figure 6.28). The Boolean intersect gave me just the bottom jaw portion of the iguana object.

Back in Layout, I did a negative displacement map on the subdivided cube object to create a template for the top portion of the inside of the mouth. I did another Save Transformed on the cube object, brought it into a background layer of Modeler, lined it up in the same spot where the previous mouth_template was, and then did a Boolean-subtract. This subtracted the bottom jaw portion of the iguana and left behind the rest of the iguana object with the upper portion of the inside of the mouth carved out (refer to Figure 6.29).

For the mouth in a closed position, I saved the lower jaw portion and the upper body/ mouth portion of the iguana as one object. To create the open mouth iguana object, I brought both the lower jaw and the upper portion of the iguana into Layout. I used bones to open the mouth. I then saved the lower jaw object in layout by using Save Transformed. In Modeler, I brought in both objects and saved them together as one object. It was then just a matter of using morph targets between the two objects to open and close the mouth.

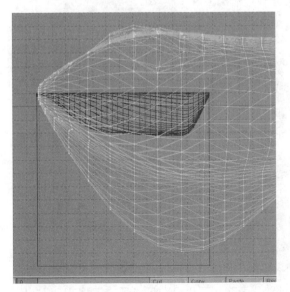

Figure 6.28 Boolean intersect for bottom jaw.

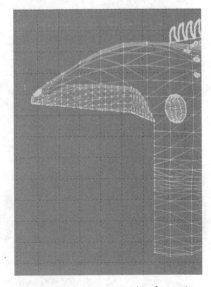

Figure 6.29 Upper inside of mouth carved out.

Case Study: Modeling Organic Characters Using LightWave's Metaform

By Bill Fleming

All images copyright 1997 Bill Fleming/Komodo Studio. Images created by Bill Fleming, 3D Chaotician, Komodo Studio.

Figure 6.30 Frankenstein's Monster. 89,000 polygons (tripled), 8 hours to model and surface. Head is surfaced with image maps, body is procedural. Created for a promotional animation.

I created these three characters in LightWave 5 using Metaform. Metaform gives you better control of the modeling process, because it doesn't exhaust your video resources. You can simply create the low resolution model and periodically Metaform it to check the results.

Many people prefer to use MetaNURBS, but I have found this is not the best way to create organic characters in LightWave. The MetaNURBS function tends to be very sluggish when working with high-detail models. Unless you have a 30MB video card, you are

Figure 6.31 Robby the Rabbit. 35,000 polygons (tripled), 6 hours to model and surface, fully procedural surfacing. Created for an animated short film.

Figure 6.32   Tommy the Gangster. 125,000 polygons (tripled), 15 hours to model and surface. Head is surfaced with image maps. The body is procedural. Created for fun.

better off working with Metaform. Another drawback to using MetaNURBS is the ridiculous exaggeration you have to apply to create features. Metaform works much better, because you can work with more polygons. This means your low-resolution model closely resembles the final Metaform output—it just lacks the smoothing.

When using Metaform, I build a low-resolution version of the model, then apply Metaform to add the detail and smooth the mesh. I typically start with the character's head. Always try to use quad polygons with Metaform. You can use tri's and even larger point counts with the MetaformPlus plug-in, but the effect of Metaform is more natural with quads. I create the head from a simple six-sided cube. I Metaform it twice to add polygons and smooth the cube, then center it along the X axis and cut it in half. I prefer to model a character one half at a time, then mirror it and merge the points along the seam. I create features by dragging the points on the cube until they resemble the outline of the feature, then smooth shift the polygons to add depth to the feature.

USING SMOOTH SHIFT

Always set the smooth shift value to zero. A larger setting will create nonplanar polygons if the source polygons are not parallel to an axis. Once you have smooth shifted them, you can drag, scale, and move the new polygons to the desired placement.

For example, I create a nose by dragging points on the front of the mesh until the outline looks like a nose. Then, I smooth shift those polygons to extrude the nose mesh. I add detail to the features by selecting groups of polygons and smooth shifting them. After I smooth shift them, I move the polygons and scale them until I get the look I want. Typically, I'll put the mesh through two instances of Metaform to add polygons for detail. My models usually end up being around 100K polygons, after I triple them.

PREVENTING NONPLANAR POLYGONS

Always triple the polygons before you import them in Layout. You can get many nonplanar polygon errors in organic shapes when using quad polygons.

I create features such as ears, body, and so forth separately and manually weld them to the main mesh. I never use the Boolean operations to add body parts—that process creates a non-uniform mesh which is very difficult to edit and impossible to Metaform. A non-uniform mesh is also very difficult to animate with Bones since it causes unusual pinching problems. You are better off manually welding the points of the two objects. This will keep the polygons as quads, which will allow you to properly Metaform the object.

Mapping Patches Onto Polygons

Now that you have a figure that is nearly a black cloud of vertices, you probably wouldn't want to weight them for animation. You've got a virtual maquette, and you can now take a cardinal surface and use magnet points to snap vertices to the shape you're now digitizing.

Snap points on the cardinal surface to points on the maquette, add or subtract detail as necessary. Now, you can focus on the properties of the new surface without worrying at all about defining its shape.

It isn't all that often that you need a single NURBS surface for a naked humanoid, so costuming is your friend. Of course, if you're making a superhero like Doctor Manhattan from *The Watchmen*, you'll want to use active blends to connect trimmed surfaces.

Why, Where, And What To Trim

You may want to build a torso and arms (worrying about the pelvis and neck/head later) out of a closed cardinal sphere with its open poles at the wrists. You'll need to watch your curve controls to make sure that the remaining longitudinal edge is placed properly, for two reasons. If you place that edge across the neck area on the top or the pelvis area on the bottom, you won't be able to trim the sphere where you need to attach those parts. Also, UV mapping of textures is easier if you use a natural-looking place for what amounts to a seam. Try the line at the bottom edge of the pectorals, and follow out to the inside of the arm.

Strategies For NURBS Hand Modeling

Place the NURBS sphere on its side, with one pole opened for the thumb. Trimming at the wrist and four fingers, making sure the start/end edge is in the palm—a life line. Fingers are open cylinders, connected with active blends. Use relational modeling to close fingers with a finger-nail (rather than trimming a hole in the finger for the nail and giving yourself mapping troubles with the convergence to a pole at the tip of the fingers also). Scaling -1 on X for the other hand introduces inversion problems on objects with trims on the surface, so curve controls need to be used to fix that.

Vertex And Face Density And Placement

No matter how powerful your computer, you will always be negotiating a balance between rendering speed, level of detail, hard drive space, and memory requirements. As the old joke goes, if you're not running out of memory, your scene isn't complicated enough.

Part of that balancing act is determining how many polygons you need and how many you can afford. More polygons will generally respond to mesh-deforming animation tools with better interpolation and will also render curves more smoothly. Fewer polygons will redraw faster, use less memory, and be easier to edit when necessary.

One way to control the complexity of a character's objects is to place the polygons exactly where you need them. Some parts of a character need very few polygons and other areas need more. Shoes, mid-sleeves, or mid-legs with little or no motion or deformation can get by with fewer polygons, while joints and flexible masses of soft tissue will require more subdivisions.

The following section discusses modeling approaches for features common to most characters.

Eyes: Realistic

For animating dilated pupils, you have two basic choices: a set of image maps with a variety of pupil sizes or a pupil opening that can be animated with either a bone or Replacment setup. I personally prefer to assign a bone to the points defining the circumference of the pupil and rotate the bone. This makes the opening close like a mechanical or camera iris, but it swirls any image map applied to the iris polygons.

If you're willing to compromise, the eyeballs modeled for the Chapter 9 projects are adequate for a learning exercise. The pupil and iris are modeled as ordinary surfaces, and the eyeball itself is just a pair of slightly modified nested spheres. An hour's tweaking could turn them into really nice eyes, if you're up to the challenge.

You can set up the eyes to simply rotate using keyframes, but I think that's inefficient for the animator. I prefer setting up eyes to use inverse kinematics to automatically track a null object. This makes it easy for the animator to keep the character's eyes lined up with another object in the scene. See Chapter 11 for details.

Eyelids: Realistic

The simplest approach is to treat the eyelids as hemispheres and allow them to interpenetrate the face. The seam along the penetration will show but appropriate texture maps can partially disguise it. This makes animation a breeze.

Eyes: Cartoon

You can model the iris and pupil for a caricature as the same corneal bulge you'd use on a realistic eyeball, but I prefer a simple flattened sphere object, imbedded just less than halfway in the sclera. This shape is more forgiving of alignment problems. If you position it a little too high or too low in the sclera, the difference is not glaringly obvious. Most cartoon characters can get by with a simple black pupil, but others look better with an iris. You will rarely need realistic refraction in a cartoon pupil, so I recommend using image map sequences to animate any pupil dilation. If you are using a solid black iris, you can simply scale it.

PROJECT 6.2

Model And Set Up A Cartoon Eye

1. Modify a copy of your character's head to give it cartoon eyes, or create a new character head from scratch. Delete the eyeball and eyelid surface points. Add a new ovoid surface for each sclera. Define the sclera as a surface.

2. Model an iris and pupil. Define them as a separate surface.

3. Set up the new eyes. You will probably have to set up the iris so it can be moved in or out as well as rotated around the sclera's center, to keep it on the eye's surface.

This isn't as easy to animate as the spherical eyeball, but you can create some great classic cartoon effects with it.

Eyelids: Cartoon

If the sclera shape of a cartoon eye is irregular or distorted, a morph or weighted shape sequence of hand-modeled target objects is the only reliable way to conform the eyelids to the eyeballs.

Start modeling the eyelids with the fully closed version. It's easier to compress the longer, complete eyelid to cover only a third of the eye than to stretch a one-third eyelid over an irregular eyeball shape. Fortunately, most eyelid movement is nearly a straight, vertical line and rapid enough that in-between errors are very small. Relatively few target objects are required, even if you build a model library that includes all the emotional reactions. If you keep the face symmetric, you should be able to model just one side's eyelids, then scale the entire library by -1 to create a matching library for the other side.

Model Cartoon Eyelids

PROJECT 6.3

Model a simple set of eyelids to match the eyes you created in the preceding project. The minimum library includes objects for the following eyelid positions: fully closed, just above halfway open, normal rest position, and wide open.

Modifying Models For Morphing

Modeling for Replacement animation is possibly the most restrictive task a modeler or TD has to perform. The rigid requirements of identical point and polygon count and distribution automatically exclude most of your modeling tools. If you make a mistake and add or delete a point, the difficulty of re-matching the point order pretty much guarantees that you've ruined the object. You should therefore limit your modeling operations to tools that move points without adding or deleting them.

Which tools you can use depend on your modeling software. In LightWave, you can safely use all the Modify panel functions in Modeler: Move, Rotate, Size, Stretch, Drag, Shear, Twist, Taper 1 and 2, Bend, Magnet, Vortex, and Pole 1 and 2. If you are careful and consistent in setting them up, you can get away with using Patch, Skin, Morph, and other functions in the Multiply panel. Be warned, any change in the settings will produce an object with incompatible point and polygon counts and ordering. You can also use MetaNURBS, if the source object and the Freeze polygonal detail settings remain the same.

One advantage morph modeling has over other forms is that (depending on your software) you get to use setup and animation tools, as well. Some programs enable you to freeze animated changes to the model, automatically creating a compatible morph target. In LightWave, the Save Transformed function will save a copy of the currently selected object from the current frame, including all position, attitude, size, Metamorph, Bones deformation, and displacement map changes to the object's geometry. This means you can use nearly any Layout function to modify an object, then save those changes in a permanent snapshot that will morph perfectly with the original object. This opens up a lot of opportunities that would be difficult or nearly impossible in Modeler. Before you get too excited, there is a drawback to using Layout for creating model libraries. The UV mapping coordinates are not saved with the same deformations. If you apply a map to an object, deform that object with Bones or other Layout tools, and save it in its deformed state, the map will not match the original. The only available workaround is to use the original object as the root of the MTSE or Metamorph chain. Because the mapping coordinates and other surface parameters are not transformed, the mapping and surfaces of the rest of the object libraries don't matter.

Problems like this make it doubly important that you keep a clean copy of the original object somewhere safe. You will be using working copies all the time to create new objects, and it's entirely too easy to inadvertently save over the original. There's nothing like trying to reconstruct an original from a lot of transformed copies to remind you to be more careful.

PROJECT 6.4 Building Morph Targets Using LightWave's Save Transformed

This project shows how I built the desk lamp morph targets used in Chapter 11 and demonstrates one way to model morph targets using Bones deformation and the Save Transformed function. The goal of this project is to build 31 compatible morph target objects. These objects can then be used with Replacement animation tools to animate the original object. (See Chapter 11 for details on Replacement animation tools.)

1. Clear the scene. We don't want anything interfering with saving clean transformed copies of the original object, and we don't need any elaborate lighting setups to help us with this particular set of transformations.

2. Load the DESKLMP.LWO object from this book's CD-ROM. This will be our original object. All the Metamorph target objects will be deformed versions of this lamp. Make sure it is positioned at the origin, 0, 0, 0. It is usually easier to manage objects that are modeled around the origin, and all the copies you are about to make will automatically inherit any displacement.

3. Adjust your views to give an adequate side view of the lamp, as in Figure 6.33.

4. Click on the Objects button. The Objects Panel appears.

5. Click on the Object Skeleton button. A panel appears with the heading *Skeleton for "Desklmp.lwo."*

6. The Current Bone button shows the word *none*, because there are no Bones in the scene yet. Click on the Add Bone button. The Current Bone button changes to read *Bone*. Click on the Rename Bone button. The Bone1 Name Panel appears. Type in the new name "BaseBone," and press Enter.

7. Repeat Step 6 to add the first SpineBone, then press p twice, to close the Skeleton and Objects panels. You will see the two new Bones you just added, with both their axes at the origin and so closely overlapping that they look like a single Bone.

8. Click on the Bones button. The name of the Bone you most recently created appears in the Selected Item pop-up, and the Bone is highlighted in the current view. Now is a good time to save the scene, just in case.

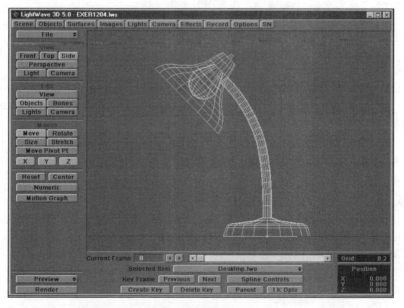

Figure 6.33 Side view of DESKLMP.LWO, before transforms.

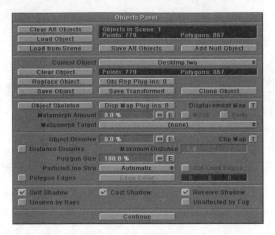

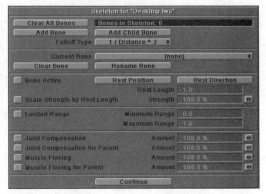

Figure 6.34 Objects Panel, with DESKLMP.LWO selected as Current Object.

Figure 6.35 Skeleton panel for DESKLMP.LWO.

9. Choose BaseBone from the Selected Item pop-up list. Select Rest Length from the Mouse area, and press N to call up the numeric data entry panel for Rest Length. Change it to 0.4, and press Enter to accept the change.

10. Select Rotate from the Mouse area, and press n again to call up the numeric Rotate panel. Change Pitch to 90, but leave the Heading and Bank settings at zero. Press Enter to close the panel and accept the changes.

11. Select Move from the Mouse area, and press n again to call up the numeric Bone Position panel. Change the Y value to -0.02, but leave the X and Z settings at zero. Press Enter to close the panel and accept the changes.

    These changes should put the BaseBone in about the position shown in Figure 6.36.

12. Create a keyframe for BaseBone at frame 0, then press r to set the Bone's rest position. While BaseBone is still active, press p to call up the Skeleton panel.

    For the models we are about to make, you will want the lamp base to remain absolutely solid while the neck does the bending. You can lock down the vertices near a Bone by setting the Bone's Minimum value.

13. Turn on the Limited Range toggle button. Change the Minimum Range to 0.1 and the Maximum Range to 0.5. Press Enter, then press p to save the changes and close the panel.

    These changes mean that any vertex in the lamp that is closer than 0.1 units to the BaseBone will not be influenced at all by any other Bone, and that any vertex between 0.1 units and 0.5 units will be affected by both BaseBone and any other Bone(s) with an overlapping area of influence.

14. Repeat Steps 9 through 13 for SpineBone. Set the Rest Length to 0.044. Position the SpineBone at coordinates 0.0, 0.081, 0.0, with a Pitch of 266 degrees and Heading and Bank of zero. Leave Limited Range off. You should end up with something like Figure 6.37.

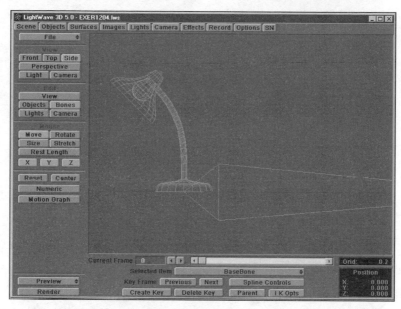

Figure 6.36   Side view of DESKLMP.LWO, with Bones added.

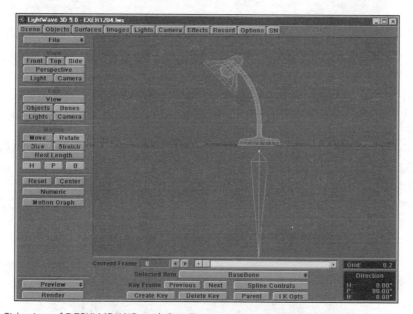

Figure 6.37   Side view of DESKLMP.LWO, with BaseBone positioned and Rest Length set.

Obviously, one SpineBone won't be enough, if you want a smooth bend to the lamp's neck. Let's add a few more SpineBones.

15. With SpineBone selected, press p to call up the Bones panel. Click on the Add Child Bone button.

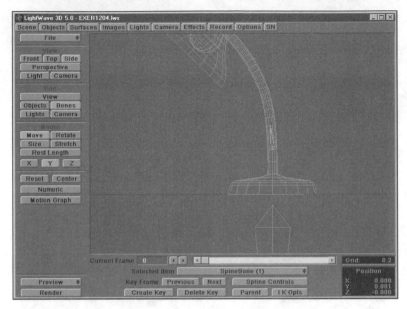

Figure 6.38 Side view of DESKLMP.LWO, with SpineBone positioned and Rest Length set.

This adds another Bone, but automatically Parented to SpineBone and with all SpineBone's settings. The new Bone is also automatically given the Parent Bone's name, with a number after it in parentheses. You should see *SpineBone(2)* listed as the Current Bone in the Skeleton panel, as in Figure 6.38.

16. Click on the Add Child Bone button four more times, to add a chain of Child Bones up to SpineBone(6). Make each new Child Bone inactive, and close the Skeleton panel when you are finished.

17. Change the Rest Length of the last Child, SpineBone(6), to 0.036. Change the pitch of SpineBone(2) and SpineBone(6) to 5 degrees, and SpineBone(3), SpineBone(4), and SpineBone(5) to 10 degrees. This should keep them close to the centerline of the lamp neck, as in Figure 6.39, with the tip of SpineBone(6) near the centerline of the lamp shade.

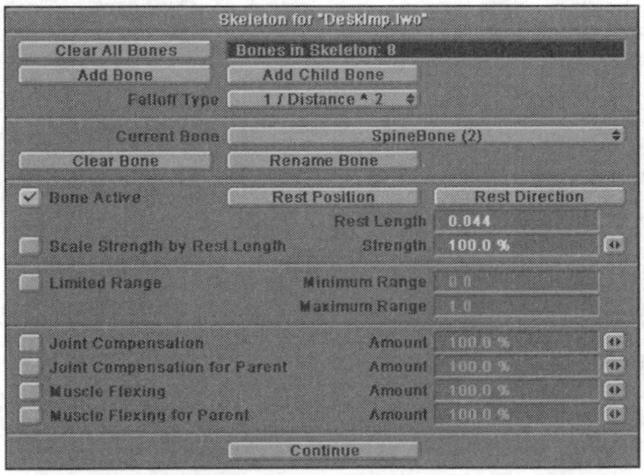

Figure 6.39 Skeleton panel after adding a Child Bone to SpineBone.

18. Set a keyframe at frame 0 for everything. Activate all the Child Bones again, and save the scene.

19. Select SpineBone(6), and open the Skeleton panel again. Add another Child Bone, but change this one's name to ShadeBone.

20. You want ShadeBone to keep the lamp shade rigid while the neck is bent by the SpineBones, so set ShadeBone's Limited Range to On, and Minimum and Maximum both to 0.09. This radius will include the entire shade, as shown in Figure 6.40. Set the Rest Length to 0.4, the same as BaseBone. Make sure ShadeBone is still inactive, and close the Skeleton panel.

21. Set ShadeBone's Pitch to -90 degrees, but keep Heading and Bank at zero. Make a keyframe for ShadeBone, then press r to activate the Bone. Make a keyframe for all items at frame 0, and save the scene again.

At this point, you should have a fairly well-articulated desk lamp. You can bend the lamp neck by progressively rotating each SpineBone a few degrees at a time. BaseBone keeps the lamp base rigid, and ShadeBone does the same for the lamp shade.

As easy as that posing sounds, there may be times you want a particular angle to this lamp and you don't want to bother adding Bones and posing it. You can avoid that hassle by posing the lamp now, and using the Save Transformed function to take snapshots of each pose for later use. Let's give it a try.

22. From frame 0, create a new keyframe for all objects at frame 30. Move to frame 30.

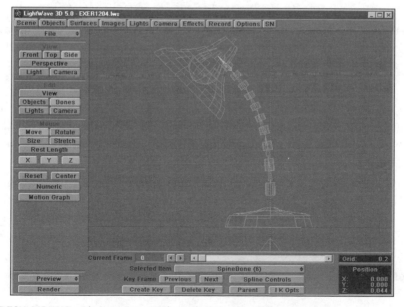

Figure 6.40   DESKLMP.LWO with SpineBone(1) through SpineBone(6) in position.

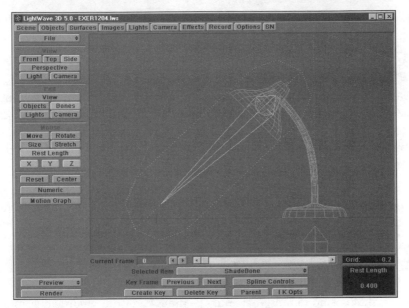

Figure 6.41 ShadeBone Limited Range includes the entire lampshade.

23. Bend the neck of the lamp over until it makes a smooth curve and the edge of the shade nearly touches ground level (see Figure 6.41). Be careful to change only the Pitch values for the SpineBones.

24. Create a new keyframe for all objects at frame 30. Save the scene file again.

25. Make a preview, and examine it critically. If the motion of the lamp bending over is not as smooth as you want it to be, readjust the SpineBones, and perhaps add some intermediate keyframes. Keep tweaking until you are happy with the preview results.

26. Create a new subdirectory in your default Objects directory to contain the new objects you are about to create.

27. Go to frame 0. Click on the Objects button. The Objects Panel appears. Because there is only one object in the scene, the lamp, Desklmp.lwo appears on the Current Object button.

28. Click on the Save Transformed button. A panel appears, warning you to change the file name for the new object to avoid overwriting the original. Save the new file in the directory you created in Step 26, with the name REPLAC00.LWO. Press Enter to close the File dialog, press p to close the Objects Panel, and press the right-arrow key to advance to the next frame.

29. Repeat Step 28 for frames 1 through 30, saving each object with the prefix REPLAC and the appropriate two-digit frame number.

You should end up with 31 compatible Metamorph target objects. If you would like to try them out, follow the directions in any or all of Projects 3.1 through 3.5, using your new objects instead of the objects provided on this book's CD-ROM.

As you can see, once you have a Boned object, it's relatively easy to create Metamorph targets from it by using the Save Transformed function.

Using SIMILAR

One of the difficulties with character animation using Metamorph objects is that modeling each object is time-consuming. Using object libraries is a big step forward, but you still have the problem of multiple actors in a scene. You don't want your characters to be identical; you want them to have unique, readily identifiable differences. But how can you afford the time to model even the most basic phonetic and emotional head objects for every new actor?

Together with Glenn Lewis, I've worked out one solution. Following this procedure lets you make manual changes to just one model, then a batch file and a utility program produce duplicates of all the compatible objects in your library with all your changes included.

Creating SIMILAR Batch Files To Build Custom Object Libraries

1. Select the baseline, or "normal," object from a library of morph objects.

For this example, I'll use the Strong Man normal head from Crestline Software's HU-MANOID model library. You can use any compatible objects you like—just make the file name substitutions in the following directions, where appropriate.

If you have no other Metamorph libraries available, you might use the REPLACXX series of desk lamp objects created in the preceding project or from the Chapter 11 directory on this book's CD-ROM.

2. Modify the normal object by using the Modeler and Layout tools that are legal for Metamorph objects.

Don't delete or add any points, because you must maintain exact point counts and arrangements for the objects to Metamorph properly.

To make my new character different, I enlarged the chin, sloped the forehead while exaggerating the eyebrow ridge, pushed the cheekbones out, and hollowed the cheeks. I also dragged the nose out and down slightly, then narrowed it. The end result was a decidedly unpleasant-looking character. That's Charley, in Figure 6.42.

The key to the rest of this process is a utility program called SIMILAR.EXE, written by Glenn Lewis. SIMILAR works with a number of file formats, including LightWave 3D. Basically, SIMILAR looks at the differences in point positions between objects A and B, and extrapolates those changes onto object C to create the new object, D. For example, the command line

```
SIMILAR normal.lwo anger.lwo charley.lwo charangr.lwo
```

compares the normal head to the ANGER morph object, then applies those changes to CHARLEY to produce Charley with an angry expression (see Figure 6.43).

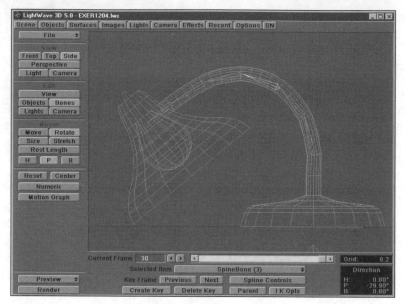

Figure 6.42 DESKLMP.LWO posed using SpineBones.

The following FACECOPY.BAT batch file I've written uses SIMILAR to create duplicates of all the Strong Man head objects, modified according to the changes in the head model named CHARLEY. This allows you to make whatever changes you like to CHARLEY, then automatically produce all 15 HUMANOID head objects with the same parameters:

```
REM FACECOPY.BAT
REM USES SIMILAR.EXE TO CONVERT HUMANOID HEADS TO CHARLEY PATTERN
SIMILAR.EXE NORMAL.LWO FEAR.LWO CHARLEY.LWO CHARFEAR.LWO
SIMILAR.EXE NORMAL.LWO ANGER.LWO CHARLEY.LWO CHARANGR.LWO
SIMILAR.EXE NORMAL.LWO STERN.LWO CHARLEY.LWO CHARSTRN.LWO
SIMILAR.EXE NORMAL.LWO SURPRISE.LWO CHARLEY.LWO CHARSURP.LWO
SIMILAR.EXE NORMAL.LWO SADNESS.LWO CHARLEY.LWO CHARSAD.LWO
SIMILAR.EXE NORMAL.LWO SMILE.LWO CHARLEY.LWO CHARSMIL.LWO
SIMILAR.EXE NORMAL.LWO GRIN.LWO CHARLEY.LWO CHARGRIN.LWO
SIMILAR.EXE NORMAL.LWO CRYING.LWO CHARLEY.LWO CHARCRYG.LWO
SIMILAR.EXE NORMAL.LWO 1CLOSED.LWO CHARLEY.LWO CHARCLOS.LWO
SIMILAR.EXE NORMAL.LWO 2PARTED.LWO CHARLEY.LWO CHARPART.LWO
SIMILAR.EXE NORMAL.LWO 3PRTOPEN.LWO CHARLEY.LWO CHARPRTO.LWO
SIMILAR.EXE NORMAL.LWO 4OPEN.LWO CHARLEY.LWO CHAROPEN.LWO
SIMILAR.EXE NORMAL.LWO 5WIDE.LWO CHARLEY.LWO CHARWIDE.LWO
SIMILAR.EXE NORMAL.LWO 6GAPE.LWO CHARLEY.LWO CHARGAPE.LWO
SIMILAR.EXE NORMAL.LWO 7PUCKER.LWO CHARLEY.LWO CHARPUCK.LWO
```

To create other characters, you'll need to use a text editor to edit the batch file.

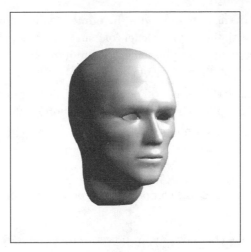

Figure 6.43 Strong Man normal head object modified to create Charley.

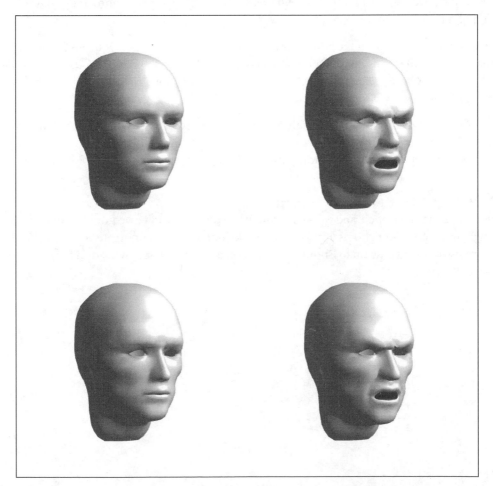

Figure 6.44 Normal compared to Anger, and the differences applied to Charley to produce an angry Charley.

3. Replace **CHARLEY** in the batch file with the name of your character, and **CHAR**, in the objects' names, with the first four letters of your character's name. You also need to replace the Strong Man normal, phoneme, and emotion object names with the appropriate object names from the library of your normal baseline.

   For example, to create a character named VICTORIA, first replace **CHARLEY.lwo** with **VICTORIA.lwo**, then replace **CHAR** with **VICT** throughout the batch file.

4. Copy FACECOPY.BAT, SIMILAR.EXE, DOS4GW.EXE, the object you modified in Step 2, and the object library to be used as a baseline to a temporary working directory.

5. Run the batch file.

   You should get a complete set of compatible morph objects, all with the changes you modeled in Sep 2.

If you later decide to make changes to your object, simply make the changes to the normal model, and run your modified FACECOPY.BAT again. It's fast enough that I've used it just to make minor tweaks. And every time you add an new object to your character's repertoire, you can add a line for it to the batch file.

SIMILAR can be used to make other morph objects, too. For example, you can put long fingernails on hand objects, or modify them into claws for that Halloween look. You can even modify torso objects to have collars, plackets, lapels, and buttons for an easy approach to clothing your characters.

SIMILAR and related utilities are available from Glenn Lewis, 8341 Olive Hill Court, Fair Oaks, CA 95628. Some of his programs are also available for the Amiga, so please specify which disk formats you prefer. For further details, see the GLEWIS directory on this book's CD-ROM.

Moving On

If you've read this chapter and worked through the projects, you've acquired a good familiarity with character modeling tools. If you expect to do high-end work or are just curious about what the professionals use, go on to Chapter 7 for a look at digitizers, scanners, and the software that goes with them.

TOOLS

Modeling characters for animation requires that you go beyond the standard tools. You need to know how to digitize a maquette or life cast, work with laser-scan data, and make a heavy mesh more efficient to set up and animate.

Chapter 5 discusses procedures for sculpting a character maquette from Sculpey or other modeling clays. Sculpting is appropriate for caricature or creature modeling, but not for digital stuntmen. Sculpting a perfect replica of a recognizable actor is an art in itself. If you need to make a photo-realistic character from a live subject, you'll be better off using either life casting or laser scanning techniques.

Making casts from life is a craft with a centuries-long history, and the procedures are well-defined. The only refinements have been the development of new casting materials that make the process faster, easier, and more reliable for the artist, and less stressful on the subject. You can still make an acceptable cast from plaster of paris applied directly to the subject's face, but much better options are available.

The following section is a quick, practical overview of the basic life casting process for a face. However, if you are planning to make a life cast, I recommend you contact Monster Makers. This company carries just about any tool, material, or guide you may find useful in making life casts or life-size maquettes in clay, plastic, latex, or plaster. Their primary business is making latex masks for motion picture special effects, so their expertise in full-head life casting is extensive. They are very knowledgeable and helpful, and can guide you through the myriad of choices to find the procedures and materials that are right for your project. Even if you choose to make a traditional plaster cast with materials from your local hardware store, you should consider buying one of the Monster Maker books or videos as a guide. You can contact them at:

Monster Makers
7305 Detroit Ave.
Cleveland, OH 44102
Tel: 216-651-7739
Internet: www.monstermakers.com

Casting From Life

One of the best modern materials for life casting is alginate, a two-part liquid mixture that rapidly hardens into a tough, rubbery coating. There are several trade names for alginate, each product having different hardening and mixing qualities that suit it for specific jobs. Alginates are kinder to the subject's skin than plaster, set more rapidly, are less prone to air bubbles, and retain finer details. Alginate is also much nicer to facial hair; plaster tends to just pull it all out, including eyebrows, unless you thickly coat the hair with Vaseline. I deliberately trimmed my beard and hair very short before these casts were taken, and the alginate gave a faithful reproduction without pulling much hair. In fact, several areas around the chin and hairline were so completely penetrated by the alginate that the skin was reproduced perfectly while the hair wasn't reproduced at all. More commonly, you will have to cast subjects with longer hair. For these situations, you should carefully fit a bald cap over the subject's hair and tape it down without deforming or stretching the subject's skin.

Even though alginate comes off most surfaces cleanly, I recommend that you do all the molding and casting over a concrete floor, or that you put down a large tarp. These processes get messy, and a slip or spill can be disastrous in the wrong environment. A basement, garage, or industrial space is best. Office and computer environments are definitely off limits, as dust and liquids can damage or destroy equipment, furniture, and carpeting.

There are several ways to apply alginate. My personal preference (based on previous mistakes) is to use several layers. The first is a thin, slower-setting mix, painted on in a thin layer to avoid distorting the subject's face with the weight of the alginate. It's surprising how much the human face can distort under just a little pressure. For example, you should never take a life cast of a reclining subject if you can possibly avoid it. Gravity pulls down any loose mass of flesh, with an effect similar to a facelift. The change will be obvious to your audience, so you should always take a life cast in the same attitude you will use the final model. Similar problems result if you load a single, heavy layer of alginate onto a subject. The alginate itself can pull the cheeks down, stretch the eyebrows down over the eyelids, and generally make your subject look half-melted. Look at Figure 7.1 for an example of the distortion in a plaster positive cast from a mold made with a single heavy layer of alginate.

A thin first alginate layer also enables you to test the placement and securing of breathing tubes. You want to use tubes large enough for the subject to breathe easily, but not so thick that they distend the nostrils or markedly deform the lips. I recommend using plastic soda straws if

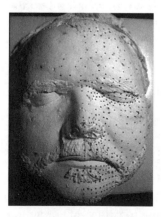

Figure 7.1   Casting Mistake #1: Plaster life cast showing the distortion of a too-heavy alginate application.

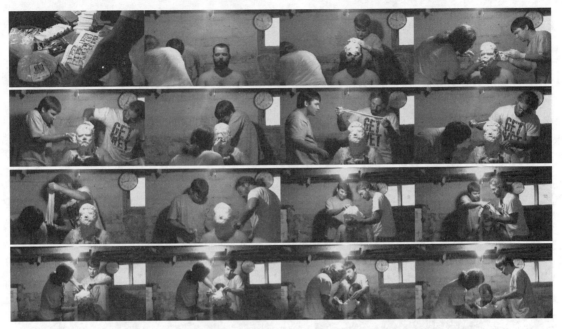

Figure 7.2 Making a life cast for a full head: assembling materials, applying alginate, applying plaster bandages, slitting back of mold, peeling mold off subject. Slitting the back of the mold to remove it makes it more difficult to get an accurate reproduction of the head's shape.

possible, as they separate easily from both alginate and plaster. Aside from the practical aspect of keeping your subject breathing, there is an important factor of trust and comfort, too. If your subject gets panicky or claustrophobic because they imagine they can't breathe, they will tear off the mold, and you will have to start all over.

From the subject's point of view, you can't blame them. I had my breathing tubes inadvertently blocked for about half a minute during the second mold for this chapter, and I was seconds away from ripping off the alginate when they finally cleared the tubes. Never joke around about the procedure, don't let anyone else do so, and keep up a cheerful, steady, loud chatter with your subject. Even with earplugs and a thick layer of alginate and plaster, they can hear you. Also, you might consider keeping a pad of paper and a pencil handy for them to write messages for anything more complex than "Yes" (thumbs up) or "No" (thumbs down).

Once the first layer of alginate is setting up, you can add a second, thicker layer. Reinforce the thinnest areas, especially around the nose, eyelids, lips, and breathing tubes, where the subject's movement may have disturbed the first layer. While the alginate layers are setting up, add layers of plaster bandages. The alginate remains rubbery and flexible—the plaster bandages will set up hard and rigid, supporting the alginate in the general shape of the subject's head. Layer the plaster bandages thickly enough to reinforce the alginate layers, making the whole assembly rigid. Too little plastering will allow the mold to spread out under the weight of the casting material, deforming the final cast (see Figure 7.4).

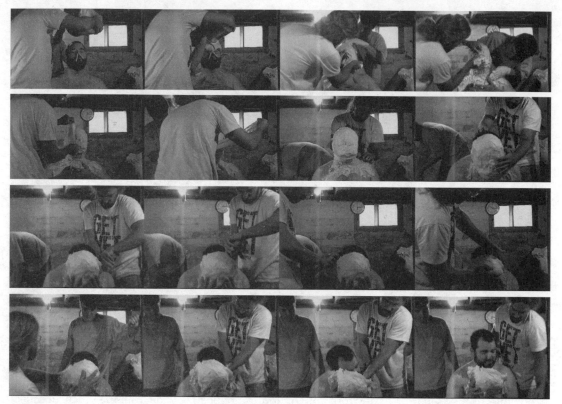

Figure 7.3 Making a life cast for a face: applying alginate, applying plaster bandages, peeling mold off subject. Casting the face alone makes it easier to reinforce for a more accurate mold.

If I had this to do over again, I'd invest (imbed) the alginate mold in a box full of freshly mixed plaster and let the plaster set up to support the mold. Mold rigidity is less critical if you will be making a lightweight plastic positive, but plaster is very heavy and will spread any mold that isn't solidly reinforced. The procedures and materials recommended in the Monster Makers guides describe how to make a lightweight plastic full-head cast. For the above figures and the rest of this chapter, I made two face casts plus separate ear casts (see Figure 7.5), using alginate for the negative molds and ordinary plaster of paris for the positives.

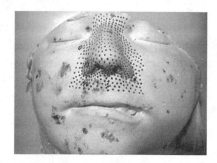

Figure 7.4 Casting Mistake #2: Results of alginate mold spread out under weight of plaster. No, my face isn't really that wide.

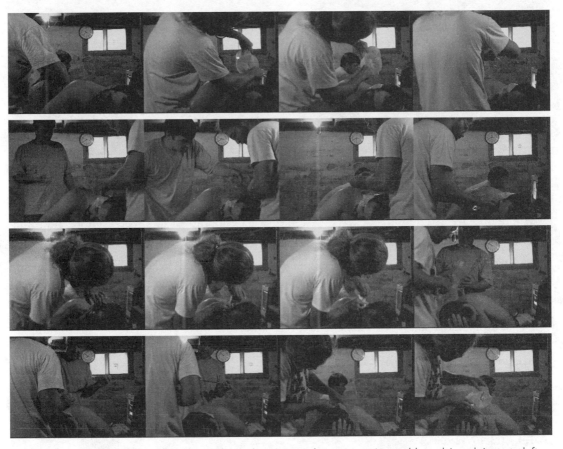

Figure 7.5 Making separate ear casts: applying alginate to right ear, removing mold, applying alginate to left ear, removing mold. Separate casts produce more accurate results with less tearing and distortion than casting the ears in the same piece as the face.

If you will be storing your casts for any length of time before digitizing them, be careful. Plaster is very porous and sensitive to many kinds of contamination. The packing material I used to ship the casts absorbed moisture from the air, encouraging mildew to grow in the plaster wherever the packing touched it. Fortunately, it only caused discoloration by the time I caught it, but if the surface had become pitted, the casts would have been a total loss.

Digitizing With The MicroScribe-3D

The most common tool for digitizing maquettes or casts is Immersion Corporation's MicroScribe-3D digitizing arm (see Figure 7.6). You will find at least one of these devices in most creature and effects shops, animation studios, and game developers worldwide. It's a simple, robust machine that works with a variety of software on most computer operating systems, including Macintosh, SGI, and Windows. If you get a chance to work with one, take advantage of it. Experience with any digitizing tool is a valuable addition to your resume. If you are running your own shop, you should consider how much modeling you do and whether investing approximately $3,000 in a digitizer can save you time and labor costs over freehand modeling. If

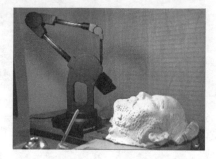

Figure 7.6 Immersion MicroScribe-3D with a plaster face cast ready to digitize.

Figure 7.7 MicroScribe-3D stylus positioned to capture a data point.

you're already using maquettes as a design and client approval tool, you're more than half-way to an animatable computer model via the MicroScribe.

The MicroScribe-3D works by reporting the exact XYZ coordinates of its stylus tip to the computer via the serial port. You simply hold the stylus tip against the surface of the object to be digitized and trip a foot pedal or press a key to capture each data point, as shown in Figure 7.7.

Depending on the software you use, this can produce a point cloud, a series of contour lines or splines, a polygonal mesh, or a NURBS surface. For more information about the MicroScribe-3D, you can contact Immersion at:

Immersion Corporation
2158 Paragon Drive
San Jose, CA 95131
Tel: 408-467-1900
Fax: 408-467-1901
Internet: www.immerse.com

Before you start digitizing, you need to fix the digitizer and the cast or maquette firmly to your work surface. If either the MicroScribe-3D or the cast moves during digitizing, you'll have to reorient the cast and digitizer by already-captured reference points, or start over and piece the model together in the computer. Neither option is very efficient, so nail everything down before you start. The MicroScribe has a standard threaded hole in the base, just like a camera, so you can use tripods and other mounting hardware. My personal preference is for a Craftsman Workmate portable folding workbench. It has a lot of predrilled holes in the top, plus you can adjust the height of the working surface. To stick the cast or maquette in place, I like to use Power Putty. This is the same type of silicone putty as Silly Putty, but it comes in different color-coded hardnesses. The green Power Putty is the stiffest and will keep even a heavy full-head plaster cast in place. You just pull off a bit and mash it into the corner of the work surface and cast, as shown earlier in Figure 7.6. When you're done, the putty comes off without staining the plaster or carrying off fragments of the cast. It's clean and reusable. You can find Power Putty in martial arts or fitness stores, where it's sold as a hand-grip exerciser.

The first step in preparing a cast for digitizing is to think carefully about what you'll be doing with the finished model. If all you need is a low-polygon model for a realtime game, you won't need to capture many points. If you'll be animating a digital stuntman in close-up for a feature film, you'll have to capture much more detail. Most digitizing applications fall somewhere between these two extremes. The critical measure is the profile of the model. You can simulate face-on surface details with shaders or maps (see Chapters 8 through 10), but you don't want straight lines and sharp angles to be clearly visible in your character's profile. You need to digitize enough points from the cast that the model's profile will appear smooth and rounded in the final rendering. This takes a certain amount of experience to judge accurately. It's difficult to re-digitize without starting completely over, so you should get as much practice as possible on noncritical test objects before you have to digitize a challenging maquette under a tight deadline.

For practice, you should digitize a series of simple tests before you try to digitize an entire cast. I recommend starting with the subject's nose, because it usually provides a set of short and long curves as a good representative sample, and it is unobstructed in profile. Start with one point each at the outer corners of the nostrils, the tip of the nose, the base of the nose at the top of the philtrum (those two lines on your upper lip), and the top of the bridge. This will form a rough pyramid. This is the simplest level of digitizing. Import the model into your rendering software, and render it in profile at several different resolutions. Compare it to the cast or reference photos. How high a resolution can you render before the polygons of the model become obvious? Digitize the nose again, adding points along the wings, bridge, and nostrils. Render the new model, and see how much higher resolution you can use before the model starts to show its flaws. Repeat this process until you've found a level of detail that produces smooth profiles at your project's finished resolution. That's the level of detail you will need to use for digitizing the entire cast.

You can save a lot of time and effort, and make a lighter, more efficient model, if you plan ahead and place each point carefully. For example, you may need to space points less than a millimeter apart near the corner of the nostril or eyelid to capture the tight curves there. The forehead, temple, and cheek may have broad, flat areas where you can space points a centimeter or more without losing detail (see Figure 7.8).

You need to examine the cast, visualizing each point connected to each adjacent point. If you are making a polygonal model, you should visualize each point connected to its neighbors with straight lines. Start with a single point, perhaps in the center of the forehead. How far away can you make a second point, connected to the first point by a straight line, without

Figure 7.8 Vary the spacing of data points to suit the curvature of the surface. Flat areas need few points, while curved areas need more.

missing any important details in the cast? Once you've placed the second point, repeat the process for a third point, and so on until you've covered the entire cast with a mesh of points.

The actual digitizing process depends on your software. I've used Wrap and WrapLite, Rhino, and Sculptor ProTools with the MicroScribe-3D, and each program has its strong and weak points.

4D Vision Sculptor ProTools

For digitizing simple polygonal meshes, Sculptor ProTools (Figure 7.9) has the simplest, most user-friendly workflow. If you are only concerned with getting an efficient polygonal mesh into your animation software as rapidly as possible with a minimum of additional learning time, this is the way to go. You simply launch the program, select the Devices|Immersion|New Model menu option, and choose a data rate and COM port for the digitizer. Power users can customize scale and other settings, but the defaults work just fine for a life cast. Once the device is online, you simply select the Devices|Immersion|Add To Model menu option and start adding data points. Sculptor is not sensitive to point order, so, any time you back yourself into a corner, you can end the line and start up again somewhere else, without slowing down or interrupting your workflow.

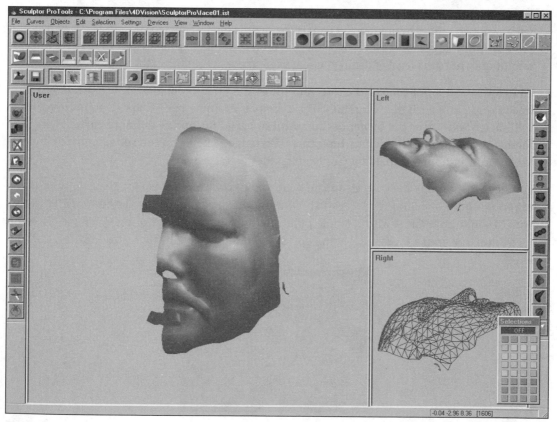

Figure 7.9   Sculptor ProTools with digitized half-face.

Sculptor uses keyboard equivalents for most of the navigation functions, so you can zoom in or out and rotate the model without taking your hand off the stylus. The F3 key turns on the Snap to Point option, which is really useful when you're stitching together adjacent polygons. This option detects when the stylus tip is within the given range of an existing point, and automatically uses the existing point for the new polygon rather than create a redundant new point. The Page Up/Page Down keys increase and decrease the range of the Snap, so you can play with the range interactively to find the setting that's best for a particular area. It's really slick to be able to reduce the Snap incrementally as you digitize into a tight area, then step the Snap back up as you move into an open area. With very little practice, I was able to get up to four valid points per second, the fastest of any of the software I tested.

The most significant advantage of the MicroScribe and other manual digitizers over laser, optical, or sonar scanners is that manual digitizing enables a skilled operator to get efficient, complete surfaces where a scanner can't. For example, most scanners have serious problems with involute surfaces or overhangs. The back of the ears and the underside of the chin, nose, and eyebrows are typical problem areas of the human head. Take a look at Figure 7.10 for a laser scan of my left ear, showing the inaccuracy of data capture for the back of the ear.

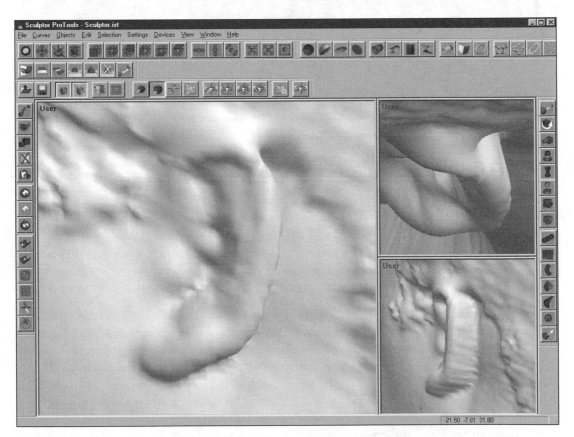

Figure 7.10   Laser scan inaccuracy for back of ear.

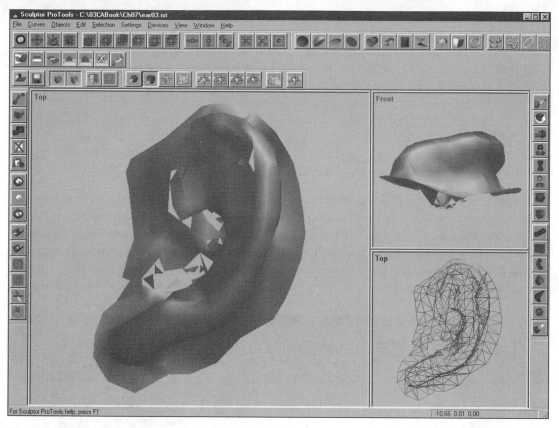

Figure 7.11 MicroScribe-3D accuracy for back of ear.

In contrast, the MicroScribe stylus is easy to maneuver to capture accurate data from the back of the ear and most other undercuts or involute surfaces (see Figure 7.11).

The only problem areas for the stylus are those that are difficult to reach, such as the inner recesses of the ear and the underside of the inner cartilage, where there just isn't room to maneuver the stylus. Neither laser scanner nor digitizer can accurately capture all surfaces. You will always have to do some patching and cleanup to finish the model. Digitizer data is generally easier to clean up, as it doesn't generate spurious data. You just have to play connect-the-dots to close up the gaps.

Sculptor uses a proprietary native file format but exports in many common 3D formats, such as 3DS, DXF, OBJ, IGES, COB, IOB, STL, and LWO. In addition to simple polygonal meshes, Sculptor enables you to convert data points to NURBS surfaces for use in more advanced animation and rendering software. The half-face digitized model pictured earlier in Figure 7.9 is available in several formats in the Chapter 7 directory on this book's CD-ROM, so you can load it into the software of your choice to examine it. There is also a demo version of Sculptor in the 4D Vision directory on this book's CD-ROM.

Robert McNeel & Associates' Rhinoceros

Rhino is a very powerful and flexible modeling program being developed by Robert McNeel & Associates. As of this writing, they are still making the software available as a free beta release, which you can download from their Web site at **www.rhino3d.com**. They plan to make Rhino a commercial product as soon as the beta cycle is complete, so I suggest you download it at your earliest opportunity. The publishers are also soliciting your feedback on the beta release, so you're welcome to contact them via email at **rhino@mcneel.com**.

Rhino is definitely intended for the power user. In addition to the standard menu and icon interface, Rhino enables you to directly enter command-line instructions. This is not the most intuitive approach, but I can see its value for the experienced power user. One very nice feature is that Rhino allows you to completely customize the keyboard equivalents, so you can automate your most often-used functions with a handful of keys. This is especially important to the digitizing process. If you try to rely on the standard menu options and icon buttons, you'll be putting down the stylus and using the mouse and keyboard every few minutes. With the right keyboard equivalents, you can manage the digitizing process with one hand, keeping the stylus moving with the other. I suggest you keep track of the functions you use most often, then draft a list of keyboard equivalents that makes sense for your personal working style. At first, you may only have a few keyboard equivalents, but, over time, your preferences will change. Within a week of starting to use Rhino, I had built a full complement of keyboard equivalents and was using complex series of operations without having to slow down or think about them. With practice, using Rhino with the MicroScribe is nearly as fast as with Sculptor.

Starting the digitizing process with Rhino takes a bit more effort than with other software. Rhino requires you to go through a 13-action calibration and orientation process each time you begin using the MicroScribe. I can understand that this is useful to a power user with an odd digitizing setup, but they really should have a default setup that enables most users to get right to digitizing.

Rhino is designed to work with NURBS, and has a slight edge in creating splines and NURBS surfaces directly from the MicroScribe data. As you can see in Figure 7.12, Rhino makes it possible to generate complex surfaces, like the human ear, from a relatively small number of splines. Making these splines is simply a matter of choosing the Sketch Curve function, then dragging the stylus tip along the curved surface.

You need to be very careful when using any of the Sketch functions, as any slip or skip of the stylus will generate data points out in the air, making an inaccurate model. I found it best to practice following the new path with the stylus at least once before enabling the Sketch Curves function. Tracing the path in soft plaster forms a slight groove, making it easier to follow the second time. It also enables you to anticipate any odd bumps or irregularities in the cast, so you can slow down and prevent errors. The drawback of plaster's softness is that you have to Sketch by dragging the stylus tip. If you push the stylus, the steel tip will dig into the plaster, damaging the cast and halting the Sketch operation. On the other hand, if you are working from a maquette or plastic cast with a harder surface, you will need to be that much more

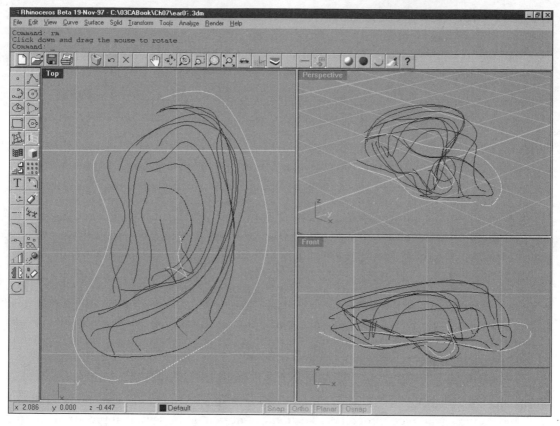

Figure 7.12 Ear digitized with Rhino as a set of Sketch Curves.

careful not to let the stylus slip during a Sketch operation. Despite these drawbacks, the Sketch functions make digitizing much faster than the point-by-point process.

Once you have digitized either the points or curves to define the entire model, you can use Rhino's surfacing tools to create NURBS surfaces or polygonal meshes. For most parts of a face cast, the standard lofting operations will give good results. For tricky areas like the involute curves of the ear, you will need to select and loft curves one at a time. Even with careful digitizing and lofting, a human ear will end up with errors that you will have to correct by hand (see Figure 7.13).

Rhino has a number of modeling tools that can make it easier to create complex organic shapes for characters. Even if you use one of the integrated software packages that includes a decent modeler, you should consider adding Rhino to your toolbox. It can export to a variety of file formats, including IGES, Wavefront OBJ, AutoCAD DXF, 3D Studio, LightWave, Raw Tri-angles, POV-Ray mesh, Moray UDO, STL, VRML, Adobe Illustrator, Windows Metafile, Renderman, and Applied Geometry (.ag), so Rhino is almost guaranteed to work well with your animation software.

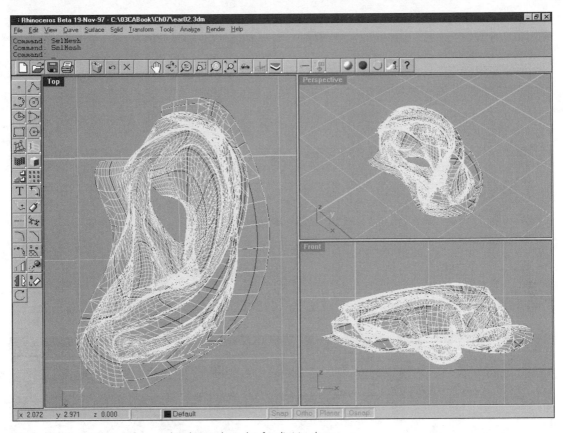

Figure 7.13   NURBS surface and polygonal mesh of a digitized ear.

Wrap And WrapLite

Wrap is a 3D modeling program published by Raindrop Geomagic, Inc. WrapLite is a stripped-down version of Wrap developed specifically to work with the MicroScribe 3D digitizer. You can find more information about both programs from the publisher's Web site, **www.geomagic.com**, including demo versions of the software and HTML versions of the manuals. Using WrapLite with the MicroScribe is simple and, with a little practice, the fastest way of getting raw model data into your computer. The catch is that it's also the fastest way to generate a lot of spurious data. Your first few models will have mistakes, and finding procedures to eliminate the sources of common mistakes requires some trial and error.

Initializing the MicroScribe with WrapLite is easier than with Rhino and only slightly harder than with Sculptor. In addition to the standard COM port and baud rate options, WrapLite enables you to choose the Autoplot distance. This is the minimum distance (measured in either inches or millimeters) you must move the stylus before the software will register a new data point. Increasing the Autoplot value produces a coarser, lighter mesh, and reducing it produces a more accurate but heavier mesh. You should practice digitizing the same object with several different Autoplot settings. Observe how different settings affect your initial capture and any optimizations or tweaks you need to produce a finished model. One setting may produce a raw mesh faster but require much more effort to clean up, while a different setting may demand more time for raw digitizing and very little for tweaking. Each subject and project will be different. You should collect enough empirical data so that you can make the right choice when you're under a tight deadline.

The first part of a WrapLite digitizing session is the Point Phase. In this mode, WrapLite gathers data points very much like Rhino's Sketch function. You choose the Digitizer icon button (see top left of Figure 7.14), position the stylus on the subject, hold down the left foot pedal (or keyboard equivalent), and drag the stylus across the subject. You don't have to follow a straight line. You can scribble in any direction you like. WrapLite doesn't turn the data into lines immediately. It keeps them as points only, so you don't have to worry about crossing over or repeating an area. When you want to move the stylus to a different area, you let up on the foot pedal, reposition the stylus, and press the pedal again to continue creating points. After a little practice, I found it easy to make short sketching strokes across the subject, coordinating the pedal motion with lifting and repositioning the stylus. This process is much faster than selecting single points with the stylus. However, it is more prone to collecting erroneous points. If the stylus tip digs into the soft plaster or skips over a slight bump, you'll get points out in the air

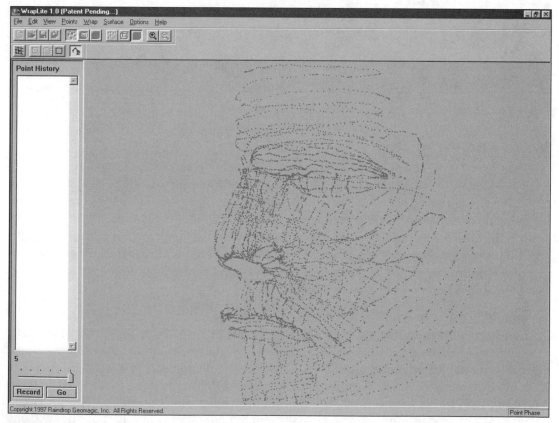

Figure 7.14 Point Phase results in WrapLite.

rather than accurately on the surface of the subject. To prevent digging in, you should drag the stylus rather than pushing it. To prevent skips, you should move the stylus slowly, with a moderate amount of pressure against the surface. You should also pay close attention to your coordination of stylus movement and the foot pedal. If you lift the stylus while the pedal is still depressed, you'll make little curlicues at the end of the digitized paths. You can stop at any time to select and delete bad points, then continue digitizing until you have good coverage of the subject. Figure 7.14 shows the results of a single Point Phase session.

Once you have all the raw points you need to define your model, you can use WrapLite's editing tools to crop, erase, or resample the raw points. When you've cleaned up the points, the next step is the Wrap Phase. This is an automated connect-the-dots routine that builds a continuous polygonal surface from the point data. This constitutes the heart of Wrap's operation. You start the wrap process by choosing the Compute Wrap icon or menu option. The software then begins a lengthy series of calculations to build the surface. This will take some time, comparable to a complex rendering. A window with a progress bar appears, so you can judge whether to hang around or take a break. Once the wrap is completed, you'll have something like Figure 7.15. The display options enable you to see any combination of points, edges, or faces, with sharp or smooth shading.

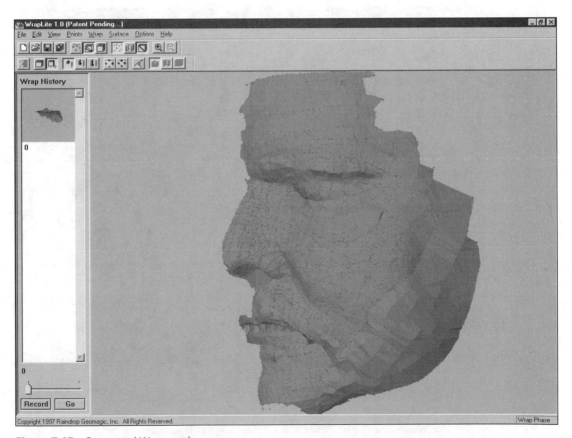

Figure 7.15 Computed Wrap results.

Once you have a basic wrap, you can use various push, drill, and selection tools to further refine the model. These aren't as complete as the tools you'll find in a general-purpose modeling program, but they are well-suited to editing digitized data sets. The next step is the Surface Phase, where WrapLite's status as a power tool really shows. You can apply the Relax Surface and Surface Refinement functions in sequence to smooth out areas of the mesh, increase the density, and reallocate points along the prominent contours of the model. You might create results like Figure 7.16 and 7.17, the product of several iterations of both functions.

The advantage to using these tools is that you can let the software search for the most efficient contours to describe the model. You can crank up the complexity of the model to virtually saturate the surface with points, then use these tools to shift all the points into a closer approximation of the model's contours. This interpolation actually produces a more detailed model of the subject's curves than the raw data you captured. It's like an expert system for your digitizer. When you optimize this mass of data, you'll end up with a more accurate yet efficient mesh than you could ever digitize by hand, even with years of experience.

You need to understand how your 3D software optimizes a mesh in order to get the results you need from a WrapLite model. Most mesh optimization routines remove redundant points based

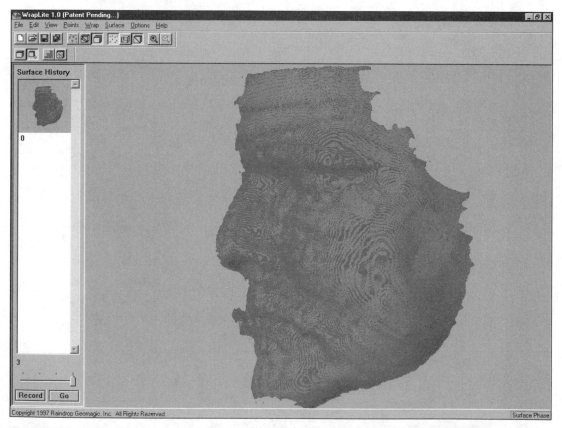

Figure 7.16 Results of applying Relax Surface and Surface Refinement to the model in the preceding figures.

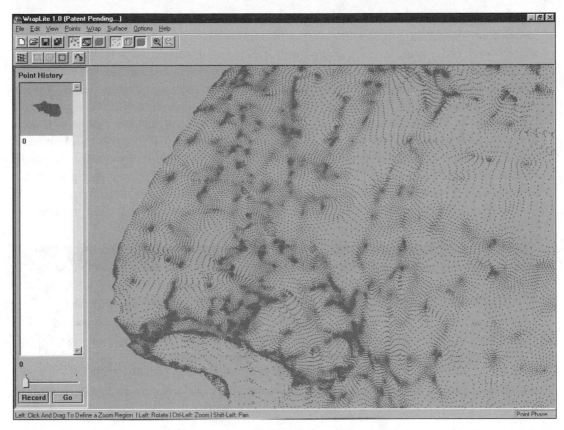

Figure 7.17   Close-up of part of Figure 7.16.

on either *proximity* (points too close together are merged) or *planarity* (points lying inside a plane are merged with its perimeter). You should run a planar optimization first. This will get rid of redundant points in broad, flat areas like the forehead and cheeks, while retaining fine detail around curved areas, such as the eyes, nose, and lips. Proximity optimization is a more sensitive process. Each iteration removes a certain amount of detail, so you need to find a balance between perfectly accurate/too complex and approximated/easy to use. Start with the smallest merge distance possible. After each iteration, render a close-up of an area, like the corner of an eye or lip, where you need lots of detail. When you notice a loss of important detail, undo the last optimization, and save the model. Of course, you should also keep a backup of the original model plus copies at each level of optimization, just in case you end up needing more detail than you originally planned.

While its digitizing and processing functions are powerful, WrapLite's navigation tools are not very good. In fact, they're the weakest part of the whole program. The program has a single perspective view window (see preceding figures). You control all zoom, rotate, and pan actions by dragging the mouse with the left button and either the Alt, Shift, or Ctrl keys held down. This arrangement makes the use of a standard mouse difficult, and the use of a tablet, touchpad, or other pointing device nearly impossible. To make matters worse, all movements are based on the workspace's global coordinates. If you zoom in to a specific area of the model and try to rotate it, the model will rotate on the axes of the entire workspace. The most common result is that the area being examined will rotate completely out of view. If you make rotations in more than one axis, it becomes very difficult to figure out which direction you should drag the mouse to rotate the model. Panning is the only navigation tool that seems to be reliable and intuitive. WrapLite is also missing a Zoom Extents or Zoom Selected function, a basic navigation tool that nearly all 3D modelers include. Tools like this become more important as models grow larger and screen redraw rates fall. Since WrapLite is designed to deal with masses of raw data (the most complex models of all), these features should be paramount. Positioning the model for this section's figures was a very frustrating series of experiments. There is really no excuse for this. Most 3D modeling software has a friendly, intuitive way of navigating a model within the 3D workspace. There are plenty of examples of successful approaches to this problem, so I hope Rainbow Geomagic corrects these flaws in their next release.

CHOOSING DIGITIZING TOOLS

When you choose a digitizing tool, you need to keep the entire modeling, setup, and animation process in mind. A tool may be efficient for one part of the process but generate lots of unnecessary work in another part. You need to find an approach and a set of tools that is most efficient for the process you are following. There is no one solution, no magic bullet, suitable for all character animation.

Whichever software you choose to drive your digitizer, the basic processes and skills remain the same. These are assets you need to develop through practice.

Digitizing Practice

Capturing enough detail to render an accurate profile is only the first step in producing a usable model. You also need enough extra detail—enough flexibility in the model to set up and animate it. This means you have to add details based on your experience in setup and animation, which is a completely different set of criteria from the static rendered profile test. For example, most life casts are made with a closed mouth. Few subjects would let you coat their teeth and tongue with alginate. This means the corners of the mouth will be compressed. You need very few points to accurately reproduce this area—if it were to always stay compressed. However, you generally need to model the mouth so it can open wide, express emotion, and form words. This means you have to understand how that area of the model will need to expand and distort from the original digitized geometry, and where you will need to add extra points to make it possible. This is something you have to learn by trial and error. To make it as easy as possible, I recommend that you concentrate on one facial feature at a time. Again, start with the nose. Practice digitizing, setting up, and animating the nose by itself until you can accurately and efficiently mimic the deformation of wrinkling and furrowing the bridge and flaring and pinching the nostrils. After you've learned to do this with one model, you can apply that experience, with minor modifications, to almost all other humanoid facial models.

MESH LAYOUT PRACTICE

Your first few attempts at laying out an efficient mesh will probably not be satisfactory. I recommend using a soft lead pencil, as it won't permanently mark the plaster. You can rub off most of the markings and start over or make changes as necessary. Once you feel more confident about your mesh layout, you can move up to water-based felt-tip markers, which will soak into the plaster and make permanent marks (see Figure 7.18).

If you have the opportunity to choose your own first practice subject, I highly recommend you start off with a hard plastic toy or bust. Most plastics are durable, will take grease pencil or other markings easily, and can be scrubbed clean without pitting or gouging the surface. This gives you the opportunity to experiment with different patterns and complexities of dots, grids, and contour lines in order to find the approach that best suits your tools and working style. Once you have succeeded in digitizing a plastic subject, you can graduate to fired Sculpey maquettes. These are not quite as forgiving and durable as plastic, but they are not as fragile as uncoated plaster. When you believe you're ready for the nasty stuff, try digitizing a plaster cast with lots of undercuts and involute surfaces. Face casts like those in Figure 7.7 are some of the most challenging and unforgiving subjects you'll ever have to deal with. Plaster casts are fragile, heavy, and hard to re-mark, and they take etch-lines from the stylus and flake, crack, and powder at the least excuse. If you can digitize plaster quickly and well, everything else will seem like child's play.

Now that you're familiar with manual digitizing, you're ready to consider the pros and cons of the biggest modeling power tool—the laser scanner.

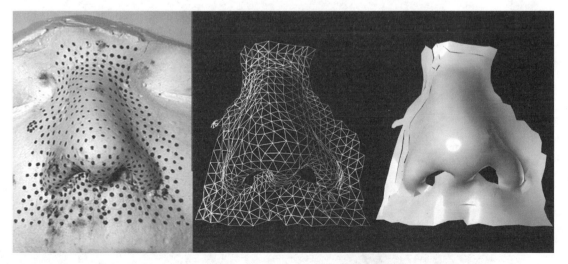

Figure 7.18 Nose marked with felt-tip pen, and corresponding digitized model in wireframe and smooth shading.

Cyberware Laser Scanners

A laser scanner is a device that bounces a low-power laser beam off the subject to precisely measure the subject's surface contours. Laser scanners are the most accurate means of capturing 3D data. Most laser scanners are built for industrial use, where they are used in reverse-engineering, prototyping, and biomedical engineering. Sales of laser scanners to entertainment production houses are a small fraction of the total market. Entertainment sales do have a higher public-relations profile, however. Laser scanners have contributed to films and television shows such as *Jurassic Park*, *The Abyss*, *Terminator 2*, *Dragonheart*, *The Mask*, *Deep Space 9*, and *Apocalypse*. The laser scanners most often used in the entertainment industry are manufactured by Cyberware, Inc. This company's product line includes tabletop models suitable for scanning small maquettes, head scanners (pictured in Figure 7.19), and full-body scanners (shown in Figure 7.20), which can capture life-size sculptures or actors.

Cyberware scanners use a 780nm infrared laser, so the beam is not visible. The power of the laser is well within safety standards, so it's safe to scan live subjects with their eyes open. At the same time the laser is scanning the subject's surface (a 17-second process), a second sensor is capturing the color map. In the 3030 HRC scanner, a 2,000-element linear CCD is paired with a cold light source (no infrared is emitted, to avoid interfering with the laser) to capture a 2K×2K color image that is perfectly matched to the captured geometry. Previous models used a lower-resolution CCD to capture less detailed color maps. If you're working in television or multimedia, the older maps are fine. If you're working in feature film, you should definitely consider the higher-resolution HRC model. Cyberware laser scanners are far more accurate than necessary for character models—the 3030 is accurate to 700μm vertically and 200μm radially. Technically, there is no question that a Cyberware scanner can capture adequate geometry and color data from your maquette or live subject.

At this time, all software for driving the scanners and processing the raw data is available only for the Silicon Graphics platform. Cyberware scanners require an SGI workstation with a mod-

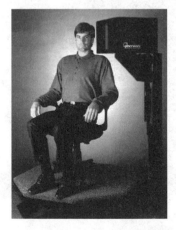

Figure 7.19 Cyberware 3030 with PS motion platform.

Figure 7.20 Cyberware full-body laser scanner.

erate amount of RAM and a decent processor. Raw scanner files are pretty large, so a bottom-end machine won't cut it. Most individuals and organizations that have occasional need for laser scanning choose to deal with a service bureau. If you only need a few scans a year or only for special projects, it doesn't make economic sense to invest $70,000-plus in a scanner that will be idle much of the time. On the other hand, some firms that have acquired Cyberware scanners have created another source of revenue by providing scanning and processing services to others. You can get more up-to-date technical, financial, and service bureau information by contacting Cyberware through their Web site or directly:

Cyberware, Inc.
2110 Del Monte Avenue
Monterey, CA 93940
Tel: 408-657-1450
Fax: 408-657-1494
Internet: www.cyberware.com

I've found the folks at Cyberware to be unfailingly polite, helpful, knowledgeable, and enthusiastic about anything pertaining to 3D scanning. It's especially nice that the company has a strong corporate interest in the arts—they are not just a bunch of techies. They are always looking for creative new ways to use their technology. Their Web site contains sample copyright-free models, documentation for most of their software, and lots of helpful tips and advice. The Cyberware vendor directory on this book's CD-ROM contains selected models and documentation from the Cyberware site. Two especially nice full-body human models are Renee and Theo, shown in Figures 7.21 and 7.22, respectively.

One problem with laser scanners is accurate capture of areas shadowed from the laser. These areas appear as holes in the mesh. Cyberware software includes several utilities for closing up these holes with various interpolation algorithms. Both these sample models have been edited with linear interpolation to remove shadow holes. A typical raw scan contains about 400K points. This is an enormous amount of data, much of which is redundant. Both samples have been decimated (surplus points removed) with automatic decimation software. This combination of processes may take half a day to a day and a half, depending on the skill of the operator and the speed of the processing workstation. I was fortunate in having Phil Dench, the author of the CySurf program, process my head scan at the Cyberware facility in Monterey. While I can't match his expertise, the following case study of my own novice efforts gives a useful comparison.

Getting My Head Examined

The first step in getting a usable scan is centering the subject. Depending on the scanner setup, the scanner head may circle around the subject, or the scanner head may be fixed and a turntable rotates the subject. In either case, it's important that the axis of rotation pass through the center of the subject's head. If the subject is off-center, you won't get as good a data set, and many of the cleanup, modeling, and mapping tools will not work as effectively. For my scan, the scan head rotated around me. A guide like a small knitting needle just above my head

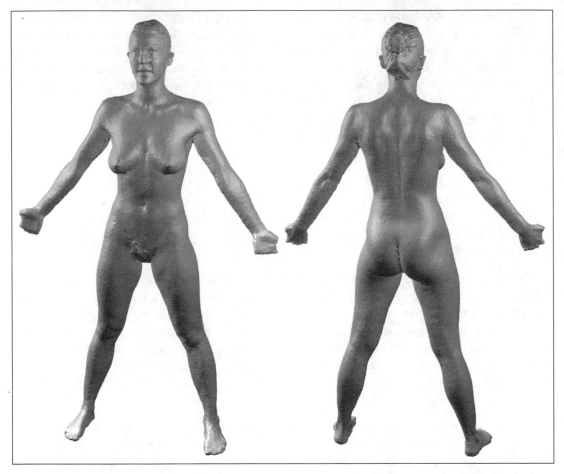

Figure 7.21 Renee. "A nude female in a neutral standing pose. It has been almost completely filled in shadowed areas, of which there were very few. There are several levels of decimation. Fingers have been removed."

marked the axis of rotation. The scanning operator (David Addleman, Cyberware's president) had me shift position until the guide was centered over the crown of my head.

The scan takes approximately 17 seconds. The subject has to hold perfectly still, or the scan data will have errors. It's like moving the original while you're making a photocopy—the information gets smeared. It's possible to correct some of these errors with the Cyberware software, but it's better to get a good scan at the beginning. It's not absolutely necessary for the subject to hold his breath during the scan, but it can't hurt. Likewise, the subject should be as calm and relaxed as possible to reduce his heart rate, because the scanner is sensitive enough to pick up the pulse in the throat. A strong, rapid pulse will appear in the raw scan as a series of vertical ridges spaced across the base of the throat.

The biggest problem for me was keeping my eyes still. At the same time the invisible laser is scanning for geometry, a bright white light is illuminating the subject for the color scan. This is distracting, and I found my eyes trying to track the scan head. To avoid this, the subject should

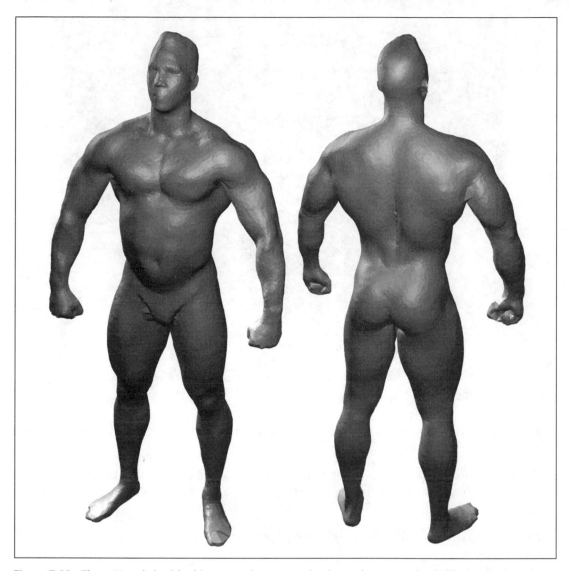

Figure 7.22   Theo. "A male bodybuilder in standing pose. It has been almost completely filled in shadowed areas, of which there were very few. Decimated and smoothed."

pick a distant reference point (preferably at eye level and straight ahead) and stare at it throughout the scan. I found that it was easier to keep my eyes open and still if I closed them for the first part of the scan (the back of the head), then held them open for the second part. It's the old paradox: If someone tells you not to blink (or yawn, or look behind you), you can't help but do it. It's easier to keep your eyes open and unmoving for 8 seconds rather than for 17.

Once the scan is complete, it takes a few minutes for the workstation to process the range (geometry) and map data and display it. You can view the raw data as either an unwrapped view (shown in Figure 7.23) or as a wrapped, or *Radial*, view (shown in Figure 7.24).

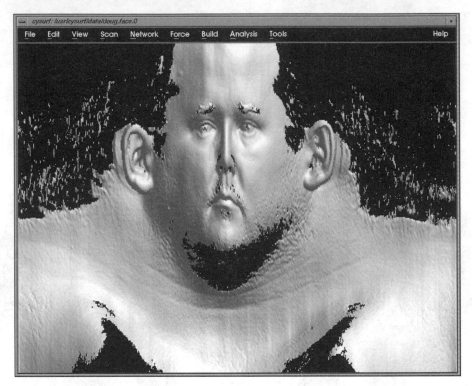

Figure 7.23 My first scan—unwrapped view.

The wrapped view is better for evaluating the overall shape, while the unwrapped view is more useful for selecting and editing the data.

Figure 7.25 shows my first scan's color map. This scan is only 512×512 resolution, but the latest Cyberware 3030 HRC scanner can produce maps up to 2048×2048, which is good enough for close-ups in feature films.

You can also choose to display the color map applied to the range data as a grayscale, as in Figure 7.26.

Viewing the wrapped view with the color map applied makes it easier to evaluate the scan and to make corrections for the next scan. For example, if you look closely at Figure 7.26, you will see that almost all the dark areas of my hair, beard, eyebrows, and even my irises have gaps. This is because the IR laser used to gather range data doesn't reflect strongly enough from dark surfaces to give a clear measurement. The result is a hole in the data wherever the subject is too dark. In addition, any undercut—the underside of the chin, back of the ears, inside of the nostrils—may not be visible to the laser or CCD, and also results in a hole in the data. The crown of the head is almost impossible to capture accurately, since the crown's surface is parallel to the laser beam and, therefore, doesn't reflect in the right direction.

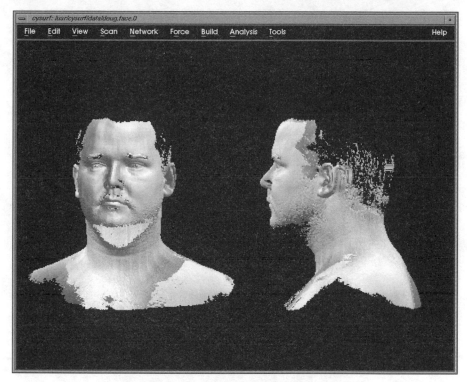

Figure 7.24 Same scan—wrapped view.

Figure 7.25 Color map.

There are several ways to solve these problems. My first solution was to shave off my beard, removing the compound problem of dark hair and undercut surface that caused most of my throat and chin to disappear. The next step was to spray my hair with a fine white powder recommended by David Addleman. It's not damaging to hair and most other surfaces, but you

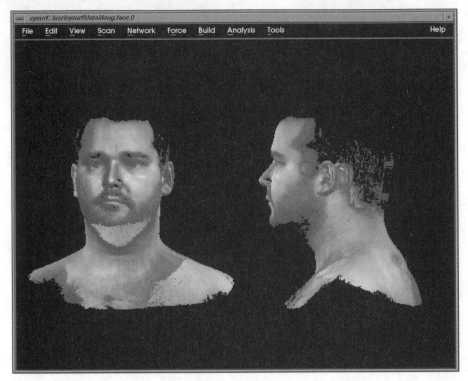

Figure 7.26 Wrapped view with color map applied.

should test it on a small area first. Spraying a patch on my forearm didn't cause an allergic reaction, so we liberally dusted my hair and eyebrows with it. If you're scanning a subject with dark surfaces, you should have some of this spray on hand. You can order it from McMaster-Carr, an industrial supply house, at the following address:

McMaster-Carr
P.O. Box 94930
Cleveland, OH 44101-4930
Tel: 216-995-5500
Tel: (Los Angeles) 562-692-5911
Fax: 216-995-9600
Internet: www.mcmaster.com
Item: 1383T9 "12oz can developer..." (approximately $7 each)

If your subject has long hair, you can either tuck the hair up into a bald cap or slick it down and tie it back in a tight ponytail. This minimizes the roughness of the hair and prevents it from obscuring the contours of the back of the head and neck. As you can tell from these figures, my hair is cut bristly short, so this step wasn't necessary for me. The last solution is to tilt the subject's head to minimize undercuts. If your subject has a hook nose or prominent eyebrow ridges, you may have to scan his head with several degrees of backwards tilt. In my case, a very slight backward tilt was enough to eliminate most of the undercut problems. My second scan came out much better, as shown in Figure 7.27.

Once you solve the major problems, you can take additional scans at no less than five-minute intervals. This time is necessary for the workstation to process and save each scan's data, and the operator to set up for the next scan. This limits how quickly you can capture different poses for morph targets. For example, in *Terminator 2: Judgement Day*, actor Robert Patrick plays a "mimetic poly-alloy" android, apparently made of liquid metal. In one scene, the liquid form of the android flows through a hole in a helicopter window, resumes human form in the left seat, then lip-syncs the words "Get out" to the chopper's pilot. Separate Cyberware scans of actor Robert Patrick were used as morph targets to animate this lip-sync sequence. The five-minute delay in setting up a new scan made it impossible to simply capture Patrick speaking the line all at once, so he had to hold each pose through a separate scan. If you watch carefully, you may be able to detect differences between Patrick's normally fluid lip movements elsewhere in the film and the discrete poses captured by the Cyberware scanner.

I hope I'm making it clear that laser scanning is an experimental process for each subject. It almost always takes some experimenting to get the desired results. If you think you can walk into a service bureau, put your subject in front of the machine, and walk out again in 10 minutes with a complete scan, you're overly optimistic. You should plan to take several scans

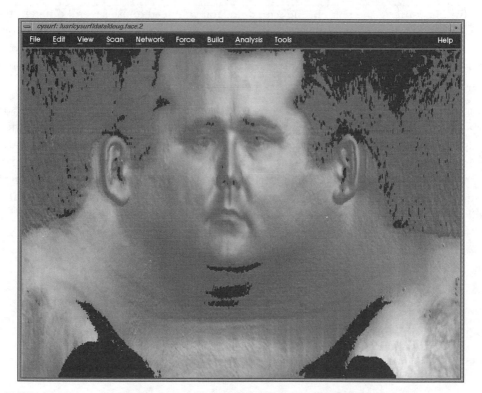

Figure 7.27   Second scan, with beard shaved, hair powdered, and head tilted back slightly.

of each subject and to spend some time with the scanner operator to tweak settings between scans. In my case, a total of seven full-head scans with varying levels of editing took just over three hours to produce with the most skilled operators in the business. You need to keep this in mind when you negotiate pricing with a scanning service bureau. Either allow for extra time to tweak scans or insist on a flat rate for each acceptable scan. Otherwise, you can end up with excessive per-hour fees, unusable raw data, or both. A good service bureau will be aware of these problems and should be willing to compromise on a fee structure that compensates them adequately while guaranteeing you the quality data that you need.

Cleaning Up After Yourself

A successful scanning session produces one or more sets of raw range and map files. These files almost always need a little cleanup to close holes in the range data caused by undercuts, dark surfaces, or a surface that's parallel to the scan. Cyberware's CySurf software provides a set of tools designed to make this cleanup as quick and easy as possible. The first step is to start CySurf. You'll see a splash screen like Figure 7.28, with the version and build information and the author's name and email address.

Load the range data, also known as an *Echo file*, for the scan you wish to clean up. Your screen should look something like Figure 7.29.

Note the black areas, the holes in the scan data. You will need to use several different tools to close them up. No one tool can do a good job on all the different types of scan errors and omissions. The first tool, Fill, is the easiest and most intuitive to use. Choose an area you want to fill in, and pan and zoom the display until you can clearly see the individual pixels of the scan data (see Figure 7.30).

Open the Edit dialog. In the Functions window, click on Fill. Left-click and drag the cursor over the hole, to paint it red. Make sure you cover all the missing areas. You can paint over the edges of the hole without doing any damage, because the Fill function won't delete or change any of the original scan data. When you execute the Fill function, the software will close up all the red-shaded areas using a straight-line interpolation, like covering the top of a container with plastic wrap. You can paint more than one hole before executing the Fill function, but it's safer to fill one hole at a time so you can Undo it if you make a mistake (see Figure 7.31).

Figure 7.28 Start CySurf.

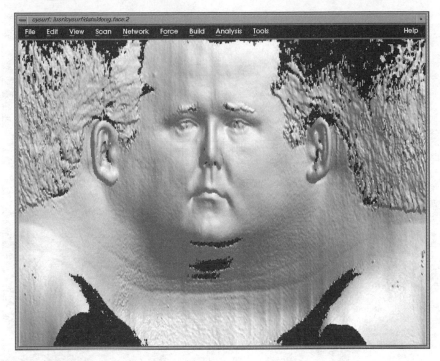

Figure 7.29 Loaded raw scan.

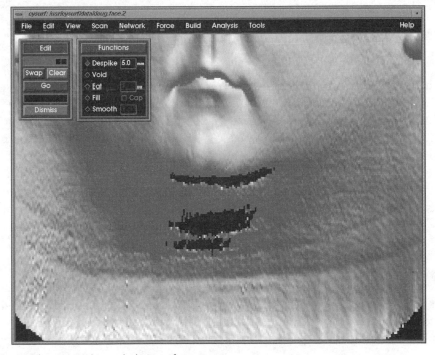

Figure 7.30 Display zoomed in on hole in surface.

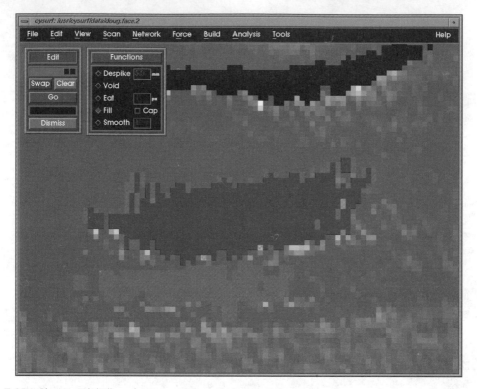

Figure 7.31 Choose Edit|Fill, and paint over the hole in the surface.

When you've painted the hole, click on Go to execute the Fill function. It shouldn't take long. Your results should look something like Figure 7.32.

Note that the original scan data has a lot of small surface detail, but the Fill area doesn't. Skin texture, surface imperfections, wrinkles, and similar artifacts can't be created by the Fill function, so the filled area is perfectly flat from one edge of the hole to another. CySurf includes embossing, sculpting, and bump mapping tools you can use to disguise the Fill areas. You can repeat the Fill process as necessary to close gaps at the front of the shoulders and small holes in the nose, ears, and elsewhere. After you've finished with Fill, the next cleanup function is Smooth. This function flattens out dimples or bumps in the surface by comparing the selected area (just like Fill) to the surrounding surface, and pushing the selected area in or out to match (see Figure 7.33). The variable next to the Smooth button sets how far Smooth looks to determine the adjoining surface level: 1 equals one pixel. The larger the number, the smoother the surface, but the longer the processing, the more surface detail is lost. If you are simply trying to smooth out scanning errors, the default setting of 1 will suffice.

The last basic cleanup function is Fill Cap. This is a special form of the Fill function that closes up the top of the head. If you simply selected the top edge of the scan and executed Fill, the straight-line interpolation of the Fill function would form a sort of cylinder coming out the top

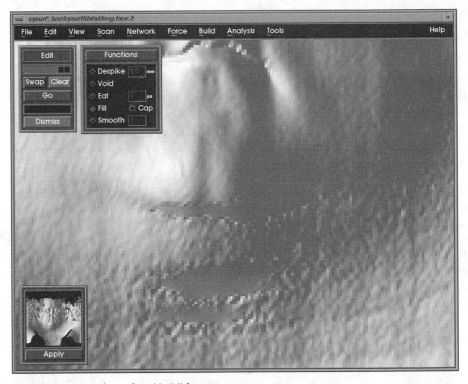

Figure 7.32 Hole in the surface after the Fill function.

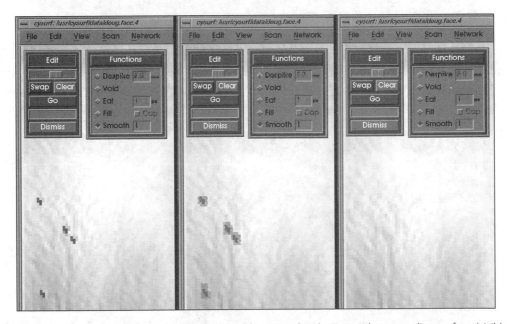

Figure 7.33 Using the Edit|Smooth function to blend bump or dimple error with surrounding surface (visible bumps, selecting bumps, and the results of Smooth function).

of the subject's head. The Fill Cap function gives you some extra controls to shape the fill, so it looks more like a normal skull rather than one of Dr. Frankenstein's creations.

Fill Cap uses both the wrapped and unwrapped views. For the first part of the process, switch to the wrapped view. You will see a set of control nodes defining a hemispherical spline patch. The Fill Cap function will fill the hemisphere, connecting the hemisphere's surface along radial lines to the existing surface. You need to position the control nodes to create the appropriate hemispherical shape for your subject's head. To do this, you will need to be able to visualize what the subject's head would have looked like if the scan data were complete. A set of front and side reference photographs comes in handy for this.

The best place to start moving the control nodes is in the front view, with the bottom nodes. Drag these nodes until they are just touching the sides of the existing surface and well below the highest remaining gaps, as shown in Figure 7.34.

Next, drag the top center nodes to the point where you want the peak of the subject's crown. Adjust the upper corner nodes to change the curvature of the hemisphere. You don't have to worry about the curves matching existing areas of the surface, because Fill Cap only fills in the missing areas. It's OK to overshoot the curve in existing areas, as long as you get the curve you need in the missing areas. There are lots of possibilities. Refer to photos of the subject if you have them, look in the mirror if you're the subject (it worked for me), or use trial and error.

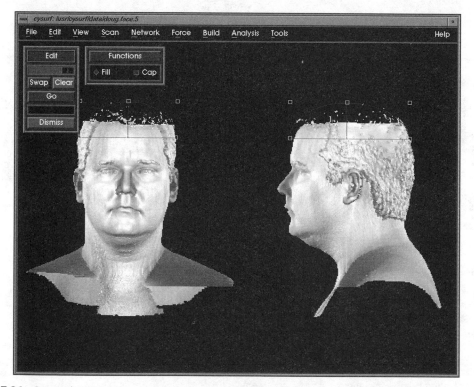

Figure 7.34   Set up the Cap spline to match the missing part of the head.

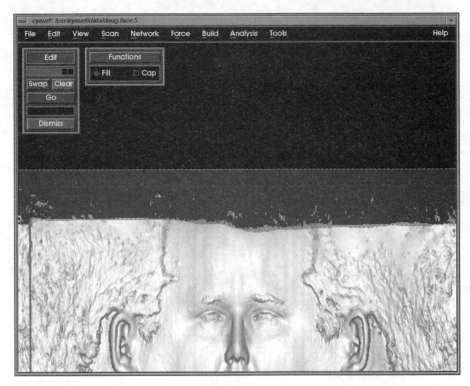

Figure 7.35   Select the Fill Cap area in unwrapped view.

The next step is to select the area to be affected by the Fill Cap function. Just as with the original Fill function, you use the unwrapped view and select the area (see Figure 7.35). You select the area more quickly if you use the cursor to trace the lower boundary of the area, then double-click above it. The entire area above the selection line will fill in. You should be cautious when using the double-click fill, though—a single pixel gap will allow it to select the entire surface.

Change back to the wrapped view. Click on Go to execute the Fill Cap function. You should get results like Figure 7.36.

You can check the accuracy of your Cap shape by applying the color map and looking for overshoot at the peak of the crown. If you refer back to Figure 7.25, you can see that the top of the color map shows the background of the scanner room, as seen over the top of the subject's head. This usually gives a contrasting color that will appear at the top of the Cap surface if it goes too far (see Figure 7.37). If you are adjusting the Fill Cap hemisphere by trial and error, you should make the peak high at first, then reduce it incrementally until the background color just barely disappears. Your results should end up something like Figure 7.36, with a crown curvature closely approximating the original subject's, and just a trace of background color along the top of the crown where it shows through the hair.

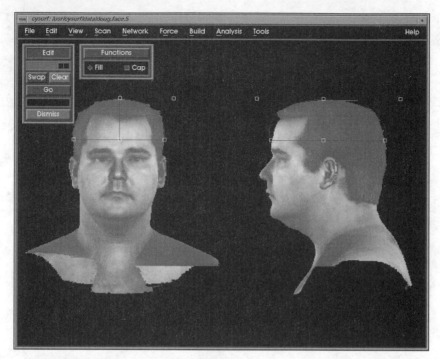

Figure 7.36 Results of using the Fill Cap function to close the missing crown of the head.

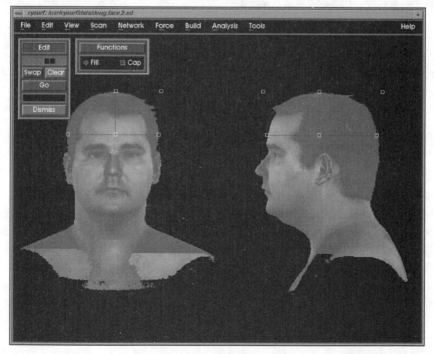

Figure 7.37 Fill Cap hemisphere set too high, showing background color at peak.

The last step in a head scan cleanup is to simplify the raw data, smoothing out irrelevant details and random spikes. In the case of my head scan, most of the irrelevant detail was in the hair (see Figure 7.38).

You can use either the Smooth or Despike functions to reduce this complexity. Smooth tends to blend out all the details at once, averaging them into the surrounding surface. Despike is similar to Smooth but only acts on certain points. If one point has a certain range value and all its neighbors have another, it's likely that the odd point is a spike. The Despike threshold is the maximum range a point can differ from its neighbors before Despike will void it out (make it a hole). If you use Despike, you'll have to go back and Fill the new holes again. The advantage of Despike is that you can decrease the threshold, execute Despike, see how much detail is left, and decide whether to continue Despiking or leave the rest of the details. This gives you a little more control than Smooth, especially if you have a very complex subject. With either function, you should be able to create something like Figure 7.39, a finely detailed face with completely smoothed hair. This makes the mesh much simpler without losing any real detail, because most of the apparent detail in a character's hair is provided by color and texture maps.

Lighten The Load

The results of the cleanup session are the complete range and map files. These aren't of much use in character animation, as they are much too heavy to set up and animate. For a full-body

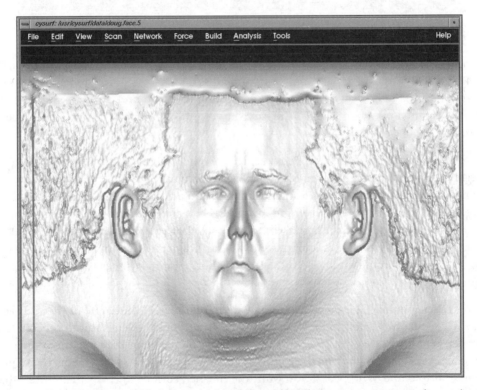

Figure 7.38   Unwrapped view of Filled, Smoothed, and Capped head, showing remaining irrelevant detail in hair.

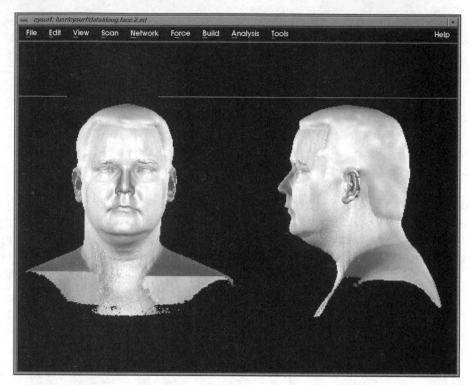

Figure 7.39 Smoothed hair on a cleaned-up mesh.

example, you can look at the file Renee250.3ds in the Cyberware directory on this book's CD-ROM. This scan has over 250,000 polygons and takes a long time simply to load. It would take a very long time and be overwhelmingly frustrating to set up and animate this mesh. Similarly, the cleaned-up model of my head, saved as a triangular mesh, is much too heavy to set up and animate (see Figure 7.40).

The solution to the problems of a heavy mesh is to simplify and optimize it. The goal of this process is to create a polygonal mesh or NURBS surface that preserves the appearance of the original scan, but is much lighter and easier to set up and animate. Using CySurf, the basic process is simple. You build a new grid, or *network*, by defining its perimeter, the number of columns and rows of points inside it, and any areas that you want to be especially detailed. CySurf then fits this new network precisely to the surface of the original scan data. The result is a light, easy-to-animate mesh or NURBS surface that accurately simulates the appearance of the original.

The first step is to load the range data you want to optimize. It should be as clean as you can make it, because any errors in the original will be duplicated in the optimized version, too. The next step is to lay out the basic network. A network is a four-point Bezier spline surface, which you place and distort by moving the control points. CySurf supports two approaches to network layout—Simple and Wrapped. If you want the finished surface to cover the entire subject in

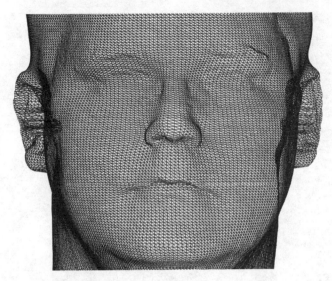

Figure 7.40 Cleaned-up head scan converted to 3DS format, showing prohibitively heavy mesh.

one piece, you should use the Wrapped network. This type of network automatically matches the seam at the back, making it invisible in the final model. You can add a Wrapped network by choosing the Network|Add Wrapped menu option, then dragging the control points to the top and bottom of the scan. You will need to do a little tweaking, especially at the top. If the network extends beyond the scan, the Bezier spline will form a little topknot. If the network doesn't go all the way to the upper edge of the scan, the model will have a hole at the top. It's literally a matter of a pixel or two, and you have to be very fussy to get the best results. Figure 7.41 shows a Wrapped network laid out over my head scan. The network control points are the eight boxes running across the top and bottom edges of the scan. The lines connecting these boxes represent the perimeter of the network. The lines and boxes in the middle of the scan are the results of the next step, adding *forces*.

Forces are lines or points you set to tell CySurf to increase the amount of detail in a specific area without making the grid more complex. Forces act like magnets, pulling the network tighter around themselves, stretching the grid so areas without forces have less detail. Point forces are easy to set—you simply position one and edit its power and range. Figure 7.41 shows point forces at the center of each eye, base of the nose, and underside of the lower lip. Line forces are a little more difficult, because you have to position at least four Bezier control points to shape the line force. Figure 7.41 shows line forces outlining the eyelids, ears, lips, eyebrows, and nose. The line forces are the curved lines. The straight lines connecting the control points are just construction lines and don't influence the network. In color, the curves are bright blue, and the construction lines and control points are black, so they're easy to tell apart. As you can see in this figure, sometimes you have to arrange control points in odd configurations to get the exact force line you need. As with any other complex process, it's a good idea to save your work before you try something new. CySurf saves the network and force data, along with the path to

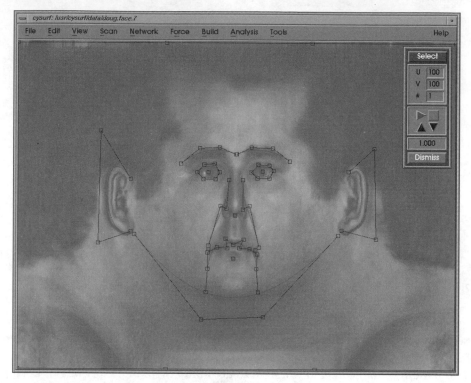

Figure 7.41 Head scan with Wrapped network and forces.

the range and color map files, in a native format called NTS. Whenever you set up a complex set of forces like those in Figure 7.41, you should save an NTS file.

The last controls you need to set are the UV, or column and row, density of the network grid. This determines the final vertex or node count of the finished model, the amount of scan detail the network can match, and the amount of processing time the surface-building process will take. Figure 7.42 shows a reasonable 100×100 grid applied over my head scan. Just for reference, the original scan data is equivalent to a 512×512 grid.

With the network, forces, and UV set, you're ready to initiate a surface build. During this process, CySurf shifts each vertex in your network grid to conform to the nearest data point on the scan, as influenced by the forces you've set. CySurf will continuously update the screen, so you can watch the changes it's making to the grid. This process is very computation-intensive and will continue to run until you stop it. The 1.000 number at the bottom of the control panel in Figure 7.41 is the *noise volume*. This variable controls how far CySurf can move each grid point from its original position. A large noise volume will allow the grid to jump all over, creating a very confusing display, while a small setting will prevent the grid points from moving at all. You need to set a relatively large number (1 is good), click on the green play arrow to start the process, then use the down arrow button (just above the number) to gradually reduce the volume. CySurf needs several iterations at each noise level to accurately fit the grid to the scan.

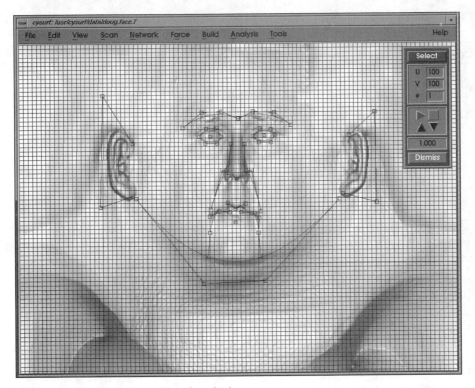

Figure 7.42 Head scan with 100x100 grid applied.

If the grid is very dense, CySurf may take a minute or so for each iteration. The most effective way to deal with this is to have something else to do while you're waiting. Read a book, balance your checkbook, whatever—pick something that you can interrupt periodically to check CySurf's progress. When you first change the volume, the grid points will jump around a lot. After they've gone through several iterations, they should settle into a smaller area, perhaps dithering between two closely spaced positions. When most of the points are stable or dithering, you can reduce the noise volume to the next level and wait for them to stabilize again. When you've reduced the volume to 0.062 or lower, your grid should be almost perfectly stable, and your results should look something like Figure 7.43. You can click on the square red stop button to end the process.

Note the effect of the point and line forces on the mesh, especially around the lips. It's much easier to set up and animate a mesh or NURBS surface if the lines follow natural contours like this—you can work with the mesh, rather than fighting it. At this point, you can export the new surface in a variety of formats. Figure 7.44 shows this model in IGES format, as loaded into Rhino.

Depending on your needs, this 100x100 mesh may be too heavy, or perhaps it's acceptable in some areas but needs more or less detail in others. You can change the UV values and repeat the surface build, or you can delete the Wrapped network and try the other approach, the

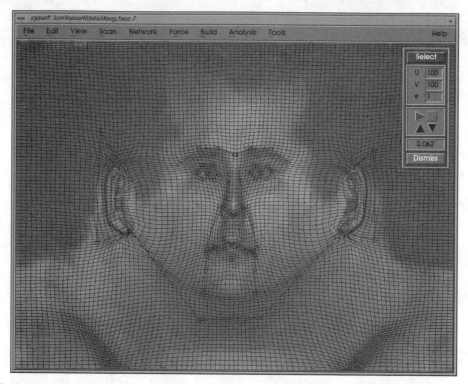

Figure 7.43 100x100 surface build.

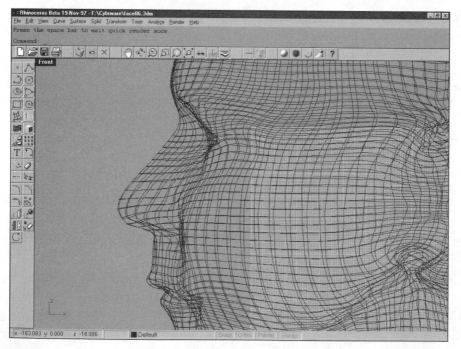

Figure 7.44 100x100 IGES model in Rhino.

Simple network. Oddly enough, the Simple approach is the more complex one. You set up a separate four-point Bezier spline surface for each area of the scan that you want to have a separate mesh density. For example, Figure 7.45 shows two networks set up over the scan's nose and upper lip, each one a 20×20 grid, using the same arrangement of forces as in Figure 7.41.

You have to be very careful to match the spline borders of each network to all its neighbors, or your final model will have gaps. The border between the nose network and the upper-lip network is an easy one—a straight line. The border between upper and lower lips, however, required some pretty extreme control point placement. When you've covered the entire scan with networks and built the surfaces, you might end up with something like Figure 7.46. This IGES model has very few points in areas that won't be animated but plenty of detail in areas like the lips and eyelids. It's also much lighter and easier to set up and animate than the original scan.

You can also use these tools to build morph targets across different scans. Simply apply the same grid and forces to several raw scans, and the resulting polygonal meshes will have compatible vertex counts and distribution. You can even morph one person into another, like the water-tentacle effects in *The Abyss*.

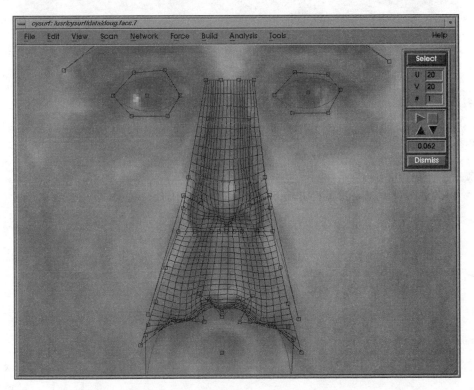

Figure 7.45   Simple 20x20 networks laid over nose and upper lip.

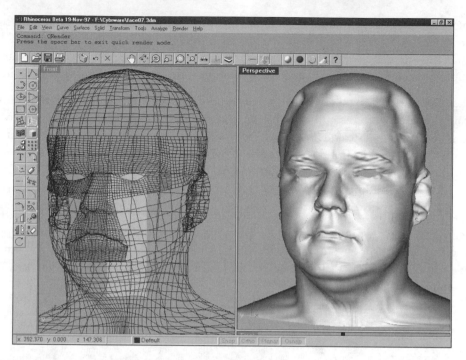

Figure 7.46 IGES model of separate network surfaces, showing grid (left) and quick render.

Moving On

You should now have a solid working knowledge of the tools and techniques available for digitizing maquettes and live subjects. Along with the character design and modeling basics from Chapters 5 and 6, this knowledge prepares you to design and build almost any character model. The next three chapters show you how to add to your models' visual appeal and realism with texture maps and shaders.

PART III

TEXTURING

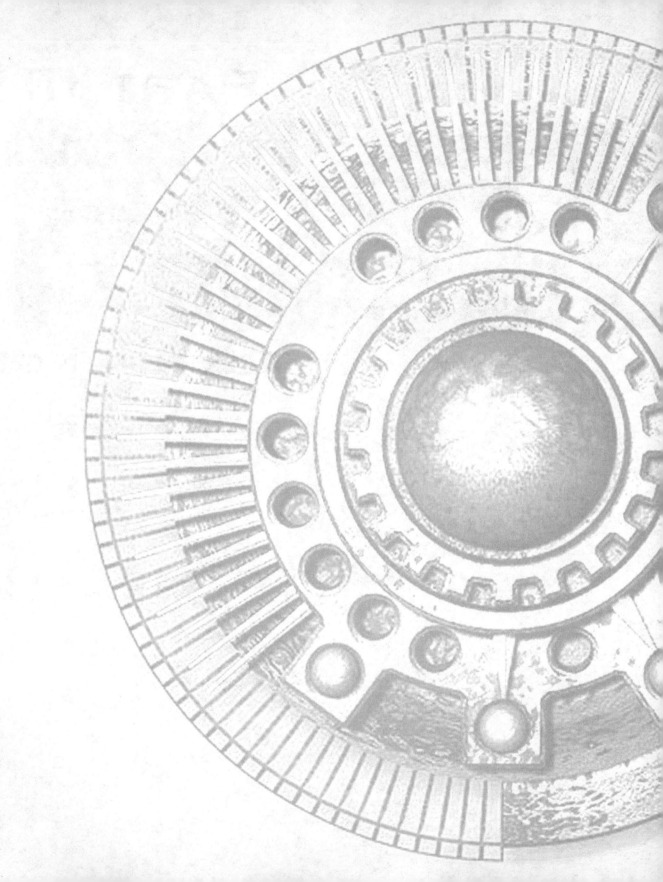

BASICS

This chapter is like a quick tour through the makeup department of a motion picture studio. Just as actors need makeup before going in front of the cameras, your models need appropriate surface materials.

This chapter offers a brief introduction to the types of materials available and a few guidelines on how you can apply them to make your characters more effective.

When you have finished modeling a character, your next step is assigning materials to the model: the coloring, textures, and shaders that add realism—or that extra touch of fantasy—for the finishing touch. Surface appearances are critical for any style of CGI character animation. A great job of texturing may not redeem a lousy piece of animation, but a lousy job of texturing can distract the audience from an otherwise excellent animation. The appearance of the character should agree with its actions. If a character moves as if made of rubber but you texture it to look like chrome, you will confuse the audience. Your texturing should help tell the story without intruding. Ideally, no one should specifically notice the maps and shaders you apply. The audience should simply accept them as a natural part of the character.

Most software refers to a combination of face attributes, texture maps, and procedural shaders as a material. This is a convenient catchall label for a large number of variables. The better programs group all the material settings and controls into a single material editor that makes it as easy as possible for you to experiment, so you can create exactly the material you need with a minimum of bother. Many programs also support material libraries. These are collections of settings that you can load, modify, and save, to speed up your work and reuse as much of it as possible.

Base Attributes

Base attributes are settings that control the model's rendered appearance without any maps or shaders. These attributes vary between programs, but generally include some form of color, specularity, ambient, transparency, and luminance.

Base color refers to the red, green, and blue (RGB) values of a material as it would appear under ambient white light, without shadows or highlights. Used alone, color is generally useful for cartoons and other primitive characters. Some software enables you to set material properties like color for each face or patch, while others limit you to setting materials for the entire object. This limits variations in base color to the same level of complexity as the model's geometry (see Figure 8.1). If you can model the character to be as complex as you need for color changes, you may be able to avoid

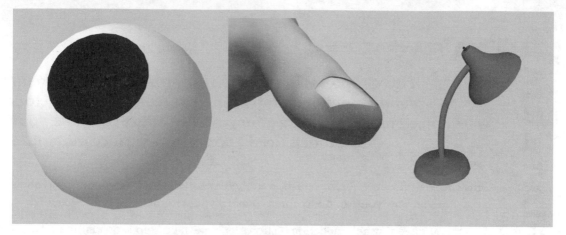

Figure 8.1 Base colors for eyeball, fingernail, and painted metal.

using texture maps or shaders. If your character requires simpler geometry with a colorfully detailed appearance, you'll need to combine base color with color maps or shaders.

Base specularity describes the intensity and extent of the *hot spot*, the area of a material that reflects the light directly into the camera lens. A tighter, brighter specularity is appropriate for shiny materials, like chitin (arthropod shells), fingernails, eyeballs, and hair. A broader, dimmer specularity is appropriate for skin, most fabrics, and matte-finished or oxidized metal (see Figure 8.2).

Base ambient values determine the color of the surface when no direct light is reflected from it. This is the color of the shadowed parts of the models shown in Figure 8.2. Depending on your software, this attribute can interact with or replace the luminance attribute. Generally, you should set ambient color to the same values as the base color, since very few materials have different shadowed and illuminated colors.

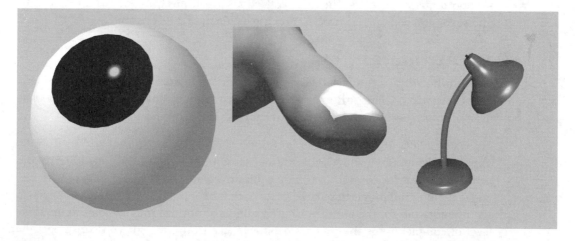

Figure 8.2 Base specularity for eyeball, fingernail, and matte-finished metal.

Base transparency controls the amount and color of light that passes through a material. Typical variables to control transparency include RGB values, to tint the light passing through, and an intensity or percentage value, to control the amount. Most characters will have very few transparent materials, but fingernails, corneas, sheer fabrics, and accessories such as eyeglasses make very good use of transparency for realistic characters. Some transparency effects will require you to model several closely spaced layers of the same objects, with outer layers having different transparency values, as in Figure 8.3.

Luminance controls the amount of self-illumination of a material. A high value makes the material appear to glow, with no shadows affecting it. This material attribute is rarely used in characters. You may occasionally have a fantasy character with glowing eyes, but a more common use is in light-emitting props, like flashlights, torches, and headlamps. If you need to simulate the highly reflective eyes of an animal in the dark, it's usually easier to set their irises or (detailed modeling!) retinas to a high luminance than to position lights and camera to catch the true reflection.

Texture Maps

Realistic characters need complex surfaces for facial features, skin, and clothing. If you are working in a more abstract style that lets you get away with solid colors and uniformly smooth surfaces, you can ignore this. But the closer you work to realism, especially when matching to live action, the more complex surfaces you will have to create for your characters. Skin must look like it has a subtle roughness, that it grew, aged, and wrinkled from use; clothing has to look like it's really made of thousands of separate fibers with a definite weave, drape, and nap; sheet materials, like polished leather and vinyl, must have the right "shine." Texture maps enable you to create these highly detailed materials while retaining the most efficient simplicity of the underlying model.

A map is an image file applied to a character or scene to override or modify the base material settings. The basic texture map types for most 3D software are color, specularity, diffusion,

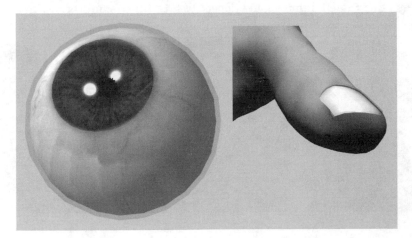

Figure 8.3 Base transparency for eyeball and fingernail.

luminance, transparency, reflection, bump, displacement, and clip. These maps control or modify the base settings of the same names. Theoretically, you could create a character that would use at least one map of each type, but most of the time, you'll only need to use a few map types.

Color And Shading Maps

Color maps modify or override the base color of the model without affecting any of the other base attributes. The left side of Figure 8.4 shows a Cyberware model of my head with a gray glossy material applied. The center shows the matching Cyberware color map. The right side shows the model with the color map applied and no other changes to the material or lighting.

Color maps are the most obvious choice for dressing up a character but don't neglect the more subtle effects you can create with the other map types. A good TD can make an object look like almost any material without using any color map at all. Conversely, even a photographic-quality color map is going to look wrong if it isn't complemented by other map types. For that reason, I recommend using color maps only as references early in the mapping process and not actually applying them to the model for rendering until last. Instead, I recommend using a light gray base color, straight 192,192,192 RGB values. Color is so overwhelming that it can distract you from getting the other settings just right, but, if a solid gray character looks good with the other maps in place, it will look great with the final colors added.

Color is also the easiest type of map to create. All consumer video, photography, and digitizing equipment is designed to capture the visible wavelengths that define surface colors, so you have a variety of tools at your disposal to gather color maps from the real world. Once that data is in your computer, even the most primitive image editing software can modify a color map. The next chapter discusses these tools and techniques in more detail, including how to create the maps shown in this chapter's figures.

Specularity maps vary or override the model's base specularity according to the map's grayscale values. These maps are necessary for mucous membranes, fingernails, claws, eyeballs, oily skin , and any other material that should appear wet, polished, shiny, or oily in some places while

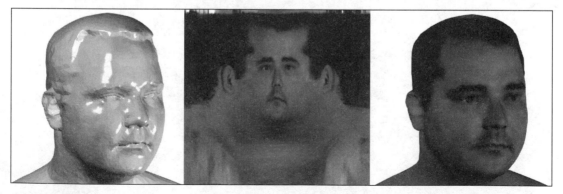

Figure 8.4 Cyberware head scan object, color map, and object with color map applied.

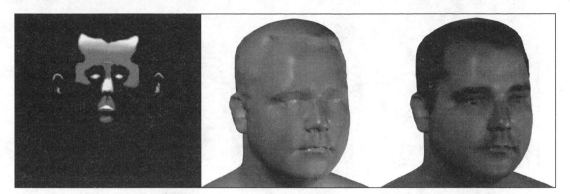

Figure 8.5   Specularity map, head with specularity map, and head with both specularity and color maps.

surrounding areas of the same material must appear dry, roughened, or matte. Human faces almost always require a specularity map. A color map alone will not reflect light properly from oily patches or taut skin while retaining the thoroughly matte areas under the cheekbones and jaw (see Figure 8.5). A uniform specularity setting is a dead giveaway that the character is CGI.

If you'd like to take a more detailed look at the effect of this specularity map, open animation file 08_05 (either AVI or MOV) from the Chapter 8 directory on this book's CD-ROM. You can use the scrub bar in your animation viewer to rotate the mapped model through a 180-degree arc while you observe the specular reflections. Note the difference in specularity between the forehead, nose, and jawline. You can compare this example with the specularity of your own face. Set up a mirror so you can see your face under a single strong light, then turn and tilt your head to reflect the light from different parts of your face. Observe the difference in strength and spread of the highlights. Chapter 9 includes an exercise on creating your own specularity maps using this technique.

Specularity mapping is also excellent for simulating the variations in woven fabric, brightening the highlights from the top of the threads and absorbing light in between the weave, as shown in Figure 8.6.

Note the dull, flat effect of the first image. It's obvious from the distribution of the reflected light that this is a flat object with a color pattern painted onto it. The second image, the specularity map, is darker where it will absorb the light and lighter where it will reflect it. The third image shows the combined effect—even though the surface is still flat, the mapped specular highlights make the material appear three-dimensional. The deepest parts of the weave are subdued, while the highest parts reflect the brightest light, simulating nylon or other gloss-finish yarn.

Diffuse maps darken the color of the model without affecting the other attributes. This type of mapping is useful for simulating dirt and other surface contaminants. Figure 8.7 shows the woven fabric color map with the grayscale map applied again, this time as a diffuse map. Now the combined effect is of dirt irregularly masking the colors of the cloth, allowing the original colors to show through where it is clean.

Luminance maps control or override the effect of base luminance, making light areas of the map appear to glow with the diffuse color of the model. This is useful mostly for special effects

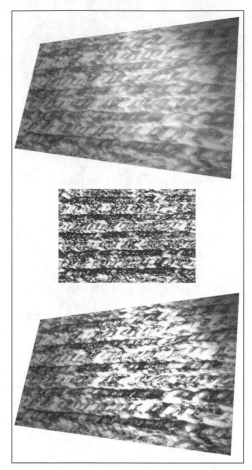 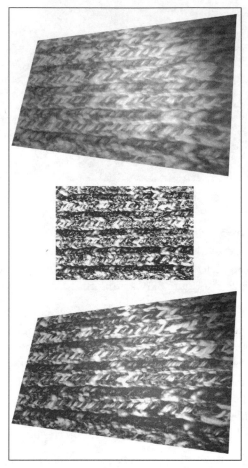

Figure 8.6 Base material with color map applied, specularity map, and base with both color and specularity maps applied.

Figure 8.7 Base material with color map applied, diffuse map, and base with both color and diffuse maps applied.

on inanimate objects. Even if a character has eerily glowing eyes, it's usually easier to create that material using base luminance than to bother with an additional map.

A transparency map controls the amount and color of light that passes through a model based on the map's RGB values. A higher, brighter setting for one of the colors permits more light of that color to shine through, making the material transparent in that range (see Figure 8.8). High values for all three colors enable light to pass uniformly, so the color of the penetrating light appears white. Transparency maps are especially useful for wing membranes, toe webbing, leaves, and other thin organic tissues that vary from fully opaque to semi- or fully transparent, based on the fine details of a map rather than modeled faces or patches.

Reflection maps should be used primarily for high-specularity surfaces, like eyeballs, fingernails, and mucous membranes, or polished accessories, like metal and glass. Even if a material is supposed to be highly polished, you should use some noise or dirt to simulate real-world

Figure 8.8 Image of leaf applied as color map and as combination color and transparency maps. Note the leaf colors in the shadow cast on the horizontal surface.

imperfections. Nothing screams "CGI!" louder than perfectly reflective chrome or glass. There are several common methods of reflection mapping, including object, environmental, and raytraced. Object reflection maps are applied only to the material and can be any map. This is especially useful when you need to cheat a scene, showing reflections of objects and sets that aren't actually there (see Figure 8.9).

GET DIRTY

The usual giveaway for CGI elements composited into live action is not enough dirt. In the real world, anything outside a sterile clean room is going to collect crud. Corrosion, contaminants, precipitated smog, you name it—dirt is everywhere. Add some rust, some dust, and some smudges and smears to your map collection. Spread some of it on your models if you have to get realistic or just to add visual appeal. Look at how your characters will move and come into contact with their environments. Any place they make habitual contact should get smudged and dirty—soles of shoes, elbows, cuffs, and knees will all collect crud over time. Keep your eyes open out in the real world, and observe and remember how materials change as they age and are abused. Take a look at an old, scuffed shoe, for instance. How would you texture a pristine CGI model of the same shoe? What color, diffuse, and specularity maps would you use? An excellent example of mapping for wear and dirt is the Sid's Room set for *Toy Story*. The book *Toy Story: The Art and Making of the Animated Film* (see the Bibliography) has a detailed explanation with examples of the maps used.

Figure 8.9 Eyeball, object reflection map, and eyeball with object reflection map applied.

Environmental reflection maps are assigned to the entire scene and render onto any material with an environmental reflection setting. You should find out exactly how environment reflections are calculated in your software. The most common method makes objects look as if they are reflecting the scene behind rather than in front of them (see Figure 8.10), and it's a dead giveaway if you are trying to achieve realism.

Automatic or raytraced reflection maps will give you the most accurate realism. The map is created by rendering an image of the scene from the mapped object's point of view, as if it were a camera with a fish-eye wide-angle lens. The drawback is that it's very difficult to cheat a scene with these reflection maps, because you have to actually build the entire scene to be reflected (see Figure 8.11).

The preceding attributes control the color and shading of the object's surfaces. The remaining attributes change the appearance of the underlying geometry, enabling you to use maps to modify the shape of your characters.

Figure 8.10 Environmental reflection map applied to an eyeball. Note that the "reflection" is of the image *behind* the object.

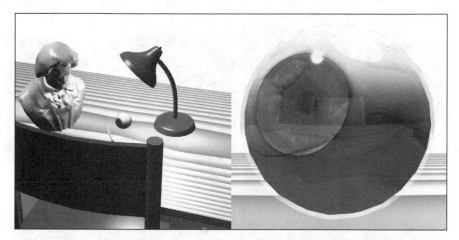

Figure 8.11 Scene with an eyeball at the center of a desk, and a close-up of the eyeball with the resulting raytraced reflection map.

Shape-Changing Maps

You can use bump maps to provide an illusion of fine surface details and imperfections that can markedly increase the realism or visual appeal of a character. These maps can make a model appear much more dimensionally complex or detailed than the model's geometry alone could achieve, without making it more difficult to set up or animate. The major disadvantage of bump maps is that the illusion of depth is only apparent face-on—the actual three-dimensional profiles of the model are unchanged. Nevertheless, there are many good applications of bump maps for both realistic and abstract characters.

Bump maps create the illusion of changes in surface depth or height based on the map's grayscale value. Bump maps generally have 8 bits (256 levels) of gray, which is plenty for most applications. You may find it useful to think of the bump map's effect as one pixel equals one vertex, as if the underlying geometry is actually made more complex by the map.

AVOIDING BUMP MAP JAGGIES

When you are creating bump maps, remember that sharp gray-value changes equal sharp 3D jaggies. The difference between one map pixel and the next creates a slope. If the difference is only a few gray values, the slope is very gentle. If the difference is between black and white, the slope is nearly vertical, and you get a 3D jagged edge in the rendered image. To avoid sharp slopes in your bump maps, you can increase the map's resolution, then apply blur or edge dither effects to smooth out any abrupt differences in gray values (see Figure 8.12).

Displacement maps are similar to bump maps but actually shift the model's geometry so the illusion of depth variations is also preserved in profile (see Figure 8.13). Note the difference in the upper and left edges between Figure 8.12 and Figure 8.13. The bump map leaves the profile unchanged, while the displacement map alters it.

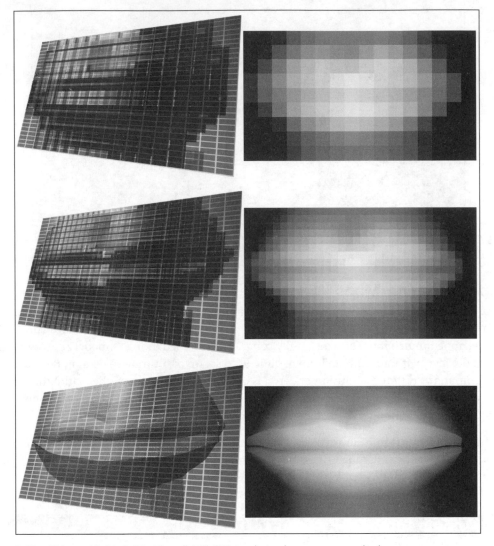

Figure 8.12 Object with 16x9, 32x18, and 640x360 resolution bump maps applied.

The major drawback to displacement maps is that the accuracy and continuity of the rendering relies on a sufficient number of vertices. If the map has more pixels than the model has vertices, the displacement becomes blocky and inaccurate. Some programs compensate for this by tessellating (subdividing) the model's faces or patches to match the resolution of the displacement map. This gives more accurate results but at the cost of a more complex model and increased processing time. If your software requires manual tessellation or a completely different mode of application for displacement maps, I don't recommend using them. Except in certain special situations where displacement maps' benefits outweigh their costs, combining an unnecessarily complex object with the hassles of map management seems to me to be the worst of both worlds.

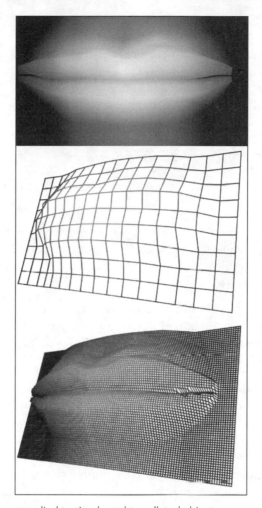

Figure 8.13 Displacement map applied to simple and tessellated objects.

Some 3D programs enable you to use a third type of shape-changing map—the clip, or *alpha*, map. This map makes parts of the material invisible to shadows, specular highlights, colors, and reflections. The effect is that of clipping out the mapped portions of the material but without modeling operations. Some software can accomplish the same effect with a combination of transparency and specularity maps. If you need to animate an opening or break in a model's surface, using a sequential or animated clip map can be a more efficient solution than modeling the effect in 3D objects. For example, if you are using bump or displacement map sequences to animate a character's mouth for lip sync, you also need to cut out the mouth opening to match the inner edge of the lips (see Figure 8.14). A matched clip map sequence will do the job perfectly and can be derived easily from the bump or displacement map sequence.

Where and how you place materials is almost as important as designing the materials themselves. A well-painted color map that's applied to the wrong part of a character doesn't do much good.

Figure 8.14   Matched color, bump, and clip maps applied to an object.

Material Placement

Ideally, the materials you apply should conform to the character's surface geometry so the material appears to be a natural part of the surface. Materials that don't follow the appropriate surface contours can make your character look like it was worked over by a wallpapering machine instead of a professional makeup artist.

Assigned materials should also move and deform along with the surface geometry when the character is animated. If you don't choose the right method of assigning a material, the material may stay in one place while the character slides out from under it. The best way to avoid these disasters is to know in advance exactly how each material must behave and what you have to do to create the effects you need. To do this, you need to understand and be able to work with your software's material placement and coordinate system.

UV(W) Mapping

You should be familiar by now with the XYZ coordinate system used to build and animate models. Most 3D software uses a second, parallel set of coordinates to control mapping. The mapping coordinates are labeled *U*, *V*, and *W*, the three letters preceding X, Y, and Z. U corresponds to the X, or horizontal, axis and V to the Y, or vertical, axis. Technically, this system is called UVW mapping, but, since the third axis is rarely used, this system is more generally called UV mapping.

This separate map coordinate system enables you to change the application of materials without having to remodel the underlying geometry. It's like pinning material onto a dressmaker's dummy. You don't have to rebuild the dummy when you make an alteration—you just move the pins to reposition the material. UV coordinates are your dressmaker's pins. UV mapping gives you the best control for assigning materials to your characters. With the right software tools, you can control material placement down to the individual vertex or patch node of your model. This is especially important if you are working with realistic characters. For example,

Figure 8.15 Color map applied to head model with UV mapping coordinates.

look at Figure 8.15. This model of my head was created by a Cyberware scanner that also recorded the surface colors. The Cyberware software assembled the model from the XYZ point data and also assigned the appropriate UV mapping coordinates.

If your software uses UV mapping, all you have to do is load the model and assign the color map using the built-in UV coordinates. You get perfect material alignment every time. This is especially important when you have complex geometry and maps that have to match precisely. UV coordinates can wrap a material all around an irregular object, getting into the undercuts and smoothly covering compound curves without inaccurate distortions. UV mapping isn't just for scanned images, either. Most of the available 3D paint software also uses UV mapping, and some of the modeling software have UV tools built in. In the next two chapters, several exercises will show you how to use UV tools to paint accurate, detailed 3D materials for your characters.

If your software doesn't support UV mapping, you have a few options that can work almost as well with a little more effort: planar, cylindrical, spherical, and repeating pattern mapping. The most basic mapping is planar.

Planar Mapping

A planar map is like the image from a slide or motion picture projector—it passes all the way through the model, as shown in Figure 8.16.

The obvious problem with planar mapping is that it can't get into undercuts, and that it smears the material along any surface that nearly parallels the line of projection. Planar mapping is therefore limited to applications where you can ensure that the projected distortions won't be visible or are not important. You can do this by assigning separate planar materials according to surface *normals*, the orientation of a face or patch. If your model is at all complex, it's very time-consuming to find all the faces that share a common direction, assign a planar material to them, and repeat the process for all the faces. It can be done, but there are better uses of your time. There are applications where planar projections are useful—transparency-mapped lighting and front projection, for instance. However, those fall under the heading of special effect rather than character animation.

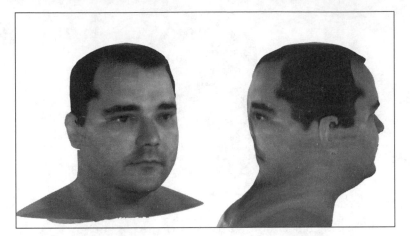

Figure 8.16 Color map applied to head model with planar mapping coordinates.

Cylindrical Mapping

Cylindrical mapping is more useful for character materials. With a little care, it can be almost as versatile as UV mapping. In principle, it's like rolling the applied material into a cylinder inside the model and projecting the material outward until it hits the surface. This takes care of the planar smearing problem in one direction, because the cylindrical projection looks accurate from every side (see Figure 8.17). The only visible distortions are at the end caps of the cylinder. In this example, the lower end cap is invisible, and the upper one is matched by flaws in the model itself. Some minor alignment problems still remain. The rear edge of the ear catches a bit of misplaced shadow that true UV mapping would place precisely.

If you can construct your characters so the ends of their cylindrical forms are concealed by other materials, you can hide the discrepancies of cylindrical mapping. For those situations where the end of the cylinder must be exposed, you'll need to spend a little extra care on designing the material to blend inconspicuously at the end cap. Project 9.2 in Chapter 9 will show you how to deal with this problem.

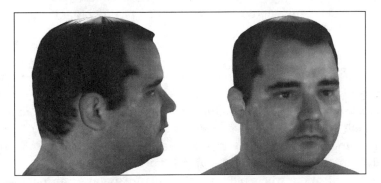

Figure 8.17 Color map applied to head model with cylindrical mapping coordinates.

Spherical Mapping

Spherical mapping takes the principle of cylindrical mapping one axis further, wrapping the material in two directions at once. This can be handy if you have a material specifically designed to be spherically mapped. However, if you are trying to adapt a planar or cylindrical material for spherical mapping, it's about as much work as tweaking two cylindrical maps. If your software doesn't have the tools to tweak the material's center and both projection axes, you'll end up with something like Figure 8.18. These results are close enough in one direction, but the second axis just causes too much distortion to be usable. Generally, spherical mapping requires spherical material design from scratch.

Repeating Patterns

Many natural materials have repeating but variable patterns. Skin creases, scales, denticles (sharkskin), and cloth all have consistent patterns that vary slightly depending on the part of the creature covered and the movement or distortion of the underlying surface. One way to deal with this challenge is to paint a huge map, large enough to cover the entire model and high-resolution enough to show all these fine details. That may not be the most efficient way, however. You may do just as well, with less work, by using a smaller map and repeating it.

There are two common ways of repeating materials. The first one is called tiling, after its similarity to laying floor tiles. This method repeats the material at regular intervals, producing results like a checkerboard or quilt, as shown in Figure 8.19.

The results of tiling are sometimes too uniform for characters. If you are working toward a certain level of realism, your characters will be more believable if they have a realistic distribution of smaller and larger patterns. In the real world, skin creases, scales, and denticles are smaller near surfaces that have to bend. These smaller divisions in the surface make it easier to flex without tearing. For the same reasons, faces or patches in CGI models are generally finer and more closely spaced where they have to flex. You can take advantage of this parallel to create natural-looking materials with repeating patterns using face mapping.

Figure 8.18 Color map applied to head model with spherical mapping coordinates.

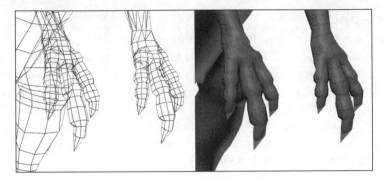

Figure 8.19 Tiled map applied to a hand model.

Face mapping is similar to tiling but with finer control. Instead of repeating the pattern the same size over and over, face mapping automatically alters the size of the pattern to match the size of the underlying face or patch (see Figure 8.20).

Look carefully at the differences between Figures 8.19 and 8.20. For the larger faces along the raptor's belly where the skin doesn't need to bend sharply, the material pattern is larger. For the smaller faces in the hands, the skin needs to be more flexible, and the material pattern is smaller. Also, face mapping makes the distribution of seams appear more natural, while the grid layout of tiling seems artificial.

You can combine face mapping with one of the other methods, as well. For example, you might use face mapping to apply bump and color materials to simulate scales on a lizard, but they'd all be the same color. To correct this, you could use planar projection for a whole-body diffuse map that would darken the upper body scales but leave the belly scales lighter. By mixing material mapping, you make it harder for your audience to spot artifacts that give away your work as CGI. The more natural variety and subtlety you put into your materials, the closer you can simulate reality. Even if your character is more stylized or caricatured, the additional detail lends a great deal of visual appeal.

There is one more way to repeat materials, but it's in another dimension entirely—the fourth dimension—time! Some software enables you to apply an animation or a sequence of images

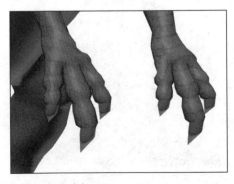

Figure 8.20 Face map applied to a hand model.

as a map or to animate the parameters of base materials. This can be very useful if used deliberately and when appropriate, and really annoying if overused or abused. Color cycling, for example, has been beaten to death and is rarely a good addition to a character animation. On the other hand, one of the easiest and most educational uses is to create mapped lip-sync sequences. This makes lip sync easier to practice and modify for the beginner, and can even be used in production if map sequences can suit the character's design. The next chapter will show you a few more examples of animated materials and how to make them.

Moving On

I hope this chapter gives you a solid foundation for designing appropriate materials for your characters. The next chapter is about the tools and techniques you can use to create and modify your own texture maps and apply them to your models.

AND APPLYING MAPS

2D maps are important to character animation in direct proportion to the realism of the characters. Learn to make and use cartoon and realistic maps, and your characters will be more effective storytellers.

This chapter covers the creation and application of 2D maps. This is the practical application of the theories described in the previous chapter and a prerequisite for the next chapter on 3D painting tools and shaders. Projects in this chapter show you how to capture textures from real-world materials, process them into maps to fit your characters, and create fantastic or caricature maps that don't yet exist outside your imagination.

If you are compositing CGI elements into live footage, you simply can't create a believable character without using maps or shaders. Simulating natural materials necessary to characters, for example, skin, mucous membranes, nails, claws, chitin, eyeballs, wrinkles, scales, feathers, fabric, leather, rubber, armor, keloids, or denticles, would be difficult or impossible without maps. Good maps also make your characters more appealing to your audience's eyes. Humans are built to appreciate visually complex textures and patterns, and, if your characters are interesting to look at (in addition to moving well), your audience will appreciate them that much more.

Real-World Texture Capture

The most efficient way to get complex, naturalistic maps is to start with nature. Most natural materials reveal their origins in growth layers, wrinkles, wear patterns, and other traces that are difficult or time-consuming to mimic by hand. If you are an accomplished 2D artist, by all means, use your talents to create your own maps from scratch. If you are less gifted, you can largely make up for it by starting with the natural world and simply working minor changes on the best raw materials.

There are at least four major ways of getting real-world images into your computer: scanners, video cameras with digitizer boards, PhotoCD, and digital cameras. Each approach is viable for creating character animation maps, but there are some tradeoffs for each one that may make a difference for your specific application.

Scanners

Scanners have been around for a relatively long time, and there are many models, prices, and feature sets to choose from. Many print shops and service bureaus also provide access to scanners, so it's not even necessary for you to own one. You can pick up a good color flatbed scanner for a few hundred dollars, and almost all the current models can be controlled directly by programs like Photoshop via TWAIN or ISIS drivers. Most scanners use either SCSI or parallel-port interfaces. If you are considering a scanner that requires a proprietary interface card, I don't recommend buying it. I recommend paying the small surcharge for a SCSI interface, because you can use the same machine on Macs, PCs, and SGIs. The advantages of scanners for mapmaking are that you can scan anything you can flatten on the glass platen, from photos to cloth to leather to raw meat, and bad scans don't cost you anything. The disadvantages are that you can't readily scan materials that are rigidly 3D, that you can't get to the scanner (or get the scanner to them), or that require special lighting that the scan head can't match.

Video

A video-digitizing board and a video camera or camcorder are very good additions to a character animator's workstation. These systems can be add-ons to your computer's main video card or a replacement for it. Generally, they have a selection of input jacks for RCA, cable, S-Video or BNC video connectors, a duplicate set of output jacks and an SVGA connector for your monitor, and record images or video directly to your computer's hard drive. In addition to digitizing still frames for maps, many boards can also digitize video sequences for match footage and motion studies. If you choose a board that also has video output, you can record your animations to videotape without any additional investment (see Chapter 20 for details). The advantages for digitizing maps are that anything the camera can see, you can digitize; you can work from VCR or camcorder tapes as well as from a live camera; you can set up whatever kind of lighting you need with a standard camera stand; and bad shots don't cost you anything. The disadvantages are that you usually can't get as high a resolution or color depth as film or scanning, you have to pay closer attention to lighting, and, if you want to do on-location capture, you need a camcorder.

PhotoCD

PhotoCD is an especially versatile means of capturing raw materials for character maps. This process requires you to shoot color film in a standard camera (usually 35mm), then have the film processed by one of Kodak's licensees onto a PhotoCD that you can put in your computer's CD-ROM drive. The PhotoCD format is supported by Photoshop and most other paint software. The advantages are that you have access to the full range of photographic lenses, filters, camera stands, lights, and setup techniques; the resolution and color depth of the PhotoCD images can match feature film requirements; you don't have to invest in any special equipment; and you "pay as you go" for the images you need. The disadvantages are that you have to wait for processing and the per-image costs can add up quickly, so it's awkward and expensive to experiment. You really need to know what you're doing before you drop off a roll of film for PhotoCD processing. When you're shooting tests, you can use slide film and have selected slides scanned or post-processed to PhotoCD—that usually costs more per image, but it can save you money over processing whole rolls for a few good shots. Several of the images in this book's Color Studio were scanned from slides. As you can see, the image quality is very good.

Ask your local film shop for details. I've generally found photo professionals to be very interested and helpful in the PhotoCD format.

Digital Camera

The most recent entry to the field of electronic imaging is the digital camera. These devices are like self-contained cameras and digitizing cards, enabling you to capture and store images for later download to your computer. The advantages are that you can see your results immediately so you can discard and reshoot bad images; you can use lights and camera stands; you can shoot on location without carrying awkward amounts of gear; and bad shots don't cost you anything. The disadvantages are the maximum number of images the camera can hold, the generally lower resolution (compared to PhotoCD or scanners), and the high cost of a good camera. For a few hundred dollars, you can get a digital camera that will produce snapshots suitable for your Web page. But if you want a camera that produces high-resolution images for television or feature film work, it will set you back several thousand dollars.

Realism

When you are called on to match live action, especially inserting a CGI character into live footage, you have to use all the realism tricks at your disposal. Materials have to be an exact match, their appearance under the matched lighting has to be identical, and, in general, you have to do your best to duplicate reality.

If at all possible, you should photograph and digitize materials onsite at the time of the live-action shoot. This gives you the opportunity to get extreme close-ups of textures and materials that may not show up clearly in the match footage. If a character is going to extrude itself from the tile floor, it's a good idea to have an exact full-color scan of that tile floor to use as a map. If you can't get shots onsite at the time, talk to the set and prop crews afterward to see if you can get shots of the materials later.

You should also shoot general coverage of the scene for use in reflection maps. Even a *clean plate* shot for the compositing effects may not be what you need for reflection mapping, but if you've got some nice clear 35mm prints, you can usually piece together a decent environment map. Make sure you make the map large enough. If a reflective object has some broad convex curves, a tiny fraction of the reflection map can stretch across quite a bit of the object.

If you have to work exclusively from the match footage, use image-processing software with an eyedropper tool to sample the footage for material colors. You will also need to sample hotspots or a white card to pick up the original light colors, because they will affect the material's appearance, as well.

Clothing

Fabric is second only to skin as an important part of your mapping palette. With the obvious variety of fabrics available, you might think that you'll have to build a huge library of fabric maps. Not so! I'm never one to discourage map collecting, but you can fake a surprising number of fabrics with a handful of basic elements. Fabrics are either woven or sheet. If it's a sheet material, like leather or vinyl, the texture is easy enough to figure out just by looking at it. If it's a woven material, simulating the texture gets a little more complex. Here are some hints:

- *Identify the weave*—Fabrics are manufactured in a wide variety of weaves, but half a dozen good bump maps will enable you to fake most of the materials you'll run across. I like digitizing shots of coarse-woven cloth, like canvas and burlap, then applying them at a very small size to simulate finer materials.

- *Identify the finish*—Fabrics can be rough and slubby, or smooth and satiny. The finish will determine what type of specularity and diffusion maps you apply. These can generally be modified versions of the bump map.

- *Identify the color*—This is where you may have to collect a lot of swatches, especially for patterned materials. On the positive side, you can create original tileable patterns and overlay them on the standard weave and finish maps to create your own fabrics.

Making Cloth Maps From Digitized Images

The three map types that most identify a fabric are transparency, bump, and specular. If you are using a video digitizer, PhotoCD, or a digital camera, it's easy to get all three. If you are using a scanner, it's a little more difficult since you have very little control over the lighting.

The first step is to set up your capture gear to get a close-up of the samples with very strong backlighting and no front lighting. My own setup is a transparent Lexan clipboard mounted in front of a floodlamp, secured in front of my camcorder. You may be able to get away with stretching a fabric sample directly in front of a light source, but that's a fire hazard, and I strongly encourage you to find another way. Figure 9.1 shows some examples of raw captures made with a Hi-8 camcorder and an ATI Turbo Pro PC2TV video card.

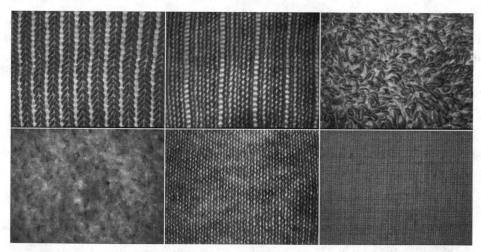

Figure 9.1 Video-captured backlit fabrics.

These captures can be used as-is for transparency maps, with lighter areas being more transparent. If you want to simulate colored fabrics, you can convert the raw captures to grayscale, then filter them with the fabric color to get a more accurate transparency appearance.

You can also use the raw capture as-is for bump maps, if the sample is not completely opaque anywhere and is uniformly colored. I recommend digitizing only white fabrics for transparency values. Any color in the weave throws off the transparency values and distorts bump values, as well. If the sample is completely opaque anywhere, you may lose necessary surface details in the blacked-out areas. You can try using brighter light sources to punch through the darker areas, but be careful not to over-light the thinnest, most transparent areas.

If transparency lighting can't give you an adequate bump map, you can try side-lighting. This works best with a camera stand with two or more positionable lights. The idea is to place the light sources so the light is cast nearly parallel to the surface to be captured. If you do it right, the highest bumps catch the brightest light, and the deeper parts of the fabric are cast in shadow, as shown in Figure 9.2.

You need to carefully balance the light so the sample is evenly lit from both sides. Any strong gradation from one side to the other will make it much more difficult to match the image's edges for a tileable map.

A little modification of the bump map will give you a good specularity map. Generally, you catch highlights from woven fabrics at the high points in the weave, with a few stray highlights from loose or protruding single fibers in the deeper parts. You can simulate this with a moderate amount of effort. Convert the bump map to grayscale, increase the contrast, and lower the brightness until the high points are in sharp relief. Then, add a noise factor to the entire map. When applied as a specularity map, the image will produce highlights from the highest "threads" plus random highlights throughout the surface, mimicking stray fibers catching the light. It's

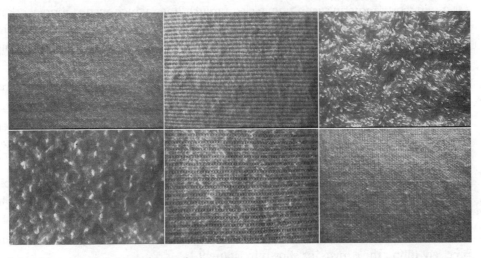

Figure 9.2 Video-captured side-lit fabrics, for bump maps.

seemingly minuscule details like this that make the difference between "a nice simulation" and "is that really CGI?"

Capturing color maps is easy by comparison. Just light your sample evenly, and, if color accuracy is important, scan a color reference chart, then follow your paint software's procedures for color calibration.

Once you have the raw images, you'll generally want to make them tile seamlessly. This is a straightforward process—it just requires patience and attention to detail.

Making Tileable Maps

This project will show you the basic process of turning a captured image into a tileable map using Adobe Photoshop. If your preferred paint software enables you to cut, copy, and paste, and to smudge or feather edges, you can use it to do the same thing.

1. Open the Cloth060.bmp image from the Chapter 9 directory on this book's CD-ROM.

2. Convert the image mode to grayscale. Turn on the Info palette. From the File menu, select Preferences|Units & Rulers, and set the units preference to Pixels. This will make it easier for you to precisely select, copy, and paste specific ranges of pixels.

3. Examine the image for vertical and horizontal *match-lines*.

   Match-lines are rows or columns of pixels that have similar patterns on both sides. If you cut and paste an image along a match-line, the seam is much harder to see, and the pasted image looks like a single image rather than a patchwork. Spotting match-lines takes practice, so I've included a lot of raw fabric scans in the Chapter 9 directory on this book's CD-ROM. After you complete this project, you should go back and repeat the process with some of the other patterns, just for practice.

   For this project, I've selected an image with relatively clean and obvious match-lines. Most real-world materials won't have clean match-lines, which means more work in cleanup and edge smudging. This example is an easy one for you to practice on. The most prominent vertical match-line is at 202 pixels from the left, and the most prominent horizontal match-line is at 215 pixels from the top.

4. Select from 202,215 up and to the left until the selected area is 128W by 216H, according to the Info palette.

   Take a close look at the borders of the selected area (see Figure 9.3). Compare the left and right edges, and the top and bottom. Note how similar they are and where they have prominent differences.

5. Copy the selection. Choose Image|Canvas Size, and increase the dimensions to double the selection's resolution, 256X and 432Y. This is to give you the necessary space to paste four copies of the selection.

6. Paste four copies of the selection into the enlarged canvas, aligning the edges and precisely filling the canvas, as shown in Figure 9.4.

7. Zoom in on the seam areas running through the vertical and horizontal centers of the image.

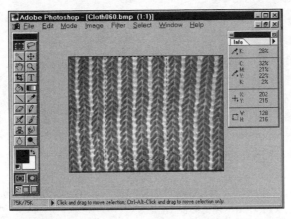

Figure 9.3 Selected area with match-lines.

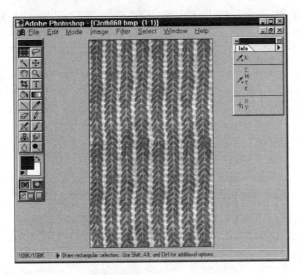

Figure 9.4 Four copies of the selection pasted together.

You need to obliterate the obvious dividing line between the pasted sections without destroying the overall pattern. In Photoshop, the tools I use most for doing this are the Smudge tool and the Blur filter. Smudge, blur, or otherwise camouflage the seams between the pasted sections. You should get results like Figure 9.5.

When you've finished hiding the seams, you should have an image that looks like a continuous piece of cloth. This is still not a tileable map—the top/bottom and right/left edges are still imperfect matches. However, the pasting and smudging has created an area that you can select with perfectly matching edges. Any selection equal to the original pasted image, that is, 128W by 216H, will automatically have matching edges.

8. Using the Crop tool, select a 128W by 216H area, not including the outer borders of the image or within smudging distance of the outer borders or the vertical or horizontal seams. If you are still using Photoshop 3, use the Select tool followed by the Crop

Figure 9.5 Before (left) and after (right) smudged portions of a pasted seam.

menu option. You want the selection's edges to run through previously uncut parts of the image. This selection will tile seamlessly.

9. Save the cropped image with a new file name. Because you'll probably be using it as a transparency map, KnitTran.bmp would be appropriate. Your results should look like Figure 9.6. If you like, you can test the tiling ability of this image by repeating Steps 5 and 6 with it.

Now that you have a basic tileable map, you can use it as a building block for finer-detail tileable maps. For ordinary tiling, you can use it as-is and simply reduce its applied scale or increase its repetition rate, whichever your 3D software requires. For face tiling, you will have to multiply the map's dimensions by copying and pasting as necessary to get an appropriate level of per-face detail. For example, if you simply applied KnitTran.bmp as-is to a character's torso using face mapping, the pattern would look very large, suitable for a sweater. If you wanted the pattern to resemble a finer knit, you might make another map with four vertical and horizontal iterations of KnitTran.bmp.

You can get acceptably realistic results simply by applying this tileable map as a transparency and bump map over an object with a base color, as in Figure 9.7.

Figure 9.6 Finished tileable map.

Figure 9.7 Tileable map applied as transparency and bump.

Creating maps for flat surfaces is relatively easy, but most characters' surfaces are curved. The next section shows you the tools and techniques that can help you map curved surfaces.

Non-Planar Mapping

Creating maps that will conform to curved surfaces is difficult enough that any tool that can make it easier is definitely worth your time to learn. Some 3D programs have features or plug-ins to assist with making maps for different mapping coordinates. The most useful for general character work is UVW mapping, but there are special cases where spherical or cylindrical mapping is useful, as well. One of the most elegant tools for spherical mapping is a Photoshop filter named Polar Coordinates.

Polar Coordinates

This filter changes the normal XY coordinates of a 2D image to polar coordinates, like a Mercator projection. The center of the image is stretched out along the top edge, and the four sides of the image are spread out to form the bottom edge of the polar image. The following project will show you how this filter can be used to assemble a spherical eyeball map from a collection of digitized images.

PROJECT 9.2 Making A Realistic Eyeball Color Map From Digitized Images

The first step is to capture a series of close-up images of your subject's eyeball. I did this by setting up a video camera with a spotlight next to it and grabbing a series of stills as I rotated my eye as far as possible in every direction. This gave me a variety of images to choose from, but you only need enough to provide overlapping coverage of the front surface of the eyeball. The images I selected are in the Chapter 9 directory on this book's CD-ROM, files eyeba008.bmp, eyeba010.bmp, eyeba012.bmp, eyeba013.bmp, eyeba015.bmp, eyeba018.bmp, eyeba020.bmp, and eyeba040.bmp, as shown in Figure 9.8.

The Polar Coordinates filter requires a consistent center for an image to be converted. You need to make sure all the images are centered around the pupil.

1. Load eyeba008.bmp. Erase all of the image except the sclera (white), iris, and pupil. Choose Image|Canvas Size, and change it to 320×320 pixels.

2. Open the Info palette. Select the color portion of the image contents, as shown in Figure 9.9.

3. Zoom in on the pupil. Grab the exact center of the pupil, and drag the selection so the coordinates readout in the Info palette reads 160,160 (the exact center of the canvas), as shown in Figure 9.10.

4. Choose Select|None, or click anywhere to drop the selection. Save the file with a new name. Repeat these four steps for the other eyeball images, being careful to center the pupil as precisely as possible. For some of the images, the pupil will appear to be an ellipse. Estimate the top-to-bottom and left-to-right centerlines of the ellipse, and select the point where they cross as the pupil's center. Your results should look like Figure 9.11.

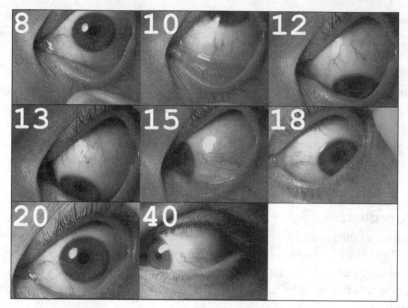

Figure 9.8 Digitized frames of eyeball to be assembled for spherical map.

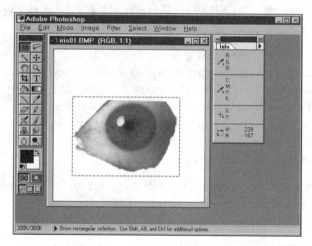

Figure 9.9 Eyeball image area selected.

You may have noticed that the first image has a strong highlight in the upper-left iris. This would look odd in the final rendering, because there would be correct highlights from the scene's lights plus this incorrect one, which would move around with the eye's motion. You need to get rid of the highlight while preserving the rest of the iris.

5. Reopen the first image. Zoom in on the highlight. Select (I'd use the Lasso tool) a similar area on the opposite side of the pupil, as in Figure 9.12.

6. Copy and paste the selection. Choose Layer|Transform|Flip Horizontal to reverse the selection left-to-right. Use the left arrow key to slide the selection over the highlight,

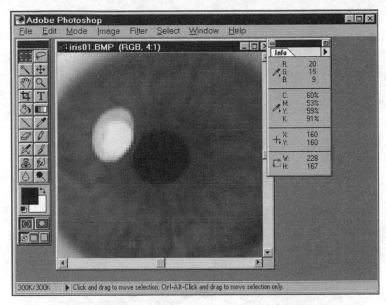

Figure 9.10 Pupil centered precisely at 160,160.

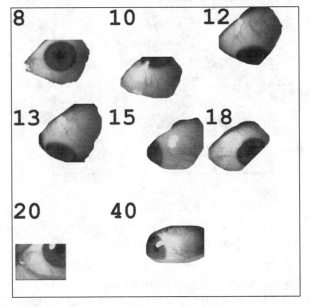

Figure 9.11 Centered eyeball images.

being careful to match the selection's edges as closely as possible to the surrounding area. Choose Image|Adjust|Brightness/Contrast, and, with Preview turned on, adjust the brightness and contrast of the selection to match the surrounding area as closely as possible. When the selection is matched, deselect it (see Figure 9.13). Save the corrected image.

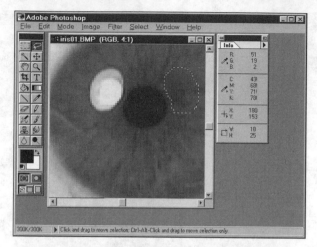

Figure 9.12 Selected mirror area for covering highlight.

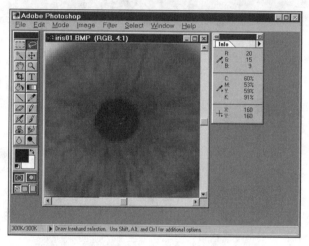

Figure 9.13 Highlight covered and selection blended in.

Now that you've got all the eyeball segments cut out and the iris highlight corrected, you're ready for the polar coordinate conversion.

7. Choose Filter|Distort|Polar Coordinates. Choose the Polar To Rectangular option (see Figure 9.14). Save the filtered file under a new name. Load each of the other eyeball segment images, and filter them to polar coordinates, as in Figure 9.15.

Polar coordinates enable you to select, paste, and modify spherical sections with the same tools and techniques as conventional 2D images without worrying about spherical distortions. If you tried to assemble the images in Figure 9.11 into a spherical map, you'd have a really hard time. With polar coordinates, it's a relatively simple matter of piecing together rectangular selections in a definite, easy-to-see relationship.

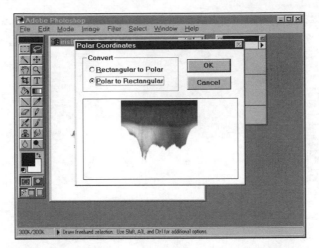

Figure 9.14   Polar Coordinates filter dialog.

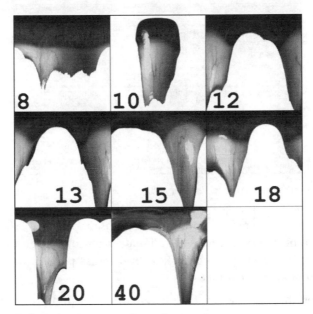

Figure 9.15   All eight eyeball segments converted to polar coordinates.

With all the eyeball segments in convenient rectangular packages, you're ready to copy and paste them into a complete eyeball map. There are a couple of tricks you can use to make the map a little smoother.

8. Open the first image (frame 8), and open the second one (frame 10) beside it, as in Figure 9.16. Use the Magic Wand tool to select the color area from 10 and paste into 8, as in Figure 9.17.

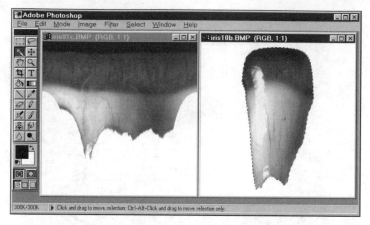

Figure 9.16 Color section of frame 10 selected using the Magic Wand tool.

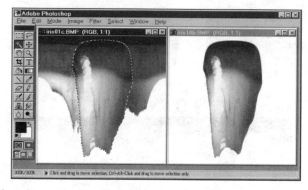

Figure 9.17 Selection from frame 10 pasted into frame 8.

Here's the fun part. There's an option for the Erase tool called Erase To Saved that erases through the current changes to an image to reveal the version of the image as it was last saved. This enables you to selectively erase parts of the pasted segment, leaving the original image intact.

9. Double-click on the Erase tool to select it, and open the Options palette. Set the Erase options to Erase To Saved, as shown in Figure 9.18.

10. You can use any of the brushes or other settings to modify the Erase tool's effects. I recommend starting with a very small dithered brush until you are familiar with the tool's effects. Carefully erase hotspots, dark areas, and other flaws from the pasted segment, allowing better areas of the first image to show through. When you're satisfied that you've combined the best of both images, save the file with a new name.

11. Repeat Steps 8, 9, and 10 to add the best parts of images 12, 13, 15, 18, 20, and 40. Fill in any blank areas with patterns sampled from nearby areas. You should end up with something like Figure 9.19.

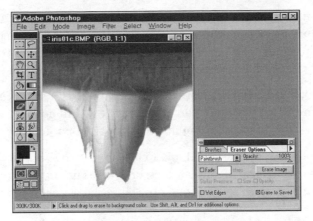

Figure 9.18 Erase To Saved option selected, and portions of the pasted image erased to reveal original image beneath.

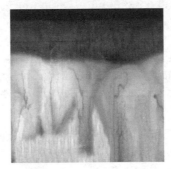

Figure 9.19 Assembled eyeball polar coordinate map.

With the eyeball segments all assembled and blended together, you're ready to convert the eyeball map from polar coordinates back to normal coordinates.

12. Choose Image|Distort|Polar Coordinates. Choose the Rectangular To Polar option. Save the filtered file under a new name. Your results should look something like Figure 9.20.

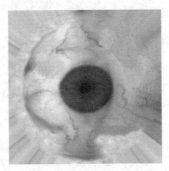

Figure 9.20 Completed eyeball map.

Ugly sucker, isn't it? Trust me, my eyeballs really don't look that bad. The overall effect is a combination of too yellow a light source for the video capture, shadows on parts of the sclera that were not revealed brightly in other segments, and no color correction. You can make a much nicer-looking eyeball map if you want to, but I figure this one is good for a monster or two.

For planar projection, this map will work as-is. For cylindrical or spherical projection, you will have to increase the size of the image canvas to provide additional map space needed to cover the back of the object without stretching the front out of proportion (see Figure 9.21).

While spherical mapping can be useful, most characters aren't shaped like basketballs. They tend to have more irregular curves and surfaces, and there's no simple geometric projection that will make those surfaces easier to paint or map. That's where unwrapped templates come in.

Working With Unwrapped Templates

There are a number of program features and plug-ins that enable you to unwrap the complex geometry of a character and roll it out flat in a wireframe view. This wireframe can serve as a template layer in Photoshop or other paint software. It makes creating an accurate map almost as easy as paint-by-numbers. When you paint colors in a face of the wireframe template, you know that those colors will map precisely to that face on the original model. Two of these template-making tools are the Unwrap plug-in for 3DS MAX and Animation:Master's Flatten function.

Unwrap For 3DS MAX

If you are using 3DS Max, I highly recommend Peter Watje's Unwrap plug-in. You can download it from **www.blarg.net/~peterw/mtutor** or contact the publisher at **peterw@blarg.net**.

Unwrap transforms the texture coordinates of the selected object into a 2D bitmap. You can specify the dimensions of the bitmap, choose whether to show hidden edges, and limit the

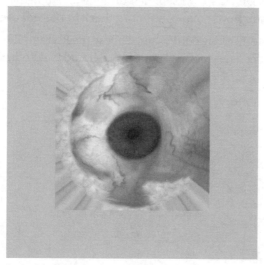

Figure 9.21   Spherical projection eyeball map.

drawn faces to those with specific materials assigned. The installation and use of Unwrap is about as simple as you can get, and very intuitive. I've found this utility to be robust and useful. In Figure 9.22, you can see a 2048×2048 unwrapped bitmap of the my head object. Unwrap version 1 didn't even hiccup at this large amount of data, and it created the bitmap in less than 20 seconds.

If you are working with someone else's models, it's helpful to create an Unwrap bitmap, apply it to the mesh as a color map, then render a few images like Figure 9.23.

This gives you a handy reference for the object geometry, and the rendered shading is much easier to interpret than a standard wireframe render. The shading provides depth cues that make it easier for you to discriminate between nearer and farther faces.

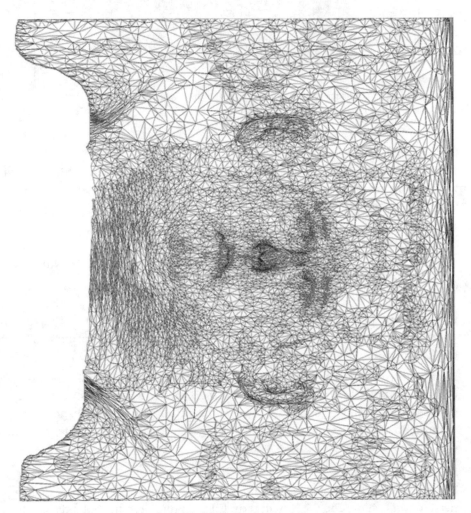

Figure 9.22   Head object processed by Peter Watje's Unwrap 1.

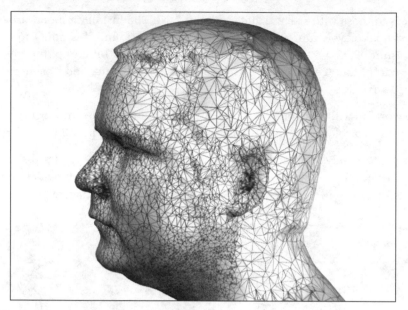

Figure 9.23 Head object re-rendered with Unwrap map.

A:M Flatten

Animation:Master has a very useful unwrap function, called Flatten, which you can use to create wireframe templates. Flatten also enables you to apply maps to objects in their flattened state, so the restored state retains the mapping coordinates.

Flattening A Spline Model

In this example, you'll flatten the Arnold head that's included with A:M, create a wireframe template from it, and apply a map to it.

1. Open the Arnold model. Open the model hierarchy so you can select a Group of control points (CPs) to flatten. Select the face group. Click on the Hide button, or press h to hide all the other CPs. This hides Arnold's hair and sunglasses, as shown in Figure 9.24.

   Flatten unwraps the selected object cylindrically around the Z axis, which is usually color-coded blue. To create Arnold's head map, you'll probably want to paint it for cylindrical mapping around an axis passing vertically through the head. The default orientation of the Z axis in A:M is back-to-front, so you'll need to rotate the Z axis 90 degrees so it's oriented up-and-down.

2. Press R, or click on the Rotate Mode button.

   The group axes have color-coded handles. To rotate the Z (blue) axis 90 degrees, you need to rotate it around the X (red) axis. Click on and drag the red axis handle until the Group Rotate boxes read 90,0,0 (see Figure 9.25).

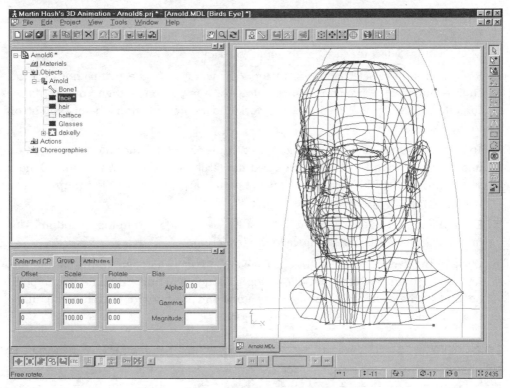

Figure 9.24 Arnold face group selected, with other CPs hidden.

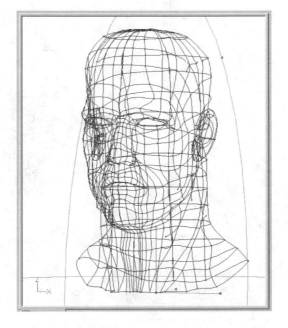

Figure 9.25 Group axes rotated so Z is vertical.

Flatten is an Action function, so you'll have to create an Action before you can use it.

3. Right-click on the Action folder to create a new Action. Press F7, or click on the Muscle Mode button. Select the face group again (see Figure 9.26).

4. Right-click on the selected group in the View window. In the menu that appears, choose Flatten. The program will calculate for a few seconds, then you should see something like Figure 9.27. Save your work under a new file name before you go on to the next step.

To create a wireframe template that you can use to paint a face map, you need an image large enough to match or exceed the resolution of the final map. Taking a screenshot of the A:M View window won't do for any but the smallest maps, so you need to render a larger wireframe.

5. Zoom in on the flattened face until it fills the View window from top to bottom. This minimizes the wasted border space in the rendering.

6. Click on the Render To A File button. The Render Panel will open. In the Output tab, set the Height and Width to produce a large enough wireframe map for you to paint on, and set the Aspect to 1. Choose a file name and directory for the rendering. In the Quality tab, choose Wireframe. Click on Start.

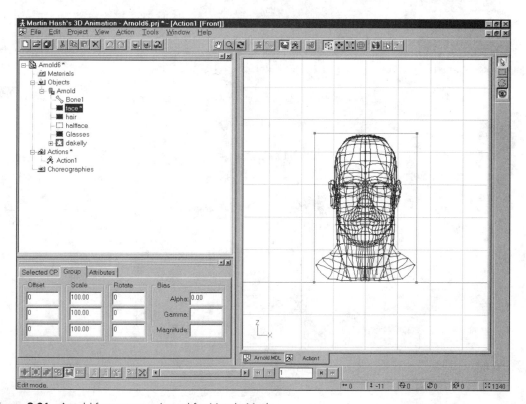

Figure 9.26 Arnold face group selected for Muscle Mode.

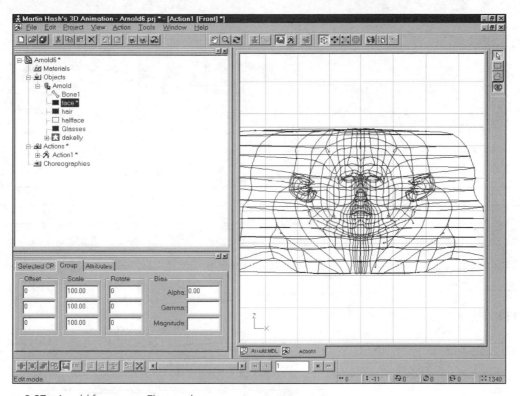

Figure 9.27   Arnold face group Flattened.

Wireframes render very quickly, so you should be able to open the wireframe template in your paint software almost immediately. Your results should look like Figure 9.28.

At this point, you can paint the map any way you like. As a quick-and-dirty sample for this project, I scaled, distorted, and tweaked my head's cyberscan map to fit the wireframe template (see Figure 9.29). The next step is to apply the finished map to the flattened group.

7. Right-click on the Arnold model in the hierarchy. Choose Import|Decal from the menu. Choose DAKArnl2.bmp from the Chapter 9 directory on this book's CD-ROM. The map will be appended to the hierarchy under the Arnold model, with a red-and-white star to show that it's a map.

8. Right-click on the DAKArnl2 star in the hierarchy. Choose Position from the menu. The map will take a few moments to load, then you'll see it in the View window with an outline and handles, ready to position, as shown in Figure 9.30.

9. Move the corner and middle handles to position the map. Zoom in as necessary to get the eyes, nose, and mouth lined up properly. The map was painted directly over the flattened template, so you should be able to get a pretty good fit simply by moving the handles to the borders of the model, as shown in Figure 9.31.

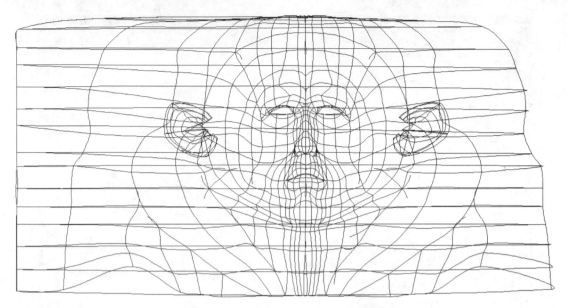

Figure 9.28 Arnold face wireframe template.

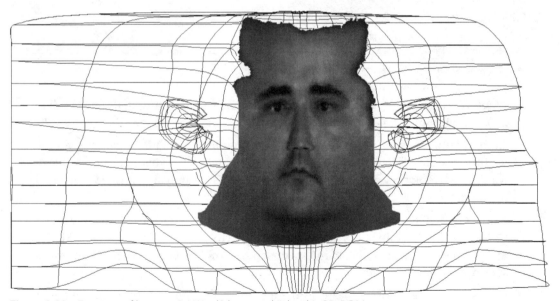

Figure 9.29 Face map, file name DAKArnl2.bmp on this book's CD-ROM.

10. Save the model and the scene. Save Action1 as something suitable, like Flatten1.act. Delete the action from the hierarchy to return the face group to its original shape. Make the other parts of the model 100 percent transparent, then render an image from the Bird's Eye view, like Figure 9.32.

As you can see in Figure 9.32, a map digitized from one face can easily be adapted to a completely different model, as long as you have an accurate template to work from.

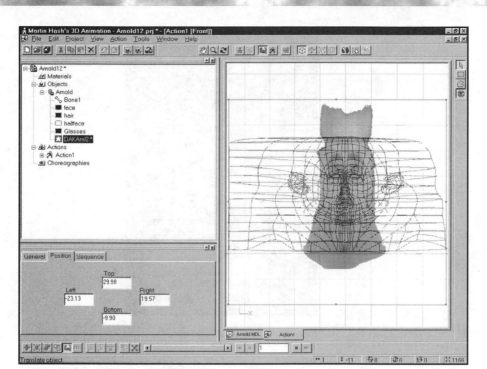

Figure 9.30 Face map loaded and ready for positioning.

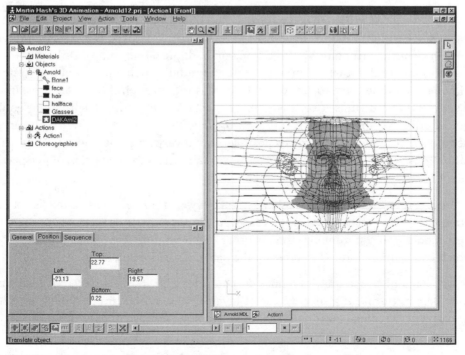

Figure 9.31 Face map positioned to match flattened group.

Figure 9.32 Final rendering of the face map applied to the Arnold model.

Unwrapped mapping templates are very useful for character creation, but not all 3D software has either a built-in or plug-in unwrap function.

Alternatives To Unwrap

If you're stuck without an unwrap, you can either buy 3D paint software (see Chapter 10 for details) or try using orthographic projection and multiple planar maps. Orthographic projection simply means that there is no perspective or parallax—no foreshortening or distortion of the image due to the convergence of light rays passing through the camera lens. Blueprints and engineering drawings are orthographic projections, and many 3D programs enable you to render orthographically, too. If your software doesn't provide this option, you can cheat it by setting the camera as far away as possible, with a very long zoom lens setting. This combination makes the objects look just as close but minimizes the distortion of perspective (see Figure 9.33).

If you render a series of wireframe images in this way, you can use them as guides for painting a series of planar maps. If you apply six separate planar maps in the form of a cube surrounding the model, you can minimize the smearing that planar projection usually causes (no face or patch can be more than 45 degrees off the plane of the applied map).

Now we'll present a case study of a housefly character (shown in Figure 9.34) created by Mike Comet, demonstrating the effective use of layered color, bump, transparency, and specular maps painted to match Unwrapped mapping templates.

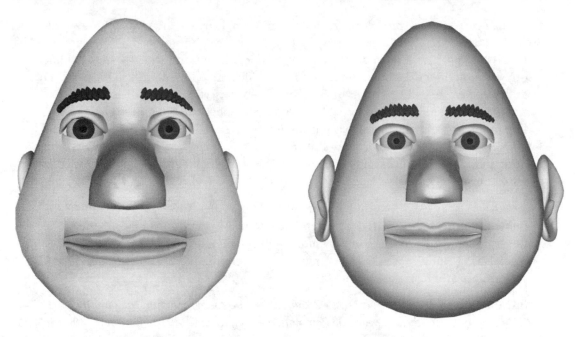

Figure 9.33 Face rendered with close-up focal length (left) showing perspective distortion and with long focal length (right) simulating orthographic projection.

Figure 9.34 Mike Comet's Housefly.

Case Study: Mike Comet's Housefly

By Mike Comet

I created the fly in 3D Studio MAX. For both maps, I applied the UVW mapping coordinates and used Peter Watje's Unwrap plug-in to create a wireframe template. I used that as a reference layer in Photoshop, and painted on top of it.

For the eyes, I drew a small circle in Photoshop. Then, I copied and pasted it in a honey-comb pattern by hand. Then, I copied that larger pattern and stamped it down around the existing pattern. Then, I grabbed the new larger pattern and repeated it until I had a large enough image. Later on, I needed to make the map a little larger, so there are a few visible seams where the patterns are not completely perfect. I applied the map using MAX's Shrink-Wrap UVW method. This is similar to Spherical, but it doesn't pinch the map at the poles, so the map looks fine all around the eye. I used the color image on the left of Figure 9.35 as the color map. The grayscale image on the right was used as both a bump map and a shininess strength (that is, specular) map. The specular color was set to a light orangish-red.

For the wings, I used a simple planar projection map. After Unwrapping the model, I painted over the template in Photoshop. I then took the color map and converted it into a transparency map for the wings by making the detail lines white instead of black. The upper half of Figure 9.36 is the color map; the lower half is the transparency map and was also used for a shininess strength map.

Mike Comet is an Animator and Artist working at the video game company Volition, Inc. in Champaign, IL. He started in computer animation during the late '80s on his Amiga 3000.

Figure 9.35 Housefly eye color, bump, and shininess strength maps.

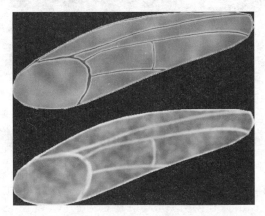

Figure 9.36 Housefly wing color (top), transparency, and shininess strength (bottom) maps.

Currently he maintains the CG-Character Animation Mailing List Frequently Asked Questions (FAQ). He tends to annoy his co-artists by suddenly singing strange lyrics out loud for no apparent reason, talking about his hammered dulcimer (a folk instrument), wanting to get a dachsund, or some strange combination of the above.

Mapping With Layers

You can add a lot of visual appeal or realism to a character if you apply a set of matched maps for at least color, bump, and specularity. Sometimes, you can use the same image for several different types of mapping, but, more often, you will need to create modified versions. When you are using more than one image, it's important that the images line up properly—it's sloppy and obvious when the bumpy texture of an eyebrow sticks out from under its coloring!

Make A Head Specularity Map

This project demonstrates how the layers feature of Photoshop can be very useful in creating matched maps.

Your first requirement is a mirror and strong directional light. It will be best if you can move them around to get the necessary angles to reflect light brightly from every part of the subject's face. I recommend that you practice on yourself—you'll have much more patience for this process than some hapless friend or relative. A clamp-on worklamp with a small spotlight bulb works well, or a fully-equipped makeup table.

1. Print a copy of the color face map, and select a highlighter felt-tip pen that gives good contrast on the print.

2. Use the mirror and light to locate the shiniest spot on the subject's skin. This is usually near the hairline or across the bridge of the nose. You are looking for smooth, taut, oily skin. This area is the reference for the white end of the map gradient. Mark it with the highlighter. Mark the perimeter of the shiny area with spots. When you've completely outlined the shiniest area, fill it in solidly with the highlighter.

3. Locate the areas of medium shininess, and mark them with a pattern of dots. Leave the least shiny, matte areas blank. When you have marked the entire face appropriately, keep the marked print by your computer for reference during the next step.

4. Load the color face map in Photoshop. Choose Window|Show Layers to open the Layers palette. Add a new layer, and name it Specularity. Use the paint bucket tool to fill the Specularity layer with black. In the Layers palette, set the Specularity layer to around 50 percent opacity, so you can see the face map through it (see Figure 9.37).

5. Refer to the print you highlighted earlier. Use the Airbrush tool with an appropriate brush size to make the shiniest areas white. I suggest starting with a smaller brush and working your way up to larger brushes as you feel comfortable with them.

6. Change the airbrush color to the next level of gray, and apply it to the areas marked on the print as half-shiny. Leave the blank, matte areas black.

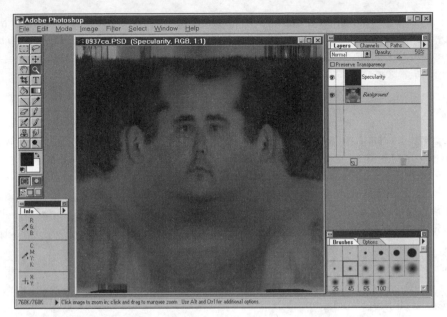

Figure 9.37 Layers for creating a matched specularity map.

7. Go over the entire image, blending edges between levels of gray so there are no sharp dividing lines. You should end up with an image like Figure 9.38. When you're finished, delete the color image layer, and save the grayscale Specularity layer as an image file with a new name.

 ## Make A Head Specularity Map

If you want more realistic detail and have the equipment, you can make a more accurate specularity map by assembling digitized images of the subject's skin.

1. Capture close-ups with strong side-lighting to show the skin's texture.

2. Assemble the digitized images with blended seams to match the color map, using the same techniques as for the eyeball map in Project 9.2.

3. Change the assembled map to grayscale, then equalize and compress it to average 128,128,128 gray.

4. Copy this grayscale image as a new layer over the color map in place of the solid black Specularity layer from the preceding project.

5. For the shiniest areas, use the Airbrush tool with a white color, the Lighten option, a small diffuse brush, and very light pressure, around 5 percent. This will enable you to "fade out" the highlighted areas of the Specularity layer while leaving the finer details of wrinkles and other surface imperfections.

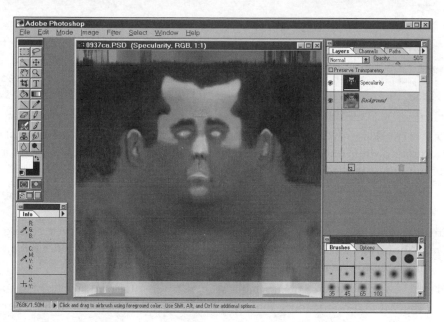

Figure 9.38 Completed specularity map.

6. For the matte or least shiny areas, use the airbrush tool with a black color, the Lighten option, a small diffuse brush, and very light pressure again, around 5 percent. This will darken the brushed areas without obliterating details.

7. You can leave the remaining areas—the moderately shiny ones—at the original equalized gray. When you're finished, delete the color image layer, and save the grayscale layer as an image file with a new name.

The final results should show a realistic variation in specularity due to follicles, pores, and other skin details from the original digitized images. So what do you do if you don't have photographs or a Cyberscan map to use as a reference? At some point (especially with fantasy characters), you'll have to create a skin map from scratch. The next section shows how.

Skin 'Em

Unless you're animating the Invisible Man, you're going to have to texture your character's skin. A variety of skin maps is the core of your image collection. You can start off with high-resolution images of leather, which seem to be popular in clip-art and background collections. Converted to grayscale and applied at smaller sizes, well-grained leather does very nicely as human skin. For more bizarre characters, keep an eye out for images of snakeskin and reptile hides, and, for the truly disgusting characters that populate some role-playing games, you might skim through a dermatology textbook or two for the "worst case" photos.

Wrinkle Map Sequences

In addition to more general skin maps, you may want to add bump maps to specific locations like the hands and eyes. Knuckles, palms, and eye corners tend to wrinkle deeply when flexed. If the character's style leans toward realism, you need to simulate this, too. Unfortunately, not all 3D packages allow you to animate a bump map's depth, so you may have to create an image sequence.

1. Paint a knuckle wrinkle bump map. Look at your own knuckle for a model. Make the background white and the folds grade down to black in the middle. Design it for planar mapping, applied from the top of the hand.

   As an alternative, you can digitize close-ups of your own knuckles in flexed and relaxed positions and use these images as templates, as in Project 9.5.

2. Create a range of knuckle wrinkle bump maps with decreasing contrast, ending with a map that is almost all white. In Adobe Photoshop, you can use the Blur filter and the Brightness setting to gradually spread out and lighten the wrinkles.

3. To test the bump maps, create an image sequence from numbered copies of the maps, and apply it to a hand model, matching the lightest images to the greatest bending angles of the knuckle joints.

Setting up animated bump maps can be as tedious and demanding as lip sync. Animating wrinkles should be one of your finishing touches, after all the action has been finalized. You may find it useful to print a copy of the rotation graph for the mapped joint, and correlate specific angles with particular bump maps, creating a sort of exposure sheet for the knuckle.

Rendered Maps

There's another way to get detailed, well-graded bump or displacement maps for characters—model them first! Some 3D software has a fog type of rendering effect that gradually darkens or lightens the scene based on the distance from the camera. Used carefully, this feature can produce a grayscale image that is finely shaded by depth. If you animate the objects, you can even render bump image sequences. This can be very useful in situations where texture maps are acceptable but complex models or setups aren't. For example, you might want a set of displacement mouth maps that you can use for quick-and-dirty lip-sync tests, which can be a much faster process than setting mouth poses for a full character setup.

Rendering Bump/Displacement Maps With Fog

This project shows you how to use the Fog feature in LightWave's Effects panel.

1. Open a new scene and load a character with a modeled face. Set the Camera to look straight on at the character's lips, and change the Camera panel resolution to crop out everything but the lips and their associated surfaces. Your Camera view should look something like Figure 9.39.

2. If you want matching color maps for the bump maps, you should render them now.

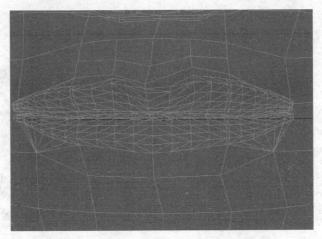

Figure 9.39 Camera view of modeled lips.

3. In the Surfaces panel, change the visible surfaces to a matte white, with no specularity or reflection and 100 percent diffusion.

4. In the Lights panel, turn off all the lights. Set Ambient Light to 100 percent.

5. In the Effects panel, set Background Color and Fog Color to black. Select Linear for Fog Type. Set the Maximum Fog Amount to 100 percent. Set the Minimum Fog Amount to 0 percent. Set Minimum Fog Distance to the distance between the Camera and the nearest visible point of the object. Set Maximum Fog Distance to the distance between the Camera and the farthest visible point of the object.

These settings create a black fog that darkens the parts of the object farther from the Camera. If you turn on the Show Fog button in the Options panel, Layout will draw a black circle representing the Maximum Fog Distance. This can be a big help when you're trying to get the Fog to cover just the right area. The resulting images will show white at the "highest" parts of the object and black at the lowest. You should end up with a rendered image like Figure 9.40.

You can also render inverted bump maps by changing the object's surfaces to black, and the background and Fog to white.

Mapping Cartoon Faces

Very simple character head objects can use animated maps instead of modeled features to provide facial details. This approach works best for cartoon-style caricatures and is best for features that do not protrude very much in profile. You can generally get away with mapping eyes and mouths, but you are better off modeling noses. This technique is especially handy for lip sync; if you are a good 2D artist, you can probably paint a set of lip-sync mouth maps faster than you can model and set up a single mouth object. You may want to consider doing tests for a new character with drawn maps for experimental features, and model them when your ideas have firmed up a bit.

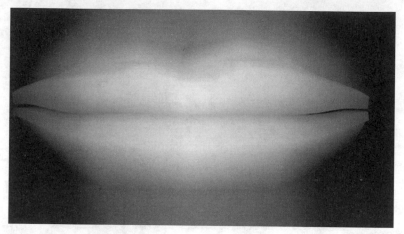

Figure 9.40 Rendered bump map of modeled lips.

Paint A Mouth

The simplest approach to facial feature mapping is to paint just the color image maps to be applied to the character's lower face. You can use any paint software that enables you to use foreground and background layers to paint over rendered images. Make sure you keep backup copies of any drawing templates you create. Just as with objects, there will always be additional demands on a character's dramatic and spoken range as the project progresses. If you can reuse the original mouth templates, it will be much easier for you to create more maps or to revise the existing libraries.

1. Set up a scene to render a close-up wireframe of the character's face, centered on the mouth. Render a wireframe that you can use as a painting template.

2. Crop the image to include only the area below the nose and above the chin. Save the cropped image.

   When you paint mouths for lip sync, you should consider keeping them compatible with the Magpie lip-sync software described in Chapter 15. Try to keep the proportions of the cropped image close to square; Magpie requires 128×128 BMP images. Even if you use higher-resolution maps for the finished animation, creating a duplicate set of thumbnail images for Magpie does not take very long and can be a great time-saver for the person doing the lip-sync exposure sheets.

3. Use the cropped map template as one layer, and paint your maps in another layer, as in Project 9.6. You can use the lines of the original modeled mouth (if any) as guides, or you can paint something completely original.

4. Paint an image of the mouth closed and at rest, a default image with no strong emotional message. Save the new layer as a separate image.

5. Repeat Step 4 to create image maps of the mouth for the basic emotional and lip-sync mouth shapes: smile, grin, frown, fear, disgust, stern, crying, sad, disdain and AI, CDGK, closed, D, E, FV, LTH, MBP, O, U, and WQ.

You can refer to the default mouths supplied with Magpie for examples of the lip-sync shapes. Figure 9.41 shows a complete model sheet. You might also look in either Levitan's or Blair's books from the Bibliography. Both contain good mouth model sheets.

6. If you like, make 128×128 resolution BMP format thumbnails for each lip-sync image, to use with Magpie.

7. Paste together a model sheet of all the thumbnails, and write the file names of the full-size maps under each image, as in Figure 9.41. This is another item for the character model sheets you'll need when you're ready to animate.

PROJECT 9.9 Bump It

The goal of this project is to create bump maps that match the color maps you painted in the preceding project. A properly executed bump map gives a sense of depth to the object and smoothes out some of the disparity between the drawn maps and the modeled object.

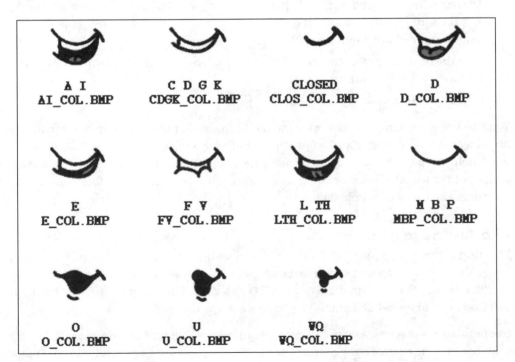

Figure 9.41 Magpie default mouth maps.

1. Load the first color map into one layer of your paint software. Add a new layer, and name it Bump. You can either save and load a duplicate of the color map into the Bump layer, or start off with a clean slate.

2. Paint over the mouth opening (if any) in the Bump layer with solid black. Cover the teeth or tongue with very dark gray.

3. Draw pure white lines down the middle of the lips, tracing the highest points of the mouth.

4. Trace the perimeter of each lip in medium gray, defining where the slope of the lips drop back toward the level of the face.

   If you need a reference, look back to Figure 9.40. This image is a depth-cued rendering of a set of modeled lips. You're trying to paint the same sort of gradient for the lip shape you defined in your color map.

5. Create gradient fills or airbrush smooth transitions between the white "high" lines and the medium gray perimeter lines.

6. Paint a white line around the perimeter of the map. Create a gradient or airbrushed fill between the outermost perimeter line and the borders of the map.

   This is to smooth the mapped area back to the normal height of the unmapped area. The smoother your gradients, the better your bump maps will look. As shown in Chapter 8, if the jump between adjacent gray levels is too large, the bump map will create a jagged, stepped appearance.

7. Save the new layer as a separate image. You don't have to create Magpie-compatible thumbnails for the bump maps.

8. Repeat for the remaining color maps.

You can test your bump map by applying it and the matching color map to a modified head object with no modeled lips, just a flat area suitable for mapping. If you are feeling ambitious, you might try painting displacement maps that bulge the character's cheeks or wrinkle the corners of the mouth. You may be surprised to see just how much of the face you can successfully animate using only painted maps.

Clip And Save

The ultimate mapping for a mouth is a matched set of color, bump or displacement, and clip maps. Color and bump maps provide the surface appearance, and the clip map cuts away the mouth opening to create an unmistakably 3D effect. Of course, if you apply a clip map, you will also have to model and animate a set of teeth and a tongue.

Clipping occurs precisely where the luma (brightness) value for the map drops below 50 percent. Because the edge of a clip map can't be dithered, if you use a low-resolution clip map, any curved or diagonal edge will show jaggies. If the bump map you are matching has a dithered edge, you can make the clipped edge smoother by duplicating the bump map, doubling or quadrupling its resolution, and converting it to a black-and-white bitmap. Because it has a lower bit depth, this image will save space even though it's several times the resolution of the color and bump maps. The clip map will also make the clipped edge jaggies much smaller, and will still precisely match the bump and color maps in proportion.

1. Open a copy of one of the bump maps you created. Quadruple its resolution. Save it under a new name.

2. Change the mouth opening to pure black. Change the remaining areas to pure white. In Adobe Photoshop, one way to do this is to lighten the entire image about 60 percent, then use the Magic Wand tool to select the mouth opening, varying the range of the wand to get exactly the selection you want. With black as the foreground color, use Fill. The mouth opening should be solid black. Use the Brightness and Contrast settings to keep the mouth opening dark, and lighten the rest of the image below 50 percent gray.

3. Change Mode to Bitmap, using 50 percent threshold, to turn the image into a black-and-white clip map. Save the modified image as a bitmap.

When you apply the clip map, be careful to position it to match the surface of the mouth area as closely as possible, and limit the mapping depth so the clipping doesn't go clear through the object. If a modeled tongue or teeth are part of the mapped object, you will have to be especially precise with the mapping dimensions or you'll clip them, too.

Hold It

If you choose to animate any part of a character using image sequences, you must pay careful attention to transitions. There is no automatic interpolation between images as there is for morphing objects, so maps are inherently more jerky and difficult to smooth. Smooth interpolation is especially important for emotional transitions, which can take several seconds. Held vowels are also prime candidates, as there is usually a slow transition from the first extreme pose to the more relaxed hold. Either of these situations will be unacceptably jerky with only the basic extreme pose maps. If you need a smoother transition, your only option is to create interpolated image maps. It's more work, but the difference in your lip sync and other transitions will be well worth it.

Environment Maps

If your character has any reflective surfaces, like eyeglasses, eyeballs, or highly polished accessories, using environment reflection maps can save you a lot of rendering time over raytracing. It's possible to make a reasonably accurate environment reflection map with a few quick renderings and a little cut-and-paste image editing, and the results will be difficult to distinguish from true raytracing.

Make An Environment Reflection Map

If possible, render an image of the scene with raytraced reflections. This image will be useful as a reference for aligning the finished reflection map and as a comparison to judge the effectiveness of mapping versus raytracing. If you can't raytrace the image first, you'll have to be more knowledgeable and aware of the factors you're dealing with. It's easy to make a time-wasting mistake, so take the time now to render a good reference image.

1. Place the camera at the center of the reflective object in the scene to be reflected. Hide, make invisible, or delete the reflective object itself (otherwise the camera will give you a nice view of its interior). If possible, set the object to cast shadows but remain otherwise invisible.

2. Set the camera field of view (FOV) to 60 degrees.

3. Rotate the camera horizontally at 60-degree increments in six sequential frames, giving full 360-degree coverage like a cylinder surrounding the object.

4. In the seventh and eighth frames, point the camera straight up and straight down, with the camera FOV set to 120 degrees. These renderings will cap the ends of the cylinder made by the previous six frames.

   If your software supports it, you can save out the motion and focal length files for the camera and quickly reapply it to other scenes. This can partially automate the setup for making environment maps.

5. Render all eight frames.

6. In your paint software, load the first rendered image. Change the canvas size to six times the width of the image, to provide room to paste in the other five horizontal images (see Figure 9.42).

7. Load each of the horizontal images in order, and position them carefully to match the vertical seams, as shown in Figure 9.43. Save the assembled image.

8. Open the top image. Apply the Filter|Distort|Polar Coordinates filter, with Polar To Rectangular selected (see Figure 9.44). If you are not using Photoshop, check your program's documentation to find a similar feature.

Figure 9.42 Canvas size increased to hold horizontal images.

Figure 9.43 Horizontal images assembled.

As described earlier in the eyeball mapping project, this filter changes an image from flat XY coordinates to a sort of Mercator projection, spreading out the periphery of the image as the lower border and stretching the center of the image to cover the top border. This enables you to paste the bottom of the filtered image to match the top of the assembled horizontal images.

9. Change the top image size to six times its original width, to match the width of the assembled horizontal images, as shown in Figure 9.45.

10. Activate the assembled horizontal image. Change its canvas size to provide room to paste the top image above it, with the existing image in the bottom of the canvas.

11. Copy the entire top image, and place it in the blank canvas area, but do not deselect it. You will probably have to slide the top image back and forth to match its lower border with the top of the lower images. When the borders match as closely as possible, deselect the top image. This will most likely leave a gap at one side or the other, as shown in Figure 9.46.

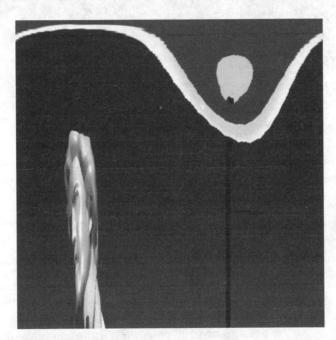

Figure 9.44 Top image filtered to polar coordinates.

Figure 9.45 Top image scaled to match width of horizontal images.

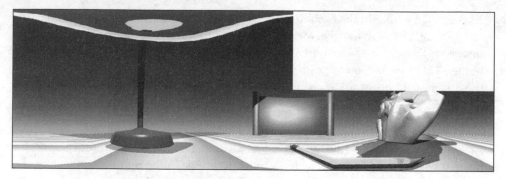

Figure 9.46 Top image pasted to match horizontal images.

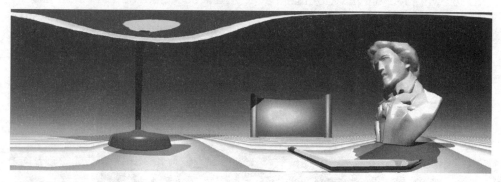

Figure 9.47 Second copy of top image pasted to fill in gap.

It may help you to think of these images as continuous cylinders—the sides are just arbitrary seams, you can cut and reassemble them anywhere, and the overall image will have the same effect.

12. Paste in a second copy of the top image. Position it to fill the gap, as shown in Figure 9.47.

13. Repeat the preceding five steps for the bottom image, but flip the filtered image vertically before you copy-and-paste it. The center of the original image must form the bottom border, rather than the top.

The final step is centering the map so the seam in the cylinder is in the direction your software expects it. This is where the reference image you raytraced comes in handy; if you didn't make one, try to estimate what object or reference point is at 180 degrees behind the Camera. That's your *centerline* for the finished reflection map. In the example scene, the center of the reflection should be pretty much in line with the center of the chair back, so that's your centerline.

14. Select the entire image, and copy it. Move the selection to the side until the centerline is centered in the canvas.

15. Paste in another copy of the image, and move it to fill the remaining space. Your results should look like Figure 9.48.

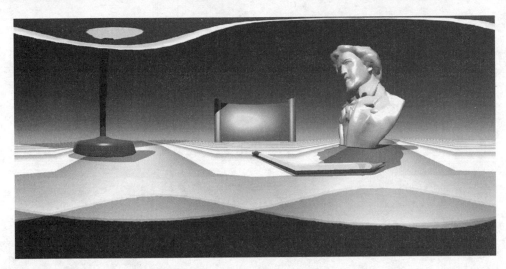

Figure 9.48   Centered environment reflection map.

Figure 9.49   Results of raytraced reflection and an environment reflection map in the same scene. Which is which?

When you apply this environment reflection map, the results can be very close to a true raytraced image. Figure 9.49 shows a mapped reflection and a raytraced one. Can you spot the difference?

Keep in mind that this cheat only works if the object is not moving too much within the scene. Reflective object rotations are OK, but translations would change the rendered perspective of the surroundings so the reflections would have to be raytraced.

Moving On

You should now have a good idea of how to make the 2D maps you'll need for your characters. The next chapter will show you how to use material power tools: procedural shaders and 3D paint software.

TOOLS

10

If you are creating characters to appear in high-resolution media, if you have tight deadlines, or if you are a perfectionist, you'll want to use these tools.

This chapter will give you an overview of 3D paint software and procedural shaders. These tools can make your *texturing* work easier and can produce results that would be difficult or impossible to achieve with more basic material tools.

3D Paint Tools

3D paint software is a valuable tool for character animation for several reasons. A minor consideration is that few 3D modeling packages have incorporated the advanced painting tools you can find in 2D software, such as Photoshop or Painter. A good financial reason is that production teams with a limited budget can have an artist painting character maps on a computer that doesn't also require the expensive, dongled 3D modeling and animation software. It's slightly more important that 3D paint tools can sometimes compensate for absent mapping functions in 3D animation software. For example, LightWave has no UV mapping support, but, in 3D paint software, you can make a cylindrical or planar map that will approximate a UV map's adherence to the model. The most significant reason, however, is that 3D paint software can provide a more intuitive and efficient interface, especially for traditional artists making the transition to the computer.

Working with a computer has an inherent drawback for the 3D artist. The nature of 3D applications in the essentially 2D interface of most desktop computers creates a cognitive gap between how your mind works and how the computer requires you to act. Lifelong experience has conditioned you to reach for, grasp, and manipulate 3D objects. You can unconsciously manipulate tools to meet the surface of these objects, either alone or in coordination between your object-grasping and tool-wielding hands. You don't have to think about it—you just do it. A standard desktop computer provides only visual feedback, and only through a 2D "window." It does not provide feedback to your sense of touch, true 3D stereoscopic vision, or kinesthetic sense. Whenever you work with a computer, you willingly cut off five-and-a-half of your six senses, at least three of which a sculptor or painter would regard as indispensable. One empirical measure of this is the fact that you can use every feature of most software with only one eye and two fingers. Considering the handicaps, it's amazing we have any decent 3D art at all!

2D software used for painting 3D model maps has generally made these handicaps worse. When you attempt to paint on an unwrapped or flattened wireframe template, instead of a moderately clear and intuitive 2D image, you see a warped and distorted projection. An untrained eye has difficulty associating this map with the original model. This difficulty makes the already-steep learning curve for 3D character creation just a little more vertical.

Publishers have developed 3D paint software in an attempt to restore some of the intuitive ease-of-use of conventional painting and sculpting tools. The general concept is that you should be able to select a tool that has an effect identical (or at least reasonably similar) to its real-world counterpart, use it with the same strokes (both motion and pressure), and get the results you intuitively expect. Several software publishers made the attempt, and a few have succeeded to a remarkable extent.

Hardware

Hardware vendors are also making valuable contributions to artist-friendly computer interfaces. One of the most cost-effective investments you can make is a pen-and-tablet like those manufactured by Wacom, shown in Figure 10.1.

These devices replace (or supplement) your mouse with a powered tablet and a stylus shaped like a pen, with a blunt plastic tip and a push-button in place of an eraser. When you move the tip of the stylus over the tablet just like an ordinary pen, the computer's cursor follows along. Advanced versions also sense the angle of the stylus, which end you're using, and how hard you're pressing. If the paint software supports these features, the feel and results are as close as

Figure 10.1 Wacom pen-and-tablet

you're going to get to a real-life artist's media. An added bonus is that you're less likely to suffer repetitive stress injuries, because the angle of your wrist and fingers is much more relaxed and natural. As of this writing, you can find good tablets like the Wacom 6×8 ArtZ II through mail-order houses for under $300. I've found that they also make work easier in 3D modeling and animation software, as long as the mouse-emulation drivers work properly. As with any purchase, try to evaluate it before you buy, and make sure it will pay for itself in boosted productivity, higher quality, or reduced aggravation. Wacom's contact information is as follows:

WACOM Technology Corporation
501 S.E. Columbia Shores Blvd., Suite 300
Vancouver, WA 98661
Tel: 360-750-8882 (800-922-9348 U.S. only)
Fax: 360-750-8924
BBS: 360-750-0638—300 to 14400 baud, 8 bits, no parity, 1 stop bit
Email:
  Sales: sales@wacom.com
  Tech. Support: support@wacom.com
Internet: www.wacom.com

A relatively new entry to interface hardware is the 6D trackball. This device takes a variety of forms, depending on the manufacturer. Spacetec produces two models in the Spaceball line: the Spaceball 2003b (MSRP $895), intended primarily for Unix machines; and the newer Spaceball 3003 (MSRP $695), for Windows NT. The 2003b is equipped with eight discrete function buttons, while the 3003 uses two buttons and a pop-up function menu. The 3003 is also more sensitive. The original 2003 required a pretty healthy push, while the newer machine responds to a lighter touch. Figure 10.2 shows both devices.

The Spaceball consists of a tennis ball-sized sphere mounted on an ergonomically designed platform. You use it by resting your wrist on the platform and gently grasping the ball around its equator. The ball itself does not move, but responds to slight fingertip pressure. As you apply gentle pushing, pulling, or twisting motions to the ball, the 3D model moves in those same directions on screen. The greater pressure you apply, the faster the model moves or rotates. The

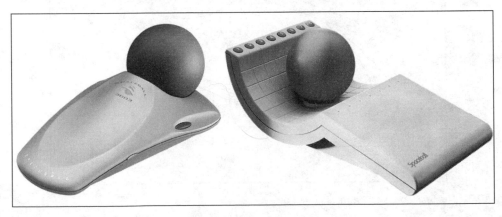

Figure 10.2 Spacetec Spaceball 3003 (left) and 2003b.

Spaceball provides six degrees of motion—translation in the X, Y, and Z axes, plus rotation in the pitch, bank, and heading axes, as shown in Figure 10.3.

The Spaceball is not intended to replace your mouse or other pointing device, but to work with it. You control the mouse or stylus with your dominant hand and the Spaceball with your other hand. Using both devices closely mimics the way you manipulate objects in the real world—you hold, move, and turn a workpiece with one hand, and apply a tool to it with the other.

You can learn to operate a Spaceball very quickly. Nonetheless, you should try out a Spaceball before you hand over the money or buy it from a vendor that provides a no-questions return policy for a reasonable trial period. You should spend as much time as possible using the Spaceball on real work, the kind of stuff you do on a regular basis, then decide whether it makes your work sufficiently easier or faster to justify the investment. I haven't heard of anyone who hates the Spaceball, but I have heard from artists who bought it, like it, but only use it once in a blue moon. As with any investment, make sure you'll get a good return on it. Spacetec's contact information is as follows:

Spacetec IMC Midwest Regional Office
2400 Lakeview Drive
Bellbrook, OH 45305
Tel: 937-848-5814

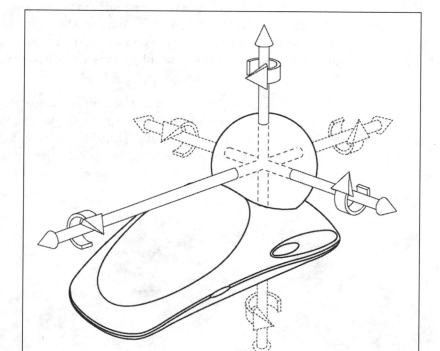

Figure 10.3 The Spaceball's six degrees of motion.

Fax: 937-848-4804

Email: tstauter@spacetec.com

Detailer

Detailer is a 3D paint package from MetaCreations, available for the MacOS, Windows 95, and NT 4. It requires a minimum of 16MB available RAM but, as usual, more is better. It installs from a CD-ROM with a serial number, but after installation, there is no dongle or other copy protection.

Detailer's manual is written in a basic, easy-to-read style that is especially appropriate for traditional artists. The only assumptions are that you understand the basics of your operating system's interface. If you know how to use a mouse (or pen-and-tablet) and know the difference between a menu and a window, you're ready for this manual. The authors have kept the computer jargon to a minimum and always introduce new concepts in relation to the artist's more traditional tools. This is the most thorough, user-friendly set of documentation I've ever seen. The only quibble is that the index, while adequate, does not have any *See* or *See Also* references. If you don't know exactly what a function is called in Designer, you have to leaf through the book until you stumble across it. A few entries for the most common synonyms would have been a nice touch.

In general, the manuals for Fractal Design products have been outstanding. I hope this standard will continue now that Fractal and MetaTools have been consolidated under the MetaCreations label.

Detailer can currently import and export models in DXF, 3DMF, 3DS, and Ray Dream Studio formats. More import/export plug-ins are in the works. Contact MetaCreations at **www.metacreations.com** for the latest updates. Each of the current import/export plug-ins has limitations or special considerations that you should be aware of.

In all model formats, Detailer does not support more than 240 objects per model. Each object can have one each of the five supported map types texture (color), bump, highlight mask (specularity), reflection mask (environment reflection), and glow (ambient)—essentially a single map with multiple layers. Because Detailer only allows one map per object, you must create any blending or overlapping within a single map. This is a significant shortcoming when compared to 3D programs that enable you to layer many maps on a single object. It is especially limiting if you are building single-mesh characters to minimize seams and visible object joints. If your entire character is one mesh, Detailer limits you to one map, as well. If your character will appear in close-up, that single map may have to be enormous to both cover the entire character and provide enough details for the close-up shots. You may have to model separate versions of the character, cut off at the boundaries of the camera field, just to keep the map resolution within your system's memory resources.

On the positive side, Detailer supports all the mapping coordinate systems covered in Chapter 8: pass-thru (planar), cylindrical, spherical, cubical, and implicit (UV). Detailer also supports environmental reflection mapping through the reflection mask.

Detailer is very sensitive to model size when applying bump maps, because the Bump Map Scaling slider has a fixed range. If your model is more than 20 units across, you may not be able to set the slider high enough to view surface relief. MetaCreations's suggested workaround to this is for you to scale down your object in your original modeler, then re-import it. I'd suggest MetaCreations change the scaling slider to something more open-ended.

DXF format doesn't include UV mapping coordinates, so you can't use implicit mapping directly. However, UV mapping is so important to creating character maps that you should try to find a workaround. If you are using a model format that does not yet have a Detailer plug-in, you may be using DXF as the "lowest common denominator" to get your models into Detailer. If this is the case and your modeler supports UV mapping, you can try converting the imported model to native Designer format. This will enable you to use implicit mapping. When the map is complete, take it directly to your modeler (you can ignore the DXF model reconversion), and apply it to your original model with UV mapping coordinates. Try this with a simple object and map before you pour hours of work into an important model—it may or may not work for you.

3DMF meshes can have holes, which won't be reproduced when you load the model into Detailer. You'll get a warning when Detailer attempts to load the model. If you choose to continue, Detailer will drop the hole when it imports. Detailer also discards NURBS, general polygons, and primitives. When you are saving models in 3DMF format from your modeling software, you should try to select options that convert any remaining splines to polygons. This will give you a better chance of importing a complete model into Detailer. The 3DMF format allows you to specify a color for each face of an object. Detailer assigns one color to the entire mesh object. Detailer also ignores 3DMF specular and specular control objects. Internally, Detailer manages specularity via modifications to the diffuse color settings and exports only the diffuse color settings. 3DMF assumes all mapping coordinates to be implicit, so, if you want your exported maps to be accurate, you should only work in implicit mapping mode if you will be exporting to 3DMF format.

At the moment, 3DS import is only available in the Windows version of Detailer. 3D Studio objects may import to Detailer with inverted normals. You can repair this by using Detailer's Invert Normals command, CTRL+Shift+J. Bump maps in 3D Studio are black=low, white=high. Detailer reverses the values. To correct this, you can either invert the completed bump map in 3D Studio or use Detailer's Negative Polarity checkbox in the Materials|Objects palette.

Detailer imports and exports a good selection of popular map file formats, including TIFF, JPEG, BMP, PICT, and RIFF. It also imports and exports Photoshop 2.x and 3.x formats, and for 3.x it supports Photoshop layers. This is an exceptionally useful feature, given the ubiquity of Photoshop in the graphic arts and the utility of multiple layers in building matched character maps. Just for good measure, some Photoshop plug-in filters are also compatible with Detailer. The manual has a few guidelines for evaluating and loading plug-ins, but they mostly boil down to "try it, and see if it works."

Detailer supports up to 32 levels of Undo for most of the paint tools, but there is no Undo at all for navigation functions. If you use the Grabber (pan) or Trackball tools to move around in the

3D View, you won't be able to Undo back to the previous angle and position. If the 3D View alignment is important, as when you are creating a pass-through map, you should make a note of the exact rotation and position values in the Control window before you make any navigation changes. This is a serious omission, Undo should work for *everything*. No Undo for a critical function is a very nasty surprise for a new user.

Detailer works well with Wacom tablets, but it doesn't support Spaceball or other 3D controllers at this time.

As you create character maps, you will develop a collection of favorite textures, brushes, patterns, and other tools that you use most often. Detailer enables you to store these tools in libraries. These libraries consume RAM, and the more tools they contain the more RAM they require. You can conserve RAM and work more easily if you set up libraries that contain only the tools you actually use. If you create libraries that hold every possible tool you might ever consider using, you won't have enough system resources to hold them all.

If you plan to use background images, be aware that Detailer tiles backgrounds from the top left corner and does not scale or stretch them to fit. If you want to see the entire background image, you have to size the 3D View window to meet or exceed the resolution of the image. This can eat RAM quickly. At Detailer's required 52 bytes per pixel, a 640×480 24-bit color image requires 15MB. If you don't have a lot of RAM, don't plan on working in large 3D views or with several models open at once.

Feedback time on contrast/brightness changes takes long enough that it interferes with productivity. Instead of dragging the slider, you should click on the bar at the setting you think you'll want. The refresh rate seems to be faster for a click than for a drag, although it's still nothing to brag about.

You can use a Detailer tool called a Floater for building complex character maps. Floaters are independent map layers that you can move around without affecting the layers underneath them, like a decal on the surface of a model before you glue it down. You can create small Floater maps of the different parts of a skin texture: wrinkles, folds, zits, scars, moles, and so on. As you add each Floater to the model, you can move them around without affecting the other maps. This makes it easy and intuitive to position details on the irregular surface of a character. Once you have placed the Floaters to your satisfaction, you can save the map in Detailer's native RIFF or Photoshop 3.x format, and the program will convert the Floaters to layers. You can either flatten the layers in the Photoshop file into a single image (for compatibility with 3D software that does not support layered maps) or save it for further editing.

If your character will evolve through the production process (and what character doesn't?), you should keep backups of the work-in-progress, with all Floaters intact and separate in Detailer's RIFF format. If you have to change something on the one-map finished character, you can always reload the Floater version and tweak the separate maps, then save out the changes with no lost effort.

The first part of your typical workflow in creating a character map might go something like this:

1. Import the model.
2. Add base map(s).
3. Add and paint Floaters.
4. Arrange Floaters.
5. Save maps in RIFF format.

   This gives you a complete character map but with the flexibility of the Floaters preserved for making revisions. The next step is to convert all these Floaters into a map your 3D software can use.

6. From the Floater List palette, choose Drop All. This drops all the Floaters onto the base map(s).

7. Save the base map(s) in a format your 3D software can use (TIFF or TGA are most often supported).

   If you need to edit the Floater placement, simply reopen the RIFF format, make the changes, drop all, and save the modified maps again.

The Align In Register With button in the Set Mapping Options dialog automatically aligns the new map with the map you choose. This is an easy and precise way of keeping different map types in perfect alignment.

In Chapter 9, you saw how useful a flattened-out object mesh can be as a template for painting maps. Detailer also provides this function, with a few extra touches. The View Mesh icon is a patch of small triangles at the upper-right corner of each map window. Click on this icon, and the object's mesh overlays the map. You can choose a mesh color to contrast best with the map. If the mapping type is Pass-through, the mesh looks like a normal view of the model from the direction the map is applied. If the map type is Implicit, the mesh looks like the Unwrap or Flatten maps in Chapter 9.

The two most significant limits to Detailer are speed and memory usage. Character maps for television and film work, and even for the high end of video games, require a resolution that Detailer finds difficult to handle. The 52-bit/pixel memory penalty makes Detailer much more expensive to run, as measured by the minimum resources necessary for a given map. More importantly, the screen refresh, stroke update, and interface response time in general are poor. The larger the map or more complex the model, the slower Detailer runs. On a 200MHz Pentium with 64MB RAM running WinNT, a single color map at 512×512 resolution slowed Detailer to a near-standstill. The first few times this happened, I assumed the system had hung up and used Task Manager to end the task. When I let it run its course, it took nearly three minutes to refresh the screen. My conclusion is that Detailer v.1.02 is usable only for low-resolution maps and models. This is adequate for lower-end multimedia and Web applications, but, if you are painting character maps for video or film resolution, Detailer is simply not up to snuff.

You're welcome to try it for yourself—there's a demo version of Detailer in the MetaCreations directory on this book's CD-ROM.

Case Study: Mapping An Iguana In Detailer

By Kim Oravecz

When I created the iguana (see Figure 10.4) in LightWave, I modeled him so that he would be one seamless mesh. I did not want any seams at the joints. Unfortunately, I could not texture map him as one whole seamless texture. LightWave 3D does not support UV mapping, so I had to use many separate cylindrical textures on him: one for each finger/toe, one for each arm and leg, one for the body/tail section, and then one for the head. The dewlap and ears are planar image maps, the spikes are done with LightWave's fractal noise, and the eyes are spherical image maps.

One little trick I'd like to share with you is how I was able to put all of these maps on my iguana without any seams showing where the different maps meet. For each texture, I created what I called a *seam alpha map*. Basically, it is just a black-to-white gradient image map that I use in the alpha channel of the image map. Where the alpha map is black, the image map will be transparent on the object. Then as the alpha map goes from black to white, the image map becomes more opaque. I would make sure the black portion of the alpha map coincided with where the seam of the texture map would be. Figure 10.5 is an example of one of these seam alpha maps that I used on my iguana's head. This particular map faded out the seam between the body/tail section and the head/neck area of the iguana. I created a similar alpha map for the body/tail surface where the top of the map met with the neck/head area.

I was able to create the fine detail on the iguana head by using Detailer. To be honest, I don't know if I could have created such a nice head texture without that program. At this

Figure 10.4   Iguana mapped in Detailer.

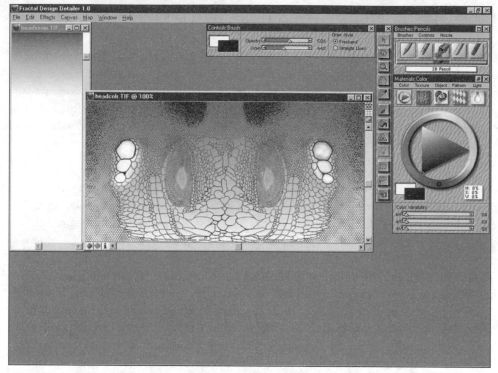

Figure 10.5 Seam alpha map and matching color map for iguana's head.

time, Detailer does not directly support the LightWave object file format, so I had to export the head portion of the object in DXF format.

In LightWave Modeler, I had named all of the surfaces of my iguana: head, body_tail, left_arm, left_leg, and so forth. To create the image map in Detailer, I would delete all of the polygons that were not associated with the texture map I was creating, then save the remaining portion of the object as a DXF file. For example, for the head texture map, I deleted all of the polygons except for the ones that had the surface name of Head_surf. I then oriented it in Modeler so it would come into Detailer in the proper orientation with the nose facing down and the top of the head facing toward the right side of the face view. What orientation you will need to save your object in for Detailer depends on the orientation you will use to bring your object into layout. In this case, the iguana object was oriented on the Z axis with the nose facing positive Z in Layout.

In Detailer, I hand painted the scales on the iguana's face using a very small airbrush tool. I used photographs of one of my pet iguanas as a reference. I ran into some strange problems along the way when painting the scales. I think because there was some pretty fine detail in the mesh, especially around the eye areas, that I could not paint the detail exactly as I wanted it. Sometimes I would put a line down in an area and Detailer would go nuts and continue that line all the way around the object. I would then just have to avoid that one little area. Also, sometimes Detailer would make a very fat line where I was trying to put a very line thin. But all in all, I really like the Detailer program and would not hesitate to recommend it, despite the little problems I ran into. They were by no means "show stoppers."

I created the very fine scales on the neck area on my Amiga in a program called Forge with Essence textures. One of the textures in the Essence volumes is called *scales*. Luckily, it creates them as a seamless tile pattern and allows you to save them out as image maps. I tweaked the parameters in Forge until I got a scale pattern that I liked and rendered it out to a TIFF image file. Then, in Detailer, I filled whatever portion of the image map I had not drawn in myself with the seamless scales texture.

In Detailer, you can paint directly on the object mesh and watch it appear on the 2D image map or you can paint directly onto the 2D image map and watch it appear on the object mesh. I found myself switching back and forth between both methods. In Detailer, you can have it show the flattened-out polygon mesh on the 2D image map as a guide when painting. I found that really came in handy.

I then saved out that image map as a TIFF through Detailer and then brought it into Photoshop as a layer. I created the color portion of the image map in Detailer as well and then brought it into Photoshop as a second layer. I made the white portion of the scales image map transparent so that you could see the underlying color image layer. I used Photoshop for combining the two image maps because of Photoshop's layering capabilities. Detailer has something it calls Floaters to be used for layering, but I have yet to get the hang of working with Floaters. It was just easier for me in Photoshop. I then flattened the image in Photoshop to make it one image map.

I also created the ear texture in Detailer (see Figure 10.6). I used the plain black-and-white head image map as a bump map.

The last map I created for the head was the specular map. On an iguana's head, the white scales on the sides of the face and under the chin (not including the dewlap) are very smooth and shiny. The scales on top of the head and back toward the neck area are not as smooth and shiny. So, I needed to create a specular map to apply to the head. I created the map in Photoshop by having the scales layer underneath the specular map image to use as a guide to where I needed to paint the black and gray portions of the image. I ended up with the specular map shown in Figure 10.7.

Figure 10.6 Iguana ear map.

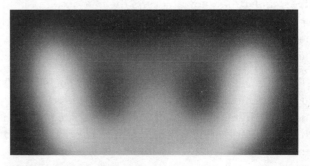

Figure 10.7 Iguana specular map.

Name:	Kimberly Oravecz
Contact:	kimo@en.com
Dimensions:	2D, 3D, time and space
Education:	Many math, programming and computer graphics classes too numerous to mention. Self-taught Lighwave artist.
Ambition:	To make the world a better place through detailed character modeling and texture mapping.
Turn ons:	Awesome 3D characters, seamless texture maps, Morph Gizmo and Metaforming with someone I respect.
Turn offs:	Anticipated actions without proper follow-through and non-planar polygons.
Biggest joy:	A 3D-rendered animation with finely detailed characters lit to perfection with an impeccable sense of timing and weight.
Goal:	To bring joy into peoples lives by creating cutting edge 3D characters and animations for film and television.

4D Paint 2

4D Paint is designed to work as a plug-in with 3DS MAX and Softimage, and as a standalone application with a limited number of 3D model formats. I had problems with most of the 3DS format models I attempted to load directly into 4D Paint. I was able to import the same models into MAX then export them as 3DS format, after which 4D Paint had no trouble importing them. I suspect that 4D Paint is a little too strict in its interpretation of the 3DS format. This could be a significant problem for users who don't have MAX or who want to work with 4D Paint on a non-MAX system while the dongled machines are busy with modeling and animation tasks.

This package doesn't demand too much of your RAM—loading the Cyberscan model of my head and the matching color map in Chapters 8 and 9, 4D Paint used a total of just over 15MB of system RAM. Quadrupling the file size of the map to 1024×1024 increased RAM usage to 25MB. 4D Paint is fairly efficient in using system resources, at least in comparison to other 3D paint software.

4D Paint's documentation assumes you already know how to use 3DS MAX's mapping functions, understand how to access the plug-ins, and know your way around MAX's menus and options without full-page screen shots and diagrams. That isn't an unreasonable expectation, because this package is a serious professional tool. If you haven't exhausted the basic capabilities of the core application, why are you considering adding more bells and whistles?

4D Paint's manual leaves a little to be desired. It doesn't have the flair or polish of the Designer manuals, but at least the information you need is in there, somewhere. The organization of the manual can make learning a challenge. The manual is utilitarian and more appropriate for the computer-literate technician than the traditional artist. If you're not completely comfortable with the Windows environment plus at least one 3D modeling and rendering package, you're going to get lost. First things first, you'll learn 4D Paint more rapidly and with less hassle if you understand the basics. If you've skipped ahead to reach this chapter, I suggest you go back and read Chapters 8 and 9.

If you're going to learn 4D Paint as quickly and efficiently as possible, I recommend you use each of the resources 4D Vision has thoughtfully provided. First, print out the readme and other text files that come with the latest version. It's especially useful to print out and read the TIPS.TXT file. This is a more effective way of learning these tips than waiting for them to pop up one at a time when you start the program. Those pop-up tips are just a sneaky way of getting users to actually read some of the documentation. If you're one of those who don't read manuals—yes, I'm talking about you!—you should also check the 4D Vision Web site for updates, FAQs, and other helpful items. Once you've exhausted the short and easy reading material, it's time to dig into the manual. I recommend you work through the first chapter, mostly for the introductory tutorial, then jump to the Tutorials chapter. The middle of the manual is mostly technical reference and is organized more for looking up specifics than shortening the learning curve. If you really want to master this software, by all means, read the manual cover-to-cover. I didn't find a single page without a useful tip or explanation. Last of all, don't forget the Help files. Just press F1 whenever you get lost, and you'll probably find the answer in 4D Paint's Help.

4D Paint can render color, bump, self-illumination (luminosity), and shininess (specularity) maps, and works in 3D mode by default. You can call up the Bitmap View, which shows the 2D maps, and paint in those if you like. However, you'll get faster response time and a more intuitive workflow if you stick with the 3D Main View as much as possible.

4D Paint supports Wacom pressure- and tilt-sensitive tablets and the Spacetec Spaceballs, and the manual includes specific advice about installation and setup for these devices. This combination can provide the most intuitive interface you'll find outside a virtual reality research lab, for a combined cost of about $1,000. If the feel of the interface is important to your mapping, you should definitely choose 4D Paint over other software that does not support these input devices. After working with 4D Paint with my Wacom tablet, I won't go back to anything that requires a mouse or doesn't handle the tilt and pressure data. By comparison, painting with the mouse is like painting with a bar of soap with an oversized brush stuck through it. You simply don't have the fine control and precise sense of where each pixel is going. 4D Paint's fast screen redraw is also an advantage with the Spaceball. You have more immediate feedback and can use lighter and more precise movements to position the model. If the screen redraw lags behind the controls, you have to back-and-fill to reposition the model, which defeats the purpose of more intuitive input devices.

The user interface has several thoughtful touches. You use the left mouse button for the usual painting, selection, and dragging tasks. Clicking on the right mouse button (or stylus equivalent) calls a pop-up menu for the Brush, Eraser, and Color Sampler (eyedropper) tools, plus the Color Picker dialog and the Zoom Extents and Light To Front functions. These are the options you'll use most, so 4D Vision has made it possible for you to do the majority of your map painting without taking your hand off the mouse or putting down your stylus. You can access the Position Toolbar functions with single-key equivalents, which also means you can keep a grip on your mouse or stylus while changing modes. Reasonably enough, the equivalents are Z for Zoom, R for Rotate, and P for Pan. Less intuitive are W for Zoom Region (drag-select zoom area) and Alt+Z for Zoom Extents (fit all objects in Main View), but they're easy to learn and you won't make any fatal errors with reflexes learned from other software. Most of the standard menu options have the keyboard equivalents you would expect in the Windows environment, and almost all of them are shown in the menus. They're not mentioned at all in the manual, however, an omission guaranteed to annoy users who are trying to learn the software as rapidly as possible.

4D Paint's organization and nesting of options are excellent. You can get to any feature with a click or two, yet the interface is clean and compact enough that you can actually work with it in 640×480 resolution (see Figure 10.8). This is an important factor if you'll be using it as a Softimage or 3DS MAX plug-in. If you can use it comfortably in a corner of the screen while the parent application is still active, you can tighten the feedback loop and make your work go much faster. If a paint package insists on occupying your entire screen, you'll spend more time toggling between applications and less time actually painting.

4D Paint enables you to paint on as many layers as you've got system resources for. This is comparable to Detailer's Floaters but is not compatible with Photoshop layers. If you need to work with layers in Photoshop, you'll have to export each map as a separate image, then import them as layers within Photoshop. It's a clumsy and time-consuming process, so I suggest you stick with one or the other rather than trying to integrate them. The color picker, shown in Figure 10.9, enables you to set grayscale values for the bump, luminosity, specularity, and opacity brushes at the same time you set the color for the diffuse brush. This is a nice touch.

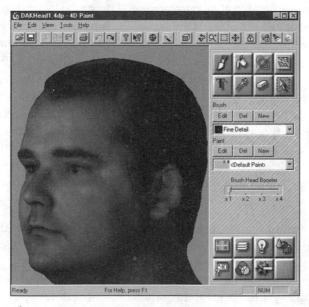

Figure 10.8 4D Paint interface.

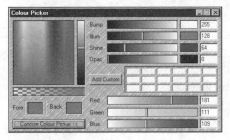

Figure 10.9 4D Paint Colour Picker.

As I mentioned in the section on Detailer, painting on layers gives you a great deal of flexibility to create detailed organic maps that you can edit with a minimum of fuss or wasted effort. You can use a base layer for the character's basic color, then add layers for wrinkles, skin defects, folds, scars, and whatever else makes the character interesting and unique. Combined and exported as a single map, the result is easy to manage in your animation software. Preserved as layers in 4D Paint's native project format, it's easy to modify and edit. The only disadvantage is that 4D Paint's native project format is not terribly efficient. If you want to preserve all the layers and other information (which I strongly recommend!), you have to save a .4DP project file. This is actually a file folder containing a proprietary project file plus PCX images of all the contributing maps. The original color map for my head was just over 3MB and the model another 573K—the project folder weighed in at 7.7MB. These project folders can get very large very quickly, but, if you want to be able to edit your character's maps, it's the only way to go. I suggest you pay extra attention to backups and documentation, since misplacing a file from the project folder can be disastrous.

I'm really impressed with the quality of information 4D Paint saves in the project file. It's not just the maps, models, and a few settings—it's the whole interface, including brushes, lights, and most importantly, View Bookmarks. This last element is a serious professional advantage for 4D Paint users. If you have a complex model with many maps, there are areas of the map that you will have to tweak repeatedly as the character evolves. Adjusting the Main View with the zoom and rotate tools takes time. Bookmarks enable you to save multiple Main View settings with descriptive names like Left Palm Close-up or Right Facial Profile. Selecting one of these from the Bookmark Controls panel is a snap, and it can give a welcome boost to your productivity. The more complex your characters and maps, the more you'll appreciate this feature.

Overall, I have been very impressed and happy with 4D Paint. It's a program you can grow with, as open-ended as your own computer system. You'll run out of ideas before you run into software limits, and that's exactly the kind of tool you need if you're working in character animation.

Check out the 4D Vision directory on this book's CD-ROM for a free demo version of 4D Paint and other software, plus a gallery, showing what other artists have been able to create with it.

Meshpaint 1.6

Meshpaint definitely comes in a distant last when measured for real utility in mapping characters. You can't interactively paint bump or specularity maps, because they aren't rendered in the working view. It's dead slow, in many instances actually slower than Detailer (although, to be fair, it consumes far less memory). I wouldn't even call this interactive—it's more like act, wait, react.

Meshpaint doesn't provide a true WYSIWYG (what you see is what you get) interface. If you cut and paste a map like the eyeball exercise in Chapter 9, Meshpaint will produce inaccuracies due to the difference between what it shows you on screen and where it actually places the pixels in the map. This is extremely counterproductive and annoying, and intolerable in a production environment.

Meshpaint doesn't provide enough levels of Undo to encourage creativity. You can't really get into experimenting with different effects while you're painting if you have to mentally keep track of how many strokes you can undo. The workaround for this is to save a lot of increments of your work, but that interferes with the creative flow, too.

Meshpaint does not support layers, either proprietary or Photoshop compatible. This lack alone relegates the software to hobbyist levels or worse. It's ridiculous to confine complex character maps with wrinkles, folds, and other surface details to a single layer. You'd have to redo so much work that it would be more efficient to paint the whole thing in Photoshop layers in 2D, over an Unwrapped or Flattened template.

Meshpaint was one of the earliest 3D paint packages, but others have passed it by. Positron has been making announcements about a version 2 for some time. As of this writing, I understand they are considering reserving their patented technologies for internal and for-fee use, rather than building it into software. If a major revision of Meshpaint is ever published, I'll be happy to see it resume its place as a viable tool for 3D artists. Until then, I have to say, you can do a lot better for the money.

trueSpace3, 3D Paint, And 3D Bump

trueSpace3 has a set of 3D paint tools built in, but they're not in the same league as 4D Paint or Detailer. The only practical use I can see for them is to demonstrate the advantages and pitfalls of 3D paint in general. These features are simply not up to the task of creating character maps.

The number of brush shapes and options is too low. There is only a handful of brush widths, and even counting the Airbrush tool (which doesn't act like any other airbrush tool you've used), you don't have a lot of options. The 3D Bump tool is even worse—you have a handful of choices for bump depth, but the effect creates visible dent artifacts, as if the bump was created with repeated blows of a ball-peen hammer. Both the paint and bump tools are too low-resolution to produce workable results without a lot of redundant retouching.

Painting on one area of a surface can cause small motions in paint already applied to other areas. The paint doesn't necessarily stay where you put it—a major flaw. Also, you cannot use either 3D paint or 3D bump to modify an existing map. TS3 will either overwrite it or not paint on the object at all. The 3D paint and bump files are stored in folders separately from the mesh and scene. If you want to move them to another machine or share them across a production team, you have to manually track and move all the map files.

> ### TRUESPACE3 DOES NOT PLAY WELL WITH OTHERS
>
> The file format for trueSpace3's 3D paint functions is proprietary, and there is no way to export a finished texture as a map to be applied and rendered in other software.

3D paint and bump redraw times are nothing to brag about. If you are used to quickly sketching a rough, then editing more slowly, don't bother to try it in TS3. If you drag the paintbrush rapidly across the side of an object, you'll get a collection of disconnected paint spots. When you stop moving the cursor, the screen redraws everything to show you a continuous, unbroken line. Meanwhile, you've been waiting, and the delay has broken you out of your creative groove.

In short, TS3's 3D paint and bump tools are fun to play with for a little while, but you'll never want to rely on them for paying work. If you use TS3 for other reasons, I suggest you use one of the 3D paint packages mentioned earlier in this chapter to create your character maps, even if you end up using them within TS3.

Cyberware Color Scans

The Cyberware scanning process, as described in Chapter 7, is fast and painless as a means of acquiring 3D surface data. The current hardware can also capture 24-bit color map data as it measures the surface geometry. The Cyberware software also creates UV mapping coordinates for 3DS and other UV-supporting formats, automatically. That's what produced Figure 10.10, the UV color map of my head.

Figure 10.10   Unretouched Cyberscan of the author's head.

There's only one real drawback to this technique: the older scan hardware has limited resolution, precisely one pixel per data point. This produces maps with only 512×512 resolution, when a film or television shot may require a much higher resolution map for close-ups. However, the Cyberscan map is especially useful as a template for creating more detailed maps. If you unwrap or flatten a model as discussed in Chapter 9, you can apply a Cyberscan map as a layer underneath it, then paint in yet a third layer with both color and mesh available as templates. If you're trying to match a live subject, you can't beat a Cyberware map as a template. If you really need an original high-resolution map, you should use Cyberware's newer HRC scanner, which captures color maps at 2K×2K resolution.

Shaders

A shader is a program or set of instructions used with your 3D software's renderer to modify the rendered image. Shaders are often used to color or transform the surface of models, including animated characters. Shaders and maps can produce similar results, but they do it in very different ways. A map changes a surface one pixel at a time. The renderer "sees" the map's value for a particular area, calculates the effects of light and shadow, and adds the resulting value to the appropriate place in the rendered image. A shader changes the surface by calculation. The renderer "sees" that the shader controls a particular area, asks the shader for the surface's value, and the shader calculates it.

This points out the two deciding factors between maps and shaders: speed of rendering and resolution of finished image. A map can be preloaded into RAM for fast access, and, because all its values are present at all times, the renderer can calculate the surface values very quickly. The limitation of maps is that the quality of the final rendering depends on the resolution of the map. If you have too small a map the pixels stretch across the screen and become obvious. Too large a map and you need a more expensive computer to render the image. Shaders have a complementary set of strengths and limitations. Shaders must calculate the appearance of each pixel in the final image. There is no shortcut, preloading, or cheating that can bypass the rendering calculations. However, shaders take up very little memory, and they can render to any resolution you choose without increasing demands on anything but CPU cycles. For example, a map of a character's face might look acceptable for long shots, but, in close-ups, the map's pixels would appear blocky and obvious. A shader designed to duplicate the map's effects would maintain a smooth, accurate appearance, even if the camera zoomed in until the character's nose filled the frame.

Shaders have the same advantage over hand-painted maps that desktop publishing has over hand-setting type. Shaders, being programs, can use the computer's calculating power to rapidly repeat a simple set of actions to create an arbitrarily complex result. If you have ever seen a Mandelbrot or Julia set, you've seen a simple example of what a shader can produce. Just a few lines of code can sometimes produce naturalistic, complex textures that can draw and hold your audience's eye.

Shaders are especially useful for surfaces that are too complex to model or paint efficiently and that repeat a pattern based on factors that you can derive or define. For example, the pattern of veins in a leaf is complex in the end result, but a small number of rules determine the direction of growth, the frequency and angle of each fork, and the decreasing width of each vein. If you program these rules into a shader, you could apply it to a leaf-shaped flat surface and produce a highly detailed, photo-realistic veined leaf. Animated characters' skin, clothing, hair, fur, scales, and other complex, rule-based surfaces are excellent subjects for shaders.

Because shaders are so useful, many 3D programs include a library of shaders as part of the package. For example, the imp's skin in Figure 17.1 is an application of LightWave's Vein shader. With a smaller interval and different color and bump settings, it makes a good human skin, too. Third-party software publishers also market plug-in shader libraries for most of the popular programs. One of the most popular new shader types as of this writing are fur and hair, both of which are notoriously difficult to either map or model.

3D Studio MAX: Digimation's Shag:Fur Plug-in

Digimation's Shag:Fur plug-in for 3D Studio MAX is a good example of a hair/fur shader. It provides a set of controls suitable for producing realistic or fantastic effects, and is powerful but straightforward to use.

The Shag:Fur package consists of a single diskette and a spiral-bound manual. The installation is easy, and Digimation's email authorization was quick. The 60-page manual is split evenly between reference and tutorial sections. This is one of the best plug-in manuals I've had the pleasure to use. It is well-illustrated, laid out logically, and the instructions are in plain English. I hope this is an ongoing practice for Digimation, and one that other 3D software publishers will emulate.

You can work through the manual's examples in a few hours, including time for playing with settings and admiring your results. Shag:Fur is one of those visually fascinating programs that makes interesting images straight from the default settings. You really have to make an effort to create an ugly, boring image. The following project presents a quick overview of Shag:Fur's functions as they apply to character animation.

Adding Realistic Hair To A Human Head

PROJECT 10.1 This project will reuse my Cyberscanned head model and matching color maps from preceding chapters. As noted in Chapter 7, I had to shave my beard and mustache in order to get a more accurate model. This project shows you how to restore the missing facial hair, and to enhance the existing hair to create a more realistic effect.

1. Use image-editing software to restore facial hair to the color map. I used Photoshop to copy, paste, distort and blend the beard from image file BEARD1.TGA into image file EDITED.TIF. It's not possible to simply cut-and-paste from one Cyberscan map to another, because minor differences in centering the subject will cause major distortions in the final map. You're welcome to try this editing yourself, or simply use my results, image file BEARD3A.TIF.

2. Use image-editing software to create a negative, high-contrast grayscale image of the color map. Figure 10.11 shows each stage in this process, and my final results. Starting from BEARD3A.TIF, I converted it to grayscale, inverted it, then adjusted the contrast and brightness. As used by Shag:Fur, black areas of the map will have no visible fur strands, white areas will have dense strands of maximum length, and gray areas will have fewer, shorter strands in proportion to their darkness.

3. Load file HEADHAIR.MAX, or import the head model from the 3DS format file in the Chapter 10 directory on the CD-ROM. It might save you some time if you copy the map files from the CD-ROM to your MAX default map directory.

4. Select the head model. You want the Fur shader to affect the entire geometry, not just a subset of the faces. You'll control the appearance of the Fur strands with maps, not geometry. You will usually want to control strand length and density separately from the model's surface materials, so you'll need to apply more than one Material ID to the model.

5. Click on the Modify tab, and select the Edit Mesh modifier. Switch from Vertex to Face sub-object mode. Scroll down to the Edit Surface Parameters sub-panel. Change the Material ID number from 1 to 2. Now the model has 2 sub-material IDs.

6. Open the Material Editor. Choose one of the Materials slots. Click on the Get Material button, then choose Multi/SubObject and click on OK. This will call up the Multi/SubObject main panel, with 6 default slots.

7. Change the Number of Materials spinner to read 2. You will only need two materials, one for color and the other for hair.

8. Assign the color map to Material 1. Assign the grayscale hair map to Material 2. Your results should look something like Figure 10.12. Assign the material to the head model. This completes the setup for the model and maps. The next step is to set up the Shag:Fur parameters.

9. Choose Rendering|Environment. In the Environment dialog box under Atmospheric, click on Add. Choose Shag:Render. Click on Add again, and choose Shag:Fur. This sets up the Shag:Fur rendering engine, and opens the plug-in's rollout. You should see something like Figure 10.13. Note that you can see Fur strands in the viewports. These are just approximations, to give you some idea of the distribution, size and angle of the final rendered strands.

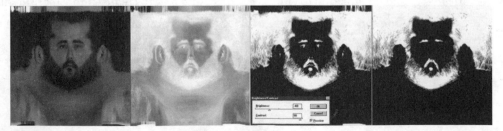

Figure 10.11 Conversion of color image to high-contrast negative grayscale.

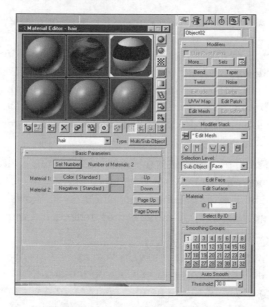

Figure 10.12 Sub-Object and Material Editor settings for color and hair maps.

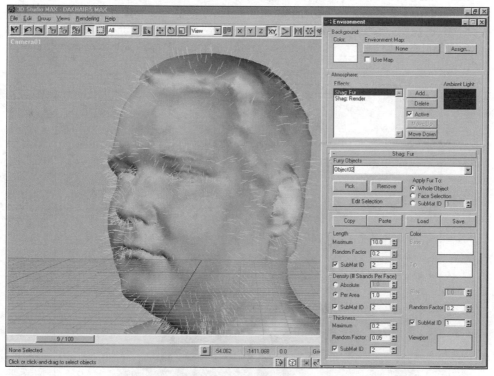

Figure 10.13 Screenshot of Camera01 view, plus upper half of Shag:Fur Environment settings for scene DAKHAIR5.MAX.

10. Under the Apply Fur To menu, choose Whole Object. Change the other values in Shag: Fur's rollout to match Figure 10.13. For more natural-looking fur, you'll want to use each control's Random Factor. This keeps the rendered strands from looking too perfectly uniform, a dead giveaway that it's computer-generated. The settings pictured give a reasonably natural variation to the color, density, length and direction of the fur. If you render an image now, you should get an effect like Figure 10.14. Note that because Shag:Fur is a rendered atmospheric effect, you can't render fur in any view except the Camera.

11. There is one remaining problem with this setup: all the hair on the head looks identical, even the direction and angle of the individual strands. In reality, groups of follicles will point in different directions. For example, human eyebrows generally point laterally outward and up, following the curve of the forehead. In Figure 10.14, the eyebrows look like bristle brushes.

12. This step shows how to apply Vectors to achieve a more natural appearance. Zoom in, all viewports, on the left eyebrow region. Click on the Create tab and click the Helpers icon. Choose Shag:Fur from the General dropdown, and click on the Vector button. This opens the Vector Parameters sub-panel, shown in Figure 10.15.

13. In the Front or Left viewport, click on the middle of the left eyebrow and drag up and to the right, following the general line of the forehead, to create Vector01. This is the direction, or vector, you want the strands to follow. You will probably need to use the Move and Rotate tools to position and orient Vector01. You should end up with something like Figure 10.16.

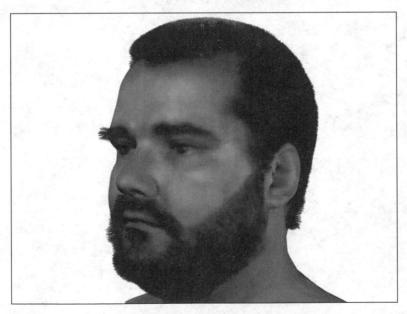

Figure 10.14 Shag:Fur rendering showing unrealistic effect of straight strands oriented parallel to surface normals.

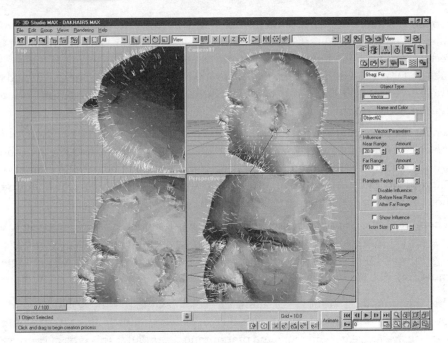

Figure 10.15   Viewports and Vector Parameters default sub-panel.

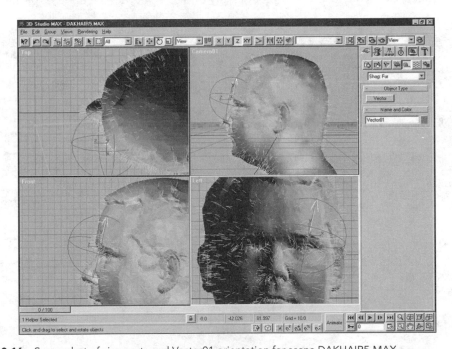

Figure 10.16   Screenshot of viewports and Vector01 orientation for scene DAKHAIR5.MAX.

14. Reopen the Rendering|Environment dialog, if you closed it. In the lower half of the Shag:Fur panel, you will see a set of controls labeled Leaning. Click on the Select Lean Vectors button, and choose Vector01 from the Select Vector Helpers file dialog, then click on OK. Set Leaning Amount to 1.0 for full effect, Random Factor to 0.3, and Max Angle to 89. If you choose an angle greater than 90, the fur strands may become ingrown and disappear.

15. Repeat the preceding settings for the Bending controls. Play with the Bending Amount control, and watch the viewports (Figure 10.17). Shag:Fur redraws the placeholder strands each time you change a setting, so you can see a good approximation of the length, lean and bend of the final rendered strands. This is a very nice feature, although it can get addictive. It's just too much fun to play with!

16. When you have the settings you want, render the Camera view. Rendering takes a little longer than with a simple mapped model, but remember that the computer has to perform a lot of calculations to simulate all those strands. You should end up with something like Figure 10.18.

Note that the individual strands vary slightly, by color, length, thickness, density, and lean and bend angles. With a little more tweaking, you can get very realistic effects that would be difficult or expensive to create with modeling or mapping techniques. This type of complex effect is where shaders can really boost your productivity and give you new creative inspiration.

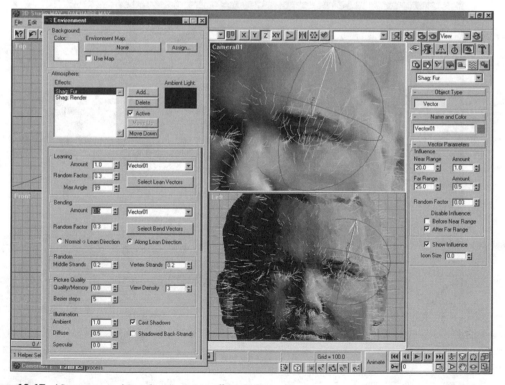

Figure 10.17 Viewports and Bending/Leaning effect on strands.

Figure 10.18   Rendering of Vectored eyebrow strands.

PAINTING HAIR

If you use Shag:Fur or other shader that relies on a map for any control settings, you can use a 3D paint program to control that shader. For example, once you have set Vectors for follicle directions, you can manipulate all other controls with maps. You could use 4D Paint to edit the hair map in the preceding project, then reload the map in MAX and re-render the scene. In effect, you can literally draw hair onto your models, using all the painting tools available to achieve 3D hair effects. The only drawback is the slower rate of interaction in comparison to ordinary map editing.

Programming Shaders

Creating new shaders is a very technical subject, well beyond the scope of this book. Generally, shader development is the domain of the technical director and other programming staff. If you're not that technical, you can simply use built-in or plug-in shaders or stick to maps. To write good shaders, you need a working knowledge of at least one programming language, a fairly deep understanding of mathematics, and the creative and problem-solving abilities to implement a purely mathematical function into a working, robust shader program. It's not an overly common set of talents, so good shader programmers can always find work. If you'd like to try programming shaders yourself, there are several resources that can get you started.

RenderMan is a shader programming language developed by Pixar long before they produced *Toy Story*. While they have pulled RenderMan from the desktop software market, several shareware and commercial products still support the RenderMan scene-description format. RenderMan shaders don't look bad on a resume, either. The basic book on the subject is Steve

Upstill's *The RenderMan Companion*, from Addison-Wesley. At the time of this writing, there was also a nice overview of shaders and a RenderMan tutorial written by Michael J. Hammel at **http://zenith.yok.utu.fi/lg/issue17/bmrt-part2**.

For a more authoritative source on shader methodology and design, try Stephen F. May's "RenderMan Notes," hosted at The Ohio State University's Computer graphics Research Group at **www.cgrg.ohio-state.edu/~smay/RmanNotes**.

If you develop an ongoing interest in shaders and the more technical end of computer graphics, I suggest you consult the ACM SIGGRAPH references in the last chapters of this book. You may find Transactions On Graphics especially interesting, as it's the place many shader algorithms are first published. If you find a particular renderer or programming language that interests you, try searching for a Usenet newsgroup devoted to it. You can usually find a plethora of free advice, worth every bit of what you pay for it. Aside from the technical assistance and directions to pertinent books and Web sites, the platform and software flame wars can do wonders for your vocabulary of invective. Which, in turn, is handy for the next time you try to write a shader under a tight deadline.

Moving On

If you've worked through all the chapters up to this point, you should be able to produce working storyboards, soundtracks, exposure sheets, and textured character and set models. The next chapter introduces you to the last step before the animation begins—character setup.

PART IV

SETUP

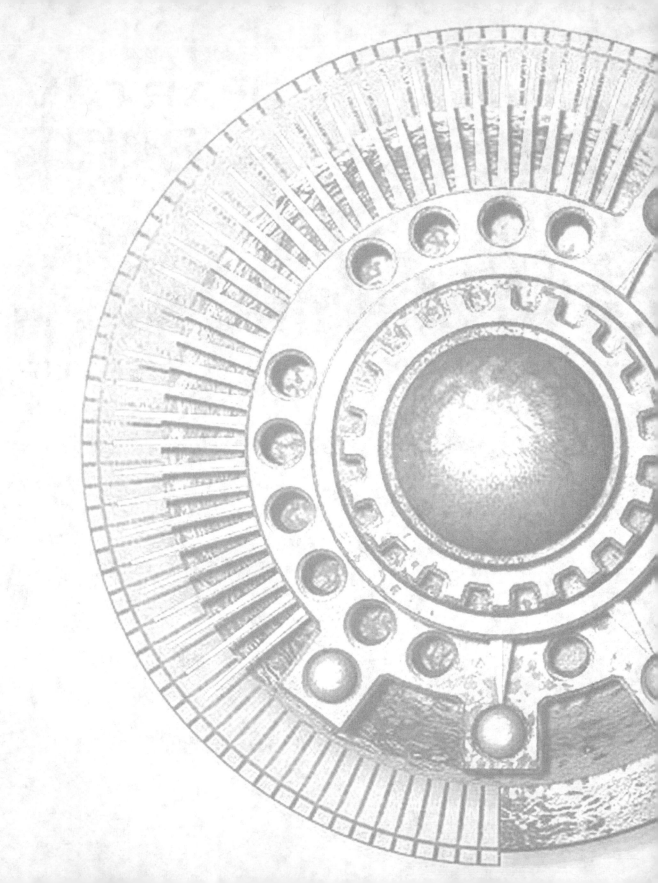

SETUPS

Setups are the flesh and bone of animated characters. You need to understand how animation works before you can set up a character, and you need to understand how a character is set up before you can animate it.

A *setup* is a scene file containing everything necessary for an animator to bring a character to life. This can include objects, hierarchies, constraints, expressions, lights, cameras, and just about any other item or function used in your animation software. A setup can be as simple as a few objects arranged in a hierarchy or as complex as several photo-realistic humanoid characters with full musculoskeletal structures and a plethora of constraints and expressions.

Before you can build a setup, you need to understand how an animator will use it. This chapter shows you the basic principles behind character animation, with projects that guide you through the process of setting up simple characters. The next two chapters show you progressively more complex setups, from primitive caricatures up to realistic emulation of muscle, skin, cloth, and hair. Each setup chapter has a companion animation chapter. Chapter 14 shows how to use this chapter's setups to practice basic animation techniques.

Animator-Friendly Setups

Character animation is hard. You should try to use your setups to make it as easy as possible. The ideal setup is one that the animator can open up and immediately start posing the character, with a minimum of confusion, bother, or wasted effort. A good setup can make a character intuitive and efficient to animate. A bad setup, or one the animator doesn't understand, can ruin a project—maybe even a career. You will either be animating the little monster yourself (in which case, you will have no one else to blame for a frustrating setup) or setting it up for another animator (in which case, they can focus all their frustration on you). Either way, it's in your best interest to make your setups as animator-friendly as possible.

Character setup can also be a way into the animation profession. If your animation skills are not yet up to professional standards, you may still be able to find work doing setups. Most professional animators I've interviewed prefer not to do setups. There is a constant migration, from setup person to junior animator, that leaves entry-level setup positions open. Make sure your demo reel, resumé, and other materials show off your setup skills!

Learn From Others' Mistakes—It's Much Cheaper!

As I note in this book's introduction, there are many similarities between CGI character animation and the more traditional forms used in the past century. I've always believed in the wisdom of learning from other people's experience and mistakes, because it is much cheaper and less painful. That said, let's take a look at what we can learn from the masters of character animation.

Setting up for 3D CGI animation has more in common with clay or puppet animation than with 2D drawn animation, for a number of reasons. In three-dimensional animation, you must set before the camera models of everything the audience will see, whether you use CGI, clay, or puppets. You have, in compensation for this extra effort, a great deal of freedom in moving your camera to compose your shots. The correctness of perspective and depth, so difficult to attain with drawn animation, is also integral to 3D, whether physical or CGI. Last, 2D animation generally relies on the laborious redrawing of anything that must appear to move. This is a huge burden. Enormous resources have been poured into developing production shortcuts to reuse as much hand-drawn artwork as possible. In 3D formats, you have the comparative luxury of reusing almost everything in nearly every frame; changes between frames are incremental or piecemeal, rather than substantial or total.

This is only to say that puppet or clay traditions have more bearing on setup techniques for CGI character animation. After the setup is complete, the efficient CGI animator's workflow more closely resembles that of a traditional 2D animator. For staging, timing, general workflow, and other animation principles discussed in Part V, we will rely heavily on the much larger (and somewhat more relevant) body of work supporting 2D character animation. Where the traditional animator would draw a handful of key poses, the CGI animator sets a handful of keyframes. Where the traditional animator would flip his sketchpad to judge the action, the CGI animator renders a wireframe preview. Where the traditional animator would add, delete, or reshuffle drawings to vary the timing of an action, the CGI animator cuts, copies, and pastes keyframes along the timeline. As Ken Cope points out in the Foreword, neither traditional 3D nor 2D character animation techniques are wholly or exclusively applicable to CGI, but both have much to contribute.

So, what does puppet animation have to offer for CGI setup?

First, let's get the terminology straight. There really isn't an official name encompassing puppet, clay, and related forms of animation. The phrase *stop motion* is used by a lot of people in the industry. However, this term was originally used for a larger body of special effects that were performed in the camera, including optical dissolves, split screens, and other effects that have nothing to do with animation. The alternatives of *dimensional animation* and *puppet animation* have their drawbacks. More recently, market forces have bred neologisms, such as Claymation™ and Go-Motion™ in an effort to differentiate one studio's or animator's techniques from the others. For the sake of consistency, I will use the term *puppet animation* to refer to puppet, clay, and all other forms of physical 3D animation. If the term offends you, feel free to scratch it out and insert your own favorite term—but only after you've purchased this book!

There are two major divisions in puppet animation techniques: *replacement* and *displacement*. Each has advantages and disadvantages, depending on the needs of a particular animation sequence. They are often combined in hybrid replacement/displacement animation, which can use the strengths of one technique to shore up the weaknesses of the other.

Replacement Animation Techniques

Replacement puppet animation uses a complete model for each pose, swapping out the model for each change, sometimes for each frame. The models are generally cast or similarly mass-produced in batches of one pose, then deformed, sculpted, or otherwise modified to create the individual poses. As you can imagine, this method requires a large number of models for even simple actions. The advantage is that the actual staging and shooting of the animation proceeds very quickly, because the entire sequence of models has been determined in advance and they can be rapidly swapped out during photography.

For a non-character example of this technique, you can look at the peach glop in *James and the Giant Peach* (1996).

One of the few examples of this technique being used for a complete character in a feature film is the *Tyrannosaurus Rex* in *The Beast of Hollow Mountain* (1956). The replacement models of *T. Rex* were used for walking and running sequences—the cyclical actions were a good match for the strengths and limitations of replacement puppet animation.

The current crop of animation software has a number of tools that can be used for replacement animation. Each has strengths and weaknesses. You can benefit from learning and practicing as many of them as possible, because you never know which one will be perfect for that rush job the boss is about to dump on you.

CGI replacement tools generally fall into two categories: *simple replacement* and *morph*. Simple replacement changes one model out for another, all at once and with no modifications. This is the closest approximation to the traditional replacement technique and has the traditional drawback of requiring a new model for each frame of motion. Morph, short for metamorphosis, is more properly called *model interpolation*. The original meaning of metamorphosis in special effects was the gradual transformation of one 2D image into another. Because the final effects of metamorphosis and model interpolation are visually similar, the mass media have used the term morph to describe both, and common usage has made that misinterpretation stick. Morph replacement animation also changes one model for another, but gradually, by interpolating the position of each vertex or control point in the original model to match those of the target model. This is the effect made popular by the changing faces of the water tentacle in *The Abyss* and the shape-changing T-1000 in *Terminator 2*. Morphing has since been used in many CGI animations. Nearly all animation software includes some type of morph tool.

This chapter covers basic setups for both simple replacement and morph animation techniques. Later chapters cover advanced replacement animation for lip sync, facial animation, and other complex actions.

Simple replacement tools can be divided into two groups: *manual replacement* and *model sequence replacement*.

Manual Replacement

At the most basic level, you can mimic single-frame replacement animation by using a manual replacement function to swap out models while stepping through each frame of the animation.

A typical replacement process might look like this:

1. Load the scene file for a shot. Position the camera, lights, sets, and props according to the storyboard sketches and director's notes for the shot.

2. Load the first character model.

3. Render the current frame.

4. Replace the character model with the next character model, according to the exposure sheet.

5. Render the current frame with a one-frame increment in the image file name.

6. Repeat Steps 4 and 5 until all frames for the shot have been rendered.

Alternatively, you could load all the models into a scene at once, then animate their visibility, transparency, or scale values to make them invisible until they are called for:

1. Load the scene file for a shot. Position the camera, lights, sets, and props according to the storyboard sketches and director's notes for the shot. Create a dummy or null at the character's location.

2. Load all the character models. Parent them all to the dummy, so their positions all match precisely.

3. Set all the character models to be either invisible, 100 percent transparent, or scaled small enough that they are not visible.

4. Make the first character model visible.

5. Render the current frame.

6. Make the current character model invisible again, and make the next character model visible, according to the exposure sheet.

7. Render the current frame with a one-frame increment in the image file name.

8. Repeat Steps 6 and 7 until all frames for the shot have been rendered.

Using Manual Replacement

Either of the preceding techniques produces a numbered image sequence for later assembly or compositing. It's possible to create character animation this way, but I have to ask, "Why?" Manual replacement combines the worst of traditional puppet animation and CGI. As with puppet animation, you can't tweak or edit the timing. It's all done straight-ahead, frame by frame. If you need to modify an action, you have to animate the sequence all over again. As with all CGI, you have to build everything you'll set before the camera and in a much less intuitive medium than clay and wire. Because it is so simple but has no advantages and nothing unique to contribute to the education of a beginner, I'm not providing a detailed project for this technique. If you ever have an animation job that requires manual model replacement, you'll be able to figure out the necessary details for your particular software package.

If you still want to experiment with this technique, you can use the replacement models provided for the next project. The Chapter 11 directory on this book's CD-ROM contains 31 models of a simple gooseneck desk lamp, each bent to a slightly different angle. You should be able to apply them to either manual replacement technique listed earlier.

MODEL FORMATS FOR THE PROJECTS

I have provided duplicate polygonal models in 3DS, DXF, and LWO formats on this book's CD-ROM. If your software can't use one of these formats directly, you should at least be able to import and translate the models to your software's native format. DXF is most commonly acceptable but does not include color, origin, or shading information, so I suggest you try the 3DS format if possible. You should also batch-convert all models from this chapter's CD-ROM directory when you begin this chapter's first project. This will save you time and distractions as you work through the projects. To avoid confusion, throughout the following text, I have omitted the usual three-letter file type extension for model names. Whenever a project's directions ask you to type a model's file name, you will need to append the appropriate file type extension for the model file format you are using.

As I stated earlier, simple replacement animation depends on having one complete model for each frame of motion. For example, suppose you created a replacement animation using 30 model replacements, and each model was only slightly different from the next. If the animation takes only 30 frames, you would have enough replacements for a smooth animation, as shown in animation file ECA1101.AVI on this book's CD-ROM. If you tried to stretch this same animation out but still only changed models 30 times, you would see jerks, or *strobing*, each time the pose changed, as you can see in animation file ECA1101B.AVI on this book's CD-ROM. The first 30 frames of the animation are identical to ECA1101.AVI, but the remaining 60 have only one model for each two frames of animation. Because the models are not really connected from frame to frame (the way morph or deformation models are), there are no in-between poses for the animation software to render. Even motion blur won't help, since the model is not actually moving during the in-between frames. This is one reason other techniques are generally more useful than single-frame replacement animation.

One potential advantage to the simple replacement technique depends on how large and diverse your library of models is and, oddly enough, is related to 2D rather than 3D animation traditions. The 2D technique known as *straight-ahead action* consists of drawing each pose as you come to it, working out timing and posing on the fly. This results in a zany, impromptu look that is more difficult to produce in a preplanned sequence. Animating using manual replacement enables you to exert the same freedom as straight-ahead action, limited only by the range of models you have available to throw into the mix.

CHARACTER MODELS FOR STRAIGHT-AHEAD ANIMATION

If you work with a particular character over any length of time, creating models for expressions and actions as you go, you may eventually collect enough models to make manual replacement animation feasible.

Another major disadvantage of this approach is that the animation is not readily edited or repeated. Just as straight-ahead action leaves no key drawings with which to connect revised actions, manual replacement animation loses the preceding scene information every time you save the scene with a replacement model.

Model Sequence Replacement

The model sequence process works a lot like manual replacement but is simpler to keep track of and easier to reuse. Model sequence animation is like lining up all the models you are going to use on a shelf, in order, with duplicates where necessary. You just work down the row, swapping out the next model in line without having to think about it. The only difference is that the shelf you use is a directory on your computer, and the software does the replacement for you.

Software That Doesn't Support Simple Replacement

Unfortunately, of the 14 animation programs reviewed, only LightWave 3D includes a procedure for loading sequences of models. It's possible to create your own sequence managers for MAX or Houdini, but that level of programming is beyond the scope of this book. The remaining software seems to completely overlook simple replacement animation. However, several programs do support some form of morphing, as later projects demonstrate.

LightWave 3D 5.5

LightWave 3D uses a plug-in called *ObjSequence* for model sequence replacement. Setting up this plug-in is very much like setting up an image sequence. You make copies of the object file for each frame where you want it to first appear and name the copy to match the frame number. For example, if you want the object REPLAC05.LWO to appear in frames 25, 37, and 42, you duplicate the REPLAC05.LWO file three times and name the copies REPLA025.LWO, REPLA037.LWO, and REPLA042.LWO.

This approach is easy to use because LightWave 3D doesn't require you to specify an object for each frame in a sequence. It holds the last used object until the next higher number in the sequence is reached. For example, if the file order is:

1, 2, 5, 10, 11

the displayed file sequence will actually be:

1, 2, 2, 2, 5, 5, 5, 5, 5, 10, 11

Obviously, this can save you a great deal of work in laying out an object sequence. You only have to specify the changes, not the holds!

PROJECT 11.1 Animating A Desk Lamp With LightWave's ObjSequence Plug-in

The approach we're going to use is simple, requiring only a bit of typing. There are only 31 objects to choose from, so we'll simply write a *batch file* (a text file containing a list of DOS commands) to make the required number of copies of the object files, numbered in the order we want them to appear. The completely manual approach would be to use your system's Copy and Rename functions for each and every file, which would get tedious very quickly.

1. Set up a new directory for the sequence objects.

2. Copy the REPLAC00.LWO through REPLAC30.LWO objects to the new directory.

3. This project is going to be fairly simple, so we won't bother with an exposure sheet. All we will be doing is making the lamp bend forward, then bend more slowly back up to its original position. This means the first 30 frames will call for the objects in their original numerical order, and the last 60 frames will call for them backwards, at two-frame intervals. You might want to write this out, to help you visualize it.

4. Using Windows Notepad or another text editor, create a new batch file named for this project (PR1101.BAT). Type:

```
REM BATCH FILE FOR PROJECT 11.1
```

for the first line, and save it in the new directory along with the objects.

5. The first frame of the animation calls for the REPLAC00.LWO object file. Add a second line to the batch file, reading:

```
COPY REPLAC00.LWO OmBJSQ000.LWO
```

This command will duplicate the original object with a new name. This means the original object will appear in frame 0 of the animation. Note that the ObjSequence plug-in requires the file name to end in a three-digit number sequence.

6. Select the second line (including carriage return), copy it, and paste it as many times as the first object is called for, which in this case is only twice. For some animations, you may end up duplicating a single object several dozen times. You should end up with this:

```
REM BATCH FILE FOR PROJECT 11.2
COPY REPLAC00.LWO OBJSQ000.LWO
COPY REPLAC00.LWO OBJSQ000.LWO
```

7. Select the number part of the new file name in the third line. Type the number of the next start frame for this phoneme object. Because we are animating one ping-pong

cycle with a total of 90 frames, and objects in the last half of the animation are all held for two frames, this object should appear in frames 0, 89, and 90:

```
REM BATCH FILE FOR PROJECT 11.2
COPY REPLAC00.LWO OBJSQ000.LWO
COPY REPLAC00.LWO OBJSQ089.LWO
```

Note that we don't have to make a copy for frame 90, as the plug-in holds the last object until a higher number comes along.

8. Repeat these steps for the rest of the objects. When you're done, you should have a list to make 61 copies, thus:

```
REM BATCH FILE FOR PROJECT 11.2
COPY REPLAC00.LWO OBJSQ000.LWO
COPY REPLAC00.LWO OBJSQ089.LWO
COPY REPLAC01.LWO OBJSQ001.LWO
COPY REPLAC01.LWO OBJSQ087.LWO
COPY REPLAC02.LWO OBJSQ002.LWO
COPY REPLAC02.LWO OBJSQ085.LWO
COPY REPLAC03.LWO OBJSQ003.LWO
COPY REPLAC03.LWO OBJSQ083.LWO
COPY REPLAC04.LWO OBJSQ004.LWO
COPY REPLAC04.LWO OBJSQ081.LWO
COPY REPLAC05.LWO OBJSQ005.LWO
COPY REPLAC05.LWO OBJSQ079.LWO
COPY REPLAC06.LWO OBJSQ006.LWO
COPY REPLAC06.LWO OBJSQ077.LWO
COPY REPLAC07.LWO OBJSQ007.LWO
COPY REPLAC07.LWO OBJSQ075.LWO
COPY REPLAC08.LWO OBJSQ008.LWO
COPY REPLAC08.LWO OBJSQ073.LWO
COPY REPLAC09.LWO OBJSQ009.LWO
COPY REPLAC09.LWO OBJSQ071.LWO
COPY REPLAC10.LWO OBJSQ010.LWO
COPY REPLAC10.LWO OBJSQ069.LWO
COPY REPLAC11.LWO OBJSQ011.LWO
COPY REPLAC11.LWO OBJSQ067.LWO
COPY REPLAC12.LWO OBJSQ012.LWO
COPY REPLAC12.LWO OBJSQ065.LWO
COPY REPLAC13.LWO OBJSQ013.LWO
COPY REPLAC13.LWO OBJSQ063.LWO
COPY REPLAC14.LWO OBJSQ014.LWO
COPY REPLAC14.LWO OBJSQ061.LWO
COPY REPLAC15.LWO OBJSQ015.LWO
COPY REPLAC15.LWO OBJSQ059.LWO
COPY REPLAC16.LWO OBJSQ016.LWO
COPY REPLAC16.LWO OBJSQ057.LWO
```

```
COPY REPLAC17.LWO OBJSQ017.LWO
COPY REPLAC17.LWO OBJSQ055.LWO
COPY REPLAC18.LWO OBJSQ018.LWO
COPY REPLAC18.LWO OBJSQ053.LWO
COPY REPLAC19.LWO OBJSQ019.LWO
COPY REPLAC19.LWO OBJSQ051.LWO
COPY REPLAC20.LWO OBJSQ020.LWO
COPY REPLAC20.LWO OBJSQ049.LWO
COPY REPLAC21.LWO OBJSQ021.LWO
COPY REPLAC21.LWO OBJSQ047.LWO
COPY REPLAC22.LWO OBJSQ022.LWO
COPY REPLAC22.LWO OBJSQ045.LWO
COPY REPLAC23.LWO OBJSQ023.LWO
COPY REPLAC23.LWO OBJSQ043.LWO
COPY REPLAC24.LWO OBJSQ024.LWO
COPY REPLAC24.LWO OBJSQ041.LWO
COPY REPLAC25.LWO OBJSQ025.LWO
COPY REPLAC25.LWO OBJSQ039.LWO
COPY REPLAC26.LWO OBJSQ026.LWO
COPY REPLAC26.LWO OBJSQ037.LWO
COPY REPLAC27.LWO OBJSQ027.LWO
COPY REPLAC27.LWO OBJSQ035.LWO
COPY REPLAC28.LWO OBJSQ028.LWO
COPY REPLAC28.LWO OBJSQ033.LWO
COPY REPLAC29.LWO OBJSQ029.LWO
COPY REPLAC29.LWO OBJSQ031.LWO
COPY REPLAC30.LWO OBJSQ030.LWO
```

9. Save the batch file, and make a backup copy! It's fairly easy to rebuild the directory structure if you accidentally delete some object files, but if you lose this batch file, you'll have to go back and type it all over.

   Also, once you have a particular object sequence worked out (and some of them can be very complex), you can apply it to any compatible set of objects. Just use your text editor's Find and Replace functions to change the source file names in the batch file. This can save you the time and bother of having to retype the whole thing from scratch.

10. Make sure you've got plenty of disk space available. Multiply the number of lines in your batch file by the size of the largest file you are duplicating to get the total required. When you are ready, execute the batch file.

11. Now you get to do some preemptive quality control. Browse the object sequence directory. Did the files end up where you expected them to? Are all the file numbers you expected actually there? Open up a few files in Modeler as a spot check, and compare them with the batch file. This quality control is not so crucial for this project, but it's a good habit to develop. It's much better to catch any mistakes now than after rendering an entire animation.

12. Load the ECA1101.LWS scene file in Layout. When it loads this scene, LightWave will look for the first desk lamp object in directory Objects\CH11. You can simply copy the Chapter 11 directory from this book's CD-ROM to your default Objects directory on your hard drive or redirect LightWave to look in this book's CD-ROM directory. After the scene loads, click on the Objects button at the top left of the Layout window to open the Objects panel.

13. Click on the Replace Object button. The Replacement Objects File dialog appears. Select the first object file in the sequence, OBJSQ000.LWO, and press Enter to close the Replacement Objects File dialog and return to the Objects panel. The Current Object button now shows the file name OBJSQ000.LWO (see Figure 11.1).

14. Click on the Obj Rep Plug-ins button just beneath the Current Object button. The Object Replacement Plug-ins panel appears, with the Plug-in 1 drop-down option reading (none), as shown in Figure 11.2.

15. Drag down the Plug-in 1 drop-down button, and select LW_ObjectSequence. Click on Continue to close the Object Replacement Plug-ins panel and return to the Objects panel. The Obj Rep Plug-ins button will now show one plug-in loaded.

16. Click on the Close Panel button at the bottom of the Objects panel to close it and return to Layout.

17. Create a keyframe at frame 0, then create another one at frame 90, for all items. Save the scene. In Layout, frame 30 should look like Figure 11.3. You may have to render the frame to update the ObjSequence plug-in.

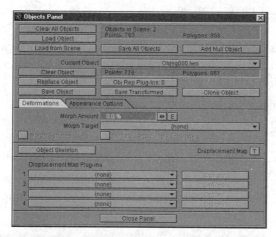

Figure 11.1 OBJSQ000.LWO, the first object of the sequence, is loaded in the Objects panel.

Figure 11.2 Object Replacement Plug-ins panel, with no plug-ins loaded.

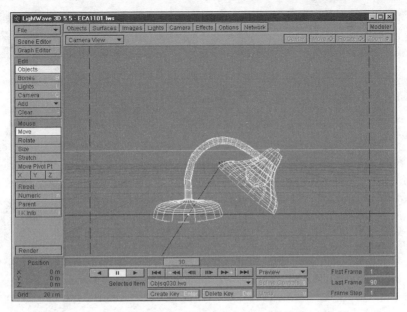

Figure 11.3 Scene at frame 30, with lamp fully flexed.

18. Make a preview for all 90 frames. Play it back at a variety of speeds, and observe it closely. Is the action smooth enough? Did any objects get out of order, causing strobing?

    Note that the motion of frames 1 through 30 is apparently smoother, even though frames 31 through 90 are using the exact same objects in reverse order. This is because the first 30 frames are animated *on ones*, that is, every frame has an increment of motion. The last 60 frames are animated *on twos*, because each object replacement is held for two frames. This is just long enough to be perceptible as strobing to most people, if the movement is large enough.

19. Manually delete alternating object files between OBJSQ031 and OBJSQ089 (33, 37, 41, and so on), then return to Layout and redraw the preview animation.

    Now, you can see how jerky the last part of the preview becomes when it's animated on fours.

    Most cel or 2D animation, especially Saturday morning cartoons aimed at children, is animated on twos and sometimes even as high as fours, in order to save money. 2D seems to be able to get away with longer intervals without strobing. Puppet animation, with the higher realism of sets and modeled characters, generally can't even get away with animating on twos, because the audience is expecting smoother, more realistic motion.

    You need to keep this in mind when planning an animation sequence. If you are thinking about using one of these replacement techniques, remember that you will have to have an object for each and every frame, or your audience will begin to see strobing.

20. If you like, render the animation in AVI format.

Note: You need an object for each and every frame, or your audience will begin to see strobing.

You should end up with an AVI file similar to the example file in the Chapter 3 directory on this book's CD-ROM, ECA1101C.AVI (see Figure 11.4).

21. Play back the sample animation on your own while you read and think about the following critique.

The model sequence technique apparently shares the strobing problem of the manual replacement technique. The advantages of a model sequence seem to be simplicity, repeatability (just run the batch file again), and editability (just edit the batch file to copy as many models to as many frame addresses as you need).

One major disadvantage of the model sequence approach should be obvious. If you've got a long shot, with a lot of action, the number of copied files is going to get very large very quickly and demand a lot of hard disk space. The rule of "one model, one frame" is an expensive one to observe when individual model files grow large. If this becomes a problem, you may have to render the animation in segments, limited by how many models your system can store at one time. Also, as with all replacement techniques, you are limited to the models you have on hand. If you need a new pose, you will have to model one or have your TD model one for you.

While not exactly a drawback, it is especially important with this approach to keep your files organized. If you mess up a directory name, you can end up with one model being systematically replaced with the target models for another!

Incidentally, this technique is an excellent one for generating an animation or a series of stills of all the models in a library—a handy reference when you have dozens or even hundreds of models to choose from!

Figure 11.4 Frames 1, 15, 30, 50, 70, and 90 from ECA1101C.AVI animation of Project 11.1 results.

Model List Replacement

The model list replacement process works a lot like the model sequence, except you don't have to change or duplicate the model files. You still get to write up which model you want to appear in a particular frame in advance, and the software does the replacement for you. The difference is that the model sequence loads the models in numerical order, but you can tell the model list to load any file in any order you like.

Software That Doesn't Support Model List Replacement

As with the model sequence technique, LightWave 3D seems to be the only software currently on the market that supports model list replacement animation.

PROJECT 11.2 Animating The Desk Lamp With LightWave's ObjList Plug-in

This approach is also a simple one, again requiring only a bit of typing, with the same 31 desk lamp objects to choose from. We'll simply write a properly formatted text file that calls for the object files in the order we want them to appear. If you are used to working with exposure sheets, this is a piece of cake.

1. The Object Replacement List text file has to have a particular format. Use Windows Notepad or your favorite text editor to create a new text file, with the first line:

```
#LW Object Replacement List
```

This header must be used for every Object Replacement List.

2. Each object replacement requires two lines in the text file. The first one sets the frame where the replacement is made. The second provides the full path and file name of the replacement object. We want the animation to start at frame 0, with the lamp at its normal position, so add these two lines to the text file:

```
0
c:\newtek\objects\ch11\replac00.lwo
```

3. To add a little variety, this time let's make the desk lamp stop part way through its bend, come back up slightly, then continue down to nearly touch the ground. To do this, objects 0 through 20 will need to be in their usual order, then repeated in reverse order back to object 10, then forward again all the way to object 30, like this:

```
#LW Object Replacement List
0
c:\newtek\objects\ch11\replac00.lwo
1
c:\newtek\objects\ch11\replac01.lwo
2
c:\newtek\objects\ch11\replac02.lwo
```

```
3
c:\newtek\objects\ch11\replac03.lwo
4
c:\newtek\objects\ch11\replac04.lwo
5
c:\newtek\objects\ch11\replac05.lwo
6
c:\newtek\objects\ch11\replac06.lwo
7
c:\newtek\objects\ch11\replac07.lwo
8
c:\newtek\objects\ch11\replac08.lwo
9
c:\newtek\objects\ch11\replac09.lwo
10
c:\newtek\objects\ch11\replac10.lwo
11
c:\newtek\objects\ch11\replac11.lwo
12
c:\newtek\objects\ch11\replac12.lwo
13
c:\newtek\objects\ch11\replac13.lwo
14
c:\newtek\objects\ch11\replac14.lwo
15
c:\newtek\objects\ch11\replac15.lwo
16
c:\newtek\objects\ch11\replac16.lwo
17
c:\newtek\objects\ch11\replac17.lwo
18
c:\newtek\objects\ch11\replac18.lwo
19
c:\newtek\objects\ch11\replac19.lwo
20
c:\newtek\objects\ch11\replac20.lwo
21
c:\newtek\objects\ch11\replac19.lwo
22
c:\newtek\objects\ch11\replac18.lwo
23
c:\newtek\objects\ch11\replac17.lwo
24
c:\newtek\objects\ch11\replac16.lwo
25
c:\newtek\objects\ch11\replac15.lwo
26
c:\newtek\objects\ch11\replac14.lwo
```

```
27
c:\newtek\objects\ch11\replac13.lwo
28
c:\newtek\objects\ch11\replac12.lwo
29
c:\newtek\objects\ch11\replac11.lwo
30
c:\newtek\objects\ch11\replac10.lwo
31
c:\newtek\objects\ch11\replac11.lwo
32
c:\newtek\objects\ch11\replac12.lwo
33
c:\newtek\objects\ch11\replac13.lwo
34
c:\newtek\objects\ch11\replac14.lwo
35
c:\newtek\objects\ch11\replac15.lwo
36
c:\newtek\objects\ch11\replac16.lwo
37
c:\newtek\objects\ch11\replac17.lwo
38
c:\newtek\objects\ch11\replac18.lwo
39
c:\newtek\objects\ch11\replac19.lwo
40
c:\newtek\objects\ch11\replac20.lwo
41
c:\newtek\objects\ch11\replac21.lwo
42
c:\newtek\objects\ch11\replac22.lwo
43
c:\newtek\objects\ch11\replac23.lwo
44
c:\newtek\objects\ch11\replac24.lwo
45
c:\newtek\objects\ch11\replac25.lwo
46
c:\newtek\objects\ch11\replac26.lwo
47
c:\newtek\objects\ch11\replac27.lwo
48
c:\newtek\objects\ch11\replac28.lwo
49
c:\newtek\objects\ch11\replac29.lwo
50
c:\newtek\objects\ch11\replac30.lwo
```

4. Save the list file. You should also save a backup copy, if you intend to do any editing of the original list.

5. In Layout, load the ECA1101.LWS scene file again.

6. Open the Objects panel. Make sure REPLAC00.LWO is listed as the Current Object.

7. Click on the Obj Rep Plug-ins button just beneath the Current Object button. The Object Replacement Plug-ins panel appears, with the Plug-in 1 drop-down reading (none).

8. Drag down the Plug-in 1 drop-down list, and select LW_ObjList. Click on the Options button to call up the Object Replacement List dialog.

9. Select the List text file you saved in Step 4. Open the selected text file, and return to the Plug-ins panel.

10. Click on Continue to close the Object Replacement Plug-ins panel and return to the Objects panel. The Obj Rep Plug-ins button will now show one plug-in loaded.

11. Close the Objects panel, and return to Layout.

12. Create a keyframe at frame 0 for all items. Save the scene.

13. Make a preview of frames 1 through 50.

   Note the abrupt stop the lamp makes at frames 20 and 30, when it reverses direction. This is because we did not put in any ease-out, a technique we'll cover in more detail in another chapter. For now, all you need to concentrate on is the basic replacement technique. We'll fine-tune it later.

14. If you like, render the animation in AVI format. You can also try rewriting copies of the list file, to create other variations on the basic bending motion of the desk lamp.

15. Play back the sample ECA1102.AVI animation from the Chapter 11 directory on this book's CD-ROM, as in Figure 11.5, or your own results, while you read and think about the following critique.

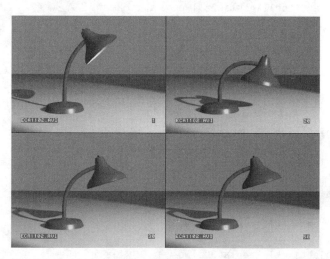

Figure 11.5   Frames 1, 20, 30, and 50 from ECA1102.AVI animation of Project 11.2 results.

The Object List technique shares the strobing problems of the Replace Object and ObjSequence techniques. One object per frame for any changes is still necessary to prevent visible jerks.

However, you don't have to create a duplicate object for every frame. You can choose a series of objects by their original file names, repeatedly and in any order you like. This saves hard drive storage space and makes file management a lot easier. Also, making changes to the sequence or timing of objects only requires the editing of the list file—you don't need to clear off the previous setup's objects and re-execute a batch file. This means you can work faster, especially when experimenting.

The odds are good that you will never have to use simple replacement techniques, but understanding them and their good and bad points will give you a better perspective to judge other CGI character animation tools. If you don't understand the problems of simple replacement animation, you won't fully appreciate the advantages of morph replacement techniques. The common problems of simple replacement are:

- The requirement of an extensive and varied library of models.
- Visible strobing in the animation if a model is replaced on twos or higher.

Morphing solves the second problem and goes a long way toward reducing the first one. Morph replacement tools come in two types: *simple morph* and *morph sequence*.

Simple Morph

Just as for other replacement techniques, when you use morph replacement, you specify a beginning model and the model that is to replace it. But instead of popping directly from one model file to the next, the morph function calculates an in-between position for each vertex or control point for every frame. This makes the changes very smooth, even when the model and target are hundreds or thousands of frames apart. It also means that models designed to be used with morphing must share the exact same number of vertices or control points. This makes creating complex morph models more of a challenge.

Unfortunately, morph doesn't know that models sometimes move in arcs. When you provide the two models to morph, all the software can do is calculate a straight-line change, or interpolation, in the position of each point relative to that point's counterpart in the target model. This can cause problems, as the following project demonstrates.

PROJECT 11.3 Desk Lamp Animation With Simple Morph

This project shows you how to create a very basic morph setup, one that will produce a smooth, gradual interpolation of a model's shape from one morph target to another. It also demonstrates some of the problems and restrictions that are part of the morphing process. Simple morphs can be very useful for changing the shape of complex organic models. As a later *hybrid setup* project shows, you can also combine a simple morph of some character parts with other setup techniques for the rest of the character. Faces and hands are especially good candidates for morph techniques, so this is a project you should study carefully. When you understand how morphing works, you can better judge when to use it and when to choose another approach for your character setups.

Software That Doesn't Support Morphing

Animation:Master 5 does not use polygons for either modeling or animation, so it does not support morphing. However, A:M's tools for creating, saving, and animating deformations of spline patches can be used to produce effects similar to morphing. Poser 2 does not support morphing. Ray Dream Studio 5 does not support morphing, but can achieve some of the same effects with animated deformation tools. Strata Studio Pro 2 does not support morphing. TrueSpace3 does not inherently support morphing, although its animated deformation functions can produce similar effects and there is at least one morphing plug-in available (see Chapters 13 and 16 for details). Extreme 3D 2 does not support morphing, but it does support shape animation by vertex editing, metaform, or deformation tool.

3D Studio MAX

3D Studio MAX 1.2 and 2 have a special Compound Object type known as a *Morph Object*. This object starts with a base object and then adds other targets with the same number of points. You can then animate the object morphing between each shape one at a time. These procedures should be the same for MAX 1.2 and 2.

1. Load the PROJ1103.MAX file from this book's CD-ROM.

   This file has two lamp objects or targets already loaded for you. If you want to start from scratch, these models are REPLAC00.3DS and REPLAC30.3DS, also on this book's CD-ROM. The red lamp you see in your User viewport is the default lamp object. The green wireframe colored lamp is bent at 100 percent, as shown in Figure 11.6.

2. Select the red lamp. Choose the Create tab at the right of the screen.

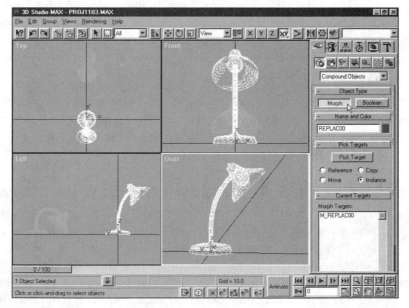

Figure 11.6 PROJ1103.MAX.

3. In the Create panel, click on the Geometry button. From the pull-down menu below, choose Compound Objects. This will bring up the Object Type panel that allows you to create a morph object, as well as other compound objects, such as Booleans.

4. Click on the Morph button. A panel drops down with the options for a morph object, as shown in Figure 11.6. The object you have selected when you click on this button becomes a morph object. Its shape becomes the default target and is automatically placed in the Current Targets window.

5. The next step is to load in the other targets. There are four radio buttons: Reference, Move, Copy, and Instance. Leave Instance selected, which is the default. Click on the Pick Target button (*not* the Pick Targets rollup!). The button turns green, waiting for you to click on a valid target object.

6. Select the green wireframe lamp, REPLAC30, by clicking on it or choosing it from the Pick Object list. In MAX 1.2, you won't see any change, but in MAX 2, you will notice the red lamp now changes to look bent as the green one does. REPLAC30 now appears in the Current Target list, with the prefix M_ to show that it is a morph target.

7. Click on the Pick Target button to turn it off. Save your file with a new name.

   The lamp object is now set up to be animated using a morph. Now, you'll test the setup by setting keyframes for the morph to animate the lamp's bending action.

8. Choose the Modify tab. The morph modifier stack appears.

9. Make sure you are on frame 0. You can either click on the Go To Start button at the bottom of the screen or drag the time slider all the way to the left.

10. Click on the Animate button to turn it on. It will turn red when active.

11. Select M_REPLAC00, the unbent lamp, from the Current Target list.

12. Click on the Create Morph Key button. This sets the morph to start at frame 0 with the unbent lamp.

13. Drag the Time Slider to frame 30, or type in "frame 30" in the frame edit box, and press Enter. Select M_REPLAC30, the bent lamp target, from the Current Targets list. Click on the Create Morph Key button. This sets the morph to go to the bent position at frame 30, so the lamp bends, as shown in Figure 11.7.

14. Go to frame 60. Select M_REPLAC00 from the Current Target list again. Click on the Create Morph Key button. This sets the morph to return to the unbent position at frame 60.

15. Save the file. Scrub the Time Slider, or choose Play. The lamp smoothly morphs between each target, creating a bending action.

   If you render the animation, you should end up with something like 1103aMAX.AVI on this book's CD-ROM. This doesn't look right. The shade, in fact the entire upper part of the lamp, seems to be shrinking in the middle of the animation!

   Remember what I mentioned earlier about morph only handling straight-line changes? If you draw a line connecting the frame 0, frame 30, and frame 60 positions of any vertex in the lamp, you will draw a perfectly straight line. Even though the lamp's

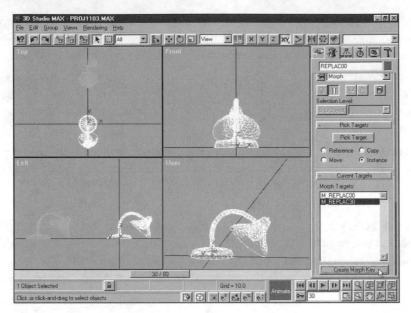

Figure 11.7 Lamp bent at frame 30.

neck is bending, moving the shade in an arc, morph is taking each point on the shortest path between two points—a straight line. As you can see, this distorts the object and produces unrealistic actions. The lamp looks like it is melting from one position to the next.

To avoid this problem, you need to use morph targets that are fairly close in shape to the preceding object. The difference between REPLAC00 and REPLAC30 is pretty extreme, but REPLAC00 and REPLAC05 are much closer in shape.

16. Use File|Import to replace REPLAC30 with REPLAC05.3DS, and repeat the preceding steps to rebuild the morph. Render the new animation.

   This one turned out much better. There is not much arc between the original model and the -05 morph target, so morph's straight-line interpolation is almost undetectable.

17. Repeat Step 16, using models REPLAC10.3DS, -15, -20, and -25, to see how much distortion you can get away with.

   Later in this chapter, Project 11.4 shows you an alternative solution to morph interpolation problems, the *morph sequence*.

Alias

The *Learning Alias V8* manual includes a good introduction to simple morphing. Lesson 18, "Animating with Metamorphosis," shows how to construct two models with the necessary identical CVs and isoparm patches, then use the Set Keyshape function to morph between them. If you are using Alias and have not worked through this lesson, I suggest you do so now and return to this project afterwards. Lesson 18 is a good enough introduction to the Set Keyshape function that describing it in detail here would be redundant.

Set Keyshape is an adequate morph tool if you are working with a single model, but if you have a library of morph targets, ShapeShifter is more useful. ShapeShifter enables you to morph more than one target and to blend morph targets to create subtle, complex results with simple controls. For each target, Alias creates a control object. The X-axis movement of this control determines the amount of morphing from the original, or *base*, object to the control's target. You can animate the morph by animating the motion of the control object.

ShapeShifter's operation is described in detail in pages 269 through 274 of *Animating in Alias* and explored as a tutorial in Lesson 24 of *Learning Alias*. As usual, the Alias documentation is thorough, clear, and well worth your time. However, it fails to make the point that morphing is not suitable for all circumstances and that there are limits to what it can do. The following project shows you how to use ShapeShifter to set up a basic morph and demonstrates some of the limitations of the morph technique. After you have completed this project, you will have a better idea of when to set up a character with morphing and when to use another approach.

1. Open files REPLAC00.DXF, REPLAC05.DXF, and REPLAC30.DXF from the Chapter 11 directory on this book's CD-ROM. Make sure GROUP is set to ON in the DXF options, so each desk lamp model will open as a single group. This will make selection easier.

2. Arrange the objects in the Perspective window so REPLAC00 is in the middle, bracketed by the other two, and track, tumble, and dolly until all three are visible in profile. You need a clear side view of all three objects to see the best results from this project.

3. Select Anim|Set Key Shape|Options. Click on ShapeShifter in the Interpolation section of the option box (see Figure 11.8). Turn on Create Control Geometry and Create Slider Geometry. These two settings will automatically create interactive control handles for the morph.

4. Set Slider Position Z to -1.0. This will position the control object just below the desk lamp, where it will be visible but out of the way. Leave the other settings at their defaults, and click on Go.

5. Click on the REPLAC00 lamp to select it as the base object.

6. Click on REPLAC30 to pick it as the morph target object.

7. At the prompt for the control object name, type "REPLAC30". If the Control Name option was set to From Target, the control will automatically be named REPLAC30.

   You should now see a triangle and rectangle, arranged as a slider control, just below the REPLAC00 object. You can now use this control to morph the base object.

8. Select Pick|Object, and click on the triangle control. Select Xform|Move, and click-drag with the middle mouse button to slide the control halfway across the rectangle. Release the mouse button to update ShapeShifter's effect.

   In the Perspective window, you should see the REPLAC00 desk lamp object bend halfway down. Unfortunately, it also seems to be badly distorted. What in the world

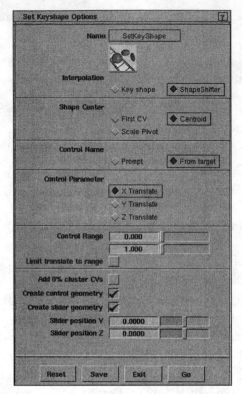

Figure 11.8 Set Keyshape options.

is going on here? The shade, in fact the entire upper part of the lamp, seems to be shrinking!

9. Drag the slider all the way across the rectangle. The lamp returns to normal proportions, but bent to match the shape of REPLAC30.

Remember what I mentioned earlier about morph only handling straight-line changes? If you draw a line connecting the start, middle, and end positions of any vertex in the lamp during this morph, you will draw a perfectly straight line. Even though the lamp's neck appears to be bending, moving the shade in an arc, the ShapeShifter morph interpolation is taking each point on the shortest path between two points—a straight line. As you can see, this distorts the object and produces unrealistic actions. The lamp looks like it is melting from one position to the next.

To avoid this problem, you need to use morph targets that are fairly close in shape to the preceding object. The difference between REPLAC00 and REPLAC30 is pretty extreme, but REPLAC00 and REPLAC05 are much closer in shape.

10. Repeat Steps 6 through 9, but click on REPLAC05. You should end up with a second slider, just under the first one.

11. Move the first slider back to its original position, then drag the new slider halfway over.

Compare the amount of distortion in Step 11's results to that produced in Step 8. 11's turned out much better. There is not much arc between the original object and the -05 target object, so ShapeShifter's straight-line interpolation is almost undetectable. If you like, try adding objects REPLAC10, -15, -20, and -25 with their own ShapeShifter controls, just to see how much distortion you can get away with.

Infini-D 4

Infini-D 4 only supports morphing for its internal SplineForm Workshop and 3D text models. It is not compatible with the DXF or 3DMF models that Infini-D can import. This Object Morphing function is essentially similar to an animated deformation tool and is of little use to character animation. If you have Infini-D, you should refer to the "Object Morphing" tutorial on page 314 of the *User's Manual* for details.

LightWave 3D 5.5

The LightWave 5.5 manuals don't have a lot of information about using the Metamorph function, so here's a more detailed project.

1. Load the ECA1101.LWS scene file into Layout again. Open the Objects panel.

2. Load object file REPLAC05, and set the Object Dissolve value (in the Appearance Options tab) at 100 percent, and press Enter to accept the change. This keeps the object invisible during renderings. We don't want to see it, we just want to use it to change the original object.

3. Repeat Step 2 for object files REPLAC10, REPLAC15, REPLAC20, REPLAC25, and REPLAC30. These are the different morph target objects you'll be using.

4. Select REPLAC00 from the Current Object drop-down list. This is the object the morph will start with.

5. Open the Deformations tab. In the Morph Target drop down list, select REPLAC30 as the target object (see Figure 11.9). This is the object the morph will go toward.

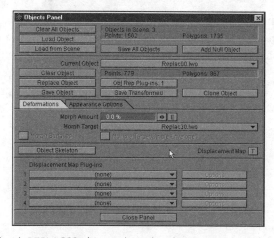

Figure 11.9 Objects Panel with REPLAC00 object selected and REPLAC30 as morph target.

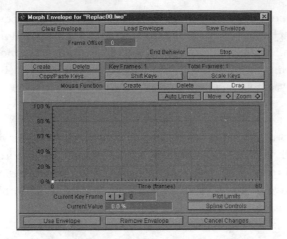

Figure 11.10 Morph Envelope panel for REPLAC00.

6. Click on the E button to the right of the Morph Amount data field to open the Morph Envelope panel, as shown in Figure 11.10.

The Morph Envelope controls how quickly and to what extent the morph will take place. This is a very important and powerful animation tool, and we really can't do it justice in this chapter. The tweaks you can perform with the Envelope controls will be detailed later on. For now, we'll just make the transformation happen smoothly over 60 frames.

7. Click on the Create button just above the Copy/Paste Keys button (not the Create button next to the label Mouse Function). The Create Key At Frame panel appears. Type "60", and press Enter to accept the input, close the panel, and return to the Morph Envelope panel.

Notice the new yellow dot at frame 60. This represents the keyframe you just created, and shows that it is currently selected.

8. While the keyframe at frame 60 is still selected, type "100" in the Current Value field at the bottom center, and press Enter. This will put the keyframe dot at the top-right corner of the Envelope graph, as shown in Figure 11.11.

This straight-line graph means that the morph will go smoothly from 100 percent REPLAC00 to 100 percent REPLAC30, over the course of 60 frames.

Figure 11.11 Envelope graph for REPLAC00, after editing.

9. Click on the Use Envelope button at the bottom left to close the Envelope panel and return to the Objects panel. Close the Objects panel, and return to the Layout window.

10. Make a wireframe preview of frames 1 through 60. Play the preview. Your results should look like Figure 11.12.

   What in the world is going on here? The shade, in fact the entire upper part of the lamp, seems to be shrinking in the middle of the animation!

   If you draw a line connecting the frame 0, frame 30, and frame 60 positions of any vertex in the lamp, you will draw a perfectly straight line. Even though the lamp's neck is bending, moving the shade in an arc, morph is taking each point on the shortest path between two points—a straight line.

   To avoid this problem, you need to use morph targets that are fairly close in shape to the preceding object. The difference between REPLAC00 and REPLAC30 is pretty extreme, but REPLAC00 and REPLAC05 are much closer in shape.

11. Open the Objects panel again, and select REPLAC05 for the morph target object. Close the Objects panel, and make another preview. Your results should look like Figure 11.13.

Figure 11.12 Frames 0, 30, and 60 from morph straight-line interpolation between very different targets.

Figure 11.13 Morph straight-line interpolation between more similar targets.

This one turned out much better. There is not much arc between the original object and the -05 target object, so Metamorph's straight-line interpolation is almost undetectable.

12. Repeat Step 11, using objects REPLAC10, -15, -20, and -25, to see how much distortion you can get away with.

Later in this chapter, Project 11.4 shows you an alternative solution to morph interpolation problems, the *morph sequence*, or in LightWave terminology, *Multiple Target Single Envelope*, MTSE.

Softimage 3D

Softimage uses the term *shape animation* to describe morphing. Pages 91 through 99 of the *Animating* manual give a brief explanation of this process. As with most software, each morph target must have the same point count and distribution as the original model. You build morph targets (like the desk lamps) by tagging and moving points on an object, then saving a *key shape* with the SaveKey|Object|Shape command. Once you have built a library of shapes, you can assign them to a compatible object with the Shape|Select|Key Shape command.

Morphing in Softimage has some significant advantages over the approaches used by other software. Most morphing software only supports straight-line, or linear, interpolation from one target to another. This causes the unwanted distortion shown in preceding figures in this project.

Softimage addresses this problem with Cardinal interpolation, which moves the model's vertices along curved trajectories. Using the Shape|Shape Interp command to choose Cardinal can eliminate most (if not all) distortion of an arcing morph.

Softimage also provides controls to morph between multiple targets simultaneously, as in a *morph sequence*, or to blend several targets together by weighting. These concepts are covered later in this chapter and in Chapter 13.

Morphing Problems

The morph technique eliminates the strobing problems of the manual replacement, model sequence, and model list techniques. Instead of popping directly from one model file to the next, the morph function calculates an in-between position for each point for every frame. This makes the changes very smooth, even when the model and target are hundreds or thousands of frames apart.

Unfortunately, morph can't read your mind. You know that a bending lamp should move in an arc, but morph doesn't know that. When you provide the two models to morph, all it can do is calculate a straight-line change, or interpolation, in the position of each point relative to its counterpart in the other model.

One way to compensate for this problem is to use enough targets, closely spaced, that the straight-line interpolation is not noticeable to your audience. This is most important with actions like a character's curling fingers or bending arms, where the points describe relatively large arcs between their start and end positions. Morphing for facial animation generally doesn't have this problem, as the arcs are much shorter and straight-line interpolation works just fine. For this and other reasons, facial animation is one of the most common uses for morph and its big brother, morph sequence. In most software, you can use morph settings to precisely control the transition between models. This gives you the power, for example, to animate a face precisely 65 percent of the distance from an "anger" model to a "rage" model, to get the exact emotional nuance you want for your animated transitions.

Even if you have to use more targets to disguise straight-line interpolations, you will still use fewer targets for morphing than you would have for an equivalent model list, model sequence, or manual replacement animation. Morph requires four or five targets for a smooth desk lamp bend. The other techniques described need 30.

One obvious limitation is that morph is designed to transform from one model to another. What do you do if you want a whole string of different targets within a single animation, as in lip sync? That's what the next function, morph sequence, is all about.

Morph Sequence

We'll wrap up the replacement animation part of this chapter with one of the most versatile and powerful replacement tools—morph sequence. I use this tool for most replacement animation by preference, because I believe it provides the best combination of control, ease of use, power, and flexibility. There are a few replacement animation tricks you can't perform with a morph sequence, but not many.

Morph sequence enables you to chain together a number of morph target models, then control the morph between the default model and any of the targets. This is incredibly powerful, because you can manipulate the morph sequence controls to interactively insert the exact percentages of each morph target exactly when you want them.

For example, if you have a model library of heads for the basic phonemes and emotions (anywhere from 15 to several dozen models), you can load them all in a morph sequence chain, then make the head lip sync and run through any emotional transition within the library's range.

MORPH SEQUENCES IN THE MOVIES

Two prominent examples of morph sequence animation are the face-mimicking water tentacle in *The Abyss* and the T-1000 in *Terminator 2: Judgment Day*. In the latter, actor Robert Patrick plays a "mimetic poly-alloy" android, apparently made of liquid metal. In one scene, the liquid form of the android flows through a hole in a helicopter window, resumes human form in the left seat, then lip syncs the words "Get out" to the chopper's pilot. Separate Cyberware scans (see Chapter 7) of Patrick's head were used as morph targets to animate this lip-sync sequence.

Needless to say, morph sequence figures prominently in lip sync and facial animation projects in later chapters. For now, you can concentrate on the basics.

PROJECT 11.4 Desk Lamp Animation Setup With Morph Sequence

This project shows you how to set up a basic morph sequence between seven desk lamp morph targets. This demonstrates one method of working around the problem of morph distortion in broad angular actions. You can apply the principles of morph sequence animation to lip sync, hand gestures, or any other repeated change to the shape of a complex model.

Software That Doesn't Support Morph Sequence

As I noted in the preceding project, there are several programs that don't support morphing. The same software generally doesn't support morph sequences, either. Animation:Master 5, Extreme 3D 2, Poser 2, Ray Dream Studio 5, Strata Studio Pro 2, and trueSpace3 do not support morph sequence replacement animation.

3D Studio MAX 2

This project shows you how to set up a morph sequence in 3D Studio MAX, plus some powerful morph weighting features available in MAX 2. Most of the steps are minor revisions of those in Project 11.3, so you should find these procedures familiar.

1. Reload your results from Project 11.3. Your scene should contain models REPLAC00, REPLAC05, and REPLAC30.

2. Import REPLAC10, -15, -20, and -25.3DS, so the scene has a total of seven desk lamp models in varying degrees of bending. Move all but REPLAC00 to one side, out of view of the rendering viewport. You should end up with something like Figure 11.14.

3. Select REPLAC00, and click on the Create tab. In the Create panel, click on the Geometry button. From the pull-down menu below, choose Compound Objects.

4. Click on the Morph button. REPLAC00 is now the base model of the morph sequence. Click on the Pick Target button (*not* the Pick Targets rollup!). The button turns green, waiting for you to click on a valid target object.

5. Select the next lamp, REPLAC05, by clicking on it or choosing it from the Pick Object list. REPLAC05 now appears in the Current Targets list, with the prefix M_ to show that it is a morph target.

6. Repeat Step 5 for the remaining desk lamp models.

7. Click on the Pick Target button to turn it off. All seven lamp models are now set up as morph targets. Save your file with a new name. Now, you're ready to animate the morph sequence.

8. Click on the Modify tab. The morph modifier stack appears.

9. Make sure you are on frame 0. Click on the Animate button. Select M_REPLAC00, the unbent lamp, from the Current Target list.

10. Click on the Create Morph Key button. This sets the morph to start at frame 0 with the unbent lamp.

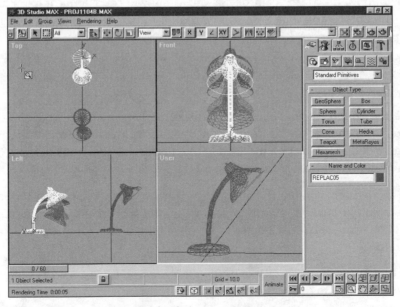

Figure 11.14 Seven desk lamp morph targets loaded.

11. Drag the Time Slider to frame 5, or type "5" in the frame edit box, and press Enter. Select M_REPLAC05, the second lamp target, from the Current Targets list. Click on the Create Morph Key button. This sets the morph to go to 05's position at frame 5.

12. Repeat Step 11 for frames 10, 15, 20, 25, and 30, each time selecting the corresponding morph target.

13. Repeat Steps 11 and 12 in reverse for frames 35, 40, 45, 50, 55, and 60, working backwards from morph target REPLAC25 to REPLAC00.

14. Save the file. Scrub the Time Slider, or choose Play. The lamp smoothly morphs between each of the seven targets, creating a bend-and-recover action.

If you render the animation, you should end up with something like 1104MAX.AVI on this book's CD-ROM. Compare this animation to 1103aMAX.AVI. Note the absence of linear interpolation-induced deformation in the morph sequence animation. Because each interpolation is only between very similar models, errors in interpolation are very small. In most situations, morph sequence animation makes linear interpolation errors invisible to the audience.

You may have noticed in the preceding morph projects that there was no way to specify a percentage of the target to use in the Morph Modifier panel. That is, at any keyframe you had to use one target at its 100 percent value. In MAX 2, there are advanced options in Track View for *weighting* morph objects, giving you much finer control.

15. Open the Track View. Expand the Objects|REPLAC00|Object (Morph) hierarchy until you see the Morph controller for REPLAC00. Note that there is a key dot on every frame where you set a morph key. Click in the dark gray area before the first key dot to deselect all key dots.

The default for the Morph controller is Cubic, but you can change it to a Barycentric type. The Barycentric controller gives you a lot more power to tweak and fine-tune your morph sequences.

16. Select the Morph controller. Click on the Assign Controller button at the top of the Track View. The Assign Morph Controller dialog will appear. Choose Barycentric Morph Controller, and click on OK.

17. To see the options available in the Morph controller, you need to open a Key Info dialog. To open the Key Info dialog for a frame, you can either right-click on the keyframe dot, or left-click on the dot and then click on the Properties button. Open the Key Info dialog for frame 5, as in Figure 11.15.

Note the *TCB* (tension, continuity, bias) spline control options. You can set continuity to 0 for linear interpolation between morph targets, or control ease-in/ease-out timing by adjusting the other TCB parameters. See Chapter 14 for more information on spline and keyframe editing and timing.

The lower half of the dialog is a list of the available morph targets plus a percentage spinner. You can select a target in the list, then change its percentage, or *weight*, using the spinner. MAX

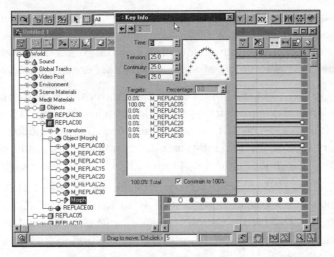

Figure 11.15 Barycentric Key Info dialog of Track View, showing frame 5 of REPLAC00 morph sequence. The Cubic controller does not include the target list or percentage controls.

will automatically compensate by increasing or decreasing the amount of the other targets. For example, if you lower one of the targets below 100 percent, the other targets will automatically divide the surplus evenly among themselves. This can be annoying if you are trying to distribute the weight among only a few of the targets. The easiest way to do this is to turn off the Constrain To 100% checkbox, set all the targets to the values you want (totaling 100, of course), then turn the checkbox back on. You can even go below 0 or greater than 100 percent, and MAX will do its best to extend the shape of the object.

This yields a pseudo-weighted morphing result. The reason I say *pseudo* is that weighted morphing utilities (such as those commonly used for lip sync) allow any channel to be 100 percent at any time. Thus, several channels may be 100 percent at a particular keyframe, or several may be 0 percent. If you try this with MAX's Barycentric morph controller, you'll get weird effects like the whole model scaling up or warping oddly. Those other utilities also ignore vertices that aren't affected in a target, but MAX insists on morphing everything. Barycentric morphing control means you can adjust percentages on keyframes with a little more finesse. However, it's still not the best tool for morphed lip sync when compared to true weighted morphing plug-ins, such as Morph Magic or Smirk.

Infini-D 4

Infini-D only supports a single morph between internal SplineForm Workshop or 3D text models. It does not support morph sequence replacement animation.

LightWave 3D 5.5

The Multiple Target Single Envelope (MTSE) plug-in is LightWave's morph sequence tool. MTSE is one of the most versatile and powerful replacement tools in LightWave. It provides you with a very good combination of control, ease of use, power, and flexibility. There are a few replacement animation tricks you can't perform with this tool, but not many.

MTSE enables you to chain together a number of morph target models, then control the morph between the default model and any of the targets by using a single effect Envelope. This is incredibly powerful, as you can manipulate the spline controls of the Envelope graph to interactively insert the exact percentages of each morph target exactly when you want them.

For example, if you have a model library of heads for the basic phonemes and emotions (anywhere from 15 to several dozen models), you can load them all in an MTSE chain, then use the Envelope spline to make the head lip sync and run through any emotional transition within your model library's range. That's a little complex for a first setup, so this project concentrates on the simpler task of animating the desk lamp without the distortions of the simple morph.

1. Load the ECA1101.LWS scene file you saved at the end of Project 11.3. It should contain object files REPLAC00, REPLAC05, REPLAC10, REPLAC15, REPLAC20, REPLAC25, and REPLAC30. These are the morph sequence target objects you'll be using. All but REPLAC00 should be set to 100% Dissolve so they are invisible when not selected.

2. Select REPLAC00 from the Current Object drop-down list. This is the beginning object for the morph sequence.

3. In the Morph Target drop-down list, in the middle of the Deformations tab, select REPLAC05 as the target object. This is the object the first morph in the chain will go toward, as shown in Figure 11.16.

4. Select REPLAC05 from the Current Object drop-down list. This is the second object in the morph sequence chain.

5. In the Morph Target drop-down list, select REPLAC10 as the target object. This is the object the second morph in the chain will go toward. Do you see the pattern you are following?

6. Repeat Steps 4 and 5 for morph sequence object pairs 10 and 15, 15 and 20, 20 and 25, and 25 and 30.

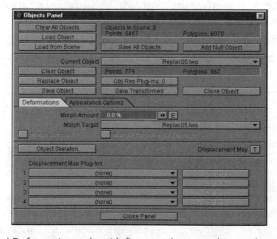

Figure 11.16 Objects panel Deformations tab, with first morph target object selected.

7. Select REPLAC00 from the Current Object drop-down list. Click on the E (for Envelope) button next to the Morph Amount data field to open the Morph Envelope panel (see Figure 11.17).

8. Click on the Create button just above the Copy/Paste Keys button (not the Create button next to the label Mouse Function). The Create Key At Frame panel appears. Type "60", and press Enter to accept the input, close the panel, and return to the Morph Envelope panel.

9. While the keyframe at frame 60 is still selected, type "600" in the Current Value field at the bottom center, and press Enter. Click on Auto Limits to resize the graph.

   The morph values for morph sequence target objects are increased by 100 for each object in the chain. If there were only two targets, the top of the scale would be 200 percent. With six targets, the top end is 600 percent. 0 through 100 percent controls morphing to the -05 object, 101 through 200 percent controls morphing to the -10 object, and so on (see Figure 11.18).

   This straight-line graph means that the morph will go smoothly from REPLAC00 to REPLAC30 over the course of 60 frames.

10. Click on the Use Envelope button at the bottom left to close the Envelope panel and return to the Objects panel. Click on the Multiple Target/Single Envelope button. This activates the MTSE chain you just set up. Close the Objects panel, and return to the Layout window.

11. Make a wireframe preview of frames 1 through 60. Play the preview.

    Pretty smooth, huh? That's only using seven objects, and the motion over 60 frames is just as smooth as using 30 objects with ObjSequence or ObjList over 30 frames. Now, let's have a little fun, before we wrap this up and move on to displacement animation.

12. End the preview. Open the Objects panel again. Click on the E button next to Morph Amount to open the Morph Envelope panel again.

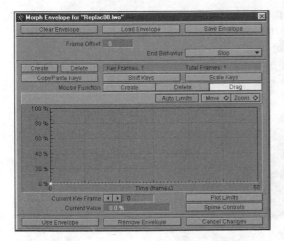
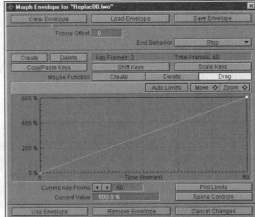

Figure 11.17 Morph Envelope panel for REPLAC00.

Figure 11.18 Envelope graph for REPLAC00, after editing.

13. Click on the Load Envelope button at the top center. From the Chapter 11 directory on this book's CD-ROM, select the file STAGGER.LWE. This is a quick little envelope I made just for fun. Press Enter to close the file dialog and return to the Morph Envelope panel, shown in Figure 11.19.

14. Click on the Use Envelope button at the bottom left to close the panel and return to the Objects panel. Close the Objects panel, and return to Layout.

15. Make a new preview. Play the preview. If you like, render an AVI. Your results should look something like ECA1104.AVI, frames from which are shown in Figure 11.20.

Boing! Isn't that fun? Fiddle with the envelope; create your own—this is a good way to learn something while amusing yourself. This particular envelope was based on something I remembered about a pendulum's period being constant, but the amplitude decreasing over time due to friction. This desk lamp is a flexible pendulum with a lot of friction and a short period.

As you can see, MTSE is powerful and at the same time relatively easy to use. The control it provides is pretty fine and can be accurately tweaked by direct numerical entry, but is still malleable enough for freehand animation work. A very nice combination. The down side is that MTSE is a bit of a RAM hog if your models are at all complex. All your target models are loaded at all times, so extensive target libraries can really tax your system.

While morph sequence and morph animation require fewer models than model list, model sequence, and manual replacement, you still need a good-sized model library to have a decent dramatic range for character animation. Add the fact that compatible models pretty much have to be modified from the same base model, thereby limiting the modeling tools you can use, and it's pretty much a bed of roses—you have to take the thorns with the blooms.

Displacement Animation

Displacement animation is the process of posing joints or bones to change a character's appearance. This approach usually requires only one complete model (in contrast to replacement animation) and is much better suited to animation of major skeletal actions, like arm and leg motion. Displacement animation is probably more familiar than replacement animation to most people, because popular characters such as Gumby and King Kong were displacement puppets.

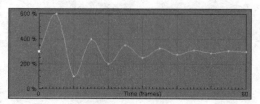

Figure 11.19   Morph Envelope panel with STAGGER.ENV envelope loaded.

Figure 11.20 Frames from ECA1104.AVI, of desk lamp animated using MTSE with Envelope STAGGER.ENV.

Traditional displacement animation requires a model that is jointed or flexible enough to be posed, but rigid enough to hold the pose while it is being photographed. Clay, rubber, urethane foam, and similar materials are often used for the external appearance of the displacement puppet, but these materials don't hold a pose very well under hot studio lights. That's why almost all displacement puppets have a metal skeleton, called an *armature*, that provides more rigid support. The design and construction of the armature is critical to the puppet's successful use, and there are many rules, guidelines, and trade secrets to building a good armature.

Displacement animation using 3D animation software is similar in many respects. The exterior appearance of many models, especially the organic shapes favored in character animation, is not readily animated. The geometric structure needed to form the surface details doesn't lend itself well to the deformations—bending, stretching, and swelling—necessary to character animation. Accordingly, most 3D animation software includes a number of functions designed to replicate the effects of an armature.

The simplest form of armature is to string together separate objects, placing them in a linked, or *parented*, hierarchy. This is a lot like assembling a marionette or a bare armature, because all the joints are exposed and very mechanical in action. If joints must have a realistic appearance, the objects must be modeled with mating surfaces, just like an armature's. Ball-and-socket, lap hinge, and other joint constructions are typical.

If a more organic armature is required, the most common approach is a *bones* setup. A CGI bone is a method of distorting the shape of a model in a controlled fashion within a defined area. During setup, a series of bones are added to a model to form a skeleton. Some bones may actually be placed outside the model's surface, but, in most cases, they are placed approximately where you would put a physical armature, through the center of the body and limbs.

Each bone in a model's skeleton influences the points in its immediate area and can also be used to influence the rest of the model, kind of like a configurable magnet. Bones can also be used to control purely muscular distortion, such as tongues, tentacles, worms, and other invertebrate structures. This is a difficult job with even the best traditional armatures and nearly impossible with other types of CGI hierarchy tools.

As you might have guessed, bone setups are powerful character animation tools, but it does take some extra effort to master their full range. Let's take a look at the more basic parent functions first.

Transformation

The most basic form of Displacement animation is a collection of rigid models, joined together like the pieces of a traditional armature or puppet so they can rotate at the joints. Most animation software has a parent or link function that can duplicate this effect, enabling you to assemble complex puppet-like characters. You can animate these hierarchies of objects by posing or *transforming* them, rotating, moving, and scaling each object to change the character's appearance.

There are several advantages to transformation animation using parented hierarchies. You have very accurate control of the positioning and posing of each child object, since there is no approximation or distortion as with replacement or bones. You can animate as much or as little as you need; each object's motions can be interactively tweaked at each frame, or simply bracketed with a single keyframe at each end of the animation. Finally, there is no need to create extensive libraries of morph models.

The disadvantages are that parent hierarchies are limited by a rather mechanical joint appearance that needs to be disguised if used to animate organic models, and that transformation animation takes longer than some other approaches. For example, using a parented hierarchy, the animator must pose the character for each key frame. Using replacement animation, the animator could much more quickly select from a sequence of pre-built poses, which might have been constructed by a modeler or TD. When you choose a setup method, you are also choosing who does how much of the work.

A pure transformation hierarchy is an excellent setup for practicing animation. It is fast and simple to set up, the screen redraw is usually the fastest of any setup your software can handle, and it doesn't require model libraries or any other complicating elements. What you see in the scene is what you have to work with. To animate it, you simply select an object, transform it to the desired appearance, set a keyframe, and go on to the next object. This simplicity enables you to use the most basic (and inexpensive) 3D animation software. Once you choose to animate with deformation or replacement techniques, you limit yourself to the (generally more expensive) software that supports those features.

Desk Lamp Setup With Parented Objects

PROJECT 11.5

This project shows you how to set up a parented hierarchy based on the replacement animation desk lamp used in the preceding projects. This demonstrates the basics of parented hierarchy setup, with a relatively small number of objects, and provides you with a setup you can animate in some of Chapter 14's timing projects. Parented hierarchies are the basis of all skeletal animation, so no matter how complex your setups eventually become, the basic techniques you'll learn in this project will still apply.

The desk lamp is a useful setup for a number of reasons. First, it's traditional, in a field that has few traditions because it's so young. *Luxo Jr.*, a short film directed by John Lasseter and produced at Pixar Animation Studios, stars a pair of animated swing-arm desk lamps. It was nominated for the 1986 Best Animated Short Film Oscar. Everybody in the industry is familiar with it, and it's one of the earliest examples of CGI animation with real character. It seems like everybody animates a desk lamp at some point, and it's a good training exercise. Second, Pixar chose *Luxo Jr.* as a subject for very good technical reasons: the lamp model's geometry can remain rigid, so you don't have to use deformation tools to animate it. The hinge points are obvious from the lamp's structure, and your audience will expect it to move mechanically around those joints, so it's much easier to model and set up than a more organic character. Third, the visual simplicity of a desk lamp forces you to animate it well, since there are no fancy textures or deformations to hide behind. If you can successfully complete the timing projects in Chapter 14 using this desk lamp setup, you will have thoroughly learned the essentials of timing. If you tried those same projects with a fully articulated humanoid character, you'd get so distracted by extraneous trivia that you'd miss the basic principles. Finally, the four simple objects that make up the desk lamp can be loaded and manipulated in even the slowest and most limited animation software.

Generic Setup

1. Load lamp objects LampBase, LowStrut, HiStrut, and Shade from this book's CD-ROM. As I mentioned earlier, I have provided the objects in 3DS, DXF, and LWO file formats. Use whatever format is easiest for your software.

   Each object has an obvious center of rotation, plus a pivot point for attaching child objects:

   - *LampBase*—Bottom center of base, center of pivot cylinder
   - *LowStrut*—Center of space between bottom of struts, center of pivot cylinder

- *HiStrut*—Same as LowStrut
- *Shade*—Center of neck stub as marked by jack

For any center that isn't obvious, I've placed a diamond-shaped *jack* as a marker. Jacks or null objects are often used as markers in modeling and animation. If your software supports objects with no faces, you can delete the diagonal edges of the jack to make it invisible in rendered images. The loaded objects should look something like Figure 11.21.

2. Link the objects in the order: LampBase, LowStrut, HiStrut, Shade. You should end up with something like Figure 11.22. The exact process you'll follow depends on your software. Refer to the software-specific parenting procedures following these general directions.

   Generally, you should parent an object from its default loading position and rotation, before you move or rotate it. If you parent it afterwards, some software will recalculate position and rotation changes from the new parent's origin, and the results will probably not be what you intended.

3. Pose the assembled lamp in a default position like Figure 11.23.

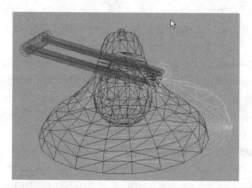

Figure 11.21　Desk lamp objects loaded and ready for parenting.

Figure 11.22　Desk lamp objects parented into hierarchy.

Figure 11.23   Desk lamp posed in default position.

The default position for any character setup should be the pose that is most common or natural for that character. The idea of a default pose is to save the animator time. Ideally, the animator should be able to load a scene, select the character, and immediately proceed to creating the first pose. For most characters, the pose in which you initially set up the hierarchy is not the best default pose. For example, if you left the desk lamp stretched out flat, just as you parented it, an animator would have to transform it into a more natural pose before they could begin animating it. This wastes time every time they open the original setup file. It's more efficient for you to take a few minutes now and create a default pose that will be useful (or at least not annoying) every time the file is opened.

4. Test the lamp's range of movement by transforming (rotating) LowStrut, HiStrut, and Shade in the pitch axis. In Chapter 14, you'll be animating this setup to create actions like those shown in Figure 11.24. Can your lamp setup be transformed to create each of these poses?

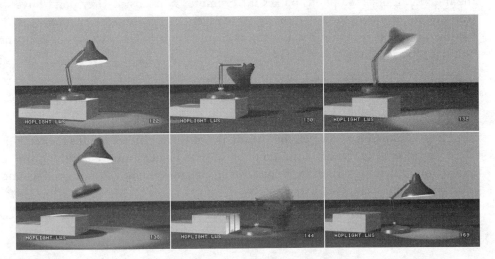

Figure 11.24   Test poses for desk lamp.

3D Studio MAX

Objects can be setup in a hierarchy very easily with 3D Studio MAX.

1. Load the four 3DS lamp object files. The objects' pivot points should already be set correctly. If you import the DXF files, they will not contain correct pivot information.

2. Click on the Select And Link button in the top toolbar.

3. Select LowStrut, the object you wish to become a child, and drag the mouse from the selected object over onto LampBase, the desired parent object. The icon will change when it is over a valid object to link to. Then, release the mouse button. The selected object is now linked to (is a child of) the object you dragged to.

4. Repeat Steps 2 and 3 to link HiStrut to LowStrut and Shade to HiStrut. Your results should be something like file PROJ1105A.MAX on this book's CD-ROM.

   You can customize what the child object inherits from the parent and limit how it moves within the hierarchy, by using the Hierarchy panel.

5. Choose the Hierarchy panel, and then click on the Link Info button.

   For most object types there is an Inherit subpanel where Move, Rotate, and Scale on each axis can be turned on and off independently. Using these settings, you can tell an object to only inherit the parent's movement on the X axis, or inherit all movement but no rotation, and so on. In the Locks subpanel, you can restrict or lock off the child's movement, rotation, or scaling within the hierarchy. This is where you'll limit the links you just built, to make sure the desk lamp can't come apart or move inappropriately.

6. With the Shade selected, check every box in the Locks subpanel. Uncheck the Rotate X box. This is the only axis you'll want the lamp shade to pivot around.

   With all Move And Scale and two of the three Rotate locks active, the Shade can't do anything on its own but pivot on the X axis. This is exactly what you want. Limiting the individual object's options makes the animator's job easier. They don't have to worry about grabbing the wring control or inadvertently pulling the hierarchy apart. Ideally, once you've set up a character, it should be impossible to take it apart or damage it accidentally.

7. Repeat Step 6 for HiStrut and LowStrut. LampBase should remain unlocked.

   Now the lamp should be posable by three rotations, one on each X axis of the three children, plus complete move, rotate, or scale animation of LampBase.

   The Pivot subpanel is also under the Hierarchy panel. This area contains the controls to set up the orientation and location of an object's pivot point. Determining this is critical for setup and animation, because an object's movement, rotation, and scaling is all based on the location of its pivot.

8. To adjust an object's pivot point, select the object, open the Hierarchy Panel, then click on the Pivot button.

9. Click on Affect Pivot Only. Use the regular Move, Rotate, or Scale transforms to adjust the pivot point relative to the object.

You may want to move the pivot point of the LampBase, either to the bottom of the base for easier alignment with the floor or to the apparent center of gravity (CG) of the base, to make rotations easier.

RESET TRANSFORM—PLAY IT SAFE

Sometimes, you may notice an object skewing oddly when it is rotated. Objects should have *Reset Transform* applied (Utilities Panel ⏐ Reset Transform ⏐ Reset Selected) before linking. Otherwise, scaling differences between parent and child may result in skewing or shearing when the child object is rotated. If you ever see a shearing problem, you should unlink the affected object, apply a reset transform, and then relink it. However, the object may need modification once it has been messed up. It's best to play it safe and reset all transforms before you link the objects.

Infini-D 4

The manuals that come with Infini-D cover the concepts of linking hierarchies briefly but adequately. Infini-D supports a number of link types:

- *Free link*—Enables the child to move and rotate independently of the parent, while inheriting the parent's rotation and movement.
- *Pivot link*—Nails down the child's rotation, but allows it to move freely.
- *Position link*—Immobilizes the child's movement but leaves rotation free.
- *Full link*—Locks both rotation and movement to the parent.

Personally, I find Infini-D's choice of labels confusing. I think choosing something called Pivot means the child should be able to pivot. It would have been less confusing if they'd call these things locks or switched the names around to be more intuitive.

You can build a parented hierarchy using the Link tool, as described in Chapter 8 of the *Infini-D User Manual*. The basic procedures is, in modeling mode, select a Child object, choose the Link tool, then select the Parent object. However, I believe it is easier and faster to link up a hierarchy in the Sequencer, as described in pages 307 through 308 of the *User Manual*. You can simply drag a Child object on top of the desired Parent to create a link. After linking, children are automatically indented under the parent. This is good visibility for quickly navigating through the hierarchical structure.

To choose a link type when creating links in Sequencer, hold down the following modifier key(s) while creating the link:

- *Free link*—No modifiers
- *Pivot link*—Option (Mac) or ALT (Win)
- *Position link*—Shift. This is the link you will use most often when building a puppet-style hierarchy of rotationally jointed objects.

- *Full link*—Option+Shift (Mac) or ALT+Shift (Win)

What Infini-D calls constraints are more accurately termed *limits*. True constraints are discussed in Chapter 12 and are unfortunately not supported by Infini-D. You can set rotational and positional limits in the Constraints tab of the Modifiers tab (marked by the hammer and screwdriver icon, B in the Quick Reference card) of the Command floater.

Chapter 7 in the *Tutorial Manual* includes a simple example of linking objects. The entire *Tutorial Manual* is a good introduction to Infini-D's basic functions. If you haven't already worked through all the tutorial exercises, I recommend you stop now and come back to this project when you are more familiar with Infini-D.

1. Load the four DXF-format lamp objects. Because the DXF format doesn't include proper centering, you'll need to reset the centerpoint for each object. Select the first object. In the Control floater, choose the Info tab, then choose Offset from the pop-up list. The Offset fields will replace the Scale fields. Enter the offset coordinates necessary to reset the centerpoint. Repeat for each object.

2. In Sequencer, hold down the Shift key, select LowStrut, and drag it on top of LampBase. This creates a Position link, which will enable you to rotate the LowStrut around its link to the LampBase.

3. Repeat Step 2 to link HiStrut to LowStrut and Shade to HiStrut.

4. Select LowStrut. In the Command floater, choose the Modifiers tab, then choose the Constraints sub-tab.

5. Click on the Rotate button. Set the Minimum and Maximum values to zero for the Y and Z axes, but leave the X axis unchanged. Click on the Move and Scale buttons, and for each tab, set all three axes to zero.

   This enables the child object to rotate freely in one axis but prevents it from inadvertently rotating, scaling, or moving when it shouldn't.

6. Repeat Step 5 for HiStrut and Shade. Leave LampBase as is, without any limits. The rest of the hierarchy will automatically inherit changes to LampBase.

   If all went well, you should be able to pose the hierarchy for the test pictured in Figure 11.24. Once you've confirmed that (or fixed any problems), the setup is ready for use in Chapter 14.

LightWave 3D 5.5

Parenting objects in LightWave is relatively simple.

1. Load the four LWO objects into Layout. The desk lamp objects already have their pivot points set correctly.

2. Select the first child object, LowStrut.

3. Click on the Parent button. When the Parent Object dialog appears, choose LampBase from the drop-down list. Click on OK to accept LampBase as LowStrut's parent.

4. Move LowStrut up to align its pivot point with the center of the pivot cylinder part of LampBase. Set a keyframe at frame 0.

   This sets up LowStrut to follow LampBase's motions and to rotate around the center of the pivot cylinder. Try rotating LowStrut on the Pitch axis, just to test. While you're at it, you might want to turn off Heading and Bank axes, just to avoid inadvertent changes.

5. Select HiStrut, and parent it to LowStrut.

6. Move HiStrut so its pivot point aligns with the center of the pivot cylinder part of LowStrut. Set a keyframe for HiStrut at frame 0.

7. Select Shade, and parent it to HiStrut.

8. Move Shade so its pivot point aligns with the center of the pivot cylinder part of HiStrut. Set a keyframe for Shade at frame 0.

   That's all there is to it. Save the scene file with a new name. You'll be using it in Chapter 14, Project 14.20.

Once you've set up a hierarchy, LightWave allows you to load the whole setup into any scene with the Load From Scene option in the Objects panel. Being able to save and reload entire Parent object hierarchies makes it much easier to reuse complex setups and actions. Once loaded, you can edit them just as when you first created them. Just as with replacement models, the longer you work with a setup, the more actions you will have available for reuse. Keep this in mind while you are working, and save as a separate scene any actions that you think you might be able to use again.

Using the Load From Scene function brings in the whole enchilada, whether you wanted it or not. If you think you might want to load just part of an action, save a duplicate of the original setup and delete all the extraneous stuff. It'll save you time later on, when you might really need it.

Poser 2

The only parenting you need to do with Poser is replacing a body part with a prop, as detailed in Chapter 6 of the Poser 2 manual. Other than that, Poser hierarchies come ready-built. Unfortunately, you can only work with existing hierarchies. This is handy for Poser's purpose of easy humanoid posing but not very useful for non-humanoid characters. If you are using Poser, you should read through the remaining projects and text, but you won't get to a project you can play with until the full Puppet setup and animation.

Ray Dream Studio 5

Chapter 13 of the RDS manual gives a comprehensive introduction to building and navigating hierarchies. It's only 17 pages—short but well-illustrated. You should definitely read through it before trying to complete this project using RDS.

RDS supports eight basic link types. For this desk lamp, you'll only be concerned with the Axis link, which allows simple rotation around a single axis.

1. Import the four DXF objects. Because DXF doesn't preserve origin information, you'll need to relocate the default origin (or *hotpoint*, as RDS calls it) according to the preceding descriptions of the objects and their rotations.

2. Choose the Selection tool. Select the first object. Drag the object's hotpoint (the small 3D sphere in its center) to the location of the desired pivot point. Repeat for the remaining objects.

3. In the Hierarchy window, drag LowStrut's icon onto LampBase's icon. This creates the basic link. Now, you need to adjust the child's position and the new link's properties.

4. Position the first child object, LowStrut, according to Figure 11.22. You want its hotspot to be in the center of the LampBase pivot cylinder.

5. Select the child object. Choose Windows|Properties, then click on the Links tab, and choose the Axis link type. Select the X axis to be active and to Rotate Free, and click on Apply.

6. Repeat Steps 3, 4, and 5 to link HiStrut to LowStrut and Shade to HiStrut. You should end up with something like Figure 11.22.

   Test your setup's posability. Can you move it to duplicate each pose shown in Figure 11.24? If so, your setup is ready for you to use in the animation projects in Chapter 14. Save the file, and go on to the next setup project.

Strata Studio Pro 2

Setting up and animating characters in SSP can be challenging. What SSP refers to as a link is actually just a pass-through of animation data from parent to child objects, and does not limit or constrain the movement or rotation of the child at all. You have to set up a separate set of locks for the child object, in the Transform tab of the Object Properties panel, to keep the child from going astray during animation. Personally, I think this is a major flaw in SSP, but this program was obviously not designed with character animation in mind.

1. Import the four DXF files.

2. Select the first object. Hold down the Command key, and drag the object origin point (the small blue diamond) to the pivot position for the selected object. Repeat for the other three objects.

3. Double-click on the Link tool from the Tools palette. The default settings should be that all four Inherit boxes are checked, meaning the child will inherit Scale, Offset, Rotate, and Move changes to the parent. If any boxes are not checked, check them before you proceed to the next step.

4. Choose the Link tool. Select LowStrut, then drag the Link cursor to LampBase. This creates a child-parent link between the selected objects. Repeat for HiStrut to LowStrut and Shade to HiStrut.

   All objects should now be linked in the correct hierarchy. The next step is to position them accurately.

5. Move LowStrut, HiStrut, and Shade to match LampBase's position, as shown in Figure 11.22.

   Finally, you need to limit or lock each child object so it doesn't get away from its parent.

6. Select LowStrut. Choose the Transform tab from the Object Properties palette. For Move, check Lock Position Setting. For Scale, check Lock Scale Settings. For Rotate, choose Object for the rotation center, and enter "0 to 0" for rotation limits in the Y and Z axes. You can leave the X rotation axis blank, or enter "0 to 360". Repeat this step for HiStrut and Shade.

   Save your results. You should now have a lamp setup that you can pose like the one shown in Figure 11.24. Test it. When you're satisfied with the setup, pose it like Figure 11.23, and save it for use in Chapter 14.

trueSpace3

Setting up a parented hierarchy in trueSpace is fast and easy to learn, as long as you follow the directions in Chapter 11 of the manual or the online help files. Here's a quick summary:

1. Load the desk lamp objects.

2. Arrange the objects into the default position.

3. Select the endmost child object.

4. Activate the Add Joint tool you want to use. For this project, you'll only need a hinge joint, but trueSpace has nine types:

   - *Add 0D Fixed Joint*—Rigid connection.

   - *Add 1D Slide Joint*—A translational joint that can move along only one axis.

   - *Add 1D Hinge Joint*—A rotational joint that rotates only around one axis.

   - *Add 2D Slide Joint*—A translational joint that can move only along a single plane.

   - *Add 2D Spherical Joint*—a ball-and-socket joint like the human shoulder.

   - *Add Shaft Joint*—1D translational and 1D rotational joint. The shaft can slide in and out and also rotate around its own long axis.

   - *Add Custom Joint*—A joint whose degrees of freedom you define (see Building the IK object).

5. Pick the parent object.

6. Reposition the joint. After you create a joint, you can relocate it with the Edit Joints tool. By default, the joint is located at the center of the child and parent intersection. If the parent and child objects do not intersect, the joint is placed at the child vertex closest to the parent object. Refer to the obvious center of rotation of each Puppet object or use its built-in jacks to align each joint with its parent and child objects.

When you create an IK joint, trueSpace automatically creates a positional constraint or *nail*, represented by a narrow green triangle, and places it on the parent object. You have to use a nail to set one fixed anchor in each IK chain. This anchor remains stationary as you move the rest of the IK chain. For example, nailing a foot to the floor enables you to move the rest of the character while IK ensures that the leg bends properly. The nail remains attached to the IK object, unless you drag it onto a different object. The nail's location on the constraint object doesn't matter.

You can open the Joint Attributes panel by right-clicking any IK tool except Disconnect Joint. It also opens whenever you select the Add Custom Joint tool.

The panel specifies the current joint's range of motion. The X, Y, and Z buttons are for translation (movement), and the Pitch, Yaw, and Roll buttons are for the rotational degrees. You can enable and disable each axis individually by selecting or deselecting its button in the panel. You can also specify each axis' limits numerically with the Min, Max and Stiff settings. The Stiffness setting enables you to control the amount of friction of the respective axis. In an IK chain, the stiffest joint is the one that is last to move. For example, if the knee is much stiffer than the ankle, the ankle may be forced to its full rotational limit before the knee starts to move.

Head And Eyes Setup With Parented Objects

PROJECT **11.6**

This project shows you how to add eyeballs and eyelids to a head model using the parent functions you learned in the preceding project. In addition, this project introduces inverse kinematics (IK) and tracking functions that can help you automate eye movement. You'll be using the same procedures as you did for the lamp, with just a couple of new wrinkles. If you haven't already completed Project 11.5, I suggest you do it now. The abbreviated directions in this (and following) projects may seem cryptic if you aren't familiar with the preceding projects.

Giving your character eyes opens up a whole new range of acting capabilities. Aside from emotional expressions and other intentional communication, the eyes can convey an extraordinary amount of unintentional information. Any parent, teacher, or police officer can tell you how a miscreant's eyes move when they are lying. A loud noise, bright light, or rapid motion also produces an involuntary reaction, which is usually readable in eye movement.

If you animate your character to mimic these natural motions, you'll be taking a big step toward convincing your audience. You'll also be able to use those motions to tell the audience what is going on, in a subtle and natural way, and so advance your story. This technique is especially important with animals or creatures that have little facial expression and eye movement and body posture are about all you have to work with.

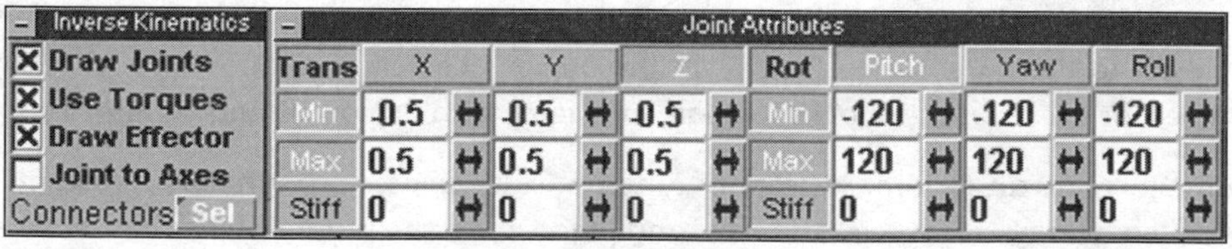

Inverse Kinematics		Joint Attributes										
☒ Draw Joints	**Trans**	X		Y		Z		**Rot**	Pitch		Yaw		Roll
☒ Use Torques	Min	-0.5	↔	-0.5	↔	-0.5	↔	Min	-120	↔	-120	↔	-120 ↔
☒ Draw Effector	Max	0.5	↔	0.5	↔	0.5	↔	Max	120	↔	120	↔	120 ↔
☐ Joint to Axes	Stiff	0	↔	0	↔	0	↔	Stiff	0	↔	0	↔	0 ↔
Connectors Sel												

Figure 11.25 The Joint Attributes panel for trueSpace 3.2.

To set up this character's head, you'll be loading four objects: the head, one eyeball (duplicated for left and right), and two eyelids. Again, I have included DXF, 3DS, and LWO versions of the models in the Chapter 11 directory on this book's CD-ROM.

Generic Setup

1. Load objects Face, Eyeball, LEyelid, and REyelid. Depending on your software, you may have to load Eyeball twice or duplicate it within your scene.

   Each object, as for the desk lamp, has an obvious or marked center of rotation. The Face object, which will act as parent to the other four, also has marked centers for the child objects to be attached.

2. Following the same procedures as in Project 11.5, position and parent the eyeballs and eyelids within the Face object. Use the jacks (in the eye sockets) as centering guides. Both the eyelids and eyeballs should be set up as direct children of the Face object. Your results should look like Figure 11.26.

3. Since the eyeballs and eyelids will be following the head as a parent, they don't need to move on their own. Set movement limits, if available, to lock down the position of the eyeballs and eyelids relative to the Face parent.

4. The eyeballs need to pivot on both pitch and heading axes, but the eyelids only need to pivot on the pitch axis. If your software supports it, lock off rotation on the bank axis for both eyelids and eyeballs, and also lock off heading rotation for the eyelids.

5. Save your results.

Play with the eyeballs and eyelids, creating expressions and making the eyes track imaginary objects. Pay special attention to trying to synchronize the eyeballs so they appear to be looking at the same object.

If you do this for a while, you will quickly tire of repeatedly posing one eyeball, then matching the rotation for the other eye. Imagine trying to do this for a long shot, in which your character intently watches the erratic and convoluted flight of a mosquito!

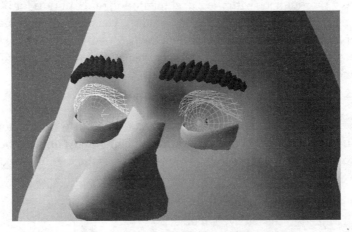

Figure 11.26 Scene with Face, Eyeball, LEyelid, and REyelid hierarchy set up.

The sensitivity of your audience to *sightlines*, the apparent direction of the eyeball, makes your job harder. We learn almost from birth to deduce exactly what someone is looking at by observing tiny variations in the angle of their eyes. Your smallest mistake in aligning the eyes can shatter your character's credibility.

Of course there is a better way to do this. Most 3D animation software has a function called *inverse kinematics*, which can make an object in a hierarchy point consistently and precisely at another object.

Inverse kinematics (IK) is, in simplest terms, a tool for posing a hierarchy in reverse. Normal kinematics is what you do with a parented or boned hierarchy, for example an arm and hand: rotate the shoulder, then rotate the elbow, then rotate the wrist, then rotate the fingers, until you get the fingertips to point at or touch what you want them to. This is tedious and counter-productive for most character animation.

Inverse kinematics, as the name implies, inverts this process. You drag the fingertip to point or touch what you want it to, and the IK software figures out the appropriate angles for all the joints. "Magic!" you say, but of course there's a catch. For the arm, or any hierarchy with two or more joints, there are several possible poses that will put the fingertip in the same position.

Think about it, and try this experiment: Touch your finger to the end of your nose, and see how much your arm can move while keeping your finger in place.

What usually happens when trying to use IK is that the hierarchy flops all over the place, and you spend a lot of time confining it to a reasonable set of poses. Some software handles IK very well but, generally the lower you go, the worse the IK flail becomes. However, IK is really useful in certain situations, and we'll be spending more time with it in other chapters. In this project, we'll be working with a very simple hierarchy having only one joint, so there will only be one IK solution for any pose, and IK flail won't happen at all. The following steps show you how to use IK to keep both eyeball objects pointed at a single target.

3D Studio MAX 2

Kinetix did a very thorough job with the 2 documentation and tutorials for IK. Considering the variety and complexity of controls and settings, I suggest you work through the *Tutorial* manual, especially Chapters 18 and 19, and read through the pertinent sections of the *User's Guide*. After you've completed the IK tutorials, add a Dummy object to your Face setup as an IK target for the eyeballs, and save the scene for use in Chapter 14.

LightWave 3D 5.5

There are some problems in LightWave with setting an object to track a target directly. The usual approach is to add a null object to the end of the hierarchy, and set the null to track the target. This also gives you better control over how the rest of the hierarchy reacts to the target's movement.

1. Add a null, and change its name to EyeNullLeft.
2. Parent EyeNullLeft to the left eyeball object.

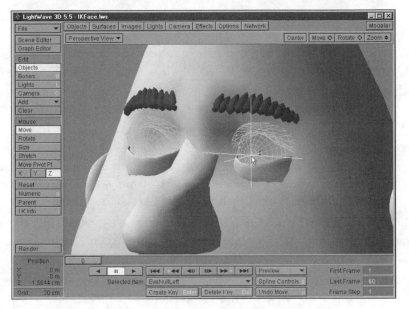

Figure 11.27 EyeNullLeft null positioned in front of left eyeball.

3. Make sure the null is still the Selected Item. Position the null (represented by a three-axis crosshair) directly in front of the pupil of the left eyeball, as in Figure 11.27.

4. Create a keyframe for the null at frame 0. Save your work.

5. Repeat Steps 1 through 4 to add Parent, and position a null named EyeNullRight to the right eyeball.

6. Add a null named EyeTarget, and position the null in front of the character's nose.

   The next step will be to limit the IK effects on the head hierarchy. You want the eyes, not the entire head, to track the target.

7. Select the Face object. Click on the IK Info button at the lower left of the Layout window. The Inverse Kinematics Options panel appears.

8. Click on the Unaffected By IK Descendants checkbox, then click on Continue to save the change and close the panel.

   This tells the head to ignore any IK effects from the Parented nulls, eyelids, or eyeballs. It will only move according to its own key frame settings.

9. Select EyeNullLeft. Click on the IK Options button at the lower right. The Inverse Kinematics Options panel appears again. Click on the Full-time IK checkbox at the upper left.

   This tells the IK routine to run constantly, updating the position of the affected objects whenever you make a change. In general, it's a good idea to use full-time IK whenever possible. You may eventually run into some complex situations when you won't want full-time IK but, for now, make it a habit to enable it.

You also have the option to set rotation limits for the selected item for the Heading, Pitch, and Bank axes. These limits tell the IK process that it can't rotate the selected item past the defined angles, and it will have to pass along any further rotation to another item in the IK hierarchy.

Just for practice, let's set some rotation limits for the eye to keep this character from trying to look out the back of his head.

10. Select the left eyeball, and click on the IK Info button again. Click on the Heading Limits checkbox, and set the Heading Minimum to -50 and Maximum to 50. Click on the Pitch Limits checkbox, and set the Pitch Minimum to -20 and Maximum to 40. Click on the Bank Limits checkbox, and set the Bank Minimum to -0 and Maximum to 0. (You don't want the eyeball spinning around its pupil, do you?) Repeat for the other eyeball.

These limits are just rough approximations. The limits you use will change depending on the shape of the character's face and the range of expression you need to animate. Now, both eyeballs are set to follow the EyeTarget.

11. To test the IK, select the EyeTarget null, and move it around in all three axes. The eyeballs should rotate to look at the null, as in Figure 11.28.

12. Save the scene under a new name.

If all went well, you now have a head with eyes that are much easier to animate.

trueSpace3

You don't have to use IK to get eyes to follow a null in trueSpace 3.2. The built-in Look At function enables you to aim any object at any other. This is essentially the same as the Aim At constraints discussed in Chapter 13.

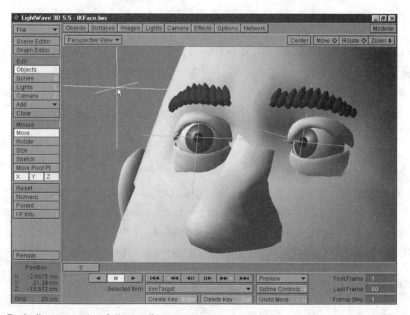

Figure 11.28 Eyeballs targeted to follow null.

Look At points the constrained object's Z axis at the target object, so construct your eyeball models with the Z axis protruding from the pupil and centered on the center of the eyeball itself. To set up the Look At, simply select the eyeball object, select Look At, and select the target.

Alternate Eye Setups

Parented eyeballs and IK goals are my personal preference for animating eye movements, but there are other methods that are appropriate for different circumstances. For realistic animation, you should mimic the actual physiological structure of the creature's eyes as closely as possible. You can adapt the projects you just completed for most of these situations, and the tutorials in Chapter 9 show how you can apply maps to create photo-realistic eyes from very simple models.

For cartoon or caricature animation, all bets are off. Extreme caricature animation will call for squashing, stretching, and generally distorting the eyes (see Figure 11.29) demands that pretty much rule out the nice, neat Parent and IK approach.

If you can get away with an iris and pupil that don't distort much, you can use a fixed *sclera*, or white, that is part of the head object, then simply animate the pupil and iris as a separate or Parented object. You may even be able to use IK goals, if the eyeball won't change its curvature much. If the eye will be distorting a lot, this approach can be more trouble than it's worth, since precisely matching the iris to the surface of a distorted eyeball can be tedious and time-consuming.

One way to overcome the problems of a grossly distorted eyeball is to use an image or image sequence to map the iris and pupil. This is definitely not interactive, requiring about the same level of pre-planning as lip sync. If the eyes need a lot more flexibility—especially if you are trying to imitate the style of Tex Avery—I recommend that you treat them as any other object to be animated using replacement or displacement methods.

Replacement animation of eyes is very straightforward, using the techniques you learned earlier in this chapter. You can probably get along with a morph target library of a dozen or so eyes. If you build them properly, you should be able to use one set for both left and right eyes. Simply model the baseline eye with the iris and pupil in the middle of the sclera. Make sure the edges of the iris and pupil have enough vertices to avoid showing straight edges, even in close shots.

Figure 11.29 Extreme take from *The Physics of Cartoons*, showing distortion of eyes.

Save a duplicate of the eye. Select and move the vertices defining the iris and pupil so the iris' rim is tangent to one edge of the sclera. Save this as one of your morph targets. Repeat this for each target object, moving the iris and pupil to another point along the edge of the sclera. I recommend building the up, down, left, and right models first, then continuing to split the angles between targets until you are satisfied that you can animate a morph to any required eye position. Alternatively, you can set up an eye animation in advance, using an object or morph sequence.

Puppet Setup With Parented Objects

PROJECT 11.7

This project builds on the experience you have accumulated in the preceding projects, and provides a preview of the complexity of a full humanoid character. This character setup will require 15 separate objects, plus a few null or dummy placeholders, to build a complete Puppet. With this setup, you should be able to animate most human actions well enough for practice. Later setups will build on this one, adding details to the head and hands to increase this character's dramatic range.

The Puppet used in the following exercises, and pictured in Figure 11.30, was originally modeled by Jim Pomeroy of Arlington, Texas, in December of 1991, and released by him into the public domain. Thanks, Jim!

I've made just a few modifications, mostly scaling the Puppet up to more average human dimensions and tweaking a few pivot placements. This Puppet is about as simple as you can get within the limits of human proportions and joint structure. It uses only 15 small objects and two nulls in a parented hierarchy, and no bones or other deformation setups at all.

There are several reasons to use such a simple model:

- Screen redraw is a lot faster than if you had the same objects animated by bones. Redraw times with hierarchical characters can quickly get out of hand, especially when you are

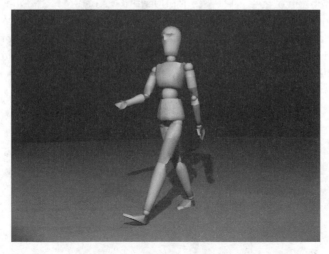

Figure 11.30 Puppet character.

down to trial-and-error tweaking of fine detail. You will be more productive and learn more easily if you can minimize your waiting time.

- This Puppet can be loaded by just about any system that can run 3D animation software. The polygon count is very low, and the memory requirements are minimal. This also translates into faster redraws, less waiting, and more effective learning.

- There are fewer distractions in a simple character. If the Puppet had bandoleers, fighting knives, and Uzis dangling off a combat harness, you could spend all your time just animating the overlapping action of the bells and whistles. Keep it simple, and concentrate on the lesson at hand. When you've mastered the animation of a simple character, you can apply the same principles to a complex one—then spend extra time on the frills and gewgaws.

- This Puppet is also easier to keep track of than a more complex or boned object. The parented joints clearly show the physical limits of their rotations. The shin should obviously pitch no more than 110 degrees relative to the thigh, and so on. The necessary notes a TD might deliver with this character are relatively brief.

There are a few disadvantages to this Puppet. It has no fingers or toes, so subtler gestures or a more refined heel-and-toe stride aren't possible. The low polygon count and minimal structure mean that there is no provision for object-level squash-and-stretch deformation. Any squash or stretch must be animated by posing the joints. The Puppet also lacks some crucial joints for expressive characters, as it has no independent shoulder joints and therefore can't even shrug without literally coming apart at the seams.

This project is good practice for another reason. This Puppet is a grossly simplified form of a humanoid character but still requires extended attention to detail to set up and animate. You should think of this as practice in stretching your attention span. One of the most important assets for an animator is an extremely long attention span and the willingness to follow through a long sequence of painstakingly detailed work. This Puppet isn't all that hard to set up, but it will prepare you for more advanced setups ahead in Chapters 12 and 13.

1. Load objects Chest, Head, Hips, Lfoot, Lhand, Llowarm, Lshin, Lthigh, Luparm, Rfoot, Rhand, Rlowarm, Rshin, Rthigh, and Ruparm. As before, I have provided these objects in 3DS, DXF, and LWO format, in the Chapter 11 directory on this book's CD-ROM. Most of the objects have obvious centers of rotation and child attachment, and I have added jacks to those that don't.

2. Using the techniques you learned in Project 11.5, arrange the objects in a parented hierarchy. If your software supports rotational limits, you should also set limits for these objects according to the following notes.

   These character notes are intended to help you pose the Puppet in simple walk and run cycles. The recommendations for joint constraints and usage may not be appropriate for animating other actions.

   All surfaces are set to a default material. This is a simple parented hierarchy of objects. There are no bones, morph, or other deformation setups. The numbers preceding each note refer to the object's place in the animation hierarchy. You may also want to consider using these numbers as a load order, if your software locks objects into the scene in the order they are first added.

1: *Puppet_Ground_Null*—This null controls the position of the character in the XZ plane. This null and the Puppet_CG_Null are the root level of the animation hierarchy and should be roughed out first for almost any action. You should always position the Puppet_Ground_Null at ground level, and on uneven terrain, you should position it at the height of the grounded foot or other grounded body part. This null is separate from the Puppet_CG_Null, so you can animate the vertical and horizontal components of the character's movement on different keyframes. You should not rotate or scale this object. You may find it helpful to think of the Puppet_Ground_Null as a support rod for the Puppet and the Puppet_CG_Null as a clamp that can only travel up and down the rod.

1: *Puppet_CG_Null*—This null controls the Y-position and 3-axis rotation of the character as a whole. It is located at the approximate center of gravity of an equivalent real-life human. This null and the Puppet_Ground_Null are the root, or first, level of the animation hierarchy. You can animate this null in the Y axis to keep the contact foot (or other contact body part) on the ground and rotate it on the appropriate axes for free-fall tumbling. If you need to rotate the character while it is in contact with the ground, rotate the Hips object.

2: *Hips*—This object includes the lower abdomen, the ball joint that forms the pivot for the Chest object, and the ball joints of the two Thigh pivots. This is the parent object of the character's body. This is the second level of the animation hierarchy, and you should animate it immediately after the CG and Ground nulls for almost any action. The pivot point is located at the center of gravity (CG). You can rotate this object a few degrees on the bank and heading axes to enhance leg motions, but anything more than that will look really strange unless accompanied by a balancing movement of the rest of the character.

3: *Chest*—This object includes the ribcage, the ball joint for the Head object, and the two ball joints for the UpArm objects. This is the third level of the animation hierarchy, and the parent for the upper half of the body. You should animate the Chest's action completely and to your satisfaction before beginning on the head or arms. You can animate the Chest to pitch nearly 60 degrees, as for a deep bow, and bank 40 or so. You should not animate heading more than 30 degrees without some complementary action of the Hips.

4: *Head*—This object is part of the fourth level of the animation hierarchy. Generally, you can animate the rotation of the Head with the inverse values (-3.4=3.4 and so on) of the same axes of rotation of the Chest, simply to keep the Head level and pointed in the original direction. Since the Head tends to follow the eyes, in more complex actions, the Head is a good candidate for IK and tracking setups, as explained earlier in this chapter and in Chapter 12.

4: *LUpArm, RUpArm*—The upper arms are also parts of the fourth level. You can animate these objects' headings with the inverse heading value of the Chest to keep the arms pointing in the right direction. You should keep pitch values between -160 and 70, and bank values between -30 and 135 degrees.

4: *LThigh, RThigh*—The thighs are also parts of the fourth level. You can animate these objects' headings with the inverse heading and bank values of the Hips to keep the legs pointing in the right direction. You should keep pitch values between -120 and 45, and bank values between -20 and 45 degrees, unless you are animating a gymnast.

5: *LLowArm, RLowArm*—The fifth level of the animation hierarchy includes the lower arms and lower legs. These joints are simple hinges, and you should only animate them in the pitch axis. You should animate other rotations using the hand or upper-arm objects. The lower-arm objects can pitch between 0 and -120 degrees relative to the upper-arm objects.

5: *LShin, RShin*—You should animate the shins between 0 and 110 on the pitch axis, relative to the thigh objects. Animate the feet or thigh objects for other rotations.

6: *LHand, RHand*—For these exercises, you only need to animate the hands through small angles on the pitch axis as overlapping action to the swing of the arms. The hands are set to 15 degrees bank rotation to give them a more natural line with the rest of the body. The pitch limits are -60 to 60, but 5 to 10 degrees are enough for the overlapping action. The fingers and toes for this character are not articulated, so the hands and feet represent the sixth and last level of the animation hierarchy.

6: *LFoot, RFoot*—You can reasonably animate the feet from -45 to 70 degrees on the pitch axis, but much shallower angles are sufficient for these exercises. You should not use the other two axes of rotation unless they are necessary to match the feet to odd terrain angles. Keyframing the foot rotations should be your next-to-last step in posing the hierarchy, as any change in higher layers will change the alignment to the ground. Generally, you should align the feet by eye with the ground surface, and keyframe them as often as necessary to keep them from penetrating or floating over the ground. Keyframes for a foot that is not in contact with the ground can be spaced as for overlapping action, similar to the pitch animation of the hands.

When you've finished parenting, limiting, and testing the Puppet setup, you should write up any additional notes pertinent to your particular software. You'll be using the Puppet extensively in Chapters 14 and 15, and your notes will come in handy.

Poser 2

As mentioned earlier, Poser hierarchies come ready-built. One of the figures provided with the software is the Mannequin, a jointed character very much like the Puppet described above. You can use it (or the skeleton, stick figure, male or female Poser figures) for all the full-figure animation projects in Chapters 14 and 15.

Poser has optional built-in IK for the arms and legs, making the job of posing the figure much easier. One interesting and useful feature in Poser's IK is that the end effectors act as positional constraints (see Chapter 12 for details). For example, to make the Mannequin execute a deep knee bend, you simply drag the torso downward. The feet remain planted at floor level, and the knees bend. This IK feature makes character animation much faster and more intuitive. Most other character animation packages (including the expensive ones) only offer this kind of functionality after a complex setup.

For *forward kinematic* (FK) animation in Poser, you can use default rotational limits or set your own. The same joint ranges listed for the Puppet, above, will work for the Poser Mannequin.

If you've worked through all the projects so far, you should have a solid grasp of Displacement animation using rigid skeletal structures. You should also have some idea of the limits of this type of setup, and the need for something a little more squashable.

Deformation

Deformation is a subset of displacement animation, based on displacement-style skeletal joints but associated with the deformable geometry of a model. This combination can enable you to animate a seamless mesh using setups similar to those you built for the swing-arm desk lamp and the Puppet. This gives you the smooth characters of Replacement animation, with the fine interactive control of Displacement.

Most CGI character animation today is done with some form of Displacement Deformation setup. You need to understand how to set up deformations, if only to remain competitive in the industry. You will also find that deformations broaden the range of styles you can use and stories you can tell, enabling you to set up and animate anything from extremely abstract caricatures to photorealistic digital stuntmen.

There are as many approaches to deformation as there are software packages that support it. Each program handles deformation setup in a slightly different way. However, there are two general approaches that can serve to categorize the available tools: *parametric* and *bones*.

Parametric deformation is usually based on placing a cage of control points around the model to be deformed, then animating the cage's controls. The software interpolates the cage's deformation in applying it to the model. This approach is only loosely connected to the original model and can be quickly revised without damaging the rest of the setup. However, parametric deformation does not provide as detailed a level of control as bones. Parametric deformation is generally most useful for squash-and-stretch and similar overall distortions, when a character (or part of one) appears to deform under outside influences. Parametric deformation can be used to create muscular or skeletal deformation, but it's not well-suited to the task.

Bones deformation is based on inserting and binding a skeleton of control handles to the character's geometry. This can be easy or extremely difficult to set up, depending on your software. Some software requires you to actually assign the mesh to specific bones vertex-by-vertex, while others use a more volume-effect approach. The end result, when it works, is that you can animate the deformation of the model by animating the bones as if they were a traditional puppet armature and the mesh an overlay of foam rubber. Bones enables you to create a more precise setup, which the animator can use to interactively tweak even the lift of an eyebrow or angle of a fingertip. The disadvantage is that the closer binding and control of a bones setup makes it that much more difficult to revise or adapt to changes in the model. In some software, reconnecting a bones skeleton to a revised mesh is so complex that it's more efficient to start over. More about this issue is discussed in Chapter 12. For now, the next few projects will show you the basics of Deformation setups.

Parametric Deformation

The most common use for parametric deformation is to animate shape changes for an entire character. This is especially useful for animating squash-and-stretch, deformations of a character under outside influences like gravity, acceleration, and impact. Setting up a parametric deformation for a squash-and-stretch should be a basic part of your repertoire.

Ball Setup For "Gumdrop" Squash Deformation

PROJECT **11.8**

This project shows you how to set up a simple parametric deformation to change a sphere into a gumdrop shape, as if the sphere is soft and has impacted a hard floor. This is an important part of one of the classic animation exercises, the bouncing ball. It would be much simpler to set up a sphere to scale on the vertical axis. However, simple scaling does not give an accurate deformation of either the top or bottom of the sphere. This scaling looks cheap and is a dead giveaway, even to an untrained audience. To avoid this, the animator needs to be able to squash the sphere out flat where it contacts the floor, while leaving the top of the sphere nearly untouched. The animator also needs to control this deformation accurately on a frame-by-frame basis, to coordinate the movement of the sphere with its deformation to match contact with the floor.

3D Studio MAX 2

3D Studio MAX 2 comes with a FreeForm Deformation (FFD) Modifier. This modifier allows an object to be manipulated by placing a cage or control lattice around it. By moving or animating the points on the lattice, the object itself is affected in a similar fashion like Figure 11.31.

Load up Bounce01.max as a sample. This is a sample sphere animated to bounce. In addition, it has a 4×4×4 FFD Modifier applied to it. The ball squashes when it is on the ground and resumes its shape when in the air. This is done by turning on animate while adjusting the FFD control points. You will notice the top of the ball kind of jiggles when it is in the air. This is because I did not adjust the tangent types for those points to be linear for the in-between frames. You can adjust the tangent types in Track View by right-clicking on the keyframe for each point (ugh).

Once you've set up the gumdrop squash, save it for use in the bouncing ball project in Chapter 14.

trueSpace3

You can set up a parametric deformation in trueSpace using Local Deformation, as described on pages 164-166 of the manual. Basically, you just click on the cross-section intersection you want to modify and drag it to create the new shape.

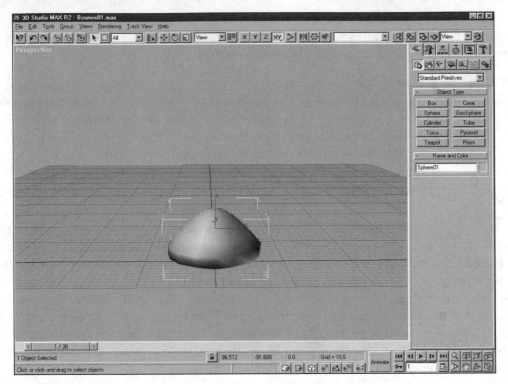

Figure 11.31 Parametric (FFD) deformation of sphere, simulating ball's squash against floor.

Animation procedures for local deformation ar e covered on pages 314 through 320, which describe how to use the deformation keys:

1. Deform the object.
2. Set the keyframe for the object's deformation.
3. Go to the next keyframe.
4. Repeat the first three steps until you have a complete sequence of shapes.

Once you've set up the gumdrop squash, save it for use in the bouncing ball project in Chapter 14.

Bones Deformation

A traditional puppet can have visible rotating joints like those you emulated in the Puppet setup. It can also have a flexible outer covering over a jointed *armature*, or inner skeleton, allowing the puppet's skin to deform without visible seams. Some animation software's bones functions can duplicate this effect, enabling you to assemble complex characters that simulate the appearance of bone, flesh, and skin.

Bones can be placed individually or in hierarchies, to deform a single joint or provide a flexible armature for an entire creature. Bones are a very powerful tool, and especially useful for the major skeletal joints. Also, the complete model, bones, and motions can be loaded (in some software, anyway) from a previously saved scene, just as with a parented object hierarchy.

Probably the most popular use of bones is in the animation of skeletal joints, but bones can also be used to animate loose flesh or slack muscle, which is especially useful for overlapping action (see Chapter 14). Depending on your software, you may be able to adjust the handling of geometry shared between two or more bones to emulate the flabbier behavior of less muscular tissues. For especially loose masses, you can borrow motion files from the character's CG, delay it a few frames, and apply it to the "flabby" bones to create a first approximation of overlapping action.

Designing for boned animation is one of the easier modeling tasks. Bones are relatively tolerant of your modeling procedures, and they don't care much in what order you created the points they will be pushing around. Your biggest challenge in modeling for bones will be planning a model that the bones won't warp into garbage, and that can reach the range of motions the animator needs without using umpteen-zillion bones to do it. As mentioned in Chapters 5 and 6, the more polygons around a boned joint, the smoother the deformation will appear. If you don't have enough polygons in the area, you may end up with sharp corners where you don't want them.

Designing for a joint's range of motion is a matter of balancing the overlapping influence of the adjoining bones so the result looks plausible. Note that I did not say *realistic*, just *plausible*. Bones are useful and powerful tools, but I don't know anybody patient enough to animate the handful of controls you'd need to realistically emulate each and every perceptible muscle in the human body. If you want photorealism, you are better off trying Replacement animation with a whole lot of very detailed sculpting or laser digitizing.

Your primary concerns for bone setup are to make sure the model has enough points in the affected areas, and that the bones have the optimum position and settings for the deformation required. You also need to run a few basic tests, and document the results to hand over to the animator.

Ball Setup For "Shmoo" Deformation

This project will show you how to set up bones to distort muscular masses that in reality wouldn't have a skeleton. This technique can be applied to facial animation, squash-and-stretch, and almost any situation where a character must deform in a precisely controllable manner. This project is deliberately set up to be the simplest possible example of bones deformation, but the principles shown here apply just as well to a fully articulated humanoid setup. It's just more of the same, like setting up the Puppet after setting up the desk lamp.

The goal of this project is to deform a sphere into an animatable approximation of one of Al Capp's Shmoos. If you're not a Li'l Abner fan, think of Flubber. The idea is to have a sphere that can deform enough to show a little self-motivation, if not personality.

1. Open a new scene. Create a sphere.

2. Add a single bone to the sphere, starting at the sphere's center and extending upwards about two-thirds of the way to the sphere's top.

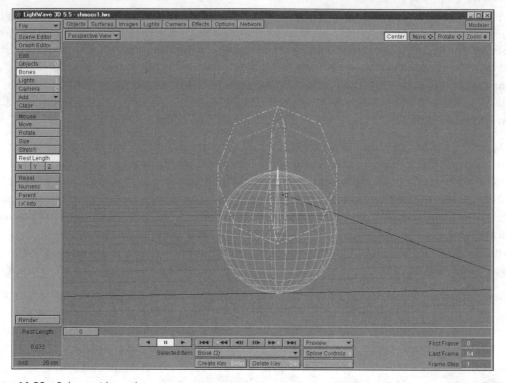

Figure 11.32   Sphere with two bones as set up.

3. Add a second bone as child of the first bone, extending upwards just past the top of the sphere. You should end up with something like Figure 11.32.

4. Modify the influence of the bones to affect only the upper hemisphere. You want a combination of influences that produces results like Figure 11.33.

   You should experiment with the bone settings, pushing the limits and finding out how your software handles bone interactions. This is probably the simplest bone setup you'll ever work with, so make your mistakes now!

3D Studio MAX 2

Default MAX bones leave something to be desired. You have to use the Linked X-Form modifier. When a bone moves, all vertices affected move 100 percent by that bone. Vertices can only be assigned to one bone. You might as well set up a simple parented object hierarchy, since you're still going to have visible seams.

However, there are two plug-ins for MAX that enable nicer bone setups. One is the Physique section of the Character Studio plug-in published by Kinetix. The other is BonesPro MAX, published by Digimation.

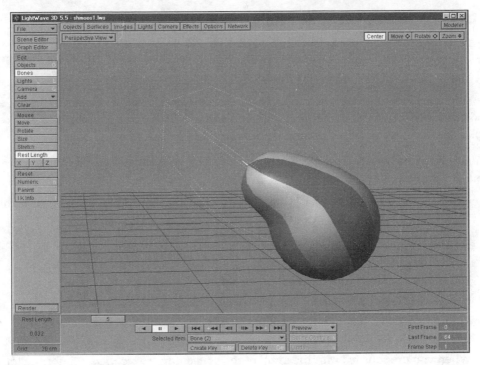

Figure 11.33 Sphere with two bones in action.

The Physique bones allow only one-to-one vertex-bone assignments. However, MAX 2 now allows FFDs to deform the mesh. Thus, you can assign an FFD control point to a bone, so when the bone moves, the FFD is affected and the object changes more smoothly. Physique offers other unique options, such as muscle bulging and tendons to help pull the mesh smoothly.

BonesPro MAX is favored by many MAX animators, and it's more similar to LightWave in usage. It can be both a Modifier or a Space Warp (In version 1.2, only the SpaceWarp was available). You can use a box object as a bone to affect the mesh. Each bone has a strength and falloff setting that allows you to customize the *pull*, or influence, of each bone. In addition, you can manually exclude or include vertices for each bone, and vertices can be affected by more than one bone. This makes it excellent for smoothly deforming polygonal meshes. Because it is just a deformation tool, it doesn't have things like muscle bulging built in, but you can manually scale bones to get this effect.

You can see how a single bone can be used to distort a model's surface with a great deal of control. Bones can pull in, push out, and generally shove the mesh around. As you may have surmised, this kind of bone animation is extremely useful for animating facial expressions. You can place bones to manipulate eyebrows, pucker lips, even set bones to nail down a dimple while the rest of the face bulges. It's very flexible, and you'll be using bones a lot in the following chapters.

Give 'Em A Hand!

PROJECT 11.10

Here's a more challenging project in applying bones to a model. It's the classic cartoon character glove, with three fingers for easier animating, and the high style of three stitched lines on the back and a rolled cuff.

The original model was modeled in LightWave with MetaNURBS. The low-frequency source model is HANDLOW.LWO, and, as usual, you can find it in this chapter's directory on this book's CD-ROM, if you feel like fooling around with it.

You're pretty much on your own with this one. If you worked through the Shmoo project, I think you can handle it.

1. Open a new scene. Load the LGlove model from the Chapter 11 directory on this book's CD-ROM. As usual, it's available in 3DS, DXF, and LWO formats.

2. Add, position, and set the parameters for the bones required to pose the hand. Give it three knuckles for each finger.

   You might refer to Figure 11.34 for an idea or two about bone placement.

   One special concern is the opposable thumb's transverse bulge. This is a real pain to animate properly. If your software supports any kind of muscle bulge feature, this is a good place to try it out.

3. When you are satisfied with the setup of the boned hand, save the setup for use later in this chapter. In the following section on Hybrid animation, you'll be adding the articulated hand to the Puppet setup.

Depending on your software, you may have a feature that enables you to save a posed deformation as a new model. In LightWave, this is the Save Transformed function, available in the Object panel. You can use this function to start building a library of hand poses for morph and morph sequence animation. Most of Preston Blair's books have a wonderful page full of cartoon hand

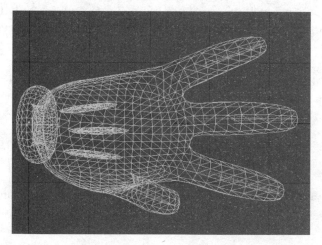

Figure 11.34 Cartoon glove with bone setup.

poses. Brian Lemay's textbooks go into even more detail. You can make right hand duplicates of all the left hand models by making a copy, then scaling it by -1 on the X axis.

You might want to try setting up the cartoon glove as a parametric deformation exercise. It's good experience to solve problems in as many different ways as you can. Each solution has its advantages and disadvantages. One of your strongest assets as an animator or setup person is your ability to solve problems quickly, efficiently, and reliably. The more practice you have, the more valuable you'll be, and the better position you'll be in for negotiating a raise, promotion, or the next creative opportunity.

Case Study: Softimage Cartoon Glove

By Ken Cope

This cartoon glove, Figure 11.35, was an exercise exploring trimmed NURBS connected with active blends, bones driven by position and up vector constraints, and the use of expressions to drive the finger rotations.

Expressions were also used to mirror and offset the animation to the other hand by a number of frames, Figure 11.36. For more about expressions, see Chapters 15 and 16.

Closed curves projected onto the surface of the sphere for the wrist hole, finger holes, and base of the thumb were trimmed.

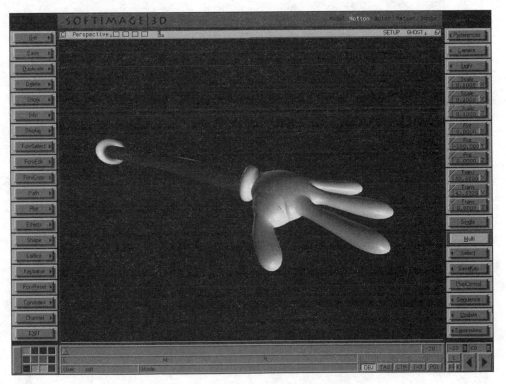

Figure 11.35   Cartoon glove modeled in Softimage.

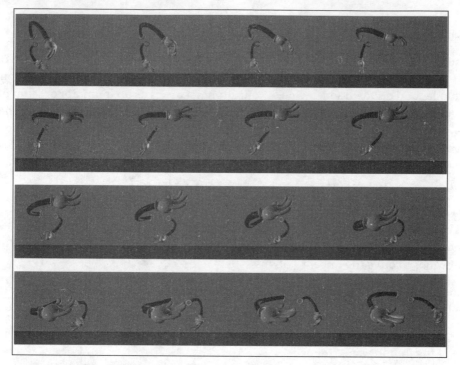

Figure 11.36 Frames showing mirror and offset of hand animation using expressions.

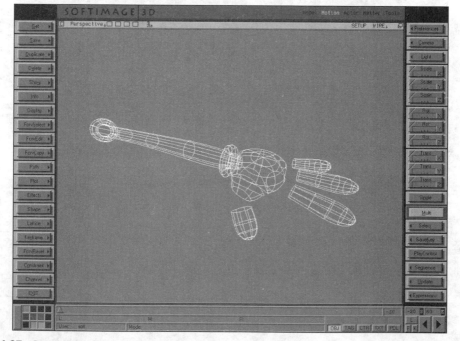

Figure 11.37 Projected curves trimmed.

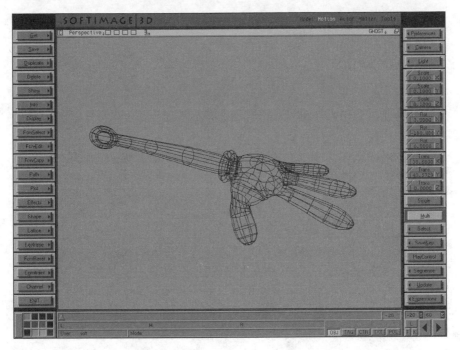

Figure 11.38   Active blends connecting trimmed parts.

The additional thumb base and then a wrist gasket and digits were connected with active blends.

Once the 2D IK chains (bones) were in place, Figure 11.39, they were position constrained with a heirarchy of null objects, one at each joint, Figure 11.40.

As with any envelope in Softimage that you wish to have driven by bones, make sure that only the objects that you want deforming the envelope are in the heirarchy. One of the easiest ways to create an up vector constraint is to toggle it automatically on during IK chain creation. If that's what you do, be sure to cut them from the chain root and place them in a separate heirarchy containing the position constraint nulls.

These nulls were driven with expressions (on more nulls, elsewhere), so that setting a keyframe for the base knuckle would be applied to each subsequent knuckle by a percentage. The pair of rubberhose arms and gloves shown in Figure 11.35 are available for you to play with in the Chapter 11 directory of the CD-ROM.

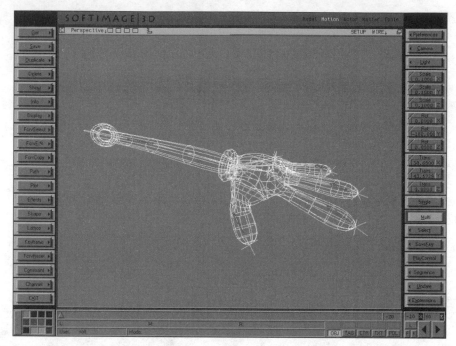

Figure 11.39 IK chains (bones) in place.

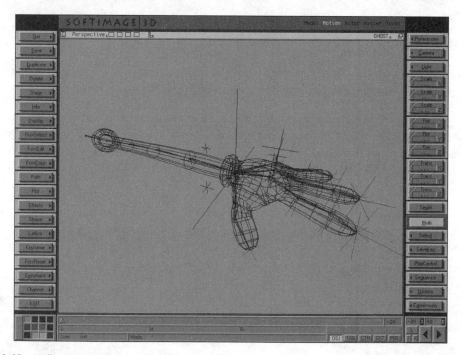

Figure 11.40 Nulls as position constraints.

Hybrid Animation

Hybrid puppet animation is, as you might expect, a combination of displacement and replacement techniques. Most puppet animation now being done in professional studios is a mixture of techniques. As in any business with deadlines and budgets, it's whatever gets the job done.

Generally, the gross skeletal animation is best handled with a displacement armature. In animation software terms, that means either parent (if joints can show) or bones (if it has to look seamless). There are a few special circumstances—long repetitive sequences, perhaps—where replacement techniques can be used for the whole-body motions, but generally this is done with displacement.

Replacement pieces really shine when there is fussy, detailed yet repetitive animation to be done. Lip sync is a prime candidate—if a character needs to speak, it's a lot easier to swap head or face parts from a library of phonemes than it is to pose the 20 or more deformation controls necessary to shape a decent-looking mouth. Sometimes, hands are also animated with replacement model parts, as they are smaller than the rest of the armature and the fine wire of their skeleton tends to break more often.

The usual technique, then, is to build displacement armatures with pegs or keys at the extremities, the neck, wrists, and so on, to which the replacement bits are readily attached and removed. A wonderful example of this technique is *The Nightmare Before Christmas*. The protagonist, Jack Skellington, had approximately 180 replacement heads, covering every permutation of lip sync and emotional expression. His displacement armature, by comparison, had about 18 joints (not including the hands, which used flexible wire rather than machined joints).

Hybrid replacement/displacement animation has its advantages. As with straight replacement, it gives faster layout of fine detail in sequences. As with bones and parent hierarchies, you can reuse poses and action sequences. Consistent use over time will build a growing range of retrievable poses. Since only part of the character must be modeled for replacement animation, there can be far fewer total models to make and track, plus more flexibility in whole-figure posability using bones and parenting.

Of course, hybrid replacement/displacement animation has its disadvantages. Changes in replacement head and hand poses must be created and managed as separate models or morph targets. This requires tracking and storage of a larger number of models than would a pure displacement method. Additionally, the complex mix of replacement and displacement techniques requires that your software be capable of handling both approaches. Several major software packages can't do this on their own and require you to buy plug-ins.

Puppet Setup With Deformation Hands

The goal of this project is to set up a hybrid animation figure, with a displacement body and deformation hands. Basically, you'll be using the Puppet you set up in an earlier Project, and substituting posable hands for the rigid mittens of the original setup.

1. Reload the Puppet setup, and save it under a new file name.

2. Merge the Cartoon Glove setup into the Puppet scene.

3. Replace Lhand (and Rhand, if you created a matching glove setup) in the Puppet hierarchy with the root of the Cartoon Glove setup.

4. Save the new setup, you'll be using it in Chapter 15.

   You can also substitute parametric deformation hands or even a morph sequence. As I said before, it's good experience to solve problems in as many different ways as you can.

3D Studio MAX 2

Because modeling and animation are so tightly integrated in MAX, it is easy to mix and match the above mentioned animation methods. A character's body might have a bone system applied to it. Then, the head might be a separate mesh. This head mesh could actually be a morph object that is parented to the neck bone of the body hierarchy.

This should be somewhat obvious to advanced users. You basically set up each part as separate entities, then link the pieces together. Alternatively, one object could be both a morph object and also have bones applied to it at the same time. You might make a morph object, then, later in the modifier stack, you could add a bone setup. You can then go down into the morph section of the stack to animate that or animate the bones, as well.

Morph sequence hands would require Morph Magic for easy use. You could probably use the default morph stuff as described above though.

Default Setups

Whether you are making an entire animated film yourself or just doing setup work for a team of animators, you should try to make the animator's job as easy as possible. One of the ways you can save the animator a lot of time and effort is to set up default scenes for each character. This is especially important on long projects with lots of shots, and group projects with more than one animator handling the same characters. It's a good way of keeping to standards and preventing conflicts. This section shows you how to set up a basic default scene for a complete character.

A default scene contains a character with all its associated textures, bones, hierarchies, plug-ins, morph libraries, and view lights set up and ready to animate. A good rule of thumb for including items in a default scene is: If the animator has to set it up before she can start animating the character, then include it. If not, you can let it slide unless the animator specifically asks for it.

Unless the animator tells you otherwise, pose the character in a typical default posture. While there are technical advantages in most software for setting up using the jesus, leonardo, or spread-eagled-on-the-ground positions, the animator shouldn't have to stand the character up every time they reload the scene. Also, for dramatic reasons, a character's hands are usually carried at or above the waist, so it saves time for the animator if you pose your characters' arms this way by default (see Figure 11.41). You should do all this in the default scene.

Figure 11.41 Default pose, minimizing startup work for the animator.

Animators can work faster and more efficiently if they can get a clear picture of the part of the character they are posing without having to tweak a view every time. Depending on your software, you may be able to set up viewport presets, extra cameras, or lights to enable the animator to quickly switch between close-up views of parts of the character.

LightWave 3D 5.5

LightWave allows you to use each light as a view, so you can simply add a set of inactive lights, assigned to the various Bones or models that require close-up views, so the animator can change views by changing lights. You can add as many lights as you need, and, once they are set, you never have to tweak them. Also, anytime you use Load From Scene to import the character, you can import all the View Lights at the same time.

Setting up these View Lights for a Parented model hierarchy is no problem, you just Parent the View Lights to the appropriate models. Boned models are a little more difficult. The easiest way to set up View Lights for a Boned hierarchy is to use Dynamic Realities' Lock & Key motion software. Animation software's ParentBone motion software can do most of the same job, but the setup is unacceptably tedious and counterproductive.

> **VIEW LIGHTS**
>
> Have at least one View Light covering each area the animator will need to see in detail. Generally, anywhere there are a lot of active Bones or an especially tricky piece of a hierarchy, you'll want to set a View Light. A typical character might need face front, right face, left face, left hand, right hand, left foot, right foot, and perhaps full-body front and full-body side View Lights.

Keep in mind that lights are always displayed in selection lists in the order they are added to the scene. You should use Load From Scene to add the character before any other lights are added, so the View Lights are at the top of the selection menu and are easiest to find. If you work with OpenGL, you should leave one active Distant Light (the default scene light will do) at the top of the list. OpenGL can only use the top eight lights in the scene's list, so you could easily end up with all eight eligible slots filled by inactive View Lights. Once you start setting active lights for the character (see Chapter 17), you should put the first key light at the top of the list. All these considerations mean you should carefully plan your View Lights before you start building the scene.

> ## VIEW LIGHT OPTIONS
>
> Set View Lights for black, 0 percent Light Intensity, Lens Flares and Shadow Maps disabled, No Diffuse and No Specular, and Shadow Type off. Remember to give them appropriate names that you can recognize quickly in the Lights selection list.

Lock & Key combos move the keyed item precisely to the lock item's coordinates. For most View Lights, you will want to offset the light from the lock item. For example, a key Light locked to the root Bone of the character's head, with no offset, would be located at the pivot of the HeadBone. This view from inside the character's head wouldn't be terribly helpful in posing the face.

The simplest way to do this is to set combos to key a Null model to each lock item, then Parent the View Lights to the appropriate Null models. For example, the head and face would only need one Null, locked to the Head Bone. The three View Lights, face front, left, and right, would all be Parented to the Null, and positioned and rotated to give the intended view.

If It Slows You Down, Throw It Out

Another important rule for setups is: Exclude anything that slows down the animator. If images, shaders, complex lighting setups, and highly detailed objects are included, they'll slow the animator down. If they're not important to creating the animation, hold them out until after the animation is complete, and add them just before the final rendering. Try to minimize bones or other deformation setups that slow down screen refresh. Fast feedback for the animator is more important than making pretty pictures, especially during the first rough-out of an action.

The simplest object hierarchy character setups are the CGI equivalent of drawing stick figures. They may not look like much compared to a finished rendering of a boned and deformed model, but they're a quick-and-dirty way of testing poses and actions, and they're easy enough to make that you can afford to throw them out and experiment more.

Chapter 12 describes setups that enable the animator to work with a bare-bones skeleton to animate, then link a complex model to the skeleton after the animation is complete. If your software supports this approach, you should definitely try it out. It can make an enormous difference in the quality of the finished animation, because it provides more practice and experimenting time during the entire length of the project.

Create A Default Scene

1. Load the last Puppet setup you created, complete with deformation hands.

2. Add preset views for detailed areas of the setup. Use lights, cameras, or viewport presets, as required by your software.

3. Pose the character in the default pose shown earlier in Figure 11.41.

4. Save the setup with a new file name.

This default scene will make it much easier to use this character in the projects in Chapters 14 and 15. You just have one thing left to do—document the setup.

Write It Up

If you're working with other animators or it's a long project, you should document the character's default scene including the view and name of each light. At minimum, you can make a model sheet by assembling a screenshot from each preset view, like Figure 11.42, and hand-write your notes around the images. Include this with the modeler's notes and any other documentation for the character. This documentation makes it faster and easier for other animators to understand your setup, and it's a good memory-jogger for you, too. If there are any special quirks in the setup, like extra controls or odd hierarchies, write that up, too. The career you save may be your own!

Document The Default Scene

Write up the lights, positions, and views for the default scene you just set up. Include notes on joint ranges, bones, parametric deformation controls, and morph target libraries. You should write down anything that isn't obvious from just looking at the setup. When in doubt, write it up. Others may not think something is obvious, while you've been staring at it so long it's engraved on your retina.

You should now be able to set up and document a default character scene that is faster and easier for an animator to use. Many of these setup tips apply as well to sets, especially complex ones with moving parts or lots of materials.

Moving On

If you've completed each project in this chapter, you have set up the necessary default scenes for the animation projects in Chapter 14. You can either jump ahead to Chapter 14 for some animation practice or continue learning about setups by going to Chapter 12.

CONSTRAINTS

A humanoid character is too complex to efficiently animate by manually keyframing every control. This chapter shows how to link controls to one another using *constraints*. A constraint setup enables the animator to use a small fraction of the total controls to pose the character faster, more intuitively, and with more consistent results.

In the early days of computer graphics, objects could only be moved or rotated by themselves, without any reference to other objects. If, for example, you wanted to lift a character's hand, you would have to move the hand to where you wanted it to go, translate and rotate the forearm until the wrist connected with the hand, rotate the upper arm until the elbow connected with the forearm, somehow try to keep the torso attached to the shoulder, and so on.

Then, hierarchies were developed. When an object is in a hierarchy, it picks up the sum of all transformations (rotation, scale, and translation) that have occurred to its parent, the parent of its parent, and so on. This was a great improvement. But then you'd rotate and translate the hips (and maybe scale them), and do the same up the line to rotate the shoulder, the upper arm, the elbow, and then the hand. If you wanted the hand to be in a particular place, you would have to keep in mind that all the other transformations came before it. This is called *forward kinematics*, or FK.

Inverse kinematics changed that to a certain extent. Like nearly everything in computer graphics, inverse kinematics was developed for another purpose, and that purpose was almost always related to engineering. Whenever possible, NASA preferred to simulate things on a computer before actually trying to do something in space. If NASA had a crane arm on the Space Shuttle, and wanted to pluck a satellite out of its orbit and put it in the cargo bay, imagine trying to rotate the joints on that crane arm this way and that until finally it connected with the satellite. What was needed was a way to tell the crane arm to go precisely to the point in space where the satellite was, and backward calculate the joint rotations to get the end of the crane to the satellite. This backward calculation was called inverse kinematics (often abbreviated to IK), a catchy name that has stuck ever since. Of course, this has other implications as well for engineering in all fields. It isn't a big stretch to actually use IK for measuring torque or simulating how the suspension of a car works.

In many ways, our human musculoskeletal system resembles a very complex machine. IK is a pretty handy way of representing some of the goal-based movements that humans and other creatures (including those only in our imagination) might be inclined to perform. But for both forward and inverse kinematics, it's obvious that—where apparent solid objects are concerned, particularly those that are going to be manifested in physical objects in the real world—limits on movement must be placed on joints to reflect the realistic movements of real-world objects and their limitations. These limits on rotation and translation were the first and simplest type of *constraints*.

Constraints

Constraints are pretty easy to demonstrate on one's own body. Bend an arm at the elbow, and, at some point, it simply can't rotate anymore. The skin stops it, or the muscle, or an actual limitation on the design of the joint itself. In the Space Shuttle example discussed earlier, the crane arm is moving relative to the shuttle itself. Presumably, the travel of the shuttle would be precisely matched to that of the satellite, so it's just a matter of reaching out and grabbing the satellite. But that is simply too limited to represent the movement of everything. You can demonstrate how inadequate this representation is by placing your hand on a desk or table firmly, and moving your body toward the desk or away from it. Your hand stays on the desk and, for the most part, doesn't rotate, and the chain of your arm from your wrist to your shoulder rotates to accommodate it. We'll start with the hands instead of the feet, because it's easier for a person to look at an arm on his or her own body and analyze the movement than the legs.

If you've been following along, your hand is now in a space related to the desk, and it's relatively unaffected by the overall contortions of the rest of the body. Moreover, as the body is moved, watch your elbow. The bends at the elbow and shoulder are constantly being evaluated and recalculated. In this case, the position of the hand is constrained to the desk, as is the orientation of the hand. (While it could be said that the rotation of the hand is being constrained, and in a world that always yielded to dictionary definitions it would be true, the term *orientation* is used because rotation was already co-opted to define the local rotational limits of objects.) A way was needed to represent this relationship of the desk to the hand. Various schemes that would act like nailing the hand to the desk were initially devised to handle the problem. But this specific solution doesn't address the problem of sliding the hand across the desk or any of the more general problems encountered by extremities.

But suppose the hand could be fastened to an object outside the body's hierarchy, and that object could be placed on the unmoving desk. The hand would stay attached to the object, yet it could be moved along the desk without interpenetrating and the body could contort in all sorts of ways, yet it would still appear that the hand was on the desk. The object that the hand is attached to would be positionally and orientationally constraining the movement of the hand. It would be, in effect, a remote control for the hand. This object, which is usually a null object or a bone, is referred to as a *constraint* (regardless of the other definitions and uses of the term constraint). A constraint object can be placed in its own hierarchy, and a constraint object can itself be constrained to other objects, including other constraints. When we refer to "*a constraint*" or "*the constraint*" in this chapter, it will be a reference to a *constraint object*, unless further described as a *positional constraint* or *orientation constraint*.

No Floating

One of the signatures of the motion of marionettes is the way they float. Everything overshoots a little bit or a lot, with nothing changing its rate of acceleration or deceleration abruptly, unless it hits an obstacle. This look might be fine if you're animating Diver Dan, but it identifies the work of a beginner in computer graphics. Avoiding the floaty, underwater ballet look requires experience and understanding of timing for animation. The long learning curve will be painfully steep, if your character setups do not allow you both to apply your timing, and to readily revise it.

You could see this in so many early CG films. Struggling with tools made for anybody but an animator, the aspiring filmmaker would pose the character and drop keys on every joint at once. Then he'd drop a key on the next pose 8, 12, 16, 24 frames later, and then the computer would "do all the poses between for free!" Characters that were supposed to be walking would be peddling invisible bicycles instead, while their feet rotated through the ground with even, unbroken timing, every part of the body moving to the next pose at the same unvarying tempo.

Characters were hard to pose in the first place, particularly if the animator used only the least common denominator of forward kinematics. Sure, starting with the hips and working out to extremities was fine for the first pose, but what about the next one? Think of all the poses you could have generated if you hadn't spent most of your time doing back flips, just to make sure nothing moved when you altered the position of the parent of a foot or a hand. Even when an animator stuck to a careful plan, and structured the animation from the torso on out, getting a sign-off at every step, it would be costly to incorporate new inspiration in the middle of a scene. If the animation needed revision, it needed redoing. Too often, a director, grateful that the feet touched the ground at all, approved scenes where the torso just floated through weightlessly.

At least it moved, so animation it must be!

Some who noticed it wasn't looking very good tried the motion capture end-run around animation. Worse yet, it became conventional wisdom that you couldn't learn how to animate using a computer, so big studios started giving shots only to animators who had proven chops with pencils or stop motion. In some shops, animators worked out the entire scene in pencil, reducing the job of computer animator nearly to one of data entry. Pencil animation is costly, especially when reduced to pre-production for computer animation.

Some of the higher end packages, notably Softimage and Alias, allowed for the efficient incorporation of constraints to drive IK skeletons. IK had been an improvement over FK, but still required one to drop a key on every joint in the skeleton at the same time. IK by itself did not make it much easier to avoid floatiness for the simple reason that it still required special effort to layer events with uneven timing. I might be moving my head at one rate, my hand at another, and be doing something entirely different with the rest of my body, such as pushing away from the desk on a rolling chair. To suggest something as simple as weight involves moving the center of mass of the body faster on the way down than on the way up, and at the right time. Delay that up and down motion of the hips a frame or two, in a simple revision that leaves the rest of the action untouched. You'll have given your character more weight, and you'll have used constraints to solve your float problem.

Constraints allow one to position something when and where you want it, in isolation from what the rest of the body is doing. If feet are constrained to a position on the floor, it is far easier to animate the appearance of weight shifting from one leg to the other merely by moving the hips. If I move my hand to my chin, I think only about what my hand is doing and where my chin is. I shouldn't have to work much harder in an animation package. I'll check on what my elbow is doing later, in a refinement pass, especially when I only need to deal with a small set of handles that allow me to finesse that hand motion clearly and intuitively.

One will never learn why and when to do this for computer generated character animation if it is prohibitively difficult to animate and revise your work to competitive standards. Wouldn't you rather learn from your mistakes in time to apply that hard-won knowledge to your scene? If you can't afford to change something that looks wrong, you'll have to pay the price of signing your name to it anyway. If the work you've done so far has kept you from working in places where properly crafted setups are created for you, then you'll have to learn how to do it for yourself. It's among the best investments you can make in yourself, and in your craft.

Positional Constraints

As previously described, a positional constraint constrains the position in space of another object. Our first example of how this works is a simple demonstration.

DIFFERENT (KEY)STROKES FOR DIFFERENT FOLKS

We'll be using Windows instructions, so when we use the term *right-click*, Power Mac users will have to use the key combination that brings up submenus from the various windowing environments. That should be the only difference in methodologies. If we instruct you to click on something, for Windows users it is assumed to be a left click, and, of course, the Power Mac users only have one button.

Set Up A Positional Constraint

This project shows you how to set up a basic positional constraint. This is an important building block for the more complex setups later in this chapter.

Animation:Master

1. In Animation:Master, create a new project, and open a modeling window. Import the Sphere High object from the Primitives directory. Throughout this project, please use only the Front view.

2. In the Project Workspace, click on the + beside the Sphere High name to open its hierarchy. Under the Sphere High name, you'll see a bone named *Bone1*. Rename it *Sphere*.

3. Click on the Bones button, or press F6 to put the modeling window into Bones mode. Using either the Add Bone button or the Add Bone hotkey (a), add a bone to the right of the sphere, as shown in Figure 12.1. The sphere and the new bone should be physically separated in an obvious way. If they aren't, move them so that they are.

4. The new bone probably has the default name. Change its name to *Translator*.

5. Add a new action. The default action name will be *Action1*. Double-click on the Action1 icon in the Project Workspace window to open a new Action window.

6. Press F8, or click on the Skeletal button to change the Action window to Skeletal mode.

7. Click on the center of the sphere. Keeping the cursor in the center of the sphere, right-click.

Simply right-clicking on the item you want to affect is adequate in simpler situations, but on more complex objects, it's a good idea to see what you've selected before you change anything. Selecting and then right-clicking is a good safety habit to develop.

8. Under the submenu New Constraint, select Translate To. You should now have an eyedropper cursor. Point the eyedropper at the base of the Translator bone that you created earlier, and click on it.

If everything was executed flawlessly, the sphere should have snapped to the position of Translator. Now, select Translator, and move it. The sphere should move with the bone. Now, rotate Translator. There should be no effect on the sphere. Translate Translator and the sphere should move with it. Move Translator, just to the right of center screen, as shown in Figure 12.2.

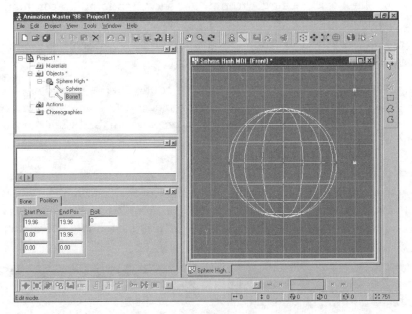

Figure 12.1 Sphere and new bone.

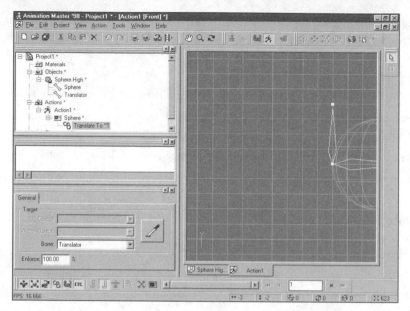

Figure 12.2 Sphere constrained to Translator bone.

If things did not proceed according to plan, then look in the workspace, under the Sphere bone, for the handcuff icon, which is the A:M icon for a constraint. The handcuff icon should have the label *Translate To Translator*. If it doesn't, it will display *Translate To*. This is simple to fix. Click on the Translate To. In the Properties box, there's a pull-down box. Simply click on the down arrow, and select Translator. The constraint should now properly jump to the position of the Translator bone.

9. Save the project with a new name. You will need to use it again for the following projects.

You have just constrained the Sphere model to the position of the Translator bone. This positional constraint enables you to move the Sphere model by moving the Translator, without affecting any other parameters of the Sphere. You can play with this by selecting the Translator and moving it around the Action window. The Sphere follows along, automatically.

3D Studio MAX 2

In addition to the default linking for hierarchy setup (covered in Chapter 11), 3D Studio MAX enables objects for IK to be bound to a positional constraint. This is known as *Binding*, and the object it is constrained to is called the *Follow Object*. This functionality is available in both 1.2 and 2.0.

NEW IK MODE

MAX 2.0 has a NewIK mode. In this mode, you can still use Follow Objects, but typically *End Effectors* are used. These End Effectors are essentially the same as Follow Objects but are a part of the bone system in MAX.

End Effectors and New IK are discussed later. For now, we will look at Binding objects for use with Interactive and Applied IK.

1. Load up the IK-Cons1.MAX file from the Chapter 12 directory on this book's CD-ROM. This scene has two dummy objects, with a sphere below one and a teapot below the other. The objects are not parented or linked in any way. You can try moving each one around independently. When you're done experimenting, use Undo, or reload the scene to get back to the initial state (see Figure 12.3).

2. Select the Green Sphere. Open the Hierarchy panel. Sphere01 should appear in the item list at the top of the panel. Click on the IK button in the top center of the Hierarchy panel to open the Inverse Kinematic options panel.

   The second subpanel is labeled *Object Parameters*. There are options for Bind Position and Bind Orientation. These sections enable you to select which axis to bind for both position and rotational constraint. They default to all axes but are disabled. In the middle of the panel is the Bind To Follow Object button.

3. Click on the Bind button under the Bind To Follow Object section. The button will turn green.

4. In the Front viewport, click and drag from the green sphere up onto the top-left dummy, the one directly above the green sphere. When the Bind cursor is over a valid bind object, it changes to a pushpin cursor. When the pushpin cursor is visible, release the mouse button. The dummy object you selected should briefly flash white.

   Back in the Hierarchy panel, note the name of the dummy object. *DummyGreen* now appears in the Bind To Follow Object section, indicating it has become the Follow Object. The box for Bind Position has been checked, as well (see Figure 12.4).

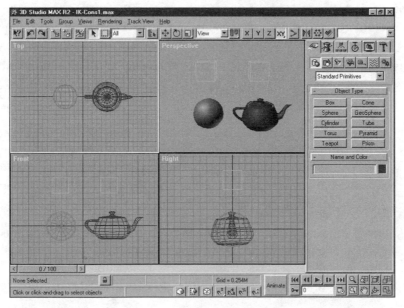

Figure 12.3   IK-Cons1.MAX initial state.

Figure 12.4 Bind Object settings for green sphere.

5. Click on the Bind button to turn off Bind mode.

   Now, we must enable the sphere to move or slide with IK.

6. The Sliding Joints subpanel is located near the bottom of the Hierarchy panel. Click on the Sliding Joints panel title to open it, if it is not already.

7. Click on Active for all three X-Axis, Y-Axis, and Z-Axis checkboxes to turn on sliding for the sphere.

8. On the top toolbar, click on the Select And Move button. Click on the left GreenDummy object, and move it.

   The sphere doesn't move! Don't worry. That's what is supposed to happen. The sphere's constraint isn't active yet, because Binding To Follow Objects won't work unless the IK toggle mode is active in MAX.

9. On the top toolbar, click on the Inverse Kinematics On/Off toggle to turn on IK mode.

10. Now, select and move the dummy object. The sphere moves along with the dummy, as if it is linked (see Figure 12.5).

You have just constrained the Sphere01 model to the position of the DummyGreen dummy. This positional constraint enables you to move Sphere01 by moving the dummy, without affecting any other parameters of Sphere01. You can play with this by selecting DummyGreen and moving it around in any viewport. The Sphere01 model follows along, automatically.

LightWave 3D 5: Lock & Key

One of LightWave's most egregious shortcomings is in the matter of constraints. LightWave does have a number of built-in constraint tools. IK, for example, works pretty well as a look-at constraint. However, LightWave lacks an adequate position or orientation constraint. Dynamic Reality's *Lock & Key* plug-in provides both position and orientation constraints to LightWave.

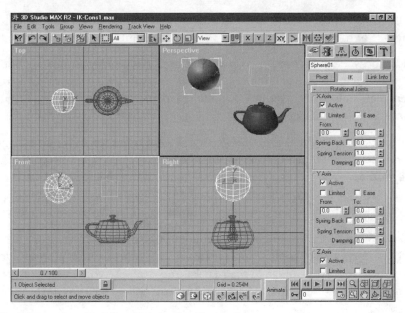

Figure 12.5   Green sphere positionally constrained to DummyGreen.

Constraints are referred to as Locks, and the constrained items as Keys. The set of a Lock with a Key is called a Combo. Once the Combo is set, the Key moves or rotates to match the Lock. This is easy enough to remember, if you think about it: a key belongs in a lock, and a key is a lot lighter and more moveable, so it makes sense that the Lock stays put and the Key is drawn to it.

Now for the tricky part. Lock & Key requires that a Key be the root of the hierarchy. This seems to require that the root of your character (generally near the center of gravity) would be constrained to the floor, or wherever the Lock was located. Huh? That doesn't seem very useful, does it? That's why Lock & Key also allows you to specify an Offset, a child somewhere in the character's hierarchy that acts as a substitute Key for the root. For example, if a character's root was between its hips, and a Combo assigned it as a Key to a Lock located on the floor, the character would end up hip-deep in the floor. However, if you set the character's foot as the Offset, the foot would be constrained to the Lock, and the character would be standing on the floor. Once you understand these basics, setting up a hierarchy to use Lock & Key is straightforward, relatively simple, and tolerant of errors.

First, you should plan how you want your character to interact with its environment. Do you need it to walk on floors or other surfaces? How about leaning against a wall, or resting its hands palm-down on a table? Sitting in a chair, maybe? For any surface that you want to constrain to another surface, you need to place Offsets. If the character is composed of Parented objects, you'll need to Parent nulls to the objects and position them on the surface you want to match the Lock. For a foot, you might set nulls at the bottom rear of the heel and under the ball. For a hand, the center of the palm generally works. If you want the character to sit properly, set an Offset...well, you get the idea. If the character is set up with Bones, you can set null

Bones at the appropriate places in the hierarchy, positioned just as you would a null object Offset. The size of the Bone or null doesn't matter, the Combo is calculated from their centers.

Second, add Locks to your scene. You can use one Lock and simply animate it, or (for example) place a null for each footstep or handhold, and not animate the Locks at all. The approach you take depends on how you prefer to work and the demands of the action. Stay flexible, and experiment with different approaches.

Third, use Lock & Key to set Combos between your character's Keys (or Offsets) and the scene's Locks. Each time you set a new Combo or animate a Lock, you will not see your results until you make a keyframe, move to another frame, then return to the keyframe. This step is necessary to trigger LightWave's *evaluation*, to retrieve the updated scene information from the Lock & Key plug-in. Don't forget to set the keyframe before the evaluation, or LightWave will forget your changes!

Once you've completed the Combo setup, you can animate your character using any other tools you like—forward kinematics, inverse kinematics, other Motion plug-ins, you name it—and the Keys will stay constrained to their Locks. You can pose your character doing anything from a simple walk to a hula dance, and the constrained feet will stay perfectly planted.

Orientation Constraints

Orientation constraints make one object assume the orientation of another. We have a simple project to add to the previous one to demonstrate this.

 Set Up An Orientation Constraint

12.2 As with Project 12.1, this basic orientation constraint setup is very simple, but it is a building block for more complex setups.

Animation:Master

You should still have the Project 12.1 file open. If you closed it, open it again.

1. Go to the Model window. Make sure that you are in Skeleton mode.

   It's important to be at the top of the model hierarchy (which should be Sphere High or Model1) for the next step. We want the new bone you are about to add to be equal in the hierarchy to the other two objects in the scene.

2. Press A, left-click, and drag to add a new bone to the left of the sphere, drawing upwards so the rotation pivot is on the bottom.

3. This new bone is named by default. Rename it *Orientor*, as shown in Figure 12.6.

4. Return to the Action window. Select Sphere.

5. Right-click to get the New Constraint submenu. Select Orient Like.

6. Under the Sphere, there should now be an Orient Like handcuff icon followed by a space in quotes. Click on Orient Like " ", go to the Properties window, and, next to Bone, arrow down to Orientor.

   Because you just turned on the rotation constraint, the Sphere should have immediately rotated to mimic the rotation of the Orientor bone, as shown in Figure 12.7.

7. Click on Orientor, and move the cursor to the top of the bone. The cursor will change to the rotation icon. Click and drag the cursor to rotate Orientor. The sphere rotates with it. Move Orientor, and the sphere does nothing. But whenever Orientor is rotated, Sphere will mimic Orientor's rotational orientation.

This is such a simple setup, we need to make it a little more challenging.

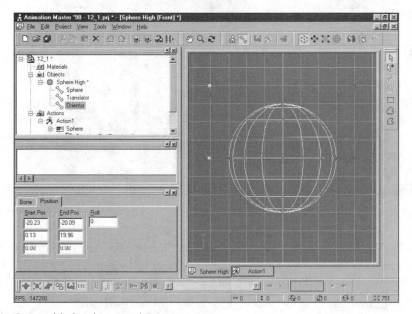

Figure 12.6 Bone added and renamed Orientor.

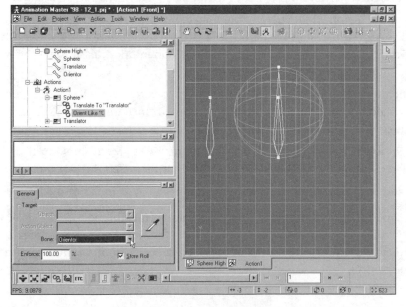

Figure 12.7 Sphere rotationally constrained to Orientor bone.

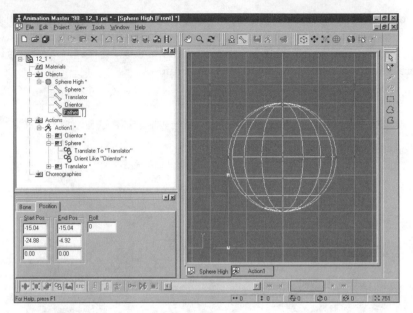

Figure 12.8 Father bone added to Model window and renamed.

8. Go back to the Model window. Select the Sphere High or Model1 object, make certain that you're in Bones Editing mode, and draw yet another Bone, perhaps 1/4 screen from Orientor. Rename it *Father*, as in Figure 12.8.

9. In the Project window, select the Orientor bone in the Objects hierarchy, and drag-and-drop it on top of the Father bone. Orientor should now be a child of Father within the Objects hierarchy, located beneath it and indented, with a connecting dotted line.

10. Return to the Action window. Note that Sphere has rotated a bit. Ignore that for now. Instead, select Father, and rotate it. Note two things: Orientor is swinging around broadly, and Sphere is rotating with Orientor's orientation, as if Orientor was still rotating on its own axis (see Figure 12.9).

11. To further demonstrate the power of orientation constraints, we'll return to the Model window. Add another bone that starts well below Translator and ends slightly below Translator's pivot. Rename it *Mom*.

12. In the Project window, drag-and-drop Translator under Mom, making it a child of Mom. Drag Mom to the top of the model hierarchy, if it isn't already there.

13. Return to the Action window. Select Mom, and rotate it as in Figure 12.10.

The sphere should swing from side to side, positionally constrained to Translator, while it remains rotationally constrained to the orientation of Orientor. Again, these constraints enable you to completely separate one means of moving an object from another, giving you much more flexible control.

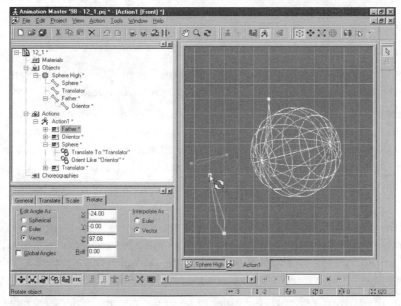

Figure 12.9   Rotating Father moves Orientor, and Sphere rotates to match.

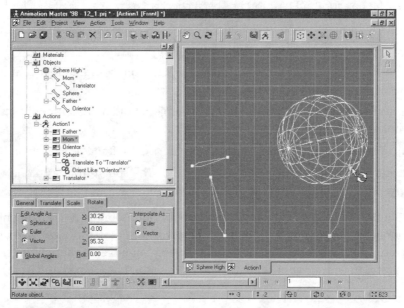

Figure 12.10   Rotating Mom moves Translator, and Sphere moves while remaining constrained to Orientor rotation.

3D Studio MAX 2

Just like Binding To Follow Objects for positional constraints, objects can have rotational bindings, as well. This project is very similar to the preceding MAX project, but it's aimed at rotational rather than positional constraint setup.

1. Load up the IK-Cons1.MAX file, the same one you used for the positional constraint project.

2. Select the Blue Teapot.

3. Open the Hierarchy panel on the right side of the screen. Click on the IK button in the top center of that panel to open the inverse kinematic options.

   The second subpanel is labeled *Object Parameters*. There are options for Bind Position and Bind Orientation. These sections enable you to select which axis to bind for both position and rotational constraint. They default to all axes but are disabled. In the middle of the panel is the Bind To Follow Object button.

4. Press the Bind button under the Bind To Follow Object section. The button will turn green.

5. In the Front viewport, click-and-drag from the blue teapot up onto the top-right dummy, the one directly above the blue teapot. When the Bind cursor is over a valid bind object, it changes to a pushpin cursor. When the pushpin cursor is visible, release the mouse button. The dummy object you selected should briefly flash white.

6. Back in the Hierarchy panel, note the name of the dummy object. *DummyBlue* now appears in the Bind To Follow Object section, indicating it has become the Follow Object. The box for Bind Position has been checked, as well.

7. Click on the Bind button to turn it off.

8. Uncheck Bind Position, and check Bind Orientation.

9. From the top toolbar, choose Select And Rotate. Click on the right BlueDummy object, and rotate it.

   The sphere doesn't rotate. As with the earlier project, binding to follow objects doesn't work unless the IK toggle mode is active in MAX.

10. On the top toolbar, click on the Inverse Kinematics On/Off toggle to turn on IK mode.

11. Select and rotate the DummyBlue object again. The sphere rotates along with the dummy, precisely mimicking the dummy's rotation.

Note that Binding To Follow Objects is very different from normally linking an object in MAX. With positional bindings, you can limit the distance an object will move, whereas, with normal linking, you cannot. With orientation, bindings objects can have rotational limits, as well. This puts more power in your hands to create a character setup that is faster and easier to animate.

LightWave 3D 5: Lock & Key

LightWave, as mentioned in the preceding Position Constraints project, lacks an adequate orientation constraint. Dynamic Reality's *Lock & Key* plug-in adds orientation constraints to LightWave. Constraints are referred to as Locks, and the constrained items as Keys. The set of a Lock with a Key is called a Combo. To create an orientation constraint, check the Lock Rotation box in the Combo Editor. Once the Combo is set, the Key rotates to match the Lock.

1. Plan how you want your character to interact with its environment. Place Offsets. Parent nulls to the character's objects and position them on the surface you want to match the Lock. Set null Bones at the appropriate places in the character's Bone hierarchy, positioned just as you would a null object Offset.

2. Add Locks to your scene.

3. Use Lock & Key to set Combos between your character's Keys (or Offsets) and the scene's Locks. Check the Lock Rotation box in the Combo Editor to create an Orientation Constraint. Set a keyframe, move to another frame, then return to the keyframe to trigger LightWave's *evaluation*, retrieving the updated scene information from the Lock & Key plug-in.

A Quick Break

If you're wondering where all this is leading, we'll be using most of these constraint types in the Swing-arm Lamp project, and every one of them in the Arm projects. Please hang in there.

Aim Constraints

Aim constraints do exactly what it sounds like they do—they aim one object (or bone, null, camera, or other item) at another object (or whatever). This enables you to precisely match the rotation of one item to the motion of another.

Set Up An Aim Constraint

PROJECT 12.3

The aim constraint is a very useful and powerful function, and you will probably find yourself using it several times within even the simplest character setup. As with rotational and positional constraints, the aim constraint described in the following project is a standard building block for the more complex setups later in this chapter.

Animation:Master

By now, you know the drill, and it's back to the...

1. Model window. Add a new bone, well above the bone we named Father. Rename it *Aimee*.

2. Drag Aimee to the top of the hierarchy so it isn't a child of any other bone, as shown in Figure 12.11.

3. Go to the Action window. Select Father, right-click to add a New Constraint, and this time pick Aim At. The eyedropper cursor will appear, ready for you to select the item that Father is supposed to aim at.

4. Click the eyedropper cursor on Aimee, or pick Aimee from the Aim At " " Properties window. Father immediately rotates to point at Aimee.

5. Now, move Aimee around. Father points at Aimee, Orientor swings around with Father, and the Sphere rotates. You can select Mom and aim it at Aimee, too.

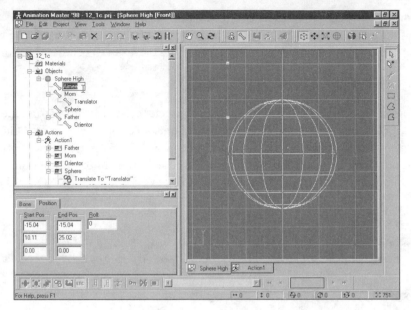

Figure 12.11 Aimee bone added to top of the Sphere hierarchy.

With just one active control—the Aimee bone—you can manipulate every other bone and model in the scene. Play with Aimee a little, and see what complex interactions you have created.

If you want to delete a constraint, simply go to the Project window, click on the handcuff icon of the constraint that you want to delete, and press the Delete key.

3D Studio MAX 2

Every object in MAX has a controller type. Controllers are used to animate objects to move, rotate, or scale, as well as controlling changes to other variables, such as color. By default, most objects created in MAX have a Bezier-position controller, a TCB-rotation controller, and a Bezier-scale controller. These three controllers are part of the generic Transform type controller, called the *Transform: Position/Rotation/Scale*.

MAX provides another type of transform controller known as a *Look-At Controller*. This controller replaces the previously listed types and makes an object orient itself so it always points at the designated target. The local Z axis of the object points towards the target by default, although you can change that to a different axis, if you like.

The goal of this project is to set up a Look At controlled object, MAX's term for an aim constraint. This first set of steps is for MAX 2.0, immediately following are some additional steps for MAX 1.2.

1. Load up LookAt0.MAX. This scene consists of a dummy object, Dummy01, and a green rectangular box, Box01. We will constrain the green box to aim at the dummy object.

2. Select the green box.

3. By default, the box has the standard Position/Rotation/Scale controller. To change this, open the Motion panel at the right of the MAX screen.

4. The first subpanel (which is closed by default) is the Assign Controller panel. Click on the Assign Controller header bar to expand the panel if it is not open.

5. You will see a hierarchical list containing the controllers mentioned earlier. Click on the top Transform: Position/Rotation/Scale controller.

6. Just above the controller list is the Assign Controller button, with an icon of a green triangle and a small black arrow. The Assign Controller button becomes active (un-grayed) when you select a controller from the hierarchy. Click on the Assign Controller button. This brings up the Assign Transform Controller dialog box, as in Figure 12.12.

7. From the list, choose Look At, then click on the OK button to close the dialog.

   The Box01 object immediately changes its orientation. The list on the Assign Controller panel now shows the Look At controller with its sub-controllers. Note that this has a Bezier position and Scale controller as before, but the Rotation controller has changed type, from a TCB to a Roll Angle. There is now also a Look At Parameters subpanel, immediately under the Assign Controller subpanel.

8. Expand the Look At Parameters subpanel, if necessary. Click on the Pick Target button. It turns green while waiting for you to pick the target object.

9. In the Right viewport, click on the dummy object. After you click on the dummy, the Pick Target button un-highlights, and the name of the dummy object appears in the Look At Target space in the subpanel (see Figure 12.13).

10. Choose the Select And Move tool from the top toolbar. Try moving the dummy object. Note that the Box01 object continually reorients itself so that it looks at the dummy. You can also move the Box01 object, and it will continue to orient itself to look at the dummy.

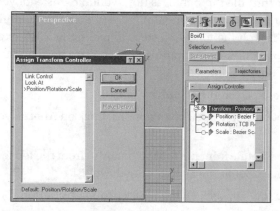

Figure 12.12 Assign Transform Controller dialog and Assign Controller Motion subpanel.

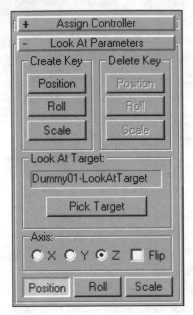

Figure 12.13 Assign Transform Controller dialog and Assign Controller Motion subpanel.

You may have noted that Box01 seems to be aiming backwards. The box appears to be pointing away from the dummy object, rather than at it. This is because the Look At controller works by making the positive local Z axis face away from the target. If this causes you any trouble, you can check the Flip box in the Look-At Parameters subpanel of the Motion panel. This will make the object look down the positive Z Axis instead of the negative Z Axis, and your Look At constraints will actually look at their targets.

3D Studio MAX 1.2

If you are using MAX 1.2, the procedures for setting up an aim constraint are exactly the same as for MAX 2, except that the flip option is not available. Instead, you can make the Box01 object look at the target, using any orientation you want, by rotating the aim-constrained object's axes. Work through the following steps to realign Box01's axes. If you use MAX 2.0, you may also wish to try this, as it explains how you can easily adjust the mesh of an aim-constrained object to orient a different way.

1. Select the green box. Open the Hierarchy panel.

2. Click on the Pivot button to open pivot options. Click on Affect Pivot Only. The button turns on.

3. Choose Select And Rotate from the top toolbar. Also from the top toolbar, choose Local from the Reference Coordinate System drop-down list.

4. Still from the top toolbar, click on the Restrict To Y Axis button.

5. In the Top viewport, rotate the box 180 degrees, until it faces the dummy. You may want to turn on the Angle Snap Toggle to help you get the precise angle.

Note that the pivot stays oriented in the same direction (because it's controlled by the Look At controller), but the mesh rotates. This is the opposite of what Affect Pivot Only usually seems to do.

6. Turn off the Affect Pivot Only button.

7. Choose Select And Move, and try moving the dummy and box one at a time. The box now orients itself down its length, pretty much the result of the preceding MAX 2 procedure.

Roll Constraints

This constraint type controls the rotation of a bone around the long axis, or the axis that lines up from the pivot to the end effector of the bone. In Softimage, this is called the *Up Vector Constraint*. In A:M, it's called *Aim Roll At*.

A note to Softimage users: Use the Up Vector Constraint to determine the plane in which a 2D IK chain will rotate. If you create a simple two bone bending knee joint, having toggled Skeleton: Automatic Up Vector Cns, a null will appear parented to the chain root. In the schematic window, in motion mode, you will see a yellow line that indicates a relationship to the first joint. The triangle defined by the chain root, the end effector, and the Up Vector constraint is the plane in which the first and second joint will bend. Rotating the chain root will rotate the Up Vector, and acts the same as would a knee rotated by the hip. If the end effector and the Up Vector Constraint are in the wrong position relative to each other, the joint will rotate on the same plane, but flip 180 degrees. This is not a problem that's hard to avoid, just one to be aware of in advance.

Something else to watch out for is the danger of assigning an envelope to an IK chain that contains an Up Vector Constraint as a child of the chain root. Like any other null object that is part of a hierarchy that has had an envelope assigned to it, that null will deform the object as it moves. If you haven't assigned an envelope to a hierarchy composed exclusively of null objects in Softimage yet, you're missing the fun. Try a flour sack exercise or a wildly deforming bouncing ball that way, and come back for the rest of this paragraph. You should be sure to cut the Up Vector Constraint from the chain root, and then parent it to the null object to which the chain root is position constrained. It will still rotate the plane on which the joint bends, but since it is no longer part of the hierarchy, it will not act like the depth charge for which nulls can so handily be used.

In creating a structure of constraints, outside and apart from the IK chain hierarchy, you have added a meta-level to the degree of control you can have over your character. You can use forward kinematics, or inverse kinematics, or neither, as you choose. You need never drop a key on the bones, using them more as a way to distribute the weighting of vertices and other aspects of skin deformations. You can more easily control the position and rotation of the joints with constraints alone. Unshackled by the physical proximity of bones that typically dictate parenting, you can arrange the relative position of these constraints in a heirarchy in any way convenient to you. A character's shoulder position constraints can be parented to a null that lets you shrug them both at the same time, no matter what you told the head, hips, and hands to do with their constraints. All of those are siblings too. Make those constraints follow a path, if you'd like to make your character's fingers spell out a word in midair without spending weeks on the project.

PROJECT 12.4 Set Up A Roll Constraint

The roll constraint is most often applied to keep parts of a character from twisting or rolling uncontrollably as they track an aim constraint. The roll constraint is not usually an animation control by itself. It is more like a safety limit on other constraints. As with preceding constraints, the roll constraint described in the following project is another standard building block you will use in the more complex setups later in this chapter.

Animation:Master

1. Reload or reopen the scene you saved from the preceding A:M project.

2. Add another new bone at the top of the hierarchy, and name it *Roller*. It doesn't matter where you place this bone, but I suggest you put it somewhere out of the way, separate from the six bones already in the scene. Make sure Roller is equal with all of the other top bones in this hierarchy and not a child of anything other than the main model.

3. Go to the Action window. Right-click on Father, choose New Constraint|Aim Roll At, and direct the new constraint at Roller.

4. This setup is a little trickier than the others, and you'll need a slightly different viewpoint. You need to rotate the scene a little (in the Action editor), say about 45 degrees. Press T for Turn, or click on the Turn button in the top toolbar, then drag in the Action window to rotate the view.

5. Select Roller, and move it a bit off the plane now occupied by nearly everything else in our simple demo scene, as in Figure 12.14.

6. Return to the Front view. If you move Roller around the scene, you'll note Father rotates on its axis to follow Stroller, Orientor rotates like a moon with Father, and, of course, Sphere picks up Orientor's rotational orientation.

ANIMATION:MASTER OFFSETS

A:M has a feature in its IK/Constraint system that is unique. After initiating your constraints, you may get translations and rotations that you don't want. A:M allows you to select the object and rotate it and translate it, yet still maintain an allegiance to the constraints. The channels it creates when you do this are called *Offsets*. Offsets can be animated, which can save you the trouble of adding additional bones or null objects to compensate for unwanted rotations or translations caused by the implementation of constraints. In short, Offsets enable you to work around a setup problem without rebuilding or starting over.

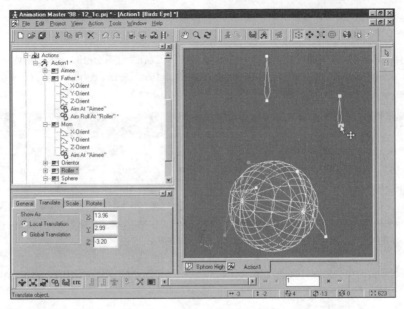

Figure 12.14   Moving Roller off-plane from the other items in the scene.

3D Studio MAX 2

There is no roll constraint equivalent in MAX. Kinetix should add roll constraints as soon as possible, since this is a very useful function for character animation.

(DON'T) DO THE TWIST

Gimbal lock is a common problem for CGI software. If the target of an aim constraint passes directly over the axis of the constrained object, that object will abruptly roll 180 degrees.

LookAt3.MAX (or LookAt3.AVI) shows an example of gimbal lock. The blue box is aim constrained to the dummy object. The small green box is parented to the main box to show the orientation more clearly. As you play back the animation, the dummy object orbits the blue box, while the blue box aims at the dummy. However, when the dummy passes directly above or below the box, the box rolls 180 degrees in a gimbal lock.

In many cases, this is a bad thing. Imagine if that box was a bone controlling how part of a mesh deformed. When it rolled, the mesh would suddenly twist and contort at that point. If your software can produce gimbal lock, you need to find a reliable technique to avoid or prevent it.

The only solution to gimbal lock if you use MAX's Look At controller is to manually roll the object yourself, creating another animation variable that you'll have to keep track of. This creates more work for the animator, and the goal of a good setup is to minimize work for the animator.

It's possible to use MAX 2's New IK system to create Look-At functionality with an Up-Vector constraint, mimicking most of a roll constraint's functions. This requires a special NewIK controller type, which can only be applied to the built-in MAX bones.

NEW IK WITH BONES PRO

Bones Pro can use any item as a bone. You can also parent any simple block object to the MAX bones. Whenever you use the New IK system with BonesPro, you basically end up with a two-layer hierarchy. The first layer is the MAX bones with the New IK. On top of that are custom blocks you parent to each piece. You don't actually move or animate the blocks, they inherit the animation from the IK bones. You use these blocks with BonesPro to deform the mesh.

This project demonstrates one method for creating bones with roll constraints using the New IK.

1. Load up the IKLookAt1.MAX file. This scene consists of three boxes and three dummy objects. Take a moment to select each one and view their names.

   The red box is a parent object. This object can move around and will provide a way to move the Look At box when we're done. The blue box is the object that will actually look at the target dummy. The green box is just a marker on the blue box, so we can see its orientation more clearly.

   The small dummy at the end of the blue box is used to extend the hierarchy of the bones. The Look At IK bones we make need to know where the end of the blue box is. The large dummy at the end will be the Target object. The small dummy on top will be the Up Vector target. To save you time, I've parented the Up-Vector dummy to the Tip dummy, then to the blue box, and finally to the red box for you. The green box and target dummy should be unlinked from anything else.

2. The first thing we will do is create the NewIK bone system. Open the Create panel.

3. Click on the System button to open the Systems subpanel. Under the Object-Type subpanel, click on the Bones button. Now, you're ready to create MAX bones.

   In many cases, you can click-and-drag to create bones. However, MAX 2.0 also enables you to convert preexisting hierarchies to the internal bone system. It will automatically create the bones for you and parent each piece of your original hierarchy to the proper bone. This is usually easier to do, because it is easier to align boxes instead of the bone objects. We already have our dummies and boxes linked, so we'll use this conversion method, called *AutoBoning*.

4. Click on the Pick Root button. The button highlights, ready for you to click on the root of the hierarchy. The Assign To Root checkbox should be off, all other checkboxes should be on, as in Figure 12.15.

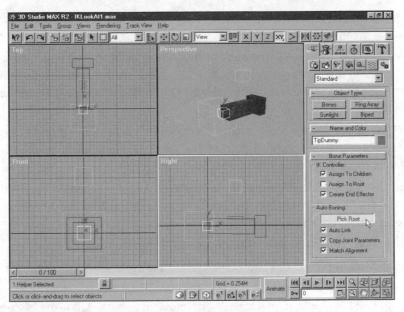

Figure 12.15   IKLookAt1.MAX scene, ready to AutoBone object hierarchy.

5. In the Right viewport, click on the red box, which is the root of our hierarchy. MAX automatically creates a series of bones. They start from the red box, go through the end, then up to the UpVector Dummy(see Figure 12.16).

6. Now, we'll change some links. From the top toolbar, choose Select And Link mode.

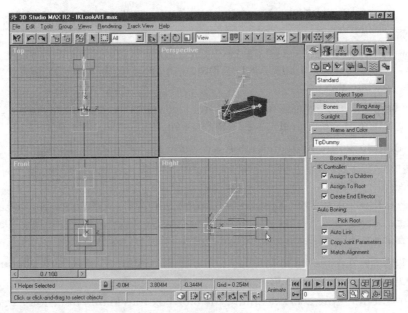

Figure 12.16   IKLookAt1.MAX after Auto-Boning object hierarchy.

7. Click on the green box, and drag the mouse over onto the blue box to parent it. This makes the green box a marker on the blue, so we can see its orientation more clearly.

8. Click on Bone01. This is the first bone at the right edge of the red box, and it appears as just a diamond. Don't accidentally select bone02, which actually runs through the red box. Drag from bone one to the red box. This makes the red box the parent of our hierarchy.

9. Select UpDummy. On the toolbar, click on the Unlink Selection button to un-parent it from the bone system. For safety, turn off the Select And Link mode by choosing Select And Move mode from the toolbar.

    We will now set up our constraints for our IK system. As noted earlier, in the NewIKsystem this is done with End Effectors instead of Binding To Follow Objects. By default, an End Effector is created at the end of the chain.

10. Select Bone03. This is the bone that runs though the blue box.

11. Open the Motion panel. This shows the options for the IK Controller type for Bone03.

    Towards the bottom of the panel are the options for End Effectors. You have options to create an End Effector that affects position, rotation, or both. These are essentially the same as the Bind constraints described earlier. There is also a button to link and un-link the Effector from another object. You can use these options to easily move another object within the hierarchy, instead of having to manually select and move the End Effectors themselves.

12. Click on the Position:Create button. This creates a position constraint. You probably can't see it, but this creates a blue cross that appears at the end of the bone.

13. Click on the Link button. The button highlights, waiting for you to select the End Effector's parent.

14. In the Right viewport, click on *LookAtDummy*. The Link button turns off as the dummy object blinks briefly. The label LookAtDummy appears in the End Effector Parent space of the End Effectors panel.

15. Select Bone04. This is the bone that goes from the end of the TipDummy to the UpVector Dummy. The Motion panel should still be open.

    Note that the Position:Create button is already grayed-out. By default, End Effectors are made for the end of the hierarchy. We will now link this End Effector to the UpVector Dummy.

16. Click on the Link button. Again, the button highlights, waiting for you to select the End Effector's parent. Select UpDummy to link the End Effector to it. The label *UpDummy* appears in the End Effector Parent space of the End Effectors panel.

    As a test, try moving the UpDummy or the LookAtDummy. Make sure you undo any movements before you continue.

    When you move the LookAtDummy, the blue box tries to aim at it. You can also see the End Effector (the blue crosshair) pull away from the bone with the LookAtDummy, as shown in Figure 12.17. Moving the UpDummy causes the blue box to roll and thrash in weird, unpredictable ways.

The next step is to set up some constraints, to make Bone02 aim at the LookAtDummy and make Bone03 roll towards the UpDummy.

17. Select Bone02. This is the bone that runs through the red box.

18. Open the Hierarchy panel, then click on the IK button to bring up the IK options subpanel.

The last subpanel in the Hierarchy panel is the Rotational Joints subpanel. This allows you turn IK object rotation on and off, and set limits and options for IK object rotation. By default, all axes are enabled for rotation.

19. Uncheck the Z-Axis Active box.

20. Select Bone 03. This is the bone that runs through the blue box.

The same Hierarchy And Rotational Joints panel should still be open. By default, all axes are active for this bone.

21. Uncheck the X-Axis and Y-Axis Active buttons. Bone03 will only be allowed to Roll, that is, rotate around its Z axis.

Next, we need to parent the blue box to Bone03. By default, it is parented to Bone02.

22. Select the blue box. Choose Select And Link from the top toolbar. Drag from the blue box to Bone03 to link it. If you find it difficult to select Bone03, you can also use the Select By Name button from the toolbar, select Bone03 by name, then click on the Link button.

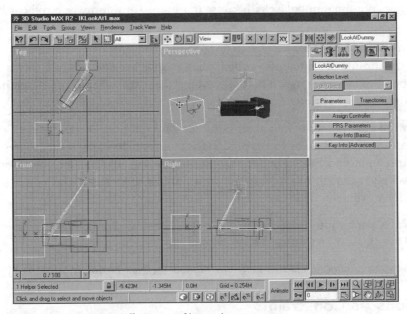

Figure 12.17 Moving LookAtDummy affects rest of hierarchy.

Test the setup so far. Choose Select And Move, and try moving the UpDummy, the LookAtDummy, and the RedBox. Try selecting UpDummy in the Top viewport, and moving it in a wide orbit around the blue box. Note how the blue box rolls so the green marker box always aims at UpDummy. Things are somewhat working—we just need to tell the IK system to use that End Effector with less pull, so it only uses it for the roll.

Make sure you undo any moves before continuing.

23. Select Bone04. This is the bone that goes from the TipDummy to the UpDummy. Open the Hierarchy panel if it's not yet open.

    Near the top of the panel is the Object Parameters subpanel. This has options for binding to follow objects. These options also affect End Effectors with the New IK system. Under the Position section, there is a Weight entry. It defaults to 1. By adjusting the value, you can control the amount of pull each End Effector has. A lower number has lower pull, while a higher value has higher pull.

24. Change the position Weight to 0.1. Now, try moving the UpDummy, LookAtDummy, and RedBox. You should have a setup that behaves like IKLookAt2.MAX.

It is best if you keep UpDummy close to Bone04 and LookAtDummy, because UpDummy still affects the blue box in ways besides roll. You might even want to parent the UpDummy to the LookAtDummy, because this would allow you to simply move and rotate the LookAtDummy to get the desired rotation of the blue box.

You can also compare the animation in IKLookAt3.MAX. This is similar to the animation back in LookAt3.MAX where the dummy moves around the box. Note that in the IK version, the blue box does not flip (gimbal lock), because it uses the UpDummy as a roll constraint.

Rotation Constraints

Rotation constraints are often also called *limits* or *spherical limits*. While this is useful when using FK bone/joint hierarchies, it becomes even more useful when using IK methods, because the joint angles are calculated for you.

Most software provides some way to set limits for joint rotation. TrueSpace even allows you to set the tension of a joint, so as you approach the rotational limit the joint progressively resists. This feature can be very helpful in getting IK to respond intuitively. A tensioned joint can be set up to behave very much like a real one, with muscles, ligaments, and bones interacting to constrain its movement.

In LightWave, joint limits are set in the IK Options panel, and are absolute values. Refer to the head and eye IK setup in Chapter 11 for details.

Please refer to the *Animation:Master Reference Manual* for the tutorial on Spherical Limits in A:M.

Expressions As Constraints

Expressions can horrify artists, once they learn that the full phrase is "mathematical expressions." Fear not, you can put down that voodoo crucifix. Even the irrationally math-phobic can readily learn to take advantage of expressions to make the process of animation less painful and far more efficient. You'll use expressions for everything from setting the way a bicep should bulge whenever its elbow bends, to creating elegant widgets for controlling multiple events with one mouse click. Proper use of expressions will simplify and maximize your control of the figure to be animated.

There will always be a tradeoff between macro and micro control of a character. Expressions are handy for getting your character close to where you want it in a rough first pass, so that a few choices put the things you care about into place. You can iteratively refine your poses and timing with secondary modifiers. It's easy to go overboard, with so many actions triggered by your input that you have no way to prevent the occurrence of automatic events. Setting up a character so that its hips will always remain at the centerpoint of the two feet is fine until you need the hips to be somewhere else. When it's finger-twiddling time, I'll do it expressively rather than crack one explicitly named knuckle at a time, and get on with my life.

For example, say you need to create a lashing cat's tail. Supposing there are more segments than you want to keep track of individually, you can use expressions in a variety of ways that each simplify and magnify your control over that tail while you're animating.

Typically, you'll use some or all of a null object's Scale, Rotation, and Translation channels to "remotely control" the affected element, in this case, the segments of the cat's tail. One approach is to take the (animator's) input value of one of the null's channels, such as its X rotation value, and use that to drive the X rotation of the root segment of the cat's tail. As you rotate the null in X, the cat's tail will simultaneously rotate in X, although the tail will be stiff as a board. Copy and apply that expression to each subsequent tail segment. When you rotate the null, every segment of the cat's tail will rotate simultaneously on its X axis, curling up rapidly. Use the null's other Y and Z rotation channels the same way, and you'll have quite a thrashable tail.

There are many ways to modify this basic setup for maximum simplicity and versatility. Add a modifier to each expression using your null's X Scale value to multiply the null's X Rotation value. While the X scale value is 1.0, the rotation value will not change. When less than 1.0, each segment will rotate. I've included a simple example file in Softimage 3.7 including some additional ideas in that regard, using all nine channels of the null object to control the cat tail.

An Elementary Overview

In the computer environment, we generally structure a skeleton hierarchically from the hips to the extremities. The feet and hands inherit any motion of the hips, unless one uses some method of constraining their position, outside of the skeleton structure, so that they stay where placed no matter where we move other parts of the body.

A stop-motion animator can secure feet or hands where they need to stay while adjusting the spine for that perfect line of action. It's as simple and elegant a solution as pushing the hips down while the floor prevents the feet from moving. You could say the feet were constrained by the floor. With pencils, an animator can retrace the position of the feet until choosing to move them. When altering the placement of the hips to improve a given pose, the pencil animator never has the computer animator's problem of the rest of the character spinning whichever way the hips do. What we need is a way of working that will allow us to capitalize on the freedom from real-world physics, and from the necessity of redrawing the entire character for each new frame, without giving ourselves even thornier problems. If we're busy worrying about how to plant a character's feet on the ground, it will be impossible to focus sufficiently on a performance.

You've seen the kinds of motion that initially led many of the earlier generations of animators to dismiss the computer as a serious medium for quality work. Stiff, mechanical movement was the norm. Characters floated, lacking the semblance of weight. The torso would glide in a straight line while the feet pedaled an imaginary unicycle through the ground plane. Hips, heads, hands, and feet bobbed about in strange little multiply-dependent epicycles, inheriting the motion of their parents rather than fluidly tracing out the intentional arc of any actual hand or foot. If, through some miracle of patience and perseverance, the feet successfully maintained contact with the ground without skating, you could forget about readjusting the hips without having to discard hours of work. Naturally, you'd moved the hips up and down, but the notion of experimentation with when and how was out of the question. When that was the best that a good animator was expected to be able to do, no wonder motion capture seemed like a good idea.

To animate without using constraints typically yields such unsatisfactory results that there is little chance of achieving a good walk without doing nearly all the work in pencil beforehand and essentially rotoscoping. That approach begs the question of animating in the computer at all; it reduces the task to a dry keyboard exercise after the pencil work is complete. Dropping a keyframe on every bone at every frame makes the subsequent task of revising the animation non-trivial, to say the least. By then, the opportunity to effectively exploit iterative refinement in the computer environment is lost.

Some animators, after tiring of covering the monitor with grease pencils and holding their heads just so while adjusting a pose to match a maze of smudges on the screen, try animating simple boxes as position holders for feet. After reposing the hips, they struggle to match the foot placement to its shoebox for each frame. This approach yields moonwalking, jittery feet, the tendency to avoid challenging animation problems by framing the feet out of the shot entirely; even designing floating characters with no feet. While one can move a character without having set it up with constraints, it's nearly impossible to effectively animate that way.

Time spent chasing undesirable artifacts is time better spent animating.

It's easy to animate the foot's desired position independently of the foot's hierarchical relationship to the skeleton, by explicitly translating a positional constraint rather than the foot itself. It is a far more effective use of resources to let the computer map the constraint's position onto that of the foot so that it stays where you want it to, while you adjust other parts of the pose.

Once you achieve fluency with constraint-based character setups, the problems that stifled your creativity before will no longer be an issue at all. Animating a walk will be easy to experiment with and push further, even on tight deadlines. When you can work out a quick first pass on the feet and hips, the torso, head, and hands, you can play back your rough approximation while your original plan is still fresh in your mind. You can see to what extent moving the hips from side to side was a good idea, and readily change it if it wasn't.

Setting up a constraint structure allows you to move parts of the body without altering the rest of the pose. A dancer routinely uses what's called isolation to move a shoulder or hips without affecting the position of other parts of the body. Without constraints, you wouldn't dare to try such a thing after you'd already posed the feet.

Without modifying any other part of your animation, you can change the personality of a character by selecting the part of the body with which your character leads when he walks. Does he puff out his chest like a manly man or does he lead with his pelvis canted forward like some deviant hipster? What if he rounds his shoulders forward, dragging his arms with his chest caved in? If he's a heavy character, you can see the effect of moving his torso down for a few more frames although his legs have already begun to push his mass back up.

Subtle revisions can completely change a character from being a weightless floater to one whose mass is apparent entirely from the way he moves. When your director suggests that you change just one thing, you can readily and cheerily incorporate the suggestion without painfully introducing new artifacts. Even better, you won't need to offer some explanation about how prohibitively hard it would be to change it, so you'll have to try that the next time, if there is a next time. The process will be one of iterative discovery and refinement, rather than the desperate effort to complete something that you can even use at all.

These days, there is no compelling reason to do it the hard way. The little additional time it takes to properly organize a constraint structure, as a routine part of the procedure of setting up a character for animation, is nothing compared to the time you'll save while animating.

If you are using Alias or Softimage, or any equivalently fully-featured package to apply these principles, there should be little difficulty in transposing the ideas from the packages used in this chapter to describe them. I'm sure you'll come up with your own unique approach; that's what this medium is all about.

At this point, you should have an understanding of the basic constraint types and how to set them up. You are now ready to apply that knowledge to complete character setups.

Elementary Projects Using Different Constraints

The following projects show you where, how, and why to apply constraints to a swing-arm lamp and to the legs, arms, and other appendages of a humanoid character.

Swing-arm Lamp Setup

This is a basic self-contained project designed to demonstrate strategies for constraining extremities similar to the arms and legs. There are only two main components to this lamp: the shade and the base. The arm of the swing-arm lamp is an IK skeletal structure, which you will set up in this project and is simplified from the normal dual-parallel leveling structure found in lamps patterned after the Luxo brand.

Setting Up The Swing-arm Lamp

PROJECT 12.5

The goal of this project is to build a lamp that can be animated as a character. The same model can be constrained different ways, as we will explore.

Animation:Master

1. In the Project menu, open the lamp-and-shade-only.prj project file from the Chapter 12 directory on this book's CD-ROM. You will see objects representing the base and shade of the lamp, as shown in Figure 12.18.

   You may have noted that there are references in the hierarchy under lamp-and-shade-only with a box next to them labeled head, shade, bulb, and base. These are groups created during the modeling process, and they have been left in this example because it is through those groups that attributes like color and reflectivity are added to components within a model.

2. In the Project Workspace window, click on the + sign next to Objects to open the Objects hierarchy. Open lamp-and-shade-only, as shown in Figure 12.19.

3. Press F6, or click on the Bones button to enter Bones mode. Press A, or click on the Add Bones button to enter Add mode. Add five bones as pictured in Figure 12.20.

4. In the Project Workspace window, click on lamp-and-shade-only under Objects. Enter Add mode, and add a new bone in the same place that you added Bone5. Add another new bone, as pictured in Figure 12.21. Make certain your Project Workspace hierarchy looks just like the one pictured and that Bone6 and Bone7 are not children of any of the other bones.

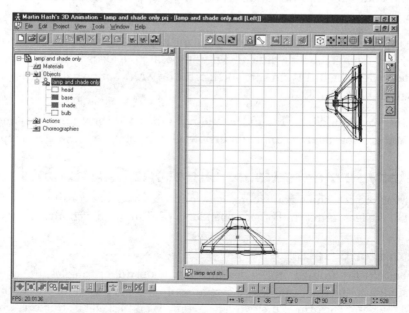

Figure 12.18   Base and shade of the swing-arm lamp.

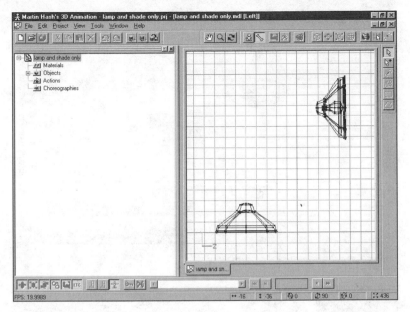

Figure 12.19 Swing-arm lamp object hierarchy.

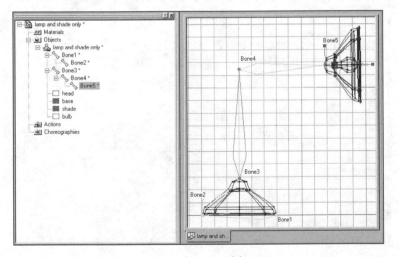

Figure 12.20 Five initial bones added to Swing-arm lamp model.

5. Now, we must assign the base and shade to their respective bones. In the Project Workspace window, select Bone2. Press G, or click on the Group button to enter Group mode. Drag a box around the control points that form the base, as in Figure 12.22. The points of the base are now assigned to Bone2.

6. Select Bone5, then repeat Step 5 to group the shade and bulb control points (see Figure 12.23).

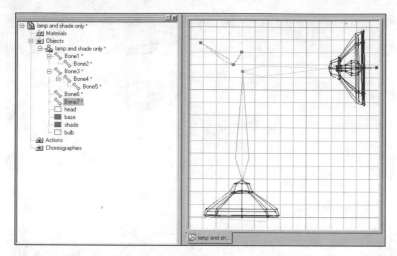

Figure 12.21 Bones 6 and 7 added to swing-arm lamp.

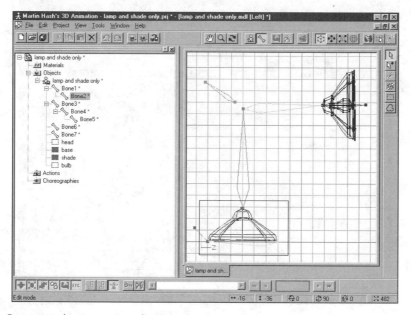

Figure 12.22 Base control points assigned to Bone2.

7. Make a folder for this project on your hard drive called *lamp tutorial*. Save the model by selecting lamp-and-shade-only under Objects in the Project Workspace window and right-clicking your mouse. Choose Save As from the pop-up menu. A Save Model As requester will pop up. Under file name, type "lamp and shade skinned.mdl", and make sure you are putting it on your hard drive in the lamp tutorial folder you just made.

8. Right-click on the project name at the top of the Project Workspace window to open the Save Project As requester. For the file name, type "lamp and shade bones.prj". For both models and projects, if you leave the suffixes .mdl and .prj off, the software will automatically add them for you.

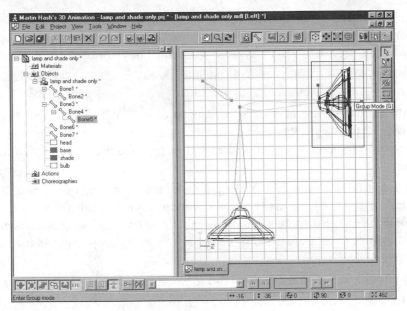

Figure 12.23 Shade and bulb control points assigned to Bone5.

9. In the Project Workspace window, right-click on Actions, and choose New Action. Change the action editing window to the Left view (number pad 4).

10. Click on Bone3 to select it. Place your cursor in the middle of the bone, right-click and select an Aim At constraint, as in Figure 12.24.

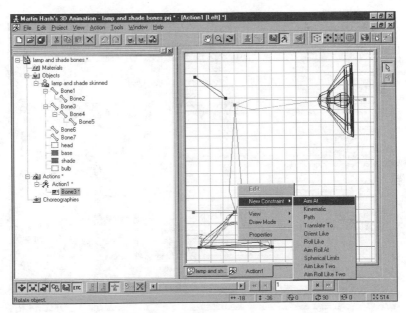

Figure 12.24 Bone3 selected for new Aim At constraint.

If you do not get the menu with the New Constraint submenu, you didn't place the cursor in the middle of the bone—try it again. You will now have an eyedropper cursor, which is used to interactively select the bone that you want to aim Bone3 at.

11. Move the tip of the eyedropper to the middle of Bone7, and click. The model will rotate to a new position because Bone3 is pointing at Bone7 (see Figure 12.25).

    An alternative method of creating an Aim At constraint is to select the Aim At constraint from the Project Workspace window under Bone3, right-click on the constraint icon to open the Constraint Properties window, then use the drop-down list to choose Bone7.

12. Now, select Bone4, right-click in the middle of the bone, and add a new Kinematic constraint. Because there are two bones overlapping in roughly the same space, and one of those will be the target of our Kinematic constraint, it's easier for you to choose the constraint target from the Bone drop-down list in the Properties window, as shown in Figure 12.26.

13. Right-click on Bone5 in the Project Workspace window.

    If Bone5 (or any other bone) doesn't appear in the Project Workspace window under the Actions, select the next bone above it—Bone4, in this case—then hit the Tab key. Navigating through the Action hierarchy with the Tab key enables you to select items that have not yet been activated in the interactive Action editing window.

14. Add an Orient Like constraint to Bone5, and, in the Properties window, select Bone6 as the constraint target.

15. Select Bone3, and add a Translate To constraint with Bone2 as the target.

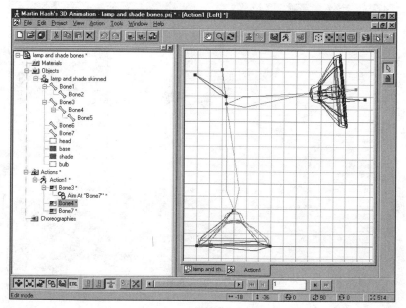

Figure 12.25 Bone3 constrained to Aim At Bone7.

Figure 12.26   Bone6 selected from drop-down list for Bone4 Kinematic constraint.

Whoa!! This can't be right! Your screen probably looks something like Figure 12.27. Bone 3 just jumped to the wrong place, didn't it?

Fear not, for this is what it was supposed to do. A:M has a feature called *Offsets*, which enables you to move an object, once you've constrained it, for an offset effect.

16. To place Bone3 in the correct place, just select it, and move it back to where it started (see Figure 12.28).

The Offset feature can be animated as well, but it can also mess up your work if you aren't careful. This is particularly true for Bone5, which overlaps Bone6.

You want to be able to select Bone6, the bone that will practically be driving all of the animation in this project, without worrying about selecting anything else by mistake. You don't want to have to look at the Project Workspace window every time to see if

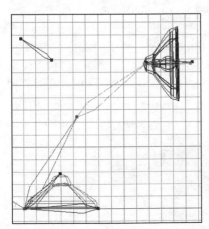

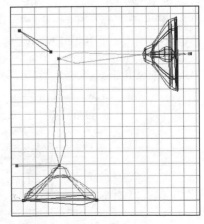

Figure 12.27   Bone3 displaced by Translate To constraint.

Figure 12.28   Bone3 repositioned using Offset feature.

you selected the correct bone, right? And because Bone5 is positionally driven by its parent, Bone4, and rotationally driven by Bone6, you don't actually need to move or rotate it directly, and, therefore, you don't need to see it in the interactive Action Edit window.

17. Now, you're ready to hide the bones you don't need to see. Under Objects in the Project Workspace window, open lamp-and-shade-skinned, and select Bone5. If you don't have the Properties window open, open it now. Click on the Bone tab. On the right side of the Properties window, you will see three checkboxes: Attached To Parent, Hide Bone, and Boolean Cutter. Attached To Parent should already have a checkmark in it, and, by pointing at Hide Bone and clicking in the box, you'll have a checkmark there as well (see Figure 12.29). Bone5 is now hidden and won't be accidentally moved when we start animating this character.

Your first constraint hierarchy is now complete. Before you go any further, you should save the Action you've set up so far.

18. Right-click on Action1 under the Actions header in the Project Workspace hierarchy, and choose Save As from the menu that appears. Save the action with the name *constraint setup.act*.

In addition to saving the hierarchy, it's a good idea to have a default version of it accessible to you while you are working. When you start playing with the lamp to see what it can do, you need a fast and easy way to return it to its original position. This safety net encourages you to experiment and learn from the setup, without having to worry about ruining it irretrievably.

A:M provides a tool for this purpose, called a *pose*. A pose appears in the Project Workspace window at the lower part of an Object's hierarchy. This is a single frame of animation that can be dragged into any action of its model at any time, so the model will assume the pose including the constraint hierarchy (with some limitations). A:M regards a pose as a single frame action, grabbed from the frame of the animation that was active when you saved the pose. You can put extra keyframes in the channels of individual components in a pose, but you can't use them at this time.

At this point, you might want to clean up the appearance of the Project Workspace window by closing some of the open components of the model, and, while you're at it, make certain that the constraint setup Action is selected, as shown in Figure 12.30.

19. To create your safety default pose, you first need to drop a keyframe. Select the constraint setup Action from the Project Workspace window. Turn on the Key Model button,

Figure 12.29   Hiding Bone5 using the Properties checkbox.

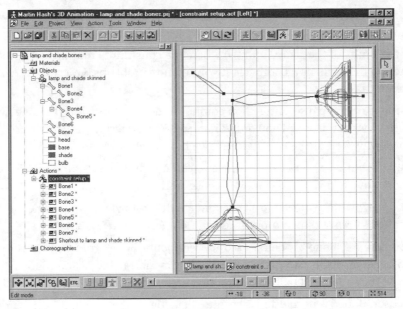

Figure 12.30   Cleaned-up Project Workspace with constraint setup Action selected.

Figure 12.31   Safety default pose saved to hierarchy as constraints no pose.

and click on the Make Keyframe button. This sets a keyframe for everything on the model. Choose the Action:Create Pose menu option, and rename the pose *constraints no pose* as in Figure 12.31.

With your newly completed setup, it's time to test the way the lamp moves when you reposition and rotate the various components. This is one of several processes that precedes animation production that falls under the general term *shakedown*.

20. Double-click on constraint setup under Actions, to open an interactive Action editing window. Select Bone6, either interactively by clicking on the bone that runs through

the lamp's shade, or by clicking on its name in the Project Workspace window. Experiment with it, move it around, rotate it, and see how the model moves.

Push the limits of the setup, and see where the constraints might cause problems in animating the lamp as a character. If you run into problems, you can always reapply the default pose.

It is time to open up a second Action editing window, so that you can have two simultaneous views of the action you are working on. The project we are about to do requires a Top view as well as the Left view that we have been working on.

21. In the Title bar area, select Window|New Window, then select Window|Tile Vertically. You now have two views to work in (see Figure 12.32).

22. Select Bone7, which will be the elbow bone. In the Front view, move Bone7 to your left, also called *screen left*, then move it screen right (see Figure 12.33).

As you can see, Bone7 is being used to steer bones Bone3 and Bone4. The fact that Bone5 is hidden doesn't stop it from functioning invisibly in the Action editor. Yet Bone5—the bone the shade and bulb are connected to that is now hidden—is unaffected.

The reason Bone5 is unaffected is because the Orient Like constraint takes precedence over the hierarchical orientation of bones Bone3 and Bone4. Note also that Bone5 doesn't move when you move Bone7. This is because you have Bone5 constrained by the End Effector of Bone4 being constrained with a Kinematic constraint targeted at Bone6. You might want to play with the way this mechanism works, selecting and moving Bone6 and Bone7 only.

You will also actively use Bone1 and Bone2 for this animation test. These bones translate and rotate the base of the lamp. After experimenting with translating and rotating

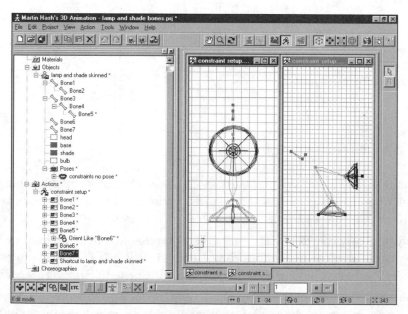

Figure 12.32 Two Action windows tiled for an animation test of the lamp setup.

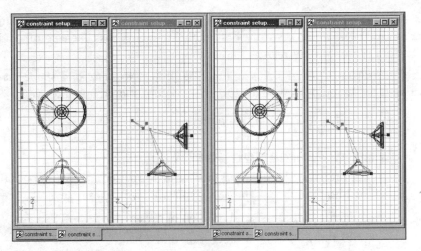

Figure 12.33   Bone7 used to steer bones Bone3 and Bone4.

the base's bones, you will want to reset the lamp in the Action editor to the default *constraints no pose* pose that you set earlier.

23. Under the Model section of the Project Workspace, under lamp and shade skinned, there is an icon that looks like a pair of big red lips. If it isn't already opened, open it now.

24. Click on the big red lips icon labeled *constraints no pose*, and hold the left mouse button down. Drag the pose into either Action editing window (see Figure 12.34), and let go of the left mouse button. The pose is applied to the setup, and the lamp should return to its original position.

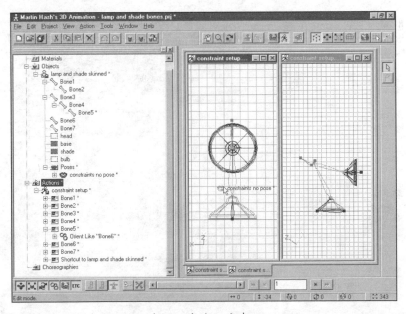

Figure 12.34   Dragging constraints no pose into an Action window.

25. You should now drop a keyframe on the entire lamp. Select Constraint Setup under Actions, and click on the keyframe button, the one that looks like a small gold key at the bottom center of the screen.

26. Save the project. Change the name of the project to *lamp and shade bones and constraints.prj*. If you don't type the .prj, the program should add it for you.

Your lamp is now ready for an animation project.

Lamp Animation Test

In this project, we'll make our new lamp jump, taking advantage of the isolation of the base and shade. The bones you will be animating are:

- Bone6 for translation and rotation of the shade
- Bone1 for translation and rotation of the base
- Bone2 for back rotation of the base (you can use either Bone1 or Bone2 for rotation of the base)
- Bone7 to add tension to the elbow of the swing-arm.

We'll follow a storyboard, which is basically a snapshot of the A:M interface at the keyframe points.

1. Frame 1 starts with the lamp as it was set up for a default pose. Leave the lamp as is (see Figure 12.35).

2. In frame 3, the lamp is anticipating the jump, building up the energy which will be released by the jump. Note that the shade is tilted up. The shade is snapping down for the *anticipation* (see Chapter 14), but it still has mass—how do we show this? We have

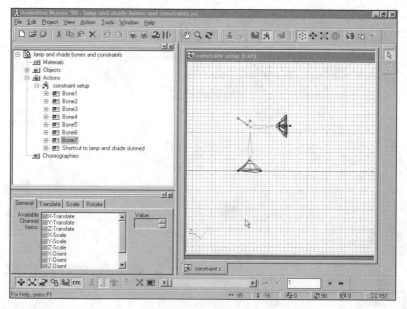

Figure 12.35 Frame 1.

the shade's mass lag behind the overall movement, hence the tilt up. Pose the lamp to match Figure 12.36.

3. Frame 5 is our deceleration key, another indication that the shade has mass, and, as you can see, the mass is catching up with the position of the arm, hence it is tilting down. Pose the lamp to match Figure 12.37.

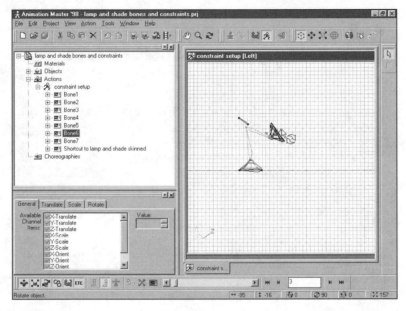

Figure 12.36   Frame 3.

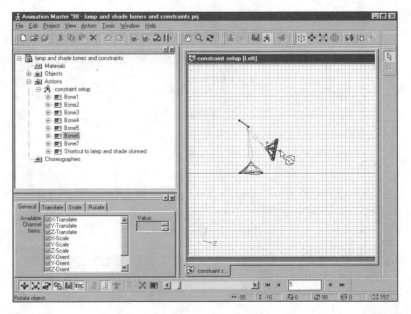

Figure 12.37   Frame 5.

4. At frame 7, the shade snaps up, flinging the mass of the shade into the air rapidly enough that, when it reaches the mechanical limit of the swing-arm, its momentum will yank the base up in the air too. Pose the lamp to match Figure 12.38.

5. The base is airborne in frame 9. Because the base is presumably heavier (more massive) than the shade, it won't rise as high as the shade. Pose the lamp to match Figure 12.39.

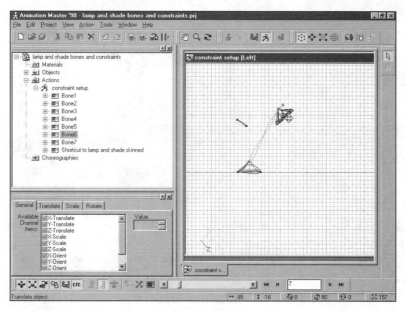

Figure 12.38   Frame 7.

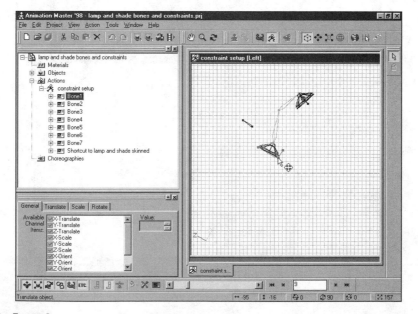

Figure 12.39   Frame 9.

6. When the base drops, it will yank the shade down, whipping it forward in frames 13 and 15, with the shade following through in frame 17. Note again that the mass of the shade is indicated by the rotation of the shade lagging behind the end of the swing-arm. Pose the lamp to match frames 13, 15, and 17 in Figure 12.40.

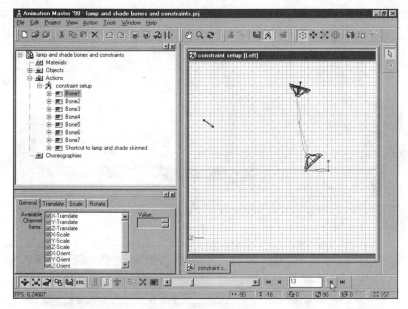

Figure 12.40a   Frame 13.

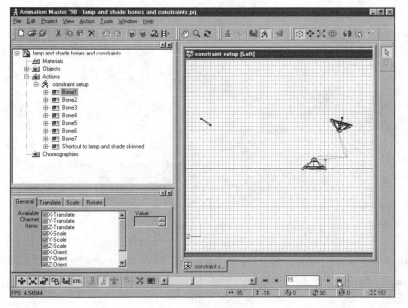

Figure 12.40b   Frame 15.

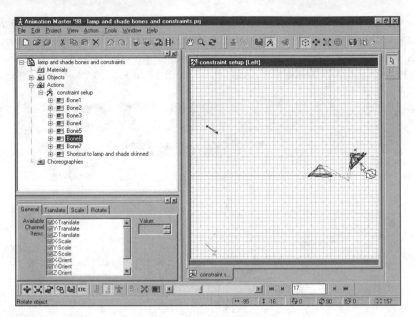

Figure 12.40c Frame 17.

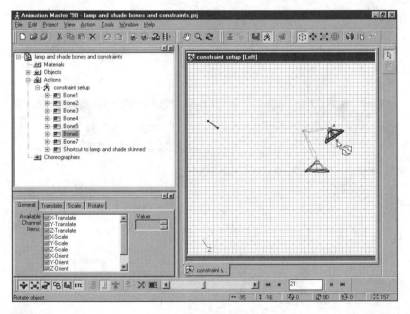

Figure 12.41 Frame 21.

7. There is a relatively slow recovery in frame 21. Pose the lamp to match Figure 12.41.

8. Following frame 21, the lamp *oscillates* (goes through several springy bounces back and forth) to the lamp's resting pose in frame 45. Pose the lamp to match Figure 12.42.

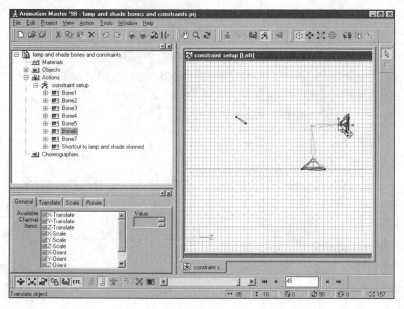

Figure 12.42   Frame 45.

Once you duplicate the frames in the storyboard, note that the swing-arm bends backward on some in-between frames. You can correct this by moving Bone7 away from the lamp, which increases the pull of the aim constraint on Bone3, more forcefully pulling the elbow in the correct direction. However, if you didn't pull the elbow of the lamp tighter and let it go the wrong way, that wouldn't necessarily be wrong. This follows a time-honored animation convention, which famed animation director Richard Williams calls *successive breaking of the joints*. For more details and projects about timing for character animation, see Chapters 14 and 15.

Your final results should look something like 12eca06.AVI, which you can find in the Chapter 12 directory on this book's CD-ROM.

Note that no matter how far away from the base that you move Bone6, the shade never moves away from the swing-arm and the swing-arm never separates from the base. You should also note that when you move the base within the limits of the swing-arm, the shade neither moves nor rotates. Yet if you move the base beyond the limits of the swing-arm, the base will drag the shade along with it. This is an important characteristic, because it is one of the options we have in constructing a leg.

After following the last project, you should know how to do the following:

- Open a Model window.
- Add a window, and select which angle you are viewing from.
- Draw a bone (Add Bone in the Bones Mode in Model).
- Attach to parent (Properties window, Bone, Attach To Parent checkbox) or detach from parent (uncheck the Attach To Parent checkbox).

- Draw a bone at the top of the hierarchy (select model name in Model section of the Project Workspace window).

- Drag-and-drop a bone in the hierarchy to a different position of the hierarchy.

- Hide a Bone (Properties window, Bone, Hide Bone checkbox), and unhide a Bone (Properties Window, Bone, uncheck the Hide Bone checkbox).

- Rename a bone or other object in Model.

- Open a new Action.

- Open an Action window.

- Add a constraint from the Action window and the Project Workspace window.

- Select the target bone for the constraint both from the Action editing window and the Properties window.

- Add a keyframe.

- Create a Pose.

- Rename a bone in Action, a pose, or a bone in a pose.

Directions for the remaining projects will be less detailed, on the assumption that you have mastered the preceding tasks. If you forget the exact details of one of these tasks, you can always come back and review these earlier projects.

Leg Setup

In the following projects, you will create a basic leg setup using the same procedures you followed to build the swing-arm lamp setup. This setup is more complex, with more bones to keep track of, but if you follow the directions carefully, you shouldn't have any problems. After the basic setup, you will apply a series of additional constraints to more closely mimic the real-life limits of a leg's musculoskeletal structure.

Basic Leg Setup

The first set of steps adds bones in a hierarchy. Once the bones are all arranged in the proper order, the next set of steps shows how to set up their constraints.

Animation:Master

1. Start by adding a new model. In the Model window, Right view, get into Bones mode, and draw the leg bones as illustrated in Figure 12.43.

2. Continue adding bones, drawing the foot bones, as shown in Figure 12.44.

3. Hide bones Bone1 and Bone2. Click on Model1 in the Project Workspace, and draw Bone5 from the base of Bone4 as illustrated in Figure 12.45.

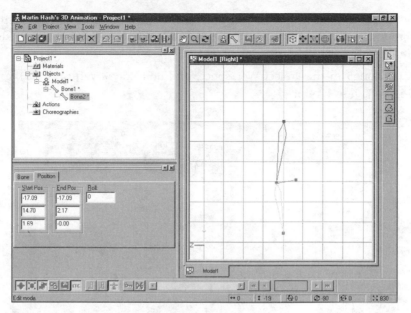

Figure 12.43   Major leg bones Bone1 and Bone2.

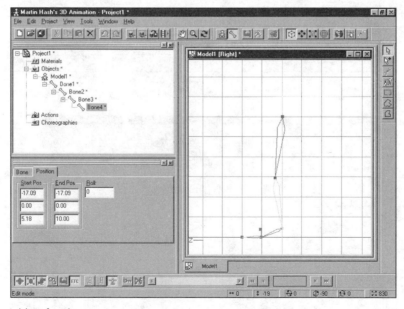

Figure 12.44   Adding foot bones.

4. Draw Bone6 vertically from the base of Bone5. Detach Bone6 from its parent (in the Properties window, the Attach To Parent checkbox should be unchecked), as shown in Figure 12.46.

5. Click on Bone5 in the Project Workspace, and add Bone7 vertically at the base of Bone4 (see Figure 12.47).

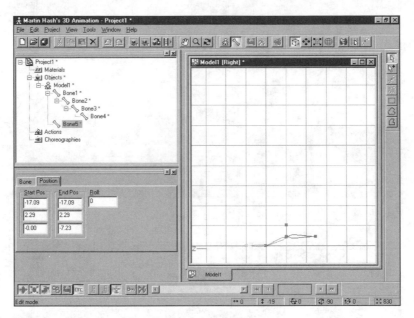

Figure 12.45 First bones hidden, and Bone5 added to Bone4.

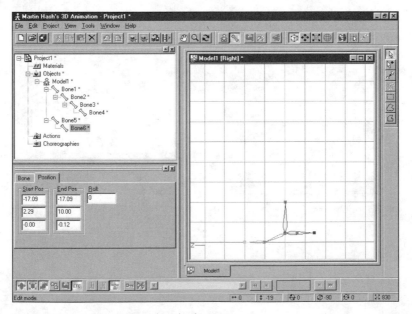

Figure 12.46 Bone6 added to Bone5, then detached.

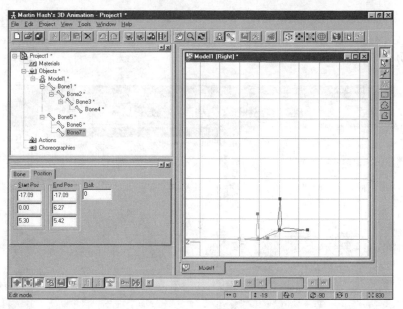

Figure 12.47 Bone7 added at Bone4.

6. Click on Bone5 in the Project Workspace, and add Bone8 vertically from the tip of Bone4, as shown in Figure 12.48.

7. Unhide bones Bone1 and Bone2. Hide bones Bone3 through Bone8, to unclutter the view.

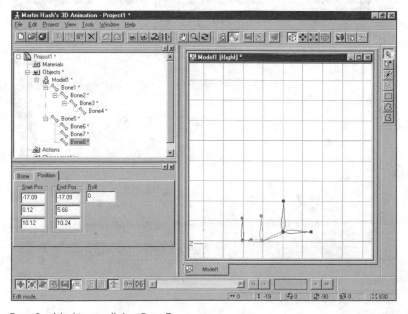

Figure 12.48 Bone8 added in parallel to Bone7.

8. Click on Model1, and draw Bone9 from the base of Bone2, as shown in Figure 12.49.

9. Click on Model1, and draw Bone10 horizontally from the base of Bone1 (see Figure 12.50).

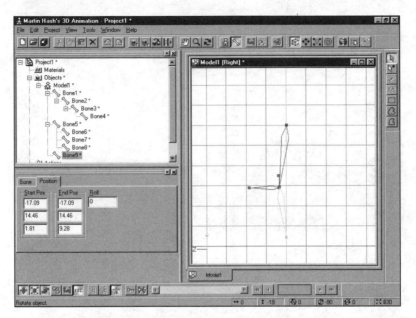

Figure 12.49 Bone9 added at root of hierarchy, and positioned at base of Bone2.

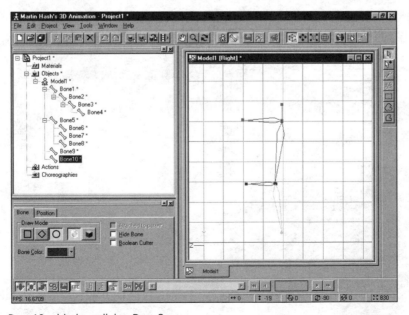

Figure 12.50 Bone10 added parallel to Bone9.

10. Unhide all the bones, as shown in Figure 12.51.

    The functions of bones Bone5 through Bone9 will be as constraints, as follows:

    - Bone5 will be the master controller for position and rotation of bones Bone6, Bone7, and Bone8.

    - Bone6 will be used to lift the heel of the foot.

    - Bone7 will be used to position the ball of the foot.

    - Bone8 will be used to lift or to leave the toe in place.

    - Bone9 will be used to steer the knee.

    - Bone10 will be used to control the location of the hip.

11. Open a new Action. Open an Action window, and select Right view.

12. Select Bone1, and add a Translate To constraint with Bone10 as the target. This attaches the thigh bone (Bone1) to the hip constraint (Bone10), so that when you move the hip constraint (Bone10), the base of the thigh bone will follow, as shown in Figure 12.52.

13. Select Bone1 again, and add an Aim At constraint with Bone9 as the target. By aiming Bone1 at Bone9, Bone 9 will steer the knee when it is moved.

14. Select Bone2, and add a Kinematic constraint with Bone6 as the target. This attaches the ankle of Bone2 to Bone6, so that when either Bone6 or its parent, Bone5, are moved, the ankle will follow.

15. Select Bone3, and add a Kinematic constraint with Bone7 as the target. This will cause Bone3 to adhere to Bone7, keeping the ball of the foot on the floor if you lift the heel using Bone6.

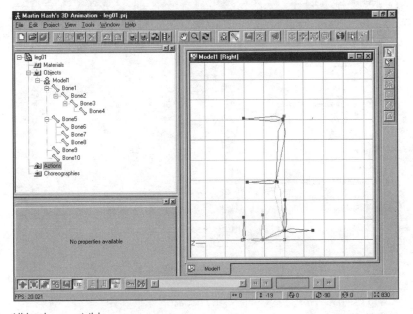

Figure 12.51 All leg bones visible.

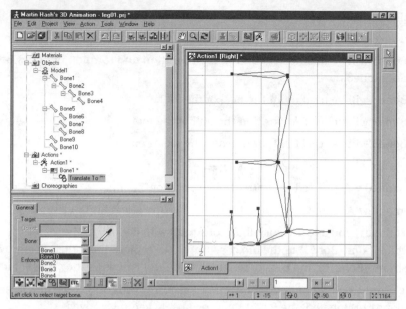

Figure 12.52 Hip-to-Thigh Translate To constraint.

16. Select Bone4, and add a Kinematic constraint targeted at Bone8. This will guide the toe of the foot to either keep the toe level or allow you to raise it.

17. Make keyframes in Branch Mode for Bone5, Bone9, and Bone10, as shown in Figure 12.53.

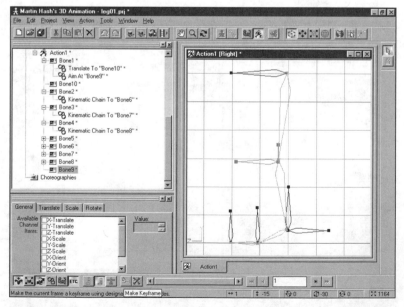

Figure 12.53 Making keyframes for Bone5, Bone9, and Bone10.

18. Now, create a new pose so that you can return back to this default position when you want to.

   This would be a good time to save your project, if you have not been doing so all along. It's a good idea to save often and save your project under different names, with numbers incrementing up, in case you need to go back a couple of steps.

   This is a complete basic leg. Now, it is time to put it through its paces in an animation test, just as we did for the swing-arm lamp.

19. In the Action window, go to frame 5.

   At the time of this writing, there is no Undo function in the Action editor for skeletal action—yet. By going to frame 5, we can always copy frame 1 to frame 5 as a backup to Undo, or use the pose that should have been created earlier.

20. Select Bone10, and move it vertically, very slowly, and observe what is happening to the leg and foot while you move it (see Figure 12.54).

   First, you will see the leg straighten. Then, the heel will lift, then the ball of the foot will lift as soon as the heel is straight above it. In all probability, you will also note some instabilities as you continue to move Bone10 vertically. These instabilities are common and are caused by continuous recalculation of the constraint relationships and their priorities. There are workarounds to address these conflicts and present unambiguous constraint relationships (fix the thrashing), which we'll cover later in this chapter.

21. Return Bone10 to its starting position, and select Bone6. Move Bone6 both vertically and horizontally toward the toe, as shown in Figure 12.55.

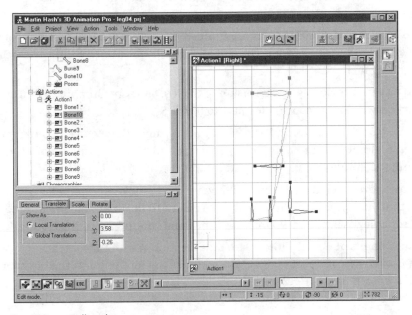

Figure 12.54   Bone10 controlling leg movement.

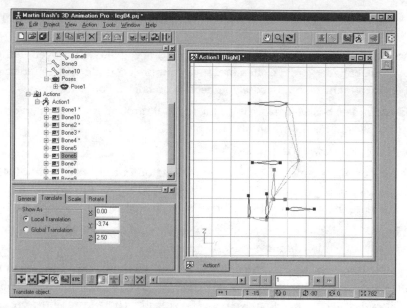

Figure 12.55 Bone6 controlling leg movement, with knee reversed.

Note that the knee has reversed. This is caused by the joint between Bone1 and Bone2 passing the base of Bone9, the Aim At constraint, causing it to aim in the opposite direction.

22. Select Bone9, and move it horizontally in the direction of the toe and a bit past the toe. The knee should be facing in the correct direction (see Figure 12.56).

    Bone6 has lifted the heel yet has maintained the ball of the foot (the base of Bone4) somewhat steadily on the floor. The ball has actually protruded a little below the floor, but not by much.

23. Revert to your previously saved version of the leg, either by dropping Pose1 back into the Action window or copying frame 1 to frame 5.

24. Select Bone5. Lift it vertically. If the knee reverses, move Bone9 toward and beyond the toe again. Rotate Bone5 on its X axis, either by grabbing its rotation handle at the tip or using the Rotate tool (r), (see Figure 12.57).

    You have now covered all the parts that you need to move to work the legs. One other thing that you might want to try is to move Bone10 down toward the ground, switch to a Front view, select Bone9, and move the bone left and right (see Figure 12.58).

    The knee points at Bone9. This looks a little unnatural with the foot facing forward, so select Bone5, and rotate it on its Y axis to make the foot point in the direction of the knee, as shown in Figure 12.59.

Compare the leg that you just constructed to the completed one on this book's CD-ROM, legcmp01.prj. Also on this book's CD-ROM is a two-legged assembly with a pelvis and anatomically named bones, twolegs1.prj. Play with these setups, compare them to the one you just built, and see if you can detect the advantages and problems inherent in each one.

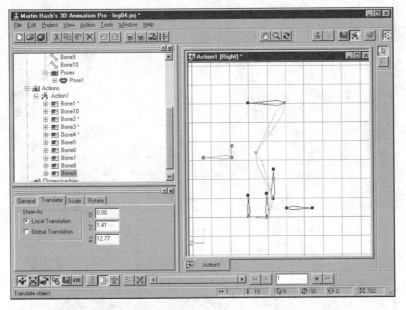

Figure 12.56   Bone9 moved to correct knee reversal.

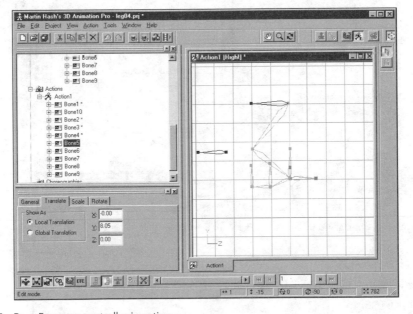

Figure 12.57   Bone5 master controller in action.

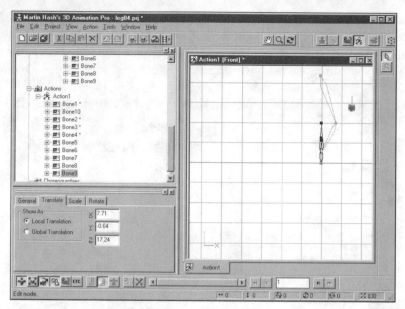

Figure 12.58 Bone10 controlling leg movement.

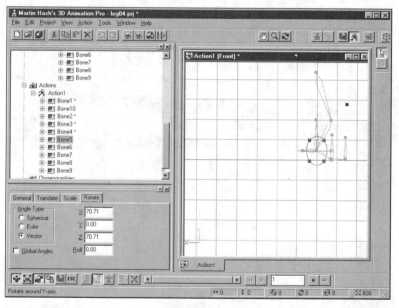

Figure 12.59 Bone5 controlling foot direction to align with knee.

3D Studio MAX 2

The following uses 3DS MAX 2.0 with the New IK system to set up a basic leg.

1. Load IKLegSimple1.MAX.

   This file has a simple block hierarchy for a character's leg, as shown in Figure 12.60. The red box is the hip, followed by the blue upper leg box, which has a protrusion so

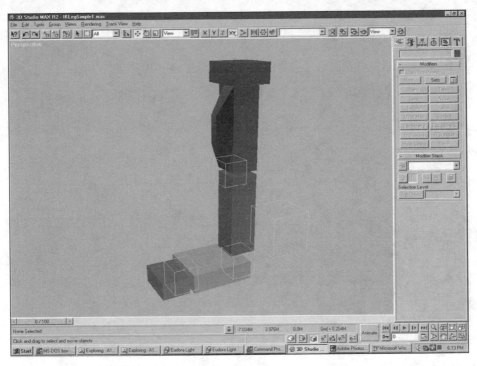

Figure 12.60 IKLegSimple1.MAX.

you can see its orientation. There are also boxes for the lower leg, foot, and toes. This leg hierarchy is already linked together. In addition, there are several dummy objects that are not linked to anything. The exception is the ToeTip-Dummy, which is linked to allow the bone hierarchy to go through the toes.

2. The first change is to create the New IK bones for the leg. Open the Create panel, and choose the Systems button.

3. Click on the Bones button to open the Bone Creation Parameters rollout.

4. Under AutoBoning, click on Pick Root. The button highlights, waiting for you to click on the topmost parent of the hierarchy.

5. In the Right viewport, click on the red Box01Hips box. This will create a bone structure through the leg boxes, as shown in Figure 12.61.

   Next, we need to create End Effectors for the bones. By default, MAX creates one only for the end bone.

6. Choose Select And Move on the toolbar. Select Bone03. This is the bone that runs through the blue upper leg box.

7. Open the Motion panel, and look towards the bottom for the End Effectors section. Under Position, choose Create. We will link each of the End Effectors to dummy objects for easier animating.

8. With Bone03 still selected and the Motion panel still up, click on the Link button. In the Right viewport, click on the KneeDummy located at the knee joint. The Link

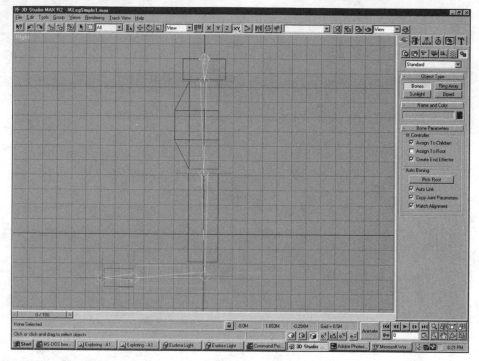

Figure 12.61 AutoBoned hierarchy.

button un-highlights, and the KneeDummy name is shown in the EndEffectorParent text area.

9. Now, we'll create and link the rest of the End Effectors. Select Bone04. Click on the Position: Create button to make the End Effector.

10. Choose Link, and then click on the HeelDummy object to link it to the dummy at the heel.

11. Click on Bone05, the one that runs through the foot. Click on the Position:Create button to make an End Effector for it.

12. Choose Link, and then click on the BallDummy to link it to the end dummy at the ball of the foot.

13. Click on the ToeTip-Dummy object. This was linked to the toe box so that MAX would create Bone06 during the AutoBone process. Unlink the ToeTip-Dummy by selecting it and then clicking on Unlink Selection from the toolbar.

14. Now, select Bone06. This bone already has an End Effector made, because it was the last child bone. Choose Link, and then click on the ToeTip-Dummy object to link it to the dummy at the end of the toes.

15. Now, we will link the dummy objects together to help animating. Select the ToeTip-Dummy, BallDummy, HeelDummy, and KneeDummy. Choose Select And Link from

the toolbar, and drag from one of these dummies over to the FootMasterDummy (to the right of the foot) to link them.

Using this setup, you can move the entire foot by moving or rotating the FootMasterDummy. In addition, you can individually move the heel, ball, or toes dummies. The KneeDummy will also move with the Foot one, as well.

16. Finally, link the first Bone01 to the red Box01Hips box. Now is a good time to save your work.

    If you try moving the red Box01Hips or any of the dummy objects around, you'll see that the IK isn't quite working yet (see Figure 12.62a and 12.62b). The knee bends the wrong way, and bones are rotating all over, such as the blue upper leg rotating inwards. Undo any changes or movements you create before you go on to the next step.

17. The first thing to do is to set some constraints. Select Bone02. This is the bone that runs through the red box and that the blue upper leg is parented to.

18. Open the Hierarchy panel, and click on the IK button. Look for the Rotational Joints subpanel on the bottom.

19. Check Limited under the X-Axis section. This will allow you to set a range in which the bone can rotate. Set the From value to -60 and the To value to 60. Check Limited for the Y- and Z-Axis sections. Set the Y limits to be from -45 through 45. Set the Z limits to be from -35 through 35.

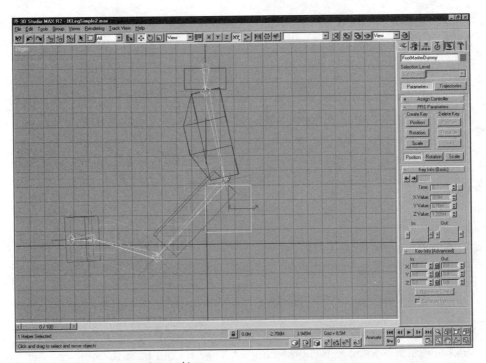

Figure 12.62a Leg IK setup not quite working.

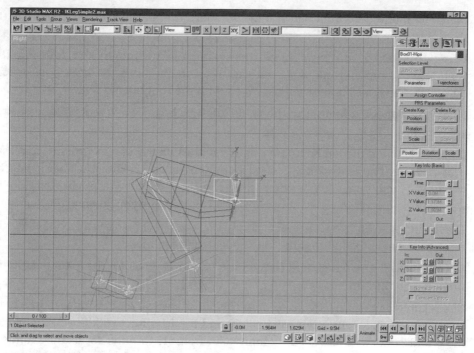

Figure 12.62b   Leg IK setup not quite working.

20. Click on Bone03. This is the one that runs through the blue upper leg. Turn off Active for the Y and Z axes. Check Limited for the X axis, and set the constraints to be from 0 through 145.

    We also need to lower the weight of this End Effector. Essentially, the End Effector at the knee will be used primarily to control the roll of the upper leg.

21. At the top of the Hierarchy panel is the Object Parameters rollout. Change the weight under the Position section to be 0.1.

22. Set the following constraints for the remaining bones. Set Bone04 constraints as follows:

    • X: -140 through -75

    • Y: -20 through 20

    • Z: -30 through 30

    Set Bone05 constraints as follows:

    • X: -70 through 50

    • Y: not active

    • Z: not active

    Remember to click on Limited for the sections that have values! Also, don't worry if the bones jump when you choose Limited. They should reset themselves when you enter the From and To values.

23. Save your work. Try moving the hip bones and dummies around.

You should be able to see the IK working somewhat better. The knee bends and tries to go toward the knee dummy. You can also move the foot, toes, and other dummy objects. The results should match that of IKLegSimple2.MAX, as shown in Figure 12.63a and 12.63b.

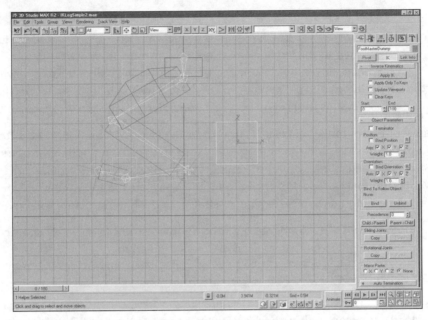

Figure 12.63a   Leg IK setup working better.

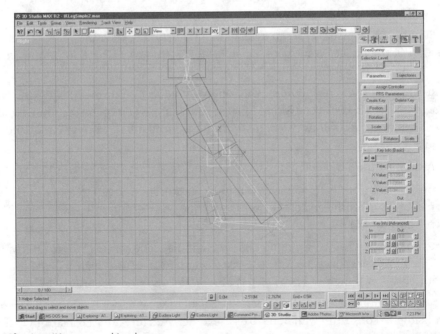

Figure 12.63b   Leg IK setup working better.

Note that if you drag the main hips down or the foot up that the heel digs into the ground. This problem is addressed in the next section. You can pretty much apply the A:M solution in MAX as well, by reversing the parenting of the foot and adding another constraint.

PROJECT 12.8 The Foot Bone's Connected To The Leg Bone?

There are several problems with the preceding leg setup. Because the foot bone is connected to the leg bone, and because in most IK systems the root bone takes precedence over the child bones, the leg forces the ball of the foot down when the leg is in certain positions, and pulls on the ball of the foot when the leg is stretched completely to its limits. Of course, it pulls the heel up first, and, sometimes, that is the arrangement you want.

But when slight unplanned movements appear in the feet in animation, it ruins the appearance that the character is rooted to the ground. What you need is a solution that leaves the foot rock steady. Like nearly everything in animation, increased control requires increased diligence. When the foot is rooted to the ground, but you pull the hip up beyond the leg's full extension, something has to give, extend, or stretch, or the bone structure will break.

As an animator, this is a small price to pay, and, in the case of cartoon-style characters, this is actually a desirable outcome that you can use to your advantage.

Animation:Master

1. If you didn't save your results from the previous project, copy legcmp01.prj from the Chapter 12 directory on this book's CD-ROM, turn off the Read-Only property, and open it in A:M. If you simply open it directly from the CD-ROM, A:M sees it as a read-only file, and you'll have trouble saving it.

2. Delete the old constraint setup by deleting the action. Delete the pose in the model section of the Project Workspace. Open a Model window. Select Bone4, and delete it. Do the same for Bone3.

3. You will now draw new bones, which by default will be named *Bone3* and *Bone4*. However, this time, click on Model1 first so that Bone3 will occupy the same hierarchy level as Bone1, and draw the bone from the toe to the ball of the foot, as shown in Figure 12.64.

4. Draw Bone4 from the ball of the foot to the ankle, as shown in Figure 12.65.

5. Draw one more bone. Its orientation is unimportant, because its purpose will be to act as a constraint for the end of the tibia (shin bone). By default, this will become Bone11 (see Figure 12.66).

6. These new bones are drawn along the center of the scene at X=0. This means that you will have to select Bone3 and use the Move tool in the Front view to slide the entire hierarchy over if the rest of your leg is offset (see Figure 12.67a and 12.67b).

7. Open an Action window, and go back to the Right view. Select Bone1, and add a new Translate To constraint with Bone10 as the target. Add an Aim At constraint to Bone1, with Bone9 as the target.

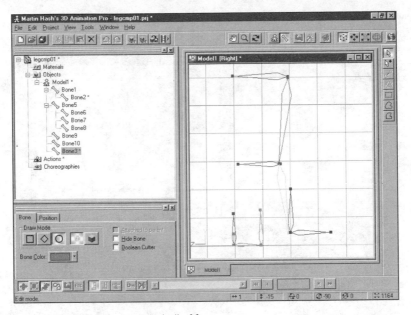

Figure 12.64   New Bone3 added, from toe to ball of foot.

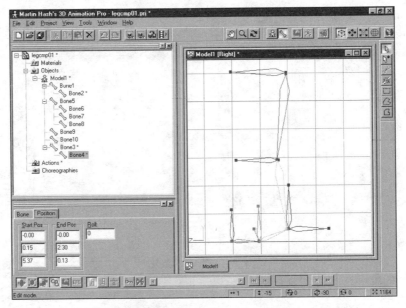

Figure 12.65   New Bone4 added, from ball of foot to ankle.

8. Select Bone2, and add a Kinematic constraint with Bone11 as the target.

9. Select Bone3, and add a Translate To constraint with Bone8 as the target. Also, add a Kinematic constraint to Bone3, with Bone7 as the target.

10. Select Bone4, and add an Aim At constraint with Bone6 as the target.

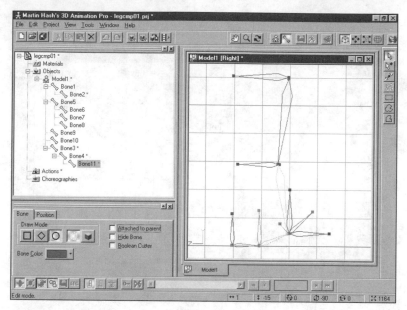

Figure 12.66 Bone11 added.

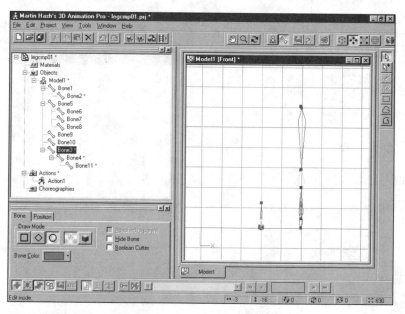

Figure 12.67a Move leg hierarchy in Front view.

This setup is now complete, so save the project under a new name. Your setup should look like Figure 12.68.

Figure 12.69 gives an indication of what this setup is capable of doing. While moving the entire foot is still done by moving Bone5, just as in the last example, the heel must now be

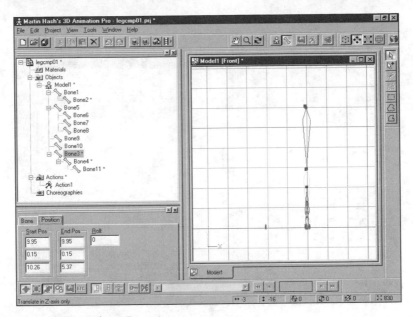

Figure 12.67b   Move leg hierarchy in Front view.

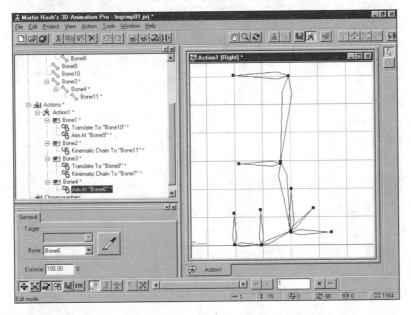

Figure 12.68   Completed leg setup.

lifted by moving Bone6. Try experimenting with this setup by selecting, moving, and rotating bones Bone5, Bone6, Bone7, Bone8, Bone9, and Bone10. Revert to the saved setup between moving the individual bones, so you can better familiarize yourself with the function of each constraint bone.

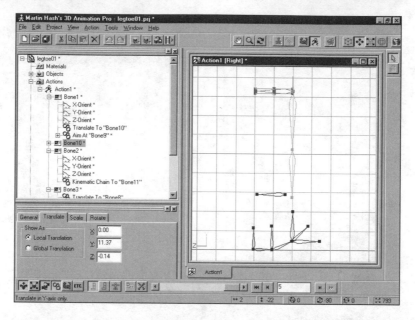

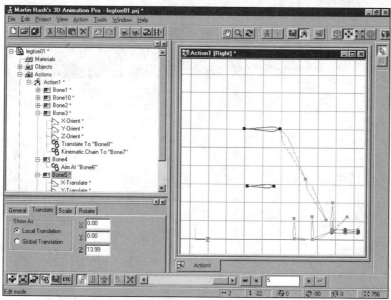

Figure 12.69 Leg setup in action.

Note that Bone2 now points at the root of Bone11, no matter how you pull the legs up by Bone10. However, Bone2 is firmly attached to Bone11 as long as the leg is not stretched beyond its limits. Also note that no matter what you do by pulling on Bone10, which is acting as the hip, it has no effect on the foot. If you pull the heel up with Bone6, it does not significantly alter

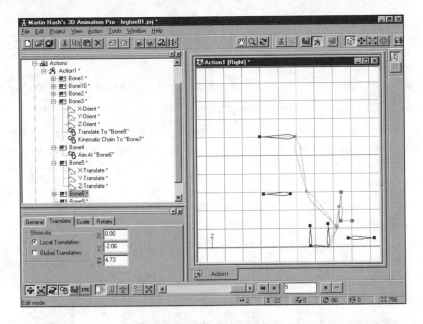

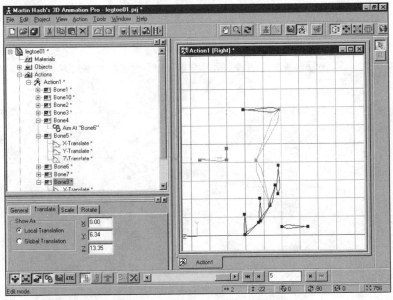

Figure 12.69 (continued) Leg setup in action.

the position of Bone3. Finally, Bone6 no longer has the priority it did in the previous project, and so it has more of an effect on the general direction of the heel, but will no longer drag the ball of the foot and the toe along with it.

This is by far the most forgiving and flexible of the general leg setups possible.

3D Studio MAX 2

This project essentially duplicates the modifications just described for the A:M leg setup.

1. Load IKLeg1.MAX.

   This is a setup similar to the previous project's, but with three important changes:

   • The IK for the leg is already set up for you, but only as far as the heel.

   • The foot boxes have been reverse-parented, with their axes moved for that. To see this more clearly, select and rotate the ToeTip-Dummy (but make sure you Undo your changes when you're done). Note how it rotates around the toe tip with the foot following.

   • There is a small FootEndDummy at the end of the foot. This is the smaller dummy overlapped with the HeelDummy.

   What we will do is create a NewIK system for the foot, with the toe tip as the base of the hierarchy. The heel end of the foot will be used as a constraint for both the leg (as is already set up) and the foot. We'll start by making the bones for the foot.

2. Open the Create panel, and choose Systems. Click on the Bones button.

3. In the AutoBoning subpanel, click on the Pick Root button. In the Right viewport, click on the ToeTip-Dummy. You should now have a bone structure set through the foot, as shown in Figure 12.70.

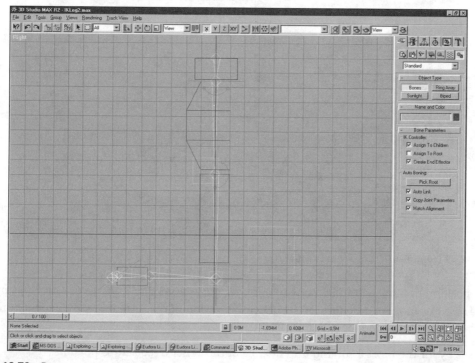

Figure 12.70 Bone structure in the foot.

4. Next, we will create an End Effector for the ball and set up limits for the ball and foot. Choose Select And Move from the toolbar. Click on Bone07. This is the bone going through the toe box.

5. Open up the Motion panel, and find the End Effectors section on the bottom. Click on Create under the Position section to make an End Effector. Click on Link, and then choose the BallDummy object as the parent.

6. Open the Hierarchy panel, and click on the IK button. In the bottom Rotational Joints section, set Limited for the X Axis with From set to -40 and To set to 75. Turn on Limited for the Y and Z axes also. Set them to -20 to 20 and -30 to 30, respectively.

7. Select Bone06. This is the small bone at the left end of the toes between the ToeTip-Dummy and the Toe block. Don't accidentally choose the root Bone05. You may want to zoom in to make an accurate selection or use the Select list in the top toolbar. Turn off Active for the Y and Z axes. Turn on Limited for the X axis, and choose -200 to -30. Don't worry if the bones move before you enter these values—after the settings are entered, the setup will reset itself.

8. Choose Select And Link, and click on the FootEndDummy at the heel area. Choose Unlink Selection from the toolbar. Drag from the FootEndDummy to the HeelDummy to link to it.

9. Select Bone08. This is the bone that runs through the main foot. Open the Motion panel, and find the End Effector section near the bottom. Click on Link, and then choose the small FootEndDummy.

10. Now, select Bone05. Choose Select And Link, and parent it to the ToeTip-Dummy.

11. Select the ToeTip-Dummy, and parent it to the FootMasterDummy. These last two steps allow you to move the foot by moving the FootMasterDummy.

12. Save your file. It should be the same as IKLeg2.MAX, which you can find in the Chapter 12 directory on this book's CD-ROM.

    Try moving the dummies and the red hip block. Now, when you move the hips down, the feet stay locked, as shown in Figure 12.71.

    You can also move the FootDummy, HeelDummy, or BallDummy to adjust the foot angles. For example, raising the heel dummy raises the heel, while the ball of the foot remains locked, as shown in Figure 12.72.

    However, if you move the hips or leg area too far away from the feet, the heel area pulls apart (which is good), but the feet remain locked, as shown in Figure 12.73.

Before animating with this or any other NewIK system, you should choose Lock Initial State in the Motion panel when your setup is complete. IKLeg3.MAX has a sample animation using this setup.

Unfortunately, because MAX doesn't have a real roll constraint for IK, it's very difficult to get the upper leg to point in the right place without also affecting how the leg is bent. For this reason, it's important to keep the KneeDummy relatively close to the leg itself.

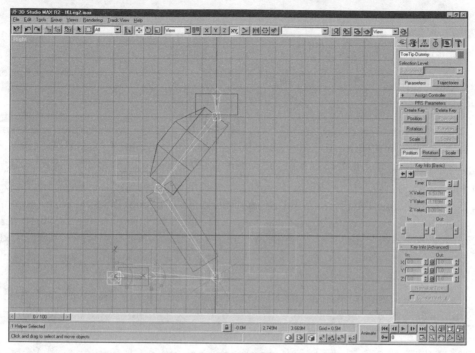

Figure 12.71 Feet stay in position when the hip is lowered.

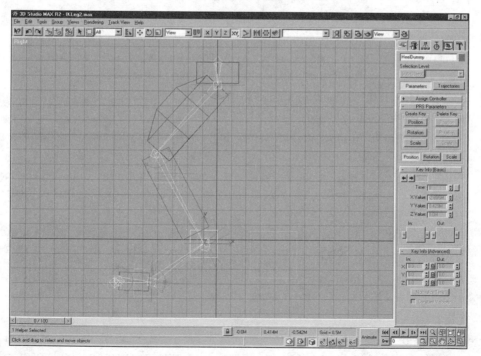

Figure 12.72 Ball of foot locked down.

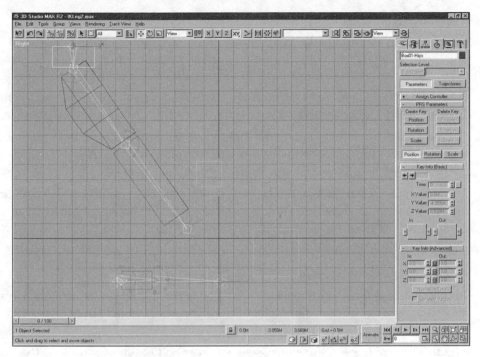

Figure 12.73   Limits to setup. Nothing's perfect!

In addition, this current setup causes the foot to wobble a bit. You may want to adjust some dampening or spring options for the foot (Bone07) and increase the range of the toe rotation (Bone06). All in all, this is a nice setup.

PROJECT 12.9 Pivoting On The Ball Of The Foot Instead Of The Heel

If you are setting up a dancer or other character that spends a lot of time standing on its toes but is otherwise human, you can modify the previous setup by simply moving the foot's positional constraint to the location of the ball of the foot. This way, when the character pivots on its toes, the ball of the foot remains the center of rotation, and you don't have to do a lot of compensating. However, if the character does a lot of conventional running or walking, you will have to work harder by moving the heel's constraint, just to keep the heel from going through the floor all the time.

There are other examples of characters that pivot on the ball of their feet. For example, the hind leg of nearly every quadruped, any kind of bird, all bipedal dinosaurs, and goat-legged mythical creatures. In these cases, what appears to be a backward facing knee is actually the ankle, and you can include that ankle in the pivot from the ball of the foot, or you can exclude it from that rotation.

Animation:Master

This project shows you how to shift the foot constraint to optimize animating movement rooted at the ball of the foot, rather than the normal human movement from the heel. A completed example of this is provided in the Chapter 12 directory on this book's CD-ROM, legbal01.prj.

1. Open your saved leg from the previous project, or load legtoe01.prj from the Chapter 12 directory on this book's CD-ROM.

2. Open a Model window, and go to the Right view. Select Bone5, and move the pivot from the heel to the ball of the foot. Do not use the Move tool, because this will move not only Bone5, but Bone6 through Bone8, as well (see Figure 12.74).

3. Select the End Effector for Bone5, and move it under the heel, making Bone5 horizontal once again. This can also be accomplished by selecting Bone5, placing the cursor in the middle of the bone, and moving it (see Figure 12.75).

4. Move Bone2, Bone6, and Bone11 to the position shown in Figure 12.76.

This is a good time to save your work.

Test the setup. Open an Action window, and go to the Right view. Select Bone5, and move it around as in Figure 12.77. Move Bone6 and Bone7 around as in Figure 12.78.

This setup is fine as far as it goes, and it could be used for many types of animation with this type of leg. But sometimes, you want the ball of the foot to act as the heel would on a normal leg, and, for this, it requires a rearrangement of the constraint hierarchy in the model.

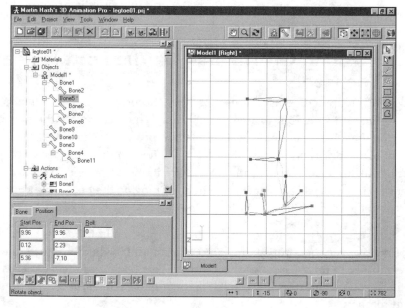

Figure 12.74 Moving pivot of Bone5.

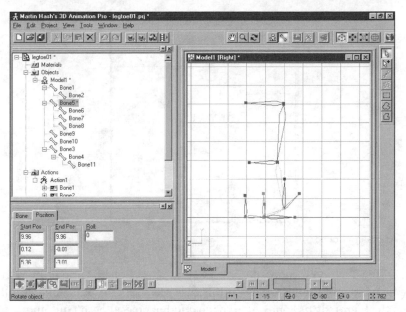

Figure 12.75   Moving End Effector of Bone5.

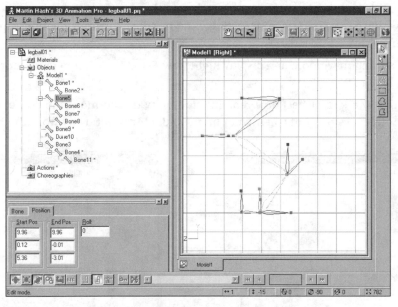

Figure 12.76   Positioning Bone2, Bone6, and Bone11.

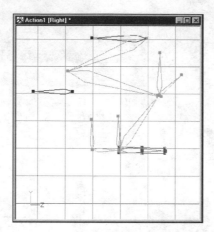

Figure 12.77   Animating Bone5.

5. Open a Model window, choose Right view, and select Bone6. Drag it up to the model name at the top of the hierarchy, in this case Model1. This puts Bone6 on the same level in the hierarchy as Bone1, so moving another object doesn't automatically move or rotate it anymore.

Again, this is a good time to save, but change the name of the project because you may want to refer back to your last save. Again, the constraint relationships should remain intact.

6. Open an Action window, and display Right view. Select Bone5, and move it around, as in Figure 12.79.

Note that the former heel now remains stationary as you move the ball of the foot. Also note, however, that when you pull the ball of the foot away from the heel con-

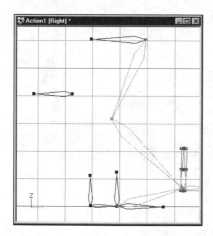
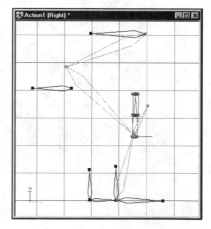

Figure 12.78   Animating Bone6 and Bone7.

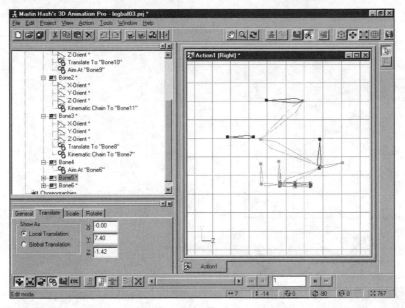

Figure 12.79 Animating Bone5 with modified setup.

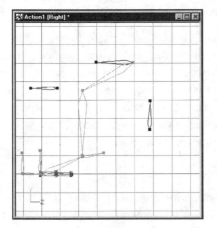

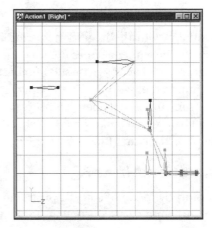

Figure 12.80 Animating Bone6 and Bone7.

straint (Bone6), the heel follows the movement of the ball regardless, as shown in Figure 12.80. Also, note that the knee has been moved forward. Otherwise, the knee will reverse direction. The heel is still controlled by Bone6 within the limits of Bone4's extension, as shown in Figure 12.81.

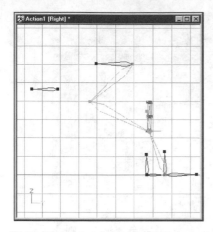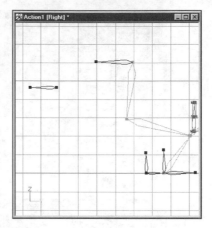

Figure 12.81   Animating the heel with Bone6, constrained by Bone4.

The Cartoon Knee

PROJECT 12.10

This setup is a bit different from the others. It is designed for a more cartoony, free-form style of animation. This can work well in conjunction with setups that can scale groups of points, and as a driver for chains of bones attached to a path. Examples of these types of setups are covered later in this chapter.

Essentially, with the free-floating, cartoon knee, there is no fixed length to the bones which make up the leg. The bones are used for orientation of the control points assigned to them, or bones parented or otherwise subordinate to them, to which control point assignments are made. This makes it easy to distort the apparent proportions of the leg. Distortions require care, because something that doesn't conserve the character's apparent volume just looks wrong, unless it's deliberate and controlled. It's a good start, however, if you're doing something wild in the vein of the Fleischer Bros., Warner Bros., or Spumco animation styles.

Animation:Master

1. Start by loading legtoe01.prj from the Chapter 12 directory on this book's CD-ROM. Select and delete the actions for Bone1 and Bone2, then in Model1 under the Objects section of the Project Workspace, delete Bone1 and Bone2.

2. If a Model window isn't open, open it now in Bones mode, and get a Right view. Click on Model1, and add a femur starting from the knee location, as illustrated in Figure 12.82. The bone is deliberately drawn short.

3. Next, draw a tibia, also starting from the knee, as shown in Figure 12.83. Pay attention to where these are in the hierarchy illustrated in the Project Workspace.

4. Open a new Action window. Select Bone1, and add a Translate To constraint with Bone9 as the target. While Bone1 is selected, add an Aim At or Kinematic constraint with Bone10 as the target.

5. Select Bone2, and add a Translate To constraint with Bone9 as the target. With Bone2 still selected, add an Aim At or Kinematic constraint with Bone11 as the target.

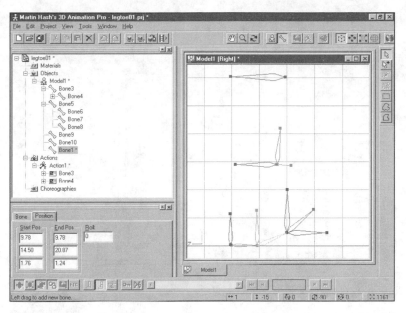

Figure 12.82 Adding the femur, Bone1.

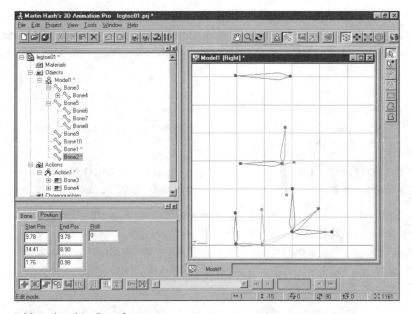

Figure 12.83 Adding the tibia, Bone2.

Your results should look like Figure 12.84. This is a good time to save the modified project under a different file name.

While your old constraints for the foot should still be active and valid, move the foot just to make sure. If they're not, refer to the second leg project presented earlier, to re-constrain the

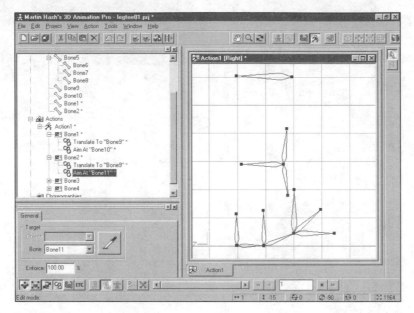

Figure 12.84 Completed cartoon knee setup.

foot. Move Bone5, Bone9, and Bone10 to see the effect of this setup. Without skin attached to these bones, the effect isn't manifestly obvious, but if a skin was attached and the geometry was relatively simple, the skin would stretch to accommodate movement in the knee.

Arm

Like the basic leg assembly, there is a basic arm assembly, which features the humerus (the bone the biceps is attached to, between the shoulder and elbow), the forearm, and a single bone representing the hand.

While the methods for handling the elbow are identical to the methods we used for the knee, there are different options for the way the hand works relative to the arm.

The strategies for dealing with elbows vary from program to program. In the following projects, we will use constrained elbows, though the simplest method has the humerus constrained at the shoulder and the forearm constrained at the wrist. With A:M, you can simply move the hand to where you want it to go, then move the elbow by directly clicking on it and simply moving the elbow effector.

While this is a fine solution at a really basic level, it generates rotational channels, and, if you look at the A:M rotational channels, you won't easily be able to tell if the elbow is pointed up or down. Since channel editing is an important part of refining a character performance, the very slightly more complicated setup of using an Aim At or Kinematic constraint at the elbow is much easier to edit later by looking at simple-to-understand translation channels. You can tell where the elbow will be pointing at a glance. This is a good example of a little more work during the setup phase saving a lot of work during the animation phase. If you are setting up characters for someone else to animate, or you will be under a tight deadline (and who isn't?), you should always take the time during setup to make the character's animation as easy as possible.

Elbows that are set up to be targeted at a constraint also aid in giving the arm (and its constituent joints and apparent muscles) the illusion of mass.

While connecting the hand to the end of the arm would seem to be a no-brainer, other options exist. Animation allows opportunities to create movement that doesn't exist in the real world. Traditional animation techniques, such as overlap and secondary motion, can also be assisted by the setup choice that you make. Finally, your setup choice can make interaction with props or the character's environment less problematic.

The basic arm is very similar to the swing-arm lamp. The main kinematic chain consists of two bones driven through IK, and a third bone (to which fingers can later be attached) that stands independent, bound to the kinematic chain of the arm only through constraints.

We intuitively know that our hands are bound to the rotational whims of the parent bones in our arms, but our minds know the position and orientation of our hands at all times. Close your eyes, and lift your hand. You can form a mental picture of the position that your hand assumes in space. In fact, when you are moving your hands in space, the actual positioning of your arm bones is usually an afterthought, determined only by the limits and torque of your bones and muscles.

So as you lift your hand to the position requested by your brain, you twist your forearm to best adapt the orientation of your hand to that prescribed by your brain. There are times (when reaching for that cereal box on the top shelf, for example), we wish that the reach of our hands could exceed the boundaries placed on them by their connections to the bones and ligaments of our arms This is why the hand in these projects is disconnected from the arm. Animation is not bound by the conventions of the physical universe (though the animator can choose it to be so). Setups should allow characters to perform as if they inhabit our universe, yet alternately perform as our imaginations let them.

The arms in the following projects are drawn straight out from the shoulder, parallel to the ground, as if the character is trying to form the letter T. This is sometimes referred to as the jesus pose by people in the entertainment industry. The rationale behind this pose is simple, and your own arm will serve as the example. Stand up, and stick your arm straight out from your side, parallel to the ground. Now, put it against your side. You have just rotated your arm 90 degrees downward. Raise your arm to stick straight out from your side again. Now, attempt to reach straight up, but don't hurt yourself. Your arm has rotated 90 degrees upward (though not exactly, as your collarbone and shoulder blade also rotated when your shoulder reached its rotational limit). In general, your arm can rotate approximately 90 degrees in any direction from the T position.

The geometry in three-dimensional characters is much less forgiving than the flesh and bone of our human arms, even when you use patches in A:M or NURBS in Softimage or Alias. Yet, this advice to create characters in a T pose often competes with the hands-at-the-sides pose that some people prefer for setup purposes. If you set up a character with the hands at the sides, the shoulder geometry would have to be constructed to allow 180 degrees of movement, just for the arm to reach up above the head. This pose also complicates other setups that can accommodate movement of the clavicle (collarbone) and scapula (shoulder blade) and simulate the deltoid (shoulder muscle).

Basic Arm Setup

PROJECT 12.11

1. Start by opening a new model and a new modeling window in Top view and Bones mode.

2. Draw the arm bones as shown in Figure 12.85.

The bend in the arm is exaggerated (as it was in the legs) for these projects. A very slight bend can be employed, but it is better to always create bones with an obvious bend in the preferred direction.

3. Add the bone for the hand, but take care to note its hierarchical position in the Project Workspace (see Figure 12.86). It should not be a child of Bone2.

4. Change to a Front view. Move all three bones to a position above the ground plane equivalent to the height of the shoulder, as shown in Figure 12.87.

5. Add the bones which will become the constraint targets, bones Bone4, Bone5, and Bone6, independent of any hierarchy (see Figure 12.88).

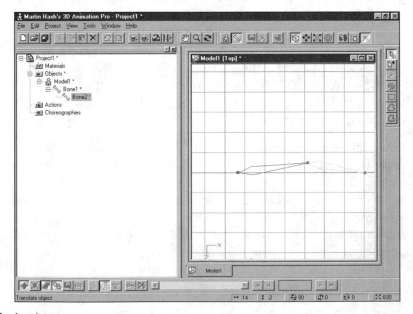

Figure 12.85 Arm bones.

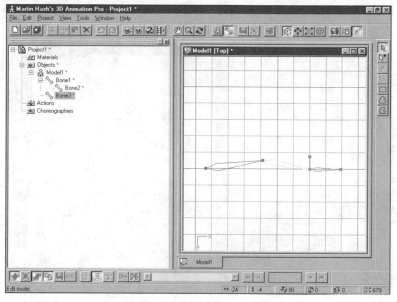

Figure 12.86 Hand bone added to the root of the hierarchy.

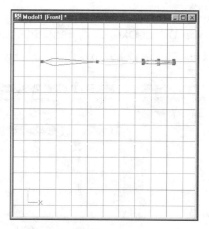

Figure 12.87 Arm bones positioned at shoulder height.

6. Return to the Top view, and, using the move tool (n), move Bone5 to the elbow position.

7. Open a new Action window, and go to the Front view. Select Bone1, add a Translate To constraint with Bone4 as the target, then add an Aim At constraint with Bone5 as the target.

8. Select Bone2, and add a Kinematic constraint with Bone6 as the target.

9. Select Bone3, and add a Translate To constraint with Bone2 as the target. Bone3 will jump to the pivot point of Bone2.

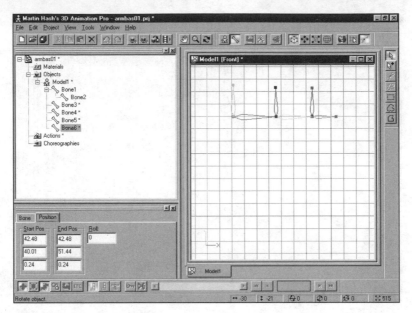

Figure 12.88 Arm bones.

10. Move Bone3 back to the tip of Bone2, both in the Front view and in the Top view. With Bone3 still selected, add an Orient Like constraint, and again select Bone2.

11. Your results should look like Figure 12.89. Save this project with a name of your choice.

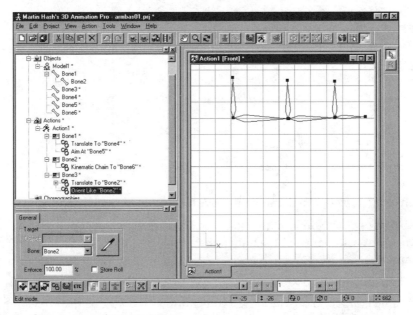

Figure 12.89 Arm bone setup with constraints.

GALLERY

In the following pages, you'll see color examples of the character animation projects presented in this book.

In addition, you'll see the work of several noted modelers, technical directors, and character animators for film, TV, multimedia, and games.

Steph Greenberg and nearly two dozen other animators created the short film, *The Physics of Cartoons*. Clips from it (and more information about how it was made) are located in the PHYSICS directory on this book's CD-ROM. This is an excellent example of traditional cartoon animation principles applied to 3D CGI.

There are three key poses for all takes: the normal pose, the squash, and the stretch. Some takes require special in-betweens, but they all use the same key poses. Slim and Tubbs do an extreme take, when they see an oncoming truck, incidentally showing off their invisible joint design. The last part of the take is a return to the *normal* pose —unless, of course, the character gets smashed flat by whatever caused the take in the first place.

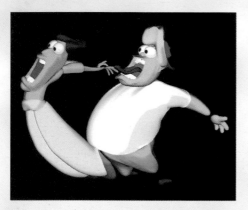 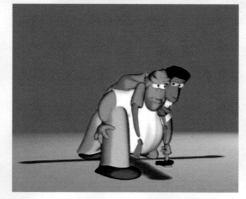

Slim and Tubbs, after meeting the truck.   Slim and Tubbs scramble for money.

Slim and Tubbs after a quick high-speed tour of an apartment building.

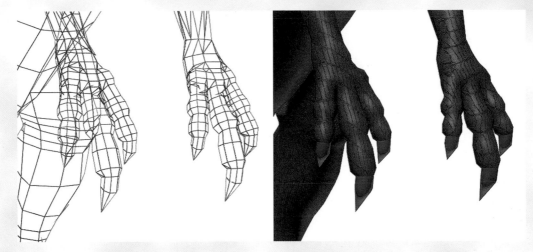

Tiled map applied to a hand model (Figure 8.20).

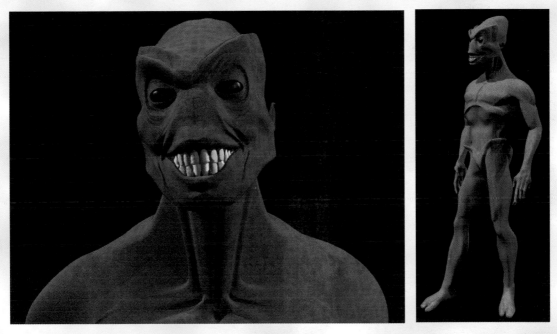

Roswell alien created by Armando Afre, using Hash's Animation:Master.
Reproduced by permission of Tom Marlin, Marlin Studios, tmarlin@marlinstudios.com.

Shag:Fur rendering showing unrealistic effects of straight strands oriental parallel to surface normals (Figure 10.14).

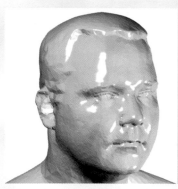  

Cyberware head scan object, color map, and object with color map applied. These are the results of the final scan, with powdered hair, shaved beard, and all possible corrections as described in Chapter 7 (From Chapter 8, Figure 8.4).

Foreground lamp character chroma keyed over digitized video background image.

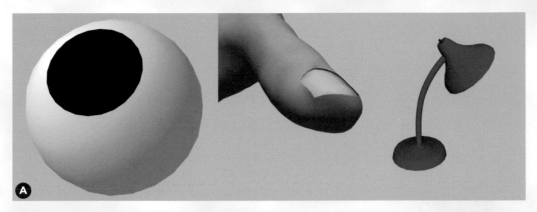

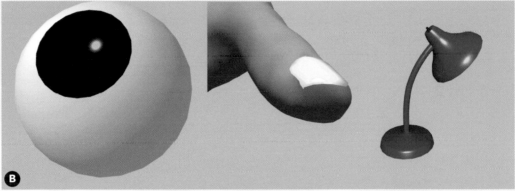

A: Base colors for eyeball, fingernail, and painted metal (From Chapter 8, Figure 8.4).

B: Base specularity for eyeball, fingernail, and matte-finished metal (Figure 8.2).

C: Base transparency for eyeball and fingernail (Figure 8.3).

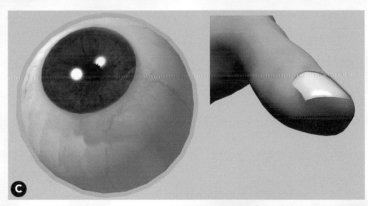

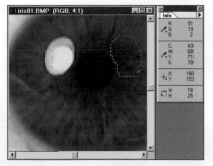

Selected mirror area for covering highlight (Figure 9.12).

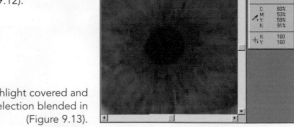

Highlight covered and selection blended in (Figure 9.13).

Kim Oravecz' "You Wanna Iguana?" with a cookie to mimic shadows of leaves (From Chapter 17, Figure 17.2).

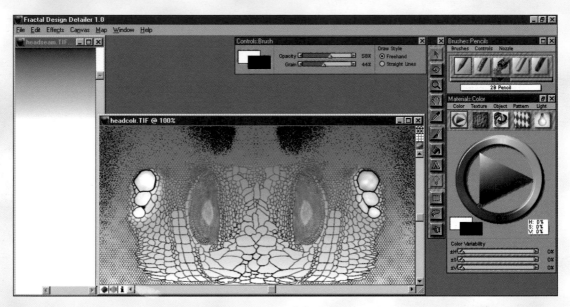

Seam alpha map and matching color map for iguana's head (from Chapter 10, Figure 10.5).

Iguana ear map (Figure 10.6).

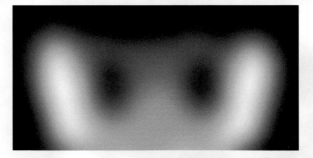

Iguana specular map (Figure 10.7).

Frog Prince, shown here in a variety of expressive poses, created by Michael B. Comet using 3D Studio MAX.

Mike Comet's Housefly (Figure 9.34).

Housefly eye color, bump and shininess strength maps.

Johnny Puma, Fantastic Frog, and Super Sloth characters created by Jeff Lew. You can contact him at jefflew@xtrabox.com.

Frankenstein's Monster (Frankie). 89,000 polygons (tripled), 8 hours to model and surface (from Chapter 6, Figure 6.29). Head is surfaced with image maps, body is procedural. Created for a promotional animation.

Robby the Rabbit (Figure 6.30). 35,000 polygons (tripled), 6 hours to model and surface, fully procedural surfacing. Created for an animated short film.

Check out the CHUBBS.MOV animation in the Komodo directory of the CD-ROM for a better look at this little demon's modeling and textures.

Tommy the Gangster (Figure 6.31). 125,000 polygons (tripled), 15 hours to model and surface. Head is surfaced with image maps. The body is procedural. Created for fun.

From Chapter 17, "Brown-Eyed Imp," modeled by Ken Cope, textured and lighted by Doug Kelly, rendered in LightWave 3D 5.5. The eyeball construction is detailed in Chapter 9, the modeling technique for the imp is described in Chapter 6, and the three-point lighting is the result of Project 17.1. The procedural skin texture is LightWave's Vein shader.

Scene from *Monster by Mistake*, showing the character animation and special effects possible with Prisms.

Gorgool from *Monster by Mistake*, created by Mark Mayerson and Catapult Productions. The maquette for Gorgool's head was modeled in Sculpey, as described in Chapter 5. *Monster by Mistake* was modeled, animated, and rendered using Prisms, published by Side Effects Software.

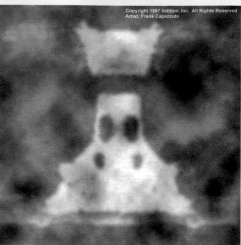

Maps for pilot character created by Frank Capezzuto, Volition, Inc.

Complete pilot character from Volition's forthcoming Freespace game.

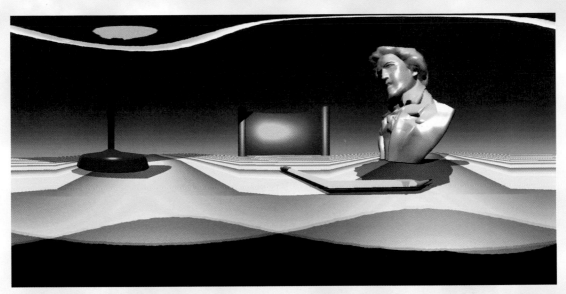

Assembled and centered environment reflection map (Figure 9.48).

Results of raytraced reflection and an environment reflection map in the same scene (Figure 9.49). Which is which?

Environmental reflection map applied to an eyeball.
Note that the "reflection" is of the image *behind* the object
(Figure 8.10).

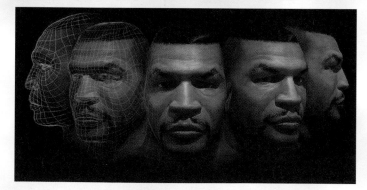

These images created by Jeff Bunker, Avalanche Software, http://www.avalanchesoftware.com, using Hash's Animation:Master software.

Excerpt from *The End*, one of several Chris Landreth self-portraits, by permission of Alias|Wavefront.

Case Study: Building A Cartoon Head In 3D Studio MAX

By Robert Terrell

Design a cartoon character face side view. Create a spline line around the outline shape of the face.

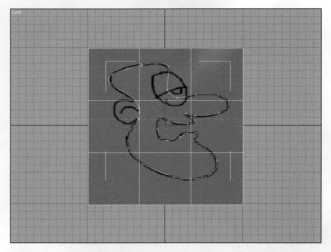

Create lines for the interior area of the face until you get it all to patch.

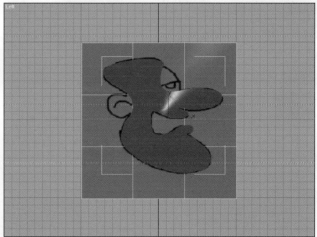

With the "Sub-Object" area selected, grab all the interior vertex points and pull them out from the centerline to create a more dimensional model.

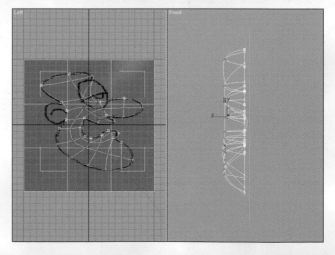

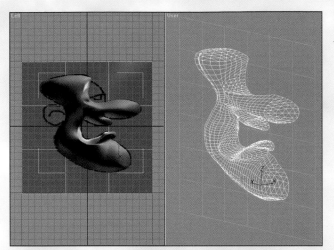

Select individual interior vertex points and move them. Use the "End result Toggle key" to check your work.

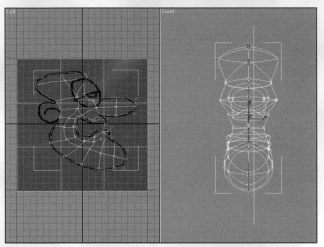

Create the other side of the head. Select the face outline spline and detach it. In the Front view, click on the "Mirror" button, select the X axis, and Clone Selection = Copy, then click on OK. Attach and weld all three objects to make them one, so you get a smooth transition between the two halves.

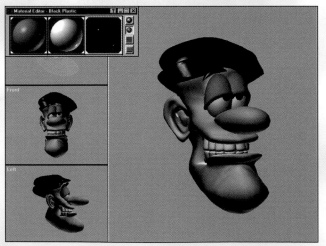

Add color, materials, or maps to your character. Eyes can be made from simple primitive shapes and spheres. By creating more individual organic shapes with splines, you can make teeth, ears, and hair if desired.

Create a body using the same tools of primitives and splines.

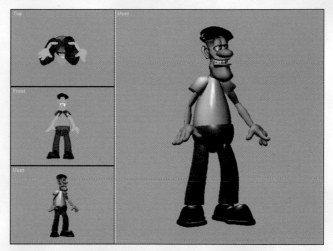

Finally, place your character into a set or interesting environment.

Captain Quazar, modeled and rendered by Bob Terrell using Animation:Master.

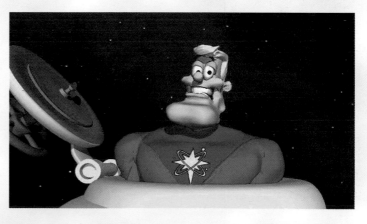

Case study images and Captain Quasar courtesy of Bob Terrell, Computoons, http://www.computoons.com.

These images are from Momentum Animation's Jurong Cobra case study in Chapter 18. This is a frame from the raw live footage, showing reference markers

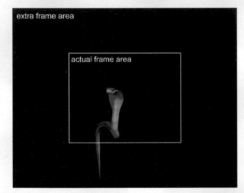

extra frame area

actual frame area

extra frame area

actual frame area

The cleaned up original footage, rendered character, and shadow layer all composited to create this final image.

Setting up this basic arm has established a constraint relationship with Bone4 anchoring the shoulder, Bone5 steering the elbow, and Bone6 determining the position of the hand. When you move Bone6, the hand maintains the orientation of the forearm but can be rotated as an addition to that orientation. This is essentially the same effect you would have gotten if you had just continued drawing Bone3 from Bone2, as a child of Bone2 in a continuous chain.

So, why take this convoluted route? Because there are times when you don't want the hand to automatically assume the orientation of the forearm. Note what happens to the arm when you select Bone5 and move it up and down, thus pointing the elbow in your selected direction. You want to be able to turn this off. For example, when a hand is on a desk, and you are pushing on the desk to rise up, you don't want the hand sliding around or rotating through the desk. When animating an overlapping action, the elbow might change direction while the hand is still moving in its previous direction for a frame or two. Yet without the ability to override the mechanical orientation of the forearm, the hand would suddenly jerk out of its intended movement, and you (as the animator) would have to manually counter-rotate it. At times like that, it is valuable to have other options. Character animation is difficult enough to do well, without adding the arcane task of compensating for parent rotation. The hand of your character need not become a rotational slave to its parent bone but adding these features will increase the up-front work for your first pass of animation.

If you've altered the setup by moving things around, revert to the saved version of the arm that you just created.

12. Select the Orient Like constraint of Bone3, which is currently targeted at Bone2, and change it to Bone6. Note that the hand has now assumed the rotational orientation of Bone6, 90 degrees from where it belongs. Rotate the hand back to its original orientation.

13. Save this setup under a different name than the previous one, then put the arm through its paces.

It has probably occurred to you that it would be really convenient if you could just switch between the two setups whenever you want. Well, you can, and we'll cover *switching constraints* later. That is another reason for having the hand separate from the forearm, because that relationship can be changed in the middle of an action, as an action is defined in A:M.

The next setup is a bit more obvious. To emphasize how these setups are related to one another, we will modify the preceding constraint arrangement instead of starting from scratch.

14. Revert to your saved version of the previous project. Open the Bone3 hierarchy in the action section of the Project Workspace, select Translate To Bone2, and change the target to Bone6. The bone will jump.

15. Open the hierarchy under Translate To Bone6, and delete the X, Y, and Z Offsets. Save this setup under a new name, and put it through its paces.

Note that the hand can now detach from the arm. If the skin were attached to the bone, the hand would stretch the length of the forearm. This is handy when binding the hand to another surface, providing a little "give" for it. This setup will result in the hand being rock steady when, for example, a character is holding on to bars in a prison, violently shaking his body back and forth, screaming, "Let me outta here! I'm innocent, I tell ya!" You don't want those fingers going through the bars just because on a frame or two the arms were pulled to their kinematic limits.

PROJECT 12.12 Kinematic Elbow Setup

There are many reasons to choose a particular setup. Sometimes, it's mechanical or the only way to do something. Sometimes, it's an arbitrary choice based on a stylistic preference, either the style of the character or the way an animator feels more comfortable working.

In the previous projects, the hand was the primary factor determining the fate of the arm's motion. The hand had full priority, with the Bone5 (the Aim At constraint) at the elbow suggesting the direction the elbow would point. But no matter how far away from the arm that Bone5 was moved, it had no pull, no force, to draw the elbow to it unless the hand allowed the arm to slacken.

Well, sometimes you want that elbow to be more steady, with the hand orbiting around it like a moon orbits around a planet. Or, sometimes you want a character to be leaning on a table with their elbows. Some animators just want to place that elbow exactly where they want it, and the hand is a second priority.

To do this setup, recall the second basic arm project, the one where the hand stays attached to Bone2 but orients to Bone6. You can do this project with the first basic arm project instead, if you prefer.

1. Open an Action window, select Front view, and open the Bone1 hierarchy. Select Aim At Bone5, and delete it.

2. With Bone1 selected, add a Kinematic constraint, with Bone5 as the target.

3. Select Bone2, open the hierarchy, and delete Kinematic Chain To Bone6. Select Bone2, and add an Aim At constraint with Bone6 as the target.

4. Save the project under a new file name, then put the arm through its paces.

Note that the constraint driving the hand could be anywhere, but it is the elbow that has control over how much the arm will extend. This becomes particularly evident when you go from an arm-pointing-down to an arm-pointing-up motion.

But, suppose that you want the setup to have the detachable hand, like the last basic arm project. Instead of using the first two basic arm projects as your basis for the Kinematic elbow, use the third project. You can also modify the previous Kinematic elbow. However you arrive at your solution, save your results as usual, but this time with the name kinelbow.prj.

Put the arm through its paces. Try all three possible Kinematic elbow setups. Note that the results of the detachable hand are even more radical than with the basic detachable hand.

If you like the possibilities offered by the basic or kinematic detachable hand for comic animation, you'll love the next project.

PROJECT 12.13

Cartoon Arm Setup

Generally, CG character animation tends to follow a conservative, animation-imitates-reality style. But if you really want to depart from that and engage in something like cartoon-style animation, a radical approach might be in order. The cartoon arm is like the cartoon knee—the elbow can float, with no fixed length to either the humerus or the forearm. This is particularly useful if you have a character with short arms who needs to reach around its body, or when animating to the camera and the arm just doesn't read well.

1. Reload the last project with the detachable hand, the one called kinelbow.prj. Delete Action1. Open a Model window, and, in the Front view, select Bone1, and delete it.

2. Switch to a Top view, and draw a new Bone1, from the elbow to the shoulder, as shown in Figure 12.90.

3. In the Front view again, move the new Bone1 back up to where the rest of the bones are, as in Figure 12.91.

4. In the Project Workspace, drag Bone1, and drop it on Model1, which will place Bone1 at the top of the hierarchy. Now, drag Bone2 on top of Bone1, to make Bone2 a child of Bone1.

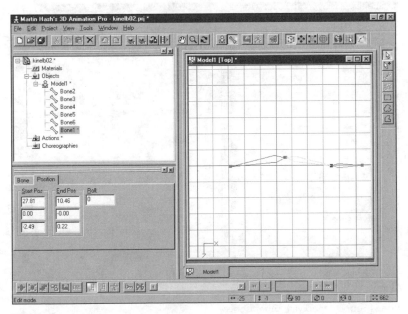

Figure 12.90   Bone1 added.

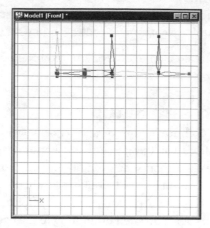

Figure 12.91   Bone1 repositioned with other bones.

5. Open a new Action window. Select Bone1, and add a new Translate To constraint with Bone5 as the target. With Bone1 still selected, add a new Aim At constraint with Bone4 as the target.

6. Now, select Bone2, and add a new Translate To constraint with Bone5 as the target. With Bone2 still selected, add an Aim At constraint with Bone6 as the target.

7. Select Bone3, and add a Translate$To constraint with Bone6 as the target. With Bone3 still selected, add an Orient Like constraint, with Bone6 as the target. Rotate Bone3 back to its initial position, as shown in Figure 12.92.

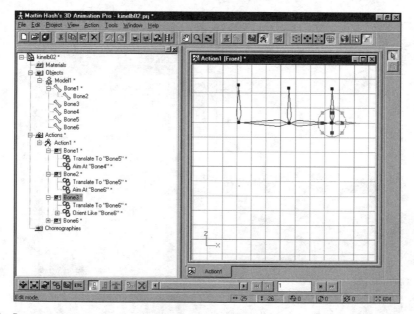

Figure 12.92   Bone1 repositioned with other bones.

8. Save this project under the name toonbw.prj.

9. Put the arm through its paces (see Figure 12.93). Then, revert back to the saved version.

10. Open a new Model window, choose Front view, and select Bones mode. Select Bone1, grab the tip of it, and shorten it. Do the same for Bone2. Your results should look like Figure 12.94.

11. Open a new Action window, or return to the one that was previously opened. Save this project as toonbw02.prj.

Put the arm through its paces now (see Figure 12.95). With the bones shortened, you get the feel for an arm with an elbow that could be anywhere. It takes some practice, discipline, and restraint to successfully use the cartoon elbow and not make it look horrible. Nobody ever said animation was easy, but we can try to make it as easy as possible.

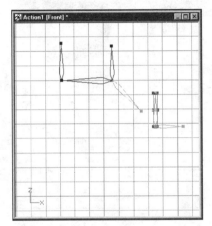 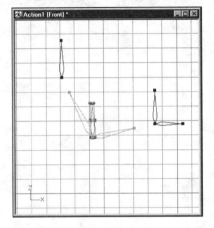

Figure 12.93   Cartoon elbow test.

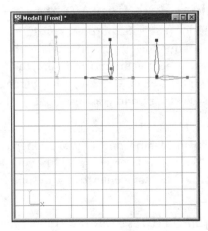

Figure 12.94   Bone1 and Bone2 shortened.

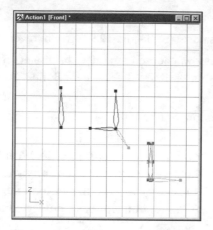

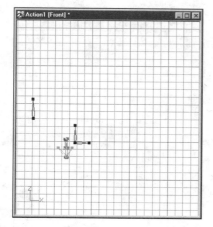 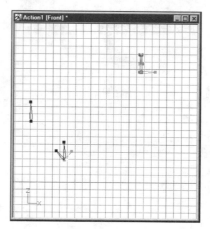

Figure 12.95 Animation test of cartoon elbow setup.

Rubber-Hose Animation: Path Constraints

Like so many tools designed for a specific purpose, constraining bones to a path can serve purposes far different than that intended by the original developer of the tool. Much like turning that $100 Makita variable-speed drill around and using the back end as a hammer because you don't want to climb down the ladder. Or using a flat blade screwdriver as a pry bar, hole punch, knife, drill, Phillips screwdriver, and yes, once again, a hammer.

In a casual conversation at a SIGGRAPH convention (the annual gathering of the tribes of CG animation, science, education, marketing, and art practitioners), Hash Inc. owner Martin Hash was once heard to remark, "Sooner or later, every tool in your toolbox becomes a hammer." This was in response to hearing how someone was using something in his software in a way that he hadn't anticipated.

While the following is being introduced as a way to do rubber-hose style cartoon animation on the arm, it has uses that go far beyond arms and, of course, legs. Although it appears complicated, once you learn it, this technique only takes a few minutes to do the initial setup.

Essentially, the reasoning behind the Constrain-To-Path setup is to simplify the animation process of moving bones in a smooth curve. Inverse kinematics generally work best when configured with a minimum number of joints, but a minimalist joint strategy often doesn't allow for the complexities of organic life. The rubber-hose arm in a cartoon character could be the neck of a giraffe, a dog's tail, the edge of a wing, or a cat's spine.

Those uses are pretty obvious once you understand the underlying concept. But this technique can also be used to control the fat on an obese character, muscles, cloth, hair (well, a ponytail at least), and can also be used to space bones apart from each other as the spline that they are attached to is compressed, bent, twisted, or stretched.

Creating the constrain-to-path rubber-hose arm is accomplished by creating a path constructed of a relatively simple spline and fastening individual bones or a chain to the spline to control the skin geometry of a character. Alias has a constraint type called *constrain to spline*, which automates this process somewhat but it also has other limitations. Nearly all software supports this to some extent.

DRY ERASE MARKERS

You will need a dry erase marker, china marker, or grease pencil to mark positions of the bones on your screen. Dry erase marker comes off your computer screen the easiest and won't cause you to rub off the anti-reflective coating on your computer screen. Expo's fine-point dry erase marker yields the best results, and having multiple colors doesn't hurt, although we won't need them for this project. Whatever you do, *don't* use an ordinary felt tip marker, because this can leave permanent marks on your screen and be very costly to clean up. If it does not say DRY ERASE on it, don't use it *under any circumstance*.

This is a pretty low-tech but effective way to add a place holder on the screen between different modes of a program, different keyframes, even different programs. Just don't move your head when you're using this technique, because the glass on your computer screen is thick enough to create a difference in the position of your marks due to the effects of parallax.

Rubber Hose Arm Setup

A:M supports realtime update of the bones that are constrained to a path, and in which the path itself is attached to and driven by simpler IK chains. This will be the approach that we will take in this project.

1. Start by loading armbas04.prj, the basic IK arm structure with the detachable hand. Open a Model window with the Top view in Bones mode.

2. At the base of each joint, take out your grease pencil or dry-erase marker, and make a cross, as shown in Figure 12.96.

3. Get into Modeling mode (F5), and turn the Show Bias Handles button on (this is the top-right icon on the top toolbar).

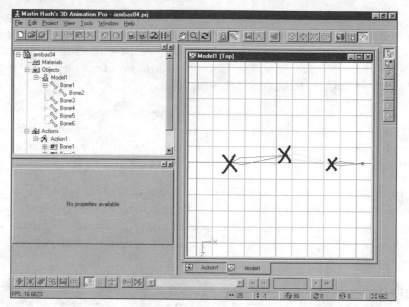

Figure 12.96 Grease pencil cross drawn at the base of each bone.

4. Add a spline with a control point on each cross. You can erase the crosses when you're done.

5. To help keep the spline direction neutral, we will adjust the gamma handles to a more neutral position. Click on the right-hand control point, and you should see the bias handle. Hold the Shift key down, click with the left mouse button, and move the mouse to rotate the gamma of the control point until it is close to that pictured in Figure 12.97. Release the Shift key, and adjust the magnitude (see Figure 12.98).

6. Repeat Step 5 for the left-hand control point.

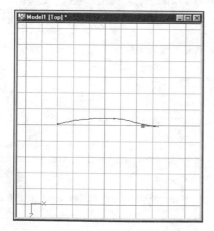

Figure 12.97 Adjusted gamma of the control point.

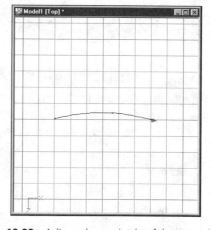

Figure 12.98 Adjusted magnitude of the control point.

7. Return to Bones mode, and hide Bone1 and Bone2.

8. Add new bones Bone7 through Bone12 in a chain, positioned along the spline, as shown in Figure 12.99. After the chain is complete, drag each child bone of Bone7 up to Model1, and drop it, thereby taking the bone out of the hierarchy, as shown in Figure 12.99.

9. Now, hide bones Bone7 through Bone12, and unhide Bone1 and Bone2.

10. We will now group the control points of the spline to the bones. Simply select Bone1, click on the Group Mode icon (g), and drag a box around the left control point (CP#1) (see Figure 12.100).

11. Repeat Step 10 for the middle (CP#2), selecting Bone2 and the right (CP#3) control point with Bone3 selected.

12. As a final check, select a Front view. If your spline is not aligned in the same plane as Bone1 through Bone3, mark crosses on the screen as you did before. Return to Modeling mode, select the control points by grouping them all together (this will not affect the bone assignment), and move them up to the crosses. When you're done, erase the crosses.

13. Return to the Bones mode, and hide Bone1 and Bone2 again. Unhide bones Bone7 through Bone12. Get into a Front view, and check to see if the bones are on the same plane. If not, move them one at a time. You don't have to mark the screen, because the constraint bones Bone4 through Bone6 mark the plane of Bone1 and Bone2. Save the project under a new name.

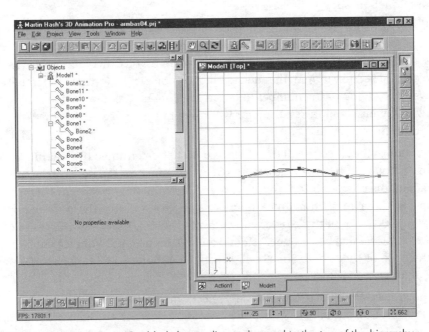

Figure 12.99   Bone7 through Bone12 added along spline and moved to the top of the hierarchy.

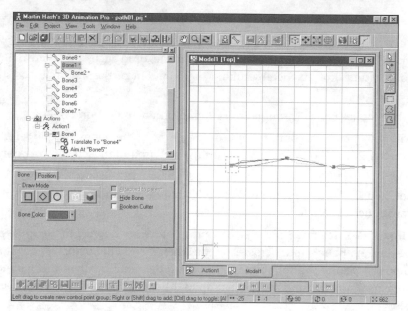

Figure 12.100 Spline control points grouped to bones.

14. It's time to open an Action window. All of your old constraint information should still be there. Just to check it, open everything up in the Project Workspace hierarchy.

15. Select Bone7, and add a Path constraint with CP#1 as the target. Do the same for bones Bone8 through Bone12.

This is where things get a little complicated. The position of a bone on a path depends on a percentage value in the Ease box of the Property window. Almost every program has some equivalent to this function, but many require you to actually move a keyframe in a channel editor. In A:M, that added bit of complexity is (fortunately) unnecessary. However, arriving at the number to put in the Ease box requires some simple math, for which your computer's calculator will come in handy if you don't feel like doing the math in your head.

The distance that a bone will travel along a path is determined by entering a number from 0 through 100 in the Ease box. 0 is at the very first control point of the spline that makes up the path, and 100 is at the very end. Because we have 6 bones of roughly the same size, we can get a ballpark figure to start with to properly space the bones by dividing 100 by 6. In this case, the increments between the bones will be 16.66. This means that the first bone, Bone7, should be at 0, because we want it to align its pivot at the base of the spline. Bone8 will be at 16.66, Bone9 33.33, Bone10 50, Bone11 66.66, and Bone12 83.33.

16. In the Project Workspace, under Bone7, select Constrain To Path "This Object" (1). In the Properties window, Bone7 already has a value of 0% in the Ease box, as shown in Figure 12.101. Select bones Bone8 through Bone12 in turn, and add the appropriate value in their respective Ease boxes.

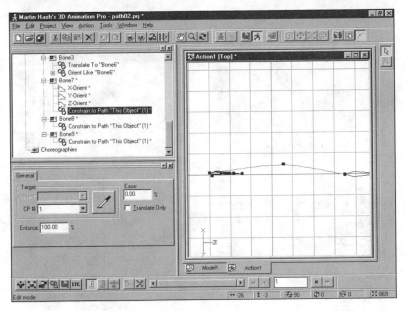

Figure 12.101 Ease setting for Bone7.

17. Select Bone7, and add an Aim At constraint with Bone8 as the target. Next, select Bone8, and add an Aim At constraint with Bone9 as the target. Continue following this pattern for bones Bone9 through Bone11.

18. Add an Aim At constraint for Bone12, with Bone6 as the target because Bone6 is the wrist constraint. Alternately, Bone3 could also have been used, particularly if you use an alternative setup with the hand attached to Bone2 or with an Orient Like constraint with Bone2 as the target.

    You may note that the bones don't quite look properly spaced. If there was geometry attached to the bones, they would be distorting it. The mathematical spacing that we entered into the Ease boxes doesn't quite match the arbitrary way in which the bones were created. But there's a fix for that.

19. Go back to bones Bone7 through Bone12, and tweak the Ease values until the bones lie more precisely along the spline. You should get something like Figure 12.102.

Roughly, Bone7 remains at 0%. The percentage for Bone8 changed to 12% from 16.66%, Bone9 to 30% from 33.33%, Bone10 to 55% from 50%, Bone11 to 70% from 66.66% and Bone12 to 89% from 83.33%. How did we arrive at these particular numbers? Well, we just tweaked them until the bones looked like they were in the right place. If this seems a bit unscientific, you might consider how scientific hand-drawn animation is: It's all done by eye. In any case, your number could be different, and you have to do this by trial and error.

When you've gotten your percentages as close as necessary for it to look right, save your project under a new name. Put this new setup through its paces by moving and rotating Bone6 (the hand) and Bone5 (the elbow) (see Figure 12.103). You can also change the curvature of the

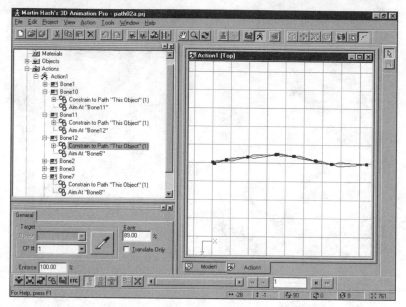

Figure 12.102 Tweaked Ease settings for bones Bone7 through Bone12.

spline by adjusting the bias handles in the Muscle mode of Action. If you bring the magnitude of CP#2 (the middle control point) down to near zero, the chain will act sort of like a regular two-bone IK chain. If you increase the magnitude of CP#2 to 150, you get a rounder chain.

So far, we've only been using this technique to do a sort of averaging type of curve between Bone1, Bone2, and Bone3 or Bone6. However, you can also animate a skew into the spline that will allow you to animate a free form curve into this arm (or whatever construct you are using this technique for). See Figure 12.104.

This last setup allows for animation of a pathed set of bones, presumably with skin attached, that still has some form of skeletal structure to it. However, an approach that is much simpler

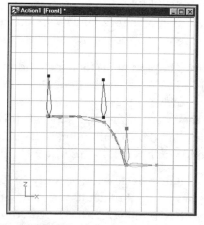

Figure 12.103 Animation test of the Rubber Hose setup.

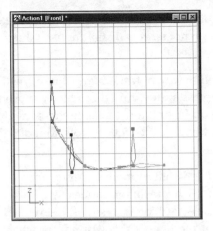

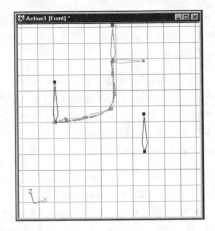

Figure 12.103 (continued) Animation test of the Rubber Hose setup.

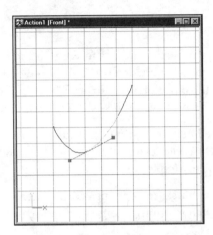

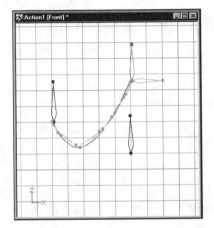

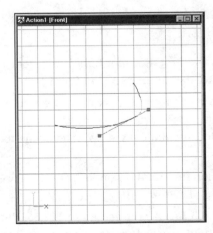

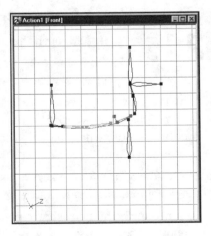

Figure 12.104 Animated skew of Rubber Hose setup.

is to delete Bone1 and Bone2 from the model and attach CP#1 to Bone4, CP#2 to Bone5, and CP#3 to Bone3 or Bone6. This will be a free-form chain not terribly dissimilar from the cartoon free-floating arm.

It should also be noted that when you pull the spline way out, the bones space themselves evenly, and, when you compress it, the bones compress evenly. And those nicely spaced Ease percentage channels, like nearly everything else, can be animated to slide the bone up and down the path. This could be useful if you use this technique for fat controls, to make the fat jiggle along the path.

If you use this technique for a tail, you might want to add one or more control points to it and, of course, the same number of constraint type bones. There are an infinitude of ways to use this path constraint technique, many of which alleviate the need for expressions, reserving the use of those tools (which aren't in the A:M programs at the time of this writing) for when more intuitive means are insufficient.

Constraint Switching

Among CG Character professionals, character setups provoke religious fervor rivaling that of platform or program preferences. This situation has largely persisted because, once you pick a setup technique, that's the way it has to be done for the duration of a project. Changing setups means scrapping everything—animation, blocking, maybe even models—and starting over.

Constraint switching can alleviate this. It is supported fully by Softimage, Alias, and A:M, and with plug-ins, in LightWave and 3D Studio Max 2. However, it can be a complex process to set up, and it would be a good idea to practice on simple examples first.

Simply put, constraint switching allows you to do two things: You can turn constraints on or off during the course of an animation, and you can switch to another constraint in the process.

Basic Constraint Switching Setup

1. In A:M, open the project armbas04.prj.
2. On frame 1, keyframe positions and rotations for Bone5 and Bone6. In the keyframe entry area, enter the number "5", and hit Enter.
3. Now that you're on frame 5, select Bone6 and move it, then click on the keyframe button. The reason we click on the keyframe button is to drop a key for both rotation and translation, where moving the bone would automatically drop a keyframe for translation only.
4. Select Bone5, and drop a keyframe for translation and rotation on keyframe 5. Pose the skeleton according to Figure 12.105 for setting keyframe 10.

So far, Bone3 (the bone that represents the hand) has been oriented to Bone6. But suppose for some reason, we want the hand to orient like the forearm. There are many reasons why you might want to do so, in particular to save time if the arm is doing many wild swings or perhaps the character is repetitively swinging its arms. This would

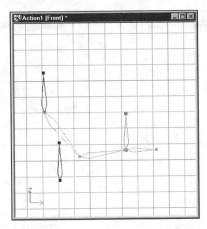

Figure 12.105   Pose for keyframe 10.

be a no-brainer if we knew that we were going to want the arm to orient to the forearm (Bone2) for the whole animation. But in this case, suppose we want to start off with the hand oriented to Bone6, but at frame 10, we want to have the hand orient to Bone2? What then?

We don't have to delete the previous Orient Like constraint to Bone6 and start a new animation.

5. Select Bone6, and add a new Orient Like constraint with Bone2 as the target (do not alter the existing Orient Like constraint, but add a new one).

6. At frame 1, give the new Orient Like constraint an enforce percentage of zero. This setting appears at the lower left of the General properties tab, in the lower-left corner of your screen.

7. Now, we need to set a key on the new orientation constraint's percentage. Turn off the Set Keyframe Translate and Rotation buttons, turn on the Key Constraints button, and drop a keyframe on frame 1.

8. Repeat Step 7 for the Orient Like constraint with Bone6 as the target.

9. Slide the keyframe slider bar to frame 5, select Orient Like Bone6, and drop a constraint key on frame 5. Do the same for Orient Like Bone2.

10. Go to frame 10, select Orient Like Bone2 (if it isn't still selected), change the enforce percentage from 0% to 100%, , and key the constraint.

11. Select Orient Like Bone6, and change the enforce percentage from 100 % to 0%, and key the constraint.

12. Set translate and rotation keyframes for Bone5 and Bone6 for frames 15, 20, 25, and 30, according to Figure 12.106.

13. At frame 35, switch back to the original orientation preference, with the Orient Like Bone6 set back to an enforce percentage of 100% and Orient Like Bone2 set back to an Enforce percentage of 0%.

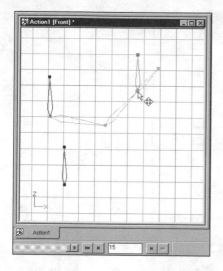 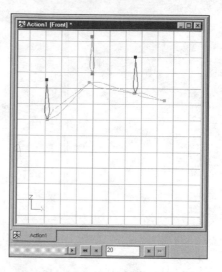

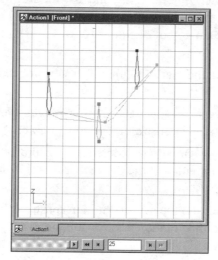

Figure 12.106 Keyframes for Bone5 and Bone6.

14. Set the position and rotation keyframes for Bone2 and Bone6 according to Figure 12.107.

15. Test the setup by dragging the keyframe slider back and forth.

    Note that from frames 1 through 9, Bone3 aligns its orientation according to Bone6 and the Orient Like offsets. At frame 10, the orientation of Bone3 is now the same as the forearm bone (Bone2). And so it remains, as we move Bone6 (the wrist) and Bone5 (the elbow) back and forth, until we get to frame 35, when Bone3 snaps back to Orient Like Bone 6. There are more graceful ways to ease into that position, such as rotating Bone6 so that as the hand switches orientation, it doesn't jump in rotation. Covering up little flaws like this is easy, compared to the tweaking you'd have to do without constraint switching.

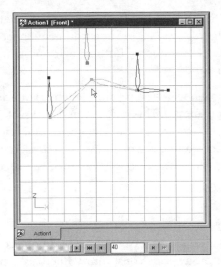 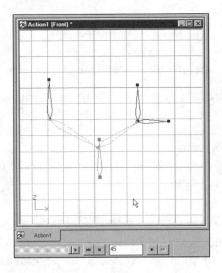

Figure 12.107 Keyframes for Bone2 and Bone6.

The next part is far trickier to explain than it is to actually do. However, some explanation in advance is necessary. Earlier in this project, we were switching how Bone3 obtains its orientation/rotation. Now, we'll do the same for Bone3's translation. The problem is that as the transition takes place between Bone3 constrained toBone6 (with a Translate To constraint), to constraining Bone3 to Bone2 (still with a Translate To constraint), Bone3 will want to jump to Bone2's pivot point. Suddenly, the hand is attached to the elbow! This could be a very ugly thing if skin was attached to the bones.

In A:M, the solution is simple. Select the bone, and move it back to the point at which the hand should join the wrist at the end of the bone. This creates what are called *offset* channels. They should only be activated when a constraint is turned on (enforce is greater than 0%).

16. Select Bone3's Translate To Bone6 constraint, and add a constraint keyframe at frame 45. Select Bone3 again, and add a new Translate To constraint with Bone2 as the target (do not change the existing Translate To constraint, but add a new one).

17. Set the new Translate To enforce percentage to 0% and add a constraint keyframe. Go to frame 1. Note that the enforcement percentage has suddenly jumped to 100% again. This is because the default behavior of A:M is to drop a 100 % enforcement percentage on all new constraints at frame 1. Set the enforce percentage of this new constraint to 0% and drop a constraint keyframe.

18. Go to frame 50, with the Translate To Bone2 constraint still selected. Change the enforce percentage to 100% and drop a constraint keyframe. Now, select the Translate To Bone6 constraint, change the Enforce percentage to 0% and drop a constraint keyframe. Note that Bone3 (the hand bone) has now translated to the elbow.

19. Select Bone3, and translate it back to the end of Bone2 (the forearm bone). Although you may be working mostly in the Front view, it's best to also check the Top view or any other relevant view at this point.

20. Select Bone6, translate it beyond the limits of the end of Bone2, and you will see that the hand stays attached to Bone2. Yet, the hand still assumes the orientation of Bone6 when you rotate it. You might want to experiment by dropping further keyframes and reorienting or switching the orientation of the hand.

Scroll through the keyframes that you have, and note how the constraint switching affects the movement of the hand when the elbow and hand are moved. This type of constraint switching can be very useful for picking up objects or having objects control the movement and orientation of the hand. This would also include a character leaning his/her hands on a desk or wall, holding the bars on a jail or fence, holding onto a steering wheel, or picking up a cup of coffee and putting it down again.

Constraint Mixing And Blending

With A:M, Alias 6 and above, and, to an extent, Softimage, you can constrain an object with more than one constraint target, and you will get an average constraint value between the two.

In A:M and Alias, you can also adjust the weight of influence of one constraint over another. Mixed or blended constraints are used to solve a variety of setup problems. They can be used to average orientations between two bones to smooth out an elbow or shoulder, they can float a bone between two other bones or nulls, so that as the bones approach or recede from each other, and the bone in the middle will always stay the same distance between them (unless weights or percentages of influence of the constraints are animated). And of course, the influence percentages or weights *can* be animated in programs that provide that feature.

PROJECT **12.16**

Mixing Translate To Constraints

We'll begin with a simple example.

1. Draw three bones as pictured in Figure 12.108.

2. Open a new action, select Bone2 (the middle bone), and add a Translate To constraint with Bone1 as the target. Select Bone2 from the Project Workspace, and add a second Translate To constraint with Bone3 as the target.

We now have a blended constraint. When Bone3 or Bone1 are moved, Bone2 will remain dynamically suspended between them. Select Bone3, and move it around. Look at the effect obtained by this simple constraint blending.

3. Select Bone2, and open the Properties window. Select Translate To Bone1. In the Properties window, the number in the Enforce box will read 100%. Change it to 60%. Note that Bone2 has now jumped closer to Bone3, because the Enforce value for the Translate To Bone3 is still set at 100%. Let's remedy this.

4. Select Translate To Bone3, and change the Enforce value to 40%.

Now, the total of the two constraint targets adds up to 100%, yet Bone2 is weighted 60 percent in favor of Bone1. Again, select Bone3, move it around, and observe the effect its movement has on Bone2. It may not be obvious, but the Enforce value is animatable.

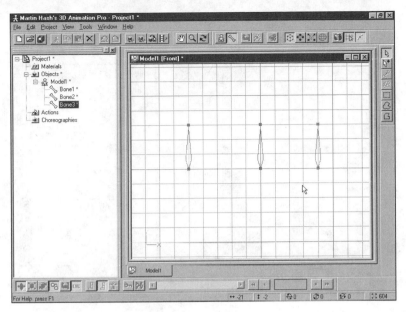

Figure 12.108   New bones.

5. Drop a keyframe for the existing constraint settings on frame 1.

6. Select the handcuff and other constraint icons in the set keyframe area, select Branch mode, and click on the keyframe button.

7. Go to frame 10. Select the Translate To Bone1 constraint, and change the Enforce value from 60% to 40%. Select the Translate To Bone3 constraint, and change the Enforce value from 40% to 60%.

   Review the default channels that we've just created, and note that the percentage channels have constant values. That is, they hold their value until the frame where the switch occurs. In A:M, this is called a *Hold* interpolation. It is called *Step* in Alias and *Constant* in Softimage. We want the constraints to be mixed and blended, that is, we want a smooth transition between the two keyframes. We must, therefore, change the Default Interpolation (located in the General properties tab) for the Enforce Percentage channels to either Linear or Spline. In this case, we'll use Spline.

8. Select the Percentage channel of the Translate To Bone3 constraint for Bone2. In the General properties tab, select Spline as the Default Interpolation.

   If we inspect the channels now, we'll see that they smoothly transfer their weights from the keyframe settings at frame 1 to the settings at frame 10, as shown in Figure 12.109. Because there are only two keyframes, the default behavior still makes the curves linear.

9. Drag the animation slider between frames 1 and 10. You should see Bone2 move between Bone1 and Bone3, without any keyframes being set on the translation of Bone2.

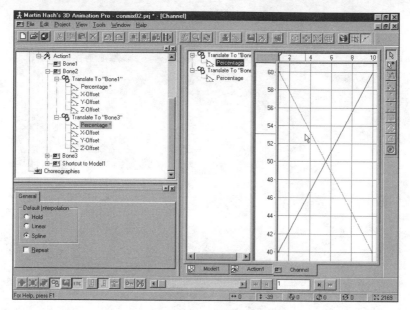

Figure 12.109 Constraint percentage channels, showing a smooth transfer between two keyframes.

This technique can be used, for example, for bouncing fat or keeping control points separated but spaced in a completely controlled manner. You might then animate the enforce percentages to give the fat some secondary motion or jiggle. You are not limited to the influence of only two bones, but mixing the influence of more bones can slow down your computer's performance.

Mixing Orient Like Constraints

PROJECT 12.17 Now that we've covered the concept of constraint mixing using translation, along with the animation of the Enforce Percentage channels, it is time to test this technique using rotation.

As with mixing Translate To constraints, mixing Orient Like constraints allows a bone to assume an equilibrium between the rotational values of two (or more) other bones. The most basic use of this technique is to smooth out rotational values at the joints (such as the elbow) so that the skin of the character appears more elastic. This also gives the appearance that the joint underneath the skin has a larger "ball" to which the skin moulds itself.

1. For this project, we can use the bones setup from the previous project. First, clear the action.

2. Select Bone2, and add an Orient Like constraint with Bone1 as the target. Select Bone2 again, and add another Orient Like constraint, this time with Bone3 as the target.

3. Now, let's test it out. Select Bone3, and rotate it. Select Bone1, and rotate it. Now, rotate Bone3 again, and note that Bone2 continually maintains an equilibrium between the two, no matter which was rotated first (see Figure 12.110).

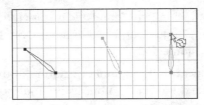

Figure 12.110 Orient Like constraint mixing. Bone2 (middle) maintains equilibrium between orientation of Bone1 and Bone3.

You can animate the values that maintain the tension between the three bones, particularly where it solves a problem that occurs during the course of the animation. You can select any ratio between the two target bones, using the enforce percentage, much as you can select gear ratios on a mountain bike. It's a good idea to experiment with this concept and practice setting up characters using it. When a nasty character setup problem lands on your desk, you want to have as many tools as possible (and as much experience with them) to help you find a solution.

PROJECT
12.18

Soft Elbow Setup

This project shows you how to modify the basic arm setup with constraint mixing, to create a soft elbow.

1. Open the basic arm example that we created earlier. In the Model window, add a new bone—Bone7—at the top of the hierarchy (under Model1), from the Top view, as shown in Figure 12.111.

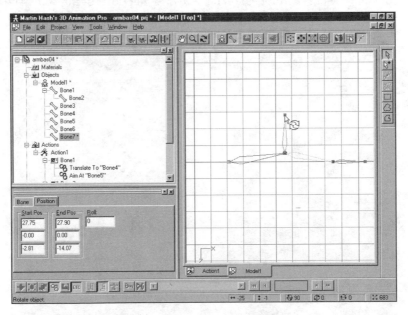

Figure 12.111 New Bone7 added to the basic arm setup.

2. Open the Action window, select Bone7, and add an Orient Like constraint with Bone1 as the target. Select Bone7 again, and add another Orient Like constraint, but this time, select Bone2 as the target.

Note that Bone7 no longer has its original orientation. If there were skin assigned to Bone7, it would be twisted 90 degrees from its original position. At this point, let's straighten out Bone7. We don't just want Bone7 to stay where it is but to follow the elbow created by Bone1 and Bone2.

3. Select Bone7 again. Add a Translate To constraint, with Bone2 as the target, so that Bone7 will fix itself at Bone2's origin and follow it wherever it goes.

4. This would be a good time to save. Let's put this setup through its paces.

5. Select Bone6, and drop a translate-only keyframe on frame 1. Go to frame 10, and move Bone6. Note that our new Bone7 rotates at half the amount that Bone2 does (see Figure 12.112). Drop a keyframe on frame 10 for Bone6.

6. Drag the frame slider back and forth between frames 1 and 10 (see Figure 12.113). Switch to a Front view, and experiment from the Front view, and again slide between frames 1 and 10. Move the elbow constraint, Bone5, and see how that affects the rotation of Bone7.

7. Save this project under a new file name for later reference.

Alternatives For Constraint Setups

While the previous tutorials explain constraint strategies using arms and legs as examples, it should be noted that these techniques can be used on other parts of the body. The cartoon arm

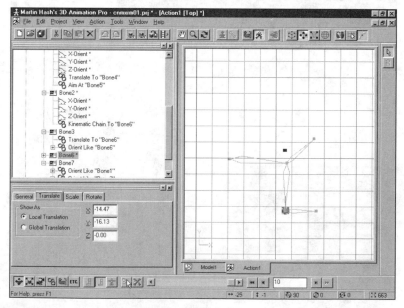

Figure 12.112   Bone6 moved, and Bone7 rotating with mixed constraints.

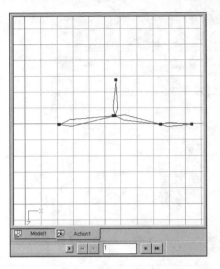
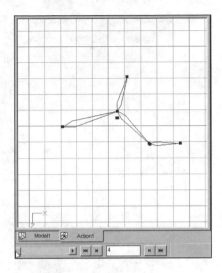
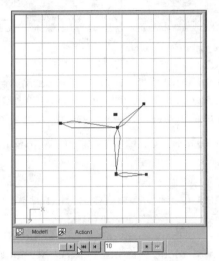

Figure 12.113 Bone6 controlling setup via constraints.

can be used for the spine of a highly flexible cartoon-style character, a horse, cats, and any other character where the general form follows a curve. On a fat character, for example, the cartoon-arm technique can be employed for the front profile of the character, allowing for control of the character's fat.

Load the jeffskel.prj from the Chapter 12 directory on this book's CD-ROM (see Figure 12.114). The first thing you should note about the jeffskel character is that the right and left arms are very different. The right arm (which is screen left) is a standard, simple skeleton. The left arm (screen right) has all sorts of complex bone structures contained within it to drive the biceps, rotate the biceps, drive the collar bone, drive the deltoid, and twist the forearm.

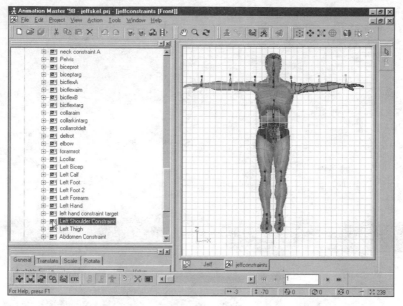

Figure 12.114 Jeffskel.prj loaded, showing different setups for right and left arms.

If you want, you can experiment with the right and left arms to see how they perform differently and preview how IK chains driving IK chains, which in turn drive still other IK chains, can be used to solve various skinning and character operation problems.

A good reason to study this skeleton isn't because it's the best example of what can be done, but because it shows how many ways setting up a character *can* be done.

Constraint Hierarchies Can Save Your Sanity

Constraints enable you to do several different tasks. They can enable you to isolate various body parts like the feet from the movement of the pelvis, the arms from the movement of the torso, or allow objects to move along with other objects without inheriting their hierarchical rotation. But these are merely the mechanical manifestation of the power of constraints.

There is also a strategic purpose that constraints can serve. Often, when starting a project (particularly one that involves other people and perhaps clients), you find yourself in a position where you have to begin animating right away, yet the final model isn't completed and the skeleton can't be finalized. For a specific example, again load the jeffskel.prj, and examine the complexity of the left arm. That complexity was developed as an approach to a particular set of problems: making the biceps rotate as the forearm points up or down, making the biceps bulge, and making the deltoid lift with the collar bone. Those demands on the skeletal structure, including methods for solving them, could not have been fully anticipated until a more complete skeleton was available. The jeffskel setup went through a *lot* of revisions.

It is common for animators to animate with a simple skeleton and character to get a general idea across, either to themselves or their clients, and then abandon any animation done at that stage. There is simply too much of a difference, between the setup for those early tests and the final setup for the initial animation keyframes to be efficiently adapted. But by developing a hierarchy which can drive a more sophisticated skeleton, and animating that hierarchy in the earliest tests, it is possible to salvage the animation. You can even transfer it from character to character, when that is a useful animation strategy.

This salvaging of animation is an enormous advantage if applied properly. If you have to wait until the models and setups are perfectly finalized before you can even begin to animate, the animation will always be under the worst time and resource crunches. If you can experiment with animation tests throughout the modeling and setup development, you will have a stock of animation that you can immediately apply to the final character. Essentially, you will be able to develop your character's movements, mannerisms, and acting throughout the project, instead of tacking them onto the end of the project like an afterthought.

This strategy of using constraints in a hierarchy of their own, to drive bones in a separate hierarchy, works for A:M, Softimage, and Alias. You may be able to apply it to other software, depending on how they handle hierarchies and constraints.

In A:M software, there is a caveat to this approach. If the bones in your initial simple hierarchy have different names than the ones in your final skeleton but the constraints have the same names, you will have to re-constrain the bones. It's not a big deal (probably around an hour of work for a typical setup), but with some planning it can be avoided altogether.

We've covered some of the methods for constraining arms and legs, so it's time to discuss the torso.

The Torso

The basis for the torso is, of course, the pelvis. It seems fairly obvious—the backbone is attached to the pelvis, and the thorax, or upper body, is attached to the backbone. Well, not so fast there, Sparky! Turn on the TV, and look at dancers and ice skaters. They often rotate or swing their hips while there appears to be no change of rotation or orientation of their upper torso. This is simply an elegant and obvious occurrence of upper torso isolation. This occurs because the body of most vertebrates is under the control of their mind and is not determined by mere mechanical linkages.

In computer animation, we all too often allow these virtual mechanical linkages to determine the fate of our animation. Besides our own human hands and eyes, the brains of our characters can be found in their animation channels. If a CG character animator noodles with the animation channel curves, more lively animation can often result. But the results of such noodling can be unpredictable, unless you build isolation into your character.

So, what do you do? One approach is to set up the entire upper torso to be driven by one null or bone with the pivot at the pelvis, with a second level of bones or nulls that can be animated independently. This may seem obvious. However, there are several different ways that these constraints can be strung together on the torso, and they in turn can be constrained to one another. You can choose setup options to either save time or just make better-looking animation.

To start, think of the upper torso and lower torso as two separate, rigid structures. The area in-between is a bit mushier and facilitates distension (like slouching) or extension (like standing at attention). The upper and lower torso are not connected with a rigid linkage, as is the common practice in CG character animation.

On the other hand, when roughing out animation or moving characters around for blocking, having to move the upper torso separately from the lower torso seems like more work than is absolutely necessary. The question you should be asking is, "Is there a way to do this so you can operate a character both ways?" Now really, would this question even be presented to you if the answer weren't yes?

PROJECT 12.19 Torso Isolation Setup

This project shows you how to set up a character's torso so the pelvis and thorax can be isolated for more efficient and better quality animation.

1. Open a new project. Add a null object under Model1 (New|Null Object). Rename the null object as *Constraints*. All bones and other nulls that will become constraints will be children of this null.

2. Under Constraints, add a bone at about pelvis height, and call it *Pelvis*, then add two more bones for the hips, as in Figure 12.115. This is the pelvis unit that will actually drive the bones to which the final mechanisms that drive the skin will be attached.

3. Add another bone under Constraints and above the Pelvis bone, in the approximate location of the pivot of the ribcage, and name this bone *Thorax* (the anatomical description of the ribcage and associated bones and cartilage).

4. Add two bones above and on either side of the Thorax, and name them *Right Shoulder* and *Left Shoulder* (if the character is facing out from the screen, then right is on the screen left and left is on the screen right) as in Figure 12.116.

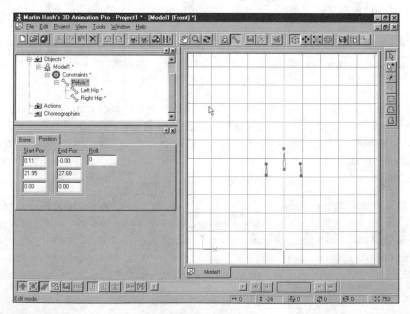

Figure 12.115 Pelvis and hip bones added under Constraints null.

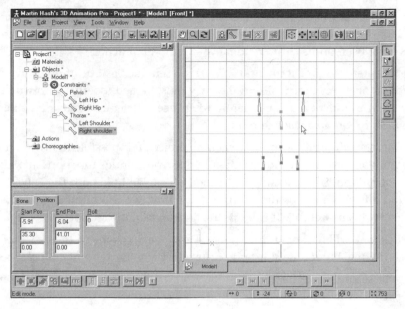

Figure 12.116 Thorax and shoulder bones added.

Now, you need to prepare the setup so that a midsection bone (which will be created later) can be targeted with a Translate To constraint to the end of the Pelvis constraint.

5. Add a new bone to the end of the Pelvis constraint. Make certain that the Attached To Parent box is unchecked, because we don't want this bone to be affected by IK dynamics. Your results should look like Figure 12.117.

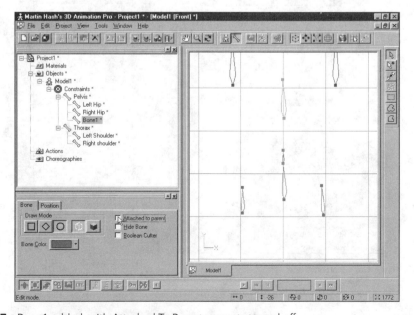

Figure 12.117 Bone1 added, with Attached To Parent property turned off.

6. Add a similar bone to the top of the Thorax, and again make sure to take the checkmark out of the Attached To Parent box. In Figure 12.118, note how these new constraint bones have been named, and rename your setup to match.

These two hierarchies (Thorax and Pelvis) represent the basic animation structures for the upper torso. For practical reasons, they must be tied together in a way that will allow them to function independently when needed, yet also move together during animation roughing or blocking stages.

As we've seen with the constraint switching project, it is possible to have a constraint setup work one way in one part of an animation but change functions in a later stage of the animation. So, we'll create a linkage which will hold both the Pelvis and Thorax, and allow them to be moved as a single unit, yet will allow them to be moved independently, as well. We'll call this the Backbone of the character.

7. The Backbone will consist of three bones. Draw the first bone in the exact location of the Pelvis bone, but a little shorter to help with visibility. Rename it *BackboneA*.

8. Draw the second bone in the same location as the pelvis target node. Rename it *BackboneB*.

The midsection bone (which will be drawn later) will be able to switch between translation to the pelvis target node and BackboneB.

9. From BackboneB, draw another short bone that starts from the Thorax's origin, and name this bone *BackboneC*.

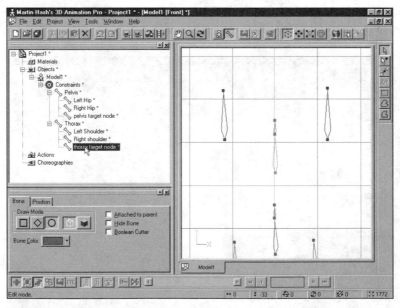

Figure 12.118 New bones added and renamed.

10. Move these two new bones underneath BackboneA in the hierarchy, as shown in Figure 12.119, and make sure that BackboneC is detached from BackboneA by turning Attached to parent off.

11. For the time being, hide the Pelvis and Thorax bone structures so you can examine Backbones A, B, and C independently.

12. BackboneB doesn't need to go all the way to the pivot of BackboneC. This would be a good time to shorten it, so it doesn't become confused with the midsection bone later on.

13. Hide the three Backbones, and make the Pelvis and Thorax structures visible again.

14. Draw the midsection bone from the origin of the pelvis target node to the origin of the Thorax. Rename the bone *Midsection*.

Here is the first crossroads in setting up this constraint hierarchy. You now have a choice:

- Drive the Pelvis, Thorax, and Midsection constraints by constraining them to the Backbone bones (which would allow you to switch those constraints off to make them independent of the Backbone).

- Place the Pelvis, Thorax, and Midsection into hierarchies with the Backbones as the parents.

Binding the torso elements together by constraining them to the Backbone is a completely legitimate technique. There are probably circumstances where you might find it to your advantage to set it up that way, but putting the torso segments into a hierarchy will actually keep the overall system simpler.

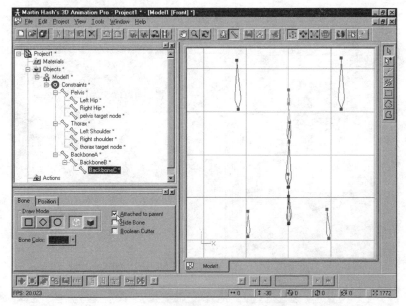

Figure 12.119   BackboneB and BackboneC positioned and arranged in hierarchy under BackboneA.

15. Drag the Pelvis structure, and drop it on BackboneA, making it a child of BackboneA. Drag and drop the Thorax on BackboneC. Finally, drag and drop Midsection on BackboneB. Your results should look like Figure 12.120.

    We now have our torso constraint hierarchy, but it's not complete until we constrain the constituent constraints.

16. Open an Action window. Select the Constraints null, and drop a translation and rotation keyframe on the entire hierarchy. This will cause the entire hierarchy to become selectable from the Project Workspace, which is a handy way to work when you have several overlapping bones or nulls.

17. Select the Pelvis, and move it. It moves independently of its parent, BackboneA. But if you were doing an animation, this would cause an undesirable bend in your character's torso. As an animator, you can certainly tweak every element that is under your control, but there are setup cheats you should definitely employ to make animating easier.

18. Return the Pelvis to its former position by deleting the translation and rotation channels.

19. Select the Pelvis. Add an Aim At constraint with BackboneB as the target. Now when we move the Pelvis, it points resolutely at BackboneB, maintaining some semblance of connection to the rest of the torso, as shown in Figure 12.121. Still, the transition between the Pelvis and the Midsection is pretty abrupt and would require some real hand tweaking to clean up all the skin folds and other artifacts.

20. Alternatively, you could try this setup: Select the Midsection, add a Translate To constraint with the Pelvis target node as the target, and add an Aim At constraint with the Thorax as the target. This setup will produce a nice curved transition, as shown in Figure 12.122.

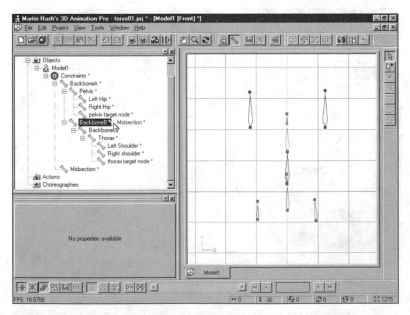

Figure 12.120 Hierarchy rearranged under BackboneA, BackboneB, and BackboneC.

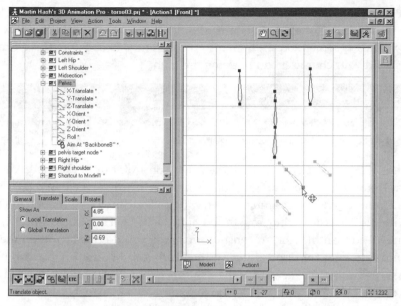

Figure 12.121   Pelvis constrained to BackboneB.

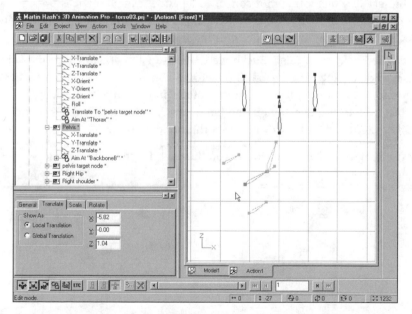

Figure 12.122   Midsection constrained for a smoother transition from the pelvis to the thorax.

There is more to this setup than meets the eye. One dead giveaway that screams "Computer Animation!" is when a character stands with its hips motionless. This is particularly noticeable when animating realistic humans or characters that interface with the real world. This setup enables you to prevent or fix the motionless hip problem. By making small, slow random alterations to the X-translation curve, you can make it appear that the character is constantly shifting the distribution of weight on its hips. This is something we humans do constantly. Exaggerate those translation curves, and your character can be doing the hula.

HIDDEN BACKBONES

The Backbone bones are hidden to avoid accidentally mis-selecting them interactively. But they are still active, even though hidden.

So, what is the downside to aiming the Pelvis constraint at BackboneB? Well, if you look at Figure 12.122 you can see that the hips are nearly vertical in relation to each other. This might not be desirable. When exaggerating the Pelvis motion in this manner, with the Pelvis departing from the baseline of the Backbone this radically, it might be prudent to turn the Aim At constraint off. You can do this by setting the enforce percentage to zero. The disadvantage is that, with Aim At disabled, you can no longer move that X-translate curve with the assurance that it will resolve itself into something reasonable. You will have to pay closer attention to exactly what is occurring in the setup and manually tweak it to remove problems.

This project demonstrates what sort of independent movement is possible with the hips. Of course, you can also move the upper torso about just as much. The setup works both ways. But, how does all this relate to the Backbone?

21. Unhide the Backbones. Select BackboneA, and translate it. Note that the Pelvis, Midsection, and Thorax all move in unison with the Backbones (see Figure 12.123). And if you rotate BackboneA, the whole thing rotates in unison with BackboneA. Not only that, but by rotating BackboneB and BackboneC, note that there is an additive rotational effect, added to the previously set rotational values.

22. Save the project under a new name. You'll need it for the next project.

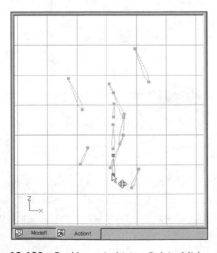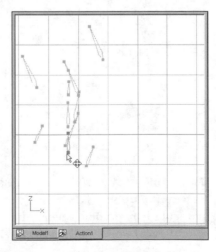

Figure 12.123 BackboneA driving Pelvis, Midsection, and Thorax.

With this setup, you really can't get too far lost. Because the Pelvis, Midsection, and Thorax are in a hierarchy with the Backbone, you can type zero values in their Translation and Rotation properties boxes to realign them with their respective parent backbone. No matter what the Backbone is doing, you still have the freedom to animate these structures any way you like. But the biggest advantages to this setup are being able to adjust the structures directly through the animation curves and having the confidence that poses won't unpredictably whack out.

Normally, when you create a constraint hierarchy, you do so with the model and first skeleton in place. But the beauty of a constraint hierarchy is that it can be moved, not only to accommodate the present character being worked on but to any character. Individual elements can be moved around as needed.

Now that we have an adequately constructed torso constraint hierarchy, we need to add the remaining elements to make it a complete and self-contained hierarchy that can be used on nearly any bipedal character. The structure of the constraint torso in many ways replicates or appears to obviate the need for a separate bone hierarchy. However, the constraint hierarchy is only a simplified way of driving the main hierarchy. The main hierarchy may be a much more complex skeletal system, designed to replicate the effects of muscle and fat as well as the mechanical effects of bones in a body.

The Legs

As mentioned earlier, part of the goal of constraint hierarchies is to maintain isolation between body parts while allowing coherent manipulation of those parts. There is no relationship in the body where this is more obviously necessary than that between the torso and the legs. The torso must remain able to move freely while the feet remain planted (or moving independently).

This becomes increasingly important when you manipulate animation curves directly. With an independent foot hierarchy, you don't have to worry about the feet shifting when you adjust the up-and-down movement of the torso.

PROJECT 12.20

Leg Isolation Setup

This project shows how to set up leg isolation in addition to the torso isolation setup in Project 12.19.

1. Reload the setup you created in Project 12.19. Before we create the constraints that drive the legs, let's reset the torso action while still maintaining the constraint relationships.

2. Select the Constraints null. Make certain that only the translation and rotation keyframe buttons are set, and select the Key Model keyframing mode. Select Edit|Delete Keyframes. You now have a neutral pose for the torso constraints with constraints preserved.

3. Open the Model window, and select a Right view. Select Constraints, and add a bone where the knee would go, at an upward angle, as shown in Figure 12.124. This makes it easier to select from a Front view. Change to the Front view, and move the knee over

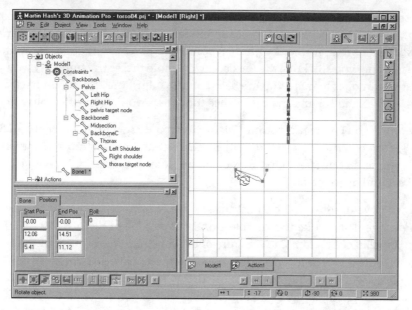

Figure 12.124 LeftKnee bone added.

to the approximate front location of a knee. Rename the object *Left Knee*. Note the Left Knee's position in the hierarchy as a child equal to BackboneA.

4. Again, select Constraints, and add a knee bone in the parallel location on the right side of the hierarchy. Rename it *Right Knee*.

5. Next, we add the foot hierarchy—Left Ankle, Left Heel, Left Ball, and Left Toe—as shown in Figure 12.125.

   The angle of the bones is designed primarily for easy selection. The ankle and heel bones should be aligned along one axis, in this case the Z axis. This way, when animating, you will always be able to tell if the foot is above or below ground by its movement on the Y axis. Well, most of the time, because in A:M, rotation occurs first and translation second. So if the Ankle is rotated on the X-axis, upward movement will be represented in both the Y and Z animation curves.

   If this is a problem, you can add another bone as the parent of the Heel, Ball, and Toe, which is a child of the Ankle, that is for the purpose of rotation only, and make the Ankle something that is used for translation only. In an effort to keep things somewhat simple, we'll go with the standard Ankle=>Heel|Ball|Toe hierarchy for the foot constraint.

6. Move the left foot hierarchy to its Front view position.

7. Create a right foot hierarchy that is a mirror-image of the left foot hierarchy. Move it to its final position in the Front view, as shown in Figure 12.126. Note the hierarchy in the Project Workspace.

We're done with the legs for now. There are no special constraint relationships in the foot and knee constraints themselves, so we won't need to go into the action editor.

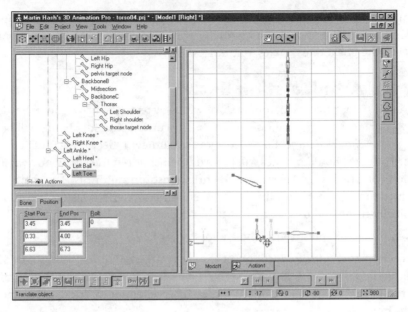

Figure 12.125   Foot bones added, from left: Left Toe, Left Ball, Left Heel, and Left Ankle. Note the bones' positions in the hierarchy.

The Arms

The arms are one of those multifunction areas where sometimes it is best for the arms to follow the translation and rotation hierarchies of the upper torso, sometimes the translation only, sometimes the rotation only, and sometimes neither.

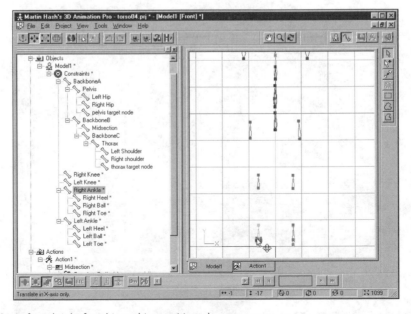

Figure 12.126   Left and right foot hierarchies positioned.

Once again, constraining the constraints comes to the rescue. Instead of making the hands and elbows a part of the upper torso hierarchy, we will instead create a hierarchy that is at the same level as the Backbone, Ankles, and Knees.

PROJECT 12.21 Arm Isolation Setup

This project's hierarchy starts with new bones, which occupy the identical space as the current Shoulder bones. The current Shoulder bones will be renamed as *Shoulder Target* bones, to more accurately reflect their function and to avoid confusion. The new Shoulder bones will have as their children the elbow and wrist constraints, the functions of which were covered in the arm constraint tutorials. This new hierarchy will then be glued to the upper torso through Translate To and Orient Like constraints, which can be strategically turned off as needed.

1. Reopen the setup you saved at the end of Project 12.20.

2. Add bones exactly in the location of the current Left Shoulder and Right Shoulder. When adding the bones, make sure that you select the Constraints null to make certain that these new bones are at a hierarchy level equal to BackboneA and the leg constraints.

3. Now, rename some constraints. Under Thorax, rename Left Shoulder as *Left Shoulder Target* and Right Shoulder as *Right Shoulder Target*. Now, rename the new bone that you just created in the location of the Left Shoulder as *Left Shoulder Constraint* and the bone at the Right Shoulder as *Right shoulder Constraint*.

4. Select Left Shoulder Constraint, and add a bone where the elbow should go (see Figure 12.127), and rename it *Left Elbow*. Do the same for the Right Elbow.

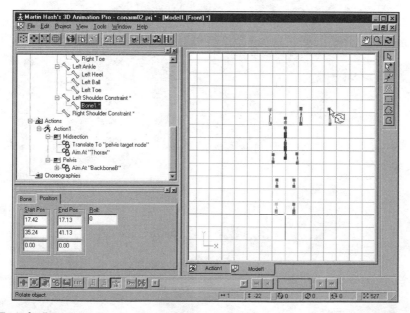

Figure 12.127 Left Elbow added and positioned.

5. Select Left Shoulder Constraint, add a bone where the left wrist would be, and rename the new bone *Left Wrist*. Do the same for the Right Wrist (see Figure 12.128).

These are all the constraints that we'll need for the arms, but we still need to tie these constraints to the torso.

6. Open the Action window. It is likely that not all the constraint bones are visible in the Project Workspace. To make them visible, select the Constraints null, and drop a keyframe on rotation and translation with the Key Model option set. Now, everything should be represented in the action Project Workspace, as shown in Figure 12.129.

7. Select Left Shoulder Constraint, and add a new Translate To constraint with Left Shoulder Target as the target. Now, add an Orient Like constraint, again with Left Shoulder Target as the target. This nails down Left Shoulder Constraint to Left Shoulder Target in both position and rotation, enforcing a perfect match. Repeat these steps for the Right Shoulder Constraint (see Figure 12.130).

8. This would be a great time to save.

Let's see how this baby handles.

9. Select BackboneA, and rotate it on the Z axis. Select the Right view, and rotate BackboneA on the X axis (see Figure 12.131).

Note that the bones of the arm constraints line up with the orientation of the body. But just to make certain that they are receiving their orientation from the Thorax, select the Thorax, and rotate it on the X axis.

10. Now, let's see what happens if we select the Right Shoulder Constraint's Orient Like constraint and crank the enforce percentage down to zero.

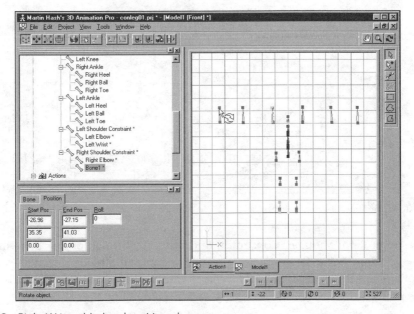

Figure 12.128 Right Wrist added and positioned.

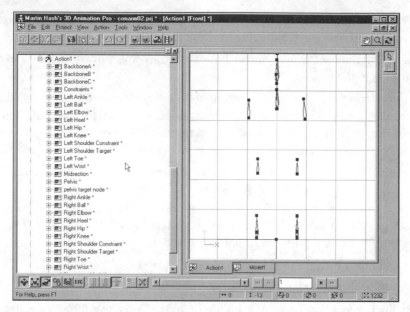

Figure 12.129 Project Workspace showing all constraints.

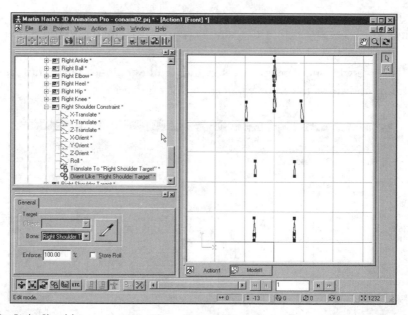

Figure 12.130 Right Shoulder constraint setup.

11. Now, select Right Shoulder Constraint, and, with Key Branch or Key Bone mode selected, click on Delete Keyframe to delete the orientation already recorded. You could also have left the translation data intact if you deselected the Key Skeletal Translations box.

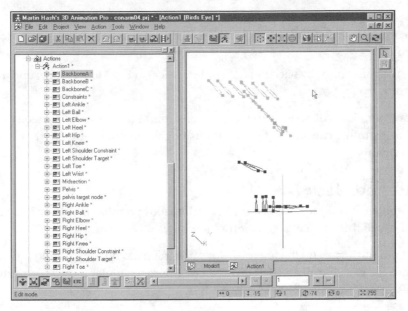

Figure 12.131 BackboneA rotated.

It should be apparent that the constraints on the right arm are now vertical, in their default orientation, as shown in Figure 12.132.

If you select the Thorax and rotate it on the X axis, you will see that the left arm, still with its orientation constraint activated, assumes the orientation of the Thorax, while the right arm steadfastly sticks with its default orientation. And if you just reactivate

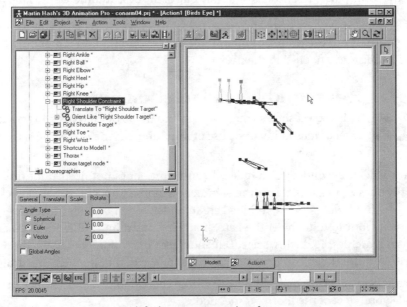

Figure 12.132 Right arm constraints in default orientation with enforce percentage at zero.

the Orient Like constraint on the Right Shoulder Constraint by setting the enforce percentage back to 100%, the right arm will resume matching the orientation of the Thorax.

12. Reset the constraints by selecting Constraints, click on Key Model mode, and delete the keyframe.

Believe it or not, that's all there is to the arm constraint hierarchy. You've seen how the elbow and wrist constraints can be used with various bone configurations. So, that leaves just one human extremity.

The Head And Neck

While we could cover things like tails and miscellaneous protuberances, the head and neck are the last pieces of this particular constraint hierarchy.

Conventional, orthodox methodology always has the head operated using forward kinematics. As far as the neck is concerned, that is the best approach under most circumstances. But, we can leave our options open by using constraints.

But, what of the head? When the body rotates, does the head not rotate? When the shoulders rotate, does the head not rotate along with them?

The answer is: *no way!* On all of our bodies, the head tends to hold itself independent right up to the physical limits of the neck. If you're looking at something, and you adjust your posture, your head stays pointed at where it was looking. If your head looks away, it's because you're thinking about something, being evasive, or are just bored and trying to find something interesting to place your gaze upon. If you bend over, you'll probably look at the floor first and continue looking in the same place. The head is arguably one of the best automated tracking devices, ever.

One thing is constant—your head stays attached to your neck. Even if you (or the character that you're animating) are drunk, although the head motion might lag behind the body, the base of the head stays attached to the neck.

Head And Neck Isolation Setup

This project shows you how to set up the head and neck to provide the same level of reusability and ease of animation as the preceding setups for the rest of the body.

1. Open a Modeling window, and hide all constraint bones not needed for this project. The only ones we need visible are the Thorax and thorax target node. Select BackboneA, B, and C, and hide them. Next, hide Left Shoulder Target and Right Shoulder Target. Next, you want to hide the entire Left Shoulder Constraint and Right Shoulder Constraint hierarchies. To do this, select Left Shoulder Constraint, hold down the Shift key, and click on the Hide Bone box. Do the same for the Right Shoulder Constraint.

This sure beats clicking and hiding everything individually. Now, there is nothing to occlude your view of the thorax target node.

2. Select a Right view, zoom into a view of the Thorax and thorax target node, and then select Constraints.

3. Draw a bone exactly on top of thorax target node, followed by two others as shown in Figure 12.133. Rename the bones as *neck constraint A, neck constraint B,* and *head target node.*

4. Select Constraints, and add a bone vertically from the base of head target node. Rename it *head constraint.*

5. Open the Action window, and select the Right Side view, zooming into the Thorax, neck, and head constraints. Select Constraints, and drop a keyframe with Key Model on, which will make the new bones appear.

6. Select neck constraint A, and add a new Translate To constraint, with thorax target node as the target. Next, add an Orient Like constraint also with thorax target node as the target.

7. Select head constraint, and add a Translate To constraint with head target node as the target.

8. Return to the model section of the Project Workspace, select neck constraint B and head target node, and turn off Attached To Parent (see Figure 12.134).

9. Save this project.

You now have a complete constraint hierarchy, which by only adjusting the location of the constraining bones can work for any bipedal character offering optimal animation flexibility. It can also work for quadruped characters, but the wrist and elbow constraints would have to be bumped up to the same level as the feet and knees.

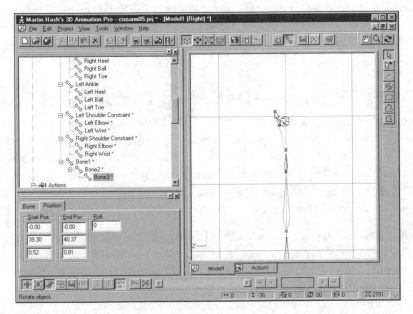

Figure 12.133 Neck bones added.

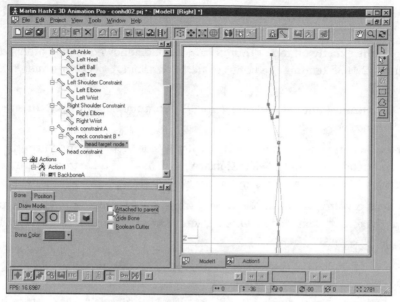

Figure 12.134 Neck and Head constraints set up.

There are a few things that can be added to this hierarchy, like eye bones that point to an Aim At constraint at a distance, and other facial sub-hierarchies like ponytails, jawbones, and maybe eyebrows, but those methodologies truly change so much from character to character that they are best handled on the character skeleton level.

Before we leave this project, let's return to the Action window, select BackboneA, and rotate it. Do the same for BackboneB and BackboneC. Note that the head constraint stays upright. It'll keep doing that, even when you rotate neck constraint A and neck constraint B, as shown in Figure 12.135. And lastly, you can, of course, rotate the head constraint by selecting it and rotating it.

Pulling It All Together—Decoding The Jeffskel Project

The Jeffskel project file (jeffskel.prj, from the Chapter 12 directory on this book's CD-ROM) is an example of a character setup that goes beyond the simplified human model that most CG animators seem to use. Jeffskel has a superstructure of constraints driving the torso, legs, shoulders, and head. In addition, this setup has a fairly complex mechanism in the left arm, which not only drives the biceps but softens the elbow, allows the arm to twist from shoulder to wrist, and incorporates a simplified working mechanism for the collarbone and deltoid muscle.

The Jeffskel character was constructed with the constraint hierarchy described in the preceding projects. The same constraints drive the right and left arms, despite the difference in complexity of their underlying structure. The implication of this is that if you animate the constraint hierarchy only and later upgrade the model and skeleton, the animation should still work just fine. This bears repeating: If you set the character up right the first time, you can make all the model and skeletal changes you want, anywhere along the line, without a bit of wasted effort.

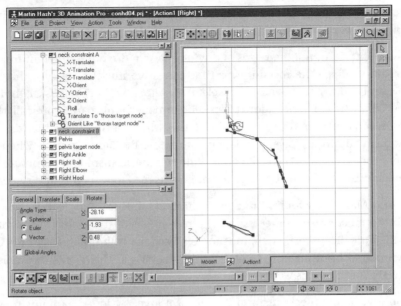

Figure 12.135 Neck and head constraints in action.

One thing left out of Jeffskel is a mechanism for the Left Wrist constraint to drive the rotation of the hand. You can modify this yourself by using the knowledge you've gained from the arm projects. In the case of the Jeffskel character, we wanted the hand to follow the rotation of the Left Forearm. The hands are constrained positionally and rotationally to bones on the ends of the Forearms. You can use constraint switching to either constrain the hand to the wrist constraints or constrain the constraint targets at the ends of the Forearms to the wrist constraints. You can even add a child bone to the Wrist constraints, with the same starting orientation as the constraint targets, which themselves have the same starting orientation as the hands. Lots of options, any one of which can save your bacon when deadlines get tight.

HIERARCHIPHOBIA

It's easy to be intimidated by complex hierarchies such as the one semi-deployed on Jeffskel. But they are always methodically constructed one step at a time, and constrained one step at a time. Take it systematically, and it's not nearly as intimidating.

It's good to keep in mind that there are two ways bones are being employed on any character. The first is as a driver for the skin. Skin-driving functions are simple on a program like A:M. You assign geometry *control points* (or *vertices* or *control vectors*, whichever term the software developer has decided to use) to a bone. In Softimage, you can assign control points to nulls. In Alias, you can create clusters of control points. But in Alias and Softimage, you can also use automatic assignment methods to attach a control point to multiple bones. This gives an effect similar to the constraint mixing project for every control point in the geometry assigned.

This concept of assigning control points is often referred to as *skinning*, and the concept of control point assignments being mixed between multiple bones, *soft skinning*.

But even with soft skinning, the needs of driving the skin are often different from simple mechanical relationships. The mechanisms that can drive muscles and fat, however, can be subordinate and additive to the standard skeletal movements. Thus, in Jeffskel, the biceps *mechanism* is subordinate first to the standard bicep=>forearm mechanism (anatomically, the humerus, the bone running from shoulder to elbow) and the twin forearm bones (the radius and ulna). The mechanism within the biceps is designed to rotate the biceps muscle when the elbow is bent, aiming the biceps muscle at the hand. Another mechanism is subordinate to the biceps rotating mechanism, designed to bulge the muscle as the elbow bends at a steeper angle.

Softimage and Alias allow for limiting the rotation of joints to a single axis, which makes the biceps rotating mechanism unnecessary. The movement of the elbow forces rotation of the bone on which the biceps rest. Then, the problem becomes isolating the rotation of the deltoid and collarbone mechanisms from the rotation of the biceps. The Jeffskel example offers some solutions to this problem, as well.

This section reveals the mechanism of the left arm layer by layer, explains how the torso is hooked up to the constraint hierarchy, and suggests ways in which bones can be hidden and unhidden to get the most out of your animation production time. The concepts contained within the Jeffskel character are fairly advanced, considering that it doesn't even get into the use of expressions in character setup.

First, a quick overview of the setup's hierarchy. There is a red bull's eye, the symbol of a null in A:M, labeled *Constraints*. This is the parent of all of the constraints contained within the constraint hierarchy as described in the preceding projects. Some of the bones within this hierarchy have been renamed to make their function clearer during setup and animation. Anything not contained within this Constraints hierarchy is the driven skeleton of the character. The skeleton is meant to be used in skinning the character, but it's not itself meant to be animated directly. Of course, once the non-constraint hierarchy has been finalized, you can animate anything you want, but you won't be able to transfer that animation to another character with a dissimilar hierarchy.

We will start out in the Model editing window, Top view.

The first layer (see Figure 12.136) is the standard basic arm bone hierarchy consisting of the Left Bicep, Left Forearm, which has Attached To Parent checked, and a bone we've named *left hand constraint target*, which is not Attached To Parent. This bone is used as a constraint target for the hand, in order for the hand to receive the orientation of the Left Forearm bone yet still remain detached. The left hand constraint target bone was put there with the concept of constraint switching the hand in mind. It is this mechanism that will be driven by the Left Wrist constraint and the Left Elbow in the constraint hierarchy.

The next layer of the arm skeletal hierarchy is designed to rotate the biceps muscle and, with it, the forearm muscles, as well. We will now unhide the bone titled biceprot. Note that roll vector is facing in the positive Z direction. Next, we unhide the bone called forarmrot. Note that the

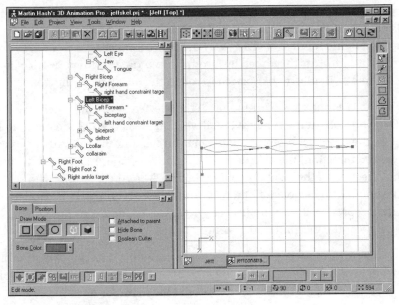

Figure 12.136 Basic arm bone hierarchy.

root of forarmrot is in the same spot as the elbow formed by the Left Bicep and Left Forearm bones. The skinning of the character will be based on this joint. Next, we unhide biceptarg, which is directly under the Left Forearm hierarchy, as shown in Figure 12.137.

The mechanical relationship of these bones is as follows: biceprot as a child of Left Bicep picks up Left Bicep's position and orientation. However, we don't want biceprot to assume Left Bicep's

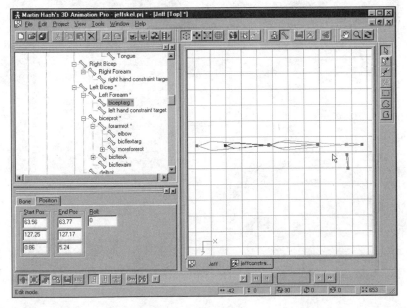

Figure 12.137 Biceps setup.

roll characteristics. Instead, we want it to point in the general direction of the hand, so when the elbow is pointing toward the ground and the hand is raised, the biceps is pointing up in the general direction of the hand as well. The way this is accomplished is by adding an Aim Roll At constraint with biceptarg as the target. By locating biceptarg slightly forward of biceprot's rotation plane, biceprot will always be coerced to roll in the direction of the hand.

We will switch to a Front view with biceprot still selected. You can barely see the roll vector because it is facing right at the camera. But, if we grab the Left Wrist constraint and move it up and to our left, then reselect biceprot again, you can see that the roll vector is now facing in a generally upward direction, the direction of the hand (see Figure 12.138). The forarmrot bone points in the direction of the hand, because it has an Aim At constraint with the Left Hand as the target. It should also be noted that the forarmrot bone has oriented its roll in a cooperative direction with biceprot, as if the joint between them was a single axis hinge. And that happens to be the purpose of the biceprot and forarmrot bones.

The biceprot and forarmrot bones will now form the platform upon which a biceps flexing mechanism will be built. The relationship of the biceprot bone to the Left Bicep and Left Forearm bones should be clear at this time, so we will hide them for now.

We return to the Model edit window, and unhide the bone directly under forarmrot, labeled *elbow*. The bone we are calling elbow has the same origin and orientation, including roll, as forarmrot. Its purpose is to soften the rotational trauma that occurs at the elbow joint on the skin. As a child of forarmrot, it will assume the orientation qualities of the forarmrot bone, including roll. Because elbow is supposed to soften the rotation at the elbow joint, we need to have its orientation and roll split between forarmrot and biceprot.

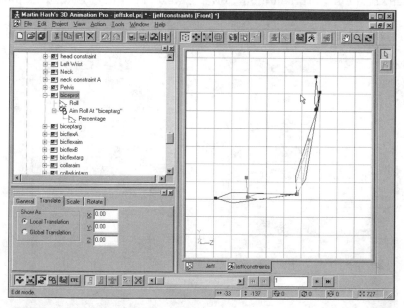

Figure 12.138 Roll vector, facing hand.

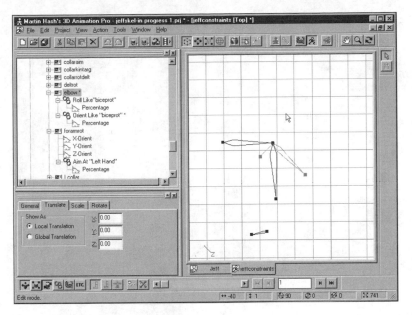

Figure 12.139 Elbow rotated by mixed constraints.

Switch to the Action edit window. Elbow assumes the orientation qualities of forarmrot, so that means that we only have to put two constraints with biceprot as the target to get a 50/50 split. All you need to do is set the enforce percentage at 50 on both the Roll Like and Orient Like constraints. If we bend the arm by moving the Left Wrist constraint, you can see that elbow has assumed a rotational orientation that is half that of forarmrot (see Figure 12.139).

Among the more conventional meat mechanisms is some way of making muscles like the biceps look like they are flexing. Most methodologies for doing this can certainly make the muscle look like it's bulging, but few work in such a way as to make the bulge move along the length of the bone, nor do they usually allow a muscle to show strain under an animator's control. This is true whether the muscle bulge is based on expressions that convert joint or bone rotation to bulging via morphs or shape animation, or whether such joint deformation is a built-in characteristic of the skinning process with the exaggeration a programmable feature.

In the case of expressions, similar control can be exerted on the muscle, but it takes mathematical sophistication. And such sophistication can be added on top of our next technique for even finer control, perhaps like bulging veins.

We'll hide elbow and unhide bicflexA and bicflexB. BicflexB is a child of bicflexA, and Attached To Parent is on. The purpose of the bicflex bones is to flex the biceps muscle. Note that bicflexA is a short bone, and bicflexB is a longer bone that terminates beyond the joint between biceprot and forarmrot. There are two constraint targets that are part of this mechanism. The first is an Aim At constraint, which we've named *bicflexaim*, and the second is the Kinematic chain target, *bicflextarg*. Note that if we bend the arm, bicflexB moves away from biceprot, as shown in Figure 12.140. It also moves to our left, much as a human biceps muscle would. This effect can be exaggerated by altering the relationship of the bones.

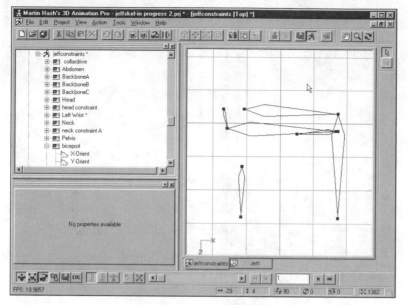

Figure 12.140 BicflexB moves as the arm bends.

In the Model window, if we lengthen bicflexA and move bicflextarg further to the right, we'll see exaggerated movement in bicflexB. With the skin showing, the exaggerated biceps looks like Figure 12.141's left image, where normally it would look more like the image on the right. In addition, the bicflexaim bone can be used to fine tune the position of the biceps, which can make it look like a load is being put on the arm, as in a character lifting a heavy object or straining to move something.

Another arm mechanism that needs to be addressed is the twisting mechanism in the forearm. If you have any detail at all in your model, you will need a mechanism that allows different parts of the forearm to rotate proportionally to the hand, which would include the wrist. In this

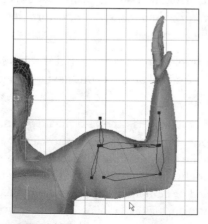

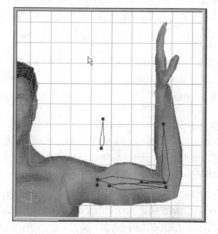

Figure 12.141 Different biceps bulges.

way, control points closer to the wrist will almost rotate along with the wrist, while points closer to the elbow will rotate less or not at all when the wrist rotates. This avoids the shearing or tearing that often results from wrist rotation on a CG character.

We will once again hide bicflexA, bicflexB, and the biceps flexing mechanism, and unhide moreforerot and wristbone. Note that moreforerot is a child of forarmrot and, as such, inherits forarmrot's orientation automatically. The same is true for wristbone as a child of moreforerot. Returning to the Action window, we look at the constraint assignment of moreforerot. We can see that it has a Roll Like constraint with Left Hand as the target. If we select Roll Like Left Hand, we see that the enforce percentage is only 50%. Because moreforerot is the child forarmrot and inherits its orientation and roll, an Enforce percentage of 50% will mean that moreforerot will only pick up 50 percent of Left Hand's roll, the other 50 percent will be its origination roll that it inherits from forarmrot.

The purpose of wristbone is to soften the rotation at the wrist bend. The axis of rotation can be at the axis of rotation of the Left hand or it can allow for trickier setups later on. In this case, we assign wristbone an Orient Like Enforce percentage of 75%. To accommodate the situation in which the hand is pulled away from the arm as we described in earlier projects, we've given wristbone a Translate To constraint to the Left Hand with an Enforce percentage of 50%. This way, the wrist rotation will accommodate a stretching arm, instead of staying at a fixed distance from the elbow.

What does this mean in practice? First, we twist the hand. We start with the hand in an upright position. Then, we twist it so that the thumb faces rearward and you can see a relatively smooth transition of points down the arm, as in Figure 12.142. If we yank the hand away from Left Forearm by constraining the hand to Left Wrist instead of left hand constraint target in a temporary modification, which during an animation would be done with constraint switching, you can see that the wristbone is floating between the Left Hand and the end of the Left Forearm bone, as shown in Figure 12.143. It still has partial rotation from the hand, which gives the wrist a flatter appearance in the wristbone area.

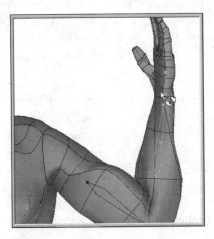
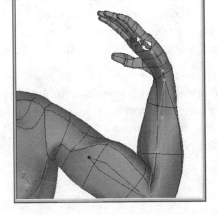

Figure 12.142 Arm twist.

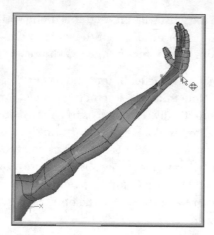

Figure 12.143 Wristbone distention.

We've saved the best of the arm mechanisms for last. The shoulder has generally been problematic for CGI since people started trying to do characters. There are numerous software-specific solutions for dealing with shoulders, many involving expressions, morphs, and IK.

The following is one IK solution that addresses many of the physical properties of the shoulder. There are certainly more anatomically correct approaches that can be taken, and the IK setup that follows can provide a springboard. The truly ambitious person doing IK setups might refer to George B. Bridgman's *The Human Machine* (ISBN: 0-486-22707-3). This book gives excellent mechanical descriptions of how the human muscular and structural mechanisms function, in a way that translates readily into CG.

First, in Model, we once again unhide bicflexA and bicflexB. Then, we unhide Lcollar and collardrive. The relationship between Lcollar and collardrive with the skin that they will help to drive can be seen in Figure 12.144.

Lcollar and collardrive comprise an IK chain that inherits position and orientation from its parent (Thorax) and terminates at the end of collardrive, where it is driven by bicflexA by having collarkintarg, a child of bicflexA, as its Kinematic target. You can see that, with the arm stretched out in its neutral, horizontal position, the shoulder is relatively flat. If you bend the arm up, the bone bends a little, pushing the deltoid up.

The next bone in this mechanism, and the bone that the skin is actually assigned to, is collarrotdelt. This bone has rather complex constraint arrangements. First, it inherits its position and orientation from collardrive, as its parent. Yet its location is between the origin of Lcollar and collardrive. To keep it floating between the two bones, we first had to give collarrotdelt a Translate To constraint with an Enforce percentage of 50%. Then, we needed to have it point at the bicflex mechanism by aiming at the collarkintarg bone as its target, so that as the biceps flexes, the deltoid muscle gets pushed up slightly but vertically. The Enforce percentage is set at 75% instead of 100% so that the deltoid muscle will rotate up slightly along with the upward

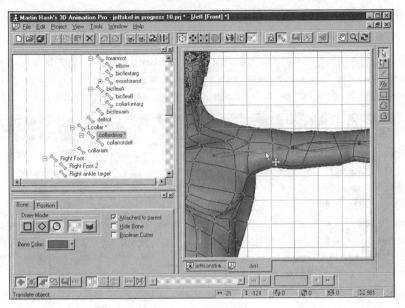

Figure 12.144 Lcollar and collardrive.

rotation of the clavicle, represented by Lcollar. Next is a Roll Like constraint with biceprot as the target, set to an Enforce percentage of 50%. This will give collarrotdelt 50 percent of the roll of the biceps, allowing a smooth transition between the biceps and the shoulder when the upper arm rotates. Last is a Spherical Limits constraint.

When we move the arm up, this shoulder setup does a pretty good job of appearing to have a rotating clavicle and a flexing deltoid muscle (see Figure 12.145). But what about when we move the arm down to the side of our character? If we have the mechanism set up without any rotational limits, then the entire shoulder will droop down. So, we added a spherical constraint

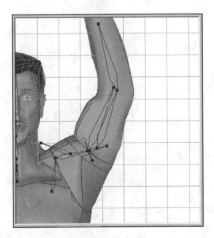

Figure 12.145 Appearance of rotating clavicle and flexing deltoid.

with minimum values of 0, -180, and -45, which keeps the collarrotdelt bone from rotating into the body, among other things, as shown in Figure 12.146.

There is one more thing about the shoulder mechanism that you should know about. We return to the Model window, select collaraim, and unhide it. Collaraim is designed to keep Lcollar aligned with the upper torso, and, as its name implies, it is used as an Aim At constraint target.

LEFT ARM FOUL-UPS

All of the setups in the left arm can get messed up in some poses. Don't panic! Keep in mind that simple procedures can be used to correct nearly every problem. Move biceptarg toward the front of the body, if the left biceps flips over because the character is reaching behind its body with the elbow facing forward. Moving biceptarg can solve many problems, but other solutions may involve moving collaraim, rotating the roll on Lcollar, rotating the roll on Left Bicep, and, as a last resort, you can always do a morph to solve a localized problem.

One potential cause of problems can occur when a bone is too long and it has an Aim At constraint that terminates midway down the length of the bone that is being aimed. The list of pathologies that can occur is endless, and the rule of the day is to try everything, and see what works.

This concludes the explanation of the jeffskel.prj Left Arm mechanisms.

The last thing we need to examine is hooking up the rest of the body to the constraint hierarchy. First, we've changed a few names. In the constraint hierarchy tutorial, we named a constraint

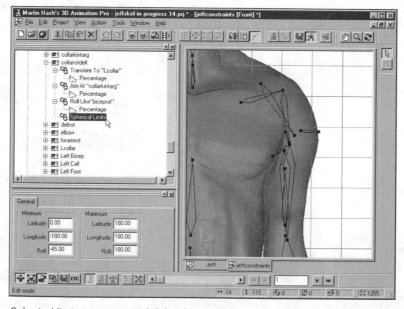

Figure 12.146 Spherical limits set to control deltoid constraints.

bone Pelvis. Here we have renamed it *Pelvis Constraint*, because it will serve as a constraint target for the pelvis bone that drives the skin. We have named that bone *Pelvis*. We have re-named Midsection as *Abdomen Constraint* and Thorax as *Thorax Constraint*. Other than the renaming, all relationships of the constraint hierarchy are identical to the constraint hierarchy projects.

We now hide all of the constraints in the torso and unhide the bones that drive the skin. Pelvis is constrained in both position and orientation by Pelvis Constraint. Abdomen is likewise con-strained to Abdomen Constraint. Thorax is similarly constrained to Thorax Constraint.

Head is constrained to head constraint, and Neck is constrained to neck constraint B. Left Thigh has a Translate To constraint with Left Hip as the target, and the Aim At constraint discussed in the leg tutorial, with Left Knee as the target. Right Thigh is similarly constrained.

So, the final question is, What should be visible for animation? The answer is that for the first pass, the major constraints should be exposed, as in Figure 12.147. This makes the first pass of animation easier. And of course, any element of the character can be selected and animated from the Project Window.

Put jeffskel.prj to the test. Compare the way the left and right sides animate. Try modifying it further using the cartoon arm on the torso. Try to duplicate the left arm setup on the right side. Try to think of other uses for the constraining techniques described. Try to find other ways to drive the biceps, collar, and shoulder.

Most of all, try to do things no one has ever done before.

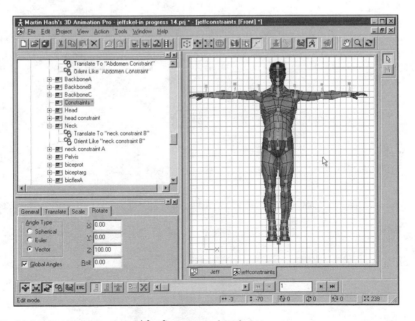

Figure 12.147   Major constraints exposed for first-pass animation.

Moving On

If you've worked through this chapter's projects, you've completed a full constraint setup for your character. If your software doesn't support constraints but you've read through this chapter, you still have a better understanding of the use of constraints—and some solid reasons to upgrade your software! In either case, you're ready to use your best character setup in the animation projects in Chapter 15. The projects dealing with full-body acting and caricature actions will put your setup to the test, and make very clear how much time and effort a good setup can save you.

If you want to continue exploring setup issues, you can go on to Chapter 13, Power Tool Setups. This chapter shows how to handle challenging technical setups such as facial animation, lip sync, cloth, hair, and soft-object physics.

POWER-TOOL SETUPS

Power tools and procedural setups, like any animation tools, are worse than useless if they get in the animator's way. As a setup person, you need to know when a power tool can save the animator work, and when it's a counter-productive geek toy.

Building setups for complex characters is a Catch-22. On one hand, you are expected to be up-to-date on the latest technological fixes, a wizard on the order of Ian Fleming's Q. On the other hand, the animator is more of an artist than an engineer, and wants a setup as intuitive as a stop-motion puppet. To balance these competing demands, you need to both keep your techno-lust in check, and protect the animator from power tool overload. Give him the most elegant, efficient setup he needs to animate the character, and save the bells and whistles for your own amusement.

The preceding chapters show you the essential tools and processes you need to create good character setups. This chapter introduces a class of optional tools, *power tools* that can (sometimes) produce more efficient setups by giving more animation control to the computer. Sometimes that tradeoff in control isn't worth it. If you are a setup person, you need to work with the animator to make sure the setup is what they need, not what you'd like to set up.

How much should you automate? It's perfectly natural for setup people to rely too heavily on the computer. It's the old hammer-and-nail dilemma: When the only tool you have is a hammer, every problem starts to look like a nail. As long as your setups are relieving the animator of the mindless drudgery associated with traditional animation production, well and good. If the setup becomes so automated or difficult to use that it begins to cramp or fight the animator's creative style, it's time to back up and take another look at who's *really* running the show. Computers are simply complex tools—don't ever let them dictate the animator's creative options. Your job as setup person is to provide the animator with a setup that is as transparent and intuitive as possible.

Some of the most useful character animation power tools have applications for facial animation, lip sync, physical simulation, and cloth simulation. This chapter shows you how to set up these power tools to make the animator's job a little easier.

Facial Animation

For most characters, you will want to set up facial animation using morphing or Displacement techniques. In some cases, you may be able to simplify animation of part or all of the face by using maps rather than animating changes in the character's geometry. Both morphing and Displacement techniques create inbetweens automatically and with finer control, so they give you a significant advantage over maps when you animate emotional transitions.

The human face is made up of many layers of muscle and other tissues, overlapping in different directions and bridging attachment points from the shoulders to the top of the skull. The goal of character facial animation is not to realistically simulate every one of these muscles, but to mimic the surface appearance produced by their combined actions well enough to tell the story. This means, you can cheat a lot in creating facial morph targets and nearly as much in setting up Displacement controls.

Because most character animation software supports some form of morphing, you will generally be setting up facial animation by creating libraries of morph targets. It's still possible to set up and animate a complex or realistic face in some software by using Displacement controls, such as bones, but these approaches are usually prohibitively difficult to animate. Morph targets are significantly faster, more reliable, and easier to animate. They are also more compatible with lip sync software like Magpie Pro, as detailed later in this chapter.

PROJECT 13.1 Displacement Facial Setup For LightWave

LightWave supports Replacement tools such as object list, object sequence, and MTSE, and shape weighting via Morph Gizmo, so you will generally be setting up facial animation in LightWave with morph targets. Once you've decided on this approach, the next decision is how to produce the necessary library of morph targets. LightWave's Modeler includes a selection of point and surface sculpting tools, so you could choose to simply reshape the basic face into the new targets. As an alternative, you could set up Bones to deform the face, then use the Save Transformed function to create a new morph target from each new Bones pose.

When you set up a skeleton in LightWave 3D to animate an organic object like a humanoid face, there is one major headache: getting the detailed control you need, without using zillions of Bones. The problem lies in how LightWave 3D handles Bone assignments. If you apply a Bone in the middle of a group of points, there is no effective way for you to limit the Bone's effects to an irregular selection of polygons and leave the rest alone. You can get around this by splitting the object into separate objects, but then you lose the Bones' advantage of seamless surfaces. You can try to nail down the unwanted points with a lot of smaller Bones, but that slows down the screen redraw, interferes with still other Bones, and clutters your scene. You might also want more than one Bone to affect a particular point. For example, the cheeks should stretch when the jaw opens but also bulge under the influence of cheek *puffers* (Bones that mimic air pressure in a closed mouth). This is a Bone setup problem that you can't easily solve using ordinary Parent/Child skeletons.

The goal of this project is to enable you to set up Bones to exclusively affect a precise selection of points. Using this technique, you should be able to mimic any combination of bone and muscle structure to deform the skin of an object. The basic steps of the procedure are:

1. In Modeler, select the points to be affected by a Bone, and define them as a surface.

2. Move the surface a safe distance from the other points. Save this *exploded* object.

3. Load the exploded object in Layout. In the first frame, apply a Bone to the defined surface, parented to the object's root Bone. Define the Limited Range Minimum and Maximum for the Bone to lock down every point in the surface.

4. In the second frame, implode the object by moving the Bone the reverse of the safe distance.

The approach I recommend is to define a separate surface for each part of a character's face. These surfaces should be bounded by the relatively immovable borders between the different parts. For example, looking at the face's anatomy tells you that the perimeter of the nose is pretty closely attached to underlying bone. So, while the nose can deform quite a bit, it can't affect surrounding tissues very much. You can, therefore, define the nose as a single surface and assign a Bone to limit its influence on the rest of the face. It's much easier to select polygons for repeated operations if they are organized by surfaces, but it's not absolutely necessary. If you have a lot of surfaces already set up for some other purpose, you can get by with manually selecting the points for each explode operation.

When you explode the separate surfaces in Modeler, the goal is to place each surface's points far enough from all other points that a Bone can include all the selected points without affecting any other points. If you do this properly, Bones assigned to a surface will not interact with any other surfaces' points or Bones. Note that Bone assignments are by point, not by polygon. A polygon will stretch as far as necessary to bridge between points assigned to different Bones.

When you assign Bones to the exploded surfaces in Layout, use identical Minimum and Maximum Limited Range values to effectively lock each point in place relative to the Bone. This enables you to implode the surface's points to their precise original positions simply by moving the Bone. If you need to distort or otherwise animate the surface, you can apply Child Bones that have a more flexible Limited Range. If the Child Bones are set in the object's exploded keyframe, they will also affect only their Parent Bone's points.

To return the object to its original shape, you must implode all the surface's Parent Bones by the exact inverse of the explosions you applied to the surfaces in Modeler. If you exploded the nose surface 2 units along the Z axis, you must implode the nose's Bone -2 units along the Z axis. When you do this, you set that keyframe as the new default pose for the object. This is a modification to the usual LightWave 3D working style of setting your default scene in frame 0 and starting the action in frame 1. Don't forget to allow for this additional one-frame offset. You can build even more layers of Bone interaction and control if you use additional frames to assemble and Bone combinations of surfaces. For each of these extra frames, the animator will have to add another offset to their x-sheet for the scene. Make sure you document this in your character notes and model sheets.

Unfortunately, you fragment all the surface mapping coordinates by using the explode-Bone-implode process. If you applied a spherical map, for example, it would render as if the sphere was mapped to the exploded version, and all the surfaces would have large sections of the map missing at their borders with adjoining surfaces.

If you need to map an object you have exploded for Boning, try to figure an acceptable way to use planar mapping. If you explode all the mapped surfaces along a mapping axis, a planar map on that same axis will not distort when you implode the object. For instance, if you created a bump map for facial wrinkles, you could apply it as a planar map on the Z axis. Knowing this, you would explode all the face surfaces along the Z axis. The imploded face would retain the correct mapping coordinates for the wrinkle map. On the other hand, the main reason for this type of Bone animation is to make Metamorph objects, in which case mapping coordinates don't matter anyway.

You can Bone an exploded object surface by surface—you don't have to do it all at once. When an exploded object is set up in Layout, you can use the Replace Object function in the Objects panel to replace it with a similar object. The point and polygon count and distribution does not have to be identical. As long as the exploded surfaces are within the Limited Ranges of the existing Bones, the scene will still work. See Figure 13.1 for an example.

This enables you to experiment with more manageable low-complexity objects before committing to the full-complexity objects for final tweaking and rendering. You can subdivide, triple, and use MetaNURBS, as long as the surfaces' points remain within the areas of the Bones you have already set in Layout. You can even modify and re-explode a derivative of the original object, if you keep careful track of which surface goes where.

The following steps will guide you through the explosion, Boning, and implosion of an example character face, using this incremental approach to work through one facial feature at a time.

1. Open Modeler. Click on Load. Select the object to be exploded, in this case HEAD1301.LWO, which you can find in the Chapter 13 directory on this book's CD-ROM (see Figure 13.2).

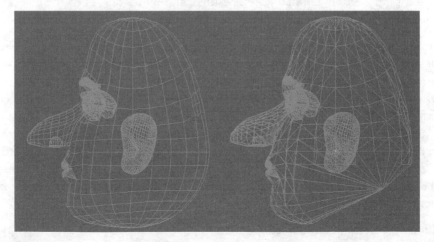

Figure 13.1 Same scene, very different objects.

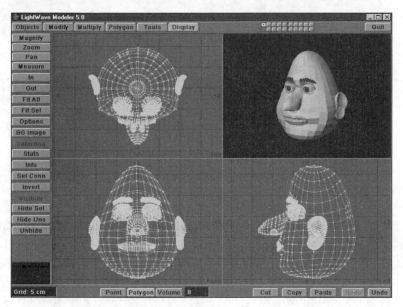

Figure 13.2 HEAD1301.LWO object loaded in Modeler.

Normally, you would next select points to define the surfaces of the object. The exact surface divisions will depend on your object. The projects later in this chapter examine some guidelines for defining surfaces. For the example object, the major facial parts have already been defined as surfaces. If you had defined new surfaces, you would now deselect all points and save the surfaced object with a new name as the baseline reference object.

2. Click on Display. Switch to Polygon selection mode. Click on Stats. Select the surface name Fred-Ear from the panel list. Click on + to select the surface's polygons. The panel closes automatically.

Your screen should look like Figure 13.3.

3. Click on Modify, click on Move, then click on Numeric. Move the selected points, using the Numeric panel, at least twice the part's maximum dimension away from the remaining parts, as in Figure 13.4.

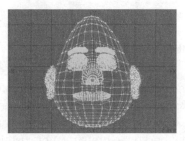

Figure 13.3 . Fred-Ear surface selected.

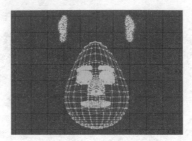

Figure 13.4 Fred-Ear surface moved.

This is enough of a safety margin for you to create a Bone that affects the entire selected surface, without including any other surfaces of the object. It's almost always best to err on the side of caution, but spreading the surfaces out over larger distances makes it more difficult to get a look at the whole object in either Layout or Modeler.

4. Write down the numbers you type in the Numeric panel as soon as you complete each move. You will need these numbers later in the process to reassemble the object accurately. I strongly recommend that you move the surfaces by round numbers (0.1000, 0.5000, and so forth), so they are easy to remember, and type in all four digits to prevent rounding errors.

5. Click on Object, then click on Save As. Save the exploded object with a new name.

   Make sure you keep an intact copy of the original object. I tend to save a copy of the object after exploding each surface, so, if something goes wrong, I never have to go back further than the previous surface.

6. Close Modeler. Open Layout. Open scene file CH13001.LWS, which you can find in the Chapter 13 directory on this book's CD-ROM. This scene is set up with the original, unexploded version of the head object, just to save you the trouble of setting Camera angles and lights.

   When you are creating a new character, I recommend setting up the head in a separate scene like this until you have worked out all the Boning problems. The head is usually more complex than the rest of the body combined.

7. Open the Objects panel, and replace the head object with the last exploded version you saved in Modeler.

8. Open the Skeleton panel. Add a root Bone for the head, with the pivot set to 0,0,0. Leave it as a null Bone for now, with Rest Length 0.0001 and Strength 0.0%. Your scene should now look like Figure 13.5.

   What you're going to do next is set a Bone for one surface, with Limited Range values that will lock down all the points in the surface. We'll refer to these types of Bones as *surface Bones*. The goal is to be able to move the surface Bones and know that the surface's points will follow along exactly, without any distortion. Later, you can add Child Bones to each surface Bone to enable you to animate more detailed surface distortions.

   To start off, you'll set up the Bones for the left and right ears. This is about the simplest part of most characters. For many humanoid characters, you won't have to Bone the

Figure 13.5 Head with root Bone set.

ears at all, because they're just immobile lumps on the side of the head. In this case, you'll set up the ears so they can wiggle front-to-back.

9. Open the Skeleton panel again. Select the root Bone. Click on Add Child Bone.

10. Rename the new Child Bone as EarsRootBone. Turn off Bone Active. Close the Skeleton panel.

11. With the EarsRootBone selected, click on Move. Turn off the X Axis and Z Axis buttons, and drag the EarsRootBone up along the Y axis until it is in the middle of the ears, according to the Side view (see Figure 13.6).

12. Create a key for the EarsRootBone at frame 0. Press R to set the rest length and position and activate the Bone.

13. Open the Skeleton panel again. With EarsRootBone selected, click on Add Child Bone. Rename the new Bone LeftEar. Turn off Bone Active. Set Rest Length to 0.01 and Strength to 100%. Close the Skeleton panel.

Figure 13.6 Side view of EarsRootBone position.

14. Move the LeftEar Bone to the center of the left ear surface of the exploded object. Create a keyframe for LeftEar at frame 0. Press R to set the rest length and position and activate the Bone.

15. Open the Skeleton panel again. With LeftEar selected, turn off Bone Active. Turn on Limited Range, and set the Minimum and Maximum to 0.06. Turn on Bone Active, and close the Skeleton panel.

    The dotted outline of the LeftEar Bone's influence should contain all the points in the left ear surface of the head object and no points from other surfaces (see Figure 13.7). If this is not the case, repeat Step 15 to correct the Limited Range settings.

16. Repeat steps 13 through 15 for the other ear, naming the Child Bone RightEar.

17. Go to frame 1. Select EarsRootBone.

18. Refer to your notes from Step 4, the explode operation in Modeler. How far did you move the ears surface? Click on Move, then click on Numeric. Enter the negative value of the ears' previous move, and click on OK.

    This should move the ears back to their precise original position. If it's off a little, try to find the cause of the error to make sure you don't repeat it for the rest of the surfaces.

19. Create a key for EarsRootBone at frame 1.

    So far, all you've apparently done is move the ears around and insulate the rest of the surfaces from the effects of the ear Bones. Now, you get to the good part—setting Child Bones to move and deform the surface, without affecting the rest of the object.

    Presumably, you'd like the character to be able to wiggle his ears. If you tried to do that with a Parented hierarchy, the pivot would look very mechanical. If you tried it using an ordinary Bone set around the ear, the side of the head would deform, as well. Exploding, Boning, and imploding the object solves this problem, enabling you to restrict smooth Bones deformations to a well-defined part of an object.

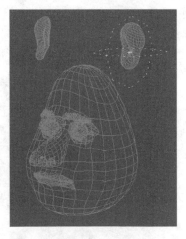

Figure 13.7 LeftEar Bone activated.

The goal of the next few steps is to add a Null Bone as a pivot, near the center of the ear, and place a normal Child Bone at the rear edge of the ear. This will enable you to bend the ear forward or back by changing the Heading angle of the null Bone. The Child Bone's influence will be stronger near the back of the ear, while the LeftEar Bone will keep the ear securely anchored near the front.

20. Go to frame 0. Open the Skeleton panel again. With LeftEar selected, click on Add Child Bone. Rename the new Bone LeftEarHinge. Turn off Bone Active and Limited Range. Set Rest Length to 0.0001 and Strength to 0.0%. Close the Skeleton panel.

21. Move the LeftEarHinge Bone towards the front of the left-ear surface of the exploded object, as in Figure 13.8. This is the line where the deformation of a bent ear should stop, where the flesh and cartilage of the ear grows out of the head.

22. Create a keyframe for LeftEarHinge at frame 0. Press R to set the rest length and position and activate the Bone.

That's the hinge—now for the *bender*.

23. Open the Skeleton panel again. With LeftEarHinge selected, click on Add Child Bone. Rename the new Bone LeftEarFlap. Turn off Bone Active. Set Rest Length to 0.01 and Strength to 25%. Turn on Scale Strength By Rest Length. Close the Skeleton panel.

24. Move the LeftEarFlap Bone to the rear edge of the left-ear surface. Pitch the Bone up 90 degrees, so the long axis is vertical and aligned (more or less) with the rear edge of the ear, as in Figure 13.9.

25. Create a keyframe for LeftEarFlap at frame 0. Press R to set the rest length and position and activate the Bone.

26. Open the Skeleton panel again. With LeftEarFlap selected, turn off Bone Active. Turn on Limited Range, and set the Minimum to 0.06 and Maximum to 0.06. Turn on Bone Active, and close the Skeleton panel.

Figure 13.8 LeftEarHinge Bone position.

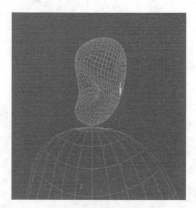

Figure 13.9 LeftEarFlap Bone in position.

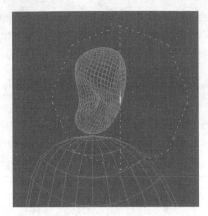

Figure 13.10 Influence of LeftEarFlap Bone.

The dotted outline of the LeftEarFlap Bone's influence should contain the entire ear surface, as in Figure 13.10.

27. To test the ear's flexibility, go to frame 1, and experiment with the Heading angle of the LeftEarHinge Bone. How far can you rotate it before the ear deformation becomes unusable? What are some good Heading values, as in Figure 13.11? Document these experiments—you will need them later when you make up the model sheet for this character's head.

28. Repeat Steps 20 through 27 for the other ear. Save the scene.

You should end up with a head that can be animated to wiggle its ears. While of questionable usefulness, this exercise is the simplest example of a procedure you can repeat to set up every other facial feature.

After you have set the Bones for a surface, you can make the character easier to animate by opening the Scene panel and hiding any Bone that should not be animated. This will keep the Layout view cleaner, so the animator can find the right Bone faster and with less confusion. Hide each of the surface Bones, plus the Bones like LeftEarFlap

Figure 13.11 Bent ear examples.

that are active but not designed to be animated directly. The remaining Bones, like LeftEarHinge, should be color-coded for contrast and remain visible.

When you've had more practice, you can build more efficient skeletons by adding the animatable Bones first, so they display near the top of drop-down lists and the null Bones are out of sight near the bottom. For now, simply accept that you will have to do a certain amount of scrolling in the selection lists to locate the Bones you want.

29. Repeat the preceding steps to define the surface, explode, Bone, and implode the eyebrows, nose, eyes, and eyelids for the head object. You should end up with something like Figure 13.12.

The mouth is the trickiest part of a Displacement setup for facial animation. In life, the mouth's influences are bounded by the rigid septum of the nose above and the equally rigid attachments to the chin and jawline below. Between these extremes, the musculature of the mouth is almost completely free. This shows us where to begin to model and Bone the mouth—Parent the upper mouth to the root of the head and the lower mouth to the jaw. This takes care of the grosser movements required for lip sync and extreme emotions. Leaving the larger motions to a Parent Bone also leaves you more flexibility in setting Child Bones to animate the subsidiary surfaces.

The next level of the animation hierarchy is the lips. Generally, you can get away with leaving the upper surface of the upper lip and the lower surface of the lower lip to fend for themselves. The tension between the Bones controlling the lips and the Bones nailing down the jawline and upper face stretches the intervening polygons enough for most expressions. The lips proper need a fair number of Bones to provide an acceptable degree of control, but laying them out is intuitive enough that it's not very difficult.

Before you begin adding Bones to the lips, you should consider ways to reduce the animator's workload without sacrificing flexibility. A labor-saving technique that is good for the lips is to alternate short chains of Bones with IK goals the Bones are

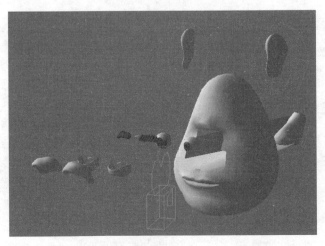

Figure 13.12   Head with Bones for upper-facial animation.

targeted to. This means, you only have to animate the root Bones and the IK goals, and the Child Bones help smooth out the lips' curves automatically. This can reduce the number of animation controls for a mouth by a factor of two, at least, and perhaps a factor of four. One of the worst things you can do in creating a character's face is to simply set an independent Bone for each cross-section of the lips, forcing the animator to endlessly noodle for even the simplest lip sync. Keep it simple!

Keep in mind that the corners of the mouth will have to move somewhere between the lower jaw's position and the rest of the face, but not exactly halfway. The lower lip usually stretches more with the jaw opening, and the upper lip stays relatively close to the upper face. The lips also should be able to pucker outwards or suck in, especially for pronouncing Ps, Vs, and Fs.

30. Follow the procedure again to surface, explode, Bone, and implode the lips and mouth area. Make the upper mouth a Child of the head's root Bone and the lower mouth a Child of the jaw Bone.

31. Add enough Bones to the lips that you can animate it to lip sync and express basic emotions. Try to minimize the number of Bones or Nulls an animator will have to use. You might end up with something like PROJ1301.LWS on this book's CD-ROM, as shown in Figure 13.13.

32. Test the mouth for effective range of motion. Try a pucker, open wide, smile, fricative, and sibilant.

Once you're satisfied with the facial animation setup, you're ready to use it in the next section.

Building Morph Target Libraries

Most characters will need a basic repertoire of facial expressions and the ability to lip sync the language of the vocal track. This gives you a baseline library of morph targets that you should

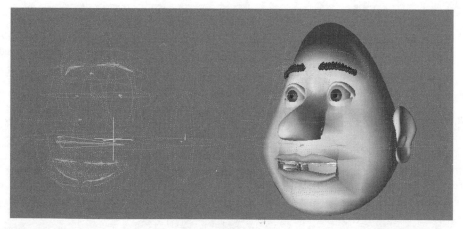

Figure 13.13 Full facial animation setup including mouth. Bones and nulls are on the left, and the FACEBONE model is on the right, from PROJ1301.LWS.

build for each new character. Once you have the baseline library, you can add to it, when necessary, to expand the dramatic or linguistic range of the character. Depending on the flexibility of your software, you may be able to get by with a very small library. If your software is not as versatile in weighting or mixing morph targets, you may have to build a larger library.

You have several options for defining a baseline library. One is to simply copy an existing library, either from an existing character, a commercial data set such as Humanoid, or the sample set (if any) provided with your lip-sync software, such as Magpie Pro. Another is to consult reference sources on traditional animation, human facial expression, or acting, and create a library to cover the range of expressions illustrated. If you choose the latter approach, either the Faigin or Lemay books listed in the Bibliography are excellent resources.

Weighted Shape Interpolation

By Ken Cope

Simple shape interpolation is not the only approach available in many packages. Although it may be the simplest, most straightforward approach, it loads a lot of work onto the modeler and the animator. Morphing from one shape to the next requires you to craft every shape you'll use. People tend to hold expressions while talking, such as smiling or frowning. Do you want to create all your target shapes smiling, and then create them all over again for a frown, and again for any other transitory expression? If you can blend or weight more than two shapes at the same time, you need only create a few targets for mouth shapes, for eyelids and brows, and a few others for overall expressions. Weighting shapes is a powerful approach, so long as you understand what to expect from it, and why.

Simple and weighted shape interpolations differ greatly from each other. Suppose you start with a neutral face A, with lips slightly parted and eyes open, then modify duplicates to create two more shapes, B, with the eyes closed, and C, with an open mouth. Simple interpolation to the closed eye shape B would not change the mouth shape, the mouth would remain closed. Simple morphing to the open mouth shape C would open the eyes again. When you interpolate back to the eyes closed shape B, the mouth shuts. The result of fifty percent of B and C is a half-lidded drooler. Using only those three shapes, you would not be able to close the eyes while keeping the mouth open—unless you used weighted shapes.

Weighted shape interpolation starts with a neutral shape and considers each target relative only to the neutral shape, not to the other target shapes. Only the differences from the original neutral shape matter for each new target. You modify the neutral by layering more interpolations from other targets. Each interpolation remains separate: the open mouth target does not modify the position of the eyes in the neutral pose, so the eyes don't change. The eye blink pose does not change the mouth vertices, only the mouth targets modify the mouth vertices. With weighted shape interpolation, your character can babble and blink incessantly without costing nearly so much of your modeling, setup, and animation time.

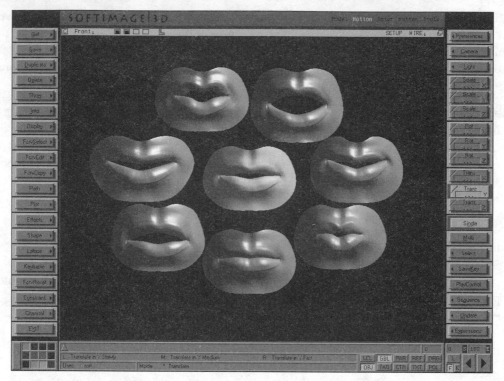

Figure 13.14 Weighted shape setup for mouth.

Take a look at Figure 13.14. The neutral starting shape is central, and all targets define deltas from this original. Relative to their original location in the central shape, vertices move on a vector (straight line) toward a new target shape, weighted or blended by a percentage with any other specified target shapes. That percentage includes negative values, and values past 100% (yes, *Spinal Tap* fans, you can go *past* 11).

Look at **A** in Figure 13.15. If a target shape's vertex is one unit in positive Z from its original on the neutral shape, morphing 100% to that target moves the vertex one unit

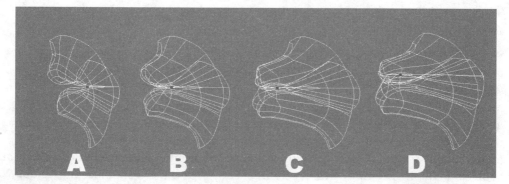

Figure 13.15 Weighted shape interpolation of a single vertex.

forward, **B**. Morphing 200% would move it forward two units, **C**. A negative value will move it in the opposite direction on the same vector. When you blend in an additional target that raises the same vertex one unit in positive Y (relative to the original shape), the vertex moves up from its new position, **D**, without changing its Z value, the last one you chose. The vertices of each target shape move relative to their position in the starting shape, even if you used other targets to animate those vertices to a new shape.

Although you can still simply blend from one target shape to the next, that does not take full advantage of the power of this approach. While modeling, don't forget that for every shape you create, you're also creating its opposite, Figure 13.16. Create a raised smile by taking a copy of the original shape, **A** and translating the mouth vertices only in Y, raising the corners of the mouth slightly higher, **B**. Using a negative value yields a frown, **C**.

Pursing the lips (Figure 13.17, **A**) widens the mouth when using its opposite, **B**. Note that this is the product of less than 20 units' change from A to B. Use a light touch, or the weighted interpolations can perform unpleasant exaggerations on your shapes.

Keep track of the direction you send your shapes while you model, so that you don't encounter any areas flying off in directions you don't want. Modeling a raised smile so that

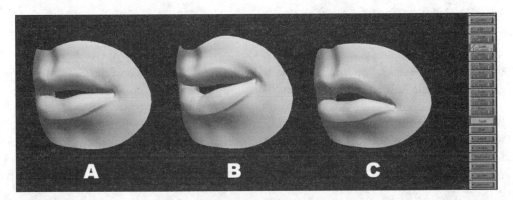

Figure 13.16　Weighting a smile.

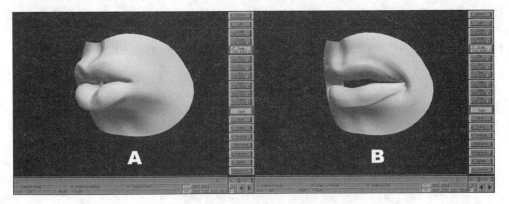

Figure 13.17　Pursing lips, A, at 40, and opposite, B, at 27.6.

it also pushes back into the face will pout it out away from the face when sent on its opposite vector from neutral. Perhaps that's what you want, but this method magnifies the bad as much as the good. Surprises abound, some serendipitous, others not.

If you use this method, it helps to use an entire face at once. If you raise a smile, you may also want to raise the cheeks, the corners of the nose, and the bottom eyelids slightly. These fleeting changes to the overall look of the face help to keep things alive, if that's the sort of thing you're looking for. It wouldn't be easy to implement that kind of subtlety with an individual muscle setup. One rapidly loses track of which muscle to use to change an expression. Because a lot of little changes can add up fairly quickly, you'll spend time tweaking to determine just how much of it suits your taste.

Use of multiple target shapes is not limited to facial animation. You can use it for bulging biceps, flesh folds, jiggling bellies, and other fun ways of faking soft tissue dynamics. You can confuse your programmer friends by telling them you did it by running a real-time simulation that you wrote on your coffee break. Naturally, you will want to trigger those shapes by rotations or other events using expressions, since the arm will look funny the first time it bends and you forget to make the biceps bulge.

Generating Target Shapes

To this day, incredibly talented sculptors carve one face after the next, one for each slightly different expression, then draw a grid onto it with numbers for the digitizer to scribe it in, one vertex at a time. Build it, bake it, slap a grid on it and digitize it, just to raise the corners of the mouth a bit. You'd better not miss a dot, or get it out of order, or you'll have to do it over again. That wasn't a terribly sophisticated way to work even back in the eighties, the dark ages of computer graphics. Despite what the bell-and-whistle vendors will tell you, modeling tools haven't changed so very significantly in the last decade. Roll your sleeves up, the pixels, patches, polys, and verts will wash off with a little lemon and salt.

Start with a good face that you (or your client) like. Nobody will think any less of you if you sculpted it out of clay or band-sawed sections of a mannequin head, then traced them onto grid paper and typed in each vertex coordinate. I don't recommend that last method unless you're being paid by the hour on client-provided tools. If you have a computer, you may have modeled a face entirely in the computer yourself. If you have, the next section will give you no trouble at all.

The most important thing to remember is, don't alter the geometry of your neutral face or that of any of the targets once you've started generating them. If you decide you need to add just one more vertex here, or delete an isoparm there, unless you can execute exactly the same procedure on all the other targets you have generated, just don't do it. The vertex list in each target must refer to the same vertices in each of the models. Unless you're looking for unique ways for the face to crumple on the monitor, only their X, Y and Z coordinates can differ, not the number or order of the vertices in your original, hero face. The simplest way to do this is to duplicate the original and move the vertices on the copy until you have the shape you want. This is where the skills you developed using global transforms to move tagged vertices pay off.

In Softimage, Cardinal patches make your life a bit easier, with all the vertices directly on the surface. You can convert to polygons or NURBS later, unless you prefer to do this in polygons all the way through the pipeline. If you're using polygons for the face, you should use some good surface subdivision tools later so you can keep it simple at this stage. Tracking down the relevant CVs on a NURBS surface is quite a bit less intuitive than the other two approaches.

One simple reason for starting with a partially open mouth is for the convenience of the modeler. It's easier to add a target that closes it the rest of the way later, and a slack mouth is as good a definition of a neutral face as any other's. If your character is supposed to be smiling a lot, according to yours or the client's specifications, the smile is a target, not the central, neutral, anchor object. You want all of your expressions to be relative to neutral, not to a smile. If you really want to use something other than a neutral mouth shape for your central shape, such as an open mouth (it can be successfully done), remember that all of your targets will move relative to that one. Any variance from my recommended procedures that works better than what I tell you is encouraged—but don't say I didn't warn you.

Asymmetry is a valuable and desirable thing, though not mandatory in the neutral target unless we're talking Quasimodo. You can create plenty of target variations on the neutral shape that are exactly the kinds of asymmetry you'll want to be able to choose from when you need it. Asymmetry does not mean making a lopsided neutral base model and forgetting about it. The idea in all cases is to provide maximum control of the character as an animator, not to lock some pose into the base model.

While those pressed for time on a rush job may opt for only a neutral mouth and an open one, you can do so much more with the neutral, open mouth and a raised smile. Don't complain that you won't have time to animate it. A good puppeteer can get quite close in real time. As a keyframer, your control is even more precise. Pursing the lips into a big, exaggerated 'ooh' mouthed pout puts you ahead of the game. Everything else is asymmetrical gravy. You only translate tagged vertices along the Y axis when creating an open mouth or raised smile target. A pursed lips target involves a lot of scaling in X, and more exaggeration than you think is appropriate when you push it forward in Z.

It's easier than you might think to move the mouth over to one side or the other of the face, as you might in a whispered aside. Think of it as creating a new neutral mouth, just with one corner near the middle and a naso-labial crease formed on the other side, but still, a neutral mouth. This is an important idea to grasp. The raised smile target translates in Y from wherever the neutral mouth vertices happen to be, based on where other targets have placed them. Create a target by grabbing all the vertices of a copy of the neutral mouth and translating it down an inch. Layering in that target will simply slide all of the dialogue you've previously animated down to the chin as that target reaches one hundred percent. The lips will purse from wherever you place the mouth.

You should also bear in mind that there are no rotations as such, with shape deformation. All movements are linear, unless modified by another target, as shown in the bending desk lamp projects in Chapter 11. Vertices defining the open eyelid, and its position when closed, interpolate at fifty percent along a straight-line vector somewhere inside the eyeball. You can create an additional half-lidded target, and adjust your f-curves to slide those lid vertices forward as the lid moves from either extreme. You may still need to add a target at each third, or just use another method for blinks, like cluster rotations, which Softimage documents sufficiently in their manuals.

While you may find it easy to create a target by tagging all the vertices of the mouth and rotating them on Z, the interpolation from neutral when you animate will not be a rotation. Worse, its negative value won't be a rotation in the opposite direction. You must remember that each vector is a straight line through the neutral and the target, and an interpolation goes only along that vector. Wishful thinking won't make it turn left at Albuquerque.

For moving a neutral mouth target around on a face, you don't have considerations as critical as matching a lid to the surface of an eyeball. If you do want to slide one corner of the mouth back and over for some sort of smirk, check out how that neutral smirk looks blended at fifty percent from only the neutral. If teeth are poking out, copy that shape, fix it, and blend it in as a new target on your way to the extreme. Few targets require what is in essence a breakdown pose to get to them, but they are easy to add if you need them.

Eyebrows are fun. Raise one, the other or both. Furrow them, arch them, and make them dance around like the love child of Spock, Shields, and Yarnell. They won't rotate around the brow unless you add a target to do so, if you really think anybody will see it. Just be sure to apply any brow targets to a copy of the neutral, not to copies of previously modeled targets.

Any stunt shapes, like puffing the cheeks like Dizzy Gillespie, should be modifications to the central, neutral mouth shape. Have I hammered that one home enough yet? Give yourself a few extra degrees of control, such as raising only one corner of the mouth, then the other on a separate target. You can move that corner up and down, wherever you need it to be, from wherever it happens to have moved.

Stack-em up

When you've settled on your neutral face and you're going to create your first target, duplicate the neutral, name the new one something descriptive, and translate it up by however many units you need to clear the first target. As long as you don't freeze the transform, you can move your targets wherever you like while you're making them, or after you're finished. It's easy to keep track of them all as either a stack in Y, or a row in X, Figure 13.18.

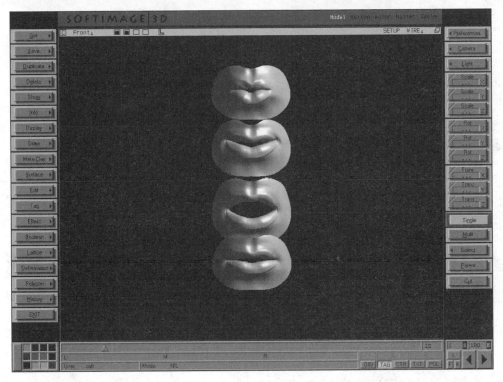

Figure 13.18 Stacking targets.

While moving the verts to make additional targets, you may want to leave it overlayed on the neutral so you can see just how far you've moved it, relative to the neutral. If you prefer, you can always pop it down and overlay it to check your work. On a raised smile, first raise the corners, and then tag the rest of the vertices of the mouth, raising them all at once. Then tag more of the surrounding vertices and raise them along, and add or lose a few as you go, to make sure the skin does what it ought to in such a move. Don't just move it all up in a solid mass without considering what the skin around the mouth would do. The lips should maintain their basic shape, especially if you're not going to change the corners of the mouth, but are creating the target primarily to move the mouth around the face.

As a last step in preparation for setting up your targets for animation in Softimage, organize your shapes into groups of seven that you expect to use together, with two groups of three, and a loner. We're going to drive the interpolation shapes using expressions tied to the three scale, three translation and single rotation channel of a null object, so you'll have rapid access to seven targets per null. We'll use only one rotation channel because gymbal lock would change the value of the other two rotations if we also used them. This way, up to three shapes at a time are conveniently accessible from your three-button mouse. If you want to get fancy, you can obtain a midi device for under $400, the Peavey PC1600 midi controller, and perform that keyboard concerto for facial animation that

Steph Greenberg first proposed. Hey, you can even buy a midi Theremin from Robert Moog that you can hook up to Softimage, using it to animate with hand gestures of your own devising to 50s monster movie soundtracks. This notion is almost as profound as it is weird. It may be the first excuse you've ever had to buy a Theremin and write it off as a business expense.

PROJECT 13.2 Expression Setup For Facial Animation

One of the most powerful setups you can create for facial animation is an expression tying weighted shape interpolation to mouse movement. This project shows you how to set up expressions to control the weighting of seven targets with a three-button mouse. This project may seem a little tedious, but don't worry, you'll do this so often you'll be doing it in your sleep.

1. Obtain a null primitive, and name it something imaginative, like "dialogue."

2. Place a value of 30 in each of the fields for scaling, one in X, Y, and Z. Place a value of 30 in the fields for translation in X, Y, and Z. Place a value of 30 in the field for X rotation, leaving Y and Z rotation values set to zero, because of the dreaded gymbal lock.

3. You may assign your favorite color to the null if you want to tell it apart from any others of the same dimensions. If you like, it could be a star or a box or a pony, as long as it doesn't slow down your screen refresh and you promise not to render it, we only want it for its channels. Set it aside for now.

4. Go into the motion module. Adjust your time line pointer so you can advance it one frame at a time and (important) park it on frame zero.

5. Select your central, neutral, anchor shape. Select Shape|Shape Interp|Weighted Interp. Next, select Shape|Select Key Shape, and click on the target that will be your neutral object, weighted shape zero.

6. Advance the time line pointer to frame one, and click on the next object. At this point, the first mouth will pop to the identical shape of the object you just clicked. Don't worry about it for now.

7. Advance the pointer to the next frame (2), and click on the next object. Repeat for the remaining objects. When you run out of objects, click the right mouse button to end the mode.

8. Select Shape|Shape List. You should see a dialogue box with a list of objects starting with Shape0, Shape1, etc. corresponding to how many objects you clicked (less one, because you started with zero). Your task is to make certain you toggle the button from Average to Additive.

Take a brief break to play with the time slider, and watch the mouth pop to each target shape as you move it to weighted shape0, shape1, and so on, corresponding to where the pointer is on the time slider.

9. Make sure your neutral shape is still selected. Select Expressions|Edit. Select Fcurves, then scroll down and pick Weighted shape 0, or wshp_0.

10. In the Expression box, type an open parenthesis.

11. Select Scn Elements and pick your null handle, the one you named "dialogue," or something even cuter. The Expressions box should now contain the open parenthesis and the name of the null object you just selected, followed by a period.

12. Select Fcurves again. Select trans, and close the parenthesis. The expression box should now read: (dialogue.trans) If you like, you may pick Validate to make sure you've entered a valid expression.

13. Pick Next to move on to expression number two. Pick Fcurves again, scroll down, and notice that wshp_0 is now grayed out. Select wshp_1.

14. In the Expression box, type an open parenthesis. Then, select Scn Elements and pick your null handle. The Expressions box should now contain the open parenthesis and the name of the null object you just selected, followed by a period.

15. Select Fcurves again. Déjà vu all over again? Good, you're learning. This time, instead of picking trans, pick scalx. In the expression box, type -30)/10 after the part that should have read: "(dialogue.scalx", so that it now reads "(dialogue.scalx-30)/10". You may select Validate at this point, if you're superstitious.

16. Yank the string: -30)/10 into the buffer by highlighting it and selecting Copy. You'll paste it onto the last part of all the rest of the weighted shapes. Select Next to move on to expression number three.

You can do this more than one way. You may have caught on that you can type or paste some of the values into the fields without the necessity of using all the dialog boxes, if that's the sort of thing you like to do. Instead of picking Fcurves for the next weighted shape each time, make sure that the affected element is the original mouth and its next weighted shape, and type it yourself in the affected elements field. After the name of the affected element and the dot, you can type wshp_ followed by the appropriate number. The only thing that's going to change in the Expression box is the name of the channel you'll be using to drive that weighted shape. Or you can continue to use the dialog boxes, particularly to make sure that scalx and rotx and etrnx are typed correctly. Copy and paste them, replacing each x with y and z where appropriate.

Weighted shape 0 we punted by tying it to a channel called trans. We won't assign values to it in animation; that's the shape we start with and default to when none of the other targets are active. Weighted shape 1 has been assigned to the scale X channel. We want weighted shape 2 to be assigned to scale Y, shape 3 to scale Z, shape 4 to rotate X, shape 5 to explicit translate X, shape 6 to explicit translate Y, and shape 7 to explicit translate Z. If you have more shapes, shape 8 would be assigned to the scale X channel of a new null, and so on down the line. However you want to get it in there, for a null object named dialogue, the expression box for weighted shape 5 should read "(dialogue.etrnx-30)/10", and the next one will look identical except the letter x will be a y. Once you've filled in all the fields, you can close the expressions dialogue box, and delete all the target shapes except for the first one. You *have* saved them in a previous file, of course, if you want to change them around at all, haven't you?

If you're still confused, I've provided an example on the CD-ROM with all the fields filled in correctly for a central mouth shape and seven targets. You'll get the hang of it soon enough.

17. At last, we animate. Select the null object, the one you named dialogue. This is now a handle for your puppet. You remember you changed the values in the fields you're using to 30. When all the channels are at 30, none of the targets is active.

18. In the motion module, highlight the Scale box by hitting the "x" hotkey on your keyboard. Just like a regular scaling operation, the left mouse button is X, the middle is Y, and the right button is Z. Now, though, they're mapped to drive target shapes 1, 2, and 3.

19. Using the left mouse button, move the x value to 40, which is 100% of shape one, the open mouth target.

Your character's mouth should now open. If you move past 40, the mouth will open even wider than you modeled it. If you move it back down, the mouth will close at 30. On its way to 20, or negative 100%, it will close and then commence to swallow itself as the upper and lower lips pass through each other. Of course, if you want to play with the target assigned to the x rotation channel, you'll have to select that, and the same for the three targets attached to the translation channels. You should spend some time just seeing what the different combinations do; it'll take some getting used to.

If you want to set a keyframe for a value of that particular shape, set a keyframe for scale X. You can move all three mouths tied to the scale channels at the same rate at the same time. Remember to set keyframes only on the target shapes you want. Don't hit save keyframe, scaling, all, unless that's what you want. Quite a lot of setup work to get to something so simple to animate, eh?

Dialogue With Weighted Shapes

When a neutral is modified by just 3 targets, open, raised smile, and pursed lips, you can get a lot more workmanlike dialogue lip-synched than you'd think. Note that it will take some experimentation with this approach to pull the most from it as an animator. The shapes you want as an animator more often come from combinations of simpler targets.

Try something simple at first, like drawing out the word "Meow." The mouth closes, **A**, with either a closed mouth target or a negative value of the open for the consonant, **B**, then reveals teeth as the mouth broadens into a raised smile, **C**. Keeping the raised smile target, you may want to introduce a slight negative value of the pursed lips target, **D**, to widen the smile.

While opening the mouth for the "ow," as seen in Figure 13.20 **A**, use the negative value of the smile to move the mouth down while it opens, **B**. Then fade out the open mouth in favor of the pursed lips, **C**, but keep bringing that raised smile from the negative back up,

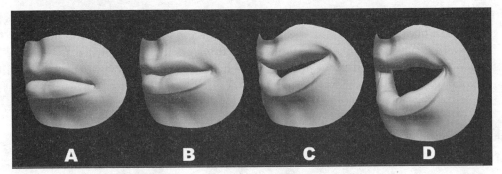

Figure 13.19   First syllable of "Meow."

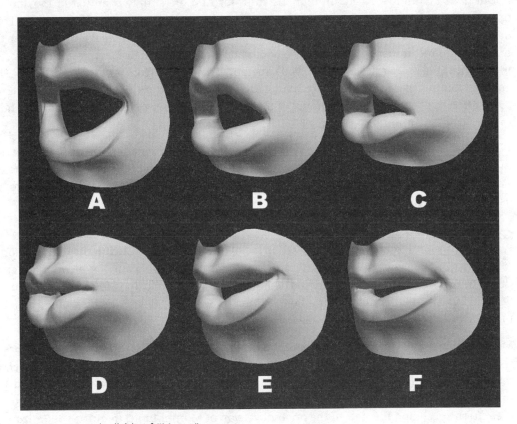

Figure 13.20   Second syllable of "Meow."

D, and keep it there, **E**, while fading out the pursed lips, **F**. When you act it out in front of a mirror, you can see it, and feel which targets to use.

If you feel compelled to hit every imaginable phoneme, you might spend some time animating to some old Lenny Bruce routines. If you can read the lips of your cute cuddly corporate icon mouthing the seven words George Carlin can't say on the air, you're ready for anything, maybe even a guest spot on *South Park*.

The temptation is to go overboard at first, nailing every phoneme. Get it out of your system, a little goes a long way. Use weighted shapes for the broad strokes, refining if you have to. In general, dialogue is the last thing to think about, after you've acted everything out with the body and the attitude of the head. You can use a few extra targets just to exaggerate the mouth moving around the face and hitting some emotive expressions before you even think about synchronizing just a few carefully selected phonemes.

Animation:Master

A:M doesn't support morphing, but Displacement setups are easy enough to use that you're not at a disadvantage. Facial animation setups for A:M are simply a matter of moving the appropriate control points to reshape the character's face, then saving the changes as a Pose, as described in the A:M manual and online Help files (look under *Creating Poses*). If you use the approach (as recommended in Chapter 6 of this book) of creating new faces from a generic face model with consistent muscle groups, you can apply Poses saved from different characters. This enables you to accumulate large libraries of facial poses with a minimum of wasted or duplicated effort. Depending on the amount of facial variation between characters, you may have to do a little fine-tuning to get some poses to fit some characters.

When you create a new pose, you should take a screenshot or render an image of it, then add that image to the character's model sheet, labeled with the name of the Pose. If you are using Magpie Pro as a lip-sync tool, you should also render a 320×240 bitmap of the new Pose to use as a thumbnail image. See the section on Magpie Pro, later in this chapter, for details.

3D Studio MAX: MorphMagic

For a simple morph sequence, you can set up facial animation in MAX with the built-in morph tools described in Projects 11.3 and 11.4. If you want to do more complex blending of emotional transitions or lip sync, you should definitely consider purchasing MorphMagic, a plug-in designed specifically for facial animation. Written by Sandeep Shekar and distributed by Platinum Pictures, this plug-in is available for both MAX 1.2 and 2.

MorphMagic shows a page of 10 targets at a time, and you can just flip through the pages to see more targets. You can enter a numeric value for each target's weight, use the slider, or manipulate it with splines. Overall, MorphMagic is very nice. It allows you to go beyond 100 percent or less than 0 percent if you want to push your morph targets. The only disadvantages are refresh speed and file size. In the original version of MorphMagic, there's no optimization. So if you have a head with 50,000 vertices and make 10 targets, you now have 10 times the data stored. MorphMagic files can be painfully big.

If you keep the original morph target around, you can make changes. For example, suppose you have three heads: a default, a smile, and a frown. You select the default and apply the MorphMagic modifier, then add in the smile and frown targets. You could then delete those smile and frown meshes from your max file. However, if you keep it around, you can actually make changes to the target, and they will be reflected in the morph object. So if you tweak the frown, you'll actually see the target change. You can later delete the frown, of course, and MorphMagic will store that info. So, the file doesn't shrink (or grow).

You have to make sure that the control splines don't go wacky. It's easy to get bad peaks in the interpolation with close keys that change a lot, as in lip sync. You'll have to go into Track View and add tangent controls to fix these problems. One good feature is that MorphMagic caps the interpolation at the limits you set. For example, if the Open target is only allowed to go from 0 to 100 and there's a spot where the interpolation spline dips down to -230, MorphMagic will actually stop at 0. This is good, because you won't have as much to fix.

You might want to try creating a low-resolution setup for faster animation. When the animation is complete, merge in the real (high-resolution) head. You can use Track View to copy and paste each target track from the low-resolution dummy over to the high-resolution head. Thus, the animator gets a lot of speed in screen refresh.

MorphMagic has a feature called *Progressive Morphing* that helps eliminate the straight-line morph interpolation errors you saw in 1103aMAX.AVI. This feature morphs the target's vertices along an arc path, rather than a straight line, so you can use it to morph angular skeletal actions (like fingers or limbs bending) using only two morph targets and a single slider.

MorphMagic information, including demo software, upgrades, and 10 tutorials, is available from **www.3dcafe.com/mm/mm.htm**. The examples are taken from an animated and lip-synced Bill Clinton caricature, and the site has a nice selection of stills and AVI clips. The tutorials are a very thorough treatment of setup and animation using MorphMagic for facial animation and lip sync, so anything else I write here would be redundant. Very nice work, Platinum!

For a facial animation setup using MorphMagic, you should render an image or take a screenshot of each morph target. Append these images to the model sheet for the character, and write up any pertinent notes on the MorphMagic settings affecting each target. If you will be using Magpie Pro as a lip-sync tool, you should also render 320×240 thumbnails of each target and add them to the appropriate Mouth directory, as described later in this chapter.

TrueSpace 3.2: SpaceTime Morph

Alain Bellon has developed a trueSpace plug-in that provides weight shape interpolation. This is very good news for character animators using trueSpace, since the main program doesn't support morphing of any kind. For full details, you can contact Alain Bellon at neuronal@netservice.com.mx, or visit his Web site, http://gumdrop.borg.com/~dream/index.htm.

Essentially, the SpaceTime Morph plug-in enables you to load up to 20 targets. These targets are subject to the usual restrictions of identical vertex count and distribution for morphing. Once the targets are loaded, you can adjust the weighting of each target with a slider. To create an animation, you adjust the sliders, create a key, then move on to the next keyframe and repeat the process. You can even sync an animation to a wav file.

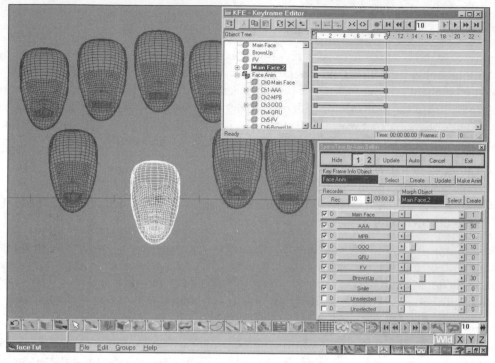

Figure 13.21 SpaceTime Morph interface.

Build A LightWave Morph Target Library From A Boned Setup

PROJECT 13.3

The Boned head you created in Project 13.1 can be used directly in animations, but it's at least as useful as a tool to create Metamorph and MTSE object libraries for Replacement animation techniques.

1. Animate the character head you Boned previously, or use PROJ1301.LWS with FACEBONE.LWO to create poses for the major phonemes and emotions.

2. Use the Save Transformed function to create and name a new morph target from each pose.

3. Save the new objects in a separate directory. Document the library with a model sheet of rendered thumbnails.

4. Depending on your approach to facial animation, you can set up either an MTSE sequence or a Morph Gizmo project (see the following section) to enable easy loading of the complete library. As you add poses, update the setup to include the new additions.

LightWave 3D 5.5: Morph Gizmo

LightWave 5.5 includes a plug-in, Morph Gizmo, that provides shape-weighting functions similar to those of Softimage or MorphMagic. The official 5.5 reference manual spends all of Chapter 16 describing how to set up and use this plug-in, so I'll just present a quick overview here.

Morph Gizmo enables you to load a base, or *Anchor*, object, then layer up to 64 groups, of 64 morph targets each, on top of the Anchor. A slider for each target determines the weight of that target's effect on the Anchor. The requirements for target objects are the same as for simple morphing or MTSE—each target must have the same vertex count and distribution as the Anchor object. Surface attributes don't matter, because only the vertex movements are used to deform the Anchor object. Any surfaces applied to the Anchor are the only ones that will appear in the final rendering. Basically, any target you create with the preceding project will work fine in Morph Gizmo (see Figure 13.22).

You animate the morph sequence by setting slider values, then creating a keyframe. The plug-in saves the combined vertex interpolation *deltas* in a Gizmo GIZ file. This file format is very small, much more manageable than a comparable MTSE or replacement scene would be. You also have the option of saving Transformed objects from any keyframe, creating new morph targets. The preview window shows the changes to the Anchor object in realtime, with or without smoothing. You can drag the scrub bar to view the animation, but, depending on the speed of your system, the playback might not be at full speed.

The only downside to Morph Gizmo is that you have to do all the animation in the interface window of the plug-in. You cannot see the changes in the normal Layout view, so you can't coordinate your facial animation with the animation of the rest of the character. This makes it harder to tweak a character's performance, because you have to change modes and rely more on the x-sheet than on visual feedback for coordination.

As with other setup methods, if you will be using Magpie Pro as a lip-sync tool, you should screen capture or render thumbnail images for each morph target, then add those thumbnails

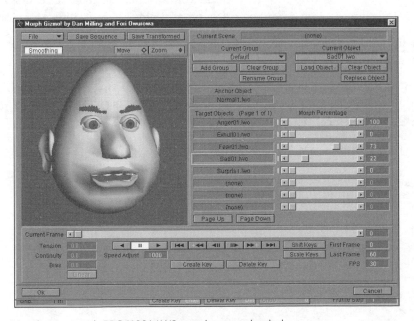

Figure 13.22 Morph Gizmo with PROJ1301.LWS morph targets loaded.

to the appropriate Mouth directory. You should also document the plug-in's setup for the animator, so she can tell which page or group to look in for a particular target.

Lip Sync

Lip sync is a subset of facial animation, so you can use the same tools and techniques described in the preceding section. Setting up a character for lip sync is essentially a process of making sure the animator has enough morph targets, maps, or Displacement poses to choose from. The last thing an animator should have to do while he's rolling hot on a long lip-sync sequence is stop and ask the setup person for another morph target or map. Anticipate the animator's needs, and you'll get a lot fewer Nerf missiles bouncing off your forehead.

The simplest form of setup for lip sync is a set of maps, to be applied to a flat surface instead of a modeled mouth. This approach makes it very easy to use software like Magpie Pro to automate most of the lip-sync process. Several projects in Chapter 9 covered the process of creating matched color, bump/displacement, and clip maps for lip sync. The only remaining setup work is adding the new maps to Magpie Pro's library.

Custom Setups For Magpie Pro

You can customize Magpie Pro to better suit your own track analysis style and needs. All you need to do is create a set of thumbnail images from your library of morph targets or maps and add those images to a Magpie Pro *expression set*. An expression set is a list of every phoneme, emotion, or action that is represented by an image file. Each image file can be used for more than one expression. For example, a single image file can be used for many of the consonant phoneme expressions. The MGE (MaGpie Expression) file controls image and channel assignments. You can edit this file directly with a word processor or interactively from within Magpie Pro.

You can find more information about Magpie Pro at its home page, **http://thirdwish .simplenet.com/magpro.html**.

The demo version of Magpie Pro, which you will find in the MAGPIE directory on this book's CD-ROM, includes a default expression set named SEGISMUNDO.MGE with 18 rendered images of a character's face, Figure 13.23:

Here's the text of the SEGISMUNDO.MGE file:

```
[Pictures]
A=a1.bmp
B=b2.bmp
C=c3.bmp
D=d4.bmp
E=e5.bmp
F=f6.bmp
G=g7.bmp
H=h8.bmp
I=i9.bmp
```

```
Closed=closed.BMP
Closing=closing.BMP
Left=left.BMP
Down=A1.bmp
Right=right.BMP
Opened=A1.bmp
Up=up.BMP
Opening=opening.BMP
Smile=happy.BMP
Angry=Angry.BMP
Sad=Sad.BMP

[Channels]
Eyes=1,138,73,189,114
Eyebrows=1,134,57,190,73
Mouth=2,72,100,154,212

[Eyes]
Closed=1
Closing=1
Left=1
Right=1
Opened=1
Opening=1

[Eyebrows]
Down=1
Up=1
Angry=1
Sad=1

[Mouth]
A=1
B=1
C=1
D=1
E=1
F=1
G=1
H=1
I=1
Smile=1
```

As you can see, the expression set is a simple, readable file that you can customize in any text editor. Be careful not to corrupt the file. If you're not completely sure of what you are doing, you should follow the directions in Magpie Pro's online Help files to create an expression set by drag-and-drop. This approach is easier but more time-consuming. Direct editing of the MGE file is a quick way to add a new expression set to your existing libraries, such as when you create a new character.

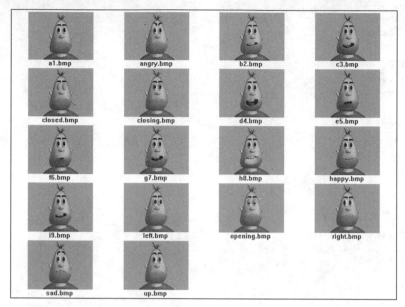

Figure 13.23 Segismundo sample expressions.

The images supplied with Magpie and Magpie Pro are good samples, but if you want to animate more accurate lip sync, you'll want to customize your own expression sets. For example, the provided sets have no transition pose for the character's mouth other than Closed. If you are animating lip sync with maps, you should also have mouths shaped for the inbetweens, or transitions, between each of the key phonemes. These inbetweens can make the difference between a jerky, distracting lip sync and one that appears fluid and natural. You can also make some of the key phonemes more specific. F and V, for instance, should have a slightly different placement of the upper front teeth against the lower lip.

Projects 9.8, 9.9, and 9.10 show how to paint matching color, bump, and clip maps for mapped lip sync. Project 13.4 shows you how to add your own maps to Magpie Pro's expression sets. If you are animating lip sync using Replacement or Displacement techniques, you will have to set up a scene with camera and lights that clearly delineate the character's mouth shape, then render 320×240 BMP files usable by Magpie Pro.

The method I use to create these images is to pose and light the basic mouth model, then create an animation using Replacement techniques that will step through every mouth model in my library. Then, I render the entire animation out to 320x240 BMP files in the appropriate Magpie Pro expression set directory. After the software finishes rendering, all I have to do is rename the image files according to the Replacement sequence notes.

PROJECT 13.4 Creating Your Own Expression Sets

If you are animating lip sync with mapped images or image sequences, creating Magpie Pro expression sets is very simple.

1. Create a new directory inside the Magpie directory, named for the new expression set you are creating.

2. Copy all the map images to a new file in the new directory, with appropriate file names.

3. Resize all the images to 320×240 pixels, and change the format (if necessary) to BMP.

4. Open an existing MGE file, using Notepad or another text editor. Save it under the name of your new expression set. This makes it easy for you to use the old MGE file as a template for the new one.

5. Edit the MGE file to add the new image file names to the appropriate expression labels.

6. Save the new MGE file to the same directory as the expression images.

7. Launch Magpie Pro, and, in the Options panel (see Figure 13.24), add the new expression set.

You may have some difficulty selecting names that accurately describe the expression represented. Unfortunately, accurate diacritical marks are not available in the standard screen fonts. To make up for this deficiency, use more letters or even complete words to describe the expressions. For example, either *e_macron* or *eee* clearly represents the long-e phoneme.

The most important consideration is that the animator is able to quickly identify and choose among the available expressions. You should print out the MGE file and a thumbnail sheet of the expression images, and add them to the documentation for the character setup.

Magpie Pro can export morph sequence files compatible with 3D Studio MAX, Animation:Master, Softimage and LightWave. To set up a character for morph sequence lip sync using Magpie Pro, you simply associate each morph target file name with the appropriate expression. Using Magpie Pro's interface, this is a three step process:

1. Highlight the expression's thumbnail image.

2. Choose Expression|Expression Properties. The Expression Properties dialog appears.

3. Click on Browse, and select the morph target that matches the selected expression.

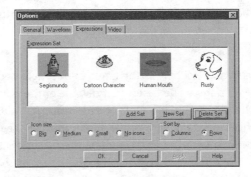

Figure 13.24 Expressions tab of the Options dialog.

Each time you do this, you add a line to the Objects section of the MGE file immediately following the Mouths section. For example, if you added a LightWave morph target for each Mouth expression in the Sigismundo set, the Object section at the end of the SIGISMUNDO.MGE file would look something like this:

```
[Objects]
A=C:\NEWTEK\OBJECTS\AMouth.lwo
B=C:\NEWTEK\OBJECTS\BMouth.lwo
C=C:\NEWTEK\OBJECTS\CMouth.lwo
D=C:\NEWTEK\OBJECTS\DMouth.lwo
E=C:\NEWTEK\OBJECTS\EMouth.lwo
F=C:\NEWTEK\OBJECTS\FMouth.lwo
G=C:\NEWTEK\OBJECTS\GMouth.lwo
H=C:\NEWTEK\OBJECTS\HMouth.lwo
I=C:\NEWTEK\OBJECTS\IMouth.lwo
Smile=C:\NEWTEK\OBJECTS\Smile.lwo
```

If you are a careful typist and understand how Magpie Pro works, you can directly edit the MGE file to add object associations more quickly. For example, if you create several characters with consistent morph target libraries, most of each character's MGE file will be identical to the others. The most significant difference is the path where the thumbnail and object files are located. If you use a text editor's find-and-replace function, you can create a new MGE file in a matter of minutes.

Lip Sync Tips For 3D Studio MAX

With 3D Studio MAX, you can use Surface Tools to model a character. Then you can create a poly mesh from that model to use with MorphMagic or Smirk. You can make morph targets by deforming the poly mesh, or (as long as the spline cage isn't changed) the splines model can be deformed, and a new poly mesh generated for each target. By basing the morph targets on the spline object, you reduce the number of controls you have to deal with and it's easier to get organic deformations.

If your character's head is going to be deformed by something like MorphMagic (MM) then you can still use Bones like Bones Pro MAX to deform it. This is straightforward, just apply both. If the head can be hidden by a seam, such as the neck ends inside the shirt, the head can be a separate object.

If you need to have the head attached to the chest and appear seamless (like a barechested strong man) there are two options. The first is to make the entire body one mesh, and make all the facial targets with the big mesh. Ugh...lots of RAM and HD space and slooow. However, if you model the neck vertices to extend well below the animated face vertices, you should still be able to make the head separate and have a seamless mesh. The trick to this is to assign a very strong weighted bone at the vertices where the neck and upper torso meet. With this setup, the vertices on both neck and upper torso will always deform exactly the same and you will never see the surfaces separate.

Physical Simulation

One of the most tempting classes of power tools for CGI character animation is physical simulation. When an animator has to manage dozens of controls, it's hard to deny the opportunity to foist some of that management off on the computer. Unfortunately, physical simulation is also one of the best ways of killing the illusion of life. Most forms of simulation end up making the character look driven by outside forces, rather than motivated from within. With the exception of a few narrow applications, physical simulation is not a good idea for character animation.

On the other hand, if your characters are to interact with a complex environment, you can save enormous amounts of time and effort by automating the behavior of that environment. Any prop, set, or other animatable element is a candidate for physical simulation. Furthermore, you have total control over the environment's parameters, so you can animate gravity, wind, mass, inertia, and other physical forces in ways that mimic the caricatured environments of classic cartoons. Suppose, for instance, a falling piano is supposed to squash flat when it lands on a character. Physical simulation software can create that effect with a standard model and a simpler setup that is also easier to animate than conventional keyframing. The lack of apparent motivation is not a problem with the falling object. In fact, motivation would spoil the effect. Thus, physical simulation is a definite asset when manipulating the character's environment but should be used only with extreme caution when animating the character itself.

There are a number of basic concepts collected under the heading of physical simulation. The most obvious is *ballistics*—the process of moving objects in paths and with velocities based on mass, inertia, and applied energy. Any falling object or missile is a good candidate for ballistics. In addition to being the most obvious, it's also one of the simplest forms of simulation. The parameters are few, well-defined, and generally intuitive, and the calculations are not terrible system hogs.

The next class of simulation is *collision detection*. This, as you might guess, is the process of calculating when one object in the scene comes into contact with another. This type of simulation has definite advantages for characters if the software enables collision detection to perform tasks such as automatically constraining the character's feet to the floor, rather than allowing them to pass through it. Collision detection plus ballistics can be used for bouncing balls and other ricochets, and for establishing the areas affected by friction and other material attributes. Collision detection can be simple, based on the crudest bounding-box approximations, or it can be refined enough to rely on the finest details in the objects' surfaces. Due to the high number of calculations necessary, the more complex the objects and the more accurate the desired results, the more computation-intensive (that is, dead slow) the simulation will be.

Material attributes are a crucial part of any physical simulation. If you want a model to look as if it's made of rubber, you need to set attributes, such as elasticity, friction, density, compressibility, and damping, to simulate rubber. Otherwise, the simulation might just as easily make the model move like porcelain. In the best simulation software, you can also animate material attributes. This enables you to change the parameters of characters or their environment during an action. This capability is invaluable for caricature, because objects must sometimes appear to be realistically solid at one moment, then turn to jelly the next.

The most advanced form of physical simulation that is of use in character animation is *soft-object deformation*. This is a process that enables you to animate an internal skeleton with the keyframe tools you're accustomed to, then turn the simulation software on to animate the meat of the character. This essentially automates squash-and-stretch and other overlapping action, within the aforesaid limits of character motivation.

Whether you are a setup person or an animator, there are several warning signs that indicate when you are applying too much physical simulation at the expense of the character's performance. The warning signs include:

- *Lack of control.* The simulation insists on making things move the way it has been programmed, rather than the way the animator wants it to.

- *Too much animator time spent tweaking the simulation parameters, rather than creating a performance.* This means there are too many controls, and the simulation is not actually saving any effort for the animator.

- *Mushy, off, or staggered timing.* Strong character performances are based on timing, hitting a pose precisely at a particular keyframe. Most simulations simply run their course, and the timing is not controllable to the frame. This tends to smear the action across a number of frames, making the action unclear and ineffective.

- *Interminable waits for screen updates or test renders.* Simulation software requires many more calculations than keyframing, even for rough previews. Most simulations also cannot be scrubbed in realtime to evaluate their results. This slows down the animator's work, often to the point where an experienced animator could keyframe the shot faster than the software could simulate it.

- *Homogenized characters.* For effective caricature using soft-object simulations, the animator must be able to animate the character's modulus of elasticity to get differential effects. Differential effects make the objects appear to change elasticity, just as a muscle reacts differently depending on whether it's taut or relaxed. Different parts of the character must have different reactions to the same forces, or the character looks like it's all made of the same stuff, like a balloon filled with meat.

Many animation programs now include basic physical simulation as part of the package. Programs that support plug-ins generally have at least one or two available for various forms of physical simulation.

3D Studio MAX: HyperMatter

HyperMatter is a plug-in for 3D Studio MAX that simulates soft-object deformation, collision, and other effects. HyperMatter enables you to animate an object's elasticity and other parameters using MAX's standard keyframe and spline controls, as shown in Figure 13.25. You can, for example, animate a character's body to have the consistency of realistic muscle during a run, then change rapidly to the consistency of gelatin as the character smashes flat into a brick wall.

Mortimer Mouse model, courtesy of View-point Datalabs.

Figure 13.25   Frame 328 from the Cannon demo file, demonstrating the automated squash possible with HyperMatter. The mice were originally identical, the left mouse has been fired out of the cannon and landed on its head.

You can blend a HyperMatter animation into a keyframed one, and turn HyperMatter effects on and off during an animation. This gives the animator complete control over how much HyperMatter animates and how much is directly controlled by the animator. This is a very good solution to the problem of balancing physical simulation software with the animator's need to control caricature.

You need to do everything you can to make the character setup as efficient as possible for animation. However, due to the way HyperMatter calculates simulations, it's possible to step through a HyperMatter animation forward, but not backward. This makes it impossible to scrub the animation to observe the effect of your revisions. Thus, HyperMatter is not responsive enough to use as a primary animation setup. HyperMatter is also extremely computation-intensive. The long calculation times mean that the animator can't get feedback as fast as without HyperMatter. Because simulations for secondary action are the icing on the cake for a character's performance, the animator should always have the option to finish the character's keyframe animation before HyperMatter is set up. Generally, it's a good idea to create a setup without HyperMatter for the initial keyframe animation, then add HyperMatter to the setup after the keyframe animation is pretty well locked. If HyperMatter's results cause you to revise the keyframe animation, the changes will at least be faster to make than if you had animated both keyframes and HyperMatter together.

The HyperMatter documentation is well thought-out, detailed, and thorough. Rather than give an inadequate summary of HyperMatter's many uses, I'll refer you to the manual and encourage you to work through the whole thing. It's actually fun, and the tutorial results are amusing.

3D Studio MAX: MetaReyes Setup

PROJECT 13.5

One of the most challenging types of characters to animate is the *creature*, a character that must move as realistically as possible while remaining under the control of the animator. Examples of creature animation include the dinosaurs of *Jurassic Park* and *The Lost World*, Draco of *Dragonheart*, and the mother squid from *Men In Black*. In each case, a fantastic creature with no real-world counterpart was set up and animated to convincingly mimic reality. To achieve this, you have to set up a system to mimic the behavior of bones, muscles, fatty tissues, and ligaments that underlie and drive the appearance of the creature's skin. If you do the setup well, the animator can concentrate on creating a great performance. If you don't build the setup to support the animator's needs, no amount of tweaking will get a convincing performance out of the creature.

REM Infografica has published a number of excellent plug-ins for 3D Studio MAX, including a metaball modeler—MetaReyes. I'm discussing this plug-in in this chapter rather than Chapter 6 because one of the most uniquely useful features of MetaReyes is that you can use it to build and animate realistic muscular systems.

Metaballs (and related metablobs and metamuscles) define their shapes by the interaction of organic primitives that attract or repel each other. This interaction is fused to create a complex, organic three-dimensional surface that would be difficult to create with polygonal or spline-based modeling tools. MetaReyes takes metamuscles one step further, enabling you to create dynamic muscles that move and distort like real muscles.

A demo version of MetaReyes is available in the REM directory on this book's CD-ROM. There are several animations and pre-built MAX files, in addition to the demo program and an HTML guide to the software. These files have some useful and interesting information, if you'd like to try muscle simulation. The basic process is as follows:

1. Select skeletal items to be connected by dynamic muscle, for example, two bones in an arm.

2. Create a dynamic muscle, and link both extremes to the objects selected in Step 1.

3. Test the dynamic muscle by animating the motion of the selected bones to stretch and squash the muscle.

4. Write up the completed dynamic muscle setup for the animator. Be sure to include the limits to the bones' rotation, to avoid overextending the modeled muscle.

Take a look at animation DYNAMIC.AVI on this book's CD-ROM, showing the complex setup of human back and shoulder muscles to accurately simulate clavicle and scapula interaction, as shown in Figure 13.26. If you need to simulate accurate muscle movement, MetaReyes is definitely the way to go.

Cloth Simulation

If you've worked through the animation projects in parallel with the setup projects, you have had a fair amount of practice animating overlapping action and follow-through by now. Those

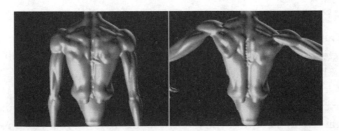

Figure 13.26 Back muscles animated using MetaReyes.

are the most important principles of animation if you are trying to do realistic clothing. Fabrics are tedious to animate, and it is nearly impossible to hand-animate a surface to precisely mimic the behavior of cloth. This is one of the areas where a simulation or procedural setup can make the difference between the impossible and the merely challenging.

Traditionally, CGI characters have dodged the problems of cloth simulation by wearing clothing that's very close to the skin (leotards and such) or rigid (armor). Related problems with skin deformation were covered over with carefully designed joints or oddly heavy accessories and jewelry. For the past several years, a number of studios and software developers have been working on the myriad of problems associated with cloth simulation, and their results have been very encouraging. Pixar's Oscar-nominated short *Geri's Game* demonstrates the high end of this effort, showcasing the cloth simulator developed by Michael Kass. Where Kass' approach addresses fine points such as warp and weft, cutting cloth on the bias, and virtual starch, the available desktop-level cloth simulators take a more lenient approach. You can expect a certain amount of rubberiness or lack of apparent weight in cloth animated with the following tools, but double-knits and silk still beat spandex and Kevlar for visual appeal.

3D Studio MAX: Infografica's ClothReyes

ClothReyes, like HyperMatter and other physical simulations, is best applied after you have finalized the keyframe animation of your characters and scenes. The calculations necessary to animate the cloth's mesh take a long time, compared to the rapid feedback of simple keyframe animation.

There is a demo version of ClothReyes on this book's CD-ROM, along with examples of MAX scene files, images, and animations created with this plug-in. The manual is slim, but offers an adequate introduction to the program's functions and some good advice about using it efficiently.

There are only a few critical considerations in setting up a ClothReyes simulation. First, there must be no self-intersection in the Hexamesh cloth model at the beginning of the animation. Once it starts, the plug-in keeps the cloth from intersecting itself, but, at the beginning, an intersection will lock up or crash the operation. Second, the cloth must be a separate surface. Closed objects are okay, but, in that case, they will behave more like rubber balls than pieces of cloth. Thus, a typical setup process runs something like this:

1. Create Hexamesh fabric objects. Be careful of the limits described earlier.

2. Select the fabric objects and all objects they are to interact with.

3. In the Modifier panel, choose ClothReyes from the drop-down list.

4. Click on Make Scene, and name the new scene. This is for the plug-in's internal use only. It doesn't actually save the whole MAX scene.

5. Select all the fabric objects, and click on Make Fabric. Edit the fabric parameters. You can choose from existing sets of parameters or create your own. This is where the animator will probably change settings, but you should create a set of usable defaults as part of the setup. Click on Close Parameters.

6. Make a test calculation. Select at least one object in the scene. Click on Start Calculation. Set a range of frames.

7. When the calculation is complete, render the animation.

If you like, you can try creating a basic setup by adding a cape, kilt, skirt, apron, or other simple mesh to one of the characters you animated in Chapter 15. If you do, document the setup, and try animating it in Chapter 16.

TOPIXCLOTH: A Cloth Simulation Plug-in For Softimage Version 3.7

This section was written by Frank Falcone and Colin Withers of TOPIX, a really cool studio in Toronto. I think we should all give them a BIG round of applause for making TOPIXCLOTH available.

TOPIXCLOTH is a free cloth plug-in for Softimage version 3.7. The cloth simulation program was developed in December 1996 for a shot in a recent Honeycomb Craver commercial where the Craver character, making his entrance as a ghost, is featured pulling a bedsheet off his head. The SGI executable is available for download along with installation instructions and demonstration files. The plug-in has been written for SGI R10000's running IRIX 6.2. Source code is included with the plug-in executable. You will require version 1.7 of the Sapphire SDK enabler available from the Softimage Web site. (*An NT version is now available, both from the TOPIX Web site and the TOPIX directory on this book's CD-ROM. DK*)

FREEWARE, COPYLEFT PROVISION, AND GENERAL SMALL PRINT

TOPIXCLOTH is released in the spirit of freeware with a "copyleft" provision: The software is released as is, without any written or implied warranty, and any further software developed and released using the code must include the original source code. The software and code cannot be redistributed without permission from TOPIX. The program and code will not be supported. TOPIX is not responsible for damage or loss of data incurred by the use of this software. TOPIXCLOTH was developed by Colin Withers and Frank Falcone for TOPIX and authored by Colin Withers.

Features

- *Practical usage*—Good at simulating a variety of cloth animation, like flags, curtains, sheets, balloons, and so forth.
- *Rugged interface*—Fast and efficient simulation calculations proven in a professional production environment.
- *Control*—Cloth stiffness/flexibility and cloth weight.
- *Dynamics*—Cloth model reacts to the forces of gravity and wind.
- *Handles*—Cloth can be dragged around or locked down via clusters.

- *Fast*—Simulation is pre-computed for quick interaction in Softimage.
- *Reloadable*—Simulation data is saved with the scene.
- *Collision detection*—Quick and dirty sphere collision models prevent cloth from intersecting other models.
- *Self collision*—Quick and dirty self collision prevents cloth from intersecting itself.
- *Iterative calculations*—Fine control for simulation accuracy.

Technical Background

In order to better understand what all the parameters in the dialog box mean, a little background is in order. The main influence for this software was a paper written by Xavier Provot, called "Deformation Constraints in a Mass-Spring Model to Describe Rigid Cloth Behavior." The cloth in the simulation is modeled to be a mesh of virtual masses with the virtual masses located at the vertices of the patch. The simulation uses the control vertices of the patch as the location of the network of virtual masses. This is why a cardinal mesh is most suited to this simulation, as the control vertices are located on the surface of the patch. The virtual mass network is linked together by three different types of massless springs.

Structural springs connect adjacent horizontal and vertical vertices, as shown in Figure 13.27. Shear springs connect vertices diagonally, and flexion springs connect every other vertex in the horizontal and vertical directions. Each spring type serves a separate purpose. Structural springs handle compression and traction stresses, shear springs handle shear stresses, and flexion springs handle stresses from the cloth bending. The position of the mesh vertices at the start frame of the simulation determines the rest length of the springs.

How It Works

The plug-in is located in the motion module of Softimage under Effects|TOPIX_cloth. The user is prompted to select a collision null, then a cloth model. The collision null is a parent to all collision spheres that should be considered by the cloth model for collision detection. This must be done regardless of whether a collision model is needed in the scene. The cloth model must be a patch, preferably a Cardinal patch (see the "Technical Background" section presented ear-

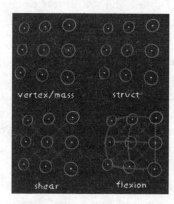

Figure 13.27 Cloth Spring parameters.

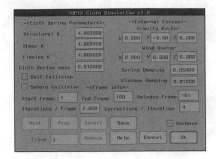

Figure 13.28 TOPIX Cloth Simulation dialog box.

lier). The plug-in then pre-computes the simulation for the frame range selected in the dialog box. The user can then see the results of the simulation by moving the frame slider in Softimage. Simulation calculations are done then buffered in memory to speed up the feedback. Further, simulation calculations are also stored with the scene and loaded up with the scene file to prevent having to recalculate the simulation every time.

Here's a summary of the parameters you can use to control TOPIX Cloth:

- *Structural K, Shear K, Flexion K*—The stiffness of the structural, shear, and flexion springs respectively. Setting a spring stiffness to zero effectively turns off that type of spring in the simulation (no speed gain is achieved in doing this, and the spring is still evaluated with a stiffness of zero).

- *Self Collision, Sphere Collision*—These two checkboxes turn on/off evaluation of self and sphere collision in the simulation. Both of these collision-detection algorithms are very ad hoc to speed up feedback. Sphere collision is computed between control vertices on the cloth mesh and the collision sphere(s), and self collision is faked by placing a virtual sphere at each vertex location in the cloth mesh and calculating the collision with other vertices in the cloth model. These fakes were appropriate for what we required but may not be appropriate for other cloth animation. The code is available, so you can rewrite this to suit your project. The simulation takes longer to compute with either or both of these turned on.

- *Start Frame, End Frame, Release Frame*—The start frame and end frame control the range of frames that the simulation is computed for. The release frame is used to turn off the handles. This disables the lock-down effect of cluster animation at and beyond this frame.

- *Iterations/Frame*—The iterations per frame is the number of intermediate steps the simulation computes between frames. Evaluating a dynamic simulation at large time steps can have adverse effects on the results of the simulation. Increasing the number of iterations per frame lowers the time that the simulation is evaluated. Putting the cloth under extreme stress (quick cartoon movement, strong forces) will require you to increase this value. A simulation computed with iterations per frame set at 2 will take twice as long as one computed with iteration per frame at 1.

- *Corrections/Iteration*—Mass spring simulations have a problem in that they appear to make the cloth look too elastic, like a rubber sheet. As you increase the stiffness of the springs to make the cloth stiffer, you must lower the time step of the simulation (increase the iterations per frame) so that the simulation does not become divergent. In order to avoid having to increase the iterations per frame (huge speed penalty), the simulation applies a constraint on each spring that it may not stretch more than 10 percent from its rest length at the start of the simulation. A spring that has become over-elongated is corrected. Increasing the corrections per iteration is a cheap way of keeping the simulation from becoming divergent (going crazy). Sometimes, more than one correction per iteration is required, as the process of correcting some springs over-elongates other springs as they are all connected together in a mesh.

- *Gravity Vector, Wind Vector*—These vectors control the direction and strength of the wind and gravity forces that are applied to the cloth model. The values plot a direction vector in Softimage Cartesian space.

- *Spring Damping, Viscous Damping*—Spring Damping is included to model the loss of mechanical energy that would occur in a real mass spring model. Values for the spring damping should not need to go greater than 0.1 (which would be approximately equal to a 10 percent mechanical energy loss). Spring Damping is also useful in damping high frequency oscillation that can happen with high spring stiffness. Viscous Damping is used to model the effect of the cloth moving in a viscous medium (water versus air). Setting the viscous damping to 1 would create the effect of cloth moving in solid concrete.

Frequently Asked Questions

Q: Why do I see little soft squares on the surface of my cloth?
A: This is what we call *surface aliasing*. If your cloth movement is very erratic, you may notice the squares. The best way to solve this is to add more points to your cloth by increasing the number of divisions (not the steps) in the source cloth mesh. Remember though, as you increase the number of points, you also effectively increase the total mass of the cloth model, thus affecting the simulation.

Q: I'm trying to animate the entire cloth model, but it doesn't seem to work.
A: Because this is a dynamics-driven program, you'll need to animate the cloth using the handles method of constrained clusters.

Q: I'm having trouble converting the resulting animation to polygons.
A: The following is a roundabout method that is rather piggish with your memory, but it works: Run the simulation. Convert the sim into shape animation using Motion|Plot|Shape. This can be very memory intensive depending on the plot frequency, the size of the cloth mesh, and the length of the sim. Duplicate the cloth model, with Shape animation toggled on in the Duplicate|Setup menu, and delete the original cloth model and sim. Now, just convert all the shape-animated cloth into polys using Effects|Convert. They should retain the same poly count and vertice numbering shape by shape (again watch division settings on Cardinal patch before you run convert—oink, oink, oink).

Q: Where is the IRIX MIPS1-2-3-4 version?
A: They are now available under the plug-in downloads.

Q: Where is the NT alpha version?
A: Still waiting for someone to send this to us.

Q: We love this so much that we'd like to give you money. Is that okay?
A: Send CASH ONLY to TOPIX c/o Colin and Frank. (Send it in a brown paper envelope marked "rent money".)

Software Limitations

- Large mesh models take longer to compute.

- Due to the efficient self-collision algorithm, moving vertices closer than their virtual collision sphere radius (which is computed by taking the average of the structural spring rest lengths) will cause the simulation to behave unpredictably.

- This cloth doesn't tear. If you grab two corners and move them apart, you will get chaotic results.

- Once you start the simulation, you can't stop it. Go get coffee.

Notes And Tips

- The cloth model must be frozen at the start of the simulation.

- The sphere collision models must be immediate children of the collision parent null.

- Pulling cluster handles too quickly will introduce stretching that is out of character with the simulation values, causing it to iterate out of control.

- Turn on both faces in the renderer.

- Linking *handles* (cluster center controls) with a chain will keep them from tearing.

- It's a good idea to randomize the points of your initial mesh in a natural way so that the simulation forces have some surface irregularities to work with (a perfectly flat patch dropped in Y with -10 gravity will have no other effect than a grid falling straight down in the Y axis).

- Don't let handles (locked cluster points) intersect with collision model(s) or self, else chaos will ensue.

- Change cloth parameters one at a time so you can see the results of the changes you make.

- It's always a good idea to give your simulation a 30 to 50 frame pre-roll to let the cloth find itself. It takes a while for the point weight properties to balance themselves with the dynamic settings of the simulation, so a pre-roll will help to reduce the bounce that occurs while this is happening. You can set the simulation start as a negative without changing the timeline start frame.

More Power Tools For 3D Studio MAX

By Mike Comet

You may wonder why I go crazy in my character setups (Chapter 12) with making Dummy objects for use with the NewIK rather than clicking on the bone and moving the End Effectors that way. This is because NewIK requires you to use the internal MAX bones. However, these Bones do not really have volume and it can be difficult to see exactly how they are spinning. In addition, applications like BonesPro MAX work better with boxes or rectangles as Bones. By using dummies I can hide the entire NewIK bone system and just view the custom boxes/rectangles and end effector dummy objects. This way, I know I won't mess up the hierarchy and the volume boxes used by Bones Pro give a better indication of what is going on when I'm animating.

Bones Pro MAX

The default MAX bones do not allow you to do smooth deformations. The plug-in of choice in my opinion is BonesPro MAX, published by Digimation. This plug-in allows you to use an object (usually a rectangle or low detail section of your character) as a bone to deform a mesh. It has options for things like weighting bone strength and falloff and setting vertex inclusion and exclusion. Bones can share vertices, an effect that results in very nice smooth deformations. By using vertex exclusion you can also get hard creases and other effects.

In MAX 1.2, the BonesPro plug-in was a SpaceWarp. This meant it always appeared at the top of the modifier stack. If you had an object and wanted to have other modifiers below it, you could do it, but if you wanted to modify your object afterwards you were out of luck. In MAX 2.0 the BonesPro plug-in is available both as a SpaceWarp (for compatibility) and as a modifier. By using the modifier version you can make drastic changes to your model later in the stack, even after animating.

One reason you would want to do this is squash and stretch. You could animate a character's body with the BonesPro modifier as the base deformation. You could then add an FFD modifier to a section of the character and animate the FFD's to get very specific squash and stretch (as opposed to just scaling the bone). Previously, you would have had to add more bones for more control, or add the FFD earlier and animate the FFD without actually seeing the character in its deformed pose.

The BonesPro plug-in also includes three other useful utilities for character animation:

- Convert a hierarchy to boxes of a set width. The boxes are automatically parented to each other. This means you can convert a MAX bone hierarchy to a set of linked rectangles.

- "Snapshot" plug-in that makes a copy of a mesh exactly as it appears in an animation, even if modified by a space warp. This is primarily useful for making a collapsed mesh copy of a pose.

- A modifier called "Blend." This is a modeling tool that makes Booleaned joints of an object smooth out. For example, imagine you had two spheres slightly intersecting and Booleaned them together. If you used the Blend modifier on that object you would end up with a smoothed water droplet type look. If you're doing polygon-based modeling this plug-in is great because it can help fix joint creases and it doesn't add any vertices to the mesh as mesh-smooth does.

Character Studio

If you've looked through the IK tutorials. you'll quickly realize that nice IK setups can be quite a job to create. Enter Character Studio. Character Studio is basically two independent plug-ins sold in one package. The first is Biped, which enables you to create a pre-linked and setup hierarchy of a two legged creature. It has FK, IK, and dynamic attaching for the hands and feet built in and preset. It also enables you to animate with footsteps by placing what look like dance instruction drawings in MAX and having the character follow those steps.

For those who want to animate without footsteps (or those that find dancing babies annoying), Biped works in a *Freeform* mode. In this mode, Biped lets you animate with Forward Kinematics or IK just like a normal hierarchy. By using the dynamic parenting options you can lock feet to the ground, hands to objects (like a character picking up a ball) and so on. It's essentially a supercharged IK system all ready to go.

Note that many animators consider using footsteps a crutch, and if you're working on a demo reel, you would be well advised to use Freeform mode, or to forgo Biped altogether. While Biped does allow you to customize the number of neck, leg, arm, and even tail links (within reason) it is limited to two legs (hence the name Biped). So if you're looking for a nice pre-made IK system for say a horse, you'll have to build it yourself or link two bipeds together in some fashion.

Another caveat with Biped is the fact that you cannot scale bones when animating. This means no squash or stretch. However, if you use custom bones, you could parent them to the respective Biped structure and then scale them when needed (although the joints wouldn't really connect properly then).

One positive note about Biped is that you can parent any object to it. So, you can use custom bones parented to Biped bones for BonesPro. Or if you wanted to make a three-legged monkey, you could set up one leg using IK and use Biped for the rest.

The second section of Character Studio is the "Physique" plug-in. Physique is a deformation tool like BonesPro. Although it's designed to work with Biped, you can actually use it with any hierarchy you create. Unlike BonesPro, however, vertices can be assigned to only one bone. In MAX 1.2 this made it very difficult to get smooth deformations for mesh based characters.

In MAX 2.0, however, the Physique plug-in now utilizes FFDs. Essentially you assign FFD control points to the Physique bones. This FFD is then used to the modify the mesh object, which results in much smoother joints. In addition, both the 1.2 and 2.0 version have *tendons*. Tendons allow you to attach a ring of points to a bone other than the one they're assigned to. This allows for effects like pectorals lifting up when the arms are raised, even though those vertices are assigned to a spine bone.

Physique also has a feature known as *muscle bulging*. This enables you to create cross sections along your bones, then edit the curves of each cross section based on where the bone is rotated. So when you rotate a forearm, the bicep area will bulge automatically. This is a very powerful tool. You can create as many cross sections and rotation targets as you like, even along different axes, and Physique will happily connect them for you.

The Character Studio bundle provides a quick way for someone to get started with character animation. You have a nice bone system all ready as well as a tool to deform the mesh when animating. Personally, I prefer using BonesPro as the deformation tool and Biped as the bones system. However, with the addition of spline-based models such as NURBS, Character Studio may be a better choice.

Combination Plate: Using BonesPro and Biped Together

It is not difficult to utilize the BonesPro MAX plug-in together with the Biped utility. You can simply use the Biped structure as bones, or, more preferably, make custom box bones and simply parent them to the Biped. The trick is to use Biped in Freeform mode. Because BonesPro requires a setup frame (usually frame 0) where the mesh and the bone structure are aligned together, Freeform mode is desirable. The reason for this is that with Freeform you can line up the Biped to your mesh and set key frames on frame 0. If you use footsteps, you can line things up, but as soon as you start creating new Footsteps, the Biped will suddenly jump to the location of the first steps and will rotate the spine and arms around it. This makes it difficult to use with BonesPro as you may constantly have to go back to adjust the first pose.

If you insist on using BonesPro with Biped Footsteps, you have two choices. You can always go back and realign your Biped on frame 0 to match your mesh. Alternatively, you can create an entire custom hierarchy for deforming your character with BonesPro. After your Biped animation is completely tweaked, you can unlink your custom hierarchy, but leave their positions at frame 0. Then you link each piece to the Biped character. Finally, on frame 1, align each piece with the Biped bone it is parented to. The result is that the bones are parented to the Biped, and on frame 0 are aligned to the mesh, then on frame 1 are animated to move to the correct location on the Biped, so the deformation takes place correctly. Ugh—Freeform mode is by far the easiest choice. Either way, make sure all the pieces of your Biped have a key set on Frame 0 (or whatever frame is the BonesPro rest frame) and that they're aligned to the mesh you want to deform.

Tips And Tricks For BonesPro MAX

BonesPro MAX offer a lot of control for setting up characters. The following are some tips and helpful reminders that may help you with setup problems:

- I almost always set my initial bone Falloff and Strength to 50 and 3, respectively. This is different from the default 100/1 setting it uses. The 50/3 setting essentially tightens up the control of each bone usually resulting in better looking deformations.
- Vertex exclusion/inclusion. For almost every setup I manually set vertices. I typically find that even with the 50/3 setting, bones that you don't think will affect certain areas

will affect them. To manually set vertices, I select all the bones and tell them to exclude all vertices. Then I go back bone by bone and select and assign vertices in each bone's range, as well as about 50 percent into adjacent bone areas.

- I have noticed (with MAX 1.2) that sometimes vertex exclusions will not work right if you don't use a simple rectangle or box object. Although BonesPro will allow you to select objects other than boxes, it may be better to stick with actual rectangles for BonesPro bones. If you want to animate a bone that has more detail you can always parent multiple layers. So you could have a really detailed bone that you animate and move, then the square bone used by the BonesPro plug-in is just parented to that and hidden during animation and rendering.

- BonesPro has a feature called *visualize* that shows a color shaded view of your object and how much influence selected bones have. However, this feature doesn't take into account any vertex inclusion/exclusion you have done, only the falloff and strength. So even if you unassign all vertices from a bone, it may still show red areas in visualize mode.

- Don't parent the mesh! Remember that you shouldn't parent the mesh that gets deformed to anything. BonesPro will automatically move it for you based on the bones.

- Reset Transform! If you are rotating custom bones around and you see them skewing, you need to go back, unlink the bones, and perform a Reset Transform operation (Utilities panel) on them. If the bones have non-uniform scaling applied, they will sometimes shear when you rotate them in the hierarchy. In general. it's a good idea to do a Reset Transform on all custom blocks in a hierarchy setup before linking. If you want the axis to be oriented a certain way, use the Affect Pivot Only option in the Hierarchy Panel.

- Multiple meshes are okay! Just because you have one bone hierarchy doesn't mean you can't use multiple meshes or BonesPro Warps/Modifiers with the same bones. For example, you may have a shirt mesh and a pants mesh and you may want to keep them separate. You may want to use the same bones, especially if the shirt hangs down a bit over the pants. All you need to do is make two BonesPro Warps or modifiers for each object, then set them up to use the same bones. You will have to set up vertex exclusions just the same, of course.

Moving On

By this time, you should have a good grasp of the issues in power tool setup and be better able to make decisions about which tools are useful and which are counterproductive.

There are several things you can do to make power tools better:

- Experiment with new tools as they become available.
- Try new ways of using old tools.

- Pay attention to feedback from animators.

- Reuse what works, and solve problems in (or discard) what doesn't.

- Give feedback to software developers and publishers, and demand better tools. Be specific about how a feature should work, how it can make a difference in your work, and why more people will buy their product if the new feature works properly.

- Most of all, practice animating, even if your primary job is setup.

With that in mind, jump ahead to Chapter 16, and try your hand at a few character animations using these setups.

PART V

ANIMATING

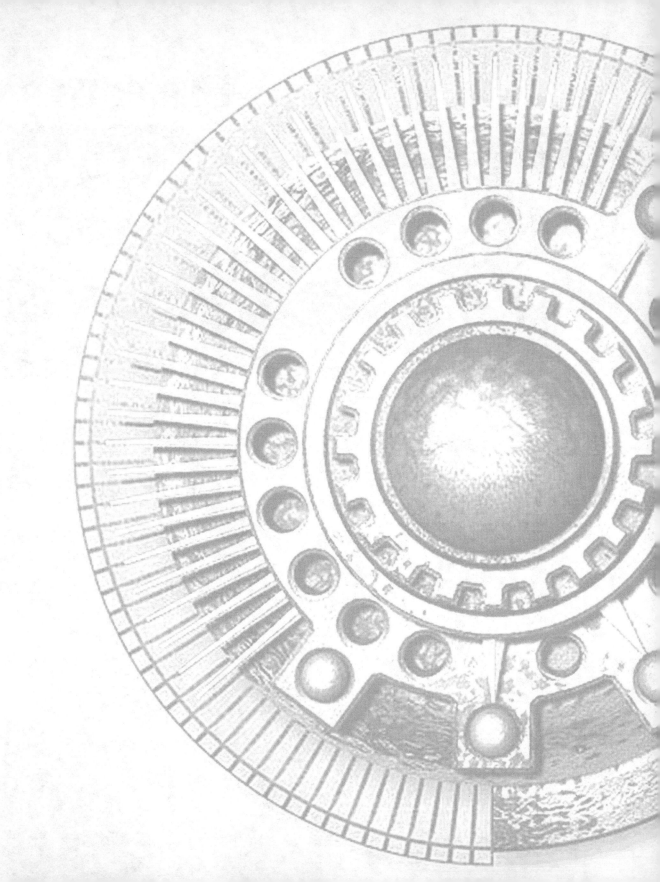

ANIMATION

To create the illusion of life, you need to animate characters with the basic principles of timing: anticipation, snap, ease, cushion, squash, stretch, follow through, overlapping action, secondary action, and holds. To animate efficiently, you need to understand spline and keyframe controls. To communicate effectively, you need to compose your shots. Finally, you need to animate your characters with uniquely characteristic actions to keep your audience entertained and interested.

This chapter is about the very basics of character animation. If you complete these projects and practice the skills you learn through them, you will have an adequate working knowledge of character animation. The remaining animation chapters of this book build on these basics, so you should take your time, practice, and master this chapter's contents before you move on.

What Is Animation?

Character animation is a deliberate, systematic and meticulous endowment of an inert symbolic object (whether pencil drawing, painting, stop-motion puppet, clay or pixels) with the appearance of thought, emotion and personality.

Character animation can imitate real life humans and animals. More generally, it is the creation from scratch of what appears to be a new life, that reminds us of life that we've seen, yet caricatures it as well. Life can be amplified upon and situational metaphors can be approached that aren't possible with live action film making. Audiences can look at their lives reflected in a world that would be filtered by their vanity were they to simply look in the mirror. All this is done through poses and seemingly magical tricks which aren't so magical once you've learned them. Learning and applying the magic tricks of the animation trade can make characters that don't just move, but with which people can identify, sympathize, empathize, laugh, be entertained, and be frightened.

Animation is a language universally understood that hardly anybody ever bothers to learn how to speak. Animators introduce new words and parts of speech all the time. Although there are very few speakers, some take to the language easily, others spend lifetimes polishing just a few phrases. Ninety-eight per cent of us consider ourselves fortunate to have learned merely how to quote a few original lines. Superior animation persuades an audience to suspend its disbelief, capitalizing upon the abstract representation of motion to communicate on an emotional level that transcends any dialect. Animation is the universal language.

An animator is a sleight-of-hand artist who draws your attention to carefully selected visual cues that best convey an idea, distracting attention frame by frame from the artifacts that distinguish and define the medium used.

An animator transcends realistic motion by abstractly representing the notion of movement, in a manner sufficiently skillful to read as *true* if not necessarily *real*.

Dictionaries define animation as both a process and as a product. Everybody wants to animate, everybody wants to bring something to life, "to imbue with life," something more easily described than done. Short of that, we want to learn what it is an animator does to achieve the *illusion* of life. Is there some mindset, some simple set of strategies for the selection of ingredients, which a skillful artist blends and bakes, resulting in some fresh animation? As the medium extends itself into the realm of computers, what distinguishes animation from an engineering approach to motion, from the simulation of physics or dynamics? How does it differ from puppetry, or from elaborate costumes and masks remotely controlled by actors?

Norman McLaren, the great Canadian animator, said, "Animation is not the art of drawings-that-move, but rather the art of movements-that-are-drawn."

In response to this, Chuck Jones says, "Animation is not drawings that move. It's drawings that move as they already exist in the director's mind."

One can learn, readily enough, which steps to take to project a shadow of any idea into dimensional space in time. One's capacity to visualize is the only limiting factor.

Much of the methodology that grew up around pencil animation was an effort to eliminate the guesswork, to codify and to observe principles that would ensure the shot would achieve its purpose. By paying attention to the ways one can break up an immense organizational nightmare into a few readily manageable steps, the technical components of animation will eventually help you to become better at visualizing.

Layout

Your first step in committing an animation to the computer is *layout*, sometimes called *blocking*. This is the equivalent of a stage production's blocking, where marks are taped on the floor to show where the characters will stand at critical points in the story. This is the next step in roughing out the animation, following directly from the storyboards. Ideally, layout consists of adding each character in its default setup to a position within the set to match that shot's storyboard sketch. At this point, you won't be doing any detailed tweaking of the character's pose, just setting its basic position and attitude.

Layout is a critical step, just as important as the storyboards. It's possible (even likely) that the storyboard artist has cheated a few sketches in ways that you can't readily lay out with the modeled sets and characters. The layout process is intended to red-flag those problems before the production makes any expensive, time-consuming mistakes.

One of the mistakes that consistently gets beginning animators (and sometimes experienced animators, too) into trouble is not doing proper layout, or not getting approvals on the layout from the client or director. Layouts, and especially camera setups, must be locked down before the characters can be animated.

Locking Down The Camera

If you don't get a lock-down on the layouts, you will have to reanimate entire sequences if the client or director decides to move the camera. In film and TV work, it's important that the actors be able to play to the camera. It's possible to get a much stronger performance and, therefore, tell a story better, if the actors' full talents are focused in one direction. You can cheat poses, facial expressions, actions, even costumes, if you can rely absolutely on what the camera can and can't see. (Can you tell if that TV anchor is wearing anything under the desk?)

This is even more important in CGI character animation. The techniques and requirements of actors playing to the camera are just as true for CGI characters as for live action. In addition, if you thoroughly examine any CGI character, you are going to find flaws and inconsistencies—it's just the nature of the current state of the art. It's very difficult to thoroughly mimic reality in a character setup, even if realism is appropriate to the style of the animation. More often, the characters will be cartoony or fantastic and have little use for an anthropometrically correct skeletal structure. The result is that character animators have to develop a bag of tricks, cheats, and workarounds to create poses and actions that hide these flaws, so the results look good to the camera. Most of these cheats fall apart if the camera angle changes even a few degrees.

If you try to animate a character to look good from all possible camera angles, you will spend a lot more time tweaking and still get the most boring, lifeless poses you can imagine. Lock down the camera during layout so you can turn your creative efforts to maximizing the dramatic or comedic effects of every pose.

One extremely difficult venue to animate for is real time, 3D games where the end user has control over the camera point of view. In this type of animation, you can't cheat the camera, you just have realistic balance, and movement which cannot trick the eye. What makes these real time 3D environments difficult to animate for is that the animation must not look pathological from any angle. It must look convincing from all possible viewing angles, and therefore takes longer to animate.

This isn't a problem for a character that is running and jumping, doing your basic locomotion and action moves. For a character that is acting and performing, it's a different story. Even a live action stage actor rarely performs theatre in the round. When an actor performs on a traditional theatrical stage, the audience begins at the proscenium, and the projection of gestures and poses directed at the audience in general still has limitations on the viewing angle.

But in real time animation that can be viewed from arbitrary angles, it is difficult to animate a character's eyes so that they can meet the viewer's eyes when the animator so desires. Poses can no longer employ graphic design techniques to lead the viewer's eye. Poses get mushed out to appear as they do in our real world by the real world physics we must observe. Bones can no longer be bent the wrong way just to make something look the way we want it to. Eyes pointed to the side in evasive mock conversation can mistakenly look a viewer in the eye with solid confidence when viewed from the wrong angle. You can't depend on close ups, specific camera heights, or cutting; absolutely none of the conventions of film making. All of these things are pathologies inherent to real time animation and the interactive environment in which they reside. You simply have to expect this from a medium in which the user controls the POV.

When you are planning animation that utilizes a more conventional linear medium, you are not bound by these limitations. Just because you are using CG for your animation does not excuse sloppy pre-production planning that imposes these limits on you. An animator or director who thinks clearly sees the shot they need in their mind. Clear thinking and planning can not only save you an enormous amount of time and trial-and-error heartaches, it can mean the difference between animation that is met with a yawn and animation that wins awards.

Camera Animation: Composing Shots For Effect

One of a director's jobs is to compose each shot, using the camera to control what the audience sees, set the mood, and advance the story. If, as an animator, you are simply handed sequences to animate, you may not have any choice in composing the shots. If you have directing authority, and especially if you are wearing all the hats, you need to know how to compose effective shots for character animation. This chapter shows you the basics.

Shot composition shows off one of CGI animation's major advantages over other cinematic forms—you have absolute control over your camera. You are not limited by the physical size and weight of a camera, nor by the tracks, dollies, and cranes required to move one. You can choose any lens you like, move the camera in any fashion and at any speed you desire, and generally indulge your creative whims without paying the exorbitant costs of more traditional cinematography.

This is not to say that you should do all those things, at least not if your purpose is to tell a story using character animation. For each camera move, ask yourself: Does it advance the story? Does it help develop the character? Does it distract the audience from the focus of this shot? Your audience is used to a more limited range of cinematography, so going to extremes with the camera may distract them from the story and characters. Keep it simple.

The first choice in composing a shot is the distance from the camera to the object, or central character, of the shot.

Keeping Your Distance

Distance affects how much information falls within the frame, how much of the frame the character occupies, and the emotional impact of any actions on your audience. Let's take a look at some of the stock distances used in traditional cinematography and note how they affect these three variables.

The Long Shot

A *long shot* contains a great deal of information. It includes the complete central character of the shot, plus a good bit of the environment surrounding the character. This is especially useful for an *establishing shot*, one that shows the audience the general environment in which the action will take place. Framing references for the long shot are generally not to human scale. Frame composition usually derives from a building or other large object, with the character (if any) being a minor focal point.

The long shot has the greatest emotional detachment from the audience. Any action composed at this distance will generally have much less impact than a closer shot. Also, minor actions will be so small a part of the screen that your audience will probably overlook them. A long shot is not a good choice for showing subtle emotional transitions or actions.

Composing A Long Shot

1. Load the Puppet character default scene you set up in Chapter 11 or some other humanoid character of your choosing. Add the restaurant building, sidewalk, and street models included in the Chapter 14 directory on this book's CD-ROM. Depending on your software, the CD-ROM may also contain usable scenes already set up for you.

2. Position the character just to one side of the restaurant door.

3. Align the camera so it is centered on the character's chest, and position the camera at least 10 meters (or equivalent) away from the character. Set a keyframe.

4. Render an image, at whatever resolution and anti-aliasing you prefer. You should get something like Figure 14.1.

Figure 14.1   Long shot.

The Full Shot

The *full shot* is an emotional step closer than the long shot. Any action shot at this distance will have a greater impact, because the audience will feel closer to it. The audience can also see more clearly the posture and the grosser expressions of the character, so you have a greater practical dramatic range for character animation.

The full shot conveys less information about the character's surroundings but can add details that are lost at the greater distance. The full shot is a good choice for establishing the character's general appearance, including props and clothing that have a bearing on the story, Figure 14.2. A long shot might show only the profile of a character in front of a building, whereas a full shot will reveal the six-gun on his hip, the silver star pinned to his vest, and the lettering over the building's doorway reading "Sheriff."

You can compose a full shot of the character by trucking the camera in (moving forward along the axis of the lens) toward the character. A full shot must always include the character's feet. If you frame the character as cut off at the ankles, you will not get a pleasing composition.

This brings us to the concept of *cutting heights*. Since most films are about people, you can usefully describe most shot compositions in relation to the human body. Over the years, directors and cinematographers have developed a set of empirical rules for composing shots relative to the actor. The standard cutting heights are under the armpits, under the ribcage, under the waist, across the upper thigh, and under the knees. If a script or director uses a term like *waist shot*, they mean a composition that ends just below the feature described.

The Medium Shot

The *medium shot* brings the audience another emotional step closer to the action. From a character's point of view (POV), this is only a couple of steps away, just beyond arm's reach. All but the most subtle facial expressions can be read by the audience, but any body language expressed using the legs is, of course, lost off screen.

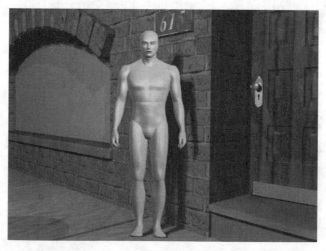

Figure 14.2 Full shot, including feet.

The audience can still pick up information about the character's immediate surroundings, but most of the screen is now occupied by the character and the audience's attention will generally be focused there.

You can compose a medium shot of the character by trucking in closer, to cut the character off at the upper thigh, as shown in Figure 14.3.

The Close Shot

The *close shot* focuses the audience's attention on the head and upper body of the character, which occupy most of the screen. This composition shows just enough of the character's body for the audience to readily perceive shrugs and general body posture. The emotional distance is arm's length, a conversational distance, so any action will have a fairly strong impact on your audience.

It will be difficult for your audience to absorb any information from the background, as most of their attention will be drawn to and held by the foreground character. Conversely, any information conveyed by the character will be that much easier for the audience to read.

You can compose a close shot of the character by trucking the camera in again, this time cutting the character off at the lower ribs, as shown in Figure 14.4.

The Specific Close Shot

The next closer distance is the *specific close shot*. The example in Figure 14.5 shows a Close Shot Head, but descriptions such as Close Shot Hand, Close Shot Window, and so on are also used. The composition is generally interpreted as including the specified object and a visual border around the object. Again referring to Figure 14.5, the head is shown with a visual border beginning well above the head and extending below the chin. The specified object occupies the entire action area of the screen.

Figure 14.3 Medium shot, upper thigh.

Figure 14.4 Close shot, through ribcage.

Figure 14.5 Close Shot Head.

This composition is very strong emotionally. The nuances of facial expressions are easy for the audience to read, and there is almost no chance of a distraction from the background. The only information the audience can observe is that expressed by the character. From a character's POV, this is a very intimate distance, used only between friends or when one character is violating the other's personal space.

You can compose a Close Shot Head of the character by trucking the camera in close enough to fill the frame vertically with the character's head.

The Extreme Close Shot

This composition is literally in your face. The audience is being force-fed the information, whether they want it or not. The audience can't see anything but the object of the shot.

Emotionally, this composition can be so strong as to be overwhelming, especially on a large screen. You should be careful not to overuse it, and keep extreme shots like this as short as possible. The emotional intensity is difficult to sustain, and you risk boring your audience with an overly close, overly simple composition. Give the audience enough time to absorb the emotional impact, then move back to a more distant shot.

You can compose an extreme close shot of the character's eyes by trucking the camera in close enough that the character's face fills the frame horizontally (see Figure 14.6).

Pick A Lens, Any Lens

The exact position coordinates you use for the camera will depend on the lens equivalent you select. LightWave's default Zoom Factor of 3.2 was used for each of the preceding examples. A higher Zoom value would require more distance between the character and the camera to achieve the same composition, and vice versa.

Depth of field (DOF) is one more variable you need to keep in mind when setting the distance for a shot. Unlike real-world cameras, CGI software, by default, has infinite depth of field, so all objects are in perfect focus. If you want to simulate the focal behavior of a real-world camera, you need to use your software's DOF, if any. When activated, DOF determines what is in focus at different distances from the camera. Objects at the exact focal distance from the camera are in sharpest focus, while those closer or farther away are progressively out of focus.

You can use DOF to minimize distractions for your audience. You can make backgrounds (or foregrounds) so blurry and out of focus that the audience ignores them. You can even set the controls so everything but the central character is out of focus. Depending on your software, you may be able to animate these settings, to shift the audience's attention without moving the camera.

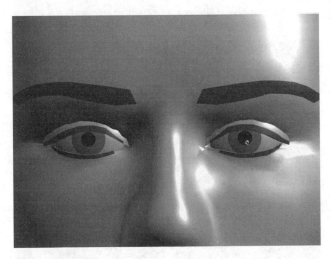

Figure 14.6 Extreme close shot eyes.

Blurry, Blurry Night

This project shows you how to set up an extreme depth of field for a medium shot of the character using LightWave 3D. The procedures are similar for most software that supports DOF.

1. Load the scene PROJ1402.LWS. Open the camera panel.

2. Set Anti-aliasing to Medium or higher. The Depth Of Field option will not work with lower anti-aliasing settings.

3. Click on the Depth Of Field button at the lower left of the panel. Set Focal Distance to 4.0. This is the distance between the camera and the character you want to be in sharpest focus.

4. Set Lens F-Stop to 0.5. This setting specifies a very shallow depth of field, producing a large amount of blurring in the foreground and background. Click Close Panel.

5. Render frame 0. You should get an image like Figure 14.7.

Note how the character in Figure 14.7 is still in sharp focus, but both the street lamp in the foreground and the brick wall in the background are blurred and, therefore, much less of a distraction.

If you need to match the DOF of a shot to live action, the Film Size feature in LightWave's camera panel can automatically emulate the settings for several real-world film and video formats.

The second part of composing a shot is selecting the camera angle.

What's Your Angle?

The basic criteria for selecting camera angles are the same as for setting the distance. You want the angle to help control what the audience sees, set the mood, and advance the story.

Figure 14.7 Shallow depth of field.

The most common camera setup is probably the *omniscient observer*, a camera positioned and angled as if it were another character in the scene. The POV is usually near or below the other character's eye levels, so the *pitch* (or elevation) angle of the camera is nearly zero.

The *heading* (or azimuth) angle varies but is rarely close to the cardinal points (0, 90, 180, 270). These angles would give head-on, perfect profile and rear views that would read as flat and artificial, because you rarely get a view like that in real life. It is usually better to keep the heading at a more natural angle, at least five degrees away from any cardinal point.

If you consistently use omniscient observer camera angles, your shot compositions will quickly become boring. If you want to keep your audience's attention, you need to spice up the mix a little with more dramatic camera angles.

Try using higher and lower camera positions, with corresponding pitch angles. There are no absolute rules governing the emotional impact of camera angles, but here are some useful rules of thumb:

- High angles, where the camera is above the character and looking down, tend to give the audience a literally lower view of the character. The character is perceived as smaller, weaker, of less importance, or being threatened. Subtlety counts for this type of composition. An extreme high angle loses the audience simply by being extreme. A relatively small high angle has the desired emotional effect without tipping off the audience.

- Low angles, reasonably enough, tend to give the audience a higher view of the character. The character is perceived as larger, stronger, of greater importance, and in closer shots can readily be perceived as threatening. Again, subtlety counts; a worm's-eye view will lose the audience, but a more subtle angle will have the desired effect.

You may have noticed I didn't mention camera angles using the third axis *bank* (or roll). That's because it's generally a bad idea to bank the camera at all, unless you are going for a very specific type of effect. Bank angles have the effect of tilting the horizontal edges of the screen frame, relative to the sets and characters. This off-kilter view can be very disturbing to the audience and is rarely used apart from action sequences or psychological thrillers.

The action shot can justify banking the camera if the character's POV is actually going through a bank angle, as in a car turning over or an aircraft doing a barrel roll. This is consistent with the action expected by the audience and will not have a strong effect—other than making the audience unconsciously lean into the angle!

The psycho thriller uses of the bank angle are more disturbing. The basic technique is to compose a more normal shot, then slightly bank the camera to skew the composition. If done subtly enough, the audience may never notice the angle. They will, however, become emotionally tense, sensing that something is not right. A variation on this technique is used to underscore a progressively more unbalanced character or setting. If you gradually increase the bank angle of any shot from the character's POV (or a shot includes the character), the audience will sense that the psychosis is becoming worse.

The best rule for camera angles in character animation is to keep it simple. Barraging your audience with lots of odd camera angles is confusing and can get in the way of telling your story. The audience will spend too much time adjusting to the new POV and miss whatever you are trying to communicate through the character. Using the same angle in several shots gives your audience a POV that they can identify quickly, so they can concentrate on the character's actions. Try to find a balance between standard shots and more unconventional compositions. Choose your camera angles to emphasize and work with, not against, the current action.

Continuity

You also need to keep continuity in mind. Look at the shot compositions you have planned to precede and follow the current one. You need to match screen position, on-screen movement, and sight lines between successive shots, or you will lose continuity.

Screen position means keeping the character in the same approximate relation to the screen frame. If the character appears on the left of the screen in one shot, he should not appear on the right in the next shot.

Matching movement means you should keep the character moving in the same direction in successive shots. If the character is walking left-to-right in one shot, he should also be walking left-to-right in the next. If the character is to change direction (Oops! Forgot something. I'll be right back!), you need to show that change of direction within a single shot.

Matching sight lines means the character should be looking in the same direction. If a character is looking out a window in one shot, the following shot should not show her staring at the tabletop. As with direction of movement, if a change is necessary, you need to show that change within a single shot. In this case, an insert shot of the character's head swiveling from the window sight line to the tabletop sight line would bridge the change nicely.

Finally, it is best to keep the camera on the same side of the action throughout a sequence. The main action should be following a *slalom*, as discussed in detail later in this chapter. You can use this slalom as a spatial dividing line for the sequence, sometimes referred to as the *line of action*. Keep the camera positioned on one side of this divider. If you jump from one side to the other, your audience will become disoriented. This is called the 180 rule, as mentioned by Sandra Frame in Chapter 3. If you shift the camera from one side to the other at the end of a sequence, you should hold the first shot a little longer to give the audience time to adjust.

Another way to cross the line of action or to easily change continuity is to use what is known as a Clean Exit. Basically, the character leaves the scene and the camera pauses for a short moment with the character totally off-screen. The next shot can be composed with more freedom without breaking continuity.

Animating The Camera

You can animate the camera in a number of ways to connect shots in a sequence. There are two major divisions of camera animation in CGI, the *move* and the *cut*. Moves are continuous transitions from one position, attitude, and lens setting to another, while cuts are abrupt changes between one frame and the next. In traditional cinematography, cuts are accomplished by editing. In CGI, you are free of the constraints of a physical camera, so you can make a cut within the animation.

Camera animation should be treated as any other technique, used only to tell the story. Inappropriate use will distract the audience and detract from your story, and is the mark of an amateur still infatuated with technological toys.

It's Your Move

A camera move is generally one of several stock types, or a combination of more than one. The stock moves are pan, tilt, dolly or truck, tracking, zoom, and rack focus The following projects will show you how to set up each of these stock moves.

Pan Camera Move

1. Reload the scene you used for the shot composing projects.
2. Rotate the camera 15 degrees to the left on its vertical axis. Leave the other two axes alone.
3. Set a keyframe at frame 1. Go to frame 30.
4. Rotate the camera 15 degrees to the right of its original position, for a total of 30 degrees. Again, leave the remaining two axes unchanged.
5. Set a keyframe at frame 30.
6. Render and play back the animation.

The pan, shown in Figure 14.8, is one of the simplest and most often-used moves, both in traditional cinematography and CGI. All you have to do is rotate the camera.

Tilt Camera Move

The tilt move is essentially identical to the pan, but on the pitch rather than heading axis.

1. Delete the changes you made in the preceding project.
2. Change the camera pitch to -5. Leave the other two axes as they are.

Figure 14.8   Beginning, middle, and end frames of a camera pan.

3. Set a keyframe at frame 1. Go to frame 30.

4. Pitch the camera up 15 degrees on its lateral axis. Again, leave the other two axes unchanged.

5. Set a keyframe at frame 30.

6. Render and play back the animation. You should end up with something like Figure 14.9.

PROJECT 14.5 Dolly Camera Move

1. Delete the changes you made in the preceding project.

2. Move the camera well back from the character. Set a keyframe for the camera position at frame 1. Go to frame 30.

3. Move the camera forward along the lens axis until the character fills the frame in a close shot. Leave the other two position axes as they are.

4. Set a keyframe at frame 30.

5. Render and play back the animation.

The dolly move, shown in Figure 14.10, mimics a traditional camera mounted on a wheeled dolly, moving down a track. You can combine the dolly move with a pan or tilt to produce a compound motion. The dolly move is also a part of the tracking and rack focus moves.

PROJECT 14.6 Tracking Camera Move

The other camera moves are pretty much independent, although you should always animate them with an eye to framing the action. The tracking move, however, is intended to follow a particular object, character, or action exclusively.

Figure 14.9 Beginning, middle, and end frames of a camera tilt.

Figure 14.10 Beginning, middle, and end frames of a camera dolly.

There are several ways to do this. The easiest is to simply parent the camera to the object or hierarchy to be tracked, then position and rotate the camera in relation to that object, as appropriate.

1. Reload the scene you've been using for the camera animations.

2. Parent the camera to the root of the character's hierarchy.

3. Offset and rotate the camera so it has a clear full shot of the character.

4. Create a keyframe for the camera at frame 1.

5. Animate the character moving along the sidewalk. Because the camera is parented to the character, it will go along for the ride.

   The simplest approach is to set a keyframe for the character's beginning and ending positions, and just let the character float. In later chapters, you'll learn how to animate walks and other *transportation animation*.

6. Render and play back the animation.

The Tracking move, displayed in Figure 14.11, is especially useful for following transportation animations like walking, running, or moving vehicles.

Zoom Camera Move

The zoom depends on your software's ability to animate the camera lens parameters. If your software does not support this, you will have to use dolly camera moves to fake it.

1. Reload the scene again.

2. Change your camera's lens setting to a minimal value that will make the character look far away.

3. Make a keyframe for the camera settings at frame 1. Go to frame 30.

4. Change your camera's lens setting to a higher value that will make the character look very close.

5. Create another camera keyframe at frame 30.

6. Render and play back the animation.

Figure 14.11   Beginning, middle, and end frames of a tracking shot.

Figure 14.12 Beginning, middle, and end frames of a zoom.

The zoom move, as shown in Figure 14.12, is another simple camera move that has been grossly overused. Avoid it wherever possible, and use dolly moves or cuts instead. If you must use a zoom, keep it to a minimum, and make sure it is essential to telling your story.

Rack Focus Camera Move

PROJECT 14.8

The rack focus is a combination of zoom and dolly camera moves, registered to each other to maintain the position and focus of the central object while the rest of the frame changes.

1. Reload the scene again.

2. Move the camera well back from the character. Set a keyframe for the camera position at frame 1.

3. Change your camera's focal length setting to a high enough value that it will frame a full shot of the character.

4. Make a keyframe for the camera lens settings at frame 1. Go to frame 30.

5. Change your camera's lens setting to a lower value that will make the character look very far away.

6. Move the camera forward along the lens axis until the character fills the frame in a full shot again, as close as possible to its proportions at frame 1.

7. Set camera position and focal length keyframes at frame 30.

8. Render and play back the animation.

The distance between the camera's first position and the second is equivalent to the distance covered by the focal length you set in Step 3. This matches the distance the camera travels to the distance the camera lens zooms.

The rack focus move (see Figure 14.13) produces a unique effect. The central object, located at the camera's focal distance, appears to remain in place and in focus. The background and foreground both appear to shift, producing a very strong disorienting effect.

This is another camera move that is prone to abuse, especially by amateurs fascinated with new toys. Use it only when it serves a valid dramatic purpose for your story. Otherwise, leave it in your bag of tricks.

Figure 14.13 First, middle, and last frames of rack focus.

Go Ahead And Cut

You may find it useful to think of a cut between shots as simply a move with zero frames between keys. The same guidelines for continuity still apply, you just have to pay a little more attention to some additional timing issues.

A cut that changes the volume of the shot or its contents creates a *visual jar* or disorientation for your audience. The *volume of the shot* is the space contained in the pyramid formed by the lens (the apex) and the four corners of the frame. The apparent volume of the shot ends at the central object or character.

A close shot of a character's head would enclose only a few cubic feet, while a long shot of the Empire State Building might contain millions. A cut between these two shots would cause an extreme visual jar due to the difference between volumes. A series of intermediate cuts, bridging from close to medium to full to long shots, would soften that shock; the difference in volume between each cut would be much smaller.

Sometimes, you will want to use the visual jar of a cut for dramatic reasons. Probably the most famous example of this is the shower scene from Alfred Hitchcock's *Psycho*, a series of such fast cuts between different contents (but nearly identical volumes) that the audience often sees what is not actually there.

More often, you need to make the cut to a shot that is simply a better composition for the following action, and your goal is just to get there as quickly as possible.

Cutting on the action is the technique of changing from one camera position to the next during the character's action. This timing of the cut relieves the visual jar, because the audience focuses it's attention on the action, not the shot composition.

You can also animate a character to presage a cut—warning the audience so they expect it—to reduce the visual jar. Animate the character to reach for or look intently at something out of frame, in the direction of the cut. The audience will follow the look or the action with their eyes, and the subsequent cut will be expected and, therefore, less jarring. This is similar to the *staging* of action discussed later in this chapter. You can also presage an action by slightly moving or zooming the camera toward the object of the action.

Cutting between angles is another way of changing the shot composition without jarring your audience. Simply keep the distance between camera and object constant, and move the camera to a new angle. The audience will only have to reorient itself to the new angle, as the volume and content of the shot will be essentially unchanged.

You can also minimize visual jar for an entire sequence of shots by creating a *master shot*. The master shot establishes the entire environment of a sequence, laying out a visual map for the audience. When you *inter-cut* a tighter *insert shot* of some part of this environment, the audience can quickly orient itself from the master shot. This is also known as an *establishing shot*. Often a master shot comes at the start of a sequence. However, directors sometimes will place the establishing shot later in the sequence to build suspense.

Updating The Story Reel—Making An Animatic

As you may recall from Chapter 4, the story reel is the first genuine test of your animation's timing and flow. The limitation of story reels is that they are made of drawings, not renderings, so you don't really have an accurate representation of the CGI animation's final appearance. It's important that you keep an accurate record of each step in your film's progress, so you can catch problems early. When you start producing finished renderings, you can selectively substitute them for the corresponding story sketches and recompile the movie. This way, the movie fills out as you make progress, and, at any time, you can view the whole thing.

CHEATS

Getting the best shot and action often means breaking the rules. In *The Physics of Cartoons, Part 1* (See the Physics directory of the CD-ROM for clips and details) we sought to use techniques that optimized the pose of the characters and the use of props for the given camera angle. Sometimes, however, the best pose would cause a chin to go through the character's chest. Props reacting to the wind had to have a minimal chance of interpenetrating with each other as they peeled off of the characters.

To obtain the desired results, the character's head might be detached from the body, and moved toward the camera by 5 virtual feet, and then scaled down so it wouldn't be out of proportion to the rest of the character. The characters had accidentally picked up a number of props, (including Hawaiian shirts, ropes, and bird cages) piled one on top of the other and held to the character by the force of the wind. Without a cheat, one or more of the props would have gone through the character's head at some point in the animation. By placing his head in front of his body, and also in front of the props, this interpenetration was no longer a potential problem.

This technique was used in the short numerous times and for various reasons. Only if we had used cast shadows would this have presented a problem. And the solution would have been other cheats such as a dummy object or exclusive light that would cast the appropriate shadow on the character's body or ground.

The key to an appropriate cheat is to see the finished shot the way that you want it in your mind, before you lay out the scene, and to create the scene in your storyboard, complete with props, exactly the way you would like to see it when it is completed. Don't leave details until later! Improvisation in 3D is much harder than it is with a pencil, even if you can't draw well. —*Steph Greenberg, Director*

Replacing Sketches In The Story Reel

This project is an extrapolation of Project 4.4 and is written for Adobe Premiere 4.2. If you are using a different editing software, read through these instructions, then consult your software's user or reference manuals to learn how to duplicate this process.

1. Start Adobe Premiere. Open the project (.ppj) file you saved when you built the story reel.

2. Choose the File|Import|File option, or press Ctrl+I. The Import dialog appears.

3. Drag-select all your test-rendered images. Click on Open to import the images.

   You shouldn't change the duration of any of the story sketches until you have added all the new rendered images. The cut-and-paste approach to editing a story reel is a very different cognitive process from the evaluation and execution of animation timing. To avoid mistakes, replace the images in one session, render the new story reel, then critique the reel's timing as a whole.

4. Arrange the new rendered images in the second video track, exactly underneath their corresponding story sketches.

5. You have two ways to make the rendered stills fit their appointed slots in the story reel. You can click-and-drag to stretch each rendering across the (approximate) number of frames. More accurately, you can double-click on the original sketch, note the time allocated, then double-click on the new image and assign it the same duration.

6. Delete the old sketches from the upper video track. As you remove each one, immediately replace it with the new rendered image from the lower video track. Repeat until all the new images are in place.

7. Render a new story reel. As mentioned earlier, you need to set the options to create a movie that can play back at full 24 fps on your system. This may limit you to a 160×120 preview, or you may be using a monster machine that can handle full-screen 24 fps playback with stereo sound and lossless compression. Use whatever works—this is just for a working preview!

   When it's complete, open the story reel, and play it. Are all the sounds still synchronized correctly? Does the story reel read well? How have the test renders changed your impression of the story compared to the original story sketches? Does the updated reel give you a better idea of the effect of timing on how the story reads? Is there anything you want to change?

   If there's something you want to change, you can adjust the timing of the individual images.

8. Double-click on the thumbnail you want to retime in the Construction window. The Clip window appears.

9. Enter a revised duration for the image, and click on OK.

10. Select and drag the thumbnails to either side of the retimed clip, if necessary, until they are all flush again.

At this point, you should ideally have all your shots blocked out, with at least one rough layout for each shot and a rendering replacing every original story sketch. In reality, there are always shots that finished early, balanced by shots that won't be done until the last minute. For most of the production cycle, the story reel is a hash of pencil sketches, rendered stills, and the occasional full-motion clip.

Once you have a layout for a shot, you can proceed to refine the timing of actions within that shot. This is the core of what a character animator does—everything else is prep work or window dressing.

Timing Is Everything

Timing makes or breaks character animation. A single frame is often the difference between an action that works and one that doesn't. To paraphrase Mark Twain, the difference between the right timing and the almost right timing is the difference between lightning and a lightning bug.

In the preceding chapters, you learned to create basic setups to move and deform characters. The following section shows you how to set the timing of those movements to get exactly the effect you want.

CGI Timing—The Basics

The basic unit of timing is the frame. The *frame rate* is measured in frames per second, or fps. Feature films are projected at 24 fps and NTSC video at 29.97 fps, usually rounded up to 30 fps for convenience. The high cost of transferring animation to film means that you will most likely be working in video formats for your first few projects. However, it is easy to use a process called *3:2 pull-up* to convert 24 fps footage to 30 fps, and more difficult to convert 30 fps to 24 fps.

With experience, you will be able to pick out a single frame's difference in an animation. You may start off being able to judge only a quarter-second or more, but with practice, you will learn to estimate and work with a twenty-fourth of a second. Even if your final output will be on video, you should use 24 fps as your baseline for timing. Most professional animators work to the 24 fps standard and will expect you to do so, if you work with them. Developing your sense of timing is a long learning process, and it's very difficult to translate that skill to a different frame rate. Even if you never work in film, you should almost always animate to 24 fps. You may work on a game or multimedia project that has a completely different playback rate, but, for those occasional exceptions, you will be better off converting your timing estimates from 24 fps to whatever, rather than trying to relearn the right timing at some arbitrary new frame rate.

There are various strategies for converting your timing. We might first consider why it's so simple to think in terms of 24 fps. An average pedestrian beat is two beats, two steps per second. That's a foot contact, on each 12th frame. Sure, some walks are slower, at 16 fps, or faster say, on 8s. That walk on 12s (one step, you should be able to infer everything of note from half the cycle) can be conveniently divided into thirds and fourths and sixths and halves.

The walk on 16s is more evenly divisible into quarters. It's no coincidence that many of the best animators are also musical in some way. Even if you have no skill in performance, your skill in appreciation will translate into timing for animation.

Think in terms of whole notes at 24 frames per second, half notes at 12, quarters at 6, eighths at 3, even sixths (4), and twelfths (2). So many traditional animators use their standard exposure sheet, divided at 8 frames for half of a foot of film, and 16 for a foot. One more half foot of film and you have a second, one and a half feet of film per second, 90 feet of film per minute. Eight frames is one third of a second, and if you're only drawing, rendering or exposing every other frame, four images get you one third of the way through a second.

If you're animating *on twos* and you've posed an extreme on frames 1, 9, 17 and 25, there are halfway (or breakdown) frames on 5, 13 and 21. This is not to say that the action represented at the breakdown frame should be an exact halfway interpolation between the two extremes. How that pose, or elements within that pose, favors one extreme or another defines a universe of nuance, interpretation, and acting. Frame 5 will be displayed (or exposed) halfway between frames 1 and 9, yet your subject's position in space may be closer to one third of the distance between 1 and 9. This breakdown pose can be said to favor 1, or to be a cushion out of frame 1. If it favors frame 9, it cushions into, or eases into, frame 9.

So frequently, a clearly readable, short scene, has two basic poses, generally indicating a transition from one clearly expressed emotional state to another. Even if you take a just a few seconds of screen time to accomplish it, you will use such fractions of a second to time, and to space, those transitions. You will internalize them so deeply you'll forget that you know them. How well you accentuate, or gloss over, little sub-events in that transition, and whether you've used sufficient frames to ensure that the idea you need to convey will register with an audience, is a measure of your skill at timing. Timing *is* animation.

Richard Williams recalls seeing Betty Boop's creator, Grim Natwick, illuminated by shafts of light, scattering dust motes as he gestured with his bony hands in a basement office. "It's all about the timing, and the spacing," said the man who survived his 100th birthday party. Even on Snow White, Disney's nine old men remembered him as the oldest guy they had ever seen.

Video, and player frame display rates, and newer formats like Showscan, pose a challenge to that convenient 24 frame structure outlined above. There are ways to think in terms of 24 fps regardless of the frame rate. While 24 and 30 fps don't factor well, 12 and 60 frames, or fields per second, do. The fact that your timeline is as infinitely sub-divisible as Zeno's Evil makes conversion a readily surmountable task. One twelfth of a second is five video fields, or five frames at sixty frames per second. The critical notion is to make sure that the poses you want to be seen are rendered, not lost in some discarded subdivision.

In video game player rates, where you must fight tooth and claw for every frame exposed per second, your best hope is for some regular maintainable rate, such as 4, 6, 8, or 10. Anything higher, such as 12 or 15, and you're golden. Your responsibility is to select the poses that most clearly convey *the idea* of the motion required. If those poses did not occur on the frames you rendered, you've dropped the ball as an animator. If you animate a sequence at the 24 frames per second rate you prefer, you cannot get away with pulling out "the extra" frames. The poses must be spaced to fit into the timing available and get the idea across. In an action game, a player's character must respond instantly to the player's button push lest he use your game as a coaster, after destroying the controller in a fit of testosterone poisoned pique. Ideally the next frame he sees will reassure him that indeed, he pushed the right button combo. With a higher frame rate, you might sneak in one or two motion-blurred frames denoting anticipation, but we shouldn't needlessly torture those suffering from attention deficit disorder.

The smoothest, most realistic animation is shot *on ones*. That is, each image is shown for only one frame. This is sometimes referred to as *full animation*. Shooting on ones is also the most expensive form of animation. More often, animation is shot on twos, where a single image is held for two frames. This cuts the cost of animation in half, because only 12 images are required for 24 frames worth of projection time.

To save money, *limited animation* is often shot on fours. Even sixes is not unheard of when a budget is tight. Other cheap tricks include animating only part of a character, while the rest of the scene is untouched; animating camera moves over still images; and reusing image sequences of standard actions, such as walks and gestures.

3D animation can't use most of the shortcuts employed in limited animation. Audiences seem more tolerant of such tricks when the animation is drawn, but, when the images are three-dimensional, the audience becomes very critical of anything not animated on ones. This is true for both puppet animation and CGI—animating on twos produces a jerky, strobing effect that destroys much of the illusion of life. Fortunately, 3D CGI animation has a few advantages of its own.

There are two major approaches to animation. The simplest, most improvisational approach is *straight-ahead*. This means just what it sounds like: The animator starts with the first frame of the animation, poses the character, then moves on to the next frame. Straight-ahead animation is most used in 2D, drawn animation, but it has a lot in common with puppet animation, too. You can improvise, exercise an intuitive grasp of timing and posing, work with a minimum of paperwork and planning, and lose lots of work with a single mistake. It's definitely not a technique for beginners.

The drawback to straight-ahead animation for CGI character work is that you create so many keyframes—one per animated variable per frame—that it is almost impossible to go back and correct errors. It is easier to simply junk an entire sequence and start over from the last good frame.

The other major approach is *pose-to-pose*. This is the approach used in most 2D animation productions. It is also much more forgiving for the beginner, although it does require more planning.

Richard Williams (the man perhaps best known for Framing Roger Rabbit), says that the best animation results from combinations of straight-ahead runs refined with pose-to-pose.

There are many job titles and terms in common use for decades among traditional animators that have become co-opted by well-meaning applications engineers, often in an effort to distinguish their feature from the same feature in a competitor's application. This has led to much mushiness in terminology, resulting in slightly different disciplines finding themselves separated by a common language.

An example is the innocuous–sounding term "key." In the Disney studio, and most other shops, the Key Assistant Animator works with the Animator to carefully refine the most critical poses in the scene. Even animators debate exactly which ones should be "keyed" extremes. Sometimes they are poses nearly identical to those drawn originally by a layout artist, who may have generated three drawings to further flesh out one storyboard panel. At the animator's discretion, he may incorporate those actual poses, though far more often he does not. Frequently, they are the drawings that most clearly and evocatively convey the emotional state of the character. These are not always the same drawings that the Key Assistant Animator is said to key. Even worse, Key poses are not uniformly the drawings that are typically considered extremes! Only since the introduction of animation software has the term keyframe come to mean any value set in time by the animator.

An animated character's acting and timing is defined by its extreme poses. An extreme pose is where an action changes speed or direction. Filling in from one extreme pose to the next are *breakdowns* and *inbetweens*. *Breakdowns* are frames that show how poses are at variance with those that would be yielded by even interpolation between the extremes. In traditional 2D animation, extreme poses are defined by the animator. In the clean-up process, they are redrawn (for the incorporation of refinement in drawing technique and conformity among different artists' drawing styles, appropriate level of detail, and for Ink and Paint)by a senior artist, the assistant animator.

The assistant is careful to incorporate any corrections or refinements to the scene based on the drawings done by the artist who keyed the scene. Suppose the Lead Animator, Andreas Deja, says Mickey Mouse should be drawn two and a half heads tall, and Mark Henn likes to animate The Mouse five heads tall. The Key will make changes based on Mark Henn's drawings until the Key's drawings are two and a half heads tall. The Assistant will have to pay special attention to arcs, and carefully preserve any changes in volume and proportion that were made by the Key, so that they may be continued in the drawings for which the assistant is responsible.

The assistant animator may also draw the breakdown pose, though that may be left to a breakdown artist. Each remaining inbetween is drawn by an even more junior artist, known as an inbetweener. Computers are not that good at performing the inbetweener's job in 2D drawn animation, unless the animator is using a program such as Animo in the first place. Inbetweeners with no more skill or imagination than to trace lines evenly between lines sometimes find work using *digital ink-and-paint* software.

If the above job stratification sounds a bit convoluted, don't worry too much. There are many with years of experience in the 2D process that still fight about just how critical each of those roles may or may not be. The important thing to remember is the notion of extremes, breakdowns and inbetweens. You will be dropping keys on any part of, or all of, all three types of poses. In classical, or full animation, it can be said that there is no such thing as an inbetween. Some parts of the same pose may be extreme, others a breakdown, and other parts delegated to rote inbetweening. You make as much of an animation decision to allow the computer to interpolate evenly, as you do when you decide to break it down "out of inbetween."

The great advantage of CGI animation is that the computer generates every inbetween. The animator keys extreme poses, ranging anywhere from every frame (for fast, complex action) to fewer than one in 24 (for slow or repetitive actions). The rest of the frames, or parts of poses where no keys were dropped, are interpolated and rendered automatically. This is a huge savings in the most expensive production commodity, the animator's time. If the computer system is powerful enough, the animator can tweak a key pose and generate a new *pencil test* sequence faster than a skilled traditional animator could draw one.

CGI pose-to-pose animations can also be revised piecemeal, without starting over and losing everything as in traditional cel or clay animation. A skeleton of bones or parented objects can be animated one layer at a time, perfecting hip action, for instance, before investing any time in animating the rest of the legs. Also, you can save each revision of an animation as you work and reload it if something goes wrong with a later version. This safety net encourages animators to experiment and try different compositions, actions, and timing. This is one reason CGI animation is more forgiving of, and easier for, the beginning animator.

A number of elements contribute to good timing. To be a competent character animator, you need to learn them all. You also need to learn how to apply them to each animation so they work in harmony.

The upcoming projects introduce one element at a time, building up to a project that ties them all together.

Mass And Energy

CGI objects have no mass or energy of their own. They are simply illusions displayed on your computer screen. To appear real in an animation, CGI objects must move in ways that simulate the mass and energy of the real-world materials they represent.

The mass of an object limits how fast it can be moved by a given amount of energy. An inflatable beach ball, for example, has very little mass, so a small amount of energy—a finger snap—can move it rapidly. The same amount of energy applied to a bowling ball would produce a much slower movement. Energy can be expended to change an object's speed, direction, or shape. This energy can come from outside (another character's action, the wind, an Acme falling anvil) or inside, from the character's own muscles.

Gravity, for all practical purposes related to character animation, is a form of energy that constantly tries to force objects towards the largest mass in the neighborhood, typically the ground. (This definition is not scientifically correct, but this is not a physics textbook.)

The behavior of an object is also governed by *inertia*, the tendency of objects to keep doing what they've been doing. If a large rock is just sitting there, it will continue to sit there until some other object acts to change it, perhaps by levering it over, dragging it away, or even shattering it into smaller rocks.

You can mimic all of this behavior simply by controlling the timing of the action. For example, let's look at one of the simplest actions, an inanimate object—a rock, let's say—falling to the ground. The rock is initially at rest, with no velocity relative to the ground. You can imagine a character holding it up, if you like. When the character releases the rock, it stays in midair for a tiny fraction of a second. This is due to inertia—the rock was motionless, inertia says it will remain motionless until something else acts on it.

That something else is gravity. Immediately, gravity overcomes inertia by pushing the rock toward the ground at an *acceleration* of 9.8 meters per second, per second. This doesn't mean the rock is falling at 9.8 meters per second—this means 9.8 mps is added to the rock's downward speed for every second that it falls. Given the constant acceleration due to gravity and leaving out any other influences, such as updrafts or a character's intervention, you can figure the exact position of the rock for each fraction of a second. The equation is:

$Y=Y_s-(1/2gt^2)$

where **Y** is the Y-axis height in meters, Y_s is the original Y-axis height in meters at the start of the drop, **g** is the constant of acceleration for gravity of 9.8, and **t** is the time in seconds since the start of the drop. In simpler form, it reads:

$Y=Y_s-(4.9t^2)$

If you calculate the distance for each twenty-fourth of a second, you have the positions of the rock for each frame of a second of animation.

If you now create an animation of a rock object, starting it at frame 0 with no velocity in any direction, you can set the rock's position in each frame to mimic the fall of the real rock, as shown in Figure 14.14. The rendered animation will show the rock object falling with a realistic acceleration.

Table 14.1 shows the distances for the first half-second, or 12 frames, of a standard fall.

Table 14.1 is provided as a guide to get you started. You should not type in a calculated value for every keyframe of an animation, especially for a simple action like this. There's no art or human judgment involved in that approach, and you could easily be replaced by a piece of software. Your animations will look like it, too.

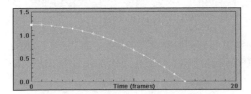

Figure 14.14   The simple timing of a falling rock.

Table 14.1 Fall Distance Per Frame At 1.0 g.

Frame	Distance
:00	0.000
:01	0.009
:02	0.034
:03	0.077
:04	0.136
:05	0.213
:06	0.306
:07	0.417
:08	0.544
:09	0.689
:10	0.851
:11	1.029
:12	1.225

If you plan to animate simulations of real-world physics, I recommend buying software to do the calculations. No sense reinventing the wheel, right? Some 3D packages have dynamics built in, such as trueSpace and 3D Studio MAX, while others require plug-ins. For LightWave, I recommend Dynamic Realities' *Impact* plug-in. It simulates gravity, collision detection, and a lot of other useful behaviors that are tedious or difficult to set up by hand.

A slightly more complicated motion you should be able to animate is the *parabola*, the arc followed by a projectile. Parabolas define the movement of a character in mid-leap, as well as the flight paths of cannonballs and hurled anvils.

A parabola is just like the acceleration curve of a falling rock, except there are two of them, connected at the top and spread apart at the base. The horizontal distance between the starting and ending points of the parabola depends on how much energy the projectile has and at what angle it is launched. A thrown rock moves up at the reverse of the rate it falls, starting off fast and slowing down until it reaches zero vertical velocity at the peak of the parabola. Then, it falls, following the same acceleration path as if it had simply been dropped from that peak's height (see Figure 14.15). The horizontal velocity of the projectile remains the same throughout the parabola—only the vertical velocity changes.

Setting up a parabola using keyframes is relatively simple. It only requires attention to detail and a little basic arithmetic.

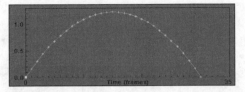

Figure 14.15 A parabola defining the path of a thrown rock.

Keyframing A Parabola

This project shows you how to keyframe a standard parabola for Earth's gravity.

1. Calculate the Y (vertical) positions for the keyframes of a straight fall beginning at the height of the parabola's peak.

   If the parabola is the exact height of one of the distances in the table shown earlier, you can simply copy the values from the table. (Hint, hint.)

2. Open the Ball scene you set up in Chapter 11.

3. Make keyframes on frames 13 through 24. In LightWave, open the Graph Editor, and select the Y Position graph and create keys.

4. Type in the calculated values for the appropriate Y-axis keyframes. Start at the peak of the parabola, and proceed down the right-hand leg, as shown in Figure 14.16.

5. Copy the values from each calculated keyframe to the corresponding keyframe on the left-hand side of the parabola, as shown in Figure 14.17.

   Presto! You have created a parabolic spline! Save the scene file under a new name. You'll be using it in the next project.

The constraints of mass, inertia, and gravity apply to animated characters as well as inanimate objects. Once a character leaves the ground (also known as *going ballistic*), the path it

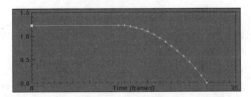

Figure 14.16 First leg of parabola defined by calculated keyframes.

Figure 14.17 Second leg of parabola defined by duplicated keyframes.

Figure 14.18 Character tumbling along a parabola.

follows is a parabola. The character's limbs may thrash or make gestures, but the *center of gravity* (CG) must remain on the parabola (see Figure 14.18).

You can create this type of action most easily by adding a null object to the scene and animating the null along a parabola. Parent the character to the null object, and position the character so its CG is centered on the null. This enables you to rotate either the null or the character for a tumbling motion. If you animate the null for both position and rotation, you have the advantage of not disturbing the keyframes used to pose the character.

PROJECT 14.11 Beach Or Bowling Alley?

This project shows you how to create a series of diminishing parabolas, first for a very bouncy object, a ball, then for a heavier object, a bowling ball.

1. Open the scene file you just saved from Project 14.10.

   Each bounce of the ball will be a little shorter than the one before, so you need to accurately model the shrinking parabolas. Fortunately, there is a quick-and-dirty way to do this without recalculating and typing a bunch of Y coordinates. The Y-coordinates of every gravity-based parabola are identical near the peak. The only differences are in the length of the legs. Therefore, you can cut and paste the top of a parabola to create shorter ones. This creates an automatic diminishing bounce. The only choice you have to make is how many keyframes you cut off the bottom of the preceding bounce. If you cut off more frames, you create the appearance of a heavier, less bouncy object. This is like setting the *modulus of elasticity* for the object's material. It should not vary within the same action (except for comic effect), so keep track of the number of frames you delete and be sure to use the same number for each bounce.

   Depending on how your software handles cut-and-paste operations on keyframes, you may need to be careful to cut off one more frame on the trailing (lower frame number) side of the parabola than on the leading side. The last frame of the preceding parabola should become the first frame of the new one.

2. Copy the middle keyframes of the parabola, leaving out the two beginning and two ending keyframes. This will make the ball rather bouncy, so it will appear light and resilient in the finished animation.

3. Paste the copied frames onto the end of the parabola. The duplicated frames are pasted in place at their original Y-axis values. You need to shift them vertically so the last keyframe is at zero on the Y axis.

4. Go to the last keyframe of the new parabola. Make a note of its Y-axis value. You want to subtract this value from all the copied keyframes, so the last keyframe is at 0.0.

5. Shift the Y-axis values for the copied keyframes downward (negative) by the Y-axis value of the last copied keyframe.

The new parabola is shifted to rest on the Y axis (see Figure 14.19).

If you like, you can render and play back an animation to see how the bounce looks.

6. Repeat Steps 3, 4, and 5 until the progressively smaller bounces fill the graph to frame 72. Edit the graph as necessary to make sure the last keyframe Y coordinate is zero, to match the first keyframe. Save the scene under a new name. You should end up with a graph like the one displayed in Figure 14.20.

7. Load another copy of the ball model. In frame 0, position it a couple of diameters along the X axis to one side of the other ball, so you can see it clearly. Create a keyframe for the new ball.

8. Repeat Steps 2 through 6 for the duplicate ball. This time, chop off more keyframes to make the bounces even shorter. Try to make a graph like Figure 14.21. This is more like a bowling ball than a bouncing ball, wouldn't you say?

9. Render and play back the animation.

Figure 14.19 First derived smaller parabola.

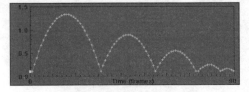

Figure 14.20 Ball spline.

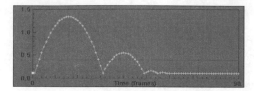

Figure 14.21   Bowling ball spline.

Photographers sometimes capture a complex motion by leaving the camera shutter open and using a high-speed flash to illuminate the action many times per second, a technique called *stroboscopic* photography. This is useful for showing a series of actions within a single image. I use a 3D rendering trick to simulate this effect for several figures in this book. If you tracked the camera during a stroboscopic rendering of this animation, you might get a final image like Figure 14.22.

CAVEAT ANIMATOR

The animator today has the tremendous advantage of being able to examine the profiles of such a Newtonian ballet, in a variety of curve editors. After a while, one can readily see just what it is that signifies such motion in graphical form. It should become just as easy to read as your own notes to yourself, and without even having to watch the motion displayed, you should be able to accurately predict what would be seen when rendered. Tweaking just a few parameters, a highly realistic motion will look even more convincing in the right number of frames. Too often, that which is real, is not entertaining enough, or is insufficiently communicative, to be of any value to the filmmaker. If the audience doesn't get the idea intended by the shot, it doesn't matter if it was real. *Your job is to tell a compelling lie.* If it looks right, it is right. It's *all* cheating.

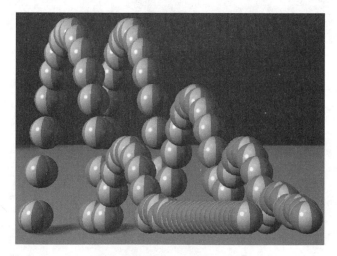

Figure 14.22   Stroboscopic image of bouncing different masses.

Timing With Splines

Traditional puppet animators making the transition to CGI have a tendency to drop a key on every frame, nailing down the character before moving to the next frame. This works, but it's a real mess to revise or edit. There's just too much data, so you end up throwing it all out and starting over. This isn't very efficient and doesn't take advantage of the computer's assets as an artist's tool.

A curve defined by lots of keyframes, as you saw in the preceding projects, resembles a connect-the-dots picture. Just as with modeling, you can also create a curve by using fewer points and connecting them with splines. Most 3D animation software uses some form of spline to interpolate (in-between) curves between keyframes. If you learn to use your software's spline motion tools, you can animate faster, with fewer keyframes and better control. You will also be able to revise and edit your animations much more easily, which makes it possible for you to experiment more to find just the right timing and poses.

The best spline controls are a matter of personal preference, but there are a few basics you should look for when choosing software. The paramount requirement is proper control handles. It doesn't matter if you're using Bezier, cardinal, or whatever variety of splines, as long as you have adequate control. You should be able to completely and interactively control the in-and-out slope and curve of the spline at every control node. You should also be able to flatten out a segment or nail down a value, without restricting what you can do with the rest of the spline.

If the software puts limits on what you can do, it's not up to the job. If the software requires data entry or other technical actions, it will distract you from the essentially creative act of timing. The goal of character animation software should be to make timing as intuitive as posing a traditional armature, combined with the jog/shuttle wheel of a good VCR. That's the essence of what you're doing, after all—setting poses, then playing with their timing. Good spline tools can come close to this ideal, but bad ones can make you feel like you're beating your head against a wall.

The shape of an animation channel is of paramount importance to the way it in-betweens. An entry and exit to a keyframe on an animation curve, on the spline of the curve, must be independently adjustable on both entrance and exit. You must be able to break the slope of that curve. Even where you can't break the slope of the curve, it must be adjustable under the animators control to determine its contour.

An experienced 3D animator can select a handful of curves on a piece of animation for hand editing. Keyframes for individual actions like "y" rotation, or "x" translation can be moved around to break synchronous timing. A section of a curve that starts up on a steep slope, and then slowly levels off, for example, will give a snap and cushion to the animation. A section of a curve that appears not to change values between keyframes will "hold". If an animator changes the value of the keyframes so that there is a small change in value during what was a hold, the animator will get a moving hold.

Many programs like Alias and Softimage provide the tools to adjust the "tangents" of the curves on the animation channel splines. That adjustment alters the slope of those curves.

Programs like Animation:Master go one step further, providing the tools to change the magnitude of those curves, to expand them out, make the curves wider, or contract them in, to make the curve more peaked.

3D Studio MAX

MAX has several different controllers available for position and rotation. By default, the position and scale controller is a Bezier Spline. With this controller type MAX will automatically create smooth interpolation between keyframes. You can also change the tangents at each keyframe. There is a custom tangent type that allows you to rotate the tangents. MAX also has several preset in and out tangent types that enable you to quickly set a key to have a linear, hold, ease in/out, or bounce type of interpolation. In *Track View* you can click on a key frame and then choose *Properties* or right click on a keyframe to set its tangent type. There is also a *Function Curves* mode that allows you to see and edit the curve directly. This includes adjusting tangents and sliding or moving keys around. Figure 14.23 shows Track View in Function Curve mode with a custom tangent keyframe. Note that you can also adjust tangent types for the currently selected object in the *Motion Panel* in MAX.

For rotation, MAX defaults to Tension/Continuity/Bias (TCB) controllers. This enables you to set ease, smoothness and other controls similar to the Bezier type, but won't allow you to edit or view a function curve. To edit the curve, you need to change the controller type to Euler Rotation. This breaks the rotation out into separate X,Y, and Z rotations created by Bezier interpolation. Each axis can have its own independent controls. This controller is useful for making a custom expression controller for a rotation, and also for improving applied or interactive IK. Because each X, Y, and Z channel is now Bezier controlled, you can also use all the tangent types for each rotation key. Figure 14.24 shows a rotation curve for an object with the Euler rotation controller. The keyframe selected has a hold in type and linear out type set for the Z-Axis rotation.

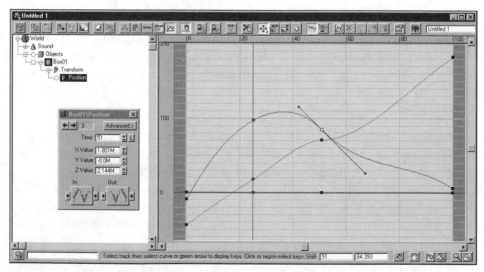

Figure 14.23   Track View in Function Curve mode with a custom tangent keyframe.

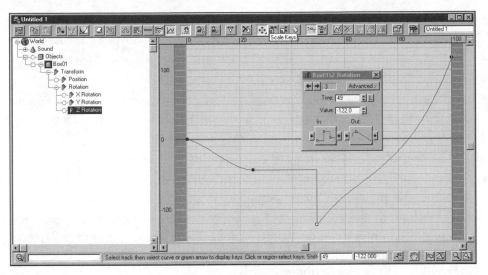

Figure 14.24 Euler Rotation curve with hold in and linear out for Z axis.

LightWave 3D's built-in spline control tools leave much to be desired. They don't have the conventional Bezier spline control handles used throughout the rest of the industry and familiar to many artists from 2D graphic software, such as Illustrator. There is no graphic handle for editing spline controls, only the numerical entry fields in the Graph Editor's Spline Control subpanel. These controls are very rudimentary by character animation standards, and they tend to require more keyframes and provide less accurate control than other software. Nevertheless, it is possible to do acceptable character animation timing with LightWave's spline control tools.

The Bias control pushes the bulge of the spline to one side of the selected keyframe, as shown in Figure 14.23. A negative value pushes the curve back, and a positive value pushes it forward.

Tension, shown in Figure 14.24, controls the apparent speed or rate of change of an object in the vicinity of the keyframe. Higher tension bunches up the adjoining frames, bringing their values closer to the keyframe. There is less change between these frames, so the motion appears slower. A lower tension has the opposite effect—objects appear to move more rapidly near the keyframe.

Continuity (see Figure 14.25) controls the curvature of the spline as it passes through the selected keyframe. A negative value takes away all curvature, making the spline cut a sharp corner. A zero value pushes the curvature of the spline outward, so it is nearly flat as it passes through the keyframe. A positive value pushes the spline into inverted entry and exit curves around the keyframe.

Figure 14.25 -1, 0, and +1 values for Continuity.

Curves Ahead

This project shows you how to duplicate the realistic bouncing motion from Project 14.11 by using fewer keyframes combined with the spline tools.

1. Open the finished scene file you saved from Project 14.11.

2. Load a second copy of the ball. In frame 0, position it a couple of diameters on the X axis to one side of the other ball, so you can see it clearly. Create a keyframe for the new ball.

3. Add keyframes at the peak and end of the parabola for the new ball.

4. Use your software's spline motion tools to smooth the parabola into a close approximation of the original keyframed parabola.

   You may have to add keyframes in between 0 and 12 and 12 and 24 to get a better parabola. Keyframes for splines work best when placed where there is the most change in direction. Instead of choosing frames exactly halfway up each leg, try frames where the change in the curve is stronger.

PLACING SPLINE HANDLES

Keyframes for splines work best when placed where there is the most change in direction.

If you are using the calculated keyframe values from the table, the spline settings are a no-brainer. All three keyframes have a zero bias, because the parabola is symmetric. The beginning and ending keyframes should be as sharp as possible, broken if your software supports *breaking splines*. The center keyframe should have strong continuity. This makes the bottom of the bounce a sharp corner and the peak of the parabola nearly flat. The tension settings should be the same as the continuity, to slow the motion near the peak keyframe and accelerate it near the bottom keyframes.

5. Render and play back the animation. Compare the first bounce from Project 14.11, and the one you just created. If they are not an exact match, go back to Step 4, and try again.

6. You should end up with a parabola like the one in Figure 14.26. When you are satisfied with the ball's bounce, save the motion (if your software supports this). You may find a use for it later.

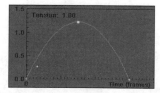

Figure 14.26 A spline-modeled parabola.

Squash, Stretch, And Motion Blur

Squash is used to show the effects of rapid deceleration and of energy expended to compress the shape of an object (see Figure 14.27).

Stretch is used to show rapid acceleration and energy expended to lengthen the shape of an object (see Figure 14.28).

To maintain the visual volume of an object, squash and stretch are usually synchronized on tangent axes. That is, if an object stretches in one axis, it must also squash in the other axes to maintain its original volume. This particular rule can be broken for extreme cartoon-style effects, but it's usually more effective when simply exaggerated. If you intend to break this rule

Figure 14.27　Squash frame from a bounce cycle.

Figure 14.28　Stretch frame from a bounce cycle.

for comic effect, you should establish the rule very firmly before you break it. The sudden, unexpected change in the rules is the source of the humor.

The easiest way to create squash in CGI is to simply scale the object, as shown in Figure 14.27. However, this makes the animation look subtly wrong to most viewers, and to an experienced animator, the problem is obvious. The part of the character that impacts the surface should deform more strongly, squashing out flat, while the opposite surface should hardly deform at all. You can produce much more accurate and pleasing results by deforming the character proportionately, as if it was actually impacting a surface and deforming to suit. There are several ways to deform all or part of a character, as you learned in Chapter 11. They take a little more work in setup and animation than a simple scaling, but the results are definitely worth it. The same is true of stretch, although the problem is not as obvious. Stretch is usually applied to show the effects of acceleration rather than physical contact, so there isn't any opposing surface to show where the stretch isn't accurate. 2D traditions use stretch to prevent *strobing* (changes between frames that are too extreme), catch the audience's eye, and destroy the illusion of smooth movement. The CGI artist can use *motion blur* instead of stretch to maintain visual continuity and prevent strobing.

Motion blur occurs when an action is faster than a camera's shutter speed—the action appears blurred between the beginning and ending positions of the moving objects. Most CGI software simulates motion blur by interpolating and rendering extra frames in between the actual numbered frames. The rendering engine then composites these extra images together, using a slight transparency. Anything that moves has a number of ghost images that combine to create a blur.

PROJECT 14.13 One Standard Bounce, Please

The first part of this project shows you how to add stretch to an animation of a bouncing ball to prevent strobing.

1. Reload the last bouncing-ball scene file you created in the preceding project.

2. Select the ball. Go to frame 1. Rotate the ball to align its vertical centerline with the parabola. Set a keyframe.

3. Repeat Step 2 for the keyframe at the peak and end of each parabola. You should end up with an animation of a ball that rotates perfectly in sync with its bouncing.

4. Add stretch to the ball for the up and down legs of the parabola. Increase the ball's Y-axis size by 150 percent, and reduce the size proportionally for the Z and X axes. I used 75 percent. Leave the ball's proportions normal at the peak frame.

5. Add squash to the hit frames, the beginning and end of the parabola. Decrease the Y-axis size, and increase the size proportionally for the Z and X axes.

6. Save the file under a new name. Render and play back the animation.

You should get an animation like Figure 14.29.

Now, try the same effect, using motion blur instead of stretch.

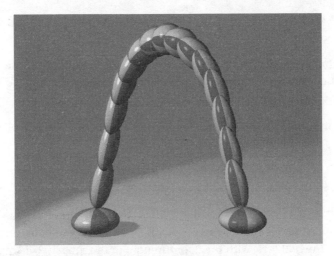

Figure 14.29 Bouncing ball with stretch and squash. Note the overlap of the stretched ball images, which prevents strobing.

7. Reload the scene file you just saved.

8. Remove the stretch from the ball along the up and down legs of the parabola, leaving the ball's proportions normal at the peak frame and along each leg. Only the squash at the beginning and ending frames should remain.

9. Turn on the motion blur rendering options for your software, and crank them up to the highest settings.

10. Render and play back the animation.

You should get an animation like Figure 14.30.

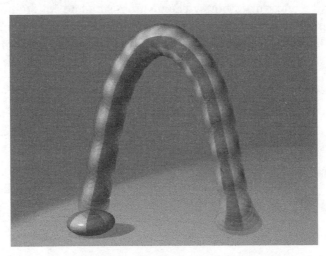

Figure 14.30 Bouncing ball with motion blur. No stretch is necessary. Squash is still used to show deformation of the ball against the floor.

Compare the effect of motion blur to the effect of stretch. Which animation would you prefer to watch? Which looks more realistic?

Motion blur is almost always better than stretch for smoothing rapid motion. It is more realistic, and most character animation software renders it automatically, so it is easier for the animator. Stretch is still useful but mostly for exaggerated action.

Finally, add an accurate deformation to the squash positions, instead of the cheesy-looking scale.

11. Reload the scene file from the preceding steps in this project.

12. Remove the squash from the ball's keyframes.

13. Add the squash deformation setup you learned in Chapter 11.

14. Begin the squash in the frame where the ball first touches the floor, and keep the flattened part of the ball level with the floor throughout the squash. Un-squash the ball as it leaves the floor, so when it stops touching the floor, it is perfectly round again.

15. Render and play back the animation.

You should get an animation like Bounce01.avi on the CD-ROM, as shown in Figure 14.31.

Squash and stretch tells the audience a lot about the material of an object. Different parts of a character should have different amounts of squash and stretch. A hard wingtip shoe, for instance, should not squash or stretch nearly as much as a flabby potbelly.

Squash and stretch can also be very effective in showing a character's internal energy, as shown in the next two projects.

Ease-in, Ease-out

Objects in the real world can't abruptly change from standing still to moving very fast. Any object that has mass needs a little time to get up to speed. The more mass, the longer the acceleration, or the more energy is required. The same is true for slowing down, changing direction, or distorting the object's shape.

In animation, a gradual change that leads into an action is called an *ease-in*. Coming out of an action gradually is called an *ease-out*.

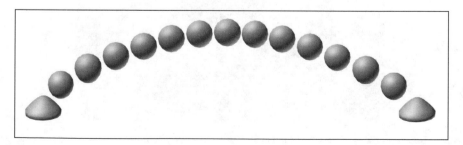

Figure 14.31   Bouncing ball with accurate squash.

I'd always heard it as easing into or out of an extreme—to cushion into a pose is to favor it on your way into it, and to ease out of it is to favor the pose you've held for a time before moving at the rate you're building up to. Yes, you can think of it the way you described, but in practical terms, I think my usage states it more clearly, but I'm biased.

The precise timing of an ease tells the audience just how massive the object is and how much energy it is using to perform the action. The quickest way to understand ease and how to apply it is to study and experiment with your software's spline motion tools.

Figure 14.32 shows two motion splines. One shows a constant speed between the start and end positions, and the other shows an acceleration curve, or ease-in, at the beginning, and an ease-out, or deceleration, at the end. Note that the object still moves from the first position to the second in the same amount of time—it just moves faster in the middle and slower on each end.

Get The Ball Rolling

PROJECT 14.14

1. Reload the original ball setup scene. Remove any keyframes you may have set during the bouncing-ball projects.

2. Select the ball, and activate your spline controls.

3. Create keyframes for the ball's pitch (elevation) rotation at frames 0, 1, 20, and 40.

4. Set X position values for the new keyframes. The ball is to start from a standstill at frame 1, then ease in to its maximum speed at frame 20 and roll off screen in three complete rotations to frame 60. In LightWave, the ball is 0.111 units in radius, which means that it can travel 0.6974 units ($2\pi r = 2 \times 3.1416 \times 0.111$) for each complete rotation. That's a total of 2.092 units to travel. Your software may use different units of measure, but the formula is the same. Let's start the ball off at -0.5 on the X axis for both frames 0 and 1, pass through 0 at frame 20, and roll right to 1.592 in frame 60. Your settings may vary.

5. Adjust the spline controls for each keyframe. You want the last section, between frames 20 and 60, to be at the maximum speed, a constant. Most software enables you to turn on a linear interpolation option, to make the spline a straight line between frames 20 and 60. Adjust the spline controls for frames 1 and 20 so the end of the curve

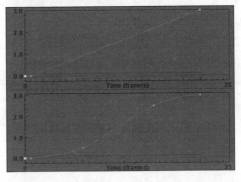

Figure 14.32 Splines for linear (top) and ease-in/ease-out (bottom) motion.

Figure 14.33 X-Position spline for rolling ball's ease-in.

nearest frame 20 closely matches the slope of the line from 20 to 60. If the slope changes abruptly at frame 20, the ball will jerk noticeably at that frame. See Figure 14.33 for one possible solution.

6. Set the ball's rotation keyframes. You want the ball to start off at 0 degrees and make three full rotations by frame 60, for a total of 1080 degrees. Frame 60 should, therefore, be set to -1080 degrees (or 1080, depending on the orientation of your software and the direction you are rolling the ball), and frame 0 and 1 left at 0 degrees.

   Determining a value for frame 20 is a little more of a challenge. The distance from 1 to 20 is 0.5 units, the total distance from 1 to 60 is 2.092, a ratio of 0.239. Multiply that by the total of degrees rotated, and you get 258.12, the number of bank rotation degrees to set for frame 20. Don't forget to make it a negative rotation. Again, the sign and value of these settings may vary according to your software and setup.

7. Save the scene under a new name. Render and play back the animation.

   Your results should look something like Figure 14.34. If the rolling contact with the floor does not exactly match the lateral travel of the ball, go back and tweak a few keyframes until you have an acceptable match.

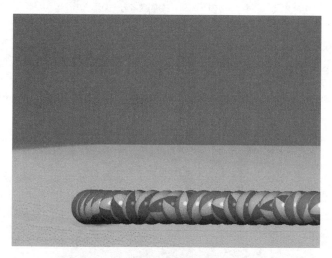

Figure 14.34 Stroboscopic rendering of ease-in for a rolling ball.

Easy Does It

This project is an example of how a frame or two difference in timing can have a great effect on the animation.

1. Reload the scene file you saved from the preceding project.

2. Move the key at frame 1 to frame 10. This compresses the ease-in into half the time, making the acceleration much more sudden.

3. Adjust the spline controls for frames 1 and 20 so the end of the spline nearest frame 20 closely matches the slope of the line from 20 to 60. As noted in the previous project, if the slope changes abruptly at frame 20, the ball will jerk noticeably at that frame.

4. Save the scene under a new name. Render and play back the animation.

   Your results should look something like Figure 14.35.

Notice how the different rates of ease made the ball seem to roll itself forward with greater energy. See what a difference a few frames make? Character animation timing is very sensitive to small differences, and you need to practice enough to understand and use them.

Don't overdo the ease-in and ease-out. It is tempting to use spline interpolation to make the whole action a smooth curve, like a lazy integral sign, as in Figure 14.36.

Spline interpolation is a wonderful tool. It's unique to computer animation and can save you a lot of effort if you use it properly. But if you overuse it, your animations will look just like all the other beginners' out there. Splines like this will give you soft, mushy actions, as if the characters are moving underwater. Usually, you'll want your animations to have more snap.

Snap

Snap is the animator's term for action that is quick, lively, and full of energy. To create an action with more snap, use splines more like the one shown in Figure 14.37.

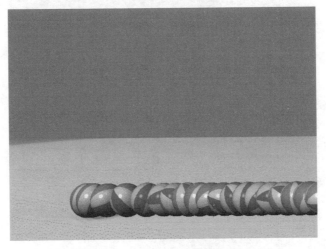

Figure 14.35   Stroboscopic rendering of faster ease-in for a rolling ball.

Figure 14.36 Spline for lazy, mushy movement.

Figure 14.37 Spline for snappy movement.

Remember that it takes more energy to accelerate and decelerate an object more quickly. To have more snap, the ease-in and -out curves of a spline should be shorter and sharper.

Take a look at animation file SNAP.AVI, located in the Chapter 14 directory on this book's CD-ROM. The upper ball has a spline like Figure 14.36, and the lower ball has a spline like Figure 14.37. Compare the motions of the lower ball and the upper ball (see Figure 14.38). Which looks more lively? Which looks more sluggish? Which one has more personality, and which one looks like a computer animated it?

Judging the balance between ease and snap takes practice. Take advantage of every opportunity you can to play with the splines, testing trade-offs and noting what values work for specific situations and moods. There are no hard-and-fast rules for this aspect of timing—you have to develop your own judgment.

Anticipation

Anticipation is an action in one direction intended to prepare the audience for a much larger action in the opposite direction. A baseball pitcher's windup is an example of anticipation.

You anticipate every time you prepare to take a step. Try this: Stand with your weight balanced evenly on both feet. While concentrating on your posture and balance, take one slow step

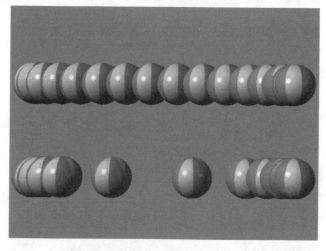

Figure 14.38 Stroboscopic image from SNAP.AVI, showing snap (bottom) and mush (top).

BEATING THE COMPUTER TO THE PUNCH

Pixar co-founder Ed Catmull was working with an early 2D animation program in the 70s at N.Y.I.T. Two extreme poses and an arc would be defined, and the program would do the rest. This worked great for pronking deer. An animation student from next door, James Davis, was brave enough to play with the propellor heads. He drew a boxer with his arm held bent up at his side, and his final pose, the arm straight out in a punch. Dr. Catmull and the others liked what they saw, but had their attention elsewhere when James put in an anticipation pose, the arm rearing back, telegraphing the punch. When others were brought over to see what was done earlier, the programmers were surprised to see an action gone so far out of arc and demanded to know what James had done to make their program behave that way. Look how far the collaborative mode among animators and programmers has brought us all since then.

forward. If you pay attention, you'll notice that you lean back and to one side as you raise your foot, then lean forward and to the other side as you put your foot down. That is an anticipation and action. You moved backward a little, in order to move forward even more.

Roll 'Em Again

This project shows you how to apply anticipation to the rolling ball.

1. Reload the scene file you saved from the preceding project.

2. Shift keyframes 1 through 60 by 10 frames, leaving frame 0 intact. This adds 10 frames of no action onto the front of the animation, because frame 0 is still nailing down the initial position and rotation of the ball.

3. Create a new key for the ball at frame 5. Move it to -0.557 on the X axis.

   This is an appropriate distance for an anticipation movement. You could push it farther for an exaggerated move or make it more subtle for a realistic move. This is somewhere in between.

   You can find appropriate values for an anticipation by moving to the symmetrical frame on the other side of the motion's origin. For example, this motion begins at -0.5 X at frame 0. The ball is located at -0.5 X again as it passes frame 11, after the anticipation. The anticipation is centered on frame 5. Frame 11 is 6 frames after frame 5, so move 6 frames further along after frame 11, to frame 17. Make a note of the rotation and position values at frame 17. In this case, 29.4 degrees and -0.443. Note that these values will not be accurate if you have the bias spline control set to anything but zero for any of these frames. You can use bias settings later, but, at this time, you need the spline segments to be evenly balanced between the keyframes. As noted earlier, these settings will vary depending on your software and setup, but the basic principles apply.

4. The X-axis position is (0.500-0.443), or 0.057. Subtract this from the resting X-axis position of -0.5 to get -0.557. The ball's rotation at frame 17 is -29.4. All this requires is

a change of sign, as the ball is rolling in the opposite direction. Set the rotation for the ball for keyframe 5 to 29.4 degrees.

Frame 5 should now have the correct position and rotation values. The only remaining tweak is to smooth out the acceleration curves, to create the proper ease-in.

5. Revise the spline controls for frames 0, 5, 11, and 30, so the anticipation is smooth. The end of the curve nearest frame 30 must closely match the slope of the line from 30 to 70.

As noted earlier, if the slope of the spline changes abruptly at any keyframe, the ball will jerk noticeably at that frame.

You should end up with a spline like Figure 14.39.

6. Save the scene under a new name. Render and play back the animation.

Your results should look something like Figure 14.40.

PROJECT 14.17 It Lives!

So far, all the animations have given the impression that some invisible hand, or maybe the wind, moved the ball. The ball itself seemed inert, as if it is being acted upon by outside forces but not taking any action of its own.

Now, let's try combining anticipation with squash and stretch, to make the ball seem alive and capable of moving itself.

Figure 14.39 Spline showing anticipation.

Figure 14.40 Ball anticipates, then rolls.

1. Load the deformable ball scene you set up in Chapter 11.

   This is the same as the file you saved from the preceding project, except the ball now has a bone or other deformation setup to stretch it into a shape like one of Al Capp's Shmoos (see Figure 14.41).

2. Set the deformation keyframes to stretch the ball upwards during anticipation, then squash down and stretch forward during the start of the forward roll, then back to normal as the top of the ball reaches the ground. See Figure 14.42 for examples.

   Your deformation splines for the ball should look something like Figure 14.43.

3. Save the scene under a new name. Render and play back the animation.

   Your results should look something like Figure 14.44.

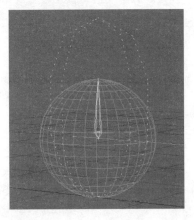

Figure 14.41　Example deformation setup in ball, using a bone.

Figure 14.42　Ball deformation during anticipation and start of roll.

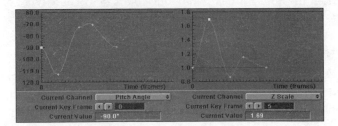

Figure 14.43　Bone Z Scale and pitch Angle spline for ball.

Figure 14.44   Ball appears to motivate its own anticipation and roll.

This shows how a very minor change in an animation can make the difference between an object that is animated and one that has the illusion of life. Your characters should always appear to be motivating themselves, to be acting from internal forces. Your characters should never look like someone is pulling their strings.

Follow-through

Follow-through is almost exactly like anticipation, but on the other end of the action. You already acted out an anticipation. Let's do it again, but instead of starting a walk, let's stop one. Take a couple of steps, just enough to get up some momentum. Stop suddenly.

Did you notice how your body swayed forward a bit, until your muscles could bring you to a complete stop? Did you rise up on your toes a little or have to brace one foot ahead of the other? Either of these actions would be a shock absorber, dissipating some of your forward motion.

You can watch another example of follow-through if you repeat that walk-and-stop exercise while carrying a cup of liquid. Not hot coffee, you don't want to scald yourself! Watch the liquid when you stop suddenly. That slop-up-and-fall-back is a contest between inertia, gravity, and the extra energy you put into your stopping action.

Your animated characters will have to perform the same kind of actions. If they simply stopped dead, they would look weightless and artificial. If your characters are to appear to have mass, they must overshoot the goal a little, then bounce back to it. These types of actions are called *follow-through.*

PROJECT 14.18   Whoa, Nellie!

By this time, you should have had enough practice modifying splines that you don't need step-by-step directions. The goal of this project is to create a complete set of splines for anticipation, stretch, ease-in, snap, ease-out, squash, and follow-through.

1. Load the scene file you saved at the end of the preceding exercise.

   The goal for this shot is to make the ball roll backwards and stretch in anticipation, then squash and ease-in to a forward roll with plenty of snap, ease-out to a stretch in follow-through, then squash back to a hold position.

   As a guide, Figure 14.45 contains the splines used to make one version of this animation. You don't need to duplicate these graphs exactly. It will be a better project if you create a different timing that still achieves the goal of the shot.

2. Set position keyframes to move the ball across the camera's view, making at least two full revolutions. Start at frame 0 with the ball at rest position, then move it back in anticipation, then forward again. Make sure you put some snap in the middle of the motion. Finish it by easing-out past the final hold position in a follow-through, then sliding back to the hold.

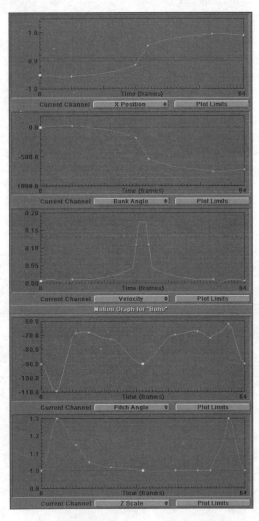

Figure 14.45 Splines for one version of this animation.

You might end up with something like the X Position graph in Figure 14.45, but then again, feel free to make up your own interpretation.

3. Set rotation keyframes so the ball rolls in contact with the ground, not sliding or spinning. Don't forget the reverse rotations for the anticipation at the beginning and the follow-through at the end. Again, you can refer to Figure 14.45 for one possible solution.

4. Save the scene with a new name. Render and play back the animation to check the motion so far.

5. Set the deformation keyframes as appropriate, to accentuate the anticipation and follow-through motions. See Figure 14.45 for an example.

6. Save the scene again. Render and play back the animation.

Your results may look something like [EXER0509]SHMOO.AVI on this book's CD-ROM, or Figure 14.46.

Depending on your software, you can also tweak the deformation keyframes in the camera view, if you find it easier to work this way rather than using a spline editor. I personally prefer to tweak squash and stretch in close-up views, to get the best feel for the amount of distortion.

Moving Holds

A 3D character cannot hold still for very many frames before it loses the illusion of life. If the character must stay in one place or position for a number of frames, you should create a *moving hold* to keep the character alive.

A moving hold is a series of tiny, subtle motions that mimic the behavior of a real living creature. Your audience perceives these clues unconsciously and automatically accepts the illusion that the animated character is alive.

Figure 14.46 Ball rolls, then follows through with ease-in, ease-out, stretch, and squash.

For example, most creatures breathe. You can imitate this subtle movement for a moving hold by stretching and squashing the character's torso (or whatever it uses for a lung casing) in the appropriate rhythm. Eyelid blinks, shifting of weight from one foot to the other, and small twitches of the hands are other useful actions you can add to a moving hold. If the scene setup permits, you can even create a slightly modified copy of the entire character, and create a moving hold by performing repeated morph changes between the original and the copy.

Move That Hold

This project shows you how to add subtle motions to an object to create a moving hold.

1. Reload the scene file you saved from the preceding project.

2. Add four new deformation keyframes at 65, 80, 95, and 110.

3. Animate a slight swell-and-shrink of the ball, peaking at frames 80 and 100 and dropping at 65 and 95, as if the ball is breathing.

4. Save the scene with a new name. Render and play back the animation.

5. Critique the action, and make revisions to the breathing action until you are satisfied with it.

   You may want to render the animation at a higher-than-usual resolution, so you can evaluate the subtlety of the breathing motion more easily.

6. Animate a very slight forward-and-back wobble, for frames 65 through 100, rotating the ball about 5 degrees, as if the ball is preparing to roll again.

7. Save the scene again. Render and play back the animation. Critique the action, then make revisions to the timing and amplitude of the wobble until you are satisfied with it.

You can generally add moving holds to a sequence after the main action is complete. If a moving hold requires special setups or models, you need to lay out the moving holds in your storyboards and all the ensuing design processes, just like any other action. In this example, you could just as easily have used the ball's scale and rotation keyframes to achieve a very similar effect.

Show A Little Character

This project shows you how to combine all the preceding timing principles to animate a desk lamp hopping. This project is patterned after John Lasseter's exposition of *Luxo Jr.'s* hop, in the 1987 SIGGRAPH paper referenced in the Bibliography.

1. Load the desk lamp scene file you set up in Chapter 11.

   The lamp's base is very heavy. The lamp can only lift it with a strong, quick jerk, so the base will leave the ground with no ease-in at all. For the same reason, the base falls back to the ground very quickly, and does not rebound at all. It behaves like a solid, heavy, rigid piece of metal.

2. Add and drag keyframes to create a spline like Figure 14.47 for the lamp, to make it move in a parabola on the Y axis. Turn linear interpolation on for the motion keyframes at the takeoff (frame 20) and ending (frame 60) keys for the Y axis, so the lamp base leaps up and slams down abruptly. Adjust the spline for the X axis so it is straight throughout.

Note that the lamp is only airborne for eight frames, just over a quarter second. If you keep the core of the action short and fast, the overall action will usually have more snap.

3. Create pitch (elevation) axis keyframes to rotate the base during the lamp's hop. Use ease-in and ease-out so the hop starts toe-last and ends heel-first. Make the lamp base flush to the ground, with zero pitch, at both the takeoff and landing keyframes. The maximum pitch angles should be just before and just after the peak of the hop, as in Figure 14.48.

4. Refer to your notes on the lamp's bending setup you created in Chapter 11. The following procedure will differ depending on the setup technique you chose for the bend.

If you chose a morph sequence setup, such as LightWave's Multiple Target Single Envelope, a 0 MTSE percentage will stretch out the lamp neck, while a 600 percent setting will bend the neck so the shade nearly touches the base. 300 percent, reasonably enough, is the middle or resting position for the lamp.

If you chose the object hierarchy setup, you will have to set rotation keyframes for the individual parts of the hierarchy to create the bend poses. Depending on your software, you may be able to copy keys from one frame to another, which makes it much easier to repeat a pose later in an animation.

You already set the movement and rotation values, so the lamp's base should be going where you want it to. The challenging part of this project is to use the bend setup to give the lamp the illusion of life.

5. Create and modify bend keyframes so the lamp bends (squashes) in anticipation, stretches out just before the takeoff keyframe, returns to rest position in mid-hop, compresses immediately after landing in follow-through, and vibrates slightly in a moving hold to the end of the animation. If your bend setup enables you to use a single spline to control the depth of the bend, you should end up with something like Figure 14.49.

6. Create keyframes for a *tracking shot* for the camera, to make it line up with the lamp at the beginning and end frames of the animation. This makes the animation *hook up* for a seamless repeating cycle.

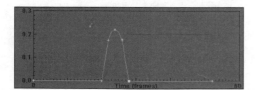

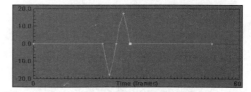

Figure 14.47 Y-position spline for hopping lamp.

Figure 14.48 Spline for lamp's rotation on the pitch axis.

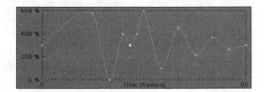

Figure 14.49 MTSE envelope for lamp hop.

7. Save the scene with a new name. You'll be using it in the next project. Render and play back the animation.

You can modify the timing of the bend and motion splines to change the character of the lamp. Drag out the number of frames between hops to make a more tired or melancholy lamp, or scale down the interval and the hop itself for a more energetic lamp.

Secondary Action

When a character has loose parts or appendages that are not held rigidly to the main body, these parts must demonstrate to the audience that they also have mass and energy of their own. A hound's floppy ears, for example, will continue to drag behind after the dog begins to run, and after the dog stops, the ears will flop forward under their own inertia. The ears' motion is a *secondary action*.

The usual guidelines for squash-and-stretch and follow through apply to overlapping action just as to the main action. Anticipation, snap, and ease don't apply because they mimic motivated action, and the secondary action is completely passive.

Up to this point, you've been animating objects with only one part or with parts firmly fixed. Now, let's try something just a little more loosely constructed.

PROJECT 14.21 Adding Secondary Action To The Lamp

This project shows you how to add a loosely attached object to your main object and animate the additional part using secondary action.

1. Open the scene you saved from the preceding project.

2. Load the TAGRING and PRICETAG models from the Chapter 14 directory on this book's CD-ROM.

The TAGRING model is modeled after the flexible plastic O-rings sometimes used to attach price or ID tags, and the tag is modeled after a very common retail sales tag profile. I could have modeled a loop of string instead of the O-ring, but the string's flexibility would have required a much more complex setup, and the extra complexity might have distracted you from the point of this project. If you want to try that approach on your own, please do so—it's an excellent practical exercise in modeling, setup, and animation.

3. Parent TAGRING to the desk lamp, and position it on the lamp's neck, as shown in Figure 14.50. Create a key for it at frame 0. You won't be moving or rotating the O-ring again, so lock off all its motion channels, if possible.

You want the price tag and O-ring to remain visibly attached to the lamp, but you also need as much space as possible for the price tag to move. If you used a morph sequence setup to bend the lamp, you should position the O-ring near the base of the lamp's neck, where any gaps caused by the neck's bending will be small and less noticeable.

4. Parent the PRICETAG to the TAGRING, and position and rotate PRICETAG, as shown in Figure 14.50. Create a key for it at frame 0.

You should have a scene like Figure 14.50, with the price tag hanging naturally off the loop in the plastic O-ring.

This arrangement of the tag and O-ring enables you to animate the price tag using only rotation keyframes. The pivot point of the tag is inside the loop of the O-ring, so pivoting the tag simulates the constraints of a real tag. If you want to push the simulation further, you can reposition the tag anywhere along the O-ring's loop, as long as you keep the tag's pivot point within the loop and keep the tag from penetrating the lamp or O-ring.

Note the angle of the tag in Figure 14.50. The thickness of the O-ring loop and the profile of the paper tag prevent the tag from hanging straight down. The tag can never be rotated to less than 5 degrees of bank angle without penetrating the O-ring. The allowable range of motion for the tag is 5 to 165 degrees bank, 45 to -4 degrees

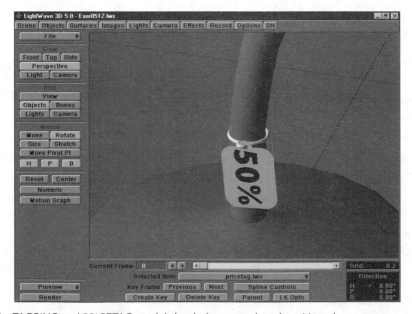

Figure 14.50 TAGRING and PRICETAG models loaded, parented, and positioned.

pitch, and 30 to -30 degrees heading. Any angle exceeding these limits will probably push the tag into the O-ring, the lamp itself, or both.

5. Make a series of keyframes for the PRICETAG model. Rotate the tag around its heading, pitch, and bank axes to create secondary actions.

The tag has no motivation or life of its own. Any movement of the tag must be initiated by the lamp or an outside force, such as wind or gravity.

You need to keep four factors in mind when animating the price tag's secondary action—lamp motion, inertia, gravity and air resistance:

- *Lamp motion* is the prime mover for the tag. The tag goes along, willy-nilly, following the lamp's position changes. This helps you choose where to set keyframes for the tag. One at each of the lamp's Position keyframes is a good start. The tag does not, however, follow along with the lamp's bending, if you are using a morph sequence setup.

- *Inertia* takes over when the lamp is not actively dragging the tag. At the top of the lamp's parabola, for instance, the tag changes from following the lamp's lead to following its own parabola. Since the center of gravity (CG) of the tag is below its pivot point, the tag shows inertia by swinging up towards the direction it had been traveling.

- *Gravity* pulls the tag down whenever the lamp motion and the tag's inertia are not strong enough to resist it. At rest, gravity keeps the tag firmly resting at 5 degrees of bank, as noted earlier.

- *Air resistance* is a factor due to the low mass and relatively large surface area of the tag. As the tag moves under the influence of the three preceding factors, it should also appear to be pushed around by the resistance of the air it passes through. For example, if the tag is descending under the influence of gravity (rotating in the bank axis), the tag may wobble in the heading and/or pitch axes.

If you are eyeballing the angles, it's much easier to work in a perspective view with the tag centered and OpenGL or other realtime shading options turned on, as in Figure 14.50. Adjust the view settings to give you a clear view of the tag's edges and where they may be intersecting other models. Figure 14.51 shows one possible solution for the price tag's secondary action.

6. Save the scene with a new name. Render and play back the animation.

You should end up with an animation similar to Figure 14.52 or the [EXER0512] SECOND.AVI animation located in the Chapter 14 directory on this book's CD-ROM.

Critique your animation. Does the tag move lightly enough in comparison to the lamp? Does the lamp seem heavy and the tag lighter? Does the tag flutter enough to give the impression of a loose joint, or does it seem to be rigidly hinged? If the answers aren't what you intended, go back and revise the angles and timings for the tag (and perhaps the lamp as well) until you are satisfied.

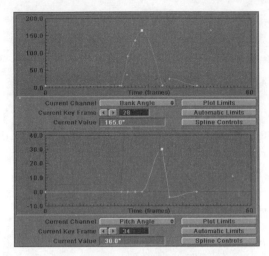

Figure 14.51   Rotation splines for the price tag's secondary action.

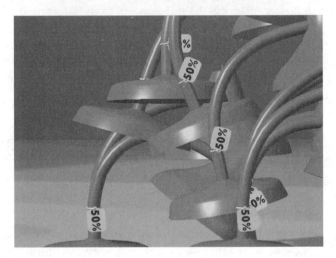

Figure 14.52   Secondary action of a pivoting price tag.

Secondary action can be set up and animated with just about every tool you learned in Chapter 11. Bones techniques are especially useful when parts of a seamless character model must second the main action.

Overlapping Action

Overlapping action and secondary action are sometimes confused or even used interchangeably. They are not synonyms, and the difference between them is literally the difference between a dead character and a live one.

When a character has appendages that are not held rigidly to the main body, but are still driven by their own volition, these appendages must demonstrate to the audience that they have mass, energy and motivation of their own. A hound's tail, for example, will tend to drag behind after the dog begins to run, and after the dog stops, the tail will tend to flop forward under its own inertia. Unlike the ears, however, the tail has its own bone and muscle structure. Instead of simply following the dictates of gravity and inertia, the tail will wag, lift or droop in addition to its inherited secondary actions. The tail will never move on precisely the same frame as the dog's hips, so the tail's action *overlaps* the hips' and the tail's aggregate motion is therefore an *overlapping action*. Overlapping action can precede the main action as well as follow it. Secondary action, as the name implies, can only second, or follow, the main action.

The usual guidelines for anticipation, snap, ease, squash-and-stretch, and follow through apply to overlapping action just as to the main action, because overlapping action is also motivated by the character.

If you'd like a challenging project, try adding a very short power cord to the desk lamp. Animate it first as a limp appendage using secondary action. Then animate it again, but make it move as if the lamp uses it as a sort of tentacle or monkey-tail that it can move of its own volition. Just for fun, you might consider giving the lamp the nervous habit of flicking its price tag with its plug.

A Nod Is As Good As A Wink: Eye And Head Motion

This section shows you how to apply some of the techniques you learned earlier in this chapter to mimic natural motions. A logical place to start is the character's eyes and head, the most expressive and closely watched parts of a character. Along the way, this section shows you how to partly automate natural eye motion using inverse kinematics.

The first tool you can get rid of, at least for character animation, is your straight edge. It won't be of any use to you, because nothing in the natural world moves in a straight line!

Throw 'Em A Curve

Now, you are probably thinking of movements that describe a straight line. Sorry, but you're mistaken. Straight-line movement is an illusion. Any simple projectile—whether bullet, spacecraft, or Olympic high-jumper—moves in an arc, defined by its velocity, mass, the force of gravity, and the resistance of the air. Over a short distance, the trajectory may appear flat, but it is actually a curve. Generally, the slower the movement, the more pronounced the curve. Billiard balls on a near-perfect table will still exhibit a little bit of table roll, and anything moving in three dimensions is even more prone to follow a curved path.

This is true for any unguided movement: Given the starting parameters, you can calculate the curve the object will follow and the impact point, using a class of mathematics called *ballistics*. You can also animate this kind of movement by using software that simulates physical laws, or *dynamics*. One such program is a plug-in for LightWave 3D called Impact!, which simulates ballistics and models *collision detection*, the interaction of physical objects based on their elasticity, movement, and mass. Other animation software has dynamics built in.

If any part of an animation calls for accurate physical effects like these, use whatever tools are available to automate as much of the process as possible. It's like photography versus oil painting—if you want it accurate, use technology, but if you want it artistic, use human judgment. Animating dozens of billiard balls realistically bouncing downstairs is simply a matter of plugging in more numbers, using the right software. If you try to animate all that by hand, you won't impress anybody (animating it in a caricatured style is another matter entirely!).

Adding feedback to the equation, however, changes most movements from a simple parabolic arc to a more complex *slalom*. A slalom is the path followed by any system, natural or machine, that can correct its movement toward a goal. Guided missiles and torpedoes, a hawk swooping down on a field mouse, your feet as you walk toward a doorway, and your hand as you reach for the doorknob are each following a slalom path. Almost every action you take describes a slalom.

The basic components of a slalom are a starting point, a goal, and the limits that trigger feedback correction. Let's take walking toward a door as a simple two-dimensional example.

You start out across a large space, perhaps a plaza or parking lot. You identify the building you wish to enter, and begin walking toward it. For the first step or two, you are following a nearly straight line. As you get closer, you notice the door you wish to enter by, and turn toward it, bending your path slightly to the right. This adds a little bit of curve to your path, beginning the slalom. As you get even closer, you glance down to make sure you aren't going to stumble over an obstacle. When you look up again, you find that you have stepped a little too far to the right and correct your path to the left to line up with the door again. This process of making tiny corrections to your path continues until you actually pass through the doorway, at which point, you are right on target—or you bruise a shoulder on the door frame, if you aren't paying close enough attention!

The corrections when you are farthest away are mostly approximations, but your estimates are more accurate the closer you are to the target, and each following correction is that much smaller. In this case, you are basing most of your correction limits on visual cues. Your first goal is the building—as long as your planned path appears to intersect the building, that's good enough. Once you spot the door, the limits become much tighter, and you correct your planned path to intersect the door. As you approach even closer, you plan to walk through the middle of the doorway, and correct your path accordingly. The result might look like Figure 14.53.

Slaloms are not just for movement through three-dimensional space, either. Any natural system that rotates around one or more axes will also describe a slalom. For example, the hawk I cited earlier describes a separate slalom with its head as it dives. It keeps its eyes on the mouse by making small, rapid corrections to the angle of its head and eyeballs. If you plotted these rotations on a graph, they would describe a slalom, with larger corrections at the beginning and very small corrections nearer to the goal.

What appear to be static poses can make use of slaloms, too. If you hold a heavy object at arm's length, and try to keep it level with your shoulder, every joint in your arm and shoulder will be describing small slaloms. Every time a small twinge or weakness in one muscle causes a

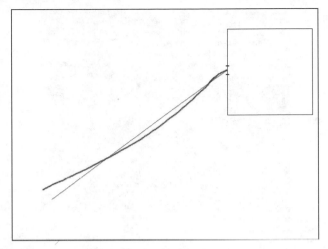

Figure 14.53 Walking toward a goal produces a simple two-dimensional slalom.

joint to vary from the target, another muscle will compensate. This is feedback, and feedback expressed mathematically describes a slalom.

So what, you say? So you must animate your characters to follow slaloms, or their actions will seem mechanical and dead, and you will lose that illusion of life you've been working so hard to maintain. Traditional animators have known and practiced this for years, although they have used other terms, such as *arcs* or *natural paths,* to describe these types of motion.

Fortunately, most 3D software uses splines to define motion paths, so it is relatively easy to make objects follow slaloms. Let's try animating an object with a slalom motion.

A Slalom Head Turn

PROJECT 14.22

1. Load the head scene file you set up in Chapter 11.
2. Go to frame 0. Turn the head 30 degrees to the right. Set a keyframe.
3. Go to frame 15. Turn the head 30 degrees to the left (60 degrees, total). Set a keyframe.
4. Save the scene with a new name. Render and play back the 15-frame animation. Your results should look something like Figure 14.54.

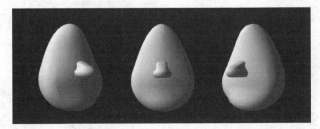

Figure 14.54 Frames 0, 7, and 15 of the head-turn animation.

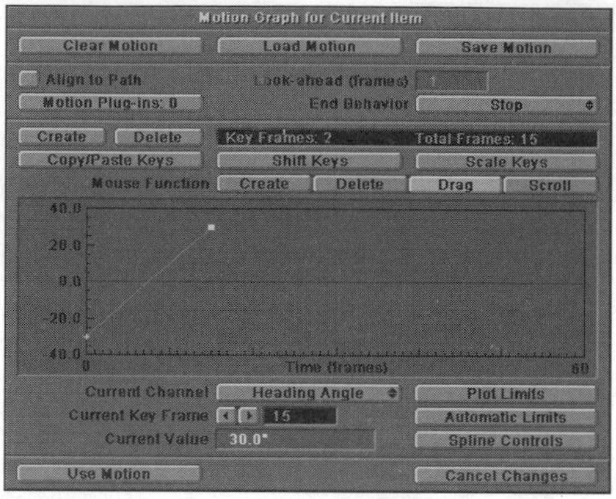

Figure 14.55 Heading Angle spline.

The head moves kind of like a tank turret, doesn't it? This is very mechanical, not lifelike at all. Let's find out why.

5. Take a look at the rotation spline for the animation. You should see something like Figure 14.55.

   Note that the spline is a straight line, not a slalom or curve.

6. Add a new key at frame 7, keeping the rotation set to 0 degrees, to keep the spline straight as in Figure 14.56. 0 is exactly halfway between the -30 degrees of the head's original rotation and the +30 degrees you set in frame 15.

   Now, you'll add some rotation in the pitch axis, to turn the straight line of the rotation spline into a slalom.

7. While you are still at frame 7, change the pitch to -5.0 degrees, as in Figure 14.57.

   Most software automatically interpolates this spline as a smooth curve between the old endpoints and the new midpoint you just created. With good spline control tools,

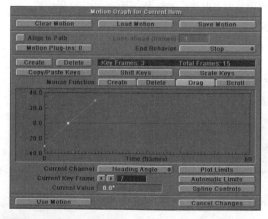

Figure 14.56 Rotation spline with new key at frame 7.

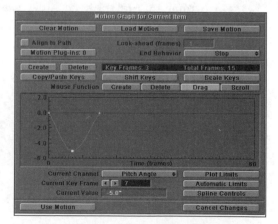

Figure 14.57 Pitch angle keyed to -5 degrees at frame 7.

it is possible to shape a curve using only endpoints and the spline controls. With poor spline controls, it is usually easier to add keyframes. Let's see how changing the pitch changed the animation.

8. Save the scene with a new name. Render and play back the 15-frame animation. Your results should look something like Figure 14.58.

This looks a little more natural, doesn't it? Just adding a few degrees in another axis is enough to give a more natural appearance. Experiment with the pitch keyframe setting. How subtle can you get, and still make the head rotation seem more natural? How extreme can you get, to make the head rotation seem caricatured and overacted?

In head movements, the slalom rule generally expresses itself as a few curves leading from the starting position to the goal, with the swell of the largest curve pointing down. The only general exception to this rule is when the character is looking toward something well above the horizon line, in which case the largest curve will swell upwards. The smaller curves are near the starting position and the goal, and represent the anticipation before and the follow-through after the main action.

As in the project you just completed, the character's head will generally pitch down slightly as the head rotates side-to-side, then come up to the goal pitch angle at the end of the rotation. For simplicity's sake, the origin pitch and the goal pitch in this project were the same. If you like, repeat the project with different origin and goal pitch angles, and see what effects you can create.

The Eyes Have It

Although it is possible to animate a character with no facial features at all, it's much easier to get your audience to identify with a character if it has eyes, eyelids, and the range of expression that they make possible. Reflexive eye movement is also fairly easy to mimic and can be a great asset to directing your audience's attention and selling a shot.

The following projects show you how to animate eyeballs and eyelids within a head model, using the parented hierarchy setup you created in Chapter 11, as seen in Figure 14.59.

Giving your character eyes opens up a whole new range of acting capabilities. Aside from emotional expressions and other intentional communication (which we'll cover in Chapters 15 and 16), the eyes can convey an extraordinary amount of unintentional or unconscious information. Any parent, teacher, or police officer can tell you how a miscreant's eyes move

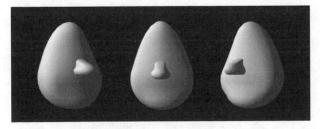

Figure 14.58   Frames 0, 7, and 15 with pitch added to heading.

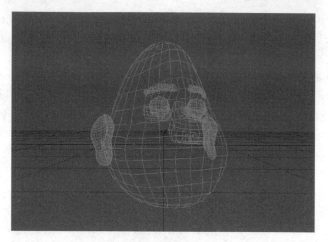

Figure 14.59   Scene with head and eye hierarchy set up.

when they are lying. A loud noise, bright light, or rapid motion also produces an involuntary or unconscious reaction, which is usually readable in eye movement.

If you animate your character to mimic these natural motions, you'll be taking a big step toward convincing your audience. You'll also be able to use those motions to tell the audience what is going on, in a subtle and natural way, and so advance your story. This technique is especially important with animals or creatures that have little facial expression, and eye movement and body posture are about all you have to work with.

You've already animated the head to follow a slalom. Now let's do the same with the eyes.

Eyeballing A Slalom

1. Select the left eyeball. Go to frame 0.
2. Change the eyeball's heading to -30 degrees, to match the heading of the head object.
3. Set two more keys for the left eyeball, changing the heading to 0 degrees at frame 7 and 30 degrees at frame 15.
4. Go back to frame 7. Change the pitch rotation to -5.0 degrees. Set a keyframe.
5. Repeat Steps 1 through 4 for the right eyeball.
6. Save the scene with a new name. Render and play back the animation.

You should end up with an animation like Figure 14.60.

You probably noticed that simultaneous rotation of the head and eyeballs is neither convincing nor realistic. The eyes can move much more rapidly than the entire head. Their purpose is to track rapid movement, to scout ahead of the slower movements of the head and body. When a creature with eyes is nervous or keyed-up, the eyes tend to flicker all over the landscape. If you tried to do that with the entire head, you'd appear to be giving your character whiplash.

Figure 14.60   Keyframes 15, 7, and 0, with eyeballs rotated.

A more realistic approach is to animate the eyes' rotation in advance of the head's. If the character is to look up and to the right, the eyes should follow a slalom up and to the right just before the head begins to follow its own slalom. In other words, the eyes should always lead the head. Let's give it a try.

7. Select the head, and add rotation keys at frames 5, 12, and 20.

8. Go to frame 5. Change the heading to -30 degrees, the same as frame 0. Turn on linear interpolation for the spline segment between frames 0 and 5.

   This keeps the graph between frames 0 and 5 flat, so the head will not move at all. If you left linear interpolation turned off, most software's default interpolation would make a curve between the keyframes, which would make the head rotate slightly between frames 0 and 5.

   This is a good trick to remember. Any time you need an object to hold perfectly still, set the keyframes at the beginning and end of the hold to identical values, and turn on linear interpolation. You can do what you like to the rest of the spline, while the segment between those keyframes remains straight.

9. Delete the keys at frames 7 and 15. Go to frame 12. Change the heading to 0 degrees. Go to frame 20. Change the heading to 30 degrees. The graph should now be a straight line between keyframes 5 and 20, as shown in Figure 14.61.

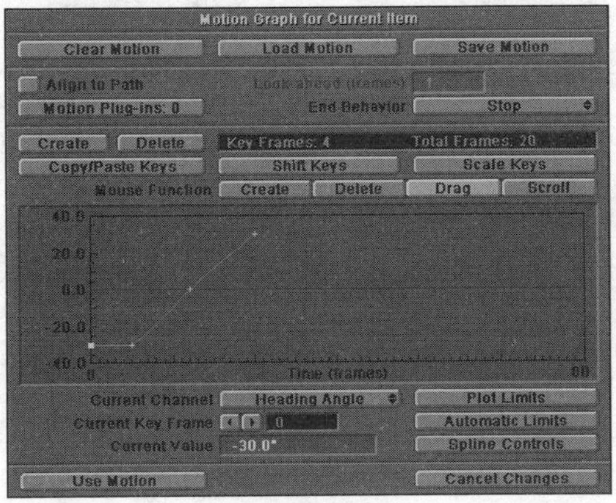

Figure 14.61   Modified rotation spline for head model.

10. Go back to frame 0. Change the pitch to 0 degrees, and set the key. Repeat for frames 5 and 20.

11. Go to frame 12, and set pitch to -5.0 degrees. You should get a spline like Figure 14.62.

12. Save the scene with a new name. Render and play back the animation.

The head should hold still for five frames, then perform the same slalom rotation you animated before. If not, see if you can figure out what's wrong (and fix it) by looking at the splines. The five-frame pause gives you enough time to animate the eyes turning before the head. The next step, reasonably enough, is to animate the eyes leading the head motion.

13. Select the left eyeball again. Go to frame 0. Change the heading to 0 degrees, to match the heading of the head object.

14. Delete the keyframes at 7 and 15.

15. Add a key at frame 5. Change the heading to 40 degrees, which is a fairly extreme rotation for normal eye movement.

16. Add a key at frame 20. Change the heading to 0 degrees to bring the eye back into alignment with the head. You should end up with a heading graph like Figure 14.63.

17. Go back to frame 5. Change the pitch to -5.0 degrees. You should end up with a pitch graph as shown in Figure 14.64.

18. Repeat Steps 13 through 17 for the right eyeball.

19. Save the scene again. Render and play back the animation.

You should end up with an animation like Figure 14.65.

This is a more natural motion for the eyes, but something is still missing. The eyelids should always frame the iris, the colored part of the eyeball surrounding the pupil, unless you are trying to show fright, rage, rolling of the eyes, or another extreme effect.

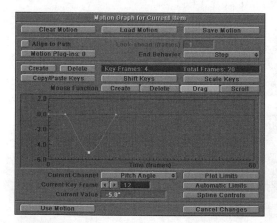

Figure 14.62 Modified pitch graph for head object.

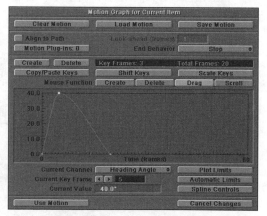

Figure 14.63 Modified heading graph for eye object.

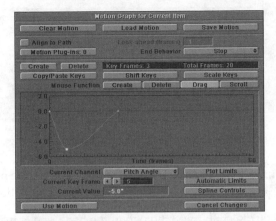

Figure 14.64 Modified pitch graph for eye object.

Figure 14.65 Keyframes 0, 5, 12, and 20, for eyes leading head motion along slalom.

In most cases, you can get away with animating eyelids in just the pitch axis. This makes it very easy to pose the eyelids—just lock off the heading and bank axes, and use the mouse. It's usually best to set the key positions for eyelids with the mouse rather than the numeric panel, because you will generally be trying to match the edge of the eyelid to the edge of the iris.

The edge of the eyelid should just cover the upper curve of the iris (see Figure 14.66). You should not be able to see the white, or *sclera*, completely surrounding the iris unless you are animating a very surprised look. The eyelid should not cover more of the iris unless the character is squinting in pain, anger, or bright light. The pupil itself always remains visible between the upper and lower eyelids, unless a blink or squint closes the eye almost completely.

PROJECT 14.24 Keep A Lid On It

1. Select the left eyelid. Go to frame 0. Change the pitch rotation to align the bottom edge of the eyelid with the top of the iris, as in Figure 14.66. When you are satisfied with the result, create a keyframe.

2. Go to the next keyframe for the left eyeball.

3. Repeat Steps 1 and 2 until all the keyframes for the eyeball have a matching keyframe for the eyelid.

4. Repeat Steps 1 through 3 for the right eyelid.

Figure 14.66 Positions of the upper eyelid over the iris: No, Yes, No.

5. Save the scene with a new file name. You will be using it for the next project. Render and play back the animation. You should end up with an animation like Figure 14.67.

That's a lot better, isn't it? Keep in mind that when the head or eye turns, the eyelid will often cover more of the upper part of the iris in a partial blink. The faster the turn, the more of the iris is covered, until a snap turn produces a full blink.

By now, you are probably tired of repeatedly posing one eyeball, then matching the rotation for the other eye. Imagine trying to do this for a long shot, in which your character intently watches the erratic and convoluted flight of a mosquito!

The sensitivity of your audience to *sightlines*, the apparent direction of the eyeball, makes your job harder. We learn almost from birth to deduce exactly what someone is looking at by observing tiny variations in the angle of their eyes. Your least mistake in aligning the eyes can shatter your character's credibility.

Of course, there is a better way to do this. Most animation software suitable for character animation supports a function called *inverse kinematics*, IK, which can make an object in a hierarchy point consistently and precisely at another object.

Animating With Inverse Kinematics And Goals

If you worked through all the setup projects in Chapter 11, you should have a setup of the head and eyeballs that has an IK goal named EyeTarget, a null or invisible object set up for the eyeballs to track automatically (see Figure 14.68).

Figure 14.67 Keyframes 20, 15, 5, and 0 of eyelids matching eyeball rotation.

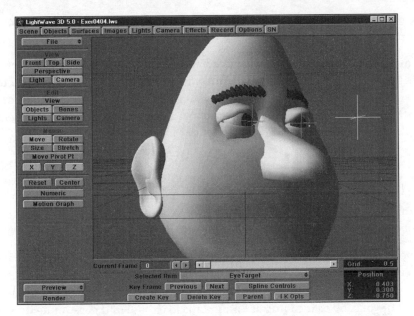

Figure 14.68   EyeTarget null positioned in front of nose.

You can animate the EyeTarget like any other object, and the eyes will follow along. You can use the EyeTarget to rotate the eyes along slaloms more easily and quickly than by setting separate sets of keyframes.

It is also much easier to mimic realistic eye movement. Researchers have compiled a lot of data about how humans and animals move their eyes in different circumstances and environments. One branch of this research is *eye-gaze tracking*. Figure 14.69 is from one of the most-often cited sources in this field, Alfred L. Yarbus' 1967 book, *Eye Movements and Vision*. You can find out more by looking it up on the Web or in your local library.

The eye-gaze track on the right represents three minutes' examination of the picture on the left. If you duplicated this eye-gaze track in a series of EyeTarget keyframes during a three-minute animation, and positioned the test image at the appropriate distance in front of the face, you could accurately mimic the original subject's perusal of the image. Why you'd want to, I don't know, but the point is that you could.

Figure 14.69   Test image and resulting eye-gaze track.

From this and related research data, we can extract a few general guidelines that are useful in character animation.

When confronting a new situation, such as entering an unfamiliar room, the eyes will case the area. This probably evolved as a survival trait—the first caveman to spot the bear tended to get out of the cave alive. What first attracts the eye is motion, especially a living creature. If nothing is moving, the eye tends to explore the lighter areas first, looking at TV screens, windows, and lamps. After that, the eye examines the darker areas of the scene.

If the roving eye finds a living creature, the first reaction is to look at the creature's eyes. From there, the eye's path depends on the type of creature. If it is armed, the eye is drawn to the immediate threat, whether gun, knife, fang, claw, or tentacle. If the creature appears unarmed and has an expressive face, the eye tends to rove between the hands and face, cross-checking and corroborating information gathered from both areas.

Please note that these are gross generalizations, and there are always exceptions and modifications depending on the situation. We all know people who would overlook a bus unless it hit them, and others who would ignore a roomful of purple baboons for the television set in the corner. Part of your job as a character animator is to expose and accentuate those differences, to show your audience, via animated eye movement, what your character is thinking about and what their likes, dislikes, and habits are.

PROJECT 14.25 A Reading Test

1. Use the IK eyeball scene you set up in Chapter 11 to animate the character reading an invisible page of text.

   The EyeTarget should move left-to-right along the width of a printed line, at a reasonable reading distance for the character, then zip right-to-left and down a little to the beginning of the next line.

2. If you'd like to add a little personality, insert keyframe pauses and back-and-forth stutters into the middle of lines, as if the character is having trouble reading an unfamiliar word.

   You can leave the head immobile, pitch it down slightly to follow the eyes down the page, or combine pitch and heading so the head follows along with each line. Moving the head more nearly matching the eyes will convey the laborious reading of a semiliterate character, while a minimal pitch and no heading changes at all can convey the actions of a speed-reader.

Blinkin' Good

Unless you are animating a zombie movie, your characters will need to blink. Blinks are one of the unconscious signals that can help convince your audience that a character is alive.

Blinks are especially important for three-dimensional CGI character animation. One of the problems of this medium is that an absolute hold, where all movement stops, immediately destroys the illusion of life. This is not true for other animation media. In fact, limited animation and camera-motion animation can get by with almost no on-screen movement.

As mentioned earlier, if a character needs to pause for a moment, to remain believable, it must do so in a *moving hold*. This is a hold as a human actor might perform it, with all the tiny motions of breathing, muscular twinges, nervous tics, shifting weight—and the occasional blink.

The mechanics of a blink are deceptively simple. The upper eyelid closes until it meets the lower lid, then rises again to its normal position. The pupil should also follow the lower edge of the lid as it closes and follow it up again as it opens.

Ah, but how fast? For how long? Timing—both its placement within the longer sequence and the speed of the blink itself—makes a great deal of difference in how a blink helps or hinders the credibility of the character.

Then, too, the blink must relate to the animation of the eyes, the face, and the rest of the character. A random blink in the middle of a staring match destroys the tension, while a quick blink at a sudden action can really sell the shot. Remember, your audience will watch your character's eyes more than any other part of the scene.

Your character should blink quickly when alert, slowly when sleepy or stupid, repeatedly when surprised, and partially or fully, depending on speed, when the head changes direction. Sections of Chapters 15 and 16 on facial animation include more examples.

Winkin', Blinkin', And Nod

If you completed all the projects so far, you should have learned to use the slalom path, linear and interpolated splines, parented eyes and eyelids, and IK goals. Now, you'll get a chance to put them all together.

Rather than a step-by-step set of instructions, this project is more like the assignments you'll get as a professional character animator. All you will get is a brief description of the action for a single shot, and it's up to you to interpret it.

The character you've been working with is asleep, head nodding forward. He is startled, and wakes suddenly. His eyes blink rapidly as they roam, looking for the source of the disturbance.

His eyes lock onto the source of the noise—a fly! (Don't worry. It's invisible—you don't have to animate it.) He stares at it intently, in a moving hold.

The fly takes off, and the character tracks it with his eyes and, with less accuracy, his head. The fly swoops and circles erratically, getting closer to the character's face with each pass.

Finally, the fly swoops in and lands—on the character's nose! He goes cross-eyed trying to see the fly, and blinks repeatedly in disbelief.

He shakes his head violently, apparently dislodging the fly.

Now, how would you end the sequence? Would he fall back to sleep? Just sit there blinking? Keep looking for the fly? You decide! Animate the whole shot, and keep the results in a safe place for future reference.

How did you decide on the timing for the blinks? What effect would it have on the whole piece if you put the blink keyframes closer together or spaced them farther apart?

Did you remember to move the head and eyes on slaloms? Did the eyes always lead the head? Did you keep the eyelids lined up with the iris of each eye?

Was the action convincing? Did you believe in the character? Did he seem alive?

This is the kind of short project that you will want to revisit as your animation skills improve. With each new tool you learn, you will probably think of an embellishment or refinement you'd like to add. It's exactly this kind of practice that will hone your skills and help you become a better character animator.

Most of the preceding projects have included some initial timings or at least a hint or two about the appropriate range of timings. As a professional animator, you need to be able to write up actions on an exposure sheet without mocking them up in your software first. This is for your own development and discipline, and so you can communicate effectively with other production team members.

X-Sheet Practice

X-sheet shorthand varies from studio to studio, and even from animator to animator, but there are a few general conventions. The start or stop of an action is usually marked with an X, especially if it must match a *hit* on the sound track. A hold is marked with a straight line between the Xs. An action is represented by a curve, and an anticipation before an action is a loop. A repeated action, such as a walk or run, is drawn as a series of curves connecting Xs located in each heel-strike frame.

PROJECT 14.27 Write It Up

This project gives you some practice in writing up an x-sheet.

1. Make a lot of copies of the blank x-sheet from Chapter 4.

2. For each project in this chapter, write up x-sheets for the different timings you used. It is not necessary to mark each keyframe. The start, stop, anticipation, follow-through, and a brief written description of each action are adequate.

3. Critique your x-sheets. Could you recreate the animation from just the exposure sheets and a sketch of a keyframe in the sequence? That's pretty much what you're expected to do as an animator, working from an x-sheet and a story sketch or two.

It's a good idea to keep practicing x-sheet markup as you work through the next two chapters. X-sheet shorthand should be second nature by the time you're done.

ANALYZING 2D CARTOONS WITH SPLINES

This is an experimental technique I came up with as a study aid. So far, it has worked for me, but I will be interested in hearing about your experiences with it. The basic idea is to analyze the timing of existing character animation by translating the character's on-screen motions to keyframed splines in your software. This enables you to compare the timing of masterpieces of character animation, from all animation styles, in the context of your particular software.

1. Digitize a favorite sequence of character animation. Look for a sequence with a single, clearly depicted character in a series of strong poses with excellent timing. If the character interacts with their environment or other characters, the conversion process gets much more complex.

2. Load the digitized animation sequence as a backdrop in your animation software.

3. Add a set of nulls or small marker objects to the scene, keeping them all within a plane parallel to the background image. That is, you want to restrict the nulls so they have no in-and-out axis movement, strictly up-and-down, left-to-right as you look at your screen.

4. Name each null for a joint or location on the character.

5. Go to the first frame of the action being analyzed.

6. Match each null precisely to the named joint or location in the current frame. Set a key for every null.

7. Go to the next frame. Repeat Step 6, until all frames of the background animation have been keyed.

8. Open your software's spline editor, and examine the timing of each null, just as you'd critique your own timing.

Keep in mind that this movement is strictly 2D, and that you won't be able to accurately match the nulls to hidden movement (in puppet animations) or cheated drawings. The idea is to use this process to create a set of splines worth studying, not to precisely reproduce the timing of a Tex Avery or Ray Harryhausen.

If you've completed the preceding projects, you now have a solid grounding in basic timing and in mimicking lifelike head and eye movement. Now that you've got the essentials of character movement under control, the next step is to apply it. One of the simplest tests of character movement is to animate the camera.

Characteristic Camera Movement

You can animate the camera as a character's point of view (POV). This makes the camera an actor, giving it the ability to help tell a story.

You can use point-to-point spline interpolation to animate a camera for a character's POV. This will give a very Steadicam-style movement. However, real people don't run around with a Steadicam for a neck, and neither should your 3D camera.

Choosing an appropriate style of camera movement can add a great deal to your animations. For example, let's use a short involving two characters: one extremely active and zany (Speedy) and the other placid and lethargic (Sleepy).

When shooting from Speedy's point of view, you need to zip the camera around much more rapidly and in more directions than when shooting from Sleepy's point of view. Otherwise, your audience will not be as quick to identify whose viewpoint they are sharing at a particular moment, and your story will not get across as effectively. Handled properly, character-based camera styles can be a major storytelling tool.

Even for something as basic as an architectural walkthrough, there are human perceptual factors you can use to make a stronger impact. The idea is to make the audience feel as though they are in the scene. If you run the camera straight down the centerline of every hallway, do perfect 90-degree pans around every corner, and keep a dead-level line of sight, you won't do that. Instead, you'll make the audience feel like they've been dumped on an amusement park ride with a hefty dose of Quaaludes.

So, how do you make the camera more human? Researchers in various branches of psychology and medicine have been developing tools for what they call *eye-gaze tracking*, the mapping of the movements of the subject's eye. As mentioned previously, the extensive body of work on the subject can be boiled down to a handful of general rules that are applicable to character animation.

Just as these rules can be used to animate the rotation of a character's eyeballs, they can be applied to the animation of the camera. Keep in mind that these are generalizations and are not to be followed without judgment or exception.

If there is a person or creature in the scene, the character's first focus is the eyes, followed by the rest of the face. The hands are next, unless two or more people are facing each other. In that case, the scan typically goes back and forth between the faces, attempting to correlate their interaction before moving on to the rest of the scene.

After faces and hands, objects are examined in order of brightness and contrast. A bright object on a dark tabletop will attract the eye, as will an open window in a dim room. Television sets, brightly lit pictures on the walls, anything moving, and other details will attract attention for longer periods of time. Blank, unchanging areas will be dismissed with a quick glance. Lower-priority items with many details may be revisited later, after other elements of the scene have been examined.

Finally, the eye roves to clues needed for navigation. Occasional glances at the floor, followed by slight corrections in the direction of travel, mimic the way people actually walk. These corrections are the defining points for slaloms.

If the camera is going to go through a door, the camera needs to dip to locate the knob or handle, then quickly return to nearly eye level as the door opens.

Keep in mind that you shouldn't exactly mimic the rapid eye movement of a real person, unless you want a particularly frantic and disorienting effect. Real eye movements can be very rapid without disorienting the observer, because the observer is in control of their own eyes and is expecting the rapid shifts. Your audience is not in control and needs more time to recognize the character's surroundings. Instead of mimicking the quick, angular rotations of a real eye-gaze track, you should animate your character POV tracks to be more gradual and rounded. You should also use a little ease-in and ease-out for all the major camera moves for a character POV, and don't forget to use slaloms.

PROJECT 14.28 Animating The Camera For Character POV

This project shows you how to animate the camera to mimic a character's point of view.

1. Load the STREET scene file from the Chapter 14 directory on this book's CD-ROM. If your software's scene format is not available, import the STREET.DXF or 3DS model into a new scene. This model is a brick storefront with a sidewalk and street attached.

2. Position the camera at roughly eyeball-height above the sidewalk at the left side of the storefront. Rotate the camera to look down the sidewalk, past the storefront. Create a keyframe for the camera at frame 0.

3. Go to frame 90. Move the camera down the sidewalk to the opposite side of the storefront. Set a keyframe.

4. Save the scene. Render and play back the animation.

   This makes the camera move smoothly down the sidewalk, at an appropriate height for an average human character. Now, you'll add a null object for the camera to look at as it moves. This makes it much easier to control the camera angle, rather than manually setting three rotation axis values for each keyframe.

5. Add a null to the scene. Name the null CamTarget.

6. Move CamTarget to the surface of the sidewalk, just in front of the storefront doorway. Set a key for CamTarget at frame 0.

7. Set the camera to look at CamTarget. Save the scene.

   At this point, you have a scene where the camera travels at character eye level down the sidewalk, looking at a null object, CamTarget. In frame 0, the CamTarget is positioned to direct the camera towards the sidewalk just past the doorway (see Figure 14.70).

   Consider what details in this scene would attract the attention of the character during a 14-frame walk. Would he look at the ground? How about the lamppost? Perhaps the shop doorway?

8. Make a list of three to six points of interest for the character. Number them in the order the character would look at them.

9. How long (for how many frames) would the character look at each point of interest? Write this number on the list next to each point of interest.

10. Using a copy of the blank exposure sheet from Chapter 4, write up the points of interest in order from first to last, spacing them according to the numbers you wrote in Step 9.

Figure 14.70 Camera looking at null goal.

11. Select the CamTarget. Refer to the exposure sheet you just created. Each point of interest is going to be a keyframe. The first point of interest should be at frame 0.

12. Move the CamTarget to the point of interest. Make a keyframe for CamTarget at the current frame. Refer to the exposure sheet for the next point of interest.

13. Repeat Step 12 for each point of interest on your exposure sheet.

    You should end up with a 90-frame animation of the camera looking at several points of interest as it travels down the sidewalk.

14. Save the scene. Render and play back an animation.

Most 3D software will automatically create a slalom running through each of the keyframe null positions you set up, so you won't jerk the camera around too sharply. You can use spline controls to change the shape of the slalom. You can make the slalom even smoother, or tighten it up to make the ride a little rougher.

This brings us to fine tuning. Just how rough is too rough? If you are animating a sedate walk down a corporate corridor, you want the movement to be just a little rougher than Steadicam style. If you are animating a character running down a flight of stairs and want a real documentary feel to it, bang that camera around a lot!

It's A Dog's Life

PROJECT **14.29**

1. Repeat the preceding project, but this time start the camera at about 20 centimeters above the sidewalk. Make up another point-of-interest list, but this time for a small dog.

2. Try to remember everything you have ever observed about a dog's behavior. In what are they most interested? How do they approach it? Do they follow a direct path or a more roundabout, wandering path? How close do they get to what interests them?

How much time do they spend looking at (and sniffing) it? How do they move, and how does their POV change while examining it?

3. Make up an exposure sheet that is at least three seconds (90 frames) long. This will give you a little more time to develop the character. Mark both the points of interest and the camera positions on the exposure sheet. Make an effort to convey the character and behavior of the dog by the way the camera and the CamTarget move.

4. Animate the camera and CamTarget according to the exposure sheet.

5. Render and play back an animation.

6. If you are not satisfied with the camera's characterization of the dog, go back to your exposure sheet, and tweak it a little. Try using spline controls to make the camera or CamTarget slaloms smoother or rougher.

7. When you are satisfied with the timing, save the scene, and render the animation. Play back the animation.

Does the animation seem to be a dog's-eye view? Does this seem like the behavior of a dog? Ask someone else, preferably a dog owner, to look at the animation. What is their reaction? If you get a laugh, consider your animation a success!

Don't Stop Now!

Practice, practice, practice! Try every project with variations in timing, note what works and what is communicated differently with each change.

A piece of advice I have heard quoted by several traditional artists is, "Everyone has a hundred thousand bad drawings inside them. The sooner you get them out of your system, the better." I'd like to extend the spirit of that quote to CGI character animation. I believe knocking out a hundred thousand keyframes (not just rendered frames!) should be enough experience to make you a really good character animator.

Moving On

At this point, you should have a solid understanding of the essentials of timing for character animation. You have practiced with some basic setups and found you can create a sense of life and character with a minimal amount of complexity.

In the next chapter, you'll apply the tools you've learned to more complex character setups. From the handful of variables for animating the desk lamp, you'll be stepping up to animating dozens or more for a bipedal walk and other humanoid actions.

USING CONSTRAINTS

The best setup in the world is useless unless you can make your characters act through posing and timing. This chapter shows you how to pose your characters for best effect, mimic weight and balance, create walks, runs, and other *motion cycles*, and use the *animation hierarchy* effectively. You'll also learn to analyze and caricature motion, including the classic cartoon repertoire of takes, sneaks, staggers, and zips.

The first part of this chapter explains how to compose your character within the frame so the action reads clearly and with the strongest dramatic effect. The next section shows you how to animate basic walks for bipedal characters of humanoid proportions. Later sections explore runs, other gaits, and non-human and caricatured *motion cycles*. This chapter also introduces the concept of the *animation hierarchy*, the division of the character into levels of a hierarchy for the creation of keyframes. This chapter also provides a guide to materials that can help you develop skills for analyzing and reproducing motion, and resources for animal and human motion studies. One of your goals in this chapter is to learn how to extrapolate your observations of natural motion to create caricatured animation. Along the way, projects will show you how to animate actions from the repertoire of classic cartoon animation, including takes, sneaks, staggers, and zips. You'll also learn the concept of *staging* for foreshadowing action.

Posing Characters Within The Shot

You can set up an acceptable camera distance, angle, and movement yet still have a composition that is boring or hard to read. The success of the shot's composition depends as much on the character's pose as on the camera setup.

You should keep two concepts in mind when evaluating your character's poses: *line of action* and *twins*. Your key poses should always have a strong, clear line of action, and you should avoid twins like the plague.

Line Of Action

Line of action is a pretty simple concept. The line of action should grow from the visual base of the character, up through its centerline, and out to the goal of the action. If this line is bent too sharply or in different directions, it is more difficult for your audience to read the pose, as you can see in Figure 15.1.

Figure 15.1 A line of action splitting toward two goals is harder to read.

Each part of a character's pose should add something to the main line of action. If part of the character is jutting out at an angle, that part breaks up the visual flow of the pose, as in Figure 15.2.

In 2D drawing, the line of action can be drawn first, and the character sketch built around the line. You can do the same for storyboard sketches, if the sketch represents a key pose. In 3D, it's generally more useful to add the line of action afterwards, as an analysis and critique for making changes. Figure 15.3 is the result of an animator applying a line of action. Compare this to the two previous poses. The head and torso point toward the same goal as the arm. A much smoother arc can be drawn from the character's feet up through the body centerline and out through the arm.

Figure 15.2 A jagged pose with parts of the character interfering with the line of action.

Figure 15.3   A pose with a clearer line of action.

Twins

Twins is a label used to describe perfectly symmetric poses. Beginners often compose a character in a twins pose, lining up each joint as if the character were a soldier standing at attention (see Figure 15.4).

A perfectly symmetric pose is highly unnatural and will make your character look boring, mechanical, and dead.

The first step to preventing twins is to avoid head-on camera angles. Even if a character is posed symmetrically, an angled camera will show enough variation between left and right that the pose will hold the audience's interest (see Figure 15.5).

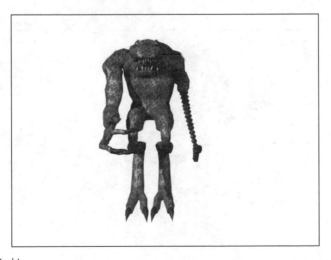

Figure 15.4   Twins. Yuck!

Figure 15.5   A stronger pose, but still a touch of the twins.

The second step is to make sure that the left and right sides of your character are never perfectly matched. Even if a pose seems to require symmetry, make it just a little off—slide one foot forward a few centimeters, or tilt the hips and shoulders in alternate directions. Whatever is necessary, as long as the resulting pose looks imperfect enough to be natural.

Testing Poses In Silhouette

As you probably noticed, poses of complex or heavily textured characters are often hard to analyze. Camouflage still works, I guess. What you need is a tool that masks all that extraneous stuff and leaves just the pose itself. One such tool is the *silhouette*, a simple black-and-white outline or negative image of the character, with no details internal to the outline (see Figures 15.7, 15.8, and 15.9).

Figure 15.6   A much more dynamic pose, without a trace of the dreaded twins.

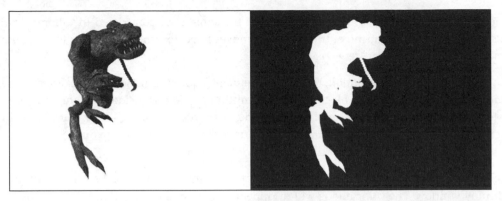

Figure 15.7 A very confusing pose. There's a lot of information inside this outline that you just can't see.

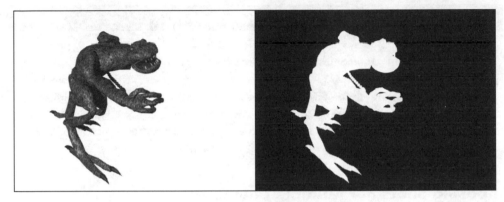

Figure 15.8 Better than the first pose but still a little cluttered and confusing.

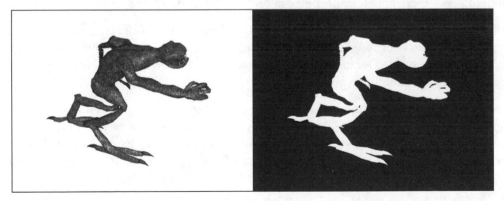

Figure 15.9 A much better pose, very easy to read.

It's important to test your key poses in silhouette. If the action does not read well as an outline, your audience is probably going to have to rely on much more subtle clues to understand what the character is trying to do or say. That takes more time, makes your audience work harder, and is generally poor animation practice. On the other hand, an action that reads well in silhouette will only get better and stronger when you add color, depth, and surface details.

Figures 15.7, 15.8, and 15.9 are examples of the same pose considered in different camera setups. The heavy texturing of the character makes the color images difficult to read, but the matching silhouettes are very easy to evaluate.

In traditional drawn animation, testing in silhouette requires making another drawing or tracing of the pose in question, blocking out or omitting the details inside the character's outline. Most 3D animation software enables you to do essentially the same thing, automatically, by rendering an alpha channel image. Another advantage to CGI is that you can render an alpha-channel animation, to test an entire action in silhouette.

In 3D Studio MAX, you can simply render the current frame, then click the Alpha button in the display window. The color image will disappear, leaving the alpha channel visible as a clear silhouette.

> ### EASY SILHOUETTE CHECKING WITH LIGHTWAVE
>
> Set the Record panel to save a sequence of alpha images. Render frame 0, just to save a single alpha channel image. In the Images panel, load the frame 0 alpha image as a sequence. In the Options panel's Layout View layer, activate the background image feature. In the Effects panel's Compositing layer, choose the alpha sequence as the Background Image. Whenever you need to check a silhouette, simply render the frame you want, then get an unobstructed view of the alpha channel image by opening the Scene panel and choosing the Hide All Objects option.

Composing Shots For Multiple Characters

If you are animating a crowd scene or the interaction between two or more characters, you should apply these principles of composition to the individuals and to the group as a whole.

Evaluating the distance, angle, depth of field, and movement of the camera, the character's and groups' lines of action, and especially avoiding twins and checking silhouettes, are just as important for groups as for individuals. Animating a solo character is generally a piece of cake compared to coordinating a group.

For every important action, you need to clear enough space around the character so that the action reads well in silhouette. The space between characters must be appropriate to the action, neither too far nor too close. If the characters take turns in leading the action, getting good poses can require a constant reshuffling of the composition. This is another instance where you will need to experiment a lot and develop your own judgment.

Composition For Direct Playback And Game Design

If you are animating for computer games, multimedia, or any other application that will play back through a computer, there are a few more factors you need to keep in mind.

At the current state of technology, most desktop computers can't play back full-frame video without skipping frames. The problem is that a computer can only push so much information through the system, and most video sequences contain much more information than a computer can handle at full speed.

There are several approaches to solving this problem. One is, of course, to get a faster computer. In time, this will be the solution for most people, and this text will be obsolete. For now, other options are within the reach of more people.

There are several techniques for compressing a video or audio/video stream for computer playback. Three of the more common are MPEG, AVI, and QuickTime. Each has its advantages and disadvantages, zealots and critics, but they all share a few important attributes.

The amount of information in an animation is not necessarily all the information about each pixel in each frame. That is what is called an *uncompressed stream* and can run about 30 megabytes per second for a broadcast-quality image. Most compression techniques take advantage of the fact that most of the pixels in frame 1, for instance, will be identical to the corresponding pixels in frame 2. These duplicated pixels do not have to be recorded all over again, just their locations. The minority pixels, the ones that show a change, or *delta*, have to be recorded completely. Do you see the implications? If a video clip has very low deltas, it can be compressed a great deal. If the deltas are high, the clip may be near its original, uncompressed size.

So, how do you ensure low deltas? Simple—don't move the camera.

Ouch. No camera movement. No cuts or transitions, either. The whole screen is one big delta when you do that. This is why a lot of early computer animation was (and is) boring. The playback penalty simply ruled out any use of dramatic camera movement or cutting. This limitation just isn't acceptable any more. So, what else can you do?

You can lower the size of the animation file by limiting the number of colors. If you cut a 24-bit video clip down to 8-bit, you just trimmed two-thirds of the file. The down side is that you will see *banding*, an abrupt borderline between adjacent color areas, because there are not enough different colors to seamlessly shade the borders.

You could cut back the frame rate, too. If you only have to display 15 frames per second instead of 30, you've cut the data stream in half again. The disadvantage is that motion starts to look choppy, and, below about 10 frames per second, you can do better with flip-books.

You can also reduce the resolution. Using 640×480 pixels takes up a lot of screen real estate; 320×240 is one-quarter the data, but still acceptable to most audiences. Even smaller resolutions are acceptable for animations designed to accompany text or occupy small screen windows in a computer game.

What it usually comes down to is a combination of all these techniques. If you need fast action, cut down the color depth, and lock down the camera, but keep the frame rate high. If you want a talking head with good color reproduction, lock down the camera, lock down the subject, use a compromise frame rate, and boost the color palette back to 24-bit. If you want to move your camera or do a lot of cuts and edits, you'll have to sacrifice something else.

Take A Walk

This section concentrates on the animation of basic walks for bipedal characters of humanoid proportions and introduces the concept of the *animation hierarchy*, the division of the character into levels of a hierarchy for the creation of keyframes.

Step By Step

A motion cycle is an action that you can repeat by connecting duplicates end-to-end, such as walking, running, hammering a nail, or any other repetitive action. Cycles require special attention to the *hookup*, the matching of beginning and ending frames to eliminate jerks or strobing when you *loop* the action or play it repeatedly. You generally use cycles in what is referred to as *transportation animation*, walking or other means of moving the character around within the shot.

Walk and run cycles are not difficult to animate once you understand the basics, but they are a core requirement for character animation. A prospective employer may even ask you to animate a simple walk (along with the classic bouncing ball project), just to ensure that you know what you're doing. It may be to your advantage to practice the following projects until you can do a simple walk by reflex and an emotional or characteristic walk with a minimum of thought.

People *do* lurch and limp, what they *don't* do is repeat cyclic motion with the precision of a computer, at least not for very long. Even in Saturday morning TV, we tried to limit ourselves to two and a half repetitions of any cycle. Once you've noticed the cycle, your eye is drawn to the dissimilarities, any hitches in your gitalong, as it were.

In the sparse occasions in feature animation where characters walk for any period in time, it is usually broken up with a lot of specific pieces of business. One that comes to mind is Mrs. Brisby being led by Mr. Ages down to the Council of Rats. He's doing all sorts of things with his crutch while gesturing and looking back and talking to Brisby. She's taking all these hesitant steps, and scurrying from every little rustle that startles her, while goggling at all the pretty lights. This is all over a sloping and terraced path. Nothing is up long enough to be a cycle per se, though cycles indeed were designed, and referred to by the animators. Rather than seeing "A Walk," you are seeing their characters revealed in the way they move.

As far as the problem of resolving undesirable lurches, you can go to some trouble to build your walk in such a manner that guarantees symmetry at first, so you'll be able to introduce asymmetry only where you want it. Give yourself at least half the duration of the cycle lead up both before and after your walk's frames. If its a 24-frame walk, make sure that that a keyframe in the middle appears the appropriate distance before the first frame and after the last frame. You

"I think walks are terrific exercises. They are technical by nature, but are key to describing character and attitude."
Chris Bailey

may be chasing down artifacts of curve shapes not matching because they started only on the first frame of the walk, thus missing the curve that the identical pose on frame 24 had leading up to it. Frame 24, of course, needs the curves after it that frame 1 had. Naturally, this affects the interpolated frames rather than the keyed ones. You also might work out a method to make sure motion from one side can be mirrored and offset to the other with a minimum of effort, either by shell-script or through the use of expressions.

Still, it's much easier to build a shot that has objectives for the character to accomplish, something for it to do. Without acting, your walk will be anexercise in which you'll quickly discover the degree of control you have (or don't) over your character.

Animation Hierarchy

The *animation hierarchy* does not refer to the hierarchical organization of parts to form a boned or parented character. The animation hierarchy refers to the division of the character into levels of a hierarchy for the creation of keyframes.

This concept is unique to CGI character animation. In cel and puppet animation, the entire character is posed completely for every frame of film, then the pose is modified as a whole for the next frame. No matter how many layers of cels are used for different character parts or how many replacement parts are socketed into a puppet, the complete character has to be assembled in front of the camera for every frame of film exposed. At the most basic physical level, every frame is a keyframe for cel and puppet animation.

Most 3D animation software enables you to set a different sequence of keyframes for each object and bone in a character. You can use as few as one or two keyframes to move the hierarchical root, the character's CG (center of gravity), along a shallow slalom. In the same shot, you can keyframe a part in the lowest level of the hierarchy (perhaps the character's toes) a dozen times, none of them on the same keyframe as the CG. This enables you to move, rotate, and scale each part of a character along its own slalom, creating smooth action with the absolute minimum of keyframes.

So, what's the big deal about a hierarchy? Think about this: Every part of a character is a dependent of the hierarchy, right back to the CG. If a part moves, every part below it in the hierarchy moves along. If a part above it moves, it has to move along. Each part of the character also has to interact with the character's world. Feet must contact the ground properly, hands must grasp and move objects, and so on.

Now, what happens if you spend hours posing a character's hands just right, setting dozens of keyframes to make precise contacts—then, you discover you didn't pose the hips correctly, and the whole figure must be reposed? Short of hiring another animator to do the shot over, you have to chuck out all your work on the hands and start from scratch. Discouraging. Not to mention costly, especially if you are on a tight deadline or budget.

On the other hand (pun intended), if you had animated according to the character's animation hierarchy, you would have found the error in the hips before you even started on the hands.

Which leads to the next question: How do you use the animation hierarchy? Very simple. Start at the root, and animate each level of the hierarchy completely before going down to the next level.

For most characters, this means you start with the CG. You need to plan where you want the character to travel, and then keyframe the CG to follow that *slalom*, the feedback curve that describes all natural, directed motion.

Walking has been described as a fall interrupted by the interposing of a limb. This observation has a special significance for CGI animation. You have already learned how to animate a fall using a spline-based parabola. You can use the same parabola, slightly modified, to describe the repeated falls of a walking character's body.

The first step (oh, the puns never end!) is to determine how high and low the character's CG will move and the distance between the ends of the parabola. To calculate these distances, you need to understand the key poses for a walking character.

Best Foot Forward

There are only three basic key poses in a walk: *heel strike*, *squash*, and *passing*. These poses are repeated in sequence for each side, to give a total of six key poses for a complete bipedal walking cycle.

The heel strike, shown in Figure 15.10, is the primary pose for the walk. The leading leg is straight, the ankle joint holds the foot at nearly a right angle to the leg, the trailing foot is solidly planted and flat to the ground, and the character's CG is evenly balanced between the feet. The arms are also at the limit of their forward and backward slaloms, balancing the opposite legs. For a natural walk, the heel strike is the low point in the CG's parabola.

The heel strike is kind of like a pole vault, converting the forward inertia of the body into an upward arc, with the straight leg defining the arc's radius.

The heel strike pose also determines the *stride length* for the character's walk, that is, the distance the character travels with each step. This is the distance between the ends of the CG's parabola. If you want the character to travel a specific distance in a certain number of frames, you must pay close attention to stride length when planning the animation.

The squash pose, shown in Figure 15.11, is just what it sounds like—the leading leg bends at the knee, squashing down slightly to absorb the impact of the heel strike. If you didn't include the squash pose and kept the leg straight from heel strike to passing, the character would walk very stiffly, like an extra from a bad monster movie.

In the squash pose, the trailing foot's toes barely touch the ground, with none of the character's weight on them, and the sole of the trailing foot is angled 70 degrees or more to the ground. This pose is the prime candidate for exaggeration in a caricatured walk, as detailed later in this chapter. Cartoon squash positions are often the CG's low point, giving the walk much more bounce between heel strike and passing poses.

Passing pose, shown in Figure 15.12, is where the leading leg straightens out again, boosting the CG to its highest position. The passing CG height is the peak of the CG's parabola.

Figure 15.10 Heel strike pose.

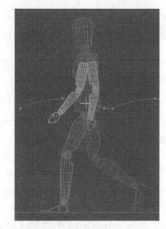

Figure 15.11 Squash pose.

Figure 15.12 Passing pose.

The trailing leg is bent at nearly its sharpest angle, raising the foot high enough that the toes clear the ground as the leg rotates forward.

Simply copying these basic poses onto a series of keyframes will not produce a natural-looking walk. The results will be stiff, artificial, and lifeless. Look at the [6EXAMPL1]15WALK01.AVI animation file, located in the Chapter 15 directory on this book's CD-ROM. This animation has only six keyframes, one for each of the basic poses for left and right sides. This is obviously not enough detail for either a realistic or caricatured motion.

Compare [6EXAMPL1]15WALK01.AVI to the [6EXAMPL2]15WALK02.AVI animation, which has more keyframes but is still derived from the basic three poses. To produce these results, you need to set the timing and spline controls for each object in the character's hierarchy, using anticipation, ease-in, snap, ease-out, and follow-through.

The following projects lead to the goal of a natural-looking humanoid walk cycle, as shown in the [6EXAMPL2]15WALK02.AVI animation. Along the way, you'll learn how to apply the concepts introduced in Chapter 14 to a more complex action.

Steppin' Time

The following project is longer than previous ones because all the explanatory notes about walks in general are inserted between the steps. Take your time, think about the notes, and save your work every now and then.

To set each motion's timing appropriately, you need to understand the *dynamics* of a walk, the motions that connect each key pose. Different parts move at different rates, accelerating and decelerating in a complex balancing act that you must learn to mimic.

It's often useful to divide the motions of a character among as many different objects as possible. This enables you to animate the height of the Puppet above the ground by changing the CG's Y position, then animate the figure's travel along the ground by moving to another control, typically the root of the hierarchy. Keeping the two motions separate gives you more control over where you put your keyframes and how you set the parameters for each spline.

For a simple walk, you can determine the position of the CG by the geometry of the legs and hips relative to the ground. Because the character geometry is fixed, it is possible to set the height of the Puppet's CG in advance, with a fair degree of accuracy, for the entire walk cycle.

In the heel strike pose, the legs form an equilateral triangle with the CG at the apex. This height is one keyframe for the Puppet's CG. According to my measurements for the heel strike pose in Figure 15.10, the vertical (Y axis) distance from the sole of the Puppet's foot to its CG is 0.867, and the stride length is approximately 0.75. Therefore, the distance traveled in a full two-step walk cycle is 1.5. Different setups or software or a deeper or shallower pose would give different numbers, but let's stick with the example for now. Measurement of the other poses gives 0.954 for the CG height at passing and 0.913 at squash.

Animating A Basic Walk

1. Open the default Puppet scene file you set up in Chapter 11.

2. Select the Puppet's root. Set the root's X position to 1.5 at frames 0 and 1, and 0.0 at frame 33. Set the spline controls to Linear at frame 33.

These keyframes will make the Puppet's root travel 1.5 units over the 33 frames of the walk cycle. This is a very mechanical approximation of the motion for the finished walk, with no anticipation, ease, or follow-through. You'll refine it later.

It is generally not an effective approach to try to pose the entire character in precise relation to the ground, if you don't have foot constraints set up as in Chapter 12. With an unconstrained hierarchy, every little tweak, from the CG on down, changes the position of the feet relative to the ground. You'll find it much more productive to tweak the character's CG position at the end, after you have finalized all the other adjustments.

The three basic key poses for this walk cycle are each mirrored—used on both the right and left sides of the character—once, for a total of six key poses. The spacing for these poses is: Heel Strike Left, frame 1; Squash Left, frame 6; Passing Left, frame 11; Heel Strike Right, frame 17; Squash Right, frame 22; Passing Right, frame 27. Heel Strike Left, from frame 1, is duplicated in frame 33 to produce an accurate hookup.

Later in this chapter, we'll explore how you can vary the spacing of the key poses to change the character of the walk. The spacing used in this project produces an ordinary brisk walk when played back at 30 fps.

3. Select the Puppet's CG. Set its Y position to 0.867 in frames 0, 1, 17, and 33, the heel strike keyframes. Set it to 0.913 in the squash frames, 6 and 22. Set it to 0.954 in the passing frames, 11 and 27. You should end up with a spline like the spline shown in Figure 15.13.

You may have to adjust the tension, especially at the peaks and valleys. I set the tension to 1.0 in frames 11 and 27, and -1.0 in frame 17. The scene should now resemble Figure 15.14. The white line represents the motion of the Puppet.

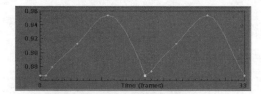

Figure 15.13   Y-Position spline.

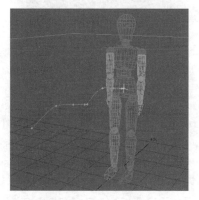

Figure 15.14   Puppet with keyframes set for Puppet's CG and root.

4. Save the scene with a new file name. Render and play back the animation.

   Look at the motion of the hips, chest, and head. Does the bouncing action seem appropriate for a walking character?

   It's a little distracting to have the figure's arms and legs dragging along before they are posed. Let's limit the view to just the parts you're actually working on.

5. Hide the entire Puppet hierarchy, then manually reselect the CG and root and the hips, chest, and head. You should end up with something like Figure 15.15.

6. Render and play back the animation. You should get something like Figure 15.16.

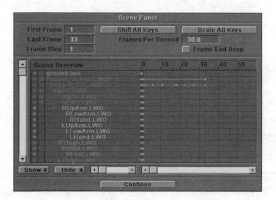

Figure 15.15   Scene panel after hiding the lower levels of the animation hierarchy.

Figure 15.16 Frame 1 after hiding the lower levels of the animation hierarchy.

It's a lot easier to evaluate an action when just the pertinent parts are visible, isn't it? Keep this in mind, and hide or show objects as you need them.

You should animate each level of the hierarchy so it reads perfectly before you begin to animate the next lower level. If you don't remember this rule, you will waste a lot of time revising poses you shouldn't have been animating in the first place.

The second level in the animation hierarchy includes the hips and chest. Before you go any further, save the scene under a new name. You should develop the habit of saving the scene file every time you make significant changes to a motion.

The hips are the driving force behind walks and runs. Just try walking without using your hips, sometime. If you manage to stay on your feet, you'll look like an arthritic penguin. Be sure to send the tape to *America's Funniest Home Videos*.

The hips rotate around the CG. At the heel strike poses, the hips rotate on the axis of the Puppet's spine, effectively giving a little more length to the stride by pushing the leading leg forward and the trailing leg backward. At the passing poses, the hips bank to raise the trailing leg slightly, giving it more ground clearance as it swings forward. The hips can also rotate on the pitch axis to give a forward lean to the character, especially when it is moving quickly.

All these movements should be kept as subtle as possible. Each of these rotations acts from the center of the character and can, therefore, have a disproportionate effect on the extremities. A single degree of pitch in the hips, for example, can move the feet several centimeters.

7. Select the hips. Make keyframes at frames 6, 11, 17, 22, 27, and 33. Set the hips to bank at the passing poses, 3 degrees at frame 11 and -3 degrees at frame 27. Set the other frames to bank 0, and set Spline Controls to Linear for frames 22 and 6 to keep the bank flat for the other poses. You should get a spline like the one shown in Figure 15.17.

The Linear settings are needed to flatten out the spline between frames 1 through 6 and 17 through 22, because that's where the feet are on the ground. The hip action is a smooth slalom during the passing pose, then—Boom!—the heel strike literally stops it flat.

Figure 15.17   Hips bank spline, showing maximum and minimum values for passing poses.

8. Set the hips' heading to help lengthen the stride by rotating 10 degrees at the left heel strike frames 0, 1, and 33, and -10 degrees at right heel strike frame 17. Drag the intervening keyframes to make a smooth slalom, as in Figure 15.18.

9. Set the hips' pitch to 5 degrees for each keyframe. This tilts the figure forward, to lean into the walk. A slower walk could use a smaller angle, while a faster walk needs a larger one.

10. Render and play back the animation.

How does the hip action look? Does it seem natural? Try a different view.

You can try changing the peak bank values a degree or two in either direction. More bank tends to produce a more feminine walk, while less bank makes it more robotic. Reducing the heading values makes the character walk like a windup toy, while increasing them stretches the stride as if in preparation for a run.

Hip action can be the toughest part of animating a character. It is usually very subtle, and attempts to analyze it from life seem prone to trigger all sorts of bizarre reactions from informal test subjects. Be discreet. (If you can't be discreet, have a good excuse handy.) Whenever possible, study your own actions, then try to find confirmation of your conclusions in film or video motion studies. Good hip action can be a matter of a fraction of a degree, so still photos or video sequences that you can rerun and study in detail are extremely valuable tools.

Once the hips are animated to your satisfaction, the chest is relatively easy. You can animate the chest by using the hips settings as a guide to setting up a *dynamic balance*.

During a walk, the upper and lower parts of the body are in dynamic balance—the combination of mass, inertia, and energy in the lower body is equaled by the mass, inertia, and energy in the upper body—so the body as a whole is in balance. This is different from static balance, in which opposing parts are in balance at rest. Dynamic

Figure 15.18   Hips heading spline, showing maximum and minimum values for heel strike poses.

balance means the parts are constantly changing and reacting to change to actively maintain the balance.

For this project, dynamic balance means that for every clockwise heading rotation of the hips, the chest heading must rotate counterclockwise. It's pretty simple, really. You need to keep in mind that the chest rotations are measured from the hips, the chest's parent, so you need to double the angle in reverse to get the same effect. That is, if the hips are at heading 10 degrees, and you set the chest to heading -10 degrees, the chest will just be facing straight ahead again. Set the chest heading to -20, and the chest will rotate as far to one side as the hips do to the other.

11. Select the chest object. Set each heading keyframe to twice the negative value of each corresponding hips heading keyframe. You should end up with a spline like the one shown in Figure 15.19.

12. Set each chest bank keyframe to the exact negative value of each corresponding hips' bank keyframe. This keeps the shoulders level. Keep the pitch keyframes set to 0. You should end up with a spline like the one shown in Figure 15.20.

13. Render and play back the animation.

Do the hips and chest rotate properly? Does the motion seem natural? Does the action look alive, or is it mechanical and dead? Are the upper and lower body in dynamic balance? If the animation is working, you should be able to visualize arms and legs following the motions of the hips and shoulders.

Save the scene file again, if you haven't already. You've completed level two of the animation hierarchy for the Puppet. The next level includes the head, upper arms, and thighs.

The head is already visible, so let's start there. The head is a hierarchical dead end, because it isn't a parent to any other objects and it doesn't have to align or make contact with any other parts of the scene. For a simple walk, all the head has to do is

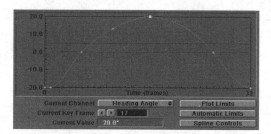

Figure 15.19   Chest heading spline.

Figure 15.20   Chest bank spline.

look straight ahead until animated to do otherwise. Note that if you set up the Puppet with constraints as detailed in Chapter 12, this would be handled automatically.

14. Select the head object. Set each heading keyframe for the head to the exact negative value of each corresponding chest heading keyframe. This keeps the head pointing in the direction of the Puppet's travel. You can set the head's pitch keyframes to the negative of the hips' pitch, if you want the Puppet to walk with its head up. You can leave the head's bank keyframes set to 0. You should end up with a spline like the one shown in Figure 15.21.

15. Render and play back the animation. Does the head remain looking forward, counterbalancing the motions of the chest and hips?

After this point, the X-position animation of the root is more trouble than it's worth. You will find it easier to compare poses and analyze motion if the Puppet remains centered in all the views. To do this, you will need to change the root's keyframes to a constant value.

16. Select the root. Change its X position to 0.0 at keyframes 0, 1, and 33.

Whenever you render and play back the animation, the Puppet will now appear to be walking in place. Later, we'll restore and fine-tune the root's spline.

Now for the fun part! Animating the thighs is nearly as hard as animating the hips, although it usually requires less judgment. Most of the thigh animation is dictated by the hips, another fraction is guided by the three key poses, and the rest depends on you to add anticipation, ease, snap, and follow-through.

17. Make the right thigh and left thigh visible again.

18. Set the heading and bank rotations of right thigh and left thigh to counter the heading and bank angles of the hips in each keyframe.

You don't need to set the Linear option for any bank keyframes as you did for the hips, because the thighs' motion should have more ease. You should get heading splines like those shown in Figure 15.22, and bank splines like the splines shown in Figure 15.23.

This just gets you back to zero with the thighs. Entering inverse angles like this is probably the most noncreative part of character animation, but it beats mousing everything around by hand and eyeballing poses that would probably become glaring errors in the finished animation. When you can get away with animating "by the numbers," it's smart to take advantage of it.

Figure 15.21 Heading spline for Puppet's head.

Figure 15.22 Heading spline for right thigh and left thigh.

Figure 15.23 Bank spline for right thigh and left thigh.

The thighs must be heading in the direction of travel, or the character will appear to waddle. The combined bank angle of hips and thighs should be near 0, or the character may appear knock-kneed, bowlegged, or listing to one side. This would be good for caricature (again, see later portions of this chapter), but it's not so good for a normal, plain-vanilla walk.

19. Render and play back the animation. Do the thighs head and bank properly? If not, go back and compare the splines. Did you forget something?

    The next step in posing right thigh and left thigh is to set the pitch angles for the heel strike, squash, and passing poses. The poses are repeated exactly on the left and right sides, so you only have to create one side's poses and copy those settings to the other side's corresponding keyframes.

20. Adjust the right thigh's pitch in keyframe 17 to match the leading thigh's angle in Figure 15.10, the heel strike pose. I used an angle of about -26.5 degrees, but your results may vary. Set left thigh to the negative of right thigh's pitch. Both thighs should have the same amount of pitch in the heel strike poses. When you are satisfied with your results, copy the pitch values to the opposite thigh in keyframes 0, 1, and 33.

21. Adjust the right thigh's pitch in keyframe 11 to match the lifted thigh's angle in Figure 15.12, the passing pose. I used an angle of about -39 degrees. When you are satisfied with your results, copy the pitch value to keyframe 27 for the left thigh. The opposite thighs in both keyframes 11 and 27 are easy ones—set their pitch to 0.

22. Adjust right thigh's pitch in keyframe 6 to match the leading thigh's angle shown in Figure 15.11, the squash pose. I used an angle of about 9.5 degrees. Adjust left thigh's pitch in keyframe 6 to match the trailing thigh's angle shown in Figure 15.11. I used -24.8 degrees. When you are satisfied with your results, copy the pitch values to the opposite thighs in keyframe 22.

You should end up with pitch splines like those shown in Figures 15.24 and 15.25.

Note the shape of the right thigh spline. Frame 1 shows the thigh trailing as the opposite heel strikes. The right thigh eases-in to frame 6, where it reaches maximum velocity. It passes through frame 11 as it begins to ease-out, then follows through to the heel strike pose at frame 17. The sharper curves between frames 1-6 and 11-17, and the relatively straighter segment between frames 6-11, give the action a fair amount of snap. This gives the impression of a quick, energetic movement. The heavy muscles of the upper leg are only moving themselves and don't have to support the body's weight or accelerate its larger mass.

Figure 15.24   Pitch spline for left thigh.

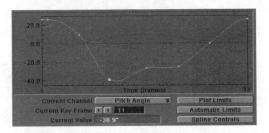

Figure 15.25   Pitch spline for right thigh.

The spline for the rest of the cycle is the other side of the story. The thigh is now the prime mover for accelerating the whole body. It's hard work to move all that mass, so the thigh rotates in a smooth, efficient acceleration curve, close to a 45 degree angle, between frames 22 and 33.

The timing and control of each thigh pitch keyframe can make the difference between a stroll, strut, march, and many other types of walk.

You could also change the walk dramatically by leaving each key value right where it is but edit the tension, bias, and continuity of each keyframe to smooth out these curves. This approach would give you the typically over-interpolated, mushy, boring action that just screams, "The computer animated this!"

23. Render and play back the animation. Do the thighs pitch properly? Do they ease-in and ease-out at acceptable rates? Is there enough snap in the motion?

    When you are satisfied with the motion of the thighs, it's time to move on to the last parts of the animation hierarchy's fourth level, the upper arms. Save the scene again before proceeding with the next step.

24. Make the right upper arm and left upper arm visible.

25. Set the heading rotations of the right upper arm and left upper arm to counter the heading angles of the chest in each keyframe.

    You should get heading splines like those shown in Figure 15.26.

    This rotates the upper arms' headings back to zero, relative to the overall position of the Puppet. The upper arms should usually be heading in the direction of travel, but when you are animating an energetic walk, you may want them to head slightly inwards for balance.

Figure 15.26   Heading splines for the right upper arm and left upper arm.

26. Render and play back the animation. Do the upper arms have appropriate headings?

27. Pitch the right upper arm and left upper arm according to the three key poses in Figures 15.27, 15.28, and 15.29.

    How would you set the ease-in, snap, ease-out, and follow-through of the upper arms? These limbs do not have to carry any weight other than their own, and they are much more like ideal pendulums swinging to counterweight the legs.

    If you reasoned that the right upper arm and the left upper arm should move in near-perfect slaloms, you should have come up with splines like those shown in Figures 15.27 and 15.28.

    At this point, you have a torso with one level of stump for each limb, the head included.

28. Render and play back the animation.

    Look very closely at this animation. Render more animations, from each principal view and whatever perspective angles and zoom factors you find useful. You want to make absolutely sure that the action so far is to your liking. Changing your mind later is a good way to waste time and effort, not to mention your patience.

    When you are satisfied with the action, save the scene again, and proceed to the fifth animation hierarchy level, the shins and lower arms.

29. Make the lower arms visible.

    The lower arm joint—the elbow—is a simple hinge, and it generally only rotates in the pitch axis. This level of the animation hierarchy is a piece of cake!

30. Pitch the lower arms according to the three key poses shown in Figures 15.10, 15.11, and 15.12.

    As with the upper arms, you can animate these objects in near-perfect slaloms, to result in splines like those shown in Figures 15.29 and 15.30.

31. Render and play back the animation.

    How does the full arm motion look? You have plenty of leeway with the timing of the arm swings. You can tweak the spline control tools a lot, as long as the arm positions match the three key poses.

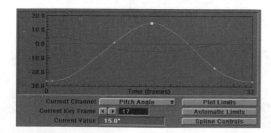

Figure 15.27 Pitch spline for RUpArm.

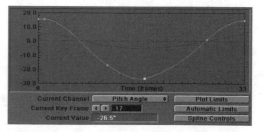

Figure 15.28 Pitch spline for LUpArm.

Figure 15.29 Pitch spline for right lower arm.

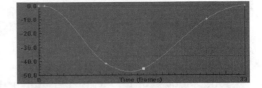

Figure 15.30 Pitch spline for left lower arm.

This is a good place to introduce another phrase borrowed from traditional animation—*successive breaking of joints*. This technique is a little like overlapping action, but it applies specifically to the hierarchy of joints in a character. Basically, when a higher joint starts to rotate, there should be a slight lag before the lower joints start to rotate as part of the same action. In practical terms, this means the rotation of a child object should begin, peak, and end some time after the parent performs the same actions.

There is a very easy way to do this in most 3D software. Simply pose the *successive joint*, the next child down the hierarchy, on the exact keyframes as its parent object. When you have completely animated the action, use the shift function of your software's keyframe editing tools to delay the child's rotation a frame or two behind the parent's. The rotations of each joint will break in succession, down through the animation hierarchy.

32. Shift all the keyframes for the right lower arm and left lower arm back (toward frame 33) by one frame. Render and play back the animation again.

    What difference did the successive breaking of joints make? Try shifting the lower arm keyframes back another frame or two. Increase and decrease the shift until you get a feel for timing this technique.

    When you have a timing you like, save the scene again, and proceed to pose the shins.

33. Make the shins visible.

    The shin joint—the knee—normally moves as a simple hinge and can only rotate in the pitch axis. This action is relatively easy to animate, but you have to pay extra attention to the timing of the heel strike-to-squash transition. This is supposed to be a reaction to the mass of the Puppet striking the ground, and the shin and thigh squash to cushion the impact. The squash should be a little faster than the rebound.

34. Pitch the right and left shins according to the three key poses shown in Figures 15.10, 15.11, and 15.12.

    You should end up with splines like those shown in Figures 15.31 and 15.32.

Figure 15.31 Pitch spline for right shin.

Figure 15.32 Pitch spline for left shin.

35. Render and play back the animation.

    How does the full arm motion look? Is there enough snap to the forward motion, leading into the heel strike?

    You must hold the straight leg of the heel strike (the shin's zero-degree pitch angle) long enough for it to register visually with the audience, or the adjoining poses (pre-heel strike and squash) will blur together and the step will appear mushy. It's a good idea to keep the leg straight for at least two or three frames.

    This is one of the critical parts of a walk—a mushy heel strike looks tired or lazy, while a very sharp snap can define a march or strut. The depth and snap of the squash also say a lot about the amount of muscle tone and tension in the leg, and the character as a whole.

    When you are satisfied with the action, save the scene again, and proceed to the sixth and last animation hierarchy level—the hands and feet.

36. Make the hands visible.

    The wrist is a *universal joint* and can rotate in both pitch and heading. For this project, you only need to use the pitch axis.

37. Pitch the right and left hands according to the three key poses shown in Figures 15.10, 15.11, and 15.12.

    As with the upper and lower arms, there are no critical alignments to the ground or other objects. Because this is the end of the hierarchy, there are no dependent actions to plan for, either. You can animate these objects in near-perfect slaloms with very few keyframes, and use successive breaking of joints, just as you did for the lower arms.

38. Shift the hand rotation keyframes down a frame or two, for successive breaking of joints.

39. Render and play back the animation.

    How does the timing look? Try shifting the keyframes back and forth a few frames, and compare the effect of each shift on the overall action. This is a relatively loose and free-swinging action, so you do not need to add much snap to the hands' extremes.

    You should end up with splines like those shown in Figures 15.33 and 15.34.

40. When you are satisfied with the hand rotations, save the scene file again.

    You're almost done! Just the feet are left to pose, then you can make the final tweaks to polish off the action.

Figure 15.33 Pitch spline for right hand.

Figure 15.34 Pitch spline for left hand.

41. Make the feet visible.

    The ankle is also a universal joint and can rotate in both pitch and bank axes, but for this project you only need to use the pitch axis.

42. Pitch the right and left feet according to the ground and the three key poses in Figures 15.10, 15.11, and 15.12.

    For keyframes where the foot is on the ground, it's more important to match the foot to the angle of the ground than to the precise angle of the pictured poses.

    Flatten the foot to the ground immediately after the heel strike pose, so the joint appears flexible and lifelike. If the foot is held at an angle to the ground after the heel strike, the ankle joint appears stiff and unnatural. Just try walking that way once, you'll feel what I mean. The muscles that run up the front of your shin act as shock absorbers when you run or walk. Holding a bent ankle after a heel strike will quickly exhaust them, and the lack of shock absorption will pass a lot more heel-strike shock to the rest of your body.

43. Render and play back the animation.

    How does the timing look? Do you get a sense of the mass of the Puppet and the springiness of the leg muscles? You may want to go back and tweak the entire thighs, shins, and feet hierarchy to get better leg motion.

    If you haven't set up constraints, you'll probably have to add a number of keyframes to keep the feet level to the ground. Whenever the feet are lifted free of the ground, you can use fewer keyframes and create smoother slaloms, but matching feet to the ground tends to produce splines like those shown in Figures 15.35 and 15.36.

44. When you are satisfied with the Foot rotations, save the scene file again.

    You've just finished the overall motion for the Puppet hierarchy. Congratulations!

No Skating Allowed

Now, it's time to go back and tweak the position of the roots of the hierarchy, to keep the Puppet lined up properly with its environment. If you set up constraints as described in Chapter 12, the following steps are unnecessary.

One of the major problems with unconstrained CGI character animation is keeping the feet aligned with fixed points on the ground. If this is not done precisely, the figure can appear to *skate* (slip the foot forward) or *moonwalk* (slip the foot backward), while the character moves as if walking normally. Even the best animators occasionally make a mistake on foot slippage.

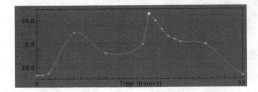 

Figure 15.35 Pitch spline for right foot.   **Figure 15.36** Pitch spline for left foot.

There is even one example in *Toy Story*, where Bo Peep is walking away from Woody and her foot slides a bit. Nobody's perfect.

In software that does not support constraints (such as standalone LightWave 3D), your best defense against foot slippage is a lot of keyframes. The combined hips-thighs-shins-feet hierarchy produces an undulating Y-position sequence that is difficult to match with a simple spline. This complex movement for the Puppet CG's Y axis is loaded on top of the root's Z and X axes, which makes it even harder to match the root's motions to a simple spline. The brute-force solution is a lot of keyframes. The following procedure is written for LightWave, but you can also apply it to most 3D animation software.

45. Go to frame 0. Select the right foot. Turn on the Center option, and use the Front view. Change the Zoom Factor to 20 or so, and turn off the Center option. Select the Puppet's CG. Your view should look like Figure 15.37.

46. Modify the Y position of Puppet's CG only. Leave the X and Z Move buttons turned off. Drag the null up or down until the sole of the right foot is level with the ground. When you have an exact alignment, save the keyframe.

47. Repeat Step 46 for all the existing keyframes where RFoot is on the ground.

48. Step through each frame, starting at frame 0. Locate the biggest discrepancies, and try using Spline Tools on the nearest keyframes to smooth out the problems.

49. For large alignment problems that you can't fix with Spline Controls, add a new keyframe in the middle of the problem area, as close to halfway between adjoining keyframes as you can get. Adjust the new keyframe to fix the problem.

50. For any frames where there is still noticeable bouncing, try turning on the Linear option between closely spaced keyframes.

51. As a last resort, keep adding keyframes as necessary, up to every frame being a key.

52. Turn the Center option back on, and select the left foot. Go to the first frame (probably frame 3) where the left foot is planted. Turn off the Center option, and select Puppet's CG.

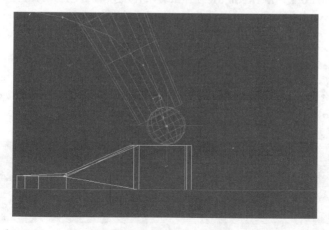

Figure 15.37   Zoomed-in Front view for tweaking Foot/Ground match.

53. Repeat Steps 46 through 51 for the right foot.

    Tweak, tweak, tweak. Gee, this is fun. (Not!)

54. When you are satisfied with the Y-position motion, save the scene. You should end up with a motion similar to the motion shown in Figure 15.38, but you may have more or fewer keyframes.

    You should now have a Puppet that only walks on the top of the ground, not bouncing over or wading through it. But, it still skates and moonwalks a bit. On to the root, in this case, Puppet_Ground_Null.

    When you tweak the Puppet_Ground_Null, you move it in both the X and Z axes. To make it easier to judge the alignment, you can position another null object at a consistent point for both Front and Side views, and flip back and forth between them.

55. Go to frame 0. Select RFoot. Turn on the Center option, and use the Front or Side view. Change the Zoom Factor to 20 or so, and turn off the Center option. Add another null object, or use the Measuring_Null. Position the null, in both Front and Side views, in the center of the ankle sphere. Make a keyframe for the null.

    Technically, you could also use the Top view, but it's pretty cluttered for most of the frames, and you'd have to hide the rest of the Puppet hierarchy.

56. Go to frame 3, and use the same procedure to reposition the null in the center of the LFoot ankle sphere, in both Front and Side views. Make a keyframe for the null.

57. Repeat Step 56 for each frame where the ground foot changes and for the frame before it. My keyframes are 1, 2, 3, 17, 18, and 33, as shown in Figure 15.39. Yours may be slightly different. Turn on the Linear option for each keyframe, to make the null snap directly to the next position without any interpolated movement.

    Your next step is to drag the Puppet_Ground_Null around to align the Measuring_Null with the center of the ankle sphere in each frame. This is just like Steps 46 through 54, but this time the positioning is in two axes.

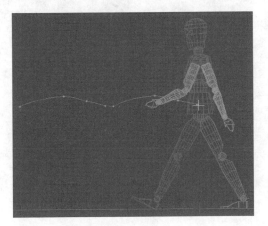

Figure 15.38 Tweaked motion for Puppet's CG object.

Figure 15.39 X Position spline for Measuring_Null, tracking the ankle joint.

58. For each keyframe, drag the Puppet_Ground_Null around in the X and Z axes to align the Measuring_Null with the center of the grounded foot's ankle sphere, as shown in Figure 15.40.

59. Use the procedures in Steps 46 through 54, to refine the Puppet_Ground_Null's movement to eliminate the Puppet's skating and moonwalking.

    You can try adjusting both the X and Z values at the same time, flipping between Front and Top or Side views, or do all the Xs and then all the Zs—whatever you prefer will work.

    You're trying to define a slalom to match the combined effects of all the joint rotations back through shin, thigh, and hip, in pitch, bank, and heading axes. Don't feel discouraged if you need to keyframe every frame for most of the action, it's just the nature of the beast.

    You may end up with splines like those shown in Figures 15.41 and 15.42.

60. Render and play back the animation.

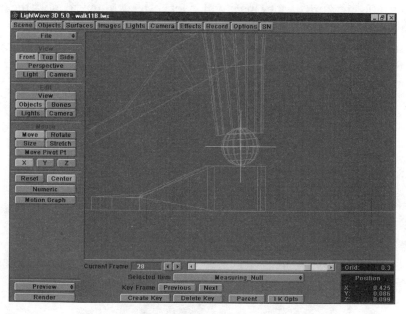

Figure 15.40 Measuring_Null aligned with ankle sphere.

Figure 15.41   X-position spline for Puppet_Ground_Null.

Figure 15.42   Z-position spline for Puppet_Ground_Null.

Critique the finished walk. You shouldn't have to make major changes at this point. If you have to go back and tweak anything you don't like, start with the root of the problem and follow the corrections down through the animation hierarchy. You'll most likely have to revise at least the keyframes for every object lower in the hierarchy and certainly for the Puppet_Ground_Null and Puppet's CG.

Now, you need to tweak the hookup frame. You'll have noticed that frame 1 and 33 are identical at this point. If you rendered an animation from 1 through 33 and looped it, the animation would stutter at the 1-33 hookup, because the same pose would appear for two successive frames. What you need to do now is delete either frame 1 or frame 33 for a seamless hookup. Deleting frame 1 is probably a bad idea, as you don't know what LightWave 3D's automatic interpolation between frame 0 and frame 2 will look like. It's easier to delete frame 33.

61. Go to frame 32. Select the Puppet's root. Click on Create Key. In the Create Motion Key panel, click on Selected Item And Descendants. Click on OK.

    Most of the objects in the Puppet had interpolated values for frame 32. This step makes those interpolated values into keyframes, which means their values will not change when you delete frame 33 in the next step.

62. Go to frame 33. Click on Delete Key. In the Delete Motion Key panel, click on Selected Item And Descendants. Click on OK.

63. Open the Scene panel. Change the Last Frame to 32. Click on Continue.

    The animation now runs from frame 1 through frame 32, and the hookup should play back without a stutter.

64. Render and play back the animation.

    This should be the finished walk cycle. How does it look?

    When you are satisfied with the walk cycle, save the scene file again. Save the splines for the Puppet's CG and Puppet_Ground_Null, too. You'll be deleting them for the next project, and you may want to be able to reload them for reference.

65. Select Puppet's CG. Open the Motion Graph panel, and click on Save Motion. Save the motion file with a name like WALKY01.MOT, so you can figure out what it means later. Close the Motion Graph panel. Repeat for the Puppet_Ground_Null's motion.

Looping The Loop

The last step in building a motion cycle is making it cyclical. Most 3D software has a set of options in the spline controls that govern the end behavior of motions. You can set a motion to stop and hold at the last value of the spline, reset to the first value, or repeat the entire spline endlessly for the entire scene. In this case, you want each part of the Puppet to repeat its actions.

66. Set each spline's end behavior to repeat. Save the scene again.

    With every object in the Puppet hierarchy set to repeat, the Puppet will continue to execute the walk cycle for an animation of any length. Try it!

67. Render and play back an animation of frames 1 through 64.

    You'll note that the lateral and vertical motions of the Puppet did not repeat. The rotations of the various objects were designed to be looped, but the XYZ motions of the nulls were designed for just one linear motion. If you want to use them as well, try the cut/copy/paste functions in your software's spline tools to assemble longer, repeating versions of these motions.

You can use this scene as a stock action scene. Document it, and file it away. Whenever you need a walk cycle, reload and edit it to suit.

It's good animation practice and a basic test of a new character to create and save a variety of walk cycles for every character you build.

This is a long project, but I hope you got a lot out of it.

Some Important Extras

If you're going to make a character walk, you'd better know how to make it start and stop, too. Unless, of course, you have an idea for an animated film that's nothing but walking. (Never mind, it's been done: Ryan Larkin's *Walking*, the definitive work on the subject.)

Starting a walk means accelerating all the Puppet's parts from a standstill to full walking speed. To start the forward movement, you must anticipate by leaning the Puppet back, then forward into the first fall, and bring the leading leg forward as if from a passing pose. Accelerate the body forward into the first step by rotating the trailing arm forcefully to the rear, and continue into a normal heel strike position. You can proceed from there with a normal walk cycle.

 ## Starting Out

1. Load your best walk cycle.

2. Add 20 frames onto the beginning of the cycle, to give you time to move the Puppet from standing still into the walk.

    Because you shifted the original starting frame, you need to create a new start at frame 1.

3. Copy a key for all items from frame 0 to frame 1.

Figure 15.43 Puppet in standing pose, before beginning walk.

Figure 15.44 Puppet in anticipation pose, just beginning walk.

4. Go to frame 1. Set up the default standing pose for the Puppet at frame 1, as shown in Figure 15.43.

5. Duplicate the Puppet keyframes from frame 1 through frame 14. Go to frame 14, and pose the Puppet as shown in Figure 15.44.

   Duplicating the nearest pose can save you effort in posing, as some of the objects' rotations will stay the same from one keyframe to the next.

   Frame 14 is the anticipation key pose that precedes the fall into the walk. The hips tilt back, shifting the Puppet's balance and enabling the leading leg to come up and slightly forward. The opposite arm also comes forward, preparing for the forward shift in balance of the next key pose. The same-side arm comes forward slightly less, preparing for an energetic backward swing.

6. Duplicate the Puppet keyframes from frame 14 through frame 18. Go to frame 18, and pose the Puppet as shown in Figure 15.45.

   Frame 18 is the falling key pose. The hips have come back to level, the leading leg and arm are more fully advanced toward the heel strike pose, and the trailing arm is strongly thrust back to add more forward acceleration.

7. Tweak the splines, and shift the keyframes lower in the hierarchy, to get the appropriate ease-in, snap, and ease-out for the motions leading into the first heel strike.

   The trailing arm is especially important if the start is a rapid one. The backward swing of the arm helps push the upper body forward, accelerating it to a walking pace. You may want to shift the keyframes for the arm, and pay special attention to the ease-in and -out in the spline. One possible solution is shown in Figure 15.46.

   Frame 21 is the heel strike, the transition to a normal walk cycle, which you can leave as is.

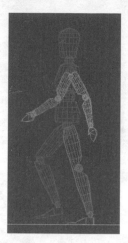

Figure 15.45 Puppet falling forward, leading to first heel strike position.

8. Edit the first squash pose, frame 26, to bend a little deeper. Change the leading foot, shin, and thigh pitch angles. You may have to adjust the trailing leg's shin, just to keep the trailing toes above the ground.

   This cushions the first heel strike impact and provides more visual bounce to the first full stride. A change of gait like this—from standing still to a walk—is visually jarring to your audience—make sure you anticipate, follow through, and generally make the action as easy to read as possible.

   If the timing seems a little off, try shifting the anticipation or falling keyframes. The procedures for tweaking keyframes to eliminate foot slippage are the same as in earlier projects.

9. Save the finished scene under a new name. You'll be using it for the next project.

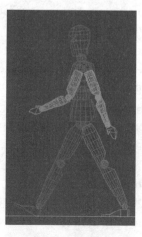

Figure 15.46 The left upper arm spline, showing anticipation and quick acceleration into the first step.

Somebody Stop Me!

PROJECT 15.3

Stopping a walk means decelerating all the Puppet's parts from full walking speed to a standstill. Stopping forward motion requires you to make the squash position deeper, using the thigh and shin as a spring to absorb most of the Puppet's forward inertia.

Because the Puppet is not continuing into another step, you should bring the trailing leg only up to level with the leading leg, not past it. You should also reduce the forward rotation of both arms and exaggerate their backward rotations.

Keep the upper body leaning backwards against the Puppet's forward inertia until the character is nearly at a full stop. Then, pitch it forward slightly in follow-through.

If the walk is an especially vigorous one or the stop very sudden, you might pose the Puppet to rise up its on toes before settling back into the *hold*, the standing pose. Keep the Puppet's CG behind its toes at all times, to maintain the appearance of balance.

1. Reload the scene file you saved at the end of the preceding project. Go to frame 26.

   This is the squash pose for the leading left leg, which is close enough to the stopping squash pose that using a duplicate can save some posing.

2. Copy a keyframe for all items from frame 26 through frame 57.

   This adds a squash pose following the heel strike pose at frame 52.

3. Copy a keyframe for all items from frame 1 (the default standing pose for the Puppet) to frame 67.

   You now have a smooth default interpolation from the heel strike at frame 52 to the standing pose at frame 67, as shown in Figure 15.47. Your next task is to modify that interpolation to make a more realistic stop from a walk cycle.

4. Go to frame 53. Tweak the left foot's pose so it is level with the ground.

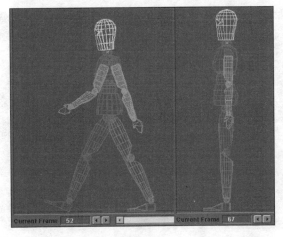

Figure 15.47 Heel strike, frame 52, and standing, frame 67.

The foot still has to flatten to the ground immediately after the heel strike, but, if you simply duplicated frame 27, it would introduce a lot of other keyframes that you don't need.

5. Go to frame 56. Pitch the hips back about 5 degrees, shifting the mass of the upper body backwards to help the Puppet slow down. The hips don't need another keyframe until frame 67, although you should tweak the spline a bit to get a smooth deceleration. Pitch the right thigh so it continues to swing forward and the right shin so the right foot clears the ground, as shown in Figure 15.48.

6. Go to frame 57. Pose the left shinbone so it reaches its maximum pitch, about 32 degrees. This makes the squash pose deeper to absorb some of the Puppet's forward inertia, slowing it down (see Figure 15.49). From about -25 degrees at this frame, the left femur should rotate almost linearly to 0 degrees at keyframe 65.

7. Go to frame 60. The right femur should already nearly match the left, but you need to create a pitch keyframe for the right shinbone, so the right foot still clears the ground. Pitch both arms so they are nearly aligned. They should be moving backwards, as in Figure 15.49, to counterbalance the rise of the hips and upper body from the squash position of frame 57.

8. Go to frame 63. Create a pitch keyframe for the right shinbone so the right foot clears the ground. This is the peak pitch for the right shinbone. After this frame, you will be lowering the foot to flat contact with the ground.

9. Go to frame 65. Create pitch keyframes for the right femur, the right shinbone, and the right foot so the right foot is parallel to the ground and moving down towards flat contact with the ground.

10. Create follow-through, and hold keyframes between frame 67 and 75, to soften the rigid "attention" pose of the Puppet.

11. Save the scene file under a new name. Render and play back the animation.

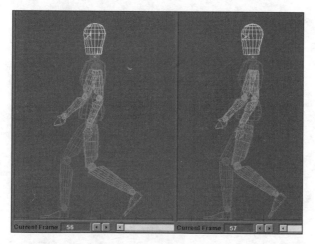

Figure 15.48 Frames 56 and 57 Puppet poses.

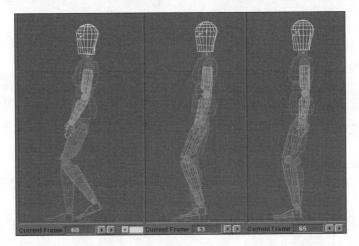

Figure 15.49   Frames 60, 63, and 65 Puppet poses.

You will probably note some uneven decelerations between keyframes. Select each item in turn, and take a look at its spline for pitch rotation. Use the spline controls to smooth out the graphs, but make sure you leave a little snap (a short, sharp curve, near the last frames). It'll make the Puppet snap to attention. Snapping the character into a key pose generally makes the action look better.

If the timing seems a little off, try shifting the follow-through or deceleration keyframes for different objects, keeping in mind the guidelines for overlapping action and successive breaking of joints. The procedures for tweaking to eliminate foot slippage are the same as in the first walk cycle projects.

When you're done tweaking, you should have an animation something like EXER0604.AVI, which you can find in the Chapter 15 directory on this book's CD-ROM.

By working through this section, you've mastered the basic principles of hierarchical animation, dynamic motion, motion cycle construction, and starting and stopping an action. Now, you're ready to apply the principles you used for walk cycles to animating run cycles and multilegged animal gaits.

Run For It

The two major differences between walks and runs are foot contact with the ground and strength of poses. Walkers, by definition, always have at least one foot on the ground. Runners may have both feet off the ground for the majority of the run cycle. This midair time, and the actions required to produce it, are the key poses of run cycles. Run poses are also much stronger visually than walk poses. Both cycles show the same actions, but almost every joint rotation is more extreme in a run.

The run cycle starts off just like the walk—with a fall forward. Instead of simply rotating one leg forward to stop the fall, a running character must also thrust upwards by flexing the trailing leg and foot, as in Figure 15.50. Note the bends in the trailing leg and foot, which straighten

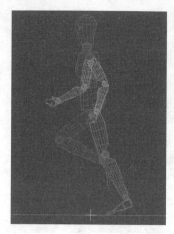

Figure 15.50 Thrust pose of a run cycle.

to propel the runner forward faster than a simple fall. This is the *thrust*, or push-off, pose of the run cycle.

Instead of falling back to a more upright posture after the cycle is started, a running character must maintain a forward lean during the entire run cycle. A faster run requires the character to lean forward farther, pushing the upper body ahead of the center of gravity (CG). This continuous "fall" helps convert the thrust of the driving leg from vertical to horizontal movement. It's also the reason running is more hazardous than walking—if runners stop suddenly, they have to quickly get their feet under their CG, or they fall down. A walker is stable at every heel strike position. There are no stable poses in a run cycle.

The result of the thrust pose is the midair pose, as shown in Figure 15.51. Both feet are well off the ground, and the character is ballistic. From the time the trailing foot leaves the ground until the leading foot makes contact, the running character is following a parabola.

The height and width of the parabola can say a lot about the character. A short, broad parabola is the mark of a serious runner or sprinter, who converts most of their energy into forward motion. A high, narrow parabola shows the character is very springy, spending more energy on moving up than moving forward.

You can exaggerate this to create a very lively, bouncy character (see the following chapter for details). The up-and-down motion of the walk cycle is limited by the arc of the character's pivoting legs. The only limit for a run cycle's vertical motion is the amount of energy you allocate your character. Just make sure that any extra energy you animate into a thrust pose is balanced by an extra-deep squash on the other end of the parabola. What goes up, must come down.

The midair pose makes your job of animating a running character a little harder, as you can't rely on foot placement to keep the character properly positioned in the scene. For the midair part of the run cycle, you'll have to figure the trajectory of the character just as you did for the falling objects in Chapter 14. The pose itself is a simple extrapolation from the preceding thrust pose to the following squash pose. The trailing leg recoils from the full extension of the thrust

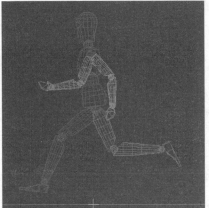

Figure 15.51 Midair pose of a run cycle.

Figure 15.52 Squash pose of a run cycle.

and starts to bend forward again. The leading leg stretches out toward the ground, remaining slightly bent to absorb the anticipated impact.

The third pose is the squash (see Figure 15.52). Because everything happens faster in a run, several of the walk poses are compressed into one run pose. The important elements of the walk cycle's passing position, heel strike, and squash poses all happen at once in the run cycle squash pose. The leading foot makes ground contact and bends to absorb the impact, and the trailing leg folds so the foot clears the ground as it kicks forward to pass the leading leg.

The runner's foot can make contact either heel-first, as in the walk, or on the ball of the foot. The faster the run, the more likely the character is to run on the balls of their feet. If the character heel-strikes, you should put a little extra deceleration in their forward motion. The jar of the heel strike slows a runner down perceptibly. When running characters brake to a stop, they literally dig in their heels. You might try to animate this, based on the stopping and starting projects in the last chapter.

A running character's arms make pretty much the same motions as a walking character's. The difference is a matter of degree. The runner's extremes are a little farther out, and the speed of transition between extremes is faster. A runner does not move faster by throwing their arms out wider. Instead, a runner keeps their arms folded more closely, making them shorter and easier to move, and moves them more rapidly. A short arm can dynamically balance a longer, heavier leg by moving faster. When you animate a runner's arms, use all the snap you can and avoid ease-in and -out like poison, for it will surely kill your character.

Animate A Running Puppet

1. Open the Puppet scene file you set up in Chapter 11.

   This scene file should include the complete Puppet character, parented, lighted, and ready to animate, just as you used it earlier.

2. Follow the same procedures you learned earlier to pose the Puppet to match the key running poses shown in Figures 15.50, 15.51, and 15.52. Repeat the poses for the opposite side, making six keyframes in all.

   This is where you really start developing your judgment. How far apart should you place your key poses? Use pose copying and shifting procedures to move your key poses around. Experiment with different timings, and keep notes on what works best for you.

3. Look at the splines for each object. Look for patterns, especially for patterns that need a little help.

   You should be developing a sense of what a spline should look like for a sharp, snappy motion versus a gradual, smooth one. You should also be developing your judgment of when each type of motion is appropriate.

4. Calculate and set keyframes to define the parabola the Puppet travels during the mid-air part of the run cycle.

   Remember, the Puppet's CG should follow a parabola precisely, no matter what the rest of the character is doing.

5. Starting at the root of the animation hierarchy, tweak the motion of each object to make the run cycle more lifelike. Follow the usual procedure of rendering wireframe or preview animations to check your progress.

   Look very closely at the hip and chest action before you jump to any conclusions. As I pointed out earlier, the hip and chest rotations are among the smallest in the whole character, but they affect everything else and are a real pain to revise. Keep to the animation hierarchy, and most of your mistakes will be small.

   One of the noticeable differences in timing between walks and runs is the kick forward of the trailing leg. In a run, this kick is very fast, with a lot of snap. You might try a straight linear interpolation over two or three frames, just to see how extreme you can get before the Puppet starts moving like he sat on a high-voltage line. On the other hand, the thrust pose is accelerating the entire body weight up and forward, so there's a lot of effort to move a large mass. A more gradual acceleration for the trailing leg's extension, with more ease-in, is appropriate here. The same goes for the squash position. The idea is to absorb the impact gradually, using the leading leg as a spring to ease-in to the flexed pose, then straighten again in an ease-out to the thrust position.

   There are some considerations for the runner's attitude, as well. If the character's head is kept high, looking ahead rather than at his path, the usual perception is that the runner has plenty of energy and is nowhere near his limits. If the runner's head is low, he is more likely to be going all-out or near exhaustion. Then again, maybe he's just watching for loose change on the sidewalk.

6. When you've got a run cycle you are happy with, save the scene under a new name. You'll probably find other uses for it.

   If you're feeling adventurous, you can animate the Puppet through a running jump by exaggerating the leg compression of the thrust pose, stretching out the midair pose (make it follow a larger parabola), and exaggerating the compression of the squash pose at the landing. The same exaggeration principles apply to running hurdles and stairs, too.

Animate Puppet Changing Gaits

In a preceding project you animated the Puppet character to accelerate, walk, and stop. In this project, you'll animate the Puppet to change from a walking gait to a fast run.

1. Load one of the multiple-cycle walks you created in a preceding project.

2. Go to the heel strike position for the second step of the cycle. Modify it to have a deeper bend and forward lean, to match the squash position of the Running project.

3. Continue with the remaining key poses for a fast run, as in the Running project. If you want to animate a fast run, make sure the Puppet runs on its toes, that the heel never makes contact with the ground, and that the hips are pitched at a more extreme angle.

You now have a better understanding of how to create walk and run cycles for bipedal humanoids. The following section tells where you can find information to help you mimic other natural actions, both for humanoids and other creatures.

Seeing Is Believing

A recurring question for character animators is, "How does a [creature to be animated] move?" The answer is sometimes found in a book or journal, often on file footage, recently even on CD-ROM, but always in nature. If you start building and animating a creature without studying it live, if you trust your assumptions and preconceptions, you will most assuredly end up scrapping most of your work. If you don't like wasting time and effort, do a little research before you start pushing pixels. And when you need the real data, go back to the source.

There are two broad categories for the information you need: anatomy and *kinesiology*, the studies of creatures' physical structures and the ways they move. You can get a lot of anatomical information from zoology and comparative anatomy textbooks, which any good library or bookstore should be able to find for you. I keep a few general zoological references around, but, when I'm working on a new creature, I usually head to a library and research it from the most up-to-date sources.

The kinesiology information is a little harder to come by. Most of the research is done on humans or on "economically significant" animals.

- The best sources of information are films and videotapes of animals and humans performing a variety of actions against measurable backgrounds, called *motion studies*.

- Still images of the same subjects are second best, but when collected in books like Eadweard Muybridge's (see Bibliography), they have the advantages of portability and independence from viewing equipment.

- A distant third in usability are the scholarly analyses, derivations, and explanations published in the scientific literature. Most of these studies ignore or omit at least some of the raw data necessary to the animator. Even if someone ran a study on the creature you're working on, there's no guarantee that they gathered or published the data you need.

The ideal study would include (at least) three-axis position data for each joint in a fully articulated skeleton, plus a complete analysis of muscle, fat, and ligament arrangements and their effect on surface appearances. In reality, what you're likely to find are very crude profile views of the creature, with the approximate locations of the major joints marked inconsistently between successive frames.

Until recently, access to most of this information was limited to people who could use film libraries or visit a zoo. The availability of consumer videotape players, and the production of nature videotapes by organizations like the National Geographic Society, have put the study of animal and human motion within reach of any aspiring animator. The development of the computer as a mass-market educational tool has also expanded the motion study resources you can acquire.

> **MOTION STUDY RESOURCES**
>
> **My favorite motion study materials include the classic works by Eadweard Muybridge, a variety of National Geographic videotapes, several Discovery Channel videotapes, the other books on animal motion listed in the Bibliography, and an excellent CD-ROM, "How Animals Move," authored by R. McNeill Alexander and distributed by Maris Multimedia and The Discovery Channel.**

I recommend that you invest in a laser disc player, one with a digital freeze frame. You can use this to repeatedly view motion studies (the Muybridge work is available on laser disc from Voyager), single-framing, and looping segments without damaging either your player or a tape. A DVD player may also be a viable choice in the future, but, as of this writing, there aren't enough pertinent titles available.

If you can't get a laser disc player, a video digitizer board for your computer can be the next best thing. Digitize clips of your favorite animation or nature videotapes, and loop them to play back on your computer. As long as this is for private, educational use, it's within the fair use limits of copyright. Just don't do something ill-advised like posting the clips on the Internet. It's illegal, and it's disrespectful to the people who produced the video in the first place.

If you get into digitizing reference material, sooner or later, you are going to be tempted to try a process called *rotoscoping*. This is easy to do with most 3D software. You just load the clip as an image sequence and assign it as a background layer. Set up a character that matches the one in the background, pose the character to match each frame of the background, and presto, you have a rotoscoped "animation." Only it isn't character animation, and it produces really crummy-looking action. Anybody who's watched a little animation can tell when something's been rotoscoped. Most professional animators hate it.

I mention rotoscoping only as a learning tool. One of the longer learning processes in CGI character animation is the interpretation of splines. An experienced animator can read them like large print, having the experience to know when a spline isn't showing enough snap, ease, or whatever. If you are just starting out in CGI animation, you need all the help you can get for learning to read and analyze splines. If you digitize some of your favorite animated or live-action clips, and rotoscope the Puppet or other characters over them, you can build yourself a set of splines to study and learn from.

If all these sources on motion studies don't help, you can always fall back on real-life simulation. When in doubt, act it out. You will find it easier to animate actions if you first act them out yourself. Get in the habit of walking through an action, testing the different approaches a character might take. If you feel silly at first, get over it. Professional animators at the major studios do this all the time. Jumping on and off desks and walking around with a board nailed to your sneakers seems to be normal, acceptable behavior for character animators. Wearing a tie to work, however, can get you blacklisted.

On All Fours

Aside from bipedal humanoids, the largest class of creatures you are likely to animate are the four-legged variety. They present some interesting problems for character animators—creating motions contrary to bipedal intuitions, visualizing actions you are unable to act out accurately, keeping twice as many legs locked to the ground, and animating a lot more gaits than you'd use for two-legged critters.

Basic anatomy accounts for the first two problems. Humans walk on the equivalent of the palms of their hands, on the metatarsal bones that form the arch of the foot. Many quadrupeds, in contrast, move on the equivalent of their toes. Cows, deer, and other hoofed animals actually walk around on tip-toe. Dogs and many other mammals walk on the balls of their feet, with the digits spread for balance. You can come close to emulating this without joining the ballet—just stand barefoot and lift both heels off the ground at once. This feels very awkward, but the change in tendon and muscle layout makes trotting and running more efficient for the animals.

When it comes to preventing moonwalking or skating, the solution for four legs is the same as for two: tweak, tweak, tweak. Or, use software that supports constraints.

The gait "problem" isn't really a problem. You just need to know what's available, and what's reasonable in certain circumstances for certain creatures. There are six common four-legged gaits—walk, pace, trot, canter, transverse gallop, and rotary gallop:

- The *quadruped walk* is similar to the human walk. Each foot is grounded for more than half the cycle. The usual order of foot placement is left fore, right hind, right fore, left hind.

- The *pace* is an odd gait used naturally only by camels and some breeds of dog. It can also be taught to other animals. In the pace, the legs move together on each side, that is, both left feet would move forward together, then both right feet. This produces a unique rocking motion.

- The *trot, canter,* and *gallop* are similar to the human run, where each foot is grounded for less than half the cycle. The feet move in diagonal pairs in the trot, left fore with right hind and right fore with left hind. In the gallop, the fore and hind feet move separately, that is, if the forefeet are grounded, the hind feet are in motion, so the spine can bend and add longer reach and more muscle to the stride. The canter is like a slow gallop crossed with a trot, in which the grounding of the fore and hind pairs overlaps.

- The *rotary gallop* is the fast gait of cats and some other animals, in which the spine curls up and stretches out to lengthen the stride and increase the animal's speed.

The exact sequence and range of motion for each gait varies according to the animal. If you have to animate one of these gaits, your best bet is to observe or acquire photos of an animal similar to the one you are animating and work out the poses from the above guidelines and the creature's individual proportions.

There is also a rare gait called a *pronk*, in which all four legs extend simultaneously in a sort of four-legged pogo. In nature, certain antelope and deer are known to pronk. In animation, one of the most memorable examples is Chuck Jones' Pepe le Pew. This gait can be very amusing when used sparingly, but only when appropriate to the character. Otherwise, stick to the more common gaits.

Animate A Walking Cow

This project originally used the cow object included on the LightWave 3D CD-ROM. If you don't use LightWave, you can try setting this up with any four-legged animal model you have handy, using the same techniques you learned in Chapter 12.

I've set up a very basic arrangement of the minimum bones necessary to animate a four-legged walk or other simple gait. The bone names are fairly self-explanatory. All the bones have been set up to animate only in the pitch axis. This is not perfectly anatomically correct, but it's good enough for this project. The bones have also been laid out in order, shoulder to hoof, then next leg, so navigating through the skeleton is as easy as possible.

1. In Layout, load scene file COW.LWS [EXER0702.LWS] from the Chapter 15 directory on this book's CD-ROM. The scene file will look in the default NEWTEK\OBJECTS\ANIMALS for the cow object. If it is not there, you will have to specify the correct path and directory.

2. Set keyframes for the entire cow and all dependent items at frames 0, 1, 13, 17, and 21. The first two frames are a baseline reference, the last three are the minimum keyframes for the walk cycle.

3. Pose the cow in frame 13 to match Figure 15.53. This is the heel strike pose for the front feet.

4. Pose the cow in frame 17 to match Figure 15.54. This is the squash pose for the front feet.

   Most of the shock-absorbing squash is accomplished by rotating bones that are concealed in the shoulder of the cow. This makes pose details hard to see in the rendered animation, but they're there.

5. Pose the cow in frame 21 to match Figure 15.55. This is the passing pose for the front feet.

Figure 15.53   Heel strike pose for walking cow.

Figure 15.54   Squash pose for walking cow.

Now for the fun part. This particular motion repeats on a 20-frame cycle, that is, the left front hoof's setting in frame 13 is identical to that of the right front hoof's setting in frame 33. Also, the entire animation is designed to loop after frame 40, so you can "wrap around" keyframes that go over 40.

6. Duplicate the settings of the left front leg in frame 13 for the right front leg in frame 33. Repeat this alternating duplication of settings for the rest of the animation. For frame 21, duplicate the settings to frame 1 (21+20=41, 41-40=1).

When you're finished, you should have a decent approximation of the original walk cycle. Unfortunately, there's no easy solution to this object's difficulty with coordinating rear and front pairs—that requires full spine, pelvic, and shoulder skeletons to

Figure 15.55   Passing pose for walking cow.

mimic whole-body flexibility. This means the vertical and lateral movements of the cow object will not match the original's, so you can expect the foot placement not to match the ground, either.

Don't be discouraged if the cow doesn't walk the way you want it to. Coordinating the fore and hind legs of an object like this is a difficult job, as the next project illustrates.

 ## Try To Tune Up A Rotoscoped Cow

This project presents you with a partially completed cow walk cycle, rotoscoped from one of the motion study sources mentioned earlier in the chapter. The front legs seem to be animating all right, as shown in the animation file Front.AVI, which you can locate in the Chapter 15 directory on this book's CD-ROM.

1. Load the Front.AVI file, and play it. It isn't the greatest—it could use some more stabilizing bones to smooth out the muscle action—but it works. More importantly, the feet lock to the ground and don't skate all over.

   The down side to this setup becomes obvious when you look at the rest of the cow.

2. Load the Whole.AVI file, and play it. Yuck! What is going on with the back legs?

Both the front and back leg bones were rotoscoped to motion capture footage on four-frame key intervals and are fairly reliable. The difficulty seems to be that there is no provision for spine or pelvic movement, so the body of the object is just a rigid block. Even a seemingly rigid creature flexes its spine and pelvis when moving, especially if it is as heavy as a cow. If the pelvis and spine moved accurately, the rear legs might be correct as is.

Possible approaches to repairing this animation include:

- Add bones to emulate the pelvis and spine, then manipulate the rear legs of the object to coordinate with the front legs.

- Tweak the existing bones in the rear legs to match the front legs, and just forget about matching the rotoscope footage exactly.

If you'd like to give it a try (and are using LightWave), load COW2.LWS [EXER0703.LWS] in Layout, and give it your best shot.

Animate A Cat's Rotary Gallop

Arguably, the toughest character animation job is to animate a feline. Most other animals have a fairly rigid bone structure, but cats are extraordinarily flexible. They have only a vestigial collarbone, and their forelegs simply attach to an overlapping nest of muscles. Their spines are only a little less flexible than a snake's, enabling their heads to face 180 degrees from the direction of their hind feet. They also have the most extreme of rotary gallops, with the spine alternating convex to concave on each stride. But, they're *so* much fun to watch!

If you'd like to try this project from scratch, here are a few guidelines.

- Research your subject. Start with the appropriate references in the Bibliography, and see where they lead you.

One additional reference you may want to check is an article by John T. Manter in the *Journal of Experimental Biology*, volume 15, number 4, (1938) "The Dynamics of Quadruped Walking." This report includes X-Y plane data for a domestic cat's legs during a walk, plus a lot of other information about force analysis. Unfortunately, it completely ignores lateral displacement, so it's only about half the data you need for a complete animation.

Big cats move just like little cats, only heavier and slower. You can get a good idea of how a tabby moves by watching documentary footage of lions and tigers. Cheetahs are a little harder to translate, because of the difference in rear leg geometry. My personal favorites are the panther and mountain lion, as their hides are more closely attached. Tigers, especially, have skin that slides all over, making it hard to analyze the underlying muscle motion.

- Narrowly define your goal. One complete stride of a domestic cat's legs is plenty. You don't even need to do the whole cat.

- Keep it simple. Use something like the Puppet to start with. After you have a clear idea of the skeletal measurements, you can model an object and use bones to animate it more smoothly.

If you can set up and animate even a rough approximation of a feline gallop, you will have a serious example of work to put on your demo reel. Cats are *hard*.

You should now have a decent grounding in mimicking natural motion. Your goal in the next section is to learn how to extrapolate your observations of natural motion to create caricatured animation. Along the way, projects will show you how to animate actions from the repertoire of classic cartoon animation, including takes, sneaks, staggers, and zips. You'll also learn the concept of *staging* for foreshadowing action.

"The continuous detailed analysis of all kinds of motion is basic to any animator's ability to re-create it or, better still, to transform it for his or her own purposes."
Steven S. Wilson, Puppets and People

An Art Of Essences

The art of character animation is not the literal reproduction of realistic movement. Simple reproduction can be automated, and anything that can be automated is not an art. The basic art of character animation is the same, whether expressed in CGI, clay, or cel. It is distilling the essence of movement, then creating it again in a new form, obviously different and just as obviously true in essence.

The first step, then, is to observe. As explained earlier, you must observe in detail exactly how an action is performed in real life before you can understand it well enough to re-create it as an animation. You must understand the forces acting on each part of the character—the mass, inertia, and energy that are expressed in acceleration, deceleration, and deformation.

Develop the habit of watching people and animals move. Anywhere you go, there are lessons to be learned about movement. Keep your eyes open, and, when you notice an especially fine movement (incredible grace running for the bus, a particularly elegant gesture in conversation), try to figure out why it was so good. Make notes, and try to animate the Puppet to achieve the same effect.

This is part of training yourself to really see. Your brain is very good at categorizing information as it comes in, pigeonholing it into classifications like "dangerous," "familiar," "food," and so on. This enables you to walk through a crowded shopping mall without having a nervous breakdown—most of the flood of information is immediately classified as unimportant noise, so you can ignore it all and carry on a conversation with your companion.

The down side to this sorting process is that you miss a lot of the details in everyday life. You need to retrain your brain to sort information about human and animal movement into a "pay attention and analyze this" pigeonhole. With practice, you can watch a person walk and be able to reproduce the exact amount of knee flex for the squash, the precise speed of the kick forward to the heel strike, even the extent of the counterbalancing shoulder action. This analysis is the essence of mimicry and the beginning of animation.

What Makes A Chicken A Chicken?

Once you can analyze and reproduce movement, you are halfway to caricaturing it. The idea of caricature is to make something more like itself. In caricaturing movement, this means exaggeration of not just the individual key poses but also the acceleration, deceleration, and deformation that connect the poses. If a character walks with a certain amount of knee bend in squash, a caricatured version will bend the knee even farther, making the squash deeper.

The real art to caricature is the judgment of what is essential and what is not. The heart of an action may not be the broadest movement, the largest change, or the most visible deformation. It may be the smallest nuance that defines that action. For example, let's take a look at a basic emotional transition, from a pose of neutrality—simply standing, relaxed but alert—to a pose of aggressive anger, almost a boxer's stance. Act this transition out yourself. Create your own interpretation, and analyze the changes between the neutral and anger poses.

You probably raised your arms, brought your hands up in front of your body, and clenched your fists. You may have also taken a half step forward, shifted your balance into a stronger stance, and perhaps pitched your head forward so you could glare at your opponent from lowered brows. This would be a typical "looking for a fight" pose.

So, what's the most important part? Which of these changes is the essence of anger? The motion of the arms is certainly the largest angular change, over 90 degrees to bring the hands up to waist level. The change in stance would probably be second, because the smaller angular changes of both legs plus the resulting forward movement of the body add up to a large perceived motion. Possibly the smallest motions are the forward pitch of the head and the closing of the hands into fists.

Guess what? The hands and head are the essential, defining motions for anger. How to prove this? Drop back to the neutral pose, and use just the head pitch and glare. Not quite anger, but maybe severe annoyance. Now, clench your fists, but keep them at your sides. Bingo! If you took this pose in a bar, either your friends would try to calm you down or the person you were facing would be getting ready to rumble. This is *repressed anger*, a version of anger that minimizes the grosser body movements but communicates almost the same information. Pure aggressive anger is ready to throw a punch; repressed anger is aggressive anger restrained— just barely—by better judgment, but still ready to explode at the next provocation.

But the grosser body pose still has something to say, doesn't it? Try this: Assume the aggressive anger pose, then open your hands so your open palms face your imaginary opponent, and pitch your head level or a little bit back, so you are looking straight ahead. Same body pose, just the hands and head are different, but it's the difference between starting a fight and trying to stop one.

The point to this exercise is that you can't assume any part of a movement is the essence. You have to look at the gestalt of the movement first, then start picking apart the individual elements. Until you develop the judgment that comes with experience, you would do well to analyze every element of every pose you look at, and compare them to similar elements of other poses as we just did with anger, neutrality, and placation.

"In the fields of observation, chance favors only the mind that is prepared."

Louis Pasteur

Try varying one element, one variable, at a time (using the ol' scientific method again) and evaluating the change in expression. Like most forms of systematic research, this can be slow going, but when you eliminate all the wrong answers, you are left with the right ones. Also, when you are forced to work through every possible permutation, you often stumble across valuable information that you weren't even looking for. Keep your eyes and mind open.

Mountains From Molehills

After you have identified the essence of a movement, the remaining question is how to exaggerate it. This breaks down naturally into two parts: the key pose and the transition. The key pose can be caricatured as if it were a drawing, so you can apply the guidelines used by artists working in 2D media to create a stronger pose, a more expressive silhouette, a smoother line of action, and a clearer definition of character. The goal is to make a key pose look even more like itself.

The caricature of a transition is a matter of timing and emphasis. This is another area where the importance of experience, judgment, and inspiration define animation as an art, not a science. You can exaggerate each of the principles of movement you learned in earlier chapters to create a caricature movement. You can push anticipation farther away from the main action, deform squash and stretch even further, delay overlapping action keys farther from the main action, and shorten snap to fewer frames.

The only principle you shouldn't usually exaggerate is ease. Caricatures look best when they are very snappy, the antithesis of ease. Too much ease makes an animation floaty, as if the character is performing underwater.

Subtlety is for live action. If you want an action to read well as a caricature, exaggerate more than you think you should. You learn from your mistakes, if you're smart. This is a time when you can learn most rapidly by deliberately making mistakes. Push the exaggeration of an action to a really outrageous extreme, both in key pose and transition. Try to do it wrong, to exaggerate too much. Examine each element of the action, and push it to the virtual limits of the character. If a part of the character is supposed to squash, mash it flat. If part is to stretch, draw it out to a needle shape. If a joint is to bend, fold it as far as it will go. If the joint is to extend, make it perfectly straight. Shorten each snap to a linear transition across a single frame.

When you're done exaggerating this action, it should be so extreme even Tex Avery would disown it. So, what's the point? This is an investigation, a search for the right amount of exaggeration. The low end is perfectly natural movement, the kind you could rotoscope or motion capture straight from life. You know you don't want to go any further in that direction. When you animate an action that is too exaggerated, you establish a high end. Together, the high and low ends define the limits of your search, which is the first step in the process of solving the problem.

You may find it's not possible to exaggerate an action too much. That's the fun part of cartoon-style animation. Sometimes, the absolute virtual limit is the exact effect you want. Sometimes, the antagonist does end up as a perfectly flat grease spot on the wall, and sometimes, the protagonist does stretch clear across the screen in a zip exit.

This is another time a laser disc player can come in handy. Rent or buy laser discs of classic Warner Brothers cartoons, and single-frame through the most extreme actions. It's amazing what you can get away with in a cartoon.

A Caricature Walk

You can thoroughly caricature an action the same way you originally animated it, starting at the root of the animation hierarchy and proceeding through the layers, exaggerating as you go. If you've already worked through the projects earlier in this chapter, you should be comfortably familiar with the key poses and transitions of walks, runs, and other motion cycles. Let's look at how you might exaggerate a normal walk cycle to create a caricature walk.

The easiest key pose to exaggerate is the squash. The limits to this pose are defined by the structure of the character: no squash at all is just a character walking with straight legs (Thud! Thud! Thud!), and maximum squash doubles up the knee joint so the character's hips are nearly on its heels. The variations on squash are mostly in the timing: How fast and far is the snap to the ease-in? How slow is the ease-in to full squash? How fast is the snap out of full squash? Almost all the exaggeration in the squash is concentrated in the knee joint, because the hips are nearly level and the foot is constrained to be flat on the ground.

The passing position uses banked hips to help increase ground clearance for the trailing foot, so the hip is eligible for exaggeration, as well. You can exaggerate the normal passing position to elevate the character in a bounce. You can also exaggerate both knees to a deeply flexed position and coordinate the rotations of the knees, thighs, and hips to maintain a constant distance between the hips' pivot and the ground. This will remove any up-and-down motion from the character's CG, mimicking a waddling duck-walk.

The heel strike provides lots of opportunities for exaggeration but must also be handled more carefully to produce the right effect. The heel strike is the result of a fast forward rotation of the trailing upper leg, with the trailing lower leg folded at least high enough that the foot clears the ground during the upper leg's forward rotation. This enables you to exaggerate the speed and angle of the hip, the speed and angle of the upper leg, the speed and angle of the lower leg, and the speed and angle of the foot, all in the same motion.

For example, you could rotate the upper leg very quickly up past the final heel strike angle, whipping the lower leg out straight at the same time, and point the toe at the leg's maximum extension. Hold that pose for a frame or three while the rest of the body continues to lean forward. Then, rotate the upper leg down rapidly, to slap the foot flat on the ground. That's basically a goose-step. Ugly, inefficient, and stupid, but it makes a loud noise. Hmmm. Sounds like a metaphor for certain political systems.

Animate The Puppet Doing A Caricature March

PROJECT 15.9

1. Load one of the Puppet walk cycles that you created earlier in this chapter.

2. Exaggerate the key poses and transitions to animate the Puppet doing a caricature march.

Here are a few guidelines, which you should supplement by acting out a marching action yourself—or perhaps watching the Rose Bowl parade—and trying to analyze what's going on:

- The trailing leg should move rapidly through the passing position and kick out straight before the heel strike.

- The foot should form a right angle or even pull the toes back toward the knee a bit, until the heel hits the ground. This exaggerates the slap of the foot flattening to the ground immediately following the heel strike.

- Lean the hips and chest back a few degrees.

- Keep the Puppet's head high or even pitched back a bit.

- Pose the arms to keep the hands high, the elbows out, and the arms pumping vigorously, with plenty of snap to balance the motions of the legs.

You might put some John Phillips Sousa on the CD player while you work on this, just to put yourself in the mood.

Animate The Puppet Doing A Caricature Sad Walk

PROJECT 15.10

1. Reload the basic walk scene you used to start the preceding project.

2. Exaggerate the key poses and transitions to animate the Puppet doing a caricature sad walk:

- Pitch the hips back a few degrees, and the thorax or chest forward a few degrees, effectively curving the spine and making the Puppet slump.

- Pitch the head forward, and keep the eye-tracking null on the ground.

- Keep the arms limp and without volition. Animate them using overlapping action, as if they were a pair of scarves tacked to the shoulders.

- Lift the legs as little as possible, and make the stride very slow and short. Either keep the feet nearly parallel to the ground and shuffle them, or drag the toes along the ground through each passing position.

- The feet should be very close to the angle of the ground at the heel strike position, so there is very little distance for the foot to slap down.

- Use longer, more gradual anticipations and ease-ins, but shorten the ease-outs as if the character is too exhausted to effectively absorb the impact of the action.

Sync Caricature Action To A Soundtrack

The goal of this project is to match a caricatured walk to sound effects and a piece of music composed and mixed especially for it. The music is the opening sequence of "Easy Come, Easy Go," the film used as an example throughout this book.

1. Following the procedures detailed in Chapter 4, analyze the sound clip 00-00-00.WAV on this book's CD-ROM, and transcribe it to exposure sheets.

   Pay special attention to marking hits for the sound of footsteps. Use the appropriate *slip* so the finished action will read well with the soundtrack.

2. Animate a sad, slow walk, as in the previous project, but match the frame after the heel strike position to the footstep hits in the exposure sheet.

   Refer to the script in Chapter 2 and the storyboards in Chapter 3 for guidelines on camera angles and shot composition.

3. When you are satisfied with the animation, render it.

4. Using the AV editor of your choice, dub the sound file over your animation.

QUICK AUDIO FOR ANIMATION TESTS

If you are using Adobe Premiere or another AV editor that lets you save a project, you can set up a dub project where the WAV file is in place and an image sequence prefixed "TEST_" is in the first video track. Just render your wireframes or other quick tests to overwrite the original TEST_ files, and you can load and run the Premiere project file to automatically dub the test animation. This is a little slower than most software's preview or wireframe mode, but it produces more accurate sync, and you can save your work.

If you match the first footstep and your track analysis is accurate, all the other footsteps should match, as well.

Sneaks

The sneak is a time-honored part of the repertoire of any classically trained animator. What fun would an animated story be if no character snuck up on another? The comic potential for consequences befalling the sneaker or the intended victim are so rich, a sneak practically guarantees your audiences' full attention.

There are two basic classes of sneak: fast and slow.

The Fast Sneak

The fast sneak is essentially a compressed, fast walk on tiptoes. The hips and chest are pitched toward each other, as in the sad pose described earlier, to curve the spine and compress the body. The sneaker is trying to look as small as possible. The head is angled forward, and the eyes should either fixate on the intended victim, or rove the scene nervously with the head following the eyes' lead.

The legs are bent throughout the sneak. If the sneaker straightened her legs, she would be a larger target. The stride is very short, with the thighs and knees rotating as little as possible. The feet are pitched downward, so only the toes make contact with the ground, and are also picked up higher than a standard walk, as if to avoid tripping over something.

The short stride, bent posture, and quick movement contribute a greater amount of up-and-down movement to the fast sneak, so the sneaker often appears to bob rapidly. The arms are carried high and the elbows are held close to the body. The arms do not swing to balance leg movement but are instead held ready to pounce.

Animate The Puppet Doing A Fast Sneak

PROJECT 15.12

1. Load the basic Puppet scene file you set up in Chapter 11.

   The sneaks are different enough from normal or caricature walks that you are probably better off starting from scratch than trying to adapt one of the actions you animated earlier.

2. Create a fast sneak passing pose at frame 1.

   The lifted foot should be level with the opposite knee, and the character's CG should be directly above or slightly in front of the grounded toes. The lifted thigh can be horizontal, or slightly above it, for a really exaggerated sneak.

3. Create a fast sneak heel strike pose at frame 7.

   The toe should be planted slowly, not just slapped down, and the sneaker should immediately lean forward to move the CG toward the leading foot.

4. Create a fast sneak squash pose at frame 15.

   As the CG moves over the leading foot, the leading knee must bend more to absorb the weight without being forced to drop the heel. The trailing foot lifts off the floor, again easing slowly (to avoid creaking floorboards).

5. Save the scene with a new file name. Render and play back the animation. Ignore the default interpolation for now. How does the timing of the key poses look? Are the keys too close together or too far apart? Use your software's keyframe editing tools to adjust the key poses' intervals.

6. Add keyframes and adjust the splines to add snap, anticipation, overlapping action, and follow-through to the sneak, just as you did for the walks and runs earlier in this chapter.

7. When you are satisfied with the animation, save it under a new name.

The Slow Sneak

The slow sneak is an elongated, slower walk, only partially on tiptoes. The action is a more rolling, fluid gait, with the intent being to cover as much ground as possible, as smoothly and quietly as possible. The hips and chest are pitched toward each other, and the head is angled forward in the squash position, to curve the spine and compress the body. In the heel strike position—actually a toe strike, but let's not quibble—the angles are reversed to make the entire body a convex arc from head to leading toe.

The eyes, again, should either fixate on the intended victim or rove the scene nervously with the head following the eyes' lead. The legs range from a compressed pose as the trailing leg squashes, to a full extension as the lead toe stretches toward the next footstep. The stride is quite long, at least equal to the normal walking stride. The feet are picked up higher in passing position than a standard walk, to avoid tripping. The long stride and slower movement smooth out the movement, but the deeper squash position still exaggerates vertical motion.

Animate The Puppet Doing A Slow Sneak

PROJECT 15.13

1. Reload the default Puppet scene file, just as you did for the preceding exercise.

2. Create a slow sneak passing pose at frame 1.

   The lifted foot should be level with the opposite knee, and the character's CG should be directly above or slightly in front of the grounded foot, which is flat on the ground. The lifted thigh is not quite horizontal. The body should be nearly vertical, making the transition from the forward to the backward lean.

3. Create a fast sneak heel strike pose at frame 15 and supporting keys immediately following.

   The toe should be planted slowly, as if testing the floor for creaks. The body is leaning backward at full extension, counterbalancing the extended leg. After contact, the foot should be rolled slowly ball-to-heel to make full sole contact with the ground. As the leading heel touches the ground, the sneaker begins to lean forward to move the CG toward the leading foot.

4. Create a fast sneak squash pose at frame 30.

   As the sneaker leans fully forward and the CG moves over the leading foot, the leading knee must bend more to absorb the weight. The trailing foot lifts off the floor, again easing slowly (to avoid creaking floorboards).

5. Save the scene with a new file name. Render and play back the animation. How does the timing of the key poses look? Are the keys too close together, or too far apart? Use your software's keyframe editing tools to adjust the key poses' intervals until you are satisfied with the timing.

6. Add keyframes, and adjust the splines to add snap, anticipation, overlapping action, and follow-through to the sneak, just as you did for the walks and runs earlier in this chapter.

7. When you are satisfied with the animation, save it under a new name.

Staging

Staging is the posing of a small action to foreshadow the character's next major action, preparing the audience to read it. Examples of staging are looking intently at the object of the action;

pointing the hands toward the object, as if targeting it; and aligning the body to face the direction of the action. In real life, people tend to unconsciously stage their actions. Good negotiators and salespeople know this. You put your hands in your pockets when you really want something, to hide their involuntary twitching toward the object of your desire.

In animation, you should make your characters look at or point toward the object of the fore-shadowed action in the reverse of the usual animation hierarchy order: eyes, head, hands, limbs, torso. You should also vary the lead timing of the eyes, depending on the nature of the following action. The more violent the action, the faster (shorter) you should make the staging.

Staging A Reach

Stage the Puppet leaning on a street lamp.

1. Load the default Puppet scene file with more detailed head and movable eyes, which you set up in Chapter 11. Add model STREET.DXF, from the Chapter 15 directory on this book's CD-ROM.

Your scene should now contain the Puppet character and a one-piece set including storefront, sidewalk, street, and street lamp.

2. Pose the Puppet beside the street lamp, in easy arm's-length leaning distance.

3. Animate the eyes first, to glance toward the street lamp.

4. Follow the motion of the eyes with a slight head turn.

5. Animate the hand nearest the street lamp to lift from the wrist, pointing the fingertips toward the post.

6. Animate the nearer arm to lift and the Puppet's body to lean toward the street lamp. Maintain the angle of the hand until the palm is parallel to the street lamp's surface.

7. Continue the Puppet's lean until the palm makes contact with the street lamp. Complete the leaning action with an elbow bend for squash, follow through, and rebound to a moving hold.

8. Animate the eyes and head to face the camera again.

9. Experiment with the timing and transitions for each key pose until you are satisfied with the animation.

Do you see how staging an action can help sell a shot? How the audience will read it better if they are prepared by a character's foreshadowing of the next action?

If you want to try a more humorous treatment of this project, have the Puppet glance toward the post, then nonchalantly look back toward the camera. As it leans toward the post, animate the wrist and arm to just barely miss the post. The Puppet should not react at all until its hand is several inches past the post. Improvise a fall. You may want to read through the next section to pick up some tips on weight and balance, so you can better pose the Puppet's off-balance fall. Have fun with this one!

Balance And Mass

These two factors are closely related, but you must handle them in completely different ways. You must animate balance with realism. Mass requires some of the most extreme exaggeration. Your characters must always keep their visible supports under their CG, or the audience will wonder why they don't fall over. When a character's CG shifts, as when it picks up a heavy object, you must pose the character to place its feet under the new center of gravity.

Mass, on the other hand, simply begs for exaggeration. If you want to animate a character struggling with a heavy load, you can use every trick in the book: bent posture, squash-and-stretch arms, exaggerated anticipation, very slow accelerations upward, and dangerously fast ones downward, just to name a few. The comic uses of differential application are fun to play with, too. Cool characters can appear to lift anything effortlessly; uncool characters can get squashed flat trying to move those same items.

PROJECT 15.15   Animate The Puppet Picking Up Objects

1. Reload the default Puppet scene file you set up in Chapter 11. Add a variety of primitive objects, of sizes suitable for the Puppet to handle one- or two-handed.

2. Animate the Puppet picking up objects and moving them to different parts of the scene.

    You can use constraint switching, as explained in Chapter 12, to keep an object aligned with the Puppet's hand.

    Assign any mass you like to the different objects, but be consistent. A small object can be very heavy (plutonium is apparently easy to come by in cartoon-land), but it must remain heavy for the entire animation.

    Pay attention to staging, shifting CG, and appropriate posing of legs and arms to brace the masses and maintain balance. Don't forget to add anticipation, overlapping action, follow-through, and, especially, squash-and-stretch.

Takes, Double-Takes, And Extreme Takes

A take is a character's overreaction to a surprise. The nature of the surprise can determine the appropriate extent or type of take, and the shot composition will determine whether you need to animate a full-body take or just a head take.

There are three key poses for all takes: the normal pose, the squash, and the stretch. Some takes require special inbetweens, but they all use the same key poses:

- A standard take starts out with a *normal* pose, as shown in Figure 15.56.
- The character presumably sees something to induce surprise. This causes the *squash* pose. The character's eyes squeeze shut as if to block out the sight, and the head and possibly the entire character recoils from the source of the surprise. Depending on the animation style and the construction of the character, this can be a literal squash (see Figure 15.57).

- The next pose is the *stretch*, the reaction to the squash position. The character stretches out, eyes wide—just the opposite of the squash—commonly with an extremely surprised expression, as shown in Figure 15.58.

- The last part of the take is a return to the *normal* pose. Unless, of course, the character gets smashed flat by whatever caused the take in the first place (see Figure 15.59).

Anticipation is very important to a take. For every action in a take, there should be a very pronounced anticipation in the opposite direction.

THE PHYSICS OF CARTOONS

Steph Greenberg and two dozen other animators created the short film, *The Physics of Cartoons*. Clips from it (and more information about how it was made) are located in the PHYSICS directory on this book's CD-ROM. This is an excellent example of traditional cartoon animation applied to 3D CGI.

PROJECT 15.16 Animate The Puppet Doing A Take

1. Reload the default Puppet scene file you set up in Chapter 11.

2. From frame 1, set a key for all items at frames 4, 8, and 13.

3. Leave frame 1 as the normal pose. In frame 4, squash the character for a full-body take or just the head for a head take. Close the eyelids tightly. Clench the arms and legs tightly to the body. Make a keyframe to save the changes.

4. In frame 8, invert all the changes you made to frame 4, doubled. Stretch out everything you squashed, and open the eyelids wide. Fling the arms and legs out wide. Save the changes.

Figure 15.56 Normal pose. Frame 1571 from *The Physics of Cartoons*.

Figure 15.57 Squash pose. Frame 1591 from *The Physics of Cartoons*.

Figure 15.58 Stretch pose. Frame 1600 from *The Physics of Cartoons*.

Figure 15.59 These characters won't just be returning to normal pose. Frame 1609 from *The Physics of Cartoons*.

5. Leave frame 13 alone as the return to the normal pose. Save the scene with a new file name. Render and play back the animation.

You should experiment with the timing of the key poses and the splines connecting them. Try different amounts of snap in the transitions. How brief can you hold a pose before the audience can't read it? How long can you hold a key pose, and what's the minimum animation needed in a moving hold to keep the character from going dead? How far from the root's keyframes can you push keyframes for the overlap of the extremities?

A double-take is a regular take with a head shake between the squash and the stretch, as if the character is trying to deny what they see.

PROJECT 15.17   Animate The Puppet Doing A Double-Take

1. Reload the scene you saved in the preceding exercise. Shift all the keyframes from the stretch pose down about 15 frames, to give you room to insert a head shake.

2. Insert a head shake between the squash pose and the stretch pose. Make the shake very abrupt and snappy, with very little ease.

If you'd like a little more of a challenge, you can try to animate the double-take depicted in Shots 4, 5, and 6 of the storyboards in Chapter 3.

PROJECT 15.18   Animate The Puppet Doing An Extreme Take

This should be fun.

1. Reload the default Puppet scene file you set up in Chapter 11.

2. Given the limits available in this character's setup, see how close you can come to duplicating the extreme stretch pose of the take depicted in Shot 18 of the storyboards in Chapter 3. Just how much stretch can you use before the character comes apart?

3. Try to create a matching squash pose.

Staggers

In animation, a stagger is when a character or object oscillates rapidly between two extreme poses, often in alternating frames, to give the appearance of vibrating from a shock or other overwhelming force. If one part of the character is affected more strongly by the impact, the remaining parts can be animated in overlapping action to emphasize the stagger. Stagger techniques can be very effective and, like takes and sneaks, are borrowed from classic cartoon animation.

You have several ways to create staggers in most 3D animation software. You could simply move the staggered object on alternating frames, using linear interpolation, and gradually diminishing the distance the object is displaced as the stagger tapers off. This should work well, as long as motion blur is turned off or its percentage is set low enough that the key poses are visible.

If you want more detailed differences between the staggered poses, you could create separate extreme key poses on two successive frames—one odd, the other even. Then, duplicate each pose to alternating frames, keeping one pose on odd frames and the other on evens. When all the stagger poses have been duplicated, you work down the keyframes, incrementally reducing the extreme poses toward the "normal" pose at the end of the stagger. This is probably the most tedious method, but it does give very precise control—you can even animate gestures and lip sync during the course of the stagger.

You could also create three morph target objects with the two extreme poses plus a normal pose. If you set the objects up in a morph sequence with the normal pose as the baseline, you could simply vary the morph to create any sort of stagger pattern you wanted. One drawback to this technique is that morphing requires straight-line transitions. Any difference in the poses that required a rotation or bend is going to look really bad in the inbetweens.

PROJECT 15.19   Animate The Puppet Staggering

1. Refer to Shot 15 from the storyboards in Chapter 3, where Fred gets hit by a windblown $1000 bill.

2. Reload the default Puppet scene file.

3. Choose one of the preceding methods for creating a stagger, and try to animate an action like that depicted in Shot 15 as applied to the Puppet character.

Zip Pans

A zip pan is exactly like a stagger, except the camera gets oscillated instead of the character. This is very effective for animating earthquakes or high-speed character impacts with immovable objects. To create one in your software, simply edit the spline for the camera to create a single-framed zigzag line in the axis of the camera's vibration.

PROJECT 15.20   Animate The Puppet Hitting A Wall

1. Load the default Puppet scene, and add the STREET.DXF model, as you did for the earlier project.

2. Animate the Puppet hitting the storefront wall, from extreme squash-and-stretch and rebound to moving hold. Make sure you include the overlapping action of the arms and legs, because they would rebound faster and flop around while the main body was still stuck to the wall.

3. Animate a zip pan of the camera, synchronized to the impact of the Puppet against the wall.

4. Experiment with the timing and duration of the zip pan, to discover what works for you.

Sorting Out The Animation Hierarchy

The animation hierarchy is not always going to start with the hips, CG, or even the body of a character. Sometimes the center of a composition is one of the extremities. In cases like this, the center of the composition temporarily becomes the root of the character's hierarchy. Reasoning from earlier statements about animating from the root of the hierarchy outwards, it seems logical to pose models in the current order of importance. The root of the animation hierarchy can change, even within a single shot. If the character's hand is the center of the composition, you should pose the hand first and make the rest of the figure follow naturally from the hand. This is where a good constraint setup can make the animator's job easy—or nearly impossible.

Get Unreal!

One of the most challenging fields in CGI character animation is motion picture special effects. Creatures like *Dragonheart*'s Draco, *Jurassic Park* and *Lost World*'s dinosaurs, and *Alien Resurrection*'s swimming horrors, represent the state of the art in fantastic creature creation and character animation. In each case, the goal was to make the audience believe that the creatures on the screen were alive. To achieve this, the character designers had to work out all the details of anatomy and kinesiology that would affect how the creatures looked and acted. In the case of *Jurassic Park* and *Lost World*, they were able to extrapolate from the work of generations of paleontologists. For the other two, sheer fantasy was to be brought to life.

If you want to do the same, you need to study anatomy, physiology, zoology, anthropometry, kinesiology, and a host of other disciplines. Not enough to get a degree, mind you, just enough to soak up the basic principles and learn where the really good references are. You can always look up the details of the *orbicularis oculi*, but at least you'll know what to ask for. Once you understand how the underlying structure—the muscles, tendons, and other tissues—all contribute to the way a creature looks and moves, devising a realistic-looking simulation of a completely fantastic character does not seem so impossible.

Getting Your Point Across: Acting By Proxy

This section shows you how to apply acting technique to character animation, covering posing, gesture, mannerisms, and emphasis. Animating for emotional communication requires at least as good a sense of timing as stage acting. In fact, acting classes are a pretty good idea for an animator—they break down inhibitions about performing and can acquaint you with a lot of references on physical expression that apply as well to animation as to live action.

There are many resources available on acting technique. These resources can help you define a mood or attitude with a pose. The essential truths of acting, whether on stage or through character animation, are based on natural, observed behavior. If you want to become a better animator, study candid photos and films of people who are not acting but reacting to real-world situations. I strongly encourage you to take movement classes of any kind, but acting or mime classes are generally best for animation purposes.

Show Some Character

A character is defined by its actions. To define a character, you will have to animate some sequence of actions that tells your audience who this character is.

STEPH GREENBERG'S 3 STAGES OF CHARACTER ANIMATION, OR, WHAT SEPARATES PASSABLE ANIMATION FROM GREAT ANIMATION

1. Characters move without pathologies that make you think, "Something's just not moving right here." This first bar is a pretty hard one to reach.

2. Characters must be able to show believable emotion, even if it is just through body language. If it's only through body language, you're pretty damn good.

3. Characters must have a distinct personality. Say you have identical twin characters, one good, one evil. You must be able to tell which one you are looking at just in silhouette. This last one is really, really hard. Think of Lasseter giving those desk lamps (Luxo Jr. and Sr.) personalities. You could tell which was which, even if they had switched bodies. Or if Buzz and Woody had a brain switch, you'd be able to tell it was Buzz inside Woody's body.

The basis of all action is posture, the broadest stroke of establishing mood. A change in posture, with all else remaining the same, can completely change the effect of a scene.

Posture can be defined as the line from the feet to the head, but I prefer to include the upper arms and, sometimes, the entire body, as well. The eyes always lead a change in posture, preparing the audience for the following action. If the character becomes sad, the eyes drop first; if happy, the eyes open wider and sparkle.

As you learned in earlier chapters, you must work to create consistently strong poses. You can judge this by testing them in silhouette, as described earlier in this chapter. Make this testing a habitual part of your workflow, so it becomes second nature.

You must time transitions so the audience has a chance to read them, but not so long that the audience is bored and their attention wanders. Never start an action within the first quarter-second of a shot—you must allow your audience at least that much time to adjust to the new camera angle and contents of the scene before they are ready to read an action. If you start an action too early in the shot, your audience may miss it entirely.

If the scene setup has been done well, your job as animator will be much simpler. You can use the standard scene views to relate the character to its environment, and use the dedicated detail views (see Chapter 11 for details) to see the close-ups you'll need when you pose the face or hands of a complex character.

"Get everything to read just in the acting, the pantomime, then when you stick the face on, it'll only plus that."
Pete Docter, The Making of Toy Story

Don't forget to follow the animation hierarchy when animating changes in posture. The same rules apply for saving time, effort, and aggravation, whether you're animating a simple walk cycle or a very complex dramatic performance.

PROJECT 15.21 What A Moody Guy!

The goal of this project is to create a series of strong, dramatic poses.

1. Reload the default Puppet scene file.

2. From frame 1, create a keyframe for all objects at frame 30.

Let's suppose the character starts off in a normal pose, then is given some very sad news by an opponent we don't see. Suppose the opponent then threatens the character, frightening him. Next, the opponent ridicules the character, causing the character's fear to transition to anger. Finally, the character's anger causes the opponent to leave, and the character exults in his victory. That's four major emotional poses: sadness, fear, anger, and exultation.

3. Pose the character in frame 30 in an expression of sadness. Remember to pose the character in order, using the animation hierarchy. Set the hips first, then the chest, and so on.

You have a number of options for figuring out what a sad posture looks like. You can find a full-length mirror and look at yourself while acting sad. You can find a movie or news video that shows a real person or a good actor looking sad. You can look for a sad pose from a traditional cartoon or comic strip. You can ask someone else to act sad for you. You can look up an example of a sad pose in one of the references cited earlier.

If you can't find your own example of a sad posture, here are a few suggestions: Slump the chest forward, and tilt the hips back. For this character, this is the closest pose to curving the spine and slumping the shoulders. Make the arms hang straight down, as if the character has neither the energy nor the inclination to do anything else with them. Pitch the head forward, and track the character's eyes to look at the ground in front of him. It's difficult to avoid a twins pose when mimicking sadness—the general lack of energy in the character seems to preclude any difference between the sides. To avoid the appearance of twins, rely on three-quarter camera angles for sad poses.

4. Make a key for the character at frame 30, to save the sad pose. Repeat Step 2 to create a "normal" key at frame 60.

5. In frame 60, pose the character to express fear.

Again, try to extract the essence of a fearful pose from your own observations.

A fearful pose is a natural progression, both emotionally and physically, from the posture of sadness. The concave slump of hips and chest is held a little deeper, and the knees bend to lower the body even further. The arms are posed with the elbows held close to the body and bent sharply to bring the hands, open and palm-forward, in front of the chest as if to ward off an attack. A little jitter in the hands protecting the body will add to the expression.

The head is pitched back, looking up, and the eyes tracked to the object of the fear. In this case, pick a point where an opponent's face would be, a few steps in front of the character you are posing. To avoid a twins pose, tweak bank and heading to turn the head slightly away from the direction of the eyes, move one foot a little behind the other, and raise one hand slightly above the level of the other.

6. Make a key for the character at frame 60, to save the fearful pose. Repeat Step 2 to create a "normal" key at frame 90.

7. In frame 90, pose the character to express anger.

An angry pose is a very strong dramatic change, from a passive, weak pose that folds the character in on itself, to a strong, aggressive pose that extends the character to full height and toward the object of the anger. Straighten the alignment of the hips and chest, and pitch the hips forward, so the entire character is leaning toward the imaginary character with a ramrod-straight spine.

Trail one foot farther back, and advance the other as if in the first step of an attack on the opponent, keeping the character's CG between the feet for proper balance. Rotate the arms to bring the hands down to waist level, and clench the hands into fists. Keep the eyes tracked on the opponent's face, but rotate the head to match the eyes' alignment, with a little extra pitch to make the jaw jut out aggressively.

8. Make a key for the character at frame 90, to save the fearful pose. Repeat Step 2 to create a "normal" key at frame 120.

9. In frame 120, pose the character to express exultation.

You're on your own for this one. I'm sure you can come up with something.

10. Evaluate all four poses in silhouette. Look for strength, readability, and no twins. Tweak the poses as necessary.

11. When you are satisfied with the four dramatic poses, save the scene under a new name.

You've got a logical series of solid, dramatic poses. Now, let's see you connect them with appropriate inbetweens and timing.

PROJECT 15.22   Timing Transitions

1. Render and play back the animation from the preceding project.

Your software automatically creates smooth interpolations between the key poses you set. This action looks too smooth, more hydraulic than human or caricature. The changes all happen at the same time, too. There is no overlapping action, anticipation, or follow-through. You need to change that by setting more keyframes that add anticipation, snap, moving holds, overlapping action, and follow-through to the animation. These are the same procedures you learned earlier in this chapter and in Chapter 14.

2. Hide all of the hierarchy except the hips (or pelvis, depending on your naming preferences).

You'll be using the animation hierarchy again, posing the root of the hierarchy throughout the animation before proceeding to the next level.

3. Add keyframes, and use the spline control tools to animate a sharper snap between key poses and to add a very slight motion around each key pose to produce a moving hold.

The largest part of the transition from one pose to the next should occur over just a few frames, starting with an abrupt change at the end of the preceding pose's moving hold. An ease to a moving hold should occupy the rest of the interval. Remember, if your character holds perfectly still for even a few frames, it will lose the illusion of life and become dead.

Consider how long the transition between two key poses should take. The transition between fear and anger, for example, should happen much faster than that between normal and sadness. How long does it take you to get angry when someone plays a nasty trick on you? Relocate the key poses to shorten or lengthen a transition.

Keep in mind that the root of the hierarchy carries the load of moving the entire character. The pitch or heading of the hips has to give the impression of driving the mass of the whole character, so don't use quite as much snap for the root of the hierarchy as you would for the higher, less massive levels.

4. Save the scene with a new file name. Render and play back the animation. Critique the animation of the hips, and make revisions until you are satisfied with this level of the animation hierarchy.

5. Make the next level of the hierarchy visible.

6. Repeat Steps 3 and 4 for this level of the hierarchy.

When you add keyframes, make sure they aren't all on the same frames as the keys for other parts of the character. Different parts of a character should reach their extreme poses at different times. If all the parts peak together, the animation loses continuity. Always keep some part of the character moving, especially during long moving holds.

For each higher level of the animation hierarchy, make the snaps a little sharper, the eases a little shorter. Each level has less mass to move and can, therefore, speed up and slow down faster. The higher levels of the animation hierarchy can also vary more during a moving hold. A 5 degree twitch in a finger is not nearly as noticeable as a 5 degree twitch in the chest.

7. Repeat Step 5, then Steps 3 and 4 again, for each level of the hierarchy.

8. When you are satisfied with the entire animation's timing and all the additional keyframes, save the scene. Render and play back the animation.

You should end up with a series of dramatic transitions that have strong poses; read well; show appropriate anticipation, snap, overlapping action, and follow-through; and hold well without going dead. Don't be discouraged if your first try at this animation isn't as good as you hoped—timing emotional transitions well takes lots of practice. Make up other sequences of emotional transitions, and animate them for practice. Pivotal scenes from plays or movies are excellent source material for animating emotional transitions.

Gestures And Mannerisms

Body language and hand gestures are an international language. Although some gestures have special meanings in certain countries or regions, there are many gestures that have almost universal meanings. Your characters will seem much more lively and self-motivated if they use gestures and body language to emphasize the message of their posture.

You can build up a repertoire of gestures by your own observations, but I recommend studying one or more of the available books on the subject. Desmond Morris' *Bodytalk* is one of the more accessible works on the subject and includes notes on regional usage.

Mannerisms are a personal version of gestural communication. A particular motion, gesture, or posture may have a special meaning when expressed by one character but not when used by another. Mannerisms are only effective in repetition. If one of your characters displays a mannerism, it will probably not be interpreted correctly by your audience the first time they see it. With repetition, the audience can associate the mannerism with the character and understand the intended message. Over time, a mannerism can become a character's identifying characteristic. One has only to think of the phrase, "What's up, Doc?" to realize how powerful a mannerism can become.

Both gestures and mannerisms should help to further define the character. Whenever you pose a character, ask yourself, "Could another character hold that pose to get that effect?" If the answer is yes, the pose doesn't help define the character—it's weak and should be changed. A gesture, mannerism, or other action should specifically and exclusively define the character performing the action.

The hands are a rich source of expression. Most gestures involve at least one hand, and many require both. The average character's hands have more joints than the rest of the body combined, even when using the classic three-fingered cartoon character gloves. The most important guideline for animating character hands is to avoid mittens, the tendency to clump all the fingers side-by-side in an undifferentiated lump. Even if an illustrated gesture shows the fingers aligned, it's a good idea to express some individuality by moving one of the fingers slightly out of line.

The hands are closely watched, ranking right behind the eyes and face in attracting your audience's attention. You should therefore practice animating hands, and pay at least as much attention to fine-tuning them as you do to the rest of the character's body. Also, try to keep the hands above the waist, unless you intend the character to look exhausted or sad.

Get Over Here!

PROJECT 15.23

The goal of this project is to apply what you've learned about posture, gesture, and mannerisms to animate a unique performance for the character.

1. Reload the default Puppet scene file again.

   Frame 1 shows the character in a normal posture.

2. For the first keyframe, pose the character to show an imperious, pompous attitude.

   Use your imagination. I'm sure you can think of a suitable model.

3. Make additional keyframes at appropriate distances. Pose the character to summon another (unseen) character, using hand gestures and posture to communicate the action and define the character.

   Typical poses might include: a forceful pointing movement with fully extended arm in the direction of the unseen character, a withdrawal of the extended arm, and a second forceful pointing movement down towards the pointing character's feet, as if to say, "You! Get over here!" as one would summon a dog.

   Pay special attention to the nuances of the hand pose. Don't forget to stage the action by pointing the hand first.

4. Animate the character waiting impatiently for the summoned character to respond.

   Animate whatever waiting twitches you prefer. Toe-tapping, clenched fists on hips, or crossed arms are all good indicators of impatience.

5. Animate the character directing the summoned character.

   Lots of pointing fingertip jabs should communicate the idea adequately.

6. Animate the character dismissing the summoned character.

   This is comparatively easy, you can use a backhanded flipping hand motion as dismissal, while the rest of the character is animated to be looking elsewhere, bored. Remember to keep an upright, imperious posture throughout the animation.

7. Save the scene with a new file name. Render and play back the animation. Tweak the moving holds, timing, and other settings as necessary. When you are satisfied with the animation, save the scene.

Come Here, Please

PROJECT 15.24

1. Repeat Project 15.23, but this time create a more persuasive character.

   This is a variation on a theme: Animate the character to summon, direct, and dismiss an unseen subject in a cajoling way. Spend more time on the directing part, using lots of encouraging and even imploring hand gestures.

2. Save the scene with a new file name. Render and play back the animation. Tweak the moving holds, timing, and other settings as necessary. When you are satisfied with the animation, save the scene.

Would You Care To Step This Way?

PROJECT 15.25

1. Repeat Project 15.23 again, but this time create an extremely diplomatic and polite character.

The character should spend a good amount of time bowing and making other polite, considerate gestures. The key pose groups might be described as invitation, ingratiation, negotiation, and farewell.

2. Save the scene with a new file name. Render and play back the animation. Tweak the moving holds, timing, and other settings as necessary. When you are satisfied with the animation, save the scene.

Timing Is Still Everything

Timing actions to emphasize lip sync dialog is the best way to sell a shot. If the action is timed well, even poor lip sync looks acceptable. If the action is not timed to emphasize the dialog properly, even excellent lip sync will not look very good.

When you are working with a lip sync exposure sheet, one approach to accents is to listen to the track, and mark each syllable that the voice talent emphasized. You can animate physical gestures like head nods to emphasize the dialog. These forms of emphasis always precede the actual syllable.

Try it yourself. Read a particularly dramatic bit of prose or poetry while watching yourself in the mirror, and you will see that you nod or lift your head well before the sound you are accenting.

You will probably need to experiment at first, but a good starting offset is three to six frames. Simply write the emphasis (*nod* or *lift*) in the Action column of the exposure sheet, the desired number of frames in advance of the lip sync frames.

A Dramatic Reading, *Sans* Mouth

PROJECT 15.26

1. Play back the Finest Hour WAV clip on this book's CD-ROM. Note the emphasized syllables, and mark them on the exposure sheet from Chapter 4.

2. Transpose all the emphasis marks from three to six frames, to allow for physical emphasis to precede the sound.

3. Load the default Puppet scene file again.

4. Animate the character according to your modified exposure sheet.

   Because the character does not yet have a mouth, you will need to convey the desired emphasis by head and body motions alone.

5. Using Adobe Premiere or the editing software of your choice, dub the provided soundtrack over the rendered animation to check the sync.

6. When you are satisfied with the quality of the finished piece, save the file under a new name.

Moving On

If you have learned (and continue to practice) the principles of character animation described in this and the preceding chapter, you should have a solid repertoire of performances. Don't neglect these basics, even after you've moved on to the complexities and challenges of animation power tools, as shown in the next chapter.

ANIMATION

Power tools and procedural setups, like any animation tools, are only as good as the animator applying them. You need to know when a power tool will save you work without reducing the quality of the final animation, and when the power tool will drag down the quality of your work. Power tools are seductive, and you need to have a well-developed suspicion of inflated claims or inappropriate applications.

The preceding chapters show you the essential tools, processes, and skills you need to create good character animation using computers. Chapter 13 introduces a class of optional tools, power tools that you can use to create animation with less effort (sometimes) by giving more animation control to the computer. Sometimes, the trade-off in control isn't worth it, but, sometimes, the right power tool can make a difficult or impossible shot feasible.

As an animator, you need to strike a balance somewhere between posing individual vertices frame-by-frame and winding up behavioral actors. Most animators will agree that hand-animating every particle in your character's universe is too much control. Most animators will also agree that directing a behavioral actor to go through a sequence of preset motions is not truly character animation. There is a vast gray area between these two extremes, and you will have to choose your own boundaries.

How much should you automate? Computers are like fire—powerful tools but terrible masters. In CGI character animation, as in many computer-dominated fields, there is a strong tendency to rely too heavily on the computer. It's the old hammer-and-nail dilemma again. As long as the computer is relieving you of the mindless drudgery associated with traditional animation production, well and good. If the computer begins to cramp or fight part of your creative style, it's time to back up and take another look at who's *really* running things. Computers are simply complex tools—don't ever let them dictate your creative options.

Some of the most useful character animation power tools have applications for lip sync, facial animation, cloth simulation, and physical simulation. This chapter shows you how to animate these phenomena effectively, building on the power-tool setups detailed in Chapter 13 to improve the quality of your animation.

"Doc" Greenberg's Pathology 101

By Steph Greenberg

These are the top 15 pathologies I find in character setups. If you can diagnose and repair these pathologies as early as possible in the animation process, you'll save a lot of time and effort (not to mention frustration) for everyone.

- Feet sliding when at least one foot should be planted firmly on the floor. This is still an incredibly common animation pathology, even though the tools to prevent it have been around for almost a decade.

- Inability to point knees in a particular direction, and keep them pointed in that direction, regardless of what the lower torso or feet are doing. The direction of the knee is part of the physical motion that not only defines a character, but can also indicate the physical load being borne by that character.

- Constantly having to correct the rotation of the feet to keep them pointed in a chosen direction. This is an indication of improperly isolating the foot at the ankle joint from the rest of the leg hierarchy.

- Inability to point elbows in a particular direction, and keep them pointed in that direction without frequent correction and additional keyframes. Correcting this pathology accommodates arm snap and "successive breaking of joints," as taught in animator Richard Williams' master classes.

- Inability to isolate the position of hands for a chosen animated arc independent of the rotation or movement of the torso. This results in additional use of dry erase markers or grease pencils to mark where the hand should be, and the subsequent creation of what should be superfluous keyframes.

- Inability to isolate the rotation of the hands for a chosen gesture from the rotation of the torso, forearm and elbow. This pathology requires additional keyframes when none should be necessary.

- The necessity of reposing the entire torso hierarchy to change the tilt of the pelvis between poses and during secondary animation. All that should be needed is the adjustment of a bone/joint's channels.

- Lack of head isolation, creating the necessity of altering the head rotation to compensate for additional or secondary animation, particularly rotation of the upper torso, between main poses just to keep the head rotation arcs the way they were intended.

- Failure to create a collarbone for use when the arm is raised beyond the point where the humerus (the bone that goes from the shoulder to the elbow) is parallel to the ground plain.

- Failure to create a skin/bone relationship that allows the shoulders to appear natural when a character:
  - Scratches his/her/its own back without aid of optional tools or instruments
  - Reaches across his/her/its chest to hold the other arm's shoulder (as if in pain) and massage it

- Reaches up for the top shelf in the pantry

- Reaches down to tie its shoes.

- Failure to build in a character's ability to place a hand on a desk and keep the hand planted, or slide it across simply, even when the body is involved in other contortions.

- Failure to account for the meat inside of the skin and plan some way for it to move independently of the torso.

- Failure to provide a way for a character to stand on its toes and keep the ball of the foot planted without constant re-keyframing of the inbetweens on the foot.

- Failure to create a mechanism to lift the toe and keep the heel and ball of the foot planted.

- Failure of a way to animate the upper torso completely independently of the leg mechanisms other than reaching the stretch limits of the bones.

Diagnosing setup pathologies, along with prescribed remedies, is something gained through logical deduction, gut instinct and experience. The setups described in Chapter 12 can be deployed to solve many of these problems occurring in different situations, and can be combined with solutions described in other chapters, even adapted across different software platforms within the allowances of the software features.

It is often helpful to write down the problem, describing it in as much detail as is possible, since within defining a problem the solution can often be found. Sometimes it helps to have some Erector Set pieces to screw together and make a primitive physical model to analyze. Popsicle sticks, Legos, cardboard, and those thick straws from fast food restaurants can help, too.

People who can create complex setups and solve their pathologies are in demand, and it's worth the investment in time to learn how to look at setups as a challenge both to your creativity and problem solving skills.

Steph Greenberg is a 3DCGIMD, CGI Character Orthopedic Surgeon, Chiropractor, and Podiatrist.

Lip Sync

Lip sync is generally the finishing touch, the last tweak to the animation that makes a big difference. The pantomime and composition may get your main point across, but it's the subtlety of the facial animation that really sells the shot to your audience. It's amazing what you can do with a well-arched eyebrow, instead of a whole-body shrug or gesture.

It seems that everybody who learns character animation is initially excited about doing lip sync. OK, we'll work through lip sync first (animators have to know how to do it), then move on to more important things.

Why this attitude, you ask? Good question! Lip sync is arguably the least creative of character animation tasks. You are slavishly following the frame-by-frame timing of the voice talent, and you have little leeway in which to be creative with the timing. Your audience is sensitive to glitches in lip sync and will often criticize an otherwise fine animation job based on a few mismatched frames.

Furthermore, because the process is so closely coupled to the sound track, a lot of R&D work has been done recently on completely automating it. For example, the proprietary software used by Mainframe Entertainment to animate "Reboot" and "Beast Wars" uses a component called *GRIN* that automates lip sync. Other animation houses probably have similar software in use or development. The CGI software industry has typically added new functions to desktop software within a few years of their high-end proprietary development. Currently, Miguel Grinberg is attempting to automate at least part of vocal track analysis with his Magpie Pro software. My advice, therefore, is not to spend a lot of time mastering lip sync. If not already, it most likely will be automated by a plug-in for your favorite animation software very soon.

This is not to say you shouldn't work through the projects in this chapter. At the least, you'll understand what the old hands are talking about when they complain about doing lip sync the old-fashioned way.

Lip sync starts, as does everything else in animation, with a lot of foresight and planning.

Plans And Maps

You don't even need to think about animating for lip sync until the script and storyboards are finalized, the voice talent has recorded all their tracks, and the director and editor have pieced together the takes they want for the final soundtrack. Once the soundtrack is locked, at least as far as the dialog is concerned, the track can be analyzed, and the exposure sheets written up (see Chapter 4 for details).

What you will be given on the exposure sheets is a frame-by-frame phonetic breakdown of the vocal track, along with all the other information about action, camera directions, and so on. For this set of projects, you can ignore everything but the phonetic breakdown.

Lip sync is one of the skills that transfer directly from traditional stop-motion or cel animation to CGI. There is a 70-year body of work on synchronizing sound to animation, most of it already available to the animator in book or video form. There is little call for cut-and-try experimenting when it comes to lip sync.

Just about every book on cel or cartoon animation has a section on lip sync, usually including a model sheet of basic drawings for the mouth. These drawings can be adapted directly as image maps for the following projects. The image maps reproduced in Figure 13.15 are provided with the Magpie Pro track analysis software.

If your TD has not already made up a phonetic map library, or you are doing everything yourself, you can either use the map library provided on this book's CD-ROM or create your own maps. If you choose to roll your own, refer to Chapter 13 for details on their construction and application.

Project 16.1 explains how you can use image sequences to animate the phonetic mouth shapes, painting the mouth as you might paint an Easter egg. This is the easiest way to do facial animation, but it's not without drawbacks.

Animating with image sequences generally provides the lowest level of realism in animation. Stylistically, this method lends itself to a number of approaches. The burden of realism or style is lifted from the TD or sculptor building the objects and transferred to the artist drawing the maps. The map artist can therefore employ almost any drawing style, ranging from the harshest minimalist abstractions to the softest, most realistic textures possible. With the right image processing software and a good deal of patience, it is possible for a talented graphic artist to turn a primitive egg shape into a photo-realistic human face and head (see Chapter 9).

That goal is beyond the purpose of the projects in this chapter. We'll concentrate on a very simple approach—the standard cartoon mouth shapes applied to the Face object you animated in Chapter 14.

You can use a color image sequence to change the surface colors of the object, painting on the mouth shapes. If the background of the color maps is not the exact shade of the object, you may need to apply matching alpha maps to make the background of the color maps transparent, depending on your software.

These image sequences can be used alone, if it suits the style of the animation. This is the simplest approach, but it will not change the profile or give any impression of a third dimension to the mouth. Also, any specularity or diffusion spot will continue to reflect from the open mouth, spoiling the effect, as in Figure 16.1.

Figure 16.1 Head with color and alpha mouth image maps applied.

The next step in complexity—a precisely matched bump or displacement image sequence—gives the lips the appearance of some depth. A bump map permits the use of a simpler object, but it will not alter the profile of the object and is less realistic. If you use a displacement image sequence, it will alter the profile of the object. The trade-off is that the object must have a finely divided geometry in the area to be mapped, or the mouth will appear to have unsightly jags. With the combination of color, alpha, and either bump or displacement image sequences, any specularity or diffusion spot will still reflect from the open mouth, as in Figure 16.2.

The last level of image sequence mapping is the addition of a matched clip image sequence. The clip map cuts away the surface of the object where the mouth is open, to reveal the teeth, tongue, and inner mouth surfaces, as shown in Figure 16.3.

Obviously, the border between the inner edge of the lips and the opening of the mouth must be carefully drawn, or the lips will appear jagged or uneven. While it is possible to dither and otherwise cheat the resolution of both color and bump images, the clip images should be the highest resolution consistent with memory resources.

With the clip image sequence, the highest level of mapped realism is possible. If the bump or displacement map is drawn correctly, the clip should occur exactly where the surface is distorted to a 90 degree angle, and the clipping will take effect exactly where the surface would disappear if it were modeled in three dimensions. The only giveaways will be at this abrupt edge of the lips. If the camera is positioned at an angle approximately tangent to the lips, the inner surface of the object's face may be visible. You should avoid these camera angles if you use clip mapping.

Figure 16.2 Head with color, alpha, and bump mouth image maps applied.

Figure 16.3 Head with color, alpha, bump, and clip mouth image maps applied.

"You pays your money and you takes your choice"; every cheat and trick used in animation has its down side. Your challenge as an animator or TD is to make those choices depending on the demands of the job at hand.

Timing For Lip Sync

Timing good lip sync isn't just a matter of sticking an *a* map in the frame where the exposure sheet is marked *a*. Different phonemes are held for different lengths of time and transition to and from other phonemes in different ways. Here are a few rules to keep in mind:

- *Snap open, close slow*—The mouth should snap open quickly in a single frame, two at the most, to full extension for vowels. It should close much more slowly to hold the vowel.

- *Hold for emphasis*—Hold important or emphasized vowels longer, just as you hold an important pose.

- *Shut up with inbetweens*—Use transition or inbetween maps when closing the mouth slowly from a held phoneme.

- *Explosive plosives*—Ts, Ds, Bs, and Ps cannot be held. Snap them out in a frame or two, or your character will look mush-mouthed.

- *Speed kills*—Don't try to keep up with a very fast speaker, or your audience won't catch it. If the mouth actions become too frenetic, use inbetweens rather than full poses for alternating mouth actions.

- *Watch yourself*—Just as discussed in the preceding chapter, you are your own best model. Keep a mirror handy. Most professional animators keep a nice-sized mirror propped right next to their monitors when doing facial animation. When in doubt about a mouth action, pronounce it yourself, and observe what your face does.

With all these guides firmly in mind, let's move on to the real thing—animating lip sync!

Animating Lip Sync

This lip-sync process depends on the program you use. Your software may not require you to specify a map for each frame in a sequence. LightWave holds the last-used map until the next higher number in the sequence is reached. For example, if the file order is

1, 2, 5, 10, 11

the displayed file sequence will actually be

1, 2, 2, 2, 5, 5, 5, 5, 5, 10, 11

Obviously, this can save you a great deal of work in laying out a lip-sync image sequence. You only have to specify the changes, not the holds.

The approach we'll use is simple, albeit tedious at times. Because there are only a handful of phoneme image maps to choose from, we'll simply make a bunch of copies of these image files, numbered in the order we want them to appear. For example, if the phoneme image for *o* appears in the exposure sheet at frames 5, 18, and 24, we'll make three copies of the file O_COL.BMP, renamed LIPC0005.BMP, LIPC0018.BMP, and LIPC0024.BMP. When LightWave 3D loads the images from the sequence for frames 5, 18, and 24, the *o* phoneme map copies will be loaded.

One more drawback of this approach should now be obvious. If you've got a long shot, with a lot of speaking, the number of copied files is going to get very large very quickly and demand a lot of hard disk space. If this becomes a problem, you may have to render the shot in segments, limited by how many phoneme image maps you can store at one time.

While not exactly a drawback, it is especially important with this approach to keep your files organized. If you mess up a directory name, you can end up with one character lip synching another's lines. Comical, sure, but the audience will be laughing at you, not your animation!

Cooking Up A Batch

This project shows how to create batch files to make the image sequence mapping process easier.

1. Set up a directory for the shot, named SHOT0065, if you haven't already. (It's a good idea to keep copies of every file you will need for a shot in the shot's own directory.) Create a subdirectory for the character, named SHOT0065\WINSTON. Create four subdirectories within the character directory: \COLOR, \BUMP or \DISPLACE, \CLIP, and \ALFA.

   Creating separate subdirectories is an easy way to manage more than one character in a shot. You don't have to worry about overwriting or deleting map or object files that are needed for another character.

2. Copy the color, bump or displacement, clip, and alpha channel map libraries for the character to the new character directory. For this project, use the map library located in directory CH16\MOUTHS on this book's CD-ROM.

   These maps are derived from the Default mouth set originally bundled with Magpie 1.

3. Get the shot's exposure sheet from your director, or, if you are doing it yourself, follow the breakdown procedures outlined in Project 4.9. For this project, we'll work from the six-page sample exposure sheet provided at the end of Chapter 4.

   The exposure sheet contains the analysis of a phrase from one of Winston Churchill's more famous speeches. The words of the quote are: "So bear ourselves that if the British Empire and its Commonwealth last for a thousand years, men will still say, this was their finest hour."

4. Starting with the first phoneme color map in the library, count how many times it is called for in the exposure sheet, and list or mark each starting frame number. Repeat this process for each phoneme color map. Some may not be used, especially in a brief shot.

5. Using Windows Write or other text editor, create a new batch file named for the shot and character (WINS0065.BAT), and save it in the shot\character subdirectory, SHOT0065\WINSTON.

6. The first marked frame of the sample exposure sheet, frame 30, calls for the phoneme *s*. According to the Magpie Default set notes, the *s* phoneme is represented by the image file labeled *CDGK*. This is kind of a catch-all mouth shape for most of the consonants. Edit the first line of the batch file to read:

```
COPY CDGK_COL.BMP COLOR\LIPC0030.BMP
```

This command duplicates the *s* color image into the Color subdirectory. This means the phoneme color map for the *s* sound will be applied to the character in frame 30 of the animation.

7. Select the first line (including the carriage return), copy it, and paste it as many times as the first map is called for. You should end up with something like this:

```
COPY CDGK_COL.BMP COLOR\LIPC0030.BMP
COPY CDGK_COL.BMP COLOR\LIPC0030.BMP
COPY CDGK_COL.BMP COLOR\LIPC0030.BMP
COPY CDGK_COL.BMP COLOR\LIPC0030.BMP
COPY CDGK_COL.BMP COLOR\LIPC0030.BMP
COPY CDGK_COL.BMP COLOR\LIPC0030.BMP
COPY CDGK_COL.BMP COLOR\LIPC0030.BMP
COPY CDGK_COL.BMP COLOR\LIPC0030.BMP
COPY CDGK_COL.BMP COLOR\LIPC0030.BMP
```

8. Select the number part of the new file name in the second line. Type the number of the next start frame for this phoneme map:

```
COPY CDGK_COL.BMP COLOR\LIPC0030.BMP
COPY CDGK_COL.BMP COLOR\LIPC0065.BMP
```

9. Repeat the number editing for the rest of this phoneme map's frames:

```
COPY CDGK_COL.BMP COLOR\LIPC0030.BMP
COPY CDGK_COL.BMP COLOR\LIPC0065.BMP
COPY CDGK_COL.BMP COLOR\LIPC0072.BMP
COPY CDGK_COL.BMP COLOR\LIPC0179.BMP
COPY CDGK_COL.BMP COLOR\LIPC0239.BMP
COPY CDGK_COL.BMP COLOR\LIPC0265.BMP
COPY CDGK_COL.BMP COLOR\LIPC0279.BMP
COPY CDGK_COL.BMP COLOR\LIPC0326.BMP
COPY CDGK_COL.BMP COLOR\LIPC0340.BMP
COPY CDGK_COL.BMP COLOR\LIPC0403.BMP
```

```
COPY CDGK_COL.BMP COLOR\LIPC0438.BMP
COPY CDGK_COL.BMP COLOR\LIPC0460.BMP...
```

10. Repeat these steps for the rest of the phoneme color maps. When you're done, you should have a fairly lengthy list of files to be copied. Save the batch file.

11. You really don't want to have to go through this whole process again to match up the clip and bump or displacement maps. Here's an easy way to do it: Save the batch file again, under a new name. The exact name isn't important—this will only be a temporary file. Use the Replace function in the temporary file to replace *LIPC* with *LIPB* and *_COL.* with *BUMP.* (or *DISP.*). Note the period included in the search term. If you leave the period off, you'll end up with a lot of lines looking like:

```
COPY CDGK_BUMP.BMP BUMPO\LIPB0030.BMP
COPY CDGK_BUMP.BMP BUMPOR\LIPB0065.BMP
COPY CDGK_BUMP.BMP BUMPOR\LIPB0072.BMP
COPY CDGK_BUMP.BMP BUMPOR\LIPB0179.BMP...
```

12. Use the Replace function again, but replace *COLOR* with *BUMP*. Save the file, in case you need it again.

13. Select all, and copy. Reopen the original batch file, go to the end of the file, and paste.

    You should now have two sections of batch file—the first copying all the color maps, and the second copying the corresponding bump or displacement maps:

```
COPY CDGK_COL.BMP COLOR\LIPC0030.BMP
COPY CDGK_COL.BMP COLOR\LIPC0065.BMP
COPY CDGK_COL.BMP COLOR\LIPC0072.BMP
COPY CDGK_COL.BMP COLOR\LIPC0179.BMP...
COPY CDGKBUMP.BMP BUMP\LIPB0030.BMP
COPY CDGKBUMP.BMP BUMP\LIPB0065.BMP
COPY CDGKBUMP.BMP BUMP\LIPB0072.BMP
COPY CDGKBUMP.BMP BUMP\LIPB0179.BMP...
```

14. Repeat the preceding steps, replacing *LIPC*, *BUMP.*, and *BUMP* in the temporary file with *LIPP*, *CLIP.*, and *CLIP*, respectively. Copy the revised section and paste it to the end of the batch file. Repeat again, replacing *LIPC*, *BUMP.*, and *BUMP* in the temporary file with *LIPA*, *_ALF.*, and *ALFA*, respectively.

    Now, you have all the copy instructions for every phoneme map you want to use in this shot:

```
COPY CDGK_COL.BMP COLOR\LIPC0030.BMP
COPY CDGK_COL.BMP COLOR\LIPC0065.BMP
COPY CDGK_COL.BMP COLOR\LIPC0072.BMP
COPY CDGK_COL.BMP COLOR\LIPC0179.BMP...
COPY CDGKBUMP.BMP BUMP\LIPB0030.BMP
COPY CDGKBUMP.BMP BUMP\LIPB0065.BMP
```

```
COPY CDGKBUMP.BMP BUMP\LIPB0072.BMP
COPY CDGKBUMP.BMP BUMP\LIPB0179.BMP...
COPY CDGKCLIP.BMP CLIP\LIPP0030.BMP
COPY CDGKCLIP.BMP CLIP\LIPP0065.BMP
COPY CDGKCLIP.BMP CLIP\LIPP0072.BMP
COPY CDGKCLIP.BMP CLIP\LIPP0179.BMP...
COPY CDGK_ALF.BMP ALFA\LIPP0030.BMP
COPY CDGK_ALF.BMP ALFA\LIPP0065.BMP
COPY CDGK_ALF.BMP ALFA\LIPP0072.BMP
COPY CDGK_ALF.BMP ALFA\LIPP0179.BMP...
```

15. Make a backup copy of this batch file! It's fairly easy to rebuild the directory structure if you accidentally delete some files, but, if you lose this batch file, you'll have to go back to the exposure sheet and start all over.

16. Make sure you've got plenty of disk space available. Multiply the number of lines in your batch file by the size of the largest file you are duplicating to get an upper-limit estimate of the total storage required. When you are ready, execute the batch file.

    If all goes well, the batch file makes copies of the appropriate color, alpha, bump, and clip maps and places them in their respective subdirectories, one of each type for each phoneme keyframe numbered in the batch file.

17. Now, you get to do some preemptive quality control. Browse the subdirectories in the shot directory. Did the files end up where you expected them to? Open up a few files from each directory as a spot check, and compare them with the exposure sheet. It's much better to catch any mistakes now than after rendering the entire shot.

18. In your animation software, load the Face scene file you set up in Chapter 11 and animated in Chapter 14.

19. Load the color image sequence you just created.

20. Load the alpha image sequence.

21. Load the bump or displacement image sequence.

22. Load the clip image sequence.

    You now have all four matching image sequences loaded and ready to apply.

23. Apply all four image sequences to the Face surface, aligning them in the space under the character's nose.

24. Set the black of the alpha image to cover the object with the color map, and set the white areas of the alpha image to let the object color show through.

    Figure 16.3 shows the texture centered below the nose, at the surface of the mouth area. I used trial and error to find the correct values for this project. You'll have to test different values to fit your own setup and software.

25. Test render a few frames at a high enough resolution that you can check for map misalignments. Compare the maps in the rendered frames to the exposure sheet callouts to make sure they match.

26. If all the spot checks are OK, test render the entire shot in 1/4 screen resolution as an AVI. Be careful to use the same frame rate as the x-sheet. This is for the next step in checking, before you commit the time to rendering at full resolution and antialiasing.

27. Open Adobe Premiere, or whatever other editing software you are using. Load the rendered AVI file, and dub the lip-sync WAV file over it. Save the results to a new AVI file.

28. Play back the dubbed file to see if the lip sync reads accurately. Make sure the playback is locked to the frame rate at which you animated it.

If you have to revise just a few of the maps' timing, you can edit the batch file manually. Just make sure you change all four file types to the same frame numbers, or the maps won't match up! You should also delete the old duplicate image files manually, as the new numbers will be different and some of the older files would probably not be overwritten by the new set.

If you have to slip the entire shot, use your software's offset function. If you don't have one, you'll have to slip the soundtrack in Premiere.

In LightWave, using a positive Frame Offset value is like slipping the image sequence ahead. Add an Offset of 5, and the sequence image for frame 15 will be used in frame 10 of the animation. Conversely, using a negative Offset value is like retarding the image sequence. A value of -5 means frame 15 of the sequence will be used for frame 20 of the animation.

Usually, you will want to push the image sequence ahead, so the screen has a chance to show the lip image before the audience hears the phoneme. Some animation houses slip the images ahead of the audio track three or four frames as a matter of standard procedure. Nobody seems to know why, but it works for the audience.

If you have to slip large sequences but not the entire shot, you are probably better off deleting the alpha, bump, and clip sections of the batch file; editing the color section; then repeating Steps 11 through 14.

This may seem tedious the first couple of times you try it, but, with a little practice, it becomes second nature. This is one of the first jobs you can hand off to an assistant. It's a no-brainer after the first few iterations, but the quality control in the last steps trains the eye to spot details.

You might have noticed another advantage of this process. If a set of maps needs to be changed for any reason, it is relatively easy, right up to final rendering. Just delete the duplicate maps from the four map subdirectories, replace the master maps in the character directory with the updated maps, and re-execute the batch file. No problem. Just make sure the person who requested the changes thinks you sweated blood to make them!

You should now have a solid grasp of the principles of lip sync. Play around with the Face a little more, making it say anything you like. Follow the procedures in Project 4.9 to break out your own exposure sheets from digitized sound samples, and Chapters 9 and 13 to create additional mouth maps for caricatured mouth actions.

As with most skills in character animation, you can learn the basics of lip sync very quickly, but honing and polishing your timing and caricature skills is a lifetime pursuit.

Lip sync for either Replacement or Displacement animation uses the same principles. Each has the advantage of providing its own inbetweens, which means you only have to model or pose the actual keyframes. If you really like doing lip sync, you can repeat Project 16.1 using these techniques.

Magpie Pro

Magpie Pro is a track analysis program written by Miguel Grinberg. The THIRDWAV directory on this book's CD-ROM contains a demo version of the program. Magpie Pro is copyrighted shareware, and you may evaluate it for a period of no more than 30 days. After this time, you must either register and pay for it or remove it from your system.

Failure to comply with this condition is a violation of international copyright law—not to mention being very rude to Mr. Grinberg, who graciously makes this software available to animators worldwide. If you use it, please pay for it.

For details on registering and free updates, please refer to the information files in the THIRDWAV directory on this book's CD-ROM.

To run Magpie Pro, you need a PC-compatible computer running Windows NT or Windows 95, 16MB RAM, about 5MB free hard disk space, a true color graphics display, and an MCI device capable of playing 8- or 16-bit WAV audio files. Magpie Pro has many improvements and additional features over Magpie 1.0, including a live-action reference video window, multiple simultaneous expression sets, whole-word libraries, and speech recognition to automate first-pass lip sync, Figure 16.4. Magpie Pro also supports export formats for Softimage, 3D Studio MAX, LightWave, and Animation:Master. To take full advantage of these export formats, Magpie Pro now includes a spline editor you can use to tweak transitions between expressions. These new features put Magpie Pro solidly in the professional animator's must-have toolkit.

Track Analysis Basics

Track analysis is not really difficult, just painstaking. There are a relatively small number of *phonemes*, or unique sounds, used by all spoken human languages. Track analysis is the art of transcribing exactly when each phoneme occurs in a voice track.

I highly recommend keeping a good dictionary handy while analyzing vocal tracks; it can save you a lot of time while you are developing your track-reading skills. Any good dictionary will have a pronunciation guide. This will list all the phonemes for the dictionary's language and explain the letters and diacritical marks used in phonetic spelling. I recommend that you use the following cheat until you can rely on your own skills.

Make up a copy of the script for the vocal track, double- or even triple-spaced so you can write legibly under or over each word. Look up each word in the dictionary. Copy the phonetic spelling of each word under the normal spelling in the script. Now, you know exactly what phonemes you need and in what order.

Track Analysis Using Magpie Pro

PROJECT 16.2

This project shows you the basics of track analysis using Magpie Pro. We'll be using a digitized sample from a speech by Sir Winston Churchill, THISHOUR.WAV, which you can find on this book's CD-ROM. The phrase is: "This...was their finest hour." You can complete the following project more easily if you transcribe this phrase in phonetic spelling before you begin.

1. Follow the instructions for installing Magpie Pro, which you can find in the THIRDWAV directory on this book's CD-ROM (see Figure 16.4). You should immediately add the character expression set you created in Chapter 13, so you have phoneme expressions to work with. When installation is complete, start Magpie Pro.

   The Waveform pane displays the sound file you will be analyzing. Magpie Pro opens up by default with no sound file loaded.

2. Open the THISHOUR.WAV audio file from the Chapter 16 directory on this book's CD-ROM.

   Opening up a new WAV file automatically loads a clean session for you to work on.

3. Click on the Play button to hear the WAV file.

   Each pair of vertical lines in the Waveform pane brackets a single frame.

4. Select the second frame from the left by clicking on it once. The frame turns red. Double-click on the frame to hear it play.

   You can tell from your phonetic transcript (and from listening carefully) that the sound at this frame is a soft *th* sound, the first phoneme of the word *this*.

Figure 16.4 The Magpie Pro interface with a demo file loaded.

5. The Magpie Pro interface refers to phoneme images as expressions. Double-click on the expression labeled TH.

   Magpie Pro copies the expression labeled TH to the second frame of the Exposure Sheet pane. The TH image appears in the Preview pane.

6. Repeat Steps 4 and 5 for all the other frames, listening carefully and matching the sounds to your phonetic transcript.

At any time during this process, you can use the different Play buttons to play the entire sound, only the selected frames, or everything up to or following the selected frames. As the sound plays back, the images matching the expressions you selected will also play back in the Preview window.

What you will be doing is looking—and listening—for characteristic shapes in the waveform that correspond to phonemes. Human speech is made up mostly of clicks, buzzes, and hisses. For example, a sharp spike—a click—can represent a plosive sound such as P and B. The word *baby* would therefore have two spikes, and you would mark the frames next to those spikes with the letter B. Buzzing phonemes like M or N show up as relatively even zigzags with very similar individual waveforms, sustained over a number of frames. Hissing Ss or Cs look a lot like static, just a little louder.

Rather than go into a rambling theoretical discussion of all the different phonemes and how they are produced, I'm going to encourage you to experiment and develop your own rules. This all goes back to the principles discussed in Chapter 15—you can take someone else's word for it, or you can observe and draw your own conclusions. Observing speech is a wonderful way to lose your preconceptions about how people communicate.

If you are working with a large audio file, you may need to use the Zoom In and Zoom Out tools to see frames more clearly.

Find the plosives and clicks in the audio file. Look for peaks or other sharp changes within the word. Select and play them back until you can identify their start at a particular frame.

You can select more than one frame in the Waveform pane by dragging the mouse. All the selected frames will turn red. Double-clicking on a phoneme in the Mouth pane will assign that Mouth to all the selected frames.

Find the buzzes and hisses. These will appear as relatively even areas, drawn out over several frames. Select all the affected frames, and assign the appropriate Mouth shape.

The remaining phonemes will probably be mostly vowels. They tend to fill in everywhere but the clicks, buzzes, and hisses. They are also the most visible mouth shapes to animate, because they are held longer and generally require more facial distortion.

7. When you are satisfied with your results, save the file.

Magpie Pro saves the session, including expression settings and the path to the original audio file, in a Magpie Pro format with the extension .MGP.

As you can see, Magpie Pro's combination of visual and audible feedback is a great help to track analysis. The features added since the original Magpie—voice recognition, spline controls, shape weighting output, and so on—make this program even more valuable to the character animator. To contact Miguel Grinberg—preferably to tell him how much you like Magpie Pro, but also for technical support—you can send him email at mgrinberg@impsat1.com.ar.

Now, let's leave lip sync and use facial expression projects to learn about other facial animation techniques.

Facial Animation

Animating facial expressions makes lip sync look like a walk in the park. Conveying emotions, especially complex transitions and slow, subtle changes, is a much tougher proposition. As I stated in Chapter 15, animating for emotional communication requires at least as much judgment and sense of timing as acting on the stage.

While you can animate emotions using layers of image sequences, this requires such a large number of inbetween maps and such care in their timing that you will lose most of mapping's usual production advantage. As both morphing and bones techniques create inbetweens automatically and with finer control, they give you a significant advantage when you animate emotional transitions.

The human face is made up of many layers of muscle and other tissues, overlapping in different directions and bridging attachment points from the shoulders to the top of the skull. The goal of character facial animation is not to realistically simulate every one of these muscles, but to mimic the surface appearance produced by their combined actions well enough to tell the story. Refer to Chapters 6 and 7 if you want more detail on how to model an expressive face. For the purposes of this chapter, I'm just going to summarize the functions a CGI face has to emulate.

Most of a human face attaches closely to the underlying bone structure. The cheeks and lips have a great deal of freedom because they are only attached to bones at their outer edges, and their muscles and skin are flexible and elastic. Other areas of the face can't move as freely, because they are on a shorter leash, so to speak. The jaw and the skull proper are the two major divisions for animating the human face. The face from the upper lip upwards is mostly attached to the skull. From the lower lip downwards and back to the angle of the jaw, the face is attached to the jawbone. This is a good start for defining the animation hierarchy for the face. The skull is the root, the jawbone is the second layer, and all other animation controls will be attached to either the skull directly or through the jawbone.

The visible function of most facial muscles is pushing skin around, changing the shape of the face in small increments. The jaw and eyeball muscles are notable exceptions, because they rotate through comparatively large angles. To animate skin deformation, you can either use a lot of overlapping bones to deform the object or model the changes in a series of objects and use Replacement techniques to animate them. The following projects will show you how to animate facial expressions using both approaches.

The Sample Face

The following setup description is based on LightWave 5.5. If you set up a face of your own in Chapter 13, you should already be familiar with the controls and limits of the setup. If you haven't worked through Chapter 13 yet, you may want to go back and at least read through it before proceeding.

LightWave 3D 5.5

In the Chapter 16 directory on this book's CD-ROM, you'll find a sample object and scene of a basic articulated head, PROJ1602.LWS. This scene is the bare minimum necessary to create most facial expressions. Even so, the number of bones required may significantly slow down screen redraw if your system's CPU is running much below 166MHz. Figure 13.13 is a screen shot of PROJ1602.LWS, with all Bones made visible.

Here is a brief description of the animation controls and limits for this scene. As an animator, you should get similar summaries from the TD or setup person with every character you animate. Animating can be a lot easier if you understand where each control for a character is located and what it is designed to do.

There is only one light in the scene—a spot aimed at the character's face and Parented to the head. This enables you to switch Views to Light and always have a consistent, face-on view of the character. When you animate a full character, you may prefer to have more lights preset for other useful views (refer to Chapter 11 for details).

The scene uses a combination of nulls and Bones to control the shape of the Head object. The nulls are used as IK targets for multiple chains of Bones. So, instead of having to pose four or eight Bones you can just move a null, and the associated Bones will follow along. All posable nulls and Bones are Parented to the head, so you can create keyframes using the Selected Item And Descendants option to save an entire facial expression. You can also create keyframes for the MouthUp and MouthLow Bones and the MouthParentNull and their descendants to keyframe the mouth and leave the rest of the face alone.

I automated the eyes as much as possible. The eyeballs are IK targeted on a null, which can be moved as described in Chapter 14 to animate most eye movements. The eyelids are also IK targeted to the same null but with Pitch Limits limits for realistic action—limited pitch rotation, and no rotation at all on the heading and bank axes. This means you just move the null, and the eyeballs and eyelids follow along. When you need to change the angle of the eyelids, pitch the LUpEyeLidHandle and RUpEyeLidHandle +20 degrees for a wide-eyed expression, -25 degrees for a sleepy or drunk expression, and -55 degrees for fully closed, as in a blink or wink. Return the UpEyeLidHandles to 0 degrees pitch to resume normal IK tracking.

The eyebrows are very simple—just two Bones each. The inner Bone is the Parent, so you can move it along the Y-axis to move the entire eyebrow. For this object, I recommend no more than 0.015 up on the Y axis and rather less than that down. Because the forehead and brow ridge for this character have pronounced slopes, you will need to bring the eyebrows forward as well as down for some expressions, or the eyebrows will disappear inside the head. Changing the Pitch of the outer Bone bends the eyebrow—simple, but adequate for most eyebrow actions. I'd keep the Pitch angle within 80 degrees of the outer Bone's rest direction.

The left ear has a Hinge Bone, which can change Heading to flap the ear. This is silly, but useful as an example in Chapter 13. If you're feeling ambitious, you might set up similar Bones for the right ear.

The JawBone is Parent to the face below the lower lip. You can Pitch the JawBone about -30 degrees before you start getting gross distortions, but -5 to -10 degrees is plenty for most expressions. Reset the JawBone to 0 degrees Pitch to close the mouth. The JawBone controls the lower half of the cheeks, as well. When the jaw gapes, the polygons along the border between JawBone and HeadRoot stretch out to bridge the distance. A more advanced face would have additional Bones placed to puff the cheeks out or bulge the cheekbones under the eyes. As I stated earlier, this scene is the simplest I could design that is consistent with a full expressive range.

MouthUp is the Parent Bone for the upper-lip Bones. MouthLow is the equivalent for the lower-lip Bones. The upper teeth are fixed to the skull, and the lower teeth are fixed to the JawBone. The controls for the lips are evenly divided between nulls and Bones. There is a null at the left and right corners of the mouth, and one null each at the midpoint of the upper and lower lips. One Bone is positioned between each of these nulls, in the middle of the top left (LipUpLeft), top right (LipUpRight), lower left (LipLowLeft), and lower right (LipLowRight) quadrants of the mouth.

These Bones and nulls are visible, but there are another 16 hidden Bones that actually control the shape of the lips. The visible lip Bones are the Parents of two separate chains, and each chain is IK targeted at one of the adjoining nulls. The effect is that when you move a null, the hidden Bones keep the nearest section of lip lined up toward the null. Move a Bone, same thing. So, by animating eight control nodes (four Bones, four nulls), you're controlling twice that many Bones.

Keep the changes small to start with. Most of the nulls and Bones around the mouth can only move 0.02 units along the Y axis before serious rendering errors appear. It doesn't require much movement to create a convincing expression. You can also Pitch the four Lip Bones to suck in or push out the lips, which is useful when you try to pose an F or V for a lip-sync sequence.

Obviously, this object has room for improvement. Both mouth corners should be remodeled so the upper and lower lips share a common point, to keep the corner from pulling apart when the JawBone is at full gape. The area around the lips is not subdivided enough or in the right pattern to deform without rendering artifacts. In a real animation production house, this character would have been sent back to the TD or setup person for repairs. It's good enough for these projects, though, and, if you like, you can repair this object by taking it through Chapter 13 again.

Creating And Reusing Facial Poses

The human face has an enormous dramatic range, with nearly infinite gradations of expression. To attempt even a brief summary of facial expression in this space would be futile. Instead,

I recommend that you consult one of the facial expression works listed in the Bibliography. And, as I've noted before, one of your most useful study guides is a mirror beside your monitor. When you want to create an expression, act it out, and observe yourself.

Even though the full range of human facial expression is too large to catalog, there are a relatively small number of types or classes of emotional expression. Sadness, anger, joy, fear, disgust, and surprise are the basics. You may find it useful to create one facial pose of each type, then experiment with variations between the poses to create a library with more dramatic range.

Keep in mind that a library of standard emotional poses is only the starting point for developing a character's expressions. You shouldn't use the same expression on any two characters. Each character should have idiosyncrasies, minor variations on the common pattern, that make each expression uniquely suited to the character.

If your software enables you to reload poses from stock scenes, or to copy and paste poses from one frame to another, you can use a stock scene of lip sync and emotional poses as a starting point for all your facial animations. This can be as big a time-saver as a morph sequence setup, if you manage it right.

In LightWave, you can add facial setups to a scene with the Load From Scene function in the Objects panel. As long as all the posing controls are Parented to or Boned in the object, you can copy or delete a pose using the Selected Items And Descendants keyframe option. To do this for lip sync, you should set up the first 11 frames (after the three-frame setup described in Chapter 13) in the standard lip-sync poses. You can then make an entire lip sync sequence by copying the appropriate keyframe poses to the keyframes called out on the x-sheet, very much like you did with the image map sequence.

PROJECT 16.3   It's The Moody Guy Again

This project is an extension of the projects in Chapter 15, but it's designed for the face rather than the entire body.

1. Load scene file PROJ1602.LWS from the Chapter 16 directory on this book's CD-ROM.

   To review from Chapter 15, let's suppose the character starts off in a normal pose then is given some very saddening news by an opponent we don't see. Suppose the opponent then threatens the character, frightening him. Next, the opponent ridicules the character, causing the character's fear to transition to anger. Finally, the character's anger causes the opponent to leave, and the character exults in his victory. That's four major emotional poses—sadness, fear, anger, and exultation.

2. Using the Bones and null controls for the sample Head object, animate the character from normal through sadness, fear, a quick burst into anger, and finally a victorious exultation. Figures 16.5 through 16.8 may give you some ideas for what poses to use.

3. Experiment with the timing and spline controls (tension, continuity, and bias) for each transition, and observe the overall effect. Which transitions do you have to stretch out? Which work better when shortened?

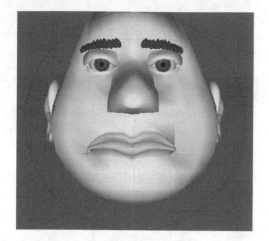

Figure 16.5 Key pose for sad.

Figure 16.6 Key pose for fear.

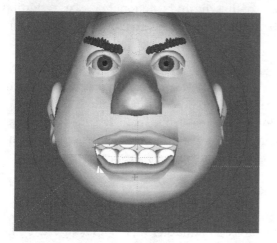

Figure 16.7 Key pose for anger.

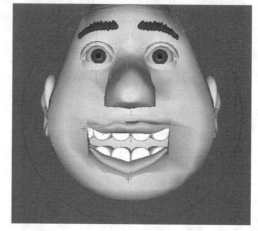

Figure 16.8 Key pose for exultation.

4. When you're satisfied with the timing of each transition, save the scene file under a new name.

Timing is still everything. When you set the timing for an emotional transition, you must hold each stage in the transition just long enough for the audience to read it and no longer. The best acting job in the world is useless if it flashes by so quickly the audience can't see it or drags on so long the audience is bored and their attention wanders. The timing of a transition alone can make a big difference in how your audience perceives a character. Imagine a character taking several seconds for a transition from confusion to comprehension. You might think this character is a little slow. On the other hand, compress this same transition to a half-dozen frames, and the character appears to be very bright, even inspired. Timing emotional transitions is another skill that takes time and practice to develop. Experiment, practice, and experiment some more. You can never have too much experience in timing character animation.

Avoid twins in posing the face, just as you would for the character's body. A perfectly symmetric face is rarely found in nature, and few human expressions are balanced. The smirk, sneer, lopsided grin, and wink are just a few of the stronger examples of one-sided facial expressions. Even blinks can be slightly offset to good effect, as you might observe in the early parts of *Toy Story*.

The principle of overlapping action applies to emotional transitions, too. You should offset the keyframes of each facial feature. If the eyes, mouth, and other features all peak at the same frame, the transition will look artificial. The action of the eyes generally leads the transition, just as it leads other actions, with the mouth following last. The mouth is controlled less by reflex and instinct than by volition. So, while the eyes immediately react to a situation, it takes a conscious decision by the character to move the mouth. This is why a surprised person's mouth may hang open—they simply don't think about doing something with it. Therefore, keep the eyes under tight control. The eyes should be the first part of the face to animate, and, even in extreme situations, the eyes are the last part of the face to lose control—eyes rolling up in the head as the character loses consciousness, for example. The mouth lags behind and represents conscious decisions rather than reflexes. The mouth can lie more easily, but it's often betrayed by the more truthful actions of the eyes.

A facial pose should precede the sound or phoneme the action is supposed to emphasize. In lip sync, for example, the lower lip should curl under the upper teeth several frames before the F sound occurs. The lead time for emotional transitions is even longer. If a head movement or facial expression is intended to emphasize a word, the entire action should end just when the word begins.

For example, look at the x-sheets at the end of Chapter 4 while listening to the FINESTHR.WAV sound clip. The word *this* has a strong vocal emphasis. You might choose to emphasize this word with a strong facial expression, as well, and perhaps a nod of the head. This visual emphasis should completely precede the sound. The nod and the facial transition to a strong key pose should end just at the first frame of the *th* phoneme, at which time the lip-sync poses should dominate. If you lap the action over the sound, the action will look stilted and poorly rehearsed. If you run the action and sound at the same time, it will look out of sync. If you run the action after the sound, it will look like a first reading by a very poor actor. When you are animating for lip sync or emotional transitions synched to a soundtrack, a good rule of thumb is "Deeds before words."

Be selective in what you emphasize. If you bob the character's head at every lip-synched syllable, the character will look spastic. When you first look at a lip-sync x-sheet, look for the emotional or dramatic high and low points of the passage, and start off with just those for emphasis. If you need emphasis, you can add poses to support the major points. But, it's better to start off with too few emphases in the action than too many.

Lip Sync Using Bones

1. Reload scene file PROJ1602.LWS.

2. Create a series of 11 poses, comparable to the Magpie Pro's lip-sync images, in frames 4 through 15.

3. Save the modified scene file as PHONEME1.LWS.

4. Using the lip-sync poses you just created and the x-sheets from Project 16.1, lip sync the Finest Hour sound clip with a dramatic reading. The easiest way to do this is to select the Head object, move to the first lip-sync pose frame, and create a keyframe for Selected Item And Descendants for each keyframe called for in the x-sheets. This will, however, create lots of unnecessary keyframes for the eyes and other parts of the objects that are not involved with lip sync. A more careful procedure is to create the keyframes for the MouthParentNull, MouthUp, and JawBone. This is, of course, slightly more work.

5. Add eye and head movements to the animation, using the principles of leading discussed in Chapter 14.

6. Save the scene file under a new name.

7. Set the beginning frame of the animation to frame 16, the first frame of the actual lip sync. Render an animation, from frame 16 to the last frame of the lip sync.

8. Dub the FINESTHR.WAV file over the rendered animation. How did you do? Is the emphasis on the correct frame for each action?

Morph Sequence Revisited

Depending on your software, morph sequence or shape weighting may be the easiest and most flexible means of animating lip sync.

If you haven't figured it out already, you can use the Save Transformed function to create a series of Metamorph target objects from a boned head animation. If standard poses are acceptable, it's much easier to experiment with timing transitions using an MTSE Envelope than individual bone motion graphs.

1. Reload the scene file you saved from Project 16.3. Select the Head object.

2. Go to the first key pose, normal, and open the Objects panel.

3. Click on Save Transformed, and save the object as NORMAL1.LWO.

4. Close the Objects panel.

5. Go to the next key pose, and repeat Steps 2, 3, and 4 for the remaining key poses. You should end up with objects for normal, sad, fear, anger, and exultation.

6. Reload the final scene file you saved from the last Moody Guy project in Chapter 15.

7. In the Objects panel, replace the existing head with the NORMAL1.LWO object. You may have to adjust the Y-axis offset to preserve whatever keyframes you made for the original head.

8. Follow the procedures you learned in Chapter 11 to set up an MTSE sequence, with NORMAL1.LWO as the base object and the sad, fear, anger, and exultation objects as the targets.

9. Edit the MTSE envelope to vary the timing for each key pose, and observe the overall effect. How well can you match the MTSE sequence to the body animation you created in Chapter 15? How much does the face add to the emotional message of the animation?

10. Save the finished scene file under a new name.

Note that by using MTSE objects for the whole head, you can vary the timing only for the entire expression, rather than the individual Bone control poses, and that the eyes are locked in position and no longer tracking a Null. If you plan to create MTSE objects, you may want to use Parented eyeballs and eyelids that will not be included by the Save Transformed function.

If you want the convenience and speed of animating a Boned face separately but still want the flexibility to tweak it along with the entire body, you can use the Load From Scene function to merge two or more complete animations. This enables you to create a separate animation for each Bone Child object (for example, the head and each hand), and then merge them with the body animation. At that point, the entire animation for body and head is accessible for tweaking. You still have complete control. Unfortunately, the screen redraw times and the length of Selected Item and Scene panel lists get rather unwieldy. Again, character animation with LightWave 3D is a matter of choosing your trade-offs.

In some situations, you may be able to combine bone or morph animation of a head object with image sequences for the mouth. This hybrid approach allows a greater dramatic range and more interactive control for the rest of the face, while making it easier for you to coordinate lip sync. You can set up the image map sequence at the beginning, as soon as you have an x-sheet, and animate the character's face to match the maps. Most of the controls for a fully boned face are around the mouth, so a hybrid head can be much simpler to set up and a great deal faster to animate, especially on slower computers. The disadvantage of this approach is that the character's style must be compatible with a painted-on mouth, as shown in the first part of this chapter.

If they are appropriate for your character, bump maps to add wrinkles can be a nice finishing touch to smiles and other expressions that crinkle up parts of the face. You are generally better off adding the wrinkle maps at the very end, after the action has been finalized. At that time, you can add wrinkle notes to the x-sheet, specifying the depth of the wrinkles at particular frames. With these notes, you can create a batch file to duplicate bump maps of different wrinkle depths. This is just like lip sync—maybe we should call it *crinkle sync*.

Morph Gizmo

Morph Gizmo is an extension to the concept behind MTSE. You can load several metamorph objects in a chain and control how much each object is weighted for each frame. The great leap forward for Morph Gizmo over MTSE is that the plug-in automatically detects what part of an object is different from the base object and only acts on those points. For example, suppose you raised the left eyebrow of a character and used Save Transformed to create a new object, then did the same for the right eyebrow, and loaded both modified objects into Morph Gizmo with the original object. Morph Gizmo enables you to control the percentage of change between the base object and either or both new raised-eyebrow objects. The rest of the character does not change, because only the eyebrow points were different from the base object. Even better, once you have set up the gizmo file, you don't have to load the morph targets. Morph Gizmo stores only the *deltas*, the changes in position for each affected vertex, so the file size is very small.

You can create a library of objects that each contain a single facial feature at an extreme pose, then combine them in Morph Gizmo to give you completely independent, highly interactive control over every facial feature of a character. You can set the morph percentage, or *weighting*, for each target interactively using a slider control. Morph Gizmo is the facial animation tool of choice for LightWave character animators.

Repeat Project 16.5, but use Morph Gizmo. You can create your own morph targets by using Save Transformed from the key poses in the final scene from Project 16.5, then load them into Morph Gizmo and mix them. Morph Gizmo provides much more flexibility, enabling you to mix facial expressions with phonemes and balance extreme expressions with more subtle ones. It's especially useful to be able to animate individual features morphing at different rates. For example, you might animate a transition from sadness to anger where the eyebrows lead and the mouth is the last part of the face to change.

Physical Simulation

As stated in Chapter 13, physical simulation is one of the most tempting classes of power tools for CGI character animation. Unfortunately, physical simulation is also one of the best ways to kill the illusion of life. You must be careful, as an animator, not to let setup people restrict your ability to animate by chaining too much control to simulation engines.

This is not to say you should never use simulation software. If you need a half-ton of tribbles to pour out of a storage bay, bouncing all over the place, only a lunatic would suggest hand-keyframing every furry tumble. At the same time, only a way-gone propeller-head would suggest unadulterated physical simulation for a character like Wile E. Coyote. You need to make intelligent, informed, appropriate choices. Toward that end, if you have not already read through the "Physical Simulation" section in Chapter 13, you should do so now.

3D Studio MAX: HyperMatter

HyperMatter is a plug-in for 3D Studio MAX that simulates soft-object deformation, collision, and other effects, enabling you to animate an object's elasticity and other parameters using MAX's standard keyframe and spline controls.

If you'd like to learn and see more, I recommend that you visit the Kinetix home page at **www.ktx.com** and peruse the animations, images, and tutorials there. You can also find a nice selection of HyperMatter-assisted animations at **www.2n.com/demosa.htm**, the home of Second Nature, HyperMatter's developers.

If you have HyperMatter, I suggest you first work through the exercises in the manual. Once you've completed those, you'll be ready for the following challenge.

Fred Goes Splat!

1. Refer to the story sketches in Chapter 3's storyboard that show Fred being ejected from the restaurant and slamming face-first into a street lamp.

2. Using the humanoid character of your choice and the street scene models provided, set keyframes to animate your character to match the storyboard's actions.

3. If you like, you can add animation controls to the street lamp to make it shudder slightly under the character's impact. You might also consider adding a stagger to the camera, as detailed in Chapter 14. Play back the pertinent section of the soundtrack for timing clues and inspiration.

4. When you're satisfied with the keyframe animation of the character and set, add HyperMatter controls to make the character squash and wrap around the street lamp.

5. Experiment with different settings for elasticity, compressibility, damping, and resilience.

   At the most extreme, the character's limbs should stretch clear out of the frame, and the head and torso should spread around the street lamp like a water balloon. At stiffer settings, you can minimize the distortion, so the character appears as solid as wood. Find an appropriate medium between these two extremes.

6. When you are satisfied with the results, render the animation. Using Adobe Premiere or other editing software, synchronize the appropriate clip from the soundtrack with your animation.

Cloth Simulation

Cloth simulation setups are best applied after you have finalized the keyframe animation of your characters and scenes. The calculations necessary to animate the cloth's mesh take a long time, compared to the rapid feedback of simple keyframe animation. You should also be aware of any cloth control handles available to you, so you can tweak the movement of the cloth to suit the composition of the shot, rather than passively hoping for a good-looking result.

Animate A Cloth Simulation

The point of this project is to add a simple cloth to an existing character and adapt it to the character's movement.

Infografica's ClothReyes

There is a demo version of ClothReyes on this book's CD-ROM, along with examples of MAX scene files, images, and animations created with this plug-in. Follow the HTML guide for the demo, or, if you already own ClothReyes, refer to the manual. If you created your own setup in

Chapter 13, you should have followed these basic guidelines:

- No self-intersection in the Hexamesh cloth model at the beginning of the animation.
- The cloth must be a separate surface.

1. Load the scene you set up in Chapter 13.

2. Select the fabric objects and all the other objects they are to interact with.

3. In the Modifier panel, choose ClothReyes from the drop-down list.

4. Click on Make Scene, and name the new scene. This is for the plug-in's internal use only—it doesn't actually save the whole MAX scene.

5. Select all the fabric objects, and click on Make Fabric. Edit the fabric parameters to create a specific effect, or use the defaults from the setup. Click on Close Parameters.

6. Select at least one object in the scene. Click on Start Calculation. Set a range of frames.

7. When the calculation is complete, render the animation.

Try resetting the fabric parameters, and recalculate the animation. What settings seem to work best for minimizing stretchiness, and what adds a sense of weight to the animated cloth?

Softimage 3.7 And TOPIXCLOTH

If you are using Softimage 3.7, refer to Chapter 13 for instructions on animating cloth with the freeware TOPIXCLOTH plug-in. The plug-in is located in the TOPIX directory on this book's CD-ROM.

PROJECT 16.8 Efficient Blocking With Magpie Pro

This is a technique first proposed by Rick May, and commented on and revised by many members of the CG-CHAR mailing list. Once you've mastered the basics of posing and timing, this approach may help you to produce better animation faster and with less effort. Depending on your working style, you may also find it more intuitive. According to industry experts, this approach encourages a higher level of refinement, and hence better finished animation, right from the beginning.

1. From your storyboards and bar sheets or x-sheets, block out all the key poses for a shot. You may find it useful to sketch these key poses or act them out.

2. In your animation software, block out your character to match each key pose, in order, spaced 10 frames apart. Ignore timing for now, the point is simply to make all the key poses.

3. Render a 320×240 bitmap of each key pose. These images are compatible with Magpie Pro's Preview window.

4. Import the rendered key poses into Magpie Pro as a new expression set, following the procedure detailed in Project 13.4.

5. Use Magpie Pro to set the timing between your key poses.

Magpie Pro's quick editing and real-time playback enable you to experiment with your timing much faster and more easily than almost any character animation software. If you have a foley or dialog track, you can digitize it, load it as a WAV file, and sync your key poses to the audio. If you have reference video of the dialogue actor, you can digitize that, too, and load it as an AVI that Magpie Pro will sync to the Preview playback.

6. Print the exposure sheet. If you have created an expression set that includes links to your animation software's key poses, you can also export the animation file directly from Magpie Pro. This is possible for Softimage, 3D Studio MAX's MorphMagic plug-in, LightWave's Morph Gizmo Pro plugin, or Animation:Master's Pose library, depending on how you set up your character and the expression set.

7. Import the timing from Magpie Pro, or shift the key poses manually to match the printed x-sheet.

8. Tweak the timing, using the principles of the animation hierarchy described in Chapter 15. Pay special attention to anticipation, follow through, and overlapping and secondary actions; these movements rely on keyframes leading or following the key poses, so the Magpie Pro timing won't provide any of these actions.

9. If you want lip sync, create it as described in preceding projects using Magpie Pro, and simply dump it on top of the character's other actions.

10. Tweak the emotional facial animation and eye movements last. Generally, the x-sheets are superfluous at this point. Just wing it.

Probably the most important advantage of this approach is that you can make a rough timing story reel, synched to the audio track, within an hour of blocking out the poses. This can be invaluable for client feedback and approval. This approach is also closer to the traditional cel animation process, in which you can get quick feedback on rough timing by flipping the key pose drawings, before the inbetweens are done. In addition, the x-sheet can be shared or edited much more easily than the full character setup in the animation software.

If you don't have Magpie Pro, you can still use this approach but with a little more effort. You need to use animation software that enables you to shift an entire character's keyframes from one frame to another, as easily as possible. You also need to set keyframe interpolation for everything to *constant*, *step*, or *linear*, depending on your software. This makes the rendered or previewed action snap from key pose to key pose, just as with the Magpie Pro approach.

If you are using Animation:Master, this approach is especially useful. In the current version of A:M, it's difficult and counterintuitive to shift an entire character's keyframes. However, if you save the entire character as a new Pose, you can use either Magpie Pro or A:M's LipSync to apply those Poses to the appropriate frames, as set by the x-sheet.

If you are using LightWave, you may want to consider plug-ins such as Con-Motion or KeyPro that enable you to more easily edit and shift keyframes for an entire character. Currently, LightWave does not enable you to easily shift keyframes for a complex setup including Bones and objects that are not part of the same hierarchy.

Once you've set the key poses, you have to tightly control how the computer inbetweens if you want good animation. Eventually, you should let the computer interpolate motion between the keyframes. Otherwise, you might as well be doing stopmo with clay. However, you should keep the keys, extremes, and breakdowns as tightly-controlled as possible. Left to any of the stock solutions, like standard splines or linear interpolation, computers do lousy inbetweens and tend to make everything floaty. Once you reset the splines from constant (or step or linear) to something like a plateau spline, you should adjust the tangents on the main expressive objects like hands, head movements, and torso bending, as well as offset some frames to create successive breaking of joints.

Motion Capture

I'd like to put in a few words about *motion capture*, a.k.a. *mocap*: it's not character animation, it almost always looks like a guy in a rubber suit, you can't do really exaggerated actions because they'd kill the actor, the raw data is a horrendous mess to try to edit into something usable, and it is neither cheaper nor faster than hand-keyframed animation, assuming the same level of finished quality. The basic principle of motion capture is to collect streams of realtime data during a performance. The basic principle of character animation is to deliberately plan, create, and revise a sequence of poses. The two approaches are antithetical at best.

Three professional animators, Jeff Hayes, Steph Greenberg, and Ken Cope, have named motion capture "Satan's Rotoscope" due to the insidious way mocap vendors are trying to market it as a replacement for trained animators. There are historical parallels between mocap and the Rotoscope process patented by the Fleischers; both have been touted as a replacement for skilled animators, produced lousy results that stuck out like a sore thumb when combined with traditional animation, produced disasters at the box office, and offended animators forced to work with them. Rotoscoping eventually died out of feature film production, once it was obvious the audience could tell the difference; mocap may go the same route. Satan's Rotoscope doesn't even have the advantage of enabling you to capture classic 2D animation the way rotoscoping does. Mocap is a legitimate tool that supports the nature of other art forms: performance capture for dance and virtual filmmaking, yes; digital puppeteering and animatronic programming, sure; character animation, absolutely not. Maybe someday the technology will evolve to be a useful adjunct to character animation, but for now I advise you to just say no.

For a more detailed debunking of mocap myths, I now turn you over to Steph Greenberg and Ken Cope.

On Mocap

By Steph Greenberg

Motion capture isn't animation.

Computer graphics is a new medium, with new possibilities. It can be used in realtime simulation, it can be used as a special effect in film, characters can be created that look plausibly real like the T-Rex in *Jurassic Park*, and characters can be created that look like classic cartoons, like those in *Marvin Martian in the 3rd Dimension*. Toys that almost look real can be brought to life, as in *Toy Story*, insects and arachnids can be given human anthropomorphic personalities. CG animated pigeons can be rendered to look like Japanese water colors, as in PDI's *Brik-A-Brak*, and odd looking, gas emitting aliens can be rendered to look like crayon drawings on textured paper as in PDI's *Gas Planet*.

No medium has yielded so many possibilities since Edweard Muybridge shot a sequence of stills to prove to the governor of California that a horse did not always have one foot on the ground. When played in sequence, the images looked like a horse running. Not many people realize that this was also the first filmed animation, since it was not a single pass of a horse running by his cameras that yielded this wonderful illusion, but several passes combined until the appropriate poses could be photographed of the horse running to make it look right. A conscious effort had to be expended to make the illusion of the horse running complete, rather than an imposition of verisimilitude that would have borne unsatisfactory results. But this conscious effort was employed to make the horse "look right" and to show all four hooves off the ground, and not to establish personality. It was editing to faithfully recreate reality.

Drawn animation proceeded this event by many years, by some accounts centuries, but it wasn't until 1915, decades after the invention of motion picture photography, that Windsor McCay created the first animated character with a personality, with *Gertie the Dinosaur*.

The dawn of computer graphics and animation was a little less straightforward. Equipment originally designed for flight simulation was subsequently subverted to use for the purpose of entertainment. While some crude personalities were created in computer generated imagery around 1981, it wasn't until mid 1980s shorts like *Tony DePeltrie* and *Oilspot and Dipstick* came out that the complexity of creating personalities and telling stories was brought to computer generated imagery (CGI). And it was extremely hard to do so, took some real skill, and it was clear that it was the job of artists to bring their creativity to the illusion of a computer rendered personality.

The skill to bring inert, individual frames to life had existed in drawn form since *Gertie the Dinosaur* was born in 1915, and had undergone a great deal of development in drawn animation in the succeeding years. All sorts of techniques and styles emerged from the pencil, joined by a similar development of techniques moving physical objects, clay, and foam models among other things, created frame by frame by individuals and organizations, all in the service of bringing things which existed in the minds of the animators to life.

Intrepid individuals and organizations brought these techniques to the new computer animation medium. John Lasseter may be a household name to any who pursue a career in computer character animation now, but his vision to use the computer to bring characters to life using traditional, pencil-originated tricks of the trade with a little stop motion thrown in, wasn't intuitively obvious to the people at the large, traditional institution in which he was employed at the time.

Computer character animation has a fundamental basis of movement that resides in joint rotations, and a character at its most basic is moved by rotating the constituent segments from which the character is built, or in the modern world, rotating dummy objects that can look like bones, to which the vertices or control points that constitute a "skin" are attached by various schemes. Whether a character is animated by forward kinematics or inverse kinematics (see Chapter 12), this is still the basis for the way characters are animated in the CGI world, with morphs and other deformation techniques subordinate to these rotations and translations.

By the late 1980s, the technicians and programmers, the high priests of CGI, had seen the work of animators like Lasseter, but didn't have the time or state of mind to learn traditional techniques. And so they sought shortcuts to bringing characters to life that had a basis in the technical life they understood, instead of the arcane world of doing things frame by frame. They didn't particularly like the existence of a club to which they couldn't qualify for membership without investing years of their time in pursuit of a craft which they weren't interested in, so they started a new club. And they would invite the members of the club consisting of animators, but only in the service of their technology, not with technology in the service of the animators.

At this point, the tools for animating characters tend to diverge. What the technicians and programmers developed was a way of recording movements in the real world time in which we all exist, called real time or realtime, and playing these rotations and translations back by imposing the rotations on a hierarchical computer rendered character. Entire human or animal samples could be captured in this manner with the proper, again military derived, instrumentation. This is a form of tele-puppeteering that is commonly called "motion capture." Other types of tele-puppeteering were developed at the same time, such as the hand puppet control for Jim Henson's *Waldo* and the devices used by DeGraf-Wahrmen on films like *Robocop*.

By the late 1980s, you had one group of people deploying traditional animation techniques, as well as developing new techniques for crafting personalities with precise timing, generally using keyframes, or hand set frames where characters were deliberately posed on very specific frames, with some limited but again deliberate computer inbetweening. This was a slow and painstaking process, but the result was the appearance of unique life and personality. The second group had as its goal, circumventing the slow and painstaking process for one with more immediate and straightforward results.

This was not an unprecedented development. A device which could be used for tracing live action called The Rotoscope had existed since the 1920s, and had been used as both a tool and way of circumventing the painstaking process of hand drawn animation ever since. Ralph Bakshi's *Fire and Ice* was an entire feature length film shot in live action with costumed actors in Spain, and hand traced in the US. Even this shortcut wasn't economical enough, so some processing of the live action footage was then used for some of the final footage of the film. In animation circles as well as other filmmaking circles, it isn't highly regarded.

But motion capture was different. No longer was the image being captured and manipulated, but the basic underlying rotational and translational movement was being recorded and imposed on characters. To the purveyors of this process, the end result was the same as hand keyframed animation, but faster and cheaper. The temptation to use this process and call the end result "animation," has led to the pejorative term, "Satan's Rotoscope," because Satan is considered by many to be the master of temptation.

The qualitative difference is obvious to even the most untrained eye. The movement you get when you capture the motion on a human is human movement. It also doesn't take into account the meat of the character, except in the most ludicrously elaborate of capture methodologies, and these are rare indeed. The timing of a hand keyframed character by skilled and practiced animators is tailored specifically to that character. The timing of a character possessed by captured human information is rooted in real world human construction and real world physics.

What this means is that motion capture, or performance capture as it is referred to by some, is really more closely related to what Edweard Muybridge was attempting to achieve, and all subsequent filmmakers, than it is to the deliberate and highly skilled art form of animation. And this is as it should be, since the crude motion capture of today will constitute the dominant form of recorded entertainment eventually, when the two dimensional medium of film is succeeded by some future medium. Even if film is not succeeded as the premiere exhibition and ultimate recording medium, the inherent advantages of having all performances available in the computer, for costuming, appearance, stunt work, and any number of traditional reasons, is becoming manifestly obvious, and it is only a matter of achieving the duplication of real appearances and the reduction of the process to something as simple as pushing a button that stands as the bottleneck to this happening.

Numerous times, inexperienced management will make the presumption that a basic performance can be captured, imposed on a character, and then edited to give the appearance that the character was hand animated. However, when motion is captured it generates information that is translated to keyframes, on the basis of every single rotational axis, every single translation, sometimes at the rate of several keyframes per second. The resulting animation curves are arbitrarily shaped, and the peaks and valleys of these curves occur in greatly differentiated places. An animator, faced with attempting to analyze and alter the recorded performance is faced with this immense overload of recorded information, forced to make choices on how to decompose this into data that can be more easily manipulated by selectively deleting keyframes.

This is an intimidating task, one which a trained artist is generally unsuited to performing. By the time this tangled mass of channels is unwound and rewound, the amount of work that has occurred amounts to more than animating the character from scratch by manually manipulating the character deliberately in the first place. And the performance of the character, which always lacks the snap of a skillfully animated character, becomes further mushed out.

The most spectacular proposal and failure involving motion capture was the theme park short, *Marvin Martian in the 3rd Dimension*. This 3 dimensional, stereoscopic 13 minute short was initially supposed to be inexpensively produced using motion capture. The producers were assured by the technicians involved that it could be done. The characters involved were Daffy Duck, Marvin Martian, and K-9, all classically animated characters, animated by artists using pencils in the late 1940s and 1950s. Matching the look of the hand painted, outlined characters, created in CGI to get the stereoscopic effect, was supposed to be the most difficult challenge of the project. After at least a year of the project was squandered attempting to make the captured human motion match the classically animated personalities of the characters, and after a huge amount of the initial budget was squandered on this attempt, it was determined that a more traditional approach was needed. The solution arrived at was nearly animating the entire thing by drawing it with pencils, to be duplicated by the CG character animators. The amount of time wasted left only a fraction of the original production schedule to complete the film, and this forced the producers to farm out the film to outside companies. The resulting cost of the short was at least five times the original budget, and some reports place it as high as eight times the original budget. Forcing motion capture into a production best done by skilled animators resulted in an unmitigated disaster, averted only because the company involved had the resources to pour more money into the project than was initially budget by nearly an order of magnitude. A very costly mistake. One that could destroy a smaller company.

An example of the concerns of a skilled and practiced animator is the concept of silhouette. While in CGI a camera can be placed arbitrarily, when dealing with character performances including live action filmmaking where the image is recorded, characters are performed for the particular resulting angle in the finished version of the film. Actors always perform to the camera, even if they aren't facing it, and are conscious of how their performance is being projected. Even stage actors are conscious of projecting to the audience, the concept of beyond the proscenium. In animation, it is important for a character's performance to "read" in silhouette, which means that even if you can see no interior details of a character, such as a black image of the character on a light background, you can still see whether the character's performance is up to snuff in the scene. This performance tends to be camera specific, and the animator deliberately crafts the performance to the resulting angle that the viewer is expected to see the character in. When a character is drawn, all sorts of cheats, like the size of Daffy's beak, can be employed. When a CG version of Daffy is animated by hand, the CG animator can distort the size and or location of his beak to achieve the same goal, in a deliberate and planned fashion. Strong poses that are a signature of Daffy's character as Duck Dodgers, can be adapted to the CG medium. But with motion capture, all of these things become inextricably intertwined with the underlying human motion that is completely incompatible with the animated world in which Daffy exists. In the same manner, any character created in CG can have qualities that completely defy the real world, in appearance and movement, and captured human motion force fed to such a character vastly limits its possibilities.

While animation for real time 3D games necessarily bypasses the concept of silhouette, the rules for that medium are different because characters are usually not actors, acting out a story, but rather are broken down into various locomotion and action activities that can be pieced together arbitrarily. These games may be the basis of a larger medium, for which motion capture becomes the filmmaking medium of the future. In this case, participation is more important than character or storytelling, and for many of these games, motion capture fits the need well. Time will tell whether this type of medium will be a dominant medium in the future, or will coexist with others as it becomes more complex, the appearance more real, the activities of the characters more varied.

But for the purpose of linear story telling, with unique characters, hand keyframed animation is the standard to beat. Nearly anyone promoting the idea of making a feature with computer generated characters attempts to associate themselves with the success of *Toy Story*, a film entirely keyframed by animators, under the direction of traditional animator and director John Lasseter. At the same time that they are invoking *Toy Story*, many are also claiming that through the use of Satan's Rotoscope, they will be able to make it faster, cheaper, and with fewer people in a shorter timeframe than was needed for the creation of *Toy Story*. The fact is that anyone who says this either doesn't know anything about animation, or has limited experience with motion capture. Whatever the results of such an attempt, it will certainly be different, more like a feature made entirely with CG costumes than something which is animated, and the promoters of such a production are simply trying to associate themselves with *Toy Story* to capitalize on the hard won success of that film, hustle up investment capital, and confuse the marketplace.

There are other issues involved in the politics of using motion capture as well. Live action directors, comfortable with directing actors and performances in realtime, may not have the patience or knowledge to direct characters from the brain of an animator. Specific performers, like Andre Agasse or Michael Jackson, may be easier to bring to a CG character in a tight time frame than to have an animator study them and animate them accordingly, particularly where clients must approve the resulting character performances. In such cases, it is clear that in a commercial sense, capturing the actions of those performers leads to a more streamlined approval process and hard to deny fact that the character is in fact puppeteered by the name brand performer. An animator at a high skill level could certainly add subtleties that performance capture is inadequate to transmit to a character, but it can also add uncertainty to a situation that might have both a tight production schedule and budget.

Yet, a company like Digital Domain, which has highly sophisticated motion capture technology and technicians and craftsmen that are among the best in that business, also employs skilled animators who can hand keyframe characters from scratch. The blockbuster, *Titanic*, in which computer generated characters are to appear as realistic as possible, has both motion captured performances imposed on CG characters, and hand keyframed characters crafted by animators.

The bottom line is simple. If someone offers you a job as an "animator", but you are actually working strictly with motion capture, the results of your work will not be considered animation by a company that is looking to hire animators who know how to bring a character to life from scratch. If you are adding hand keyframed animation to a motion capture based character, all an animation company will see is the motion capture. When people see the results of motion capture, all they will see is the human underneath the computer generated character, with the same life as one of those "walk around characters" at a theme park.

On Mocap

By Ken Cope

Puppetry isn't animation, either.

A large part of the reason computer animation is being done at all is because programmers used computers to apply captured movements to modeled geometry in the computer. Every time somebody wanted to move something, an entirely new approach and discipline coalesced to complete a job in six weeks or less. Witness point tracking may have already been around before it was used to capture the movement of an actress for a can commercial during the Superbowl, but it instantly became the fast way to input "realistic" movement into the computer.

John Lasseter hooked up with Ed Catmull and others at Pixar, back when it was still part of ILM. He got the chance to apply his animation skills, and his appreciation for the stop-motion puppetry of George Pal, to the wet clay of computer animation. In those days, flying logos amidst chrome and glass spheres were all you had to spin to be a computer animator. The folks at Pixar had already deeply explored cel animation in the 70s. Much of that work reached fruition when they forever changed the way Disney produces its animated feature films (the ones in which trees and graphite are transmuted alchemically into pixels) by the end of the eighties.

Catmull's team studied the comparative utility of ways to emulate the factory methods of studios like Disney; they knew just how vital an artist was to the equation. Much of that research resulted in identifying which aspects of production were done more effectively with computers, and which were better left to an artist. They learned both about keyframing, and about how bad computers were at inferring two-dimensional interpolative poses from flat drawings. Just what should the lines do when something appeared from behind something else in a series of drawings, say a shoe moving from behind the other leg? Compared to those types of problems, 3D was a much easier way to explore the technologies they were using to trigger and time computer animated figures.

By the late eighties, computers had gotten so responsive that puppeteers could integrate them into their repertoire changing little about the way they were used to working. Jim

Henson's team was able to use simple control devices and see the performance as they crafted it with help from PDI. Digital faces and masks were ubiquitous. Mike (of *Spike and Mike* fame) Gribble's face was cyberscanned and puppeteered with a *waldo* (a teleoperation system, labeled with a character's name from a Robert Heinlein novel), and became a standard demo on Silicon Graphics workstations. Developed at deGraf/ Wahrman, Mike the talking head became a prototype for the digital face of Cain in *Robocop II*. Even Felix the Cat got the puppet head treatment. Real-time puppetry is everywhere from trade shows to game shows to Super Mario 64; it's finding new venues on the Web in VRML.

So, we can digitize human motion and apply it to digital characters, and puppeteers can do what they always have done, in yet another environment. Shouldn't computer animation be a realtime medium, especially as the speed and power of computers is making it harder to tax them to their full potential? Moore's law is beginning to look like a timid suggestion. A reasonable approximation of a neighborhood holodeck has better odds of appearing soon than does the establishment of a permanent colony on the Moon. Digitize those humans and puppeteers. Declare animation to be a task best done on the computer, by computer operators, whose work should now be referred to as animation!

Perhaps some of the problems have found their solutions. The allure of human motion is infinite; who doesn't like puppets? When I work in the digital environment generating characters that exist nowhere else, I frequently ask myself if puppetry or mocap or hand animation might not be a better solution for the problem. Even dynamic simulation of hair and drapery promise to give animators more time to explore other challenges, now that less time needs to be spent chasing down distracting artifacts. Problems that don't suggest an obvious solution are the only ones worth solving.

So why don't Pixar, and PDI, along with every aspiring animator who just bought a system I would have signed Faustian bargains for five years ago, just throw in the towel and call it quits? Because they know how little they have scratched the surface of animation. Look how far we've come from *Tony de Peltrie* to *Geri's Game*. The field is going to be inventing itself for decades to come.

Animators, and those who truly appreciate animation, strive for characters that come to life; beings that transcend the medium employed to summon them from thin air. The best animators reveal secrets about what it means to be alive. An animator does not merely transcribe motion. The abstract idea of motion is part of a rich vocabulary used to instantly convey an abstract perception more convincingly than can words alone. Ironically, some people can more readily believe in the "reality" of film than they can forget the artifice of a play with live actors. What could be more real than sharing the air breathed by live human beings? The undeniable truth of their very presence betrays the lie we so desire to believe. Human motion artifacts in abstract CG characters burst the bubble of illusion as harshly as their absence strains credulity in GG characters purporting to be real humans. Similarly, it's hard to forget the human operating the puppet. We look carefully to spy out the devices used, and the location of the man behind the curtain, but are disappointed if we find him before the magic has worked its spell. Even cartoons made of pulp, graphite, and pixels have their origins betrayed by the hand of an animator, or even worse, by the hands of one too many. Hand animation is a standard no less daunting than the motion of a human, or of a puppet.

Animation, particularly computer animation, subsumes and contains just about all of the disciplines. Jim Henson didn't program Waldo C. Graphic anymore than Michael Jackson puppeteered his Ghost Skeleton. There is more that you can learn from Henson's puppetry and from Jackson's dance than there is to learn from digitizing their performance. If anybody tries to convince you that what you'll learn by transcribing another's performance into the computer is how to be an animator, that what you're doing is animation, you are being done a disservice. At best, you are paying for computer experience (cheaper by the minute) with time stolen from the exploration of methods in wide use to create characters that behave neither like humans nor remotely-operated puppets. Whenever you decide you want to learn how to animate, how to craft a performance of your own, you're going to have to set aside Satan's Rotoscope to do so.

There is much animation out there to inspire, and the bar was set high long before there were computers. CG-Character Animation has its own unique problems and standards, and you will find passionate debate and equally compelling arguments on every side of every aspect of it, as you will among deeply passionate people. Acting and dancing and being in your body is part of being a performer. Transcribing those performances is a job for specialists whose work nobody will describe as animating.

As more puppeteers become involved with computer animation, there will be more ways to get physically involved with the means at your disposal to perform. Puppetry is a discipline every bit as deep and unforgiving as animation. How an animator and a puppeteer use time most neatly defines the gulf between the two. A puppeteer rehearses and extemporizes, becoming both juggler and dancer as the self is subsumed in a few ephemeral moments of performance; recording only the happiest of accidents to raw streaming data. An animator might have been that puppeteer, while working out what might be done, but then sets out to craft and obtain control over every nuance of the performance, from outside time, simultaneously performing and composing. A puppeteer's performance is so much raw channel data for editing and filtering. The animator's performance is the composition of a score, with notes, holds, and intervals that convey the essence of a predictable performance. The animator's role is to ensure the placement on cue of any subtlety on every mark, created with a script so versatile that its revision is a simple task. A puppeteer must perform again with the hope that this time is close enough for jazz.

Is Ludwig Van Beethoven more important than Miles? Should we criticize Mozart for not making his music fast enough, when Bach could sit down and whip out a fugue on demand? Should the cathedral builders withhold a musician's access to pipe organs if they don't improvise as well as they compose? You'd better learn it all; if you aspire to being an animator, you'll need all the help you can get.

Moving On

If you have worked through all the chapters and projects up to this point, you've learned enough about character animation to model, set up, and animate your own characters in your own film. The next chapters show you how to wrap up that work, creating a complete film or demo reel.

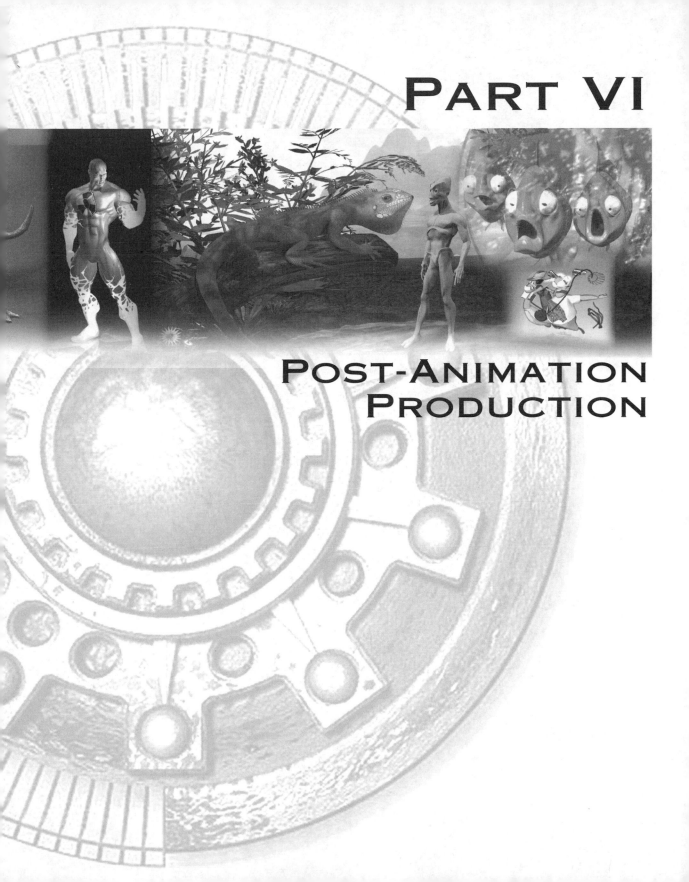

PART VI

POST-ANIMATION PRODUCTION

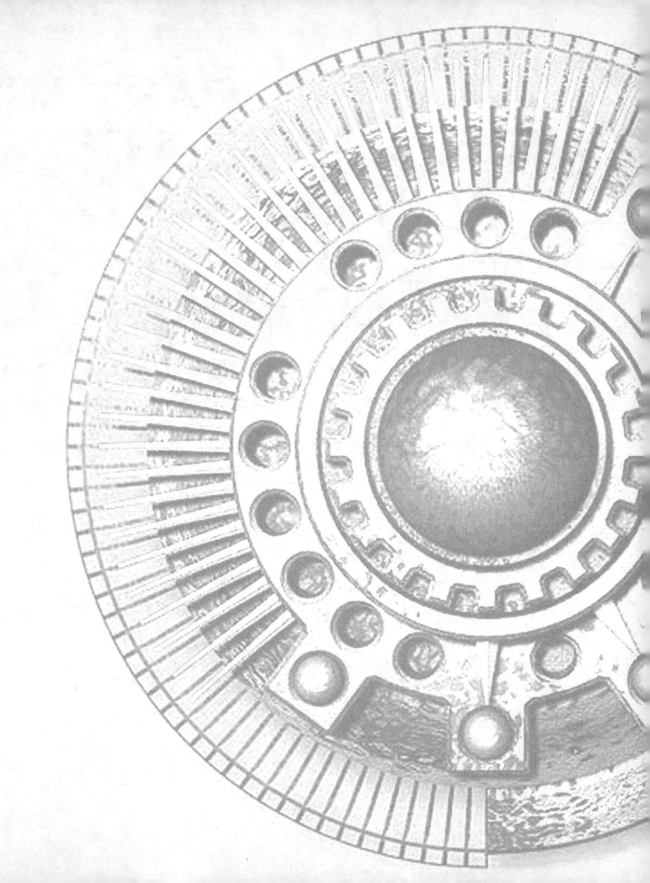

RENDERING

All your test renderings are no more than dress rehearsals. Your final lighting and rendering are opening night: here are the results you will place before your audience.

If you avoided twins, staged actions, balanced your compositions, and posed for strong lines of action, it's all worthless if the lighting and rendering doesn't reinforce the point of your animation. You need to set up lighting just as carefully as you pose and time your characters. You need to render your animation as carefully as you modeled, textured, and set up your characters. What you produce at this stage is going to be seen by your audience, so attention to detail is paramount.

Lighting Design

Lighting design is a whole profession in itself, and much has been written elsewhere on creating good lighting designs with 3D software. Therefore, this chapter concentrates on lighting tips specifically for character animation. Appropriate lighting can help tell your story, while poorly designed or inappropriate lighting can obscure or ruin it.

You can save time and effort if you set up lighting last, after all camera and character animation has been finalized and approved. You will be modifying the lighting to support the animation, so if there are revisions to the action, you will have to revise the lighting as well. There's no sense doing a job over if you don't have to.

A useful way to light the shot before turning it over to the animators is to add one light above and to one side of the camera, with intensity from 50 through 100 percent, and set ambient light values around 50 percent. This makes the whole scene clear enough for the animators to see what they're doing, reduces the setup's complexity, and keeps shaded-mode redraws and test rendering times to a minimum. After the animation is final, you can set up a more aesthetically pleasing and dramatically useful lighting design.

Basic Three-Point

The standard three-point lighting setup of *key* light, *fill* light, and *rim* (or *back*) light works just fine as a starting point for character lighting:

- *Key light*—Illuminates the strongest part of the character's face or action, and casts the strongest shadows.

- *Fill light*—Softens the shadows to bring out the remaining areas.
- *Rim light*—Outlines the character's profile.

The usual photographer's three-point setup is a key light high and to one side of the camera and a fill light low and to the other side, both pointing toward the subject, and a rim light high in back of the subject and on the same side as the fill light, pointing toward the camera.

Three-Point Lighting For Imp

PROJECT 17.1

This project shows you how to set up the basic three-point lighting for a humanoid character.

1. In the 3D software of your choice, import the model IMP.DXF from the Chapter 17 directory on this book's CD-ROM. You won't have to animate the Imp, this is just for lighting tests. Add materials and background color, if you like.

2. Turn off ambient light. Set up a 100 percent white key spotlight, and add a 50 percent blue fill spotlight. If your software allows it, set this spotlight to diffuse only, with no specular highlights. Add a 200 percent white rim spot. If possible, set this spotlight for full specular highlights with no diffuse lighting. Arrange the lights in a standard studio photographer's three-point, with all three spots targeted on the Imp model.

3. Render an image. You should end up with something like Figure 17.1.

Setting The Mood, Telling The Story

The three-point setup is adequate for illuminating the character, but it doesn't do much for telling the story. Lighting can set the mood of a shot, highlight an action, and even foreshadow a character's behavior.

Light for the story, light for the character, but never light to show off. Your audience will rarely care that you can light every form of lens flare known to cinematography or that you can simulate light refracting through a lava lamp. The audience wants you to tell them a story. No one should notice your lighting. It should be completely taken for granted. If the lighting stands out enough to be noticed by a nonprofessional audience, you've been soloing when you should have been harmonizing.

You can help establish the mood of a shot by carefully selecting and balancing the lighting colors. Generally, warm lights (daylight and firelight; warm whites to reds) as keys make for a positive mood, accented by cooler fill and rim lights. Cooler lights (night and moonlight; cool whites to blues) as keys, especially in an overall darker shot, can create a sense of foreboding unless they are strongly balanced by warmer fill and rim lights.

You also need to consider the effect of colored lights on the character's textures. Complementary colors in light and surfaces can go black or otherwise produce unintended effects.

Shadow is at least as effective as light in setting a shot's mood. What you do not light is often more important than what you do light. Your audience's eye is drawn to the bright areas of the

Figure 17.1 Imp illuminated with a standard three-point setup.

frame. Keep the character in the light while shading the rest of the scene, and the audience will keep their eyes on your character. Go easy on the shadows, not only to minimize rendering time but for simplicity in the shot composition. I usually prefer to leave all but one light's shadows off. Only one light in a scene is the best one to create a shadow that helps tell the story or define the character—find that light, and turn its shadow on. Whenever possible, use shadow mapping instead of raytracing. Shadow mapping generally gives you better control and shorter rendering times, although it does consume more RAM. Also, if you use only one light's shadow mapping, that shadow will be colored by the other lights, producing an elegantly realistic effect.

I'm Ready For My Close-Up, Mr. DeMille

If you can, start off with lighting the character. In a minimalist stage production, it's just the actor and the lights, right? It's the same principle here. You can create a good story with just the character shot against a plain background, but the lighting still has to show that character to the audience. A completely dark stage doesn't have a lot of dramatic range. There will be times you have to start with the lighting of the set, but try to put the character first whenever you can.

You shouldn't plan to set up a character's lighting just once for an entire sequence. To get the right effect, cinematographers and gaffers usually re-light the subject for each change in camera angle and shot composition. This is especially important when lighting a character's face. A perfectly good lighting setup for one camera angle may give a completely wrong effect from another angle. You will also want to set up lighting for any other character action. Bringing up the intensity of a supplemental key light on a hand, just before the hand gestures, can be as strong a precursor for the audience as the traditional staging motion.

LIGHTING STEREOTYPES THAT WORK

Good people are lit from heaven, bad people are lit from hell. Key lighting a character's face from a low angle is a common technique in horror and mystery films when a sinister effect is desired. Keep the key light high for more sympathetic characters, and nearly overhead for that angelic, haloed effect.

The eyes are the windows to the soul. If the audience can't see your character's eyes, the animator will have a harder time communicating emotional transitions and the character's mental processes. The character's eyes should show a bright specular spot unless they are unhappy or otherwise emotionally down.

Lights used in cinematography specifically to bring out that spot are called *eyelights*. You can set up good eyelights by parenting a pair of tightly focused spotlights to the camera (with enough offset to get a good reflection angle) and targeting them at the eyeballs. If your software allows it, turn off the diffuse component of the eyelights while retaining their specular component. This can make lighting the rest of the face much easier, because you don't have to worry about the eyelights overwhelming the rest of the lights.

The eyelights should be tight enough to only illuminate the eyeballs, themselves, and must have an animation control for intensity so you can dim them when necessary, as during a blink or when the character transitions to a "down" emotional expression. Literally, the light should go out of their eyes. It doesn't take much light to get that sparkle in the character's eyes. Start off with a very low intensity, and work your way up to the lowest value that gives you an acceptable specular highlight.

Projecting Shadows

If you need to match real-world lighting, you may sometimes have to match shadows cast across the character by lights and shadowing objects outside the frame. This can be challenging, but, if you do it successfully, it is one of the most effective techniques for making your CGI creations blend seamlessly with reality.

Many 3D rendering programs enable you to project a map with a light. In cinematography, a cutout or filter used this way is called a *cucaloris*, or *cookie*. Two common examples of this are a horizontal pattern of light and dark stripes to mimic window blinds and a vertical pattern to mimic prison bars. Figure 17.2 shows another example of cookie lighting. Compare the effect of the image on the top, with no cookie, to that on the bottom, using a cookie to mimic the dappled pattern of leaves casting shadows on the iguana.

If you need to match shadows in live-action footage, you'll need an accurate (or at least plausible) cookie map to project. If possible, you should try to capture important shadow profiles on the live-action set. One way to do this is to position your still camera in line between the primary

Figure 17.2 Iguana with basic lighting (top) and a cookie to mimic shadows of leaves (bottom).

shadow and the light source, pointed at the shadowed surfaces. Your camera will see precisely the shadow outline that you need to project, so you can edit the digitized photograph into a cookie map. If possible, keep your camera entirely within the shadows cast by other objects. If you can't do this, you may have to take several photos, with your camera's shadow occluding different parts of each shot, so you can assemble a cookie map from the clear parts.

The cookie map will be projected across the scene and may appear at several times its original size, so you should use the highest-resolution PhotoCD format available. If you are projecting color, such as sunlight filtered through green leaves, you will need to maintain the full 24-bit color depth. If you are simply projecting solid shadows, you can save most of the file size by converting the map to 8-bit grayscale, but you shouldn't cut it down to a 1-bit black-and-white mask unless you want all the shadows to be razor-sharp. Grayscale edges in the cookie map will automatically give you the soft-shadow edges you need to match real-world lighting.

Miscellaneous Tips

Here are a few more lighting ideas you may find useful:

- When you're ready to start lighting the finished animation, turn down the ambient light to five percent or less. Ambient light may be good for sunny outdoor scenes, but too much will wash out a shot and leave it looking flat. You can create a more natural look by using soft lights for area lighting. For a nice soft fill light, use a distant light with full diffuse but no specular component.

- Don't use lens flares in character animation. Most cinematographers are very careful to prevent lens flare, so why should you deliberately add it? It has also been overdone so much that lens flares on a demo reel are usually interpreted as an amateur's touch.

- If you have a lighting setup that you use often, set up a scene with just those lights, parented to a null object at the origin. Many programs enable you to merge elements from other scenes, so you can easily load the null and its parented lights into your current project. Also, it helps to name your lights in case you want to tweak them later. WarmKeyLight is a lot easier to understand than Light003.

- Experiment with lighting every chance you get. Lighting often takes as much time as staging the scene. A lot of that time goes to the numerous test renders needed to get things lit exactly right. If you've practiced lighting, you'll be able to get closer to the final setup on your first rough, and you won't have to waste time on test renders when your deadlines are tight.

Software Lighting Specifics

The following are some tips, references, and warnings about setting up lights in specific 3D animation software.

3D Studio MAX 1.2

Chapter 20 of the MAX manual (Chapter 17 of the MAX2 User Guide), "Lighting Your Scene," does a very thorough job describing both the workings of the software's lighting features and the theory and practice of lighting design. If you are using MAX and you haven't yet worked through this part of the manual, you're not getting your money's worth.

Setting up eyelights in MAX is easier and faster than in many other packages due to a couple of handy features. You can create excellent MAX eyelights in four steps:

1. Add a Spotlight, either Free or Target (MAX manual pages 20-13 through 20-25, or MAX2 17-6, 7), and name it Eyelight. Target Spotlights are better if you need to track the character's head movements. Free Spotlights are slightly easier to deal with if the head won't be moving much during the shot.

2. In the Eyelight's General Parameters rollout, click on the Exclude button, then set the Exclude options to keep the Eyelight from illuminating any surface in the scene other than the eyeballs (MAX manual page 20-21, or MAX2 17-15). This prevents any excess light from making a raccoon mask on your character's face.

3. MAX has a slick way of orienting the Eyelight so the light's hotspot is reflected from exactly where you want it on the eyeball. Select the viewport you want to render, select the Eyelight, and click on the Place Highlight icon from the Align flyout (MAX manual page 20-17, or MAX2 17-9). Drag the cursor over the surface of the eyeball until it's over the place you want to reflect the highlight. MAX will automatically reposition and align the Eyelight.

4. The final touch for the Eyelight is to set the Spotlight Hotspot and Spotlight Falloff. The most interactive (and I think, fastest) way to do this is to set one of the views to the Eyelight. Because you've already used Place Highlight to orient the Eyelight to the eyeball, the eyeball will be centered in the Eyelight view. After you select the Eyelight, you can use the Spotlight Hotspot and Spotlight Falloff controls to interactively set the size of the Eyelight cones. You can choose to make the Hotspot small enough to highlight only one eyeball, or broad enough to cover both eyeballs at once, depending on the demands of the shot.

Alias

If you have Alias and you haven't worked through the *Learning Alias* manual, you should have your head examined. The "Lighting" and "Rendering" sections, including Lessons 12 and 13, introduce most of the features and functions you are likely to use, and point you to detailed resources elsewhere in Alias's massive documentation. This is one of the few manuals I have seen that actually provides illustrations of lighting effects. Well done!

Setting up eyelights, cookies, and three-point lighting in Alias is simply a matter of following the official manual's introductory lessons and then adapting what you've learned to lighting your character.

Electric Image Animation System 2.7.5

As noted in earlier chapters, EIAS is one of the most feature-laden 3D programs on the market, and the interface reflects that—most of the dialog boxes look like the cockpit of a 747. The good side is that all the options are right out there in the open where you can see them. The bad side is that the interface can be intimidating, even overwhelming, for a beginner. If you are new to EIAS, just take it one gadget at a time, follow the tutorials, and you'll get results in no time.

The manuals support the software's complexity and power with a good supply of tutorials and explanatory text. Unfortunately, between the version 2 manuals, the 2.5 supplements, and the 2.7.5 supplements, you have to go through 6 manuals to find the information you need. If you are running into problems with a new feature, you should start with the 2.7.5 documents and work your way backwards, to make sure you're not learning the outdated features and procedures. I suggest you track down and mark outdated information in the older manuals as you learn the latest procedures.

If you're new to the program, I can't recommend strongly enough that you work through the *Tutorial* manual before you do anything else. The first exercise includes detailed setup information for most of the light types, and it takes you through the lighting process step-by-step as painlessly as possible. If you're still not confident in your control of the lighting features after completing the tutorials, try reading through Chapter 11 of the *Reference* manual. This doesn't have the step-by-step organization of the tutorials, but it may answer your remaining questions. Once you've got the basics of EIAS 2 lighting, you're ready to tackle the new toys.

One of the newest features in EIAS's Light Info Window is Shadow Color. This is useful for compositing characters into live-action footage, as you need to match both the color and density of the live-action shadows for a seamless effect. Version 2.5 added a Shadow Darkness feature, enabling you to set the density of shadows for the second half of the shadow-matching requirement.

Another new kid on the 2.7.5 block is the Enable Illumination checkbox. When checked, this turns on the diffuse component of the light. If you uncheck this box while leaving Enable Highlight checked (immediately above it in the window), you can render specular highlights without washing out the rest of the surface. This is exactly the feature you need for bright eyelights without a raccoon mask. It also makes setting up the eyelight spotlights much less fussy, giving you more room for error without spoiling the results. You can simply use the Look At Object tool to make the eyelight track the eyeball object, and keep the eyelight cone down to a reasonable size. If there's a little highlight reflected from the wet edge of the eyelid, it will look perfectly natural.

Extreme 3D 2

Extreme 3D supports ambient, distant, omni, and spot lights. You can control color and intensity for all light types. Omni lights have position and falloff parameters, distant lights have orientation and shadows, and spot lights have all the preceding plus light cone and atmospheric effects.

A nice touch is that you can set the intensity of a light to a minimum of -20, creating a negative light that subtracts light from overlit areas. This is a very handy tool for cheating lights around characters, enabling you to brightly light the character while darkening their immediate surroundings. This brings the character into more prominent relief, drawing your audience's attention and helping you tell the story. This may also help you set up eyelights, because Extreme 3D does not allow you to exclude light from objects or to turn off the diffuse component of a light. I recommend that you simply keep your eyelight spotlights as small and tightly linked as possible, and use small negative lights if necessary to remove any stray highlights on the rest of the character's face.

One of the enhancements in version 2 is that objects with transparency settings can now cast transparency effects in their shadows. This means you can create cookie objects with detailed transparency maps for effects like those in Figure 17.2.

The Extreme 3D manual takes the interesting and effective approach of presenting lighting and materials together, describing the interaction of light with surface attributes to create the final rendered appearance. The level of writing is appropriate to an audience that is comfortable with personal computer operation. The authors introduce new terms and concepts in logical order, with examples, and avoid unnecessary jargon. This is a nice piece of documentation, and you should definitely read through it before attempting any lighting setups.

Unfortunately, the light animation tools are buried in terminology that differs from the rest of the 3D software industry. If you want to make a light track a null, you create a *watch link* to a *construction object*—there isn't a single entry in the index or table of contents about tracking, look-at, or other more common terms. One of the most frustrating things about learning to use Extreme 3D is trying to figure out what the publisher decided to call a particular feature or function. I recommend that you read the manual with a highlighter or pen in hand and mark odd terms with synonyms and *See Also* references in the index. Macromedia should have done this, but the manual is worth this salvage effort. At least it forces you to read the entire manual more carefully!

Houdini 2

Houdini is in a class by itself. Most other software allows the neophyte to get by with crude or limited animations, using just the basic default settings for any feature they haven't learned yet. You can't do that with Houdini—you have to know what you're doing.

Houdini 2 is the most technically powerful and demanding software reviewed in this book. It's not impossible, or even difficult, for a new user to learn. It simply requires you to commit time to actually reading and understanding the manuals. The staff at Side Effects Software has done a laudable job in compiling the *Reference* and *Tutorial* manuals for Houdini 2. The text is phrased as simply as the subject matter permits, and jargon is defined clearly when it first appears. In fact, Houdini incorporates so many lighting models and the manuals explain them so well, they would make good references for an advanced course in computer graphics.

Setting up eyelights, cookies, and three-point lighting in Houdini is a piece of cake, once you've learned to control the software's exhaustive range of options. If you attempt to set up lighting in Houdini without cracking the manuals, you'll get no sympathy from me.

Infini-D

The tutorial and reference manuals for this software do a good job of introducing the user to Infini-D's lighting features. Most of the information is contained in Chapter 16, "Working With Lights." It doesn't have much to say about general lighting principles, but the examples, figures, and tutorials are thorough and well-written.

Infini-D supports distant, point (omni), and spot lights that behave pretty much like the same light types in other software. In addition, Infini-D has a Tube light that mimics the linear pattern of a fluorescent tube. Fluorescents are generally useful for illuminating sets rather than characters, so I won't suggest that you use the Tube light very often.

You have a few choices about shadows: none, soft-edged, and hard-edged. You can also turn off shadows for each object in a scene, which overrides the light setting. Basically, if either the object or the light is set for no shadows, you won't get one. If you want a shadow, both the object and the light must have shadows turned on.

Setting up eyelights in Infini-D isn't terribly difficult, because you can use the Target Spotlight to keep a narrow spot locked on the eyeballs. Unfortunately, you can't disable the diffuse component of the light, so you'll have to keep the spot narrow enough that it won't bleed over and give your characters raccoon masks.

Infini-D supports Masks (cookies) and Gels for spotlights, and pages 257 through 258 in the manual include a quick tutorial on how to set them up.

Martin Hash's Animation:Master

A:M's manual contains only four pages describing lights. Out of a 380-page manual, this is a little skimpy considering the importance of the subject. There is little discussion of lighting principles, and you are expected to figure out how to change most of the settings based on verbal descriptions rather than screenshots or diagrams.

A:M does not have a lot of special-effects lighting options, beyond those indispensable to character animation. Light types include Klieg (spot), Bulb (omnidirectional), and Sun (parallel). You can turn off shadows for all three types and can choose shadow maps rather than raytracing for the Klieg type.

If shadow positions are important to your lighting setup, you can save time by turning on shadows for the preview renders. This is slightly faster than performing a Render To File every time you move a light. The fastest working method I've found is to use Progressive Render Mode, then right-click and drag to select the rendered area. This enables you to choose the shadowed area alone, so the rendering feedback is as fast as possible. You can reach the Rendering Shadows setting by calling up the Options dialog from the Tools menu, then choosing the Rendering tab.

The A:M manual does not list any limits, or even hints, about the intensity values for lights. You can go much higher than 100, so it's possible to re-create overexposures and glare with a single light source. This greater range makes it easier to set up some lighting effects in A:M than in other software that claims more powerful lighting tools.

You also have the option of turning off the specular (highlights) or diffuse (ambient) components for each light. This is especially useful in creating eyelights, as you can simply turn off the diffuse component so you don't have to worry about excess eyelight creating a raccoon mask on your character's face. Because you have better control over what lights are reflected or ignored, you don't have to spend as much time and effort on limiting the width and falloff of spotlights.

A:M does not support lights that project maps. If you need a cookie for complex shadows or a stained-glass color projection, you have to create a model with the appropriate color, transparency, or cookie-cut maps and position that model in front of the light. This is more like real-world light rigging, but it's definitely more time-consuming and trickier than other software approaches to the same set of problems.

Poser 2

Don't expect to create subtle lighting designs with Poser. The only light type it supports is distant, meaning all the characters and props in a scene will have exactly the same lighting. There are no spotlight cones or falloff, so you can't create the tight lights necessary for eyelights or dramatic shadows. You can set and animate light color, intensity, and direction, and can turn shadows on or off, but that's it. Also, you have precisely three lights in every scene. You can turn some off, but you can't add any more. Essentially, you are limited to basic three-point lighting, with key, fill, and backlight being your only tools.

The only way I've found to create more complex lighting in Poser is by using one or more cookies for the entire scene. You can model a 2D object in another modeling program, then import it to Poser. This cookie prop can cast shadows mimicking spotlights and other light sources. The cookie has to be large enough to shadow the entire scene, because the distant light is evenly distributed. If you need a guide to create the cookie model, try rendering an image from the light's point of view.

Fortunately, Poser plays well with others. You can export Poser characters in a variety of formats. You might consider exporting a Poser model for each key pose, then set up a replacement animation of those models in software with more versatile lighting options.

Poser's manual is adequate and laid out well. It's a perfectly good introduction to figure lighting, within the limits of the software, and the illustrations include enough screenshots and rendered examples that beginners should find Poser a very easy starting point.

Ray Dream Studio 5

Fractal Design's manuals, as I mentioned before, are generally excellent. They are carefully targeted to their audience of artists, with a minimum of technical jargon. Unfortunately, that sometimes leads to oversimplification or errors. For example, the RD5 manual states that ambient light "is the equivalent of daylight in a real world scene." Sorry, but ambient light in the real world is the result of all the *reflections* of light from the sun and other sources, not the direct sunlight itself. A page later, the authors correctly state that Distant lights, with parallel rays, are similar to sunlight. The message here is that RD5's manuals are a friendly and useful introduction to the software's wealth of tools, but, if you want to thoroughly (and correctly) understand the theory, you'll need supplemental reading material.

The first half of Chapter 14 in the RD5 manual covers the available lighting types and gives some good advice about the most rendering-efficient setups. RD5 makes it easy for you to set up the most efficient default lighting for animation—you simply can't change the default Preview lighting! If you're determined to slow down your Preview in exchange for more complex lighting, you can use Shaded Preview or Better Preview modes to view the effect of the scene's lights. You still can't see shadows or rendered effects, but that's what test renders are for.

Ambient light is one setting for the entire scene, and it's limited (as are all lights and shadows) to the range 0 through 100 percent. This means you can't overexpose a scene with a single light but have to add more lights until you get the desired effect. This approach works for many lighting situations, but matching real-world glares and hot spots will be much more difficult and time-consuming.

In addition to the aforementioned Distant light, RD5 supports Bulb (point-source) and Spot lights. Bulb lights have Range and Distance Falloff settings in addition to the basic color, brightness, and shadow parameters. Spot lights add Half Angle and Angular Fall-off, to enable you to simulate the umbra and penumbra of a real-world shadow. Spot lights are the only ones whose effects depend on direction as well as placement and distance, so it's natural that Spots be the only lights with a Point At function to orient them towards a specified object. With all these parameters, setting up a Spot can get confusing. RD5 has a handy Direct Manipulation option that displays control handles on the Spot in the Perspective view for Position, Brightness, Half Angle, Angular Fall-Off, Light Aim, and Light Cone Cross Section. This is a lot to keep track of at first, but, once you've had a little practice, it is a lot simpler and faster than working through layers of menu options and dialog boxes.

RD5 seems to favor raytracing as the solution for every rendering problem. I don't recommend this approach, as raytracing is overkill for most character animation and it dramatically increases rendering times (see the "Rendering" section of this chapter for details). That's why I recommend that you always override the default Ray-Traced Shadows setting in each light's Properties palette and change it to Soft RTD Shadows.

RD5 refers to projected maps as Gels, from the stage-lighting term for a color filter. RD5 Gels can be full color or grayscale maps or 1-bit masks. They can be stills or image sequences, and can be applied as single images or tiled across the Perspective view. In addition, RD5 has built-in Gel shaders that project vertical or horizontal stripes, vertical or circular gradients, or a Formula shader you can define.

Ray Dream Studio 5 does not have the most powerful or versatile lighting options among the software reviewed here, but it is certainly adequate for most character animation. Most importantly, it is easy to learn and use and, therefore, a good first choice for the beginner or student.

Softimage 3D

Softimage, like Alias, makes further detailed information on lighting superfluous. The *Quick Start* manual provides an easy, step-by-step introduction to the basics, and the *Self-Training Workbook* completes it. For specific information, you can refer to Chapter 2 of the *Defining Materials and Textures* manual, or the two-volume *Reference Guide*.

Setting up eyelights, cookies, and three-point lighting in Softimage is simply a matter of working through *Quick Start* and the *Self-Training Workbook*, then adapting what you've learned to lighting your character.

Strata Studio Pro 2

SSPro supports ambient, directional, point, and spot lights. The *User* and *Reference* manuals form an adequate introduction to the lighting tools, if you don't mind digging a bit. The information for any function appears to be scattered among several locations, and the index is not always accurate. Be prepared to run into a blind alley or two if you have to depend on the index or table of contents.

You can make eyelights in SSPro by adding a spotlight, as described on pages 49 through 50 of the *User* manual. Once you have placed the eyelight, you can target it at the eyeball. You can turn off shadows, minimize the spot angle and falloff, and increase intensity to 100 percent for a hard, bright highlight. Keep the spot diameter small to avoid lighting a raccoon mask on the character's face.

SSPro refers to projected maps as Gels. You can apply a color or grayscale map as a Gel to any spotlight or point light. This is the easiest way of making a cookie in SSPro.

trueSpace3

The manual for trueSpace3 is a little skimpy on how to set up lights and contains nothing on lighting theory. You'll need to read pages 258 through 262 in the manual, then rely on these tips and the general guidelines earlier in this chapter when you start lighting your characters.

trueSpace3 supports three light types: infinite (distant), local (omni), and spot. As with most 3D software, the spotlight is the type most suited to lighting characters. You can set color, intensity, falloff, and cone angle. You can also make a number of shadow settings, choosing from raytraced or shadow mapping and specifying the size and fuzziness of the shadow map. trueSpace3 has a helpful option, Image Dependent, that automatically scales the shadow map resolution based on the resolution of the rendered image.

If you need cookie or projected transparency lighting effects in trueSpace3, you'll have to do it the hard way and actually build a shadowing object. If you want to project a color transparency, you'll be limited to raytraced rendering, because shadow mapping won't show object transparencies.

You can set up eyelights in trueSpace3 by using spotlights with the Look At command described on page 325 of the manual. Since trueSpace3 doesn't allow you to turn off the diffuse component of the light, you'll need to keep the spot tight on the eyeballs to avoid lighting a raccoon mask on your characters.

Lights Out

With these tips firmly in mind, you should be able to light any character's action to good effect. The next section will show you how to get the best images possible, considering your computer, budget, and schedule.

Rendering

The goal of this section is to point out some of the tips and tricks you can use to minimize rendering time. This is especially important in a production environment, but even hobbyists like to see their animations as quickly as possible. Sometimes you have to choose between rendering time and image quality, but many of the following techniques can be used without reducing quality. If you can reliably get good images out of a system faster than anyone else, you'll never be unemployed for long.

Your Computer

The first thing you should do to shorten rendering time is get a bigger, faster machine. Just kidding! Although you can never have too much RAM, hard disk space, or processing speed, most of us have to work in the real world. Fantasies about the ideal rendering monster system won't improve your work. On the other hand, if you can produce really outstanding work on a rinky-dink machine, your problem-solving skills and can-do mindset will be valuable assets even when you're wrangling a 20 teraFLOP network.

Most 3D software follows the same steps every time it renders an image. It loads the objects, maps, and other files required for the current frame into RAM, calculates the image, and saves the image to storage. You can add optional steps (post-processing plug-ins, image file compression, and so on) to this process, but most of them slow it down. Each step in the rendering process is a potential bottleneck. Learn the bottlenecks of your particular system's RAM, storage drives, and CPU, and how to work around them.

If you have plenty of hard disk space but little RAM, you can split up scenes into more manageable layers, render each layer as an image sequence, and composite the layers together (see Chapter 20 for details). This enables you to render complex scenes that would otherwise overload your machine. If you don't have enough RAM and you try to render the scene anyway, your software will treat part of your hard disk as if it were RAM (a swap file), and move bits of the scene to and from your hard disk as necessary. This repeated disk accessing is sometimes referred to as *thrashing*. As you may imagine, this really slows down the rendering process, and doesn't do your hard disk any good, either.

If you have plenty of RAM but loading files from the hard disk seems to take up a lot of time, you might try allocating a RAM disk. (The exact procedure will depend on the hardware platform you are running.) If you load some or all of the scene's files to the RAM disk, your software can load them for rendering much faster.

If you are thinking about upgrading or purchasing a machine, pay as much attention to the bus speed as to the CPU speed. The bus speed determines how fast a program can push data around your system, from hard disk to RAM to CPU, and back again. If the bus speed is significantly lower than the CPU speed, you may not be getting all the performance you should. The CPU may render images fast enough, then sit there wasting cycles waiting for the next batch of data from the bus.

BUYING THE FARM

If you've got a lot of rendering to do on a regular basis, you may want to consider building a small render farm. The advantage of this lies in rendering on inexpensive stripped-down systems while keeping your more expensive animation workstation free for your creative use. In Win95/NT, a render farm node might consist of a moderately fast motherboard and CPU, sufficient RAM for rendering your largest scene without thrashing, a minimal video card, a floppy disk drive, a network card, and a hard drive just large enough to hold the bare-bones operating system plus your rendering software and the current scene files. As of this writing, you should be able to put together a rendering node like this for less than half the price of a full system. You can even adapt old, semi-obsolete computers as nodes. Who cares if they're slow, if they're cranking out images nonstop? Many hands make light work!

Files

Most 3D software can render much faster if the object and image files for a scene are designed to load and render efficiently. Here are a few simple guidelines that can speed up your rendering.

For images, keep it simple. If an image is going to occupy a quarter of the screen at the camera's closest distance, and your output resolution is 640×480, any resolution higher than 160×120 will be wasted. Design your color, bump, and other maps to suit the resolution at which you will actually render them. The same goes for color depth. It's just wasting RAM and disk space to use a 24-bit color image for a bump map, when only 8-bits worth of luminance information is used. Make a habit of asking yourself, "How much detail is the audience able to see?" Whenever possible, use image maps instead of procedural shaders, since maps render much faster. One approach is to apply a shader to an object, render an image of it, and apply the rendered image as a map to the original object.

For objects, again, keep it simple. If an object is going to appear small or in the background of a shot, replace it with a simplified version. Save the full zillion-polygon versions for extreme close shots where all the detail will show. If you will be using a character in a number of different shots, you may be able to save a lot of rendering time by creating different versions of the object for different camera distances. Even if an object is seen only in close shots, if it is very complex, you may find it worthwhile to model alternate versions with back surface polygons deleted. If a shot only shows the character's face, loading the polygons that form the back of his head is a waste of time.

Shadows

After you've finished laying out a scene and have done your test renders, take a good look at where the shadows are falling. Note which models have to cast shadows, receive shadows, or shadow themselves. For each model, turn off the shadow options that aren't needed.

Just as for models, turn off shadow options for lights that don't need them. Use only the minimum lights necessary to the scene. More lights always cause a longer render but do not always produce better-looking results. If you must set up a complex lighting scheme, try separately lighting layers of a scene to save rendering time (a rendered layer applied as a background image needs no lights).

Use shadow maps rather than raytraced shadows whenever possible. They render faster and generally look better because of their soft edges. You can fake shadows, too. If you are really pressed for rendering time, you can model shadow objects. For example, if a table has a shadow below it, make a dark transparent polygon shadow and place it beneath the table.

Render Modes

One of the options that beginners tend to waste a lot of time on is *raytracing*. This rendering algorithm generates images by calculating the path between each screen pixel and each light source in the scene. Although raytracing produces more realistic images than some faster algorithms, raytracing is a real brute-force overkill solution for most images. Other than the gee-whiz factor of creating complex scenes, do you really need photo-realistic glass, chrome, or other raytraced surfaces? You should keep in mind that potential employers will have seen a lot more CGI than you have and are thoroughly sick of raytraced reflection studies. They will be more interested in a good application of shadow, reflection, and projection maps to achieve a realistic effect with more finesse. If you have a lot of obviously raytraced stuff on your demo reel, it won't say much about your ability as a TD to fake a "look" without resorting to brute-force rendering. It's better to dazzle them with your skills, not your tools.

You should always try to keep enough RAM available to render the scene in one segment. Split the rendering into foreground and background layers, if necessary, and you'll still save time overall. Select an appropriate anti-aliasing level. Overdoing it for a particular resolution just wastes time. Motion blur can be increased to cover a number of problems but can also increase rendering times. If you plan to use a lot of motion blur, you may want to split the scene into layers again. You can generally render a background layer without motion blur, but the foreground characters should have as much motion blur as they can handle.

If you are rendering an animation to put on a demo reel or otherwise impress someone, you might try rendering it in widescreen. You will actually be rendering a smaller size image, but it looks like a letterboxed film, so people tend to think of it as higher quality work.

Output File Formats

If you will be compositing any layers of animation and have plenty of hard disk space, you should save the rendering as a numbered sequence of image files. Your renderer won't have to run compression for an AVI or QuickTime animation after rendering, and the rendered images will look a lot nicer than the compressed animation frames. Choose an image format that your compositing software can load in numbered sequence.

If you have the file space to spare, I recommend rendering animation files with zero compression at first. You can always use an editing program or video utility to compress the finished file. If you render to a compressed file and something goes wrong, you will have to re-render the entire sequence. If the file is uncompressed, you can edit it or insert re-rendered sequences without losing image quality to repeated compressions.

Watching The Kettle Boil

Some rendering software gives you the option of watching the rendering in progress. This is a bad thing, generally. It encourages you to waste time watching the screen, and it costs time for every pixel rendered. Instead of simply saving the data to the image file, the software has to translate it into a form it can present in the display window, then update the display. This can be a significant fraction of the actual rendering time. You should only use this option when you are experimenting with lighting and rendering options. When you are ready to render the completed animation, turn this option off.

Software Rendering Specifics

The following are some tips, references, and warnings about rendering in specific 3D animation software.

3D Studio MAX 1.2

Chapter 34 of the MAX manual (MAX2 Chapter 30) covers rendering issues adequately but briefly. There aren't any earth-shattering revelations here. The text barely touches on issues of rendering speed and image quality. Your best bet is to work through the manual to learn the available options and settings, try my general recommendations from earlier in this chapter, then experiment to find what works best for you.

MAX version 1.2 allows you to render an animation without specifying a file name to save it. This means you can render an entire animation before you realize it can't be saved, and you've wasted all that rendering time. Although the manual contains a warning about this, the program itself should ask you to confirm this setting before it begins rendering. I hope Kinetix repairs this oversight as soon as possible.

MAX enables you to render quick animation tests, or *animatics*, by omitting most frames and then playing back the abbreviated animation at a reduced frame rate to match. For example, you can set the Every Nth Frame option to 15, then render an AVI with a frame rate of 2 fps, to play the animation back at the equivalent of 30 fps. This is a quick way to create a rendered sequence to substitute for a sketch in your story reel, as shown in Chapter 4 of this book.

MAX is multithreaded and supports multiple processors. It also supports network rendering, although you won't find it written up in the manual. Instead, read the max_nr.hlp file—it's a step-by-step tutorial in configuring your own render farm. Kinetix has made this a no-brainer. MAX's network rendering software requires just one machine on the network to have a valid MAX dongle attached, then it farms out the work to the rest of the nodes using standard Win95/NT and TCP/IP networking protocols. It's even robust enough to recall a job from a stalled machine and submit it to another one. Rendered images can be directed to a shared network drive or stored on each node's local drive. In all, MAX has a robust, versatile, and simple approach to network rendering.

There are a number of third-party plug-in renderers available for MAX. The least useful for character work are the raytracers. I suggest you save your money, because MAX's native capabilities with reflection maps can duplicate nearly any reflection or refraction effect in a fraction of the time. If you have to match a lot of live-action footage, you might look at some of the radiosity renderers (such as RadioRay), as the best of them can produce truly photo-realistic lighting effects. More to the point for character animation are the cel shaders, which mimic the effects of hand-drawn 2D cel animation. Currently available MAX cel renderers include CartoonReyes from Infografica, and Illustrator and ComicShop from Digimation.

Alias

As mentioned earlier, Alias has done a superlative job on their introductory Learning Alias manual. The same lessons used to introduce lighting concepts also cover rendering, including optimization and trade-offs to minimize rendering time. Read the *Learning Alias* manual, then apply those lessons to your character animation. For more technical details, refer to the *Rendering in Alias* manual. If you run into problems, the official manuals' *Global Index* will put you on the right track.

Electric Image Animation System 2.7.5

The EIAS *Starter* manual presents a good basic overview of the rendering process. The language is precise, concise, and dense but rewards careful reading. This isn't a browse-over-lightly, this is a read-and-think-about.

The *Starter* manual also give you your first look at the Render Control window, unfortunately without any accompanying explanation of what all those bells and whistles are supposed to do. If you're feeling a little panicky when you see this, turn immediately to the *Tutorial* manual, and work through the first exercise. The directions are simple, and you'll be confidently setting up the Render options by page 13. It's not a bad idea to work through the entire *Tutorial* manual before you tackle anything else in EIAS. You'll get up to speed quicker and certainly experience a lot less stress.

With version 2.5, anti-aliasing options expanded dramatically. You can choose levels from 4×4 to 64×64, and sampling levels from 1×1 to 64×64. For most character animation applications, you can keep these levels fairly low. When you need to render promotional stills or film resolutions, crank 'em up. If you're locking down the camera, you might consider rendering the background Groups at high anti-aliasing and sampling rates, then rendering the character and any moving models with lower sampling. Motion blur makes most anti-aliasing of moving models redundant.

The 2.5 release also marked the debut of Renderama, EIAS's new network rendering manager. This program can distribute your animations for rendering across an AppleTalk or TCP/IP local network or the Internet. The documentation (about a quarter of the 2.5 update manual) starts from the very basics of network operation and covers everything you'll need to know to wrangle your own distributed or local render farm. Got any friends on the Internet that don't keep their Macs busy all the time? Put 'em to work!

Extreme 3D 2

Extreme 3D includes the rendering options you would expect based on its lighting and animation capabilities. You can select anti-aliasing level, object smoothness, a variety of shadow options, and types of alpha channel rendering. Chapter 6 in the manual covers rendering issues fairly well.

If you've set up a transparency-mapped object as a cookie, make sure you turn on Transparency in Shadows in the Final Render Setup.

You should make a few test renders with Front Faces selected. If your models have been constructed properly, their face normals should all be oriented to point outward. Front Faces tells the software to only render one side of the faces, so the rendering goes much faster. If your character's normals are not aligned properly, they'll show up in the test render as holes in the model. If this happens, you can either try to flip the offending normals or turn off Front Faces and accept longer rendering times.

The manual's section on network rendering is an adequate overview of the process and discusses the major issues of running an Extreme 3D render farm. The approach is reasonably simple, as network operations go. You submit a rendering job from your primary workstation to the server, then you resume your other work while the server manages the details of parceling out jobs to the nodes and keeping track of the incoming rendered images. A nice bonus is that you can have a mix of MacOS and Win95 machines on the network, and they can all render images for the same scene files (except the platform-specific formats AVI, QT, and PICT).

Houdini 2

Houdini 2 has one of the most versatile and powerful sets of rendering tools on the market. It also complies with the usual trade-off between power and ease of use—it's a real challenge to learn! Fortunately, Side Effects Software has done their usual thorough job on the two-volume *Reference Manual*, and the *Tutorial Manual* will at least give you a few easy-to-follow examples so you can actually render something. If you want to dig into optimization, network rendering, and other advanced rendering functions, you'll need to spend a lot of time with the Houdini manuals. On the positive side, I think working through all that information will give you the equivalent of a Master's degree in computer graphics.

Infini-D

This software comes with some of the most helpful and extensive rendering documentation I've seen. Three full chapters in the reference manual plus some very well-done exercises in the tutorial manual cover introductory through advanced rendering features. A very nice job by the publisher. If you read the manuals, plus the general guidelines in this chapter, you should have no trouble at all with optimizing your Infini-D renderings.

Infini-D does support true raytracing, but you should avoid it for the sake of shorter rendering times. Infini-D supports enough reflection mapping features that you should be able to fake reflections and refractions without resorting to brute-force raytracing.

Like MAX, Infini-D enables you to render quick animation tests, or animatics, by omitting most frames, then playing back the abbreviated animation at a reduced frame rate to match. In the Animation tab of the Render Setup dialog, you can set the Render Every Nth Frame field to 15, then render a QuickTime animation with a frame rate of 2 fps, to play the animation back at the equivalent of 30 fps. This is a quick way to create a rendered sequence to substitute for a sketch in your story reel, as shown in Chapter 4 of this book. You can even type in a list of the specific frames you want to render, to produce just the key frames of the animation.

One feature of Infini-D's rendering is of particular interest to animators matching live footage. ShadowCatcher objects (see pages 378+ of the Infini-D manual) render only where they are shadowed. This makes it much easier for you to accurately render your characters and their shadows for compositing into live footage.

At this time, Infini-D does not support any form of network rendering. All you can do is load separate copies of the software on each machine, manually choose which frames each computer is to render, and point their outputs to a shared directory.

Martin Hash's Animation:Master

The A:M manual's section on rendering is brief but adequate. The software doesn't have as many bells and whistles as some other programs, but the essentials are there. The rendering option dialogs are straightforward and laid out well, so you should have no problem relating them to the general guidelines presented earlier in this chapter.

If you need to render complex optical effects that A:M doesn't support directly, you can render image sequences with alpha channels and add the other effects in compositing software. This is the fastest way of putting A:M characters into complex post-processed, raytraced, or radiosity-rendered environments.

If at all possible, light your scenes with Kliegs so you can use Shadow Mapping. If you can render exclusively with shadow maps rather than raytracing, you can save up to 60 percent of your rendering time. (Based on my tests, your results may vary.)

At this time, the network rendering engine for Animation:Master is still in development. Check Hash's Web site at **http://www.hash.com** for details as they become available.

Poser 2

Poser's rendering capabilities are on a level with it's lighting tools—bare minimum for the intended task, but functional and robust. The rendering options include resolution, anti-aliasing, background, and whether you want to render shadows and materials. Poser cannot render alpha channels, so you have to render images with a background color and use chroma keying to composite them.

Poser can render numbered image sequences and AVI or QuickTime animations, and also supports AVIs and QuickTime animations as background images. Poser's rendering quality is adequate, considering its lighting limitations. Even after you've graduated to more advanced character animation software, you may want to keep Poser around for quickly rendering storyboards, animatics, or layout and blocking experiments.

Ray Dream Studio 5

Chapter 17 of the RD5 manual does a thorough job of introducing the new user to the concepts of rendering. The manual also presents the issues and workable solutions for optimizing the process, depending on the demands of the particular project. The middle of the chapter covers lighting effects you would do well to avoid, specifically the wide variety of lens flares, glows, and other optical effects suitable for space opera but detrimental to character animation.

RD5 enables you to set the optical properties of each model and to choose from Draft, Ray Tracer, Adaptive, and Natural Media rendering modes. This can markedly speed up rendering, if you set every model to No Reflections, No Refractions, and choose the Adaptive renderer. This renderer adapts the rendering method for each area of the image, using ray tracing where necessary and the faster A-Buffer where possible. If you have one or two reflective models in a scene, this renderer can give you the optical effects you need for those surfaces while rendering the remainder at top speed.

The Adaptive renderer also enables you to globally turn off features such as Reflection, Refraction, Bump maps, Transparency, and anti-aliasing that lengthen render times but may not be necessary for every image. Used with care and forethought, this collection of features can enable you to render images with a fine balance between quality and speed.

The interaction of many renderer settings and the idiosyncrasies of character animation make it impossible for me to recommend any hard-and-fast setups for RD5 rendering. I suggest that you choose representative frames from your finished animations, and render a series of tests to determine the options that work best for you. If you pursue a consistent style of character animation, you will quickly find a set of rendering options that you can apply to all your later renderings. RD5 enables you to save your own settings as presets for the Render menu, including camera, rendering frame range, and effects. This is especially handy if you have a collection of different settings that you use often.

One of the most interesting and novel features of the RD5 renderer is that you can choose output quality based on rendering time. This sounds like a nice bit of magic, especially for professionals on a deadline. However, the rendering time is only estimated. Because sequential frames in an animation can vary widely in rendering time, the aggregate render time for a lengthy animation can be significantly longer than the original estimate. If time is important, I suggest you render the most time-consuming frame of the animation first, and set the render options based on that time rather than RD5's default estimate.

RD5 supports alpha channel rendering for easier and more accurate compositing (see Chapter 18) and G-buffer rendering for post-processing and special effects based on scene geometry. These extra channels add significantly to the size of the rendered files, so don't enable them unless you need to.

RD5 doesn't have a standalone render engine, but you can create a batch queue that a single machine can render unattended. This might prove useful for a primitive render farm. You would have to load a copy of RD5 (check with MetaCreations for site licensing) on each node, and each node would only render its own queue.

Softimage 3D

As mentioned earlier, Softimage has covered introductory issues very well in their *Quick Start* manual and *Self-Training Workbook*. The same lessons used to introduce lighting concepts also cover rendering, including optimization and trade-offs to minimize rendering time. Read the *Quick Start* manual, then work through the *Self-Training Workbook*. Apply those lessons and the general guidelines earlier in this chapter to your character animation. For more technical details and examples, refer to the *Rendering* manual. If you run into problems, the two-volume *Reference Guide* will give you all the answers you are likely to need.

Strata Studio Pro

Chapter 8 of the SSPro *User* manual provides a good introduction to the available rendering options. Several rendering methods are supported, including raytracing, scanline, and Raydiosity (sic). For most characters, scanline rendering will be accurate enough and will significantly reduce rendering time.

Several of the rendering methods have a set of Expert options. These typically include shadows, reflections, refraction, and transparency. Depending on the requirements of your scene, you can save rendering time and RAM by turning off most or all of these options. Pages 51 through 68 of the *Reference* manual include all the technical details and trade-offs.

SSPro can render an alpha channel for any 32-bit image file format. This is an important feature if you will be compositing layers or matching live footage.

SSPro does not yet support network rendering, but you can queue up a number of rendering jobs or run them in the background while you continue to use other software.

trueSpace3

The trueSpace3 manual plays a little joke on the inattentive reader. The chapter entitled "Rendering" is actually about materials settings, while most of the rendering functions are described in Chapter 3, "View Group." Other than that, the documentation is adequate and covers most of what you'll need to understand to optimize your renderings.

trueSpace3 has relatively few output file formats: BMP, AVI, JPEG, FLC, and TGA. This last format is the only one that can be rendered at 32 bits to include an alpha channel. If you will need to composite your character over other layers or live footage, you have exactly one choice for rendering output.

You can use true raytracing to render your images, but the trueSpace3 manual is conscientious about pointing out raytracing's disadvantages and some workable alternatives. trueSpace3 has a fistful of options that can save or cost you rendering time, including resolution, anti-aliasing levels, depth of field, motion blur, raytracing depth, fog, and Photoshop-compatible post-processing filters.

At this time, trueSpace3 does not support any form of network rendering. You can load separate copies of the software on each network node, manually choose the range of frames each computer is to render, and point their outputs to a shared directory.

Further Study

If you are interested in the technical theory behind rendering, you can find out more by reading some of the computer graphics textbooks cited in the Bibliography. The ACM SIGGRAPH publications mentioned in Chapter 21 are also good resources, once you have a basic grounding in CGI theory.

Moving On

In this chapter, we've covered the basics of lighting your characters and a number of simple tricks to render your animations faster or more efficiently. The next chapter shows you how to use compositing software to add dissolves and special effects, and to composite your CGI characters over background footage using move matching.

EFFECTS

Compositing is a means to add your CGI creations to live-action footage, or to combine effects you couldn't render in one pass. Add compositing to your personal toolkit, and you'll more than double utility and effectiveness of all your other tools.

Compositing is the process of adding parts of one image to another. In photography, compositing refers to procedures on a single image. In video and film work, it usually means performing similar compositing operations on a sequence of images.

Compositing was originally done using *optical printers* and several layers of film, one layer for each piece of original footage, matte, or special effect. Each layer would add *film grain* to the composited footage, so there were limits to how many layers you could composite without losing image quality. Digital compositing does not add film grain, so you can composite as many layers as you want without sacrificing image quality. This is a mixed blessing. If you are matching live action digitized from film, you may need to overlay a film grain effect on your CGI images. Otherwise, they may look too clean and stand out from the live action footage they are supposed to match.

Film and video work uses compositing for several functions. You can composite parts of a duplicate background, or *clean plate*, to cover unwanted parts of the image to salvage footage that might otherwise have to be reshot. This is often used to conceal safety lines and other equipment in live action. You can also composite shot transitions, such as dissolves, wipes, and special effects. If you have to split CGI scenes into layers to speed up rendering or stay within your computer's capacity, you can reassemble the scene with compositing. While these other applications are useful, the most important use of compositing in the context of this book is adding an animated character to digitized backgrounds or live-action footage.

Compositing Software

Several commercial software packages are available for editing and compositing animations, including Adobe's Premiere and After Effects and Eyeon's Digital Fusion.

Premiere

Premiere is an audio and video editing program that can handle most file types and sizes appropriate to desktop machines. It can perform most of the video and audio editing, simple transition effects, and compositing you'll need for working with exclusively CGI footage. Premiere is widely available, often at significant discounts. A stripped-down trial version is bundled with some video editing hardware. The reference manual and tutorials that ship with the full version is an adequate introduction to basic compositing and editing, and you shouldn't have any major problems with it. One significant caveat is that Premiere does not support true 3:2 pulldown (see Chapter 20), so if you animate to 24 fps and want to output at 30 fps, you'll get some nasty strobing effects.

After Effects

After Effects is a "big brother" to Premiere, with more advanced video editing features that enable it to handle the integration of live action and CGI elements. Unfortunately, the audio tools are a step down from Premiere's. The Production Bundle of versions 3 and higher has two features critical to CGI compositing—motion tracking and motion stabilizing—which are discussed later in this chapter. Again, the documentation is up to Adobe's usual competent standards, although the motion tracking section is minimal enough that I'll supplement it with a tutorial later in this chapter. As with Premier, After Effects does not render correct 3:2 pulldown, so 24 to 30 fps conversions will have temporal artifacts.

Digital Fusion

Digital Fusion is a video-only editing program designed specifically to handle the large file sizes and special formats of film and high-end video work. The basic package includes all the tools you'll need to match CGI elements to live-action footage. Also, I find the Digital Fusion interface much easier to learn and faster to use than either of the Adobe products. The interface gives you on-the-fly feedback as you add each edit or effect, greatly speeding up the experimental process and making you more productive.

If you ever intend to work in film formats, you should consider Digital Fusion. At the time of this writing, plug-ins are in development for other packages, but Digital Fusion is the only desktop editing software that natively supports the Cineon film-scanner format. This means that you don't have to go through a laborious and time-consuming conversion process to get Cineon files into your computer. It also means you can work with Cineon's full 10-bit logarithmic color depth, so you don't have the headaches of color compression and correction on both input and output.

A fully enabled demo version of Digital Fusion 1 is in the Eyeon directory on this book's CD-ROM. The only limitation to this demo is the pair of Eyeon logos superimposed on the final rendering. You won't be able to use the results for commercial work, but you can experiment with and learn all Digital Fusion's functions. The Help files reproduce many pages from the full version's documentation, so you can read them to learn about most of the program's features. There wasn't enough space on the CD-ROM for all the tutorial AVIs and sample footage, but the Intel and Alpha software is all there, and you can substitute your own footage in the tutorial Flows.

The Basics

Compositing software has nearly as many bells and whistles as 3D animation software. As with 3D, you don't need to understand or use them all in order to produce decent character animation. Therefore, this chapter provides a brief overview of the most necessary and often-used compositing processes.

Dissolve

The most basic compositing effect is the *dissolve*, a gradual transition from one shot to the next. You can vary a dissolve from a long, slow transition for dramatic effect to a very short dissolve that is almost a cut. A *match dissolve* is a transition where the beginning and end scenes are roughly the same but a visible difference helps tell the story. This is a popular cinematic technique, but it has been used so much, it has become cliché. Even though it still works, you should use it sparingly.

PROJECT 18.1

Match Dissolve In Digital Fusion

This project shows you how to set up a match dissolve.

1. Open a new Flow. Add a Loader (see Figure 18.1), double-click to make it active, and load the image sequence 18_A0000.TGA from the Chapter 18 directory on this book's CD-ROM.

If you would like to create your own image sequence, set up a street scene with a daylight lighting pattern, and animate the camera to dolly along the sidewalk from right to left. Render at least 128 frames, to give yourself room for a smooth dissolve.

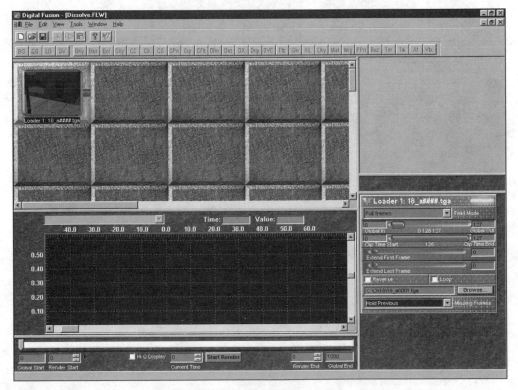

Figure 18.1   Loader 1 controls, with 18_A0000.TGA sequence loaded.

2. Copy and paste Loader 1 into the cell below it, creating Loader 2. Double-click on Loader 2 to activate it, and, in the control panel, load the image sequence 18_B0000.TGA. Change the Global In setting to 100. The dissolve will start at frame 100, so you don't need to show any of the second sequence until that frame.

   If you would like to make your own version of the second image sequence, repeat the previous setup, but substitute night lighting and animate the camera moving in the opposite direction, as if retracing its path.

3. Add a Dissolve (DX) tool to the Flow, to the right of Loader 2. Connect Loader 1 to the second input of Dissolve 1, as in Figure 18.2.

4. Right-click on the Operation bar in the Dissolve controls, and choose Bezier Spline from the drop-down menu (see Figure 18.3).

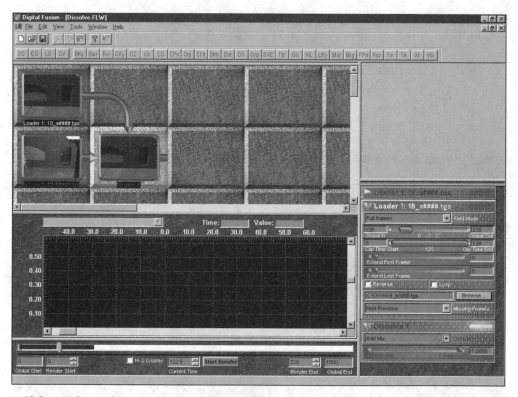

Figure 18.2 Loaders and Dissolve set up in Flow.

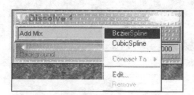

Figure 18.3 Opening a Bezier Spline for the Dissolve controls.

5. The default spline is a horizontal line having 1.0 value throughout the animation. You need to click on the spline to add control points at frames 100, 128, and 228.

6. Move the spline control points to create a spline like Figure 18.4, where the Dissolve starts off at 1.0 (full background image sequence) and transitions smoothly to 0.0 (full foreground image sequence) during frames 100 through 128.

7. When you are satisfied with the spline, right-click on the Dissolve 1 control slider. Choose Connect To|Dissolve 1:Operation:Value from the drop-down menu, as shown in Figure 18.5. This tells the Dissolve function to follow the value of the spline you just made.

8. Add a Saver to the Flow, and render the complete animation to the end of the second image sequence. If you used the example image sequences, this should be frame 228. Your results should be something like DISSOLVE.AVI, in the Chapter 18 directory on this book's CD-ROM.

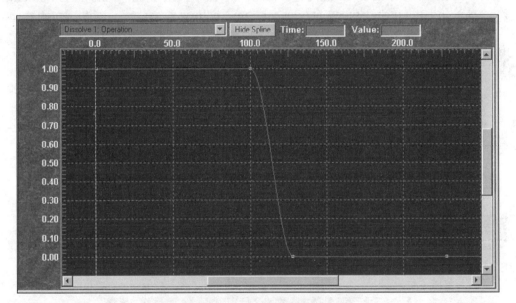

Figure 18.4   Dissolve Spline.

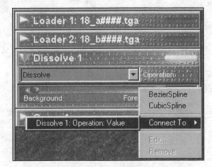

Figure 18.5   Choose Connect To|Dissolve 1:Operation:Value.

This match dissolve from day to night lighting tells the audience that time has passed. As I said before, this is cliché, but it still works. If you'd like a more dramatic match dissolve exercise, you can set up a daylight scene with a walking character. Set up the camera in a tracking shot that allows the character to walk gradually out of the frame. For the second shot, set up the character to walk back into the frame, as if returning from a long walk, with the nighttime lighting setup showing that time has passed.

Chroma Key

Chroma key is a technique used for seamlessly combining part of one image with another image by selectively excluding specified colors. This is commonly referred to as *blue screen*, from the color most-often used as a key, or *green screen*, from the second most-common color. You have probably seen chroma keying as used by television meteorologists, where they stand in front of a colored panel and the weather maps are chroma keyed around them. If the person mistakenly wears clothing that includes the key color, you can see the weather map right through them.

PROJECT 18.2 Key Compositing

This project shows you how to use chroma key. It uses single images, but the same procedures apply to image sequences or animations.

1. Render a character against a solid blue background. I use either fully saturated 0,0,255 blue or, for NTSC-legal video, 0,0,240. You should get an image like Figure 18.6.

2. Open a new Flow. Add two Loaders, the first for the foreground image you just rendered and the second for the PORCH.BMP background from the Chapter 18 directory on this book's CD-ROM.

3. Add a Merge (Mrg) tool to the Flow, and connect both Loaders to it so the foreground image merges over the background, as shown in Figure 18.7.

4. Insert a Blue/Green Keyer (BKy) or Chroma Keyer (CKy) between the foreground image and the Merge tool. Right-click on the Merge tool, and choose View On|Small.

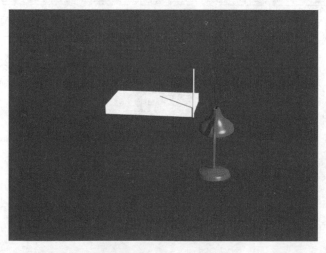

Figure 18.6 Foreground character rendered against color background.

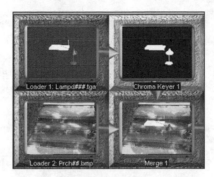

Figure 18.7 Loaders, Merge, and Keyer added to Flow.

5. Click on the Blue/Green Keyer to make it active. Click and drag a selection box in the Small view over an area you know is part of the background (key) color. In this example, any of the four corners of the image will do. The foreground object appears on top of the background, with a rough edge.

6. Drag more boxes over the blue-tinted stray pixels that form the rough edges of the foreground object. Be careful not to select part of the foreground object. Each time you select a pixel, all pixels of that color will be added to the matte. The edge of the object should become visibly cleaner as you matte out the stray pixels.

7. Use the Scale menu option and scroll bars to zoom in and move around the Small display, looking for stray pixels, Figure 18.8.

Figure 18.8 Keyer settings and clean foreground object in Small display.

Figure 18.9 Foreground character chroma keyed over background image.

8. When you are satisfied that you have added all stray pixels to the matte, add a Saver to the Flow, and render the composited image. You should get results like Figure 18.9.

Computers are very good at rendering bluescreen backgrounds and making every pixel exactly the same color. This is nearly impossible to reproduce in real life. If you ever composite live-action blue screen footage into an animation, you'll have to deal with a range of shades due to uneven lighting or discolored paint or filters. Digital Fusion's Chroma Key and Blue/Green Key controls enable you to adjust for variations in lighting and key colors to produce a clean matte. The color you select for a key should not appear in any of the lights, objects, or textures in the foreground image. Blue is commonly used, but almost any color will work.

Alpha Channel

If you need to composite a CGI character into a complex live-action background, the matched lighting or reflection maps may not leave you a clear choice of color for a chroma key. For these situations, most 3D software enables you to render an alpha channel, a separate 8-bit layer of the image that exactly silhouettes the scene's objects in grayscale. Figure 18.10 shows a ren-

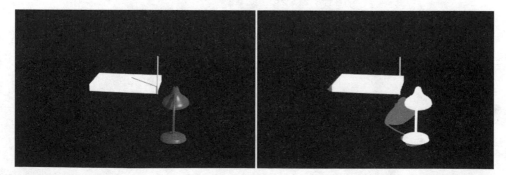

Figure 18.10 Rendered image and corresponding alpha channel.

dered image with its grayscale alpha channel. Alpha channel compositing uses this grayscale layer as a filter to combine the foreground image with a separate background.

Normally, the alpha channel is invisible in 32-bit (24-bits color+8-bits alpha channel=32 bits) images. The extra layer is only visible in programs like Digital Fusion, Photoshop, or other applications that enable you to look at layers separately. Some 3D software renders the alpha channel as a separate image file, which gives you another image sequence to keep track of. It's easier if you can render single 32-bit images that include the alpha channel.

Alpha Channel Compositing

PROJECT **18.3**

This project shows you how to composite layers using an alpha channel.

1. Open a new Flow. Add two Loaders, the first for the foreground image ALPHA.TGA and the second for the PORCH.BMP background, both from the Chapter 18 directory on this book's CD-ROM.

ALPHA.TGA was rendered on a black background with black shadow-catching objects in order to get deeper shadows.

2. Add a Merge (Mrg) tool to the Flow, and connect both Loaders to it. Right-click on Loader 1, and choose View On|Small to put ALPHA.TGA in the Small display.

3. Right-click in the Small display, and choose Display|Alpha, as shown in Figure 18.11. This changes the Small display from the default color channels of the image to the alpha channel.

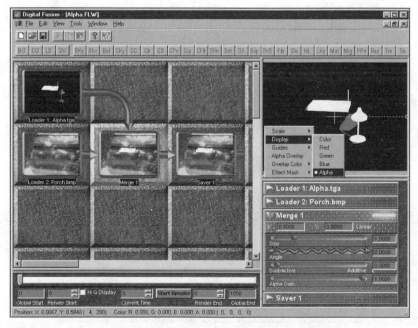

Figure 18.11 Flow layout, Merge control settings, and alpha channel in Small display.

4. Edit the Merge control settings to match those shown in Figure 18.11, so the foreground image merges cleanly over the background.

   Note that using the alpha channel gets rid of the painstaking pixel selection you had to do for the Chroma or Blue/Green Keyers. This is why rendering alpha channels for all your character animations can be a great timesaver.

5. Add a Saver to the Flow, and render the composited image. You should get results like Figure 18.12.

Alpha channels give you cleaner, more accurate mattes than color keying. The alpha channel is rendered at the same time as the color layers, so all anti-aliasing, blur, and other rendering effects match precisely in the alpha channel. If you render low-resolution tests, you can be confident that the alpha channels will work exactly the same when you render at full resolution. This is especially important when you have to re-render a sequence to make a change or correction. If you use alpha channels to composite several layers, you only have to re-render the changed layer, then re-composite it with the unchanged layers.

Dealing With Live Action

Compositing your CGI character animation onto live action footage requires some additional processes. If done carefully and well, the results can make the CGI elements indistinguishable from the live action. I find this to be one of the most fun and rewarding forms of character animation—bringing CGI creatures into the real world.

Documenting The Set

Before you shoot the live action, you need to thoroughly document the set. After the shoot, you will need to re-create those parts of the set that your character will touch, shadow, or be shadowed by. Trying to do this after the fact, when all you can measure are images from the live

Figure 18.12 Rendered objects composited over background with alpha channel.

action footage, is much harder. Take a few notes, measurements, and photographs now, and you'll save yourself many headaches later.

The first priority is reference points. You need to choose or create several visual references that will be easy to pick out in each frame of the footage. You will use these reference points to stabilize and match camera motion and may also have to use them to create models of shadowed or shadowing surfaces. A good reference point contrasts strongly with its surroundings and shows a consistent profile throughout camera moves. In the sample footage, the sidewalk, steps, and door provided a number of excellent reference points (see Figure 18.13).

If you can't find a good set of reference points, you may have to make your own. Ping-pong balls painted Day-Glo green work well, and you can tack them temporarily to the set or props with putty. A solid, non-natural color from the Day-Glo palette makes is easy to mask the reference marks out of the footage during compositing. Spherical reference marks provide a more consistent appearance through most camera moves, making tracking and motion stabilizing much easier. An excellent example of this technique is shown on *The Making of Jurassic Park* videotape or laserdisc, in the Gallimimus stampede sequence (see Bibliography).

Your second priority is to measure the set, including the reference points and any surfaces your character will touch, shadow, or be shadowed by. You will need to model these reference points and surfaces and add them to your character's scenes, so you can animate the character to match. I've found the most reliable way to keep track of set measurements is to take a series of photographs or digitized video prints of the set and then write my notes and measurements directly on the prints. If you can't mark up the photos, try grease pencil on a transparent overlay. Figure 18.14 shows my notes for the porch steps in the sample footage.

You should also measure the position of any local (other than sunlight) light sources and (very important!) the starting position and attitude of the camera's focal plane. Get the lens settings, too. If you are working with a commercial film crew, you can get some of these measurements

Figure 18.13 Frame from sample footage.

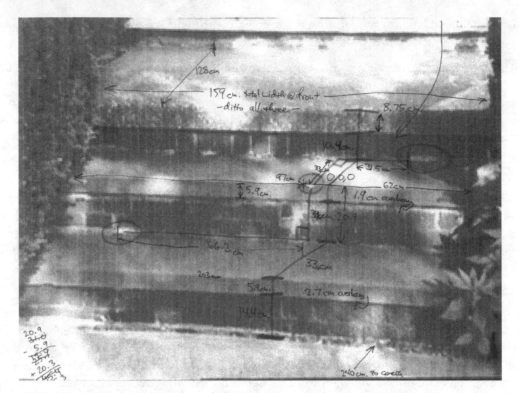

Figure 18.14 Measurements and notes on reference photo.

from the focus puller. It's a good idea to cross-check your measurements. It's much easier to re-measure on the set than to locate and correct measurement errors during post-production.

Once you've got the data you need for modeling, you can start collecting what you'll need to match the lighting, shadows, and colors. The first step is a *clean plate,* an image of the empty set with lighting just as it will appear in the final footage. This is the visual reference you will consult on questions of shadow and highlight density, falloff (the shadows' soft edges), and color, Figure 18.15. You may also use a series of clean plates, taken in different directions, to build environment reflection maps (see Chapter 9).

The second step is to repeat the clean plate shoot with reference lighting objects in the frame. I like to use a set of plastic foam objects that are light, rigid, and easy to move around on the set. You can make your own easily with inexpensive materials from any craft shop. The only criteria are that you be able to extract shadow and highlight colors, and deduce the angle of light sources from the reference shots. My own rig is a plastic foam block topped by a 1-centimeter grid, with a wooden dowel gnomon at one corner and a white plastic foam lighting ball (see Figure 18.16).

Just place the reference lighting objects in the frame, preferably as close as possible to the character's anticipated position, and take another clean plate (see Figure 18.17).

Figure 18.15 Clean plate.

Figure 18.16 Closeup of lighting reference object with gnomon and white ball.

Figure 18.17 Lighting reference object with gnomon and white ball.

Figure 18.18 CGI lighting reference objects and character composited into clean plate.

The goal of all this is to be able to produce an exact match between CGI elements and the clean plate, as in Figure 18.18. Note the exact match of shadow angle and density between the reference image and the final composite.

CGI Set Matching

Once you've taken all the measurements and reference photos, you can use them to build shadow surfaces and lighting setups in your 3D software. If you've taken good measurements, you can do this by the numbers and very quickly.

PROJECT 18.4 Duplicating Shadow Surfaces

The goal of this project is to make a duplicate model in the computer of every surface that the character will cast a shadow on. This is necessary for the software to render the character's shadow so it will accurately match the footage.

1. Refer to the measurements in Figure 18.14 to build a 1:1 scale model of the porch steps in the software of your choice.

In case you can't read my scrivenings, here are the important measurements for building the model:

- The top slab is 128 cm deep, 8.75 cm thick, and 159 cm wide. All remaining elements are also 159 cm wide.

- The top riser is inset 5 cm and is 10.4 cm high.

- The middle slab is 33 cm deep and 5.9 cm thick.

- The middle riser is inset 1.9 cm, and the top of the middle slab is 20.9 cm above the top of the bottom slab.

- The bottom slab is 33 cm deep and 5.9 cm thick.

- The bottom riser is inset 2.7 cm and is 14.4 cm high.

If you don't want to build the model, you can import one of the versions (PORCH.DXF, PORCH.3DS, or PORCH.LWO) I've provided in the Chapter 18 directory on this book's CD-ROM. I have also provided models of some of the lighting reference objects (LITEREF, LITEGRID) that appear in this chapter's figures. You'll need to add a matte white sphere to complete the next exercise, but then, you wouldn't want me to do it all for you, would you?

2. In your animation software, load file PORCH.BMP as the backdrop image.

3. Lay out the models according to the measurements and the background image of the clean plate. Add markers for the reference points noted in Figure 18.14.

Pay especially close attention to the position of the LITEREF object. The corner with the gnomon should be precisely 97 cm from the left corner of the middle slab, and the front edge of LITEREF should be flush with the front edge of the slab. I aligned the reference object with a chip in the concrete, which I measured as a reference mark and wrote up on Figure 18.14.

If you are using LightWave, you can load file PORCH.LWS from the Chapter 18 directory on this book's CD-ROM to see an example of how I set up the matching scene.

Match Scene Lighting

PROJECT 18.5

The goal of this project is to match the angle, intensity, color, and falloff of the light sources in the footage. It's relatively easy in this case, because the only direct light source is the sun, the shadows are distinct, and the ambient light is consistent throughout the character's area of movement.

1. In the scene you set up in Project 18.4, add a single light source at a long distance from the porch model. Position the camera to look down at the LITEREF/LITEGRID grid, as in Figure 18.19.

2. Look at Figure 18.16 for reference. Move the light source around, and re-render the camera view until the end of the rendered shadow appears at exactly the same grid coordinates as the shadow end in Figure 18.16.

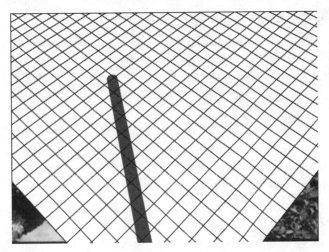

Figure 18.19 LITEREF/LITEGRID as rendered by CGI camera.

3. Change the light falloff (if your software has this feature) to mimic the falloff of the gnomon's shadow in Figure 18.16.

   The next step is to match the color of the light. This isn't just matching the color of sunlight—you have to match the color distortions produced by the video camera and the digitizing process, too. The most reliable way to do this is to sample the final rendering and compare it to the same areas of the footage.

   You'll need to keep Photoshop or other image processing software open while you render and re-render the scene. If you don't have enough system memory to do this, the process will get tedious very quickly.

4. Set the light to pure white. Render a frame. Open the frame in Photoshop.

5. Use the Photoshop eyedropper to sample the image at the highlight of the white sphere. Make a note of the RGB values. Take another sample at the center of the darkest part of the shadow behind the sphere but still on the LITEREF object's surface.

   These two samples give you the brightest and darkest color values for the light.

6. Repeat Step 5 on reference image LITETEST.TGA, which you'll find in the Chapter 18 directory on this book's CD-ROM.

   I found the highlight sample of this image colored 239,232,238, and the shadow behind the sphere colored 14,16,16. Your results may vary.

7. Change the light's color values to match the sample you took from LITETEST.TGA. Re-render the image, and check the identical sample areas. Readjust the light and re-render until you are satisfied that the rendered color of the reference objects closely matches the original colors.

CGI Animation To Matched Set

Now that you've successfully matched the shadow surfaces and the light angle, falloff, and color, it's time to animate a character to match the clean plate. Animating to a single image is much easier than trying to match an entire image sequence. It also enables you to tweak the animation without being distracted by the movement of the camera.

PROJECT 18.6 Animate CGI Character To Shadow Objects

This project shows you how to use the shadow objects as a guide to animate your character. If you do this right, the character will appear to be interacting with the real-world surfaces you duplicated with the shadow objects.

1. Adapt a character animation from one of the earlier exercises to make the character walk, hop, or slither up the porch steps. For this example, I chose to use the hopping desklamp from the animation projects in Chapter 14.

2. Keep the character to the middle or right edge of the stairs, so its entire shadow falls only on the porch object surfaces. You didn't model the shrubbery as a shadow surface, so you won't get rendered shadows for them, either.

3. Match the character's foot placement to the upper surface of each slab. Be careful that the foot does not penetrate or float over the surface but meets it precisely, as in Figure 18.20. If your software supports it, you should use constraints to keep the feet from sliding.

4. When you are satisfied with your animation of the character, render the complete animation with an alpha channel.

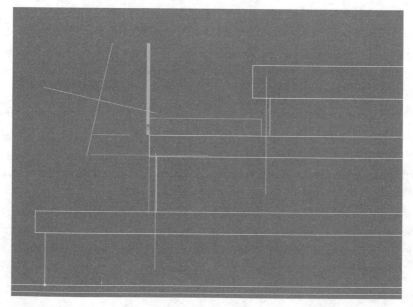

Figure 18.20 Desklamp aligned with porch step.

5. Composite the complete animation over the PORCH.BMP background image, using the procedure depicted in Project 18.3.

You should get results something like animation PORCH.AVI (Figure 18.21), which you can find in the Chapter 18 directory on this book's CD-ROM.

Move Matching

If you've worked through each of the preceding projects, you've got a pretty good handle on the process of compositing CGI elements onto still background images. This was pretty much the state of the compositing art until *Jurassic Park*. All CGI compositing was done with footage from a locked-down, immobile camera, because it was simply too difficult and expensive to match elements to a moving camera. When Steven Spielberg challenged the JP effects team to allow him to shoot from a hand-held camera, they came through with the basic techniques used in most effects houses today.

You've already learned the essentials of the process: measure the set, build matching shadow surfaces, and animate the CGI character to the modeled surfaces. The next step is to animate the CGI camera to precisely mimic the movements of the footage camera. The final step is to composite the rendered elements over the moving footage.

Figure 18.21   Frames from PORCH.AVI sample animation.

The primary hassle of match moving is tweaking rough footage. A hand-held camera, even on a Steadicam, changes location and attitude on every frame. For example, look at the images in Figure 18.22. This was shot with a hand-held camcorder, with no Steadicam or dolly. It's very rough.

This means that without other assistance, the match mover has to hand-animate the camera in all three axes of rotation and all three coordinate axes, for each frame of footage. Ouch!

But of course, there's good news. (You knew it all along, didn't you?) Necessity drove clever innovators to develop a technique called *motion stabilizing*, that removes most of the frame-by-frame camera motion and smooths out the remainder. The end result is like having the world's best camera dolly but without having to set up, tear down, or have extra grips—all the freedom of a hand-held camera with the ease-of-use of a dolly or Steadicam.

Before we can dig into motion stabilizing, we have to get footage into the computer. You have a plethora of choices here. It seems that every day another video card manufacturer is coming out with another video digitizing board. Prices keep dropping, and capabilities keep increasing. If you have a genuine business need for it, you can easily cost-justify a broadcast-quality capture and playback system like DPS's PVR or Hollywood.

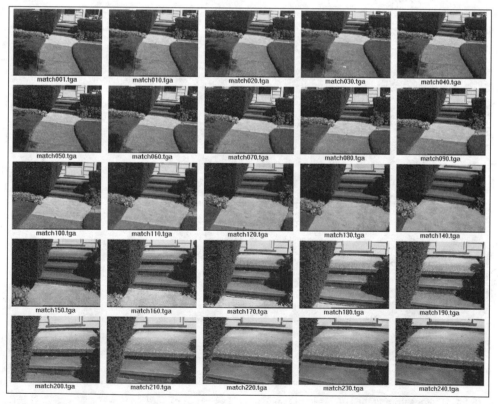

Figure 18.22 Frames from example match footage.

If you are working in film, you will probably need to go through a service bureau, like Cinesite. This is the opposite end of the film output process described in Chapter 20, and you'll be working with the same group of professionals. Expect to spend big bucks, though. Fees of $3 or more per scanned frame are typical.

If you have more limited needs or resources, there are a number of video cards that will drive your monitor, accelerate rendering and animation playback, and digitize video and/or audio, as well. I can recommend ATI's PC2TV or All-In-Wonder cards as good, under-$300 entry-level choices, but the field is crowded and fast-moving enough that you will need to do your own research just before you buy.

The example footage of my front sidewalk and porch was shot on Hi8, then digitized through an ATI Pro Turbo PC2TV video card at 30 fps. This card streams the video data directly to the computer's hard disk, so it requires a fast drive with adequate free space. I then saved it out as an image sequence (files MATCH001.TGA through MATCH265.TGA), which you can find in the Chapter 18 directory on this book's CD-ROM.

Motion Stabilizing With Digital Fusion

This project shows you how to remove most of the jitter and wobble from live footage. If you can stabilize your footage first, move matching becomes much easier.

1. Open a new Flow.

2. Add a Loader. Choose the image sequence to be stabilized, Figure 18.23 (MATCH001.TGA).

3. Add a Tracker operator to the right of the Loader.

4. Open the Large display. Right-click on Loader 1, and choose View On|Large from the pop up menu. Right click on Tracker 1, and choose View On|Small from the pop-up menu.

5. Double-click on the Tracker operator to activate it, and open the function controls (see Figure 18.24). A white crosshair will appear in both the Large and Small displays.

6. In the Large display, left-click and drag the white crosshair to the left edge of the door's threshold.

7. You may need a closer view to position the crosshair accurately. Right-click on the display, then choose Scale and a magnification value from the pop-up menu. You can use the scroll bars at the bottom and right edge of the display to center the desired area.

8. Click on the Select Pattern checkbox in the Tracker controls. This makes the Small display zoom in on the area around the crosshair.

Whatever appears in the Small display is the pattern the Tracker will look for. You want the pattern to be unique and easy to pick out from its surroundings, so the Tracker can do an accurate job. The larger the pattern and the higher resolution the

Figure 18.23 DF screen with match footage loaded and ready for Tracker setup.

Figure 18.24 Tracker controls.

image, the better. This sample footage is about the worst case. The individual frames are only 320×240, so you only have a few pixels to make a pattern.

9. Use the Size slider in the Tracker controls to zoom in or out so a recognizable pattern fills the Small display. You may have to reposition the Tracker crosshair, too. You should end up with something like Figure 18.25.

10. This pattern is going to be difficult enough for the Tracker to follow, so set the Accuracy control to High. Fortunately, the background of the pattern area is white, and the contrast between light and dark areas is good, so you can set the Color control to Full Color.

11. Turn off the Select Pattern checkbox to lock in the pattern settings.

If everything is working properly, you should be able to move to another frame in the sequence and see the Tracker crosshair remain centered in the pattern area. If not, go back and try again. If your image sequence has extreme camera movement, you may not be able to get the Tracker to work smoothly throughout the sequence. You can solve this problem by breaking the sequence up, resetting the Tracker each time it loses track of the pattern. You may also have to use more than one pattern, if the objects or camera movement occlude the first pattern. Once you get the Tracker crosshair moving properly, you're halfway to stabilizing the footage. Save your work before you go any further.

12. Copy and paste Loader 1 to the space below it as Loader 2, starting a second row in the Flow.

13. Add a DVE tool to the right of Loader 2. Double-click on the DVE tool to activate its controls.

14. Right-click on the Offset bar in the middle of the DVE controls. Choose Connect To| Tracker 1:Steady Position from the pop-up menu (see Figure 18.26). This tells the DVE to follow the Tracker motion path but to smooth it out a bit.

15. Add a Saver tool after the DVE, save your changes, then render the stabilized image sequence. Save the Flow. You'll need it again for Project 18.9.

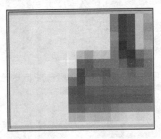

Figure 18.25 Tracker pattern for threshold edge.

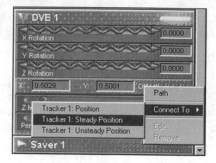

Figure 18.26 DVE settings to follow Tracker.

Choose an image or animation file format that you can load as a backdrop in your 3D software. Most programs can accept TGA files (my personal preference), but your software might not.

Figure 18.27 shows a few example frames from a stabilized image sequence. Note that the area under the Tracker crosshair remained almost perfectly steady in all images.

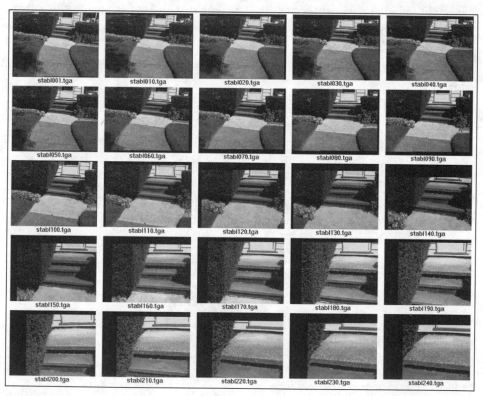

Figure 18.27 Sample stabilized images.

Move Matching

PROJECT 18.8

1. Now, you can go back to Project 18.6 and repeat it, using the stabilized footage instead of the still background image, with the additional step of animating the camera position.

2. Add a null object at the position of the Tracker crosshair relative to the shadow surfaces, according to the measurements you used to build the surfaces in Project 18.4. Set the camera to track the null object. If your software supports it, you can save a lot of effort by constraining the camera to look at the position of the Tracker crosshair. If the Tracker is accurate, this camera look-at constraint can automate the match of the pitch and heading rotation axes, and make the remaining matches a lot easier. If your software doesn't enable you to track the camera to a null object, you'll have to animate the camera completely by hand.

3. Set up a hierarchy of null objects, one for each remaining axis of rotation or movement. If your software supports camera tracking, you'll only have to set up nulls for Bank rotation, and X, Y, and Z movement. Lock off all movement or rotation for each of these nulls, except for the single axis they are intended to use. Give them descriptive names like BankNull, XMoveNull, YMoveNull, and ZMoveNull. The results should allow you to separately set keyframes for movement and rotation of the camera on each axis. This enables you to set the minimum number of keyframes necessary to match move the camera, and keeps keyframes on one axis from interfering with already-matched movement in the other axes. For example, if the original footage was shot from a dolly or crane, the Bank axis might have been locked throughout the shot. You could simply set a beginning and end keyframe on the Bank axis, then ignore it for the rest of the match move process. If the Bank axis was tied to the others, you'd have to make sure the correct Bank value was set for every camera keyframe throughout the sequence. That's a lot of extra work, especially when you're looking at thousands of frames.

4. Position and rotate the camera at the beginning and end frames of the sequence so the background image matches precisely with the shadow surfaces. I recommend you start with the Bank axis. Because the footage and shadow surfaces both have strong vertical and horizontal lines, it's relatively easy to judge whether they're on the same angle. Also, the Bank axis is usually the one with the least keyframes, because rapidly tilting the camera is generally not good cinematic technique. Nail down the easy stuff first, the axes with the fewest keyframes.

5. Next is the distance (usually Z axis) from the camera to the shadow surfaces. It's pretty easy to judge when the size of the porch model matches the size of the porch image, even if they aren't perfectly centered.

6. Once you've nailed the distance, you can match either the vertical or lateral axis, depending on the shot and your personal preferences. Take the easy one first. If you have a shot with lots of horizontal lines, set the vertical axis next. Each horizontal line provides a reference mark for the vertical axis, and vice versa. In the example footage, the strong horizontal lines of the porch steps make the vertical match a lot easier.

Whichever axis you choose to do first, nail it down and then do the same for the remaining axis.

7. At this point, you should have the beginning and end frames matched precisely to the shadow surfaces. To efficiently set keyframes for the rest of the sequence, you have to find where the splines for each axis peak and change direction. The easiest way to do this is to select an axis, then step through the sequence one frame at a time, paying careful attention to the difference between the existing setting for that axis and the true setting as represented by the background image. You are looking for the peak difference, the frame where the existing setting is as far off as possible. At that frame, you set a correcting keyframe for that axis, then continue stepping through the sequence looking for the next-largest tracking error. On a smooth camera move, you may be able to set a handful of frames describing a simple slalom. On a jerky handheld move like this example, you will probably have to set many more keyframes. Worst case, you may have to use linear interpolation and set a key for every frame.

8. When you've matched the camera to your satisfaction, render and composite the animation as an image sequence, as you did in Project 18.6.

The next step will be to put all that live-action camera jitter back in, restoring the appearance of a hand-held camera and making the CGI element that much more realistic.

PROJECT 18.9 Motion Destabilizing

This project shows you how to reverse the effects of the stabilizing you did in Project 18.7. This destabilizing restores the live-action appearance to the composited footage, so it doesn't appear overly smooth like a SteadiCam or motion-control camera.

1. Reload the Flow you saved from Project 18.7. Save it with a new name before you start making the following changes.

2. Select Loader 2, and change the image sequence to the stabilized one you rendered at the end of Project 18.7.

3. Double-click on the DVE tool to activate its controls. Right-click on the Offset bar in the middle of the DVE controls. Choose Connect To|Tracker 1:Unsteady Position from the pop-up menu. This tells the DVE to *invert* the Tracker motion path, restoring the jitter that the Steady Position removed.

4. Drag Loader 1 and Tracker 1 to the row underneath Loader 2 and DVE 1. Add a Chroma Keyer (CKy) to the right of the DVE. Add a Merge (Mrg) tool two spaces to the right of Tracker 1, and connect both Loaders to it so that the stabilized image merges over the original footage. Drag the Saver to the right of the Merge. Your Flow should look something like Figure 18.28.

5. Right-click on the Chroma Keyer, and choose View On|Large. Click on the Chroma Keyer to make it active. Move to a frame that shows the black border that the stabilization added to the image.

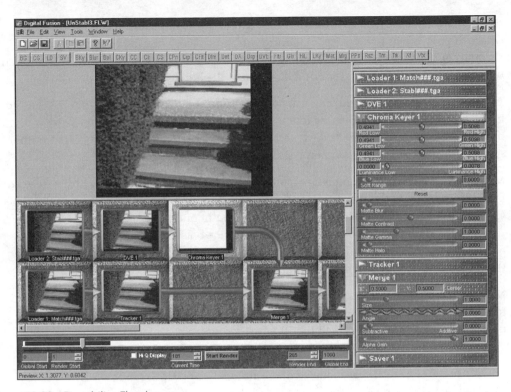

Figure 18.28   Destabilize Flow layout.

6. Click and drag a selection box in the Large view over part of the black stabilization border. This masks the stabilized image, so the black border becomes transparent in the Merge, and the underlying original image shows through. Your Chroma Keyer and Merge settings should be similar to those in Figure 18.28.

7. Save your changes, then render the destabilized image sequence.

If all goes well, the final rendered animation should show your character accurately composited to the steps, with the original jerky camera motions and the correct lighting and shadows. Don't be disappointed if your first attempt doesn't turn out as well as you'd hoped. Like most processes in character animation, move matching takes practice and attention to detail. Try again, and I think you'll be pleasantly surprised at how quickly your results improve.

Case Study: Move Matching The Jurong Cobra

By Dylan Crooke, Momentum Animations

The COBRA.MOV animation, which you'll find in the Momentum directory of this book's CD-ROM, was created as an advertisement for Jurong Reptile Park. This animation is a composite of a CGI snake character over live footage of a complex jungle location shot just outside of Melbourne. The live action camera was mounted on a crane and could move along almost any axis. The final shot chosen was complex and almost an orbit of where the cobra was to be placed. Lighting was matched by placing a white and a chrome sphere in the scene and shooting them directly after the main shots. This allowed us to get a good idea of the color and direction of the light.

The live footage was dumped onto our computers from digital Betacam via a DPS Perception VR (Video Recorder). The raw footage was then deinterlaced, partially to give it a more filmic look and also to make it easier to paint out reference markers placed in the scene by Technical Director Domenic DiGiorgio, Figure 18.29.

Most of the scene was measured as accurately as possible by Technical Assistant Stephen Evans at the time of the live action shoot. He was then responsible for fully modeling the CGI scene. Steven also worked out a neat way to paint out the reference points: he motion-tracked each point and placed part of the image back on top of the point, covering each nicely with a feathered edge. The results were seamless and you would never know there were once about half a dozen markers in the shot.

Move matching the camera was tricky. Because the movement was so unusual it proved to be almost impossible to track accurately. The more I worked on the camera path the more of a mess I made. It seemed that the best results were achieved by using fewer keyframes for the camera. Unfortunately, it still wasn't a perfect match.

The 3D snake character was modeled and animated using Hash's A:M V5. The CGI layers were rendered as 32-bit TGA files using the alpha channel as a matte, Figure 18.30. Additional color grading and noise filters were also applied to further integrate the snake into the scene. The cobra's shadow was created by making the snake inactive (invisible to the CGI camera) but still casting shadows, and making the scene totally white. When this was rendered, a grayscale image was produced that could be used as a shadow layer in the final composite, Figure 18.31.

We finally settled on a 2D solution to the move matching problem. We rendered the footage, motion stabilized it, then motion tracked the stabilized footage to the live action layer. In this case, the cobra was coming from the bottom of the screen, so extra image area around the frame was required. The frame size was doubled to allow extra image if needed. The final render had only four camera key frames.

I rendered a single point from the scene, one of the reference markers near the bottom of the snake. Just a single dot that moved around the screen as the camera moved. This footage was then motion stabilized by locking on to the dot. This stabilized footage was a dot totally still in the middle of the screen with the frame moving all over the place around it, the usual result of motion stabilizing.

This "still" dot was then motion tracked to the reference dot in the scene. The footage was replaced with the CGI snake animation and that was how we got a perfect motion match. Then the foreground rock was masked out so the snake would appear to be behind it. The shadow footage was composited on the same layer as the snake,

Figure 18.29   Frame from raw live footage showing markers.

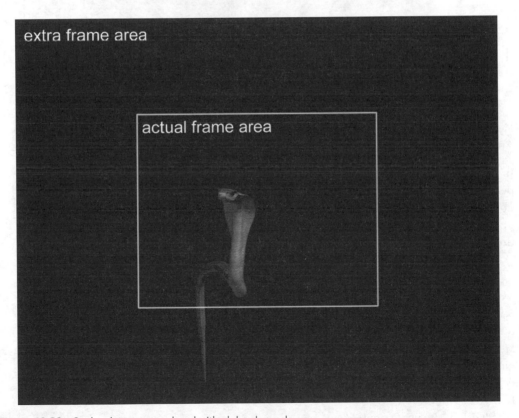

Figure 18.30   Snake character rendered with alpha channel.

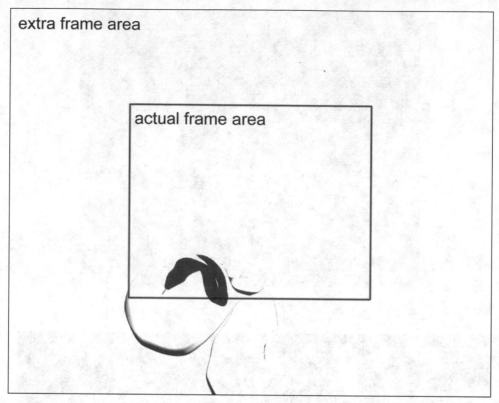

Figure 18.31 Snake shadow.

Figure 18.32, compositing and motion tracking/stabilizing was achieved using Adobe After Effects.

In theory, this technique has a problem in that even though the image is locked, the perspective will not be totally right. That is exactly the case, but it isn't nearly as notice-able as a badly locked composite. It worked for this project but may not work for all applications. It certainly saved us a lot of time, very important with the three week timeline for four commercials.

For more information, you can contact Dylan Crooke at:

Momentum Animations
6 Salisbury St
North Caulfield 3161
Melbourne, Victoria
Australia
Phone: +61 3 9500 1142
Fax: +61 3 9500 1194
Email: dylan@momentumanimations.com
Internet: www.momentumanimations.com

Figure 18.32 Final composite.

Moving On

If you have completed all the exercises in this chapter, you should now be able to composite your characters over other CGI layers, backgrounds, and live footage. This gives you an enormous creative range for your own films. Even if you work in an environment where someone else does the compositing work, your mastery of the jargon and technology will make it easier for you to understand their job and, therefore, make you a more productive and valuable member of the team.

FINISHING TOUCHES

Good title design and readable credits add to the professional appearance of your animations. Take the time to do them right, especially for your demo reel or an independent short.

There are a few finishing touches you should consider for your completed character animation. Depending on your audience, you may want to add titles, end credits, bars and tone, and perhaps even some post-process effects, like film grain. None of these are crucial to your character animation per se, but, when done well, they do add a more professional polish.

If this is just for your demo reel, minimal contact information and technical credits are enough. If you plan to distribute your work through any public channels, you should create minimal titles and credits at the very least. If you are considering broadcast or animation festival submissions, you should do the whole nine yards.

Title Design

Even a great animation won't look quite as good without titles. Even a bad animation looks a little more professional with good titles. Titles are cheap, quick to create, and easy to animate (compared to characters, anyway), but you still have to put some thought into them. They should at least conform to basic principles of typographic design, because your audience has to read them. These rules are few, simple, and easy to follow.

Keep each title card on screen long enough for your audience to read it, at least one second for every five words. Don't dally, though. Leaving a title card in place for too long can lose your audience's attention, not to mention subtracting from the time you are allotted to actually tell your story. If you are titling for a demo reel, you should keep your titles down to the minimum time—the reviewer will probably fast-forward through them if they last longer than 10 seconds.

Don't move your titles around too much. Zooming titles that fly all over the screen are the hallmark of an amateur. There are some "professional" title designers out there who should be ashamed of the titles they've done for feature film and television. Flash, glitz, and a virtuoso animation performance are just annoyances if they don't help you get your message across. A prime example of this is the horrendous title and credit work for *Spawn*, in which even the expected and well-known names in the credits are almost impossible to read because of the rapidly oscillating text and poorly contrasting colors. It looks like the optical printer's gate had been left unlocked, and the film just went through any which way. If it was designed to be disturbing, it succeeded, but if the titles were meant to be read, the design failed. Hold still, and let the words in the titles speak for themselves!

Don't get fancy with shaders and textures for titles. Brushed metal and polished chrome are very much passé and the mark of an amateur. The only circumstances under which you should texture a title are when the texture ties the titles directly to the story, the texture is not obtrusive or distracting, and the text will remain easily legible. A very nice example of this is the ribbon texture for the word *Beauty* in the title sequence of Disney's animated remake of *Beauty And The Beast*. The final effect is subtle, attractive to the eye, unobtrusive to the text, and links to the story thematically by its similarity to Belle's hair ribbons.

If you're absolutely positive that you want to animate your titles, at least make them animate legibly in the direction the audience will be reading them. If you bring letters on screen from right to left like a TV streamer, the audience can read them as they appear. This enables you to minimize the title's on-screen time and doesn't annoy your audience. If you bring the letters on screen in reverse order, the audience can't read them until the last (first) letter appears. Unless there's a thematic reason for doing things backwards, this is just an annoying affectation.

Many fonts are unsuitable for modeling and animation, or for reliable reproduction in video or film. The first disqualification is the minimum width of a stroke. Many typefaces that are designed for print have fine *serifs*, the thin strokes that cross the ends of the major strokes in a letter (see Figure 19.1). By comparison, sans serif typefaces have no minor strokes, and tend to reproduce much more evenly for both film and television.

Keep your delivery medium in mind when you choose a title font. When reproduced on film, fine serifs are very sensitive to the timing of film development and can close up or bleed out. They are also sensitive to the projection environment, when low projector light can cause serifs to disappear into the background. In video, a serif that is too fine may disappear entirely or break up into a multicolored fringe effect. This is caused by the video monitor's attempt to reproduce a single line of contrasting pixels—computer monitors are built for this, but the typical consumer television isn't anywhere near that precise. Any misalignment of the video monitor's three color guns

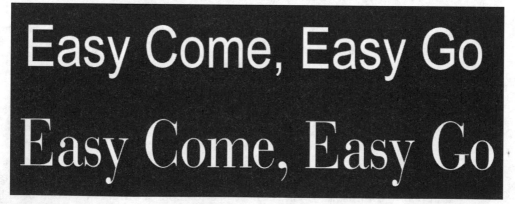

Figure 19.1 Sans serif and serif fonts.

will give the contrasting pixels a border of red, blue, and green. If the text moves at all, this multihued border will also appear to *crawl*, the illusion of secondary movement produced as pixels are handed off unevenly from one row of screen phosphors to the next.

Keep your letters open. This is closely related to the problem of serifs. Some fonts have such small letter openings that they can close up completely when reproduced on film or video. Letters like *b*, *d*, and *o* have less frequent problems with occluded openings, but letters like *e*, *a*, and *g* have smaller openings and can run into problems more easily. Letter openings are important visual cues for your audience, so choose your title fonts to make them easy to see (see Figure 19.2).

Make sure the title letters differ enough for the audience to read them easily. Some fonts are so heavily stylized that the letters appear almost identical, forcing the reader to search for more subtle clues to identify them. Figure 19.3 shows examples of good and inadequate differentiation.

Figure 19.2   Open and closed fonts.

Figure 19.3   Good and bad differentiation.

Keep your ascenders and descenders as reading cues for your audience. Ascenders and descenders are the strokes that go above the midline or below the bottom of some letters. Lowercase *b*, *d*, *h*, *k*, and *l* have ascenders, and *g*, *j*, *p*, *q*, and *y* have descenders. These are strong visual cues that make it easier for your audience to read your titles quickly and easily. Some stylized fonts compress the ascenders and descenders into the midline space, distorting the shape of the letter. These fonts are harder for your audience to read (see Figure 19.4), so you should avoid them. The same is true of font cases. If upper- and lower-case characters are difficult to tell apart, or if you run titles in all caps, small caps, or all lowercase, your audience will have a harder time reading your titles. Keep your text simple and legible, and leave the storytelling and showing-off to your characters.

Use italics with caution and moderation. A typeface that leans in odd directions is difficult to read. Choose an italic angle (if any) less than 30 degrees and preferably less than 15. Inclining the angle of a letter's major strokes changes its appearance enough to make it harder to identify. If you choose to use an italic font, at least keep the angle consistent. Once the audience identifies the italic angle, it's a little easier to read until the angle changes again. If a stylized font changes the inclination of each letter, it's confusing and difficult to read. See Figure 19.5 for examples.

Keep your titles consistent. Once you have selected a good font, use it for all your titles. Changing fonts in the middle of a title sequence requires your audience to readjust all over again, in effect reducing readability and wasting screen time. Stick to one font throughout your titles.

Finally, keep in mind that your audience presumably is interested in your animation, not the number of oddball fonts (Figure 19.6) you keep on your computer. Don't select a strange font just because it caught your eye. You don't want your audience to be so distracted with your titles that they miss the beginning of your animation. Choose title fonts carefully!

Choose your title colors carefully. Sometimes appropriate colors can be a nice touch, but more often they are a bad idea. Your primary goal is to ensure that your audience can read the titles, and poor color choices can reduce the visual contrast to the point where the letters blend into

Figure 19.4 Normal ascenders and descenders compared to vertically compressed fonts.

Figure 19.5   Normal and italic fonts.

Figure 19.6   Good and bad font choices for titles and credits.

the background. At the other extreme, clashing color choices can create a disturbing effect that is not only illegible but causes a majority of the audience to look away from the screen. In general, plain white letters on a black background are the best title colors you can use.

If you are superimposing titles over a background image, try to select a light primary color that contrasts pleasantly with the dominant hues of the background. If the background image changes markedly, which is common with live footage or strong camera movements, you may have problems getting consistent visual contrast between titles and background. In these situations, it's generally a good idea to use drop shadows or a darker outline to completely separate the superimposed titles from the background. The main title sequence from *Silence Of The Lambs* is an excellent example of simple, strongly contrasting superimposed titles. Throughout a long sequence of camera moves and widely varying backgrounds, the titles never lose contrast.

Be careful where you put your titles in the frame. For best results in all media, titles must be limited to the video text-safe area. Most televisions cut off the outer edge of the picture with a bezel over the tube's edges or rounded corners in the tube itself. Even if you are working in film, it's smart to title with eventual TV broadcast in mind. Keep your titles in the safe area, or the work will have to be re-titled for broadcast—and you won't necessarily have control of the new titles!

Many 3D programs now provide built-in video text-safe guidelines:

- *LightWave*—Click on Show Safe Areas in the Layout View tab of the Options panel. The Camera view will show two concentric rectangles with rounded corners. The outer one is the action-safe area, and the inner one is the text-safe area.

- *Animation:Master*—Open the Properties window for the Camera choreography, choose the Attributes tab, and turn on the Text Safe checkbox.

- *3D Studio MAX*—You can use the keyboard shortcut Shift+F, or right-click on a viewport label, then choose Show Safe Frame from the pop-up Properties menu. You can modify the size of the safe area by choosing the Views|Viewport Configuration menu option, then choosing the Safe Frames tab in the Viewport Configuration dialog that appears.

- *Alias*—Select Layouts|Perspective, then Display|Tgl Cut-In to display the Toggle Cut-In Options box. Turn on the TV toggle. If you want to customize the safe-area overlay, pages 387 through 390 in the *Alias Overview* manual describe the available options.

- *Softimage*—Choose the ruler icon from the Perspective window to open the Layout dialog box. Turn on the Field Guide checkbox. For information on customizing the safe title and safe action field guides, refer to page 32 of the Softimage reference guide and to the *Installation Guide* for instructions on editing the .softimage file.

PROJECT 19.1 Main Titles

This project gives you a few guidelines for creating your main title sequence, but, because titles can vary so much, the creative details are left up to you.

1. Build text objects for your main titles.

   If you haven't created text objects before, you should work through the appropriate basic exercises for your software. Remember your typography, and don't make the text hard to read.

   - *LightWave*—Try the first part of Modeler Tutorial #5 in the user guide for release 5.0, or pages 15.12 through 15.16 in the user guide for release 5.5.

   - *3D Studio MAX*—Pages 10-13 in volume 1 of the user's guide summarize the basics of creating text.

   - *trueSpace3*—Pages 211 and 212 of the manual show you how to create text objects.

   - *Softimage*—Pages 153 and 154 of the *Modelling* manual describe how to create and save custom fonts. The *Reference Guide* has more detailed information on the SaveEffectsFont (pages 1229 through 1230) and GetEffectsFont (pages 838 through 839) features.

   - *Alias*—Pages 150 through 153 of the *Nurbs Modeling* manual cover the basics of modeling text objects. The modeling tutorial in the *Learning* manual (pages 165 through 168) and especially the Alias flying logo tutorial (pages 287 through 303) are also useful.

- *Extreme 3D*—Page 156 of the manual briefly describes how to use the text tool to create closed spline curve objects that can be turned into 3D objects using other modeling tools.

2. Animate the text objects for your main title sequence. If you want a real challenge, why not animate a character putting the title together or otherwise interacting with the letters?

LENS FLARE GEEKS NEED NOT APPLY

As you lay out the animation, be creative, but don't move the camera around, don't use chrome textures on the text objects, and don't use lens flares or any other techniques that scream "Beginner!" This is not some cheap cable TV flying logo. This is supposed to be the introduction to your best work. Trust me, a cheesy title practically guarantees your demo reel will be ejected immediately. This is the consensus of a number of professional animators who have to review demo reels on a regular basis.

Are all your titles legible at the resolution your audience will be viewing them? Do they detract from the value of your animation or add to it? When in doubt, keep it simple—your character animation should be able to speak for itself.

End Credits

This project shows you how to lay out your technical end credits. There are two common ways to handle end credits: the scroll and the dissolve. I prefer the dissolve, just because the text holds still and is therefore easier to read.

1. Use whatever graphics software you prefer to create a series of black-and-white images, one for each credit. Make them the same size as the final resolution of your demo reel, and use antialiased text, if you can. Make a solid black image to use at the beginning and end of the credits.

   I used Adobe Photoshop to create the credits images for *Easy Come, Easy Go* located in the Chapter 19 directory on this book's CD-ROM. They look like Figure 19.7.

Figure 19.7 Director's credit card from *Easy Come, Easy Go*.

If you use any of the provided sample materials to create your own demo reel, please include the appropriate credit images (or your own versions, with the same phrasing) in your demo reel's end credits.

The remaining steps show how LightWave's Foreground Dissolve and Image Sequence functions make dissolving credits very easy to create and modify. If you are using a different program, you can usually duplicate this effect. Just apply the credit image files to a series of simple plane objects, position the objects in front of the camera, set the background color to black, and animate the transparency values of the objects to make the titles appear and then dissolve in the proper sequence.

If you prefer, you can also easily create title sequences in Digital Fusion, Premiere, After Effects, or most other editing and compositing programs.

2. Figure out the beginning frame for each credit. Remember to leave at least 30 frames (1 second) for each 5 words. You can use more, but try not to let your credits drag out longer than your animation.

3. Rename each credit image with its starting frame number, TITL0000.IFF, TITL0050.IFF, and so on.

4. Open Layout. Open the Images panel and load the image sequence TITL0000.IFF.

5. Open the Effects panel, and select the Compositing tab. Choose TITL0000.IFF as the Foreground Image.

6. Click on the E (for Envelope) button next to Foreground Dissolve to open the Foreground Image Dissolve Envelope panel. Create an envelope like Figure 19.8, where the foreground image sequence is normally at 0 percent but transitions to 100 percent just

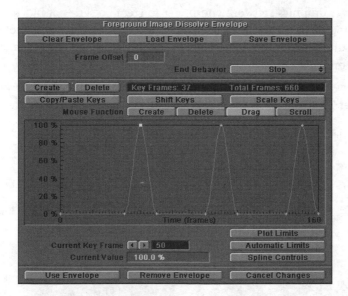

Figure 19.8 Foreground Image Dissolve Envelope.

before and after the credit images change. You can do this most efficiently by copying and pasting the first set of transition keyframes to each of the other transitions.

7. Set the Record and Camera panels to render the credits in the same aspect ratio as the original images. Render the complete animation.

This is a low-memory method of creating titles or credits, because only one image map has to be loaded in RAM at a time.

Finishing Touches

Here are a few last-minute additions you may want to consider before you transfer your finished work to film or video.

Bars And Tone

If you have put a lot of effort into sound synchronizing, color composition, and lighting for your character animation, you will want that effort shown to best advantage in the final product. If you are transferring your animation to videotape, you should consider adding a few seconds of SMPTE color bars and the standard 400 hertz tone to the beginning of your tape. This standard reference enables the video engineer to optimize for color, image quality, and sound level at the time of broadcast or projection.

Most 3D software includes a color test chart in the sample maps collection. If yours doesn't, you can try the SMPTE.GIF image file in the Chapter 19 directory on this book's CD-ROM. For the audio tone, you can download one of the shareware test tone generators or use the 400HZTON.WAV file, also on this book's CD-ROM.

Film Clutter

If the content of your animation would benefit from it, you might consider a number of post-process effects that reproduce artifacts of the film projection process. This can be useful for matching perfectly clean CGI animation to naturally grungy real-world footage. You can also use it to give your animations the appearance of a silent film, an old home movie, or a historic newsreel.

Film grain adds the visual artifacts typical of the chemical film process. This is the most subtle of the effects and is the most basic film-simulation effect. If you are compositing your CGI elements into live footage, you will need to add film grain to make the CGI look as if it belongs in the shot. If you are creating a completely CGI world for your characters, adding film grain will make it more believable to the audience.

Dirt and scratches can be overdone very easily—use them sparingly and only when they'll help you tell your story or increase your work's verisimilitude to the original effect you're trying to mimic.

Antique or stylized leaders can help prepare your audience for a "period" reproduction or parody. If your animation fits one of these categories, by all means, use the appropriate leader. If you want to maintain the illusion, you should also use a matching trailer, even if it's just the words *The End* in graceful script.

Reference footage or pre-digitized video clips for these and other effects are available from a number of vendors, including Artbeats, the publishers of some very good texture collections. You can request a sample Artbeats CD-ROM to evaluate their video clip collections from their Web site at **www.artbeats.com**, or call them at 541-863-4429. I've purchased a number of their products and always found them to be a good value.

Moving On

Once you've worked through this chapter, you should have the completed titles, credits, and post-process effects you need for the next chapter. Chapter 20 will show you how to put all the pieces of your animation together and transfer them to videotape, film, or other publishing medium.

FINAL OUTPUT

Even the best character animation is worthless if an audience can't see it. How you record, distribute, and play back your animations will depend on your resources and your target audience.

This final production chapter will show you how to finish off your demo reel. You'll learn the basics of transferring your finished animation to videotape or film.

Frame Rates

The number one criteria for reproducing your animations is frame rate. As you have learned in earlier chapters, the essence of an animation performance is in the timing. A difference of a single frame can make or break the believability of an action. Therefore, you should choose a medium that enables you to set a consistent frame rate, so you can animate specifically for that rate with the assurance that what you animate is what your audience will see.

For film or video, the frame rate is fixed by the standards of the technology. Feature films are projected at 24 fps, NTSC video at 29.97 fps, and PAL video at 25 fps. You don't have to worry about the distribution side of those formats. You just set your animation software to the appropriate frame rate, and the medium does the rest.

For other reproduction methods, you will have to do a little more work. Some computer animation formats, for example, allow you to specify a frame rate for playback. These rates can be modified by the end user, and are limited by the speed and transfer rate of the user's system, but generally play animations the way you intended them. Other computer animation formats and the purely mechanical animation formats do not allow you to specify a frame rate. All you can do in these circumstances is animate for an average range of frame rates and hope that most of your audience will fit within that range.

The least expensive medium for your animations is the one you used to create it—your computer.

CG All The Way

You can store small animations on diskettes, larger ones on Zip or Jaz disks, or even burn 650MB at a time onto CD-R, depending on your system's resources. The advantages are cost and time savings. The disadvantages are that your audience will have to have a computer compatible with yours, including animation playback software, system memory and speed, and removable media drive. This can severely limit your audience.

Your physical distribution medium can be diskette; high-capacity disk, such as Zip, Bernoulli, or Jaz; or CD-ROM. You may also choose to publish your animations on the Internet via the Web or FTP. You should base your publishing decisions on the audience you want to reach. Decide what format or venue your audience will prefer, then adapt your production to your audience. If you choose a physical distribution medium, no one will see your animations unless you send them a copy. On the positive side, you can make your animations as long, active, and colorful as you like. If you choose to publish your animations on the Internet, you will have to keep them short and compressed enough to be easy to download, which can severely crimp your creativity.

Once you've selected your distribution channel, you need to decide in what format to record your animation files.

File Formats

There are a number of video compression formats and *codecs* (compressor/decompressor) in common use. Each of them has advantages and disadvantages. At the moment, there is no clearly superior codec or file format for all-purpose digital video.

FLC or FLI, generally called *flicks*, are older animation formats originally supported by Autodesk. They have limited capability to sync to sound, and their playback rates, resolution, and bit depth leave something to be desired. However, they have been around a long time, and there are many free and shareware utilities for building and playing them on even the oldest PCs. One of my favorites is Dave's Targa Animator, available from many DOS and Windows FTP sites.

GIF is a temporarily useful format but may not remain so since it's no longer possible to write legal software that supports it. Fortunately, there are several good free or shareware utilities that can assemble a series of images into the GIF89a sub-format. This format can be displayed by Web browsers as an inline animation that takes up very little space and downloads quickly. This is the format commonly used for animated headers, buttons, and other decorations on Web pages. The format's main disadvantage for character animation is that you cannot control the frame rate at all, so the playback over the Web depends entirely on the connection speed. The GIF89a format is appropriate mostly for short loops of a dozen frames or less.

QuickTime (QT) is an audiovisual compression format initially pushed by Apple and still a part of the MacOS, but it is now also available on a variety of platforms. QuickTime players and Internet browser plug-ins are bundled with many software packages or available for free download. Choosing this format to distribute your animations is a fairly safe decision. There are several codecs available for QT, including Radius's Cinepak, which seems to be a favorite among animators.

AVI, which stands for Audio Video Interleaved, is the official video format for the Microsoft Windows platform. It's not supported on as many platforms as QT, but the larger installed base of Windows machines makes AVI a viable video distribution format. The Cinepak codec is also available for AVI, but the Intel, Microsoft, or other codec may better suit your needs. I suggest you experiment with every codec available to you, and draw your own conclusions based on tests with your own animations.

MPEG is a family of formats originally designed to compress live-action video. With this goal in mind, MPEG excels at irregular, near-chaotic images like human faces in motion, and performs less competently with abstract, linear patterns like amateurish CGI. The good news is that the closer your animations get to the complexity of the real world, the better MPEG is at reproducing them. A significant advantage of the MPEG format is that it is public domain, so there are a variety of hardware and software solutions from competing vendors, and the prices range from free to quite reasonable. Later in this chapter, we'll run through a project using the MPEG-1 format to transfer character animations to videotape.

Mechanical Playback: Flipbooks

Flipbooks are the second most basic form of animation players (the flipping disk is the first), and have been used for so long we don't really know when the first one was made. They're simple to use, portable, and don't require any other equipment to view. At least one professional animator uses flipbooks as business cards, and Disney recently revived the practice of publishing flipbook excerpts from its animated films. They're also fun to give away or trade with other animators, and it's often handy to have one to help explain your work to non-animators.

The disadvantage to flipbooks for character animation is that you can't control the playback frame rate—it's entirely up to the skill and preference of your audience. Depending on how you produce them, flipbooks can also be somewhat more difficult and expensive to produce than videotapes, diskettes, or CDs.

The cheapest way to create a flipbook from your animations is to set up a table in a spreadsheet or word processor. The following project shows you how to create your own flipbook template in Microsoft Word.

Make Your Own Flipbook

1. Create a new folder, and render at least 40 frames of an animation into it, in BMP format. For this example, I created the folder C:\CAPTURE3 and rendered images MATCH001.BMP through MATCH040.BMP into it.

2. In Word, open a new document. Set the page margins to the maximum printing area for the printer you will be using. Select All, and set the font to something like Courier 10 point. This will be the label font for the individual frames of the flipbook, so you will want to keep it small.

3. Choose the Table|Insert Table menu option. Set the table to 4 columns and 10 rows. This will give you space in each cell for an image about the size of a postage stamp.

4. Set the alignment of the entire document to Right Justify. This will keep the images at the right margin of each cell, leaving the extra space at the left edge for the staples or other means of holding the flipbook together.

5. Click in the top-left cell to select it. Choose the Insert|Picture menu option, and choose the first rendered image in the directory you created. In the Insert Picture dialog, turn on the Link To File checkbox at the lower right. Directly underneath it, turn off the Save Picture In Document checkbox. Click on OK.

This sets up a link between the cell in the Word table and the image file in the new directory. The image itself will not be included in the Word file, just the path and file name information, so the document remains small even when you link it to very large images. This also means that every time you open, print, or even scroll around the table, the images will be reloaded fresh from the directory. You can even leave Word open while you render new images, and, as they're completed, they'll replace the old images in the table.

6. Click in the same cell, in the empty space to the left of the image you've just linked. Type in the last three digits of the image file name. Save the document.

7. Repeat Steps 5 and 6 for the remaining 39 cells in the table. You should end up with something like Figure 20.1.

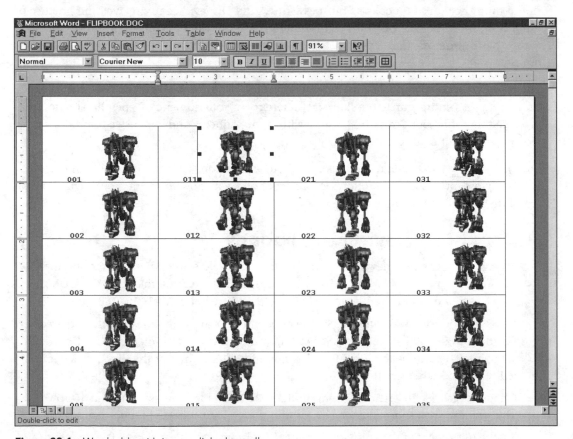

Figure 20.1 Word table with images linked to cells.

8. When you've finished all 40 cells, print off the page on some heavy card stock. Cut the frames out along the lines, stack them up in order, and staple them together. That's all there is to it!

Now that you've got the flipbook template set up, it's very fast and easy to make a flipbook of your current animation. Just set the rendering to the path and file name root you linked to the Word table cells, and you can print off a flipbook sheet faster than you can render a single frame. If you're feeling ambitious or have a use for larger flipbooks, you can try increasing the size of the cells or making multipage tables that contain more than 40 cells. As a general rule, flipbooks get awkward to use after about 200 sheets, so don't go overboard without testing first.

Flipbook Software

If you run a Macintosh or PowerMac, you can take advantage of a software product named Flipbook (how original!), specifically designed to print flipbooks. Flipbook is published by S. H. Pierce & Company (Tel: 617-338-2222) and is available through several mail-order software distributors. This is a handy little utility that converts QuickTime movies, PICS animation files, or PICT image sequences into a printed layout on pre-perforated flipbook paper.

Advanced Flipbook: The Mutoscope

If you get hooked on flipbooks, you might be interested in a 19th-century super-flipbook called a Mutoscope. The heart of this device is a cylinder with a large series of flipbook cards mounted around its circumference. It's as if the card deck is so large that it can wrap around with its last card next to the first. Figure 20.2 shows a picture of one type of Mutoscope, plus an opened view of a slightly different model.

The viewer looks through the eyepiece and turns a crank. The crank turns the cylinder, which rotates the edges of the cards against a stop. The stop holds the cards in view, just as your

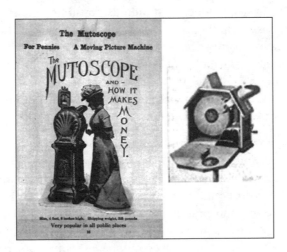

Figure 20.2   Mutoscopes.

thumb does with a flipbook, until the crank is turned enough to flip the card over and reveal the next one. It's a mechanically simple device, and, if you're handy with tools, you can probably build one yourself.

Mutoscopes can be large enough to hold thousands of cards, so you can get many seconds of animation onto a single cylinder. The original machines are now collector's items, and the cards are bought and sold just like baseball cards. If you are interested in seeing a working Mutoscope, there are several in the Main Street Arcade in Disneyland and in some of the older amusement parks, like Cedar Point in Sandusky, Ohio.

Film

If you are an independent filmmaker, you should stick with video formats until you can find financial backing for film transfer. If you carefully archive all your animation scenes, objects, and related files, you can always go back and re-render to higher resolution for film. Film output is expensive, but it definitely gives the best-looking results. Unless you can afford your own film recorder with a pin-register camera back, you will be sending your rendered images to a service bureau to be transferred to film. I recommend against trying to save money by transferring to 16 mm. Go with 35 mm. The price difference in film is relatively small compared to the transfer charges for the recorder. Also, if you are trying to get into film festivals or sell your animation, 35 mm prints have a wider potential audience.

If you need to do a film transfer, I strongly recommend you spend some time talking with the professionals at Cinesite or other service bureaus before you make any binding decisions. They're the ones with the expertise, and they can save you a great deal of time, money, and aggravation.

Video

You have several options for recording and showing your finished demo reel on videotape. There are three levels of video production standards: consumer, industrial, and broadcast. For most individual purposes, including demo reels, consumer grade will do fine. The most commonly accepted format in the United States and UK is VHS. Character animation studios usually have a selection of machines capable of playing back just about any format, but, if you're looking for work, you don't want to put your potential employer to any extra bother. If you have access to industrial or broadcast equipment, make your master reel on the best format you can handle, but make VHS dubs to mail out with your résumé.

Transferring animation to video is relatively inexpensive, but cutting corners with cheap compression boards can really hurt the final appearance. The most cost-effective solution at present for industrial or broadcast standards is to use a special hard drive recording device, then dump the finished piece to broadcast-quality videotape. Many of these hardware solutions also work with your choice of editing and post-processing software, such as Digital Fusion, Premiere, After Effects, or Razor. I've had good experience with DPS's Personal Animation Recorder (PAR) and Perception Video Recorder, but there are a number of competing products you may want to investigate as well. The market is constantly changing, and new products with lower price tags and more features are coming out all the time. At the moment, you're still looking at several thousand dollars to get true broadcast quality video, so you may be better off finding a service bureau or fellow animator who has equipment you can borrow or lease.

If your system's output resolution justifies it, rent a broadcast-quality recording deck for a day to make your master tape. You can usually get a BetacamSP deck for under $200 a day in most major cities. Do all your prep work before you pick up the deck—you don't want to have to pay for another day because you couldn't find a cable or a blank tape.

> ### SHORT TAPES SAVE REELS
>
> **Buy short, 5- or 10-minute videotapes in bulk for your demo reels. This keeps studio staff from taping reruns of Gilligan's Island over your demo reel. This can mean the difference between getting a job and getting lost in the shuffle. If your reel stays on a shelf because no one bothers to tape over it, yours may be the only tape sitting there the next time they need to hire someone.**

Buying lots of tapes is important, too. You have to look at demo reels as résumés. Make lots, send out lots. You're going after some pretty high-paying jobs, either as a TD or animator. Would you worry about the price of each sheet of paper if you were getting your résumé duplicated? What fraction of your first year's income are you willing to spend on a résumé that gets you the job? You'll be sending out quite a few demo reels before you get that first job, so resign yourself to spending the money or working a barter. Nothing ventured, nothing gained.

If you can't afford film or professional video, you may be able to record a low-budget demo reel using direct computer playback. This is currently very limited by trade-offs in resolution, speed, color depth, or all three, but it's cheap. You use a relatively inexpensive device called a scan converter to convert your computer's video signals to something acceptable to your consumer-grade VCR. Generally, the cheaper the converter, the lousier the videotaped images. The bottom end is around $250 as of this writing, and upper-end converters cost more than a DPS PAR. Don't despair if this is all you can afford. Several studios have assured me that they look for the quality of the animation, not the professional polish on the tape production. Make sure the playback is at the same rate as you animated it, the images are relatively clear, and the tape tracking doesn't wander all over the place, and you should be all right.

Cheap Demo Reels: Inexpensive Video Transfer

If disk recorders, single-frame VTRs, or scan converters are too expensive for your budget, I have some good news for you. Recent developments in video cards have significantly lowered the entry level for consumer-grade video transfer. With a little effort and a very small amount of money, you can put all your animations onto videotape from your own PC. The results of this process aren't anywhere near broadcast quality, but they're good enough to display your character animation skills.

I've written the following project for PC-compatibles running Windows 95. The programs used are mostly DOS command-line utilities, but they all work within Win95's MS-DOS window.

Similar solutions do exist for other platforms and operating systems, so you can use this project as a guide to finding a solution that fits your system. I have deliberately limited this project to free or shareware programs, with the exception of the drivers and utilities bundled with ATI video boards. My experience has been with the ATI Pro Turbo PC2TV, but other ATI video cards with MPEG acceleration should be able to give you similar playback rates. I haven't tested boards from other manufacturers, but any board that accelerates MPEG playback and provides NTSC video output may give you acceptable results. I paid just under $250 for the Pro Turbo when it first shipped, but I've seen prices as low as $150 for other ATI boards. They aren't limited to TV output, either. This series is a pretty nice video board overall, and I recommend them if the specs suit your needs. For details, check out **www.atitech.com**.

PROJECT 20.2 Transferring Your Animation To Videotape

The basic process is to render and edit your animation to produce a series of still images, convert those images to a format compatible with an MPEG encoder, encode the images into an MPEG video stream, encode the sound into an MPEG audio stream, multiplex the MPEG video and audio streams together, and play the finished MPEG movie through the ATI board to produce 30 fps NTSC video to your VHS VCR.

1. Render a sequence of TGA images to 352×240 resolution, 24-bit color depth, at 30 fps for best NTSC video recording through the ATI output. Render the files to the path C:\RENDER\TEST0000.TGA, if you want them to be compatible with the example commands in this project.

I like to keep all the current project files in the RENDER directory to avoid confusion. At several points in this process, you will nearly double the hard disk space required to store working files. Make sure you have plenty of room! 352×240 may seem like low resolution, but it's not actually much lower than a typical consumer VHS deck can reproduce, and it's adequate for showing your timing and poses. When you're a working professional, you can afford broadcast-quality video transfers. If you're a beginner, I'm sure you have more pressing demands for your cash!

It's a good idea to append at least 30 frames of SMPTE color bars, then another 30 frames of black at the beginning of the first video sequence. You can either append these during editing or render them at the beginning of the image sequence. If you plan to append other sequences on videotape, you should also end each rendered sequence with 30 frames of black. This will give you a little more slack in matching your assemble edits, especially if you are using a consumer-grade VCR that doesn't make clean edits.

Because some pixel-size detail is lost in the MPEG compression, it's a waste of rendering time to use too much anti-aliasing. Motion blur or a post-process soft filter is a good idea, as either one may help smooth over the occasional dropped frame. If your rendering software supports it, turn on NTSC color saturation limits. Without these limits, rendered colors may oversaturate the video output and create glaring artifacts on your videotape.

2. Edit and assemble the image sequence and soundtrack. If you rendered the TGA sequence just as you want it on videotape, you can skip ahead to Step 5. Otherwise, load

the image sequences, AVI clips, and WAV files, into a new project in your editing software.

This project uses Adobe Premiere, but you can do most of this with shareware programs, too. You can save effort by setting up a default project for producing MPEGs, with the following parameters:

- No compression
- TGA numbered sequence output (TEST0000.TGA)
- 30 fps output 352×240 output resolution
- C:\RENDER output path
- Very low-resolution AVI Preview with full audio

3. Edit the source files together to get the final effect you want on the videotape. Make a thumbnail AVI Preview to check the sound sync, video f/x, and transitions. 160×120, one of Premiere's presets, is usually adequate and will give 30 fps playback on any MPC2-compatible computer.

4. Output edited images as continuous TGA numbered sequence. When the project is edited to your satisfaction, save it with a new file name. Output the video as a 24-bit, 352×240 TGA image sequence to path C:\RENDER\TEST0000.TGA.

5. If the project has a soundtrack, you will need to output the sound as a single WAV file, synchronized at 30 fps, at the audio quality you want on the videotape, to path C:\RENDER\SOUNDTRK.WAV. In Premiere, you can do this by opening the thumbnail AVI Preview as a Clip and using the File|Export|Waveform menu option to create the WAV file.

Once you have the WAV file, you need to convert it to MPEG. Cool Edit is a shareware sound editor with a plug-in to encode MPEG audio streams. You can download a trial version and the MPEG plug-in from **www.syntrillium.com/cool.htm**.

6. Load the WAV file in Cool Edit (make sure you have the MPEG encoder plug-in installed), and use File|Save As to convert it to C:\RENDER\TEST.MP2.

Make sure the bitrate, mode, and sampling rate are compatible with your machine's playback capabilities. To test your machine's playback rates, you can try loading sample MPEGs and watching (and listening) carefully for dropped frames or slow playback. Windows's Media Player or the ATI Player will both give you information about an MPEG's audio and video streams, including the actual playback rate. As an example, the audio stream for the "Balls & Blocks" MPEG on the CD-ROM is Layer 2, 224Kbps, 44.1KHz 8-bit Mono, and it played back without a hitch on my system.

The MPEG video encoder requires YUV images for input. You can use the freeware program DISPLAY, written by Jih-Shin Ho, to quickly and easily batch-translate the TGA files to YUV format. You can download DISPLAY from the author's site at **http://bicmos.ee.nctu.edu.tw/Display** or from a software repository at either **http://**

www.simtel.net/simtel.net/msdos/graphics-pre.html or **http://oak.oakland.edu/ simtel.net/msdos/graphics-pre.html**. Look for files disp189a.zip and disp189b.zip.

Here's the basic syntax for using DISPLAY.EXE, excerpted from the DISPLAY.DOC file included with the software:

```
(c) For command-line batch conversion :
display --batch | -b <output_format> [--bw|--grey|--color|--true|--same]
[--stay] [--dialog | -g] [--report|-r <report_file>] [--effect]
[--width|-w <image_width>] [--height|-h <image_height>]
[--skip <bytes>] [-i]
input_file | input_file output_directory | input_file output_file |
input_files output_directory
output_format: Standard extensions. Like gif, bmp ... (see section (6))
bw,grey,color,true: B/W dither, Grey scale, 8bit full color,
24bit true color.
same: The same color format as input image. If input is 24-bit image,
output is saved as true color image (if possible). Otherwise output
is saved as 8bit full color image.
The default color type for batch conversion is 8bit full color.
-g: DISPLAY will let you change the setting of output_format if there
is any.
+ --stay: Don't exit DISPLAY after viewing.
+ --effect: Perform default special effects (in config.dis) on images.
+ --skip: Number of bytes to skip before reading .GRY and .RGB images.
+ -w & -h: For images format without information header(YUV,RGB,GREY).
+ -i: Don't initialize screen.
```

7. Use DISPLAY.EXE to convert the rendered TGA sequence to YUV format. Type the command line:

```
display -byuv --same -w352 -h240 c:\render\test*.tga c:\render
```

This command produces a YUV file sequence in path C:\RENDER, with the same color depth (352×240 resolution) from the original Targa images in the path C:\RENDER with file name root TEST. This is suitable for a YUV sequence to compress into an MPEG-1 stream using MPEG2ENC.EXE. This conversion only takes about two seconds per image, but long sequences add up. On a 133MHz Pentium, it can take 90 minutes to convert the 1,800 frames necessary for one minute of NTSC video. It's like an extension of the rendering process. Be patient, and make sure you have plenty of disk space.

Retyping the command line is tedious and error-prone. You can save time by always rendering your image sequences as C:\RENDER\TEST0000.TGA and making a DOS batch file to execute the command line.

8. When the YUV translation is complete, move the original TGA files to another drive for storage or back them up and delete them. If the next step goes wrong, you may

need them again, but, if you're making a long MPEG, you will probably need the storage space the TGA files are occupying.

Your next step is to use the MPEG2ENC.EXE utility to compress the YUV sequence into an MPEG-1 stream. MPEG2ENC.EXE is a free MPEG video encoder released by the MPEG Software Simulation Group. You can download an archive, including the encoder and decoder executables, plus the source code, from **www.creative.net/~tristan/MPEG/mssg/mpeg2v12.zip.**

MPEG2ENC.EXE requires command-line instructions and a fairly complex parameter file. Several sample parameter files are included with the software archive, along with documentation that describes the function and options for each parameter. I've experimented with these files a bit and found some parameters that work well with the ATI boards. For this project, the parameter file will look something like Figure 20.3. This file, MPEGTEST.PAR, is also on the CD-ROM.

The important variables for this project are:

- *Line 2*—Set for TEST0000 file name root.
- *Line 7*—Set for YUV format.
- *Line 8*—Set for 412 frames in the YUV image sequence. You will have to change this value to the frame count of each animation, but most of the other values should stay the same once you find the settings that work for your system.
- *Line 9*—Set for the first frame of the YUV image sequence, TEST0001.YUV.
- *Line 13*—Set to encode an MPEG-1 file. 0 produces an MPEG-2 file.
- *Line 15*—Set for the horizontal resolution of the incoming images, 352.
- *Line 16*—Set for the vertical resolution of the incoming images, 240.
- *Line 17*—Set for normal 1:1 aspect ratio. This is the aspect ratio of the incoming images and should match the original rendered aspect ratio.
- *Line 19*—Set for the bitrate your computer can sustain. For example, ANIM1.MPG from the ATI CD-ROM has a bitrate of 1125000 bps, and plays back smoothly. Your machine's performance may vary. If the playback stutters, try reducing this number.
- *Line 20*—Set for the default MPEG-1 buffer size of 20.
- *Line 31*—Set for the horizontal resolution of the output MPEG file, 352.
- *Line 32*—Set for the vertical resolution of the output MPEG file, 240.

If you really love getting technical, you can read the documentation included with the encoder plus the background materials available at **www.mpeg.org** and tweak all the parameters to suit yourself. The command line will be easier to type if you keep a copy of the parameters file in the same directory as the project files, in this case C:\RENDER.

9. Type the command line:

```
mpeg2enc mpegtest.par test.mpg
```

```
           MPEG-1 Test Sequence, 30 frames/sec, for ATI PC2TV playback
Line 2 ──── test%04d /* name of source files, i.e., TEST0000 */
           - /* name of reconstructed images ("-": don't store) */
           - /* name of intra quant matrix file ("-": default matrix) */
           - /* name of non intra quant matrix file ("-": default matrix) */
           stats.doc /* name of statistics file ("-": stdout ) */
Line 7 ──── 1 /* input picture file format: 0=*.Y,*.U,*.V, 1=*.yuv, 2=*.ppm */
Line 8 ──── 412 /* number of frames */
Line 9 ──── 1 /* number of first frame */
           00:00:00:00 /* timecode of first frame */
           15 /* N (# of frames in GOP) */
           3 /* M (I/P frame distance) */
Line 13 ─── 1 /* ISO/IEC 11172-2 stream */
           0 /* 0:frame pictures, 1:field pictures */
Line 15 ─── 352 /* horizontal_size */
Line 16 ─── 240 /* vertical_size */
Line 17 ─── 1 /* aspect_ratio_information 1=square pel, 2=4:3, 3=16:9, 4=2.11:1 */
           5 /* frame_rate_code 1=23.976, 2=24, 3=25, 4=29.97, 5=30 frames/sec. */
Line 19 ─── 1125000.0 /* bit_rate (bits/s) */
Line 20 ─── 20 /* vbv_buffer_size (in multiples of 16 kbit) */
           0 /* low_delay */
           1 /* constrained_parameters_flag */
           4 /* Profile ID: Simple = 5, Main = 4, SNR = 3, Spatial = 2, High = 1 */
           10 /* Level ID: Low = 10, Main = 8, High 1440 = 6, High = 4 */
           1 /* progressive_sequence */
           1 /* chroma_format: 1=4:2:0, 2=4:2:2, 3=4:4:4 */
           2 /* video_format: 0=comp., 1=PAL, 2=NTSC, 3=SECAM, 4=MAC, 5=unspec. */
           5 /* color_primaries */
           5 /* transfer_characteristics */
           4 /* matrix_coefficients */
Line 31 ─── 352 /* display_horizontal_size */
Line 32 ─── 240 /* display_vertical_size */
           0 /* intra_dc_precision (0: 8 bit, 1: 9 bit, 2: 10 bit, 3: 11 bit */
           1 /* top_field_first */
           0 0 0 /* frame_pred_frame_dct (I P B) */
           0 0 0 /* concealment_motion_vectors (I P B) */
           1 1 1 /* q_scale_type (I P B) */
           0 0 0 /* intra_vlc_format (I P B)*/
           0 0 0 /* alternate_scan (I P B) */
           0 /* repeat_first_field */
           1 /* progressive_frame */
           0 /* P distance between complete intra slice refresh */
           0 /* rate control: r (reaction parameter) */
           0 /* rate control: avg_act (initial average activity) */
           0 /* rate control: Xi (initial I frame global complexity measure) */
           0 /* rate control: Xp (initial P frame global complexity measure) */
           0 /* rate control: Xb (initial B frame global complexity measure) */
           0 /* rate control: d0i (initial I frame virtual buffer fullness) */
           0 /* rate control: d0p (initial P frame virtual buffer fullness) */
           0 /* rate control: d0b (initial B frame virtual buffer fullness) */
           2 2 11 11 /* P: forw_hor_f_code forw_vert_f_code search_width/height */
           1 1 3 3 /* B1: forw_hor_f_code forw_vert_f_code search_width/height */
           1 1 7 7 /* B1: back_hor_f_code back_vert_f_code search_width/height */
           1 1 7 7 /* B2: forw_hor_f_code forw_vert_f_code search_width/height */
           1 1 3 3 /* B2: back_hor_f_code back_vert_f_code search_width/height */
```

Figure 20.3 MPEGTEST.PAR parameter file.

This produces a 412-frame, 352×240 resolution, 24-bit color MPEG-1 file, C:\RENDER\TEST.MPG. This will take a while, usually several seconds per frame on a P133. Again, this is like an extension of the animation rendering process. Make sure you have adequate hard disk space, start the process, then go do whatever you usually do during a long render.

The next step in the process is to use the MPLEX.EXE utility to multiplex the MPEG video and audio streams. MPEG1 Systems Multiplexer, MPLEX.EXE, is a freeware utility written by Christopher Moar that combines video and audio MPEG streams. To download it, link to **www.visiblelight.com/mpeg/software/windows.htp** or download directly from **www.powerweb.de/mpeg/util/msdos/mplex11.zip** or **www.powerweb.de/mpeg/msdos.html**.

Install it somewhere in your default path. I chose to put it in the C:\RENDER directory with the rest of the MPEG stuff. The command-line controls are relatively simple:

```
MPLEX <input stream> [<input stream2>] <output system stream>
```

10. Type the command to produce a synchronized-sound MPEG-1 stream, C:\RENDER\TESTSND.MPG:

```
mplex test.mpg test.mp2 testsnd.mpg
```

11. To test the new MPEG file's playback, you'll need to hook up your VCR to your ATI board's video output. Hook up a TV or monitor to the VCR's output, so you can preview what will be going onto the tape. Use the ATI Desktop controls to adjust the video output position and size to completely fill your TV monitor.

It's OK if the TV bezel cuts off a little bit of the image's margin on each side, but you don't want a distracting black border around your animation.

12. Launch and set up Media Player (with the ATI MPEG driver) or the ATI Player for full-screen playback to videotape. If you use the ATI Player, press F2 to hide the Player controls during full-frame playback.

If the MPEG file works, rename it, and make a backup copy, so you won't accidentally overwrite it with your next MPEG.

If your MPEG files won't play back at 30 fps, try re-encoding them with a lower bit rate by changing Line 19 in the parameters file. The lower the bitrate, the lower the image quality, but you have to work within your system's limits.

With the MPEG acceleration of the ATI board, I've been able to get some pretty good-looking videotape. You can't expect a client to pay you for the VHS-quality playback you'll get from this process, but it's good enough to build your animation demo reel. The most important factor is getting an accurate, consistent frame rate so the reviewer can assess your timing. The slightly smeared edges and color artifacts of MPEG-1 compression aren't going to harm your work, at least as far as most animation studios are concerned.

Moving On

If you've worked through the entire book, you should now have a solid understanding of character animation and a pretty good demo reel. Congratulations!

The next three chapters will give you lots of tips and advice on how to use your demo reel to get a job, how to keep it, and how to start up your own animation business.

PART VII

TAKING CARE OF BUSINESS

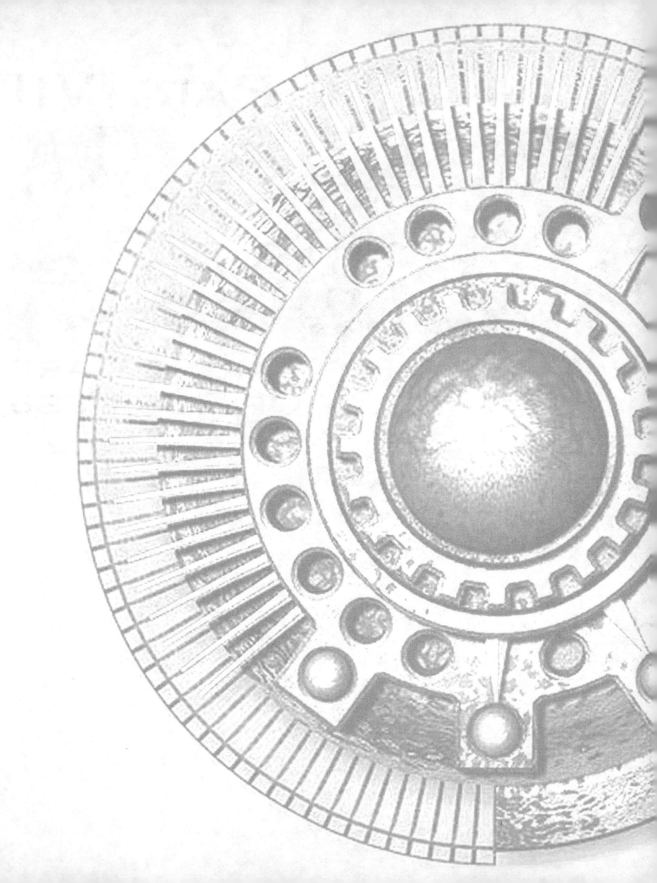

STARTING OUT

When you're trying to break into the business, you need to know what employers are looking for and where to find animation industry information.

This chapter is intended to provide information you can use to start or continue your career in character animation. This information is as accurate as I could make it, but this industry is moving fast and the details change all the time. I encourage you to check Coriolis' online updates (see Appendix B for the URL) before taking any irrevocable actions—like mailing your last copy of your demo reel to an out-of-date address!

Animation is not a career choice you should make lightly or on the spur of the moment. Most successful animators I have interviewed have always had an interest in animation, and many wanted to be animators from early childhood. If you have been attracted to CGI character animation by recent publicity on high salaries and many job opportunities, think again—this is a job you do because you love it, not because you get paid a lot to do it. The "high" salaries are not enough to compensate you for long hours and grueling work if you don't sincerely love what you're doing.

Self-Education

Trying to teach yourself character animation is a long, slow road, fraught with peril and liberally pitted with potholes. The only signposts along the way are the contacts you make and the feedback you receive from your fellow students and colleagues. It's not a choice for the weak or fainthearted.

Fortunately, there are more resources for the self-taught animator today than at any previous time. This book and others like it, focusing on one or more software packages, are good places to start. Books on traditional animation (see the Bibliography) are excellent sources of information, if you don't mind translating their techniques into 3D CGI. For more timely information, there are magazines and professional journals in a variety of related fields. These are the journals I use myself—long on information, short on fluff, and generally reliable to get the story straight:

- *3D Artist* is the best collection of tutorials and hands-on information for artists using desktop 3D software. The focus is on what works, the tutorials are generally written by artists actually working in 3D for a living, and the product reviews are honest. There is usually at least one article on one of the desktop character animation packages, and tutorials for any software are often written to be applicable elsewhere.

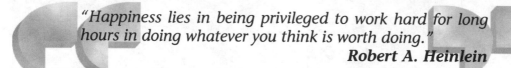

"Happiness lies in being privileged to work hard for long hours in doing whatever you think is worth doing."

Robert A. Heinlein

Columbine Inc.
P.O. Box 4787
Santa Fe, NM 87502
ISSN: 1058-9503
Internet: http://www.3dartist.com

- *ACM Transactions On Graphics* is a quarterly academic research journal dealing with the algorithms and other theoretical arcana behind graphics programming. Techniques first published here sometimes take years to show up in commercial desktop software. Smart TDs read this journal and work out their own implementations to stay ahead of the commercial pack.

ISSN: 0730-0301
Internet: http://www.acm.org/pubs/tog

- *Computer Graphics* is a sister publication to *Transactions*. The contents are more about implementations and tutorials, and the annual *SIGGRAPH Conference Proceedings* are always a worthwhile collection of eye candy and solid information.

Association for Computing Machinery
11 West 42nd Street
New York, NY 10036
ISSN: 0097-8930
Internet: http://www.siggraph.org

- *Animation Magazine* is a trade journal covering traditional and CGI animation. Industry news, help wanted, bios, retrospectives, and business-related articles are a big help to novices and old pros alike. This one's definitely worth a subscription.

Animation Magazine
30101 Agoura Court, Suite 110
Agoura Hills, CA 91301
Email: Animag@AOL.com
ISSN: 1041-617X
Internet: http://www.imall.com/stores/animag

- *Cinefex* is the trade journal of the feature film special effects community. Slick and heavily illustrated, this quarterly publishes long, in-depth, nuts-and-bolts articles on f/x techniques. Stopmo, miniatures, CGI, you name it—if it ends up on the big screen, Cinefex shows how it's done. Even the issues that don't include CGI articles have lots of useful information for character animation, and the advertiser's index reads like a who's who of houses you'd like to work for.

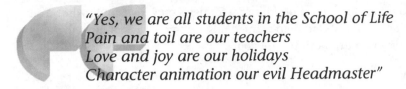

"Yes, we are all students in the School of Life
Pain and toil are our teachers
Love and joy are our holidays
Character animation our evil Headmaster"

Jim Studt

Cinefex
P.O. Box 20027
Riverside, CA 92516
ISSN: 0198-1056
Tel: 800-434-3339

- *Computer Graphics World* covers pretty much what the title says. You'll find articles here about hardware, software, and other technical issues, and the industry news leans more toward hardware and software vendors than animation houses. The downside is that space constraints force tutorials to be less detailed than one would prefer.

CGW
10 Tara Blvd., 5th Floor
Nashua, NH 03062-2801
ISSN: 0271-4159
Internet: http://www.cgw.com

- *Game Developer* is a slim magazine that is short on animation-specific articles but long on contact info and industry buzz for the game community. If you're looking for a way to break into the character animation business, game developers are often less picky about your demo reel than feature animation houses. If you're not already a gamer, read the back issues so you understand the problems and can talk about them intelligently at your job interview.

Miller Freeman Inc.
600 Harrison Street
San Francisco, CA 94107
ISSN: 1073-922X
Internet: http://www.gdmag.com

- *NT Studio* is a magazine dedicated to production tools for Windows NT platforms. Topics include industry news, tutorials, and hardware and software reviews for LightWave 3D and other packages. If you're working on—or even considering—the NT platform, it's worth reading.

NT Studio
201 E. Sandpointe Avenue, Suite 600
Santa Ana, CA 92707
Tel: 714-513-8400
Fax: 714-513-8612
Internet: http://www.ntstudio.com

- *Post* is a post-production trade journal useful primarily for news on who's doing what. You should at least scan the promotional and help-wanted ads scattered throughout the magazine for production houses that may want to hire you.

Testa Communications
25 Willowdale Avenue
Port Washington, NY 11050
Tel: 516-767-2500
Fax: 516-767-9335

A FAQ, or Frequently Asked Questions list, is a document containing questions and answers that are often asked of a discussion group or help desk. Just about every major newsgroup, mailing list, or Web site has a FAQ. Smart vendors compile their own FAQs for technical support and make them freely available via the Internet.

Reading FAQs has got to be the easiest, cheapest way in the history of the world to fake being an expert. Contrariwise, jumping into a newsgroup or mailing list and asking the Number One Question from that group's FAQ instantly labels you as a dweeb too dumb to pour sand out of a boot.

Check out the FAQs listed in Appendix B for a hoard of useful information on animation and computer graphics.

Schools

Choosing to attend a school to learn character animation is a big decision. You'll be dedicating several years (depending on the program) and anywhere from a few thousand to tens of thousands of dollars. Make sure you'll be getting your time and money's worth!

The most important factor in choosing a school is the faculty. You are better off with great teachers and lousy equipment than with lousy teachers and state-of-the-art computers. Any computer store can sell you the hardware and software. Experienced animators who can also teach are much more difficult to find. If possible, use your network contacts to find teachers with solid reputations, then get into whatever program they're teaching. If you take this approach to its logical extreme, you might consider tracking down a really good animator and negotiating private lessons. Your best resource in making this decision is the school placement office. Animation schools like to brag about the studios that have hired their students, so ask for the names and contact information of well-placed graduates. Most animators will be happy to discuss their educational adventures, such as which teachers to seek out, which ones to avoid, and pitfalls in the curriculum that you should sidestep.

To help with your research, I suggest you consult the out-of-date but still useful *Complete Guide to Animation and Computer Graphics Schools* by Ernest Pintoff, listed in the Bibliography. A more timely but shallower and less analytical resource is GWEB (**http://www.gweb.org/schools-index.html**). This is a World Wide Web-based electronic trade journal for the computer animation and graphics industry. The site includes links to most of the major animation schools.

Practice

Practice, practice, practice! An animator animates! Whether you are in school or studying on your own, you should try to animate something every day, for as many hours as you can afford. Keep a default character setup handy, so you can just load it up and start animating whenever you have the time. If you don't have an original action in mind, go back and reanimate any of the exercises from Part V. The more practice you have on the basics, the more easily you'll be able to animate the hard stuff. Set a goal for yourself to animate so many seconds per week. Over time, you'll get faster. Raise the goal, and keep challenging yourself. Resist the temptation to animate schlock just to make your goal. You should insist on every shot being the best you can do at that time. Don't throw away any of your finished practice efforts—these animations are a record of your progress as an animator. Append everything to your archive reel, so you can show it to mentors, fellow students, and potential employers.

Harold Harris, creative director at TOPIX, told me he was dismayed at the small quantity of animation shown by animation school graduates. Some of them had as little as two or three minutes to show for their entire school career. He said a good animator should practice enough to have 10 minutes of quality animation on their archive reel. If you animate something every day, completing as little as 10 seconds a week will enable you to assemble a 10 minute archive reel in just over a year. If you've got three times as much animation to show as the other candidates for a job, you'll definitely have an advantage. Get to work on it!

Best Foot Forward: Your Demo Reel

Completing the step-by-step exercises in this book will not get you a job. You need to go beyond this, to put together a presentation that tells potential employers that you can breathe life into any model they hand you. This presentation will be your demo reel.

You should be keeping all your material, including textbook exercises, on an archive reel. You can take this to an interview, where you may have the opportunity to discuss your learning experiences and techniques. All those bits and pieces of work in progress will help convince a potential employer that you actually did the work on your demo reel.

For your demo reel, select at least three minutes of your best work from your archive reel. You can get by with less than three minutes if your work is very good, but you should have a reasonable explanation ready if you're under two minutes. Don't go over five minutes. Reviewers will have decided in the first few minutes whether they want to talk to you—anything over five minutes is probably not going to be looked at.

Put your absolute best 10 to 30 seconds of character animation at the beginning of your reel. At least one supervisor told me he'll hit the fast-forward button if he doesn't see something interesting in the first 10 seconds. Remember, these people sometimes have several hundred reels to go through, so don't waste their time or test their patience!

If you have a lot of material you want to show, resist the urge to do an MTV-style montage of fast cuts. Some reviewers won't mind this, but it annoys others, and you won't want to risk that. If at all possible, arrange your pieces in some logical order to minimize the jarring effect of cuts.

Put your name and contact information at the beginning and end of your reel. Keep your titles simple and legible, and, if possible, incorporate some character animation into them. Perhaps you can animate a character pushing the titles on screen or otherwise interacting with the letters. Don't put a date on your reel, and don't explain what software you used in your animations, either. Some houses will automatically turn you down if you don't use their favorite software. On the other hand, if you apply to a house that relies on the same software you used to produce your reel, it is pretty easy to put an explanatory printed insert in the cassette case. Your philosophy should be to let your work speak for itself, and don't give the reviewer any irrelevant information they could use to weed you out. One exception to this is credit for others' work—make sure everybody who contributed to the work on your reel is credited on the insert, with details of who did what on which pieces. It's a lot better to volunteer this information up front than to be answering awkward questions at an interview.

Depending on how good your material is and how paranoid you are, you may want to rig your demo reel so nothing can be lifted from it by unscrupulous persons. One simple technique is to run an animated streamer through the middle of each scene, traveling behind your main characters but in front of the sets and background. The streamer can say something like "Doug Kelly's Demo Reel—Not For Commercial Use." If you use color cycling in the streamer or vary its transparency values, it is very difficult to remove. If you choose to do this, make sure the "protection" you employ doesn't protect you from becoming employed! Keep it as subtle and unobtrusive as you can.

Animation houses are going to be looking for some very specific elements in your reel. They want to see that you can do the work you are applying for, not just that you have the potential to be able to do it someday. If your demo reel doesn't show what they are looking for, you can expect a polite letter to the effect that, "We have no requirement for your services at this time."

So, what do you need to show? That all depends on what job you are applying for.

Character Animation Demo Reel

If you want to be a character animator, then show character animation in your demo reel. The animators who review your reel are going to be looking for a clear understanding of squash-and-stretch, anticipation, secondary motion, timing, and the other animation concepts you worked through in Part V. Beyond that, they will be looking at the whole effect of your work. Do your characters seem motivated? Do they act convincingly? Do they appear to be thinking? Can the viewer understand what the character is expressing?

You don't necessarily have to show off texturing, lighting, and other rendering details. If you are looking for character animation work, you can show your ability just as well with simple wireframe skeletons. A 30-second wireframe of excellent character animation beats 3 minutes of mediocre raytraced walk cycles, any day.

Make sure that the playback speed on your videotape is high enough. 30 fps is best, but you can get by with 24 or even 12. Any speed lower than that, and the reviewer really can't get a fair idea of your timing. This shouldn't be a problem. Today, even most low-end video cards can play back animation at 24 fps or better. If you're looking for work in the U.S., use standard VHS videotapes. You can buy inexpensive 10- or 15-minute videotapes in bulk at very reasonable prices. (The short length keeps people from taping soap operas over your reel.) That's what everybody in the industry uses, and, if you're the only one in the stack with a CD-ROM, Zip, or floppy disk, the reviewer is unlikely to make the extra effort to look at your work. Even if he does, he is going to expect more from you than from the tapes that made his job a little easier.

A good rule of thumb is to pretend that the reviewer is busy, irresponsible, disorganized, and forgetful. Make your reel fast and easy to view, hard to lose, and easy to remember and to locate on a crowded shelf or in a box of other tapes. Rewind the tape before you send it, and pop out the no-erase tabs. Unique or colorful labels with your name and contact information on the spine, face, and ends of the cassette will help. If your tape has a label and the rest of the shelf is just blank black plastic, you've improved your chances. Remember, it can take months before a busy studio gets to your reel, or they may be keeping you in mind for an upcoming job. Make sure they can find your reel when they remember you!

You can also jog the reviewer's memory by putting a thumbnail image on your demo reel labels. A strong pose of a character from the reel is best, but a personal logo or other simple graphic will work, too. You are sending your reel to people with good visual memories and perhaps only so-so verbal skills. Make it easy for them to remember and identify your reel!

Technical Director Demo Reel

If you are looking for work as a technical director, your reel should focus on character construction and rendering. You need to be familiar with modeling, texturing, and animation tools from the technical side. You'll also need strong problem-solving skills and usually some programming knowledge and experience. Unlike animators, you will want to put examples of work in progress in your demo reel and portfolio. Include shots of your best models rendered in wireframe and close-ups of the especially tricky parts. You may want to include prints of some of your best images, as you can get better quality than videotape, and the reviewer can examine them at leisure.

It's a good idea to have duplicates of models, setups, and other electronic files to show at an interview. If you've written any custom shaders, modeling plug-ins or utilities, or any other examples of useful code, bring them along, too. Just don't leave any files on the demo machine or leave the disk—most interviewing companies will be scrupulously honest, but there are always a few bad apples who will try to use your work without paying for it.

Your lighting samples should show a solid understanding of the basic principles. Subtlety is usually better than an overwhelming light show. It's better to show that you can work well with a few lights to establish mood, appeal, and direct the viewer's eye than to overwhelm the scene with a technically challenging but poorly designed profusion of lights. Any effects shots should go well beyond any tutorial you may have read. As a TD, you will be expected to solve new problems, not just use others' solutions. Show that you understand your tools well enough to push their limits.

If you're interested in one of the more technical houses, they'll more than likely require you to know Unix. The minimum hardware you'll need to run Unix is generally a lot more expensive than the minimum hardware you need to run Win95, WinNT, or MacOS. So, what do you do if you don't have the money for a Unix box? The consensus of professional TDs and supervisors at various animation houses is that you can train yourself for Unix by running Linux on a desktop PC. This is a freeware operating system, the majority of the commands you'll be using are identical, and you can learn the differences very quickly. There are also several good books and a ton of online resources on the subject. If you'd like to learn more about Linux, you can find lots of information and other links at **http://www.ssc.com/linux/resources/ftp.html**.

Quality, Not Quantity

What you leave off your demo reel is at least as important as what you put on. You are only as good as the worst piece on your reel. If you want to be employed as a character animator, leave the flying logos, bouncing checkered balls, zooming spacecraft, architectural walkthroughs, tunnel flythroughs, and game rides on your archive reel. And even if it looks like good character animation, leave off the dinosaurs. Everybody has seen dinosaur animations by now, and they are definitely old hat. The same goes for monster animations; most game monsters show very little in the way of acting (I see you! I kill you!), and unless they show very good posing and timing, you're better off without them.

BEST FOOT FORWARD
You are only as good as the worst piece on your reel.

If you're shooting for one of the top studios, you can leave off the "transportation" animation as well. The bar has been raised in the past few years. Previously, a good walk cycle could get you a job. Now, you should only include a walk or run cycle if it is technically proficient and shows character. Otherwise, cycles tell very little about your abilities as a character animator.

Don't ever put the results of an exercise or tutorial on your demo reel. That includes the exercises in this book! Supervisors or directors at animation studios have seen every demo, exercise, and tutorial a zillion times by the time they get to your tape, and you can guarantee an instant ejection and trashing if you put the 3D Studio MAX "drunken baby" or similar over-used demo on your reel. Keep your reel original!

It should go without saying that *original* means your own work, but some people still haven't gotten the message. Character animation is a very small professional community, and everybody sees the good demo reels sooner or later. I've heard similar stories from just about every reviewer about really stupid plagiarists who assemble "their" demo reels from other people's. It's especially stupid when the reviewer finds their own work, or a friend's, with the plagiarist's name on it. Of course, the reviewer immediately tells all their industry friends about it, and the plagiarist can't get work anywhere. Plagiarism is an excellent way to cut your career off at the knees. Don't do it!

As I stated in Chapter 1, one of the most liberating things about desktop animation software is that you really can do it all yourself. There are software tools that can assist you in doing screenwriting, storyboard and layout art, modeling, texturing, audio digitizing, track breakdown, animation, rendering, record keeping, financial and scheduling project management, music composition and recording, audio and video mixing and editing, title design, and film or video recording.

The question is, do you want to handle it all?

It may be to your advantage to work with a complementary partner or group to produce a joint demo reel. If your talents are in the area of technical director, working with an animator can build a reel that is more coherent, entertaining, and demonstrates that you work well as part of a team. On the other hand, as an animator, you will find that working with a good technical director gives your reel an extra polish that puts it above the competition.

Whatever your approach, if you follow this book's guidelines in putting together a coherent, story-telling demo reel, you will have a good chance at landing a job interview.

So, how can you improve your chances? Sending in a demo reel "cold" is a common approach, but this has some drawbacks since the most popular studios receive hundreds of reels. At some studios a non-animator, often a secretary, filters out the absolute trash before any of the creative or supervisory staff get to see it. This can occasionally result in a reel being trashed for reasons having nothing to do with the talent of the animator—the "filters" simply don't know what they are doing.

If you are sending a demo reel, it is a good idea to get the email address, fax, or phone number of a senior animator or director at the studio, and send them a polite message that you would like to send in your reel. If they agree, tell them exactly when you are sending it, and, if they give you permission, add their name to the Attention line. This way, the reel is more likely to be put aside for someone who knows what they are looking at, and the person you contacted may even ask to see the reel before the filter gets to it.

Remember that your contact person is doing you a favor. Be polite. Don't call them at home. Don't nag. Send a follow-up thank-you note. And never broadcast whatever personal contact information they give you!

Résumé, Portfolio, And Cover Letter

Do include a résumé and cover letter with your demo reel. Keep it businesslike, neat, and correct. If you submit a résumé with typos, it does not speak well for your attention to details. Run a spell-checker—that's what word processors are for! Creative layouts are OK, but make sure both the letter and résumé are easy to read. Some supervisors are getting along in years, and their eyes aren't what they used to be. Tiny or confusing typography is counterproductive.

Stress your schooling and/or industry experience. Include your outside interests, especially physical pursuits like martial arts, dance, or acting that contribute to your talents as an animator.

The better studios have gotten past the sweatshop mentality, and are looking for people with balanced lives. The burnout rate on workaholics is too high to support in the long run.

In your cover letter, stress the position you are applying for, and why you want it. Show that you understand what the job entails, and why you want to work for this particular studio.

If you have other artwork, sending in a duplicate portfolio is acceptable to many studios. Call or write ahead to make sure it's OK, and if possible, put as much of it on your video demo reel as possible. The simplest approach is to borrow a camcorder, and do a pan-and-scan coverage of your 2D art or sculptures with close-ups of the fine details. If you do send a portfolio, make sure it's a duplicate. Color photocopies are perfectly acceptable, and most studios can't guarantee to return materials. Don't ever send your only copy of anything!

Interviews

You got the call to come in for an interview. Great! Now calm down. That's the first rule in surviving an interview. Yes, it's a stressful part of life, but nobody has ever been executed for a poor interview in the animation business. You'll live through it.

Right now, you are in a very good position for doing well in an interview. The demand for competent, talented character animators is still high, and most production studios are doing anything they can to lure new hires. That puts more control in your hands (just don't abuse it), so relax and just be yourself. The interviewer has every reason to try to hire you—they will be looking for reasons to hire you, not to turn you away.

If the interview requires air travel, the company should arrange and pay for your travel and lodging. Never fly to an interview on your own nickel; if the company won't pick up the tab, they're not serious. If it's just a short drive or a cross-town trip, you'll be expected to handle it on your own.

DON'T "DRESS FOR SUCCESS"

Most animation houses are very casual places, and the few that aren't are nasty places to work. Typical attire is jeans and T-shirts. If you show up for an interview in a suit or other business attire, that's two-and-a-half strikes against you. I know several people who were hired after interviewing in ripped jeans and grungy T-shirts, but that's pushing it a little. Casual but clean is your best bet.

You probably were asked to come in for an interview because of your demo reel. If your reel was an accurate representation of your talents, the interview is going to be relatively easy for you. The interviewer will probably ask some technical questions about your work and may ask to see some rough work-in-progress examples from your archive or story reel. This is just a check to make sure you actually did the work on your reel.

Your interview portfolio should include examples of every step in the process for your demo reel: story, script, story sketches, character designs, bar sheets/exposure sheets, model documentation, test renders, et cetera. You don't have to bring the complete set of everything, just representative samples. Don't just whip the samples out first thing—that's a little pushy, and there's always the chance you'll show them something they don't like. Just keep your portfolio case in plain sight and wait for the interviewer to ask to see it. If they ask a technical question about something on your reel that is best explained by one of the samples, go ahead and show it.

Aside from the technical interview, they will be trying to assess whether you will fit in with other employees. I've heard stories from several studios about very good technical hires that just didn't work out. The persons in question could do the work, and were in fact very talented, it's just that they couldn't work well with the other members of the team or in that particular studio's culture.

The interview is also a chance for you to ask questions about the working environment. In most shops, the interview includes a tour of the facilities and introductions to many of the other team members. Use this time to ask questions about the work environment. How much creative input do people in your position have? Who will you be reporting to? How long does a typical project last? What's your potential career path within the studio? What's a typical day like? How long do people work, and at what hours? Is the daily routine regimented or free-form? Is there a lot of informal cross-pollination of ideas, or do people pretty much stay in their cubicles? Where do people go for lunch? Is the local take-out any good, or do a lot of people pack lunches? This isn't as trivial as it sounds—you'll be spending an hour a day (at least) with these people at one or more meals, and if the gang's favorite take-out is something you're violently allergic to, you'll be miserable.

Read the cartoons on the walls, especially the work areas of people who'll be working closely with you. If there's nothing on the walls and the interviewer tells you "Dilbert" has been banned, I'd look elsewhere. On the other hand, if it looks like the interior was inspired by the Marquis de Sade, you may be happier somewhere else. One popular litmus test in the animation industry is *The Spirit of Christmas* or its spin-off series, *South Park*. If you haven't seen this short animation, try to find a copy. Are you offended by it, or do you think it's the funniest thing you've ever seen? If you feel strongly about it, ask (at an appropriate time on your tour) if they have a copy lying around. If they get all stiff and say that sort of material is inappropriate, you get an idea of their tolerance for off-color humor. If they enthusiastically pull up a copy on the nearest workstation, and tell you the animation has its own directory on the main fileserver, again you have a better picture of their comedic standards. Either way, you can tell if you'll fit in.

Getting Hired

So you get a phone call, or the interviewer asks when you can start. Congratulations! But don't quit your current job just yet. Think about the offer at least overnight. They shouldn't get upset if you tell them you need to sleep on it. Also, you should ask for a letter or fax, on company letterhead, spelling out the terms of their offer. I learned this one the hard way: I accepted a verbal offer of employment from a fairly large company, relocated across the continent, then was informed that the position had been eliminated in a reorganization.

Nothing was in writing, so I didn't have a leg to stand on, legally. Don't let that happen to you—get the offer in writing!

Are they offering enough compensation, both pay and benefits? Will you be able to cover your living expenses plus savings, IRAs, and other financial needs? There's nothing wrong with making a counter-offer, if their offer is too low. Benefits like vacation time, overtime, and comp time are negotiable, too. Unless the studio is very large and has ironclad labor contracts, everything is on the table. If your annual two week trip to Yosemite is more important than an extra $3,000 in salary, negotiate for the extra time off.

Before you sign an employment contract, read it carefully, and run it past a good entertainment lawyer. Not the family lawyer, an entertainment specialist. There are some serious land mines in entertainment law that can make your life miserable if you're not aware of them. For instance, some studios insist on a non-compete clause, which means that if you quit you can't work anywhere else in the industry for a number of years. There's some question as to whether this practice is even legal, but the threat of a lawsuit can definitely dampen your chances of being hired elsewhere. Even if you decide to go ahead and sign a restrictive contract, you should at least know what you're in for. If you have questions, I suggest you contact MPSC Local 839 (listed in the "Unions" section, later in this chapter) for advice.

Not Getting Hired

So you don't get a phone call. Don't just sit there, send out some more demo reels! The best way to wait for that one perfect job is to go out searching for others. The worst way is to sit by the phone, waiting for the call that never comes. At the end of each interview, ask when you can expect to hear from them again. Wait this amount of time before you call, but then you should definitely call them back. Remember that the people who looked at your demo reel and who interviewed you are also the ones doing the work, and they do get swamped. Dealing with clients takes precedence over hiring new staff, but that doesn't mean they don't want you. Jogging their memory can make a big difference in how long it takes to hire you, or at least let you know that you should be looking elsewhere. You may also be just the right person for a job opening they'll have in six months, so stay in touch.

If you get a definite turndown, don't take it personally, and don't give up. Use this opportunity to ask the interviewer (politely, of course) for a critique of your demo reel and/or interview. If the decision was based on the quality of your work, ask what you need to improve and for

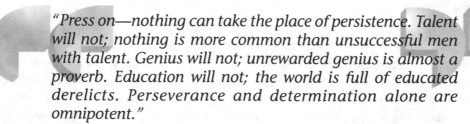

"Press on—nothing can take the place of persistence. Talent will not; nothing is more common than unsuccessful men with talent. Genius will not; unrewarded genius is almost a proverb. Education will not; the world is full of educated derelicts. Perseverance and determination alone are omnipotent."

Calvin Coolidge

advice about additional training or practice. If the decision was based on personal compatibility, ask if they can recommend any shops that might be more suitable. The animation community is a very small one, and most of the players know one another. It never hurts to ask for a referral!

Networking

Speaking of referrals, you should try to build up your list of contacts in the business. Keep track of everybody who's seen your demo reel, interviewed you, or spoken with you at SIGGRAPH, ASIFA, or other animator's gatherings. If possible, collect their email and other contact information, and keep it up-to-date. Get on the Internet, if you aren't already. The minimum service packages available from most Internet service providers are very reasonable and a worthwhile investment. Watch the industry press and the appropriate mailing lists and Usenet newsgroups for announcements or gossip about upcoming projects, and use that contact information to let them know you are available. Whenever you update your demo reel, send out notices to the appropriate people, asking if they'd like to see it.

This is very important: Do *not* simply add all these people to a personal mailing list and send them a lot of trivial form letter email. When you have new information to distribute, send an individual email to each person. If you reuse most of the text, at least make enough changes that the message is not an obvious form letter. Unless you are already on a first name basis with the recipient, you should make your emails as formal and structured as a cover letter for a résumé. Keep the message brief, make your points clearly and succinctly, and be polite. Each message you send to a potential employer is the same as showing up on their doorstep unannounced—you'd better have a good reason for doing so, and it had better be in their best interest to hear what you have to say. Being an inconsiderate nag can get you on everybody's filter list, meaning they'll never listen to you again. Use your best judgment!

If you want to survive in this business, stay in touch with your colleagues. The animation business is still project-based; only the largest studios (and not all of those) keep animators on staff when there is no paying work for them. Many animators follow the work, staying at a studio through a project, then moving on to another project at another studio. Others may stay at a studio for years, working on whatever comes by and hanging on through the dry spells. For either approach, it's a good idea for you to stay informed about who's working where, on what project, and for how long. Even a large studio may have to suddenly cancel a project and lay off the animation team, for business reasons having nothing to do with the merits of the project. The July '97 closing of Warner Digital is a case in point. If you're well-connected and up-to-date, you'll be able to find another job immediately, but if you've been out of the loop for a while, you'll have a harder time of it.

CG-CHAR

One of the best places to start networking is the Computer Generated Character Animation listserv. This is a closed mailing list, maintained by and for character animators working in the CGI medium. It has been around since early 1996, and at last count had over 1,000 subscribers. The tone of the list has varied over time, from a hard-core group of experienced profession-als to a more student-and-novice tone as of this writing. It's not a moderated list, but if you misbehave, you'll be unsubscribed. It's a lot like a medieval guild hall, where novices, journey-men, and masters all meet informally to share information and socialize.

The CG-CHAR home page is a collection of resources by and for subscribers of the CG-CHAR listserv. Galleries of art, works in progress, book reviews, shareware, and job postings are there now, and plans for the future include complete listserv archives and interactive chats.

To quote the founder of the listserv, Rick May, "The CG (computer generated) Character Ani-mation List was created for artists and TD's to share information and ideas on creating computer assisted character animation. We are hoping to discuss not only software and (a little) hard-ware, but techniques and ideas. Although we are applying our artistry through the computer—we welcome postings from people with cel or stopmo experience. A lot of people creating CG char-acter work nowadays have cel or stopmo backgrounds anyway—techniques learned from these disciplines are always helpful. Traditional animators could also benefit from our list—perhaps learning how to use the computer in their animation work."

For more information, email Rick at **rick@cg-char.com** or visit the Web site **http://www.cg-char.com**.

ASIFA

ASIFA, Association Internationale Du Film d'Animation, is "devoted to the encouragement and dissemination of film animation as an art and communication form." This is another great place to network, but since it includes all forms of animation, you may find it less focused on your needs than CG-CHAR. It has over 1,100 members in 55 countries. The United States has the most members, 280, and Canada is a close second with 250.

ASIFA produces a newsletter, annual calendar, and animation school list. It also maintains an employment database and a film archive. The ASIFA Workshop Group runs animation work-shops for children in over 30 countries. ASIFA membership is open to all individuals interested in animation. For more information, contact ASIFA International at **http://www.swcp.com/~asifa/asifaint.htm** or ASIFA Hollywood at:

ASIFA Hollywood
725 South Victory Boulevard
Burbank, California 91502
Tel: 818-842-8330
Fax: 818-842-5654
Internet: http://www.awn.com/asifa_hollywood

CGA—Computer Game Artists

This is a fledgling organization (**http://www.vectorg.com:80/cga**) of and for game artists. It's an excellent place to build up your network if you are interested in character animation for games. You have the opportunity to get in on the ground floor and help build it!

Mentoring

Whether you're a student, self-teacher, amateur, or professional, you can use a good mentor. Mentoring can include occasional career advice, a fresh pair of eyes to critique your work, frequent tutoring, and even collaboration. It all depends on what you need and what your mentor can provide. There are lots of ways a more experienced person can assist your growth as an animator.

Finding a mentor will take some effort on your part. If you are working in an animation studio, you may have coworkers willing to act as mentors. If you're a student, one of your teachers may be able to give you the extra time outside of class. If you're on your own, try meeting senior animators or technical directors through the networking resources listed in this chapter. If you hit it off with one of them, ask if they'd be willing to mentor you.

Women In Animation

If you happen to be female, this organization is specifically chartered to address the special concerns of women in this business. To quote from their Web site, "Women In Animation is a professional, non-profit organization established in 1994 to foster the dignity, concerns and advancement of women in any and all aspects of the art of animation. Women In Animation was formed by a number of prominent women in all areas of animation, from producers to academics to the former publisher of Animation Magazine. Every major studio in Hollywood is represented, as well as most independent studios and New York-based members of the animation industry."

The Web site has a lot of useful information about meetings and workshops on a variety of animation-related topics. Highly recommended.

Women In Animation
P.O. Box 17706
Encino, CA 91416
Tel: 818-759-9596
Internet: http://www.women.in.animation.org

Kellie-Bea Rainey has assembled a useful site (**http://www.animation.org/women/noframes**) showcasing Women In Animation with interviews and photos, a mentoring match-up system, lots of related links, and a questionnaire for those who would like to contribute. This is definitely worth visiting for anyone who'd like a candid look inside the industry.

SIGGRAPH

This is the Special Interest Group of the ACM that deals with computer graphics, from scientific visualization to entertainment. The annual SIGGRAPH conference is the major CGI event of the year. If you're at all interested in computer graphics as a profession (or even a serious hobby), don't miss it. This is where the software and hardware vendors and studios pull out the stops. SIGGRAPH is held in Southern California every other year, and in alternate years rotates from city to city. SIGGRAPH '97 was held at the Los Angeles Convention Center. You can find future venues at the SIGGRAPH Web site. Don't miss it!

Association for Computing Machinery
11 West 42nd Street
New York, NY 10036
Internet: http://www.siggraph.org

Unions

The following is a quote from the Local 839 Web site:

"What is Local 839? Simply put, we are a union of artists, writers and technicians making animated films. We've been around since 1952 helping animation employees get decent wages, better working conditions...and a little respect."

"Animators are among our members. Writers of TV cartoons hold MPSC union cards. Digital painters, computer animators and modelers are part of the MPSC. We negotiate contracts, create résumés, provide legal and negotiating advice to artists and technicians working for the largest and most profitable animation companies in the world."

For more details, contact:

MPSC Local 839 IATSE
4729 Lankershim Boulevard
North Hollywood, CA 91602-1864
Tel: 818-766-7151
Fax: 818-506-4805
Email: mpsc839@netcom.com
Internet: http://www.primenet.com/~mpsc839/

Potential Employers

Following is a list of major animation and special effects houses that have advertised recently for TDs or animators. As always, contact information is subject to change without notice. Sending a reel is the best approach, but this has some drawbacks, because, as mentioned earlier, the most popular studios receive hundreds of reels.

• Blue Sky Studios/VIFX does CGI animation for TV and feature film, including *Joe's Apartment* and *Alien:Resurrection.*

Blue Sky Studios, Inc.
One South Road
Harrison, NY 10528
Tel: 914-381-8400
Fax: 914-381-9791
Internet: http://www.blueskyprod.com

- Digital Domain, James Cameron's effects production house, is easily one of the most popular "dream jobs" in the industry. The corporate culture is...interesting. They did effects for *True Lies* and *Titanic*.

Digital Domain
300 Rose Avenue
Venice, CA 90291
Tel: 310-314-2934
Email: digital_hiring@d2.com
Internet: http://www.d2.com

- Dream Quest Images, a division of the Walt Disney Company, does feature film digital visual effects.

Dream Quest Images
Attn.: Geoff Brooks-Talent Recruiting
2635 Park Center Drive
Simi Valley, CA 93065
Tel: 805-581-2671
Fax: 805-583-4673
Email: talent@dqimages.com

- DreamWorks Animation is part of DreamWorks SKG, the start-up studio headed by Steven Spielberg, Jeffrey Katzenberg, and David Geffen.

DreamWorks Animation
Attn.: Michele Henderson
P.O. Box 7304 #132
North Hollywood, CA 91603
Email: animhr@dreamworks.com

- Industrial Light + Magic, or ILM, is a division of Lucas Digital Ltd. and does effects work for Lucasfilm and other studios, as well. They animated numerous aliens for *Men in Black*, Draco for *Dragonheart*, and tornadoes for *Twister*, but their line of award-winning effects goes back to the original *Star Wars*.

Lucas Digital
HR Dept.
P.O. Box 2459
San Rafael, CA 94912
Tel: 415-662-1800

- MetroLight looks for TDs and animators who are comfortable in a Unix, high-end environment. If you have exclusively desktop PC experience, you will need programming skills or something extra to convince them.

MetroLight Studios, Inc.
Attn.: Résumés
5724 W. 3rd St., #400
Los Angeles, CA 90036
Tel: 213-932-0400
Fax: 213-932-8440
Email: resumes@metrolight.com
Internet: http://www.metrolight.com

- ORIGIN Systems is a major game developer, with too many credits to list. They use LightWave 3D, among other software.

ORIGIN Systems, Inc.
Attn.: Human Resources
5918 W. Courtyard Dr.
Austin, TX 78730
Email: nvargas@origin.ea.com

- Pacific Data Images does feature film digital visual effects using proprietary software. PDI has been around for a long time. Recent work includes the 3D Homer and Bart in *The Simpsons* Halloween special and the aliens in *The Arrival*. *Ants* is currently in production.

Pacific Data Images
Attn.: CG Animation Search
3101 Park Boulevard
Palo Alto, CA 94306
Tel: 415-846-8100
Fax: 415-846-8101
PDI Job Hotline: 1-800-655-8779
Internet: http://www.pdi.com

- Pixar Animation Studios produced *Toy Story, Tin Toy, Luxo Jr.*, and the Listerine and Gummi Savers TV ads. As if you didn't know.

Pixar Animation Studios
Attn: Recruiting
1001 West Cutting Blvd.
Richmond, CA 94804
Tel: 510-236-4000
Fax: 510-236-0388
Job Hotline: 510-412-6017
Email: hr@pixar.com
Internet: http://www.pixar.com

- Square L.A. produced best-selling role-playing games Final Fantasy and Chrono Trigger.

Square L.A.
4640 Admiralty Way
Suite 1200

Marina del Rey, CA 90292-6621
Tel: 1-888-470-8273
Fax: 310-302-9550
Email: hr@sqla.com
Internet: http://www.sqla.com

- Sony Pictures Imageworks does digital visual effects. One major project in the works is *Dinotopia*. They accept reels, résumés, and portfolios.

Sony Pictures Imageworks
9050 W. Washington Boulevard
Culver City, CA 90232
Fax: 310/840-8888
Email: resumes@spimageworks.com
Internet: http://www.spiw.com

- Tiburon Entertainment develops games for Electronic Arts, including Soviet Strike and Madden NFL '97. They're expanding.

Tiburon Entertainment
HR Department
P.O. Box 940427
Maitland, FL 32794-0427
Fax: 407-862-4077
Email: sharksmail@tibent.com
Internet: http://www.tibent.com

- Walt Disney Feature Animation is going digital in a big way. Currently, they are gearing up for production of *Dinosaur*.

Walt Disney Feature Animation
Attn.: Human Resources HR 7.6
500 S. Burbank Street
Burbank, CA 91521-8072
Fax: 818-544-5400
Email: resumes@fa.disney.com

- Windlight Studios did the animated Gymnast Barbie ads. They specialize in long-format computer character animation, and use motion capture for some of their work.

Windlight Studios
Attn.: Human Resources
702 North First Street
Minneapolis, MN 55401
Email: hr@windlight.com

Moving On

If you've got the talent and you've followed the guidelines in this chapter, you should be well on your way to landing a job in character animation. The next chapter has some tips for coping with an animator's life when you're working in someone else's studio.

BEING AN EMPLOYEE

Once you've landed a job in animation, you'll have to work to keep it. You'll also need to look after yourself, if you want to avoid being underpaid, exploited, obsolete, or disabled.

If you've landed your first animation job, congratulations! You're on your way in a career with lots of opportunities for personal growth, increasing public recognition, and artistic satisfaction. Not to mention that at least some of your work will be just plain fun! Seeing your work in public for the first time, whether in a video game, on TV, or on the silver screen, will be a rush you won't forget. Most senior animators I've talked to still get opening-night jitters when they attend premieres—it's a thrill that won't fade, as long as you care about your work.

Now What Do I Do?

So, what is your job? No matter what your job title or description reads, your number one job is getting the work done. That means doing your own assigned work, plus working well with others, taking direction, and understanding how the rest of the studio works. You're not a cog in a machine—you're a voice in the chorus, a creative artist who collaborates with professional colleagues to produce great character animation. The better you understand others' work, the better you can do your own.

Whenever possible, find out how you can make your coworkers' jobs easier. If someone else is depending on your work, ask what they need from you. If some small additional task on your part makes their part much easier, do it. Conversely, you should tactfully let coworkers know how to make your job easier. One way to do this is to show polite interest in the jobs of people who provide models, setups, and other materials for your job. If the studio has been running successfully for a while, you'll probably find out that they're way ahead of you on labor-saving tricks. However, once in a while, you'll find they're spending a lot of effort on something that isn't crucial. Handle this diplomatically. Don't say, "You've been wasting your time tweaking that model for six weeks. It'll all have to be done over anyway." Try something like, "Wow, that looks great. Why don't you let me run some animation tests on the model right now? We may be able to use it as is." This way, you've prevented further wasted effort, and the "bad news" will be in the animation tests rather than your personal observations. As a general rule, make positive reports and compliments in a personal way, but try to put negative reports and critiques in as objective a form as possible. It's just human nature—nobody enjoys criticism, even when it's constructive.

863

It's important to your career and your current project that you understand exactly where the studio priorities are. It's not unreasonable that two weeks of your time may very well be less expensive than two days (or even two hours) of someone else's. I ran into this a few years ago, when I was coordinating materials from about 60 individuals for a corporate project. I was presented with more than 20 different file formats, which meant I'd have to spend a lot of time translating them to a single common format. I tried to impose some file format standards. The project director took me aside and very reasonably explained that it was more time- and cost-effective for one person (me) to be stuck doing a week's worth of translating than to retrain 60 other employees who all had more technically demanding work to do. Sometimes doing tedious, apparently stupid work is the most effective use of your time on a project. It's nothing personal, so don't take it that way. Remember your position. You will be starting off on a very low rung, and should not try to act like you're a director. Entry-level positions, even well-paid ones, are for people who are there to learn.

One of the best things about the character animation business is that, once you're on the job, nobody cares whether you graduated from a premier school or you taught yourself by hand-drawing flipbooks. The majority of animation production studios are well-run businesses where hard work and talent are rewarded. It's a complete meritocracy. It's only your work they notice. Make sure your work says the right things about you: good, solid, on time, and with no unpleasant strings attached. If you do magnificent work but are a prima donna, every time the director sees one of your shots, he's going to remember the temper tantrum you threw while working on it. On the other hand, if you put in a lot of extra effort to make an excellent shot, every time the director sees it, she'll remember you in the best possible way. Give your employer good value for value received. Work for the hours you are paid, and give the best efforts that your talents, skills, and full attention can produce. Make them glad they hired you!

One of the smartest things you can do on your first job is to make your boss look good. If there is a problem on the project, resist the urge to blurt out the solution to all and sundry. Instead, see your supervisor privately, and float your idea as a possible solution. If it's not viable for some reason, you haven't embarrassed yourself. If it's a good idea, your supervisor can help you develop it and can share in the credit. This is good for both of you—your boss gets a solution, and you get your boss's good will. If your boss chooses to take full credit for your idea, I suggest that you let it slide as long as this is your first job. Think of it as part of paying your dues. As I mentioned earlier, the animation community is a very small one. A good recommendation from an experienced supervisor is worth a lot. You'll have lots of good ideas throughout your career, so one idea is a small price to pay to start your career on the right foot.

Most of the supervisors and managers you'll work for will be reasonable people, great to work for and helpful to your career. A small percentage of supervisors can be more difficult. If you're working for one of them, you'll have to show more self-control and be more solidly centered. Don't be a prima donna, but don't be a doormat either. Getting a paycheck doesn't mean they own you, just as being an artist doesn't mean you should abuse or rip off your employer. Be honest, reasonable, and fair, as long as your employer does the same.

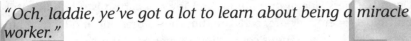

"Och, laddie, ye've got a lot to learn about being a miracle worker."

Capt. Montgomery Scott, UFP, Ret.

It's to your advantage to build a reputation of reliability. The first rule is: Don't promise what you can't deliver. You're not making a sales pitch to a client, you're telling your boss what you can and can't do. It's not good for anyone if you bite off more than you can chew. Of course, we all make mistakes sometime. If you can't deliver on a promise, go to your supervisor as soon as you've identified the problem. Work with your supervisor to find a solution. Don't just throw it in his lap and run away. And don't wait until two seconds before the deadline to ask for help.

When you're being asked to do a job that you're unsure of, be willing to say, "I don't know." Be just as willing to say, "I can try to find out." If you've really got a bad feeling about a job, or you can see major problems, don't just say "No." Instead, say, "We can do it that way, but it will cost X dollars and Y days extra." It's the supervisor's, director's, or producer's job to make the call. It's your job to provide them with your best professional assessment, then carry out their decision.

Most large studios have a cadre of "suits," the business-school graduates, attorneys, and financiers that make the business decisions. If you're lucky (or simply did your research before you took the job), the suits at your studio have also had a background or at least a solid personal liking for motion pictures and storytelling. The best situation is where former animators have built their own studio, so the top executives once had your job and understand both the creative and business side of animation. If you're stuck in a studio managed by suits who don't understand filmmaking, animation, or art in any form, you are probably not going to have a long and happy career there. A case in point is the July 1997 closing of Warner Digital. The creative part of Warner Digital was top-notch, some of the best people in the business, and their work was outstanding. Unfortunately, the suits made a series of this-quarter, bottom-line calls and decided to fold the studio.

Despite incidents like this, it's important to your career survival that you be able to cooperate with suits. Don't bite the hand that feeds you. The suits in your studio are the people who make your paycheck show up on time. If they weren't out there meeting with clients and hustling for projects to keep you and your buddies busy, you'd be out looking for another job. The bottom line is that suits who may know little or nothing about the creative process can nevertheless green-light or kill projects. It's a classic example of the Golden Rule: He who has the gold, makes the rules. If you antagonize the wrong suit, you can find yourself unemployed (the project was killed) or doing scut work (the project was bastardized), with a bunch of your co-workers alongside you. This doesn't mean you should grovel, just that you have to make your observations, criticisms, and suggestions in polite form, through proper channels, and in language suits can understand. Most suits are not inherently bad people. They don't enjoy producing schlock any more than you do. Many of them have years of training and experience in the financial and business side of animation, and their expertise is a valid contribution to the production. To get where they are, odds are that they either put in a lot of time, are very talented or very lucky, or have serious connections. Any one of these cases is sufficient reason for you to treat them with a modicum of respect. If they are making decisions which make your job harder, you should discuss that fact, privately, with your supervisor. If you point out that a change they've asked for will require weeks of expensive overtime and a missed delivery date, they will most likely see reason. If you rant and rave and call them names, you'll do yourself more harm than good, and they're not likely to listen to you in the future. Be professional, be reasonable, and, if the suits won't reciprocate, keep your demo reel and résumé updated—you'll probably need them sooner rather than later.

Maintaining Your Space—And Yourself

If you are a typical animator, you will spend more time at work than away from it. With that in mind, make sure you are going to be comfortable. Windows? What windows? Get used to the idea of not seeing the sun very much. Sunlight glaring off your monitor's screen and the cost of commercial office space mean you will usually be working in a windowless cubicle or sharing a room with other animators or TDs.

You'll probably spend more time decorating your cubicle than you spend furnishing your home. Animators are famous for cluttering their workspace with toys. It may be a good idea to arm yourself—there have been hair-raising reports of Nerf wars in some shops. Try to keep a sense of humor. When deadlines are tight and nerves are thrumming, the catharsis of a good Nerf™ battle can save your production team's sanity.

Make sure you take care of yourself physically. CGI animators, like other computer workers, are prone to Repetitive Stress Injury (RSI), including carpal tunnel syndrome, Dequervaine's, and related maladies. Set up your workstation to provide proper support, and, if you have already injured yourself, follow the directions of your therapist. A lot of animators use wrist braces and ergonomic supports. Get yourself a good chair with proper back support. After searching unsuccessfully for decent workstation furniture, I finally designed and built my own. It's a standing-height work surface for my keyboard and tablet, with my monitor at eye level, and a matching draftsman's stool. I alternate standing and sitting on about a 20-minute cycle, to keep from stiffening up over the course of a 16-hour workday.

Take especially good care of your eyes. Staring at a monitor for hours can exhaust the focusing muscles of your eyes, getting them in a rut that can affect your ability to change focus rapidly. Try to have a brightly colored object within view at least 20 feet away, and periodically (every 15 minutes or so) look up and focus your eyes on it. Looking out a window is best, but, if your

"Animation can be a bit of an endurance sport, physically and mentally, and you have to make sure you're up to it."
Phil South

work area is too enclosed, set up a mirror on the far wall to double your line of sight. If you ever have any doubts about the effect your job is having on your vision, talk to your optometrist or ophthalmologist.

Even if you love your job, you need to keep a balanced perspective. Set aside some time, on a regular basis, to keep up your personal life.

Collecting Your Due

The intangible rewards of a job you love are wonderful, but you've got to pay the bills, too. Don't ever work for free. Negotiate comp time, overtime pay, a percentage of the project, or even stock options, but don't agree to work uncompensated overtime. If there's a real crunch on to finish an important job, management should at least agree to give you an equivalent amount of time off (with pay!) after the crunch is over. Mandatory unpaid overtime happens to be against the law. The Fair Labor Standards Act (FLSA), passed in 1938 and enforced by the U.S. Department of Labor, requires premium pay for work in excess of 40 hours per week. If management attempts to end-run this law by telling you you're salaried and therefore exempt, here are some of the other criteria the Department of Labor will apply: setting work schedules; requiring employees to keep time sheets; docking pay for partial days worked; paying overtime for "extra" hours worked; reporting pay on an hourly basis; and using the same disciplinary system for exempt and nonexempt employees. Essentially, if the studio wants you to work and be paid like management, they have to treat you like management. Penalties are serious, including back pay and punitive damages. Usually, employers who try to require unpaid overtime are simply new to running a business and don't understand the situation. Once in a great while, you'll have an employer who knowingly and systematically breaks this law. I suggest you find work elsewhere and perhaps send a letter to the Department of Labor after you're safely employed again.

Benefits

Take advantage of company benefits that improve your quality of life. When you're hired, the HR (Human Resources) department should provide you with a list of official benefits. At least one shop has an on-site masseur, which is great for muscle cramps and RSI, the character animators' occupational hazards. If you wear corrective lenses and have optical health insurance, you should consider getting the new prescription glasses designed especially for computer work. Some studios also have discount purchase programs for everything from movie tickets to groceries to computers. Take advantage of what you can, and, if you think of a good benefit for you and your coworkers, suggest it. Good benefits are cost-effective ways for your employer to stay competitive, and they'll usually appreciate your suggestions.

Even if this is your first job as an animator, you should start planning for your retirement. There are entirely too many horror stories of traditional animators having to work into their 80s or dying broke because they didn't plan for retirement. Don't let that happen to you. The nature of the business is that you will probably move around a lot, being a "project gypsy," or being headhunted from one studio to the next as your skills and reputation improve. There is also the fact that CGI character animation is a very young industry, and even the oldest shops have not been around very long. Shops tend to open, have a more or less successful run, then close, just like any other small business. If your career is going to last 25 to 40 years, you can't count on retiring from the first studio you work for.

The ephemeral nature of the industry means you need a retirement plan that you can take with you. Plans administered through a union are one option. IRAs and other savings plans that you run for yourself are another. Social Security will probably be broke or completely overhauled by the time you can collect from it, so don't count on that. If you have no idea how to invest money over the long term, I suggest you consult a personal financial planner. Your banker or insurance agent may be able to help, but they'll have an understandable bias toward the products they'll try to sell you. My personal recommendation is investment in income properties like real estate or intellectual property. If you build up a portfolio of marketable assets, you can practically guarantee a steady cash flow from leasing or licensing without having to work very hard after your retirement. This is the strategy followed by some of the wealthiest people in the entertainment business. For details, I recommend *Fortune* magazine.

Screen Credit

There is one benefit you will probably not be able to negotiate for your first job, but you should get it as soon as you can and then never let it go. It's screen credit. This isn't just about vanity, it's about money. If you have a string of screen credits on your résumé, and the people who watch credits (most of the industry, plus the fans) recognize your name, that's worth serious cash when you negotiate your next contract. It's also the way your name gets attached to the industry's awards—they go to the people named in the credits, not necessarily the people who did the work. If you're ever going to cash in on your professional reputation, make the lecture circuit, try to get an independent project green-lighted, or publish your memoirs or even a technical book, your screen credits are even more important than your demo reel. You should start collecting screen credits as soon as you have the leverage to demand them—you don't need to wait until your current contract is up.

> ### RENEGOTIATION IS NOT A BAD THING
>
> After you've been working for a while, and especially if you are doing exemplary work, it's a good idea to think about changes you'd like to make. More money is always nice, but think about additional vacation time, company sponsorship of private projects, or more creative input/control. Everything is subject to renegotiation, but you've got to be willing to leave for greener pastures if management won't give you what you need. Don't even think about trying to bluff, they'll call you on it, every time.

Professional Development

CGI character animation is an art that you'll never completely master. It's a lifelong pursuit, a process of honing your skills toward a perfection you can reach for but never grasp. There's always something new to learn, some new method or fine-tuning of an older method that will get you closer to your goal. You should always be developing your skills and professional knowledge. Never rest on your laurels. Always be learning, always be curious about what's around the bend, technically and cinematically.

The resources listed in the preceding chapter will continue to serve you well throughout your animation career. Learn from others' work at every opportunity. See every film or TV program that includes character animation, and collect laser disks of the best examples. Try to keep up on the literature, keep an eye on the most useful listservs and newsgroups, and don't miss SIGGRAPH if you can possibly avoid it. If you're working in games, the Computer Games Development Conference is another must-see. You can find details online at **http://www.cgdc.com**.

If traditional art training will help you hone your skills, you should investigate the opportunities available in your community. Most art schools have open life drawing classes where you can practice for a small fee. Classes in related disciplines such as sculpture, photography, filmmaking, or industrial design may be available, too. Opportunities tend to be more plentiful in larger cities, but you can find an art teacher willing to tutor in even the smallest town. If you're a union member, the local chapter may offer classes or referrals to other members who can be of assistance. Keep an eye out for special seminars, too. According to the animators I've talked to, Richard Williams' master classes are more than worth the fee, lodging, and airfare. Classes in martial or theater arts or sports that require discipline in movement are excellent training for character animators—and they get you away from the monitor and keyboard for a while.

Speaking of which, you should habitually pull out all the stops on your tools. Learn absolutely everything you can do with the software and hardware you have access to. Go beyond the manuals, books like this one, and the conventional solutions others rely on. Find new solutions to problems that haven't even been recognized yet. When you have the time and budget to make your own projects, that intimate familiarity with your tools will pay you back manyfold.

The path you follow to develop yourself depends entirely on the type of work you like to do. If you enjoy being a generalist, you may want to stay with smaller studios. Conversely, if you are working for a larger studio, you may find it difficult to get assignments outside your narrow job description.

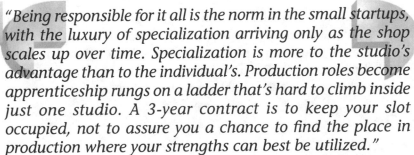

"Being responsible for it all is the norm in the small startups, with the luxury of specialization arriving only as the shop scales up over time. Specialization is more to the studio's advantage than to the individual's. Production roles become apprenticeship rungs on a ladder that's hard to climb inside just one studio. A 3-year contract is to keep your slot occupied, not to assure you a chance to find the place in production where your strengths can best be utilized."

Ken Cope

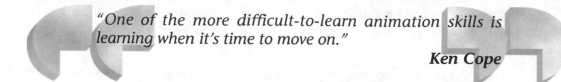

"One of the more difficult-to-learn animation skills is learning when it's time to move on."

Ken Cope

You may choose to stick with one studio through many projects or follow the most interesting work from studio to studio. You may decide to remain an animator, or, with experience, you may find that you prefer to direct or even produce. If you can't find personal satisfaction at any studio, you may even choose to branch out on your own.

Side Projects

Odds are good that you became interested in animation because you want to tell stories, to make characters come to life. At some time in your career, you are going to want to take on a side project, a personal film to scratch the storytelling itch you can't indulge at your regular job. Some studios are very supportive of side projects, providing facilities, budgets, and personnel to assist you. Others don't support side projects, but don't forbid them, either. Some studios actively discourage side projects with a myriad of sanctions, legal and otherwise.

Despite what your employer or their lawyers may say, what you do on your own time is yours, unless your contract states something to the contrary. If you develop valuable ideas—character designs, scripts, any kind of intellectual property—you should be very careful not to use any company resources. If you so much as borrow a company pencil, the company may have a legal claim on the properties you develop. If you do it on your own time, in your own place, on your own equipment, it belongs to you. Just make sure you can prove all this in a court of law.

This is why it's important to own your own equipment and software. With appropriate tools at home, you can pursue side projects without official support or sanctions. You can choose to use the same software tools as in your regular job or branch out and experiment with other solutions. In either case, the skills you hone at home will make you a better animator at work, too. Reasonable companies understand this and encourage it. If your company doesn't, you might want to reexamine your reasons for continuing to work there.

Even if you're deliriously happy with your current position, you should keep your demo reel and résumé up to date. Every time you finish a nice shot, especially when you wrap up a major project, add those bits to your archive reel. If the new material justifies it, update the editing of your demo reel. You never know when an opportunity is going to knock, and a prepared demo reel can make the difference between grabbing the brass ring and missing it clean.

Moving On

I hope this chapter has provided you with some sound advice, and that it will make your first animation job a little easier. If you've been in the business for a while or are just curious about your future options, the next chapter describes some of the advantages and pitfalls of going into the character animation business for yourself.

Running Your Own Shop

If you really love doing the best work you can, making your own creative decisions, setting your own rules, and working on your own schedule, you may want to work for yourself.

Working for yourself is potentially the most rewarding career path for an animator, both financially and creatively. However, being a great animator doesn't automatically qualify you to run a business. It's a set of skills, talents, and attitudes that can be very different from the creative side of animation. If you don't have it, you're better off working in another person's shop.

Working as an independent is not the best option for every animator. Being an employee of an animation studio or game developer has several advantages: you don't have to manage the business, you can concentrate on your animation, and you (usually) get a steady paycheck and benefits. The pay, however, can be a fraction of what you could make on your own.

Independent animators are generally either freelance, subcontractors, or consultants. To succeed as an independent animator, you need the basic know-how of any successful small business owner: accounting and finance, customer relations, legal risk management, and estimating, for starters. As a person, you need to be self-starting, diplomatic, persistent, entrepreneurial, thorough, and organized. That's all in addition to your skills and talent as an animator. Do you see why most animators are not in business for themselves?

Freelance animating is usually work-for-hire, which means you are essentially a temporary employee on a project basis. Freelancing can make you very good money, but you will also have to market your services and pay more attention to business matters than a regular employee would.

Being a subcontractor is like running your own production house, with a little less responsibility and a lot less creative control. Your client, the main contractor on the project, will hand you a piece of work and tell you when the finished product is due. Where, when, and how you do the work is usually up to you. With this freedom comes added risk—if you don't deliver as contracted, the client (and sometimes even their client) can sue you for damages. Think about production insurance, and don't promise what you can't deliver.

Being a consultant can be lucrative and relatively low-risk, but you need a solid reputation and a lot of friends and colleagues in the business who know the quality of your work and will recommend you when a problem arises. Don't plan to start off as a successful animation consultant. You can only get there after a lot of solid professional work and sustained networking.

Running a production house is the next rung up the ladder. To succeed at this level, you need a reputation that will bring in clients, the management and people skills to attract and retain talented personnel, and the discipline and tenacity to keep it all running smoothly. The financial rewards can be huge, in proportion to the risks you run while building up your studio. The less tangible rewards are good, too. If your studio wins an award, you can be the one on stage stammering through a laundry list of thank yous.

Growing A Business

More than half of all small business start-ups fail in the first three years. It's up to you to make sure you're not one of them. One of the most sensible strategies is detailed in a book I highly recommend, Paul Hawken's *Growing A Business*. The central concept is that each business has an optimal growth rate and path, and attempting to hurry or force it will only cause trouble. If you read this book and think carefully about your own business, the next logical growth opportunity will usually become obvious.

Setting Goals

Whether you read Hawken or not, you should keep an eye on your goals. Set a goal for your business. It shouldn't sound like one of those pompous corporate mission statements. It should be something that's personally important to you. "Create the best character animation in the tri-state area," "Make enough money to retire by age 40," or "Prove to my parents that I'm not a waste of space" are all perfectly good goals, although you might not want to put those last two on your company letterhead.

Once you've made a goal for yourself, make a list of tasks you'll need to accomplish to reach your goal. Write the goal across the top of the page, and list the tasks under it. Don't get stressed out about making a perfect or exhaustive list. Again, these should be simple statements describing milestones to your goal. If your goal is to produce award-winning animations, you'll need to work at tasks like "study and learn from other animators," "finish animations to the best of my ability," and "practice and improve my animation skills every day." Keep this list of tasks where you can refer to it. If your workspace is private or you don't mind clients reading it, you might put it on the wall where you can see it as you work.

When you need to make a decision about your business—a new project to accept or decline, a software or hardware purchase, an offer to include your work in an exhibition, whether to hire employees—refer to your goals and your list of tasks. Which choice will get you closer to your goal? Are you making progress on the tasks? Is your goal still the one you want, and do you still believe these tasks will get you there? Over time, your tasks and even your goal will change. This is a natural part of the growth of your business. The important thing is that you are constantly aware of your goal, so you can work toward it without wasting yourself on distractions and tangents.

Personnel

You're it. Until you have signed contracts for work you simply don't have time to do, you should be your only employee. Once you've got a surplus, you can think about hiring independent contractors to pick up the slack. There are very good reasons many businesses are choosing to use contractors rather than employees—it's just too expensive to keep full-timers around, costing you salary, benefits, and overhead if they're not going to be working full time. On top of that, you have the problems of recruiting, training, and retaining good talent in a field that is absolutely vicious about headhunting.

Independent contractors are a good compromise between your one-person shop and the next Pixar. You can bring them together for a large project, and, if you can keep the projects coming in, you can keep the team together. You'll have to pay careful attention to the legalities, however. The IRS has been clamping down on employers who just relabel everyone a contractor. If they're supposed to be independent, you have to treat them as independent—which means you can't dictate when and how they work—just what they're supposed to turn in. You need to be comfortable with delegating authority and trusting your contractors to deliver on time. If you can't, you're probably better off sticking with solo work or growing your business through a partnership with other animators.

Financing Your Business

We live in a capitalist society, so, whatever your personal beliefs, you need to be conversant with and competent in financial matters, or your business will not succeed.

The first step is to calculate the bare necessities for your business. This means figuring out just what you need to create the products your clients will pay for. It does not include luxuries like new office furniture, top-of-the-line entertainment systems, or a new car, even though you can make a case for those items being business expenses. When you are starting a new business, you should start on a shoestring. It keeps your mind focused, minimizes distractions, and keeps you in touch with financial reality. It also minimizes the financial fall you may take if your business fails and maximizes your profit margin if you succeed.

Your bare necessities will probably include a space to work, a computer, at least one software package capable of character animation, and a means of delivering the finished animations to your clients. That's it. Everything else is extra, and you should avoid adding anything to your necessities list unless it can pay for itself immediately. You need furniture? Stack boards and milk crates, or visit the local thrift or secondhand shops. You need office supplies? Buy them as needed for specific projects until you can justify maintaining an inventory. If you go out and buy a filing cabinet, file folders, stapler, printer, paper, letterhead, business cards, answering machine, tape dispenser, paper clips, matching envelopes, et cetera, ad nauseam, you will be tying up hundreds of dollars before you even have a client. You don't need to instantly recreate the office environment you chose to leave!

DON'T WASTE, BUT DON'T SKIMP

Your computer should run well, with enough free memory and mass storage that you're not wasting animation time trying to coax an overtaxed machine. If there are software tools that will honestly make you more productive, find a way to finance them as reasonably as possible. Some tools are valuable enough that you can make a good business case for charging them to your credit card—but it takes a pretty big return to justify investment at a 17 percent interest rate!

Your computer and primary software package will probably be your largest start-up costs. If your cash flow is very tight, you should consider leasing your computer. If you add up all the lease payments, this probably seems very expensive. Look at it another way: Instead of having several thousand dollars tied up in a piece of equipment, you pay a few hundred dollars per month for the same capability while using that big chunk of money as working capital. This might enable you to (for instance) rent a broadcast-quality VTR to do your video transfers, where you might otherwise have had to work with prosumer- or consumer-grade hardware. For a really big rendering job, you can contract with a render farm to get faster turnaround. Both these options mean you can charge more for the job with a smaller investment. Leasing isn't completely risk free. You should make sure there's an escape clause that enables you to get out of the lease if your business doesn't fly, and don't neglect insurance on the equipment.

When you start calculating cost/benefit ratios and getting quotes on equipment and services, you should consider how you want to make the transition from your current job to running your own business. If you have an inexpensive home workspace, you aren't risking much. You can experiment, working evenings and weekends as an animator while maintaining your day job. You can keep track of your expenses, and, when the animation is bringing in enough to pay your bills, you can drop the day job and animate full time. If the animation never does bring in enough to support you, you've still got the day job, and you haven't wasted a lot of time and money in setting up a home office. On the other hand, if you sink your savings into a lease on commercial office space and buy new furniture and the latest top-of-the-line animation workstations, a failing business could push you into bankruptcy. This is why you should start a business on your own, financially. Don't borrow, don't go looking for venture capital, and don't take on well-heeled silent partners. One of the worst mistakes you can make is being in debt to people who don't understand the animation business. Borrowing puts you in the hole from the first minute. Interest starts accruing before you even have clients. Venture capitalists aren't in business to sponsor the development of great animation—they're in it to make money as quickly as possible. If you don't produce, they will have no compunction about auctioning off your assets and suing you for their losses. Silent partners are rarely either silent or truly partners. Sooner or later, they will stick their noses into the business, and you will then find out that the people who kick in the cash expect to dictate how the business is run.

Your number one asset is your talent as an animator. No amount of cash can compensate for a lack of talent, but talent can demand lots and lots of cash, if you handle it right. You are the only person who should be in control of your business.

Pricing

Once you've decided to take the plunge and animate full time, it's even more important to have a clear financial picture of your business. The longer you've been part-time animating, the better your baseline of financial records. You need to add up all your fixed expenses: rent, leases, service contracts, utilities, telephone, finance charges, insurance, the whole nine yards. This is your overhead, the amount you have to bring in just to keep breathing. Add on what you need to match the discretionary income you are used to or want to get used to. Don't delude yourself into believing a.) you can live like a king, with clients paying the bills, or b.) you can live really cheap, to keep your expenses low. Be as realistic as possible, and don't forget to include whatever you've been contributing to your savings or retirement plan. Increase this figure by your new withholding rate, including Social Security, income taxes, and all the other fun stuff you'd rather not have to pay. This total is your *nut*, what you need to collect from clients in order to break even and maintain your standard of living.

The production expenses go on top of this and are based on what the job actually requires in addition to your overhead. Extra equipment rental, blank media, subcontracted services, couriers, insurance riders—all the stuff that you've been learning about while you've been part-timing. These figures are going to be different for every job you do and are the ones most likely to change during a project, due to client decisions or unforeseen problems.

Now that you know what you need to charge for your work, you have to decide how to bill it to your clients. My personal preference is to quote an hourly rate only for very small jobs, a daily rate for projects taking up to two weeks, and my lowest rate for projects over two weeks. For the shorter projects, I pad out my time to compensate for the sales and client setup time, which seem to be nearly the same for tiny jobs as it is for big ones. Remember that every minute you spend meeting with, traveling to, or telephoning your client is also part of your working time. If you can't get away with billing every minute of that time directly, you need to find some way to cover it in the project's overhead or you'll be losing money.

BUSINESS IS BUSINESS

For details on invoices, collections, taxes, and accounting practices, I highly recommend Bernard B. Kamoroff's *Small Time Operator*. In my opinion, it's the best single source on the administration of small businesses, just as Hawken is best on small-business philosophy.

Even if you are just starting out as an animator, resist the temptation to do work "on spec" or for free, just to build up your demo reel or reputation. If the potential client is a nonprofit organization, insist on some sort of compensation, whether it's free tickets or other services, access to equipment, or a tax-deductible receipt for services rendered (calculated at your full rates, of course). If the client is a for-profit, insist on either a cut of the gross, a barter for services or product, or a contract for your standard rates. Any other arrangement will most likely add your name to the long list of animators who have been ripped off by unscrupulous or inexperienced clients. If you really need the advertising, I suggest you do a *pro bono* PSA (public service announcement) for a local nonprofit or charity that will arrange to give it a lot of airtime. This work goes under the accounting category of promotional business expense, so you at least earn a nice tax deduction.

Insurance

Working for yourself is enough of a risk, you don't need to raise the stakes by neglecting to insure yourself against problems that are beyond your control. You should maintain insurance on yourself, your family, and possessions as if you were still working for someone else. Most homeowners or renters insurance will not cover the replacement costs of computers adequate for professional character animation, so you should consider additional insurance appropriate to your business. Ask your current insurance agent if you can add a computer rider to your current policies. You may be able to get a better deal than with a completely separate policy.

Take a careful look at your assets. Your computer(s), software, reference books, videos, and AV and office equipment are important to your business. If you lose them to theft or disaster, you need to replace most of them before you can continue generating income. One approach is to insure everything for replacement value and keep an updated list of your business assets on file with your insurance agent. You might also consider operational insurance that will pay for emergency leases on critical equipment until you can purchase your own replacements. The cheapest computer insurance is a regular set of system backups, stored offsite so you can get your new or repaired system up and running as quickly as possible.

Don't neglect insurance on yourself in addition to the standard life, health, and disability. If your business depends on your talents and performance, you may want to consider key man insurance sufficient to keep your business going if you are ever laid up and unable to perform. You should maintain a baseline of insurance on yourself and your business assets from the start. Figure the insurance premiums into your overhead, because they don't change according to the amount of income the business brings in. There are other forms of insurance that you should research and price before you actually need them. If a particular project is going to require you to purchase additional insurance, you need to include those charges in calculating your bid.

If you are doing film or television work, you should consult an insurance broker or agency that specializes in production insurance. They will be familiar with your needs and will be able to point out contingencies and risks you might not think of. They will also be able to quote reasonable rates. An ordinary small-business insurance agent might respond to your list of expensive electronics with a disproportionately high premium. If a production requires you to lease equipment in addition to your usual layout, you should get riders or additional policies to cover them from the time you take delivery to the time you return them. If you rent rather than buy a piece of equipment, odds are that it will be too expensive for you to replace easily!

If your product is going to be shown in public, you should consider Errors and Omissions (E&O) insurance. This covers you against libel, slander, and copyright or trademark infringement. It doesn't give you permission to infringe on people, but it does protect you against honest mistakes. If you have employees, make sure they're covered in the policy, too. Getting E&O insurance usually means having a good entertainment attorney help you fill out the forms, so the expense includes the policy's premium plus your attorney's fees.

If you are making the leap to film or high-end video production, you may want to insure negatives, master tapes, or other original elements. You may also want insurance against flawed equipment, processing, or media. Remember the disclaimers on videotapes? If a bad tape drops out in the middle of your final delivery, the manufacturer won't do anything more than hand you a new blank tape. If a deadline, payment, or original element is at risk, always keep duplicates, but buy the insurance too.

If the amount of work requires you to hire independent subcontractors or employees, you'll have a lot of insurance regulations to comply with. Depending on where you work, you may have to pay for state disability benefits, Workman's Compensation, Social Security, and so forth. One more reason to think long and hard before hiring employees!

Advertising

If you're working freelance or subcontracting, get yourself a good agent. An agent only makes money if you do, and a good one will get you far more than you could negotiate for yourself. Agents also network for you, keeping track of where the work is and who's doing what—an invaluable resource when you are hired project-by-project. If you are a consultant, you're probably going to be doing your own networking, although having an agent might not hurt.

If you're running your own studio, you need to get your name and services in front of the people who write the checks. My own experience has been that word-of-mouth advertising has the best return on investment. This doesn't mean sitting in your office and waiting for friends to throw you work. It means making sure all your friends, acquaintances, colleagues, and clients have current copies of your demo reel, business card, brag sheet, and schedule of services. Take your best contacts out to lunch now and then (networking, remember?), and let them know you'll appreciate any business they can throw your way. This is also crucial to planning for growth. You need to stay in touch with people who can supply you with labor, expertise, and equipment when you get a large or rush job that's beyond your capacities. If you've got a solid network of colleagues, you can put together a larger production team much more rapidly and with a better chance of success.

If you really feel you must advertise conventionally, do try to keep your expenses down, and target your ads to the market you're trying to reach. Direct mail, ads in industry newsletters, and bartered services for advertising (especially for local-access cable TV or your neighborhood movie theater) are low-budget strategies that have a good chance of paying off.

Protecting Yourself

It's a sad fact that just about everyone in this industry has a horror story about a client or employer who exploited them. This doesn't mean there are a lot of dishonest clients out there. The real villains are few and far between, and they quickly develop reputations in the industry.

You can avoid them by using your network of colleagues to do your own background check. A more common problem is the client who doesn't understand the business, gets in over their head, then decides that stiffing the animator is a viable solution to their problem. It's up to you to protect yourself from this kind of unpremeditated rip-off.

Disclaimer: I'm not an attorney, and nothing in this book constitutes legal advice. This information is based on my personal experience and that of the animators I have interviewed. Every situation is different, and, while I believe these tips can be useful, you should definitely consult your own attorney before agreeing to do anything for a client!

Dealing With Clients

Ah, clients. Where would animators be without clients? Broke and unemployed, but probably less stressed.

The client/animator relationship is a simple one. They have money, which you need. You can create animation, which they want. Try not to lose sight of this basic fact, especially when a difficult client's headgames cloud the issue.

The best way to deal with client problems is to prevent them from occurring. Make sure you have a good contract that spells out all the details. Nothing is impossible, just expensive. If the client is willing to pay for it, you should be willing to do it. If a particular piece of work is going to be unpleasant, quote them a high price and long delivery schedule. If they're willing to pay your asking price, at least you'll be compensated well for work you don't enjoy.

If an approval deadline is approaching and you have not heard from the client, call them. Stay in touch. More client delays are due to oversight than intentional stonewalling or indecision. Make sure the client knows the deadline is coming up, and that you are ready to go. When your own deadlines are looming, don't talk to the client. Filter your incoming calls with an answering machine, and reply to the client's answering machine after-hours, when you won't have to speak to them directly. Every time you interact with the client, they see it as an opportunity to make changes. Even if you convince them not to make changes, those negotiations are coming out of your production time. Stick to the approvals spelled out in your contract, and don't let the client micromanage you.

When you are presenting materials for approval, make sure there is one obvious glitch to fix. Clients are like editors; they need to feel useful. Don't bring other problems to their attention; just fix them. Pointing out a problem to a client can get them started on a whole chain of revisions. Anticipate changes you think the client will request, but if you finish them ahead of time, hold the changes in reserve. In fact, you should always hold work in reserve. If you finish work ahead of schedule, don't try to deliver it. The client will just ask for more changes, right up to the original deadline. Deliver work exactly when it is due, no sooner and no later.

Dealing with a client when a problem occurs is the acid test of your diplomacy skills. Even the best clients can be difficult, just because they don't understand your business or your problems. If the client is reasonable, your best approach is to explain the problem—and your proposed solution—in plain English and with just enough detail to get your point across. If the client is unreasonable, your only defense is your contract.

Remember, they have money, which you need. You can create animation, which they want. If they are difficult, pad the bid on the next job enough to pay for the aggravation. If a client becomes more trouble than they are willing to pay for, just politely turn down the job.

Contracts

A contract is simply an agreement between people to do things for each other. You agree to give me a videotape with a certain animation on it, and I agree to give you a certain amount of money. That's the principle, anyway. Contracts get complicated when the job, your risks, or the client's wishes get complicated. But complex or simple, you need to understand and stick with the essentials of contracts.

GET IT IN WRITING

A good contract should be all or nothing: if you aren't willing to put everything in writing, you shouldn't have a contract at all.

A good contract must spell out the precise terms of the entire relationship between the people involved. Leaving anything out or relying on verbal agreements, handshakes, or memoranda is just begging for trouble. If a negotiating point is important enough for the client or you to agree to it, it's important enough to write into the contract. If changes in the relationship require changes to the contract, you should amend it in writing, too. There is standard language for contracts that spells out exactly how you can make agreed-on changes, ranging from initialed handwritten notes on the original contract to the renegotiation and redrafting of the whole thing.

I have signed contracts with people who would rather have seen me arrested and jailed. We were able to build all our expectations into the contracts in sufficient detail that, despite extreme personal differences, we were able to deal with each other in a businesslike way so that each of us gave and received a fair deal. The product was delivered on time and within budget, and I got paid in full, with no lawsuits, threats, or unpleasantness. Contracts are a good thing!

FAMILY BUSINESS IS STILL BUSINESS

A contract is even more important when you are doing business with family or friends. Spelling out all the details ahead of time can save you major headaches, loss of friendship, and even broken families. If you find out during negotiation that the other parties can't or won't agree to terms you find necessary, it's better to call off the deal right then, with no hard feelings and no losses on either side. Once you have a contract, you've got to stick with it, or you risk losing your business.

So, what should a good animation contract include? The first items are the ground rules for the contract: who the parties are, what the purpose of the contract is, how the contract can be modified, and under what laws the contract will be enforced (usually the state or country where you live). This is all standard legal stuff.

The next critical item is the escape clause. This is an explicit description of how each party can cancel the contract without getting sued. You need one of these to protect yourself in case you get sick or otherwise can't complete the project or the client becomes completely unreasonable. The client needs this clause in case the project becomes unnecessary, their business changes, or you become completely unreasonable. In either case, you need a set of rules that determines when the contract can be canceled, how each party notifies the other about cancellation, whether or how much you get paid for work already performed, and what completed work, if any, you turn over to the client. A worst-case starting point is for you to keep all your work, return any money the client has paid you, and call it even. It's up to you and your attorney to negotiate better terms, like guarantees of payment for out-of-pocket expenses and work already completed.

Next is the description of the work you will perform, usually described in terms of deliverables. This can include videotapes, film, prints, data files, or just about any other tangible media. The more specific the description, the better for you. If the contract reads "videotape," and you budget for a VHS master but the client insists that you deliver on BetacamSP, you'll probably end up eating the bill for the more expensive master. You need to be very specific about working files, too. It's in your interest to deliver only the finished product and to retain all working files. This way, if the client wants to reuse any of the characters or setups, they have to contract with you. If the client won't agree to let you keep the working files, charge extra for the buyout (see the "Intellectual Property" section, later in this chapter). Deliverables can come from the client, too. If you need their logo, stock footage, or other proprietary data, the client has to provide it before you can get started. Again, be very specific. If all you have is a CD-ROM drive, that 9-track tape they hand you can blow your budget.

Compensation is another set of clauses you to need scrutinize closely. You should never start a job for less than 25 percent of the total, and, if you'll have extra expenses, you should get that money up front. It's common to get 50 percent up front, 25 percent at the halfway point, and the final 25 percent on delivery. Here's an important safety tip: Never hand over the final tape, print, or film until you have payment in hand. If the client insists on seeing the final product before paying you, give them an approval tape with SMPTE timecode across the bottom. They'll be able to see the whole piece, they just can't broadcast it. When they pay you, give them the tape without the timecode.

Do You Like Getting Paid?

Never hand over the final deliverable until you have payment in hand.

That brings up the subject of schedules. Most clients will be insistent that the final deliverable be in their hands by a particular date and time. They will be much less concerned about providing you with the data or approvals you need. It's up to you to make a contract that will keep everybody on schedule or compensate you when the client ignores it. The first item should be your start date. Make it a dependency—you agree to start work the day you receive all the client's promised deliverables. That puts the ball in their court. If they delay the project, it's not your fault. In fact, you should consider making every date in the schedule a dependency. Your deadlines should be something like "20 business days following receipt of approved storyboards," rather than "no later than February 12." This encourages the client to keep track of the project, and can dramatically reduce your stress levels. If waiting for the client may cost you money (loss of other opportunities, storage fees, rentals, and so forth), include a schedule of additional charges to make up your losses. Time is money, after all. And turnabout is fair play. Expect the client to insist on late delivery penalties ranging from progressive forfeiture of your fee to a whopping payment to them if you make them miss a TV advertising slot. Don't sign anything that could wipe out your business, unless you really enjoy high-stakes gambling.

The potentially stickiest part of the contract is the schedule of approvals. It's rare for a client to simply tell you what they want, hand you the money, and accept what you deliver. Most clients will want to see work in progress, and all of them will want to make changes. To save time, money, and sanity all around, all parties should agree on these approvals and schedule them in the contract, then stick to them. Typical approvals for character animation include story, storyboards, character design, rough animation tests, test renderings, and final animation, not necessarily in that order. You must get the client to sign off on each of these deliverables before you do any more work. If you're halfway through animation and they want to change the character design, you've just wasted a lot of effort. If you suspect (or know, from prior experience) that a client will drag their feet on approvals, add on "held work" fees that are high enough to compensate you for your waiting time. If a client wants to make changes after approvals, your contract should spell out exactly what fees must be paid for you to do the work over. You won't be able to tell the client they can't make changes, so you have to make it in their own financial interest to keep their vacillation to a minimum.

Intellectual Property

Intellectual property is a legal category that includes copyrights, patents, and trademarks. If you are creating anything, you will be dealing with at least one of these critters. Unless you invent a new process or gadget, you won't be concerned with patents. Most commonly, you will be dealing with the copyrights for the animations you produce. If you create original characters or work with clients' properties, you'll also need to understand trademarks.

"So what?" you say, "I just want to get paid for my animations." Sure, you can say that. And you can spend your declining years watching reruns of your best work, eating your heart out because you'll never see another dime while the copyright owners are raking in the money. Intellectual property is big money, and, as a character animator, you are one of the people who creates it in the first place. If you're smart, you'll do your best to hold on to as many intellectual property rights as you can.

Copyrights are used for artistic, literary, dramatic, or musical works. In theory, you could have five distinct types of copyrights in a particular animated film: the character design, the script, the complete film, the musical score and the recorded soundtrack. You, as the creator, have secured copyright protection the moment you record a work in a fixed form. That includes drawings, renderings, videotape, film—you get the idea. It's not necessary for you to register a work for you to have copyright protection, but registration does beef up the protection a bit. Secured copyright gives you the exclusive right to display or perform the work or to reproduce and distribute copies to the public. Nobody else can do this, legally, without your permission. Like patents, a copyright is a license to sue rather than a guarantee of compliance.

To register a copyright, you must first get a copy of the appropriate forms from the Register of Copyrights in Washington, D.C. Each type of copyrightable work has a different forms; make sure you get the right one. The forms are very simple, mostly your contact information and a description of the work. When you've completed the forms, you send the forms, copies of the work (not your only original!), and a filing fee (usually $20) to the copyright office. You don't have to register right away, but, like most forms of legal protection, it's a good idea. After a few months, you'll receive official notice that your copyright has been registered.

Whenever you create a new work, you should immediately tag it with the standard copyright notice, e.g.: Copyright © 1997 Douglas A. Kelly. Displaying this notice doesn't make any legal difference, but it might persuade the more timid plagiarists to steal elsewhere. One odd bit for the notice: if you are copyrighting a revised work, the date should be hyphenated to include both first and most recent copyright dates, e.g., Copyright © 1994-1997 Douglas A. Kelly would be appropriate for a book published in 1997 that included material I first copyrighted in 1994. This is for tracking the expiration of copyright, which is measured from the earlier date. Something you create yourself is copyright for your lifetime plus 50 years. Something you hire or contract for, and for which you buy out the copyright of the creator, is good for 75 years.

If you are creating copyrightable works as an employee or under a work-for-hire contract, your employer retains the copyright. If you are an independent contractor, you retain copyright unless your contract specifically states otherwise. Don't just give this away, for goodwill or any other purpose. The copyrights and trademarks in a marketable character design can be worth far more than you ever made from the original animation. If your client insists on retaining the copyrights, make sure they pay you extra for it. You might also consider negotiating a licensing or royalty arrangement, where if the characters generate income over a certain amount, you get a percentage. This is a very reasonable approach. If the character doesn't make any money, the client doesn't owe you anything more, but, if the character is very profitable, you get cut in on the deal. In this as in most contract negotiations, make sure you've got an attorney who will negotiate the best deal for you.

If a client tries to grab your copyrights without paying extra, you have a number of big sticks you can wave. A registered copyright permits you to file a federal copyright infringement suit, which would be very expensive for your client to fight. Second, if they've been accounting for you as an independent contractor and now they claim you're an employee (so they can keep your copyrights), they may be in big trouble with the IRS for evading employer taxes.

Choosing An Attorney

Yes, you need an attorney. Starting your own animation business without a lawyer is like walking around the Old West without a six-gun—you are just begging to be robbed. *Never* sign a contract without having qualified legal counsel review it, especially if you want to remain on good terms with the other parties to the agreement. A good attorney will draft a contract in which everything is spelled out as clearly as possible. Cobbling something together on your own or, worse yet, blindly signing something the other party drafted, is a recipe for disaster. A bad contract can literally cripple your business, stop your career, and generally ruin your life. A good contract can save you from even the worst run of bad luck or broken promises. I usually draft my own contracts, but I still run them past my attorney and cheerfully pay his fee. It's the cheapest form of business insurance you'll ever buy.

Just as you wouldn't choose a dermatologist to treat a brain tumor, don't go to the family lawyer when you need an entertainment law specialist. Family law, or even standard business practice, is a far cry from what you'll be doing. Furthermore, make sure the entertainment attorney knows the specifics of animation contracts and has successfully represented animation clients. This is a highly specialized niche of the entertainment industry, and there are issues common to animation that rarely crop up in other parts of the industry. I've seen a contractor's attorney actually revise a production subcontract in my favor, just because he didn't know the business well enough to look out for his client's interests.

Word of mouth is probably your best bet at locating a competent animation attorney. Even if you search through bar association listings or consult animation union representatives, you will finally be relying on personal recommendations to narrow down your search. This is another area where your professional networking will pay off. The wider your circle of colleagues, the more opinions and experience you will be able to draw on in selecting an attorney.

Once you have a name, call for an appointment to discuss your needs. Make sure the initial meeting is free. You should never retain an attorney or agree to pay any kind of fee without that first face-to-face meeting. I've been burned on this point, myself. I once paid an up-front fee to an attorney and was thereafter foisted off on a series of assistants and never saw the attorney again. Needless to say, I changed representation almost immediately, but my fee was gone.

In hindsight, I could have saved that fee by doing a little basic research and asking a few pertinent questions. Where did he go to law school? What's his specialty, and how long has he been practicing it? How many other clients does he have? (That's an important one; if he has hundreds, it's a bucket shop and you'll be lucky just to get your calls returned.) Can you have a few client's names as references? After your meeting, call these references and ask their opinion of the attorney. Does the attorney return phone calls promptly? Does he answer questions understandably, or give you the brush-off? Have the contracts been well-written? Has the attorney been conscientious in preventing trouble before it happens? When trouble does happen, has his in-court representation been successful?

The factual, professional part of the meeting is only half the issue. You should also find out if you and the attorney will be able to trust each other and work together. One of the worst mistakes you can make in any business is to hide something from your attorney, and one of the most unpleasant things that can happen is to be stuck with untrustworthy or offensive counsel during a difficult legal process. The best lawyer in the business is useless if you can't share critical information with him. Unfortunately, an attorney will rarely give away the fact that he is unreliable or obnoxious in the first meeting. You'll just have to go with your instincts. If you feel something is not right, trust that feeling, and seek counsel elsewhere.

When you are satisfied with an attorney's credentials and personality, you can secure his services by signing a retainer agreement. This can be a straight fee-for-services contract, a percentage of your net income, or a combination of the two. You can find out more about comparable fee schedules and percentage arrangements by contacting your state's bar association. If you don't have many contracts to review or draft, the flat rate is probably best. If the number of contracts picks up, you may find it more cost-effective to cut your attorney in for a share of the net in exchange for as-needed legal counsel.

Legal Self-Care

Retaining a good animation attorney is no excuse to ignore the legal aspects of your business. The more you know, the safer you are. At the least, you'll be better able to judge when to call your lawyer.

There are a number of resources specifically designed for the legal needs of the small business operator. One of the best is Nolo Press, an organization dedicated to legal self-help books for individuals and small organizations. If you have access to the Internet, I highly recommend Nolo's Web site at **www.nolo.com/index.html**.

Another source of excellent free advice and lots of links to pertinent books is Nolo's Small Business index **www.nolopress.com/ChunkSB/SB.index.html**.

These books are well-written, thorough, and easy to read. Most of them include tear-out forms for the most common business needs. It has been my experience that if you read the appropriate Nolo Press books, you'll be almost as well-prepared as your attorney.

When It Isn't Fun Anymore

Most small business owners will reach a point when they question getting into the business. It's perfectly natural. It's just that you've been working too hard for too long. Take a break! Pace yourself. It's good to work hard, but you also need to take full days away from work on a regular basis. Between jobs, right after sending a deliverable to a client, when you've hit a creative block—whenever the "fresh" mind will do you the most good.

If you are dissatisfied with your career choice over a longer period of time, perhaps it's the work you're doing. If it's just a succession of jobs for clients, it can be very difficult to sustain your enthusiasm. Think about developing your own content, working on your own short film, or otherwise having a purely personal creative project. Some of the best studios in the business do this for their employees, encouraging them to experiment, learn, and recharge their creative batteries between commercial projects. The results may not be commercially viable, but you can always submit them to the screening rooms at SIGGRAPH or the animation festivals. If nothing else, it's a rewarding hobby that also provides a nice tax deduction.

Moving On

This chapter provides a quick overview to some of the most critical issues facing the independent character animator. I hope some of this advice will save you the painful lessons others have learned the hard way and make your own business ventures that much easier. I also hope you will find encouragement here, and go out and build your own career. Good luck!

PART VIII

APPENDIXES

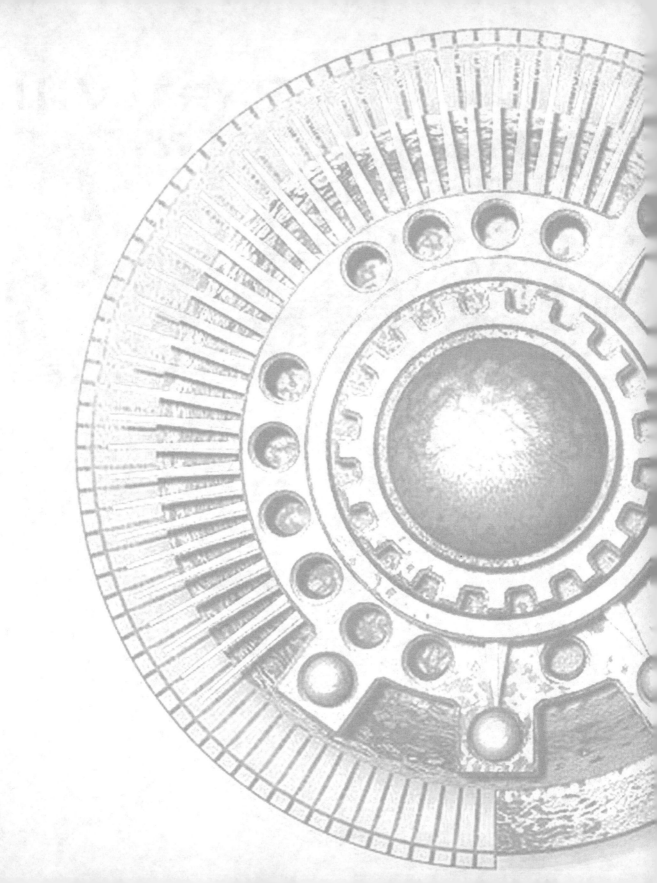

GLOSSARY

16mm—a smaller film size for educational and film festival use.

3:2 pulldown—a process to convert 24 fps film footage to 30 fps for television.

35mm—the standard film size for motion pictures in wide release.

Academy field ratio—a standardized ratio for the film frame. Created in 1930, it began at 1:1.33 (height versus width), and currently stands at 1:1.85.

Academy leader—a length of film appended at the beginning of a reel to assist the projectionist in framing and focusing.

acceleration—increase in velocity.

action—any visible change in a scene; movement, rotation, size, or deformation of an object.

action axis—see *line of action*.

algorithm—a procedure or set of rules for solving a problem. An algorithm is implemented by a programmer to create software.

aliasing—the stairstep pattern seen along the edge of a curve or diagonal border when presented in a raster display, as in a computer monitor or print. See *antialiasing*.

alpha (software)—the first draft of a computer program, before the faults have been corrected.

alpha channel—a grayscale or black-and-white rendering of a scene, used as a matte in compositing.

altitude—rotation on the X, or left-to-right horizontal axis. In most 3D software, it's the Pitch rotation.

animation—any technique which makes inanimate objects move on the screen.

animation cycle—see *cycle, motion*.

animation hierarchy—the sequence of levels, from root to outer extremities, followed to efficiently animate a complex character. See Chapter 12 for examples.

animator—the person who sets the frame-by-frame timing and posing of the objects in a scene.

antialiasing—a technique for blending color values near an aliased border to visually smooth it out for raster display. In most 3D software, this requires rendering multiple passes and blending aliased areas.

anticipation—a brief action in the opposite direction, preceding and foreshadowing the main action.

aperture (lens aperture)—in cinematography, the size of the lens opening divided by the focal length, expressed as an f-stop, e.g., f/8, f/11.

arc—see *slalom*.

armature—an internal skeleton designed to support and hold the pose of the outer material of a stop-motion puppet.

aspect ratio—the ratio of width to the height of a film frame. In CGI, it also refers to the ratio of the resolution and takes into account the aspect ratio of the individual pixels.

AVI—Audio Video Interleaved, a playback compression format designed for the Microsoft Windows operating systems.

azimuth—rotation on the vertical or Z axis. In most 3D software, the Heading rotation.

back light—see *rim light*.

back projection—in cinematography, projecting footage onto a screen placed behind the action as a means of compositing in the camera.

background—an image or sequence rendered behind all the objects in a scene.

backplane—an object sized and positioned to act as a background.

ball and socket joint—a rotational joint having three degrees of freedom. The human hip is a ball and socket joint with limited range of movement.

ballistics—the branch of mathematics describing the behavior of falling bodies.

banding—borders between areas of similar color or brightness, visible because the image does not contain enough colors to shade the border more smoothly. *Dithering* can make banding less noticeable.

bank—rotation on the front-to-back horizontal axis.

bar sheet—diagrams similar to sheet music, used to set the broad timing for long sequences of animation.

beta (software)—the next generation of software after alpha, ideally with fewer faults but not yet ready for public release.

beta tester—an optimist who believes he or she can do production work with faulty software. One who tests beta software.

Betacam—a family of VTR formats developed by Sony.

BG—in cinematography, abbreviation for background.

bit—the smallest unit of information processed by a digital computer, a 1 or 0. Bits are grouped into *bytes*.

blocking—in stage or cinema direction, setting marks or positions for actors in a scene.

bluescreen—see *chroma key*.

bouncing ball—basic animation exercise demonstrating timing, squash, and stretch.

breakdown drawings—see *inbetweens*.

bug—an error in computer software that produces an unintended result, a.k.a. *fault*.

byte—a group or word of bits, a unit of digital data. Computer file sizes are usually measured in thousands (Kb) or millions (Mb) of bytes.

CAD—Computer Aided Design; the use of computers and graphics software to design products, partially automating traditional drafting and engineering tasks.

camera—a machine designed to expose photosensitive film to a focused image for a controlled period of time, to create an image on the film. In cinematography, a machine to perform this operation repeatedly for successive frames to create a motion picture. In most 3D software, the point from which the scene is rendered, emulating a physical camera.

camera animation—animation performed exclusively with the camera, as pans, dollys, zooms, or other changes, while photographing a scene or image with no other action.

camera back—the part of the camera that holds the film. Motion picture and film recorder camera backs can hold many feet of film.

camera body—the main part of the camera between the back and the lens, containing the shutter and film transport. Film recorder and stop-motion camera bodies have very accurate pin registration for the film sprocket holes, to ensure that each image is recorded in precisely the same position.

camera shake—see *zip pan*.

cameraless animation—animation that is drawn or etched directly on film stock.

caricature—exaggeration of the peculiarities or unique attributes of a person or thing. In character animation, the exaggeration of the essentials of a motion to create unrealistic but truthful action.

cel—acetate sheets used in cel animation.

cel animation—animation drawn or painted on transparent acetate sheets, and layered with foreground and background cels or images. Named after the celluloid sheets used in the early development of the technique.

center of gravity—abbreviated CG, the center of an object's balance.

CG—see *center of gravity*.

CGI—Computer Generated Imagery, any graphic image created with the assistance of a computer.

character—in CGI, an object which displays volition and personality in a scene.

character animation—in CGI, the process of timing and posing a character object to create the illusion of life.

character model—in CGI, an object or collection of objects to be animated as a character.

charts—in traditional animation, graphic notes or diagrams to show the timing for *inbetweens* or camera motion. In most 3D software, splines, fcurves or motion graphs.

cheating—repositioning objects between shots to improve a composition without tipping off the audience that the scene has been changed.

chroma key—keying a composite layer by color, typically blue or green. See also *bluescreen*.

clay animation—stop-motion cinematography of clay or other plastic material that is manually deformed by the animators for each pose. Clay can be used alone or supported by an armature.

clean plate—a live-action shot with no actors in it, to be used in compositing CGI effects.

cleanup—adding changes to a storyboard that has gone through its first round of revisions.

climax—in drama, the most important *crisis* in the story.

close-up—literally, a shot of the subject face alone. Generally, considered to be any close shot.

code—part of a program as written by a programmer. "Fixing that *fault* only took a few lines of code."

collision detection—an algorithm used in some CGI software to detect when one object intersects another. Can be used to automate animation tasks such as bouncing balls.

color depth—the number of bits used to store color information for each pixel in an image. 1-bit is black and white, 8-bit can be color or grayscale having 256 different values, and 24-bit has 8-bit values for red, green and blue, approximating the color depth of a television screen.

color key—see *chroma key*.

commercial—a brief advertisement, generally intended for television. Typically 15, 30, or 60 seconds in length. Also known as a *spot* or *ad*.

compression—removing redundant information from a data file to make it smaller, often used for storing or playing back images and animations. Different algorithms and software have different definitions of "redundant."

computer—a machine capable of running a program to produce the intended result. A machine that can't run a program correctly is sometimes referred to as a boat anchor, e.g., "Your 286 is a boat anchor as far as LightWave is concerned."

computer animation—animation timed and posed by a human and *inbetweened* and rendered by a computer. If a non-animator is ignorant enough to say something like, "The computer does all the work," the nearest animator is entitled to whup them upside the head with a blunt instrument.

computer graphics—see CGI.

conflict—in drama, the collision between character and circumstance that drives the story.

constraint—an object or null in a setup that controls or influences the movement or position of another object or null.

coordinates—in geometry and CGI, a set of numbers that describes a location from the origin of the local system. In most 3D software, XYZ coordinates are used to describe the location of an object in world coordinates, and the location of each point in an object's local coordinates.

coverage—additional camera angles and setups rendered to give the editor more leeway in assembling the final cut. Almost never used in traditional animation, and rarely used in CGI animation.

crane—vertical movement of the camera, a.k.a. *boom*.

crawl—very slow camera move intended to build tension. a.k.a. *creep*.

creeping titles—a.k.a. *scrolling titles*. Titles that move across the screen, typically from bottom to top, making it easier for the audience to read credits that are displayed briefly.

crisis—in drama, a decision point where a character's actions determine the direction of the story.

crossing the line—shifting the camera to the opposite side of the line of action, which can confuse the audience if not handled carefully.

CRT—acronym for cathode ray tube, a common type of computer or video display.

CU—in cinematography, close up. See also *close shot*.

cut—the act of moving from one shot to another through the editing process.

cutting height—in cinematography, the height where the bottom of the frame intersects the actor(s).

cutting on the action—changing from one camera position to the next during the character's action. This relieves the *visual jar*, because the audience focuses its attention on the action, not the shot composition.

cycle—see *motion cycle*.

default scene—a 3D default scene contains a single character with all its associated textures, bones, hierarchies, constraints, plug-ins, and lights set up and ready to animate.

delta—a change in color or luminance values for each pixel from one frame of an animation to the next. Large deltas make animations more difficult to compress for direct computer playback.

depth of field—the area in which objects are in focus. See Chapter 14 for exercises demonstrating depth of field.

dialogue—any soundtrack, script, or storyboard incorporating an actor's vocal performance.

digitizer—a device, often a computer peripheral, for converting analog signals to digital data. In CGI, typical source materials are 3D models, film or video footage, or still images.

direct to video—a growing market segment of videotape sales and rentals of films that have never been theatrically released. A potential opportunity for independent animators.

director—the person who oversees the big picture of the production, and who generally has final creative control over the look, story, timing, and editing of an animated film.

displacement—a class of animation techniques based on posing or deformation of a single object. Contrast with *replacement*.

display buffer—a section of RAM that contains the current image.

dissolve—a special effect shot transition where the first shot gradually fades out and is replaced by the second shot fading in. See *wipe*.

dither—scattering pixels of one value over the border into an area of a different value, to visually blend the two areas together. See *banding*.

dolly—camera move as if on a *dolly*, truck, or other horizontally mobile platform, a.k.a. *track*, *truck*.

dope sheet—see *exposure sheet*.

double-bounce walk—see *walks*.

double-take—see *takes*.

drawn-on-film—see *cameraless animation*.

dubbing—the process of correcting mistakes in dialogue or soundtrack by rerecording . In animation, the process of adding sound to the silent animation.

dynamic balance—constantly hanging but balanced equilibrium between mass, inertia, and energy in a character. If the combination of mass, inertia, and energy in the lower body is equal to the mass, inertia, and energy in the upper body, the body as a whole is in dynamic balance.

dynamics—the motions that connect each key pose. Different parts move at different rates, accelerating and decelerating in a complex balancing act.

ease-in—gradual acceleration from the preceding hold or beginning of an action to the snap, the fastest part.

ease-out—gradual deceleration from the snap to the end of the action.

ECU—in cinematography, extreme close up.

edge—a line connecting two points, the boundary between one polygon and the next.

editor, film editor—the person who assembles shots in sequence and synchronizes the soundtrack(s) according to the director's instructions.

effects—see *special effects*.

effects animation—animation created to mimic phenomena such as fire, smoke, clouds, rain, or anything else that moves but is not a character or *prop*.

effects track—a soundtrack containing sound effects, rather than music or dialog.

elevation—a side or front view of a set design.

ELS—in cinematography, extreme long shot.

encoder—see *scan converter*.

ergonomics—design of objects to fit the user's shape and actions, to prevent injury, and to increase comfort and efficiency.

establishing shot—shows the audience the general environment in which the action will take place.

exposition—in drama, necessary background information communicated to the audience, usually by dialog, sometimes by a title sequence or insert shot, that would be difficult or impossible to convey by a character's actions.

exposure sheet—a form filled out by the animator with frame-by-frame information for character action, lip sync, backgrounds, and camera.

expression—short for "mathematical expression." Using one object or control to manipulate another object or control by way of an algorithm or set of rules.

extreme take—a gross distortion of a character to show surprise.

eye movements—animation of the eyes and eyelids, used to define the character and foreshadow actions.

eyelights—in cinematography, lights set up specifically to bring out a highlight spot in an actor's eyes.

fade—a *dissolve* to or from a solid color, usually black or white.

fade in—the process where an image gradually appears from a blackened screen by lightening up to scene.

fade out—the opposite of *fade in*.

fair use—the doctrine of copyright prevalent in the U.S., that a free duplicate of a copyrighted work may be made for personal educational use.

fairings—see *ease-in, ease-out*.

fault—an error in a computer program that produced unwanted or unintentional results. Less scrupulous developers may document the behavior of a fault and call it a feature.

fcurve—short for *function curve* or *spline*.

FG—in cinematography, foreground.

fill light—a light used to soften shadows and make hidden details visible without washing out the key light.

film grain—tiny imperfections in an image produced by the crystals in film emulsion.

film recorder—a system that uses a camera to record digital images from a high-resolution CRT or laser. For motion picture film, the camera must have a pin-register film transport.

flicker fusion—the visual phenomenon that blends a rapid series of still images into the illusion of continuous motion. The frame rate at which flicker fusion occurs varies widely, from as low as 15 fps to over 100 fps. See also *showscan*.

focal length—the length of a camera lens assembly, measured from the rear nodal point to the focal plane. After all, it's not the size of the lens, it's how you use it.

focal plane—a.k.a. *film plane*. The plane behind the camera lens where the image is in sharpest focus.

focus—the sharpness and clarity of an image.

focus pull—animating the depth of field to match the area of sharp focus to an object's movement.

foley—sound effects recording by professional noisemakers.

follow through—animation to mimic inertia during deceleration. A character coming to a rapid stop must overshoot the target slightly to show follow through.

foot slippage—unless the grounded foot is the root of the animation hierarchy, changes to a character's pose can cause the foot to slip forward or backward inconsistently with the character's overall motion. A forward slip is called skating, a backward slip is called moonwalking.

footage—in cinematography, exposed film from a camera, measured in feet.

fps—acronym for frames per second, the rate at which images are projected to create the illusion of motion in film, video, or other media. See also *frame rate*.

frame—in cinematography, the boundaries of the projected image.

frame rate—the speed at which separate images are viewed in a motion picture or other device for creating the illusion of motion. See also *sound speed, silent speed, flicker fusion, fps.*

frame-accurate—a VTR with a tape transport that can accurately record a single frame or field at a time. Used until recently to record animation to tape, now largely replace by digital recorders.

fricative—a class of *phonemes* including f and v.

front projection—projecting an image into a scene from the front, used to composite in the camera. Contrast with *rear projection.*

full animation—animating a complete character on ones or twos, the highest quality of *cel animation.* See *limited animation.*

function curve—long form of *fcurve.* A spline used to animate a function.

gag—a visual joke or humorous situation.

going ballistic—an uncontrolled emotional outburst. In animation, when a character leaves the ground in a ballistic trajectory or parabola.

good take—a live action shot or soundtrack recording good enough to be used.

graphics—see computer graphics.

hardware—computer equipment that you can see and touch, in contrast to software, which is intangible.

heading—see *azimuth.*

heel strike position—a character's pose in a walk cycle where the leading heel first contacts the ground. One of three key poses for a standard walk cycle. See also *squash position, passing position, motion cycle.*

held cel, hold cel—in cel animation, an image duplicated for a number of frames.

Hi-8—a consumer video format developed by Sony and popular for camcorders, providing higher image quality than 8mm or VHS.

hidden line removal—an algorithm that removes lines not visible to the camera from a wireframe rendering, producing a cleaner image.

hinge—the simplest rotational joint, having only one degree of freedom.

hit—a musical beat or sound effect used to synchronize the action.

hold—a pose or shot repeated over a number of frames.

hold, moving—a pose held by a character for a number of frames, animated to vary slightly to keep the character visually alive.

hookup—match the beginning and ending poses in a motion cycle so the cycle can be looped. See *loop, motion cycle*.

hot spot—specular highlight on an object's surface where a light source reflects directly into the camera's lens.

inbetweener—in traditional 2D animation, the junior or assistant animator who draws the *inbetweens*.

inbetweens—frames between key poses that show the smallest incremental changes.

index of refraction—a number representing how much a material bends or refracts the light passing through it.

inertia—the tendency of objects to keep doing what they've been doing.

ink and paint—the transfer of original drawings to ink on acetate sheets, and filling the outlined areas with the correct colors.

inking—the first step in *ink and paint*.

input—communicating information to a computer.

input devices—peripherals designed to make it easier to communicate information to a computer. Common examples include the mouse, keyboard, *pen and tablet*, scanner, and *digitizer*.

insert shot—a shot filmed or rendered separately from the master shot, usually a closeup for exposition or from a character's POV, and edited into the main shot.

inter-cut—shots edited together in a sequence.

inverse kinematics—usually abbreviated IK. A class of algorithms for determining the posing of a hierarchical chain by the positioning of the end links. Drag a finger, the arm follows along.

iris—the colored portion of the eye surrounding the pupil.

iris out—in cinematography, a transition in which a circular *matte* shrinks until the entire frame is obscured. *Iris in* is the reverse.

joystick—an input device usually relegated to games, but occasionally useful in CGI.

key animator—a.k.a. lead animator. The senior animator trusted with creating the *key poses*.

key drawings—in cel animation, drawings of the *key poses*.

key light—the primary light in a scene, providing most of the illumination.

key pose—one of the extreme positions of a character that defines an action.

key sounds—points in the soundtrack used to match the animation, e.g., footsteps.

keyframe animation—setting key poses and interpolating between the keys to create animation. Contrast with *procedural animation*.

lateral—a sideways camera move.

leica reel—see *story reel.*

level—status in an animated character's hierarchy, determining when in the animation process a part is posed. Generally, the root of the hierarchy is posed first, and the extremities last.

limited animation—animating on fours or more, or holding the majority of an image while animating a small part of it. A lot of television animation is limited.

line of action—*1. re* posing characters; an imaginary line drawn through the character's center and any limbs protruding beyond the body's silhouette. Ideally, there should only be one line possible for a key pose, and the line should have a pronounced curve that directs the audience's eye to follow the action. *2.* In cinematography, the main line (or slalom) of the action. The camera should stay on one side of the line of action during a sequence, to avoid confusing the audience.

line test—see *pencil test.*

*lip sync*_coordinating a character's facial animation to a sound track to create the illusion that the character is speaking.

live action—footage shot in the real world.

local coordinates—in most 3D software, XYZ values are calculated from the pivot of a object, rather than the origin of the entire virtual world.

lockdown—in puppet animation, a fastener inserted into a puppet's foot to keep it in place on the set. In cinematography, securing the camera so it does not move during a shot. In most 3D software, setting several identical values with linear interpolation in adjacent frames of a motion graph, to prevent any undesired movement.

long shot—a shot in which the entire figure, as well as a good deal of the background, is visible.

loop—repeat a motion cycle within a shot. See *hookup, motion cycle.*

LS—in cinematography, long shot.

luma key—similar to *chroma key*, but composites images based on luminance or brightness rather than color.

master shot—a shot that establishes the entire environment of a sequence, laying out a visual map for the audience. A camera setup wide enough to encompass an entire scene, designed to be intercut with closer shots.

match—see *move matching, dissolve.*

match dissolve—a dissolve from one image to a similar image, to show the passage of time or other gradual change or to smooth the transition.

match-lines—rows or columns of pixels within an image that have similar patterns on both sides, used for creating seamless tileable maps.

matte—a mask used to block part of an image for compositing.

MCU—in cinematography, medium close up. See also *medium close shot*.

metamorphosis—see *morph*.

mittens—the tendency to pose all of a character's fingers side-by-side in an undifferentiated lump. Closely related to *twins*.

mocap—abbreviation of *motion capture*.

model interpolation—technically correct but generallly unused name for *morph*.

model sheet—in cel animation, a collection of drawings showing the character in a variety of poses. In CGI animation, screen shots or test renders of the character from several angles and in a variety of poses, with notes from the technical director on animation controls, constraints, and limits for the character.

modeling—in CGI, creating objects by manipulating points, edges, and faces.

modulus of elasticity—a number representing the ability of a material to return to its original shape after being deformed.

moonwalk—see *foot slippage*.

morph—a process that changes one model for another gradually, by interpolating the position of each vertex or control point in the original model to match those of the target model.

motion blur—motion occurring while the camera shutter is open produces a blurred image; CGI can reproduce this effect by rendering and compositing images of a moving object's position between frames.

motion capture—a.k.a. *mocap*; a.k.a. *Satan's Rotoscope* Ken Cope, Jeff Hayes, Steph Greenberg.

motion cycle—an action that you can repeat by connecting duplicates end-to-end, e.g., walking, running, hammering a nail, or any other repetitive action. See *loop, hookup*.

motion study—detailed, sustained analysis of the movement of a subject, necessary to realistic or caricature animation.

mouse—input device, common but not well suited to character animation. See also *pen and tablet*.

mouth action—see *phoneme*.

move matching—matching the CGI camera movements and settings to live action footage, in order to render CGI elements that will merge seamlessly with the live action.

moving hold—a pose that a character must maintain for at least several frames, with slight changes to avoid losing the illusion of life.

MPEG—a lossy compression format popular for direct computer playback of animation and live action.

MS—in cinematography, *medium shot*.

natural path—see *slalom*.

noodle—*tweaking* settings back and forth and repeatedly creating previews long past the point of diminishing returns.

NTSC—the standard for television signals used in the U.S.

NURBS—Non-Uniform Rational B-Splines.

object animation—traditional stop-motion animation of objects instead of puppets or clay.

omniscient observer—in cinematography, a camera directed as if it were an invisible, all-seeing actor in a scene.

on-axis cut—abrupt change in camera setup on the long axis of the lens, either closer to or farther from the subject.

one-shot—one subject fills the frame, a.k.a. *single*.

ones, twos, or fours—the number of frames exposed for a single composition. The fewer the frames, the smoother and more expensive the animation.

optical printer—a machine that produced a film print by combining two or more prints, used for transitions and other compositing effects.

opticals—effects produced by an optical printer.

origin—the center of the coordinate system, where X, Y and Z all equal 0.

OTS—in cinematography, over the shoulder.

out of sync—soundtrack running behind or ahead of the animation.

out take—a shot that is not included in the final print of the film.

overlapping action—animating a part of the character to show flexibility, mass, and inertia separate from the character's main body.

overlay—see *foreground layer*.

PAL—a standard for television signals used in the U.K. and Europe.

palette—the range of colors available to a display device. A 24-bit palette can reproduce as many shades of color as the average person can see.

pan—abbreviation of panorama. Horizontal camera rotation around a fixed point; a Y-axis rotation.

pan, truck—a pan executed by moving the camera sideways rather than rotating it.

pan, zip—a caricatured camera motion representing a fast stop, as if the entire camera is vibrating rapidly.

parabola—a mathematical curve describing the path of a projectile in a gravity field.

passing position—one of the three main poses for a walk or run, in which the trailing leg is rotated past the supporting leg. See also *walk cycle*.

pen and tablet—a more artist-friendly substitute for the standard computer mouse, which simulates the behavior of a pen on paper, a.k.a. *stylus*.

pencil test—a preliminary rendering of an animation used to test an action, often created without color, maps, or background objects. Originally sketched with pencil, shot on film, and viewed as a negative image. See also *preview*.

pencil test reel—see *story reel*.

performance capture—see *motion capture*.

peripherals—additional equipment for a computer, e.g., external hard drives, *pen and tablet*, *film recorder*, or *digitizer*.

persistence of vision—see *flicker fusion*.

personality—the collateral effect of animated actions, creating the illusion that a character has unique motivations, volition, and thought processes.

phoneme—a.k.a. *mouth action* or *phonic shape*. The shape of the mouth when pronouncing a particular sound.

pin registration—securing the film precisely in an animation camera or *film recorder* with a set of pins, to ensure that each frame is registered exactly like all the others.

pitch—in most 3D software, the left-to-right rotational axis. A character's head nods on the pitch axis. Also, the presentation of a storyboard, related to a salesperson's presentation.

pixel—contraction of *picture element*. The smallest individual dot visible on a computer monitor. Rows and columns of pixels together make an image.

pixilation—stop motion animation created by posing living actors frame-by-frame.

plan—a top or overhead view of a set design.

point—one set of XYZ coordinates that defines the end or intersection of an edge, a.k.a. vertex.

point of view—see *POV*.

polygon—a surface defined by three or more edges and three or more points, a.k.a. *face, surface*.

pose—in most 3D software, the total of all bone and object translations and transforms for a character in a particular keyframe.

pose-to-pose—animating by setting all the key poses first, then going back over the animation and tweaking the *inbetweens*.

POV—abbreviation of point of view. A camera directed to show the scene as it would appear to one of the characters.

premise—a very brief summary of the point of a story, generally a sentence or two at the most, e.g., "easy come, easy go."

preview—a rapidly rendered part of an animation, created as a test.

procedural animation—movement or other animation that is controlled by an algorithm, e.g., Dynamic Realities' *Impact* plug-in. Contrast with *keyframe animation*.

propeller head—a term applied to CGI artists who come from a more technical, especially computer science, background. Can be comradely or pejorative, depending on usage.

pull-back—see *zoom*.

puppet—a jointed or flexible figure designed either to be animated or manipulated in a real-time performance.

puppet animation—stop-motion animation techniques using jointed or flexible puppets.

push-in—see *zoom*.

rack focus—directing the audience's attention by animating the depth of field to change the area of sharp focus. See Chapter 9 for project involving this concept.

RAM—Random Access Memory, the type of memory used to hold program information for fast access. Equivalent to having information on your desk, rather than filed in a drawer. CGI requires a lot of RAM.

range of movement—the limits to which a character can be posed before they distort unacceptably. Part of the information that the TD should write on the character's model sheet.

raster—data generated or displayed one row of points at a time, adding rows to create a matrix or image. In CGI, the data is usually an image or scanner dataset.

raytracing—a class of CGI rendering algorithms that calculates the value of each pixel by mathematically tracing the path of a ray from the pixel through all the reflections and refractions it would encounter in a scene.

real-time—"live" or in a 1:1 temporal ratio, in contrast to animation or computer time.

rear projection—projecting images or sequences on a screen behind the actors in a scene, to composite the image and live action in the camera.

repeat—see *loop*.

replacement—a class of animation techniques in which objects or parts of objects are sequentially replaced to create the illusion of changing shape or pose. Contrast with *displacement*.

resolution—the number of *pixels* in an image, usually expressed as the width by the height, e.g., 640×480.

rev. (revision)—in software, a new or improved edition of a program, presumably superior to, or at least not as flawed as, the preceding revision.

reveal—moving the camera to gradually expose more of a scene.

reverse angle—cutting from one camera angle to another nearly 180 degrees from the first. See Shots 5 through 9 in the example storyboards.

rim light—a light used to highlight the edges or rim of the subject.

room tone—the ambient or background sound and acoustic nature of a space where recording is done. Room tone is recorded for dubbing into blank spaces in the track, since completely blank spots in the soundtrack would be noticed by the audience.

Rotoscope—a technique originally patented by the Fleischer studio, in which live action footage was traced over to create cel animation. See also *Satan's Rotoscope*.

rough cut—the first complete edit of the film that still needs to be fine tuned.

RSI, RMI, CPS—Repetitive Stress Injury, Repetitive Motion Injury, Carpal Tunnel Syndrome. Occupational hazards of animation workers, that can permanently disable the victim's hands. Prevention is the best cure.

rubber hose construction—a style of character design in which the limb has no fixed joint, it simply bends in an arc to connect the torso to the hand or foot.

run cycle—action of a running character that has hookup frames suitable for looping.

Satan's Rotoscope—a.k.a. motion capture. Term coined by Ken Cope, Jeff Hayes, and Steph Greenberg.

scene—in 3D software, a file containing all the camera, object, and rendering settings necessary to create a series of images. In cinematography, a collection of shots in the same set and in a close temporal series.

sclera—the visible white portion of the human eyeball, surrounding the iris.

script—the written plan for a film, including dialog and some stage direction. The precursor to the storyboard.

sentence measurement—transcribing the timing of each take in a vocal recording session, to be used in selecting takes for track analysis.

sequence—a number of shots, in order, that tell part of the story.

set—the place where a scene is shot.

setup—in cinematography, the positions of actors and camera; in CGI, the links, constraints, and expressions created to make animation of a character easier.

short—film with running time between 2 to 20 minutes. Classic cartoon shorts usually ran between 6 and 7 minutes.

shot—the basic unit of film. A continuously exposed unedited piece of film. In CGI, an uncut sequence of frames.

shot on twos—in traditional animation, exposing two frames of film for each change in the animation, so a 24 fps projection speed will only show 12 new images per second.

shot volume—the space contained in the pyramid formed by the lens (the apex) and the four corners of the frame. The apparent volume of the shot ends at the central object or character.

Showscan—a projection system combining 65 fps frame rate and a widescreen format to enhance perceived realism.

sibilant—a class of phonemes including the consonants s and z.

SIGGRAPH—the Association for Computing Machinery's Special Interest Group on Computer Graphics. See Resources for details.

sightlines—an actor or character's line of vision, from the center of the eyeball through the pupil to the point being observed.

silent speed—16 fps, the minimum required to prevent *strobing*.

silhouette—the filled outline of a character in strong contrast to the rest of the scene, usually black and white. Useful for evaluating poses. In most 3D software, created by rendering an alpha channel image.

skate—see *foot slippage*.

skeleton—the arrangement and hierarchy of bones in a 3D character that enables the animator to pose it. See also armature.

slalom—the path followed by any system, natural or machine, that can correct its movement toward a goal.

slip—moving the soundtrack forward or back in relation to key sounds, deliberately modifying the sync so the action reads better.

slow-in, slow-out—see *ease-in, ease-out*.

snap—rapid, energetic changes within an action, the opposite of *ease*.

sneak—a caricatured action of attempting to move quietly on tiptoe.

software—the set of instructions or programs used to control a computer.

sound effects—see *foley*.

sound speed—24 *fps*.

soundtrack—the dialogue, music, and sound effects from a film.

special effects animation—smoke, water, or other non-character visual effects, generally animated in most 3D software by a specially designed plug-in.

speed lines—in traditional animation, drybrush lines drawn to show the path of a quickly-moving object or character. Superseded in CGI by *motion blur*.

sprocket hole—an evenly spaced series of holes matching the sprocket that pulls film through a camera or projector.

squash and stretch—exaggerated distortion of an animated object, intended to emphasize compression (squash) in deceleration or collision and elongation (stretch) in acceleration.

squash pose—in a take, the key pose in which a character or their face is most compressed in recoil.

squash position—in a walk cycle, the key pose in which the body is at its lowest and the supporting leg is bent to absorb the impact of the *heel strike position*.

stagger—a caricatured rapid oscillation of a character, especially after striking or being struck.

staging—animating a character to foreshadow the main action, making it easier for the audience to read.

static balance—balance achieved with no ongoing adjustments or changes in mass, inertia, or energy. See also *dynamic balance*.

still shot—a.k.a. *lockdown*, a shot in which the camera does not move.

stop motion—action created by stopping the camera, making changes to the scene or camera settings, and starting the camera again. Originally used to create dissolves and other optical effects in addition to animation, now generally used to describe clay or puppet animation.

story reel—an animation composed of story sketches synchronized to the soundtrack. Usually, each sketch is replaced with finished sequences as production proceeds.

storyboard—a sequence of story sketches depicting the major actions and layout for each shot. Often pinned to a large board or wall for group review and critique. See Appendix F for an example.

straight ahead action—in 2D animation, drawing each pose as you come to it, working out timing and posing on the fly. Contrast with *pose-to-pose*.

stretch—deforming all or part of a character to show acceleration. Contrast with *squash*.

stretch pose—in a take, the key pose immediately following the squash, in which the character's recovery from the squash is exaggerated beyond the original pose.

stride length—the distance a character travels with each step.

strobing—changes between frames that are too extreme, that catch the audience's attention and destroy the illusion of smooth movement.

stroboscopic photography—capturing a series of images on a single film frame by leaving the shutter open and firing a sequence of flashes or strobes, often used to capture a complex or rapid motion.

studio animation—animation produced by specialists within a larger organization, so the product is more of a team effort than an individual creative achievement.

stylus—see *pen and tablet*.

successive breaking of joints—when a higher joint starts to rotate, there should be a slight lag before the lower joints start to rotate as part of the same action. This means the rotation of a Child object should begin, peak, and end some time after the Parent performs the same actions.

sweatbox—projection room in an animation studio used to review and critique animation. Term originated at Disney studios due to lack of air conditioning, and was retained and used elsewhere due to the animator's stress levels during critiques.

sync—short for synchronization, the matching of sound to action on film or videotape.

synchronization—see *sync*.

synopsis—a brief summary of a script.

tablet—see *pen and tablet*.

take—a character's recoil of fear or surprise. See also *stretch pose*, *squash pose*.

telephoto lens—a camera lens assembly constructed so its focal length is significantly longer than its physical length.

television animation—animation designed for the limitations of the television cutoff and safe-titling areas and (sometimes) for the higher frame rate.

television cutoff—the outside border of the television image that is visible on studio monitors but is not displayed by many home televisions.

television safe-titling—the area within the television image that is safe for titles and other written communication.

test—see *pencil test*.

three-shot—three subjects fill the frame.

thumbnail—a smaller version of an image, used for convenience or, in CGI, to save memory.

tie-down—in traditional 3D animation, usually a threaded rod with a keyed head that locks into the bottom of a character's foot. The animator passes the rod through a hole in the stage and tightens it down with a wingnut, securing the puppet in place.

tilt—vertical equivalent of pan. See *pan*.

time encoding—adding time code to a videotape to enable accurate measurement and reference down to the frame and field. Generally using the SMPTE standard HH:MM:SS:FF.

time sheet—see *exposure sheet.*

track analysis—the transcription of a vocal track to a series of phonemes in an exposure sheet. a.k.a. *track breakdown.*

track breakdown—see *track analysis.*

track reader—the specialist who performs *track analysis.*

transfer—in cinematography, a moving object carries the audience's attention across the frame. a.k.a. hand-off. In editing, duplicating images or sound from one media format to another.

transform—in CGI, a change in shape, size, or attributes. Contrast with *translate.*

transition—in drama, a visible change from one dominant emotional state to another. In editing or cinematography, the effect or cut used between shots.

translate—in CGI, to change position. In general computer usage, changing data to a different file format, as when importing a 3DS or DXF file and saving it in another model format.

transport—the mechanism in a VTR used to move the tape past the recording and playback heads. A very accurate and expensive transport can reliably position the tape to within one frame, enabling single-frame recording for animation.

transportation animation—walking or other means of moving the character around within the shot.

traveling shot—a camera move that follows a character or other action.

treatment—a short form of a script, used by some studios when considering a production.

trucking, truck pan—see *dolly.*

tweak—to make fine adjustments or changes to settings. See also *noodle.*

twins—posing a character to appear symmetric in the frame. To be avoided, as it makes the character look stiff and lifeless.

two-shot—two subjects fill the frame, a.k.a. *double.*

twos—see *shooting on twos.*

U-matic—an industrial videotape format, rarely used in consumer or entertainment venues.

union shop—a studio or production house that has signed an agreement with a union to hire only members of that union. Non-union workers can (sometimes) still get a job there, but may have to joint the union to keep it.

universal joint—rotational joint having two degrees of freedom.

user friendly—a matter of opinion regarding the utility of computer software, as people have different cognitive and working styles. Hostile for some is friendly for others.

vector graphics—images drawn on a screen by lines connecting points. Good for outlines and wireframes, not good for color images of solid objects.

vertex—in most 3D software, a point.

VGA-to-NTSC converter—an adapter which converts the VGA output of a computer to the NTSC standard video signal used by most video equipment. Inexpensive ones have inferior video signals; you should test them before buying or renting. See also *encoder.*

VHS—a consumer-grade videotape format using half-inch tape in a cassette, having a maximum resolution of approximately 400 lines.

visual jar—a sudden change in shot volume or camera orientation that momentarily disorients the audience.

voice track—the part of the soundtrack that contains dialog.

voice-over—an offscreen voice dubbed over footage, which does not need to be lip synched. A fast and cheap way to make changes after animation is completed.

VTR—a Video Tape Recorder of any format, usually VHS, S-VHS, or BetacamSP. Frame-accurate VTRs can be used to record animations as they are rendered, one frame at a time, under computer control.

walk cycle—a walk action that has hookup frames suitable for looping.

WAV—a file format for digitized sound, commonly used with the Microsoft Windows operating systems.

wide angle lens—a lens having a focal length shorter than the diagonal measure of the image at the focal plane.

wide-screen—a film format designed for a higher aspect ratio, producing panoramic images.

wild wall—a wall or other object in a set that can be deleted or moved when not in camera range to make room for lighting or camera movement.

wipe—a special effect shot transition where the first shot is gradually replaced by the second shot, with a relatively sharp dividing line. A wipe can go from any direction, but typically moves top-to-bottom or left-to-right. See *dissolve.*

wipe the frame—passing a foreground object in front of the camera at the moment of a cut, usually used to smooth a transition.

wire frame—an abbreviated representation of an object, showing just the edges defining the object's polygons. Computers can draw wireframes very fast, so they are widely used for previews and tests.

workstation—marketing term for a more powerful personal computer system.

world coordinates—a coordinate system of measuring translation from a single origin for all items.

WS—in cinematography, wide shot.

x-sheet—see *exposure sheet*.

XYZ—coordinate axes of three-dimensional space; in most 3D software, the Y-axis is up-and-down, the Z axis is front-to back, and the X axis is side-to-side.

zip pan—see *pan, zip*.

zoom—using a lens capable of various focal lengths in order to change a shot.

THE CD-ROM

This appendix is a summary guide to the CD-ROM inside the back cover. The CD-ROM itself contains an HTML version of this appendix, INDEX.HTM, that you can open with any Web browser.

Contributors And Other Links

If you have any questions, problems, or just want to chat, email me at dakelly@earthlink.net. For online updates to this book, plus news about my other projects, check out my homepage at: **http://home.earthlink.net/~dakelly/index.htm**.

You can contact Ken Cope through his home page, Ozcot Studios, at: **http://www.ozcot.com**.

You can send email to Sandra Frame at **SFrame13@aol.com**.

4D Vision

4D Vision is the publisher of several software packages useful to character animation. This directory contains a subset of their Web site, a gallery of art created with 4D Vision products, and demo versions of their 4D Paint and Raygun programs. Due to technical difficulties at press time, a demo version of Sculptor Pro Tools was not included, but is available directly from their Web site at **www.4dvision.com**.

Adobe

This directory contains tryout versions of Photoshop 4.0, Premiere 4.2, After Effects 3.1, and the free Acrobat 3.0 viewer for reading PDF files.

Caligari

This directory contains the Trial Version of trueSpace 3, plus a video clip of an animated desk lamp created in trueSpace. For more information, contact the publisher at **www.caligari.com**.

Ch02

This directory contains the installation archive for ScriptMaker, a shareware screenwriting template for Microsoft Word 6.0.

Ch03

This directory contains:

- The individual story sketches for the "Easy Come, Easy Go" storyboard in TIFF format

- An AVI clip with each sketch as a single frame
- A subdirectory of the old story sketches
- EASYSHO2.DOC, the script as expanded to each shot description
- SKETCH.PDF, a blank story sketch template in Acrobat format

Ch04

This directory contains:

- Complete soundtrack WAV files for "Easy Come, Easy Go"
- Lip sync project WAV files
- Exposure sheet templates in Word and Acrobat formats for both 24 and 30 fps

Ch06

This directory contains desk lamp models required for the Chapter 6 projects in LightWave, 3D Studio MAX, and DXF formats.

Ch07

This directory contains a variety of facial models created with Cyberware laser scanners and the Immersion MicroScribe 3D digitizer.

Ch08

Animation clip 08_05.AVI, showing the author's Cyberscanned head model with color and specularity maps applied.

Ch09

This directory contains files required for Chapter 9's projects, including:

- Digitized images of a variety of fabrics
- A series of images of the author's eye
- A facial color map adapted to a different model

Ch10

This directory contains files required for Chapter 10's projects, including:

- A cyberscan color map of the author's head
- A cyberware model of the author's head
- An edited color map of the author's head, defining areas of facial hair
- 3D Studio MAX scene for setting up Digimation's Shag:Fur hair shader

Ch11

This directory contains files required for Chapter 11's projects, including:

- Desklamp one-piece model and replacement/morph target models, in LightWave, 3D Studio MAX, and DXF formats
- Puppet character objects, in LightWave, 3D Studio MAX, and DXF formats
- Cartoon glove model, in LightWave, 3D Studio MAX, and DXF formats
- Project scene files in LightWave and 3D Studio MAX format
- Animation clips in MPEG format

Ch12

This directory contains files required for Chapter 12's projects, including:

- Cartoon glove Softimage database
- Project scene files in Animation:Master, LightWave, and 3D Studio MAX format
- Animation clips in MPEG format

Ch13

This directory contains files required for Chapter 13's projects, including:

- Facial and lip sync models and replacement/morph target models, in Softimage, LightWave, 3D Studio, and DXF formats
- Lip sync mouth maps
- Project scene files in LightWave and Softimage format
- Animation clips in MPEG format

Ch14

This directory contains models, maps, and scene files for the street scene and Puppet character required for Chapter 14's projects.

Ch15

This directory contains several example animation clips in MPEG format.

Ch16

This directory contains models, maps, setups, and WAV files required for Chapter 16's lip sync projects.

Ch17

This directory contains the Imp character, ready to set up for the Chapter 17 lighting projects.

Ch18

This directory contains files required for Chapter 18's projects, including:

- Sets and character models
- Digitized video footage to match camera movement
- Clean plate stills to match lighting and shadows
- Project scene files
- Project flows for Digital Fusion

Ch19

This directory contains images to be used as title and credit cards for "Easy Come, Easy Go."

Ch20

This directory contains an MPEG version of Allen Coulter's short animated film, "Balls & Blocks," plus a Word template for creating flipbooks and a parameter file for compiling MPEG clips.

Shortly before press time, an improved shareware utitily was released that makes the tedious parts of MPEG compression obsolete. I highly recommend the AVI to MPEG converter programmed by John Schlichter and available from **www.mnsi.net/~jschlic1/avi2mpg1/ avi2mpg1.htm**. Tom Holusa has added a nice graphical user interface, so it's just a matter of selecting an AVI file and clicking *Start*. Combined with an MPEG playback board like ATI's All-In-Wonder, this is an excellent and inexpensive way to get your character animations to videotape.

Comet

This directory contains several animations created by Michael B. Comet, who contributed projects and images to a number of chapters in this book. To see more of his work, check out the last page of this book's Color Studio, Mike's page in the Artist Directory, or cruise his Web site at **www.comet-cartoons.com**.

Computoons

This directory contains a mirror of Robert Terrell's heavily-animated Computoons Web site, including video clips from 3DO's *Captain Quazar* and a full version of *Nightwalk*. It's worth browsing; Bob gives a very thorough behind-the-scenes look at his studio's projects.

Cyberware

A selection of Cyberscanned models of humans and objects, with a short description file. For more models and information, go to **www.cyberware.com**.

Digimation

This directory contains a tryout version of Bones Pro MAX. Digimation also publishes Shag:Fur and other 3D Studio MAX plug-ins useful for character animation. Check out their Web site at **www.digimation.com**.

eyeon

This directory contains a fully-functional demo version of eyeon software's Digital Fusion compositing program. The only difference from the commercial version is that the eyeon and Digital Fusion logos are automatically composited on the final rendering, so you can't use it for commercial work. You can use this software to complete the compositing projects in Chapters 18 and 19, creating match moves, optical effects, and titles. The demo version also includes several tutorials that show off the software's more advanced functions. For more information, check out the eyeon Web site at **www.eyeon.com**.

Glewis

This directory contains an HTML file and a collection of images demonstrating some of the capabilities of SIMILAR, EMPH, and other utilities Glenn Lewis has written to assist with morphing objects in a variety of file formats. You can also check out his Web site at **http://www.c2.net/ ~glewis/** for his latest projects.

Hash

This directory is a real jackpot. First, take a look at FLUFFY.MPG, a complete version of Doug Aberle's award-winning animation created with Animation:Master. Then install the trial version of Animation:Master 98, which you can use to complete the projects in Chapter 12 and elsewhere in this book. To complete your education in the use of Animation:Master, you'll want to read the V6 Tutorials Acrobat file, the online help, and the HTML Help pages. You can practice setup and animation with the sample character models in the MODELS subdirectory until you get around to building your own.

JeffLew

This directory contains QuickTime clips and a variety of images of Jeff Lew's work. I especially recommend the DRAGON.MOV clip for its demonstration of weight and balance.

Komodo

This directory contains a QuickTime clip that provides a 360-degree view of Bill Fleming's "Chubby" character. For more details on Komodo Studio and Bill's modeling techniques, refer to the Komodo page in the Artist and Studio Directory appendix, and to Bill's case study in Chapter 6.

Magpie

This directory contains a fully-functioning demo version of the lip sync program Magpie Pro, plus the original shareware 0.9 version of Magpie. Each program includes a selection of lip sync or facial expression maps, plus tutorial files to supplement the projects in Chapters 13 and 16. For more information about Magpie Pro, email the author, Miguel Grinberg, at **mgrinberg@impsat1.com.ar**, or visit Third Wish Software and Animation's Web site at **thirdwish.simplenet.com**.

MetaCreations

This directory contains demo versions of Detailer and Painter, both of which you will find useful in completing the projects in Chapters 8, 9, and 10. For more information, visit MetaCreation's Web site at **www.metacreations.com**.

Momentum

This directory contains the COBRA.MOV match move animation described in the case study in Chapter 18. Momentum Animations is also developing characters for a CGI animated feature film. For details, visit their Web site at **www.momentumanimations.com**.

Physics

This directory contains several MPEG clips from the award-winning short film, *The Physics of Cartoons, Part One*, directed by Steph Greenberg. An HTML file in this directory contains basic information about the film's production. For more information, visit the film's official homepage at **www.animation.org/physics/**.

REM

This directory contains a mirror of REM Infografica's Web site, including many video clips and images created with their 3D Studio MAX plug-ins. In addition, demo versions of CartoonReyes, ClothReyes, MetaReyes, and JetaReyes are included.

TOPIX

This directory contains the installation archive for the NT version of the Softimage cloth simulation plug-in, TOPIXCloth, written by Frank Falcone and Colin Withers. If you use this software, please contact them through the TOPIX Web site at **www.topix.com** and let them know what you're doing with it.

BIBLIOGRAPHY

Ablan, Dan. *LightWave Power Guide*. Indianapolis, IN: New Riders Press, 1996. ISBN: 1-56205-633-6.
Good general coverage of LightWave's features, with excellent tutorials and a few items on character animation.

_____. *Inside LightWave 3D*. Indianapolis, IN: New Riders Press, 1997. ISBN: 1-56205-799-5.
A major improvement over Ablan's previous book, with much more professional-level detail and contributions by a handful of other LightWave experts. If you own the software, you should definitely own this book, especially since the official 5.5 manuals have fewer tutorials than the older versions.

Arijon, Daniel. *Grammar of the Film Language.* Hollywood, CA: Silman-James Press, 1991. ISBN: 1-879505-07-X.
An exhaustive guide to the visual narrative techniques that form the "language" of filmmaking regarding the positioning and movement of players and cameras, as well as the sequence and pacing of images. Heavily illustrated with line drawings. In print for nearly twenty years in several languages. Highly recommended.

Bacon, Matt. *No Strings Attached: The Inside Story of Jim Henson's Creature Shop.* MacMillan, 1997. ISBN: 0-02-862008-9.
History, techniques, problem-solving, and lots of illustrations from the best puppeteers in the business. Includes behind-the-scenes from *Dark Crystal, Labyrinth, Pinocchio,* and other projects. Animators have a lot to learn from puppeteers, and this is an excellent place to start.

Barba, Eugenio, and Nicola Savarese. *A Dictionary of Theatre Anthropology: The Secret Art of The Performer*. ISBN 0-415-05308-0.
An academic approach, heavy on theory and a little long-winded, but an incomparable resource of photographs and analysis to worldwide physical expression, dance, and acting. Not a substitute for acting classes, but close.

Bell, Jon A. *3D Studio Max f/x: Creating Hollywood-Style Special Effects*. Durham, NC: Ventana, 1996. ISBN: 1-56604-427-8.
If you need a quick set of tutorials on making good-looking images with MAX, this is the book for you. Not much directly pertinent to character animation, but a solid reference for everything else.

Blair, Preston. *Cartoon Animation*. Wilton, CT: Walter Foster, 1994. ISBN: 1-56010-084-2.
The best collection of caricature motion studies in a form easily adapted to 3D computer animation. Especially useful for character design regarding head and hands.

Blacker, Irwin R. *The Elements of Screenwriting*. New York, NY: Collier Books, 1986. ISBN: 0-02-000-220-3.
One of the best, and certainly the most compact, source about writing for film or video. This book is the absolute minimum necessary for the amateur to understand the mechanics of writing usable scripts. Not a bad reminder for the experienced screenwriter, either!

Blinn, Jim, Mark Henne, John Lasseter, Ken Perlin, and Chris Wedge. "Animation Tricks." *ACM SIGGRAPH Course Notes* 1 (1994). P.O. Box 12114, New York, NY 10257. Annual.
A collection of short lectures from some of the top working professionals. These tips and tricks are the hard-won lessons of experience. Required reading.

Bogner, Jonathan, prod. and Mike Bonifer, dir. *The Making of Toy Story*. Burbank, CA: Walt Disney Co., 1995. Videocassette.
A little light on the animation side and proportionally heavier on the celebrity voice talent, but some good quotes and a little behind-the-scenes at Pixar. Originally shown on The Disney Channel around *Toy Story*'s opening.

Bordwell, David, and Kristin Thompson. *Film Art: An Introduction*. 4th ed. New York: McGraw-Hill, 1993. ISBN: 0-070-06446-6.
A more historical and theoretical, if shallower, approach to Arijon's subject, with stills and sequences from Hollywood and foreign films. Also covers sound and film criticism.

Bridgman, George B. *Constructive Anatomy*. Dover. ISBN: 0-48621-104-5.
One of the most often-cited resources for drawing from life, written and illustrated in a way that is especially useful for 3D modeling and character setup.

Brown, Curtis M., Bonnie Dalzell, and Robert W. Cole. *Dog Locomotion & Gait Analysis*. Hoflin Pub Ltd., 1986. ISBN: 9-99784-732-6.
A detailed and thorough breakdown of canine movement, including structure and physiology. Very useful for studying all kinds of animal motion; once you learn the details for dogs, you can apply the same principles to most mammals and many other species as well.

Chan, Alan. *The FX Kit for Lightwave*. Lancaster, CA: Lightspeed, 1995.
Writing and publication quality are spotty, but this 300+ page collection of tutorials (and its version 5.0 Addendum) are a useful supplement to the NewTek 5.0 and 5.5 manuals.

Cook, David A. *A History of Narrative Film*. 3d ed. New York: W. W. Norton, 1996. ISBN: 0-393-96819-7 (pbk).
A good basic history of film, especially cinematic technique and influences.

Culhane, Shamus. *Animation: From Script To Screen*. New York: St. Martin's Press, 1990. ISBN: 0-312-05052-6.
An ex-Disney animator with sixty years industry experience describes the whole animation process, including production details, setting up a studio, storyboards, character animation, business issues, and more. One of the "traditional" craftsmen who has embraced the computer as a labor-saver for the animator.

De Leeuw, Ben. *Digital Cinematography.* AP Professional, 1997. ISBN: 0-12208-875-1.
Excellent coverage of lighting and camera work for CGI, tied to the real-world equivalents. Profusely illustrated.

Egri, Lajos. *The Art of Dramatic Writing.* New York, NY: Simon & Schuster, 1960. ISBN: 0-671-21332-6.
The best source on how to write an interesting, dramatic story. Lots of guidelines for developing convincing characters.

Faigin, Gary. *The Artist's Complete Guide to Facial Expression.* New York, NY: Watson-Guptill Publications, 1990. ISBN: 0-823-01628-5
Useful for modeling and animating facial expressions, especially the more realistic. For the exaggerated or caricatured, refer to Blair.

Feher, Gyorgy. *Cyclopedia Anatomicae.* Illustrated by Andras Szunyoghy. Black Dog & Leventhal Publishers, Inc. 1996. ISBN: 1-884822-87-8.
A monster of a book, probably more information than you'll need to design your characters. Always a fascinating browse, you'll continue to stumble over interesting bits for years.

Frierson, Michael. *Clay Animation : American Highlights 1908 to Present.* Twayne's Filmmakers Series, 1994. ISBN: 0-80579-328-3.
Mostly a history, but some useful tips that can be applied to CGI. An excellent companion to Wilson's *Puppets and People.*

Giambruno, Mark. *3D Graphics and Animation: From Starting Up to Standing Out.* New Riders Publishing, February 1, 1997. ISBN: 1-56205-698-0.
Lightweight and definitely aimed at the beginner, this book attempts to cover many of the same areas as the one you're reading now. Browse it before buying, to see if it will have anything new for you.

Halas, John. *The Contemporary Animator.* Boston, MA: Focal Press, 1990. ISBN: 0-240-51280-4.
Excellent survey of the art up to 1990. Dated in areas pertaining to computer graphics, but a wealth of information on the various styles and techniques of animation. Worth tracking down for the glossary alone.

Hawken, Paul. *Growing a Business.* Fireside, 1988. ISBN: 0-67167-164-2.
The best single source on how to start and grow a small business. Learn from other people's mistakes, and save yourself a lot of pain, money, and time.

Hayward, Stan. *Scriptwriting for Animation.* Focal Press, 1978. ISBN:0-24050-967-6.
Animation here means 2D cel work, but there are some useful tips that still apply. Out of print; check your local library.

Hoffer, Thomas W. *Animation: A Reference Guide.* Westport, CN: Greenwood Press, 1981. ISBN: 0-313-21095-0.
Exhaustive reference and critical bibliography on the genre. Probably more information than you'd normally want, but if it's about animation and it existed prior to 1979—it's in here.

Itten, Johannes. *The Elements of Color*. Van Nostrand Reinhold Company. ISBN:0-442-24038-4. Standard reference for art classes. If you need help on composing colors for sets, characters or lighting, this chunk of theory may be what you need. If you won't use it very often, try the library; the hardcover edition is expensive.

Jones, Chuck. *Chuck Amuck: The Life and Times of an Animated Cartoonist*. 1st ed. New York, NY: Farrar Straus Giroux, 1989. ISBN: 0-240-50871-8.
This and *Chuck Reducks* comprise the autobiography (to date) of one of the best-loved classic cartoon directors. Bugs, Elmer, Daffy, and the rest of the WB gang acquire a little more life when you read this book. It's also a valuable peek inside the workings of the Hollywood system. Don't think the bozos aren't still in charge.

Jurgens, Jo. *Animated Conversations-Interviews with the World's Greatest Animators*. Forthcoming. When Jo finally finds a publisher, don't miss this one. I've read a couple of excerpts, and it's going to be a gold mine for the professional animator or animation fan.

Kamoroff, Bernard B. *Small Time Operator: How to Start Your Own Small Business, Keep Your Books, Pay Your Taxes, and Stay Out of Trouble!* 22nd Ed. Bell Springs Pub, 1997. ISBN: 0-91751-014-3. Precisely what the title says. 'Nuff said.

Kanfer, Stefan. *Serious Business: The Art and Commerce of Animation in America from Betty Boop to Toy Story*. 1997. ISBN: 0-684-80079-9. Illustrated, color and b/w, hardbound.
This is more about the business than the art, and is a sweeping chronicle that actually turns out to be a fairly fast and enjoyable read. Well researched and comprehensive, if a bit too encyclopedic; it's hard to trace that many strains of cartoon DNA through so many studios and pogroms. This is a good overview of the history of the business that you had to be nuts to want to get into until fairly recently. You really ought to know this stuff and if you don't, this is a good source for it.

Katz, Steven D. *Film Directing: Shot by Shot*. Studio City, CA: Michael Wiese Productions, 1991. ISBN: 0-941188-10-8.
Excellent resource on the creation and use of storyboards for directing a film.

_____. *Film Directing—Cinematic Motion: A Workshop for Staging Scenes*. Studio City, CA: Michael Wiese Productions, 1992. ISBN: 0-941188-14-0.
Less important (for animation, anyway) resource on the actual composition techniques used in directing a film. Staging, choreography, blocking, and so on, plus meaty interviews with professionals like John Sayles and Ralph Singleton. A good complement to Arijon's book, with a different perspective.

Kelly, Doug. *Lightwave 3d 5 Character Animation F/X*. Durham, NC: Ventana, 1997. ISBN: 1-56604-532-0.
My first book, including some of the information in the one you're reading now, but with more detail on specific LightWave procedures.

_____. "Natural Camera Movement." *3D Artist*, 18 (1995): 33. P.O. Box 4787, Santa Fe, NM 87502. Irregular. ISSN: 1058-9503.
How to avoid the Steadicam Syndrome in CG animation.

Klein, Norman M. *7 Minutes: The Life and Death of the American Animated Cartoon.* 1993. ISBN: 0-86091-396-1. Illustrated b/w softbound.
This is a dense book. Klein taught at Cal Arts and the book is a lot more scholarly than the Kanfer tome, but of far more interest to anybody who wants to know what made the shorts work. There is plenty of theory and film nerd de-construction, yet because of its subject, informs more than abstracts. I expect that familiarity with the ideas the author explores in this book will help anybody make better short animated films. There is a lot of insightful and comprehensive comparison, context and chronology. A lot of basic cartoon structures are illuminated as they go from fresh to formula. Highly recommended.

Lemay, Brian. *Advanced Layout and Design Workbook.* Oakville, ON: 1997. ISBN: 09-9699419-2-7.

_____. *Designing Cartoon Characters for Animation.* Oakville, ON. ISBN: 0-9699419-1-9.

_____. *Layout and Design Made Amazingly Simple.* Oakville, ON: 1993.
Lemay, an instructor at Sheridan, has done an incredible job in these three volumes. These detailed, exhaustive books make Blair's pale in comparison. Unfortunately, these are at present only available direct from the author, but are well worth the extra effort. Send queries to: Brian Lemay, Suite 1422, 1011 Upper Middle Rd., Oakville, ON, L6H 5Z9.

Lasseter, John. "Principles of Traditional Animation Applied to 3D Computer Animation." *Computer Graphics.* 21:4 (1987), 35–44. Association for Computing Machinery, 1515 Broadway, 17th Floor, New York, NY 10036. ISSN: 1069-529X.
Lasseter translates the principles of animation taught at Disney (see Thomas and Johnston) to 3D computer animation, and also introduces the concept of layering or "hierarchical" animation. Solid gold; if you skip everything else in this list, get a copy of this paper.

Lasseter, John, and Steve Daly. *Toy Story: The Art and Making of the Animated Film.* New York, NY: Hyperion Press, 1995. ISBN: 0-7868-6180-0.
A wonderful collection of production art and interviews with the principal creators, both at Pixar and Disney. A must-have for 3D CGI enthusiasts and professionals.

Laybourne, Kit. *The Animation Book.* New York: Crown, 1979. ISBN: 0-517-52946-7.
Beginner's guide to most of the film-based techniques, from drawing on film to sand and clay stop-motion.

Lee, Stan, and John Buscema. *How to Draw Comics the Marvel Way.* New York, NY: Simon & Schuster, 1984. ISBN: 0-671-53077-1.
Useful as a study guide for constructing humanoid characters, strong poses, and dramatic scene composition. 2D drawing exercises translate well to 3D modeling.

Levitan, Eli. *Handbook of Animation Techniques.* New York, NY: Van Nostrand Reinhold, 1979. ISBN: 0-442-26115-2.
Focused on production for television advertising, this is a very nuts-and-bolts volume. While technically dated, it contains solid production advice which should be taken seriously by anyone trying to do business in animation. Direct and written in plain English, with a minimum of philosophizing.

Lewis, Verin G. "Storyboarding." *3D Artist*, 18 (1995): 32–33. P.O. Box 4787, Santa Fe, NM 87502. Irregular. ISSN: 1058-9503.
Concise argument for the necessity of storyboarding commercial 3D animation and a brief overview of storyboard production.

LightwavePro Compilation Book. Sunnyvale, CA: Avid Media Group, 1996.
A collection of 100 tutorials from LightwavePro magazine. Worth acquiring, even though there isn't much on version 5.0.

London, Barbara, and John Upton. *Photography*. 5th ed. New York, NY: Harper Collins, 1994. ISBN: 0-673-52223-7.
Useful for chapters on lighting, composition, color, lenses, and film vocabulary, all of which are readily adapted to 3D computer animation.

Lund, Bill. *Getting Ready for a Career As a Computer Animator*. 1997. ISBN: 1-56065-549-6.
One more in a series of vocational guidance books from this author. Some good advice, but be aware that he's not an industry insider. Better than nothing, but do your own research before you blow serious money on an animation school.

Malkiewicz, Kris. *Film Lighting: Talks with Hollywood's Cinematographers and Gaffers*. New York, NY: Prentice Hall Press, 1986. ISBN: 0-671-62271-4 (pbk).
This is the working expertise of an impressive collection of lighting professionals. Not exactly an easy read, but lots of information. Derived almost entirely from live-action production, a lot of the hardware specifics won't apply to CG work, but the principles are the same.

Martino, Stephen Michael. *Storyboard Design for Computer Generated Animation*. Master's thesis. Columbus, OH: Ohio State University, 1989.
Well written and adequately illustrated, this is one thesis that won't put you to sleep. The author had previously worked as a designer and animator at Cranston/Csuri in Columbus and as a director at Metrolight Studios in Los Angeles. Storyboard examples include Dow "Scrubbing Bubbles," and KTLA, NBA, and HBO logos, among others. Solid practical advice on dealing with clients, too.

Morris, Desmond. *Bodytalk: The Meaning of Human Gestures*. New York, NY: Crown Publishers, 1994. ISBN: 0-517-88355-4.
A readable popular version of somewhat scholarly research on informal gestural communication. Excellent resource for animators, either for practice or to build up a library of reusable motions.

Morrison, Mike. *Becoming a Computer Animator*. Indianapolis, IN: Sams, 1994. ISBN: 0-672-30463-5.
A brief history of computer animation and assessment of technology as of 1994. Basic tutorials using an early version of Caligari's trueSpace. Covers finding employment and an overview of animation schools. There is one chapter each on television, feature films, visualization, forensic, and game animation. Includes a CD-ROM of animation clips and (now seriously dated) software demos.

Murch, Walter. *In the Blink of An Eye*. Silman-James Press, 1995. ISBN: 1-87950-523-1.
Mostly about film editing, but also contains valuable information about why people blink.
Another one to browse at your library or bookstore.

Muybridge, Eadweard. *The Human Figure in Motion*. New York, NY: Dover Press. ISBN: 0-486-20204-6.

_____. *Animals in Motion*. New York, NY: Dover Press. ISBN: 0-486-20203-8.
Muybridge took carefully measured sequences of photos of animal and human movement in the late 1800s. These sequences are a great help for anyone trying to make something move realistically, or to derive the essentials of an action for caricature.

Parke, Frederick I., and Keith Waters. *Computer Facial Animation*. 1996. ISBN: 1-56881-014-8.
An exhaustive, very scholarly compilation of research and applications of facial animation. A difficult read, but even the figures and captions will give you a lot of information that isn't available anywhere else. If you make a living with lip sync or facial expressions, you need to have this book on your reference shelf.

Peck, Stephen Rogers. *Atlas of Facial Expression: An Account of Facial Expression for Artists, Actors, and Writers*. New York, NY: Oxford University Press, 1987. ISBN: 0-195-04049-X.
Excellent technical reference on the facial structure and the uses of muscles in emotional and vocal communication.

Pintoff, Ernest, et al. *The Complete Guide to Animation and Computer Graphics Schools*. 1995. ISBN: 0-82302-177-7.
Useful but out-of-date. Double-check phone numbers, addresses, placement rates, accreditations, and policies before you mail out any applications or make other expensive plans.

Plantec, Peter M. *Caligari Truespace2 Bible*. 1996. ISBN: 1-56884-841-2.
Adequate general introduction to the software, but nothing of value to character animation. The section so-labeled should not have seen print.

Reese, Andrew. *Looking Good in 3D*. Durham, NC: Ventana. ISBN: 1-56604-494-4.

Reese, Andrew. *3D Modeling & Animation Marketplace: The Definitive Guide to the Multimillion Dollar 3d Industry*. 1997. ISBN:1-57610-157-6.

Reese, Stephanie. *Character Animation with 3D Studio Max*. ISBN: 1-57610-054-5.
The Reeses do their usual workmanlike job in each of these books. If the topic is of interest to you, they are generally worth your money.

Ruff, Barry, and Gene Bodio. *Softimage Design Guide*. Scottsdale, AZ: Coriolis, 1997. ISBN: 1-57610-147-9.
An excellent book, and I'm not just saying that because the same production team worked on this one. Very dense with lots of useful information about software that has few other third-party books.

Thomas, Frank, and Ollie Johnston. *Disney Animation: The Illusion of Life*. New York, NY: Abbeville Press, 1981. Reprinted Hyperion Press, 1995. ISBN: 0-7868-6070-7.

Referred to as "the animation bible" due to its size and the value of its contents. The Disney "rules of animation" and many other useful rules-of-thumb are included. Recently reprinted, with some loss of color and image quality since the '81 edition, but still well worth the price.

Thompson, Frank T. *Tim Burton's Nightmare Before Christmas: the Film, the Art, the Vision: With the Complete Lyrics From the Film*. 1st ed. New York, NY: Hyperion, 1993. ISBN: 1-562-82774-X.
A really good behind-the-scenes book, about one of the most technically challenging puppet animation films ever. This is an excellent idea-generator for replacement modeling and armature construction that applies to CGI as well as traditional methods.

Vince, John. *3D Computer Animation*. New York, NY: Addison-Wesley, 1992. ISBN: 0-201-62756-6.
Introductory technical animation theory for programming. Recommended for TDs.

Watt, Alan, and Mark Watt. *Advanced Animation and Rendering Techniques*. New York, NY: Addison-Wesley, 1992. ISBN: 0-201-54412-1.
An excellent technical text, covering important implementation theory and details. Recommended for TDs.

Weil, Jerry, Neil Eskuri, Andy Kopra, John McLaughlin, and Kathy White. "Tricks of the Trade: Computer Graphics Production." *ACM SIGGRAPH Course Notes* 5 (1995). P.O. Box 12114, New York, NY 10257. Annual.
A goldmine of production rules-of-thumb collected from technical directors at different production houses. Recommended for TDs, animation supervisors, and anyone else who needs to produce CGI animation on time and within budget.

Whitaker, Harold, and John Halas. *Timing for Animation*. 1st ed. New York, NY: Focal Press, 1981. ISBN: 0-240-51310-X.
An absolute treasure trove of information on timing. Difficult to find, but well worth it.

Wilson, Steven S. *Puppets and People*. London: Tantivy Press, 1980. ISBN: 0-498-02312-5.
A history, filmography, and a smattering of basic nuts-and-bolts for the motion picture techniques of compositing live-action with stop-motion puppets. Examines the work of Willis O'Brien, Ray Harryhausen, Phil Tippett, and others. Lots of photos, and because the physical models tend to decay or be salvaged for parts, a collection of information hard to find elsewhere. Worth looking for, if only to use the extensive bibliography pointing to primary sources in the industry press.

Zaloom Mayfield Productions, prod. *The Making of Jurassic Park*. Universal City, CA: Amblin Entertainment, 1994. Videocassette.
A good collection of behind-the-scenes information and interviews, featuring Steven Spielberg, Stan Winston, Phil Tippett, Dennis Muren, Michael Lantieri, Mark Dippe, Steve Williams, and others. Includes a sequence on the techniques used for matching animation to live-action footage from a moving camera, plus the use of animal motion studies. Originally broadcast on NBC.

STUDIO DIRECTORY

This appendix contains pages of contact information and samples of work created by some of the artists and studios who have contributed to this book. If you are planning to hire an animator or studio, this appendix gives you a convenient sample of the talent available. If you are an animator looking for work, this appendix gives you an idea of the level of talent and skill required to work for the contributing studios.

ALIEN FROM "THE ROSWELL OMEN"

ORIGINAL SCULPTURE BY BRIAN WADE

MODELED, ANIMATED AND RENDERED
IN Animation:Master BY

ARMANDO AFRE
PIXELSHOP(TM)
MANDO@IONIX.NET
HTTP://WWW.PIXELSHOP.COM

FOR

TOM MARLIN
MARLIN STUDIOS
TMARLIN@MARLINSTUDIOS.COM
WWW.MARLINSTUDIOS.COM/STUE

Jared E. Bendis

"Jack Of All Trades, Master Of None"

The Bunny Picture

Problem Solving

Courseware Designer

Custom System Building

Custom Business Networking

Web Site Design

Working on first CG Animated short "Its Good To Fit In"

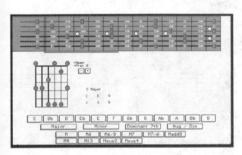

creen Shot From "Chordware for Guitar"

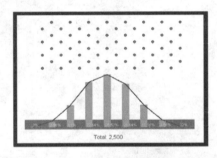

Screen Shot From "Monte-Carlo Bell Curve"

Design and Knit Custom Photo Sweaters
Shown Here: The "Doug Kelly"

phone: (216) 226-8787
email: jaredjared@earthlink.net
http://home.earthlink.net/~jaredjared/

Check out Catapult Productions'
Monster By Mistake! website at
http://www.MonsterByMistake.com
or email Mark Mayerson at
mayerson@sidefx.com

For Prisms and Houdini information, contact:
Side Effects Software
477 Richmond Street West, Suite 1001
Toronto, Ontario, Canada M5V 3E7
tel: (416) 504 9876 fax: (416) 504 6648
http://www.sidefx.com   donna@sidefx.com

Michael B. Comet

I started out in grade school on my own by doing flipbooks
and stop motion stuff with an old Super 8mm camera. At the
same time I was programming little graphics apps and games
in BASIC. Eventually I got Imagine and Later Lightwave 3D
on my Amiga 3000. I ended up creating characters and
animations for a freelance game and a Sci-Fi CD-ROM. Neither
of them have been published...sigh. In addition, I moved
onto C++ and UNIX and ended up writing my own little modeler
and renderer as well as some personal shaders for Lightwave.

Currently I work as an animator for Volition, Inc. doing character work for our
game's cutscenes with 3DSMAX (and some custom software). I'm responsible for
body and facial setup and animation. Plus I do modeling, texturing, lighting
and other art related tasks.

I tend to enjoy doing funny cartoony type animations, and find a lot of the old
Warner Bros. shorts really inspirational. I also look up to Chuck Jones, both
for animation and story telling. Watching a lot of Disney cartoons as a kid
also caused me to want to be an animator.

Besides classic cartoons I'm also a fan of anime. I
actually studied Japanese for a few years and hope to
travel there in the future. Plus I just can't seem to
eat enough sushi! I find medieval music and related
topics interesting...I play a hammered dulcimer in my
spare time. One of my goals in life is to move into a
place that allows pets so I can buy a dachsund. Oh yeah
that and to trick people into thinking I'm actually sane.
(Is there such a thing as a normal animator?)

If you'd like to find out more about me check out my web page at:
http://www.comet-cartoons.com/   or E-mail me at: comet@comet-cartoons.com
http://www.soltec.net/~comet/   or: mbc@po.cwru.edu

Insanely Yours,

Michael Comet
Keeper of the Llamas

COMPUTOONS®
3D CHARACTER DESIGN AND ANIMATION

http://www.computoons.com

I am a freelance 3D animator providing characters ranging from cartoon-like to photo-realistic starting from initial sketches to final 3D animation. I use Animation Master, LightWave and 3D Studio MAX for my 3D work. I'm currently based in Boston, and work remotely for most clients.

me of my recent clients include:

Reelfx Inc. - TX
Kimberly-Clark Corp. - WI
Thrustmaster Inc. - OR
Hash Inc. - OR
Sybex Inc. - CA
DarkForge - MA

Contact Info:
Jeffrey Lew
(617) 859-9648
jefflew@xtrabox.com
http://3dagency.simplenet.com

Kimberly D. Oravecz

35382 Stevens Blvd
Eastlake, OH 44095

voice: (440) 942-691(
e-mail: kimo@en.con

"You wanna iguana?"

- Created in Lightwave 3D v 5.0
  - Texture maps created with Detailer 1.0,
    Photoshop, Forge and procedurals
  - Plants created with Lparser
  - Background image created in Bryce 2
- All other models created by me
  in Lightwave

"The undersea world of Jacques Seahorse"

- Created in Lightwave 3D v 5.5
- Texture mapping done with Detailer 1.0,
  Photoshop and procedurals
- All objects created by me in Lightwave

"Tooki Tooki"

I created this image on my Amiga 4000
in Alpha Paint. The image was hand
painted, nothing was scanned in. I used
a photo from a book as a visual reference.

What I enjoy doing most is creating very detailed organic objects along with the detailed texture maps, especially animals and plants. I plan to study more on animation in the future as well.

Freelance work has included: assisting in the photography of birds and bird cages for an ad that runs monthly in Bird Talk magazine for a local pet store, several calligraphy jobs, and I have recently completed a flying logo project for Ernst & Young, LLP.

I currently work for Avery Dennison as a Digital Printing Technician, where I create graphic in Photoshop and Corel Draw and perform various tests on a variety of wide-format digital printers.

reflections of fantasy...

Mark Riddell

135 Reding Road
Ancaster, ON
Canada
L9G 1M9

905.648.0255
mrriddel@cgl.uwaterloo.ca
http://www.cgl.uwaterloo.ca/~mrriddel/

Specializing in digital character animation
Strong traditional skills
Experience with unix administration

Rick Knowles

602-1297 Marlborough Court
Oakville Ontario
Canada
L6H 2S1
(905) 337-3921

rdknowle@cgl.uwaterloo.ca
http://www.cgl.uwaterloo.ca/~rdknowle

Computer animator and graphic designer
Traditional skills specializing in pencil and charcoal

TOPIX / MAD DOG

35 McCAUL ST.
TORONTO, ON
CANADA
M5T 1V7

416 971 7711
www.topix.com

Mad Dog Digital
A DIVISION OF TOPIX

Honeycomb craver "geezer mansion"
client: kraft
animation: Topix
post production: Mad dog digital

David Bowie "little wonder"
director: floria sigismondi
post production: Mad dog digital

Since it's foundation in 1987, Topix has specialised in character
animation and special fx, type and broadcast design and film
titling for commercial advertising, feature films and the
broadcast markets. In 1995 Topix launched Mad Dog Digital,
a high end flame-based post production and effects studio.

Paramount pictures "harriet the spy"
director: bronwen hughes
animation: Topix
post production: Mad dog digital

Alliance films "the sweet hereafter"
director: atom egoyan
animation: Topix
post production: Mad dog digital

"Media television"
client: city tv
animation: Topix

"On the road"
client: panasonic
post production: Mad dog digital

"Face of technology"
client: comdisco
animation: Topix

Marshmallow munchies "runner"
client: heritage brands
animation: Topix
post production: Mad dog digital

"Lifesavers: let the good times roll"
client: hershey canada
animation: Topix

"Zwilling"
client: henkel knives
animation: Topix
post production: Mad dog digital

Volition, Inc.

2212 Fox Drive, Suite G
Champaign, IL 61820
E-mail: personnel@volition-inc.com

WHO WE ARE

Volition is a computer game developer located in Illinois,
creators of the hit games Descent and Descent II. Volition's
staff includes a full complement of talented artists and
programmers.

The working environment is very relaxed and all of the employees
are avid gamers. We offer competitive salaries and a complete
benefits package.

WHAT WE LOOK FOR IN A DEMO REEL

We get a number of reels and portfolios from artists
who are applying. Artists have a wide range of
responsibilities, although it's not uncommon to focus
on an area one enjoys the most.

The following is a list of general skills that we look
for when reviewing demo reels:

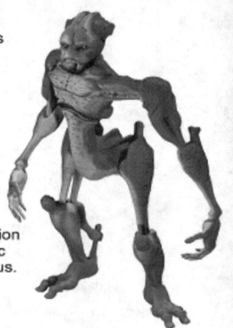

- Modeling skills, including realtime low polygon
  modeling as well as high detail models.

- Solid texturing and lighting skills. The ability
  to create realtime textures is a plus.

- Character animators must show proficiency in motion
  skills with an emphasis on keyframing and dynamic
  posing. A traditional animation background is a plus.
  Knowledge of 3D character setup is desirable.

- Traditional drawing ability and design skills.

VENDOR DIRECTORY

This appendix contains pages of contact information, specifications, and samples of work created using software and hardware products described in this book. This information is provided by the respective vendors, and I make no warranties as to its accuracy. If you are considering a purchase, this appendix is a convenient directory of the available character animation products. For details and up-to-date information, please contact the vendors directly.

  # 4D Paint™

'Almost like holding an object in my hand to paint it with a real brush'
Dave Sieks - Game Developer Magazine

4D Paint is the world's most advanced interactive real-time 3D paint environment system for Windows NT and 95. 4D Paint is a must have for game developers, character animators, industrial designers or anyone doing professional 3D work.

The 3D artist can now paint color, bump, opacity, self-illumination, and shininess or any combination directly onto the surface of a 3D object with a single brush stroke. For example it is possible to paint the complex color and surface texture of fish scales directly onto a 3D model of a fish and see the results while painting. For added flexibility in painting and positioning 2D Paint and texture effects onto a 3D model, it is possible to overlay the object's unfolded mesh onto any paint or other layer as your positioning guide. 3D artists can then paint in 2D and 3D simultaneously in either 3D or unfolded mode.

Compatibility:
3D File Import: .3DS, LWO*, DXF*, Alias triangle*.
Supports imports and manages multiple object and material definitions.

32 Bit Bitmap Import & Export: .jpg, .bmp, .tif, .pic, .tga, and many others.

Cut & Paste: Import 2D bitmaps from other applications.

Multiple Layer Support: Every channel can have multiple layers of paint. Each one is independent of the other with adjustable opacity.

3D File Export: .3DS, LWO*, VRML 1.0 & 2.0,* Renderman.*

Direct Interface: 3DS MAX™, AutoCAD Rel 14™, Softimage™ and Rhino 3D™

Tools:
Unfold 3D meshes to a 2D map instantly

Painting 2D and 3D Simultaneously.

Unlimited Undo. (Depends on memory)

Paint and Rendering:
Paint on Multiple Channels: (Simultaneously)
Bump, Color, Glow, Shininess Opacity and Alpha.

Render & Paint Realtime:
Color, Bump, Glow, and Shininess*

Real media paint tools: 4D Paint comes standard with a huge library of special effects paints, brushes and a texture library. The paint system is designed to closely emulate the experience of painting with real brushes and paints.

Lighting: Realtime 3D Lighting of models. Multiple light sources for rendering.

Ray traced rendering output:* Highest quality image output for 2D Print applications. Incorporate your 3D work with 2D presentations or print media.

Control Inputs: Wacom pressure and tilt* sensitive tablets, 3D Spaceball.

Minimum Requirements: 32MB, 800 X 600 X 16 bit color graphics, Pentium processor, 30 MB disk, Windows 95 or NT 4.0 and a CD-ROM drive.

Recommended: Pentium Pro +, 64-128 MB Ram and 1280 X 1024 X 24 Bit color graphics.

Note: Items marked with a * are specific to 4D Paint 2.0
Some features mentioned are not available in 4D Paint Goya 1.5. For a full list of features for each version of 4D Paint please refer to the web site.
Specifications are subject to change without notice. (Generally for the better) Please refer to the web site for the most current specifications.
Sample images courtesy of Giant Pictures NZ., ECG Taiwan, AniMagicians USA., Formworks, NZ.

Contacts:
Intl. e-mail 4dvisasia@4dpaint.com
Ph 64 9 3094 906

www.4dpaint.com

USA e-mail sales@4dvision.com
4D Vision LLC
PH 800 252 1024

www.4dvision.com

Cyberware

Cyberware manufactures a variety of instruments for 3-dimensional scanning. Pioneered by Cyberware, the laser- and video-based technology can scan complex objects in only seconds. Cyberware makes standard and custom design laser scanners for many different applications. Some of these applications include industrial design, animation, anthropology, and medicine.

Cyberware software is responsible for all of the data acquisition and many post-processing tasks. The CyDir software controls the scanning process and all of the motion platform commands, as well as the automatic assembly of multiple scans into a single file. CyDuce will produce very efficient polygonal models by reducing the number of nonessential vertices in a model. CySculpt provides the capability to efficiently edit, reshape, repair, refine, and prepare a surface for rapid prototyping. The CySurf package provides a means of converting digitized data into NURBS surfaces quickly and easily. CySlice is used to convert more complex models into IGES NURBS slices using a simple interface.

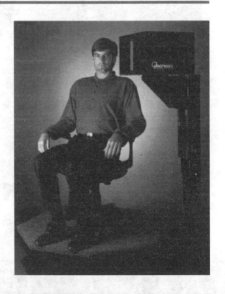

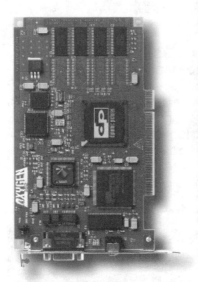

eyeon

Digital Fusion began its evolution as a DOS application and has since been completely rewritten from the ground up to fully take advantage of the Windows NT platform. It now has one of the most sophisticated software architectures for post production work running on Windows NT workstations. Digital Fusion is object-oriented and fully multi-threaded with a custom GUI (Graphical User Interface). Not only is it a program that is multi-processor aware, taking advantage of all of the latest system architectures, but one that is easy to learn and use.

eyeon Software's Digital Fusion brings the high-end post production studio to the NT workstation, with Ultimatte Matting technology, the mind-bending 5D Ltd. MONSTER Plugins (previously only available on Flame and Flint) and now MetaCreations Final Effects all available as optional plugins with Digital Fusion Version 2. Digital Fusion not only delivers speed and power, it gives you the creative freedom you thought was out of your reach.

With Digital Fusion new nonlinear time line layout, eyeon Software continues to revolutionize the post production environment with Digital Fusion Version 2. This nonlinear Compositing System gives you the flexibility to work with unlimited layers, while remaining resolution independent. Want the power to put it all together? With Digital Fusion's visual flow diagram, flexible interface

and non linear time line you have a powerful overview of the creative process.

70 Valleywood Drive Markham, Ontario Canada L3R 4T5

TIMELINE EDITING
Non linear time line edit. Clip list system. Drag, drop, cut, trim, effect direct on timeline

MULTIPROCESSOR
True Multithreaded, Multiprocessor support DEC Alpha and Pentium Pro Optimization.

MMX ACCELERATED
Pentium II multimedia instruction optimized to boost performance.

OBJECT ORIENTED
Flexible object oriented drag and drop design. Powerful intuitive flow creation for users

RESOLUTION INDEPENDENCE
Any Resolution Images can be mixed and matched Independently into a final output.

DIGITAL FILM
4k res 64bit Film Version Direct in & out to Kodak Cineon format.

DPS DIGITAL VIDEO
Direct support and control of DPS Hollywood, Perception and PAR Boards.

DIGITAL VIDEO
PAL & NTSC Video with full field processing direct interface to digital video systems.

IMAGE TRACKING
Automated target tracking, steadying, stabilizing. Unlimited number of tracking points.

DISPLAY LAYOUT
Compose directly on images. Effect and layer automatically.

SPLINES
Advanced Bezier Spline control of all aspects of every image processing function.

ADVANCED WARP
Corner and perspective pinning. Apply drips, Vortex, Refraction, Deform effects.

SUPERIOR CHROMA KEYER
Halo Reject Color Spill, Color Correction, Soft Edge and Matte Shape Control.

TIME INTERPOLATION
Full Spline Control of temporal sequences. Slow Down and Speed Up, with Spline Curves.

PLUGINS
Digital Fusion® advanced 64bit API kit. 5D Monster Plugins.

SYSTEM REQUIREMENTS
Windows NT 400 system DEC Alpha or Intel Pentium. Minimum system 64mb ram, 16bit display, 2Gb disk, CD-ROM.

RECOMMENDED SYSTEM
Multiprocessor,1280 x 1024 24bit Display, 128+ mb ram. DPS Hollywood or Perception. Windows NT4.0.

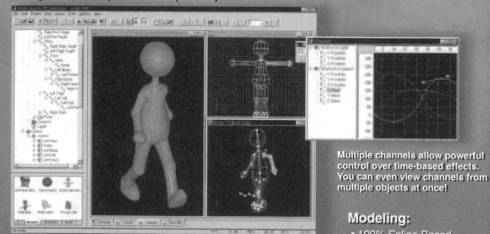

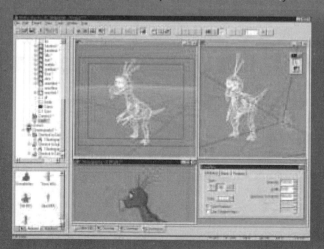

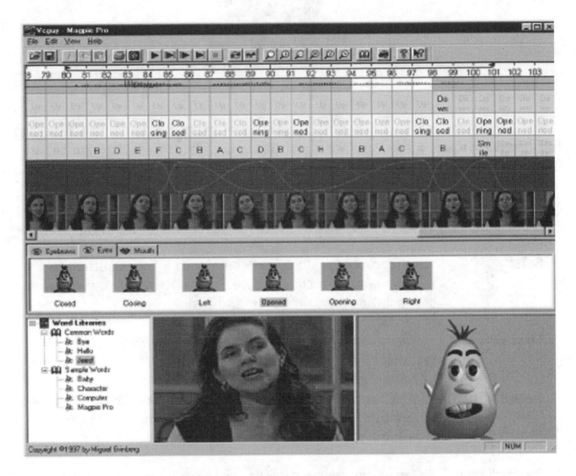

Discover the power and flexibility of

MAGPIE PRO

The professional tool for audio track breakdown and timing animations

http://thirdwish.simplenet.com

MICRO MADNESS

making ideas fly

Since 1991, Micro Madness has served the entertainment sector as an SGI reseller and full service systems integrator. We specialize in the film, video, and animation industries. Let us help you with our unsurpassed depth of knowledge and resources.

Micro Madness is the single source for all of your advanced graphics computing needs.

Sales Our focused product line contains the top solutions in the industry. And our consultative approach helps you select the best solution for your needs and budget.

Consulting We provide a wide range of services to meet your technological demands.

Networking Whether you are planning an enterprise-wide solution or a re-integrating your existing hardware, our consultants can determine the most effective solution for you.

Renderfarm Our in-house twenty-four processor Onyx computer is the ideal timesaver for all your rendering needs.

Rentals We maintain an extensive inventory of leading edge hardware available for short- and long-term rental.

Please visit us at our website for more information:

19 West 21 Street, Suite 706
New York, NY 10010
212-741-4177

http://www.madness.net

SOFTIMAGE|3D

SOFTIMAGE|3D is a powerful cross-platform modeling, animation, and rendering package designed for use in professional 3D production environments. Typically used in the Game, Commercial/Broadcast, and Film/Video marketplaces, Softimage has consistently set the standard by which other 3D systems are measured. In addition to its modeling, animation, and rendering features, SOFTIMAGE|3D offers a unique artist-oriented workflow which allows it to be used as the basis of a professional animation environment. The "Extreme" version of SOFTIMAGE|3D adds advanced modeling, rendering and particle/dynamics capabilities, as well as Meta-Clay density-based organic modeling. Available for both Silicon Graphics and Windows NT®-based systems, the SOFTIMAGE|3D system ships with an extensive library of particle effects, mental ray™ shaders, and motion capture files.

The mental ray renderer for SOFTIMAGE|3D is the highest-quality renderer in the industry, offering exceptional photorealism and advanced effects. mental ray™ supports distributed rendering across Intel, Alpha and MIPS RISC-based workstations and servers for Windows NT-based and Silicon Graphics systems, allowing customers to configure cost-effective, hardware independent "renderfarms".

Softimage also provides a complete suite of developer tools. The SOFTIMAGE®|SDK is a cross-platform software development environment that makes it easy for customers and third party software developers to create their own plug-ins and enhancements for SOFTIMAGE|3D. Softimage also provides platform-specific tools for games developers, such as exporters for the SONY Playstation, Nintendo 64, SEGA Saturn, and Direct X platforms.

For further information on the SOFTIMAGE|3D product line, as well as our next-generation products, make contact:

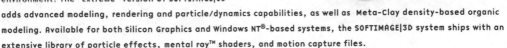

SOFTIMAGE®

━━━━ softimage.com/dk_book ━━━━
1 800 387-2559x8860   1 514 845-1636x8860

Hippo images by Jeremy Birn at Palomar Pictures, www.3drender.com

SoulBlade ©NAMCO Limited

3D

O

P

CHARACTER ANIMATION IN DEPTH

CREATIVE PROFESSIONALS PRESS

Left Brain Meets Right Brain: Creativity Meets Technology

*"**3D Studio MAX f/x** is nothing less than the instructional tour de force for using 3D Studio MAX to create completely professional Hollywood-style animation effects."*

— *Alex Kiriako,* Assoc. Editor, 3D Artist Magazine

Design and Create

Master Your Tools

| Intermediate Designer and Artist | Advanced Designer and Artist |

SERIES	MAIN FEATURES	DETAILS	CONTENT FOCUS	AUDIENCE
F/X AND DESIGN Design and Create	The ideal creative professional's practical "show and tell" guide. Focuses on creating impressive special effects and presenting unique design approaches. Provides numerous step-by-step projects that designers, animators, and graphics professionals can really learn from and use. Highly "visual" editorial approach with special tips, techniques and insight from graphics professionals.	8" x 10" format High-quality paper and printing 300 to 400 pages 32 to 96 pages of full color plates CD-ROM $49.99 (U.S.) $69.99 (CAN) CD-ROM features interactive design projects and special effects, professional quality art, animation, and resources.	3D tools, graphics creation and design tools, Web design tools, multimedia tools, animation software: Photoshop, Illustrator, 3D Studio, AutoCAD, Director, Softimage, Lightwave, Painter, QuarkXPress	Animators, graphic artists, 3D professionals, layout and production artists. The ideal books for the working creative professional.
IN DEPTH Master Your Tools	Comprehensive guides for creative power users, professionals, animators, and design experts. Focuses on presenting in-depth techniques to show readers how to expand their skills and master their tools. Jam-packed with "insider" tips and techniques and hands-on projects to help readers achieve real mastery. Ideal complement to the *f/x and Design* series.	7 3/8" x 9 1/4" 600 to 800 pages 16 to 64 pages of full color plates CD-ROM $49.99 to $59.99 (U.S.) $69.99 to $84.99 (CAN) CD-ROM features tools and resources for the "design" professional and power user.	3D tools, graphics creation and design tools, Web design tools, multimedia tools, animation software: Photoshop, Illustrator, 3D Studio, AutoCAD, Director, Softimage, Lightwave, Painter, QuarkXPress	Animators, graphic artists, 3D professionals, layout and production artists. Perfect for the working power user.

Creative PROFESSIONALS PRESS™

Creative Professionals Press offers the graphic designer, Web developer, and desktop publisher the hottest titles in the design industry today! Whether you're a professional working for a design studio or a freelance designer searching for the latest information about design tools, Creative Professionals titles address your design and creative needs. The *f/x and design* and *In Depth* series are highly interactive and project-oriented books that are designed to help the intermediate to advanced user get the most out of their design applications and achieve real mastery.

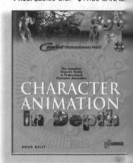

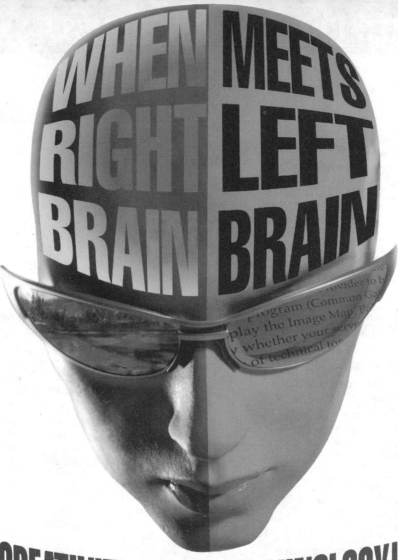

CREATIVITY MEETS TECHNOLOGY!

What you see in your mind's eye, Creative Professionals Press books help you create. Let our books guide you to the cutting edge of today's graphics and tomorrow's unpredictable visual explorations.

Thorough, carefully structured direction along with real-world applications, interactive activities, extensive full-color illustrations, and hands-on projects take you to places you've only imagined. When right brain meets left brain, creativity meets technology. And when creativity meets technology, anything is possible.

Creative PROFESSIONALS PRESS™

f/x and design Series • In Depth Series • Looking Good Series

800.410.0192 • **Int'l Callers: 602.483.0192**

www.coriolis.com

Available at Bookstores and Computer Stores Nationwide

CORIOLIS